1500
Best Bars, Cookies, Muffins, Cakes
& More

Esther Brody

Robert
ROSE

1500 Best Bars, Cookies, Muffins, Cakes & More
Text copyright © 2008 Esther Brody
Photographs copyright © 2008 Robert Rose Inc.
Cover and text design copyright © 2008 Robert Rose Inc.

The recipes in this book were previously published in *500 Best Muffin Recipes*, published in
2003 by Robert Rose Inc.; in *250 Best Cakes & Pies*, published in 2003 by Robert Rose Inc.;
in *500 Best Cookies, Bars & Squares*, published in 2004 by Robert Rose Inc.; or in *250 Best
Cobblers, Custards, Cupcakes, Bread Puddings & More*, published in 2004 by Robert Rose Inc.

For complete cataloguing information, see page 576.

Disclaimer
The recipes in this book have been carefully tested by our kitchen and our tasters. To the best
of our knowledge, they are safe and nutritious for ordinary use and users. For those people
with food or other allergies, or who have special food requirements or health issues, please
read the suggested contents of each recipe carefully and determine whether or not they may
create a problem for you. All recipes are used at the risk of the consumer.

We cannot be responsible for any hazards, loss or damage that may occur as a result of
any recipe use.

For those with special needs, allergies, requirements or health problems, in the event
of any doubt, please contact your medical adviser prior to the use of any recipe.

Design and Production: Kevin Cockburn/PageWave Graphics Inc.
Proofreader: Sheila Wawanash
Indexer: Gillian Watts
Cover Photography: Colin Erricson
Interior Photography: Mark T. Shapiro
Food Styling: Kate Bush
Prop Styling: Charlene Erricson

Cover image: Raspberry Coconut Bars (page 298)

We acknowledge the financial support of the Government of Canada through the Book
Publishing Industry Development Program (BPIDP) for our publishing activities.

Published by Robert Rose Inc.
120 Eglinton Avenue East, Suite 800, Toronto, Ontario, Canada M4P 1E2
Tel: (416) 322-6552 Fax: (416) 322-6936

Printed and bound in Canada

1 2 3 4 5 6 7 8 9 TCP 16 15 14 13 12 11 10 09 08

Contents

Introduction

Getting Started

The secret to successful baking lies in paying close attention to the recipe. Before you begin, read the recipe carefully and assemble all the necessary equipment and ingredients. Adjust oven racks to the desired level and, 15 minutes before you want to bake, preheat the oven to the required temperature.

Preparing Ingredients

Don't make ingredient substitutions and don't double or halve the recipe unless it states that you can do so.

Use Fresh Ingredients

- Purchase ground spices in small amounts and store tightly sealed in a cool, dry place. Replace ground spices annually.
- Ensure that leavening agents such as baking soda and baking powder are still functional. Baking soda will keep for up to 1½ years in a glass jar with a tight lid or in its original container. To make sure it is still active, mix 1 tbsp (15 mL) baking soda in ½ cup (125 mL) cold water. Add 1 tsp (5 mL) vinegar. If the mixture doesn't fizz, discard the baking soda. To test whether baking powder is still active, dissolve 1 tsp (5 mL) baking powder in ⅓ cup (75 mL) hot tap water. The mixture should bubble up vigorously.
- Chocolate should be well wrapped and stored in an airtight container in a cool place. If the storage location is too warm, a gray-white color (called bloom) will appear on the surface of the chocolate. This does not affect the flavor, and the chocolate will return to its normal color when melted.
- Buy seeds and nuts from a bulk food store with rapid turnover and store them in the refrigerator.
- Keep marshmallows in the freezer.
- Check the "best before" date on ingredients such as peanut butter, sour cream and yogurt.

All About Eggs

- Always use large eggs for baking.
- Since eggs separate more easily when cold, separate the yolks from the whites as soon as you remove the eggs from the refrigerator. Cover the yolks with cold water and return them to the refrigerator until you're ready to use them. (Drain the water before using.)
- If you're going to beat the egg whites, let them come to room temperature for 5 to 10 minutes first.
- Do not leave eggs at room temperature for longer than 1 hour.

Softening Fats

Remove shortening, butter or margarine from the refrigerator to soften 1 hour before mixing unless the recipe specifies the use of cold or chilled.

Toasting Nuts

Spread nuts out in a single layer on a baking sheet and bake at 350°F (180°C) for about 7 minutes, stirring or shaking the pan once or twice, until lightly browned. To remove nut skins (such as with hazelnuts or almonds), place nuts in a clean tea towel and rub vigorously.

Making Sugar-Cinnamon Mix

In a cup, combine ¼ cup (50 mL) granulated sugar and 1 tsp (5 mL) ground cinnamon. Store in an airtight container.

Melting Chocolate

The trick to melting chocolate is to ensure it doesn't "seize." Therefore, it is important that the chocolate does not come in contact with water, which will cause it to solidify into a grainy mass. If your chocolate seizes while melting, add 1 tsp (5 mL) shortening for every 2 oz (60 g) of chocolate and stir until the mixture is smooth and creamy. Do not use butter, as it contains water.

To ensure that chocolate melts quickly and evenly on the stovetop, break it into small pieces (or use chocolate chips) and stir constantly. Chocolate should be melted over low heat in the top of a double boiler or in a bowl set over a saucepan of hot (not boiling) water. Grease your melting container with shortening before melting chocolate for easy removal.

Chocolate also melts well in the microwave. Use chocolate chips, squares or small chunks. Place in a microwave-safe bowl, cover tightly with microwave-safe plastic wrap and microwave on High for about 1 minute per ounce (the time will vary depending upon the power of your microwave and the quantity of chocolate used). Stir well until completely melted.

Using Honey Instead of Sugar

You can replace sugar with honey in most recipes. (The reverse does not hold true, however; if a recipe calls for honey, then that is what will work best.) When substituting honey for sugar, add 1/2 tsp (2 mL) baking soda for each 1 cup (250 mL) honey and reduce the amount of liquid in the recipe by 1/4 cup (50 mL). Reduce the oven temperature by 25°F (10°C), as recipes containing honey will brown faster.

Measuring

For best baking results, it is essential to measure ingredients accurately each time. Have measuring cups for both dry and liquid ingredients ready — it saves time to have large measures also. Make sure your measuring spoons are in good shape, not warped, bent or dented, as you can't get perfect measurements if they are.

Dry Ingredients

- Use measuring cups with a flat rim so they can easily be leveled off. To measure less than 1/4 cup (50 mL), use standard measuring spoons. Fill cups or spoons to overflowing, then level off using a straight-edged knife or spatula. Do not pack or bang on the table.
- If a recipe calls for "sifted flour," it should be sifted first, then measured. Otherwise, flour is not sifted before it is measured.
- If a recipe calls for "packed" or "firmly packed" brown sugar, spoon it into a measuring cup, pack it down with the back of a spoon, then level off.
- Baking soda, baking powder and cocoa powder have a tendency to pack down in their containers, so before measuring, stir to loosen.

Liquid Ingredients

- Always use a see-through glass or plastic measure with volume amounts marked on the outside.
- Place measuring cup on a flat surface and bend down so that you can read the measure at eye level.
- Make sure your measuring cup has a safety rim above the full cup mark to get an accurate measurement without spilling a drop.
- Shortening, butter or margarine that is not sold in stick form should be measured in a cup that holds the exact amount when leveled off. Press firmly into the cup so that no air holes are left. Level off and scoop out.
- To measure oil or melted fat, dip measuring spoon into the oil and then lift out carefully. The spoon should be so full that it will not hold another drop.

Mixing for Best Results

- Before mixing batter or dough, combine dry ingredients such as flour, baking powder, baking soda and salt in a bowl and mix thoroughly to ensure they are well blended.
- If a recipe calls for a melted ingredient, such as butter, shortening or chocolate, let cool slightly before adding eggs. Otherwise, the eggs may curdle.
- If a recipe calls for extracts or flavorings, mix them in after creaming the butter and sugar (and after beating in eggs, if using) so they will be well incorporated.

Preparing Pans

- If the recipe indicates the pan should be greased, I recommend using shortening. Place a dab of shortening on a piece of waxed paper and spread it in a thin, even layer over the pan. Grease pans only if the recipe specifies.
- Butter, margarine or oil may cause baked goods to stick to the pan. If you don't have shortening, instead of greasing, you can line the pan with parchment or waxed paper, cut to fit.
- If a recipe calls for a lightly greased pan, spraying it with vegetable spray is acceptable.

• •

Making Perfect Muffins

Preparing the Tins

Muffin tins can be greased or sprayed with vegetable spray, but I prefer lining them with paper baking cups.

Mixing the Batter

A key factor in producing successful muffins is the mixing. There are two common methods for mixing muffins:

The Standard Method

1. Sift the dry ingredients into a large bowl and make a well or depression in the center. Remember to mix dry ingredients together well to distribute the baking powder and baking soda evenly.
2. Combine the egg (slightly beaten), milk and oil or melted shortening (cool the melted butter or shortening first).
3. Add the liquid ingredients all at once to the dry ingredients.
4. Stir quickly only until the dry ingredients are moist. The batter will be slightly lumpy.
5. Spoon batter into prepared muffin tins.
6. Bake as directed.

The Biscuit Method

1. Cut shortening into the sifted dry ingredients until crumbly.
2. Combine the egg and milk. Add all at once to the flour mixture.
3. Stir just until moist.
4. Spoon batter into prepared muffin tins.
5. Bake as directed.

I prefer to use the standard mixing method with most of my recipes, unless the recipe states otherwise. I find it the easiest way.

Your muffins will be lighter when you mix them together quickly and lightly, as this produces the best rising effect. Use as few strokes as possible — the batter should look lumpy. I stir and mix my muffin batter with a "folding-in" movement, using a large stainless steel spoon, not a spatula as you would normally when "folding" in a recipe. When a muffin batter is overmixed, it is too smooth and flows readily, leaving the spoon in a long, ribbon-like strand. This will result in tough muffins with funnels and a pronounced peak.

Dry ingredients should be thoroughly mixed in one bowl and liquid ingredients in another bowl. As soon as you combine the two of them, you have to work quickly, stirring just to enough to moisten and combine. Then spoon immediately into muffin tins.

The batter for muffins is usually stirred but may be creamed. For a stirred batter, the dry ingredients are mixed together to evenly distribute the baking powder and baking soda. If the leavening is unevenly distributed, the muffins may have a bitter taste. For a creamed batter, the shortening and sugar are beaten together before adding the other ingredients. The muffins are usually sweeter and have a cake-like texture.

Filling the Tins

In most of my muffin recipes I fill the muffin tins right to the top, unless I am adding a filling or topping, to produce large, even-sized muffins. For smaller muffins, use medium-sized paper baking cups. The yield will be 3 or 4 muffins greater. You should reduce the baking time slightly, usually up to 5 minutes.

Any cups not filled with batter should be filled halfway with water. This will not only save the muffin pans but will add moisture to the oven, enlarging the muffins and allowing for even baking.

Once the muffin batter has been prepared and put into the muffin tins, it should go into the oven quickly. The idea is for the batter to start rising in the oven, not on the counter. That is why I prepare the muffin tins before I start mixing the recipe.

Baking

Most muffin recipes suggest baking at 375°F (190°C) or 400°F (200°C). I have found that baking at 425°F (220°C) for 20 minutes works best for many of my muffins. If the muffins brown too quickly, turn your oven down.

Muffins bake best on the middle rack of the oven. On the lowest shelf, the bottoms burn too quickly; on the highest shelf, the tops brown too soon.

I set my timer for 15 minutes, then rotate the muffin pan front to back, then bake for the remaining 5 minutes. Most ovens cook unevenly (often baking faster at the back), but I have found that this method produces a more evenly baked and browned muffin. Check the accuracy of your oven often and make any necessary adjustments.

Muffins are done when they are golden brown, firm to the touch, pull away from the sides of the pan and a toothpick inserted in the center comes out clean and dry.

Muffins can be baked successfully in the microwave using special microwave muffin pans or glass custard cups. Be sure to follow the manufacturer's directions that come with your microwave oven for proper baking time and power levels. See pages 112–117 for some great recipes.

Instead of baking muffin batter immediately, you can freeze it by spooning the batter into paper baking cups. Place cups in the freezer. When frozen, place the cups in airtight containers or freezer bags and return to the freezer. To bake, unwrap and place the paper cups and frozen batter in ungreased muffin tins. Bake in a 300°F (150°C) oven until well risen. Then increase oven temperature to 425°F (220°C) and bake for 15 to 20 minutes or until golden brown. If you wish to thaw the muffin batter first, that usually takes about an hour. Bake thawed muffins in a 425°F (220°C) oven for 15 to 20 minutes or until golden brown.

Removing Muffins from the Tin

Muffins straight from the oven are very fragile, so let the pan cool for 5 to 10 minutes before removing the muffins. The steam from the pan should loosen them. If they still stick, loosen them by running a knife around the edge of the cups. Often, you can simply turn the pan upside down and the muffins will fall out.

If you are baking fruit-filled muffins, let them cool completely before removing from the tins.

If you wish to keep muffins warm for serving, loosen them and tilt slightly to one side of the muffin tin. Place them in the warm, turned-off oven until you are ready to serve.

Storing and Reheating Muffins

- Whether I plan on freezing the muffins or eating them in the next few days, I wrap each muffin separately in plastic wrap. Once wrapped, they have a terrific shelf life of 3 to 5 days. They will stay moist and fresh and ready to go. I do not store muffins in the refrigerator, as they become stale and dry faster. Keep them on the counter or in the freezer.
- Muffins freeze well for up to 6 months if wrapped properly. To freeze muffins, cool completely first. Wrap in plastic and place on a foil or Styrofoam tray. Place tray in a large airtight freezer bag and tie securely. This double wrap prevents the freezer taste you sometimes get when foods thaw.
- Because muffins are great warm, you can reheat them by wrapping them loosely in foil and placing them in a 400°F (200°C) oven for 5 to 10 minutes. If frozen, heat for 15 to 20 minutes. Muffins can also be heated in the microwave: cover with a damp paper towel and heat for about 30 seconds or just until warm. Be careful: microwaves heat very quickly.

• •

Making Perfect Cookies

- I recommend investing in heavy-duty baking sheets. They will likely cost a bit more, but they are worth it because they won't rust and your cookies will bake more evenly. Baking sheets differ from baking pans in that they don't have sides, which allows the heat to circulate around the cookies, helping to ensure more even baking. If you don't have heavy-duty baking sheets, lower the temperature of your oven by 25°F (10°C).
- Grease baking sheets only if the recipe specifies. A general rule of thumb is that dough containing a high proportion of shortening is baked on ungreased sheets. Unnecessary or excessive greasing will cause some cookies to spread too much.
- Shortening, butter, margarine and occasionally vegetable oil all work equally well in cookie recipes. Use whichever the recipe specifies. I do not recommend the use of spreads sold in tubs for baking, as these products contain a higher percentage of water than solid fats. Cookies made from spreads will expand too much and will not brown as well as those made from more solid fats. They will also be tough and more likely to stick to the baking sheet. Don't substitute margarine or shortening when the recipe calls specifically for butter.

- If a cookie recipe calls for shortening, be aware that substituting butter or margarine will produce different results. Because butter and margarine melt more quickly than shortening, cookies made from butter will lose their shape and spread out more. Cookies made from shortening hold their shape better.
- Roll cookie dough out on a floured board unless otherwise specified.
- When making cut cookies, dip the cookie cutter in flour so it won't stick to the dough. Cut the cookies as close together as possible to reduce the quantity of leftover scraps to reroll; the more the dough is handled, the less tender your cookies will be.
- Ensure that all cookies in a batch are the same size and shape to ensure even cooking.
- Adjusting the temperature of the dough can help you get the cookie shape you want. If you want your cookies to maintain their shape during baking, chill them on the sheet for 15 minutes before placing them in the oven and increase the oven temperature by a few degrees. If you want the cookies to flatten, place them in the oven when the dough is at room temperature and lower the oven temperature by a few degrees.
- Place the baking sheet on the middle rack of your oven. Ensure that the sheet is narrower than the oven rack and doesn't touch the sides of the oven so the heat can circulate properly. For best results, bake one sheet of cookies at a time.
- Pay close attention to oven temperature, as cookies bake in a very short time and quickly become overcooked. If your oven is hotter than mine, you may need to lower the temperature by 25°F (10°C) or shorten the suggested baking time. You will get a feel for how your oven bakes after making a couple of batches of cookies.
- Begin checking to see if your cookies are done a few minutes before the time suggested in the recipe — oven temperatures vary, and every extra minute can make a big difference to the quality of cookies. Undercooked cookies are better than overcooked cookies. They should be a bit soft in the center when they are removed from the oven.

Drop cookies are done when they spring back into shape when you touch them lightly. Crisp cookies are done when lightly browned.

- Remove cookies from the sheet within 3 minutes of taking them out of the oven unless the recipe specifies otherwise. Using a lifter, transfer warm cookies to a wire rack to cool.
- Most cookies can be stored at room temperature for up to 3 weeks in an airtight container. Crisp cookies should be stored in a container with a loose-fitting lid, unless you live in a humid climate, in which case they should be covered tightly. If crisp cookies do soften, heating them in a 300°F (150°C) oven for 5 minutes will crisp them up.
- Most cookie dough can be frozen for up to 6 months, and most cookies freeze well. To freeze cookies, let cool completely and place in airtight freezer bags with a sheet of waxed paper between layers.

Making Perfect Brownies, Bars and Squares

- Use heavy metal baking pans for best results. If all you have is a glass baking dish, reduce the oven temperature by 25°F (10°C) and decrease the baking time slightly.
- Grease pans only if the recipe specifies. Unnecessary or excessive greasing will cause cakes to be gummy.
- Don't overbeat batter. When adding flour alternately with a liquid, keep the mixing to an absolute minimum, mixing only until the flour and liquid are incorporated into the batter. If using an electric mixer, beat on low speed. Overmixing will make the cake tough.
- When pouring batter into a baking pan, spread it evenly and take care to fill all corners so the baked cake will come out even. Use a spatula to spread the batter gently across the bottom of the pan and into the corners in a smooth, even layer without touching the sides of the pan.
- Once the batter is in the baking pan, bang the pan on the counter two or three times. This will eliminate any large air pockets that will create holes in the finished product.
- For bars and squares with a crust topped by a fluid batter, the crust must be baked before the batter is added to prevent it from becoming soggy. All the recipes in this book have taken this into account and are written accordingly. Follow the recipe instructions.

- The position of the baking pan in the oven influences how the product turns out. Center the pan on the middle rack of the oven. For best results, bake only one cake at a time. If you are baking multiple cakes, make sure the pans don't touch each other or the sides of the oven. And don't place one pan directly underneath another.
- Since temperatures (and therefore baking times) can vary dramatically between ovens, check for doneness a few minutes before the time indicated in the recipe. Your cake is done when a tester inserted in the center comes out clean and dry, the cake shrinks slightly from the sides of the pan, and the top springs back when touched lightly in the center.
- Most brownies, bars and squares should be cooled completely in the pan before cutting. To prevent cakes from becoming soggy, cool them in the pan on a wire rack. This allows the bottom of the pan to be cooled by circulating air.
- Sometimes it is appropriate to cut cakes before they are completely cooled. If the cake has a sticky filling, run a knife around the edge of the pan to loosen it as soon as it comes out of the oven. Crispy bars should be cut while still warm to prevent them from shattering. Then place the pan on a rack to cool.
- When cutting brownies, bars and squares, use a sharp knife and a gentle, sawing motion to avoid squashing the cake. Brownies, bars and squares can be cut into a variety of sizes. If you are trying to stretch the quantity, cut smaller sizes. As a general rule, the thicker and richer the cake, the smaller each portion should be.
- Store brownies, bars and squares in a tightly covered container or in the baking pan, covered tightly with foil. Make sure they are completely cooled before storing.

Making Perfect Cakes

- To prepare your baking pan, coat generously with shortening (unless otherwise specified) and dust lightly with flour. For chocolate cakes, I sometimes dust lightly with unsweetened cocoa powder. Pans for foam cakes are never greased.
- Use the flour indicated in the recipe. Do not substitute.
- Mix ingredients according to the instructions in the recipe. Pans should be filled about three-quarters full, as cakes will rise during baking. Spread batter evenly to the sides and fill corners. Tap the filled

pan lightly on the counter to get rid of any air bubbles that may have formed.

- Place the pan in the center of the oven, so that it is not touching the sides, and bake for the time stated in the recipe. For best results, bake one cake at a time. Cake is done when the top is lightly browned and the sides shrink away a little from the pan, or when you press lightly in the center of the cake and it springs back. I usually insert a toothpick in the center — if it comes out clean and dry, the cake is done.
- When you remove the pan from the oven, place it on a wire rack to cool for about 10 minutes. Then take a knife and loosen the cake around the edges. Invert pan onto a plate, then back onto the rack to cool completely.
- If you are frosting the cake, wait until it is completely cooled or it will become soggy. Brush off any loose pieces or crumbs. Spoon about half the frosting onto the top of the cake and, with a knife, start swirling over top. Then work toward the sides and cover them with a swirling motion. You can also get a good effect by frosting the sides before the top.
- Decorate to suit your taste, or the occasion, using colored icings, fruits, nuts, chocolate curls and so on.

Making a Perfect Pie Crust

Many people shy away from pie-making because they can't make good pastry. It is important to remember two things: keep all the ingredients as cold as possible and work the dough as little as possible.

The principal ingredients in a pie crust are flour, fat and liquid. My greatest problem was in adding the liquid to the flour-fat mixture. It is nearly impossible for a recipe to tell you the exact amount of liquid to use, mainly because flours vary. If you use too little, your crust may be crumbly instead of flaky, and if you use too much, you will end up with a tough crust. Pie dough should be soft and semi-dry — not sticky or doughy, but moist enough to hold its shape.

All-purpose flour is the most popular choice, as it makes a tender, flaky crust. It should be sifted once before measuring. The choice of fat is more varied. Lard makes excellent pastry, but most people steer away from it because we're all trying to reduce our fat intake. I like to use shortening. Whichever fat is used, it should be well chilled before you add it. Using your fingers to work the fat into the flour

sometimes works best. Pastries made with lard or shortening usually do not require chilling, but pastries made with a large amount of butter do.

Once you have found the right combination, stick with it. Trying to find this combination is what causes people to give up. As my mom used to say, just add enough that it feels or looks right. Her pies were delicious. You have to be flexible to be a good pastry maker, as the dough you have always used may, at times, handle differently because of room temperature, humidity or a slight variation in measuring your ingredients. So persevere!

- While preheating the oven, place a baking sheet on the rack where you will be baking the pie. When the pie is ready for baking, place it on the baking sheet and bake for the required time.
- Sift the flour once and then measure accurately into the mixing bowl with the other dry ingredients.
- Cut in the shortening (or fat) with a pastry blender or two knives until the pieces are the size of small peas. An experienced pie baker may want to do this by hand.
- To make your pastry extra tender and flaky, divide the shortening in half. Cut in the first half until the mixture resembles cornmeal. Then cut in the remaining half until mixture resembles small peas.
- Add liquid slowly. Sprinkle 1 tbsp (15 mL) of the water over part of the flour-shortening mixture. Gently toss with a fork and push to one side of the bowl. Sprinkle the next tablespoon of water over the dry part, mix lightly and push over to the moistened part. Repeat until all of the mixture is moistened. Gather up mixture with your fingers and form into a ball. If you are making a two-crust pie, divide the dough into lower and upper crust and form each of these into a ball.
- If using a food processor, place the flour and salt, if used, into the bowl and pulse once or twice, just to blend. Cut the cold shortening into chunks and add to bowl. Process briefly, in intervals, until the mixture resembles coarse crumbs. Add the water and pulse the dough until it holds together in a ball and feels like the right consistency.
- Turn the dough out onto a lightly floured working surface, flatten ball slightly and roll out to 1/8-inch (0.25 cm) thickness. Roll the dough from the center out to the edge, using light strokes. Never roll completely across. Dust with more flour underneath as required, but do not turn dough over. If your dough is sticky, chill for 15 to 30 minutes before rolling.

- Roll dough on waxed paper or between two sheets of waxed paper to prevent sticking. If any tears occur, do not reroll your pastry. Just patch it up.
- To transfer your pastry to the pie plate, roll it carefully over your rolling pin, then unroll over the pie plate, fitting it loosely onto the bottom and sides. You can also fold the pastry in half, place it gently into your pan, and then open up and fit into your pie plate. Lift the edges while easing into pan to avoid shrinking, but do not stretch the dough to fit.
- For a single crust, fit the dough loosely into the bottom and sides of the pan. Trim the dough ½ to 1 inch (1 to 2.5 cm) beyond the edge. Fold under and flute the edge, or press all around the rim with the tines of a fork. If your recipe calls for a baked pie shell, prick the bottom and sides well with a fork so the shell won't puff up while baking. If the crust and filling are to be baked together, do not prick the pastry.
- For a double crust, fit the lower crust into the pan. Trim it even with the rim of your pie plate and moisten the edge. After adding the pie filling, add the top crust and trim ½ inch (1 cm) beyond the edge. Tuck top under the edge of the lower crust to seal in the juices. Crimp or flute the edges, making sure the edges are hooked onto the rim of the pan. Slash the upper crust with several slits to allow steam to escape, using whatever design you wish.
- Some people like to cover the edges of the pie plate with a strip of foil to prevent overbrowning, but be sure to remove the foil about 15 minutes before the end of the baking time.
- If prebaking the crust, place a sheet of foil over the dough and put pie weights, rice or beans on the foil to prevent bubbles. Bake as directed in recipe, then remove the weights and foil, brush crust with a beaten egg and return to oven to bake for 1 to 2 minutes more, until golden.

Making a Perfect Meringue
- Use a small, deep bowl unless you are using more than 4 egg whites. Clean the bowl and beaters first to make sure there isn't any grease or oil on them.
- Separate your eggs carefully so that there is not even a tiny bit of egg yolk in the whites.
- For maximum volume, egg whites should be at room temperature before you beat them.

- Beat egg whites with cream of tartar, as this stabilizes the whites. Beat on high speed until foamy and soft peaks form when the beaters are lifted. If you don't have any cream of tartar, use 1 tsp (5 mL) lemon juice, unless you have more than 2 or 3 whites.
- When adding sugar, do so gradually, and on medium speed, adding sugar a spoonful at a time. When all of the sugar has been added, increase speed and beat until stiff but still glossy and pliable peaks form.
- Pour your hot filling into a baked, cooled crust. Set aside and let a thin film form on the filling. Spoon the meringue onto the hot filling around the edge of the crust, so that there is less chance of the meringue shrinking and weeping. Then gently spread the meringue with a spatula around the edge of the pie crust until it is well sealed. Using the spatula, spread the meringue from the edges toward the center, swirling but not making high peaks. Cover the entire pie.
- After baking, cool your meringue pie on a wire rack, at room temperature, for 3 hours before cutting. To cut slices easily, be sure to use a sharp knife. After each cut, dip your knife in hot water.

Baking Problems (and How to Solve Them)
Muffins
Muffins are too hard.
- There was too much flour and not enough liquid in the batter. Try using ¼ cup (50 mL) less flour.
- You may have stirred too long and hard. Try mixing for only 10 seconds.

Muffins are flat or spreading.
- If they are spreading out over the top of the tins, don't fill the cups as full.
- There may have been too much liquid in the batter. Try using ¼ cup (50 mL) less liquid.

Muffins are tough and soggy, with peaks in the center.
- You may have overmixed, which toughens the batter.
- Underbaking could be causing the problem, as ovens vary in temperature. Try turning up your oven by 25°F (10°C) and shorten the baking time.

Muffins rise high, but fall flat in the center.
- There was not enough flour in the batter. Increase the amount by about ¼ cup (50 mL).

- Sometimes the eggs are so large that they increase the ratio of liquid ingredients. Use large eggs but not extra-large.

Muffins do not brown.
- Your oven rack may be too high or too low. If muffins are baked on the lowest rack, they may burn on the bottom before being done on top. If muffins are baked on the highest rack, they will get too brown on top. Always use the middle rack for even browning.

Muffins are coarse-textured.
- The batter was not mixed enough and/or the muffins were baked at too low a temperature.

Cookies

Cookies stick to the baking sheet.
- Check the recipe to see if the sheet should be greased. If not, there may be ingredients in the cookies, such as raisins, that are causing them to stick. In that case, transfer the cookies to a wire rack as soon as they come out of the oven so they won't have a chance to stick to the sheet.

Cookies crumble or break when you remove them from the baking sheet.
- The sheet should be greased.
- The cookies may have been left on the hot sheet for too long after they were removed from the oven. Transfer cookies from the sheet to a wire rack within 3 minutes.

Cookies are too dry.
- Ingredients may not have been measured properly. Always measure ingredients accurately in a standard measuring cup.
- The eggs may not have been large enough. Always use large eggs for baking.
- The cookies may have been overbaked.

Cookies spread out too much.
- You may have used too much butter, shortening or liquid, or too little flour. Always measure ingredients accurately in a standard measuring cup.

Cookies run into each other instead of baking separately.
- You may have made the cookies too large and/or placed them too close together on the baking sheet. Cookies should be the size indicated in the recipe and should be placed far enough apart (most recipes suggest 2 inches/5 cm for medium-sized cookies) to allow for the appropriate amount of spreading.

- A dough that is too thin will also spread more than usual. Check to make sure you've measured the ingredients accurately.

Cookies bake unevenly.
- Use heavy-duty baking sheets.
- Make sure all the cookies are the same size and that the baking sheet is placed in the center of the oven on the middle rack. It should not touch the sides of the oven. Since the heat in the rear of the oven is usually more intense than in the front, rotate the sheet halfway through the baking process.

Cookies are too well done.
- Check to ensure that your oven temperature is not too hot, and begin checking for doneness a couple of minutes before the suggested baking time.
- Make cookies the size specified in the recipe and place them the recommended distance apart on the sheet.

Cookies are burned on the bottom only.
- The baking sheet may be placed too low in the oven. It should be centered on the middle rack.
- Use a light-colored sheet. Those with a dark surface absorb heat, which may cause cookie bottoms to brown.

Cakes, Brownies, Bars and Squares

Cake falls.
- There was too much liquid, sugar, leavening agent, butter or shortening in the batter. Check your measurements.
- There was not enough flour in the batter.
- The egg whites were beaten too much.
- The oven was not hot enough and/or the baking time was too short. Increase the temperature by 25°F (10°C) and note the results.

Cake expands over the top of the pan.
- The pan may be too small. Check the recipe for the proper size.
- There was too much batter in the pan. Batter should fill the pan only one-half to three-quarters full, depending on the cake.
- There was too much shortening, sugar or leavening agent in the batter. Check your measurements.

Cake texture is coarse and dense.
- The oven temperature may be too low. Increase the temperature by 25°F (10°C) and note the results.

- There was not enough fat in the batter or you have not creamed the shortening or butter well enough. Shortening or butter should be well beaten with sugar until the mixture is smooth and creamy.
- The batter was beaten too much after the flour was added.

Cake is too dry.
- The cake was baked for too long or at too high a temperature.
- There was not enough fat, sugar or liquid in the batter. Check your measurements.
- The batter contained too much leavening agent (such as baking powder) or flour.
- The egg whites were beaten until they were too stiff.
- Cocoa powder was substituted for chocolate without adding more fat.

Cake is heavy.
- There was not enough sugar or leavening agent in the batter. Check your measurements.
- There was too much liquid, fat or egg in the batter.
- The batter was overmixed.
- Your oven was too hot. Reduce the temperature by 25°F (10°C) and note the results.

Cracks or bumps appear on top of cake.
- There was too much flour or sugar in the batter, or not enough liquid. Check your measurements.
- Your oven was too hot. Reduce the temperature by 25°F (10°C) and note the results.
- The batter was overmixed or spread unevenly in the pan.

Cake has holes in it.
- The batter was not thoroughly mixed.
- There was too much egg in the batter — perhaps the eggs were too large, or you used too many. Always use large (never extra-large) eggs unless another size is called for in the recipe, and never add an extra egg just to use it up. Do not use 2 medium or small eggs as the equivalent of 1 large egg.

Cake crumbles when sliced.
- There was too much fat, sugar or leavening agent in the batter. Always measure ingredients accurately.
- The oven was not hot enough and/or the baking time was too short. Increase the temperature by 25°F (10°C) and note the results.
- The cake was removed from the pan before it was completely cooled.

Cake is soggy or has streaks at the bottom.
- There was too much leavening agent or sugar in the batter.
- There was too much liquid in the batter, or the eggs were underbeaten.
- The ingredients were not mixed thoroughly enough. When mixing, ensure that ingredients are blended.
- The oven was not hot enough and/or the baking time was too short. Increase the temperature by 25°F (10°C) and note the results.

Cake rises higher on one side.
- The batter was spread unevenly in the pan or the pan is slightly warped.
- The pan was set too close to another pan or to the side of the oven.
- The oven temperature is uneven or the oven rack is not level.

Cake sticks to pan.
- The pan was not greased properly. Follow the instructions in the recipe.
- The cake was left in the pan for too long. Cool in the pan only for the amount of time indicated in the recipe, then remove to a wire rack to cool completely.

Cake burns on bottom.
- The heat distribution in your oven is uneven. Rotate the pan halfway through baking.
- Your oven was too hot. Reduce the temperature by 25°F (10°C) and note the results.
- The pan was set too close to the side of the oven.

Crust is too sticky and moist.
- You used too much sugar. Check the recipe to make sure you measured correctly.
- The baking time was too short.

Crust is too pale.
- There was not enough fat, sugar or leavening agent in the batter. Always measure ingredients accurately.
- There was too much flour in the batter.
- The pan may be too large. Check the recipe for the proper size.
- There was not enough batter in the pan. Batter should fill the pan one-half to three-quarters full, depending on the cake.
- The oven was not hot enough. Increase the temperature by 25°F (10°C) and note the results.

Classic Muffins

Basic Muffins

Makes 12 muffins
- Preheat oven to 400°F (200°C)
- Muffin tin, lightly greased

2 cups	all-purpose flour	500 mL
4 tsp	baking powder	20 mL
1/2 tsp	salt	2 mL
2 tbsp	granulated sugar	25 mL
1 cup	milk	250 mL
2	eggs, beaten	2
3 tbsp	melted butter, margarine or shortening	45 mL

1. In a large bowl, sift together flour, baking powder, salt and sugar. Make a well in the center.
2. In another bowl, combine milk, beaten eggs and melted butter. Pour into dry ingredients. Mix just until blended, no more than 15 to 20 strokes. Do not overmix.
3. Spoon batter into prepared muffin tin. Bake in preheated oven for 15 to 18 minutes or until golden brown.

Variations *Apple Cinnamon Muffins: Add 1 tsp (5 mL) ground cinnamon, 2 tbsp (25 mL) butter and 1 1/2 cups (375 mL) finely chopped apples.*

Bacon Muffins: Fry 5 strips side bacon until crisp; crumble. Set aside to cool. Substitute bacon and drippings for the melted butter.

Blueberry Muffins: Substitute packed brown sugar for granulated sugar. Dredge 1 1/2 cups (375 mL) frozen blueberries in 2 tbsp (25 mL) of flour taken from basic recipe. (This prevents blueberries from sinking.) Fold berries into batter.

Cheese Muffins: Add 1 cup (250 mL) shredded sharp Cheddar cheese to dry ingredients.

Cornmeal Muffins: Use 3/4 cup (175 mL) cornmeal and 1 1/4 cups (300 mL) all-purpose flour instead of 2 cups (500 mL) all-purpose flour. Add 1 tbsp (15 mL) more granulated sugar (or omit sugar completely). Use 1 egg instead of 2 eggs.

Double Top Muffins: Place 1 cooked, dried apricot half in bottom of each greased muffin cup; fill two-thirds full with batter. Top with a crumb mixture of 1/2 cup (125 mL) firmly packed brown sugar, 1/2 cup (125 mL) softened butter or margarine, 1/3 cup (75 mL) all-purpose flour and 1 tsp (5 mL) ground cinnamon.

Dried Fruit and Nut Muffins: Add 1/2 cup (125 mL) dried fruit (raisins, figs, chopped pitted dates) and/or nuts.

Oatmeal Muffins: Substitute 1 cup (250 mL) quick-cooking rolled oats for 1 cup (250 mL) flour. Add 1/4 cup (50 mL) more flour.

Orange Muffins: Add 1 tbsp (15 mL) grated orange zest to dry ingredients. Substitute orange juice for milk.

Pumpkin Muffins: Add 1 tsp (5 mL) ground cinnamon and 1/2 tsp (2 mL) ground nutmeg to dry ingredients. Add 2/3 cup (150 mL) canned pumpkin purée (not pie filling) with the milk.

Quick Tea Cake Muffins: Increase sugar to 1/2 cup (125 mL) and eggs to 3 eggs. Reduce milk to 3/4 cup (175 mL). Bake at 425°F (220°C) for about 15 minutes.

Rice Muffins: Use 1 cup (250 mL) flour and 1 cup (250 mL) cold boiled rice. Use 1 egg instead of 2 eggs and 2/3 cup (150 mL) milk instead of 1 cup (250 mL). Add rice last, mixing in lightly. Bake for about 30 minutes.

Rich Biscuit-Style Muffins

Makes 12 muffins
- Preheat oven to 400°F (200°C)
- Muffin tin, greased

2 cups	all-purpose flour	500 mL
2 1/2 tsp	baking powder	12 mL
2 tbsp	granulated sugar	25 mL
1/2 tsp	salt	2 mL
1/2 cup	shortening	125 mL
1	egg, well beaten	1
3/4 cup	milk	175 mL

1. In a bowl, sift together flour, baking powder, sugar and salt. Using a pastry blender, cut in shortening.
2. In another bowl, combine egg and milk. Add to dry ingredients; stir until moistened.
3. Spoon batter into prepared muffin tin. Bake in preheated oven for 25 minutes.

Variations *Cranberry-Cube Muffins: Fill muffin tins one-third full. Cut 1 cup (250 mL) canned jellied cranberry sauce into 1/2-inch (1 cm) cubes. Sprinkle over batter. Spoon in the remaining batter.*

Cheese-Caraway Muffins: Add 1 cup (250 mL) shredded sharp processed cheese and 1 tsp (5 mL) caraway seed to flour mixture.

Bacon Muffins: Add ½ cup (125 mL) crumbled crisp bacon to dry ingredients.

Raisin, Nut or Date Muffins: Add ½ to ¾ cup (125 mL to 175 mL) raisins, chopped nuts or coarsely cut dates.

Quick-Bake Muffins

Makes 6 muffins
- Preheat oven to 400°F (200°C)
- Muffin tin, greased or paper-lined

1 cup	self-rising flour	250 mL
3 tbsp	mayonnaise	45 mL
½ cup	milk	125 mL

1. In a bowl, combine flour and mayonnaise. Add milk, a little at a time, stirring just until moistened.
2. Form dough into balls; place into prepared muffin tin. Bake in preheated oven for about 20 minutes.

Tip *If you don't have self-rising flour, use 1½ tsp (7 mL) baking powder to 1 cup (250 mL) all-purpose flour.*

Self-Iced Muffins

Makes 12 large muffins
- Preheat oven to 375°F (190°C)
- Muffin tin, paper-lined

1 cup	packed brown sugar	250 mL
1 cup	margarine	250 mL
2 cups	all-purpose flour	500 mL
1	egg, beaten	1
1 cup	milk	250 mL
1 tsp	white vinegar	5 mL
1 tsp	baking soda	5 mL
1 cup	dates, dredged in flour	250 mL
1 cup	raisins, dredged in flour	250 mL
1 tsp	ground cinnamon	5 mL
1 tsp	vanilla	5 mL

1. In a bowl, combine sugar and margarine; beat well. Add flour. Set aside ¾ cup (175 mL) of this mixture for topping.
2. To the remaining mixture add egg, milk, vinegar and baking soda; combine well. Add dates, raisins, cinnamon and vanilla.
3. Spoon batter into prepared muffin tin. Sprinkle with reserved mixture. Bake in preheated oven for 20 to 30 minutes.

Mom's Old-Fashioned Oatmeal Muffins

Makes 12 muffins
- Preheat oven to 350°F (180°C)
- Muffin tin, greased

1½ cups	quick-cooking rolled oats	375 mL
1 cup	all-purpose flour	250 mL
1 tsp	baking powder	5 mL
1 tsp	baking soda	5 mL
½ tsp	salt	2 mL
1 tsp	ground cinnamon	5 mL
¾ cup	packed brown sugar	175 mL
1	egg, lightly beaten	1
¼ cup	vegetable oil	50 mL
1 cup	plain yogurt	250 mL
½ cup	raisins	125 mL

1. In a bowl, combine oats, flour, baking powder, baking soda, salt, cinnamon and brown sugar. Make a well in the center.
2. In another bowl, whisk together egg, oil and yogurt. Add to dry ingredients; stir just until blended. Fold in raisins.
3. Spoon batter into prepared muffin tin. Bake in preheated oven for 20 to 25 minutes.

Golden Oatmeal Muffins

Makes 12 muffins
- Preheat oven to 400°F (200°C)
- Muffin tin, greased

1 cup	quick-cooking rolled oats	250 mL
1 cup	buttermilk or sour cream	250 mL
½ cup	vegetable oil or melted shortening	125 mL
½ cup	firmly packed brown sugar	125 mL
1	egg, beaten	1
1 cup	all-purpose flour	250 mL
1 tsp	baking powder	5 mL
½ tsp	baking soda	2 mL
1 tsp	salt	5 mL

1. In a bowl, combine oats and buttermilk; let stand for 5 minutes. Add oil, brown sugar and egg.
2. In another bowl, combine flour, baking powder, baking soda and salt. Add to oat mixture, stirring just until moistened.
3. Spoon batter into prepared muffin tin. Bake in preheated oven for 15 to 20 minutes or until golden brown.

Best-Ever Bran Muffins

Makes 18 large muffins
- Preheat oven to 375°F (190°C)
- Muffin tins, greased

2½ cups	all-purpose flour	625 mL
¾ cup	packed brown sugar	175 mL
1½ cups	natural bran	375 mL
1½ tsp	ground cinnamon	7 mL
1 tsp	ground nutmeg	5 mL
2 tsp	baking soda	10 mL
½ tsp	salt	2 mL
2	eggs	2
¾ cup	vegetable oil	175 mL
2 cups	buttermilk	500 mL
¼ cup	light (fancy) molasses	50 mL
1 cup	raisins (dark or yellow)	250 mL

1. In a bowl, combine flour, brown sugar, bran, cinnamon, nutmeg, baking soda and salt. Make a well in the center.
2. In another bowl, whisk together eggs, oil, buttermilk and molasses. Pour into flour mixture; stir just until blended. Fold in raisins.
3. Spoon batter into prepared muffin tins. Bake in preheated oven for 20 to 25 minutes.

Honey Bran Flakes Muffins

Makes 12 large muffins
- Preheat oven to 400°F (200°C)
- Muffin tin, greased

1¼ cups	all-purpose flour	300 mL
¾ tsp	baking soda	4 mL
½ tsp	baking powder	2 mL
½ tsp	salt	2 mL
1½ cups	bran flakes cereal	375 mL
1¼ cups	buttermilk	300 mL
¼ cup	vegetable oil	50 mL
¼ cup	liquid honey	50 mL
1	egg	1
½ cup	dark raisins	125 mL

1. In a bowl, combine flour, baking soda, baking powder, salt and bran flakes.
2. In another bowl, combine buttermilk, oil, honey and egg; whisk well. Pour into flour mixture; stir just until moist and blended. Fold in raisins.
3. Spoon batter into muffin tin. Bake in preheated oven for 15 to 20 minutes.

Nutritious Raisin Bran Muffins

Makes 12 muffins
- Preheat oven to 400°F (200°C)
- Muffin tin, greased

1 cup	all-bran or natural bran cereal	250 mL
1 cup	milk	250 mL
1	egg	1
3 tbsp	butter, margarine or shortening, melted	45 mL
1 tsp	vanilla	5 mL
1 cup	raisins	250 mL
1 cup	all-purpose flour	250 mL
1 tbsp	baking powder	15 mL
½ cup	packed brown sugar	125 mL
1 tsp	ground cinnamon	5 mL
½ tsp	salt	2 mL

1. In a bowl, combine bran and milk. Add egg, butter and vanilla; mix well. Stir in raisins.
2. In another bowl, sift together flour and baking powder. Add brown sugar, cinnamon and salt; mix well. Make a well in the center; add bran mixture. Stir just until blended.
3. Spoon batter into prepared muffin tin. Bake in preheated oven for 15 to 20 minutes.

Sour Cream Raisin Bran Muffins

Makes 12 muffins
- Preheat oven to 375°F (190°C)
- Muffin tin, greased or paper-lined

½ cup	butter or margarine	125 mL
¾ cup	packed brown sugar	175 mL
1	egg, lightly beaten	1
1 cup	all-purpose flour	250 mL
½ tsp	baking soda	2 mL
½ cup	bran flour or natural bran	125 mL
1 cup	sour cream	250 mL
1 tsp	vanilla	5 mL
¾ cup	raisins	175 mL

1. In a bowl, cream together butter, brown sugar and egg. Add all-purpose flour, baking soda, bran flour, sour cream, vanilla and raisins; stir just until moist and blended.
2. Spoon batter into prepared muffin tin. Bake in preheated oven for 20 to 25 minutes.

Wheat Germ Muffins

Makes 18 to 24 muffins

- Preheat oven to 400°F (200°C)
- Muffin tins, greased or paper-lined

2 cups	all-purpose flour	500 mL
2 tbsp	baking powder	25 mL
1 tsp	baking soda	5 mL
1½ cups	wheat germ	375 mL
1 cup	firmly packed brown sugar	250 mL
2	eggs	2
1½ cups	milk	375 mL
½ cup	vegetable oil	125 mL

1. In a bowl, combine flour, baking powder, baking soda, wheat germ and brown sugar; mix until well blended.
2. In another bowl, whisk together eggs, milk and oil. Pour into dry ingredients; stir just until blended.
3. Spoon batter into prepared muffin tins. Bake in preheated oven for 15 to 20 minutes.

Wholesome Wheat Germ Muffins

Makes 12 muffins

- Preheat oven to 400°F (200°C)
- Muffin tin, greased

1½ cups	all-purpose flour	375 mL
¼ cup	packed brown sugar	50 mL
1 tbsp	baking powder	15 mL
½ tsp	salt	2 mL
⅔ cup	wheat germ	150 mL
½ cup	raisins	125 mL
1 cup	milk	250 mL
1	egg	1
2 tbsp	melted margarine, cooled	25 mL

1. In a bowl, combine flour, brown sugar, baking powder and salt; mix well. Add wheat germ and raisins.
2. In another bowl, whisk together milk, egg and margarine. Add to dry ingredients; stir just until moistened. Do not overmix.
3. Spoon batter into prepared muffin tin. Bake in preheated oven for about 20 minutes.

Southern Biscuit Muffins

Makes 12 large muffins

- Preheat oven to 400°F (200°C)
- Muffin tin, greased

2½ cups	all-purpose flour	625 mL
¼ cup	granulated sugar	50 mL
1½ tbsp	baking powder	22 mL
¾ cup	chilled butter or margarine	175 mL
1 cup	cold milk	250 mL

1. In a bowl, combine flour, sugar and baking powder. Add butter; mix until crumbly. Add milk; stir just until moist.
2. Spoon batter into prepared muffin tin. Bake in preheated oven for 20 minutes or until golden brown.

Tip *Delicious with jam, jelly or honey, these muffins are just like baking powder biscuits.*

Creamy Rice Muffins

Makes 12 muffins

- Preheat oven to 350°F (180°C)
- Muffin tin, greased

2 cups	milk or water	500 mL
1 cup	white rice (not instant)	250 mL
¼ cup	butter or margarine	50 mL
¼ cup	granulated sugar	50 mL
2	eggs	2
1 cup	sour cream	250 mL
¾ cup	all-purpose flour	175 mL
1 tsp	baking powder	5 mL
¼ tsp	salt	1 mL

1. In a saucepan over medium-high heat, bring milk to a boil; add rice. Cook, covered, until thick and milk is absorbed. Set aside to cool.
2. In a bowl, cream together butter, sugar, eggs and sour cream. Add flour, baking powder and salt; mix well. Add cooled rice; stir just until blended.
3. Spoon batter into prepared muffin tins. Bake in preheated oven for about 45 minutes.

Tip *Delicious served warm with sour cream and sliced strawberries.*

Rice Pudding Muffins

Makes 12 muffins
- Preheat oven to 400°F (200°C)
- Muffin tin, greased

1½ cups	all-purpose flour	375 mL
¼ cup	granulated sugar	50 mL
1½ tsp	baking powder	7 mL
½ tsp	baking soda	2 mL
¼ tsp	salt	1 mL
1 tsp	ground cinnamon	5 mL
1 tsp	ground nutmeg	5 mL
1 cup	cooked white rice, cooled	250 mL
1	egg	1
2 tbsp	butter, melted	25 mL
1¼ cups	buttermilk	300 mL
	Confectioner's (icing) sugar	

1. In a bowl, combine flour, sugar, baking powder, baking soda, salt, cinnamon and nutmeg. Add rice.

2. In another bowl, whisk together egg, butter and buttermilk. Add to flour mixture; stir just until moist.

3. Spoon batter into prepared muffin tin. Bake in preheated oven for 15 to 20 minutes. Remove from tins; sprinkle with confectioner's sugar.

Esther's Savory Cheese Muffins

Makes 12 muffins
- Preheat oven to 425°F (220°C)
- Muffin tin, greased or paper-lined

2 cups	all-purpose flour	500 mL
3 tbsp	granulated sugar	45 mL
1 tbsp	baking powder	15 mL
½ tsp	grated lemon zest (optional)	2 mL
1	egg, lightly beaten	1
1 cup	milk	250 mL
¼ cup	melted butter or margarine	50 mL
1 cup	shredded Cheddar cheese, divided	250 mL

1. In a bowl, combine flour, sugar, baking powder and lemon zest (if using). Make a well in center of mixture.

2. In another bowl, combine egg, milk and butter; whisk well. Stir into flour mixture. Reserve 2 tbsp (25 mL) cheese for topping; add the remaining cheese to flour mixture. Mix until moist and blended.

3. Spoon batter into prepared muffin tin. Sprinkle tops with reserved cheese. Bake in preheated oven for 20 minutes or until golden brown.

Variations *This recipe originally called for ¾ tsp (4 mL) garlic salt. I don't use it, but you might want to give it a try.*

You can replace the 1 cup (250 mL) milk with ½ cup (125 mL) milk and ½ cup (125 mL) plain yogurt.

Cottage Cheese Muffins

Makes 12 muffins
- Preheat oven to 400°F (200°C)
- Muffin tin, greased

1	package (12 oz/375 g) dry cottage cheese	1
3 tbsp	granulated sugar	45 mL
2	eggs, lightly beaten	2
½ cup	melted butter or margarine	125 mL
Pinch	salt	Pinch
2 tsp	baking powder	10 mL
1 cup	all-purpose flour	250 mL

1. In a bowl, combine cottage cheese, sugar, eggs and butter; mix well. Add salt, baking powder and flour; stir just until blended.

2. Spoon batter into prepared muffin tin. Bake in preheated oven for 20 to 25 minutes or until lightly browned.

Tip *Delicious served warm with sour cream and thawed frozen strawberries.*

Variation *Use 2 cups (500 mL) dry cottage cheese and ½ cup (125 mL) creamed cottage cheese.*

Parmesan Muffins

Makes 12 muffins
- Preheat oven to 400°F (200°C)
- Muffin tin, greased or paper-lined

1	egg	1
½ cup	plain yogurt or sour cream	125 mL
1 cup	milk	250 mL
½ cup	melted butter or margarine	125 mL
2½ cups	all-purpose flour	625 mL
½ cup	freshly grated Parmesan cheese	125 mL
¼ cup	granulated sugar	50 mL
1 tbsp	baking powder	15 mL
1 tsp	salt	5 mL
½ tsp	dried basil	2 mL

1. In a bowl, combine egg, yogurt, milk and butter; whisk well.
2. In another bowl, combine flour, cheese, sugar, baking powder, salt and basil. Make a well in center of mixture; pour in egg mixture. Stir just until blended.
3. Spoon batter into prepared muffin tin. Bake in preheated oven for about 20 minutes.

Variations *Replace basil with ¼ tsp (1 mL) dried rosemary. Add ¼ cup (50 mL) yellow cornmeal to the dry ingredients.*

Replace basil with package of fine herbs from a store-bought pizza mix.

• •

Carrot Plus Muffins

Makes 18 to 24 muffins
- Preheat oven to 400°F (200°C)
- Muffin tins, greased

3 cups	all-purpose flour, divided	750 mL
1 tsp	baking powder	5 mL
½ tsp	baking soda	2 mL
½ tsp	salt	2 mL
½ tsp	ground cloves	2 mL
½ tsp	ground nutmeg	2 mL
1 tbsp	chopped candied ginger	15 mL
½ cup	granulated sugar	125 mL
½ cup	packed brown sugar	125 mL
½ cup	vegetable oil	125 mL
2	eggs	2
½ cup	apricot juice or orange juice	125 mL
1	can (14 oz/398 mL) apricots, drained (or 8 fresh ripe apricots, sliced), some slices reserved for topping	1
1 cup	grated carrots	250 mL
1 cup	grated rutabaga	250 mL
½ cup	chopped pecans	125 mL
TOPPING (OPTIONAL)		
1	package (8 oz/250 g) cream cheese, softened	1
¼ cup	apricot juice or orange juice	50 mL
½ cup	confectioner's (icing) sugar	125 mL

1. In a bowl, combine 2¾ cups (675 mL) of the flour, baking powder, baking soda, salt, cloves and nutmeg.

2. In another bowl, combine ginger and the remaining flour; mix well. Add to clove mixture.
3. In another bowl, combine granulated sugar, brown sugar and oil. Add eggs one at a time; whisk in juice. Pour into flour mixture, stirring just until moistened. Add apricots, carrots, rutabaga and pecans.
4. Spoon batter into prepared muffin tins. Bake in preheated oven for 20 to 25 minutes or until toothpick inserted in center comes out clean.
5. *If desired, prepare the topping:* In a bowl, combine cream cheese, juice and confectioner's sugar; mix well. Spread onto cooled muffins. Top each with a slice of apricot.

Tip *Rutabaga and carrots make a great combination. The result is a dense, moist muffin.*

• •

The Muffin Lady's Famous Rhubarb Muffins

Makes 18 muffins
- Preheat oven to 425°F (220°C)
- Muffin tins, greased or paper-lined

1½ cups	packed brown sugar	375 mL
¼ cup	vegetable oil	50 mL
2	eggs	2
2 tsp	vanilla	10 mL
1 cup	buttermilk	250 mL
1½ cups	finely diced rhubarb	375 mL
½ cup	chopped walnuts or pecans	125 mL
2½ cups	all-purpose flour	625 mL
1 tsp	baking powder	5 mL
1 tsp	baking soda	5 mL
½ tsp	salt	2 mL
TOPPING		
⅓ cup	granulated sugar	75 mL
1½ tsp	ground cinnamon	7 mL
1 tbsp	margarine, melted	15 mL

1. In a bowl, whisk together brown sugar, oil, eggs and vanilla; mix well. Add buttermilk, rhubarb and walnuts.
2. In another bowl, combine flour, baking powder, baking soda and salt. Add to rhubarb mixture; stir just until moist.
3. *Prepare the topping:* In another bowl, combine sugar, cinnamon and margarine.
4. Spoon batter into prepared muffin tins. Sprinkle with topping. Bake in preheated oven for about 20 minutes.

Carrot Pineapple Streusel Muffins

Makes 12 muffins
- Preheat oven to 400°F (200°C)
- Muffin tin, greased or paper-lined

STREUSEL TOPPING

¼ cup	lightly packed brown sugar	50 mL
¼ cup	chopped walnuts	50 mL

MUFFINS

1	package (15 oz/450 g) carrot raisin loaf cake mix	1
1 cup	undrained crushed pineapple	250 mL
1	egg	1
3 tbsp	vegetable oil	45 mL

1. *Prepare the topping:* In a bowl, combine sugar and walnuts; set aside.

2. *Prepare the muffins:* In another bowl, combine cake mix, pineapple, egg and oil; mix until smooth.

3. Spoon batter into prepared muffin tin. Sprinkle with topping. Bake in preheated oven for 20 minutes.

Special Carrot Puddings

Makes 12 muffins
- Preheat oven to 400°F (200°C)
- Muffin tin, greased

¾ cup	shortening	175 mL
½ cup	packed brown sugar	125 mL
1	egg	1
1¼ cups	all-purpose flour	300 mL
½ tsp	baking soda	2 mL
1 tsp	baking powder	5 mL
1 tsp	salt	5 mL
1 tbsp	water	15 mL
1 tbsp	freshly squeezed lemon juice	15 mL
1 tsp	vanilla	5 mL
2 cups	grated carrots	500 mL

1. In a bowl, combine shortening and brown sugar; mix well. Add egg, flour, baking soda, baking powder, salt, water, lemon juice, vanilla and carrots. Do not overmix.

2. Heat prepared muffin tin in oven for a few minutes. Spoon in batter. Bake in preheated oven for 20 minutes.

Tip *I serve these with meat dinners or with a green salad.*

Pumpkin Muffins

Makes 18 to 24 muffins
- Preheat oven to 400°F (200°C)
- Muffin tins, greased

1	can (14 oz/398 mL) pumpkin purée (not pie filling)	1
4	eggs	4
1½ cups	granulated sugar	375 mL
1½ cups	vegetable oil	375 mL
3 cups	all-purpose flour	750 mL
1 tbsp	ground cinnamon	15 mL
2 tsp	baking soda	10 mL
2 tsp	baking powder	10 mL
1 tsp	salt	5 mL
1 cup	raisins	250 mL

1. In a bowl, combine pumpkin purée and eggs. Add sugar and oil; mix well.

2. In another bowl, combine flour, cinnamon, baking soda, baking powder, salt and raisins. Add to pumpkin mixture, stirring just until blended.

3. Spoon batter into prepared muffin tins. Bake in preheated oven for 20 to 25 minutes.

Apple Crunch Muffins

Makes 12 small muffins
- Preheat oven to 375°F (190°C)
- Muffin tin, greased

1½ cups	all-purpose flour	375 mL
⅓ cup	granulated sugar	75 mL
2 tsp	baking powder	10 mL
½ tsp	salt	2 mL
½ cup	dry non-fat milk	125 mL
½ tsp	ground cinnamon	2 mL
¼ cup	shortening, softened	50 mL
1	egg	1
½ cup	water	125 mL
1 cup	finely chopped peeled apples	250 mL

TOPPING

⅓ cup	firmly packed brown sugar	75 mL
⅓ cup	finely chopped nuts	75 mL
½ tsp	ground cinnamon	2 mL

1. In a bowl, combine flour, sugar, baking powder, salt, milk and cinnamon; mix well. Add shortening, egg, water and apples. Mix quickly, just until blended. Spoon batter into prepared muffin tin.

2. *Prepare the topping:* In a bowl, combine brown sugar, nuts and cinnamon; sprinkle over muffins. Bake in preheated oven for 20 to 25 minutes.

Tip *I always mix batter in stainless steel bowls.*

Esther's Special Banana Muffins

Makes 12 muffins
- Preheat oven to 425°F (220°C)
- Muffin tin, paper-lined

1 cup	granulated sugar	250 mL
2	eggs	2
1/2 cup	margarine, softened	125 mL
2 cups	all-purpose flour	500 mL
2 tsp	baking soda	10 mL
3 to 4	ripe bananas, mashed	3 to 4

1. In a bowl, cream together sugar and eggs until well mixed. Add margarine; blend well. Add flour and baking soda; mix until a loose dough forms. Add bananas; stir just until moist.

2. Spoon batter into prepared muffin tin. Bake in preheated oven for 15 to 20 minutes or until golden brown. Turn pans around, back to front, for last 5 minutes of baking.

Tip *If you plan to double the recipe, use only 1 1/2 cups (375 mL) sugar.*

Banana Muffins Plus

Makes 12 muffins
- Preheat oven to 350°F (180°C)
- Muffin tin, greased or paper-lined

1 cup	granulated sugar	250 mL
1/2 cup	butter or shortening	125 mL
1	egg	1
3	ripe bananas, mashed	3
1/2 tsp	salt	2 mL
2 tbsp	orange juice or milk	25 mL
1 1/2 tsp	baking powder	7 mL
1/2 tsp	baking soda	2 mL
2 cups	all-purpose flour	500 mL
1/2 cup	semisweet chocolate chips (optional)	125 mL

1. In a bowl, cream together sugar, butter and egg; mix well. Add bananas, salt, orange juice, baking powder, baking soda, flour and chocolate chips (if using); stir well.

2. Spoon batter into prepared muffin tin. Bake in preheated oven for 20 to 30 minutes.

Banana Bran Muffins

Makes 30 to 36 muffins
- Preheat oven to 375°F (190°C)
- Muffin tins, greased or paper-lined

1/2 cup	granulated sugar	125 mL
1 cup	packed brown sugar	250 mL
1 cup	vegetable oil	250 mL
3	eggs	3
1 tsp	vanilla	5 mL
1 1/2 cups	mashed ripe banana	375 mL
3 cups	natural bran	750 mL
1 1/2 cups	buttermilk	375 mL
3 cups	all-purpose flour	750 mL
1 tbsp	baking powder	15 mL
1 tbsp	baking soda	15 mL
1 tsp	salt	5 mL
1 cup	raisins	250 mL

1. In a bowl, combine granulated sugar, brown sugar and oil. Beat in eggs, one at a time. Add vanilla and banana; mix well. Add bran and buttermilk.

2. In another bowl, combine flour, baking powder, baking soda and salt. Add to banana mixture; stir until ingredients are just mixed. Do not overmix. Fold in raisins.

3. Spoon batter into prepared muffin tins. Bake in preheated oven for 15 to 20 minutes.

Tip *Feel free to halve the recipe. Or simply freeze the muffins and use as needed.*

Banana Date Nut Muffins

Makes 12 muffins
- Preheat oven to 400°F (200°C)
- Muffin tin, greased or paper-lined

1	package (7 oz/210 g) bran muffin mix with dates or corn muffin mix	1
1 cup	mashed ripe bananas	250 mL
2	eggs	2
1/3 cup	chopped walnuts or pecans	75 mL

1. In a bowl, combine muffin mix, bananas, eggs and walnuts; mix just until blended.

2. Spoon batter into prepared muffin tin. Bake in preheated oven for 15 to 20 minutes or until done.

Variation *Use plain bran muffin mix instead of bran muffin mix with dates and add 1/2 cup (125 mL) chopped dates.*

Esther's Favorite Blueberry Muffins

Makes 12 small muffins

- Preheat oven to 400°F (200°C)
- Muffin tin, greased or paper-lined

¼ cup	butter or margarine, softened	50 mL
¾ cup	granulated sugar	175 mL
1	egg, beaten	1
1½ cups	cake and pastry flour	375 mL
½ tsp	salt	2 mL
2 tsp	baking powder	10 mL
½ cup	milk	125 mL
1 cup	fresh or frozen blueberries	250 mL

1. In a bowl, cream together butter and sugar. Add egg; mix well.

2. In another bowl, sift together flour, salt and baking powder. Add to creamed mixture alternately with milk; stir just until moistened. Fold in blueberries.

3. Spoon batter into prepared muffin tin. Bake in preheated oven for 15 to 20 minutes or until browned.

Tip *Store your favorite muffin recipes neatly by slipping them between the clear plastic pages of a photo album. They are protected from spills and can be removed easily.*

Old-Fashioned Blueberry Muffins

Makes 12 muffins

- Preheat oven to 400°F (200°C)
- Muffin tin, greased or paper-lined

2	eggs	2
1¼ cups	milk	300 mL
½ cup	melted butter or margarine	125 mL
1 tsp	grated lemon zest	5 mL
1½ cups	all-purpose flour	375 mL
1 cup	whole wheat flour	250 mL
½ cup	granulated sugar	125 mL
1 tbsp	baking powder	15 mL
½ tsp	salt	2 mL
1½ cups	fresh or frozen blueberries	375 mL

1. In a bowl, combine eggs, milk, butter and lemon zest; whisk well.

2. In another bowl, combine all-purpose flour, whole wheat flour, sugar, baking powder and salt; mix well. Make a well in the center. Pour in egg mixture; stir just until ingredients are moistened.

3. Spoon batter into prepared muffin tin. Bake in preheated oven for 15 to 20 minutes.

Blueberry Muffins with Orange Butter Topping

Makes 12 muffins

- Preheat oven to 350°F (180°C)
- Muffin tin, greased

1¾ cups	all-purpose flour	425 mL
½ cup	granulated sugar	125 mL
1 tsp	grated orange zest	5 mL
1 tbsp	baking powder	15 mL
1 cup	fresh or frozen blueberries	250 mL
1 cup	milk	250 mL
½ cup	melted butter	125 mL
1	egg	1
½ tsp	salt	2 mL
TOPPING		
2 tbsp	melted butter	25 mL
¼ cup	freshly squeezed orange juice	50 mL
¼ cup	granulated sugar	50 mL

1. In a bowl, sift together flour, sugar, orange zest and baking powder. Add blueberries; toss to combine well.

2. In another bowl, whisk together milk, butter, egg and salt. Add to flour mixture; stir quickly just until all ingredients are moistened. Spoon batter into prepared muffin tin, dividing evenly. Bake in preheated oven for 15 to 18 minutes or until golden brown.

3. *Prepare the topping:* In a bowl, combine butter and orange juice. Pour sugar into another bowl. When muffins are ready, remove from tins. Dip tops into butter mixture and then into sugar.

Jam-Filled Muffins

Makes 12 muffins

- Preheat oven to 425°F (220°C)
- Muffin tin, greased

1½ cups	all-purpose flour	375 mL
¼ cup	granulated sugar	50 mL
2 tsp	baking powder	10 mL
½ tsp	baking soda	2 mL
½ tsp	salt	2 mL
1	egg	1
½ tsp	vanilla	2 mL
¼ cup	butter or margarine, melted	50 mL
1 cup	plain yogurt	250 mL

¼ cup	milk	50 mL
	Jam or jelly	
¼ cup	nuts (optional)	50 mL

1. In a large bowl, combine flour, sugar, baking powder, baking soda and salt.
2. In another bowl, beat together egg and vanilla. Add butter, yogurt and milk; mix well. Add to flour mixture; stir just until blended.
3. Spoon batter into prepared muffin tin, filling half full. Add 1 tsp (5 mL) of your favorite jam or jelly to each; top with the remaining batter. Add nuts (if using). Bake in preheated oven for 15 to 20 minutes.

Coffee Walnut Muffins

Makes 12 muffins
- Preheat oven to 375°F (190°C)
- Muffin tin, greased

1 tbsp	instant coffee powder or granules	15 mL
½ cup	hot water	125 mL
½ cup	milk or cream	125 mL
1	egg, beaten	1
½ cup	melted shortening or oil	125 mL
1½ cups	all-purpose flour	375 mL
1 tbsp	baking powder	15 mL
⅓ cup	granulated sugar	75 mL
1 tsp	salt	5 mL
½ cup	chopped walnuts	125 mL

1. In a bowl, dissolve coffee in hot water. Add milk, egg and shortening; stir to combine well.
2. In another bowl, combine flour, baking powder, sugar and salt. Add walnuts; stir well. Add coffee mixture; stir just until moist.
3. Spoon batter into prepared muffin tin. Bake in preheated oven for 15 to 20 minutes.

Coffee Cake Muffins

Makes 12 muffins
- Preheat oven to 375°F (190°C)
- Muffin tin, greased or paper-lined

TOPPING		
⅓ cup	granulated sugar	75 mL
1½ tsp	ground cinnamon	7 mL
1 tbsp	margarine, melted	15 mL
MUFFINS		
3 tbsp	butter, softened	45 mL
¾ cup	granulated sugar	175 mL

1	egg	1
2 cups	all-purpose flour	500 mL
1 tbsp	baking powder	15 mL
Pinch	salt	Pinch
¾ cup	milk	175 mL
1 cup	raisins	250 mL

1. *Prepare the topping:* In a bowl, combine sugar, cinnamon and margarine; mix well. Set aside.
2. *Prepare the muffins:* In another bowl, beat butter. Add sugar and egg; beat well.
3. In another bowl, combine flour, baking powder and salt. Add to creamed mixture alternately with milk; blend well. Fold in raisins.
4. Spoon batter into prepared muffin tin. Sprinkle with topping. Bake in preheated oven for 20 minutes.

Coffee Raisin Spice Muffins

Makes 12 muffins
- Preheat oven to 400°F (200°C)
- Muffin tin, paper-lined

1 cup	confectioner's (icing) sugar	250 mL
2 tsp to 1 tbsp	grated lemon zest	10 to 15 mL
4 to 5 tsp	freshly squeezed lemon juice	20 to 25 mL
1 cup	brewed coffee	250 mL
1 cup	granulated sugar or packed brown sugar	250 mL
1½ cups	chopped raisins	375 mL
⅓ cup	butter or margarine or shortening	75 mL
½ tsp	ground cloves	2 mL
1 tsp	ground cinnamon	5 mL
1 tsp	ground nutmeg	5 mL
½ tsp	salt	2 mL
½ tsp	baking powder	2 mL
1 tsp	baking soda	5 mL
2 cups	all-purpose flour	500 mL

1. In a bowl, combine confectioner's sugar, lemon zest and lemon juice; mix well. Set aside.
2. In a saucepan over medium-high heat, combine coffee, sugar, raisins, butter, cloves, cinnamon and nutmeg; bring to a boil. Cook for 3 minutes. Set aside to cool.
3. When cool add salt, baking powder, baking soda and flour; mix well.
4. Spoon batter into prepared muffin tin. Bake in preheated oven for 15 to 20 minutes or until toothpick inserted in center comes out clean. Set aside to cool. Drizzle with topping.

Lemon Tea Muffins

Makes 12 small muffins
- Preheat oven to 375ºF (190ºC)
- Muffin tin, greased or paper-lined

1 cup	cake and pastry flour or all-purpose flour	250 mL
1/2 cup	granulated sugar	125 mL
1 1/2 tsp	baking powder	7 mL
1 tsp	salt	5 mL
2	eggs	2
1/2 cup	freshly squeezed lemon juice	125 mL
1/4 cup	melted margarine	50 mL
2 tsp	grated lemon zest	10 mL
TOPPING		
1/4 cup	melted margarine	50 mL
1 tbsp	freshly squeezed lemon juice	15 mL
	Granulated sugar	

1. In a bowl, combine flour, sugar, baking powder and salt.

2. In another bowl, whisk together eggs, lemon juice, margarine and lemon zest. Add to flour mixture; stir just until moist and blended.

3. Spoon batter into prepared muffin tin. Bake in preheated oven for 15 to 20 minutes. Remove muffins from pan while still warm.

4. *Prepare the topping:* In a bowl, combine margarine and lemon juice. Dip muffin tops in juice mixture; dip in sugar.

Raisin Muffins

Makes 12 muffins
- Preheat oven to 350ºF (180ºC)
- Muffin tin, greased or paper-lined

1 cup	raisins	250 mL
1 1/2 cups	water	375 mL
2/3 cup	packed brown sugar	150 mL
1/2 cup	shortening	125 mL
1	egg, beaten	1
1 tsp	vanilla	5 mL
1 1/2 cups	all-purpose flour	375 mL
1 tsp	salt	5 mL
1 tsp	baking soda	5 mL
1 tsp	baking powder	5 mL

1. In a saucepan over medium-high heat, combine raisins and water; bring to a boil. Cook for 20 minutes. Set aside to cool (keep in water).

2. In a bowl, cream together brown sugar, shortening and egg. Add cooled raisins with water and vanilla.

3. In another bowl, sift together flour, salt, baking soda and baking powder. Add to creamed mixture; stir just until blended.

4. Spoon batter into prepared muffin tin. Bake in preheated oven for about 20 minutes.

Raisin Nut Muffins

Makes 12 muffins
- Preheat oven to 400ºF (200ºC)
- Muffin tin, greased or paper-lined

1/2 cup	butter, softened	125 mL
1 cup	granulated sugar	250 mL
3	eggs	3
2 cups	all-purpose flour	500 mL
2 tsp	baking powder	10 mL
1/4 tsp	ground nutmeg	1 mL
2/3 cup	milk	150 mL
1 cup	chopped walnuts	250 mL
1 cup	raisins, dredged in flour	250 mL

1. In a bowl, cream butter. Add sugar; beat slowly until well blended.

2. In another bowl, beat eggs until light. Add to creamed mixture.

3. In another bowl, sift together flour, baking powder and nutmeg. Add to batter alternately with milk; mix well. Fold in walnuts and raisins.

4. Spoon batter into prepared muffin tin. Bake in preheated oven for 15 to 20 minutes.

Sweet Raisin Muffins

Makes 12 muffins
- Preheat oven to 425ºF (220ºC)
- Muffin tin, greased

1 cup	raisins	250 mL
1 tbsp	grated orange zest	15 mL
1 cup	boiling water	250 mL
1/2 tsp	baking soda	2 mL
1/2 cup	granulated sugar	125 mL

2 tbsp	margarine	25 mL
1	egg	1
1³⁄₄ cups	all-purpose flour	425 mL
2 tsp	baking powder	10 mL
¹⁄₂ tsp	ground cinnamon	2 mL
¹⁄₄ tsp	ground nutmeg	1 mL

1. In a bowl, combine raisins and orange zest. Add boiling water and baking soda. Set aside to cool.
2. In another bowl, cream together sugar and margarine. Add egg; beat well. Add raisin mixture; beat well.
3. In another bowl, combine flour, baking powder, cinnamon and nutmeg. Fold into creamed mixture; stir just until moist.
4. Spoon batter into prepared muffin tin. Bake in preheated oven for 20 minutes or until toothpick inserted in center comes out clean.

Spicy Raisin Muffins

Makes 12 to 18 muffins

- Preheat oven to 350°F (180°C)
- Muffin tins, greased or paper-lined

1¹⁄₂ cups	raisins	375 mL
1 cup	water	250 mL
¹⁄₂ cup	packed brown sugar	125 mL
¹⁄₂ cup	butter or margarine	125 mL
1	egg, beaten	1
1¹⁄₂ cups	all-purpose flour	375 mL
1 tsp	baking soda	5 mL
¹⁄₄ tsp	ground mace	1 mL
1 tsp	ground cinnamon	5 mL
¹⁄₄ tsp	ground cloves	1 mL

1. In a saucepan over medium-high heat, bring raisins and water to a boil. Simmer for 20 minutes. Set aside to cool. Retain ³⁄₄ cup (175 mL) water; discard rest.
2. In a bowl, cream together brown sugar and butter. Add egg and raisin water; beat well. Add raisins, flour, baking soda, mace, cinnamon and cloves; stir just until blended.
3. Spoon batter into prepared muffin tins. Bake in preheated oven for about 15 minutes.

Date Muffins

Makes 12 muffins

- Preheat oven to 400°F (200°C)
- Muffin tin, greased

¹⁄₃ cup	shortening	75 mL
1	egg, beaten	1
³⁄₄ cup	milk	175 mL
2 cups	all-purpose flour	500 mL
1 tbsp	baking powder	15 mL
¹⁄₂ tsp	salt	2 mL
1 cup	chopped pitted dates	250 mL

1. In a bowl, cream shortening. Add egg and milk; beat well.
2. In another bowl, sift together flour, baking powder and salt. Add to creamed mixture; blend well. Add dates.
3. Spoon batter into prepared muffin tin. Bake in preheated oven for about 25 minutes.

Variation *For sweet muffins add ¹⁄₄ cup (50 mL) sugar.*

Poppy Seed Muffins

Makes 12 muffins

- Preheat oven to 400°F (200°C)
- Muffin tin, greased

1 cup	milk	250 mL
¹⁄₂ cup	poppy seeds	125 mL
¹⁄₄ cup	butter or margarine	50 mL
3 tbsp	granulated sugar	45 mL
1	egg	1
1 tsp	vanilla	5 mL
2 cups	all-purpose flour	500 mL
1 tbsp	baking powder	15 mL
³⁄₄ tsp	salt	4 mL

1. In a bowl, combine milk and poppy seeds. Let stand for about 10 minutes.
2. In another bowl, combine butter, sugar and egg; beat well. Add vanilla; blend thoroughly. Add poppy seed mixture.
3. In another bowl, combine flour, baking powder and salt; mix thoroughly. Make a well in the center. Add liquid ingredients; stir just until moist.
4. Spoon batter into prepared muffin tin. Bake in preheated oven for 20 to 25 minutes. Serve warm.

Esther's Famous Poppy Seed Muffins

Makes 12 muffins
- Preheat oven to 425°F (220°C)
- Muffin tin, paper-lined

¼ cup	vegetable oil	50 mL
¾ cup	granulated sugar	175 mL
2	eggs	2
½ cup	poppy seeds	125 mL
1 cup	sour cream	250 mL
¼ cup	milk	50 mL
2 cups	all-purpose flour	500 mL
½ tsp	baking soda	2 mL
2 tsp	baking powder	10 mL
½ tsp	salt	2 mL

1. In a bowl, cream together oil, sugar and eggs. Add poppy seeds, sour cream, milk, flour, baking soda, baking powder and salt. Stir just until moist and still lumpy. The mixture will be quite thick and heavy.
2. Spoon batter into prepared muffin tin. Bake in preheated oven for 15 to 20 minutes or until toothpick inserted in center comes out clean.

Small-Batch Peanut Butter Muffins

Makes 6 small muffins
- Preheat oven to 400°F (200°C)
- Muffin tin, paper-lined

⅓ cup + 2 tsp	self-rising flour	85 mL
1 tbsp	superfine sugar	15 mL
¼ cup	skim milk	50 mL
1	egg, lightly beaten	1
3 tbsp	chunky-style peanut butter, at room temperature	45 mL
1 tsp	margarine, melted	5 mL

1. In a bowl, sift together flour and sugar. Add milk, egg, peanut butter and margarine; stir just until blended (batter will be lumpy).
2. Spoon batter into prepared muffin tin. Bake in preheated oven for 20 minutes or until toothpick inserted in center comes out clean.

Tip *These muffins are great served with any flavor jam.*

Peanut Butter Crunch Muffins

Makes 12 muffins
- Preheat oven to 400°F (200°C)
- Muffin tin, greased

TOPPING

3 tbsp	peanut butter	45 mL
¼ cup	granulated sugar	50 mL
2 tbsp	all-purpose flour	25 mL
Pinch	salt	Pinch

MUFFINS

2 cups	all-purpose flour	500 mL
1 tbsp	baking powder	15 mL
½ tsp	salt	2 mL
2 tbsp	granulated sugar	25 mL
1	egg, beaten	1
1 cup	milk	250 mL
⅓ cup	melted butter or margarine	75 mL

1. *Prepare the topping:* In a bowl, combine peanut butter, sugar, flour and salt; mix with a fork. Set aside.
2. *Prepare the muffins:* In another bowl, combine flour, baking powder, salt and sugar. Make a well in the center.
3. In another bowl, whisk together egg, milk and butter. Add to dry ingredients; stir quickly just until blended.
4. Spoon batter into prepared muffin tin. Sprinkle with topping. Bake in preheated oven for 20 minutes.

Peanut Butter Jelly Muffins

Makes 12 muffins
- Preheat oven to 375°F (190°C)
- Muffin tin, greased

1½ cups	all-purpose flour	375 mL
½ cup	packed brown sugar	125 mL
1 tsp	baking powder	5 mL
½ tsp	baking soda	2 mL
½ tsp	salt	2 mL
½ cup	smooth peanut butter	125 mL
2	eggs, beaten	2
¾ cup	milk	175 mL
1 tsp	vanilla	5 mL
¼ cup	margarine, melted	50 mL
	Grape jelly or apricot jam	

1. In a bowl, sift together flour, brown sugar, baking powder, baking soda and salt. Make a well in the center.
2. In another bowl, combine peanut butter and eggs; beat well. Add milk, vanilla and margarine; mix thoroughly. Add to dry ingredients; mix until moist.
3. Spoon batter into prepared muffin tin. Make an indentation in the center of each; spoon 1 tsp (5 mL) either grape jelly or apricot jam into each muffin. Bake in preheated oven for about 20 minutes.

Tip *The contrasting colors of grape and apricot make a sweet, colorful arrangement.*

• •

Pecan Muffins

Makes 12 muffins
- Preheat oven to 400°F (200°C)
- Muffin tin, greased or paper-lined

1½ cups	all-purpose flour	375 mL
½ cup	granulated sugar	125 mL
½ cup	chopped pecans	125 mL
2 tsp	baking powder	10 mL
½ tsp	salt	2 mL
1	egg, lightly beaten	1
½ cup	milk	125 mL
¼ cup	vegetable oil	50 mL

1. In a bowl, combine flour, sugar, pecans, baking powder and salt. Make a well in the center.
2. In another bowl, combine egg, milk and oil. Add to dry ingredients; stir just until moist.
3. Spoon batter into prepared muffin tin. Bake in preheated oven for 15 to 20 minutes.

• •

Chocolate Cheesecake Muffins

Makes 12 muffins
- Preheat oven to 375°F (190°C)
- Muffin tin, greased or paper-lined

FILLING
3 oz	cream cheese, softened	90 g
2 tbsp	granulated sugar	25 mL

MUFFINS
1 cup	all-purpose flour	250 mL
½ cup	granulated sugar	125 mL
3 tbsp	unsweetened cocoa powder	45 mL
2 tsp	baking powder	10 mL
½ tsp	salt	2 mL
1	egg, beaten	1
¾ cup	milk	175 mL
⅓ cup	vegetable oil	75 mL
	Confectioner's (icing) sugar (optional)	

1. *Prepare the filling:* In a bowl, combine cream cheese and sugar; beat until light and fluffy. Set aside.
2. *Prepare the muffins:* In another bowl, combine flour, sugar, cocoa, baking powder and salt. Make a well in center of mixture.
3. In another bowl, combine egg, milk and oil. Pour into flour mixture; stir just until lumpy and moist.
4. Spoon batter into prepared muffin tin. Add 1 tsp (5 mL) cheese filling; top with the remaining batter.
5. Bake in preheated oven for 20 minutes. Dust with confectioner's sugar, if desired.

• •

Chocolate Chipit Snackin' Muffins

Makes 12 muffins
- Preheat oven to 400°F (200°C)
- Muffin tin, paper-lined

1½ cups	all-purpose flour	375 mL
1 cup	granulated sugar	250 mL
2 tbsp	unsweetened cocoa powder	25 mL
1 tsp	baking powder	5 mL
1 tsp	baking soda	5 mL
½ tsp	salt	2 mL
¼ cup	vegetable oil	50 mL
1 tsp	vanilla	5 mL
1 tbsp	white vinegar	15 mL
1 cup	warm water	250 mL
½ cup	semisweet chocolate chips	125 mL

1. In a bowl, combine flour, sugar, cocoa, baking powder, baking soda and salt. Make a well in the center. Add oil, vanilla, vinegar and warm water. Stir just until moist. Add chocolate chips.
2. Spoon batter into prepared muffin tin. Bake in preheated oven for 15 to 20 minutes.

Variation *Before putting in oven, sprinkle chocolate chips over top.*

Chocolate Date Muffins

Makes 12 muffins
- Preheat oven to 350°F (180°C)
- Muffin tin, greased

2 cups	all-purpose flour	500 mL
4 tsp	baking powder	20 mL
1/2 tsp	salt	2 mL
1/2 cup	granulated sugar	125 mL
1/2 cup	unsweetened cocoa powder	125 mL
1/2 cup	sliced dates	125 mL
1 cup	milk	250 mL
1	egg, beaten	1
2 tbsp	shortening, melted	25 mL

1. In a bowl, sift together flour, baking powder, salt, sugar and cocoa. Add dates; mix with your fingers. Add milk, egg and shortening; stir just until blended.

2. Spoon batter into prepared muffin tin. Bake in preheated oven for 20 minutes.

Chunky Chocolate Orange Muffins

Makes 12 muffins
- Preheat oven to 400°F (200°C)
- Muffin tin, greased

1/2 cup	butter, softened	125 mL
1 cup	granulated sugar	250 mL
2	eggs	2
1/2 cup	sour cream	125 mL
	Grated zest of 2 oranges	
1/2 cup	freshly squeezed orange juice	125 mL
2 cups	all-purpose flour (or 2 1/4 cups/ 550 mL cake and pastry flour)	500 mL
1 tsp	baking powder	5 mL
1/2 tsp	baking soda	2 mL
3 oz	semisweet chocolate, chopped (or 1/2 cup/125 mL semisweet chocolate chips)	90 g
1 oz	semisweet chocolate, melted	30 g

1. In a bowl, combine butter and sugar; cream until light and fluffy. Add eggs one at a time; beat well. Add sour cream, orange zest and orange juice; mix well.

2. In another bowl, combine flour, baking powder, baking soda and chopped chocolate. Add to creamed mixture; stir gently just until blended.

3. Spoon batter into prepared muffin tin. Bake in preheated oven for 18 to 22 minutes or until top springs back when lightly touched. Set aside to cool. Drizzle with melted chocolate.

The Muffin Lady's Special Mincemeat Muffins

Makes 18 to 24 muffins
- Preheat oven to 350°F (180°C)
- Muffin tins, greased or paper-lined

3/4 cup	vegetable oil	175 mL
1 cup	granulated sugar	250 mL
2	eggs, beaten	2
2 cups	all-purpose flour	500 mL
1 cup	milk	250 mL
1 cup	all-bran cereal or whole bran cereal	250 mL
2 tsp	baking powder	10 mL
1 tsp	salt	5 mL
1 tsp	baking soda	5 mL
1 cup	mincemeat	250 mL

1. In a bowl, combine oil, sugar, eggs, flour, milk, cereal, baking powder, salt, baking soda and mincemeat; mix well.

2. Spoon batter into prepared muffin tins. Bake in preheated oven for 20 to 25 minutes.

Tip *If you don't want to use all the batter, it can be stored in the refrigerator for about 2 weeks.*

Wholesome Healthy Muffins

continued on next page

Basic Bran Muffins

Makes 12 large muffins
- Preheat oven to 400°F (200°C)
- Muffin tin, greased or paper-lined

1 cup	all-purpose flour	250 mL
1/2 cup	packed brown sugar	125 mL
1/4 tsp	salt	1 mL
1 1/2 tsp	baking powder	7 mL
1/2 tsp	baking soda	2 mL
1 1/2 cups	natural bran	375 mL
1/2 cup	raisins	125 mL
1/2 cup	chopped nuts (optional)	125 mL
2	eggs, beaten	2
1 cup	milk	250 mL
1/4 cup	light (fancy) molasses	50 mL
1/2 cup	margarine, melted	125 mL

1. In a bowl, combine flour, brown sugar, salt, baking powder, baking soda, bran, raisins and nuts (if using). Make a well in the center.
2. In another bowl, beat together eggs, milk, molasses and margarine. Add to flour mixture; stir just until moistened. Do not overmix (batter will be lumpy).
3. Spoon batter into prepared muffin tins. Bake in preheated oven for 18 to 20 minutes.

Variations *Banana Bran Muffins: Replace molasses and raisins with 1 cup (250 mL) mashed bananas. Decrease milk to 1/2 cup (125 mL) and add 1 tsp (5 mL) ground cinnamon.*

Applesauce Bran Muffins: Replace molasses with 3/4 cup (175 mL) sweetened applesauce. Decrease milk to 1/2 cup (125 mL) and add 1 tsp (5 mL) ground cinnamon or nutmeg.

Carrot Bran Muffins: Add 1 cup (250 mL) grated carrots and 1 tsp (5 mL) ground cinnamon to dry ingredients.

Easy Breakfast Bran Muffins

Makes 12 muffins
- Preheat oven to 375°F (190°C)
- Muffin tin, paper-lined

1 cup	natural bran	250 mL
1/2 cup	granulated sugar	125 mL
1 cup	all-purpose flour	250 mL
1 tsp	baking powder	5 mL
1 tsp	baking soda	5 mL
1/2 tsp	salt	2 mL
1	egg	1
6 tbsp	vegetable oil	90 mL
1 cup	boiling water	250 mL
1/3 cup	raisins or dates	75 mL

1. In a bowl, combine bran, sugar, flour, baking powder, baking soda and salt. Make a well in the center.
2. In another bowl, beat together egg and oil. Add raisins and boiling water; mix well. Pour into dry ingredients; stir just until blended.
3. Spoon batter into prepared muffin tin. Bake in preheated oven for about 20 to 25 minutes.

All-Bran Cereal Muffins

Makes 12 muffins
- Preheat oven to 400°F (200°C)
- Muffin tin, greased

1 cup	all-bran cereal	250 mL
1 cup	milk	250 mL
1	egg	1
1/4 cup	melted shortening	50 mL
1/2 cup	raisins or chopped dates	125 mL
1 cup	all-purpose flour	250 mL
2 1/2 tsp	baking powder	12 mL
1/2 tsp	salt	2 mL
1/4 cup	granulated sugar	50 mL
1 tsp	ground cinnamon	5 mL
1/2 tsp	ground nutmeg	2 mL

1. In a bowl, combine cereal and milk; mix well. Let stand until milk is absorbed. Add egg and shortening; beat well. Stir in raisins.
2. In another bowl, sift together flour, baking powder, salt, sugar, cinnamon and nutmeg. Add to cereal mixture; blend well.
3. Spoon batter into prepared muffin tin. Bake in preheated oven for 20 to 25 minutes.

Sunburst Bran Muffins

Makes 12 to 18 muffins

- Preheat oven to 400°F (200°C)
- Muffin tins, greased or paper-lined

2 cups	all-purpose flour	500 mL
1 tbsp	baking powder	15 mL
1/2 tsp	salt	2 mL
1	egg	1
1 1/4 cups	milk	300 mL
1 1/2 cups	all-bran cereal	375 mL
1/3 cup	margarine, melted	75 mL
1/2 cup	raisins (optional)	125 mL
1/2 cup	firmly packed brown sugar	125 mL
1 tsp	grated orange zest	5 mL
1/2 cup	freshly squeezed orange juice	125 mL

1. In a large bowl, combine flour, baking powder and salt. Make a well in the center.
2. In another bowl, beat egg with a fork. Stir in milk, cereal, margarine, raisins (if using), sugar, zest and juice. Mix well. Add to flour mixture, stirring just until blended and moistened.
3. Spoon batter into prepared muffin tins. Bake in preheated oven for about 20 minutes.

Buttermilk Bran Muffins

Makes 18 to 24 muffins

- Preheat oven to 400°F (200°C)
- Muffin tins, greased or paper-lined

1/3 cup	shortening	75 mL
1/2 cup	firmly packed brown sugar	125 mL
1	egg	1
1 cup	all-purpose flour	250 mL
1 tsp	baking powder	5 mL
1/2 tsp	baking soda	2 mL
1 tsp	salt	5 mL
3 cups	all-bran cereal	750 mL
1 cup	buttermilk	250 mL

1. In a bowl, cream together shortening, brown sugar and egg.
2. In another bowl, sift together flour, baking powder, baking soda, salt and bran; mix well. Add to creamed mixture alternately with buttermilk; stir just until blended.
3. Spoon batter into prepared muffin tins. Bake in preheated oven for about 20 minutes.

Bran Oat Muffins

Makes 24 muffins

- Preheat oven to 350°F (180°C)
- Muffin tins, greased or paper-lined

2	eggs, beaten	2
1 cup	packed brown sugar	250 mL
3/4 cup	vegetable oil	175 mL
2 cups	milk	500 mL
1/3 cup	bran	75 mL
1/3 cup	quick-cooking rolled oats	75 mL
1/3 cup	wheat germ	75 mL
1 tsp	baking soda	5 mL
2 tsp	baking powder	10 mL
1 tsp	salt	5 mL
2 cups	all-purpose flour	500 mL
1 cup	raisins or dates	250 mL
1/4 cup	walnuts (optional)	50 mL
1 tsp	ground cinnamon	5 mL
1 tsp	vanilla	5 mL

1. In a bowl, combine eggs, brown sugar, oil and milk; whisk until well blended. Add bran, oats, wheat germ, baking soda, baking powder, salt, flour, raisins, walnuts (if using), cinnamon and vanilla. Stir just until moist and blended.
2. Spoon batter into prepared muffin tins. Bake in preheated oven for 15 to 20 minutes.

Honey Bran Muffins

Makes 12 muffins

- Preheat oven to 400°F (200°C)
- Muffin tin, greased or paper-lined

1/2 cup	natural bran	125 mL
1/2 cup	toasted wheat germ	125 mL
1/2 cup	raisins	125 mL
1 cup	whole wheat flour	250 mL
2 1/2 tsp	baking powder	12 mL
1/2 tsp	baking soda	2 mL
1/2 tsp	salt	2 mL
1/4 tsp	ground cinnamon	1 mL
Pinch	ground nutmeg	Pinch
Pinch	ground allspice	Pinch
1	egg	1
3 tbsp	light (fancy) molasses	45 mL
1/4 cup	liquid honey	50 mL
1/3 cup	vegetable oil	75 mL
1 1/4 cups	milk	300 mL

1. In a bowl, combine bran, wheat germ, raisins, flour, baking powder, baking soda, salt, cinnamon, nutmeg and allspice; mix well. Make a well in the center.
2. In another bowl, whisk together egg, molasses, honey, oil and milk. Pour into dry ingredients; stir just until moistened (batter will be runny).
3. Spoon batter into prepared muffin tin. Bake in preheated oven for about 15 minutes.

● ●

Upside-Down Honey Bran Muffins

Makes 18 large muffins
- Preheat oven to 350°F (180°C)
- Muffin tins, greased

1 cup	liquid honey	250 mL
½ cup	water	125 mL
½ cup	walnuts	125 mL
1 cup	whole wheat flour	250 mL
1 cup	natural bran	250 mL
1 cup	all-bran cereal	250 mL
1 tsp	baking soda	5 mL
1 tbsp	baking powder	15 mL
1 tsp	salt	5 mL
2	eggs	2
1 cup	sour cream	250 mL
1 cup	raisins	250 mL

1. In a saucepan over low heat, combine honey and water; gently warm until blended.
2. Spoon 1 tbsp (15 mL) walnuts into each muffin cup; cover with 1 tbsp (15 mL) warm honey mixture.
3. In a bowl, combine flour, natural bran, bran cereal, baking soda, baking powder and salt.
4. In another bowl, whisk together eggs and sour cream; fold in raisins. Add the remaining warm honey mixture. Add to flour mixture; stir quickly just until moist and blended.
5. Spoon batter into prepared muffin tin. Bake in preheated oven for about 25 minutes. Let cool slightly; invert pan over a large plate or tray so that honey mixture is now a topping.

● ●

All-Bran Sour Cream Muffins

Makes 12 muffins
- Preheat oven to 425°F (220°C)
- Muffin tin, greased

1 cup	unsifted cake and pastry flour	250 mL
1 tbsp	baking powder	15 mL
½ tsp	baking soda	2 mL
½ tsp	salt	2 mL
¼ cup	packed brown sugar	50 mL
¾ cup	all-bran cereal	175 mL
2	egg whites	2
¼ cup	dark molasses	50 mL
¾ cup	sour cream	175 mL
3 tbsp	vegetable oil	45 mL

1. In a bowl, sift together flour, baking powder, baking soda and salt. Add brown sugar and cereal; blend well.
2. In another bowl, combine egg whites, molasses, sour cream and oil; beat well. Add to flour mixture; stir just until blended.
3. Spoon batter into prepared muffin tin. Bake in preheated oven for 15 to 20 minutes.

Tip *When making recipes that require egg whites only, drop the yolks into a pan of boiling, salted water and hard-cook them for use in salads, sandwiches, etc.*

● ●

Bran 'n' Cheese Muffins

Makes 16 muffins
- Preheat oven to 400°F (200°C)
- Muffin tins, greased or paper-lined

1 cup	all-bran cereal	250 mL
1¼ cups	buttermilk or sour milk	300 mL
1	egg	1
¼ cup	vegetable oil	50 mL
1½ cups	all-purpose flour	375 mL
¼ cup	granulated sugar	50 mL
1½ tsp	baking powder	7 mL
½ tsp	baking soda	2 mL
½ tsp	salt	2 mL
1 cup	shredded sharp Cheddar cheese	250 mL

1. In a small bowl, combine cereal and buttermilk. Let stand for 5 minutes.
2. In another bowl, beat egg. Add oil and cereal mixture.
3. In a large bowl, combine flour, sugar, baking powder, baking soda, salt and cheese. Add egg mixture, stirring just until moistened and lumpy.
4. Spoon batter into prepared muffin tins. Bake in preheated oven for 20 to 25 minutes.

Tip *To prevent a block of cheese from becoming moldy, wrap a cloth saturated in white vinegar around the cheese.*

Crunchy Cheddar Bran Muffins

Makes 12 muffins
- Preheat oven to 400°F (200°C)
- Muffin tin, greased

1 cup	all-bran cereal	250 mL
1¼ cups	buttermilk or sour milk	300 mL
¼ cup	shortening	50 mL
⅓ cup	granulated sugar	75 mL
1	egg	1
1½ cups	all-purpose flour	375 mL
1½ tsp	baking powder	7 mL
½ tsp	salt	2 mL
¼ tsp	baking soda	1 mL
1 cup	shredded sharp Cheddar cheese	250 mL

1. In a bowl, cover bran with buttermilk. Let stand until softened.

2. In another bowl, combine shortening and sugar; cream until light and fluffy. Beat in egg.

3. In another bowl, sift together flour, baking powder, salt and baking soda. Add to creamed mixture alternately with bran mixture; stir in cheese.

4. Spoon batter into prepared muffin tin. Bake in preheated oven for about 30 minutes.

Double Cheese Bran Muffins

Makes 12 to 18 muffins
- Preheat oven to 400°F (200°C)
- Muffin tins, greased or paper-lined

1 cup	boiling water	250 mL
1½ cups	all-bran cereal	375 mL
¼ cup	butter or margarine	50 mL
½ cup	milk	125 mL
1	egg	1
1½ cups	all-purpose flour	375 mL
¼ cup	granulated sugar	50 mL
1 tbsp	baking powder	15 mL
½ tsp	salt	2 mL
1½ cups	shredded old Cheddar cheese, divided	375 mL
2 tbsp	freshly grated Parmesan cheese	25 mL

1. In a medium bowl, pour boiling water over cereal and butter. Stir until butter melts. Set aside to cool. Stir in milk and egg.

2. In a large bowl, combine flour, sugar, baking powder and salt. Stir in 1¼ cups (300 mL) of the Cheddar cheese and the Parmesan cheese. Add cereal mixture, stirring just until moist and blended.

3. Spoon batter into prepared muffin tins. Sprinkle with the remaining Cheddar cheese. Bake in preheated oven for 20 to 25 minutes or until golden brown.

Cream Cheese Bran Muffins

Makes 12 muffins
- Preheat oven to 375°F (190°C)
- Muffin tin, greased or paper-lined

TOPPING

1	package (8 oz/250 g) cream cheese, softened	1
¼ cup	granulated sugar	50 mL
1	egg, beaten	1

MUFFINS

1¼ cups	all-bran cereal	300 mL
1 cup	milk	250 mL
¼ cup	vegetable oil	50 mL
1	egg, beaten	1
1¼ cups	all-purpose flour	300 mL
½ cup	granulated sugar	125 mL
1 tbsp	baking powder	15 mL
½ tsp	salt	2 mL
½ cup	raisins	125 mL

1. *Prepare the topping:* In a bowl, combine cream cheese, sugar and egg; mix until blended well. Set aside.

2. *Prepare the muffins:* In another bowl, combine bran cereal and milk. Let stand for 2 minutes.

3. In another bowl, combine oil and egg. Add to cereal mixture; mix well. Add flour, sugar, baking powder and salt; stir just until moist and blended. Fold in raisins.

4. Spoon batter into prepared muffin tin. Drop 1 tbsp (15 mL) topping onto each muffin. Bake in preheated oven for 25 minutes.

Spiced Carrot Bran Muffins

Makes 12 muffins

- Preheat oven to 400°F (200°C)
- Muffin tin, greased or paper-lined

1 cup	all-bran cereal	250 mL
1 cup	buttermilk or sour milk	250 mL
1	egg, beaten	1
¾ cup	finely shredded carrots (about 2 medium)	175 mL
3 tbsp	vegetable oil	45 mL
1 cup	all-purpose flour	250 mL
¼ cup	packed brown sugar	50 mL
2 tsp	baking powder	10 mL
¾ tsp	ground cinnamon or allspice	4 mL
½ tsp	baking soda	2 mL
½ tsp	salt	2 mL

1. In a bowl, combine bran cereal and buttermilk. Let stand for about 5 minutes. Add egg, carrots and oil; mix well.

2. In another bowl, combine flour, brown sugar, baking powder, cinnamon, baking soda, salt and bran mixture; stir just until blended.

3. Spoon batter into prepared muffin tin. Bake in preheated oven for 15 to 20 minutes or until browned.

Tip *If you want a quick and delicious icing for carrot muffins, boil a small potato and mash it. Add confectioner's (icing) sugar and vanilla.*

Spicy Bran–Sweet Potato Muffins

Makes 12 large muffins

- Preheat oven to 350°F (180°C)
- Muffin tin, greased

CRUMB TOPPING

¾ cup	crushed bran flakes cereal	175 mL
2 tbsp	butter or margarine, melted	25 mL
2 tbsp	light brown sugar	25 mL

MUFFINS

1 cup	vegetable oil	250 mL
¾ cup	firmly packed light brown sugar	175 mL
2	eggs	2
1 tsp	vanilla	5 mL
½ cup	crushed bran flakes cereal	125 mL
1 cup	all-purpose flour	250 mL
1½ tsp	baking soda	7 mL
½ tsp	salt	2 mL
½ tsp	ground cinnamon	2 mL
¼ tsp	ground ginger	1 mL
Pinch	ground cloves	Pinch
Pinch	ground allspice	Pinch
1 tsp	grated orange zest	5 mL
1½ cups	pared shredded sweet potato	375 mL
1 cup	chopped almonds	250 mL

1. *Prepare the topping:* In a bowl, combine cereal, butter and sugar. Set aside.

2. *Prepare the muffins:* In another bowl, combine oil, brown sugar, eggs and vanilla; beat on high for 2 minutes.

3. In another bowl, combine cereal, flour, baking soda, salt, cinnamon, ginger, cloves and allspice; mix well. Add orange zest. Add to oil mixture; stir just until blended. Fold in sweet potato and almonds.

4. Spoon batter into prepared muffin tin. Sprinkle topping evenly over tops. Bake in preheated oven for about 20 minutes.

Apple Bran Muffins

Makes 12 muffins

- Preheat oven to 400°F (200°C)
- Muffin tin, greased

1 cup	all-purpose flour	250 mL
1 tsp	baking soda	5 mL
1 tsp	baking powder	5 mL
½ tsp	salt	2 mL
3 tbsp	packed brown sugar	45 mL
1 cup	natural bran	250 mL
1	egg	1
1 cup	buttermilk or sour milk	250 mL
¼ cup	vegetable oil	50 mL
2 tbsp	light (fancy) molasses	25 mL
1	small apple, peeled and finely chopped	1

1. In a bowl, combine flour, baking soda, baking powder, salt and sugar; mix well. Add bran; stir well with a fork. Make a well in the center.

2. In another bowl, beat together egg, buttermilk, oil and molasses; add apple. Pour into dry ingredients; stir just until blended.

3. Spoon batter into prepared muffin tin. Bake in preheated oven for about 15 minutes.

Apple-Filled Bran Muffins

Makes 12 muffins
- Preheat oven to 400°F (200°C)
- Muffin tin, paper-lined

1/3 cup	chopped apple	75 mL
1/4 cup	chopped walnuts	50 mL
2 tbsp	packed brown sugar	25 mL
1 tbsp	butter, softened	15 mL
1/2 tsp	ground cinnamon	2 mL
1 1/4 cups	all-purpose flour	300 mL
1/3 cup	granulated sugar	75 mL
1 tbsp	baking powder	15 mL
1/4 tsp	salt	1 mL
1 cup	all-bran cereal	250 mL
1 cup	milk	250 mL
1	egg, beaten	1
2 tbsp	vegetable oil	25 mL

1. In a small bowl, combine apple, walnuts, brown sugar, butter and cinnamon. Set aside.

2. In a large bowl, combine flour, sugar, baking powder and salt.

3. In another bowl, combine cereal and milk. Let stand for 5 to 10 minutes. Stir in egg and oil. Add to flour mixture, stirring just until blended.

4. Spoon batter into prepared muffin tin, filling cups only half full. Spoon in 1 tsp (5 mL) apple filling and then top with the remaining batter. Bake in preheated oven for 20 minutes or until golden brown.

Apple Bran Streusel Muffins

Makes 12 large muffins
- Preheat oven to 400°F (200°C)
- Muffin tin, greased or paper-lined

STREUSEL TOPPING

1/4 cup	all-purpose flour	50 mL
1/4 cup	packed brown sugar	50 mL
1/2 tsp	ground cinnamon	2 mL
2 tbsp	cold butter	25 mL

MUFFINS

2 cups	all-purpose flour	500 mL
1 cup	natural bran	250 mL
3/4 cup	lightly packed brown sugar	175 mL
1 tbsp	baking powder	15 mL
1 tsp	ground cinnamon	5 mL
1 tsp	salt	5 mL

1/2 tsp	baking soda	2 mL
2	large apples, chopped	2
1 cup	milk	250 mL
1/2 cup	vegetable oil	125 mL
2	eggs	2

1. *Prepare the topping:* In a small bowl, combine flour, brown sugar and cinnamon. Using a pastry blender, cut in butter until mixture is crumbly. Set aside.

2. *Prepare the muffins:* In a large bowl, combine flour, bran, brown sugar, baking powder, cinnamon, salt and baking powder. Fold in chopped apples.

3. In another bowl, beat together milk, oil and eggs. Pour into apple mixture and stir just until blended.

4. Spoon batter into prepared muffin tin. Sprinkle with topping and bake in preheated oven for 25 to 30 minutes.

Tip *Store brown sugar, raisins, nuts, bran, etc. in glass jars to keep fresh.*

Applesauce Bran Muffins

Makes 36 muffins
- Preheat oven to 375°F (190°C)
- Muffin tins, greased

3 cups	sweetened applesauce	750 mL
2 cups	buttermilk or sour milk	500 mL
1 cup	packed brown sugar	250 mL
3/4 cup	light (fancy) molasses	175 mL
3/4 cup	vegetable oil	175 mL
1 tbsp	vanilla	15 mL
3	eggs	3
3 cups	natural bran	750 mL
6 cups	all-purpose flour	1.5 L
1 tbsp	baking soda	15 mL
1 tbsp	ground cinnamon	15 mL
1 tbsp	salt	15 mL
3 cups	raisins or chopped dates	750 mL

1. In a bowl, whisk together applesauce, buttermilk, brown sugar, molasses, oil, vanilla and eggs. Stir in bran; let stand for 5 to 10 minutes.

2. In another bowl, combine flour, baking soda, cinnamon and salt; mix well. Add applesauce mixture; stir just until blended. Fold in raisins.

3. Spoon batter into prepared muffin tins (bake in batches). Bake in preheated oven for about 25 minutes.

Branicot Pecan Muffins

Makes 18 to 24 muffins

- Preheat oven to 400°F (200°C)
- Muffin tins, greased or paper-lined

1 cup	boiling water	250 mL
2 cups	all-bran cereal	500 mL
1/2 cup	butter or margarine	125 mL
1	egg	1
1/2 cup	milk	125 mL
2 tbsp	light (fancy) molasses	25 mL
1 1/2 cups	all-purpose flour	375 mL
1 cup	chopped dried apricots	250 mL
1 cup	chopped pecans	250 mL
1/2 cup	firmly packed brown sugar	125 mL
1 tbsp	baking powder	15 mL
1/2 tsp	salt	2 mL

1. In a small bowl, pour boiling water over cereal and butter. Stir until butter melts and set aside to cool.
2. In another bowl, combine egg, milk and molasses. Stir in cooled cereal mixture.
3. In a large bowl, combine flour, apricots, pecans, brown sugar, baking powder and salt. Add cereal mixture, stirring just until moistened and blended.
4. Spoon batter into prepared muffin tins. Bake in preheated oven for 15 to 20 minutes or until golden brown.

Tip *For stale nuts, place in a 250°F (120°C) oven for 5 to 10 minutes. The heat will freshen them.*

Tangerine Bran Muffins

Makes 12 muffins

- Preheat oven to 400°F (200°C)
- Muffin tin, greased or paper-lined

1 cup	all-bran cereal	250 mL
3/4 cup	milk	175 mL
2 tsp	grated tangerine zest	10 mL
1/3 cup	freshly squeezed tangerine juice	75 mL
1	egg, beaten	1
1/4 cup	vegetable oil	50 mL
1 1/4 cups	all-purpose flour	300 mL
1/4 cup	granulated sugar	50 mL
1 tbsp	baking powder	15 mL
1/4 tsp	baking soda	1 mL
1/4 tsp	salt	1 mL
1	tangerine, divided into sections	1

1. In a bowl, combine bran cereal, milk, zest, juice, egg and oil; blend well.
2. In another bowl, sift together flour, sugar, baking powder, baking soda and salt. Add to bran mixture; stir just until moist and blended.
3. Spoon batter into prepared muffin tin. Top each with an orange section. Bake in preheated oven for 20 to 25 minutes.

Date Bran Muffins

Makes 12 muffins

- Preheat oven to 375°F (190°C)
- Muffin tin, greased or paper-lined

1 1/2 cups	natural bran	375 mL
3/4 cup	all-purpose flour or cake and pastry flour	175 mL
1 tsp	baking soda	5 mL
1 tsp	salt	5 mL
1	egg	1
1/2 cup	lightly packed brown sugar	125 mL
1 tbsp	vegetable oil	15 mL
1 cup	buttermilk or sour milk	250 mL
1 cup	chopped dates	250 mL
1 cup	hot water	250 mL
1/2 cup	lightly packed brown sugar	125 mL
1 tsp	freshly squeezed lemon juice	5 mL

1. In a large bowl, combine bran, flour, baking soda and salt.
2. In another bowl, beat together egg, brown sugar, oil and buttermilk. Pour into dry ingredients and stir just until blended.
3. In another bowl, combine dates, hot water, brown sugar and lemon juice. Add to batter, stirring just until blended.
4. Spoon batter into prepared muffin tin. Bake in preheated oven for 20 to 25 minutes.

Tip *Dates, marshmallows and any sticky ingredients can be cut easily with scissors dipped in hot water.*

Double Bran Fig Muffins

Makes 8 to 12 muffins
- Preheat oven to 375°F (190°C)
- Muffin tin, greased

¾ cup	whole wheat flour	175 mL
½ cup	natural bran	125 mL
½ cup	oat bran	125 mL
⅓ cup	wheat germ	75 mL
⅓ cup	packed brown sugar	75 mL
1 tsp	baking powder	5 mL
½ tsp	baking soda	2 mL
½ tsp	ground cinnamon	2 mL
¼ tsp	salt	1 mL
1	egg	1
1 cup	buttermilk	250 mL
¼ cup	vegetable oil	50 mL
1 cup	chopped figs, divided	250 mL

1. In a bowl, combine whole wheat flour, natural bran, oat bran, wheat germ, brown sugar, baking powder, baking soda, cinnamon and salt. Make a well in the center.
2. In another bowl, whisk together egg, buttermilk and oil. Set aside 2 tbsp (25 mL) figs; add the remaining figs to egg mixture. Pour into dry ingredients; stir just until blended. Do not overmix.
3. Spoon batter into prepared muffin tin; top with reserved figs. Bake in preheated oven for 20 to 25 minutes.

Prune Bran Muffins

Makes 12 to 18 muffins
- Preheat oven to 400°F (200°C)
- Muffin tins, greased

1½ cups	all-purpose flour	375 mL
½ cup	granulated sugar	125 mL
1 tbsp	baking powder	15 mL
1 tsp	salt	5 mL
1½ cups	all-bran cereal	375 mL
1 cup	milk	250 mL
½ cup	chopped pitted prunes	125 mL
1	egg	1
⅓ cup	vegetable oil	75 mL

1. In a bowl, combine flour, sugar, baking powder and salt.
2. In another bowl, combine cereal, milk and prunes. Let stand for 2 minutes. Add egg and oil; beat well. Add to flour mixture; stir just until moist and blended. Do not overmix.
3. Spoon batter into prepared muffin tins. Bake in preheated oven for 15 to 20 minutes or until golden brown.

Chocolate Chip Bran Muffins

Makes 12 muffins
- Preheat oven to 350°F (180°C)
- Muffin tin, paper-lined

½ cup	shortening, softened	125 mL
⅔ cup	granulated sugar	150 mL
1	egg	1
1 tsp	vanilla	5 mL
1½ cups	all-purpose flour	375 mL
½ tsp	baking soda	2 mL
3 tbsp	unsweetened cocoa powder	45 mL
½ tsp	salt	2 mL
1 cup	buttermilk or sour milk	250 mL
½ cup	all-bran cereal	125 mL
½ cup	semisweet chocolate chips or carob chips	125 mL

1. In a bowl, cream together shortening, sugar, egg and vanilla.
2. In another bowl, combine flour, baking soda, cocoa and salt. Add to creamed mixture alternately with buttermilk; stir just until blended. Add bran cereal and chocolate chips; stir well.
3. Spoon batter into prepared muffin tin. Bake in preheated oven for about 25 minutes.

Surprise Brownie Muffins

Makes 12 muffins
- Preheat oven to 350°F (180°C)
- Muffin tin, paper-lined

1¾ cups	all-purpose flour	425 mL
5 tsp	baking powder	25 mL
1 tsp	salt	5 mL
1 cup	granulated sugar (can be reduced to ½ cup/125 mL or to taste)	250 mL
⅔ cup	unsweetened cocoa powder or carob powder	150 mL
1¼ cups	natural bran	300 mL
2	eggs, beaten	2

1 cup	milk	250 mL
1/2 tsp	vanilla	2 mL
2/3 cup	vegetable oil	150 mL

1. In a bowl, combine flour, baking powder, salt, sugar, cocoa powder and bran. Make a well in the center.

2. In another bowl, combine eggs, milk, vanilla and oil; mix well. Pour into dry ingredients; stir just until moist and blended.

3. Spoon batter into prepared muffin tin. Bake in preheated oven for 18 to 20 minutes.

Old-Time Classic Oat Bran Muffins

Makes 12 large muffins

- Preheat oven to 375°F (190°C)
- Muffin tin, greased or paper-lined

1 1/2 cups	oat bran	375 mL
1 cup	buttermilk	250 mL
1	egg	1
1/3 cup	vegetable oil	75 mL
1/2 cup	packed brown sugar	125 mL
1/2 tsp	vanilla	2 mL
1 cup	all-purpose flour	250 mL
1 tsp	baking powder	5 mL
1 tsp	baking soda	5 mL
1/2 tsp	salt	2 mL
1/2 tsp	ground cinnamon	2 mL
1/2 cup	raisins	125 mL

1. In a large bowl, combine oat bran and buttermilk. Let stand.

2. In another bowl, beat egg lightly. Add oil, brown sugar and vanilla. Stir into bran mixture.

3. In another bowl, sift together flour, baking powder, baking soda, salt and cinnamon. Stir into bran mixture just until moistened. Fold in raisins.

4. Spoon batter into prepared muffin tin. Bake in preheated oven for 15 to 20 minutes or until firm to the touch.

Easy Oat Bran Muffins

Makes 12 muffins

- Preheat oven to 400°F (200°C)
- Muffin tin, greased or paper-lined

1 1/4 cups	all-purpose flour	300 mL
1/2 cup	packed brown sugar	125 mL
3/4 cup	oat bran	175 mL
1/4 cup	granulated sugar	50 mL
2 tsp	baking powder	10 mL
1/2 tsp	salt	2 mL
1/4 tsp	ground cinnamon	1 mL
1	egg, lightly beaten	1
1 cup	milk	250 mL
1/4 cup	vegetable oil	50 mL
1/4 cup	liquid honey	50 mL

1. In a large bowl, mix together flour, brown sugar, oat bran, sugar, baking powder, salt and cinnamon. Make a well in the center. Add egg, milk, oil and honey. Mix just until moist and blended.

2. Spoon batter into prepared muffin tin, filling cups three-quarters full. Bake in preheated oven for 20 to 25 minutes.

Double Good Oat Bran Muffins

Makes 18 muffins

- Preheat oven to 400°F (200°C)
- Muffin tins, greased

1 cup	quick-cooking rolled oats	250 mL
1 cup	all-purpose flour	250 mL
1 cup	oat bran	250 mL
1 tsp	baking soda	5 mL
1 tbsp	baking powder	15 mL
1/2 tsp	salt	2 mL
1/2 cup	chopped pecans	125 mL
1/2 cup	chopped almonds	125 mL
1 cup	plain yogurt	250 mL
1 cup	buttermilk	250 mL
1	egg	1
1 tsp	vanilla	5 mL
1/4 cup	butter or margarine, melted or oil	50 mL
1/2 cup	dark brown sugar	125 mL

1. In a bowl, combine oats, flour, oat bran, baking soda, baking powder, salt, pecans and almonds; mix well.

2. In another bowl, whisk together yogurt, buttermilk, egg, vanilla, butter and brown sugar. Add to dry ingredients; stir just until blended.

3. Spoon batter into prepared muffin tins. Bake in preheated oven for 18 to 20 minutes.

Tip *As a substitute for 1 cup (250 mL) buttermilk, you can combine 3 tbsp (45 mL) powdered buttermilk with about 3/4 cup (175 mL) lukewarm water.*

Honey Nut Oat Bran Muffins

Makes 12 muffins

- Preheat oven to 425°F (220°C)
- Muffin tin, greased or paper-lined

2 cups	oat bran cereal	500 mL
⅓ cup	all-purpose flour	75 mL
2 tbsp	packed brown sugar	25 mL
¼ cup	chopped nuts	50 mL
¼ cup	raisins	50 mL
1 tbsp	baking powder	15 mL
½ tsp	salt	2 mL
¼ tsp	ground cinnamon	1 mL
1 cup	milk	250 mL
2	eggs, beaten	2
⅓ cup	liquid honey or light (fancy) molasses	75 mL
2 tbsp	vegetable oil	25 mL

1. In a bowl, combine cereal, flour, brown sugar, nuts, raisins, baking powder, salt and cinnamon. Make a well in the center. Add milk, eggs, honey and oil; stir just until moist and blended.

2. Spoon batter into prepared muffin tin. Bake in preheated oven for 15 to 20 minutes or until golden brown.

Honey Date Cereal Muffins

Makes 12 large muffins

- Preheat oven to 400°F (200°C)
- Muffin tin, greased

2 cups	oat and wheat cereal (such as Kellogg's Common Sense)	500 mL
1¼ cups	skim milk	300 mL
¼ cup	liquid honey	50 mL
2	egg whites	2
3 tbsp	vegetable oil	45 mL
¾ cup	chopped pitted dates	175 mL
1¼ cups	all-purpose flour	300 mL
1 tbsp	baking powder	15 mL
¼ tsp	salt	1 mL
¾ tsp	ground cinnamon	4 mL
¼ tsp	ground nutmeg	1 mL

1. In a large bowl, combine cereal, milk, honey, egg whites, oil and dates.

2. In another bowl, combine flour, baking powder, salt, cinnamon and nutmeg. Add to cereal mixture, stirring just until well blended. Batter will be lumpy.

3. Spoon batter into prepared muffin tin. Bake in preheated oven for 15 to 20 minutes or until golden brown.

Buttermilk Oat Bran Muffins

Makes 12 muffins

- Preheat oven to 400°F (200°C)
- Muffin tin, greased

1 cup	all-purpose flour	250 mL
1 cup	oat bran	250 mL
⅓ cup	granulated sugar	75 mL
1 tsp	baking powder	5 mL
1 tsp	baking soda	5 mL
½ tsp	ground cinnamon	2 mL
¼ tsp	salt	1 mL
1	egg	1
¾ cup	buttermilk	175 mL
¼ cup	corn oil	50 mL
1 tbsp	grated orange zest	15 mL
2 tbsp	freshly squeezed orange juice	25 mL
1 cup	raisins or chopped dates	250 mL

1. In a large bowl, combine flour, oat bran, sugar, baking powder, baking soda, cinnamon and salt. Mix well and make a well in the center.

2. In another bowl, whisk together egg, buttermilk, oil, zest and juice. Pour into dry ingredients and stir just until moist and blended. Fold in raisins.

3. Spoon batter into prepared muffin tin. Bake in preheated oven for 20 to 25 minutes or until top springs back when lightly touched.

Tip *If you have leftover raisins and nuts, chop them together for a great snack and healthy treat.*

Carrot Pecan Oat Bran Muffins

Makes 18 muffins

- Preheat oven to 375°F (190°C)
- Muffin tins, greased

1 cup	all-purpose flour	250 mL
1 cup	oat bran	250 mL
2 tsp	baking soda	10 mL
1 tsp	baking powder	5 mL
½ tsp	salt	2 mL
2 tsp	ground cinnamon	10 mL
1 cup	packed brown sugar	250 mL
1½ cups	shredded carrots	375 mL
2	large apples, shredded	2
½ cup	raisins	125 mL

1 cup	chopped pecans	250 mL
¼ cup	vegetable oil	50 mL
½ cup	skim milk	125 mL
2	eggs, lightly beaten	2
1 tsp	vanilla	5 mL

1. In a large bowl, combine flour, oat bran, baking soda, baking powder, salt and cinnamon. Add sugar and mix well. Stir in carrots, apples, raisins and pecans. Make a well in the center. Add oil, milk, eggs and vanilla, stirring just until moist and blended.

2. Spoon batter evenly into prepared muffin tins. Bake in preheated oven for about 20 minutes.

· ·

Carrot Chipit Oat Bran Muffins

Makes 12 muffins
- Preheat oven to 400ºF (200ºC)
- Muffin tin, greased or paper-lined

1¼ cups	whole wheat flour	300 mL
1 cup	oat bran	250 mL
½ cup	firmly packed brown sugar	125 mL
1 tsp	baking soda	5 mL
1 cup	butterscotch chips or semisweet chocolate chips	250 mL
1 cup	grated carrots	250 mL
¾ cup	plain yogurt	175 mL
½ cup	chopped pecans	125 mL
½ cup	melted butter	125 mL
1½ tsp	grated orange zest	7 mL
2	eggs	2

1. In a bowl, combine flour, bran, brown sugar, baking soda and butterscotch chips; mix well.

2. In another bowl, combine carrots, yogurt, pecans, butter, zest and eggs. Add to dry ingredients; stir just until blended.

3. Spoon batter into prepared muffin tin. Bake in preheated oven for 25 to 30 minutes.

· ·

Vegetable Oat Bran Muffins

Makes 24 muffins
- Preheat oven to 425ºF (220ºC)
- Muffin tins, greased

4 cups	oat bran	1 L
1 cup	all-purpose flour	250 mL
2 tbsp	baking powder	25 mL
2 tbsp	cornstarch	25 mL
½ tsp	salt	2 mL

2 tbsp	ground cinnamon	25 mL
½ tsp	ground nutmeg	2 mL
2 cups	skim milk	500 mL
½ cup	packed brown sugar	125 mL
¼ cup	vegetable oil	50 mL
2	eggs	2
1 tbsp	vanilla	15 mL
2 tbsp	corn syrup	25 mL
2 cups	grated carrots, zucchini or apple, or mashed banana	500 mL
1½ cups	raisins or currants or chopped dates (or a mixture)	375 mL

1. In a bowl, combine oat bran, flour, baking powder, cornstarch, salt, cinnamon and nutmeg. Make a well in the center.

2. In another bowl, combine milk, brown sugar, oil, eggs, vanilla, corn syrup, carrots and raisins; blend well. Add to dry ingredients; stir just until moistened.

3. Spoon batter into prepared muffin tins. Bake in preheated oven for 15 to 20 minutes.

Variation *Substitute 1 can (14 oz/398 mL) pumpkin purée (not pie filling) for the grated carrots.*

· ·

Oat Bran Fruit Muffins

Makes 12 muffins
- Preheat oven to 350ºF (180ºC)
- Muffin tin, greased

2¼ cups	oat bran	550 mL
½ cup	packaged mixed dried diced fruit	125 mL
1 tsp	ground cinnamon	5 mL
1 tsp	baking powder	5 mL
½ tsp	baking soda	2 mL
¼ tsp	salt	1 mL
2	egg whites	2
1 cup	unsweetened applesauce	250 mL
½ cup	packed brown sugar	125 mL
½ cup	buttermilk or plain yogurt	125 mL
2 tbsp	vegetable oil	25 mL

1. In a bowl, combine oat bran, dried fruit, cinnamon, baking powder, baking soda and salt.

2. In another bowl, whisk together egg whites, applesauce, brown sugar, buttermilk and oil. Add to dry ingredients; stir just until blended.

3. Spoon batter into prepared muffin tin. Bake in preheated oven for 30 to 35 minutes.

Applesauce Oat Bran Muffins

Makes 12 muffins
- Preheat oven to 425°F (220°C)
- Muffin tin, greased or foil-lined

TOPPING

¼ cup	crushed walnuts	50 mL
1 tbsp	granulated sugar	15 mL
½ tsp	ground cinnamon	2 mL

MUFFINS

1 cup	oat bran	250 mL
1 cup	all-purpose flour	250 mL
¼ cup	granulated sugar	50 mL
1 tbsp	baking powder	15 mL
½ tsp	salt	2 mL
¼ cup	raisins	50 mL
2	eggs	2
1 cup	unsweetened applesauce	250 mL
3 tbsp	milk	45 mL
3 tbsp	vegetable oil	45 mL

1. *Prepare the topping:* In a bowl, combine walnuts, sugar and cinnamon. Set aside.

2. *Prepare the muffins:* In a large bowl, combine oat bran, flour, sugar, baking powder, salt and raisins.

3. In another bowl, beat eggs lightly with a fork. Stir in applesauce, milk and oil. Pour into dry ingredients. Stir just until moist and blended.

4. Spoon batter into prepared muffin tin. Sprinkle with topping. Bake in preheated oven for 20 minutes.

Tip *Here's a great way to crush nuts and avoid messy cleanups: Place nuts in a plastic bag or between sheets of waxed paper and crush with a rolling pin.*

Apple Walnut Oat Bran Muffins

Makes 18 muffins
- Preheat oven to 400°F (200°C)
- Muffin tins, greased or paper-lined

1 cup	all-purpose flour	250 mL
1 cup	whole wheat flour	250 mL
1 cup	oat bran	250 mL
1 tbsp	baking powder	15 mL
1½ tsp	baking soda	7 mL
1 tsp	ground cinnamon	5 mL
1 cup	chopped walnuts	250 mL
1 cup	grated apple	250 mL
½ cup	packed brown sugar	125 mL
1½ cups	buttermilk	375 mL
3	egg whites	3
5 tbsp	vegetable oil	75 mL

1. In a large bowl, combine all-purpose flour, whole wheat flour, oat bran, baking powder, baking soda, cinnamon, walnuts and apple.

2. In another bowl, dissolve brown sugar in buttermilk. Add egg whites and oil, beating lightly with a fork until well blended. Add to dry ingredients, stirring just until moistened. Do not overmix.

3. Spoon batter into prepared muffin tins. Bake in preheated oven for 20 minutes.

Banana Oat Bran Muffins

Makes 12 muffins
- Preheat oven to 375°F (190°C)
- Muffin tin, greased or paper-lined

1¼ cups	all-purpose flour	300 mL
¾ cup	oat bran	175 mL
1 tsp	baking powder	5 mL
1 tsp	baking soda	5 mL
¼ tsp	salt	1 mL
1	egg	1
⅓ cup	vegetable oil	75 mL
⅓ cup	lightly packed brown sugar	75 mL
1 cup	mashed ripe banana	250 mL
½ cup	buttermilk or sour milk	125 mL
2 tbsp	light (fancy) molasses	25 mL
¾ cup	raisins	175 mL

1. In a large bowl, combine flour, oat bran, baking powder, baking soda and salt.

2. In another bowl, whisk together egg, oil, brown sugar, banana, buttermilk, molasses and raisins. Add to dry ingredients, stirring just until blended and lumpy.

3. Spoon batter into prepared muffin tin. Bake in preheated oven for 20 to 25 minutes.

Banana Raisin Oat Bran Muffins

Makes 12 muffins
- Preheat oven to 400°F (200°C)
- Muffin tin, paper-lined

1 cup	whole wheat flour	250 mL
1 tsp	baking powder	5 mL
1 tsp	baking soda	5 mL
1 cup	oat bran	250 mL
½ cup	raisins	125 mL
1	egg, lightly beaten	1

¼ cup	vegetable oil	50 mL
½ cup	granulated sugar	125 mL
1 cup	mashed ripe bananas	250 mL
1 tsp	vanilla	5 mL

1. In a bowl, combine flour, baking powder, baking soda, oat bran and raisins.

2. In another bowl, combine egg, oil, sugar, bananas and vanilla. Add to flour mixture; stir just until blended.

3. Spoon batter into prepared muffin tin. Bake in preheated oven for 20 to 25 minutes.

• •

Berry Oat Bran Muffins

Makes 12 muffins
- Preheat oven to 375°F (190°C)
- Muffin tin, greased or paper-lined

1	egg, lightly beaten	1
½ cup	milk or plain yogurt	125 mL
¼ cup	vegetable oil	50 mL
¼ cup	liquid honey	50 mL
⅔ cup	sweetened applesauce	150 mL
1 tsp	vanilla	5 mL
1 cup	whole wheat flour	250 mL
1 tsp	baking powder	5 mL
1 tsp	baking soda	5 mL
1 cup	oat bran	250 mL
1 cup	berries (Saskatoon or any other)	250 mL

1. In a blender or food processor, combine egg, milk, oil, honey, applesauce and vanilla. Mix well and transfer to a large bowl.

2. In another bowl, combine flour, baking powder, baking soda, oat bran and berries. Stir into egg mixture just until blended. Do not overmix.

3. Spoon batter into prepared muffin tin. Bake in preheated oven for about 15 minutes.

• •

Lemon Banana Oat Bran Muffins

Makes 12 muffins
- Preheat oven to 400°F (200°C)
- Muffin tin, greased or paper-lined

1½ cups	all-purpose flour	375 mL
¾ cup	oat bran cereal	175 mL
1 tsp	baking soda	5 mL
½ tsp	salt	2 mL
1 cup	granulated sugar	250 mL
½ cup	margarine or butter	125 mL

1 cup	mashed ripe bananas	250 mL
2	eggs	2
½ tsp	grated lemon zest	2 mL
⅓ cup	milk	75 mL
1 tsp	freshly squeezed lemon juice	5 mL
½ cup	chopped nuts	125 mL

1. In a bowl, combine flour, cereal, baking soda and salt. Mix together well.

2. In a large bowl, cream together sugar and margarine until light and fluffy. Stir in bananas, eggs and zest.

3. In another bowl, combine milk and juice. Add to banana mixture alternately with flour mixture, stirring after each addition. Fold in nuts.

4. Spoon batter into prepared muffin tin. Bake in preheated oven for 15 to 20 minutes.

• •

Orange Oat Bran Muffins

Makes 12 to 18 muffins
- Preheat oven to 400°F (200°C)
- Muffin tins, lightly greased

1 cup	oat bran	250 mL
1 cup	whole wheat flour	250 mL
¾ cup	all-purpose flour	175 mL
½ cup	quick-cooking rolled oats	125 mL
1 tbsp	baking powder	15 mL
½ tsp	ground cinnamon	2 mL
¼ tsp	salt	1 mL
2	eggs, lightly beaten	2
2 tsp	grated orange zest	10 mL
1 cup	freshly squeezed orange juice	250 mL
½ cup	liquid honey	125 mL
⅓ cup	vegetable oil	75 mL
¼ cup	skim milk	50 mL

1. In a bowl, combine oat bran, whole wheat flour, all-purpose flour, oats, baking powder, cinnamon and salt; blend well. Make a well in the center.

2. In another bowl, combine eggs, orange zest and juice, honey, oil and milk; blend well. Add to dry ingredients; stir just until blended.

3. Spoon batter into prepared muffin tins. Bake in preheated oven for 15 to 20 minutes.

Oat Bran Raisin Muffins

Makes 12 muffins
- Preheat oven to 400°F (200°C)
- Muffin tin, greased or paper-lined

2 cups	oat bran	500 mL
¼ cup	packed brown sugar	50 mL
2 tsp	baking powder	10 mL
½ cup	raisins	125 mL
1 cup	plain yogurt	250 mL
2	egg whites, lightly beaten	2
¼ cup	milk	50 mL
¼ cup	liquid honey or light (fancy) molasses	50 mL
2 tbsp	vegetable oil	25 mL
1 tsp	grated orange zest	5 mL

1. In a large bowl, combine oat bran, sugar, baking powder and raisins. Make a well in the center. Add yogurt, egg whites, milk, honey, oil and zest, stirring just until blended.

2. Spoon batter into prepared muffin tin. Bake in preheated oven for 20 minutes.

Surprise-Inside Muffins

Makes 12 muffins
- Preheat oven to 425°F (220°C)
- Muffin tin, greased

1½ cups	all-purpose flour	375 mL
2½ tsp	baking powder	12 mL
¼ tsp	salt	1 mL
1 cup	oat bran	250 mL
½ cup	packed light brown sugar	125 mL
1 cup	milk	250 mL
⅓ cup	vegetable oil	75 mL
2	eggs, lightly beaten	2
1 tsp	vanilla	5 mL
¾ cup	apricot-pineapple jam	175 mL
3 oz	cream cheese, cut into 12 pieces	90 g

1. In a bowl, sift together flour, baking powder and salt. Add oat bran and brown sugar. Set aside.

2. In another bowl, combine milk, oil, eggs and vanilla. Add to dry ingredients; stir just until moist.

3. Spoon batter into prepared muffin tin, filling one-third full. Add 1 tbsp (15 mL) jam to each; top with 1 piece cream cheese. Spoon the remaining batter over jam and cheese, dividing evenly. Bake in preheated oven for 14 to 16 minutes or until browned.

Tip *These muffins are perfect for a special brunch.*

Quick Oatmeal Muffins

Makes 12 muffins
- Preheat oven to 425°F (220°C)
- Muffin tin, greased or paper-lined

1 cup	all-purpose flour	250 mL
¼ cup	granulated sugar	50 mL
1 tbsp	baking powder	15 mL
½ tsp	salt	2 mL
1 cup	quick-cooking rolled oats	250 mL
1	egg, lightly beaten	1
1 cup	milk	250 mL
3 tbsp	vegetable oil	45 mL

1. In a large bowl, combine flour, sugar, baking powder, salt, oats, egg, milk and oil. Stir just until moist and blended.

2. Spoon batter into prepared muffin tin. Bake in preheated oven for about 15 minutes.

Grandma's Old-Fashioned Oatmeal Muffins

Makes 12 muffins
- Preheat oven to 425°F (220°C)
- Muffin tin, greased or paper-lined

¾ cup	old-fashioned rolled oats	175 mL
¾ cup + 2 tbsp	all-purpose flour	200 mL
2 tbsp	firmly packed light brown sugar	25 mL
1½ tsp	baking powder	7 mL
½ tsp	baking soda	2 mL
½ tsp	salt	2 mL
1 tsp	ground cinnamon	5 mL
¼ cup	butter or margarine	50 mL
1	egg	1
¾ cup	buttermilk	175 mL
TOPPING		
⅓ cup	granulated sugar	75 mL
1½ tsp	ground cinnamon	7 mL
1 tbsp	margarine, melted	15 mL

1. In a bowl, combine oats, flour, brown sugar, baking powder, baking soda, salt and cinnamon; mix well. Cut in butter; mix until crumbly.

2. In another bowl, beat together egg and buttermilk. Pour into dry ingredients; stir just until blended.

3. *Prepare the topping:* In another bowl, combine sugar, cinnamon and margarine; mix well.

4. Spoon batter into prepared muffin tin. Sprinkle with topping. Bake in preheated oven for 15 to 20 minutes.

Whole Wheat Oatmeal Muffins

Makes 12 muffins
- Preheat oven to 400ºF (200ºC)
- Muffin tin, greased

½ cup	all-purpose flour	125 mL
½ cup	whole wheat flour	125 mL
1 cup	old-fashioned rolled oats	250 mL
2 tsp	baking powder	10 mL
½ tsp	salt	2 mL
2	eggs	2
¾ cup	packed brown sugar	175 mL
¾ cup	milk	175 mL
¼ cup	butter or margarine, melted	50 mL
1 tsp	vanilla	5 mL

1. In a bowl, combine all-purpose flour, whole wheat flour, oats, baking powder and salt; blend well.

2. In another bowl, whisk together eggs, brown sugar, milk, butter and vanilla. Add to dry mixture; stir just until blended.

3. Spoon batter into prepared muffin tin. Bake in preheated oven for 15 to 20 minutes.

Whole Wheat Honey Oatmeal Muffins

Makes 12 muffins
- Preheat oven to 400ºF (200ºC)
- Muffin tin, greased or paper-lined

1 cup	whole wheat flour	250 mL
1 cup	old-fashioned rolled oats	250 mL
1½ tsp	baking powder	7 mL
1 tsp	baking soda	5 mL
½ tsp	salt	2 mL
¼ tsp	ground cinnamon	1 mL
¼ cup	packed brown sugar	50 mL
1	egg	1
¼ cup	butter or margarine, melted and cooled	50 mL
¼ cup	liquid honey	50 mL
1¼ cups	buttermilk	300 mL

1. In a large bowl, combine flour, oats, baking powder, baking soda, salt, cinnamon and brown sugar.

2. In another bowl, whisk together egg, butter, honey and buttermilk. Pour into flour mixture, stirring just until moistened and blended.

3. Spoon batter into prepared muffin tin. Bake in preheated oven for 15 minutes.

Garden Oatmeal Muffins

Makes 18 muffins
- Preheat oven to 400ºF (200ºC)
- Muffin tins, greased or paper-lined

1½ cups	quick-cooking rolled oats	375 mL
1½ cups	milk	375 mL
1	egg	1
½ cup	margarine, melted	125 mL
1 cup	all-purpose flour	250 mL
1 cup	whole wheat flour	250 mL
½ cup	firmly packed brown sugar	125 mL
3½ tsp	baking powder	17 mL
1 tsp	salt	5 mL
1 tsp	ground cinnamon	5 mL
½ tsp	ground nutmeg	2 mL
1 cup	grated carrots	250 mL
1 cup	grated zucchini	250 mL

1. In a bowl, cover oats with milk. Let stand for 5 minutes. Add egg and margarine; blend well.

2. In another bowl, combine all-purpose flour, whole wheat flour, brown sugar, baking powder, salt, cinnamon and nutmeg; blend well. Add oat mixture; stir just until moist. Fold in carrots and zucchini.

3. Spoon batter into prepared muffin tin. Bake in preheated oven for about 20 minutes.

Buttermilk Oatmeal Muffins

Makes 12 muffins

- Preheat oven to 400°F (200°C)
- Muffin tin, greased

1 cup	quick-cooking rolled oats	250 mL
1 cup	buttermilk	250 mL
1	egg, beaten	1
½ cup	packed brown sugar	125 mL
¼ cup	melted shortening, cooled, or vegetable oil	50 mL
½ cup	all-purpose flour	125 mL
½ cup	whole wheat pastry flour	125 mL
1½ tsp	baking powder	7 mL
½ tsp	baking soda	2 mL
½ tsp	salt	2 mL

1. In a bowl, combine oats and buttermilk. Let stand for 50 to 60 minutes.
2. In another bowl, combine egg, brown sugar and shortening; mix well. Add to oat mixture; blend well. Add all-purpose flour, whole wheat flour, baking powder, baking soda and salt; stir just until moist and blended.
3. Spoon batter into prepared muffin tin. Bake in preheated oven for 15 to 20 minutes or until browned.

Maple Oat Muffins

Makes 12 muffins

- Preheat oven to 400°F (200°C)
- Muffin tin, paper-lined

1 cup	quick-cooking maple-flavored rolled oats	250 mL
1 cup	sour cream	250 mL
1 cup	all-purpose flour	250 mL
½ cup	packed brown sugar	125 mL
1 tsp	baking powder	5 mL
½ tsp	baking soda	2 mL
½ tsp	salt	2 mL
1	egg, beaten	1
¼ cup	vegetable oil	50 mL

1. In a bowl, combine oats and sour cream. Set aside.
2. In another bowl, combine flour, brown sugar, baking powder, baking soda and salt.

3. Add egg and oil to oat mixture; blend well. Add dry ingredients; mix together quickly just until moist. Do not overmix (batter will be lumpy).
4. Spoon batter into prepared muffin tin. Bake in preheated oven for 15 to 20 minutes.

Fruity Oatmeal Muffins

Makes 12 muffins

- Preheat oven to 350°F (180°C)
- Muffin tin, greased or paper-lined

1 cup	all-purpose flour	250 mL
1 tsp	baking powder	5 mL
¼ tsp	pumpkin pie spice	1 mL
1 cup	packaged dried fruit	250 mL
½ cup	butter or margarine, softened	125 mL
⅔ cup	granulated sugar	150 mL
6	eggs	6
1 tsp	vanilla	5 mL
⅓ cup	old-fashioned rolled oats	75 mL

1. In a small bowl, combine flour, baking powder and pumpkin pie spice. Toss 1 tbsp (15 mL) of this mixture with the dried fruit.
2. In a large bowl, beat butter and sugar on medium speed until light and fluffy. Beat in eggs and blend well. Reduce speed to low and add vanilla. Gradually add flour mixture, beating just until blended. Stir in fruit mixture and oats.
3. Spoon batter into prepared muffin tin. Bake in preheated oven for 20 minutes or until golden brown.

Apple Date Oatmeal Muffins

Makes 8 large muffins

- Preheat oven to 400°F (200°C)
- 8-cup muffin tin, paper-lined

¾ cup	quick-cooking rolled oats, divided	175 mL
1 tsp	firmly packed light brown sugar	5 mL
¼ tsp	ground cinnamon	1 mL
1 cup less 1 tbsp	all-purpose flour	235 mL
2 tbsp	granulated sugar	25 mL
2 tsp	baking powder	10 mL
1 tbsp	grated orange zest	15 mL
½ cup	freshly squeezed orange juice	125 mL
1	egg	1

¼ cup	margarine, melted	50 mL
1	small apple, chopped	1
8	dates, pitted and chopped	8

1. In a small skillet over medium heat, toast ⅓ cup (75 mL) of the oats, stirring often, for 3 to 4 minutes or until golden. Remove from heat and stir in brown sugar and cinnamon. Set aside.

2. In a large bowl, combine the remaining oats, flour, sugar and baking powder. Make a well in the center.

3. In another bowl, combine zest, juice, egg and margarine. Add to the flour mixture, stirring just until moistened. Fold in apple and dates.

4. Spoon batter into prepared muffin tin. Sprinkle with toasted oat mixture. Bake in preheated oven for 20 to 25 minutes.

• •

Lemon-Glazed Apple Oatmeal Muffins

Makes 12 muffins

- Preheat oven to 400°F (200°C)
- Muffin tin, greased or paper-lined

1¼ cups	all-purpose flour	300 mL
½ cup	packed light brown sugar	125 mL
1½ tsp	baking powder	7 mL
1 tsp	baking soda	5 mL
1 tsp	ground cinnamon	5 mL
½ tsp	salt	2 mL
¼ tsp	ground nutmeg	1 mL
1	egg	1
½ cup	milk	125 mL
¼ cup	vegetable oil	50 mL
2 tbsp	freshly squeezed lemon juice	25 mL
¾ cup	quick-cooking rolled oats	175 mL
1 cup	finely chopped apples	250 mL
½ cup	chopped nuts	125 mL
LEMON GLAZE		
½ cup	confectioner's (icing) sugar	125 mL
1 tbsp	freshly squeezed lemon juice	15 mL
1 tbsp	butter or margarine, melted	15 mL

1. In a medium bowl, combine flour, sugar, baking powder, baking soda, cinnamon, salt and nutmeg.

2. In a large bowl, beat egg. Add milk, oil and lemon juice. Stir in oats and mix well. Add flour mixture, blending well. Add apples and nuts, stirring just until moistened and lumpy. Do not overmix.

3. Spoon batter into prepared muffin tin. Bake in preheated oven for 20 minutes or until golden brown.

4. *Meanwhile, prepare the glaze:* In a small bowl, combine confectioner's sugar, lemon juice and butter. Remove muffins from tin and place on a plate. Drizzle with glaze.

Tip *When buying lemons, look for fine-textured skin. The lemon will be juicier. If there is a bit of greenish coloring, the juice will be more acidic.*

• •

Apricot Oatmeal Muffins

Makes 12 to 18 muffins

- Preheat oven to 400°F (200°C)
- Muffin tins, greased or paper-lined

¾ cup	boiling water	175 mL
1 cup	quick-cooking rolled oats	250 mL
½ cup	chopped dried apricots	125 mL
½ cup	margarine or butter	125 mL
1	egg	1
1 cup	milk	250 mL
2½ cups	all-purpose flour	625 mL
½ cup	firmly packed brown sugar	125 mL
1 tbsp	baking powder	15 mL
½ tsp	salt	2 mL

1. In a medium bowl, pour boiling water over oats, apricots and margarine. Stir until margarine melts. Set aside to cool. Add egg and milk.

2. In a large bowl, combine flour, brown sugar, baking powder and salt. Add oat mixture, stirring just until blended and moistened. Do not overmix.

3. Spoon batter into prepared muffin tins. Bake in preheated oven for about 20 minutes.

Scrumptious Blueberry Oat Muffins

Makes 12 muffins

- Preheat oven to 400°F (200°C)
- Muffin tin, greased

1 cup	quick-cooking rolled oats	250 mL
1 cup	buttermilk	250 mL
1	egg, beaten	1
1/4 cup	butter or margarine, melted	50 mL
1 cup	all-purpose flour	250 mL
1 tsp	baking powder	5 mL
1/2 tsp	baking soda	2 mL
1/2 tsp	salt	2 mL
3/4 cup	lightly packed brown sugar	175 mL
1 cup	fresh or frozen blueberries, thawed and drained	250 mL

1. In a bowl, combine oats and buttermilk. Let stand for 5 to 10 minutes. Mix in egg and butter.
2. In another bowl, combine flour, baking powder, baking soda, salt and brown sugar. Add oat mixture; stir just until blended. Fold in blueberries.
3. Spoon batter into prepared muffin tin. Bake in preheated oven for 15 to 20 minutes.

Cranberry Oatmeal Muffins

Makes 12 muffins

- Preheat oven to 350°F (180°C)
- Muffin tin, greased

1/2 cup	finely chopped walnuts	125 mL
1/2 cup	dried cranberries	125 mL
1 1/2 cups	all-purpose flour, divided	375 mL
1 tbsp	baking powder	15 mL
3/4 tsp	salt	4 mL
3/4 cup	old-fashioned rolled oats	175 mL
3 tbsp	butter or margarine, softened	45 mL
3/4 cup	firmly packed light brown sugar	175 mL
3/4 cup	milk	175 mL
1	egg	1

1. In a small bowl, toss together nuts, cranberries and 1 tsp (5 mL) of the flour. Set aside.
2. In a large bowl, combine the remaining flour, baking powder and salt. Stir in oats.
3. In another bowl, combine butter, sugar, milk and egg, blending well. Add to flour mixture, stirring just until evenly moist and blended. Fold in nut mixture.

4. Spoon batter into prepared muffin tin. Bake in preheated oven for about 20 minutes.

Orange Date Oatmeal Muffins

Makes 12 large muffins

- Preheat oven to 400°F (200°C)
- Muffin tin, greased or paper-lined

1 1/4 cups	milk	300 mL
1 cup	quick-cooking rolled oats	250 mL
1	orange, quartered and seeded	1
1	egg	1
3/4 cup	firmly packed brown sugar	175 mL
1/2 cup	butter or margarine, melted	125 mL
1/2 cup	chopped dates	125 mL
2 cups	all-purpose flour	500 mL
1 tbsp	baking powder	15 mL
1/2 tsp	salt	2 mL

1. In a bowl, pour milk over oats. Let stand for 5 minutes.
2. In a food processor or blender, process orange until finely chopped. Stir into oat mixture. Add egg, sugar, butter and dates.
3. In a large bowl, combine flour, baking powder and salt. Add oat mixture, stirring just until blended. Do not overmix.
4. Spoon batter into prepared muffin tin. Bake in preheated oven for 20 to 25 minutes or until golden brown.

Peachy Oatmeal Muffins

Makes 12 to 18 muffins

- Preheat oven to 400°F (200°C)
- Muffin tins, paper-lined

2 cups	whole wheat flour	500 mL
1 cup	old-fashioned rolled oats	250 mL
1/2 cup	natural bran	125 mL
1/2 cup	packed brown sugar	125 mL
1 1/2 tsp	baking soda	7 mL
1 tsp	salt	5 mL
2	eggs	2
1 1/2 cups	buttermilk	375 mL
1/4 cup	vegetable oil	50 mL
1 tbsp	grated orange zest	15 mL
1 1/2 tsp	ground cinnamon	7 mL
3	peaches, finely chopped	3

1. In a large bowl, combine flour, oats, bran, sugar, baking soda and salt. Make a well in the center.
2. In another bowl, whisk together eggs, buttermilk and oil. Stir in zest and cinnamon. Add to dry ingredients, stirring just until moistened. Fold in peaches.
3. Spoon batter into prepared muffin tins. Bake in preheated oven for about 20 minutes.

Variation *You could replace peaches with 2 cups (500 mL) fresh chopped pears, plums or nectarines.*

● ●

Pineapple Oatmeal Muffins

Makes 12 muffins
- Preheat oven to 350°F (180°C)
- Muffin tin, greased or paper-lined

1	can (8 oz/227 mL) crushed pineapple, with juice	1
1 cup	sour cream	250 mL
1	egg	1
¼ cup	butter or margarine, melted	50 mL
1½ cups	all-purpose flour	375 mL
1 cup	old-fashioned rolled oats	250 mL
½ cup	granulated sugar	125 mL
1 tbsp	baking powder	15 mL
1 tsp	ground cinnamon	5 mL
½ tsp	ground nutmeg	2 mL
½ tsp	salt	2 mL
1 cup	raisins (optional)	250 mL

1. In a bowl, combine pineapple (with juice), sour cream, egg and butter; blend well.
2. In another bowl, combine flour, oats, sugar, baking powder, cinnamon, nutmeg, salt and raisins (if using). Add to pineapple mixture; stir just until moist.
3. Spoon batter into prepared muffin tin. Bake in preheated oven for 30 to 35 minutes or until lightly browned.

● ●

Oatmeal Date Muffins

Makes 12 muffins
- Preheat oven to 375°F (190°C)
- Muffin tin, greased or paper-lined

1 cup	all-purpose flour	250 mL
2 tsp	baking powder	10 mL
½ tsp	baking soda	2 mL
½ tsp	salt	2 mL
1 cup	old-fashioned rolled oats	250 mL
1 cup	buttermilk	250 mL
½ cup	packed dark brown sugar	125 mL
1	egg, beaten	1
½ cup	butter or margarine, melted	125 mL
½ cup	chopped moist dates	125 mL

1. In a medium bowl, sift together flour, baking powder, baking soda and salt.
2. In a large bowl, combine oats and buttermilk. Let stand for 5 minutes. Add brown sugar, egg and butter, mixing well. Fold in dates. Add to flour mixture, stirring just until moist and blended.
3. Spoon batter into prepared muffin tin. Bake in preheated oven for 25 to 30 minutes.

● ●

Oatmeal Raisin Breakfast Muffins

Makes 12 small muffins
- Preheat oven to 400°F (200°C)
- Muffin tin, greased

½ cup	raisins	125 mL
1 cup	all-purpose flour, divided	250 mL
¼ cup	butter or margarine	50 mL
⅓ cup	granulated sugar	75 mL
2	eggs	2
⅔ cup	milk	150 mL
1 tbsp	baking powder	15 mL
¾ tsp	salt	4 mL
1 cup	old-fashioned rolled oats	250 mL

1. In a small bowl, toss together raisins and ¼ cup (50 mL) of the flour. Set aside.
2. In a large bowl, cream together butter and sugar. Add eggs one at a time, beating after each addition. Add milk.
3. In another bowl, combine the remaining flour, baking powder and salt. Pour into wet ingredients. Add oats, stirring just until blended. Fold in dredged raisins.
4. Spoon batter into prepared muffin tin. Bake in preheated oven for 20 to 25 minutes.

Tip *In baking only, you can use 1 cup (250 mL) shortening plus ½ tsp (2 mL) salt to replace 1 cup (250 mL) butter.*

Chocolate Chip Oatmeal Muffins

Makes 12 large muffins
- Muffin tin, greased or paper-lined

1 cup	old-fashioned rolled oats	250 mL
2 cups	buttermilk	500 mL
2	eggs, lightly beaten	2
1⅔ cups	whole wheat flour	400 mL
1 tsp	baking soda	5 mL
1 tsp	salt	5 mL
2 tbsp	vegetable oil	25 mL
1 cup	semisweet chocolate chips	250 mL

1. In a bowl, combine oats and buttermilk. Cover and refrigerate overnight. The next day, add beaten eggs; whisk well. Preheat oven to 400°F (200°C).

2. In another bowl, sift together flour, baking soda, salt and oil. Add to oat mixture; stir just until blended. Fold in chocolate chips.

3. Spoon batter into prepared muffin tin. Bake in preheated oven for 15 to 20 minutes.

Wheat Germ Oat Muffins

Makes 12 muffins
- Preheat oven to 425°F (220°C)
- Muffin tin, greased or paper-lined

½ cup	wheat germ	125 mL
½ cup	quick-cooking rolled oats	125 mL
1 cup	all-purpose flour	250 mL
1 tbsp	baking powder	15 mL
½ tsp	salt	2 mL
¾ tsp	ground cinnamon	4 mL
Pinch	ground nutmeg	Pinch
½ cup	packed brown sugar	125 mL
⅓ cup	shortening	75 mL
1	egg, lightly beaten	1
1 cup	milk	250 mL
1 tsp	vanilla	5 mL

1. In a bowl, combine wheat germ, oats, flour, baking powder, salt, cinnamon, nutmeg and brown sugar; blend well. Using a pastry blender or two knives, cut in shortening; mix until crumbly. Add egg, milk and vanilla; stir just until moist.

2. Spoon batter into prepared muffin tin. Bake in preheated oven for 15 to 20 minutes.

Favorite Wheat Germ Muffins

Makes 12 muffins
- Preheat oven to 425°F (200°C)
- Muffin tin, greased or paper-lined

1 cup	all-purpose flour	250 mL
1 cup	toasted wheat germ	250 mL
4 tsp	baking powder	20 mL
¼ tsp	baking soda	1 mL
½ tsp	salt	2 mL
1	egg	1
2 tbsp	butter or margarine, softened	25 mL
¼ cup	packed brown sugar	50 mL
	Grated zest of 1 orange	
¼ cup	freshly squeezed orange juice	50 mL
¾ cup	plain yogurt	175 mL

1. In a large bowl, combine flour, wheat germ, baking powder, baking soda and salt. Make a well in the center.

2. In another bowl, cream together egg, butter and sugar. Stir in zest and orange juice, mixing well. Add yogurt. Add to dry ingredients, stirring just until blended. Do not overmix.

3. Spoon batter into prepared muffin tin. Bake in preheated oven for about 15 minutes.

Orange-Glazed Wheat Germ Muffins

Makes 12 muffins
- Preheat oven to 400°F (200°C)
- Muffin tin, greased or paper-lined

ORANGE GLAZE

½ cup	confectioner's (icing) sugar	125 mL
1 tbsp	freshly squeezed orange juice	15 mL

MUFFINS

1½ cups	all-purpose flour	375 mL
½ cup	wheat germ	125 mL
¼ cup	granulated sugar	50 mL
1 tbsp	baking powder	15 mL
½ tsp	salt	2 mL
1 tbsp	grated orange zest	15 mL
⅔ cup	milk	150 mL
⅓ cup	margarine, melted	75 mL
2	eggs	2

1. *Prepare the glaze:* In a bowl, combine confectioner's sugar and orange juice; blend well. Set aside.

2. *Prepare the muffins:* In another bowl, combine flour, wheat germ, sugar, baking powder, salt and zest; mix well. Make a well in the center.

3. In another bowl, combine milk, margarine and eggs. Add to dry ingredients; stir just until moist and blended.

4. Spoon batter into prepared muffin tin. Bake in preheated oven for 20 to 25 minutes. Let cool; drizzle with glaze.

Apple Streusel Wheat Germ Muffins

Makes 12 muffins

- Preheat oven to 400°F (200°C)
- Muffin tin, greased or paper-lined

TOPPING

¼ cup	granulated sugar	50 mL
½ tsp	ground cinnamon	2 mL
⅓ cup	chopped nuts	75 mL
2 tbsp	butter or margarine, melted	25 mL

MUFFINS

1½ cups	all-purpose flour	375 mL
½ cup	wheat germ	125 mL
¼ cup	granulated sugar	50 mL
1 tbsp	baking powder	15 mL
¾ tsp	ground cinnamon	4 mL
½ tsp	salt	2 mL
1 cup	chopped peeled apple	250 mL
1	egg	1
1 cup	milk	250 mL
¼ cup	vegetable oil	50 mL

1. *Prepare the topping:* In a bowl, combine sugar, cinnamon, nuts and butter. Set aside.

2. *Prepare the muffins:* In a large bowl, combine flour, wheat germ, sugar, baking powder, cinnamon and salt. Stir in apple.

3. In another bowl, whisk together egg, milk and oil. Add to dry ingredients, stirring just until moistened.

4. Spoon batter into prepared muffin tin. Sprinkle with topping. Bake in preheated oven for 20 to 25 minutes or until browned.

Banana Wheat Germ Muffins

Makes 12 muffins

- Preheat oven to 375°F (190°C)
- Muffin tin, greased or paper-lined

2	small ripe bananas (or 1 large), mashed	2
½ cup	granulated sugar or brown sugar	125 mL
⅓ cup	vegetable oil	75 mL
1	egg	1
1 tsp	vanilla	5 mL
½ cup	wheat germ	125 mL
1½ cups	all-purpose flour	375 mL
1 tsp	baking powder	5 mL
1 tsp	baking soda	5 mL
½ cup	milk	125 mL

1. In a bowl, combine bananas, sugar, oil, egg and vanilla; beat until smooth. Add wheat germ; blend well.

2. In another bowl, sift together flour, baking powder and baking soda. Add to banana mixture alternately with milk; stir just until blended.

3. Spoon batter into prepared muffin tin. Bake in preheated oven for 20 to 25 minutes.

Blueberry Wheat Germ Muffins

Makes 12 muffins

- Preheat oven to 400°F (200°C)
- Muffin tin, greased or paper-lined

1¾ cups	all-purpose flour	425 mL
⅓ cup	wheat germ	75 mL
⅓ cup	granulated sugar	75 mL
1 tbsp	baking powder	15 mL
1½ tsp	grated lemon zest	7 mL
½ tsp	salt	2 mL
1	egg	1
1 cup	milk	250 mL
¼ cup	vegetable oil	50 mL
1 cup	fresh blueberries or frozen blueberries, drained	250 mL

1. In a large bowl, combine flour, wheat germ, sugar, baking powder, zest and salt. Make a well in the center.

2. In another bowl, whisk together egg, milk and oil. Add to dry ingredients, stirring just until moist and blended. Fold in berries.

3. Spoon batter into prepared muffin tin. Bake in preheated oven for 20 to 25 minutes.

Orange Wheat Germ Muffins

Makes 12 muffins

- Preheat oven to 400°F (200°C)
- Muffin tin, greased or paper-lined

1 cup	all-purpose flour	250 mL
¾ cup	wheat germ	175 mL
½ cup	natural bran	125 mL
1 tbsp	baking powder	15 mL
½ tsp	salt	2 mL
½ cup	packed brown sugar	125 mL
½ cup	raisins	125 mL
1	egg	1
1 cup	milk	250 mL
¼ cup	vegetable oil	50 mL
2 tsp	grated orange zest	10 mL

1. In a large bowl, combine flour, wheat germ, bran, baking powder, salt, brown sugar and raisins.

2. In another bowl, whisk together egg, milk, oil and zest. Add to dry ingredients, stirring just until moist and blended.

3. Spoon batter into prepared muffin tin. Bake in preheated oven for 15 to 20 minutes.

Tip *For plumper raisins, soak in orange juice and store in the refrigerator.*

Wheat Muffins

Makes 12 muffins

- Preheat oven to 400°F (200°C)
- Muffin tin, greased or paper-lined

1 cup	all-purpose flour	250 mL
1 cup	unsifted whole wheat flour	250 mL
2 tsp	baking powder	10 mL
1 tsp	salt	5 mL
1	egg, lightly beaten	1
¼ cup	light (fancy) molasses	50 mL
1 cup	milk	250 mL
¼ cup	butter or margarine, melted	50 mL

1. In a large bowl, combine all-purpose flour, whole wheat flour, baking powder and salt. Make a well in the center.

2. In another bowl, combine egg, molasses, milk and butter. Add to flour mixture, stirring just until blended. Do not overmix.

3. Spoon batter into prepared muffin tin. Bake in preheated oven for 25 minutes or until golden brown.

Herbed Whole Wheat Muffins

Makes 12 muffins

- Preheat oven to 400°F (200°C)
- Muffin tin, greased or paper-lined

1 cup	whole wheat flour	250 mL
1 cup	all-purpose flour	250 mL
⅓ cup	granulated sugar	75 mL
2 tsp	baking powder	10 mL
½ tsp	baking soda	2 mL
½ tsp	salt	2 mL
½ tsp	dried basil	2 mL
¼ tsp	dried marjoram	1 mL
¼ tsp	dried oregano	1 mL
Pinch	dried thyme	Pinch
¾ cup	raisins	175 mL
1 cup	buttermilk	250 mL
2 tbsp	butter or margarine, melted	25 mL
1	egg, beaten	1
2 tbsp	wheat germ	25 mL

1. In a large bowl, combine whole wheat flour, all-purpose flour, sugar, baking powder, baking soda, salt, basil, marjoram, oregano, thyme and raisins.

2. In another bowl, whisk together buttermilk, butter and egg. Add to flour mixture, stirring just until moistened and blended.

3. Spoon batter into prepared muffin tin. Sprinkle with wheat germ. Bake in preheated oven for 15 to 20 minutes.

Spicy Whole Wheat Muffins

Makes 12 large muffins

- Preheat oven to 350°F (180°C)
- Muffin tin, greased or paper-lined

2 cups	whole wheat flour	500 mL
¾ cup	all-purpose flour	175 mL
⅔ cup	packed brown sugar	150 mL
2 tsp	baking soda	10 mL
1 tsp	pumpkin pie spice	5 mL
2 cups	buttermilk	500 mL
¾ cup	raisins	175 mL

1. In a bowl, combine whole wheat flour, all-purpose flour, brown sugar, baking soda and pumpkin pie spice. Stir in buttermilk. Fold in raisins.

2. Spoon batter into prepared muffin tin. Bake in preheated oven for 35 to 40 minutes.

Honey Whole Wheat Muffins

Makes 12 muffins

- Preheat oven to 400°F (200°C)
- Muffin tin, greased or paper-lined

1 cup	whole wheat flour	250 mL
1 cup	all-purpose flour	250 mL
1 tbsp	baking powder	15 mL
1 tsp	salt	5 mL
1	egg	1
1 cup	milk	250 mL
1/4 cup	vegetable oil	50 mL
1/4 cup	liquid honey	50 mL

1. In a large bowl, combine whole wheat flour, all-purpose flour, baking powder and salt. Make a well in the center.

2. In another bowl, whisk together egg, milk and oil. Add the honey. Stir into flour mixture until moist and lumpy.

3. Spoon batter into prepared muffin tin. Bake in preheated oven for 20 to 25 minutes or until lightly browned.

Peanut Butter Wheat Muffins

Makes 12 small muffins

- Preheat oven to 400°F (200°C)
- Muffin tin, greased or paper-lined

1 1/4 cups	whole wheat flour	300 mL
1 tsp	baking powder	5 mL
1 tsp	baking soda	5 mL
1/2 tsp	salt	2 mL
1/3 cup	packed brown sugar	75 mL
1	egg	1
1/2 cup	peanut butter	125 mL
1 cup	buttermilk	250 mL
1/2 tsp	vanilla	2 mL
1/2 cup	peanut halves (optional)	125 mL

1. In a large bowl, mix together flour, baking powder, baking soda, salt and brown sugar. Make a well in the center.

2. In another bowl, whisk together egg and peanut butter. Whisk in buttermilk and vanilla. Add to dry ingredients, stirring just until moistened.

3. Spoon batter into prepared muffin tin. Sprinkle with peanut halves (if using). Bake in preheated oven for 15 to 18 minutes.

Walnut Crunch Wheat Muffins

Makes 18 small muffins

- Preheat oven to 425°F (220°C)
- Muffin tins, greased or paper-lined

1 cup	whole wheat flour	250 mL
1 cup	all-purpose flour	250 mL
1/2 tsp	salt	2 mL
1 tbsp	baking powder	15 mL
1 tsp	baking soda	5 mL
1/2 cup	packed brown sugar	125 mL
1 cup	coarsely chopped walnuts	250 mL
1 cup	buttermilk	250 mL
2	eggs, beaten	2
1/3 cup	melted butter	75 mL

1. In a bowl, sift together whole wheat flour, all-purpose flour, salt, baking powder, baking soda and brown sugar; mix well. Add walnuts; make a well in the center.

2. In another bowl, whisk together buttermilk, eggs and butter. Pour into flour mixture; stir only until moist and blended.

3. Spoon batter into prepared muffin tins. Bake in preheated oven for about 15 minutes.

Apple Whole Wheat Muffins

Makes 12 muffins

- Preheat oven to 400°F (200°C)
- Muffin tin, greased or paper-lined

1 1/2 cups	whole wheat flour	375 mL
1/2 cup	all-purpose flour	125 mL
2 1/2 tsp	baking powder	12 mL
3/4 tsp	salt	4 mL
1	egg, beaten	1
3/4 cup	milk	175 mL
1/3 cup	vegetable oil	75 mL
1/3 cup	liquid honey	75 mL
1 cup	chopped apples	250 mL

1. In a large bowl, combine whole wheat flour, all-purpose flour, baking powder and salt.

2. In another bowl, whisk together egg, milk, oil and honey. Add to flour mixture, stirring just until moist and blended. Do not overmix. Fold in apples.

3. Spoon batter into prepared muffin tin. Bake in preheated oven for 18 to 20 minutes or until a toothpick inserted in center comes out clean and dry.

Apricot Whole Wheat Muffins

Makes 12 muffins
- Preheat oven to 400°F (200°C)
- Muffin tin, greased or paper-lined

1	can (14 oz/398 mL) apricot halves, well drained	1
1 cup	all-purpose flour	250 mL
¾ cup	whole wheat flour	175 mL
2½ tsp	baking powder	12 mL
½ tsp	baking soda	2 mL
¾ tsp	salt	4 mL
Pinch	ground ginger	Pinch
⅓ cup	packed brown sugar	75 mL
1	egg	1
¼ cup	vegetable oil	50 mL
½ cup	milk	125 mL
¼ cup	dried apricots, cut into tiny pieces	50 mL

1. In a blender, purée canned apricots. Set aside.
2. In a bowl, combine all-purpose flour, whole wheat flour, baking powder, baking soda, salt, ginger and brown sugar; mix well. Make a well in the center.
3. In another bowl, whisk together egg, oil and milk. Add 1 cup (250 mL) apricot purée and dried apricots. Add to flour mixture; stir just until moist and blended.
4. Spoon batter into prepared muffin tin. Bake in preheated oven for about 15 minutes.

Orange Marmalade Wheat Muffins

Makes 12 muffins
- Preheat oven to 400°F (200°C)
- Muffin tin, greased

¾ cup	whole wheat flour	175 mL
¾ cup	all-purpose flour	175 mL
⅓ cup	granulated sugar	75 mL
2 tsp	baking powder	10 mL
½ tsp	baking soda	2 mL
¼ tsp	salt	1 mL
2 tsp	ground ginger	10 mL
2	eggs	2
⅓ cup	sour cream	75 mL
1 tbsp	grated orange zest	15 mL
⅓ cup	freshly squeezed orange juice	75 mL
7 tbsp	butter, melted	105 mL
	Orange marmalade	

1. In a bowl, combine whole wheat flour, all-purpose flour, sugar, baking powder, baking soda, salt and ginger. Make a well in the center.
2. In another bowl, whisk together eggs, sour cream, orange zest, orange juice and butter. Pour into dry ingredients; stir quickly just until moist and blended.
3. Spoon batter into prepared muffin tin. Add about 1 tsp (5 mL) orange marmalade to center of each. Bake in preheated oven for about 20 minutes.

Whole Wheat Date Muffins

Makes 12 muffins
- Preheat oven to 375°F (190°C)
- Muffin tin, greased or paper-lined

1 cup	chopped pitted dates	250 mL
1 tsp	baking soda	5 mL
¾ cup	boiling water	175 mL
1	egg	1
½ cup	granulated sugar	125 mL
1 tsp	salt	5 mL
1 tsp	vanilla	5 mL
1½ cups	whole wheat flour	375 mL
1 tsp	baking powder	5 mL
½ cup	chopped walnuts	125 mL
¼ cup	butter, melted	50 mL

1. In a large bowl, toss together dates and baking soda. Pour boiling water over top. Mix well and set aside to cool.
2. In another bowl, whisk together egg, sugar, salt and vanilla. Add to date mixture. Stir in flour, baking powder and walnuts. Add melted butter, stirring just until blended.
3. Spoon batter into prepared muffin tin. Bake in preheated oven for 15 to 20 minutes.

Tip *Store shelled nuts (and coconut) in tightly covered containers in the fridge or freezer to prevent from becoming rancid. When ready to use, heat thoroughly at 350°F (180°C).*

Raisin Bran Wheat Muffins

Makes 12 large muffins
- Preheat oven to 400°F (200°C)
- Muffin tin, greased or paper-lined

1 cup	natural bran	250 mL
1 cup	buttermilk	250 mL
½ cup	raisins	125 mL
½ cup	liquid honey	125 mL
¼ cup	light (fancy) molasses	50 mL
⅓ cup	butter, melted, or vegetable oil	75 mL
2	eggs	2
1 tsp	vanilla	5 mL
2 cups	whole wheat flour	500 mL
1 tsp	baking powder	5 mL
1 tsp	baking soda	5 mL
¼ tsp	ground cinnamon	1 mL
Pinch	salt	Pinch

1. In a small bowl, combine bran, buttermilk and raisins. Set aside to soak.
2. In another bowl, whisk together honey, molasses, butter, eggs and vanilla. Add bran mixture.
3. In another bowl, sift together flour, baking powder, baking soda, cinnamon and salt. Add to liquid ingredients, stirring just until blended. Do not overmix.
4. Spoon batter into prepared muffin tin. Bake in preheated oven for 20 to 25 minutes.

Tip *As a substitute for 1 cup (250 mL) buttermilk, you can combine 3 tbsp (45 mL) powdered buttermilk with about ¾ cup (175 mL) lukewarm water.*

Cheddar Cheese Muffins with Apple Butter

Makes 12 to 18 muffins
- Preheat oven to 400°F (200°C)
- Muffin tins, greased or paper-lined

2 cups	all-purpose flour	500 mL
½ cup	granulated sugar	125 mL
1 tbsp	baking powder	15 mL
½ tsp	salt	2 mL
½ tsp	baking soda	2 mL
2 cups	shredded Cheddar cheese	500 mL
1 cup	plain yogurt	250 mL
¼ cup	butter or margarine, melted	50 mL
2	eggs, beaten	2
APPLE BUTTER		
½ cup	butter, softened	125 mL
½ cup	apple jelly	125 mL
¼ tsp	ground cinnamon	1 mL

1. In a large bowl, combine flour, sugar, baking powder, salt and baking soda. Stir in cheese, mixing well. Make a well in the center.
2. In another bowl, whisk together yogurt, butter and eggs. Add quickly to dry ingredients, stirring just until blended and lumpy.
3. Spoon batter into prepared muffin tins. Bake in preheated oven for 18 to 20 minutes or until golden brown.
4. *Meanwhile, prepare the apple butter:* In a bowl, beat butter until creamy. Add jelly and cinnamon, blending well. Serve with warm muffins.

Cheddar Cheese Apple Muffins

Makes 12 large muffins
- Preheat oven to 400°F (200°C)
- Muffin tin, greased or paper-lined

1	egg	1
1¼ cups	milk	300 mL
¼ cup	melted margarine	50 mL
2½ cups	all-purpose flour	625 mL
¼ cup	granulated sugar	50 mL
1 tbsp	baking powder	15 mL
1 tsp	salt	5 mL
1 cup	grated apple	250 mL
1¼ cups	shredded old Cheddar cheese, divided	300 mL

1. In a bowl, beat egg lightly with a fork. Add milk and margarine; stir well.
2. In a bowl, combine flour, sugar, baking powder and salt. Add egg mixture; stir just until blended. Fold in apple and 1 cup (250 mL) of the cheese.
3. Spoon batter into prepared muffin tin. Sprinkle with the remaining cheese. Bake in preheated oven for about 20 minutes or until golden brown.

Applesauce Cheese Muffins

Makes 12 large muffins
- Preheat oven to 400°F (200°C)
- Muffin tin, greased

2 cups	whole wheat flour	500 mL
1/4 cup	wheat germ	50 mL
2 tbsp	granulated sugar	25 mL
1 tbsp	baking powder	15 mL
1/2 tsp	baking soda	2 mL
1/4 tsp	salt	1 mL
1/4 cup	butter or margarine, softened	50 mL
1 1/2 cups	shredded Cheddar cheese	375 mL
2	eggs, lightly beaten	2
3/4 cup	milk	175 mL
3/4 cup	sweetened applesauce	175 mL

1. In a bowl, combine flour, wheat germ, sugar, baking powder, baking soda and salt. Cut in butter with a pastry blender until mixture is crumbly. Add cheese.

2. In another bowl, combine eggs, milk and applesauce. Pour all at once into dry ingredients and stir just until blended.

3. Spoon batter into prepared muffin tin. Bake in preheated oven for 18 to 20 minutes.

Cheddar Bacon Muffins

Makes 12 muffins
- Preheat oven to 400°F (200°C)
- Muffin tin, greased or paper-lined

2 cups	all-purpose flour	500 mL
2 tbsp	granulated sugar	25 mL
1 tbsp	baking powder	15 mL
1/4 tsp	salt	1 mL
1/2 cup	shredded Cheddar cheese	125 mL
4 to 5	slices bacon, cooked crisp and crumbled	4 to 5
1	egg, lightly beaten	1
1 cup	milk	250 mL
1/4 cup	vegetable oil	50 mL

1. In a large bowl, combine flour, sugar, baking powder, salt, cheese and bacon. Blend well and make a well in the center.

2. In another bowl, whisk together egg, milk and oil. Pour into dry ingredients and stir just until moist and lumpy.

3. Spoon batter into prepared muffin tin. Bake in preheated oven for 20 to 25 minutes.

Variations *Increase shredded Cheddar cheese to 1 cup (250 mL). Use the added 1/2 cup (125 mL) to sprinkle over tops before baking.*

Replace milk with 1 can (10 oz/284 mL) of any cream soup such as mushroom or chicken.

Omit the bacon and substitute 2/3 cup (150 mL) chopped cooked ham. Substitute Swiss cheese for Cheddar and increase oil to 1/3 cup (75 mL).

Cheddar Brunch Muffins

Makes 12 muffins
- Preheat oven to 400°F (200°C)
- Muffin tin, greased or paper-lined

2 cups	all-purpose flour	500 mL
2 tbsp	granulated sugar	25 mL
2 1/2 tsp	baking powder	12 mL
1/2 tsp	salt	2 mL
1 1/2 cups	shredded Cheddar cheese	375 mL
1	egg	1
1 cup	milk	250 mL
1/4 cup	melted butter	50 mL

1. In a large bowl, sift together flour, sugar, baking powder and salt. Fold in cheese, making sure to coat well with flour. Add unbeaten egg, milk and butter, stirring quickly just until blended. Do not overmix.

2. Spoon batter into prepared muffin tin. Bake in preheated oven for 20 to 30 minutes.

Tip *A dull knife works much better than a sharp one for slicing cheese.*

Potato Cheese Muffins

Makes 12 muffins
- Preheat oven to 400°F (200°C)
- Muffin tin, greased or paper-lined

2 cups	all-purpose flour	500 mL
1/2 cup	granulated sugar	125 mL
4 tsp	baking powder	20 mL
1 tsp	salt	5 mL
2	eggs	2
1 1/2 cups	milk	375 mL
1/2 cup	cooled mashed potatoes	125 mL

½ cup	shredded Cheddar cheese	125 mL
⅓ cup	melted shortening	75 mL

1. In a bowl, combine flour, sugar, baking powder and salt. Make a well in the center.
2. In another bowl, beat eggs well. Add milk, potatoes, cheese and shortening; mix well. Add to flour mixture, stirring just until moistened.
3. Spoon batter into prepared muffin tin. Bake in preheated oven for 25 minutes or until lightly browned.

Tip *A great way to use today's leftover potatoes for tomorrow's lunch.*

● ●

Cheesy Mushroom Muffins

Makes 12 muffins

- Preheat oven to 375°F (190°C)
- Muffin tin, greased

3 tbsp	butter or margarine	45 mL
3 cups	finely chopped mushrooms	750 mL
1 cup	whole wheat flour	250 mL
1 cup	all-purpose flour	250 mL
1 tbsp	baking powder	15 mL
2 tsp	granulated sugar	10 mL
½ tsp	salt	2 mL
1 cup	shredded old Cheddar cheese	250 mL
¾ cup	milk	175 mL
2	eggs	2

1. In a skillet, heat butter over medium-high heat. Add mushrooms; cook quickly until golden brown and no moisture is left.
2. In a bowl, sift together whole wheat flour, all-purpose flour, baking powder, sugar and salt. Add cheese; toss to coat well.
3. In another bowl, beat together milk and eggs. Add to flour mixture; mix well. Add mushrooms.
4. Spoon batter into prepared muffin tin. Bake in preheated oven for 30 minutes.

● ●

Cheese and Mustard Muffins

Makes 12 muffins

- Preheat oven to 375°F (190°C)
- Muffin tin, greased

2 tbsp	minced green onions	25 mL
2 tbsp	minced red bell pepper	25 mL
¼ cup	unsalted butter	50 mL
1 cup	all-purpose flour	250 mL
1 cup	whole wheat pastry flour	250 mL
2½ tsp	baking powder	12 mL
½ tsp	salt	2 mL
2	eggs	2
1 cup	milk	250 mL
2 tbsp	Dijon mustard	25 mL
1 tbsp	granulated sugar	15 mL
1 cup	shredded Cheddar cheese	250 mL

1. In a saucepan over medium-high heat, combine onions, pepper and butter. Sauté until soft; set aside.
2. In a bowl, combine all-purpose flour, whole wheat flour, baking powder and salt; mix well.
3. In another bowl, combine eggs, milk, mustard and sugar; whisk well. Stir in cheese. Add onion mixture and flour mixture; stir just until moist and blended.
4. Spoon batter into prepared muffin tin. Bake in preheated oven for 20 to 25 minutes.

● ●

Beer and Cheese Muffins

Makes 12 muffins

- Preheat oven to 400°F (200°C)
- Muffin tin, greased or paper-lined

2 cups	all-purpose flour	500 mL
2 tbsp	granulated sugar	25 mL
1 tsp	baking powder	5 mL
¼ tsp	dry mustard	1 mL
1 cup	beer	250 mL
¼ cup	vegetable oil	50 mL
1	egg, beaten	1
1¼ cups	shredded sharp Cheddar cheese	300 mL

1. In a bowl, combine flour, sugar, baking powder and mustard. Make a well in the center.
2. In another bowl, combine beer, oil, egg and cheese. Add to dry ingredients; stir just until blended.
3. Spoon batter into prepared muffin tin. Bake in preheated oven for 20 to 25 minutes.

Cheesy Tuna 'n' Rice Muffins

Makes 6 muffins

- Preheat oven to 375°F (190°C)
- Muffin tin, greased

2 cups	cooked rice	500 mL
1 cup	shredded Cheddar cheese	250 mL
1	can (7½ oz/213 g) drained flaked tuna	1
¾ cup	black olives, sliced into thirds	175 mL
1 tbsp	chopped onion	15 mL
1 tbsp	dried parsley	15 mL
1 tsp	seasoned salt	5 mL
2	eggs, beaten	2
2 tbsp	milk	25 mL
¼ cup	melted butter or margarine	50 mL
1 tbsp	freshly squeezed lemon juice	15 mL
½ tsp	seasoned salt	2 mL
½ tsp	dried parsley	2 mL

1. In a bowl, combine rice, cheese, tuna, olives, onion, parsley and salt. Add eggs and milk; mix thoroughly.

2. Spoon batter into prepared muffin tin. Bake in preheated oven for 15 minutes or until lightly browned.

3. In a bowl, combine butter, lemon juice, salt and parsley; mix well. Spoon over warm muffins.

Tangy Cottage Cheese Muffins

Makes 12 muffins

- Preheat oven to 400°F (200°C)
- Muffin tin, greased

1	egg, lightly beaten	1
¼ cup	vegetable oil	50 mL
½ cup	milk	125 mL
1 cup	cottage cheese	250 mL
2 tbsp	chopped green onions	25 mL
2 tsp	finely chopped fresh dill	10 mL
½ tsp	Worcestershire sauce	2 mL
2 cups	all-purpose flour	500 mL
1 tbsp	baking powder	15 mL
½ tsp	seasoned salt	2 mL

1. In a bowl, combine egg, oil, milk, cheese, onions, dill and Worcestershire sauce; stir well. Add flour, baking powder and salt; stir just until moist and blended.

2. Spoon batter into prepared muffin tin. Bake in preheated oven for 20 minutes.

Cheese Danish Muffins

Makes 12 large muffins

- Preheat oven to 400°F (200°C)
- Muffin tin, greased or paper-lined

4 oz	cream cheese, softened	125 g
2 tbsp	granulated sugar	25 mL
1 tbsp	freshly squeezed lemon juice	15 mL
1	egg	1
1¼ cups	milk	300 mL
½ cup	melted margarine	125 mL
1 tsp	grated lemon zest	5 mL
2½ cups	all-purpose flour	625 mL
½ cup	granulated sugar	125 mL
3½ tsp	baking powder	17 mL
1 tsp	salt	5 mL

1. In a bowl, cream together cheese, sugar and lemon juice. Set aside.

2. In another bowl, beat egg lightly with a fork; add milk, margarine and zest.

3. In another bowl, combine flour, sugar, baking powder and salt. Stir in egg mixture until blended.

4. Spoon batter into prepared muffin tin, filling half full. Place 1 tbsp (15 mL) cheese mixture over each; top with the remaining batter. Bake in preheated oven for 20 minutes.

Cottage Marmalade Muffins

Makes 6 muffins

- Preheat oven to 400°F (200°C)
- Muffin tin, greased or paper-lined

½ cup + 1 tbsp	all-purpose flour	140 mL
1 tsp	baking powder	5 mL
Pinch	salt	Pinch
1	egg, lightly beaten	1
⅔ cup	small-curd cottage cheese	150 mL
1 tbsp	vegetable oil	15 mL
1 tsp	liquid honey	5 mL
2 tbsp	orange marmalade	25 mL

1. In a bowl, sift together flour, baking powder and salt. Make a well in the center.

2. In another bowl, whisk egg, cheese, oil and honey. Add to dry ingredients, stirring until moistened.

3. Spoon batter into prepared muffin tin, filling cups half full. Add 1 tsp (5 mL) marmalade to each cup and top with the remaining batter. Bake in preheated oven for 15 to 20 minutes.

Cheesy Lemony Muffins

Makes 12 large muffins

- Preheat oven to 400°F (200°C)
- Muffin tin, greased or paper-lined

1½ cups	all-purpose flour	375 mL
¼ cup	granulated sugar	50 mL
1½ tsp	baking powder	7 mL
½ tsp	baking soda	2 mL
½ tsp	salt	2 mL
1	small lemon	1
1 cup	creamed cottage cheese	250 mL
1 cup	all-bran cereal	250 mL
2 tbsp	milk	25 mL
2	eggs	2
¼ cup	butter or margarine, melted	50 mL
¼ cup	liquid honey	50 mL

1. In a large bowl, combine flour, sugar, baking powder, baking soda and salt. Make a well in the center.
2. Peel lemon very thinly to remove zest. Then remove white pith, seeds and inner membranes from the rest of the lemon. Put zest and pulp into a food processor or blender and process until smooth. Add cottage cheese and process again. Stir in cereal and milk. Let stand for 5 minutes.
3. Stir in eggs, margarine and honey. Pour into flour mixture, stirring just until moistened and lumpy.
4. Spoon batter into prepared muffin tin. Bake in preheated oven for 20 minutes or until golden brown and firm to the touch.

Cheese and Rice Muffins

Makes 12 muffins

- Preheat oven to 425°F (220°C)
- Muffin tin, greased

8 oz	dry cottage cheese	250 g
¾ cup	cooked rice	175 mL
1 tbsp	butter or margarine, melted	15 mL
1 tbsp	vegetable oil	15 mL
3 tbsp	granulated sugar	45 mL
3 tbsp	sour cream	45 mL
3	eggs, beaten	3
¾ cup	all-purpose flour	175 mL
2 tsp	baking powder	10 mL

1. In a bowl, combine cottage cheese, rice, butter, oil, sugar, sour cream, eggs, flour and baking powder.
2. Place empty prepared muffin tin in preheated oven; heat until sizzling. Remove from oven. Spoon batter into hot tin. Bake in preheated oven for 20 to 25 minutes.

Savory Yogurt Muffins

Makes 24 muffins

- Preheat oven to 375°F (190°C)
- Muffin tins, greased or paper-lined

1 cup	old-fashioned rolled oats	250 mL
⅓ cup	oat bran	75 mL
1 cup	boiling water	250 mL
1 cup	granulated sugar	250 mL
⅓ cup	vegetable oil	75 mL
2	eggs	2
2 cups	low-fat plain yogurt	500 mL
1 cup	whole wheat flour	250 mL
1 cup	all-purpose flour	250 mL
1 tbsp	baking soda	15 mL
2 cups	all-bran cereal	500 mL

1. In a bowl, combine oats, oat bran and water. Let stand for 5 minutes. Add sugar, oil, eggs and yogurt; blend well. Add whole wheat flour, all-purpose flour, baking soda and bran cereal; stir just until blended. Do not overmix.
2. Spoon batter into prepared muffin tins. Bake in preheated oven for about 15 minutes.

Tip *If you only want to use half the batter, keep the remainder, covered, in your refrigerator for up to 2 weeks.*

Variation *For every 2 cups (500 mL) batter, you can add: 1 cup (250 mL) fresh or frozen berries (blueberries, raspberries or cranberries) and 1 tbsp (15 mL) grated orange zest, 1 cup (250 mL) chopped fruit (dates, raisins, prunes, apricots), ½ cup (125 mL) chopped nuts (walnuts or almonds) and 1 tsp (5 mL) pumpkin pie spice.*

Yogurt Honey Muffins

Makes 12 muffins
- Preheat oven to 400°F (200°C)
- Muffin tin, greased

1¼ cups	whole wheat flour	300 mL
1 cup	all-purpose flour	250 mL
¼ cup	packed brown sugar	50 mL
1½ tsp	baking powder	7 mL
1 tsp	baking soda	5 mL
1 tsp	salt	5 mL
Pinch	ground cinnamon	Pinch
Pinch	ground nutmeg	Pinch
1½ cups	plain yogurt	375 mL
¼ cup	liquid honey	50 mL
¼ cup	melted butter	50 mL
1	egg	1
1 cup	raisins (optional)	250 mL

1. In a bowl, combine whole wheat flour, all-purpose flour, brown sugar, baking powder, baking soda, salt, cinnamon and nutmeg; mix well. Make a well in the center.
2. In another bowl, whisk together yogurt, honey, butter and egg. Pour into dry ingredients. Fold in raisins (if using); stir just until moist and blended.
3. Spoon batter into prepared muffin tin. Bake in preheated oven for about 15 minutes.

Orange-Glazed Yogurt Muffins

Makes 12 muffins
- Preheat oven to 400°F (200°C)
- Muffin tin, greased or paper-lined

2½ cups	all-purpose flour	625 mL
1 tsp	baking powder	5 mL
1 tsp	baking soda	5 mL
½ tsp	salt	2 mL
⅔ cup	butter or margarine	150 mL
2	eggs	2
½ cup	plain yogurt	125 mL
1 tbsp	grated orange zest	15 mL
½ cup	freshly squeezed orange juice	125 mL
ORANGE GLAZE		
3 to 4 tsp	freshly squeezed orange juice	15 to 20 mL
½ cup	sifted confectioner's (icing) sugar	125 mL

1. In a bowl, sift together flour, baking powder, baking soda and salt.
2. In a large bowl, beat together butter and sugar until light and fluffy. Add eggs, yogurt, and orange zest and juice, beating until smooth. Fold in flour mixture and stir just until blended. Do not overmix.
3. Spoon batter into prepared muffin tin. Bake in preheated oven for 15 to 20 minutes. Set aside to cool.
4. *Prepare the glaze:* In a bowl, combine orange juice and confectioner's sugar to make a fairly thick glaze. Drizzle over cooled muffins.

Apricot Bran Yogurt Muffins

Makes 12 muffins
- Preheat oven to 375°F (190°C)
- Muffin tin, greased or paper-lined

1¼ cups	all-purpose flour	300 mL
1¼ cups	natural bran	300 mL
¾ cup	packed brown sugar	175 mL
1 tbsp	baking powder	15 mL
1 tsp	baking soda	5 mL
¼ tsp	ground cinnamon	1 mL
¼ tsp	salt	1 mL
1 cup	chopped dried apricots, divided	250 mL
1 cup	low-fat plain yogurt	250 mL
¼ cup	vegetable oil	50 mL
1	egg	1
1½ tsp	vanilla	7 mL

1. In a large bowl, combine flour, bran, brown sugar, baking powder, baking soda, cinnamon and salt.
2. Set aside 2 tbsp (25 mL) of the apricots; add the remaining apricots to flour mixture.
3. In another bowl, whisk together yogurt, oil, egg and vanilla. Add to flour mixture, stirring just until blended. Do not overmix.
4. Spoon batter into prepared muffin tin. Sprinkle with reserved apricots. Bake in preheated oven for 20 to 25 minutes.

Blueberry Bran Yogurt Muffins

Makes 12 to 18 muffins

- Preheat oven to 350°F (180°C)
- Muffin tins, greased or paper-lined

2 cups	plain yogurt	500 mL
2 tsp	baking soda	10 mL
1½ cups	packed brown sugar	375 mL
2	eggs	2
1 cup	vegetable oil	250 mL
2 cups	natural bran	500 mL
2 tsp	vanilla	10 mL
2 cups	all-purpose flour	500 mL
4 tsp	baking powder	20 mL
½ tsp	salt	2 mL
1 cup	fresh blueberries or frozen blueberries, unsweetened	250 mL

1. In a bowl, combine yogurt and baking soda. Set aside.
2. In a large bowl, whisk together brown sugar, eggs and oil. Add bran and vanilla.
3. In another bowl, sift together flour, baking powder and salt. Add to bran mixture alternately with yogurt mixture. Fold in blueberries.
4. Spoon batter into prepared muffin tins. Bake in preheated oven for 30 to 35 minutes or until toothpick inserted in center comes out clean.

Tip *When a recipe tells you to fold in egg whites, fruit or other ingredients, use a rubber spatula. Gently cut down through the center of the mixture, across the bottom and up the side, heaping mixture from bottom to top. Repeat, turning bowl slightly each time.*

Lemon Yogurt Cranberry Muffins

Makes 12 large muffins

- Preheat oven to 400°F (200°C)
- Muffin tin, greased or paper-lined

⅔ cup	liquid honey	150 mL
⅓ cup	vegetable oil	75 mL
4	eggs	4
1½ tsp	lemon extract	7 mL
1¾ cups	all-purpose flour	425 mL
¾ cup	whole wheat flour	175 mL
2½ tsp	baking powder	12 mL
1 cup	lemon-flavored yogurt	250 mL
1 cup	coarsely chopped cranberries	250 mL
1 tbsp	grated lemon zest	15 mL

1. In a large bowl, beat together honey and oil until creamy. Beat in eggs and lemon extract.
2. In another bowl, combine all-purpose flour, whole wheat flour and baking powder. Add to egg mixture alternately with yogurt, beginning and ending with flour mixture. Fold in cranberries and zest, stirring just until moistened. Do not overmix.
3. Spoon batter into prepared muffin tin. Bake in preheated oven for 15 to 20 minutes.

Sour Cream–Raisin Muffins

Makes 12 small muffins

- Preheat oven to 400°F (200°C)
- Muffin tin, greased or paper-lined

1	egg	1
1 cup	sour cream	250 mL
½ cup	milk	125 mL
½ cup	raisins	125 mL
1¾ cups	all-purpose flour	425 mL
2 tbsp	granulated sugar	25 mL
1 tsp	baking powder	5 mL
½ tsp	baking soda	2 mL
½ tsp	salt	2 mL
1 tsp	ground nutmeg	5 mL

1. In a bowl, combine egg, sour cream and milk; beat well. Add raisins.
2. In another bowl, sift together flour, sugar, baking powder, baking soda, salt and nutmeg. Add egg mixture; stir just until moist and blended. Do not overmix.
3. Spoon batter into prepared muffin tin. Bake in preheated oven for 15 to 20 minutes.

Nutritious Health Muffins

Makes 30 to 36 muffins
- Preheat oven to 375°F (190°C)
- Muffin tins, greased or paper-lined

4	eggs	4
1½ cups	canola oil	375 mL
2½ cups	packed brown sugar	625 mL
1 tbsp	salt	15 mL
2½ cups	milk	625 mL
1 tbsp	baking soda	15 mL
3 tbsp	light (fancy) molasses	45 mL
½ cup	sweetened applesauce	125 mL
¾ cup	chopped walnuts (or 1 apple, peeled and grated)	175 mL
1 cup	chopped dates	250 mL
1 cup	raisins	250 mL
5½ cups	whole wheat flour	1.375 L

1. In a bowl, beat together eggs and oil. Add brown sugar; mix well. Gradually add salt, milk, baking soda, molasses, applesauce, walnut pieces, dates, raisins and whole wheat flour; stir just until blended.
2. Spoon batter into prepared muffin tins (bake in batches). Bake in preheated oven for about 25 minutes.

Cereal Breakfast Muffins

Makes 12 to 18 muffins
- Preheat oven to 375°F (190°C)
- Muffin tins, paper-lined

2 cups	all-purpose flour	500 mL
½ cup	granulated sugar or brown sugar	125 mL
1 tbsp	baking powder	15 mL
1 tsp	ground cinnamon	5 mL
¼ tsp	ground nutmeg	1 mL
½ tsp	salt	2 mL
1 cup	milk	250 mL
1	egg	1
1 tsp	vanilla	5 mL
⅓ cup	vegetable oil	75 mL
1	apple or pear, peeled and coarsely chopped	1
½ cup	raisins	125 mL
2 cups	dry cereal	500 mL

1. In a bowl, combine flour, sugar, baking powder, cinnamon, nutmeg and salt. Make a well in the center.

2. In another bowl, beat together milk, egg, vanilla and oil. Add apple, raisins and cereal. Pour into dry ingredients; stir just until moistened.
3. Spoon batter into prepared muffin tins. Bake in preheated oven for 25 to 30 minutes.

Fresh Herb Muffins

Makes 12 muffins
- Preheat oven to 400°F (200°C)
- Muffin tin, greased or paper-lined

1½ cups	all-purpose flour	375 mL
1 tbsp	granulated sugar	15 mL
1½ tsp	baking powder	7 mL
½ tsp	baking soda	2 mL
Pinch	salt	Pinch
1 tsp	garlic powder	5 mL
⅓ cup	freshly grated Parmesan cheese	75 mL
½ cup	finely chopped fresh herbs (oregano or basil)	125 mL
1	egg	1
2 tbsp	butter, melted	25 mL
1¼ cups	buttermilk	300 mL

1. In a bowl, sift together flour, sugar, baking powder, baking soda, salt and garlic powder. Add cheese and herbs; stir well.
2. In another bowl, beat egg lightly with a fork; add butter and buttermilk. Add to dry ingredients; mix quickly just until moistened.
3. Spoon batter into prepared muffin tin. Bake in preheated oven for 15 to 20 minutes.

Delicious Vegetable Muffins

Makes 12 large muffins
- Preheat oven to 350°F (180°C)
- Muffin tin, greased

2⅓ cups	all-purpose flour	575 mL
¼ cup	freshly grated Parmesan cheese, divided	50 mL
2 tbsp	granulated sugar	25 mL
1 tbsp	baking powder	15 mL
¾ tsp	salt	4 mL
¾ tsp	dried thyme	4 mL
Pinch	ground nutmeg	Pinch
1 cup	milk	250 mL
¼ cup	vegetable oil	50 mL
1	egg	1
½ cup	chopped spinach	125 mL
½ cup	grated carrots	125 mL

| 1 | green onion, chopped | 1 |
| 2 tbsp | sliced pimento | 25 mL |

1. In a bowl, combine flour, half the Parmesan cheese, sugar, baking powder, salt, thyme and nutmeg.
2. In another bowl, combine milk, oil and egg. Add to flour mixture; stir just until moist. Add spinach, carrots, green onion and pimento.
3. Spoon batter into prepared muffin tin. Sprinkle with the remaining Parmesan cheese. Bake in preheated oven for 20 to 25 minutes.

• •

Two-Tone Muffins

Makes 12 muffins

- Preheat oven to 400°F (200°C)
- Muffin tin, paper-lined

2 cups	all-purpose flour	500 mL
½ cup	granulated sugar	125 mL
1 tbsp	baking powder	15 mL
1 tsp	salt	5 mL
¾ cup	roasted diced almonds	175 mL
¾ cup	freshly squeezed orange juice	175 mL
⅓ cup	almond oil or vegetable oil	75 mL
1	egg, beaten	1
¼ cup	unsweetened cocoa powder	50 mL
1 tsp	grated orange zest	5 mL

1. In a bowl, combine flour, sugar, baking powder and salt. Add almonds, reserving some for garnish.
2. In another bowl, combine orange juice, oil and egg. Add to flour mixture; stir just until moist.
3. In another bowl, combine half the batter and cocoa. Set aside. To the remaining batter add orange zest; mix well.
4. Spoon orange zest batter into one side of prepared muffin cups, dividing evenly. Spoon cocoa batter into other side of cups, dividing evenly. Sprinkle with reserved almonds. Bake in preheated oven for 20 minutes.

• •

Cornmeal Bacon Muffins

Makes 12 muffins

- Preheat oven to 425°F (220°C)
- Muffin tin, greased or paper-lined

6	bacon slices, chopped	6
1½ cups	all-purpose flour	375 mL
1½ cups	shredded Cheddar cheese, divided	375 mL
½ cup	cornmeal	125 mL
1 tbsp	baking powder	15 mL
½ tsp	salt	2 mL
Pinch	cayenne pepper (optional)	Pinch
1	egg	1
1 cup	milk	250 mL
¼ cup	melted butter or margarine	50 mL

1. In a skillet over medium-high heat, cook bacon until crisp; drain. Set aside to cool.
2. In a bowl, combine flour, 1¼ cups (300 mL) of the Cheddar cheese, cornmeal, baking powder, salt, cayenne (if using) and bacon.
3. In another bowl, whisk egg; add milk and melted butter. Stir into flour mixture until blended.
4. Spoon batter into prepared muffin tin. Sprinkle with the remaining cheese. Bake in preheated oven for 20 minutes.

• •

Wild Rice Muffins

Makes 12 large muffins

- Preheat oven to 375°F (190°C)
- Muffin tin, paper-lined

2 cups	water	500 mL
⅓ cup	wild rice	75 mL
2	eggs	2
1 cup	milk	250 mL
½ cup	melted butter, cooled	125 mL
1½ cups	all-purpose flour	375 mL
½ cup	natural bran	125 mL
⅓ cup	packed brown sugar	75 mL
1 tbsp	baking powder	15 mL
¼ tsp	salt	1 mL
¼ tsp	ground nutmeg	1 mL
½ cup	chopped toasted pecans	125 mL
½ cup	sliced dates	125 mL
¼ cup	slivered apricots	50 mL
2 tsp	grated orange zest	10 mL

1. In a saucepan over high heat, bring water to a boil. Reduce heat to medium; add rice. Cook, covered, for 45 minutes or until tender. Drain well; set aside to cool.
2. In a bowl, whisk eggs. Add rice, milk and butter; mix well.
3. In another bowl, combine flour, bran, brown sugar, baking powder, salt and nutmeg. Add to rice mixture; blend well. Add pecans, dates, apricots and orange zest; mix just until moist.
4. Spoon batter into prepared muffin tin. Bake in preheated oven for 20 to 25 minutes or until golden brown.

Low-Fat Muffins

Old-Fashioned Bran Muffins

Makes 12 to 18 muffins
- Preheat oven to 400°F (200°C)
- Muffin tins, lightly sprayed with vegetable spray or paper-lined

1 cup	all-bran cereal	250 mL
1½ cups	skim milk	375 mL
1¼ cups	all-purpose flour	300 mL
2 tbsp	granulated sugar	25 mL
4 tsp	baking powder	20 mL
¾ tsp	salt	4 mL
1	egg	1
3 tbsp	shortening, melted	45 mL

1. In a bowl, cover bran cereal with milk. Let stand for 5 minutes.

2. In another bowl, combine flour, sugar, baking powder and salt. Make a well in the center.

3. Add egg and shortening to bran mixture; blend well. Stir into flour mixture until blended.

4. Spoon batter into prepared muffin tins. Bake in preheated oven for 25 minutes.

Easy Bran Muffins

Makes 12 muffins
- Preheat oven to 400°F (200°C)
- Muffin tin, lightly sprayed with vegetable spray or paper-lined

2 tbsp	canola oil	25 mL
¼ cup	firmly packed brown sugar	50 mL
¼ cup	light (fancy) molasses	50 mL
2	egg whites	2
1 cup	skim or 1% milk	250 mL
1½ cups	natural bran	375 mL
1 cup	all-purpose flour	250 mL
1½ tsp	baking powder	7 mL
½ tsp	baking soda	2 mL
¾ tsp	salt	4 mL
½ cup	raisins	125 mL

1. In a bowl, beat together oil, brown sugar, molasses and egg whites. Add milk and bran; blend well.

2. In another bowl, combine flour, baking powder, baking soda and salt. Add to liquid ingredients; stir just until moist. Add raisins; blend.

3. Spoon batter into prepared muffin tin. Bake in preheated oven for 20 minutes.

Variation *Ginger Bran Muffins: Add 1 tbsp (15 mL) finely chopped crystallized ginger to batter.*

All-Bran Muffins

Makes 18 to 24 muffins
- Preheat oven to 425°F (220°C)
- Muffin tins, paper-lined

1¼ cups	all-bran cereal	300 mL
1 cup	buttermilk	250 mL
1	egg	1
½ cup	vegetable oil	125 mL
2 tbsp	light (fancy) molasses	25 mL
2 tsp	vanilla	10 mL
1 cup	all-purpose flour	250 mL
1 tsp	baking powder	5 mL
1 tsp	baking soda	5 mL
Pinch	salt	Pinch

1. In a bowl, cover cereal with buttermilk. Set aside.

2. In another bowl, vigorously beat together egg, oil, molasses and vanilla.

3. In another bowl, combine flour, baking powder, baking soda and salt. Add to egg mixture; stir just until blended. Add cereal mixture; blend well.

4. Spoon batter into prepared muffin tins. Bake in preheated oven for 15 to 20 minutes.

Blueberry Buttermilk Bran Muffins

Makes 24 muffins
- Preheat oven to 375°F (190°C)
- Muffin tins, paper-lined

3 cups	natural bran	750 mL
2 cups	whole wheat flour	500 mL
¾ cup	granulated sugar	175 mL
1 tbsp	baking powder	15 mL
1 tsp	baking soda	5 mL
2	eggs, beaten	2
2 cups	buttermilk	500 mL
½ cup	vegetable oil	125 mL
½ cup	light (fancy) molasses	125 mL
1 cup	fresh or frozen blueberries	250 mL

1. In a bowl, combine bran, flour, sugar, baking powder and baking soda.

2. In another bowl, combine eggs, buttermilk, oil and molasses. Pour into dry ingredients; stir just until moist. Do not overmix. Fold in blueberries.

3. Spoon batter into prepared muffin tins. Bake in preheated oven for about 25 minutes.

Whole Wheat Banana Bran Muffins

Makes 18 to 24 muffins

- Preheat oven to 350°F (180°C)
- Muffin tins, lightly sprayed with vegetable spray or paper-lined

2½ cups	whole wheat flour, divided	625 mL
½ cup	coarsely chopped dates	125 mL
½ cup	coarsely chopped prunes	125 mL
3 cups	natural bran	750 mL
1 cup	boiling water	250 mL
1 cup	raisins	250 mL
2½ tsp	baking soda	12 mL
1 cup	buttermilk or low-fat milk	250 mL
¾ cup	liquid honey	175 mL
2	ripe bananas, mashed	2
⅓ cup	vegetable oil	75 mL
½ cup	egg substitute	125 mL
½ cup	chopped walnuts (optional)	125 mL

1. In a food processor, combine 1 cup (250 mL) of the flour, dates and prunes; process until finely chopped. In a bowl, combine fruit mixture, bran, water and raisins. Let stand for 10 minutes.

2. In another bowl, combine the remaining flour and baking soda.

3. In another bowl, combine buttermilk, honey, bananas, oil, egg substitute and walnuts (if using); blend well. Add to flour mixture; combine well. Add bran mixture; stir just until moist and blended.

4. Spoon batter into prepared muffin tins. Bake in preheated oven for 20 to 25 minutes.

Low-Fat Pineapple Bran Muffins

Makes 12 to 18 muffins

- Preheat oven to 375°F (190°C)
- Muffin tin, sprayed with vegetable spray

4	egg whites	4
1	can (8 oz/227 mL) crushed pineapple, with juice	1
½ cup	granulated sugar	125 mL
⅓ cup	skim or 1% milk	75 mL
3 tbsp	vegetable oil	45 mL
3 tbsp	light (fancy) molasses	45 mL
1½ cups	natural bran or all-bran cereal or bran flakes cereal	375 mL
¾ cup	all-purpose flour	175 mL
¾ cup	whole wheat flour	175 mL
2 tsp	baking powder	10 mL
½ tsp	ground ginger	2 mL
½ tsp	salt	2 mL

1. In a bowl, whisk together egg whites, pineapple (with juice), sugar, milk, oil and molasses; blend well. Add bran. Let stand for 5 minutes.

2. In another bowl, combine all-purpose flour, whole wheat flour, baking powder, ginger and salt. Add to bran mixture; stir just until blended.

3. Spoon batter into prepared muffin tin. Bake in preheated oven for 20 to 25 minutes.

Raisin Bran Muffins

Makes 12 to 18 muffins

- Preheat oven to 400°F (200°C)
- Muffin tins, lightly sprayed with vegetable spray or paper-lined

½ cup	whole wheat flour	125 mL
¼ cup + 3 tbsp	all-purpose flour	95 mL
6 tsp	sugar substitute	30 mL
1 tbsp	baking powder	15 mL
¼ tsp	salt	1 mL
1½ cups	natural bran	375 mL
1½ cups	quick-cooking rolled oats	375 mL
¾ cup	buttermilk	175 mL
¼ cup	frozen apple juice concentrate, thawed	50 mL
2 tbsp	vegetable oil	25 mL
2	egg whites	2
2½ tsp	liquid honey	12 mL
⅓ cup	raisins	75 mL
½ cup	hot water	125 mL

1. In a bowl, sift together whole wheat flour, all-purpose flour, sugar substitute, baking powder and salt; blend well. Add bran and oats.

2. In a blender, combine buttermilk, apple juice concentrate, oil, egg whites and honey; process until well blended. Pour into dry ingredients; stir just until moist. Add raisins and hot water.

3. Spoon batter into prepared muffin tins. Bake in preheated oven for 20 minutes or until lightly browned and firm to the touch.

Orange Currant Oat Bran Muffins

Makes 12 muffins

- Preheat oven to 375°F (190°C)
- Muffin tin, sprayed with vegetable spray

2½ cups	oat bran	625 mL
½ cup	currants	125 mL
1 tbsp	baking powder	15 mL
1 tsp	grated orange zest	5 mL
⅓ cup	granulated sugar, divided	75 mL
½ cup	freshly squeezed orange juice	125 mL
¼ cup	vegetable oil	50 mL
3	egg whites	3

1. In a bowl, combine oat bran, currants, baking powder, orange zest and ¼ cup (50 mL) of the sugar; blend well. Add orange juice and oil; stir until well blended.
2. In a bowl, beat egg whites; slowly add the remaining sugar until soft peaks form. Gently add to oat bran mixture; blend well.
3. Spoon batter into prepared muffin tin. Bake in preheated oven for about 20 minutes or until browned.

Blueberry Oatmeal Muffins

Makes 12 to 18 muffins

- Preheat oven to 425°F (220°C)
- Muffin tins, paper-lined

1¾ cups	all-purpose flour	425 mL
1 cup	quick-cooking rolled oats	250 mL
¼ cup	firmly packed brown sugar	50 mL
1 tbsp	baking powder	15 mL
½ tsp	salt	2 mL
1 tsp	ground cinnamon	5 mL
1 cup	skim milk	250 mL
1	egg, beaten	1
3 tbsp	vegetable oil	45 mL
1 cup	fresh or frozen blueberries, unsweetened	250 mL

1. In a bowl, combine flour, oats, brown sugar, baking powder, salt and cinnamon; blend well. Add milk, egg and oil; stir until blended. Fold in berries.
2. Spoon batter into prepared muffin tins. Bake in preheated oven for 20 to 25 minutes.

Cinnamon Raisin Muffins

Makes 12 muffins

- Preheat oven to 375°F (190°C)
- Muffin tin, paper-lined

2¼ cups	all-purpose flour	550 mL
¼ cup	granulated sugar	50 mL
2 tsp	baking powder	10 mL
1 tsp	ground cinnamon	5 mL
½ tsp	baking soda	2 mL
½ tsp	salt	2 mL
¾ cup	dark raisins	175 mL
1 cup + 2 tbsp	buttermilk	275 mL
1	egg, lightly beaten	1

1. In a bowl, combine flour, sugar, baking powder, cinnamon, baking soda and salt; blend well. Stir in raisins, buttermilk and egg until blended.
2. Spoon batter into prepared muffin tin. Bake in preheated oven for about 20 minutes or until lightly browned.

Johnny Appleseed Muffins

Makes 12 muffins

- Preheat oven to 425°F (220°C)
- Muffin tin, sprayed with vegetable spray or paper-lined

1 cup	whole wheat flour	250 mL
½ cup	unbleached flour	125 mL
1 cup	bran flakes cereal	250 mL
1 tbsp	baking powder	15 mL
½ tsp	baking soda	2 mL
1 tsp	ground cinnamon	5 mL
½ tsp	ground nutmeg	2 mL
½ tsp	ground cloves	2 mL
1¼ cups	unsweetened applesauce	300 mL
½ cup	fat-free egg substitute	125 mL
⅓ cup	liquid honey	75 mL
2 tbsp	vegetable oil	25 mL
1	apple, shredded	1

1. In a bowl, combine whole wheat flour, unbleached flour, cereal, baking powder, baking soda, cinnamon, nutmeg and cloves; mix well.
2. In another bowl, whisk together applesauce, egg substitute, honey and oil; blend well. Add apple; pour into flour mixture. Stir just until moist.
3. Spoon batter into prepared muffin tin. Bake in preheated oven for about 20 minutes.

Apricot Orange Muffins

Makes 12 muffins

- Preheat oven to 350°F (180°C)
- Muffin tin, lightly sprayed with vegetable spray or paper-lined

1 cup	orange juice	250 mL
½ cup	chopped dried apricots	125 mL
½ cup	raisins	125 mL
1	egg	1
1	egg white	1
2 tbsp	butter, melted	25 mL
1½ tsp	vanilla	7 mL
2 cups	all-purpose flour	500 mL
¾ cup	granulated sugar	175 mL
2 tsp	baking powder	10 mL
1 tsp	baking soda	5 mL
Pinch	ground nutmeg	Pinch

1. In a bowl, combine orange juice, apricots, raisins, egg, egg white, butter and vanilla.

2. In another bowl, combine flour, sugar, baking powder, baking soda and nutmeg. Add liquid ingredients; stir just until moist and blended.

3. Spoon batter into prepared muffin tin. Bake in preheated oven for 20 to 25 minutes or until golden brown.

Blueberry Muffins

Makes 12 muffins

- Preheat oven to 400°F (200°C)
- Muffin tin, lightly sprayed with vegetable spray or paper-lined

1¾ cups	all-purpose flour	425 mL
1 tbsp	baking powder	15 mL
½ tsp	salt	2 mL
3 tbsp	granulated sugar	45 mL
1	egg white	1
1 tsp	freshly squeezed lemon juice	5 mL
1 cup	skim milk	250 mL
¼ cup	corn oil margarine, melted	50 mL
1 cup	frozen unsweetened blueberries, not thawed	250 mL

1. In a bowl, sift together flour, baking powder, salt and sugar.

2. In another bowl, beat together egg white and lemon juice until stiff.

3. Add milk and margarine to flour mixture; blend with a fork just until mixed. Fold in beaten egg white. Add blueberries.

4. Spoon batter into prepared muffin tin. Bake in preheated oven for 25 minutes.

Orange Fig Fiber Muffins

Makes 12 muffins

- Preheat oven to 350°F (180°C)
- Muffin tin, paper-lined

1	small orange, quartered and seeded	1
¾ cup	water	175 mL
5	large dried figs, quartered	5
¼ cup	margarine, cut into pieces	50 mL
⅓ cup	frozen orange juice concentrate	75 mL
2	egg whites	2
2 cups less 2 tbsp	all-purpose flour	475 mL
1 tsp	baking powder	5 mL
½ tsp	baking soda	2 mL
½ tsp	salt	2 mL
2½ tsp	sunflower seeds	12 mL

1. In a blender or food processor, combine orange, water, figs, margarine, orange juice concentrate and egg whites. Process for 1 minute or until well blended and peel is finely ground. Transfer to a bowl.

2. In another bowl, sift together flour, baking powder, baking soda and salt. Add to orange mixture; stir just until blended. Fold in sunflower seeds.

3. Spoon batter into prepared muffin tin. Bake in preheated oven for about 35 minutes.

Carrot Orange Muffins

Makes 12 muffins

- Preheat oven to 400°F (200°C)
- Muffin tin, lightly sprayed with vegetable spray or paper-lined

1 cup	all-purpose flour	250 mL
1 cup	whole wheat flour	250 mL
2 tsp	baking powder	10 mL
1 tsp	ground cinnamon	5 mL
¼ tsp	salt	1 mL
1 tsp	grated orange zest	5 mL
⅔ cup	freshly squeezed orange juice	150 mL
½ cup	skim milk	125 mL

¼ cup	vegetable oil	50 mL
2 tbsp	liquid honey	25 mL
2	egg whites	2
1 cup	coarsely grated carrots	250 mL

1. In a bowl, combine all-purpose flour, whole wheat flour, baking powder, cinnamon and salt.
2. In another bowl, whisk together orange zest, orange juice, milk, oil, honey and egg whites (mixture will look curdled). Add carrots; pour into flour mixture. Fold with spatula just until moist.
3. Spoon batter into prepared muffin tin. Bake in preheated oven for 20 to 25 minutes or until golden brown.

• • • • • • • • • • • • • • • • • • • •

Prune Muffins

Makes 18 muffins

- Preheat oven to 375°F (190°C)
- Muffin tins, sprayed with vegetable spray or paper-lined

1 cup	prune paste	250 mL
2 cups	packed brown sugar	500 mL
2	eggs	2
2 tbsp	light (fancy) molasses	25 mL
2¾ cups	all-purpose flour	675 mL
1½ cups	natural bran	375 mL
2 tsp	baking powder	10 mL
½ tsp	salt	2 mL
1 cup	raisins	250 mL
2 tsp	baking soda	10 mL
2 cups	buttermilk	500 mL

1. In a bowl, beat together prune paste and sugar. Add eggs and molasses; beat well.
2. In another bowl, combine flour, bran, baking powder and salt. Add to prune mixture; stir just until blended. Add raisins.
3. In another bowl, combine baking soda and buttermilk; mix well. Add to batter; stir just until blended.
4. Spoon batter into prepared muffin tins. Bake in preheated oven for 20 minutes.

• •

Maple Muffins

Makes 12 muffins

- Preheat oven to 375°F (190°C)
- Muffin tin, sprayed with vegetable spray

1 cup	whole wheat flour	250 mL
1 cup	unbleached flour	250 mL
¼ cup	coarsely chopped pecans	50 mL
2 tsp	baking powder	10 mL
⅔ cup	low-fat milk	150 mL
⅔ cup	pure maple syrup	150 mL
½ cup	fat-free egg substitute	125 mL
2 tbsp	vegetable oil	25 mL

1. In a bowl, combine whole wheat flour, unbleached flour, pecans and baking powder.
2. In another bowl, whisk together milk, maple syrup, egg substitute and oil. Pour into dry ingredients; stir just until blended.
3. Spoon batter into prepared muffin tin. Bake in preheated oven for 15 to 20 minutes.

• •

Maple Pecan Muffins

Makes 12 muffins

- Preheat oven to 400°F (200°C)
- Muffin tin, paper-lined

1 cup	all-purpose flour	250 mL
½ cup	whole wheat flour	125 mL
¼ cup	chopped pecans	50 mL
2	egg yolks	2
½ cup	skim milk	125 mL
¼ cup	pure maple syrup	50 mL
2 tbsp	unsalted butter or margarine, melted	25 mL
4	egg whites	4
3 tbsp	granulated sugar	45 mL

1. In a bowl, combine all-purpose flour, whole wheat flour and pecans. Set aside.
2. In another bowl, combine egg yolks, milk, maple syrup and melted butter. Set aside.
3. In another bowl, beat egg whites at high speed, gradually adding sugar, until stiff peaks form.
4. Beat milk mixture until well blended. Add to flour mixture; stir until moist. Gently fold in egg whites until blended.
5. Spoon batter into prepared muffin tin. Bake in preheated oven for 20 minutes or until lightly browned.

Sunny Boy Cereal Muffins

Makes 12 muffins
- Preheat oven to 375°F (190°C)
- Muffin tin, paper-lined

1 cup	sifted whole wheat flour	250 mL
1 cup	Sunny Boy cereal	250 mL
½ cup	raisins or chopped dates	125 mL
½ tsp	salt	2 mL
½ cup	liquid honey	125 mL
2 tbsp	safflower oil	25 mL
1	egg	1
1 tsp	baking soda	5 mL
1 cup	buttermilk or sour milk	250 mL

1. In a bowl, combine flour, cereal, raisins and salt; blend well.

2. In another bowl, combine honey, oil and egg; mix well.

3. In another bowl, combine baking soda and buttermilk; blend well. Add to honey mixture; mix well. Add to flour mixture; stir just until moist.

4. Spoon batter into prepared muffin tin. Bake in preheated oven for about 25 minutes.

Quick Cornmeal Muffins

Makes 12 muffins
- Preheat oven to 450°F (230°C)
- Muffin tin, sprayed with vegetable spray

1 cup	cornmeal	250 mL
½ cup	whole wheat flour	125 mL
½ cup	unbleached flour	125 mL
1 tbsp	baking powder	15 mL
1 tsp	dried sage	5 mL
1 cup	skim milk	250 mL
¼ cup	fat-free egg substitute	50 mL
2 tbsp	liquid honey	25 mL
2 tbsp	vegetable oil	25 mL

1. In a bowl, combine cornmeal, whole wheat flour, unbleached flour, baking powder and sage; blend well. Make a well in the center.

2. In another bowl, whisk together milk, egg substitute, honey and oil. Pour into dry ingredients; stir until well blended.

3. Spoon batter into prepared muffin tin. Bake in preheated oven for 15 minutes or until golden brown.

Low-Cal Cornmeal Muffins

Makes 12 small muffins
- Preheat oven to 425°F (220°C)
- Muffin tin, paper-lined

¾ cup	cornmeal	175 mL
¼ cup	all-purpose flour	50 mL
½ tsp	salt	2 mL
1½ tsp	baking powder	7 mL
¼ tsp	baking soda	1 mL
¾ cup	buttermilk	175 mL
1	egg	1
2 tbsp	butter or margarine, melted, or vegetable oil	25 mL
2 tbsp	sugar substitute	25 mL

1. In a bowl, sift together cornmeal, flour, salt, baking powder and baking soda; blend well. Add buttermilk, egg, butter and sugar substitute; beat for 1 minute with rotary beater (mixture will be loose).

2. Spoon batter into prepared muffin tin. Bake in preheated oven for 20 to 25 minutes.

Herbed Brown Rice Muffins

Makes 12 large muffins
- Preheat oven to 400°F (200°C)
- Muffin tin, paper-lined

1¾ cups + 2 tbsp	all-purpose flour	450 mL
1 cup	cooked brown rice	250 mL
1 tbsp	baking powder	15 mL
2 tsp	granulated sugar	10 mL
½ tsp	salt	2 mL
¼ cup	minced fresh basil	50 mL
2 tbsp	chopped fresh dill	25 mL
1 cup	skim milk	250 mL
¼ cup	water	50 mL
1	egg	1
3 tbsp	vegetable oil	45 mL

1. In a bowl, combine flour, rice, baking powder, sugar, salt, basil and dill; blend well with a fork.

2. In another bowl, combine milk, water, egg and oil. Add to flour mixture; stir just until blended.

3. Spoon batter into prepared muffin tin. Bake in preheated oven for 20 to 25 minutes.

Fruit and Vegetable Muffins

Apple Crisp Muffins

Makes 12 large muffins
- Preheat oven to 400°F (200°C)
- Muffin tin, greased or paper-lined

1	egg, beaten	1
1¼ cups	milk	300 mL
½ cup	melted margarine	125 mL
⅓ cup	liquid honey	75 mL
1½ cups	graham cracker crumbs	375 mL
1½ cups	all-purpose flour	375 mL
1 tbsp	baking powder	15 mL
1 tsp	ground cinnamon	5 mL
½ tsp	salt	2 mL
1 cup	grated peeled apples	250 mL

1. In a bowl, beat egg, milk, margarine and honey; blend well. Add graham cracker crumbs.

2. In another bowl, combine flour, baking powder, cinnamon and salt. Add honey mixture; stir just until moist. Fold in apples.

3. Spoon batter into prepared muffin tin. Bake in preheated oven for 20 minutes.

Spiced Apple Muffins

Makes 12 to 16 muffins
- Preheat oven to 400°F (200°C)
- Muffin tins, greased

2 cups	all-purpose flour	500 mL
1 cup	bran flakes cereal	250 mL
⅔ cup	packed brown sugar	150 mL
1 tbsp	baking powder	15 mL
1 tsp	salt	5 mL
½ tsp	ground cinnamon	2 mL
¼ tsp	ground nutmeg	1 mL
2	eggs	2
⅔ cup	milk	150 mL
¼ cup	vegetable oil	50 mL
1 cup	grated peeled apples	250 mL

1. In a bowl, combine flour, bran flakes, brown sugar, baking powder, salt, cinnamon and nutmeg; blend with a fork. Make a well in the center.

2. In another bowl, beat eggs slightly. Add milk, oil and apples; mix well. Add to dry ingredients; stir quickly just until moist (batter will be lumpy).

3. Spoon batter into prepared muffin tins. Bake in preheated oven for 15 to 20 minutes.

Apple Cinnamon Muffins

Makes 12 muffins
- Preheat oven to 425°F (220°C)
- Muffin tin, greased

2 cups	all-purpose flour	500 mL
½ cup	granulated sugar	125 mL
1 tbsp	baking powder	15 mL
1½ tsp	ground cinnamon, divided	7 mL
½ tsp	salt	2 mL
½ cup	butter or margarine	125 mL
1	large apple, peeled and diced	1
¼ cup	finely chopped walnuts	50 mL
1	egg	1
⅔ cup	milk	150 mL
1 tbsp	packed brown sugar	15 mL

1. In a bowl, sift together flour, sugar, baking powder, ½ tsp (2 mL) of the cinnamon and salt. Using a pastry blender or two knives, cut in butter. Measure out ¼ cup (50 mL) mixture; reserve for topping. Add apple and walnuts to the remaining flour mixture.

2. In a bowl, beat egg. Add milk; blend well. Add to flour mixture; stir just until blended (batter should be lumpy).

3. Spoon batter into prepared muffin tin. Add the remaining cinnamon and brown sugar to reserved topping mixture; sprinkle over batter. Bake in preheated oven for 15 to 20 minutes or until toothpick inserted in center comes out clean.

Spicy Apple Bran Muffins

Makes 30 to 36 muffins
- Preheat oven to 375°F (190°C)
- Muffin tins, greased or paper-lined

4	eggs	4
1½ cups	milk	375 mL
1 cup	packed brown sugar	250 mL
½ cup	vegetable oil	125 mL
2 tsp	vanilla	10 mL
3 cups	all-bran cereal	750 mL
2 cups	grated peeled apples	500 mL
1 cup	raisins	250 mL
1 cup	chopped walnuts	250 mL
3 cups	all-purpose flour	750 mL
2 tbsp	baking powder	25 mL
2 tsp	baking soda	10 mL
1½ tsp	ground cinnamon	7 mL

| ½ tsp | ground nutmeg | 2 mL |
| 1 tsp | salt | 5 mL |

1. In a bowl, beat eggs. Add milk, brown sugar, oil and vanilla; blend well. Add bran cereal, apples, raisins and walnuts; mix well.

2. In another bowl, combine flour, baking powder, baking soda, cinnamon, nutmeg and salt. Add bran mixture; mix well. Add to flour mixture; stir just until blended.

3. Spoon batter into prepared muffin tins. Bake in batches in preheated oven for 20 minutes or until firm to the touch.

• •

Apple Streusel Muffins

Makes 12 muffins

- Preheat oven to 400°F (200°C)
- Muffin tin, greased or paper-lined

STREUSEL TOPPING
⅓ cup	packed brown sugar	75 mL
⅓ cup	chopped pecans (optional)	75 mL
2 tbsp	all-purpose flour	25 mL
½ tsp	ground cinnamon	2 mL
2 tbsp	butter, softened	25 mL

MUFFINS
1½ cups	all-purpose flour	375 mL
¼ cup	granulated sugar	50 mL
2 tsp	baking powder	10 mL
½ tsp	ground cinnamon	2 mL
¼ tsp	salt	1 mL
Pinch	ground nutmeg	Pinch
1 cup	shredded peeled apples	250 mL
½ cup	milk	125 mL
¼ cup	vegetable oil	50 mL
1	egg, beaten	1

1. *Prepare the topping:* In a bowl, combine brown sugar, pecans (if using), flour, cinnamon and butter; mix until crumbly. Set aside.

2. *Prepare the muffins:* In another bowl, sift together flour, sugar, baking powder, cinnamon, salt and nutmeg; blend well. Add apples. Make a well in the center.

3. In another bowl, combine milk, oil and egg. Add to dry ingredients; stir just until moist.

4. Spoon batter into prepared muffin tin, filling half full. Sprinkle with topping, reserving 3 tbsp (45 mL). Top with the remaining batter; sprinkle with the remaining topping. Bake in preheated oven for 20 to 25 minutes.

• •

Apple Pecan Streusel Muffins

Makes 12 muffins

- Preheat oven to 375°F (190°C)
- Muffin tin, greased

STREUSEL TOPPING
½ cup	packed brown sugar	125 mL
½ cup	chopped pecans	125 mL
¼ cup	butter, softened	50 mL

MUFFINS
2 cups	all-purpose flour	500 mL
2 tsp	baking powder	10 mL
2 tsp	baking soda	10 mL
1 tsp	salt	5 mL
1 tsp	ground cinnamon	5 mL
½ tsp	ground allspice	2 mL
Pinch	ground cloves	Pinch
1	egg	1
1 cup	packed brown sugar	250 mL
¼ cup	vegetable oil	50 mL
1 cup	sweetened applesauce	250 mL

1. *Prepare the topping:* In a bowl, combine brown sugar, pecans and butter; mix until crumbly. Set aside.

2. *Prepare the muffins:* In another bowl, combine flour, baking powder, baking soda, salt, cinnamon, allspice and cloves.

3. In another bowl, beat together egg, brown sugar, oil and applesauce. Add to flour mixture; stir just until moist.

4. Spoon batter into prepared muffin tin. Sprinkle with topping. Bake in preheated oven for 20 to 25 minutes or until browned.

Cheesy Apple Bacon Muffins

Makes 18 small muffins
- Preheat oven to 400°F (200°C)
- Muffin tins, greased or paper-lined

2 cups	all-purpose flour	500 mL
¼ cup	granulated sugar	50 mL
4 tsp	baking powder	20 mL
¾ tsp	salt	4 mL
1 cup	milk	250 mL
⅓ cup	melted butter	75 mL
1	egg, lightly beaten	1
½ cup	finely chopped apples	250 mL
¾ cup	shredded sharp (old) Cheddar cheese	175 mL
⅔ cup	crumbled crisp bacon (about 8 slices)	150 mL

1. In a bowl, combine flour, sugar, baking powder and salt; blend well.
2. In another bowl, combine milk, butter and egg; mix well. Add to flour mixture; stir just until blended. Fold in apples, cheese and bacon.
3. Spoon batter into prepared muffin tins. Bake in preheated oven for 15 to 20 minutes or until browned.

Oatmeal Raisin Applesauce Muffins

Makes 12 muffins
- Preheat oven to 350°F (180°C)
- Muffin tin, greased or paper-lined

½ cup	butter or margarine	125 mL
¾ cup	lightly packed light brown sugar	175 mL
1	egg	1
1 cup	all-purpose flour	250 mL
½ tsp	ground cardamom or cinnamon	2 mL
1 tsp	baking powder	5 mL
¼ tsp	baking soda	1 mL
¼ tsp	salt	1 mL
¾ cup	sweetened applesauce	175 mL
½ cup	golden raisins	125 mL
1 cup	quick-cooking rolled oats	250 mL
½ cup	chopped nuts	125 mL
	Confectioner's (icing) sugar (optional)	

1. In a bowl, cream together butter and brown sugar until light and fluffy. Add egg; beat well.
2. In another bowl, combine flour, cardamom, baking powder, baking soda and salt. Add to creamed mixture alternately with applesauce; blend well. Add raisins, oats and nuts.
3. Spoon batter into prepared muffin tin. Bake in preheated oven for 25 to 30 minutes. Let cool. Remove muffins from pan. Sprinkle with confectioner's sugar, if desired.

Very Ripe Banana Muffins

Makes 12 muffins
- Preheat oven to 350°F (180°C)
- Muffin tin, greased or paper-lined

1 cup	mashed overripe bananas	250 mL
⅓ cup	vegetable oil	75 mL
½ cup	granulated sugar or brown sugar	125 mL
½ tsp	salt	2 mL
1	egg	1
1 tsp	vanilla	5 mL
1½ cups	all-purpose flour	375 mL
1 tsp	baking soda	5 mL
1 tsp	baking powder	5 mL
½ cup	chopped walnuts or pecans (optional)	125 mL

1. In a bowl, combine bananas, oil, sugar and salt; blend well. Add egg and vanilla; beat well.
2. In another bowl, combine flour, baking soda, baking powder and walnuts (if using). Add to banana mixture; stir just until moist. Do not overmix.
3. Spoon batter into prepared muffin tin. Bake in preheated oven for 15 to 20 minutes.

Iced Banana Muffins

Makes 12 muffins
- Preheat oven to 350°F (180°C)
- Muffin tin, greased or paper-lined

1 cup	granulated sugar	250 mL
1 tsp	baking soda	5 mL
2 tsp	baking powder	10 mL
2 cups	all-purpose flour	500 mL
Pinch	salt	Pinch
½ cup	melted butter	125 mL
2	eggs	2
¼ cup	milk	50 mL
3	ripe bananas, mashed	3

ICING

1½ cups	confectioner's (icing) sugar	375 mL
2 tbsp	butter, melted	25 mL
1¼ tbsp	milk	19 mL
1 tsp	vanilla	5 mL

1. In a bowl, sift together sugar, baking soda, baking powder, flour and salt; blend well. Add butter, eggs and milk; stir just until blended. Add bananas.
2. Spoon batter into prepared muffin tin. Bake in preheated oven for 25 minutes. Set aside to cool.
3. *Prepare the icing:* In a bowl, combine confectioner's sugar, butter, milk and vanilla; mix well. Spread over muffins.

Breakfast Banana Chip Muffins

Makes 12 muffins
- Preheat oven to 375°F (190°C)
- Muffin tin, greased or paper-lined

¼ cup	granulated sugar	50 mL
¼ cup	vegetable oil	50 mL
1 cup	mashed ripe bananas	250 mL
1	egg	1
1 tsp	vanilla	5 mL
½ cup	all-bran cereal	125 mL
½ cup	all-purpose flour	125 mL
½ cup	whole wheat flour	125 mL
1 tsp	baking powder	5 mL
1 tsp	baking soda	5 mL
½ tsp	salt	2 mL
½ cup	semisweet chocolate chips	125 mL

1. In a bowl, combine sugar, oil, bananas, egg, vanilla and cereal. Let stand for 5 minutes.
2. In another bowl, combine all-purpose flour, whole wheat flour, baking powder, baking soda and salt. Add to bran mixture; stir just until blended. Fold in chocolate chips.
3. Spoon batter into prepared muffin tin. Bake in preheated oven for 20 to 25 minutes.

Banana Yogurt Muffins

Makes 12 muffins
- Preheat oven to 375°F (190°C)
- Muffin tin, greased

1⅔ cups	all-purpose flour	400 mL
1 tsp	baking powder	5 mL
1 tsp	baking soda	5 mL
½ cup	butter, softened	125 mL
⅔ cup	natural bran	150 mL
½ cup	chopped nuts	125 mL
1	egg	1
⅔ cup	puréed ripe bananas	150 mL
½ cup	plain yogurt	125 mL
½ cup	packed brown sugar	125 mL
1 tbsp	light (fancy) molasses	15 mL

1. In a bowl, combine flour, baking powder and baking soda. Using a pastry blender, cut in butter until mixture is crumbly. Add bran and nuts.
2. In another bowl, combine egg, bananas, yogurt, sugar and molasses. Add to dry ingredients; stir just until blended.
3. Spoon batter into prepared muffin tin. Bake in preheated oven for 20 to 25 minutes or until a toothpick inserted in center comes out clean.

Easy Banana Bran Muffins

Makes 12 muffins
- Preheat oven to 400°F (200°C)
- Muffin tin, greased or paper-lined

1 cup	all-purpose flour	250 mL
3 tbsp	granulated sugar	45 mL
2½ tsp	baking powder	12 mL
½ tsp	salt	2 mL
1 cup	all-bran cereal	250 mL
1	egg, beaten	1
1 cup	mashed ripe banana	250 mL
¼ cup	milk	50 mL
2 tbsp	vegetable oil	25 mL

1. In a bowl, sift together flour, sugar, baking powder and salt. Add cereal.
2. In another bowl, combine egg, banana, milk and oil; blend well. Add to dry ingredients; stir just until moist.
3. Spoon batter into prepared muffin tin. Bake in preheated oven for 20 to 25 minutes.

Wheat Germ Banana Muffins

Makes 12 muffins

- Preheat oven to 375°F (190°C)
- Muffin tin, greased or paper-lined

1¼ cups	all-purpose flour	300 mL
½ cup	natural bran	125 mL
⅓ cup	wheat germ	75 mL
1 tsp	baking powder	5 mL
1 tsp	baking soda	5 mL
Pinch	salt	Pinch
½ cup	butter or margarine	125 mL
½ cup	lightly packed brown sugar	125 mL
1	egg	1
⅔ cup	mashed ripe bananas	150 mL
½ cup	buttermilk or sour milk	125 mL
1 tbsp	light (fancy) molasses	15 mL
¾ cup	raisins	175 mL
⅓ cup	chopped nuts	75 mL

1. In a bowl, combine flour, bran, wheat germ, baking powder, baking soda and salt; blend well.
2. In another bowl, cream butter, brown sugar and egg. Mix in bananas, buttermilk and molasses. Stir into flour mixture until blended. Add raisins and nuts.
3. Spoon batter into prepared muffin tin. Bake in preheated oven for 20 to 25 minutes.

Banana Pineapple Muffins

Makes 12 muffins

- Preheat oven to 400°F (200°C)
- Muffin tin, greased

½ cup	granulated sugar	125 mL
½ cup	shortening, softened	125 mL
½ cup	mashed overripe bananas	125 mL
½ cup	crushed pineapple, with juice	125 mL
1	egg, beaten	1
1 tsp	baking soda	5 mL
1 tsp	baking powder	5 mL
1½ cups	all-purpose flour	375 mL
Pinch	salt	Pinch

1. In a bowl, cream together sugar and shortening. Add bananas and pineapple; mix well. Add egg (batter will look curdled). Add baking soda, baking powder, flour and salt; blend well.
2. Spoon batter into prepared muffin tin. Bake in preheated oven for 15 minutes.

Banana Nut Muffins

Makes 12 muffins

- Preheat oven to 400°F (200°C)
- Muffin tin, greased

1¾ cups	all-purpose flour	425 mL
⅓ cup	granulated sugar	75 mL
1 tbsp	baking powder	15 mL
½ tsp	salt	2 mL
½ tsp	ground nutmeg	2 mL
½ cup	chopped nuts	125 mL
1 cup	mashed ripe bananas	250 mL
⅓ cup	vegetable oil	75 mL
¼ cup	milk	50 mL
1	egg	1
2 tsp	freshly squeezed lemon juice	10 mL

1. In a bowl, combine flour, sugar, baking powder, salt and nutmeg; blend well. Add nuts; stir.
2. In another bowl, combine bananas, oil, milk, egg and lemon juice. Beat slightly with a rotary beater. Add to dry ingredients; mix just until moist.
3. Spoon batter into prepared muffin tin. Bake in preheated oven for 20 to 25 minutes.

Banana 'n' Peanut Muffins

Makes 12 muffins

- Preheat oven to 400°F (200°C)
- Muffin tin, greased or paper-lined

1½ cups	whole wheat flour	375 mL
2 tsp	baking powder	10 mL
½ tsp	baking soda	2 mL
½ tsp	salt	2 mL
Pinch	ground cinnamon	Pinch
Pinch	ground nutmeg	Pinch
½ cup	packed brown sugar	125 mL
1½ cups	mashed ripe bananas	375 mL
1	egg	1
⅓ cup	melted butter, cooled	75 mL
½ cup	coarsely chopped peanuts	125 mL

1. In a bowl, combine flour, baking powder, baking soda, salt, cinnamon, nutmeg and brown sugar. Make a well in the center.
2. In another bowl, whisk together bananas, egg and butter. Add to dry ingredients; fold in nuts. Stir just until moist (batter will be lumpy).
3. Spoon batter into prepared muffin tin. Bake in preheated oven for about 15 minutes.

Chocolate 'n' Banana Muffins

Makes 12 small muffins
- Preheat oven to 350°F (180°C)
- Muffin tin, greased or paper-lined

1/3 cup	vegetable oil	75 mL
1/2 cup	granulated sugar	125 mL
1	egg	1
1 cup	mashed ripe bananas	250 mL
1	package (10 oz/300 g) semisweet chocolate chips, divided	1
1 cup	all-purpose flour	250 mL
1 tsp	baking soda	5 mL
1/2 tsp	salt	2 mL
1/2 tsp	ground cinnamon	2 mL

1. In a bowl, whisk together oil, sugar and egg. Add bananas and half the chocolate chips; mix well.
2. In another bowl, combine flour, baking soda, salt and cinnamon. Stir into liquid ingredients.
3. Spoon batter into prepared muffin tin. Sprinkle evenly with the remaining chocolate chips. Bake in preheated oven for 15 to 20 minutes.

Pineapple Choco-Banana Muffins

Makes 12 muffins
- Preheat oven to 375°F (190°C)
- Muffin tin, greased or paper-lined

1 cup	all-purpose flour	250 mL
3/4 cup	whole wheat flour	175 mL
1/2 cup	granulated sugar	125 mL
1 cup	semisweet chocolate chips	250 mL
1 tbsp	baking powder	15 mL
1/2 tsp	salt	2 mL
1	egg	1
1/2 cup	mashed ripe banana	125 mL
1	can (14 oz/398 mL) crushed pineapple, drained, juice reserved	1
1/2 cup	vegetable oil	125 mL

1. In a bowl, combine all-purpose flour, whole wheat flour, sugar, chocolate chips, baking powder and salt.
2. In another bowl, beat egg. Add bananas, pineapple, reserved juice and oil; stir just until blended. Add to dry ingredients; stir until moist.
3. Spoon batter into prepared muffin tin. Bake in preheated oven for 20 to 25 minutes.

Lemony Apricot Jam Muffins

Makes 12 muffins
- Preheat oven to 400°F (200°C)
- Muffin tin, greased or paper-lined

1 1/2 cups	all-purpose flour	375 mL
1/2 cup	granulated sugar	125 mL
1/2 tsp	grated lemon zest	2 mL
1 1/2 tsp	baking powder	7 mL
1/2 tsp	baking soda	2 mL
1/2 tsp	salt	2 mL
1	egg, beaten	1
1/4 cup	butter, melted	50 mL
1 cup	buttermilk	250 mL
2 tsp	freshly squeezed lemon juice	10 mL
	Apricot jam	
1/4 cup	chopped almonds	50 mL

1. In a bowl, combine flour, sugar, lemon zest, baking powder, baking soda and salt. Make a well in the center.
2. In another bowl, whisk together egg, butter, buttermilk and lemon juice. Add to dry ingredients; stir just until blended.
3. Spoon batter into prepared muffin tin, filling half full. Drop a bit of apricot jam into each tin. Top with the remaining batter; sprinkle with almonds. Bake in preheated oven for 15 to 20 minutes or until golden brown.

Simplified Blueberry Muffins

Makes 12 small muffins
- Preheat oven to 400°F (200°C)
- Muffin tin, greased

1	egg	1
	Milk	
1 1/2 cups	self-rising flour	375 mL
1/2 cup	granulated sugar	125 mL
1/4 cup	butter or margarine, softened	50 mL
1 cup	fresh or frozen blueberries, partially thawed	250 mL

1. In a measuring cup, combine egg and enough milk to make 1 cup (250 mL).
2. In a bowl, combine flour and sugar. Using a pastry blender, cut in butter until crumbly. Add egg mixture; stir just until moist. Fold in blueberries.
3. Spoon batter into prepared muffin tin. Bake in preheated oven for 20 to 25 minutes or until golden brown.

Grandma's Blueberry Gems

Makes 12 muffins
- Preheat oven to 400°F (200°C)
- Muffin tin, greased or paper-lined

2¼ cups	all-purpose flour	550 mL
¾ cup	granulated sugar	175 mL
1 tbsp	baking powder	15 mL
¾ tsp	salt	4 mL
6 tbsp	butter or margarine, melted	90 mL
¾ cup	milk	175 mL
¾ cup	water	175 mL
2	small eggs	2
	Grated zest of 1 lemon	
	Juice of ½ lemon	
1½ cups	frozen blueberries, not thawed	375 mL

1. In a bowl, sift together flour, sugar, baking powder and salt. Add butter, milk, water, eggs, lemon zest and lemon juice; blend well. Using a spatula, fold in blueberries.

2. Spoon batter into prepared muffin tin. Bake in preheated oven for 25 minutes or until golden brown.

Blueberry Sour Cream Muffins

Makes 12 muffins
- Preheat oven to 450°F (230°C)
- Muffin tin, greased or paper-lined

1 cup	fresh or frozen blueberries	250 mL
2 tbsp	all-purpose flour	25 mL
¼ cup	butter or margarine	50 mL
¾ cup	granulated sugar	175 mL
2	eggs	2
1¼ cups	all-purpose flour	300 mL
½ tsp	baking soda	2 mL
¼ tsp	salt	1 mL
¾ cup	sour cream	175 mL
½ tsp	vanilla	2 mL

1. In a bowl, combine blueberries and flour; toss to coat well. Set aside.

2. In a bowl, combine butter and sugar; cream until light. Add eggs one at a time; beat well.

3. In another bowl, sift together flour, baking soda and salt. Add to creamed mixture alternately with sour cream; mix well. Add blueberries and vanilla.

4. Spoon batter into prepared muffin tin. Bake in preheated oven for about 15 minutes.

Blueberry Muffins with Crunchy Pecan Topping

Makes 12 muffins
- Preheat oven to 400°F (200°C)
- Muffin tin, paper-lined

TOPPING

⅔ cup	packed brown sugar	150 mL
½ cup	chopped pecans	125 mL
2 tbsp	all-purpose flour	25 mL
½ tsp	ground cinnamon	2 mL
2 tbsp	melted butter	25 mL

MUFFINS

½ cup	butter	125 mL
1 cup	granulated sugar	250 mL
1 tsp	vanilla	5 mL
3	eggs	3
2 cups	all-purpose flour	500 mL
½ tsp	salt	2 mL
1 tsp	baking powder	5 mL
1 tsp	baking soda	5 mL
1¼ cups	sour cream, divided	300 mL
2 cups	frozen blueberries, thawed and patted dry	500 mL

1. *Prepare the topping:* In a bowl, combine brown sugar, pecans, flour and cinnamon; mix well. Add melted butter; stir. Set aside.

2. *Prepare the muffins:* In a bowl, combine butter and sugar; cream until light and fluffy. Add vanilla; continue to beat. Add eggs one at a time; beat well.

3. In another bowl, combine flour, salt, baking powder and baking soda. Add one-third of this mixture to creamed mixture; mix well. Add half the sour cream and one-third of the flour mixture; blend well. Add the remaining sour cream and the remaining flour mixture; mix well.

4. Spoon batter into prepared muffin tin, filling half full. Add blueberries; top with remaining batter. Sprinkle with topping. Bake in preheated oven for 20 to 25 minutes.

Blueberry Almond Muffins

Makes 12 muffins
- Preheat oven to 400°F (200°C)
- Muffin tin, greased or paper-lined

2 cups	all-purpose flour	500 mL
1 cup	granulated sugar	250 mL
2 tsp	baking powder	10 mL
1/2 tsp	salt	2 mL
2	eggs	2
1/2 cup	milk	125 mL
1/3 cup	melted butter or margarine	75 mL
1 tsp	grated lemon zest	5 mL
1 tsp	freshly squeezed lemon juice	5 mL
1	package (10 oz/300 g) frozen unsweetened blueberries, divided	1
1/4 cup	sliced almonds	50 mL
2 tbsp	granulated sugar	25 mL

1. In a bowl, combine flour, the 1 cup (250 mL) sugar, baking powder, salt, eggs, milk, butter, lemon zest and lemon juice. Blend on low speed just until moist. Beat on medium speed for 2 minutes. Add 1 cup (250 mL) of the blueberries; stir well.

2. Spoon batter into prepared muffin tin. Sprinkle with almonds, the remaining blueberries and the 2 tbsp (25 mL) sugar. Bake in preheated oven for 20 to 25 minutes or until golden brown.

Blueberry Lemon Muffins

Makes 12 muffins
- Preheat oven to 425°F (220°C)
- Muffin tin, greased or paper-lined

1 cup	fresh blueberries or frozen blueberries, thawed	250 mL
2 cups	all-purpose flour, divided	500 mL
1 tbsp	baking powder	15 mL
1/2 tsp	salt	2 mL
1/4 tsp	ground nutmeg	1 mL
3/4 cup	granulated sugar	175 mL
	Grated zest of I lemon	
1	egg	1
1/4 cup	vegetable oil	50 mL
1 1/4 cups	milk	300 mL
1/2 cup	chopped walnuts	125 mL

1. In a bowl, combine blueberries and 2 tbsp (25 mL) of the flour: toss until lightly coated. Set aside.

2. In another bowl, combine the remaining flour, baking powder, salt, nutmeg and sugar; stir with a fork until well blended. Sprinkle with lemon zest.

3. In another bowl, beat together egg, oil and milk. Add to flour mixture; stir just until moist and blended. Add walnuts and berries; blend well.

4. Spoon batter into prepared muffin tin. Bake in preheated oven for 20 minutes.

Tip *If using frozen berries, thaw and gently pat dry on paper towels.*

Variation *You can make a loaf with this batter. Spoon into a greased loaf pan. Bake at 350°F (180°C) for about 1 hour and 10 minutes.*

Glazed Blueberry Orange Muffins

Makes 12 large muffins
- Preheat oven to 400°F (200°C)
- Muffin tin, greased or paper-lined

1 1/2 cups	all-purpose flour	375 mL
1 cup	whole wheat flour	250 mL
1 tbsp	baking powder	15 mL
1 tsp	ground cinnamon	5 mL
1/2 tsp	salt	2 mL
1	egg	1
1 1/4 cups	milk	300 mL
1/3 cup	vegetable oil	75 mL
1/3 cup	liquid honey or pure maple syrup	75 mL
1 tsp	grated orange zest	5 mL
1 1/2 cups	fresh or frozen blueberries, not thawed	375 mL
GLAZE		
1/2 cup	confectioner's (icing) sugar	125 mL
1 tsp	grated orange zest	5 mL
2 tsp to 1 tbsp	freshly squeezed orange juice	10 to 15 mL

1. In a bowl, combine all-purpose flour, whole wheat flour, baking powder, cinnamon and salt.

2. In another bowl, combine egg, milk, oil, honey and orange zest. Add to dry ingredients; stir just until blended. Do not overmix. Fold in blueberries.

3. Spoon batter into prepared muffin tin. Bake in preheated oven for about 20 minutes or until golden brown.

4. *Prepare the glaze:* In a bowl, combine confectioner's sugar, orange zest and orange juice; mix until smooth. Spread over warm muffins.

Tip *Omit the glaze if you are freezing the muffins.*

Black Cherry Muffins

Makes 12 muffins

- Preheat oven to 400°F (200°C)
- Muffin tin, greased or paper-lined

2 cups	all-purpose flour	500 mL
1 tbsp	baking powder	15 mL
¼ tsp	salt	1 mL
1 cup	coarsely chopped pitted black cherries	250 mL
6 tbsp	butter or margarine, softened	90 mL
⅔ cup	granulated sugar	150 mL
2	eggs	2
1 tsp	vanilla	5 mL
½ cup	milk	125 mL

1. In a bowl, combine flour, baking powder and salt. In another bowl, combine 1 tbsp (15 mL) flour mixture and cherries; toss well. Set aside.
2. In another bowl, combine butter and sugar; beat until light and fluffy. Add eggs and vanilla; beat for 3 minutes. Add the remaining flour mixture alternately with milk; beat well. Add cherries.
3. Spoon batter into prepared muffin tin. Bake in preheated oven for 20 to 25 minutes or until golden.

Quick Lemon Muffins

Makes 12 muffins

- Preheat oven to 400°F (200°C)
- Muffin tin, greased

6 tbsp	butter	90 mL
1 cup	granulated sugar	250 mL
2	eggs	2
1½ cups	all-purpose flour	375 mL
½ cup	milk	125 mL
	Grated zest of 1½ lemons	
¼ tsp	salt	1 mL
1½ tsp	baking powder	7 mL
TOPPING		
	Juice of 1½ lemons	
⅓ cup	granulated sugar	75 mL

1. In a bowl, cream together butter, sugar and eggs. Add flour, milk, lemon zest, salt and baking powder; mix well.
2. Spoon batter into prepared muffin tin. Bake in preheated oven for 15 to 20 minutes.

3. *Meanwhile, prepare the topping:* In a bowl, combine lemon juice and sugar. When muffins are done, prick tops with a fork. Drizzle with topping.

Lemon Yogurt Muffins

Makes 12 muffins

- Preheat oven to 400°F (200°C)
- Muffin tin, greased

1¾ cups	all-purpose flour	425 mL
¾ cup	granulated sugar	175 mL
	Grated zest of 1 large lemon	
1 tsp	baking powder	5 mL
¾ tsp	baking soda	4 mL
¼ tsp	salt	1 mL
1 cup	lemon-flavored yogurt	250 mL
6 tbsp	melted butter, cooled	90 mL
1	egg	1
1 to 2 tbsp	freshly squeezed lemon juice	15 to 25 mL

1. In a bowl, combine flour, sugar, lemon zest, baking powder, baking soda and salt.
2. In another bowl, whisk together lemon yogurt, butter, egg and lemon juice. Add to flour mixture; stir just until blended.
3. Spoon batter into prepared muffin tin. Bake in preheated oven for 20 to 25 minutes.

Lemon Poppy Seed Muffins

Makes 12 muffins

- Preheat oven to 375°F (190°C)
- Muffin tin, greased

1 cup	lemonade	250 mL
½ tsp	grated lemon zest	2 mL
¼ cup	poppy seeds	50 mL
¼ cup	butter	50 mL
¼ cup	granulated sugar	50 mL
1	egg	1
1 tsp	vanilla	5 mL
2 cups	all-purpose flour	500 mL
1 tbsp	baking powder	15 mL
1 tsp	salt	5 mL
GLAZE		
2 tbsp	freshly squeezed lemon juice	25 mL
2 tsp	granulated sugar	10 mL

1. In a saucepan, heat lemonade over medium-high heat. When just about to boil, remove from heat. Add lemon zest and poppy seeds. Set aside to cool.

2. In a bowl, combine butter and sugar; beat well. Add egg and vanilla; mix thoroughly.

3. In another bowl, combine flour, baking powder and salt. Add to butter mixture; mix well. Add lemonade mixture; stir to moisten thoroughly.

4. Spoon batter into prepared muffin tin. Bake in preheated oven for 20 to 25 minutes or until golden brown.

5. *Prepare the glaze:* In a saucepan over medium-high heat, combine lemon juice and sugar. Heat, stirring constantly, just until sugar has completely dissolved. With a cake tester or metal skewer, prick the surface of each muffin all over; drizzle with glaze.

• • • • • • • • • • • • • • • • • • • •

Great Lemonade Muffins

Makes 12 muffins
- Preheat oven to 400°F (200°C)
- Muffin tin, greased or paper-lined

1¾ cups	sifted all-purpose flour	425 mL
¼ cup	granulated sugar	50 mL
2½ tsp	baking powder	12 mL
¾ tsp	salt	4 mL
1	egg, well beaten	1
1	can (6 oz/175 g) frozen lemonade concentrate, thawed, divided	1
¼ cup	milk	50 mL
⅓ cup	vegetable oil	75 mL
½ cup	chopped walnuts	125 mL
	Granulated sugar	

1. In a bowl, sift together flour, sugar, baking powder and salt. Make a well in the center.

2. In another bowl, combine egg, ½ cup (125 mL) of the lemonade concentrate, milk and oil. Add to flour mixture quickly; stir just until moist and blended. Add walnuts; stir gently.

3. Spoon batter into prepared muffin tin. Bake in preheated oven for 25 minutes. Remove from tins. While still hot brush muffins with the remaining lemonade; sprinkle with sugar.

• • • • • • • • • • • • • • • • • • • •

Orange Muffins

Makes 12 muffins
- Preheat oven to 400°F (200°C)
- Muffin tin, greased or paper-lined

2	oranges, cut into 8 pieces each	2
½ cup	freshly squeezed orange juice	125 mL
½ cup	dates or raisins	125 mL
1	egg	1
½ cup	margarine	125 mL
¼ cup	wheat germ or natural bran	50 mL
1½ cups	all-purpose flour	375 mL
1 tsp	baking powder	5 mL
1 tsp	baking soda	5 mL
¾ cup	granulated sugar	175 mL
Pinch	salt	Pinch

1. In a blender or food processor, combine oranges, orange juice, dates, egg and margarine; process until well blended. Scrape down edges of blender. Add wheat germ; process again.

2. In a bowl, sift together flour, baking powder, baking soda, sugar and salt. Add orange mixture; blend well.

3. Spoon batter into prepared muffin tin. Bake in preheated oven for about 15 minutes.

• • • • • • • • • • • • • • • • • • • •

Cinnamon Nut Orange Muffins

Makes 12 muffins
- Preheat oven to 375°F (190°C)
- Muffin tin, greased

1½ cups	all-purpose flour	375 mL
1½ tsp	baking powder	7 mL
¼ tsp	salt	1 mL
¼ tsp	ground nutmeg	1 mL
¼ cup	pecans	50 mL
⅓ cup	butter	75 mL
1 cup	granulated sugar, divided	250 mL
1	egg	1
½ tsp	vanilla	2 mL
1 tsp	grated orange zest	5 mL
½ cup	milk	125 mL
1 tsp	ground cinnamon	5 mL
¼ cup	melted butter	50 mL

1. In a bowl, combine flour, baking powder, salt, nutmeg and pecans.

2. In another bowl, cream together butter and half the sugar. Beat in egg, vanilla and orange zest; blend well. Add flour mixture alternately with milk, stirring just until blended.

3. Spoon batter into prepared muffin tin. Bake in preheated oven for 20 to 25 minutes.

4. Meanwhile, in a bowl, combine the remaining sugar and cinnamon. Remove muffins from tins. While still hot, dip tops in melted butter; roll in sugar-cinnamon mixture.

Mandarin Orange Muffins

Makes 12 muffins
- Preheat oven to 400°F (200°C)
- Muffin tin, paper-lined

1½ cups	all-purpose flour	375 mL
½ cup	granulated sugar	125 mL
2½ tsp	baking powder	12 mL
¼ tsp	salt	1 mL
¼ tsp	ground allspice	1 mL
½ tsp	ground nutmeg	2 mL
1	egg	1
¾ cup	milk	175 mL
⅓ cup	melted butter	75 mL
1 cup	mandarin orange segments, each cut into 4 pieces	250 mL
2 tbsp	granulated sugar	25 mL

1. In a bowl, sift together flour, sugar, baking powder, salt, allspice and nutmeg.

2. In another bowl, beat egg. Add milk and melted butter; blend well. Add to flour mixture; stir just until moist. Add orange pieces; stir gently.

3. Spoon batter into prepared muffin tin. Sprinkle with sugar. Bake in preheated oven for about 20 minutes.

Marmalade Muffins

Makes 12 muffins
- Preheat oven to 375°F (190°C)
- Muffin tin, greased or paper-lined

	Chopped peel of 1 grapefruit	
	Chopped peel of 1 orange	
1½ cups	buttermilk	375 mL
1 cup	granulated sugar	250 mL
1 tsp	salt	5 mL
½ cup	margarine	125 mL
1¾ cups	all-purpose flour	425 mL
2 tsp	baking powder	10 mL
½ tsp	baking soda	2 mL

1. In a food processor or blender, combine grapefruit peel, orange peel and buttermilk; process until finely ground. Add sugar, salt and margarine; process.

2. In a bowl, combine flour, baking powder and baking soda. Add peel mixture; stir just until moist.

3. Spoon batter into prepared muffin tin. Bake in preheated oven for 20 minutes.

Orange Surprise Muffins

Makes 12 muffins
- Preheat oven to 400°F (200°C)
- Muffin tin, greased

3 tbsp	shortening	45 mL
2 cups	all-purpose flour	500 mL
1 tbsp	baking powder	15 mL
½ tsp	salt	2 mL
¾ cup	milk	175 mL
1	egg	1
½ cup	orange marmalade	125 mL
3 tbsp	granulated sugar	45 mL

1. In a saucepan, heat shortening over medium-high heat. Set aside to cool.

2. In a bowl, sift flour, baking powder and salt.

3. In a blender or food processor, combine milk, egg, marmalade and sugar. Add cooled shortening; blend until thoroughly mixed.

4. Make a well in the center of dry ingredients. Add marmalade mixture; stir quickly just until moist.

5. Spoon batter into prepared muffin tin. Bake in preheated oven for 30 to 35 minutes or until golden brown.

Orangeberry Muffins

Makes 12 muffins
- Preheat oven to 375°F (190°C)
- Muffin tin, greased

1	orange, cut into pieces	1
⅓ cup	shortening	75 mL
1	egg	1
½ cup	milk	125 mL
1½ cups	all-purpose flour	375 mL
¾ cup	granulated sugar	175 mL
2 tsp	baking powder	10 mL
1 tsp	baking soda	5 mL
1 cup	fresh or frozen blueberries	250 mL

1. In a blender or food processor, combine orange pieces, shortening, egg and milk. Blend until orange is finely chopped. Set aside.

2. In a bowl, combine flour, sugar, baking powder and baking soda. Make a well in the center. Add orange mixture; stir just until moist and blended. Fold in blueberries.

3. Spoon batter into prepared muffin tin. Bake in preheated oven for 22 to 25 minutes or until golden brown.

Pineapple Orange Muffins

Makes 12 muffins
- Preheat oven to 400°F (200°C)
- Muffin tin, greased or paper-lined

2 cups	all-purpose flour	500 mL
1/2 tsp	salt	2 mL
4 tsp	baking powder	20 mL
1/4 cup	granulated sugar	50 mL
1	egg	1
1 cup	unsweetened pineapple juice	250 mL
1/4 cup	melted shortening	50 mL
1/2 cup	well-drained crushed pineapple	125 mL
TOPPING		
2 tbsp	granulated sugar	25 mL
1 tsp	grated orange zest	5 mL

1. In a bowl, sift flour, salt, baking powder and sugar.

2. In another bowl, beat together egg and pineapple juice. Add shortening; blend well. Add to flour mixture; stir just until moist and blended. Fold in pineapple.

3. *Prepare the topping:* In a bowl, combine sugar and orange zest.

4. Spoon batter into prepared muffin tin. Sprinkle with topping. Bake in preheated oven for 25 minutes.

Orange Date Muffins

Makes 12 muffins
- Preheat oven to 400°F (200°C)
- Muffin tin, paper-lined

1 1/4 cups	whole wheat flour	300 mL
1 cup	all-purpose flour	250 mL
3/4 cup	lightly packed brown sugar	175 mL
2 tsp	baking powder	10 mL
1 tsp	baking soda	5 mL
1/2 tsp	salt	2 mL
3/4 cup	chopped dates	175 mL
1 tsp	grated orange zest	5 mL
2	eggs	2
1/2 cup	freshly squeezed orange juice	125 mL
1/3 cup	melted butter	75 mL

1. In a bowl, combine whole wheat flour, all-purpose flour, brown sugar, baking powder, baking soda and salt; mix well. Add dates and orange zest.

2. In another bowl, beat eggs. Add orange juice and butter; blend well. Add to dry ingredients; stir with a fork just until moist.

3. Spoon batter into prepared muffin tin. Bake in preheated oven for 15 to 20 minutes.

Orange Chocolate Chip Muffins

Makes 12 muffins
- Preheat oven to 400°F (200°C)
- Muffin tin, greased or paper-lined

1	egg	1
1 cup	milk	250 mL
1/2 cup	melted margarine	125 mL
1/2 tsp	grated orange zest	2 mL
1/4 cup	freshly squeezed orange juice	50 mL
1 1/2 cups	all-purpose flour	375 mL
1 cup	whole wheat flour	250 mL
1/2 cup	granulated sugar	125 mL
1 tbsp	baking powder	15 mL
1/2 tsp	salt	2 mL
1/2 cup	semisweet chocolate chips	125 mL

1. In a bowl, beat egg with a fork. Add milk, margarine, orange zest and orange juice.

2. In another bowl, combine all-purpose flour, whole wheat flour, sugar, baking powder and salt. Stir in egg mixture until moist. Fold in chocolate chips.

3. Spoon batter into prepared muffin tin. Bake in preheated oven for about 20 minutes.

Old-Fashioned Orange Tea Cakes

Makes 12 muffins
- Preheat oven to 350°F (180°C)
- Muffin tin, paper-lined

2 cups	sifted cake and pastry flour	500 mL
2 tsp	baking powder	10 mL
2 tbsp	butter or shortening	25 mL
1 cup	granulated sugar	250 mL
1	egg	1
1 tbsp	grated orange zest	15 mL
1/4 cup	milk	50 mL
1/2 cup	freshly squeezed orange juice	125 mL

1. In a bowl, combine flour and baking powder.

2. In another bowl, cream together butter and sugar. Add egg; beat until light and fluffy. Add orange zest; blend well. Add flour mixture alternately with milk and orange juice; beat until smooth.

3. Spoon batter into prepared muffin tin. Bake in preheated oven for 25 minutes.

Peaches 'n' Cream Muffins

Makes 12 to 18 muffins
- Preheat oven to 400°F (200°C)
- Muffin tins, greased or paper-lined

2	eggs	2
1¼ cups	milk	300 mL
⅓ cup	liquid honey	75 mL
¼ cup	melted margarine	50 mL
1 tsp	grated lemon zest	5 mL
1½ cups	all-bran cereal	375 mL
2 cups	all-purpose flour	500 mL
1 tbsp	baking powder	15 mL
1 tsp	ground cinnamon	5 mL
½ tsp	salt	2 mL
1	can (14 oz/398 mL) sliced peaches, drained and cut into cubes	1
4 oz	cream cheese, cubed	125 g

1. In a bowl, beat eggs lightly. Add milk, honey, margarine, lemon zest and cereal; stir well.

2. In another bowl, combine flour, baking powder, cinnamon and salt. Add cereal mixture; stir just until blended. Fold in peaches and cheese.

3. Spoon batter into prepared muffin tins. Bake in preheated oven for 20 to 25 minutes or until golden brown.

Peach Melba Dessert Muffins

Makes 12 muffins
- Preheat oven to 400°F (200°C)
- Muffin tin, greased or paper-lined

1 cup	diced peaches	250 mL
½ tsp	ground cinnamon	2 mL
2 cups	all-purpose flour	500 mL
½ cup	granulated sugar	125 mL
2½ tsp	baking powder	12 mL
½ tsp	salt	2 mL
½ cup	chopped walnuts	125 mL
1	egg	1
1 cup	milk	250 mL
⅓ cup	melted butter or margarine	75 mL
2 tbsp	brandy	25 mL
	Raspberry jam	

1. In a bowl, combine peaches and cinnamon. Set aside.

2. In a bowl, sift together flour, sugar, baking powder and salt. Add walnuts; blend well. Make a well in the center.

3. In another bowl, whisk together egg, milk, butter and brandy. Add peach mixture; blend well. Add to dry ingredients; stir just until moist.

4. Spoon batter into prepared muffin tin, filling half full. Add about 1 tsp (5 mL) raspberry jam; cover with the remaining batter. Bake in preheated oven for 20 to 25 minutes.

Special Pear Cheese Muffins

Makes 12 muffins
- Preheat oven to 425°F (220°C)
- Muffin tin, paper-lined

2 cups	all-purpose flour	500 mL
⅓ cup	granulated sugar	75 mL
1 tbsp	baking powder	15 mL
½ tsp	salt	2 mL
¼ tsp	pumpkin pie spice	1 mL
1 cup	shredded Colby cheese	250 mL
2	pears, peeled and cut into large chunks	2
1 cup	milk	250 mL
2	eggs	2
¼ cup	melted butter	50 mL

1. In a bowl, combine flour, sugar, baking powder, salt and spice. Make a well in the center.

2. In a blender or food processor, combine cheese, pears, milk, eggs and butter; process until pears are finely chopped. Add to flour mixture; stir just until moist and blended.

3. Spoon batter into prepared muffin tin. Bake in preheated oven for 20 to 25 minutes.

Pineapple Muffins

Makes 12 muffins
- Preheat oven to 400°F (200°C)
- Muffin tin, greased

2 cups	all-purpose flour	500 mL
½ cup	granulated sugar	125 mL
1 tbsp	baking powder	15 mL
½ tsp	salt	2 mL
1	egg	1
¼ cup	vegetable oil	50 mL
1 cup	milk	250 mL
½ cup	well-drained crushed pineapple	125 mL

1. In a bowl, combine flour, sugar, baking powder and salt. Make a well in the center.

2. In another bowl, beat egg. Add oil, milk and pineapple; mix well. Add to dry ingredients; stir just until moist.

3. Spoon batter into prepared muffin tin. Bake in preheated oven for 20 to 25 minutes.

Pineapple Coconut Delights

Makes 12 muffins
- Preheat oven to 375ºF (190ºC)
- Muffin tin, greased or paper-lined

1½ cups	all-purpose flour	375 mL
1 tsp	baking powder	5 mL
½ tsp	baking soda	2 mL
½ tsp	salt	2 mL
¼ cup	butter, softened	50 mL
½ cup	granulated sugar	125 mL
1	egg	1
1 cup	sour cream	250 mL
1 tsp	rum extract	5 mL
1 cup	drained crushed pineapple	250 mL
½ cup	flaked coconut (sweetened or unsweetened)	125 mL

1. In a bowl, combine flour, baking powder, baking soda and salt.

2. In another bowl, beat together butter, sugar, egg, sour cream and rum. Add to flour mixture; stir just until blended. Add pineapple and coconut.

3. Spoon batter into prepared muffin tin. Bake in preheated oven for 20 to 25 minutes.

Pineapple Upside-Down Muffins

Makes 12 muffins
- Preheat oven to 375ºF (190ºC)
- Muffin tin, greased

¼ cup	melted butter	50 mL
⅓ cup	packed brown sugar	75 mL
1	can (8 oz/227 mL) crushed pineapple, drained	1
1½ cups	all-purpose flour	375 mL
½ cup	granulated sugar	125 mL
¼ tsp	salt	1 mL
½ tsp	baking soda	2 mL
1 tsp	baking powder	5 mL

1 tsp	ground cinnamon	5 mL
2	eggs, beaten	2
1 cup	buttermilk	250 mL
2 tbsp	melted butter	25 mL

1. Spoon melted butter evenly into prepared muffin tin. Sprinkle brown sugar over top. Spoon pineapple over brown sugar. Set aside.

2. In a bowl, combine flour, sugar, salt, baking soda, baking powder and cinnamon. Make a well in the center.

3. In another bowl, whisk together eggs, buttermilk and butter. Add quickly to flour mixture; stir just until moist and blended.

4. Spoon batter into muffin cups over pineapple. Bake in preheated oven for 20 to 25 minutes.

5. When cool, remove muffins from pan. Serve pineapple-side up.

Tip *As a substitute for 1 cup (250 mL) buttermilk, you can combine 3 tbsp (45 mL) powdered buttermilk with about ¾ cup (175 mL) lukewarm water.*

Tropical Treat Muffins

Makes 12 muffins
- Preheat oven to 400ºF (200ºC)
- Muffin tin, greased

2 cups	all-purpose flour	500 mL
2 tsp	baking powder	10 mL
½ tsp	baking soda	2 mL
½ tsp	salt	2 mL
½ cup	packed brown sugar	125 mL
1	egg, well beaten	1
1 cup	sour cream	250 mL
1	can (8 oz/227 mL) crushed pineapple, with juice	1
⅓ cup	vegetable oil or melted shortening	75 mL
½ cup	chopped pecans	125 mL

1. In a bowl, sift together flour, baking powder, baking soda and salt. Add brown sugar.

2. In another bowl, combine egg and sour cream; mix well. Add pineapple (with juice), oil and pecans. Add to flour mixture; stir just until moist.

3. Spoon batter into prepared muffin tin. Bake in preheated oven for 20 minutes.

Favorite Raspberry Muffins

Makes 12 muffins

- Preheat oven to 400°F (200°C)
- Muffin tin, greased or paper-lined

1½ cups	all-purpose flour	375 mL
½ cup	quick-cooking rolled oats	125 mL
½ cup	packed brown sugar	125 mL
¼ tsp	salt	1 mL
2 tsp	baking powder	10 mL
1 tsp	baking soda	5 mL
1 cup	frozen raspberries, not thawed	250 mL
2	eggs	2
½ cup	buttermilk	125 mL
½ cup	melted margarine	125 mL
TOPPING		
¼ cup	butter, softened	50 mL
¼ cup	packed brown sugar	50 mL
¼ cup	quick-cooking rolled oats	50 mL
¼ cup	all-purpose flour	50 mL
1 tsp	ground cinnamon	5 mL

1. In a bowl, combine flour, oats, brown sugar, salt, baking powder and baking soda. Add frozen raspberries; blend well.
2. In another bowl, whisk together eggs, buttermilk and margarine. Add to flour mixture; stir just until moist and blended.
3. *Prepare the topping:* In a bowl, cream together butter and brown sugar. Add oats, flour and cinnamon; mix well.
4. Spoon batter into prepared muffin tin. Spoon topping over muffins evenly. Bake in preheated oven for 15 to 20 minutes.

Raspberry Almond Muffins

Makes 12 muffins

- Preheat oven to 350°F (180°C)
- Muffin tin, paper-lined

½ cup	butter (room temperature)	125 mL
¾ cup	granulated sugar	175 mL
2	eggs	2
1 tsp	baking powder	5 mL
½ tsp	baking soda	2 mL
1 tsp	almond extract	5 mL
2 cups	all-purpose flour, divided	500 mL
1 cup	plain yogurt or buttermilk	250 mL
¼ cup	raspberry preserves	50 mL
5 oz	almond paste	150 g

1. In a bowl, combine butter and sugar; cream until light and fluffy. Beat in eggs one at a time. Add baking powder, baking soda and almond extract; mix well. Fold in 1 cup (250 mL) of the flour. Add yogurt and the remaining flour; mix well.
2. Spoon batter into prepared muffin tin, filling half full. Top each with 1 tsp (5 mL) raspberry preserves and piece of almond paste. Top with the remaining batter. Bake in preheated oven for 25 to 30 minutes or until lightly browned.

Raspberry Blueberry Cornmeal Muffins

Makes 12 muffins

- Preheat oven to 400°F (200°C)
- Muffin tin, greased or paper-lined

1 cup	yellow cornmeal	250 mL
1 cup	all-purpose flour	250 mL
⅓ cup	granulated sugar	75 mL
2 tsp	baking powder	10 mL
¼ tsp	salt	1 mL
1 cup	buttermilk	250 mL
6 tbsp	melted butter	90 mL
1	egg, lightly beaten	1
1 cup	fresh or frozen blueberries	250 mL
½ cup	fresh or frozen raspberries	125 mL

1. In a bowl, sift together cornmeal, flour, sugar, baking powder and salt. Make a well in the center.
2. In another bowl, combine buttermilk, butter and egg. Add to dry ingredients; stir just until moist and blended. Fold in blueberries and raspberries.
3. Spoon batter into prepared muffin tin. Bake in preheated oven for 20 to 25 minutes or until golden brown.

Raspberry Pecan Streusel Muffins

Makes 12 muffins

- Preheat oven to 375°F (190°C)
- Muffin tin, greased

PECAN STREUSEL TOPPING		
¼ cup	chopped pecans	50 mL
¼ cup	packed brown sugar	50 mL
¼ cup	all-purpose flour	50 mL
2 tbsp	butter or margarine, melted	25 mL
MUFFINS		
1½ cups	all-purpose flour	375 mL
½ cup	granulated sugar	125 mL

2 tsp	baking powder	10 mL
½ cup	milk	125 mL
½ cup	melted butter or margarine	125 mL
1	egg, beaten	1
1 cup	fresh or frozen raspberries	250 mL

1. *Prepare the topping:* In a bowl, combine pecans, brown sugar and flour. Add butter; mix until crumbly. Set aside.
2. *Prepare the muffins:* In a large bowl, combine flour, sugar and baking powder. Make a well in the center.
3. In another bowl, combine milk, butter and egg; mix well. Add to flour mixture; stir just until moist.
4. Spoon batter into prepared muffin tin, filling half full. Add a few raspberries. Top with the remaining batter. Sprinkle with topping. Bake in preheated oven for 25 to 30 minutes or until browned.

Strawberry Cheesecake Muffins

Makes 12 large muffins
- Preheat oven to 375ºF (190ºC)
- Muffin tin, greased or paper-lined

4 oz	cream cheese, softened	125 g
¼ cup	sifted confectioner's (icing) sugar	50 mL
2½ cups	all-purpose flour	625 mL
1 tbsp	baking powder	15 mL
½ tsp	salt	2 mL
1	egg	1
1¼ cups	milk	300 mL
½ cup	lightly packed brown sugar	125 mL
⅓ cup	melted butter or margarine	75 mL
1 tsp	grated lemon zest	5 mL
¼ tsp	almond extract	1 mL
¼ cup	strawberry jam	1 mL

1. In a bowl, combine cream cheese and confectioner's sugar; beat until smooth. Set aside.
2. In a bowl, combine flour, baking powder and salt.
3. In another bowl, combine egg, milk, brown sugar, butter, lemon zest and almond extract. Add to flour mixture; stir just until moist and blended.
4. Spoon batter into prepared muffin tin, filling half full. Add 1 tbsp (15 mL) cream cheese mixture and 1 tsp (5 mL) jam. Top with the remaining batter. Bake in preheated oven for about 20 minutes or until lightly browned.

Variation *You can use any type of jam, such as apricot, peach, grape, etc.*

Strawberry Tea Muffins

Makes 12 muffins
- Preheat oven to 400ºF (200ºC)
- Muffin tin, greased or paper-lined

1¼ cups	all-purpose flour	300 mL
⅔ cup	oat bran	150 mL
1½ tsp	baking powder	7 mL
½ tsp	baking soda	2 mL
½ cup	granulated sugar	125 mL
2	eggs	2
¼ cup	butter, melted	50 mL
1 cup	buttermilk	250 mL
½ cup	strawberry preserves	125 mL
¼ cup	sliced almonds	50 mL

1. In a bowl, combine flour, oat bran, baking powder, baking soda and sugar. Make a well in the center.
2. In another bowl, whisk together eggs, butter and buttermilk. Add to flour mixture; stir just until moist and blended.
3. Spoon batter into prepared muffin tin, filling half full. Add 1 heaping tbsp (15 mL) strawberry preserves. Top with the remaining batter. Sprinkle with sliced almonds. Bake in preheated oven for 15 to 20 minutes or until golden brown.

Best-Ever Rhubarb Pecan Muffins

Makes 12 muffins
- Preheat oven to 350ºF (180ºC)
- Muffin tin, lightly greased

2 cups	all-purpose flour	500 mL
¾ cup	granulated sugar	175 mL
1½ tsp	baking powder	7 mL
½ tsp	baking soda	2 mL
1 tsp	salt	5 mL
¾ cup	chopped pecans	175 mL
1	egg	1
¼ cup	vegetable oil	50 mL
2 tsp	grated orange zest	10 mL
¾ cup	freshly squeezed orange juice	175 mL
1¼ cups	finely chopped fresh rhubarb	300 mL

1. In a bowl, combine flour, sugar, baking powder, baking soda, salt and pecans.
2. In another bowl, beat egg. Add oil, orange zest and orange juice. Add to flour mixture; stir just until moist and blended. Add rhubarb.
3. Spoon batter into prepared muffin tin. Bake in preheated oven for 25 to 30 minutes.

Carrot Cake Muffins

Makes 12 muffins

- Preheat oven to 375°F (190°C)
- Muffin tin, greased or paper-lined

1 cup	all-purpose flour	250 mL
¾ cup	quick-cooking rolled oats	175 mL
1½ tsp	baking powder	7 mL
1 tsp	baking soda	5 mL
1 tsp	ground cinnamon	5 mL
¾ cup	raisins or chopped dates	175 mL
1	egg, beaten	1
1¼ cups	sweetened condensed skim milk	300 mL
1½ cups	grated carrots	375 mL
½ cup	drained crushed pineapple	125 mL
2 tbsp	vegetable oil	25 mL
2 tsp	grated orange zest	10 mL

1. In a bowl, combine flour, oats, baking powder, baking soda, cinnamon and raisins.

2. In another bowl, combine egg, milk, carrots, pineapple, oil and orange zest. Add to dry ingredients; stir just until blended.

3. Spoon batter into prepared muffin tin. Bake in preheated oven for 20 to 25 minutes or until toothpick inserted in center comes out clean and dry.

Coconut Pecan Carrot Muffins

Makes 12 large muffins

- Preheat oven to 375°F (190°C)
- Muffin tin, greased or paper-lined

2¼ cups	all-purpose flour	550 mL
⅔ cup	packed brown sugar	150 mL
½ cup	shredded coconut (sweetened or unsweetened)	125 mL
½ cup	pecans	125 mL
½ cup	raisins	125 mL
1 tbsp	baking powder	15 mL
1 tsp	salt	5 mL
1 tsp	ground cinnamon	5 mL
1½ cups	grated carrots	375 mL
⅔ cup	milk	150 mL
¼ cup	vegetable oil	50 mL
1 tsp	vanilla	5 mL
1	egg	1

1. In a bowl, combine flour, brown sugar, coconut, pecans, raisins, baking powder, salt and cinnamon. Add carrots.

2. In another bowl, combine milk, oil, vanilla and egg. Add to flour mixture; stir just until moist.

3. Spoon batter into prepared muffin tin. Bake in preheated oven for 20 to 25 minutes.

Applesauce Carrot Muffins

Makes 18 to 24 muffins

- Preheat oven to 400°F (200°C)
- Muffin tins, greased or paper-lined

3 cups	all-purpose flour	750 mL
2½ tsp	baking powder	12 mL
1 tsp	baking soda	5 mL
½ tsp	salt	2 mL
1 tbsp	ground cinnamon	15 mL
1 tsp	ground cloves	5 mL
½ tsp	ground nutmeg	2 mL
1½ cups	packed brown sugar	375 mL
1 cup	vegetable oil	250 mL
1 cup	sweetened applesauce	250 mL
3 cups	grated carrots	750 mL
3	eggs, lightly beaten	3

1. In a bowl, sift flour, baking powder, baking soda, salt, cinnamon, cloves and nutmeg. Add brown sugar, oil, applesauce, carrots and eggs; mix well.

2. Spoon batter into prepared muffin tins. Bake in preheated oven for 18 to 20 minutes.

Spicy Traditional Pineapple Carrot Muffins

Makes 12 to 18 muffins

- Preheat oven to 400°F (200°C)
- Muffin tins, greased

1¼ cups	all-bran cereal	300 mL
1	can (14 oz/398 mL) crushed pineapple, with juice	1
¼ cup	milk	50 mL
1	egg	1
½ cup	packed brown sugar	125 mL
⅓ cup	vegetable oil	75 mL
1 cup	shredded carrots	250 mL
2 cups	all-purpose flour	500 mL
1 tbsp	baking powder	15 mL
2½ tsp	ground cinnamon	12 mL
1 tsp	ground ginger	5 mL
1 tsp	salt	5 mL
½ cup	raisins	125 mL

1. In a bowl, combine cereal, pineapple (with juice) and milk. Let stand for 5 minutes. Add egg, brown sugar, oil and carrots.
2. In another bowl, combine flour, baking powder, cinnamon, ginger and salt. Add cereal mixture and raisins; stir just until moist.
3. Spoon batter into prepared muffin tins. Bake in preheated oven for 20 to 25 minutes or until tops are firm to the touch.

Pineapple Walnut Carrot Muffins

Makes 12 to 18 muffins

- Preheat oven to 400°F (200°C)
- Muffin tins, greased or paper-lined

1½ cups	all-purpose flour	375 mL
1½ cups	shredded carrots	375 mL
¼ cup	granulated sugar	50 mL
⅔ cup	coarsely chopped walnuts	150 mL
1 tsp	ground cinnamon	5 mL
1 tsp	baking soda	5 mL
¼ tsp	baking powder	1 mL
¼ tsp	salt	1 mL
¼ tsp	ground nutmeg	1 mL
3	egg whites, lightly beaten	3
2 cups	drained crushed pineapple	500 mL
¼ cup	water	50 mL
2 tbsp + 2 tsp	frozen apple juice concentrate, thawed	35 mL
2 tbsp	vegetable oil	25 mL

1. In a bowl, combine flour, carrots, sugar, walnuts, cinnamon, baking soda, baking powder, salt and nutmeg.
2. In another bowl, combine egg whites, pineapple, water, apple juice concentrate and oil. Add to flour mixture; mix with a fork just until blended. Do not overmix.
3. Spoon batter into prepared muffin tins. Bake in preheated oven for 25 to 30 minutes.

Zucchini and Carrot Muffins

Makes 12 muffins

- Preheat oven to 375°F (190°C)
- Muffin tin, paper-lined

1½ cups	all-purpose flour	375 mL
¾ cup	packed brown sugar	175 mL
1 tsp	baking powder	5 mL
½ tsp	ground ginger	2 mL
¼ tsp	baking soda	1 mL
2	eggs, lightly beaten	2
1½ cups	shredded carrots	375 mL
1 cup	shredded zucchini	250 mL
½ cup	raisins	125 mL
½ cup	chopped walnuts	125 mL
½ cup	vegetable oil	125 mL
¼ cup	liquid honey	50 mL
1 tsp	vanilla	5 mL

CITRUS CREAM CHEESE FROSTING

1	package (8 oz/250 g) light cream cheese, softened	1
½ cup	confectioner's (icing) sugar	125 mL
1 tbsp	finely grated orange zest	15 mL
2 tbsp	freshly squeezed orange juice	25 mL

1. In a bowl, combine flour, brown sugar, baking powder, ginger and baking soda.
2. In another bowl, combine eggs, carrots, zucchini, raisins, walnuts, oil, honey and vanilla. Add to flour mixture; stir just until blended.
3. Spoon batter into prepared muffin tin. Bake in preheated oven for 15 to 20 minutes.
4. *Prepare the frosting:* In a bowl, combine cream cheese, confectioner's sugar, orange zest and juice; beat on medium speed until fluffy. Spread over cooled muffins.

Corn Carrot Muffins

Makes 12 muffins

- Preheat oven to 400°F (200°C)
- Muffin tin, greased

1 cup	shredded carrots	250 mL
1 cup	yellow cornmeal	250 mL
1 cup	milk	250 mL
2	eggs, lightly beaten	2
2 tbsp	vegetable oil	25 mL
1 cup	all-purpose flour	250 mL
2½ tsp	baking powder	12 mL
1 tsp	salt	5 mL

1. In a bowl, combine carrots and cornmeal.
2. In a saucepan over medium-high heat, bring milk to a boil. Add to carrot mixture. Let cool to room temperature. Add eggs and oil.
3. In another bowl, combine flour, baking powder and salt. Add to carrot mixture; blend well.
4. Spoon batter into prepared muffin tin. Bake in preheated oven for 20 minutes.

Cornmeal Muffins

Makes 12 muffins
- Preheat oven to 425°F (220°C)
- Muffin tin, greased

½ cup	all-purpose flour	125 mL
1 tbsp	granulated sugar	15 mL
1 tbsp	baking powder	15 mL
¾ tsp	salt	4 mL
1½ cups	white cornmeal	375 mL
¼ cup	melted butter or margarine	50 mL
1	egg, well beaten	1
1 cup	milk	250 mL

1. In a bowl, sift together flour, sugar, baking powder and salt. Mix in cornmeal. Make a well in the center.

2. In another bowl, combine butter, egg and milk. Add to flour mixture; stir until well blended. Do not overmix.

3. Spoon batter into prepared muffin tin. Bake in preheated oven for 20 to 25 minutes or until golden brown.

Buttermilk Cornmeal Muffins

Makes 12 large muffins
- Preheat oven to 400°F (200°C)
- Muffin tin, greased or paper-lined

1 cup	yellow cornmeal	250 mL
1½ cups	buttermilk	375 mL
1¼ cups	all-purpose flour	300 mL
1½ tsp	baking powder	7 mL
1 tsp	baking soda	5 mL
1 tsp	salt	5 mL
½ cup	granulated sugar	125 mL
1	egg	1
⅓ cup	melted butter, cooled	75 mL

1. In a bowl, combine cornmeal and buttermilk. Set aside.

2. In another bowl, combine flour, baking powder, baking soda, salt and sugar.

3. In another bowl, whisk together egg and butter. Add cornmeal mixture; stir well. Add to flour mixture; stir just until blended. Do not overmix.

4. Spoon batter into prepared muffin tin. Bake in preheated oven for 20 to 25 minutes.

Easy Orange Cornmeal Muffins

Makes 12 muffins
- Preheat oven to 425°F (220°C)
- Muffin tin, greased

1 cup	yellow cornmeal	250 mL
1 cup	all-purpose flour	250 mL
⅓ cup	granulated sugar	75 mL
4 tsp	baking powder	20 mL
¼ tsp	salt	1 mL
1	egg, lightly beaten	1
1 cup	milk	250 mL
¼ cup	vegetable oil	50 mL
1 tbsp	grated orange or lemon zest	15 mL

1. In a bowl, combine cornmeal, flour, sugar, baking powder and salt.

2. In another bowl, combine egg, milk, oil and orange zest. Add to cornmeal mixture; stir just until blended.

3. Spoon batter into prepared muffin tin. Bake in preheated oven for about 15 minutes or until lightly browned.

Cornmeal Sausage Gems

Makes 12 muffins
- Preheat oven to 425°F (220°C)
- Muffin tin, greased

8 oz	bulk beef or pork sausage, formed into 12 small patties	250 g
1 cup	all-purpose flour	250 mL
1 cup	yellow cornmeal	250 mL
2 tsp	baking powder	10 mL
½ tsp	salt	2 mL
1 tbsp	granulated sugar	15 mL
1	egg	1
1 cup	milk	250 mL
2 tbsp	sausage drippings	25 mL

1. In a skillet over medium-high heat, brown patties. Pour off drippings, saving as they accumulate.

2. In a bowl, sift together flour, cornmeal, baking powder, salt and sugar.

3. In another bowl, beat egg. Add milk and sausage drippings; mix well. Add to flour mixture; stir just until flour is dampened.

4. Place 1 patty in bottom of each muffin cup. Top with batter. Bake in preheated oven for 20 minutes.

Corn Muffins

Makes 12 muffins
- Preheat oven to 425°F (220°C)
- Muffin tin, greased

1 cup	yellow cornmeal	250 mL
1 cup	all-purpose flour	250 mL
2 tbsp	granulated sugar	25 mL
4 tsp	baking powder	20 mL
½ tsp	salt	2 mL
1 cup	milk	250 mL
¼ cup	shortening	50 mL
1	egg	1

1. In a bowl, combine cornmeal, flour, sugar, baking powder, salt, milk, shortening and egg; stir until well blended.
2. Spoon batter into prepared muffin tin. Bake in preheated oven for 15 minutes or until golden brown.

Oatmeal Corn Muffins

Makes 12 muffins
- Preheat oven to 400°F (200°C)
- Muffin tin, greased or paper-lined

1 cup	all-purpose flour	250 mL
1 tsp	baking powder	5 mL
¾ tsp	salt	4 mL
½ cup	yellow cornmeal	125 mL
½ cup	old-fashioned rolled oats	125 mL
1 cup	buttermilk	250 mL
1	egg	1
⅓ cup	packed light brown sugar	75 mL
½ cup	melted butter or margarine	125 mL

1. In a bowl, combine flour, baking powder and salt.
2. In another bowl, combine cornmeal, oats and buttermilk. Add egg, brown sugar and butter; beat with a spoon until well blended. Add flour mixture; stir just until blended.
3. Spoon batter into prepared muffin tin. Bake in preheated oven for about 25 minutes or until golden brown.

Golden Cheddar Corn Muffins

Makes 12 muffins
- Preheat oven to 400°F (200°C)
- Muffin tin, well-greased

1 cup	yellow cornmeal	250 mL
1 cup	shredded old Cheddar cheese	250 mL
1 cup	all-purpose flour	250 mL
½ tsp	baking soda	2 mL
½ tsp	salt	2 mL
3	eggs	3
1	can (10 oz/284 mL) creamed corn	1
1 cup	buttermilk	250 mL
¼ cup	vegetable oil	50 mL
2 tbsp	chopped fresh parsley	25 mL

1. In a bowl, combine cornmeal, cheese, flour, baking soda and salt.
2. In another bowl, whisk together eggs, corn, buttermilk and oil. Add to dry ingredients; stir well. Add parsley; stir just until blended.
3. Spoon batter into prepared muffin tin. Bake in preheated oven for 25 to 30 minutes.

Mexican-Style Corn Muffins

Makes 6 muffins
- Preheat oven to 400°F (200°C)
- Muffin tin, paper-lined

½ cup + 1 tbsp	all-purpose flour	140 mL
4 tbsp	yellow cornmeal	60 mL
2 tsp	granulated sugar	10 mL
1½ tsp	baking powder	7 mL
¼ tsp	salt	1 mL
¼ cup	skim milk	50 mL
1	egg, lightly beaten	1
2 tbsp	water	25 mL
1 tbsp	vegetable oil	15 mL
½ cup	canned Mexican-style corn, drained	125 mL
1 tbsp	chopped green chilies	15 mL

1. In a bowl, combine flour, cornmeal, sugar, baking powder and salt.
2. In another bowl, combine milk, egg, water and oil. Add to flour mixture; stir to blend well. Add corn and chilies; stir just until blended.
3. Spoon batter into prepared muffin tin. Bake in preheated oven for 15 to 20 minutes.

Double Corn Pepper Muffins

Makes 12 muffins
- Preheat oven to 375°F (190°C)
- Muffin tin, greased or paper-lined

1½ cups	all-purpose flour	375 mL
¾ cup	yellow cornmeal	175 mL
¼ cup	granulated sugar	50 mL
1 tbsp	chili powder	15 mL
½ tsp	salt	2 mL
½ tsp	baking soda	2 mL
¼ tsp	dried crushed chili peppers	1 mL
3	eggs	3
⅔ cup	buttermilk or sour milk	150 mL
2 tbsp	vegetable oil	25 mL
1 cup	corn kernels	250 mL
½ cup	chopped red or green bell peppers	125 mL

1. In a bowl, combine flour, cornmeal, sugar, chili powder, salt, baking soda and chilies.
2. In another bowl, beat eggs, buttermilk and oil. Add corn and chopped peppers; blend well. Add to flour mixture; mix just enough to moisten.
3. Spoon batter into prepared muffin tin. Bake in preheated oven for 15 to 18 minutes or until golden brown. Serve warm.

Tip *If using frozen corn kernels, thaw before adding to the batter. If using canned, drain them first.*

Chili-Pepper Corn Muffins

Makes 12 large muffins
- Preheat oven to 375°F (190°C)
- Muffin tin, greased or paper-lined

1 cup	all-purpose flour	250 mL
1 cup	yellow cornmeal	250 mL
1 tbsp	baking powder	15 mL
1½ tsp	ground cumin	7 mL
1 tsp	hot pepper flakes	5 mL
½ tsp	salt	2 mL
⅔ cup	sour cream	150 mL
⅔ cup	milk	150 mL
2 tbsp	butter or margarine, melted	25 mL
1	egg	1
1¾ cups	finely shredded sharp (old) Cheddar cheese	425 mL
⅓ cup	finely diced seeded hot chili peppers or jalapeño peppers	75 mL
⅓ cup	finely chopped green onions	75 mL
⅓ cup	canned whole kernel corn, drained	75 mL

1. In a bowl, combine flour, cornmeal, baking powder, cumin, red pepper and salt.
2. In another bowl, combine sour cream, milk, butter and egg; whisk until blended. Add cornmeal mixture; mix well. Add cheese, chili peppers, green onions and corn; blend well.
3. Spoon batter into prepared muffin tin. Bake in preheated oven for 25 to 30 minutes or until toothpick inserted in center comes out clean.

Bell Pepper Muffins

Makes 12 muffins
- Preheat oven to 400°F (200°C)
- Muffin tin, greased or paper-lined

¼ cup	butter or margarine	50 mL
¼ cup	finely chopped red bell peppers	50 mL
¼ cup	finely chopped yellow bell peppers	50 mL
¼ cup	finely chopped green bell peppers	50 mL
2 cups	all-purpose flour	500 mL
2 tbsp	granulated sugar	25 mL
1 tbsp	baking powder	15 mL
¾ tsp	salt	4 mL
½ tsp	dried basil	2 mL
1 cup	milk	250 mL
2	eggs	2

1. In a skillet, heat butter over medium-high heat. Cook red, yellow and green peppers for 3 minutes or until bright and tender-crisp. Set aside.
2. In a bowl, combine flour, sugar, baking powder, salt and basil.
3. In another bowl, combine milk and eggs; blend well. Add to flour mixture; stir just until moist. Add peppers.
4. Spoon batter into prepared muffin tin. Bake in preheated oven for 15 minutes or until golden brown.

Ham, Pepper and Onion Muffins

Makes 12 muffins
- Preheat oven to 400°F (200°C)
- Muffin tin, greased or paper-lined

¼ cup	butter or margarine	50 mL
¾ cup	finely chopped onions	175 mL
¾ cup	finely chopped ham	175 mL
2 cups	all-purpose flour	500 mL
2 tbsp	granulated sugar	25 mL
1 tbsp	baking powder	15 mL
1 tsp	coarsely ground black pepper	5 mL

½ tsp	salt	2 mL
1 cup	milk	250 mL
1	egg	1

1. In a skillet, heat butter over medium-high heat. Add onions; cook for about 2 minutes. Set aside.
2. In a bowl, combine ham, flour, sugar, baking powder, pepper and salt; blend well.
3. In another bowl, combine milk, egg and onions. Add to flour mixture; stir just until moist.
4. Spoon batter into prepared muffin tin. Bake in preheated oven for 20 to 25 minutes.

Turkey Ham, Cheese and Pepper Muffins

Makes 12 muffins
- Preheat oven to 375°F (190°C)
- Muffin tin, well-greased

¼ cup	butter or margarine	50 mL
½ cup	minced sweet onions	125 mL
¼ cup	minced green bell peppers	50 mL
1	clove garlic, minced or pressed	1
2 cups	all-purpose flour	500 mL
1 tbsp	baking powder	15 mL
1 tsp	salt	5 mL
½ tsp	freshly ground black pepper	2 mL
1 cup	milk	250 mL
2	eggs	2
1 cup	finely diced turkey ham	250 mL
½ cup	diced Cheddar cheese	125 mL
¼ cup	shelled roasted sunflower seeds	50 mL

1. In a skillet, heat butter over medium-high heat. Add onions, green peppers and garlic. Cook, stirring, for 5 to 7 minutes or until onions are translucent.
2. In a bowl, combine flour, baking powder, salt and pepper.
3. In another bowl, combine milk and eggs; beat well. Add to flour mixture; mix well. Add vegetables with drippings, turkey and cheese; stir just until moist.
4. Spoon batter into prepared muffin tin. Sprinkle with sunflower seeds. Bake in preheated oven for 25 to 30 minutes.

Onion Parsley Muffins

Makes 12 muffins
- Preheat oven to 400°F (200°C)
- Muffin tin, greased

2 cups	all-purpose flour	500 mL
1 tbsp	granulated sugar	15 mL
1 tbsp	baking powder	15 mL
1½ tsp	salt	7 mL
¼ cup	vegetable oil	50 mL
1 cup	milk	250 mL
4	green onions, chopped	4
¼ cup	chopped fresh parsley	50 mL

1. In a bowl, sift together flour, sugar, baking powder and salt.
2. In another bowl, combine oil, milk, green onions and parsley. Add to dry ingredients; mix just until well-blended.
3. Spoon batter into prepared muffin tin. Bake in preheated oven for 20 to 25 minutes or until toothpick inserted in center comes out clean.

Golden Squash Muffins

Makes 12 muffins
- Preheat oven to 400°F (200°C)
- Muffin tin, greased or lined with foil cups

2¼ cups	all-purpose flour	550 mL
⅓ cup	granulated sugar	75 mL
2½ tsp	baking powder	12 mL
¼ tsp	salt	1 mL
⅓ cup	butter or margarine, softened	75 mL
1	egg	1
¾ cup	mashed cooked winter squash	175 mL
1 tsp	grated orange zest	5 mL
1 cup	milk	250 mL
¼ cup	golden raisins	50 mL

1. In a bowl, combine flour, sugar, baking powder and salt. Using a pastry blender or two knives, cut in butter until mixture is crumbly.
2. In another bowl, beat egg. Add squash, orange zest and milk; blend well. Add to flour mixture; stir just until blended. Fold in raisins.
3. Spoon batter into prepared muffin tin. Bake in preheated oven for 20 to 25 minutes.

Best Zucchini Muffins

Makes 12 muffins

- Preheat oven to 400°F (200°C)
- Muffin tin, greased

1 cup	all-purpose flour	250 mL
1 cup	whole wheat flour	250 mL
1½ tsp	baking powder	7 mL
½ tsp	baking soda	2 mL
1 tsp	ground cinnamon	5 mL
½ tsp	ground allspice	2 mL
1 tsp	salt	5 mL
1	egg	1
¼ cup	vegetable oil	50 mL
½ cup	granulated sugar	125 mL
1 cup	grated zucchini	250 mL
½ cup	milk	125 mL

1. In a bowl, combine all-purpose flour, whole wheat flour, baking powder, baking soda, cinnamon, allspice and salt. Make a well in the center.
2. In another bowl, beat egg. Add oil, sugar, zucchini and milk; blend well. Add to dry ingredients; stir just until moist (batter will be lumpy).
3. Spoon batter into prepared muffin tin. Bake in preheated oven for 20 to 25 minutes.

Whole Wheat Zucchini Muffins

Makes 8 to 12 muffins

- Preheat oven to 400°F (200°C)
- Muffin tin, greased or paper-lined

1 cup	whole wheat flour	250 mL
½ tsp	baking powder	2 mL
½ tsp	baking soda	2 mL
1 tsp	ground cinnamon	5 mL
⅓ cup	chopped nuts	75 mL
1	egg	1
½ cup	granulated sugar	125 mL
½ cup	vegetable oil	125 mL
1 tsp	vanilla	5 mL
1 cup	grated zucchini	250 mL

1. In a bowl, combine flour, baking powder, baking soda, cinnamon and nuts. Make a well in the center.
2. In another bowl, combine egg, sugar, oil, vanilla and zucchini. Add to dry ingredients; mix just until blended.
3. Spoon batter into prepared muffin tin. Bake in preheated oven for 20 to 25 minutes or until toothpick inserted in center comes out clean and dry.

Zucchini Nut Muffins

Makes 18 to 24 muffins

- Preheat oven to 375°F (190°C)
- Muffin tins, greased or paper-lined

4	eggs	4
1 cup	granulated sugar	250 mL
½ tsp	vanilla	2 mL
1 cup	vegetable oil	250 mL
2 cups	grated zucchini	500 mL
3 cups	all-purpose flour	750 mL
1½ tsp	baking powder	7 mL
1 tsp	baking soda	5 mL
1 tsp	salt	5 mL
1 tsp	ground cinnamon	5 mL
1 cup	chopped walnuts	250 mL

1. In a bowl, combine eggs, sugar and vanilla; beat for 2 minutes. Slowly add oil; beat for 2 minutes. Add zucchini.
2. In another bowl, combine flour, baking powder, baking soda, salt and cinnamon. Add walnuts; blend well. Add zucchini mixture; stir just until blended.
3. Spoon batter into prepared muffin tins. Bake in preheated oven for 25 to 30 minutes.

Lemon Zucchini Muffins

Makes 12 muffins
- Preheat oven to 400°F (200°C)
- Muffin tin, greased

2 cups	all-purpose flour	500 mL
2 tsp	baking powder	10 mL
½ tsp	baking soda	2 mL
½ tsp	salt	2 mL
Pinch	ground nutmeg	Pinch
¾ cup	granulated sugar	175 mL
1	egg	1
½ cup	milk	125 mL
½ cup	vegetable oil	125 mL
2 tbsp	freshly squeezed lemon juice	25 mL
1 cup	grated zucchini, squeezed dry	250 mL
	Grated zest of 1 lemon	

1. In a bowl, combine flour, baking powder, baking soda, salt, nutmeg and sugar; stir with a fork until well blended.

2. In another bowl, beat together egg, milk, oil and lemon juice. Add to flour mixture; blend well. Add zucchini and lemon zest; stir with a fork just until blended (batter will be thick).

3. Spoon batter into prepared muffin tin. Bake in preheated oven for 20 to 25 minutes.

Tip *When buying lemons, look for fine-textured skin. The lemon will be juicier. If there is a bit of greenish coloring, the juice will be more acidic.*

Chocolate Zucchini Muffins

Makes 12 muffins
- Preheat oven to 400°F (200°C)
- Muffin tin, greased

1 cup	all-purpose flour	250 mL
½ cup	whole wheat flour	125 mL
⅓ cup	quick-cooking rolled oats	75 mL
1 tsp	baking soda	5 mL
½ cup	butter, softened	125 mL
½ cup	granulated sugar	125 mL
2	eggs	2
2 tbsp	sour cream or plain yogurt	25 mL
1 tsp	vanilla	5 mL
½ tsp	grated lemon zest	2 mL
2 cups	packed grated zucchini	500 mL
4 oz	bittersweet chocolate, grated	125 g
½ cup	chopped pecans (optional)	125 mL

1. In a bowl, combine all-purpose flour, whole wheat flour, oats and baking soda.

2. In another bowl, combine butter and sugar; cream until fluffy. Add eggs, sour cream, vanilla and lemon zest; beat well. Add flour mixture alternately with zucchini; blend well. Add chocolate and pecans (if using); beat well.

3. Spoon batter into prepared muffin tin. Bake in preheated oven for about 20 minutes or until toothpick inserted in center comes out clean and dry.

Tip *Try substituting carob for chocolate in some of your recipes. Carob is similar to chocolate in flavor but is lower in fat and is caffeine-free.*

Quick-Mix and Microwave Muffins

Muffin Mixes

Quick-Mix Muffins

Microwave Muffins

Muffin Mixes

Biscuit Mix No. 1

Makes about 16 cups (4 L)

12 cups	all-purpose flour	3 L
4 tsp	cream of tartar	20 mL
4 tsp	baking soda	20 mL
1/4 cup	baking powder	50 mL
1/4 cup	granulated sugar	50 mL
1 2/3 cups	powdered milk	400 mL
1 lb	lard or shortening	500 g
1 tbsp	salt	15 mL

1. In a bowl, combine flour, cream of tartar, baking soda, baking powder, sugar, powdered milk, lard and salt. Mix with fingers or a pastry blender until coarse crumbs form.

2. Store mix in an airtight container in a cool, dry place. Use as you would any commercial mix.

Biscuit Mix No. 2

Makes about 10 cups (2.5 L)

9 cups	all-purpose flour	2.25 L
1 tbsp	salt	15 mL
1/4 cup	baking powder	50 mL
2 cups	shortening (1 lb/500 g)	500 mL

1. In a large bowl, mix together flour, salt and baking powder. Add shortening, working in with a pastry blender (or fingers) until texture resembles coarse crumbs.

2. Store mix in an airtight container in a cool, dry place. Use as you would any commercial mix.

Biscuit Mix No. 3

Makes 7 1/2 to 8 cups (1.875 to 2 L)

6 cups	sifted cake and pastry flour (or 5 1/4 cups/1.3 L all-purpose flour)	1.5 L
3 tbsp	baking powder	45 mL
1 1/2 tsp	salt	7 mL
1 cup	shortening (8 oz/250 g)	250 mL

1. In a large bowl, sift together flour, baking powder and salt 2 or 3 times to distribute evenly. Cut in shortening until mixture resembles coarse crumbs.

2. Store mix in an airtight container in a cool, dry place for up to 6 weeks.

All 'Round Muffin Mix

Makes about 8 cups (2 L)

7 cups	all-purpose flour	1.75 L
1 1/3 cups	non-fat dry milk	325 mL
3/4 cup	granulated sugar	175 mL
1/4 cup	baking powder	50 mL
1 tbsp	salt	15 mL

1. In a large bowl, with a fork, combine flour, milk, sugar, baking powder and salt. Store in an airtight container in a cool, dry place.

Whole Wheat Mix

Makes about 14 cups (3.5 L)

4 cups	whole wheat flour	1 L
4 cups	all-purpose flour	1 L
1 1/2 cups	non-fat dry milk	375 mL
1 1/2 cups	granulated sugar	375 mL
1/2 cup	wheat germ	125 mL
1/4 cup	baking powder	50 mL
1 tbsp	salt	15 mL
1 1/2 cups	shortening	375 mL

1. In a large bowl, combine whole wheat flour, all-purpose flour, milk, sugar, wheat germ, baking powder and salt. Using a pastry blender or two knives, cut in shortening until mixture is crumbly.

2. Store mix in an airtight container in a cool, dry place.

Bran and Whole Wheat Mix

Makes about 12 cups (3 L)

3 cups	whole wheat flour	750 mL
3 cups	all-purpose flour	750 mL
2 1/2 cups	all-bran cereal	625 mL
1 1/2 cups	non-fat dry milk	375 mL
1 1/2 cups	packed brown sugar or granulated sugar	375 mL
1/4 cup	baking powder	50 mL
1 tbsp	salt	15 mL
1 1/2 cups	shortening	375 mL

1. In a large bowl, using a pastry blender or your fingers, mix together whole wheat flour, all-purpose flour, cereal, dry milk, brown sugar, baking powder, salt and shortening. Blend well until mixture resembles fine crumbs.

2. Store mix in an airtight container in a cool, dry place for up to 3 months.

Cinnamon Raisin Bran Muffin Mix

Makes about 13½ cups (3.375 L)

6 cups	all-purpose flour	1.5 L
4 cups	raisins	1 L
3 cups	bran flakes cereal	750 mL
3 cups	natural bran	750 mL
2 cups	packed brown sugar	500 mL
2 tbsp	baking soda	25 mL
2 tbsp	ground cinnamon	25 mL
2 tsp	salt	10 mL

1. In a large bowl, combine flour, raisins, cereal, bran, brown sugar, baking soda, cinnamon and salt.

2. Store mix in an airtight container in a cool, dry place for up to 4 weeks.

Tip *Use a packaged muffin mix, or one of your homemade mix recipes, to make a good quick coffee cake. Bake in a square pan and top with cinnamon and sugar.*

Granola Mix

Makes about 14 cups (3.5 L)
- Preheat oven to 300°F (150°C)
- Two large roasting pans

4 cups	quick-cooking or old-fashioned rolled oats	1 L
1 cup	coarsely chopped walnuts	250 mL
¾ cup	hulled sunflower seeds	175 mL
½ cup	slivered almonds	125 mL
½ cup	coarsely chopped pecans	125 mL
½ cup	wheat germ	125 mL
½ cup	natural wheat and barley cereal	125 mL
⅓ cup	sesame seeds	75 mL
1½ cups	shredded coconut (sweetened or unsweetened)	375 mL
1 cup	packed light brown sugar	250 mL
⅔ cup	vegetable oil	150 mL
⅔ cup	water	150 mL
½ cup	liquid honey	125 mL
2 tsp	vanilla	10 mL
1 tsp	ground cinnamon	5 mL
½ tsp	ground nutmeg	2 mL
1½ cups	raisins	375 mL

1. In a large bowl, combine oats, walnuts, sunflower seeds, almonds, pecans, wheat germ, cereal, sesame seeds and coconut. Set aside.

2. In a large saucepan over low heat, combine brown sugar, oil, water, honey, vanilla, cinnamon and nutmeg. Heat, stirring occasionally, for 15 to 20 minutes or until sugar dissolves. Do not let boil. Pour over dry ingredients and stir until well coated.

3. Divide batter evenly between the two pans. Bake in preheated oven for 25 to 30 minutes (or 10 minutes more if you want a crunchier texture). Set aside to cool.

4. When cool, break into pieces. Stir in raisins. Store mix in airtight containers in a cool, dry place for up to 6 months.

Just-a-Minute Mix

Makes about 12 cups (3 L)

10 cups	all-purpose flour	2.5 L
⅓ cup	baking powder	75 mL
1 tbsp	salt	15 mL
2⅓ cups	shortening (1 lb/500 g)	575 mL

1. In a large mixing bowl, combine flour, baking powder and salt, mixing well. Using a pastry blender or two knives, cut in shortening until mixture resembles coarse crumbs.

2. Store mix in an airtight container in a cool, dry place

Multipurpose Mix

Makes about 13 cups (3.25 L)

10 cups	all-purpose flour	2.5 L
½ cup	granulated sugar	125 mL
⅓ cup	baking powder	75 mL
1 tbsp	salt	15 mL
2 cups	shortening	500 mL

1. In a large bowl, combine flour, sugar, baking powder and salt, mixing well. Using a pastry blender or two knives, cut in shortening until mixture resembles coarse crumbs.

2. Store in an airtight container in a cool, dry place for up to 3 months.

Variation *Whole Wheat Multipurpose Mix: Use 5 cups (1.25 L) all-purpose flour and 5 cups (1.25 L) whole wheat flour.*

Rolled Oats Mix

Makes about 10 cups (2.5 L)

4 cups	all-purpose flour	1 L
4 cups	quick-cooking rolled oats	1 L
1½ cups	dry non-fat milk	375 mL
¼ cup	baking powder	50 mL
1 tbsp	salt	15 mL
1½ cups	shortening	375 mL

1. In a large bowl, combine flour, oats, milk, baking powder and salt. Using a pastry blender, cut in shortening until mixture resembles coarse crumbs.

2. Store in an airtight container and keep in a cool, dry place.

Corn Muffin Mix

Makes about 9½ cups (2.375 L)

4 cups	all-purpose flour	1 L
4 cups	yellow cornmeal	1 L
2 cups	non-fat dry milk	500 mL
¾ cup	granulated sugar	175 mL
¼ cup	baking powder	50 mL
1 tbsp	salt	15 mL

1. In a large bowl, combine flour, cornmeal, milk, sugar, baking powder and salt. Mix with your hands, lifting mixture and letting it fall through your fingers.

2. Store mix in an airtight container in a cool, dry place.

Quick-Mix Muffins

Plain Muffins

Makes 12 muffins
- Preheat oven to 400ºF (200ºC)
- Muffin tin, greased

2 cups	All 'Round Muffin Mix (see recipe, page 97)	500 mL
1	egg, lightly beaten	1
1 cup	water	250 mL
3 tbsp	butter or margarine, melted	45 mL

1. Put muffin mix in a large bowl. In another bowl, combine egg, water and melted butter. Add all at once to muffin mixture and stir just until moistened.

2. Spoon batter into prepared muffin tin. Bake in preheated oven for 20 to 25 minutes.

Variations *Cheese Muffins: Add a small piece of Cheddar cheese in the center of each muffin before baking.*

Jelly Muffins: Fill cups only half full with batter. Put 1 tsp (5 mL) of your favorite jelly in center of each muffin and top with the remaining batter. Bake as directed.

Easy Buttermilk Muffins

Makes 6 muffins
- Preheat oven to 400ºF (200ºC)
- Muffin tin, greased or paper-lined

1 cup	buttermilk baking mix	250 mL
3 tbsp	granulated sugar	45 mL
1	egg	1
⅓ cup	water	75 mL

1. In a large bowl, combine buttermilk mix, sugar, egg and water. Whisk together for about 30 seconds.

2. Spoon batter into prepared muffin tin. Bake in preheated oven for 15 to 20 minutes.

Variations *Buttermilk Nut Muffins: Add ¼ cup (50 mL) chopped nuts.*

Buttermilk Date Muffins: Add ¼ cup (50 mL) chopped dates.

Granola Muffins

Makes 6 muffins
- Preheat oven to 400ºF (200ºC)
- Muffin tin, greased

1 cup	Multipurpose Mix (preferably Whole Wheat, see page 98)	250 mL
⅔ cup	Granola Mix (see recipe, page 98), divided	150 mL
2 tbsp	packed light brown sugar	25 mL
½ cup	milk	125 mL
1	egg, lightly beaten	1

1. In a large bowl, combine Multipurpose Mix, ½ cup (125 mL) of the Granola Mix and sugar. Add milk and egg, stirring just until moistened.

2. Spoon batter into prepared muffin tin. Sprinkle tops with the remaining Granola Mix. Bake in preheated oven for 20 to 25 minutes or until golden brown.

Just-a-Minute Muffins

Makes 12 muffins
- Preheat oven to 400°F (200°C)
- Muffin tin, greased

2½ cups	Just-a-Minute Mix (see recipe, page 98)	625 mL
3 tbsp	granulated sugar	45 mL
¾ cup	milk	175 mL
1	egg, beaten	1

1. In a large bowl, combine mix and sugar. Add milk and egg, stirring just until moistened. Batter will be lumpy.

2. Spoon batter into prepared muffin tin. Bake in preheated oven for 20 to 25 minutes.

Tip *You can add raisins, blueberries or any other fruits, or chocolate chips — whatever you have on hand.*

Oat Muffins

Makes 12 muffins
- Preheat oven to 425°F (220°C)
- Muffin tin, greased

2¼ cups	Rolled Oats Mix (see recipe, page 99)	550 mL
¼ cup	raisins (optional)	50 mL
2 tbsp	granulated sugar	25 mL
⅔ cup	water	150 mL
1	egg, beaten	1

1. In a large bowl, combine mix, raisins (if using), sugar, water and egg. Stir just until moistened. Do not overmix.

2. Spoon batter into prepared muffin tin. Bake in preheated oven for about 20 minutes.

Oat or Bran Muffins

Makes 12 muffins
- Preheat oven to 400°F (200°C)
- Muffin tin, greased

1	egg	1
2 tbsp	vegetable oil or shortening, melted	25 mL
1 cup	soured skim milk	250 mL
½ tsp	baking soda	2 mL
⅔ cup	all-bran cereal or old-fashioned rolled oats	150 mL

1⅓ cups	homemade or packaged biscuit mix	325 mL
⅓ cup	packed brown sugar	75 mL

1. In a large bowl, beat egg. Add oil, milk, baking soda and bran, mixing well. Add biscuit mix and brown sugar.

2. Spoon batter into prepared muffin tin. Bake in preheated oven for 18 to 20 minutes.

Variation *Orange Muffins: Add a little grated orange zest, plus 2 to 3 tbsp (25 to 45 mL) sugar for a sweeter muffin.*

Grandma's Muffins

Makes 12 muffins
- Preheat oven to 400°F (200°C)
- Muffin tin, greased or paper-lined

2 cups	pancake and waffle mix	500 mL
½ cup	lightly packed brown sugar	125 mL
1 tsp	ground cinnamon	5 mL
¾ cup	milk	175 mL
1 tsp	vanilla	5 mL
1	egg, lightly beaten	1
¼ cup	vegetable oil	50 mL
¾ cup	raisins (optional)	175 mL

1. In a large bowl, mix together pancake mix, brown sugar and cinnamon.

2. In another bowl, combine milk, vanilla, egg and oil. Stir into dry ingredients just until blended. Fold in raisins (if using).

3. Spoon batter into prepared muffin tin. Bake in preheated oven for 18 to 20 minutes.

Breakfast Muffins

Makes 6 large muffins
- Preheat oven to 400°F (200°C)
- Muffin tin, greased or paper-lined

2¼ cups	Cinnamon Raisin Bran Muffin Mix (see recipe, page 98)	550 mL
½ cup	low-fat plain yogurt	125 mL
½ cup	milk	125 mL
3 tbsp	vegetable oil	45 mL

1. Put muffin mix in a large bowl. In another bowl, whisk together yogurt, milk and oil. Stir into mix just until moistened.

2. Spoon batter into prepared muffin tin. Bake in preheated oven for 20 to 25 minutes or until firm to the touch.

• •

Marmalade Breakfast Muffins

Makes 12 muffins
- Preheat oven to 400°F (200°C)
- Muffin tin, greased or paper-lined

2¼ cups	buttermilk baking mix	550 mL
2 tbsp	granulated sugar	25 mL
1	egg, lightly beaten	1
½ tsp	vanilla	2 mL
¼ cup	all-fruit orange marmalade spread	50 mL

1. In a large bowl, combine buttermilk mix and sugar. Add egg and vanilla, mixing just until blended.

2. Spoon batter into prepared muffin tin, filling cups half full. Top each with 1 tsp (5 mL) orange marmalade. Spoon the remaining batter evenly over marmalade. Bake in preheated oven for 12 to 15 minutes or until a toothpick inserted in center comes out clean.

Tip *In place of the egg, you can use ¼ cup (50 mL) egg substitute plus 1 cup (250 mL) water.*

• •

All-Bran Breakfast Muffins

Makes 24 to 36 muffins
- Muffin tin, greased or paper-lined

1 cup	bran flakes cereal	250 mL
1 cup	boiling water	250 mL
2½ cups	all-purpose flour	625 mL
2½ tsp	baking soda	12 mL
1 tsp	salt	5 mL
½ cup	shortening	125 mL
1 cup	granulated sugar	250 mL
2	eggs	2
2½ cups	buttermilk	625 mL
2 cups	all-bran cereal	500 mL
1 cup	raisins	250 mL

1. In a bowl, combine cereal and boiling water. Set aside to cool.

2. In another bowl, combine flour, baking soda and salt. Set aside.

3. In another bowl, cream together shortening and sugar. Add eggs, one at a time, beating well each time. Add dry ingredients to this mixture alternately with buttermilk; stir until blended.

4. Add cooled bran flakes mixture, all-bran cereal and raisins; cover bowl tightly. Let stand overnight in refrigerator; do not stir. Spoon batter into prepared muffin tin. Bake at 400°F (200°C) for 30 minutes.

Tip *This batter will keep for 3 to 4 weeks in the refrigerator if covered tightly.*

• •

Old-Time Six-Week Bran Muffins

Makes 36 to 48 muffins
- Muffin tin, greased or paper-lined

4 cups	natural bran	1 L
2 cups	bran flakes cereal	500 mL
2 cups	boiling water	500 mL
1 cup	butter	250 mL
1 cup	granulated sugar	250 mL
2 cups	packed brown sugar	500 mL
4	eggs	4
4 cups	buttermilk	1 L
½ cup	light (fancy) molasses	125 mL
5 cups	all-purpose flour	1.25 L
2 tbsp	baking soda	25 mL
1 tbsp	baking powder	15 mL
1 tsp	salt	5 mL
2 cups	raisins	500 mL

1. In a bowl, combine bran and bran flakes. Cover with boiling water; mix well. Set aside.

2. In another bowl, cream together butter, granulated sugar and brown sugar. Beat in eggs one at a time. Add buttermilk and molasses; mix well.

3. In another bowl, combine flour, baking soda, baking powder, salt and raisins. Add to buttermilk mixture; stir just until blended. Add bran mixture; mix well.

4. Pour batter into a container; cover tightly. Store in the refrigerator for up to 6 weeks.

5. When ready to bake, spoon batter into prepared muffin tin, filling three-quarters full. Bake at 400°F (200°C) for 20 to 25 minutes or until firm and springy to the touch.

Coffee 'n' Bran Muffins

Makes 24 muffins

- Muffin tin, greased or paper-lined

½ cup	butter or margarine, soft or melted	125 mL
1 cup	granulated sugar	250 mL
2	eggs	2
1 cup	brewed coffee	250 mL
2 cups	buttermilk	500 mL
2½ cups	all-purpose flour	625 mL
2½ tsp	baking soda	12 mL
3 cups	all-bran cereal	750 mL

1. In a bowl, whisk together butter, sugar and eggs. Add coffee and buttermilk; whisk until mixture looks curdled. Add flour and baking soda; beat to blend well. Stir in cereal. Cover bowl tightly; refrigerate.

2. When ready to bake, stir mixture well. Spoon batter into prepared muffin tin. Bake at 400°F (200°C) for 20 minutes.

Quick Cocoa Bran Muffins

Makes 12 muffins

- Preheat oven to 400°F (200°C)
- Muffin tin, greased or paper-lined

1	package (14 oz/400 g) bran and honey muffin mix	1
¼ cup	unsweetened cocoa powder	50 mL
1	egg, lightly beaten	1
¾ cup	water	175 mL
½ cup	raisins	125 mL
¼ cup	finely chopped nuts (optional)	50 mL

1. In a large bowl, combine muffin mix and cocoa, blending well. Stir in egg and water just until blended. Add raisins and nuts (if using).

2. Spoon batter into prepared muffin tin. Bake in preheated oven for 15 to 17 minutes. Serve warm.

Golden Honey Bran Muffins

Makes 48 to 60 muffins

- Muffin tin, greased or paper-lined

6 cups	all-bran cereal	1.5 L
2 cups	boiling water	500 mL
1 cup	liquid honey	250 mL
5 cups	all-purpose flour	1.25 L
2 tbsp	baking soda	25 mL
2 tsp	ground cinnamon	10 mL
1 tsp	salt	5 mL
1 cup	shortening	250 mL
1 cup	granulated sugar	250 mL
1 cup	lightly packed brown sugar	250 mL
4	eggs	4
4 cups	buttermilk	1 L
2 cups	raisins or chopped dates	500 mL

1. In a bowl, cover bran cereal with boiling water. Add honey; stir well. Set aside.

2. In another bowl, combine flour, baking soda, cinnamon and salt.

3. In another bowl, cream together shortening, granulated sugar, brown sugar, eggs, buttermilk and soaked cereal. Add flour mixture; mix well. Stir in raisins. Pour batter into a container; cover tightly. Store in refrigerator for up to 2 months.

4. When ready to bake, spoon batter into prepared muffin tin, filling three-quarters full. Bake at 375°F (190°C) for 20 to 25 minutes.

Blueberry Bran Muffins

Makes 48 muffins

- Muffin tin, paper-lined

6	eggs	6
1½ cups	firmly packed dark brown sugar	375 mL
¼ cup	light molasses	50 mL
¼ cup	liquid honey	50 mL
4 cups	buttermilk	1 L
1½ cups	vegetable oil	375 mL
1 tsp	vanilla	5 mL
2½ cups	natural bran	625 mL
2 cups	wheat germ	500 mL
1¾ cups	finely chopped pecans or walnuts, divided	425 mL
2 cups	fresh or frozen blueberries, partially thawed	500 mL
4½ cups	all-purpose flour	1.125 L
4 tsp	baking powder	20 mL
4 tsp	baking soda	20 mL
1 tsp	ground cinnamon	5 mL
¼ tsp	salt	1 mL

1. In a bowl, beat together eggs, brown sugar, molasses and honey until well blended. Add buttermilk, oil and vanilla; stir well. Add bran, wheat germ and 1¼ cups (300 mL) of the pecans. Let stand for 10 minutes; stir in berries.

2. In another bowl, combine flour, baking powder, baking soda, cinnamon and salt. Add to batter, mixing just until blended. Cover bowl tightly; refrigerate overnight.

3. Spoon batter into prepared muffin tin. Sprinkle tops evenly with the remaining pecans. Bake at 400°F (200°C) for about 25 minutes.

Tip *Batter can be stored in the refrigerator or frozen.*

• •

Pineapple Bran Muffins

Makes 24 to 36 muffins
• Muffin tin, greased

2 cups	all-bran cereal	500 mL
2 cups	buttermilk	500 mL
2	eggs, lightly beaten	2
1	can (19 oz/540 mL) crushed pineapple, with juice	1
½ cup	melted butter or margarine	125 mL
2½ cups	all-purpose flour	625 mL
¾ cup	packed dark brown sugar	175 mL
2 tsp	salt	10 mL
2 tsp	baking soda	10 mL
1 cup	toasted chopped almonds	250 mL

1. In a bowl, combine bran and buttermilk; let stand for 5 minutes. Add eggs, pineapple (with juice) and butter; stir well.

2. In another bowl, combine flour, brown sugar, salt, baking soda and almonds. Add to bran mixture; stir just until blended (batter will be lumpy).

3. Pour batter into a container; cover tightly. Store in the refrigerator for up to 3 weeks.

4. When ready to bake, spoon batter into prepared muffin tin, filling three-quarters full. Bake at 375°F (190°C) for 25 minutes.

• •

Convenient Raisin Bran Muffins

Makes 24 to 36 muffins
• Muffin tin, greased or paper-lined

1 cup	natural bran	250 mL
1 cup	boiling water	250 mL
½ cup	butter or margarine	125 mL
¾ cup	packed brown sugar	175 mL
3	eggs	3
2½ cups	all-purpose flour	625 mL
2½ tsp	baking soda	12 mL
½ tsp	salt	2 mL
2 cups	raisin bran cereal	500 mL
2 cups	buttermilk	500 mL
1 cup	raisins	250 mL
1 cup	coarsely chopped walnuts	250 mL

1. In a bowl, cover bran with boiling water; set aside for 20 minutes.

2. In a food processor, combine butter, brown sugar, eggs and soaked bran; process until smooth.

3. In a bowl, combine bran mixture, flour, baking soda, salt, cereal and buttermilk; beat well. Fold in raisins and walnuts.

4. Pour batter into a container; cover tightly. Store in the refrigerator for up to 6 weeks.

5. When ready to bake, spoon batter into prepared muffin tin, filling three-quarters full. Bake at 375°F (190°C) for 20 minutes.

• •

Oat Bran Refrigerator Muffins

Makes 48 to 60 muffins
• Muffin tin, greased or paper-lined

⅔ cup	wheat germ	150 mL
1½ cups	natural bran	375 mL
1½ cups	oat bran	375 mL
3 cups	all-bran cereal	750 mL
3 cups	boiling water	750 mL
1 cup	margarine	250 mL
1 cup	firmly packed brown sugar	250 mL
½ cup	granulated sugar	125 mL
½ cup	light (fancy) molasses	125 mL
4	eggs	4
4 cups	buttermilk	1 L
2 cups	raisins and/or dates	500 mL
3 cups	all-purpose flour	750 mL
2 cups	whole wheat flour	500 mL
3 tbsp	baking soda	45 mL
1 tsp	salt	5 mL

1. In a bowl, combine wheat germ, natural bran, oat bran and bran cereal. Add boiling water; mix well. Set aside to cool.

2. In another bowl, cream together margarine, brown sugar and granulated sugar; add molasses. Beat in eggs one at a time. Add buttermilk; mix well. Stir in raisins.

3. In another bowl, combine all-purpose flour, whole wheat flour, baking soda and salt. Add to creamed mixture; mix well. Stir in bran mixture; blend well.

4. Pour batter into a container; cover tightly. Store in the refrigerator for at least 24 hours before baking.

5. When ready to bake, spoon batter into prepared muffin tin, filling three-quarters full. Bake at 375°F (190°C) for 25 to 30 minutes.

Quick 'n' Easy Oatmeal Raisin Muffins

Makes 12 muffins

- Preheat oven to 400°F (200°C)
- Muffin tin, greased or paper-lined

2 cups	buttermilk baking mix	500 mL
½ cup	quick-cooking rolled oats	125 mL
½ cup	raisins	125 mL
2 tbsp	granulated sugar	25 mL
1	egg	1
⅔ cup	milk	150 mL
	Butter or margarine	

1. In a large bowl, combine buttermilk mix, oats, raisins and sugar.
2. In another bowl, beat together egg and milk. Pour into dry ingredients and stir until well blended.
3. Spoon batter into prepared muffin tin. Bake in preheated oven for 15 minutes.

Wheat Germ Muffins

Makes 12 muffins

- Preheat oven to 375°F (190°C)
- Muffin tin, greased or paper-lined

2 cups	wheat germ pancake mix	500 mL
½ cup	margarine	125 mL
½ cup	granulated sugar	125 mL
1	egg	1
1¼ cups	milk	300 mL

1. Pour pancake mix into a large bowl. Using a pastry blender, cut in margarine until mixture resembles coarse crumbs. Add sugar.
2. In another bowl, beat egg. Add milk and beat well. Pour into dry ingredients and stir slowly, just until moistened and blended. Batter should be lumpy.
3. Spoon batter into prepared muffin tin. Bake in preheated oven for 25 minutes.

Whole Wheat Muffins

Makes 18 to 24 muffins

- Preheat oven to 400°F (200°C)
- Muffin tins, greased

1	egg	1
1¼ cups	water	300 mL
4½ cups	Whole Wheat Mix (see recipe, page 97)	1.125 L

1. In a large bowl, beat egg slightly with water. Stir in mix just until moistened.
2. Spoon batter into prepared muffin tins. Bake in preheated oven for 15 to 20 minutes.

Applesauce Whole Wheat Muffins

Makes 12 muffins

- Muffin tin, greased or paper-lined

¾ cup	all-purpose flour	175 mL
½ cup	whole wheat flour	125 mL
1 cup	quick-cooking rolled oats	250 mL
½ cup	packed brown sugar	125 mL
1 tsp	baking powder	5 mL
½ tsp	baking soda	2 mL
½ tsp	ground cinnamon	2 mL
¼ tsp	salt	1 mL
¾ cup	buttermilk	175 mL
¼ cup	sweetened applesauce	50 mL
¼ cup	vegetable oil	50 mL
1	egg, beaten	1
¼ cup	raisins	50 mL

1. In a bowl, combine all-purpose flour, whole wheat flour, oats, brown sugar, baking powder, baking soda, cinnamon and salt.
2. In a bowl, combine buttermilk, applesauce, oil and egg; mix well. Add to dry ingredients; stir just until moistened. Fold in raisins. Cover bowl tightly; refrigerate overnight.
3. Spoon batter into prepared muffin tin. Bake at 400°F (200°C) for 18 to 20 minutes.

Tip *Batter will keep, refrigerated, for 2 to 3 weeks.*

Nutty Bran and Whole Wheat Muffins

Makes 18 to 24 muffins

- Preheat oven to 400°F (200°C)
- Muffin tins, greased

4½ cups	Bran and Whole Wheat Mix (see recipe, page 97)	1.125 L
1¼ cups	water	300 mL
1	egg, lightly beaten	1
½ cup	chopped nuts	125 mL

1. In a large bowl, combine mix, water, egg and nuts. Stir just to moisten.
2. Spoon batter into prepared muffin tins. Bake in preheated oven for 15 to 20 minutes or until toothpick inserted in center comes out clean.

Quick-Mix Cornmeal Muffins

Makes 12 muffins

- Preheat oven to 400°F (200°C)
- Muffin tin, greased

1½ cups	Multipurpose Mix (see recipe, page 98)	375 mL
¾ cup	yellow cornmeal	175 mL
2 tbsp	granulated sugar	25 mL
1 cup	milk	250 mL
1	egg, lightly beaten	1

1. In a bowl, combine mix, cornmeal and sugar. Add milk and egg, stirring just until moistened.
2. Spoon batter into prepared muffin tin. Bake in preheated oven for 25 to 30 minutes.

Quick-Mix Corn Muffins

Makes 12 muffins

- Preheat oven to 425°F (220°C)
- Muffin tin, greased

1	egg	1
1 cup	water	250 mL
2⅓ cups	Corn Muffin Mix (see recipe, page 99)	575 mL
¼ cup	butter or margarine, melted, or bacon or sausage fat	50 mL

1. In a bowl, with a fork, mix together egg and water until blended. Add Corn Muffin Mix and melted butter, stirring just to blend.
2. Spoon batter evenly into prepared muffin tin. Bake in preheated oven for 20 minutes or until golden brown.

Tip *To check baking powder for freshness, stir 1 tsp (5 mL) baking powder into ½ cup (125 mL) boiling water. If the mixture does not fizz and bubble, the baking powder has lost its leavening power and should be thrown out.*

Double Corn Muffins

Makes 12 muffins

- Preheat oven to 375°F (190°C)
- Muffin tin, greased or paper-lined

1	package (12 oz/340 g) corn muffin mix	1
1	can (16 oz/473 mL) whole kernel corn, drained	1
1	can (2¼ oz/64 g) deviled ham	1

1. Prepare muffin mix according to package directions. Stir in corn.
2. Spoon batter into prepared muffin tin. Drop a spoonful of deviled ham in center of each muffin. Bake in preheated oven for 20 minutes.

Spicy Corn Muffins

Makes 12 muffins

- Preheat oven to 400°F (200°C)
- Muffin tin, greased or paper-lined

2	eggs	2
¾ cup	milk	175 mL
2	packages (each 8½ oz/251 mL) corn muffin mix	2
1 cup	shredded Cheddar cheese	250 mL
1 cup	thawed frozen corn	250 mL
¼ cup	drained sliced pickled jalapeño peppers	50 mL

1. In a small bowl, lightly beat together eggs and milk.
2. In a large bowl, combine muffin mix, cheese, corn and peppers. Stir in milk mixture and stir just until blended. Batter will be lumpy. Let stand for 5 minutes.
3. Spoon batter into prepared muffin tin. Bake in preheated oven for 20 minutes or until golden brown.

Buttermilk Corn Muffins

Makes 6 muffins

- Preheat oven to 400°F (200°C)
- Muffin tin, greased or paper-lined

½ cup	buttermilk baking mix	125 mL
½ cup	yellow cornmeal	125 mL
2 tbsp	granulated sugar	25 mL
1	egg	1
¼ tsp	salt	50 mL
⅓ cup	water	75 mL
2 tbsp	butter, melted	25 mL

1. In a medium bowl, combine buttermilk mix, cornmeal, sugar, egg, salt and water. Mix in melted butter, blending well.
2. Spoon batter into prepared muffin tin. Bake in preheated oven for 15 to 20 minutes.

Blueberry Cornbread Muffins

Makes 12 to 18 muffins

- Preheat oven to 400°F (200°C)
- Muffin tins, greased or paper-lined

1	package (14 oz/400 g) blueberry muffin mix	1
1 cup	yellow cornmeal	250 mL
1 cup	water	250 mL
1	egg	1
1	package (10 oz/300 g) frozen blueberries, thawed	1

1. In a large bowl, combine mix and cornmeal.

2. In another bowl, mix together water and egg. Add to the dry ingredients, blending with a fork just until moistened. Fold in blueberries.

3. Spoon batter into prepared muffin tins. Bake in preheated oven for 20 to 25 minutes.

Tip *Keep muffins hot longer by lining your basket (under the cloth or napkin) with a sheet of foil.*

Bacon, Chive and Corn Muffins

Makes 12 muffins

- Preheat oven to 400°F (200°C)
- Muffin tin, greased

1	package (12 oz/340 g) corn muffin mix	1
2 tsp	minced fresh chives or dried chives	10 mL
Pinch	freshly ground black pepper	Pinch
1	egg	1
2/3 cup	milk	150 mL
1/2 cup	crumbled crisp bacon	125 mL

1. In a large bowl, combine corn muffin mix, chives and pepper. Add egg and milk and mix according to package directions. Fold in bacon.

2. Spoon batter into prepared muffin tin. Bake in preheated oven for 15 to 20 minutes. Serve hot.

Quick Banana Muffins

Makes 18 to 24 muffins

- Preheat oven to 400°F (200°C)
- Muffin tins, greased

4 cups	homemade or packaged biscuit mix	1 L
1 cup	granulated sugar	250 mL
1/2 cup	all-purpose flour	125 mL
1/2 tsp	baking soda	2 mL
4	eggs, beaten	4
1 cup	sour cream	250 mL
2 cups	mashed ripe bananas (about 4 medium)	500 mL
1 cup	chopped walnuts	250 mL

1. In a large bowl, combine biscuit mix, sugar, flour and baking soda.

2. In another bowl, combine eggs and sour cream. Stir into dry ingredients. Add mashed banana and fold in chopped nuts.

3. Spoon batter into prepared muffin tins. Bake in preheated oven for 15 to 20 minutes or until toothpick inserted in center comes out clean.

Tip *To shell walnuts, soak overnight in salt water before gently cracking. This will remove the nutmeat intact.*

Blueberry Pancake Muffins

Makes 12 muffins

- Preheat oven to 400°F (200°C)
- Muffin tin, paper-lined

2 cups	blueberry pancake and waffle mix	500 mL
1/2 cup	granulated sugar or packed brown sugar	125 mL
2	eggs, beaten	2
1 cup	milk	250 mL
1/2 cup	butter or margarine, melted	125 mL

1. In a large bowl, combine pancake mix and sugar. Add eggs, milk and melted butter. Stir just to moisten, but do not overmix.

2. Spoon batter into prepared muffin tin. Bake in preheated oven for 15 to 20 minutes or until golden brown.

Tip *If you have saved egg yolks from previous recipes, use them in place of whole eggs. Use 2 yolks for every whole egg.*

Blueberry Cinnamon Treats

Makes 48 cookies

- Preheat oven to 375°F (190°C)
- Baking sheet, ungreased

1	package (14 oz/400 g) wild blueberry muffin mix	1
2 tbsp	vegetable oil	25 mL
2 tbsp	milk	25 mL
1/2 tsp	ground cinnamon	2 mL
1	egg	1

LEMON BUTTER FROSTING

1½ cups	confectioner's (icing) sugar	375 mL
2 tbsp	butter or margarine, softened	25 mL
½ tsp	grated lemon zest	2 mL
1 tsp	freshly squeezed lemon juice	5 mL
1 tbsp	milk	15 mL

1. In a large bowl, combine muffin mix, oil, milk, cinnamon and egg. Fold in packaged blueberries.
2. Drop dough by teaspoonfuls (5 mL), 2 inches (5 cm) apart, onto baking sheet. Bake in preheated oven for 10 minutes or until edges are golden brown. Remove from baking sheet immediately.
3. *Prepare the frosting:* In a bowl, mix together confectioner's sugar and butter. Stir in lemon zest and lemon juice. Then add milk, 1 tsp (5 mL) at a time, until desired consistency is reached. Frost cookies and serve.

Blueberry Miniatures

Makes 24 to 36 miniature muffins
- Preheat oven to 400°F (200°C)
- Miniature muffin tins, greased

2 cups	homemade or packaged biscuit mix	500 mL
1 tbsp	granulated sugar	15 mL
1	egg	1
2 tbsp	butter or margarine, melted	25 mL
¾ cup	milk	175 mL
1 cup	blueberries, washed and stemmed	250 mL
1 tbsp	Sugar-Cinnamon Mix (page 4)	15 mL

1. In a large bowl, combine biscuit mix and sugar.
2. In another bowl, beat egg slightly. Stir in melted butter and milk. Add to biscuit mixture all at once and stir just until moistened. Fold in blueberries.
3. Spoon batter into prepared muffin tins. Sprinkle with Sugar-Cinnamon Mix. Bake in preheated oven for 10 minutes or until golden brown. Remove from pans and serve hot.

Blueberry Nut Muffins

Makes 12 muffins
- Preheat oven to 400°F (200°C)
- Muffin tin, greased or paper-lined

1	egg	1
½ cup	milk	125 mL
1	package (14 oz/400 g) wild blueberry muffin mix	1
½ cup	chopped nuts	125 mL

1. In a large bowl, blend together egg and milk. Stir in muffin mix just until blended. Batter should be lumpy. Fold in packaged blueberries and nuts.
2. Spoon batter into prepared muffin tin. Bake in preheated oven for 15 to 20 minutes.

Polka Dot Muffins

Makes 12 muffins
- Preheat oven to 400°F (200°C)
- Muffin tin, greased or paper-lined

1 cup	chopped fresh cranberries or frozen cranberries, thawed	250 mL
¾ cup	granulated sugar, divided	175 mL
1 tsp	grated orange zest	5 mL
1	egg, beaten	1
½ cup	freshly squeezed orange juice	125 mL
2 tbsp	vegetable oil	25 mL
2 cups	homemade or packaged biscuit mix	500 mL

1. In a bowl, combine cranberries, ½ cup (125 mL) of the sugar and orange zest. Set aside.
2. In another bowl, combine egg, the remaining sugar, orange juice and oil. Add biscuit mix and stir just until moistened. Fold in cranberry mixture.
3. Spoon batter into prepared muffin tin. Bake in preheated oven for 25 minutes or until browned.

Festive Cranberry Date Muffins

Makes 12 muffins
- Preheat oven to 350°F (180°C)
- Muffin tin, greased or paper-lined

¾ cup	chopped almonds, pecans or walnuts	175 mL
1	package (14 oz/400 g) date and orange loaf and muffin mix	1
½ cup	milk	125 mL
2	eggs, lightly beaten	2
3 tbsp	butter, melted	45 mL
1 cup	fresh or frozen cranberries, cut in half	250 mL

1. Toast nuts in preheated oven for 5 minutes or until slightly browned. Set aside.
2. Pour muffin mix into a large bowl and make a well in the center. Add milk, eggs and butter, stirring just until blended. Fold in nuts and cranberries.
3. Spoon batter into prepared muffin tin. Bake in preheated oven for 15 to 20 minutes or until a toothpick inserted in center comes out clean and dry.

Glazed Orange Muffins

Makes 12 muffins

- Preheat oven to 400°F (200°C)
- Muffin tin, greased or paper-lined

1	package (14 oz/400 g) bran with fruit muffin mix	1
1	egg	1
1½ cups	water	375 mL
¼ cup	orange marmalade	50 mL
GLAZE		
1 tbsp	grated orange zest	15 mL
⅓ cup	freshly squeezed orange juice	75 mL
¼ cup	granulated sugar	50 mL

1. In a bowl, combine muffin mix, egg and water, mixing well.

2. Spoon just enough batter into prepared tin to cover bottoms. Add 1 tsp (5 mL) marmalade to each. Fill with the remaining batter. Bake in preheated oven for about 20 minutes.

3. *Prepare the glaze:* In a small saucepan over low heat, combine orange zest, orange juice and sugar. Cook until sugar dissolves.

4. Place warm muffins on a rack with waxed paper underneath. Drizzle hot glaze over muffins.

Orange Date Nut Muffins

Makes 24 muffins

- Preheat oven to 375°F (190°C)
- Muffin tins, greased or paper-lined

1	package date-and-orange loaf cake mix	1
2	eggs	2
1 cup	sour cream	250 mL
2 tbsp	vegetable oil	25 mL
½ cup	chopped nuts	125 mL
¼ cup	lightly packed brown sugar	50 mL
¼ cup	chopped nuts	50 mL

1. In a large bowl, combine cake mix, eggs, sour cream, oil and nuts. Mix together just until moistened and blended.

2. Spoon batter into prepared muffin tins. Sprinkle with brown sugar and chopped nuts. Bake in preheated oven for 20 to 25 minutes.

Raspberry Buttermilk Balls

Makes 10 to 12 muffins

- Preheat oven to 450°F (230°C)
- Muffin tin

1	package buttermilk baking mix Raspberry jam	1

1. Prepare baking mix as directed on package. Roll out dough to ½ inch (1 cm) thick. With a floured cookie cutter or inverted glass, cut into 10 to 12 circles. Reserve the remaining dough. Place a circle in each muffin cup.

2. Make a depression in center of each cup of batter. Fill each with 1 tsp (5 mL) raspberry jam.

3. Shape the remaining dough into 10 to 12 balls and place on top of jam. Bake in preheated oven for 10 minutes or until lightly browned.

Hawaiian Hula Muffins

Makes 12 muffins

- Preheat oven to 350°F (180°C)
- Muffin tin, greased or paper-lined

2 cups	homemade or packaged biscuit mix	500 mL
¾ cup	finely crushed butterscotch-flavored hard candies, divided	175 mL
¾ cup	milk	175 mL
¼ cup	vegetable oil	50 mL
1 cup	sour cream	250 mL
1	can (13½ oz/385 g) crushed pineapple, drained	1

1. In a bowl, combine biscuit mix and ¼ cup (50 mL) of the candies.

2. In a small bowl, combine milk and oil. Add to biscuit mixture, stirring just until moistened.

3. Spoon batter into prepared muffin tin. Bake in preheated oven for 10 to 12 minutes.

4. Split warm muffins and spread bottom sections with half the sour cream. Spoon on half the pineapple and half the remaining candies. Replace muffin tops and cover with remaining sour cream, pineapple and candies.

Tip *Use reserved juice from drained pineapple to retain the bright fresh coloring of sliced apples, bananas, avocados and mushrooms. The juice prevents darkening without adding an overpowering flavor.*

Fruit Muffin Buns

Makes 12 muffins

- Preheat oven to 375°F (190°C)
- Muffin tin, greased

2 cups	buttermilk baking mix	500 mL
1 tbsp	granulated sugar	15 mL
Pinch	ground nutmeg	Pinch
¾ cup	milk	175 mL
½ cup	butter or margarine, softened, divided	125 mL
	Fruit pie filling or stewed fruit, drained	

1. In a large bowl, combine buttermilk mix, sugar and nutmeg. Add milk and stir until mixture stiffens. Turn out on a floured board and roll out to ⅛ inch (0.25 cm) thick.
2. Spread with ¼ cup (50 mL) of the butter. Fold dough in half and spread with the remaining butter. Fold again and roll into a rectangle. Cut into twelve 3-inch (7.5 cm) squares.
3. Place squares in prepared muffin tin. Spoon in fruit filling. Pull corners of dough together and pinch to seal. Bake in preheated oven for 25 minutes.

Variation *Dried Fruit Filling: Poach until soft, drain and chop 6 dried apricots, 3 dried prunes and 1 dried peach. Set aside. In a bowl, beat together 1 egg, ½ cup (125 mL) sugar, 1 tsp (5 mL) lemon juice and ½ tsp (2 mL) ground cinnamon. Stir in fruit.*

Frosted Brownie Fudge Muffins

Makes 6 muffins

- Preheat oven to 350°F (180°C)
- Muffin tin, greased

1	package (14 oz/400 g) hot fudge brownie mix	1
½ cup	creamy chocolate frosting	125 mL
½ cup	whipped cream	125 mL

1. Prepare brownie mix according to package instructions. Spoon half the batter into prepared muffin tin.
2. Before opening hot fudge pouch, squeeze until fudge is softened, about 20 to 25 times. Squeeze fudge evenly over batter in cups. Spoon the remaining batter over fudge. Bake in preheated oven for about 25 to 30 minutes. Set aside to cool slightly.

3. Warm frosting in microwave on High for 30 seconds. Drizzle over warm muffins and top with whipped cream.

Devil's Food Muffins

Makes 24 muffins

- Preheat oven to 400°F (200°C)
- Muffin tins, paper-lined

1	package (18 oz/510 g) devil's food cake mix	1
3	eggs	3
1⅓ cups	water	325 mL
½ cup	vegetable oil	125 mL

1. Pour cake mix into a large bowl and make a well in the center.
2. In another bowl, with a mixing spoon, beat together eggs, water and oil. Add to cake mix and stir just until moistened.
3. Spoon batter into prepared muffin tins. Bake in preheated oven for 15 to 20 minutes.

Tip *For an extra special treat, ice muffin tops with vanilla or chocolate icing, or put vanilla icing on half of muffin top and chocolate on the other half.*

Creamy Cottage Cheese Muffins

Makes 12 muffins

- Preheat oven to 400°F (200°C)
- Muffin tin, greased or paper-lined

⅓ cup	granulated sugar	75 mL
3 tbsp	butter or margarine	45 mL
½ cup	cream-style cottage cheese	125 mL
1 tsp	grated lemon zest	5 mL
1	egg	1
1¾ cups	homemade or packaged biscuit mix	425 mL
½ cup	milk	125 mL

1. In a large bowl, cream together sugar and butter. Beat in cottage cheese and lemon zest. Add egg, beating well. Stir in biscuit mix and milk just until moistened.
2. Spoon batter into prepared muffin tin. Bake in preheated oven for 20 minutes.

Tip *When you are creaming butter and sugar together, it is a good idea to rinse the bowl with boiling water first. They will cream faster.*

Sesame Cheese Muffins

Makes 12 small muffins
- Preheat oven to 400°F (200°C)
- Muffin tin, greased or paper-lined

1½ cups	homemade or packaged biscuit mix	375 mL
1 cup	shredded sharp processed cheese, divided	250 mL
1 tbsp	vegetable oil	15 mL
½ cup	chopped onions	125 mL
1	egg, beaten	1
½ cup	milk	125 mL
1 tbsp	toasted sesame seeds	15 mL
2 tbsp	butter or margarine, melted	25 mL

1. In a large bowl, combine biscuit mix and half the cheese.
2. In a small skillet, heat oil over medium heat. Cook onions just until tender.
3. In a bowl, combine egg, milk and onions. Add all at once to biscuit mixture and stir just until moistened.
4. Spoon batter into prepared muffin tin. Sprinkle with the remaining cheese and sesame seeds. Drizzle melted butter over top. Bake in preheated oven for 15 to 20 minutes.

Cheddar Beer Muffins

Makes 12 large muffins
- Preheat oven to 400°F (200°C)
- Muffin tin, greased or paper-lined

3 cups	homemade or packaged biscuit mix	750 mL
¼ cup	granulated sugar	50 mL
1	egg	1
1 cup	milk	250 mL
2 tbsp	beer	25 mL
½ cup	shredded Cheddar cheese	125 mL

1. In a large bowl, combine biscuit mix and sugar. Stir with a fork until no lumps remain.
2. In another bowl, whisk together egg, milk and beer. Pour into dry ingredients. Add cheese, stirring just until moistened. Do not overmix.
3. Spoon batter into prepared muffin tin. Bake in preheated oven for 12 to 15 minutes.

Tip *If desired, increase the beer to ⅓ cup (75 mL).*

Stuffed Bacon Cheese Muffins

Makes 12 muffins
- Preheat oven to 400°F (200°C)
- Muffin tin, greased

2 cups	homemade or packaged biscuit mix	500 mL
5	slices bacon, cooked crisp and crumbled	5
¾ cup	milk	175 mL
1	egg, beaten	1
12	cubes Swiss cheese (½-inch/1 cm cubes)	12

1. In a bowl, combine biscuit mix and bacon. Add milk and egg, stirring just until blended.
2. Spoon half of the batter evenly into prepared muffin tin. Add a cheese cube to each and top with the remaining batter. Bake in preheated oven for 25 minutes or until golden brown. Serve hot.

Ham and Cheddar Muffins

Makes 12 muffins
- Preheat oven to 400°F (200°C)
- Muffin tin, greased or paper-lined

2 cups	homemade or packaged biscuit mix	500 mL
2 tsp	dry mustard (or 2 tbsp/25 mL granulated sugar)	10 mL
1	egg, beaten	1
½ cup	milk	125 mL
1	can (6.5 oz/184 g) flaked ham	1
1½ cups	shredded Cheddar cheese	375 mL

1. In a medium bowl, with a fork, combine mix, dry mustard, egg and milk. Stir in ham and cheese just until blended.
2. Spoon batter into prepared muffin tin. Bake in preheated oven for 20 minutes.

Chive Dinner Muffins

Makes 12 muffins
- Preheat oven to 400°F (200°C)
- Muffin tin, greased

2 cups	homemade or packaged biscuit mix	500 mL
2 tbsp	shortening	25 mL
1	egg	1
⅔ cup	milk or water	150 mL
¼ cup	snipped chives	50 mL

1. In a bowl, with a fork, combine mix, shorter
   egg, milk and chives. Beat vigorously for 1 m
2. Spoon batter into prepared muffin tin. Bake
   preheated oven for 15 minutes.

Bacon Muffins

Makes 12 muffins

- Preheat oven to 400°F (200°C)
- Muffin tin, greased

2 cups	homemade or packaged biscuit mix	
2 tbsp	granulated sugar	
1	egg	
2/3 cup	cold water or milk	
6	slices bacon, cooked crisp and crumbled	

1. In a large bowl, combine biscuit mix, suga
   and water. With a fork, beat vigorously fo
   1 minute. Stir in bacon, mixing just until
2. Spoon batter into prepared muffin tin. Bake in
   preheated oven for 15 minutes.

Meal-in-One Muffin

Makes 12 muffins

- Preheat oven to 400°F (200°C)
- Muffin tin, greased or paper-lined

1 tbsp	butter or margarine	15 mL
2 tbsp	finely chopped onion	25 mL
2 tbsp	finely chopped celery	25 mL
2 tbsp	shredded carrot	25 mL
1	can (4 1/2 oz/128 mL) deviled ham	1
2 cups	packaged or homemade biscuit mix	500 mL
1 tbsp	granulated sugar	15 mL
1/2 cup	shredded Cheddar cheese	125 mL
1	egg	1
2/3 cup	milk	150 mL

1. In a small skillet, heat butter over medium heat.
   Add onion, celery and carrot, cooking until tender
   but not brown. Let cool. Stir in ham and set aside.
2. In a medium bowl, combine biscuit mix, sugar,
   cheese, egg and milk. Beat with a fork for 1 minute.
3. Spoon into prepared muffin tin. Make an
   indentation in the center of each and spoon in
   ham mixture. Bake in preheated oven for
   18 to 20 minutes or until browned.

Microwave Muffins

Muffins baked in a microwave oven can be ju
delicious as those made the traditional wa
difference is the speed at which they ca

Most conventional-oven recipe
adapted for use in a microwave
that you know well, at first, u
familiar with adapting reci
work out changes requi
final result should be
particular muffin
you will proba
in the micro

The r
espe
the

Deluxe Pizza Muffins

Makes 12 muffins

- Preheat oven to 400°F (200°C)
- Muffin tin, sprayed with vegetable spray

2 cups	homemade or packaged biscuit mix	500 mL
3/4 cup	milk	175 mL
FILLING		
1	jar (15 1/2 oz/458 mL) spaghetti sauce	1
1	can (4 oz/115 g) sliced mushrooms, drained	1
1	small green bell pepper, chopped	1
1	package (3 oz/75 g) sliced pepperoni, cut into quarters	1
1 cup	shredded mozzarella cheese	250 mL

1. In a bowl, blend together biscuit mix and milk to
   form a soft dough. Turn out onto a floured surface
   and knead about 20 times. Roll dough into a
   rectangle, about 1/8 inch (0.25 cm) thick. With a
   cookie cutter or inverted glass, cut out twelve
   4-inch (10 cm) circles. Press the circles into
   bottom and up sides of muffin cups.
2. *Prepare the filling:* In a large bowl, combine
   spaghetti sauce, mushrooms, green pepper and
   pepperoni. Spoon over dough circles and then
   sprinkle with cheese. Bake in preheated oven for
   15 minutes or until browned.

> **Tip** *If you do not have a cupcaker (microwave muffin pan) or glass ramekins, use the lower part of a paper cup for hot drinks. Cut it down to size and line it with a paper baking cup. Place the cups in a circle on a flat microwave-safe plate, and use as you would ramekins.*

Use large baking cups and fill them two-thirds full. If you put more batter in, they may overflow during baking and the muffins could be undercooked. The cooking time given in most microwave muffin recipes is correct for the amount of batter that fits comfortably into this size of baking cup. Cups of a different size will not yield as good results.

To ensure even cooking, give the muffin pan a half turn during the cooking period. Another technique for even cooking is to place your muffin or dish on a rack. For example, if you put 6 ramekins with muffin batter in the microwave oven, they should be arranged in a ring and their position changed during cooking time. The individual cups are not rotated. The circle of ramekins is turned for better distribution of heat energy.

When muffins are done, tiny bubbles will pop on the surface (as on the tops of pancakes when they are ready to turn). The muffins may be slightly moist on top, but when scratched with a toothpick, the dough will be done beneath the surface and the small moist spots will disappear when the muffins stand for a few minutes.

> **Tip** *For mini micro muffins, line a paper (but not recycled paper) or Styrofoam egg carton with mini paper baking cups. Fill only two-thirds full also. Microwave on High for 1 to 1½ minutes or until tops are dry.*

Being a creature of habit, I do most of my muffin baking in a regular oven and therefore don't have an abundance of recipes for the microwave oven, but I hope you will enjoy the selections here, and that you will try adapting some of your recipes.

> **Tip** *For a quick café au lait with your muffins, microwave 1 cup (250 mL) milk on High for 2 to 3 minutes. Pour in ¼ cup (50 mL) espresso or 1 tsp (5 mL) instant coffee powder or granules.*

Micro Tips

To shell nuts:
- Pour 1 cup (250 mL) nuts (Brazils, walnuts, almonds or pecans) into a large bowl. Cover with 1 cup (250 mL) water and heat on High for 3 to 4 minutes or until water boils. Let stand for 1 minute. Pour off water and arrange nuts on paper towel to cool. Use a nutcracker to shell the nuts, being careful that you aren't burned by any hot water that may still be inside the shell.

To soften brown sugar:
- Put the brown sugar in a covered container and microwave on High for 50 seconds. *Or:*
- Put the hard block of sugar into a heavy plastic bag. Add a little water, or a quarter of an apple, or a slice of bread. Tie a piece of string loosely around the opening and heat on High for 20 seconds. Check to see if sugar has softened. If not, repeat once or twice, as necessary, being sure not to let sugar melt. When the sugar has softened sufficiently, take it out of the oven and let stand for about 5 minutes. Remove apple or bread and throw away, then stir to remove lumps.

To soften cream cheese:
- For spreads and dips or for baking — microwave, uncovered, on Defrost for 1 to 2 minutes.

To bring cheese to room temperature:
- Place 8 oz (250 g) cold cheese on a microwave-safe plate. Microwave on Medium for 45 to 60 seconds, until surface no longer feels chilled.

To extract juice from a lemon:
- Microwave the whole lemon on High for 30 seconds, then roll firmly on a flat surface, using the palm of your hand.

To thaw frozen juice concentrate:
- Place frozen concentrated juice in a small bowl, (never microwave in metal can) and microwave on High for 1 minute.

To melt chocolate:
- Place chocolate in a glass measuring cup. Microwave on Medium-High for 1 minute, then stir and repeat until melted completely. It will take about 2 minutes to melt 1 cup (250 mL) of chocolate chips.

To melt butter or margarine:
- Place in a glass dish. Cover with waxed paper or a paper towel to avoid splattering. Heat on High for 30-second intervals until fully melted.

To soften butter:
- Cover 1/4 cup (50 mL) butter with waxed paper. Microwave on Defrost for 30 seconds.

To liquefy solid honey:
- Place in a glass cup or container, Cook on High for 30 seconds, then stir to dissolve the crystals; repeat procedure, stirring often, until the honey is liquid.

For spreadable crystallized honey:
- Remove lid from jar and microwave on High for 1 to 2 minutes.

To plump raisins (or other dried fruits):
- Microwave 1 cup (250 mL) raisins or dried fruits in 1/2 cup (125 mL) water, covered, on High for 2 minutes or until boiling. Let stand, covered, for 10 minutes.

Refrigerator Micro Bran Muffins

Makes 24 to 36 muffins
- Ramekins or microwave muffin pan, paper-lined

1 1/2 cups	bran flakes cereal	375 mL
1 1/2 cups	natural bran	375 mL
1/2 cup	boiling water	125 mL
2	eggs, lightly beaten	2
1/4 cup	light (fancy) molasses	50 mL
1 3/4 cups	buttermilk or sour milk	425 mL
1/4 cup	vegetable oil	50 mL
1 to 2 tsp	browning sauce (such as Crosse & Blackwell)	5 to 10 mL
1 cup	raisins, dates, currants or prunes	250 mL
2 1/2 tsp	baking soda	12 mL
1 tsp	baking powder	5 mL
1/4 tsp	salt	1 mL
1/2 cup	firmly packed dark brown sugar	125 mL
2 cups	whole wheat flour	500 mL

1. In a large bowl, combine cereal and bran. Add boiling water and stir to moisten evenly. Set aside to cool. Then add molasses, buttermilk, oil, browning sauce and dried fruit; blend together well.
2. In another bowl, combine baking soda, baking powder, salt, brown sugar and flour. Add to bran mixture and stir just until moist.
3. Spoon batter into prepared muffin pan, filling cups two-thirds full. Bake on a rack for 2 1/2 to 3 minutes on High, rotating pan once during cooking time. Let stand for 3 to 5 minutes before removing muffins from pan.

Microwave Chocolate Chip Bran Muffins

Makes 12 muffins
- Ramekins or microwave muffin pan, paper-lined

3/4 cup	milk	175 mL
1/4 cup	vegetable oil	50 mL
1	egg, beaten	1
1 cup	natural bran	250 mL
1 cup	all-purpose flour	250 mL
2 1/2 tsp	baking powder	12 mL
1/2 tsp	salt	2 mL
3 tbsp	unsweetened cocoa powder	45 mL
1/2 cup	granulated sugar	125 mL
1/2 cup	semisweet chocolate chips	125 mL

1. In a bowl, combine milk, oil and egg. Stir in bran.
2. In another bowl, mix together flour, baking powder, salt and cocoa.
3. Add sugar to the liquid mixture. Stir in flour mixture and add chocolate chips.
4. Spoon batter into prepared muffin pan, filling cups two-thirds full. Place pan on a rack in the microwave. Bake on High for 2 to 2 1/2 minutes, rotating pan halfway through cooking time. Let stand for 3 to 5 minutes before removing from pan.

Banana Oatmeal Muffins

Makes 12 muffins

- Ramekins or microwave muffin pan, paper-lined

1/4 cup	butter or margarine, softened	50 mL
3/4 cup	packed brown sugar	175 mL
1	egg, beaten	1
1 cup	buttermilk	250 mL
1 cup	old-fashioned rolled oats	250 mL
1 cup	all-purpose flour	250 mL
1 tbsp	baking powder	15 mL
1/2 tsp	salt	2 mL
1/2 tsp	ground allspice	2 mL
2	bananas, chopped	2

1. In a bowl, cream together butter and brown sugar. Mix in egg and buttermilk.

2. In another bowl, combine oats, flour, baking powder, salt and allspice; mix well. Add to the creamed mixture and stir in the bananas.

3. Spoon batter into prepared ramekins or muffin pan, filling cups one-half to two-thirds full. (If using ramekins, arrange in microwave in a circle.) Microwave on High for about 2 minutes, rotating after 1 minute. A toothpick inserted in the center should come out clean and dry. Let muffins stand for 3 to 5 minutes before removing from pan.

Banana Pecan Oat Muffins

Makes 6 to 8 muffins

- Ramekins or microwave muffin pan, paper-lined

1 cup	all-purpose flour	250 mL
1/4 cup	oat bran	50 mL
1/4 cup	packed brown sugar	50 mL
1/4 cup	chopped pecans	50 mL
1/2 tsp	baking soda	2 mL
Pinch	salt	Pinch
1 cup	mashed ripe bananas (about 3 medium)	250 mL
1	egg	1
1/2 cup	vegetable oil	125 mL
TOPPING		
3 tbsp	chopped pecans	45 mL
3 tbsp	packed brown sugar	45 mL
1/4 tsp	ground cinnamon	1 mL

1. In a large bowl, combine flour, oat bran, sugar, pecans, baking soda and salt.

2. In a small bowl, beat together bananas, egg and oil. Stir this mixture into the flour mixture just until blended. Spoon batter into prepared muffin pan, filling cups two-thirds full.

3. *Prepare the topping:* In a bowl, combine pecans, brown sugar and cinnamon and sprinkle evenly over muffins.

4. Bake on High, rotating twice, for 2 minutes or until toothpick inserted in center comes out clean and dry. Let stand for 3 to 5 minutes.

Currant Nut Whole Wheat Muffins

Makes 12 muffins

- Ramekins or microwave muffin pan, double paper-lined

3/4 cup	all-purpose flour	175 mL
3/4 cup	whole wheat flour	175 mL
1/3 cup	natural bran or oat bran	75 mL
1 tsp	baking soda	5 mL
1/2 tsp	ground cinnamon	2 mL
1/4 tsp	ground ginger	1 mL
1/4 tsp	salt	1 mL
1 cup	low-fat vanilla-flavored yogurt	250 mL
1/4 cup	vegetable oil	50 mL
1	egg	1
1/4 cup	packed dark brown sugar	50 mL
1/3 cup	chopped walnuts	75 mL
1/3 cup	currants	75 mL

1. In a large bowl, mix together all-purpose flour, whole wheat flour, bran, baking soda, cinnamon, ginger and salt.

2. In a blender or food processor, combine yogurt, oil, egg and sugar; process until smooth. Add half the flour mixture and process until blended. Scrape down sides of container and add the remaining flour mixture; process until smooth.

3. Pour batter back into bowl and stir in walnuts and currants. Spoon batter into prepared pan, filling cups three-quarters full. (Baking may have to be done in batches.) Microwave on High for 3 to 4 minutes, rotating muffin pan a quarter-turn twice. Tops should spring back when gently pressed. Let stand for 3 to 5 minutes.

Tip *For a special treat to keep kids happy while you're busy micro baking, take simple chocolate or vanilla wafers and place a marshmallow on top of each. Microwave for 15 seconds. The marshmallows will fluff up to a fantastic size and the kids love it.*

Blueberry Quick Oat Muffins

Makes 12 muffins

• Ramekins or microwave muffin pan, paper-lined

½ cup	granulated sugar	125 mL
1¼ cups	all-purpose flour	300 mL
1 cup	quick-cooking rolled oats	250 mL
1½ tsp	baking powder	7 mL
½ tsp	baking soda	2 mL
¾ cup	sour cream	175 mL
⅓ cup	margarine, melted	75 mL
⅓ cup	milk	75 mL
1	egg, beaten	1
½ tsp	vanilla	2 mL
1 cup	fresh blueberries (or frozen, thawed)	250 mL
	Sugar-Cinnamon Mix (see page 4)	

1. In a large bowl, combine sugar, flour, oats, baking powder and baking soda.

2. In another bowl, combine sour cream, margarine, milk, egg and vanilla; mix well. Stir this mixture into the dry ingredients, mixing just until moist. Fold in the blueberries.

3. Spoon batter into prepared ramekins or muffin pan, filling cups two-thirds full. Sprinkle with Sugar-Cinnamon Mix. Bake, uncovered, on High for 2½ to 3 minutes. A toothpick inserted in the center should come out clean and dry. Let muffins stand for 3 to 5 minutes.

Vegetable Corn Muffins

Makes 8 to 12 muffins

• Ramekins or microwave muffin pan, double paper-lined

1 cup	all-purpose flour	250 mL
½ cup	yellow cornmeal	125 mL
1 tbsp	granulated sugar	15 mL
1 tbsp	baking powder	15 mL
½ tsp	salt	2 mL
¾ tsp	Italian seasoning	4 mL
Pinch	garlic powder	Pinch
2	eggs, beaten	2
1 tbsp	vegetable oil	15 mL
½ cup	drained corn kernels	125 mL
⅓ cup	milk (can use skim)	75 mL
⅓ cup	chopped green bell pepper	75 mL
¼ cup	finely chopped onion	50 mL

1. In a large bowl, combine flour, cornmeal, sugar, baking powder, salt, Italian seasoning, garlic powder, eggs, oil, corn, milk, green pepper and onion. Stir just until blended. Do not overmix.

2. Spoon batter into prepared ramekins or pan. Microwave on a rack on High for 2½ to 3 minutes, rotating once halfway through cooking time. A toothpick inserted in the center of each muffin should come out clean and dry. Let stand for 3 to 5 minutes.

Whole Wheat Honey Muffins

Makes 12 muffins

• Ramekins or microwave muffin pan, paper-lined

1¾ cups	whole wheat flour	425 mL
4 tsp	baking powder	20 mL
½ tsp	salt	2 mL
1	egg, beaten	1
¾ cup	milk	175 mL
⅓ cup	liquid honey	75 mL
¼ cup	vegetable oil	50 mL
⅓ cup	chopped walnuts	75 mL

1. In a large bowl, combine whole wheat flour, baking powder and salt.

2. In another bowl, blend together egg, milk, honey, oil and walnuts.

3. Pour egg mixture into dry ingredients and stir until well moistened. The batter should be a bit lumpy.

4. Spoon batter into prepared pan, filling cups two-thirds full. (Baking may have to be done in batches.) Place muffin pan on a rack in the microwave. Bake on High for 2½ minutes, rotating pan once during cooking. Let muffins stand for 3 to 5 minutes.

All Spicy Muffins

Makes 8 to 12 muffins
- Ramekins or microwave muffin pan, double paper-lined

1½ cups	all-purpose flour	375 mL
¾ cup	granulated sugar, divided	175 mL
2 tsp	baking powder	10 mL
½ tsp	salt	2 mL
½ tsp	ground nutmeg	2 mL
½ tsp	ground coriander	2 mL
½ tsp	ground allspice	2 mL
½ cup	milk	125 mL
½ cup	butter or margarine, melted, divided	125 mL
1	egg	1
1 tsp	ground cinnamon	5 mL

1. In a large bowl, combine flour, ½ cup (125 mL) of the sugar, baking powder, salt, nutmeg, coriander and allspice.
2. In a small bowl, combine milk, ⅓ cup (75 mL) of the butter and egg. Stir into flour mixture just until moist.
3. Spoon batter into prepared muffin pan, filling three-quarters full. (Baking may have to be done in batches.) Microwave on High for 2½ to 4½ minutes, rotating halfway through cooking time. A toothpick inserted in center should come out clean and dry. Let muffins stand for 5 minutes before removing from pan.
4. Meanwhile, in a small dish combine the remaining sugar and cinnamon. Roll warm muffins in the remaining butter and then the sugar-cinnamon mixture. Serve warm.

Peanut Butter Chip Banana Muffins

Makes 12 muffins
- Ramekins, double paper-lined

1½ cups	all-purpose flour	375 mL
½ cup	granulated sugar	125 mL
2 tbsp	baking powder	25 mL
½ tsp	salt	2 mL
1	egg, lightly beaten	1
½ cup	milk	125 mL
⅓ cup	vegetable oil	75 mL
¾ cup	mashed ripe banana	175 mL
1 cup	peanut butter chips	250 mL
¼ cup	raisins	50 mL
¼ cup	graham cracker crumbs	50 mL

1. In a large bowl, combine flour, sugar, baking powder and salt. Make a well in the center and add egg, milk, oil and mashed banana; stir just until moist. Stir in peanut butter chips and raisins.
2. Spoon batter into prepared ramekins, filling each half full. Sprinkle with crumbs. (Baking may have to be done in batches.) Arrange ramekins in a circle on rack in microwave and bake on High for 2 minutes. Rotate circle of ramekins and bake for 1 minute or until done.

Apple Spice Muffins

Makes 8 to 12 muffins
- Ramekins or microwave muffin pan, paper-lined

¼ cup	shortening	50 mL
¾ cup	granulated sugar	175 mL
2	eggs	2
¾ cup	sweetened applesauce	175 mL
¼ cup	milk	50 mL
1 tbsp	freshly squeezed lemon juice	15 mL
1½ cups	all-purpose flour	375 mL
1 tsp	salt	5 mL
1 tsp	baking soda	5 mL
1 tsp	ground cinnamon	5 mL
¼ tsp	ground nutmeg	1 mL
¼ tsp	ground cloves	1 mL
¼ cup	floured raisins	50 mL
¼ cup	chopped walnuts	50 mL

1. In a bowl, cream together shortening and sugar. Add eggs and mix well. Add applesauce, milk and lemon juice.
2. In another bowl, sift together flour, salt and baking soda. Add cinnamon, nutmeg and cloves. Pour this dry mixture gradually into the liquid mixture. Add raisins and nuts and mix together.
3. Spoon batter into prepared muffin pan. Bake on High for 2 to 2½ minutes, turning halfway through cooking time. Let stand for 3 to 5 minutes.

Tip *An extra apple or two hanging around? A baked apple takes 4 minutes in the microwave. Fill the middle with ice cream and drizzle liqueur on top. A delicious dessert that looks like you spent all day in the kitchen.*

Quick Poppy Cheese Muffins

Makes 12 muffins

- Ramekins or microwave muffin pan, paper-lined

2½ cups	all-purpose biscuit mix	625 mL
1 cup	shredded sharp Cheddar cheese	250 mL
1 tsp	poppy seeds	5 mL
1	egg	1
1 cup	milk	250 mL

1. In a large bowl, combine biscuit mix, cheese, poppy seeds, egg and milk; stir just to moisten.

2. Spoon batter into prepared ramekins or pan, filling cups two-thirds full. If using ramekins, arrange them in a circle. Bake on High for 2½ minutes, rotating ramekins or pan halfway through cooking time. Let muffins stand for 3 to 5 minutes.

Orange Cinnamon Muffins

Makes 12 muffins

- Ramekins or microwave muffin pan, paper-lined

2 cups	all-purpose flour	500 mL
½ cup	packed brown sugar	125 mL
1 tbsp	baking powder	15 mL
½ tsp	salt	2 mL
½ tsp	ground cinnamon	2 mL
1 tsp	finely grated orange zest	5 mL
2	eggs	2
½ cup	freshly squeezed orange juice	125 mL
½ cup	vegetable oil	125 mL
TOPPING		
3 tbsp	granulated sugar	45 mL
1 tsp	finely grated orange zest	5 mL
½ tsp	ground cinnamon	2 mL

1. In a large bowl, combine flour, brown sugar, baking powder, salt, cinnamon and orange zest.

2. In another bowl, whisk together eggs, orange juice and oil. Pour into flour mixture and stir just until moist.

3. *Prepare the topping:* In a bowl, combine sugar, zest and cinnamon

4. Spoon batter into prepared muffin pan, filling cups two-thirds full. Sprinkle with topping. Bake, uncovered, on High for 2 to 2½ minutes, rotating pan halfway through cooking time. A toothpick inserted in the center should come out clean and dry. Let muffins stand for 3 to 5 minutes before removing from pan.

Pineapple Carrot Nutty Muffins

Makes 12 to 18 muffins

- Ramekins or microwave muffin pan, double paper-lined

1½ cups	whole wheat flour	375 mL
½ cup	packed brown sugar	125 mL
½ cup	granulated sugar	125 mL
1 cup	Grape Nuts cereal	250 mL
1½ tsp	baking soda	7 mL
¾ tsp	baking powder	4 mL
2 tsp	ground cinnamon	10 mL
1 cup	well-drained crushed pineapple	250 mL
2	eggs, beaten	2
2 cups	shredded carrots	500 mL
1 tsp	vanilla	5 mL
¾ cup	margarine, melted	175 mL

1. In a large bowl, combine flour, brown sugar, granulated sugar, cereal, baking soda, baking powder and cinnamon.

2. In another bowl, combine pineapple, eggs, carrots, vanilla and margarine. Stir into the dry ingredients, mixing just until moistened. The batter will be quite thick.

3. Spoon batter into prepared muffin pan, filling cups two-thirds full. Bake, uncovered, on High for 2 to 2½ minutes, rotating halfway through cooking time. Let muffins stand for 3 to 5 minutes before removing from pan.

Buffins, Cuffins and Puffins

Buffins

Cuffins

Puffins

Buffins

● ●

Buffins

Makes 16 to 24 buffins
- Preheat oven to 400°F (200°C)
- Muffin tins, greased

2 cups	milk	500 mL
½ cup	butter or margarine	125 mL
¼ cup	granulated sugar	50 mL
1 tsp	salt	5 mL
1 tbsp	active dry yeast	15 mL
¼ cup	very warm water	50 mL
2	eggs, beaten	2
4 cups	all-purpose flour	1 L

1. In a saucepan over medium heat, scald the milk. Add butter, sugar and salt. Set aside to cool.
2. Dissolve yeast in the very warm water. Add to scalded milk mixture. Add beaten eggs and flour, beating until smooth. Let rise for 1½ hours.
3. Beat batter down and spoon into prepared muffin tins, filling cups no more than half full. Set aside and let rise again for 30 minutes. Bake in preheated oven for 12 to 15 minutes.

● ●

Wheat Germ Cornmeal Buffins

Makes 18 to 24 buffins
- Preheat oven to 375°F (190°C)
- Muffin tins, greased

2	eggs, lightly beaten, divided	2
2 tbsp	milk	25 mL
1	package (¼ oz/7 g) active dry yeast	1
¼ cup	very warm water (not boiling)	50 mL
¼ cup	granulated sugar	50 mL
¼ cup	butter, melted	50 mL
½ tsp	salt	2 mL
¼ cup	yellow cornmeal	50 mL
½ cup	currants or raisins	125 mL
1 cup	milk	250 mL
¼ cup	wheat germ	50 mL
2¼ cups	all-purpose flour	550 mL

1. In a small bowl, combine 2 tbsp (25 mL) of the beaten egg with the 2 tbsp (25 mL) milk. Set aside.
2. In a large bowl, dissolve yeast in warm water. Let stand for 5 minutes. Mix in the remaining egg, sugar, butter, salt, cornmeal and currants. Stir in the 1 cup (250 mL) milk and wheat germ, blending well. Add flour gradually and beat until smooth. Cover loosely with a towel or waxed paper and place in a warm spot. Let rise for 1 hour or until doubled in size.
3. Punch dough down or beat well. Spoon into prepared muffin tins. Cover again and let rise in a warm spot for 30 minutes or until muffin tin is full.
4. Lightly beat the reserved egg and milk and brush over tops. Sprinkle with additional wheat germ, if desired. Bake in preheated oven for 15 to 20 minutes or until browned.

Tip *When making any recipe requiring egg whites only, drop the yolks into a pan of boiling, salted water. Use these hard-cooked yolks for salads or sandwich fillings.*

● ●

Praline Buffins

Makes 12 buffins
- Preheat oven to 450°F (230°C)
- Muffin tin

½ cup	butter	125 mL
½ cup	packed brown sugar	125 mL
	Ground cinnamon	
36	pecan or walnut halves	36
2 cups	biscuit mix	500 mL
⅓ cup	sweetened applesauce	75 mL
⅓ cup	milk	75 mL

1. Put 2 tsp (10 mL) butter in each muffin cup. Heat in preheated oven until butter is melted. Stir 2 tsp (10 mL) brown sugar and a pinch of cinnamon into butter in each cup. Add 3 nut halves to each.
2. In a large bowl, combine biscuit mix, applesauce and milk. Mix well until a dough forms. Spoon batter into muffin cups. Bake in preheated oven for 10 minutes.
3. Invert whole pan immediately onto a plate and let sit for 5 minutes, allowing syrup to run down over buffins. Remove the pan and serve warm.

Tip *To get walnut meats out whole, soak nuts overnight in salt water before cracking.*

Caraway Rye Buffins

Makes 24 buffins
- Preheat oven to 350°F (180°C)
- Muffin tins, greased

2	packages (each ¼ oz/7 g) active dry yeast	2
½ cup	warm water	125 mL
½ tsp	granulated sugar	2 mL
3 cups	all-purpose flour	750 mL
1½ cups	rye flour	375 mL
2 tsp	salt	10 mL
¼ tsp	baking soda	1 mL
2 tbsp	caraway seeds	25 mL
1 cup	low-fat plain yogurt	250 mL
½ cup	butter or margarine, melted	125 mL
2	eggs	2
1	egg white, mixed with 1 tbsp (15 mL) water	1
	Additional caraway seeds	

1. In a large bowl, sprinkle yeast over warm water and sugar. Let stand for 5 minutes to let yeast soften.
2. In another bowl, combine all-purpose flour, rye flour, salt, baking soda and seeds.
3. In another bowl, whisk together yogurt, butter and eggs. Add to yeast mixture and mix until blended. Add half the flour mixture and beat on medium-high speed for 1 minute. Add the remaining flour mixture and continue beating until well blended. Cover with a towel and place in a warm spot away from drafts. Let rise for 1 hour or until doubled in size.
4. Punch down dough. Divide evenly into prepared muffin tins. Cover again and let rise in warm spot for 45 minutes or until doubled.
5. Brush tops with egg wash. Sprinkle with caraway seeds. Bake in preheated oven for 20 to 25 minutes or until golden brown.

Baked "Donut" Buffins

Makes 8 to 12 buffins
- Preheat oven to 375°F (190°C)
- Muffin tin, greased or paper-lined

¼ cup	butter or margarine	50 mL
6 tbsp	granulated sugar	90 mL
1	egg	1
½ tsp	vanilla	2 mL
1¼ cups	all-purpose flour	300 mL
2 tsp	baking powder	10 mL
Pinch	salt	Pinch
¼ tsp	ground nutmeg	1 mL
⅓ cup	milk	75 mL
TOPPING		
½ cup	granulated sugar	125 mL
1 to 1½ tsp	ground cinnamon	5 to 7 mL

1. In a large bowl, cream together butter and sugar. Add egg and vanilla, then flour, baking powder, salt, nutmeg and milk. Mix only until blended.
2. Spoon batter into prepared muffin tin. Bake in preheated oven for 15 minutes.
3. *Prepare the topping:* In a small bowl, mix sugar and cinnamon until well blended. Remove muffins from tins and roll in topping.

Apple Doughnut Buffins

Makes 12 buffins
- Preheat oven to 350°F (180°C)
- Muffin tin, greased

1½ cups	all-purpose flour	375 mL
½ cup	granulated sugar	125 mL
1¾ tsp	baking powder	9 mL
½ tsp	salt	2 mL
½ tsp	ground nutmeg	2 mL
⅓ cup	shortening	75 mL
1	egg	1
¼ cup	milk	50 mL
½ cup	grated apple	125 mL
TOPPING		
½ cup	butter, melted	125 mL
½ cup	granulated sugar	125 mL
1½ tsp	ground cinnamon	7 mL

1. In a large bowl, sift together flour, sugar, baking powder, salt and nutmeg. Using a pastry blender, cut in shortening.
2. In another bowl, combine egg, milk and grated apple. Add to flour mixture.
3. Spoon batter into prepared muffin tin. Bake in preheated oven for 20 to 25 minutes. Remove from pan.
4. *Prepare the topping:* In a bowl, combine butter, sugar and cinnamon. Roll buffins in topping. Serve warm.

Citrus Upside-Down Buffins

Makes 8 to 12 buffins

- Preheat oven to 425°F (220°C)
- Large ramekins

2 cups	canned grapefruit sections, with juice	500 mL
1	can (10 oz/284 mL) mandarin orange sections, with juice	1
½ cup	packed brown sugar	125 mL
3 tbsp	all-purpose flour	45 mL
3 tbsp	butter or margarine	45 mL
1 cup	all-purpose flour	250 mL
1 tbsp	granulated sugar	15 mL
1½ tsp	baking powder	7 mL
¼ tsp	salt	1 mL
¼ cup	butter or margarine	50 mL
	Milk	
1	egg, lightly beaten	1
	Granulated sugar	
	Ground cinnamon	

1. In a small bowl, mix together the undrained grapefruit and mandarin orange sections (with juice). Spoon evenly into ramekins.
2. In another small bowl, mix together brown sugar and the 3 tbsp (45 mL) flour. Sprinkle over fruit and dot with the 3 tbsp (45 mL) butter. Bake in preheated oven for 15 minutes.
3. In a large bowl, combine the 1 cup (250 mL) flour, sugar, baking powder and salt. Cut in the ¼ cup (50 mL) butter.
4. In a measuring cup, add enough milk to beaten egg to make ½ cup (125 mL). Add to flour mixture. Stir until well blended.
5. Drop batter by spoonfuls over hot fruit cups to form biscuits. Sprinkle with sugar and cinnamon. Bake in preheated oven for 20 to 25 minutes or until golden brown. Serve warm.

Miniature Strawberry Buffins

Makes 36 to 48 miniature buffins

- Preheat oven to 400°F (200°C)
- Miniature muffin tins, greased

½ cup	strawberry-flavored drink mix	125 mL
¾ cup	milk	175 mL
1	egg	1
2 tbsp	vegetable oil	25 mL
2 cups	biscuit mix	500 mL
	Confectioner's (icing) sugar	

1. In a small bowl, combine drink mix, milk, egg and oil. Beat with a fork until well blended.
2. In a large bowl, combine biscuit mix and wet ingredients. Stir just until biscuit mix is completely moistened. The batter will be soft.
3. Spoon batter into prepared muffin tins, filling cups two-thirds full. Bake in preheated oven for 10 minutes or until delicately golden but not browned.
4. Remove buffins from pan and sprinkle tops with confectioner's sugar. Serve hot.

Cuffins

Cuffins

Makes 12 cuffins

- Preheat oven to 400°F (200°C)
- Muffin tin, paper-lined

⅓ cup	shortening, softened	75 mL
2 cups	sifted cake and pastry flour	500 mL
1 cup	granulated sugar	250 mL
2½ tsp	baking powder	12 mL
¾ tsp	salt	4 mL
¾ cup	milk, divided	175 mL
1	egg, lightly beaten	1
1 tsp	vanilla	5 mL

1. In a large bowl, cream shortening until well softened. Add cake flour, sugar, baking powder and salt, mixing until blended. Add half the milk and egg, mixing until flour is dampened. Add the remaining milk and vanilla and stir just until moistened and well blended (or beat for 2 minutes with a hand mixer).
2. Spoon batter evenly into prepared muffin tin. Bake in preheated oven for 20 minutes or until done.

Coconut Chiffon Cuffins

Makes 12 to 18 cuffins
- Preheat oven to 400°F (200°C)
- Muffin tins, paper-lined

2¼ cups	sifted cake and pastry flour	550 mL
1½ cups	granulated sugar, divided	375 mL
1 tbsp	baking powder	15 mL
1 tsp	salt	5 mL
⅓ cup	vegetable oil	75 mL
1 cup	milk, divided	250 mL
1½ tsp	vanilla	7 mL
2	eggs, separated	2
1 cup	flaked coconut (sweetened or unsweetened)	250 mL

1. In a large bowl, combine flour, 1 cup (250 mL) of the sugar, baking powder and salt. Make a well in the center. Add oil, half the milk and vanilla. Beat for 1 minute on medium speed. Add the remaining milk and egg yolks. Beat again for 1 minute.

2. In a small bowl, beat egg whites until soft peaks form. Gradually add the remaining sugar and beat until stiff peaks form. Fold into the batter.

3. Spoon batter into prepared muffin tins. Top with coconut. Bake in preheated oven for about 15 minutes.

Apple Spice Cuffins

Makes 12 to 16 cuffins
- Preheat oven to 350°F (180°C)
- Muffin tins, paper-lined

2	apples, peeled and diced	2
¼ cup	water	50 mL
1¼ cups	all-purpose flour	300 mL
2 tbsp	unsweetened cocoa powder	25 mL
½ cup	granulated sugar	125 mL
½ tsp	baking powder	2 mL
1 tsp	baking soda	5 mL
½ tsp	salt	2 mL
½ tsp	ground cinnamon	2 mL
½ tsp	ground allspice	2 mL
2	egg yolks	2
¼ cup	raisins	50 mL

1. In a small saucepan over medium heat, combine apples and water. Simmer, covered, for 5 minutes or until tender. Set aside to cool.

2. In a large bowl, combine flour, cocoa, sugar, baking powder, baking soda, salt, cinnamon and allspice. Add apples and egg yolks, beating until blended. Fold in raisins.

3. Spoon batter into prepared muffin tins, dividing evenly. Bake in preheated oven for about 30 minutes.

Banana Nut Cuffins

Makes 18 to 24 cuffins
- Preheat oven to 350°F (180°C)
- Muffin tins, paper-lined

2 cups	all-purpose flour	500 mL
1⅔ cups	granulated sugar	400 mL
1¼ tsp	baking powder	6 mL
1¼ tsp	baking soda	6 mL
1 tsp	salt	5 mL
⅔ cup	shortening	150 mL
⅔ cup	buttermilk	150 mL
3	eggs	3
1¼ cups	mashed ripe bananas	300 mL
½ cup	chopped walnuts or pecans	125 mL
	Confectioner's (icing) sugar	

1. In a large bowl, combine flour, sugar, baking powder, baking soda, salt, shortening, buttermilk, eggs, bananas and walnuts. Mix at low speed, scraping sides, then beat on high speed for 3 minutes.

2. Spoon batter into prepared muffin tins. Bake in preheated oven for 20 to 25 minutes. When cuffins cool, dust with confectioner's sugar.

Tip *To separate eggs, use a small funnel, cracking egg open over the funnel. The white will run through while the yoke will remain in the funnel.*

Cherry Cuffins

Makes 12 cuffins
- Preheat oven to 400°F (200°C)
- Muffin tin, paper-lined

3	eggs	3
½ cup	shortening, melted	125 mL
¾ cup	milk	175 mL
1 tsp	vanilla	5 mL
1½ cups	all-purpose flour	375 mL
1¼ cups	granulated sugar	300 mL
2 tsp	baking powder	10 mL

Pinch	salt	Pinch
1 lb	cherries, pitted and chopped	500 g

1. In a bowl, combine eggs, shortening, milk and vanilla. Mix well.
2. In a large bowl, combine flour, sugar, baking powder and salt. Add cherries and stir into egg mixture. Do not overmix.
3. Spoon batter into prepared muffin tin. Bake in preheated oven for about 25 minutes.

• •

Lemon Sugar-Topped Cuffins

Makes 12 small cuffins
- Preheat oven to 425°F (220°C)
- Muffin tin, paper-lined

TOPPING

1 tbsp	granulated sugar	15 mL
1/2 tsp	grated lemon zest	2 mL

CUFFINS

1 cup	self-rising flour	250 mL
1/2 cup	granulated sugar	125 mL
1/2 cup	milk	125 mL
1/3 cup	vegetable oil	75 mL
1 tsp	grated lemon zest	5 mL
1	egg	1
1/2 tsp	vanilla	2 mL

1. *Prepare the topping:* In a small bowl, combine sugar and lemon zest. Set aside.
2. *Prepare the cuffins:* In a large bowl, combine flour and sugar. Make a well in the center. Add milk, oil, lemon zest, egg and vanilla. Mix together until just moistened.
3. Spoon batter into prepared muffin tin. Sprinkle with topping. Bake in preheated oven for 15 minutes.

Variations *Jam Cuffins: Omit lemon zest and topping. Spoon batter into muffin tins and top each with 1 tsp (5 mL) seedless red raspberry jam. Swirl a thin knife or toothpick through batter and bake as above.*

Mocha Chip Cuffins: Omit lemon zest and topping. Reduce milk to 1/4 cup (50 mL). Dissolve 2 tsp (10 mL) instant coffee powder or granules in 1/4 cup (50 mL) hot water and combine with the milk. Fold in 1/3 cup (75 mL) mini chocolate chips and bake as above.

Sour Cream 'n' Spice Cuffins: Omit lemon zest and topping. Add 1/2 tsp (2 mL) ground cinnamon and a pinch each of ground cloves and ground nutmeg to the dry ingredients. Decrease the milk to 1/4 cup (50 mL) and combine with 1/4 cup (50 mL) sour cream. Make a topping of 1/2 cup (125 mL) chopped walnuts, 1 tbsp (15 mL) granulated sugar and 1/4 tsp (1 mL) ground cinnamon. Sprinkle on top of each cuffin and bake as above.

• •

Lemon Streusel Cuffins

Makes 18 to 24 cuffins
- Preheat oven to 350°F (180°C)
- Muffin tins, paper-lined

2 1/4 cups	sifted cake and pastry flour	550 mL
2 tsp	baking powder	10 mL
1/2 tsp	salt	2 mL
1 3/4 cups	granulated sugar	425 mL
1 tbsp	freshly squeezed lemon juice	15 mL
1 tsp	grated lemon zest	5 mL
1 cup	non-fat plain yogurt	250 mL
3 tbsp	vegetable oil	45 mL
1/2 tsp	vanilla	2 mL
4	egg whites	4

STREUSEL TOPPING

1/4 cup	firmly packed brown sugar	50 mL
1/4 cup	old-fashioned rolled oats	50 mL
1/4 tsp	ground cinnamon	1 mL

1. In a large bowl, combine flour, baking powder and salt.
2. In another bowl, beat together sugar, juice, zest, yogurt, oil and vanilla. Pour into flour mixture and beat on low speed just until well blended.
3. In a small bowl, beat egg whites until stiff peaks form. Fold into batter.
4. *Prepare the topping:* In another bowl, combine brown sugar, oats and cinnamon.
5. Spoon batter into prepared muffin tins. Sprinkle with topping. Bake in preheated oven for 35 to 40 minutes.

Tip *To substitute all-purpose flour for cake flour in a recipe, remove 2 tbsp (25 mL) of flour from every cup of all-purpose flour, and add 2 tbsp (25 mL) cornstarch.*

Lemon Cream Cuffin Tarts

Makes 36 cuffins
- Preheat oven to 375°F (190°C)
- Muffin tins, foil-lined

1	roll refrigerated sugar cookie dough	1
1	package lemon pudding and pie filling	1
1 tsp	grated lemon zest	5 mL
	Sweetened whipped cream	
	Strawberries, washed and hulled	

1. Unwrap cookie dough and cut into 36 slices. Press into bottoms and up sides of prepared muffin tins. Bake in preheated oven for 10 minutes or until golden brown. Let cool completely and then carefully peel off the foil. Set aside.
2. In a bowl, prepare pudding mix according to package directions. Stir in lemon zest and place in refrigerator.
3. When filling is chilled, spoon 1 tbsp (15 mL) into each cup. Return to refrigerator.
4. To serve, spoon some whipped cream on top. Place a whole strawberry, hull-side down, on top.

Pumpkin Nut Cuffins

Makes 12 to 18 cuffins
- Preheat oven to 375°F (190°C)
- Muffin tins, greased or paper-lined

2 1/4 cups	all-purpose flour	550 mL
1 tbsp	baking powder	15 mL
1/2 tsp	baking soda	2 mL
1/2 tsp	salt	2 mL
3/4 tsp	ground ginger	4 mL
1/2 tsp	ground cinnamon	2 mL
1/2 tsp	ground nutmeg	2 mL
1/2 cup	butter or margarine, softened	125 mL
1 1/3 cups	granulated sugar	325 mL
2	eggs, well beaten	2
1 cup	canned pumpkin purée (not pie filling) or cooked pumpkin, mashed	250 mL
3/4 cup	milk	175 mL
3/4 cup	chopped pecans or walnuts	175 mL

1. In a large bowl, combine flour, baking powder, baking soda, salt, ginger, cinnamon and nutmeg.
2. In another bowl, cream together butter and sugar until light and fluffy. Stir in eggs and pumpkin. Pour into dry ingredients alternately with milk, blending until smooth. Fold in the nuts.
3. Spoon batter into prepared muffin tins. Bake in preheated oven for 25 minutes or until a toothpick inserted in center comes out clean.

Tips *These cuffins are not very sweet, so if you have a sweet tooth, top them with your favorite frosting.*

If you are using fresh pumpkin in a recipe, a 5-lb (2.5 kg) pumpkin yields about 4 1/2 cups (1.125 L) mashed pumpkin.

Peanut Butter Cuffins

Makes 12 cuffins
- Preheat oven to 375°F (190°C)
- Muffin tin, paper-lined

2 cups	all-purpose flour	500 mL
2 tsp	baking powder	10 mL
1/2 tsp	salt	2 mL
1/2 cup	peanut butter	125 mL
1/3 cup	shortening, softened	75 mL
1 tsp	vanilla	5 mL
1 1/2 cups	packed brown sugar	375 mL
2	eggs	2
3/4 cup	milk	175 mL

1. In a large bowl, mix together flour, baking powder and salt.
2. In another bowl, cream together peanut butter, shortening and vanilla. Gradually add brown sugar, beating with a spoon until light and fluffy. Add eggs, one at a time, beating well after each addition. Add to flour mixture alternately with milk.
3. Spoon batter into prepared muffin tin. Bake in preheated oven for 20 minutes.

Tip *You can frost the cuffins with peanut butter and sprinkle with confectioner's (icing) sugar.*

Peanut Butter Chocolate Cuffins

Makes 12 to 18 cuffins
- Preheat oven to 350°F (180°C)
- Muffin tins, paper-lined

2 cups	all-purpose flour	500 mL
2 cups	granulated sugar	500 mL
3/4 cup	unsweetened cocoa powder	175 mL
1 tsp	baking soda	5 mL

1 tsp	salt	5 mL
½ tsp	baking powder	2 mL
¾ cup	shortening	175 mL
¾ cup	buttermilk	175 mL
¾ cup	water	175 mL
2	eggs	2
1 tsp	vanilla	5 mL

PEANUT BUTTER CREAM ICING

6 oz	cream cheese, softened	175 g
⅔ cup	creamy peanut butter	150 mL
¼ cup	milk	50 mL
1 tsp	vanilla	5 mL
3 cups	confectioner's (icing) sugar	750 mL

1. In a large bowl, combine flour, sugar, cocoa, baking soda, salt and baking powder. Make a well in the center. Add shortening, buttermilk, water, eggs and vanilla. Beat on low speed for 30 seconds, scraping sides of bowl. Then beat on high speed for 3 minutes.

2. Spoon batter into prepared muffin tins. Bake in preheated oven for 20 minutes or until toothpick inserted in center comes out dry. Remove from pan and cool completely.

3. *Meanwhile, prepare the icing:* In a large bowl, beat together cream cheese and peanut butter. Add milk and vanilla, beating well. Gradually add confectioner's sugar and beat until smooth. (If necessary, add additional milk until a smooth consistency is reached.) Spread over cooled cuffins.

Tip *To make this cuffin even more special, take a pastry bag with a large star tip and fill with icing. Insert the tip into the center of each cuffin. Pipe some icing into the cuffin and add a swirl on top.*

Cocoa Raisin Cuffins

Makes 12 cuffins
- Preheat oven to 350°F (180°C)
- Muffin tin, greased or paper-lined

1¼ cups	all-purpose flour	300 mL
1 cup	granulated sugar	250 mL
¾ tsp	baking soda	4 mL
½ tsp	ground cinnamon	2 mL
¼ tsp	ground nutmeg	1 mL
¼ tsp	salt	1 mL

¼ cup	butter or margarine, melted (about 1 stick)	50 mL
¼ cup	unsweetened cocoa powder	50 mL
¾ cup	sweetened applesauce	175 mL
1	egg, lightly beaten	1
½ cup	raisins	125 mL

1. In a large bowl, mix together flour, sugar, baking soda, cinnamon, nutmeg and salt. Make a well in the center.

2. In another bowl, blend together butter and cocoa. Add applesauce and pour into flour mixture. Add egg, stirring just until moistened and blended. Fold in raisins.

3. Spoon batter into prepared muffin tin. Bake in preheated oven for 20 minutes.

Old-Fashioned Chocolate Cuffins

Makes 12 to 18 cuffins
- Preheat oven to 375°F (190°C)
- Muffin tins, greased or paper-lined

½ cup	shortening	125 mL
1 cup	granulated sugar	250 mL
2	eggs, separated and yolks beaten	2
2 cups	all-purpose flour	500 mL
2 tsp	baking powder	10 mL
¼ tsp	salt	1 mL
¼ tsp	baking soda	1 mL
¾ cup	milk	175 mL
1 tsp	vanilla	5 mL
2½ oz	unsweetened chocolate, melted	75 g

1. In a large bowl, cream together shortening and sugar. Add beaten egg yolks.

2. In another bowl, combine flour, baking powder, salt and baking soda. Add to creamed mixture alternately with milk. Add vanilla and melted chocolate.

3. In another bowl, beat egg whites until stiff. Fold into mixture and blend well.

4. Spoon batter into prepared muffin tins. Bake in preheated oven for 25 minutes or until done.

Tip *In any recipe that calls for separated eggs, remember this rule: eggs separate more easily when they are very cold, but whipped egg whites gain more volume if they are at room temperature.*

Sweet Chocolate Cuffins

Makes 12 cuffins
- Preheat oven to 375°F (190°C)
- Muffin tin, paper-lined

2 cups	sifted cake and pastry flour	500 mL
2 tsp	baking powder	10 mL
½ tsp	salt	2 mL
¼ cup	butter	50 mL
3 oz	unsweetened chocolate	90 g
2	eggs, separated	2
1½ cups	granulated sugar	375 mL
1⅓ cups	milk	325 mL
2½ tsp	vanilla	12 mL
	Confectioner's (icing) sugar	

1. In a large bowl, mix together flour, baking powder and salt.

2. In top of a double boiler over hot (not boiling) water, melt butter and chocolate.

3. In a small bowl, beat together egg yolks and sugar until well blended and lemon colored. Add chocolate mixture and blend well. Pour into flour mixture alternately with milk and vanilla. Beat on low speed until blended.

4. In another small bowl, beat egg whites until stiff peaks form. Fold gently into the batter.

5. Spoon batter into prepared muffin tin. Bake in preheated oven for about 20 minutes. Remove from pan and set aside to cool. Dust tops with confectioner's sugar.

Chocolate Chip Cuffins

Makes 12 to 18 cuffins
- Preheat oven to 375°F (190°C)
- Muffin tins, paper-lined

⅓ cup	shortening, softened	75 mL
¾ cup	granulated sugar	175 mL
2	eggs	2
1 tsp	vanilla	5 mL
2¼ cups	sifted cake and pastry flour	550 mL
1 tbsp	baking powder	15 mL
1 tsp	salt	5 mL
⅔ cup	milk	150 mL
1	package (8 oz/250 g) semisweet chocolate chips	1

1. In a large bowl, cream together shortening and sugar. With a spoon, mix in eggs one at a time. Add vanilla.

2. In another bowl, combine flour, baking powder and salt. Add to the shortening mixture alternately with milk.

3. Spoon batter into prepared muffin tins, filling cups half full. Sprinkle with half the chocolate chips. Top with the remaining batter and sprinkle with the remaining chocolate chips. Bake in preheated oven for 20 to 25 minutes.

Chocolate Cream Cheese Cuffins

Makes 24 cuffins
- Preheat oven to 350°F (180°C)
- Muffin tins, greased or paper-lined

1	package (8 oz/250 g) cream cheese, softened	1
1	egg	1
⅓ cup	granulated sugar	75 mL
1 cup	semisweet chocolate chips	250 mL
3 cups	all-purpose flour	750 mL
2 cups	granulated sugar	500 mL
½ cup	instant chocolate drink powder	125 mL
1 tsp	salt	5 mL
2 tsp	baking soda	10 mL
2 tsp	vanilla	10 mL
2 tbsp	white vinegar	25 mL
2 cups	water	500 mL
⅔ cup	vegetable oil	150 mL

1. In a small bowl, mix together cream cheese, egg and sugar. Add chips and blend well. Set aside.

2. In a large bowl, combine flour, sugar, chocolate powder, salt and baking soda, mixing well. Add vanilla, vinegar, water and oil. Beat on low speed just until well blended.

3. Spoon batter into prepared muffin tins. Drop 1 heaping tsp (5 mL) cheese mixture into each prepared muffin cup. Bake in preheated oven for 20 to 25 minutes.

Variation *For a quick version of this recipe, use 1 package chocolate cake mix (the two-layer size). Mix according to package directions and bake as above. You can use chocolate pieces or chunks in place of the chips.*

Brownie Chip Cuffins

Makes 12 cuffins
- Preheat oven to 350ºF (180ºC)
- Muffin tin, paper-lined

3 oz	semisweet chocolate	90 g
1/2 cup	butter	125 mL
2	eggs	2
1 1/2 cups	packed light brown sugar	375 mL
1 1/2 tsp	vanilla	7 mL
1 tbsp	strong brewed coffee	15 mL
1 tsp	ground cinnamon	5 mL
1	ripe banana, mashed	1
1 cup	all-purpose flour	250 mL
1 cup	white chocolate chips (optional)	250 mL

1. In a small saucepan over low heat, melt chocolate with butter, stirring gently. Set aside to cool.

2. In a large bowl, whisk together eggs, sugar, vanilla, coffee and cinnamon. Add mashed banana and drizzle with chocolate, stirring lightly. Add flour, stirring just until moistened and blended. Fold in white chocolate chips (if using).

3. Spoon batter into prepared muffin tin. Bake in preheated oven for 20 to 25 minutes or until a toothpick inserted in the center comes out dry and clean.

Fudgey Cuffins

Makes 12 cuffins
- Preheat oven to 375ºF (190ºC)
- Muffin tin, paper-lined

1 1/4 cups	packed brown sugar, divided	300 mL
1/3 cup	milk	75 mL
2 oz	unsweetened chocolate	60 g
1/3 cup	shortening, softened	75 mL
1 tsp	vanilla	5 mL
2	eggs	2
1 1/3 cups	all-purpose flour	325 mL
1 tsp	baking soda	5 mL
1/2 tsp	salt	2 mL
1/2 cup	milk	125 mL

1. In a saucepan over very low heat, combine half the brown sugar, the 1/3 cup (75 mL) milk and chocolate, stirring until chocolate melts. Set aside to cool.

2. In a large bowl, cream together shortening and the remaining brown sugar until light and fluffy. Add vanilla and eggs, one at a time. Beat well after each addition.

3. In another bowl, combine flour, baking soda and salt. Add to creamed mixture alternately with the 1/2 cup (125 mL) milk, beating after each addition. Add chocolate mixture.

4. Spoon batter into prepared muffin tin. Bake in preheated oven for about 20 minutes.

Tip *Try substituting carob for chocolate in some of your recipes. Carob is similar to chocolate in flavor but is lower in fat and is caffeine-free.*

Black Bottom Cuffins

Makes 12 cuffins
- Preheat oven to 400ºF (200ºC)
- Muffin tin, paper-lined

1 1/2 cups	all-purpose flour	375 mL
1/2 tsp	baking powder	2 mL
1/2 tsp	baking soda	2 mL
1/4 cup	unsweetened cocoa powder	50 mL
1 cup	granulated sugar	250 mL
1/2 tsp	salt	2 mL
1 cup	water	250 mL
1 tsp	vanilla	5 mL
6 tbsp	vegetable oil	90 mL
FILLING		
4 oz	cream cheese, softened	125 g
1	egg, beaten	1
6 tbsp	granulated sugar	90 mL
1/2 cup	semisweet chocolate chips	125 mL

1. In a large bowl, mix together flour, baking powder, baking soda, cocoa, sugar and salt.

2. In another bowl, combine water, vanilla and oil. Pour into dry ingredients and stir well. Spoon batter into prepared muffin tin, about 2 tbsp (25 mL) each.

3. *Prepare the filling:* In another bowl, mix together cream cheese, egg, sugar and chocolate chips. Spoon 1 tbsp (15 mL) over batter and top with the remaining batter.

4. Bake in preheated oven for 20 minutes or until toothpick inserted in center comes out clean.

Puffins

Poppin' Puffins

Makes 6 to 8 puffins
- Preheat oven to 450°F (230°C)
- 6 to 8 ramekins, greased
- Baking sheet

2	eggs	2
1 cup	milk	250 mL
1 cup	all-purpose flour	250 mL
1/2 tsp	salt	2 mL
1 tbsp	vegetable oil	15 mL

1. In a large bowl, blend together eggs and milk. Beat in flour and salt. Add oil and beat another 30 seconds. Do not overmix.
2. Spoon batter into prepared ramekins, filling cups only half full. Place cups on a baking sheet. Bake in preheated oven for 10 minutes or until puffins pop. Then reduce heat to 350°F (180°C) and bake for 25 to 30 minutes or until firm and browned.
3. A few minutes before removing from oven, prick each puffin with a fork, allowing steam to escape. If you want puffins dry inside, turn off oven, keep door ajar and leave cups in for 30 minutes.

Variations *Cheese Puffins: Mix 1/2 cup (125 mL) shredded cheese into batter before filling cups.*

Stuffed Puffins: Split the puffins in half and fill with creamed vegetables, scrambled eggs or anything you like.

Whole Wheat Puffins: Replace half the all-purpose flour with whole wheat flour.

French Breakfast Puffins

Makes 12 small puffins
- Preheat oven to 350°F (180°C)
- Muffin tin, greased

1 1/2 cups	all-purpose flour or cake and pastry flour	375 mL
1 1/2 tsp	baking powder	7 mL
1/2 tsp	salt	2 mL
1/4 tsp	ground nutmeg	1 mL
1/3 cup	shortening, softened	75 mL
1/2 cup	granulated sugar	125 mL
1	egg	1
1/2 cup	milk	125 mL
TOPPING		
1/2 cup	granulated sugar	125 mL
1 tsp	ground cinnamon	5 mL
1/2 cup	butter or margarine, melted	125 mL

1. In a bowl, combine flour, baking powder, salt and nutmeg.
2. In a large bowl, cream shortening, sugar and egg, blending well. Stir in flour mixture alternately with milk.
3. Spoon batter into prepared muffin tin. Bake in preheated oven for 20 to 25 minutes.
4. *Prepare the topping:* In a bowl, combine sugar and cinnamon. As soon as puffins are ready, remove from pan. Roll in melted butter, then in sugar-cinnamon mixture. Serve immediately.

Orange Bran Puffins

Makes 12 puffins
- Preheat oven to 400°F (200°C)
- Muffin tin, greased

1 cup	all-purpose flour	250 mL
1/2 tsp	baking powder	2 mL
3/4 tsp	baking soda	4 mL
1 tsp	salt	5 mL
3 tbsp	granulated sugar	45 mL
1 cup	bran	250 mL
1 tsp	grated orange zest	5 mL
1	egg	1
1 cup	buttermilk	250 mL
1 tbsp	butter or margarine, melted	15 mL

1. In a large bowl, combine flour, baking powder, baking soda, salt and sugar. Stir in bran and orange zest.
2. In another bowl, beat egg slightly with buttermilk and melted butter. Add all at once to the flour mixture and stir just until moistened. Do not overmix. The batter will be lumpy.
3. Spoon batter into prepared muffin tin. Bake in preheated oven for 15 minutes or until golden brown. Best served warm.

Peanut Orange Breakfast Puffins

Makes 12 puffins
- Preheat oven to 425°F (220°C)
- Muffin tin or 12 ramekins, greased

2 cups	all-purpose flour	500 mL
1 tbsp	baking powder	15 mL
1 tsp	salt	5 mL
1/4 cup	granulated sugar	50 mL

1	egg, beaten	1
1 cup	milk	250 mL
1/4 cup	peanut oil	50 mL
1/2 cup	chopped salted peanuts	125 mL
TOPPING		
1/4 cup	granulated sugar	50 mL
1 tsp	grated orange zest	5 mL
1/4 cup	butter or margarine, melted	50 mL

1. In a large bowl, combine flour, baking powder, salt and sugar.

2. In another bowl, combine egg, milk and peanut oil. Pour into flour mixture and stir just until moistened. Fold in peanuts.

3. Spoon batter into prepared muffin tin. Bake in preheated oven for 15 to 20 minutes or until lightly brown.

4. *Prepare the topping:* In a bowl, combine sugar and zest until crumbly. Dip puffin tops, hot from the oven, into melted butter and then into sugar mixture. Serve warm.

Herbed Puffin Popovers

Makes 12 puffins
- Muffin tin, greased or paper-lined

1 cup	all-purpose flour	250 mL
1/2 tsp	dried thyme	2 mL
1/4 tsp	ground nutmeg	1 mL
1/4 tsp	salt	1 mL
1 cup	milk	250 mL
1/2 tsp	Dijon mustard	2 mL
2 tbsp	vegetable oil	25 mL
2	eggs	2

1. In a large bowl, combine flour, thyme, nutmeg and salt. Make a well in the center.

2. In another bowl, whisk together milk, mustard, oil and eggs. Pour into flour mixture, whisking until smooth and blended.

3. Spoon batter into prepared muffin tin. Bake in a 450°F (230°C) oven for 15 minutes. Reduce heat to 375°F (190°C) and bake for 20 to 25 minutes or until crusty and golden brown.

Tip *For this particular recipe it is best not to preheat the oven but to turn it on as you are placing the muffin tins inside.*

Cinnamon Puffs

Makes 8 to 12 puffins
- Preheat oven to 425°F (220°C)
- Muffin tin, greased

1 cup	all-purpose flour	250 mL
1/2 tsp	salt	2 mL
1 tsp	ground cinnamon	5 mL
3	eggs	3
1 cup	milk	250 mL
3 tbsp	butter or margarine, melted	45 mL

1. In a blender, combine flour, salt, cinnamon, eggs, milk and melted butter. Blend just until smooth.

2. Spoon batter into prepared muffin tin. Bake in preheated oven for 15 to 20 minutes.

Applesauce Puffins

Makes 12 puffins
- Preheat oven to 400°F (200°C)
- Muffin tin, greased or paper-lined

2 cups	packaged biscuit mix	500 mL
1/4 cup	granulated sugar	50 mL
1 tsp	ground cinnamon	5 mL
1/2 cup	sweetened applesauce	125 mL
1/4 cup	milk	50 mL
1	egg, beaten	1
2 tbsp	vegetable oil	25 mL
TOPPING		
1/4 cup	granulated sugar	50 mL
1/4 tsp	ground cinnamon	1 mL
2 tbsp	butter or margarine, melted	25 mL

1. In a large bowl, mix together biscuit mix, sugar and cinnamon. Add applesauce, milk, egg and oil. Beat with a spoon for about 1 minute.

2. Spoon batter into prepared muffin tin. Bake in preheated oven for 12 minutes or until golden brown. Let cool slightly before removing from tins.

3. *Prepare the topping:* In a bowl, combine sugar and cinnamon. Dip slightly cooled puffins in melted butter, then in sugar-cinnamon mixture.

Tip *Try making these in a miniature muffin pan.*

Apple Streusel Puffins

Makes 12 puffins

- Preheat oven to 375°F (190°C)
- Muffin tin, greased or paper-lined

¼ cup	butter, melted	50 mL
½ cup	granulated sugar	125 mL
1	egg, lightly beaten	1
½ cup	milk	125 mL
1½ cups	all-purpose flour	375 mL
1 tbsp	baking powder	15 mL
½ tsp	salt	2 mL
½ tsp	ground cinnamon	2 mL
1 cup	grated apple	250 mL
TOPPING		
¼ cup	granulated sugar	50 mL
¼ cup	chopped walnuts	50 mL
½ tsp	ground cinnamon	2 mL

1. In a large bowl, cream together butter and sugar. Stir in egg and milk. Add flour, baking powder, salt and cinnamon. Fold in apple.
2. *Prepare the topping:* In a bowl, combine sugar, walnuts and cinnamon.
3. Spoon batter into prepared muffin tin. Sprinkle with topping. Bake in preheated oven for about 20 minutes.

Red Cherry Puffins

Makes 12 puffins

- Preheat oven to 350°F (180°C)
- Muffin tin, paper-lined

2½ cups	chopped canned red cherries (reserve ½ cup/125 mL juice)	625 mL
½ cup	granulated sugar	125 mL
2 tbsp	quick-cooking tapioca	25 mL
2	egg whites	2
Pinch	salt	Pinch
¼ tsp	cream of tartar	1 mL
2	egg yolks	2
⅓ cup	granulated sugar	75 mL
⅓ cup	sifted cake and pastry flour	75 mL

1. In a saucepan over medium heat, combine cherries, cherry juice, sugar and tapioca. Simmer for 5 minutes, stirring constantly. Set aside.
2. In a small bowl, beat egg whites until foamy. Add salt and cream of tartar. Beat until stiff peaks form.

3. In another bowl, beat egg yolks until thick and lemon-colored. Gradually add sugar, beating well. Fold into egg whites. Stir in flour.
4. Spoon cherry mixture into prepared muffin tin and pour batter over top. Bake in preheated oven for 25 to 30 minutes.

Tip *Delicious served warm with ice cream.*

Lemon Nutmeg Puffins

Makes 6 puffins

- Preheat oven to 450°F (230°C)
- Muffin tin, greased

1 cup	whole wheat bread flour	250 mL
½ tsp	ground nutmeg	2 mL
¼ tsp	salt	1 mL
3	eggs	3
1 cup	milk	250 mL
1 tbsp	vegetable oil	15 mL
	Grated zest of 1 lemon	
2 tsp	butter or margarine	10 mL

1. In a bowl, combine flour, nutmeg and salt.
2. In a blender, process eggs. Gradually add flour mixture alternately with milk. Add oil and zest, blending until smooth. The batter should be thick.
3. Heat prepared muffin tins in preheated oven for a few minutes. Cut butter into 6 pieces and place a piece in each muffin cup. Return to oven until sizzling.
4. Spoon batter into prepared muffin tin. Bake in preheated oven for 25 minutes.

Tip *If you are not serving these immediately, puncture tops with a sharp knife to release the steam inside. Return pan to the turned-off oven, leaving door partially open, until you are ready to serve.*

Ginger Lemon Puffins

Makes 12 puffins

- Preheat oven to 375°F (190°C)
- Muffin tin, greased

¼ cup	butter, softened	50 mL
1¼ cups	granulated sugar, divided	300 mL
1	egg	1
1 tsp	grated lemon zest	5 mL
2 cups	all-purpose flour	500 mL
4 tsp	baking powder	20 mL

½ tsp	salt	2 mL
¼ tsp	ground nutmeg	1 mL
1 cup	milk	250 mL
2 tsp	ground ginger	10 mL
½ cup	melted butter	125 mL

1. In a bowl, cream together butter and ½ cup (125 mL) of the sugar. Beat in egg and lemon zest.
2. In a large bowl, combine flour, baking powder, salt and nutmeg. Add creamed mixture alternately with milk, beating after each addition.
3. Spoon batter into prepared muffin tin. Bake in preheated oven for 15 to 20 minutes.
4. Meanwhile, in a bowl, combine the remaining sugar and ginger. When puffins come out of the oven, immediately dip in melted butter, then in sugar-ginger mixture. Serve while warm.

Pecan Lemon Honey Puffins

Makes 6 puffins
- Preheat oven to 425°F (220°C)
- Muffin tin or 6 ramekins, greased

1 cup	all-purpose flour	250 mL
½ tsp	salt	2 mL
2	eggs	2
1 cup	milk (room temperature)	250 mL
3 tbsp	finely chopped pecans	45 mL
LEMON HONEY BUTTER		
6 tbsp	butter, softened	90 mL
6 tbsp	liquid honey	90 mL
	Finely grated zest of 1 lemon	

1. In a large bowl, combine flour and salt. Make a well in the center.
2. In another bowl, beat together eggs and milk. Pour into flour mixture, beating just until smooth. Fold in pecans.
3. Spoon batter into prepared muffin tin. (If using custard cups, place them on a baking sheet.) Bake in preheated oven for 25 to 30 minutes or until they puff up and are well browned.
4. *Prepare the lemon honey butter:* In a bowl, combine butter, honey and zest. Spread over warm puffins.

Tip *Try other flavored spreads with these puffins.*

Strawberry Drop Puffins

Makes 12 puffins
- Baking sheet, greased

2 cups	miniature marshmallows	500 mL
¼ cup	granulated sugar	50 mL
1 cup	sour cream	250 mL
1 cup	water	250 mL
½ cup	butter or margarine	125 mL
1 cup	all-purpose flour	250 mL
¼ tsp	salt	1 mL
4	eggs	4
4 cups	fresh strawberries, washed and hulled, divided	1 L

1. In a bowl, combine marshmallows, sugar and sour cream. Cover and chill for several hours.
2. In a large saucepan over medium-high heat, bring water to a boil. Add butter, stirring until melted. Add flour and salt, stirring vigorously until mixture forms a ball. Remove from heat and cool slightly. Add eggs one at a time, beating after each addition.
3. Drop batter by heaping tablespoons (15 mL), about 3 inches apart, on prepared baking sheet. Bake at 450°F (230°C) for 15 minutes. Reduce heat to 325°F (160°C) and bake for 25 minutes. Set aside to cool. Split puffins in half and remove any webbing inside.
4. In a bowl, crush 2 cups (500 mL) of the strawberries. Slice the remaining 2 cups (500 mL) strawberries. Fold all berries into chilled sour cream mixture. Spoon ¼ cup (50 mL) filling into bottom half of each split puffin. Cover puffins with tops and spread with 1 tbsp (15 mL) filling.

Tip *To keep strawberries fresh and firm, wash and remove caps (hull) just before using, not when storing, or they will absorb too much water and become mushy. Washing removes the natural protective covering. The hull protects the berry and helps preserve flavor, texture and nutrients.*

Variation *Strawberry Sundae Puffins: Fill split puffin halves with whipped cream and sliced fresh strawberries. Drizzle with a prepared fudge sauce and cover with the puffin tops. Dust lightly with confectioner's sugar.*

Double Chocolate Puffins

Makes 8 to 12 puffins
- Preheat oven to 350°F (180°C)
- Ramekins or muffin tin, greased

3 oz	unsweetened chocolate	90 g
¾ cup	milk	175 mL
6 tbsp	butter or margarine, softened	90 mL
¾ cup	granulated sugar	175 mL
2	eggs	2
1 tsp	vanilla	5 mL
¾ cup	all-purpose flour	175 mL
1½ tsp	baking powder	7 mL

1. In a saucepan over low heat, combine chocolate and milk until smooth. Set aside to cool.
2. In a large bowl, cream together butter and sugar. Add eggs, one at a time, mixing well. Add vanilla and stir in flour and baking powder. Stir in chocolate mixture.
3. Spoon batter into prepared ramekins. Bake in preheated oven for 20 to 25 minutes. Remove from oven and invert cups over a plate so that puffins are upside-down.

Tip *For an added treat, whip ½ cup (125 mL) whipping cream and gradually stir in ½ cup (125 mL) slightly softened chocolate ice cream. Spoon over the inverted puffins.*

Chocolate Peanut Puffins

Makes 12 puffins
- Preheat oven to 400°F (200°C)
- Muffin tin, paper-lined

2 cups	biscuit mix	500 mL
2 tbsp	granulated sugar	25 mL
½ cup	creamy peanut butter	125 mL
¾ cup	chocolate-covered peanuts	175 mL
1	egg	1
¾ cup	milk	175 mL
2 tbsp	vegetable oil	25 mL

1. In a large bowl, combine biscuit mix and sugar. Cut in peanut butter until mixture is crumbly. Add peanuts, mixing well.
2. In a small bowl, beat egg slightly. Add milk and oil. Pour into peanut mixture and stir just until moistened.
3. Spoon batter into prepared muffin tin. Bake in preheated oven for 20 minutes or until golden brown. Serve hot.

Parmesan Cheese Puffins

Makes 8 to 12 puffins
- Preheat oven to 425°F (220°C)
- Muffin tin or ramekins, greased

4	eggs	4
1 cup	milk	250 mL
⅔ cup	all-purpose flour	150 mL
½ cup	freshly grated Parmesan cheese	125 mL
½ tsp	salt	2 mL

1. In a large bowl, beat together eggs and milk. Add flour, cheese and salt, beating until well blended.
2. Spoon batter into prepared muffin tin. Bake in preheated oven for 35 to 40 minutes.

Cheese Puffin Popovers

Makes 6 puffins
- Preheat oven to 425°F (220°C)
- 6 ramekins, greased
- Baking sheet

1 cup	all-purpose flour	250 mL
½ tsp	salt	2 mL
2	eggs	2
1 cup	milk	250 mL
½ cup	shredded Cheddar cheese	125 mL

1. In a bowl, combine flour and salt. Add eggs, milk and cheese, stirring until just smooth.
2. Spoon batter into ramekins, filling only half full. Set cups on baking sheet.
3. Bake in preheated oven for 45 minutes or until golden brown. Do not open oven before done or the puffins will fall. Serve hot.

Potato Cheese Puffins

Makes 12 puffins

- Preheat oven to 400°F (200°C)
- Muffin tin or 12 ramekins, greased

1¼ cups	all-purpose flour	300 mL
¼ cup	granulated sugar	50 mL
1 tbsp	baking powder	15 mL
1 tsp	salt	5 mL
1 cup	instant potato flakes, divided	250 mL
1	egg	1
1 cup	milk	250 mL
¼ cup	vegetable oil	50 mL
½ cup	shredded Cheddar cheese	125 mL

1. In a large bowl, mix together flour, sugar, baking powder, salt and ¾ cup (175 mL) of the potato flakes.
2. In another bowl, combine egg, milk and oil. Beat slightly until well blended. Pour into flour mixture and stir just until moistened and blended.
3. Spoon batter into prepared tin, filling cups two-thirds full. Sprinkle tops with cheese and the remaining potato flakes. Bake in preheated oven for 15 to 20 minutes or until browned.

Tip *Keep oils in a squeeze bottle for when you need only a small amount of oil.*

Baked Salmon Puffins

Makes 4 to 6 puffins

- Preheat oven to 300°F (150°C)
- 4 to 6 ramekins, greased
- Baking pan

3	eggs, separated	3
1	can (16 oz/455 mL) salmon	1
¾ cup	bread crumbs	175 mL
1 tbsp	finely chopped onion	15 mL
1 tbsp	freshly squeezed lemon juice	15 mL
½ tsp	salt	2 mL
Pinch	freshly ground black pepper	Pinch

1. In a small bowl, beat egg whites until stiff peaks form. Set aside.
2. Drain salmon and remove any skin or small bones. Flake with a fork.
3. In a large bowl, beat egg yolks slightly. Add salmon, bread crumbs, onion, lemon juice, salt and pepper, mixing well. Fold in beaten egg whites.
4. Spoon batter into prepared ramekins. Place in baking pan with 1 inch (2.5 cm) boiling water. Bake in preheated oven for 45 to 50 minutes or until a knife inserted in the center of a puffin comes out clean.

Tip *There are all kinds of prepared dips available in supermarkets that would be great with these puffins, especially one with sour cream, dill, onion, etc.*

Tuna Mushroom Puffins

Makes 4 to 6 puffins

- Preheat oven to 400°F (200°C)
- 4 to 6 ramekins, greased

4	eggs, lightly beaten	4
2 cups	soft bread crumbs	500 mL
1 tsp	salt	5 mL
1 tbsp	prepared mustard	15 mL
1 tbsp	minced onion	15 mL
2 cups	milk	500 mL
1	can (6 oz/170 g) chunky-style tuna sauce	1
1	can (10 oz/284 mL) cream of mushroom soup (undiluted)	1
2 tbsp	butter	25 mL

1. In a large bowl, combine eggs, bread crumbs, salt, mustard, onion, milk and tuna. Pour evenly into prepared custard cups. Place cups in a large pan of hot water. Bake in preheated oven for 35 to 40 minutes.
2. In a saucepan over medium heat, combine cream of mushroom soup and butter. Spoon over puffins and serve warm.

Muffins Just for Kids

This chapter is specially written for kids. It contains recipes for muffins that kids will enjoy eating and making. The recipe that follows on this page is a basic, easy, plain muffin recipe — great for young cooks or anyone who has never baked muffins. The variations show you how to make a few changes and/or substitutions, and create a wide range of different-flavored muffins. Following this recipe are other easy-to-make muffin recipes which I hope you will try to bake — and enjoy. When baking, keep the following tips in mind.

- Make sure your oven racks are in the right position.
- Set the oven to the temperature called for in your recipe so that the oven will be preheating and ready to use by the time you have mixed your muffin batter.
- Grease your muffin tins or line them with large-size paper baking cups and set aside.
- In a large bowl, measure out all of your dry ingredients, for example, flour, sugar, baking powder, baking soda, salt, etc.
- Make a well (hole) in the centre of these dry ingredients and set aside.
- In a smaller bowl, combine your liquid ingredients, for example, milk, beaten eggs, oil, etc.
- Add the smaller bowl of liquid ingredients all at once to the larger bowl of dry ingredients and stir only until the dry ingredients are just moistened. Do not overmix.
- Spoon the batter into the tins, filling them three-quarters full, or fill the tins to the top for larger muffins.
- Bake as directed in your recipe.

To measure dry ingredients:
- Use plastic or metal measuring cups that come in sets of different sizes. Spoon the dry ingredient into the right size cup until heaping, holding the cup over the canister it came in, or an empty bowl, not over the mixing bowl you are using to prepare the recipe.
- Level the ingredient by scraping a knife across the top, allowing the excess amount to fall back into the canister or empty bowl. Do not tap the cup on the counter. Level measuring spoons containing a dry ingredient the same way.

To measure liquid ingredients:
- To measure any liquid, use a measuring cup with a spout and amounts marked on the side of the cup. Place the cup on a counter and pour the liquid into the cup, bending down to read the measurements properly.
- To measure small amounts, pour into measuring spoon until full, holding spoon away from your mixing bowl.

Fruits and vegetables:
- Always wash any fruits and vegetables before using them in your recipe.

● ●

Plain Muffins

Makes 12 muffins
- Preheat oven to 400°F (200°C)
- Muffin tin, greased or paper-lined

2 cups	all-purpose flour	500 mL
1 tbsp	baking powder	15 mL
¼ cup	granulated sugar	50 mL
½ tsp	salt	2 mL
1 cup	milk	250 mL
1	egg, beaten	1
¼ cup	vegetable oil	50 mL
½ tsp	vanilla	2 mL

1. In a large bowl, combine flour, baking powder, sugar and salt. Make a well in the center.
2. In another bowl, combine milk, beaten egg, oil and vanilla. Add liquid ingredients all at once to dry ingredients. Stir only until moistened and slightly lumpy.
3. Spoon batter into prepared muffin tin. Bake in preheated oven for 20 to 25 minutes or until golden brown.

Variations *Orange Muffins: Replace half or all of the milk with orange juice and add 1 tsp (5 mL) grated orange zest.*

Cheese Muffins: Reduce sugar to 2 tbsp (25 mL), add 1 cup (250 mL) shredded cheese to the dry ingredients, and use 2 tbsp (25 mL) of oil instead of the ¼ cup (50 mL).

Raisin Muffins: Add ½ cup (125 mL) raisins to the dry ingredients.

Blueberry Muffins: Fold in 1 cup (250 mL) fresh blueberries or ¾ cup (175 mL) thawed, well-drained frozen blueberries into the batter before spooning into the muffin tins.

Quick-Mix Muffins

Makes 6 to 8 muffins
- Preheat oven to 400°F (200°C)
- Muffin tin, paper-lined

1 cup	buttermilk baking mix	250 mL
3 tbsp	granulated sugar	45 mL
1	egg	1
⅓ cup	water	75 mL

1. In a large bowl, mix together baking mix, sugar and egg. Add water and beat vigorously with a mixing spoon for 1 minute.

2. Spoon batter into prepared muffin tin. Bake in preheated oven for 15 to 20 minutes.

Variation *Add ¼ cup (50 mL) chopped nuts to batter before spooning into muffin tins.*

Quick Breakfast Muffins

Makes 12 muffins
- Preheat oven to 375°F (190°C)
- Muffin tin, paper-lined

2 cups	all-purpose flour	500 mL
4 tsp	baking powder	20 mL
¼ cup	granulated sugar	50 mL
Pinch	salt	Pinch
1	egg	1
1 cup	milk	250 mL
2 tbsp	vegetable oil or melted butter	25 mL

1. In a large bowl, mix together flour, baking powder, sugar and salt. Make a well in the center.

2. In another bowl, whisk together egg, milk and oil. Pour into dry ingredients and stir only until moistened. Do not overmix.

3. Spoon batter into prepared muffin tin. Bake in preheated oven for 20 to 25 minutes or until done.

Tip *If you want to save time in the morning, mix the dry ingredients the night before, cover and set aside on the counter. Blend together the liquid ingredients and set aside in the fridge until the morning. Then, all you have to do for a really quick breakfast muffin is pour the liquid ingredients into the dry ingredients and bake as above.*

Spicy Spice Muffins

Makes 12 muffins
- Preheat oven to 425°F (220°C)
- Muffin tin, greased or paper-lined

2 cups	all-purpose flour	500 mL
1 tbsp	baking powder	15 mL
1 tsp	salt	5 mL
1 tsp	ground ginger	5 mL
1 tsp	ground nutmeg	5 mL
1 tsp	ground cinnamon	5 mL
1	egg, well beaten	1
½ cup	granulated sugar	125 mL
¼ cup	butter or margarine, melted	50 mL
1 cup	milk	250 mL

1. In a large bowl, combine flour, baking powder, salt, ginger, nutmeg and cinnamon.

2. In another bowl, combine egg, sugar, melted butter and milk. Add to the flour mixture, stirring just until moistened and blended.

3. Spoon batter into prepared muffin tin. Bake in preheated oven for 15 to 20 minutes.

Egg Bread Muffins

Makes as many as you want
- Preheat oven to 350°F (180°C)
- Muffin tin, greased

1	loaf of bread (white or brown) Cheddar cheese slices, about ½ inch (1 cm) thick Eggs Toppings: chopped onions, chopped tomatoes, chopped green bell peppers, chopped fresh herbs, salt, freshly ground black pepper	1

1. Arrange bread slices on a cutting board. Cut out circles the same size as bottom of muffin tin cups, using a cookie cutter or top of a glass. Make as many as you want.

2. Place circles of bread in bottom of each prepared muffin cup. Place cheese slices on top of each bread circle. Break an egg over top. Add your choice of toppings.

3. Bake in preheated oven until tops turn golden brown or longer if you want a firmer yolk. Serve immediately.

Bran Cereal Muffins

Makes 12 large muffins
- Preheat oven to 400°F (200°C)
- Muffin tin, paper-lined

1¼ cups	all-purpose flour	300 mL
1 tbsp	baking powder	15 mL
½ tsp	salt	2 mL
½ cup	granulated sugar	125 mL
1½ cups	all-bran cereal	375 mL
1¼ cups	milk	300 mL
1	egg	1
⅓ cup	vegetable oil	75 mL

1. In a large bowl, mix together flour, baking powder, salt and sugar. Set aside.
2. In another bowl, combine cereal and milk. Stir well and let stand for 1 to 2 minutes or until the cereal has softened. Add the egg and oil to this cereal mixture and beat well. Pour into the flour mixture and stir just until moistened.
3. Spoon batter evenly into prepared muffin tin. Bake in preheated oven for 25 minutes or until lightly browned.

Variation *Add ½ cup (125 mL) raisins to the batter. Substitute 3 cups (750 mL) raisin bran cereal or 2½ cups (625 mL) bran flakes cereal in place of the all-bran cereal.*

Oatmeal Cinnamon Muffins

Makes 12 small muffins
- Preheat oven to 400°F (200°C)
- Muffin tin, greased or paper-lined

1 cup	all-purpose flour	250 mL
3½ tsp	baking powder	17 mL
½ tsp	salt	2 mL
½ tsp	ground cinnamon	2 mL
Pinch	ground nutmeg	Pinch
¾ cup	old-fashioned rolled oats	175 mL
½ cup	lightly packed brown sugar	125 mL
1	egg	1
1 cup	milk	250 mL
¼ cup	vegetable oil or shortening, melted	50 mL

1. In a large bowl, combine flour, baking powder, salt, cinnamon and nutmeg. Stir in rolled oats and brown sugar; blend together well.
2. In another bowl, beat together egg, milk and oil. Add to flour mixture and stir only until moistened. Batter will be lumpy.

3. Spoon batter into prepared muffin tin. Bake in preheated oven for 20 to 25 minutes or until done.

Puffed Wheat Morsels

Makes 8 to 12 muffins
- Muffin tin, greased or paper-lined

¼ cup	butter or margarine	50 mL
¼ cup	packed brown sugar	50 mL
¼ cup	corn syrup	50 mL
3 cups	sugar-coated puffed wheat cereal (or puffed rice or corn)	750 mL

1. In a heavy saucepan over medium heat, melt butter with brown sugar and corn syrup. Cook until bubbly and slightly thick. Be careful — it gets very hot. Remove from heat, holding onto handle tightly.
2. Pour in cereal and stir quickly with a wooden spoon. Drop by spoonfuls into prepared muffin tin. Let cool before serving.

Surprise Cornmeal Muffins

Makes 12 muffins
- Preheat oven to 400°F (200°C)
- Muffin tin, paper-lined

1 cup	yellow cornmeal	250 mL
1¼ cups	cake and pastry flour	300 mL
1 tsp	baking soda	5 mL
2 tsp	baking powder	10 mL
½ tsp	salt	2 mL
½ cup	shortening or butter	125 mL
½ cup	granulated sugar	125 mL
1	egg	1
1 cup	milk	250 mL
½ cup	plain yogurt	125 mL
¼ cup	filling (such as softened cream cheese, jam etc.)	50 mL

1. In a large bowl, combine cornmeal, flour, baking soda, baking powder and salt.
2. In another bowl, cream together shortening and sugar. Beat in egg, milk and yogurt. Pour into dry ingredients and stir just until moistened.
3. Spoon half the batter evenly into prepared muffin tin. Top each with 1 tsp (5 mL) filling and then spoon the remaining batter evenly over top. Bake in preheated oven for 20 to 25 minutes or until golden brown.

Peanut Butter Cornmeal Muffins

Makes 12 small muffins
- Preheat oven to 400°F (200°C)
- Muffin tin, greased or paper-lined

1 cup	all-purpose flour	250 mL
½ tsp	salt	2 mL
1 tbsp	baking powder	15 mL
1 tbsp	granulated sugar	15 mL
½ cup	yellow cornmeal	125 mL
1 cup	milk	250 mL
1	egg, beaten	1
¼ cup	peanut butter	50 mL
1 tbsp	butter or shortening, melted	15 mL

1. In a large bowl, combine flour, salt, baking powder and sugar. Stir in cornmeal.

2. In another bowl, combine milk, egg, peanut butter and melted butter. Add the milk mixture, stirring only until moistened. Do not overmix.

3. Spoon batter into prepared muffin tin. Bake in preheated oven for 20 to 25 minutes or until done.

Corn-on-the-Cob Muffins

Makes 12 muffins
- Preheat oven to 425°F (220°C)
- Muffin tin, paper-lined

1 cup	all-purpose flour	250 mL
¾ cup	yellow cornmeal	175 mL
2 tbsp	granulated sugar	25 mL
2 tsp	baking powder	10 mL
¾ tsp	salt	4 mL
1	egg, beaten	1
¾ cup	milk	175 mL
¼ cup	butter or margarine, melted	50 mL
½ cup	cooked corn, cut off the cob	125 mL
2 tbsp	minced green onion (optional)	25 mL

1. In a large bowl, combine flour, cornmeal, sugar, baking powder and salt.

2. In a small bowl, combine egg, milk, butter, corn and green onion (if using). Pour into dry ingredients and stir just until moistened and blended.

3. Spoon batter into prepared muffin tin. Bake in preheated oven for 20 minutes or until lightly browned.

Mini Pumpkin Muffins

Makes 24 to 36 miniature muffins
- Preheat oven to 350°F (180°C)
- Miniature muffin tins, greased

1¾ cups	all-purpose flour	425 mL
½ cup	packed brown sugar	125 mL
1 tsp	baking powder	5 mL
½ tsp	baking soda	2 mL
½ tsp	salt	2 mL
½ tsp	ground cinnamon	2 mL
¼ tsp	ground nutmeg	1 mL
¾ cup	canned pumpkin purée (not pie filling)	175 mL
½ cup	vegetable oil	125 mL
⅔ cup	milk	150 mL

1. In a large bowl, mix together flour, brown sugar, baking powder, baking soda, salt, cinnamon and nutmeg.

2. In another bowl, combine pumpkin, oil and milk until well-blended. Add to flour mixture and stir just until moistened and blended. Do not overmix.

3. Spoon batter into prepared miniature muffin tins, filling cups to the top. Bake in preheated oven for 12 to 15 minutes.

Halloween Monster Muffins

Makes 12 small muffins
- Preheat oven to 400°F (200°C)
- Muffin tin, paper-lined

1½ cups	all-purpose flour	375 mL
2 tsp	baking powder	10 mL
½ tsp	salt	2 mL
1 tsp	ground cinnamon	5 mL
½ tsp	ground ginger	2 mL
¼ tsp	ground cloves	1 mL
¼ tsp	ground nutmeg	1 mL
½ cup	packed brown sugar	125 mL
½ cup	raisins (optional)	125 mL
1	egg	1
½ cup	milk	125 mL
½ cup	canned pumpkin purée (not pie filling)	125 mL
¼ cup	vegetable oil	50 mL

1. In a large bowl, combine flour, baking powder, salt, cinnamon, ginger, cloves, nutmeg and brown sugar. Mix in raisins (if using). Make a well in the center.

2. In another bowl, beat together egg, milk, pumpkin and oil. Pour into flour mixture and stir just until moistened. The batter will be lumpy.
3. Spoon batter into prepared muffin tin. Bake in preheated oven for about 20 minutes.
4. Decorate with vanilla or cream cheese frosting or whipping cream. Use raisins, chocolate chips, Smarties, carrot or green bell pepper pieces, nuts or whatever else you have on hand to make all kinds of scary monster faces on your muffin tops.

Apple Muffins

Makes 12 muffins
- Preheat oven to 400°F (200°C)
- Muffin tin, greased or paper-lined

1¾ cups	all-purpose flour	425 mL
3½ tsp	baking powder	17 mL
½ tsp	salt	2 mL
¼ cup	granulated sugar	50 mL
½ tsp	ground nutmeg	2 mL
1 cup	milk	250 mL
1	egg, beaten	1
⅓ cup	vegetable oil	75 mL
1 tsp	grated lemon zest	5 mL
¾ cup	grated peeled apple	175 mL

1. In a large bowl, combine flour, baking powder, salt, sugar and nutmeg. Make a well in the center.
2. In a small bowl, combine milk, beaten egg and oil. Add this mixture, all at once, to dry ingredients and stir just until moist. Fold in lemon zest and apple with just a few strokes. The batter will be a bit lumpy.
3. Spoon batter into prepared muffin tin. Bake in preheated oven for 25 to 30 minutes.

Apple Honey Muffins

Makes 12 small muffins
- Preheat oven to 400°F (200°C)
- Muffin tin, greased or paper-lined

1 cup	sweetened applesauce	250 mL
⅓ cup	orange juice	75 mL
¼ cup	liquid honey	50 mL
¼ cup	vegetable oil	50 mL
1	egg	1
1 cup	all-purpose flour	250 mL
¾ cup	old-fashioned rolled oats	175 mL

1 tbsp	baking powder	15 mL
½ tsp	ground cinnamon	2 mL

1. In a small bowl, mix together applesauce, orange juice, honey, oil and egg.
2. In a large bowl, mix together flour, rolled oats, baking powder and cinnamon. Make a well in the center. Pour liquid ingredients into dry ingredients and stir just to moisten. Do not overmix.
3. Spoon batter into prepared muffin tin. Bake in preheated oven for 25 to 30 minutes.

Tip *Top hot, baked muffins (or cupcakes) with a marshmallow and put back in oven until marshmallows melt and brown lightly.*

Apple Nut Muffins

Makes 12 muffins
- Preheat oven to 400°F (200°C)
- Muffin tin, greased or paper-lined

⅔ cup	unsweetened apple juice or milk	150 mL
½ cup	vegetable oil	125 mL
1 tsp	vanilla	5 mL
1	egg	1
2 cups	all-purpose flour	500 mL
¼ cup	granulated sugar	50 mL
¼ cup	firmly packed brown sugar	50 mL
1 tbsp	baking powder	15 mL
½ tsp	salt	2 mL
½ cup	chopped nuts	125 mL
1	apple, peeled and chopped	1
	Sugar-Cinnamon Mix (see page 4)	

1. In a large bowl, beat together juice, oil, vanilla and egg. Stir in flour, granulated sugar, brown sugar, baking powder and salt. Mix just until moistened. (Batter will be lumpy.) Stir in nuts and apple.
2. Spoon batter into prepared muffin tin. Sprinkle with Sugar-Cinnamon Mix. Bake in preheated oven for 20 minutes or until golden brown.

Tip *To soften rock-hard brown sugar, put a piece of cut apple in the container. Leave for 1 day, remove, and fluff up the sugar with a fork.*

Apple Cheddar Muffins

Makes 12 muffins

- Preheat oven to 400°F (200°C)
- Muffin tin, greased or paper-lined

½ cup	butter or margarine	125 mL
½ cup	packed brown sugar	125 mL
2	eggs	2
1⅔ cups	whole wheat flour	400 mL
½ tsp	salt	2 mL
1 tsp	baking soda	5 mL
½ cup	old-fashioned rolled oats	125 mL
1 cup	apple pie filling	250 mL
½ cup	finely chopped sharp (old) Cheddar cheese	125 mL
¼ cup	milk or water	50 mL

1. In a large bowl, cream together margarine and brown sugar. Add eggs and mix well. Add flour, salt and baking soda and mix. Add oats, pie filling and cheese and mix well. Stir in milk.

2. Spoon batter into prepared muffin tin. Bake in preheated oven for 20 minutes.

Tip *If children (or adults) are sick in bed, serve their meals in a muffin tin. The cups hold assorted foods, even a small glass of milk or juice, and you will avoid sliding and spilling.*

"Candy Apple" Muffins

Makes 12 muffins

- Preheat oven to 400°F (200°C)
- Muffin tin, greased
- Wooden skewers or Popsicle sticks

2 cups	all-purpose flour	500 mL
½ cup	granulated sugar	125 mL
1 tbsp	baking powder	15 mL
½ tsp	salt	2 mL
¼ tsp	ground nutmeg	1 mL
½ cup	milk	125 mL
¼ cup	butter or margarine, melted	50 mL
2	eggs	2
1 tsp	vanilla	5 mL
1	apple, chopped	1
DIP		
½ cup	liquid honey	125 mL
½ cup	packed dark brown sugar	125 mL
¾ cup	finely chopped walnuts	175 mL

1. In a large bowl, mix together flour, sugar, baking powder, salt and nutmeg.

2. In another bowl, combine milk, butter, eggs and vanilla until well blended. Pour into dry ingredients and stir until just moistened. Fold in apple. Do not overmix.

3. Spoon batter into prepared muffin tin. Bake in preheated oven for 15 to 20 minutes or until lightly browned. Let cool slightly and remove from pan.

4. *Prepare the dip:* In a saucepan over medium heat, bring honey and brown sugar to a boil. Stir until sugar is dissolved. Pour walnuts onto a plate.

5. Spear warm muffins with a skewer or Popsicle stick and dip quickly into the honey/brown sugar mixture, then into chopped nuts.

Tip *You can use a miniature muffin tin and bake for 12 to 15 minutes.*

Special Banana Muffins

Makes 12 muffins

- Preheat oven to 425 °F (220°C)
- Muffin tin, paper-lined

1 cup	granulated sugar	250 mL
2	eggs	2
½ cup	margarine, softened	125 mL
2 cups	all-purpose flour	500 mL
2 tsp	baking soda	10 mL
3	ripe bananas, mashed	3

1. In a large bowl, cream together sugar and eggs until well mixed. Add margarine and blend well. Add flour and baking soda and blend until mixture resembles a loose dough. Add bananas and stir just until moist and blended.

2. Spoon batter into prepared muffin tin. Bake in preheated oven for 15 to 20 minutes or until golden brown.

Banana Split Muffins

Makes 12 muffins

- Preheat oven to 400°F (200°C)
- Muffin tin, greased or paper-lined

2	egg whites	2
½ cup	granulated sugar, divided	125 mL
⅔ cup	flaked coconut (sweetened or unsweetened)	150 mL
2 cups	biscuit mix	500 mL

2/3 cup	milk	150 mL
2 tbsp	shortening, melted	25 mL
2	egg yolks, beaten	2
1/2	small banana, cut into 12 cubes	1/2
12	maraschino cherries, halved	12
12	walnut halves	12

1. In a small bowl, beat egg whites until soft peaks form. Gradually add 1/3 cup (75 mL) of the sugar and continue beating until stiff peaks form. Fold in coconut and set aside.
2. In a large bowl, mix together biscuit mix and the remaining sugar.
3. In another bowl, combine milk, shortening and egg yolks. Add this mixture all at once to dry ingredients. Stir just until moistened.
4. Spoon 1 1/2 tbsp (20 mL) batter into the bottom of each prepared cup. Place a banana cube, cherry half and walnut half on top of batter. Cover with 1 tbsp (15 mL) more batter. Spoon 1 1/2 tbsp (20 mL) meringue mixture on each muffin. Top with the remaining cherries. Bake in preheated oven for 15 to 20 minutes.

Banana Walnut Muffins

Makes 12 muffins
- Preheat oven to 350°F (180°C)
- Muffin tin, greased or paper-lined

1 1/2 cups	all-purpose flour	375 mL
3/4 cup	granulated sugar	175 mL
3/4 cup	chopped walnuts (about 3 oz/75 g)	175 mL
1 1/2 tsp	baking soda	7 mL
1/4 tsp	salt	1 mL
1 1/4 cups	mashed ripe bananas	300 mL
1/2 cup	melted unsalted butter (1 stick)	125 mL
1	egg	1
2 1/2 tbsp	milk	32 mL

1. In a large bowl, combine flour, sugar, chopped walnuts, baking soda and salt.
2. In another bowl, combine mashed bananas, melted butter, egg and milk. Add to dry ingredients and stir just until moistened. Do not overmix.
3. Spoon batter into prepared muffin tin. Bake in preheated oven for 25 minutes or until a toothpick inserted in center of muffin comes out dry.

Tip *For a nice thick milkshake to enjoy with your muffins, put half a banana, 1/2 cup (125 mL) each of 2% milk, plain yogurt and sliced strawberries (or blueberries) in a blender and purée.*

Easy Blueberry Muffins

Makes 12 muffins
- Preheat oven to 400°F (200°C)
- Muffin tin, greased or paper-lined

1 3/4 cups	all-purpose flour	425 mL
1/3 cup	granulated sugar	75 mL
1 tbsp	baking powder	15 mL
3/4 tsp	salt	4 mL
3/4 cup	milk	175 mL
1/3 cup	vegetable oil	75 mL
1	egg	1
1 cup	fresh blueberries (or thawed and drained frozen blueberries)	250 mL

1. In a large bowl, mix together flour, sugar, baking powder and salt until blended.
2. In another bowl, beat together milk, oil and egg. Add to the flour mixture and stir only until moistened. Do not overmix. Gently fold in blueberries.
3. Spoon batter into prepared muffin tin. Bake in preheated oven for 20 to 25 minutes. Delicious served warm.

More Blueberry Muffins

Makes 12 muffins
- Preheat oven to 375°F (190°C)
- Muffin tin, greased or paper-lined

2 cups	all-purpose flour	500 mL
2 tsp	baking powder	10 mL
1/4 tsp	salt	1 mL
1/2 cup	butter, softened	125 mL
1 cup	granulated sugar	250 mL
2	eggs	2
3/4 cup	milk	175 mL
1 1/2 cups	blueberries	375 mL

1. In a large bowl, mix together flour, baking powder and salt. Make a well in the center.
2. In another bowl, cream together butter and sugar, then beat in eggs one at a time. Gradually stir in milk. The mixture may look curdled. Pour into the flour mixture and stir just until moistened. Gently fold in blueberries.
3. Spoon batter into prepared muffin tin. Bake in preheated oven for 25 to 30 minutes or until toothpick inserted in center of a muffin comes out clean and dry.

Blueberry Breakfast Gems

Makes 12 muffins

- Preheat oven to 425°F (220°C)
- Muffin tin, greased or paper-lined

2 cups	all-purpose flour	500 mL
3 tbsp	packed brown sugar	45 mL
1 tbsp	baking powder	15 mL
½ tsp	salt	2 mL
1 cup	milk	250 mL
1	egg	1
¼ cup	butter or margarine, melted	50 mL
1 cup	fresh blueberries (or frozen)	250 mL
2 tbsp	granulated sugar	25 mL

1. In a large bowl, mix together flour, brown sugar, baking powder and salt.
2. In a small bowl, combine milk, egg, and butter; mix until well blended. Add to the flour mixture and stir just until moistened. Do not overmix. Fold in the blueberries.
3. Spoon batter into prepared muffin tin. Sprinkle sugar over tops. Bake in preheated oven for 20 to 25 minutes or until golden brown.

Blueberry Oat Muffins

Makes 12 muffins

- Preheat oven to 400°F (200°C)
- Muffin tin, greased or paper-lined

1 cup	quick-cooking rolled oats	250 mL
1 cup	water	250 mL
1 cup + 3 tbsp	oat bran	295 mL
1 tsp	baking powder	5 mL
½ tsp	baking soda	2 mL
½ tsp	sea salt	2 mL
¾ cup	packed brown sugar	175 mL
1	egg, beaten	1
¼ cup	vegetable oil	50 mL
1¼ cups	fresh or frozen blueberries	300 mL

1. In a medium bowl, combine quick-cooking oats and water. Set aside.
2. In a large bowl, mix together oat bran, baking powder, baking soda, sea salt and brown sugar. Add egg and oil and mix only until blended. Add the oats and mix only until blended. Fold in blueberries and stir only until moistened. Do not overmix.

3. Spoon batter into prepared muffin tin. Bake in preheated oven for 20 to 25 minutes or until done.

Blueberry Cornmeal Muffins

Makes 12 muffins

- Preheat oven to 400°F (200°C)
- Muffin tin, greased or paper-lined

1 cup	all-purpose flour	250 mL
1 cup	yellow cornmeal	250 mL
¼ cup	granulated sugar	50 mL
1 tsp	baking soda	5 mL
1 tsp	baking powder	5 mL
½ tsp	salt	2 mL
2 tsp	finely grated lemon zest	10 mL
1½ cups	buttermilk	375 mL
1	egg	1
¼ cup	butter or margarine, melted	50 mL
1 tsp	vanilla	5 mL
1½ cups	fresh blueberries (or frozen)	375 mL

1. In a large bowl, combine flour, cornmeal, sugar, baking soda, baking powder, salt and lemon zest.
2. In another bowl, whisk together buttermilk, egg, butter and vanilla. Pour into flour mixture and stir just until moistened. Do not overmix. Fold in blueberries.
3. Spoon batter into prepared muffin tin. Bake in preheated oven for 20 to 25 minutes or until golden brown.

Blueberry Orange Muffins

Makes 12 muffins

- Preheat oven to 400°F (200°C)
- Muffin tin, paper-lined

2 cups	all-purpose flour	500 mL
1 tbsp	baking powder	15 mL
½ tsp	ground cinnamon	2 mL
½ cup	vegetable oil	125 mL
2	eggs	2
⅓ cup	liquid honey	75 mL
¼ cup	milk	50 mL
¼ cup	orange juice	50 mL
1½ cups	fresh blueberries	375 mL

1. In a large bowl, combine flour, baking powder and cinnamon. Make a well in the center.
2. In another bowl, beat together oil, eggs, honey, milk and orange juice. Pour into flour mixture and blend just until moistened. Fold in blueberries.

3. Spoon batter into prepared muffin tin. Bake in preheated oven for 20 to 25 minutes or until golden brown.

• •

Blueberry Cheese Muffins

Makes 12 to 18 muffins
- Preheat oven to 400°F (200°C)
- Muffin tins, greased or paper-lined

1½ cups	all-purpose flour	375 mL
¼ cup	granulated sugar	50 mL
1 tbsp	baking powder	15 mL
1 tsp	salt	5 mL
1 cup	yellow cornmeal	250 mL
2 cups	shredded sharp Cheddar cheese	500 mL
2 cups	fresh blueberries, rinsed and drained	500 mL
1 cup	milk	250 mL
1	egg, beaten	1
¼ cup	butter or margarine, melted	50 mL

1. In a large bowl, mix together flour, sugar, baking powder, salt, cornmeal, cheese and blueberries.

2. In another bowl, beat together milk, egg and melted butter. Add all at once to the flour mixture, stirring just until blended.

3. Spoon batter into prepared muffin tins. Bake in preheated oven for 20 to 25 minutes.

• •

Miniature Orange Muffins

Makes 24 to 36 miniature muffins
- Preheat oven to 375°F (190°C)
- Miniature muffin tins, greased

2 cups	all-purpose flour	500 mL
1 tsp	baking soda	5 mL
1 tsp	salt	5 mL
1 tsp	grated orange zest	5 mL
½ cup	butter, at room temperature	125 mL
1 cup	granulated sugar	250 mL
¾ cup	sour cream	175 mL
½ cup	raisins	125 mL
½ cup	chopped nuts	125 mL
DIP		
1 cup	granulated sugar	250 mL
½ cup	freshly squeezed orange juice	125 mL

1. In a large bowl, combine flour, baking soda, salt and zest.

2. In another bowl, cream together butter and sugar. Add sour cream alternately with flour mixture, stirring just until moistened and blended. Fold in raisins and nuts.

3. Spoon batter into prepared muffin tin. Bake in preheated oven for 12 to 15 minutes.

4. *Prepare the dip:* In a small bowl, mix together sugar and orange juice. Dip warm muffins into dip mixture. Let cool before serving.

• •

Orange Raisin Muffins

Makes 12 muffins
- Preheat oven to 425°F (220°C)
- Muffin tin, greased

2 cups	all-purpose flour	500 mL
⅓ cup	granulated sugar	75 mL
½ tsp	salt	2 mL
¾ tsp	baking soda	4 mL
½ cup	raisins	125 mL
1	egg, well beaten	1
½ tsp	grated orange zest	2 mL
⅓ cup	freshly squeezed orange juice	75 mL
⅔ cup	buttermilk or sour milk	150 mL
⅓ cup	shortening	75 mL

1. In a large bowl, mix together flour, sugar, salt and baking soda. Add raisins.

2. In another bowl, combine beaten egg, orange zest and juice, buttermilk and shortening. Pour into dry ingredients and stir just until moistened and blended.

3. Spoon batter into prepared muffin tin. Bake in preheated oven for 25 minutes.

Tips *To make 1 cup (250 mL) of sour milk, measure 1 tbsp (15 mL) white vinegar or lemon juice into a measuring cup. Then fill to 1 cup (250 mL) with milk. Let stand about 5 minutes before using in your recipe.*

For a special treat, spread peanut butter on butter cookies or vanilla wafers. Place a toasted marshmallow between two cookies or wafers and press together slightly and — voila! — a Peanut Butter Puff.

Strawberry Jam–Filled Muffins

Makes 12 muffins
- Preheat oven to 400°F (200°C)
- Muffin tin, greased or paper-lined

1¾ cups	all-purpose flour	425 mL
½ cup	granulated sugar	125 mL
1 tbsp	baking powder	15 mL
½ tsp	salt	2 mL
2	eggs	2
⅔ cup	milk	150 mL
⅓ cup	butter or margarine, melted	75 mL
1 tsp	grated lemon zest	5 mL
½ cup	strawberry jam	125 mL

1. In a large bowl, mix together flour, sugar, baking powder and salt.
2. In another bowl, lightly beat eggs. Add milk, butter and lemon zest. Pour into flour mixture, stirring just until moistened and blended. Do not overmix.
3. Spoon half the batter into prepared muffin tin. Make a well in the center of each cup and add a spoonful of jam. Spoon the remaining batter over jam. Bake in preheated oven for 20 to 25 minutes or until golden brown.

Variation *Substitute raspberry jam (or any other favorite jam) for the strawberry.*

Peanut Butter Muffins

Makes 12 muffins
- Preheat oven to 400°F (200°C)
- Muffin tin, paper-lined

2 cups	all-purpose flour	500 mL
1 tbsp	baking powder	15 mL
½ tsp	salt	2 mL
1¼ cups	milk	300 mL
1	egg	1
3 tbsp	granulated sugar	45 mL
½ cup	peanut butter	125 mL

1. In a large bowl, mix together flour, baking powder and salt. Make a well in the center.
2. In a blender, combine milk, egg, sugar and peanut butter. Cover and blend until thoroughly mixed. Add all at once to dry ingredients and stir just until moistened. Do not overmix.
3. Spoon batter into prepared muffin tin. Bake in preheated oven for 25 to 30 minutes or until golden brown.

Peanut Butter Banana Muffins

Makes 12 muffins
- Preheat oven to 400°F (200°C)
- Muffin tin, greased or paper-lined

2 cups	all-purpose flour	500 mL
½ cup	packed brown sugar	125 mL
1 tbsp	baking powder	15 mL
¼ tsp	salt	1 mL
½ cup	peanut butter (chunky or smooth)	125 mL
2 tbsp	vegetable oil	25 mL
2	eggs	2
¾ cup	milk	175 mL
2	ripe bananas, mashed	2

1. In a large bowl, combine flour, brown sugar, baking powder and salt.
2. In another bowl, combine peanut butter, oil, eggs, milk and mashed bananas. Add to flour mixture, stirring just until moistened and blended.
3. Spoon batter evenly into prepared muffin tin. Bake in preheated oven for 20 minutes or until done.

Crunchy Peanut Butter and Jelly Muffins

Makes 12 muffins
- Preheat oven to 400°F (200°C)
- Muffin tin, paper-lined

2 cups	all-purpose flour	500 mL
½ cup	granulated sugar	125 mL
2½ tsp	baking powder	12 mL
½ tsp	salt	2 mL
¾ cup	crunchy peanut butter	175 mL
¾ cup	milk	175 mL
2	eggs	2
¼ cup	jam or jelly	50 mL

1. In a large bowl, mix together flour, sugar, baking powder and salt. Using a pastry blender or two knives, cut in peanut butter until mixture resembles coarse crumbs. Add milk and eggs all at once, stirring just until moistened and blended.
2. Spoon 2 tbsp (25 mL) batter into each prepared cup. Put 1 tsp (5 mL) jam or jelly in center of each. Top with another 2 tbsp (25 mL) batter. Bake in preheated oven for about 20 minutes.

Peanut Butter Oat Muffins

Makes 12 to 18 muffins
- Preheat oven to 375°F (190°C)
- Muffin tins, greased or paper-lined

1½ cups	whole wheat flour	375 mL
1½ cups	old-fashioned rolled oats	375 mL
4 tsp	baking powder	20 mL
1 tsp	salt	5 mL
1 tsp	baking soda	5 mL
½ cup	raisins	125 mL
1 cup	plain yogurt	250 mL
¾ cup	liquid honey	175 mL
½ cup	peanut butter	125 mL
⅓ cup	vegetable oil	75 mL
3	eggs, lightly beaten	3
1 tsp	vanilla	5 mL

1. In a large bowl, combine flour, oats, baking powder, salt and baking soda. Stir in raisins.
2. In another bowl, beat together yogurt, honey, peanut butter, oil, eggs and vanilla until smooth. Add to dry ingredients and stir just until moistened and blended. Do not overmix.
3. Spoon batter into prepared muffin tins. Bake in preheated oven for 25 to 30 minutes or until done.

Peanut Pops

Makes 8 pops
- 8-cup muffin tin
- Eight 5-oz (150 mL) paper drinking cups
- 8 plastic spoons

1 cup	finely crushed peanut brittle	250 mL
4 cups	vanilla ice cream	1 L
8 tbsp	peanut butter	125 mL

1. Place a paper cup in each ungreased muffin tin cup. Add 1 tbsp (15 mL) peanut brittle to each. Spoon in some ice cream to half fill each cup. Add 1 tbsp (15 mL) peanut butter and then the remaining ice cream. Top with the remaining peanut brittle.
2. With the back of a spoon, pack mixture down firmly. Insert a plastic spoon, bowl-end down, into each cup. Wrap each cup in foil and place muffin tin in freezer.
3. When firm, peel off foil, lift out cups and eat ice cream on a stick. Or leave cups on, pull out spoon and enjoy an ice cream sundae.

Chocolate Muffins

Makes 12 muffins
- Preheat oven to 400°F (200°C)
- Muffin tin, greased or paper-lined

1⅔ cups	all-purpose flour	400 mL
¾ cup	granulated sugar	175 mL
⅓ cup	unsweetened cocoa powder	75 mL
3½ tsp	baking powder	17 mL
½ tsp	salt	2 mL
1	egg	1
1 cup	milk	250 mL
¼ cup	vegetable oil or shortening, melted	50 mL

1. In a large bowl, combine flour, sugar, cocoa, baking powder and salt.
2. In another bowl, beat together egg, milk and oil. Pour into the flour mixture and stir just until combined. Do not overmix.
3. Spoon batter into prepared muffin tin. Bake in preheated oven for 20 to 25 minutes.

Double Chocolate Muffins

Makes 12 large muffins
- Preheat oven to 400°F (200°C)
- Muffin tin, paper-lined

1 cup	semisweet chocolate chips, divided	250 mL
1 tbsp	instant coffee powder or granules	15 mL
¼ cup	margarine	50 mL
1¼ cups	milk	300 mL
1	egg	1
2½ cups	all-purpose flour	625 mL
⅓ cup	granulated sugar	75 mL
1 tbsp	baking powder	15 mL
½ tsp	salt	2 mL

1. In a saucepan over low heat, melt half the chocolate chips, coffee, margarine and milk, stirring to blend well. Set aside. When mixture cools, beat in egg.
2. In a large bowl, combine flour, sugar, baking powder and salt. Stir in chocolate mixture, stirring just until moistened. Fold in the remaining chocolate chips.
3. Spoon batter into prepared muffin tin. Bake in preheated oven for 20 minutes or until a toothpick inserted in center of a muffin comes out clean and dry.

Chocolate Lovers' Delight

Makes 12 muffins
- Preheat oven to 400°F (200°C)
- Muffin tin, paper-lined

3 oz	unsweetened chocolate	90 g
1/3 cup	vegetable oil	75 mL
2	eggs	2
1 tsp	vanilla	5 mL
1 1/3 cups	milk	325 mL
2 cups	all-purpose flour	500 mL
1/2 cup	granulated sugar	125 mL
2 tsp	baking soda	10 mL
1 cup	semisweet chocolate chips, divided	250 mL

1. In a saucepan over low heat, melt the chocolate with the oil (or microwave on Medium for 2 minutes). Remove from heat and add eggs, vanilla and milk; blend well.
2. In a large bowl, combine flour, sugar and baking soda. Add the chocolate mixture and half the chocolate chips, stirring only until moistened.
3. Spoon batter into prepared muffin tin. Sprinkle with the remaining chocolate chips. Bake in preheated oven for 20 to 25 minutes or until a toothpick inserted in the center comes out clean.

Tip *An ice cream scoop makes filling muffin cups a breeze. To make muffins mushroom out, use an oiled scoop.*

Chocolate Chip Muffins

Makes 12 muffins
- Preheat oven to 400°F (200°C)
- Muffin tin, greased or paper-lined

1	egg	1
1 cup	sour cream	250 mL
1/2 cup	milk	125 mL
1 3/4 cups	all-purpose flour	425 mL
2 tbsp	granulated sugar	25 mL
1 tsp	baking powder	5 mL
1/2 tsp	baking soda	2 mL
1 tsp	salt	5 mL
1 cup	semisweet chocolate chips	250 mL

1. In a bowl, beat egg. Stir in sour cream and milk.
2. In a large bowl, combine flour, sugar, baking powder, baking soda and salt. Pour egg mixture into flour mixture and stir just until moistened. Fold in chocolate chips.

3. Spoon batter into prepared muffin tin. Bake in preheated oven for 20 to 25 minutes.

Chocolate Chip Banana Muffins

Makes 12 muffins
- Preheat oven to 425°F (220°C)
- Muffin tin, greased or paper-lined

2	ripe bananas	2
1 tsp	baking soda	5 mL
1 tsp	hot water	5 mL
1/2 cup	margarine or vegetable oil	125 mL
3/4 cup	granulated sugar	175 mL
1	egg, beaten	1
1 tsp	vanilla	5 mL
1 1/2 cups	all-purpose flour	375 mL
1 tsp	baking powder	5 mL
1 tsp	salt	5 mL
5 oz	semisweet chocolate chips	150 g

1. In a medium bowl, mash bananas. Add baking soda and hot water and set aside.
2. In a large bowl, cream together margarine and sugar. Add egg and vanilla; mix well. Add flour, baking powder and salt. Add banana mixture and blend together. Add chocolate chips; stir just until moistened.
3. Spoon batter into prepared muffin tin. Bake in preheated oven for 15 to 20 minutes.

Chocolate Chunk Banana Muffins

Makes 12 muffins
- Preheat oven to 375°F (190°C)
- Muffin tin, greased or paper-lined

1 cup	mashed overripe bananas (about 2 medium)	250 mL
1 cup	low-fat Miracle Whip	250 mL
1/2 cup	granulated sugar	125 mL
1/2 tsp	vanilla	2 mL
2 cups	all-purpose flour	500 mL
2 tsp	baking soda	10 mL
1/2 cup	chocolate chunks (or cut up a plain chocolate bar)	125 mL

1. In a large bowl, combine bananas, Miracle Whip, sugar and vanilla.
2. In another bowl, whisk together flour and baking soda. Fold into the banana mixture and stir just until blended. Fold in chocolate chunks.

3. Spoon batter into prepared muffin tin. Bake in preheated oven for 20 minutes or until golden brown.

Tip *You could use chocolate chips in place of the chocolate chunks. Using the Miracle Whip means you don't have to add an egg to this recipe, and the muffins are nice and moist.*

Fudgey Nut Muffins

Makes 12 small muffins
- Preheat oven to 400°F (200°C)
- Muffin tin, greased or paper-lined

1 cup	all-purpose flour	250 mL
1⅓ cups	granulated sugar	325 mL
1¼ tsp	baking powder	6 mL
½ tsp	salt	2 mL
¼ tsp	baking soda	1 mL
1 cup	milk	250 mL
3 tbsp	butter or shortening, melted	45 mL
1	egg	1
½ tsp	vanilla	2 mL
3 oz	unsweetened chocolate, melted and cooled	90 g
1	package (6 oz/175 g) semisweet chocolate chips	1
½ cup	chopped walnuts	125 mL

1. In a large bowl, combine flour, sugar, baking powder, salt and baking soda. Make a well in the center. Add milk, butter, egg, vanilla and melted chocolate; stir just until moistened and blended. Fold in the chocolate chips and walnuts.

2. Spoon batter into prepared muffin tin. Bake in preheated oven for 20 to 25 minutes or until toothpick inserted in center of a muffin comes out clean and dry.

Tips *Hey kids! Get Mom to buy your favorite cake mix. Prepare the batter as directed on the package. Use flat-bottomed ice-cream cones. Fill one-quarter full with the batter. Bake at 375°F (190°C) for 20 minutes or until done. Frost and decorate with chocolate chips, miniature marshmallows, candy, raisins or whatever you happen to have on hand.*

To avoid the mess of serving ice cream at children's parties, prepare the ice cream in balls. Put them into muffin tins and store in freezer until it is time to serve them. This makes dishing it out easier and faster and avoids the usual "He/she got more than I did!"

Hot Chocolate Puddings with Marshmallow Topping

Makes 6 puddings
- Six 6-oz (175 g) ramekins

1	package chocolate pudding and pie filling	1
2 cups	miniature marshmallows, divided	500 mL

1. Prepare pudding as directed on package. Remove from heat and stir in 1½ cups (375 mL) of the marshmallows just until mixed, not melted. Pour into ramekins. Top with the remaining marshmallows. Serve hot.

Barbecue Muffins

Makes 10 muffins
- Preheat oven to 375°F (190°C)
- Muffin tin, greased

1	package (10 oz/284 g) refrigerated buttermilk biscuits	1
½ cup	tomato ketchup	125 mL
3 tbsp	packed brown sugar	45 mL
1 tbsp	cider vinegar	15 mL
½ tsp	chili powder	2 mL
1 lb	lean ground beef	500 g
1 cup	shredded Cheddar cheese	250 mL

1. Remove dough from package and separate into 10 biscuits. With the palm of your hand or a small rolling pin, flatten each biscuit into 5-inch (12.5 cm) circles. Press dough into the bottom and up the sides of each prepared cup. Set aside.

2. In a small bowl, combine ketchup, brown sugar, vinegar and chili powder, stirring until smooth.

3. In a skillet over medium-high heat, brown the ground beef. Drain the fat and add ketchup mixture, mixing well.

4. Divide meat equally among the biscuit-lined muffin cups, about ¼ cup (50 mL) each. Sprinkle with cheese. Bake in preheated oven for 20 minutes or until golden brown. Let cool before serving.

Tip *Make mini meat loaves by patting meat mixture into muffin pan cups. Brush each generously with barbecue sauce and bake.*

Pizza Muffins

Makes 12 muffins
- Preheat oven to 375°F (190°C)
- Muffin tin, greased

1½ cups	chopped pepperoni sausage	375 mL
1	green bell pepper, finely chopped	1
1	can (10 oz/284 mL) sliced mushrooms	1
1	onion, finely chopped	1
1¼ cups	shredded cheese (such as Monterey Jack)	300 mL
½ cup	pizza sauce	125 mL
2 tsp	garlic powder	10 mL
5	eggs	5
¼ cup	vegetable oil	50 mL
1¼ cups	all-purpose flour	300 mL
1 tbsp	baking powder	15 mL

1. In a large bowl, combine pepperoni, green pepper, mushrooms, onion, cheese, pizza sauce and garlic powder.
2. In another bowl, beat eggs. Blend in oil, then flour and baking powder. Beat until smooth. Stir in pepperoni mixture and mix until well blended.
3. Spoon batter into prepared muffin tin. Bake in preheated oven for 20 to 25 minutes or until lightly browned.

Chili Muffins

Makes 8 muffins
- Preheat oven to 400°F (200°C)
- Muffin tin

1 lb	lean ground beef	500 g
¾ cup	salsa (medium), divided	175 mL
1 tsp	chili powder	5 mL
½ tsp	salt	2 mL
¼ tsp	freshly ground black pepper	1 mL
1	can (14 oz/398 mL) red kidney beans, rinsed and drained	1
½ cup	shredded Cheddar cheese (or Monterey Jack, etc.)	125 mL

1. In a large bowl, break up the beef with a fork. Mix in ¼ cup (50 mL) of the salsa, chili powder, salt and pepper. Divide evenly into 8 muffin cups. Press into the center of each to form a well and press into the bottom and up sides of each cup. Bake in preheated oven for 10 minutes or until the meat is no longer pink.
2. In another bowl, combine beans and the remaining salsa. Spoon into the muffin cups. Sprinkle with cheese. Bake for 7 to 8 minutes or until the beans are hot and the cheese is melted.

Pepperoni Muffins

Makes 12 large muffins
- Preheat oven to 400°F (200°C)
- Muffin tin, greased or paper-lined

2½ cups	all-purpose flour	625 mL
¼ cup	freshly grated Parmesan cheese	50 mL
2 tbsp	packed brown sugar	25 mL
1 tbsp	baking powder	15 mL
½ tsp	salt	2 mL
1 tsp	dried oregano or basil	5 mL
1 cup	chopped pepperoni (casings removed)	250 mL
4 oz	cream cheese, softened	125 g
1 cup	milk	250 mL
2	eggs	2
½ cup	margarine or butter, melted	125 mL

1. In a large bowl, combine flour, cheese, brown sugar, baking powder, salt, oregano and pepperoni.
2. In another bowl, beat cream cheese, gradually adding milk. Add eggs, one at a time, and beat well. Stir in margarine. Add to flour mixture, stirring just until moistened.
3. Spoon batter into prepared muffin tin. Bake in preheated oven for about 20 minutes. Serve warm.

Hamburger Muffins

Makes 18 muffins

- Preheat oven to 350°F (180°C)
- Muffin tins

18	slices white or brown bread	18
	Butter	
1 lb	lean ground beef	500 g
1 cup	canned mushroom soup	250 mL
¼ cup	chopped onions	50 mL
1	egg, beaten	1
½ cup	shredded Cheddar cheese	125 mL
1 tsp	Worcestershire sauce	5 mL
	Salt and freshly ground black pepper	

1. Trim the crusts off bread slices and flatten slightly with a rolling pin. Butter each slice on one side and place, buttered-side down, in muffin cups. Set aside.
2. In a bowl, mix together meat, soup, onions, egg, cheese, Worcestershire sauce and salt and pepper to taste. Spoon mixture evenly over bread slices. Bake in preheated oven for 35 to 45 minutes or until meat is well-cooked.

Meal in a Muffin

Makes 6 muffins

- Preheat oven to 350°F (180°C)
- Muffin tin

8 oz	boiled ham, cut into chunks	250 g
1½	slices rye bread, crusts removed and torn into pieces	1½
2 tbsp	minced green onion	25 mL
2 tbsp	chopped fresh parsley	25 mL
1	egg yolk	1
1 tbsp	unsweetened apricot jam	15 mL
1 tsp	honey mustard	5 mL

1. In a food processor, combine ham, bread, onion, parsley, egg yolk and jam; process until ground.
2. Spoon mixture evenly into muffin cups. Bake in preheated oven for 30 minutes. Remove from oven and brush tops with mustard. Return to oven and bake for 5 more minutes. Remove from cups and cool just enough to eat.

Funny Face Tuna Melts

Serves 4 to 6

- Preheat broiler
- Small baking sheet

1	can (6.5 oz/184 g) flaked tuna, drained	1
2 tbsp	mayonnaise	25 mL
1	stalk celery, chopped	1
¼ cup	shredded Cheddar cheese	50 mL
	Freshly ground black pepper	
2 to 3	English muffins, split in half	2 to 3
	Pickle slices	
	Olives	
	Tomato slices	

1. In a bowl, combine tuna, mayonnaise, celery, cheese and pepper to taste. Divide mixture evenly over each muffin half.
2. Make "funny faces" on each half, using pickle slices for eyes, olives for the nose and half a tomato slice for smiling mouths. Use any other garnishes you have on hand as well. Place under the broiler for 3 to 5 minutes or until cheese melts.

Little Miss Muffins

Serves 4

- Preheat broiler
- Small baking sheet

1	can (6.5 oz/184 g) flaked chicken or tuna, well-drained	1
¼ cup	mayonnaise	50 mL
1	tomato, peeled, seeded and chopped	1
1 tbsp	freshly squeezed lemon juice	15 mL
	Salt and freshly ground black pepper	
	Butter	
2	English muffins, split and toasted	2
1	small cucumber, sliced	1
2	slices processed cheese, each cut diagonally in half	2
1	tomato, sliced	1

1. In a bowl, mix together chicken, mayonnaise, chopped tomato, lemon juice and salt and pepper to taste.
2. Butter the toasted English muffins and put cucumber slices and chicken mixture on each half. Top with cheese and tomato slices. Broil for 2 to 3 minutes or until cheese melts.

Special Occasion Muffins

Passover Popovers

Makes 12 popovers
- Preheat oven to 450°F (230°C)
- Muffin tin, greased

½ cup	vegetable oil or shortening	125 mL
1½ cups	water	375 mL
2 tbsp	granulated sugar	25 mL
1½ cups	cake meal	375 mL
7	eggs	7

1. In a saucepan over medium-high heat, combine oil, water and sugar; bring to a boil. Remove from heat. Add cake meal; cool slightly. Add eggs one at a time; beat after each addition.
2. In preheated oven, heat prepared muffin tin. Spoon batter into cups, filling three-quarters full. Bake in preheated oven for 20 minutes. Lower heat to 350°F (180°C); bake for another 25 to 30 minutes.

Passover Apple Muffins

Makes 12 muffins
- Preheat oven to 425°F (220°C)
- Muffin tin, greased

FILLING

⅓ cup	granulated sugar	75 mL
1½ tsp	ground cinnamon	7 mL
1 tbsp	margarine, melted	15 mL

MUFFINS

4	egg yolks	4
⅔ cup	granulated sugar	150 mL
2 cups	grated apples	500 mL
½ tsp	grated lemon zest	2 mL
1 tbsp	freshly squeezed lemon juice	15 mL
1 cup	matzo meal	250 mL
½ tsp	ground cinnamon	2 mL
4	egg whites, beaten until stiff	4
Pinch	salt	Pinch

1. *Prepare the filling:* In a bowl, combine sugar, cinnamon and margarine; mix well. Set aside.
2. *Prepare the muffins:* In another bowl, beat together egg yolks and sugar. Add apples, lemon zest, lemon juice, matzo meal and cinnamon; mix well. Fold in egg whites and salt.
3. Spoon some of the batter into prepared muffin tin, filling half full. Sprinkle with filling. Top with the remaining batter. Bake in preheated oven for 15 to 20 minutes.

Passover Blueberry Muffins

Makes 12 small muffins
- Preheat oven to 350°F (180°C)
- Muffin tin, greased or paper-lined

1 cup	granulated sugar	250 mL
½ cup	vegetable oil	125 mL
3	eggs	3
½ cup	cake meal	125 mL
¼ cup	potato starch	50 mL
¼ tsp	salt	1 mL
1	package (10 oz/300 g) frozen blueberries, thawed and drained	1
	Ground cinnamon (optional)	
	Granulated sugar (optional)	

1. In a bowl, combine sugar, oil and eggs; beat well.
2. In another bowl, sift together cake meal, potato starch and salt. Add to egg mixture; stir until blended. Fold in blueberries.
3. Spoon batter into prepared muffin tin. Sprinkle with cinnamon and sugar, if desired. Bake in preheated oven for 30 minutes or until browned.

Passover Cocoa Brownies

Makes 8 to 12 muffins
- Preheat oven to 400°F (200°C)
- Muffin tin, greased

½ cup	unsweetened cocoa powder	125 mL
½ cup	boiling water	125 mL
2	eggs	2
1 cup	granulated sugar	250 mL
½ cup	vegetable oil	125 mL
½ cup	cake meal	125 mL
1 tsp	instant coffee powder or granules, dissolved in 2 tsp (10 mL) water	5 mL
½ cup	chopped walnuts	125 mL

1. In a bowl, combine cocoa and water; mix to form a paste. Set aside.
2. In a bowl, combine eggs, sugar and oil; beat until well blended. Add cocoa paste; mix well. Add cake meal, coffee mixture and walnuts.
3. Spoon batter into prepared muffin tin, dividing evenly. Bake in preheated oven for 20 to 25 minutes.

Traditional Pumpkin Muffins

Makes 12 muffins
- Preheat oven to 400°F (200°C)
- Muffin tin, greased or paper-lined

1 cup	all-purpose flour	250 mL
1 cup	whole wheat flour	250 mL
½ cup	lightly packed brown sugar	125 mL
1 tbsp	baking powder	15 mL
1½ tsp	ground cinnamon	7 mL
½ tsp	ground nutmeg	2 mL
2	egg whites	2
½ cup	milk	125 mL
1 cup	canned pumpkin purée (not pie filling)	250 mL
¼ cup	vegetable oil	50 mL
½ tsp	vanilla	2 mL
¾ cup	raisins	175 mL

1. In a bowl, combine all-purpose flour, whole wheat flour, brown sugar, baking powder, cinnamon and nutmeg; blend well. Make a well in the center.
2. In another bowl, beat egg whites. Add milk, pumpkin, oil and vanilla; blend well. Add to dry ingredients; stir just until moist. Add raisins.
3. Spoon batter into prepared muffin tin. Bake in preheated oven for 20 to 25 minutes or until browned.

Creamy Pumpkin Nut Muffins

Makes 12 muffins
- Preheat oven to 400°F (200°C)
- Muffin tin, greased or paper-lined

CREAM CHEESE FILLING

4 oz	cream cheese, softened	125 mL
2 tbsp	packed brown sugar	25 mL
1½ tsp	maple flavoring	7 mL

MUFFINS

2 cups	all-purpose flour	500 mL
¾ cup	packed brown sugar	175 mL
½ cup	chopped walnuts	125 mL
2 tsp	baking powder	10 mL
1 tsp	ground cinnamon	5 mL
½ tsp	baking soda	2 mL
¼ tsp	salt	1 mL
2	eggs	2
1 cup	canned pumpkin purée (not pie filling)	250 mL
¾ cup	evaporated milk	175 mL
¼ cup	vegetable oil	50 mL
2 tsp	maple flavoring	10 mL

NUT TOPPING

¼ cup	chopped walnuts	50 mL
2 tbsp	packed brown sugar	25 mL

1. *Prepare the filling:* In a bowl, mix together cream cheese, brown sugar and maple flavoring until smooth. Set aside.
2. *Prepare the muffins:* In a large bowl, mix together flour, brown sugar, nuts, baking powder, cinnamon, baking soda and salt. Make a well in the center.
3. In another bowl, whisk together eggs, pumpkin, evaporated milk, oil and maple flavoring until well blended. Add to flour mixture, stirring just until moistened and blended. Do not overmix.
4. *Prepare the topping:* In a small bowl, combine walnuts and brown sugar.
5. Spoon batter into prepared muffin tin. Add 1 heaping tsp (5 mL) cream cheese filling to each cup. Sprinkle with topping. Bake in preheated oven for about 20 minutes.

Tip *To keep a bowl from slipping on a working surface, place it on a folded wet towel.*

Apple Streusel Pumpkin Muffins

Makes 12 to 18 muffins
- Preheat oven to 375°F (190°C)
- Muffin tins, greased or paper-lined

STREUSEL TOPPING

2 tbsp	all-purpose flour	25 mL
¼ cup	granulated sugar	50 mL
½ tsp	ground cinnamon	2 mL
4 tsp	butter	20 mL

MUFFINS

2½ cups	all-purpose flour	625 mL
2 cups	granulated sugar	500 mL
1 tsp	baking soda	5 mL
1 tbsp	pumpkin pie spice	15 mL
½ tsp	salt	2 mL
2	eggs, beaten	2
1 cup	canned pumpkin purée (not pie filling)	250 mL
½ cup	vegetable oil	125 mL
2 cups	finely chopped apples	500 mL

1. *Prepare the topping:* In a bowl, combine flour, sugar and cinnamon. Cut in butter; mix until coarse and crumbly. Set aside.

2. *Prepare the muffins:* In another bowl, combine flour, sugar, baking soda, pumpkin pie spice and salt. Make a well in the center.

3. In another bowl, combine eggs, pumpkin and oil; stir just until blended. Add apples; blend well. Add to dry ingredients; stir just until moist.

4. Spoon batter into prepared muffin tins. Sprinkle with topping. Bake in preheated oven for 25 to 30 minutes.

• •

Orange Pumpkin Muffins

Makes 12 muffins

- Preheat oven to 400°F (200°C)
- Muffin tin, greased or paper-lined

1¾ cups	all-purpose flour	425 mL
2½ tsp	baking powder	12 mL
½ tsp	baking soda	2 mL
½ tsp	salt	2 mL
⅔ cup	packed brown sugar	150 mL
1 tsp	ground cinnamon	5 mL
¼ tsp	ground nutmeg	1 mL
Pinch	ground ginger	Pinch
Pinch	ground mace	Pinch
1	egg	1
¼ cup	melted butter or margarine, cooled	50 mL
½ cup	milk	125 mL
	Finely grated zest of 1 orange	
½ cup	freshly squeezed orange juice	125 mL
¾ cup	canned pumpkin purée (not pie filling)	175 mL

1. In a bowl, combine flour, baking powder, baking soda, salt, brown sugar, cinnamon, nutmeg, ginger and mace. Make a well in the center.

2. In another bowl, whisk together egg, butter, milk, orange zest, orange juice and pumpkin. Add to dry ingredients; stir just until blended.

3. Spoon batter into prepared muffin tin. Bake in preheated oven for about 20 minutes.

• •

Christmas Morning Muffins

Makes 12 to 18 muffins

- Preheat oven to 375°F (190°C)
- Muffin tins, greased or paper-lined

2 cups	all-purpose flour	500 mL
½ cup	wheat germ	125 mL
4 tsp	baking powder	20 mL
1 tsp	baking soda	5 mL
1 tsp	salt	5 mL
½ cup	granulated sugar	125 mL
1 tsp	ground cardamom	5 mL
½ cup	chopped almonds	125 mL
½ cup	raisins	125 mL
1 cup	glazed mixed fruit	250 mL
2	eggs	2
1 cup	buttermilk	250 mL
½ cup	melted butter or margarine	125 mL

1. In a bowl, combine flour, wheat germ, baking powder, baking soda, salt, sugar, cardamom, almonds, raisins and mixed fruit.

2. In another bowl, whisk together eggs, buttermilk and butter. Add to dry ingredients; stir quickly just until ingredients are moist.

3. Spoon batter into prepared muffin tins. Bake in preheated oven for 20 to 25 minutes.

• •

Christmas Tea Muffins

Makes 12 muffins

- Preheat oven to 375°F (190°C)
- Muffin tin, greased or paper-lined

2 cups	all-purpose flour	500 mL
1 tbsp	baking powder	15 mL
½ cup	granulated sugar	125 mL
1 tsp	salt	5 mL
¾ cup	milk	175 mL
3 tbsp	maraschino cherry juice	45 mL
¼ cup	vegetable oil	50 mL
1	egg	1
⅓ cup	chopped maraschino cherries	75 mL
¼ cup	chopped almonds	50 mL

1. In a bowl, sift together flour, baking powder, sugar and salt.

2. In another bowl, whisk together milk, cherry juice, oil and egg. Add to dry ingredients; stir in cherries and almonds. Stir just until blended.

3. Spoon batter into prepared muffin tin. Bake in preheated oven for 25 minutes.

Cranberry Tea Muffins

Makes 12 muffins

- Preheat oven to 400°F (200°C)
- Muffin tin, greased or paper-lined

2 cups	cake and pastry flour	500 mL
1/3 cup	granulated sugar	75 mL
2 tsp	baking powder	10 mL
1/2 tsp	salt	2 mL
2	eggs	2
3/4 cup	milk	175 mL
1/4 cup	melted butter	50 mL
1 cup	chopped fresh cranberries	250 mL
1 tsp	grated orange zest	5 mL

1. In a bowl, combine flour, sugar, baking powder and salt.
2. In another bowl, whisk together eggs, milk and butter. Add to flour mixture; stir quickly just until blended. Fold in cranberries and orange zest.
3. Spoon batter into prepared muffin tin. Bake in preheated oven for 20 to 25 minutes.

Traditional Cranberry Muffins

Makes 12 muffins

- Preheat oven to 375°F (190°C)
- Muffin tin, greased

1 1/2 cups	all-purpose flour	375 mL
1/2 cup	granulated sugar	125 mL
1 tbsp	baking powder	15 mL
1/4 tsp	salt	1 mL
1	egg	1
1 cup	milk	250 mL
1/3 cup	melted butter or margarine	75 mL
1 cup	fresh or frozen cranberries, thawed and drained	250 mL
1/2 cup	chopped nuts	125 mL

1. In a bowl, combine flour, sugar, baking powder and salt.
2. In another bowl, whisk together egg, milk and butter. Add to dry ingredients; stir just until moist and blended. Fold in cranberries and nuts.
3. Spoon batter into prepared muffin tin. Bake in preheated oven for 20 to 25 minutes.

Tip *Add a few teaspoons of sugar and cinnamon to an empty pie plate and slowly burn over the stove. Your home will smell like a bakery.*

Cranberry Upside-Down Muffins

Makes 12 to 18 muffins

- Preheat oven to 375°F (190°C)
- Muffin tins, greased

3/4 cup	whole-berry cranberry sauce	175 mL
1/4 cup	chopped pecans	50 mL
2 tbsp	granulated sugar	25 mL
1/4 tsp	ground nutmeg	1 mL
12	pecan halves	12
1/2 cup	butter or margarine (room temperature)	125 mL
1/2 cup	granulated sugar	125 mL
2 tsp	baking powder	10 mL
1/2 tsp	salt	2 mL
2	eggs	2
2 cups	all-purpose flour	500 mL
1/2 cup	buttermilk	125 mL

1. In a bowl, mix together cranberry sauce, chopped pecans, sugar and nutmeg. Divide evenly among muffin cups. Press 1 pecan half into center of each cup. Set aside.
2. In a large bowl, beat together butter, sugar, baking powder and salt until pale and fluffy. Beat in eggs. Gently stir in flour alternately with buttermilk, beginning and ending with flour.
3. Spoon batter gently over cranberry mixture. Bake in preheated oven for about 20 minutes. Let cool slightly and then invert muffin pan over a plate.

Cranberry Swirl Muffins

Makes 12 small muffins

- Preheat oven to 400°F (200°C)
- Muffin tin, paper-lined

1/4 cup	shortening	50 mL
1/2 cup	granulated sugar	125 mL
2	egg whites	2
1 1/2 cups	all-purpose flour	375 mL
2 tsp	baking powder	10 mL
1/2 tsp	salt (optional)	2 mL
3/4 cup	milk	175 mL
1/2 cup	cranberry sauce	125 mL

1. In a bowl, cream together shortening and sugar. Add egg whites; beat until fairly smooth. Add flour, baking powder, salt (if using) and milk; stir just until blended. Add cranberry sauce; swirl with spatula through batter.

2. Spoon batter into prepared muffin tin, dividing evenly. Bake in preheated oven for 20 minutes or until golden brown.

• •

Cranberry Streusel Muffins

Makes 12 muffins
- Preheat oven to 375°F (190°C)
- Muffin tin, greased or paper-lined

STREUSEL TOPPING

2 tbsp	all-purpose flour	25 mL
2 tbsp	granulated sugar	25 mL
¼ tsp	ground cinnamon	1 mL
2 tbsp	butter or margarine	25 mL

MUFFINS

¼ cup	butter or margarine, softened	50 mL
¼ cup	granulated sugar	50 mL
1	egg	1
1 tsp	vanilla	5 mL
2 cups	all-purpose flour	500 mL
2 tsp	baking powder	10 mL
Pinch	salt	Pinch
½ cup	milk	125 mL
2 cups	coarsely chopped cranberries	500 mL
½ cup	confectioner's (icing) sugar	125 mL

1. *Prepare the topping:* In a bowl, combine flour, sugar and cinnamon. Cut in butter until mixture is crumbly. Set aside.

2. *Prepare the muffins:* In another bowl, combine butter and sugar; cream until light and fluffy. Beat in egg and vanilla.

3. In a bowl, combine flour, baking powder and salt. Add to creamed mixture alternately with milk; stir just until moist. In another bowl, combine cranberries and confectioner's sugar; fold into batter.

4. Spoon batter into prepared muffin tin. Sprinkle with streusel topping. Bake in preheated oven for 25 to 30 minutes.

• •

Cranberry-Filled Almond Muffins

Makes 12 muffins
- Preheat oven to 375°F (190°C)
- Muffin tin, greased or paper-lined

1½ cups	all-purpose flour	375 mL
½ cup	granulated sugar	125 mL
1 tsp	baking powder	5 mL
¼ tsp	baking soda	1 mL
¼ tsp	salt	1 mL
2	eggs	2
¼ cup	melted margarine	50 mL
½ cup	sour cream	125 mL
½ tsp	almond extract	2 mL
¾ cup	sliced almonds, divided	175 mL
½ cup	whole-berry cranberry sauce	125 mL

1. In a bowl, combine flour, sugar, baking powder, baking soda and salt.

2. In another bowl, whisk together eggs, margarine, sour cream and almond extract; blend well. Add ½ cup (125 mL) of the almonds. Add to flour mixture; stir just until blended.

3. Spoon batter into prepared muffin tin, filling half full. Add 1 tbsp (15 mL) cranberry sauce to each; top with the remaining batter. Sprinkle evenly with the remaining almonds. Bake in preheated oven for 30 to 35 minutes or until golden brown.

• •

Cranberry Applesauce Muffins

Makes 12 muffins
- Preheat oven to 400°F (200°C)
- Muffin tin, greased

1¾ cups	all-purpose flour	425 mL
½ cup	granulated sugar, divided	125 mL
1½ tsp	baking powder	7 mL
½ tsp	baking soda	2 mL
½ tsp	salt	2 mL
1	egg	1
¾ cup	milk	175 mL
¾ cup	sweetened applesauce	175 mL
¼ cup	melted butter or margarine	50 mL
1 cup	coarsely chopped cranberries	250 mL
2 tbsp	all-purpose flour	25 mL
½ tsp	ground cinnamon	2 mL

1. In a bowl, combine flour, half the sugar, baking powder, baking soda and salt. Make a well in the center.

2. In another bowl, combine egg, milk, applesauce and butter; mix well. Add to flour mixture; stir quickly just until batter is moist.

3. In another bowl, combine cranberries and flour; toss well. Fold into batter.

4. Spoon batter into prepared muffin tin. Sprinkle tops with the remaining sugar and cinnamon. Bake in preheated oven for 20 to 25 minutes.

Apricot Cranberry Bran Muffins

Makes 12 muffins
- Preheat oven to 400°F (200°C)
- Muffin tin, greased or paper-lined

1¾ cups	all-purpose flour	425 mL
⅓ cup	packed brown sugar	75 mL
2 tsp	baking powder	10 mL
½ tsp	salt	2 mL
2	eggs	2
2 tsp	grated orange zest	10 mL
⅔ cup	freshly squeezed orange juice	150 mL
¼ cup	vegetable oil	50 mL
1 cup	all-bran cereal	250 mL
⅔ cup	chopped dried apricots	150 mL
¾ cup	whole-berry cranberry sauce	175 mL

1. In a bowl, combine flour, brown sugar, baking powder and salt. Make a well in the center.
2. In another bowl, whisk together eggs, orange zest, orange juice and oil. Add cereal and apricots; blend well. Add to flour mixture; stir just until blended. Fold in cranberry sauce.
3. Spoon batter into prepared muffin tin. Bake in preheated oven for 25 to 30 minutes or until golden brown.

Cranberry Banana Breakfast Muffins

Makes 12 muffins
- Preheat oven to 400°F (200°C)
- Muffin tin, greased or paper-lined

2 cups	oat bran	500 mL
½ cup	firmly packed brown sugar	125 mL
¼ cup	all-purpose flour	50 mL
2 tsp	baking powder	10 mL
½ tsp	salt	2 mL
½ tsp	ground cinnamon	2 mL
½ cup	finely chopped cranberries	125 mL
⅔ cup	cranberry juice	150 mL
½ cup	mashed ripe bananas	125 mL
2	egg whites, lightly beaten	2
3 tbsp	vegetable oil	45 mL

1. In a bowl, combine oat bran, brown sugar, flour, baking powder, salt and cinnamon. Add cranberries; stir gently.
2. In another bowl, combine cranberry juice, bananas, egg whites and oil. Add to dry ingredients; mix just until moist and blended.

3. Spoon batter into prepared muffin tin. Bake in preheated oven for 20 to 25 minutes or until golden brown.

Cranberry Honey Muffins

Makes 12 muffins
- Preheat oven to 400°F (200°C)
- Muffin tin, greased or paper-lined

⅓ cup	margarine, softened	75 mL
⅓ cup	liquid honey	75 mL
1	egg, well beaten	1
1¼ cups	chopped cranberries or thick cranberry sauce	300 mL
	Grated zest of 1 orange	
⅔ cup	milk	150 mL
2 cups	all-purpose flour	500 mL
1 tbsp	baking powder	15 mL
1 tsp	salt	5 mL

1. In a bowl, cream together margarine and honey. Add egg, cranberries, orange zest and milk; mix well.
2. In another bowl, combine flour, baking powder and salt. Add to cranberry mixture; stir just until ingredients are moist.
3. Spoon batter into prepared muffin tin. Bake in preheated oven for about 20 minutes.

Cranberry Fruitcake Muffins

Makes 12 muffins
- Preheat oven to 400°F (200°C)
- Muffin tin, greased or paper-lined

⅔ cup	all-purpose flour	150 mL
⅔ cup	whole wheat flour	150 mL
½ cup	old-fashioned rolled oats	125 mL
1½ tsp	baking soda	7 mL
1 tsp	ground ginger	5 mL
2	eggs	2
½ cup	liquid honey	125 mL
⅓ cup	orange juice	75 mL
¼ cup	vegetable oil	50 mL
1 tsp	vanilla	5 mL
1 cup	cranberries	250 mL
¾ cup	grated apples	175 mL

1. In a bowl, combine all-purpose flour, whole wheat flour, oats, baking soda and ginger.

2. In another bowl, whisk together eggs, honey, orange juice, oil and vanilla. Add cranberries and apples; stir well. Add to flour mixture; stir just until blended.

3. Spoon batter into prepared muffin tin. Bake in preheated oven for 15 to 20 minutes.

• •

Cranberry Nut Muffins

Makes 12 muffins
- Preheat oven to 350°F (180°C)
- Muffin tin, greased

2 cups	all-purpose flour	500 mL
¾ cup	granulated sugar	175 mL
½ cup	chopped nuts	125 mL
1 tsp	baking powder	5 mL
1 tsp	baking soda	5 mL
2 tsp	grated orange zest	10 mL
¾ cup	mayonnaise	175 mL
¼ cup	frozen undiluted orange juice concentrate, thawed	50 mL
2	eggs, beaten	2
2 cups	fresh or frozen whole cranberries	500 mL

1. In a bowl, combine flour, sugar, nuts, baking powder, baking soda and orange zest.

2. In another bowl, combine mayonnaise, orange juice concentrate, eggs and cranberries; mix well. Add to flour mixture; stir just until blended.

3. Spoon batter into prepared muffin tin. Bake in preheated oven for 20 to 25 minutes.

• •

Orange Upside-Down Cranberry Muffins

Makes 12 to 18 muffins
- Preheat oven to 375°F (190°C)
- Muffin tins, sprayed with vegetable spray

	Frozen orange juice concentrate	
	Granulated sugar	
2½ cups	all-purpose flour	625 mL
⅓ cup	granulated sugar	75 mL
1 tsp	salt	5 mL
1 tbsp	baking powder	15 mL
1 tsp	baking soda	5 mL
1 cup	chopped pecans	250 mL
	Grated zest of 2 oranges	
1 cup	whole-berry cranberry sauce	250 mL

⅔ cup	freshly squeezed orange juice	150 mL
1 tbsp	freshly squeezed lemon juice	15 mL
2	eggs	2
¼ cup	vegetable oil	50 mL

1. Into each prepared muffin cup, spoon 1 tsp (5 mL) frozen concentrate and ½ tsp (2 mL) sugar. Set aside.

2. In a bowl, combine flour, sugar, salt, baking powder, baking soda, pecans and orange zest. Make a well in the center.

3. In another bowl, whisk together cranberry sauce, orange juice, lemon juice, eggs and oil. Add to flour mixture; stir quickly just until blended.

4. Spoon batter into muffin tins. Bake in preheated oven for 25 to 30 minutes or until browned. Remove from oven; let stand for 5 minutes. Turn pans upside-down so orange mixture is on top. Spoon any remaining sauce over muffins.

• •

Stuffed Orange Cranberry Muffins

Makes 12 muffins
- Preheat oven to 375°F (190°C)
- Muffin tin, paper-lined

1	large orange, quartered and seeded	1
¾ cup	boiling water	175 mL
¼ cup	vegetable oil	50 mL
1	egg	1
2 cups	all-purpose flour	500 mL
2 tsp	baking powder	10 mL
1 tsp	baking soda	5 mL
½ tsp	salt	2 mL
¾ cup + 2 tbsp	lightly packed brown sugar	200 mL
¾ cup	cranberries	175 mL
4 oz	cream cheese, cut into 12 pieces	125 g

1. In a blender, combine orange pieces and boiling water; blend until almost smooth. Add oil and egg; blend well.

2. In a bowl, combine flour, baking powder, baking soda, salt, brown sugar and cranberries. Add orange mixture; stir quickly just until moist.

3. Spoon batter into prepared muffin tin, filling half full. Add 1 cream cheese piece; top with the remaining batter. Bake in preheated oven for 20 to 25 minutes or until lightly browned.

Holiday Gingerbread Muffins

Makes 12 to 18 muffins
- Preheat oven to 400°F (200°C)
- Muffin tins, greased or paper-lined

1½ cups	all-purpose flour	375 mL
1½ cups	whole wheat flour	375 mL
⅓ cup	firmly packed brown sugar	75 mL
3½ tsp	baking powder	17 mL
2 tsp	ground ginger	10 mL
¾ tsp	ground cinnamon	4 mL
½ tsp	salt	2 mL
1	egg	1
1¼ cups	milk	300 mL
½ cup	light (fancy) molasses	125 mL
½ cup	melted margarine	125 mL

1. In a bowl, combine all-purpose flour, whole wheat flour, brown sugar, baking powder, ginger, cinnamon and salt. Make a well in the center.
2. In another bowl, whisk together egg, milk, molasses and margarine. Stir into dry ingredients.
3. Spoon batter into prepared muffin tins. Bake in preheated oven for about 20 minutes.

Gingerbread Sour Cream Muffins

Makes 12 muffins
- Preheat oven to 400°F (200°C)
- Muffin tin, greased

1½ cups	all-purpose flour	375 mL
1 tsp	baking soda	5 mL
1 tsp	ground ginger	5 mL
¼ tsp	salt	1 mL
2	eggs	2
½ cup	sour cream	125 mL
½ cup	light (fancy) molasses	125 mL
¼ cup	packed brown sugar	50 mL
¼ cup	butter or margarine, melted	50 mL
	Sweetened whipped cream	

1. In a medium bowl, combine flour, baking soda, ginger and salt.
2. In a large bowl, beat eggs with a fork until light. Add sour cream, molasses, sugar and butter, blending well. Add flour mixture, stirring just until moistened and blended.
3. Spoon batter into prepared muffin tin. Bake in preheated oven for 15 to 20 minutes. Serve warm, topped with whipped cream.

Mincemeat Bran Muffins

Makes 24 muffins
- Preheat oven to 375°F (190°C)
- Muffin tins, greased

2¼ cups	all-purpose flour	550 mL
1¼ cups	natural bran	300 mL
2 tsp	baking powder	10 mL
2 tsp	baking soda	10 mL
1 tsp	salt	5 mL
2	eggs, beaten	2
¾ cup	vegetable oil	175 mL
¾ cup	granulated sugar	175 mL
¼ cup	light (fancy) molasses or packed brown sugar	50 mL
2 cups	milk	500 mL
1½ cups	mincemeat	375 mL

1. In a bowl, combine flour, bran, baking powder, baking soda and salt. Make a well in the center.
2. In another bowl, beat together eggs, oil and sugar. Add molasses, milk and mincemeat; beat well. Add to dry ingredients; stir just until moist.
3. Spoon batter into prepared muffin tins. Bake in preheated oven for 18 to 20 minutes.

Snow Muffins

Makes 12 muffins
- Preheat oven to 375°F (190°C)
- Muffin tin, greased

2 cups	all-purpose flour	500 mL
1 cup	lightly packed brown sugar	250 mL
1 tbsp	baking powder	15 mL
1 tsp	salt	5 mL
3 tbsp	margarine, melted	45 mL
1 cup	milk	250 mL
1½ cups	snow	375 mL
¾ cup	raisins or currants	175 mL

1. In a bowl, combine flour, brown sugar, baking powder and salt; mix well. Add margarine and milk; mixture will be lumpy. Quickly add snow and raisins; stir just until blended.
2. Spoon batter into prepared muffin tin. Bake in preheated oven for 20 to 25 minutes or until lightly browned.

Tip *At first, when I was given this recipe, I thought it was an April fool's joke! Before making muffins, collect fresh, clean, loosely packed snow.*

Mini Cinnamon Breakfast Muffins

Makes 24 miniature muffins
- Preheat oven to 400°F (200°C)
- Miniature muffin tins, greased or paper-lined

1½ cups	all-purpose flour	375 mL
½ cup	granulated sugar	125 mL
2 tsp	baking powder	10 mL
1 tsp	ground cinnamon	5 mL
½ tsp	salt	2 mL
½ tsp	ground allspice	2 mL
½ tsp	ground nutmeg	2 mL
1	egg, lightly beaten	1
½ cup	milk (2% or skim)	125 mL
⅓ cup	butter or margarine, melted	75 mL

1. In a large bowl, mix together flour, sugar, baking powder, cinnamon, salt, allspice and nutmeg. Make a well in the center.

2. In another bowl, combine egg, milk and margarine, beating until well blended. Add to dry ingredients, stirring only until moistened and blended. Do not overmix.

3. Spoon batter into prepared muffin tins. Bake in preheated oven for 12 to 14 minutes or until muffins are done.

Tip *For an extra-delicious muffin, melt ¼ cup (50 mL) margarine and brush over tops of warm muffins. Mix together ½ tsp (2 mL) cinnamon and 2 tbsp (25 mL) sugar and sprinkle over tops.*

Cinnamon Coffee Cake Muffins

Makes 12 muffins
- Preheat oven to 400°F (200°C)
- Muffin tin, greased or paper-lined

FILLING

¼ cup	all-purpose flour	50 mL
2 tbsp	granulated sugar	25 mL
½ tsp	ground cinnamon	2 mL
2 tbsp	butter or margarine	25 mL

MUFFINS

1⅓ cups	all-purpose flour	325 mL
1 cup	whole wheat flour	250 mL
½ cup	packed brown sugar	125 mL
1 tbsp	baking powder	15 mL
1 tbsp	ground cinnamon	15 mL
½ tsp	salt	2 mL
⅓ cup	butter or margarine	75 mL
2	eggs	2
1½ cups	milk	375 mL
½ cup	raisins	125 mL

1. *Prepare the filling:* In a small bowl, mix together flour, sugar and cinnamon. Using a pastry blender or two knives, cut in butter until mixture resembles coarse crumbs. Set aside.

2. *Prepare the muffins:* In a large bowl, combine all-purpose flour, whole wheat flour, brown sugar, baking powder, cinnamon and salt. Cut in butter. Make a well in the center.

3. In another bowl, whisk together eggs and milk until blended. Add to flour mixture, stirring only until moistened. Fold in raisins.

4. Spoon batter into prepared muffin tin, filling cups only half full. Add 1 tbsp (15 mL) filling to each and top with the remaining batter. Sprinkle any remaining filling on top. Bake in preheated oven for 20 minutes or until firm to the touch.

Tip *Cutting in butter produces a lighter, cake-like texture in these muffins.*

Morning Glory Corn Muffins

Makes 12 muffins
- Preheat oven to 400°F (200°C)
- Muffin tin, greased or paper-lined

1 cup	all-purpose flour	250 mL
¾ cup	yellow cornmeal	175 mL
3 tbsp	granulated sugar	45 mL
1 tbsp	baking powder	15 mL
1 tsp	salt	5 mL
1	egg	1
¾ cup	milk	175 mL
⅓ cup	butter or margarine, melted	75 mL

1. In a large bowl, with a fork, combine flour, cornmeal, sugar, baking powder and salt. Make a well in the center.

2. In another bowl, with a fork, mix together egg, milk and butter. Add to flour mixture, stirring just until flour is moistened. Do not overmix.

3. Spoon batter into prepared muffin tin. Bake in preheated oven for 20 minutes or until lightly browned.

Kernel Krunch Corn Muffins

Makes 12 large muffins
- Preheat oven to 425°F (220°C)
- Muffin tin, greased or paper-lined

¾ cup	unsalted butter, softened	175 mL
¾ cup	granulated sugar	175 mL
3	eggs	3
1⅔ cups	all-purpose flour	400 mL
1⅔ cups	yellow cornmeal	400 mL
4 tsp	baking powder	20 mL
½ tsp	salt	2 mL
2 cups	milk	500 mL
1 cup	drained whole corn kernels	250 mL

1. In a large bowl, cream together butter and sugar until fluffy. Beat in eggs one at a time, beating well after each addition.
2. In another bowl, combine flour, cornmeal, baking powder and salt. Add to butter mixture alternately with milk, mixing on low speed, beginning and ending with dry ingredients. Fold in corn.
3. Spoon batter into prepared muffin tin. Bake in preheated oven for 20 minutes.

Tip *Never double the amount of salt when you double a recipe. Season according to taste.*

Old-Fashioned Cornbread Muffins

Makes 12 muffins
- Preheat oven to 425°F (220°C)
- Muffin tin, greased

1½ cups	yellow cornmeal	375 mL
1½ tsp	baking powder	7 mL
1 tsp	salt	5 mL
¾ tsp	baking soda	4 mL
1	egg	1
1½ cups	buttermilk	375 mL
¼ cup	shortening, melted	50 mL

1. In a large bowl, combine cornmeal, baking powder, salt and baking soda until well blended. Make a well in the center.
2. In another bowl, beat together egg and buttermilk. Add to dry ingredients, stirring until thin and smooth. Stir in melted shortening.
3. Heat muffin tin in preheated oven. Spoon batter into hot tin and then bake for 18 to 20 minutes or until crusty and golden brown. Serve hot.

Tip *These are made with cornmeal only, no flour. It makes them crispy outside and moist inside.*

Raspberry Corn Muffins

Makes 12 muffins
- Preheat oven to 400°F (200°C)
- Muffin tin, lightly greased

¾ cup	fresh raspberries	175 mL
1½ cups	all-purpose flour, divided	375 mL
¾ cup	granulated sugar	175 mL
¾ cup	yellow cornmeal	175 mL
1 tbsp	baking powder	15 mL
½ tsp	salt	2 mL
2	eggs	2
1 cup	milk	250 mL
1 tsp	vanilla	5 mL
¼ cup	melted butter	50 mL

1. In a small bowl, gently toss together raspberries and 2 tbsp (25 mL) of the flour.
2. In a large bowl, combine the remaining flour, sugar, cornmeal, baking powder and salt. Make a well in the center.
3. In another bowl, whisk together eggs, milk and vanilla. Add to dry ingredients along with melted butter. Stir quickly just to moisten and blend.
4. Spoon 2 tbsp (25 mL) batter into each prepared muffin cup. Scatter 3 to 4 floured raspberries into each cup and spoon the remaining batter over top. Bake in preheated oven for 15 minutes or until golden brown.

Smoked Sausage Corn Muffins

Makes 12 muffins
- Preheat oven to 375°F (190°C)
- Muffin tin, paper-lined

8 oz	smoked sausage	250 g
1 cup	all-purpose flour	250 mL
¾ cup	yellow cornmeal	175 mL
¼ cup	granulated sugar	50 mL
1 tbsp	baking powder	15 mL
1 cup	buttermilk	250 mL
¼ cup	vegetable oil	50 mL
2	eggs, beaten	2

1. Cut sausage into quarters lengthwise, then cut crosswise into ¼-inch (0.5 cm) pieces. In a skillet over medium heat, lightly brown sausage. Remove from skillet and drain on paper towels.
2. In a large bowl, combine flour, cornmeal, sugar and baking powder. Add buttermilk, oil, eggs and sausage, stirring just until blended.

3. Spoon batter into prepared muffin tin. Bake in preheated oven for 15 minutes or until golden brown.

Tip *Delicious with scrambled eggs in place of toast.*

Graham Muffin Gems

Makes 12 muffins
- Preheat oven to 425°F (220°C)
- Muffin tin, greased or paper-lined

1 cup	all-purpose flour	250 mL
3/4 tsp	salt	4 mL
4 tsp	baking powder	20 mL
1/4 cup	packed brown sugar	50 mL
1 cup	graham flour	250 mL
1 cup	milk	250 mL
1	egg, lightly beaten	1
1/4 cup	butter or margarine, melted	50 mL

1. In a large bowl, mix together all-purpose flour, salt and baking powder. Add brown sugar and graham flour. Stir in milk, egg and butter until blended.

2. Spoon batter into prepared muffin tin. Bake in preheated oven for about 20 minutes.

Variation *Pecan Muffins: Add 1/2 cup (125 mL) chopped pecan nuts to the dry ingredients. Put a half pecan on each muffin top before baking.*

Afternoon Tea Muffins

Makes 12 muffins
- Preheat oven to 400°F (200°C)
- Muffin tin, greased or paper-lined

1 1/2 cups	all-purpose flour	375 mL
1/2 cup	granulated sugar	125 mL
1/4 tsp	salt	1 mL
2 tsp	baking powder	10 mL
1 tsp	baking soda	5 mL
1 tsp	ground cinnamon	5 mL
1/2 tsp	ground nutmeg	2 mL
1 1/4 cups	raisins	300 mL
2	eggs, beaten	2
1 cup	buttermilk	250 mL
2 tbsp	margarine, melted	25 mL

1. In a large bowl, mix together flour, sugar, salt, baking powder, baking soda, cinnamon and nutmeg. Fold in raisins.

2. In a small bowl, whisk together eggs, buttermilk and margarine. Add to dry ingredients, stirring quickly just until moistened. Batter will be lumpy.

3. Spoon batter into prepared muffin tin. Bake in preheated oven for 20 to 25 minutes.

Creamy Muffin Curls

Makes 12 muffins
- Preheat oven to 375°F (190°C)
- Muffin tin, greased

2 cups	all-purpose flour	500 mL
4 tsp	baking powder	20 mL
1/2 tsp	salt	2 mL
1/4 cup	shortening	50 mL
2/3 cup	milk	150 mL
3 tbsp	creamed butter	45 mL
1/2 cup	packed brown sugar	125 mL

1. In a large bowl, with a fork, mix together flour, baking powder and salt. Add shortening and then milk, blending to make a soft dough. Knead slightly and then roll out to 1/4 inch (0.5 cm) thick.

2. Spread with creamed butter and sprinkle with brown sugar. Roll up like a jelly roll. Cut into 1-inch (2.5 cm) pieces. Stand rolls on end in prepared muffin tin. Bake in preheated oven for 30 minutes.

Tip *Centers of rolls curl up and will be glazed on edges.*

Spiced Buttermilk Muffins

Makes 12 large muffins
- Preheat oven to 350°F (180°C)
- Muffin tin, greased

2 cups	whole wheat flour	500 mL
2/3 cup	all-purpose flour	150 mL
2/3 cup	packed brown sugar	150 mL
2 tsp	baking soda	10 mL
1 tsp	pumpkin pie spice	5 mL
2 cups	buttermilk	500 mL
3/4 cup	raisins	175 mL

1. In a large bowl, combine whole wheat flour, all-purpose flour, brown sugar, baking soda and pumpkin pie spice. Add buttermilk, stirring just until moistened. Fold in raisins.

2. Spoon batter into prepared muffin tin. Bake in preheated oven for 35 to 40 minutes or until a toothpick inserted in center comes out clean and dry.

Fresh Fruit Muffins

Makes 12 muffins
- Preheat oven to 400°F (200°C)
- Muffin tin, lightly greased

2 cups	all-purpose flour	500 mL
1/2 cup	granulated sugar	125 mL
1/3 cup	skim milk powder	75 mL
1 tbsp	baking powder	15 mL
1/2 tsp	salt	2 mL
1	egg	1
1/2 cup	margarine, melted	125 mL
1/2 cup	milk (2% or skim)	125 mL
1 cup	chopped fresh fruit	250 mL
1 tsp	freshly squeezed lemon juice	5 mL
1/2 tsp	grated lemon zest	2 mL

1. In a large bowl, combine flour, sugar, skim milk powder, baking powder and salt.
2. In another bowl, whisk together egg, margarine and milk until blended. Add fruit, lemon juice and zest. Add to flour mixture, stirring just until blended. Batter will be lumpy.
3. Spoon batter evenly into prepared muffin tin. Bake in preheated oven for 15 to 20 minutes or until golden brown.

Tip *The key to tender muffins is not to overmix. Just mix ingredients until no flour is visible.*

Island Fruit Muffins

Makes 24 muffins
- Preheat oven to 375°F (190°C)
- Muffin tins, greased or paper-lined

2 1/4 cups	oat bran	550 mL
2/3 cup	all-purpose flour	150 mL
2/3 cup	whole wheat flour	150 mL
1 tsp	baking powder	5 mL
2 1/2 tsp	baking soda	12 mL
1/4 tsp	salt	1 mL
1 1/2 cups	golden raisins	375 mL
1 1/4 cups	shredded coconut (sweetened or unsweetened)	300 mL
2	eggs	2
1 cup	buttermilk	250 mL
1/2 cup	vegetable oil	125 mL
1 cup	mashed ripe bananas	250 mL
1/2 cup	liquid honey	125 mL

1. In a large bowl, combine oat bran, all-purpose flour, whole wheat flour, baking powder, baking soda, salt, raisins and coconut.
2. In another bowl, whisk together eggs, buttermilk, oil, bananas and honey. Add to dry ingredients, stirring just until moistened and blended. Do not overmix.
3. Spoon batter into prepared muffin tins. Bake in preheated oven for 20 to 25 minutes or until browned.

Tip *To tint coconut, place 1 1/3 cups (325 mL) flaked coconut in a jar. Add a few drops of food coloring, screw on lid and shake well.*

Apple Almond Muffins

Makes 12 muffins
- Preheat oven to 375°F (190°C)
- Muffin tin, greased or paper-lined

1/2 cup	butter (room temperature)	125 mL
1/2 cup	granulated sugar	125 mL
2 tsp	baking powder	10 mL
1/2 tsp	salt	2 mL
2	eggs	2
2 cups	all-purpose flour	500 mL
1/2 cup	buttermilk	125 mL
1	can (8 oz/250 g) almond paste	1
1 cup	chopped peeled apples	250 mL
	Thin apple slices	
	Warmed honey	

1. In a large bowl, beat together butter, sugar, baking powder and salt until pale and fluffy. Beat in eggs. Fold in flour alternately with buttermilk, beginning and ending with flour. Stir until well blended but do not overmix.
2. Crumble almond paste over batter and sprinkle with chopped apples. Stir just until blended.
3. Spoon batter into prepared muffin tin. Top each with 2 thin slices of apple. Bake in preheated oven for 20 minutes or until a toothpick inserted in the center comes out dry and clean. Brush tops with 2 tbsp (25 mL) warmed honey.

Tip *Out of muffin pans? Use aluminum foil muffin or cupcake liners, or custard cups. Place on a baking sheet and bake as usual.*

Apple Cider Muffins

Makes 12 muffins

- Preheat oven to 400°F (200°C)
- Muffin tin, greased or paper-lined

½ cup	packed brown sugar	125 mL
½ cup	vegetable oil	125 mL
¼ cup	light (fancy) molasses	50 mL
1	egg	1
¾ cup	sweet apple cider	175 mL
2	apples, peeled and finely chopped	2
1½ cups	all-purpose flour	375 mL
¾ cup	natural bran	175 mL
1 tbsp	baking powder	15 mL
1 tsp	baking soda	5 mL
½ tsp	salt	2 mL
½ tsp	ground nutmeg	2 mL
1 cup	raisins	250 mL
½ cup	chopped walnuts	125 mL

1. In a bowl, mix together brown sugar, oil, molasses and egg. Stir in cider and apples. Set aside.
2. In a large bowl, combine flour, bran, baking powder, baking soda, salt and nutmeg. Add apple mixture, stirring just until blended. Fold in raisins and walnuts.
3. Spoon batter into prepared muffin tin. Bake in preheated oven for 15 to 20 minutes.

Striped Apple Cinnamon Muffins

Makes 12 muffins

- Preheat oven to 400°F (200°C)
- Muffin tin, greased or paper-lined

2 cups	all-purpose flour	500 mL
¼ cup	granulated sugar	50 mL
1 tbsp	baking powder	15 mL
¾ tsp	salt	4 mL
½ cup	finely chopped tart apple	125 mL
1	egg, beaten	1
¾ cup	milk	175 mL
¼ cup	vegetable oil	50 mL
TOPPING		
3 tbsp	granulated sugar	45 mL
1 tsp	ground cinnamon	5 mL
½ tsp	ground nutmeg	2 mL
1 cup	thinly sliced tart apple	250 mL

1. In a large bowl, combine flour, sugar, baking powder and salt. Stir in chopped apple.
2. In another bowl, combine egg, milk and oil. Add to flour mixture and stir until just moistened and blended.
3. *Prepare the topping:* In a bowl, mix together sugar, cinnamon and nutmeg. Add apple slices and toss to coat.
4. Spoon batter into prepared muffin tin and arrange apple slices over batter to make stripes. Bake in preheated oven for 20 to 25 minutes.

Tip *To prevent peeled or cut apples or other fruits from turning brown, brush surfaces with lemon juice.*

Applesauce Crunch Muffins

Makes 12 muffins

- Preheat oven to 400°F (200°C)
- Muffin tin, paper-lined

1½ cups	all-purpose flour	375 mL
¼ cup	granulated sugar	50 mL
1 tbsp	baking powder	15 mL
½ tsp	salt	2 mL
½ tsp	ground cinnamon	2 mL
1	egg	1
¾ cup	milk	175 mL
3 tbsp	vegetable oil or shortening, melted	45 mL
	Sweetened applesauce	
TOPPING		
⅔ cup	lightly packed brown sugar	150 mL
⅓ cup	all-purpose flour	75 mL
2 tbsp	butter or margarine, softened	25 mL

1. In a large bowl, sift together flour, sugar, baking powder, salt and cinnamon.
2. In another bowl, beat together egg, milk and oil. Pour into flour mixture. Stir just until moistened. Batter will be lumpy.
3. *Prepare the topping:* In a small bowl, mix together brown sugar, flour and butter.
4. Spoon batter into prepared muffin tin. Top each with 1 tsp (5 mL) applesauce. Sprinkle with topping. Bake in preheated oven for 18 to 20 minutes or until golden brown.

Applesauce Snackin' Muffins

Makes 12 muffins
- Preheat oven to 375°F (190°C)
- Muffin tin, paper-lined

¾ cup	all-purpose flour	175 mL
⅔ cup	whole wheat flour	150 mL
¾ tsp	baking soda	4 mL
1 tsp	ground cinnamon	5 mL
½ tsp	ground ginger	2 mL
Pinch	ground cloves	Pinch
Pinch	salt	Pinch
1 cup	sweetened applesauce	250 mL
¼ cup	packed brown sugar	50 mL
¼ cup	light (fancy) molasses	50 mL
¼ cup	vegetable oil	50 mL
2	eggs	2
1 cup	raisins	250 mL
ICING (OPTIONAL)		
⅔ cup	confectioner's (icing) sugar	150 mL
1 tbsp	unsweetened apple juice	15 mL

1. In a large bowl, combine all-purpose flour, whole wheat flour, baking soda, cinnamon, ginger, cloves and salt.

2. In another bowl, whisk together applesauce, sugar, molasses, oil and eggs. Fold in raisins. Add to dry ingredients, stirring just until moistened.

3. Spoon batter into prepared muffin tin. Bake in preheated oven for 15 to 20 minutes.

4. *If desired, prepare the icing:* In a bowl, whisk together confectioner's sugar and apple juice. Drizzle over cooled muffins.

Apricot Muffins

Makes 12 muffins
- Preheat oven to 400°F (200°C)
- Muffin tin, greased or paper-lined

1¾ cups	all-purpose flour	425 mL
2½ tsp	baking powder	12 mL
½ tsp	baking soda	2 mL
½ tsp	salt	2 mL
½ cup	chopped pecans	125 mL
2	eggs	2
¼ cup	vegetable oil	50 mL
½ cup	lightly packed brown sugar	125 mL
1	can (14 oz/398 mL) apricots, puréed	1
1 tsp	orange extract	5 mL

1. In a large bowl, combine flour, baking powder, baking soda, salt and pecans.

2. In another bowl, beat eggs lightly. Add oil, brown sugar, puréed apricots and orange extract. Add to flour mixture, stirring just until blended.

3. Spoon batter into prepared muffin tin. Bake in preheated oven for 20 to 25 minutes.

Corn Flakes 'n' Banana Muffins

Makes 12 muffins
- Preheat oven to 400°F (200°C)
- Muffin tin, greased

1¼ cups	all-purpose flour	300 mL
1 tbsp	baking powder	15 mL
½ tsp	salt	2 mL
½ tsp	ground cinnamon	2 mL
¼ tsp	ground nutmeg	1 mL
½ cup	firmly packed brown sugar	125 mL
2 cups	lightly crushed corn flakes cereal	500 mL
1	egg	1
⅓ cup	milk	75 mL
¼ cup	vegetable oil	50 mL
1 cup	mashed ripe bananas	250 mL

1. In a medium bowl, sift together flour, baking powder, salt, cinnamon, nutmeg, brown sugar and crushed corn flakes.

2. In a large bowl, combine egg, milk and oil. Stir in banana. Add flour mixture and stir just until blended.

3. Spoon batter into prepared muffin tin. Bake in preheated oven for 20 to 25 minutes.

Tip *If you have a lot of overripe bananas, don't throw them away. Save them by peeling, slicing and puréeing them in the blender with a few drops of lemon juice to prevent browning. Freeze in zippered freezer bags and keep handy for future recipes.*

Banana Crumble Muffins

Makes 12 muffins

- Preheat oven to 400°F (200°C)
- Muffin tin, greased or paper-lined

TOPPING

½ cup	banana nut crunch cereal	125 mL
1 tbsp	packed brown sugar	15 mL
1 tsp	ground cinnamon	5 mL
1 tsp	vegetable oil	5 mL

MUFFINS

1¼ cups	all-purpose flour	300 mL
1 tbsp	baking powder	15 mL
Pinch	salt	Pinch
1	egg	1
½ cup	milk	125 mL
⅓ cup	firmly packed brown sugar	75 mL
3 tbsp	vegetable oil	45 mL
1½ cups	banana nut crunch cereal	375 mL
1 cup	finely chopped bananas	250 mL

1. *Prepare the topping:* In a bowl, mix together cereal, brown sugar and cinnamon. Drizzle with oil and mix until topping is crumbly. Set aside.
2. *Prepare the muffins:* In a large bowl, combine flour, baking powder and salt. Make a well in the center.
3. In another bowl, whisk egg. Add milk, brown sugar and oil, blending well. Pour into flour mixture and stir just until moistened and blended. Do not overmix. Fold in cereal and bananas.
4. Spoon batter into prepared muffin tin. Sprinkle with topping. Bake in preheated oven for 15 to 20 minutes.

Berry Special Muffins

Makes 12 muffins

- Preheat oven to 400°F (200°C)
- Muffin tin, paper-lined

2 cups	all-purpose flour	500 mL
½ cup	granulated sugar	125 mL
1½ tsp	baking powder	7 mL
½ tsp	baking soda	2 mL
½ tsp	salt	2 mL
1	egg	1
1½ tsp	grated orange zest	7 mL
½ cup	freshly squeezed orange juice	125 mL
½ cup	butter or margarine, melted	125 mL
1 cup	coarsely chopped fresh or frozen berries	250 mL

1. In a large bowl, combine flour, sugar, baking powder, baking soda and salt. Make a well in the center.
2. In another bowl, whisk together egg, orange zest, orange juice and margarine until well blended. Add to flour mixture and stir just until moistened and blended. Fold in berries.
3. Spoon batter into prepared muffin tin. Bake in preheated oven for 20 minutes or until golden brown.

Lemon Oat Blueberry Muffins

Makes 12 muffins

- Preheat oven to 400°F (200°C)
- Muffin tin, greased or paper-lined

1 cup	all-purpose flour	250 mL
1 tbsp	baking powder	15 mL
½ tsp	salt	2 mL
¼ tsp	ground nutmeg	1 mL
¾ cup	packed brown sugar	175 mL
¾ cup	old-fashioned rolled oats	175 mL
	Finely grated zest of 1 lemon	
1	egg	1
¼ cup	vegetable oil	50 mL
1 cup	milk	250 mL
1	can (14 oz/398 mL) blueberries, drained and patted dry	1

1. In a large bowl, combine flour, baking powder, salt, nutmeg and brown sugar. Stir with a fork until well blended. Add oats and lemon zest.
2. In another bowl, whisk together egg, oil and milk. Add to flour mixture, stirring just until blended and moistened. Fold in blueberries.
3. Spoon batter into prepared muffin tin. Bake in preheated oven for 15 to 20 minutes.

Tip *A medium lemon yields about 2 to 3 tbsp (25 to 45 mL) juice and 1 tbsp (15 mL) grated zest. To always have freshly squeezed juice on hand, pour into ice cube trays and freeze. When frozen, place in plastic bags until ready to use.*

Coffee Cake Blueberry Muffins

Makes 12 muffins
- Preheat oven to 400°F (200°C)
- Muffin tin, greased or paper-lined

TOPPING

1/2 cup	packed brown sugar	125 mL
1 tbsp	all-purpose flour	15 mL
1 1/2 tsp	ground cinnamon	7 mL
2 tbsp	margarine, softened	25 mL

MUFFINS

3/4 cup	margarine, softened	175 mL
3/4 cup	granulated sugar	175 mL
1	egg	1
1 cup	sour cream	250 mL
1 tsp	vanilla	5 mL
2 cups	all-purpose flour	500 mL
1 tsp	baking powder	5 mL
1 tsp	baking soda	5 mL
1/4 tsp	salt	1 mL
2 cups	fresh or frozen blueberries, thawed and well drained	500 mL

1. *Prepare the topping:* In a small bowl, mix together brown sugar, flour, cinnamon and margarine. Set aside.

2. *Prepare the muffins:* In a large bowl, cream margarine and sugar until light and fluffy. Add egg and blend well on low speed. Stir in sour cream and vanilla. Add flour, baking powder, baking soda and salt. Stir just until moistened and blended.

3. Spoon batter into prepared muffin tin, filling cups half full. Add blueberries and top with the remaining batter. Sprinkle with topping. Bake in preheated oven for 15 to 20 minutes or until golden brown.

Blueberry Walnut Streusel Muffins

Makes 12 muffins
- Preheat oven to 400°F (200°C)
- Muffin tin, greased or paper-lined

1 1/2 cups	all-purpose flour	375 mL
2 tsp	baking powder	10 mL
1/2 tsp	salt	2 mL
6 tbsp	butter, softened	90 mL
1/2 cup	granulated sugar	125 mL
1	egg	1
1 tsp	vanilla	5 mL
1/2 cup	milk	125 mL
1 1/2 cups	fresh blueberries	375 mL

WALNUT STREUSEL TOPPING

1/4 cup	chopped walnuts	50 mL
2 tbsp	packed brown sugar	25 mL
1/4 tsp	ground cinnamon	1 mL
2 tbsp	melted butter	25 mL

1. In a medium bowl, combine flour, baking powder and salt.

2. In a large bowl, cream butter and sugar until light and fluffy. Beat in egg and vanilla. Add flour mixture alternately with milk. Stir just until moistened and blended. Fold in blueberries.

3. *Prepare the topping:* In a bowl, combine walnuts, brown sugar, cinnamon and butter.

4. Spoon batter into prepared muffin tin. Sprinkle with topping. Bake in preheated oven for about 20 minutes.

Lemon Berry Streusel Muffins

Makes 12 muffins
- Preheat oven to 400°F (200°C)
- Muffin tin, paper-lined

TOPPING

1/2 cup	all-purpose flour	125 mL
2 tbsp	granulated sugar	25 mL
1 1/2 tsp	finely grated lemon zest	7 mL
1/4 cup	butter or margarine, melted	50 mL

MUFFINS

2 1/2 cups	all-purpose flour	625 mL
1 1/4 cups	granulated sugar	300 mL
1 tbsp	finely grated lemon zest	15 mL
2 tsp	baking powder	10 mL
1 tsp	baking soda	5 mL
1	egg	1
1 cup	buttermilk	250 mL
1/2 cup	butter or margarine, melted	125 mL
1 tbsp	freshly squeezed lemon juice	15 mL
1 1/2 cups	frozen berries (any kind), coated with 1 tbsp (15 mL) flour	375 mL

1. *Prepare the topping:* In a bowl, mix together flour, sugar, zest and butter. Set aside.

2. *Prepare the muffins:* In a large bowl, combine flour, sugar, lemon zest, baking powder and baking soda.

3. In another bowl, whisk together egg, buttermilk, melted butter and lemon juice. Add to dry ingredients, stirring just until moistened and blended. Fold in berries.

4. Spoon batter into prepared muffin tin. Crumble reserved topping over tops. Bake in preheated oven for 20 minutes or until lightly browned.

• •

Lemon Pepper Muffins

Makes 12 muffins
- Preheat oven to 400°F (200°C)
- Muffin tin, greased or paper-lined

2 cups	all-purpose flour	500 mL
1/2 cup	granulated sugar	125 mL
2 tsp	baking powder	10 mL
1/2 tsp	baking soda	2 mL
1/2 tsp	salt	2 mL
3/4 tsp	freshly ground black pepper	4 mL
	Finely grated zest of 1 lemon	
1 cup	milk	250 mL
	Juice of 1 lemon	
1	egg	1
1/3 cup	butter, melted	75 mL

1. In a large bowl, combine flour, sugar, baking powder, baking soda, salt and pepper. Stir until well blended. Add lemon zest and mix until well coated. Make a well in the center.

2. In another bowl, whisk together milk, lemon juice and egg. Add to dry ingredients at once. (Milk mixture may look curdled.) Stir just until well blended. Add butter and blend together.

3. Spoon batter into prepared muffin tin. Bake in preheated oven for 15 to 20 minutes or until toothpick inserted in center comes out clean.

Tip *Freeze grated zest from lemons and oranges in small plastic yogurt cups.*

• •

Orange Tea Muffins

Makes 12 muffins
- Preheat oven to 375°F (190°C)
- Muffin tin, greased or paper-lined

1 1/2 cups	all-purpose flour	375 mL
1/2 cup	granulated sugar	125 mL
2 tsp	baking powder	10 mL
1/2 tsp	salt	2 mL
1/2 cup	butter or margarine, melted	125 mL
	Grated zest of 1 orange	
1/2 cup	freshly squeezed orange juice	125 mL
2	eggs	2
1 cup	fresh or frozen raspberries (optional)	250 mL
1/2 cup	sweetened flaked coconut (optional)	125 mL

1. In a large bowl, combine flour, sugar, baking powder and salt.

2. In another bowl, combine melted butter, orange zest, orange juice and eggs, mixing well. Add raspberries (if using) and coconut (if using). Add to flour mixture, stirring just until moist and blended.

3. Spoon batter into prepared muffin tin. Bake in preheated oven for 15 to 20 minutes (22 to 25 if using raspberries and coconut) or until lightly browned.

• •

Miniature Orange-Dipped Muffins

Makes 24 to 36 miniature muffins
- Preheat oven to 375°F (190°C)
- Miniature muffin tins, well-greased

1/2 cup	butter, softened	125 mL
1 cup	granulated sugar	250 mL
2 cups	all-purpose flour	500 mL
1 tsp	baking soda	5 mL
1 tsp	salt	5 mL
1 tsp	grated orange zest	5 mL
3/4 cup	sour cream	175 mL
1/2 cup	raisins	125 mL
1/2 cup	chopped nuts	125 mL
DIP		
1 cup	granulated sugar	250 mL
1/2 cup	freshly squeezed orange juice	125 mL

1. In a large bowl, cream together butter and sugar until smooth.

2. In another bowl, combine flour, baking soda, salt and zest. Add to creamed mixture alternately with sour cream, stirring just until blended. Do not overmix. Fold in raisins and chopped nuts.

3. Spoon batter into prepared muffin tins. Bake in preheated oven for 12 to 15 minutes.

4. *Prepare the dip:* In a bowl, combine sugar and orange juice. Dip warm muffins into this mixture.

Tip *Soften butter quickly by grating it.*

Orange Sunbursts

Makes 5 sunbursts

- Preheat oven to 325°F (160°C)
- Oblong baking dish

5	oranges	5
½ cup	snipped dates	125 mL
¼ cup	flaked coconut (sweetened or unsweetened)	50 mL
Dash	aromatic bitters	Dash
5	marshmallows	5

1. Cut tops off oranges with a grapefruit knife. Scoop out pulp and chop.

2. In a bowl, combine pulp, dates, coconut and bitters. Spoon mixture into orange shells and place in baking dish. Pour a little water around oranges.

3. Bake in preheated oven for 25 minutes. Top each orange with a marshmallow and continue baking for 8 to 10 minutes or until marshmallows are golden.

Spicy Orange and Sweet Potato Muffins

Makes 12 muffins

- Preheat oven to 400°F (200°C)
- Muffin tin, greased or paper-lined

1 cup	all-purpose flour	250 mL
1 cup	whole wheat flour	250 mL
2 tsp	baking powder	10 mL
2 tsp	baking soda	10 mL
1 tsp	ground cinnamon	5 mL
½ tsp	ground nutmeg	2 mL
½ tsp	ground allspice	2 mL
1	can (16 oz/455 mL) sweet potatoes, drained	1
⅔ cup	firmly packed brown sugar	150 mL
2	eggs	2
1 cup	orange juice	250 mL
1	carrot, shredded	1
1 tsp	vanilla	5 mL

1. In a medium bowl, combine all-purpose flour, whole wheat flour, baking powder, baking soda, cinnamon, nutmeg and allspice.

2. In a large bowl, mash sweet potatoes. Add brown sugar, eggs, orange juice, carrot and vanilla. Mix together until well blended. Add flour mixture, stirring just until moistened and blended. Do not overmix.

3. Spoon batter into prepared muffin tin. Bake in preheated oven for 15 to 20 minutes. Serve warm.

Cinnamon Pear Muffins

Makes 12 to 18 muffins

- Preheat oven to 400°F (200°C)
- Muffin tins, greased or paper-lined

3 cups	diced peeled pears	750 mL
¾ cup	granulated sugar	175 mL
½ cup	vegetable oil	125 mL
2	eggs	2
2 tsp	vanilla	10 mL
2 cups	all-purpose flour	500 mL
2 tsp	baking soda	10 mL
2 tsp	ground cinnamon	10 mL
1 tsp	ground nutmeg	5 mL
1 tsp	salt	5 mL
1 cup	raisins	250 mL
1 cup	chopped walnuts or pecans	250 mL

1. In a bowl, combine pears and sugar.

2. In a large bowl, whisk together oil, eggs and vanilla. Add pear mixture and blend well.

3. In another bowl, combine flour, baking soda, cinnamon, nutmeg and salt. Add to oil mixture and stir just until moistened and blended. Do not overmix. Fold in raisins and walnuts.

4. Spoon batter into prepared muffin tins. Bake in preheated oven for about 20 minutes.

Kiwi Raspberry Muffins

Makes 12 muffins

- Preheat oven to 400°F (200°C)
- Muffin tin, greased or paper-lined

1 cup	all-purpose flour	250 mL
1 cup	whole wheat flour	250 mL
1 tbsp	baking powder	15 mL
½ tsp	baking soda	2 mL
2	kiwifruits, peeled and chopped	2
½ cup	fresh raspberries (or frozen)	125 mL
1	egg, lightly beaten	1
¼ cup	margarine or butter	50 mL
⅓ cup	skim milk	75 mL
1 tsp	vanilla	5 mL

1. In a large bowl, mix together all-purpose flour, whole wheat flour, baking powder and baking soda. Add kiwis and raspberries, mixing well. Make a well in the center.

2. In another bowl, combine egg, margarine, milk and vanilla. Add to the flour mixture, stirring only until moistened and blended. Do not overmix.

3. Spoon batter into prepared muffin tin. Bake in preheated oven for 15 to 20 minutes.

- -

Strawberry Pecan Muffins

Makes 12 muffins

- Preheat oven to 400°F (200°C)
- Muffin tin, paper-lined

STREUSEL TOPPING

1/4 cup	all-purpose flour	50 mL
1/4 cup	finely chopped pecans	50 mL
1/4 cup	light brown sugar	50 mL
2 tbsp	butter or margarine, softened	25 mL

MUFFINS

2 cups	all-purpose flour	500 mL
1/3 cup	granulated sugar	75 mL
2 1/2 tsp	baking powder	12 mL
1 tsp	grated lemon zest	5 mL
1/4 tsp	salt	1 mL
2/3 cup	milk	150 mL
1/4 cup	butter or margarine, melted	50 mL
1	egg	1
2 cups	finely chopped fresh strawberries	500 mL

1. *Prepare the topping:* In a small bowl, combine flour, pecans, brown sugar and butter. Mix with your fingers until crumbly. Set aside.

2. *Prepare the muffins:* In a large bowl, combine flour, sugar, baking powder, lemon zest and salt. Make a well in the center.

3. In another bowl, whisk together milk, melted butter and egg until blended. Add to flour mixture and stir just until moistened. Do not overmix. The batter will be lumpy. Fold in strawberries.

4. Spoon batter into prepared muffin tin. Sprinkle with streusel topping. Bake in preheated oven for 20 to 25 minutes.

- -

Chocolate Cinnamon Muffins

Makes 12 muffins

- Preheat oven to 375°F (190°C)
- Muffin tin, greased or paper-lined

1/2 cup	butter or margarine, softened	125 mL
2/3 cup	granulated sugar, divided	150 mL
2 tsp	baking powder	10 mL
1/2 tsp	salt	2 mL
2	eggs	2
2 cups	all-purpose flour	500 mL
1 1/2 tsp	ground cinnamon, divided	7 mL
1/2 cup	buttermilk	125 mL
1 cup	semisweet chocolate chips, melted	500 mL
4 oz	cream cheese, cut into small pieces	125 g

1. In a large bowl, beat together butter, 1/2 cup (125 mL) of the sugar, baking powder and salt until pale and fluffy. Beat in eggs.

2. In another bowl, mix together flour and 1 tsp (5 mL) of the cinnamon. Slowly stir into butter mixture alternately with buttermilk just until moistened and blended. Do not overmix. Fold in melted chocolate just until blended.

3. Spoon batter into prepared muffin tin. Press pieces of cream cheese into top of batter in each cup. Sprinkle with the remaining sugar and cinnamon. Bake in preheated oven for about 20 minutes.

- -

Almond Orange Muffins

Makes 12 muffins

- Preheat oven to 375°F (190°C)
- Muffin tin, lightly greased or paper-lined

2 1/4 cups	all-purpose flour	550 mL
1/2 cup	granulated sugar	125 mL
2 1/2 tsp	baking powder	12 mL
1/2 tsp	baking soda	2 mL
1/4 cup	sliced almonds	50 mL
1/2 cup	skim milk	125 mL
1 tsp	grated orange zest	5 mL
1/2 cup	freshly squeezed orange juice	125 mL
1/4 cup	butter or margarine, melted	50 mL
2	egg whites	2

1. In a large bowl, combine flour, sugar, baking powder and baking soda. Stir in almonds.

2. In a small bowl, combine milk, orange zest and juice, melted butter and egg whites. Mix until well blended. Add to flour mixture, stirring lightly just until moistened and blended. Batter will be lumpy.

3. Spoon batter into prepared muffin tin. Bake in preheated oven for 15 to 20 minutes.

Tip *For long-term storage of eggs, crack them open into an ice-cube tray. When completely frozen, put egg cubes in a sealed freezer bag and use as needed.*

Almond Citrus Muffins

Makes 12 large muffins
- Preheat oven to 350°F (180°C)
- Muffin tin, greased or paper-lined

½ cup	whole almonds	125 mL
1¼ cups	all-purpose flour	300 mL
2 tsp	baking powder	10 mL
¼ tsp	salt	1 mL
1 cup	shredded wheat bran cereal	250 mL
¼ cup	packed brown sugar	50 mL
¾ cup	milk	175 mL
1 tsp	grated orange zest	5 mL
¼ cup	freshly squeezed orange juice	50 mL
1	egg	1
¼ cup	vegetable oil or almond oil	50 mL

1. Spread almonds in a single layer on baking sheet. Bake in preheated oven, stirring occasionally, for 12 to 15 minutes or until lightly toasted. Set aside to cool and then chop toasted almonds. Increase oven temperature to 400°F (200°C).
2. In a large bowl, combine flour, baking powder and salt.
3. In a medium bowl, combine cereal, brown sugar, milk, orange zest and orange juice. Let stand for 2 minutes or until cereal is softened. Add egg and oil, beating well. Stir in almonds. Add to flour mixture and stir until just moistened. Batter will be lumpy.
4. Spoon batter into prepared muffin tin. Bake in preheated oven for 20 minutes or until lightly browned.

Caramel Nut-Topped Muffins

Makes 12 large muffins
- Preheat oven to 400°F (200°C)
- Muffin tin

TOPPING

½ cup	firmly packed brown sugar	125 mL
¼ cup	margarine	50 mL
½ cup	chopped pecans or walnuts	125 mL

MUFFINS

2	eggs	2
¾ cup	milk	175 mL
½ cup	margarine, melted	125 mL
1½ cups	all-purpose flour	375 mL
1 cup	whole wheat flour	250 mL
⅓ cup	granulated sugar	75 mL
1 tbsp	baking powder	15 mL
1 tsp	ground cinnamon	5 mL
½ tsp	salt	2 mL

1. *Prepare the topping:* Into each muffin cup measure 2 tsp (10 mL) brown sugar and 1 tsp (5 mL) margarine. Place in preheated oven for 2 minutes to melt. Remove from oven and add 2 tsp (10 mL) nuts to each cup. Set aside.
2. *Prepare the muffins:* In a bowl, beat eggs with a fork. Blend in milk and melted margarine.
3. In a large bowl, combine all-purpose flour, whole wheat flour, sugar, baking powder, cinnamon and salt. Add liquid mixture, stirring just until moistened and blended. Do not overmix.
4. Spoon batter into muffin tin. Bake in preheated oven for about 20 minutes. Invert pan onto a plate so caramel nut topping is on top. Serve warm.

Mocha Walnut Frosted Muffins

Makes 12 muffins
- Preheat oven to 350°F (180°C)
- Muffin tin, greased or paper-lined

½ cup	butter or margarine, softened	125 mL
1 cup	granulated sugar	250 mL
2 cups	all-purpose flour	500 mL
1 tbsp	baking powder	15 mL
¼ tsp	salt	1 mL
½ cup	cold strong brewed coffee	125 mL
¾ cup	chopped walnuts	175 mL
3	egg whites, beaten until stiff	3

FROSTING

3 tbsp	butter, softened	45 mL
1 cup	confectioner's (icing) sugar, divided	250 mL
1 tbsp	unsweetened cocoa powder	15 mL
2 tbsp	strong brewed coffee	25 mL

1. In a large bowl, cream butter thoroughly. Add sugar gradually, beating well.
2. In another bowl, mix together flour, baking powder and salt. Add to creamed mixture alternately with coffee. Stir thoroughly until well blended. Add chopped walnuts. Fold in egg whites.
3. Spoon batter into prepared muffin tin. Bake in preheated oven for 25 minutes.
4. *Prepare the frosting:* In a bowl, cream together butter and 2 tbsp (25 mL) of the confectioner's sugar. Add cocoa, the remaining confectioner's sugar and coffee. Beat until light and fluffy. Spread over cooled muffins.

Peanut Butter Surprise Muffins

Makes 12 small muffins
- Preheat oven to 375°F (190°C)
- Muffin tin, greased or paper-lined

1 cup	all-purpose flour	250 mL
½ tsp	salt	2 mL
1 tbsp	baking powder	15 mL
1 tbsp	granulated sugar	15 mL
½ cup	yellow cornmeal	125 mL
1 cup	milk	250 mL
1	egg, beaten	1
¼ cup	peanut butter	50 mL
1 tbsp	shortening, melted	15 mL

1. In a large bowl, combine flour, salt, baking powder and sugar. Stir in cornmeal, mixing to blend well.

2. In a small bowl, combine milk, egg, peanut butter and melted shortening. Add to dry ingredients, stirring until moistened and blended.

3. Spoon batter into prepared muffin tin. Bake in preheated oven for about 20 minutes.

Cocoa Nut Oatmeal Muffins

Makes 12 muffins
- Preheat oven to 400°F (200°C)
- Muffin tin, greased or paper-lined

½ cup	margarine, melted	125 mL
2	eggs	2
1 cup	milk	250 mL
1 tsp	vanilla	5 mL
1¼ cups	all-purpose flour	300 mL
¾ cup	old-fashioned rolled oats	175 mL
1 cup	granulated sugar	250 mL
⅓ cup	unsweetened cocoa powder	75 mL
1 tbsp	baking powder	15 mL
1 tsp	salt	5 mL
1 cup	chopped nuts	250 mL

1. In a small bowl, whisk together margarine, eggs, milk and vanilla.

2. In a large bowl, mix together flour, oats, sugar, cocoa, baking powder and salt. Add egg mixture, stirring just until moistened and blended. Fold in chopped nuts.

3. Spoon batter into prepared muffin tin. Bake in preheated oven for 15 to 20 minutes or until a toothpick inserted in the center comes out clean and dry.

Tip *Try ice cream muffins! Soften two or three different flavors of ice cream. Fill muffin tins one-third full with one flavor. Smooth out into bottoms of cups and then layer with the other flavors. Freeze, unmold and then decorate as you wish.*

Cream Cheese Carrot Muffins

Makes 12 muffins
- Preheat oven to 350°F (180°C)
- Muffin tin, greased or paper-lined

1	package (8 oz/250 g) cream cheese, softened	1
⅓ cup	granulated sugar	75 mL
3	eggs, lightly beaten, divided	3
1½ cups	all-purpose flour	375 mL
1 tsp	baking powder	5 mL
1 tsp	baking soda	5 mL
½ tsp	ground cinnamon	2 mL
½ cup	packed brown sugar	125 mL
⅓ cup	vegetable oil	75 mL
⅔ cup	plain yogurt	150 mL
1 cup	finely grated carrots	250 mL
½ cup	finely chopped walnuts	125 mL

1. In a small bowl, whisk together cream cheese, sugar and one-third of the eggs. Set aside.

2. In a large bowl, combine flour, baking powder, baking soda and cinnamon.

3. In another bowl, combine brown sugar, oil, the remaining eggs and yogurt. Stir in carrots and walnuts. Add to flour mixture and stir just until moistened.

4. Spoon about 2 tbsp (25 mL) batter into muffin tin. Top with heaping spoonfuls of cream cheese mixture and top with the remaining batter. Bake in preheated oven for about 20 minutes.

Easy Mini Cheesecakes

Makes 12 mini cheesecakes
- Preheat oven to 325°F (160°C)
- Muffin tin, foil-lined

2	packages (each 8 oz/250 g) cream cheese, softened	2
½ cup	granulated sugar	125 mL
1 tsp	vanilla	5 mL
2	eggs	2
12	vanilla wafers	12
	Jam, nuts, chocolate curls, etc.	

1. In a large bowl, combine cheese, sugar and vanilla. Blend on medium speed until smooth. Add eggs, blending well.

2. Put 1 vanilla wafer in each cup. Spoon cheese mixture over wafers. Bake in preheated oven for 25 minutes. Set aside to cool. Remove from tin and chill in refrigerator before serving. Top with whatever you like.

Variation *For a special flavor, use ½ tsp (2 mL) rum or almond flavoring in place of the vanilla.*

Cheese Muffin Ring

Serves 6 to 8
- Preheat oven to 425°F (220°C)
- Ring mold, greased

1½ cups	sifted cake and pastry flour	375 mL
2 tsp	baking powder	10 mL
½ tsp	salt	2 mL
¾ cup	shredded cheese (any type)	175 mL
1	egg, well beaten	1
½ cup	milk	125 mL
1 tbsp	butter or shortening, melted	15 mL

1. In a large bowl, sift together flour, baking powder and salt. Add cheese and blend together well.

2. In another bowl, combine egg, milk and melted butter. Add to dry ingredients, stirring just until moistened and blended.

3. Spoon batter into prepared ring mold. Bake in preheated oven for 25 minutes.

Tip *Serve with scrambled eggs or vegetables.*

Parmesan Tomato Muffins

Makes 12 muffins
- Preheat oven to 350°F (180°C)
- Muffin tin, lightly greased

1¾ cups	all-purpose flour	425 mL
⅓ cup	freshly grated Parmesan cheese	75 mL
2 tbsp	granulated sugar	25 mL
2 tsp	baking powder	10 mL
¼ tsp	baking soda	1 mL
Pinch	garlic powder	Pinch
½ tsp	crushed dried rosemary	2 mL
Pinch	freshly ground black pepper	Pinch
1	egg, lightly beaten	1
½ cup	milk	125 mL
½ cup	tomato sauce	125 mL
⅓ cup	olive oil or vegetable oil	75 mL
	Freshly grated Parmesan cheese	

1. In a large bowl, combine flour, cheese, sugar, baking powder, baking soda, garlic powder, rosemary and pepper. Make a well in the center.

2. In another bowl, mix together egg, milk, tomato sauce and oil. Add to dry ingredients, stirring just until moistened and blended. Do not overmix.

3. Spoon batter into prepared muffin tin. Bake in preheated oven for 20 to 25 minutes or until lightly browned.

Pepper, Corn and Zucchini Muffins

Makes 12 muffins
- Preheat oven to 400°F (200°C)
- Muffin tin, paper-lined

¾ cup	all-purpose flour	175 mL
⅓ cup	yellow cornmeal	75 mL
1 tbsp	firmly packed light brown sugar	15 mL
2 tsp	baking powder	10 mL
½ tsp	salt	2 mL
½ cup	skim milk	125 mL
1	egg	1
⅓ cup	margarine, melted	75 mL
1½ cups	shredded zucchini	375 mL
½ cup	chopped roasted red peppers	125 mL

1. In a large bowl, combine flour, cornmeal, sugar, baking powder and salt. Make a well in the center.

2. In another bowl, whisk together milk, egg and melted margarine. Add to dry ingredients, stirring just until moistened and blended. Do not overmix. Stir in zucchini and peppers.

3. Spoon batter into prepared muffin tin. Bake in preheated oven for 20 to 25 minutes.

• •

Cocoa Nut Zucchini Muffins

Makes 12 muffins

- Preheat oven to 375ºF (190ºC)
- Muffin tin, greased

¾ cup	butter or margarine	175 mL
2 cups	granulated sugar	500 mL
2 tsp	vanilla	10 mL
3	eggs	3
1½ cups	all-purpose flour	375 mL
1 cup	whole wheat flour	250 mL
½ cup	unsweetened cocoa powder	125 mL
2½ tsp	baking powder	12 mL
1½ tsp	baking soda	7 mL
1 tsp	ground cinnamon	5 mL
2 cups	grated zucchini	500 mL
½ cup	milk	125 mL
1 cup	chopped nuts	250 mL

1. In a large bowl, cream together butter, sugar and vanilla. Add eggs one at a time, beating well after each addition.

2. In another bowl, combine all-purpose flour, whole wheat flour, cocoa, baking powder, baking soda and cinnamon. Add to the creamed mixture alternately with zucchini and milk, mixing well. Do not overmix. Fold in nuts.

3. Spoon batter into prepared muffin tin. Bake in preheated oven for 25 minutes.

Tip *Save margarine tubs for storing baking ingredients such as raisins, cinnamon, baking soda, nuts, etc.*

• •

Mexican Muffins

Makes 12 muffins

- Preheat oven to 400ºF (200ºC)
- Muffin tin, greased

1 cup	milk	250 mL
¼ cup	butter, melted	50 mL
2	eggs, beaten	2
2 cups	all-purpose flour	500 mL
2 tsp	baking powder	10 mL
2 tsp	ground cumin	10 mL
½ tsp	salt	2 mL
½ cup	chopped fresh cilantro	125 mL

1. In a medium bowl, whisk together milk, butter and eggs.

2. In another bowl, combine flour, baking powder, cumin and salt. Add to milk mixture and stir just until blended. Stir in cilantro.

3. Spoon batter into prepared muffin tin. Bake in preheated oven about 15 minutes or until a toothpick inserted in center comes out clean and dry.

Tip *Check spices for freshness by sniffing for aroma. The stronger the aroma, the fresher and more flavorful they will be.*

• •

Potato Pudding Muffins

Makes 12 muffins

- Preheat oven to 375ºF (190ºC)
- Muffin tin, lightly greased

12	potatoes	12
2	onions, grated	2
4	eggs, well beaten	4
1 cup	all-purpose flour	250 mL
1 tbsp	salt	15 mL
½ tsp	freshly ground black pepper	2 mL
½ tsp	dried savory	2 mL
1 tsp	baking powder	5 mL
8 tbsp	bacon fat or butter, melted	125 mL

1. Peel potatoes and grate over a bowl of cold water. Drain, pressing out as much water as possible. In a large bowl, combine grated potatoes, onions and eggs.

2. In another bowl, combine flour, salt, pepper, savory and baking powder. Add to potato mixture and mix well. Stir in melted fat.

3. Spoon batter into prepared muffin tin. Bake in preheated oven for 1 hour or until brown and crusty. Let stand for 30 minutes on a cake rack, then run a knife around edges and remove from pan.

Tip *To freeze, place muffins on a baking sheet, freeze, and then put into freezer bags.*

Mashed Potato Muffins

Makes 24 muffins

- Preheat oven to 400°F (200°C)
- Muffin tins, greased

10	potatoes	10
1 tsp	salt	5 mL
½ tsp	freshly ground black pepper	2 mL
2 tbsp	vegetable oil	25 mL
4	eggs, beaten	4
2	onions, chopped	2

1. In a saucepan of boiling water, cook potatoes until soft. In a bowl, combine cooked potatoes, salt, pepper and oil; mash until smooth. Add eggs; mix well.
2. In a skillet over medium-high heat, cook onions for about 2 minutes. Add to potato mixture; stir well.
3. In preheated oven, heat prepared muffin tins. Spoon batter into cups. Bake in preheated oven for 30 to 40 minutes.

Sweet Potato Muffins

Makes 12 small muffins

- Preheat oven to 400°F (200°C)
- Muffin tin, greased

⅔ cup	cooked sweet potatoes, well-drained	150 mL
¼ cup	butter or margarine	50 mL
½ cup	granulated sugar	125 mL
1	egg	1
¾ cup	all-purpose flour	175 mL
2 tsp	baking powder	10 mL
½ tsp	salt	2 mL
½ tsp	ground cinnamon	2 mL
¼ tsp	ground nutmeg	1 mL
½ cup	milk	125 mL
¼ cup	chopped pecans or walnuts	50 mL
¼ cup	chopped raisins	50 mL

1. In a blender or food processor, purée sweet potatoes.
2. In a large bowl, cream together butter and sugar. Beat in egg and puréed sweet potatoes.
3. In another bowl, combine flour, baking powder, salt, cinnamon and nutmeg. Add to sweet potato mixture alternately with milk and mix just until moistened and blended. Fold in chopped nuts and raisins.
4. Spoon batter into prepared muffin tin. Bake in preheated oven for about 20 minutes.

Tip *If desired, sprinkle the muffins with sugar and cinnamon before baking.*

Salmon Lunch Muffins

Makes 6 muffins

- Preheat oven to 350°F (180°C)
- Muffin tin, lightly greased

1	can (6 oz/175 mL) skinless, boneless salmon, not drained	1
2	eggs	2
½ cup	chopped celery	125 mL
½ cup	quick-cooking rolled oats	125 mL
½ tsp	baking powder	2 mL
¼ cup	evaporated milk	50 mL
2 tsp	freshly squeezed lemon juice	10 mL
¾ tsp	salt	4 mL
¼ tsp	freshly ground black pepper	1 mL

1. In a food processor, combine salmon (and juice), eggs, celery, oats, baking powder, milk, lemon juice, salt and pepper. Purée until well blended.
2. Spoon batter into prepared muffin tin. Bake in preheated oven for 30 minutes or until golden brown. Serve warm.

Tip *For a tangier muffin, add 1 to 2 drops of hot pepper sauce.*

Drop Cookies and Hand-Shaped Cookies

Drop Cookies

Hand-Shaped Cookies

Drop Cookies

Drop cookies are the most popular type of cookie, as they are so easy to make. Dropped from a spoon onto a baking sheet, they spread out as they bake. Many of the most common cookies, such as traditional chocolate chip, oatmeal, meringues and macaroons, are drop cookies. But the ingredients for drop cookies can be varied to produce a wide range of delectable treats, from fruit-filled and frosted cookies to chunky hermits.

Homemade Oatmeal Macaroons

Makes about 3 dozen
- Preheat oven to 350ºF (180ºC)
- Baking sheet, lightly greased

2	egg whites	2
¾ cup	granulated sugar, divided	175 mL
½ cup	butter or margarine, melted	125 mL
2 cups	quick-cooking rolled oats	500 mL
¼ cup	all-purpose flour	50 mL

1. In a large bowl, beat egg whites until soft peaks form. Gradually add ¼ cup (50 mL) of the sugar, beating until stiff peaks form.
2. In another large bowl, mix together the remaining sugar, butter or margarine, oats and flour. Fold into beaten egg whites until well blended.
3. Drop by level tablespoonfuls (15 mL), about 1 inch (2.5 cm) apart, onto prepared baking sheet. Bake in preheated oven for 10 to 12 minutes or until lightly browned. Immediately transfer to wire racks to cool.

Tip *Overbaked cookies can be crumbled and sprinkled over ice cream or fresh fruit or used as a topping for fruit crumbles.*

Oat Bran Raisin Cookies

Makes about 1 dozen
- Preheat oven to 350ºF (180ºC)
- Baking sheet, greased

⅔ cup	oat bran	150 mL
¼ cup	old-fashioned rolled oats	50 mL
3 tbsp	all-purpose flour	45 mL
½ tsp	baking powder	2 mL
3 tbsp	margarine, softened	45 mL
¼ cup	firmly packed brown sugar	50 mL
1	egg white, lightly beaten	1
2 tsp	water	10 mL
¼ tsp	vanilla	1 mL
2 tbsp	raisins	25 mL

1. In a small bowl, mix together oat bran, rolled oats, flour and baking powder.
2. In a large bowl, beat together margarine and brown sugar until smooth and creamy. Stir in egg white, water and vanilla, mixing until thoroughly incorporated. Add flour mixture and mix well. Fold in raisins.
3. Drop by level tablespoonfuls (15 mL), about 2 inches (5 cm) apart, onto prepared baking sheet. Using a fork or the bottom of a glass, flatten slightly. Bake in preheated oven for 12 to 15 minutes or until bottoms are slightly browned. Let cool on sheet for 3 minutes, then transfer to wire racks to cool completely.

Tip *This recipe makes a smaller batch of cookies than usual, but it can be doubled, if desired.*

Wholesome Banana Granola Drops

Makes about 4 dozen
- Preheat oven to 375ºF (190ºC)
- Baking sheet, greased

1½ cups	all-purpose flour	375 mL
½ tsp	baking soda	2 mL
½ tsp	salt	2 mL
1 tsp	ground cinnamon	5 mL
½ cup	butter or margarine, softened	125 mL
1 cup	firmly packed brown sugar	250 mL
1	egg	1
½ tsp	vanilla	2 mL
1 cup	mashed ripe bananas	250 mL
1 cup	granola	250 mL

1. In a small bowl, mix together flour, baking soda, salt and cinnamon.
2. In a large bowl, beat butter and brown sugar until smooth and creamy. Add egg, vanilla and bananas and beat until well blended. Add flour mixture and mix well. Stir in granola.
3. Drop by tablespoonfuls (15 mL), about 2 inches (5 cm) apart, onto prepared baking sheet. Bake in preheated oven for 12 minutes or until golden brown. Immediately transfer to wire racks to cool.

Tip *To keep bananas from turning brown, wrap individual bananas tightly in aluminum foil and refrigerate in the crisper drawer. This will slow down the ripening process.*

Banana Oatmeal Drops

Makes about 5 dozen
- Preheat oven to 350°F (180°C)
- Baking sheet, greased

1½ cups	all-purpose flour	375 mL
1¾ cups	quick-cooking rolled oats	425 mL
1 tsp	salt	5 mL
1 tsp	ground cinnamon	5 mL
½ tsp	baking soda	2 mL
¼ tsp	ground nutmeg	1 mL
¾ cup	shortening, softened	175 mL
1 cup	firmly packed brown sugar	250 mL
1	egg	1
1 cup	mashed ripe bananas	250 mL
½ cup	chopped pecans or walnuts	125 mL

1. In a medium bowl, mix together flour, oats, salt, cinnamon, baking soda and nutmeg.
2. In a large bowl, beat shortening and brown sugar until smooth and creamy. Add egg and mashed bananas and mix well. Add flour mixture and mix well. Fold in nuts.
3. Drop by heaping teaspoonfuls (5 mL), about 2 inches (5 cm) apart, onto prepared baking sheet. Bake in preheated oven for 12 to 15 minutes or until golden brown. Let cool slightly on sheet, then transfer to wire racks to cool completely.

Tip *For a special treat, frost these cookies with Quick Banana Frosting or Creamy Lemon Frosting (see recipes, page 547).*

Apple Oatmeal Cookies

Makes about 6 dozen
- Preheat oven to 400°F (200°C)
- Baking sheet, greased

1¾ cups	all-purpose flour	425 mL
½ tsp	baking powder	2 mL
½ tsp	baking soda	2 mL
½ tsp	salt	2 mL
½ cup	quick-cooking rolled oats	125 mL
½ tsp	ground nutmeg	2 mL
½ tsp	ground cinnamon	2 mL
½ cup	shortening, softened	125 mL
1 cup	packed brown sugar	250 mL
2	eggs	2
1 cup	finely chopped peeled apples	250 mL
1 cup	raisins	250 mL
1 cup	chopped nuts	250 mL

1. In a medium bowl, mix together flour, baking powder, baking soda, salt, oats, nutmeg and cinnamon.
2. In a large bowl, beat shortening and brown sugar until smooth and creamy. Add eggs, one at a time, mixing until well incorporated. Mix in apples and raisins. Add flour mixture and mix well. Fold in nuts.
3. Drop by rounded teaspoonfuls (5 mL), about 2 inches (5 cm) apart, onto prepared baking sheet. Bake in preheated oven for 10 to 12 minutes or until golden brown. Immediately transfer to wire racks to cool.

Tip *To test if eggs are fresh, place them in a bowl of cold, salted water. They are fresh if they sink to the bottom and stay there.*

Cranberry Orange Oatmeal Cookies

Makes about 5 dozen
- Preheat oven to 375°F (190°C)
- Baking sheet, greased

2 cups	all-purpose flour	500 mL
1 tsp	baking powder	5 mL
¼ tsp	baking soda	1 mL
½ tsp	salt	2 mL
2 cups	quick-cooking rolled oats	500 mL
1 cup	butter or margarine, softened	250 mL
1½ cups	granulated sugar	375 mL
2	eggs	2
1 tsp	vanilla	5 mL
1 cup	raisins	250 mL
1 cup	coarsely chopped cranberries, fresh or frozen	250 mL
1 tbsp	grated orange zest	15 mL

1. In a large bowl, mix together flour, baking powder, baking soda, salt and oats.
2. In another large bowl, beat butter or margarine and sugar until smooth and creamy. Beat in eggs, one at a time, until well incorporated. Mix in vanilla. Add flour mixture and mix well. Fold in raisins, cranberries and orange zest.
3. Drop by rounded teaspoonfuls (5 mL), about 2 inches (5 cm) apart, onto prepared baking sheet. Bake in preheated oven for 10 to 12 minutes or until edges are lightly browned. Immediately transfer to wire racks to cool.

Chock-Full Oatmeal Cookies

Makes about 4 dozen
- Preheat oven to 375°F (190°C)
- Baking sheet, lightly greased

2 cups	all-purpose flour	500 mL
1 tsp	baking soda	5 mL
½ tsp	salt	2 mL
1 cup	quick-cooking rolled oats	250 mL
½ cup	butter, softened	125 mL
½ cup	granulated sugar	125 mL
¾ cup	packed brown sugar	175 mL
1	egg	1
2	egg whites	2
2 tsp	vanilla	10 mL
1 cup	semisweet chocolate chunks	250 mL
½ cup	dark raisins	125 mL

1. In a medium bowl, mix together flour, baking soda, salt and oats.
2. In a large bowl, beat butter and sugars until smooth and creamy. Beat in egg, then egg whites, until incorporated. Stir in vanilla. Add flour mixture and mix well. Fold in chocolate and raisins until well combined.
3. Drop by level tablespoonfuls (15 mL), about 2 inches (5 cm) apart, onto prepared baking sheet. Bake in preheated oven for 10 to 12 minutes or until golden brown. Immediately transfer to wire racks to cool.

Tip *Always use large eggs when baking cookies.*

Peaches 'n' Cream Oatmeal Cookies

Makes about 3 dozen
- Preheat oven to 350°F (180°C)
- Baking sheet, lightly greased

1½ cups	whole wheat flour	375 mL
2½ cups	old-fashioned rolled oats	625 mL
2 tsp	baking powder	10 mL
1 tsp	salt	5 mL
⅔ cup	butter or margarine, softened	150 mL
¾ cup	granulated sugar	175 mL
¾ cup	packed brown sugar	175 mL
2	eggs	2
1½ tsp	vanilla	7 mL
3	peaches, diced	3
¾ cup	raisins (optional)	175 mL

1. In a large bowl, mix together flour, oats, baking powder and salt.
2. In another large bowl, beat butter or margarine and sugars until smooth and creamy. Beat in eggs, one at a time, until incorporated. Stir in vanilla. Add flour mixture and mix well. Fold in peaches and raisins (if using). Refrigerate dough for 30 minutes, until firm.
3. Drop by rounded teaspoonfuls (5 mL), about 2 inches (5 cm) apart, onto prepared baking sheet. Bake in preheated oven for 10 to 15 minutes or until golden brown. Immediately transfer to wire racks to cool.

Tip *Although these cookies will taste better if made from freshly picked peaches, canned peaches make an acceptable substitute out of season.*

Peanut Butter 'n' Honey Oatmeal Drops

Makes about 8 dozen
- Preheat oven to 350°F (180°C)
- Baking sheet, greased

1½ cups	all-purpose flour	375 mL
1 tsp	baking soda	5 mL
1 tsp	salt	5 mL
1½ cups	quick-cooking rolled oats	375 mL
1½ cups	crunchy peanut butter	375 mL
2 cups	liquid honey	500 mL
3	eggs	3
1 tbsp	water	15 mL
2 tsp	vanilla	10 mL
2 cups	raisins	500 mL

1. In a medium bowl, mix together flour, baking soda, salt and oats.
2. In a large bowl, mix together peanut butter, honey, eggs, water and vanilla until well blended. Add flour mixture and mix well. Fold in raisins. Refrigerate dough for 30 minutes, until firm.
3. Drop by rounded teaspoonfuls (5 mL), about 2 inches (5 cm) apart, onto prepared baking sheet. Bake in preheated oven for 12 to 15 minutes or until tops spring back when lightly touched. Immediately transfer to wire racks to cool.

Tip *When you need to measure honey or syrup, grease the cup with vegetable oil. If your recipe calls for oil, shortening or butter, measure that ingredient first, then use the cup to measure out honey or syrup.*

Golden Raisin Oat Cookies

Makes about 3 dozen

- Preheat oven to 350°F (180°C)
- Food processor
- Baking sheet, ungreased

2 cups	old-fashioned rolled oats	500 mL
1 cup	golden raisins	250 mL
2 cups	all-purpose flour	500 mL
1 tsp	baking soda	5 mL
½ tsp	salt	2 mL
1 cup	butter or margarine, softened	250 mL
1 cup	packed light brown sugar	250 mL
1 cup	granulated sugar	250 mL
2	eggs	2
2 tsp	vanilla	10 mL

1. Using a food processor, pulse oats and raisins until coarsely ground. Add flour, baking soda and salt and pulse once or twice to combine.

2. In a large bowl, beat butter or margarine and sugars until light and creamy. Beat in eggs, one at a time, until incorporated. Stir in vanilla. Add flour mixture and mix well.

3. Drop by tablespoonfuls (15 mL), about 2 inches (5 cm) apart, onto baking sheet. Bake in preheated oven for 12 to 15 minutes or until golden brown. Immediately transfer to wire racks to cool.

Tip *To soften brown sugar that has hardened, add a slice of fresh bread. Close container tightly. The sugar will be soft in a few hours.*

Peanut Butter Oat Cookies

Makes about 4 dozen

- Preheat oven to 350°F (180°C)
- Baking sheet, greased

1 cup	all-purpose flour	250 mL
½ tsp	baking powder	2 mL
½ tsp	baking soda	2 mL
1½ cups	quick-cooking rolled oats	375 mL
½ tsp	salt	2 mL
½ cup	butter, softened	125 mL
½ cup	granulated sugar	125 mL
1 cup	lightly packed brown sugar	250 mL
1	egg	1
6 tbsp	crunchy peanut butter	90 mL
2 tbsp	water	25 mL
½ tsp	vanilla	2 mL

1. In a medium bowl, mix together flour, baking powder, baking soda, oats and salt.

2. In a large bowl, beat butter and sugars until smooth and creamy. Beat in egg until incorporated. Add peanut butter, water and vanilla and mix until smooth. Add flour mixture and mix well.

3. Drop by rounded tablespoonfuls (15 mL), 2 inches (5 cm) apart, onto prepared baking sheet. Using your hand or the back of a spoon, press down slightly to flatten. Bake in preheated oven for 15 minutes or until golden brown. Immediately transfer to wire racks to cool.

Maple Walnut Oatmeal Cookies

Makes about 2½ dozen

- Preheat oven to 375°F (190°C)
- Baking sheet, greased

1 cup	all-purpose flour	250 mL
3 cups	quick-cooking rolled oats	750 mL
½ tsp	baking soda	2 mL
½ tsp	salt	2 mL
¼ tsp	ground cinnamon	1 mL
¾ cup	butter or butter-flavored shortening, softened	175 mL
1¼ cups	firmly packed brown sugar	300 mL
1	egg	1
1½ tsp	vanilla	7 mL
1½ tsp	maple extract	7 mL
⅓ cup	milk	75 mL
1 cup	coarsely chopped walnuts	250 mL

1. In a large bowl, mix together flour, oats, baking soda, salt and cinnamon.

2. In another large bowl, beat butter or shortening and brown sugar until smooth and creamy. Beat in egg until incorporated. Stir in vanilla, maple extract and milk and mix well. Add flour mixture and mix well. Fold in nuts.

3. Drop by rounded tablespoonfuls (15 mL), about 2 inches (5 cm) apart, onto prepared baking sheet. Using your hand or the back of a spoon, press down slightly to flatten. Bake in preheated oven for 10 to 12 minutes or until lightly browned. Let cool on sheet for 2 minutes, then transfer to wire racks to cool completely.

Tip *If you ever have a recipe that calls for half an egg, beat one egg lightly and use 2 tbsp (25 mL).*

Easy Oatmeal Drop Cookies

Makes about 4 dozen
- Preheat oven to 375°F (190°C)
- Baking sheet, greased

1 cup	all-purpose flour	250 mL
1 tsp	baking powder	5 mL
½ tsp	salt	2 mL
¾ cup	shortening, softened	175 mL
1 cup	lightly packed brown sugar	250 mL
2	eggs, beaten	2
1 tsp	vanilla	5 mL
⅓ cup	milk, divided	75 mL
3 cups	old-fashioned rolled oats	750 mL

1. In a large bowl, mix together flour, baking powder and salt.

2. Using two knives, a pastry blender or the tips of your fingers, cut in shortening until mixture resembles coarse crumbs. Stir in brown sugar, eggs, vanilla and half the milk. Beat until the mixture is smooth and blended. Mix together the remaining milk and oats and fold into mixture.

3. Drop by rounded teaspoonfuls (5 mL), about 2 inches (5 cm) apart, onto prepared baking sheet. Bake in preheated oven for 12 to 15 minutes or until golden brown. Immediately transfer to wire racks to cool.

Variations *Date Nut Oatmeal Cookies: Add 1 cup (250 mL) chopped dates and 1 cup (250 mL) chopped nuts to the batter along with the oats.*

Chocolate Chip Oatmeal Cookies: Add 1 cup (250 mL) semisweet chocolate chips to the batter along with the oats.

Raisin Oatmeal Cookies: Add ¾ cup (175 mL) raisins to the batter along with the oats.

Old-Fashioned Raisin Nut Oatmeal Cookies

Makes about 6 dozen
- Preheat oven to 400°F (200°C)
- Baking sheet, ungreased

1 cup	water	250 mL
1 cup	raisins	250 mL
2½ cups	all-purpose flour	625 mL
1 tsp	baking soda	5 mL
½ tsp	baking powder	2 mL
1 tsp	salt	5 mL
1 tsp	ground cinnamon	5 mL
½ tsp	ground cloves	2 mL
2 cups	quick-cooking rolled oats	500 mL
½ cup	chopped nuts	125 mL
¾ cup	shortening or butter, softened	175 mL
1½ cups	granulated sugar	375 mL
2	eggs	2
1 tsp	vanilla	5 mL

1. In a small saucepan, over medium heat, bring water and raisins to a boil. Simmer for 15 to 20 minutes or until raisins are plump. Drain, reserving liquid. If necessary, add water so liquid measures ½ cup (125 mL). Set raisins aside.

2. In a large bowl, mix together flour, baking soda, baking powder, salt, cinnamon, cloves, oats, nuts and reserved raisins.

3. In another large bowl, beat shortening or butter and sugar until smooth and creamy. Beat in eggs, one at a time. Stir in vanilla and reserved raisin liquid. Add flour mixture and mix well.

4. Drop by rounded teaspoonfuls (5 mL), 2 inches (5 cm) apart, onto baking sheet. Bake in preheated oven for 8 to 10 minutes or until lightly browned. Let cool for 3 minutes on sheet, then transfer to wire racks to cool completely.

Oatmeal Lace Pennies

Makes about 5½ dozen
- Preheat oven to 350°F (180°C)
- Baking sheet, lined with foil, bright side up

1 cup	old-fashioned rolled oats	250 mL
1 cup	granulated sugar	250 mL
3 tbsp	all-purpose flour	45 mL
¼ tsp	baking powder	1 mL
½ tsp	salt	2 mL
1	egg	1
½ cup	butter, melted	125 mL
½ tsp	vanilla	2 mL

1. In a medium bowl, mix together oats, sugar, flour, baking powder and salt.

2. In a large bowl, beat egg, butter and vanilla. Add flour mixture and mix well. (If dough seems too soft, chill for 15 to 20 minutes to firm.)

3. Drop by rounded teaspoonfuls (5 mL), about 2 inches (5 cm) apart, onto prepared baking sheet. Bake in preheated oven for 8 to 10 minutes. Let cool for 2 minutes on foil, then transfer to wire racks to cool completely.

German Chocolate Cake Cookies

Makes 3 dozen

- Preheat oven to 350°F (180°C)
- Baking sheet, greased

½ cup	butter or margarine, softened	125 mL
2	eggs	2
1	package (18 oz/510 g) chocolate cake mix	1
2 tbsp	all-purpose flour	25 mL
18	maraschino cherries, halved	18

1. In a large bowl, cream butter until smooth. Beat in eggs, one at a time, until incorporated. Mix in cake mix and flour. (Dough should be stiff.)
2. Drop by rounded teaspoonfuls (5 mL), about 2 inches (5 cm) apart, onto prepared baking sheet. Press a cherry half into the top of each cookie. Bake in preheated oven for 10 to 12 minutes. Immediately transfer to wire racks to cool.

Tip *For a treat, ice the cookies while they are still warm with Chocolate Icing (see recipe, page 548).*

Chocolate Buttermilk Pyramids

Makes about 4 dozen

- Preheat oven to 350°F (180°C)
- Baking sheet, ungreased

2 cups	all-purpose flour	500 mL
½ cup	unsweetened cocoa powder	125 mL
2 tsp	baking powder	10 mL
½ tsp	baking soda	2 mL
1 tsp	salt	5 mL
½ cup	shortening, softened	125 mL
1 cup	granulated sugar	250 mL
2	eggs	2
½ tsp	vanilla	2 mL
1 cup	buttermilk	250 mL
	Confectioner's (icing) sugar, sifted (optional)	

1. In a medium bowl, mix together flour, cocoa, baking powder, baking soda and salt.
2. In a large bowl, beat shortening and sugar until smooth and creamy. Beat in eggs, one at a time, until well incorporated. Stir in vanilla. Add flour mixture alternately with buttermilk, mixing well after each addition.

3. Drop by rounded teaspoonfuls (5 mL), about 2 inches (5 cm) apart, onto baking sheet. Bake in preheated oven for 12 to 15 minutes or until edges are lightly browned. Immediately transfer to wire racks to cool. Dust warm cookies with confectioner's sugar, if desired.

Tip *Keep a sugar shaker filled with confectioner's sugar available for dusting cookies.*

Jam-Filled Chocolate Thumbprints

Makes about 4 dozen

- Preheat oven to 350°F (180°C)
- Baking sheet, greased

1¾ cups	all-purpose flour	425 mL
1 tsp	baking soda	5 mL
½ tsp	salt	2 mL
¾ cup	butter or margarine, softened	175 mL
¼ cup	granulated sugar	50 mL
½ cup	packed brown sugar	125 mL
2	eggs	2
1 tsp	vanilla	5 mL
1½ cups	mini semisweet chocolate chips	375 mL
	Raspberry jam	

1. In a small bowl, mix together flour, baking soda and salt.
2. In a large bowl, cream butter or margarine and sugars until smooth and creamy. Add eggs, one at a time, beating until incorporated. Stir in vanilla. Add flour mixture and mix until just blended. Fold in chocolate chips and let stand for 10 minutes.
3. Drop by tablespoonfuls (15 mL), 2 inches (5 cm) apart, onto prepared baking sheet. Using your thumb, a thimble or the back of a small spoon, make an indentation in each cookie. Bake in preheated oven for 10 to 12 minutes or until golden brown. Spoon raspberry jam into each indentation and transfer to wire racks to cool.

Tip *To decrystalize jam, jelly or syrup, place jar in a pan of cold water, over low heat. Heat gently and the crystals will disappear.*

Chocolate Meringue Kisses

Makes about 4 dozen kisses
- Preheat oven to 300°F (150°C)
- Baking sheet, lined with parchment paper or foil and sprayed with nonstick spray
- Pastry bag with large star tip

¾ cup	granulated sugar	175 mL
¼ cup	unsweetened cocoa powder	50 mL
3	egg whites	3
¾ tsp	vanilla	4 mL
CHOCOLATE GLAZE		
3 oz	semisweet chocolate	90 g
1 tbsp	shortening	15 mL

1. In a small bowl, mix together sugar and cocoa.
2. In a large bowl, beat egg whites and vanilla until soft peaks form. Gradually beat in sugar mixture until stiff peaks form.
3. Using a pastry bag, press stars onto prepared sheet, about 2 inches (5 cm) apart. Bake in preheated oven for 30 to 35 minutes or until lightly browned. Immediately transfer to wire racks to cool.
4. *Prepare the glaze:* In a small saucepan, over low heat, melt chocolate and shortening, stirring constantly. Holding gently with your fingers, dip the top of each meringue into the glaze, then place on waxed paper to harden.

Tip *If meringues have fallen, crumble them into pieces and use in parfait dishes with whipped cream, ice cream and fruit.*

The Original Tollhouse Cookie

Makes about 5 dozen
- Preheat oven to 375°F (190°C)
- Baking sheet, greased

1 cup	all-purpose flour	250 mL
½ tsp	baking soda	2 mL
½ tsp	salt	2 mL
⅔ cup	butter, softened	150 mL
1 cup	lightly packed brown sugar	250 mL
1	egg	1
1½ tsp	vanilla	7 mL
½ cup	old-fashioned rolled oats	125 mL
½ cup	chopped nuts	125 mL
1 cup	semisweet chocolate chips or chunks	250 mL

1. In a small bowl, mix together flour, baking soda and salt.
2. In a large bowl, beat butter and brown sugar until smooth and creamy. Beat in egg until well incorporated. Stir in vanilla. Add flour mixture and mix well. Stir in rolled oats, nuts and chocolate chips or chunks.
3. Drop by rounded teaspoonfuls (5 mL), about 2 inches (5 cm) apart, onto prepared baking sheet. Bake in preheated oven for 10 minutes or until golden brown. Immediately transfer to wire racks to cool.

Tip *For a quick, delicious frosting, add maple syrup to confectioner's sugar and stir until thick and creamy. It's especially good on chocolate or mocha cookies.*

Dad's Favorite Chocolate Chip Cookies

Makes about 7 dozen
- Preheat oven to 375°F (190°C)
- Baking sheet, ungreased

3½ cups	all-purpose flour	875 mL
1 tsp	salt	5 mL
1 tsp	baking soda	5 mL
⅔ cup	shortening, softened	150 mL
⅔ cup	butter or margarine, softened	150 mL
1 cup	packed brown sugar	250 mL
1 cup	granulated sugar	250 mL
2	eggs	2
2 tsp	vanilla	10 mL
2	packages (each 12 oz/375 g) semisweet chocolate chips	2
1 cup	chopped nuts (optional)	250 mL

1. In a medium bowl, mix together flour, salt and baking soda.
2. In a large bowl, beat shortening, butter or margarine and sugars until smooth and creamy. Beat in eggs, one at a time, until incorporated. Stir in vanilla. Add flour mixture and mix well. Fold in chocolate chips and nuts (if using).
3. Drop by rounded teaspoonfuls (5 mL), about 2 inches (5 cm) apart, onto baking sheet. Bake in preheated oven for 10 minutes or until lightly browned. Let cool on sheet for 2 minutes, then transfer to wire racks to cool completely.

Chocolate Mint Chip Drops

Makes about 5 dozen

- Preheat oven to 375°F (190°C)
- Baking sheet, ungreased

2 cups	all-purpose flour	500 mL
¾ cup	unsweetened cocoa powder	175 mL
1 tsp	baking soda	5 mL
¼ tsp	salt	1 mL
1 cup	butter, softened	250 mL
¾ cup	granulated sugar	175 mL
1 cup	packed light brown sugar	250 mL
2	eggs	2
2 tsp	vanilla	10 mL
2 cups	mint chocolate chips	500 mL

1. In a medium bowl, combine flour, cocoa, baking soda and salt.
2. In a large bowl, beat butter and sugars until smooth and creamy. Add eggs, one at a time, mixing until well incorporated. Stir in vanilla. Add flour mixture and mix well. Fold in mint chocolate chips.
3. Drop by heaping teaspoonfuls (5 mL), about 2 inches (5 cm) apart, onto baking sheet. Bake in preheated oven for 9 to 12 minutes or until cookies are crisp. Let cool on sheet for 2 minutes, then transfer to wire racks to cool completely.

Tip *You can also substitute chocolate chips for the mint chocolate chips and add ¼ tsp (1 mL) mint extract along with the vanilla.*

Orange Chocolate Chip Cookies

Makes about 3 dozen

- Preheat oven to 350°F (180°C)
- Baking sheet, ungreased

1 cup	all-purpose flour	250 mL
¼ tsp	salt	1 mL
½ cup	butter or margarine, softened	125 mL
½ cup	granulated sugar	125 mL
4 oz	cream cheese, softened	125 g
1	egg	1
1 tsp	vanilla	5 mL
1 tsp	grated orange zest	5 mL
1 cup	semisweet chocolate chips	250 mL

1. In a small bowl, mix together flour and salt.
2. In a large bowl, beat butter or margarine, sugar and cream cheese until smooth. Beat in egg until incorporated. Stir in vanilla and orange zest. Add flour mixture and mix well. Fold in chocolate chips.
3. Drop by teaspoonfuls (5 mL), about 1 inch (2.5 cm) apart, onto baking sheet. Bake in preheated oven for 15 minutes or until edges are lightly browned. Immediately transfer to wire racks to cool.

Tip *When baking cookie dough containing chocolate bits, flouring a greased baking sheet will prevent the chocolate from sticking and burning if it comes in direct contact with the baking sheet.*

Cream Cheese Chocolate Chip Cookies

Makes about 4 dozen

- Preheat oven to 350°F (180°C)
- Baking sheet, ungreased

1	package (10 oz/300 g) mini semisweet chocolate chips, divided	1
2¼ cups	all-purpose flour	550 mL
1½ tsp	baking soda	7 mL
½ cup	butter, softened	125 mL
1	package (8 oz/250 g) cream cheese, softened	1
1½ cups	granulated sugar	375 mL
1	egg	1
½ cup	chopped nuts	125 mL

1. In a small saucepan, over very low heat, melt 1 cup (250 mL) of the chocolate chips.
2. In a medium bowl, mix together flour and baking soda.
3. In a large bowl, beat butter, cream cheese and sugar until smooth and creamy. Beat in egg until well incorporated. Beat in melted chocolate until well combined. Add flour mixture and mix well. Fold in nuts and the remaining chocolate chips.
4. Drop by tablespoonfuls (15 mL), about 2 inches (5 cm) apart, onto baking sheet. Bake in preheated oven for 10 to 12 minutes or until cookies are firm around the edges. Immediately transfer to wire racks to cool.

Tip *Try making these cookies using raspberry or other flavored chips. For an added treat, drizzle melted chocolate chips over top of the cookies as soon as they come out of the oven.*

Chocolate Chip Raspberry Cream Cheese Drops

Makes about 2 dozen

- Preheat oven to 350°F (180°C)
- Baking sheet, ungreased

2½ cups	all-purpose flour	625 mL
1 tsp	baking soda	5 mL
½ cup	butter or margarine, softened	125 mL
1½ cups	granulated sugar	375 mL
1	package (8 oz/250 g) cream cheese, softened	1
1	egg	1
1 cup	semisweet chocolate chips, melted	250 mL
1 cup	mini raspberry chips	250 mL

1. In a medium bowl, mix together flour and baking soda.
2. In a large bowl, beat butter or margarine, sugar and cream cheese until smooth. Beat in egg and melted chocolate until well blended. Add flour mixture and mix well. Fold in raspberry chips.
3. Drop by rounded teaspoonfuls (5 mL), about 2 inches (5 cm) apart, onto baking sheet. Bake in preheated oven for 12 to 15 minutes or until tops of cookies spring back when lightly touched. Immediately transfer to wire racks to cool.

Golden Coconut Macaroons

Makes about 1½ dozen

- Preheat oven to 350°F (180°C)
- Baking sheet, lined with parchment or waxed paper or foil

2	egg whites	2
½ tsp	vanilla	2 mL
2 tbsp	cake and pastry flour	25 mL
½ cup	granulated sugar	125 mL
¼ tsp	salt	1 mL
2 cups	shredded coconut (sweetened or unsweetened)	500 mL

1. In a large bowl, beat egg whites and vanilla until soft peaks form.
2. In another large bowl, sift together flour, sugar and salt. Fold in beaten egg whites, then fold in coconut, blending thoroughly.

3. Drop by rounded teaspoonfuls (5 mL), about 2 inches (5 cm) apart, onto prepared baking sheet. Bake in preheated oven for 20 minutes or until golden brown. Immediately transfer to wire racks to cool.

Variations *Cherry Coconut Macaroons: Add ½ cup (125 mL) chopped candied cherries along with the coconut.*

Chocolate Chip Macaroons: Substitute ½ cup (125 mL) semisweet chocolate chips for the coconut.

Cornflake Macaroons: Substitute 2 cups (500 mL) cornflakes for the coconut.

Hazelnut Macaroons: Substitute 2 cups (500 mL) finely ground hazelnuts for the coconut.

Ambrosia Coconut Drops

Makes about 4 dozen

- Preheat oven to 350°F (180°C)
- Baking sheet, lightly greased

2 cups	all-purpose flour	500 mL
1 tsp	baking soda	5 mL
½ tsp	salt	2 mL
½ cup	butter, softened	125 mL
1¼ cups	granulated sugar	300 mL
2	eggs	2
1 cup	shredded coconut (sweetened or unsweetened)	250 mL
1 tbsp	grated orange zest	15 mL
½ cup	freshly squeezed orange juice	125 mL

1. In a medium bowl, sift together flour, baking soda and salt.
2. In a large bowl, beat butter and sugar until smooth and creamy. Beat in eggs, one at a time, until incorporated. Add flour mixture and mix well.
3. In a small bowl, combine coconut and orange zest and juice. Fold into batter.
4. Drop by teaspoonfuls (5 mL), about 2 inches (5 cm) apart, onto prepared baking sheet. Bake in preheated oven for 10 to 12 minutes or until golden brown. Transfer to wire racks.

Tip *If you shake an egg and you hear a rattle, the egg is most likely bad. Don't use it.*

Carrot Coconut Drops

Makes about 4 dozen
- Preheat oven to 400°F (200°C)
- Baking sheet, lightly greased

2 cups	all-purpose flour	500 mL
2 tsp	baking powder	10 mL
½ tsp	salt	2 mL
½ cup	shortening, softened	125 mL
½ cup	butter, softened	125 mL
¾ cup	granulated sugar	175 mL
2	eggs	2
1 cup	mashed cooked carrots	250 mL
¾ cup	shredded coconut (sweetened or unsweetened)	175 mL

1. In a medium bowl, mix together flour, baking powder and salt.

2. In a large bowl, beat shortening, butter and sugar until smooth and creamy. Beat in eggs, one at a time, until incorporated. Stir in carrots. Add flour mixture and mix well. Fold in coconut.

3. Drop by teaspoonfuls (5 mL), about 2 inches (5 cm) apart, onto prepared baking sheet. Bake in preheated oven for 8 to 10 minutes or until golden brown. Transfer to wire racks.

Tip *If desired, these cookies may be frosted with Orange Butter Icing (see recipe, page 549).*

Hermits

Makes about 7 dozen
- Preheat oven to 375°F (190°C)
- Baking sheet, ungreased

3½ cups	all-purpose flour	875 mL
1 tsp	baking soda	5 mL
½ tsp	salt	2 mL
1 tsp	ground cinnamon	5 mL
1 tsp	ground nutmeg	5 mL
½ cup	butter or margarine, softened	125 mL
½ cup	shortening, softened	125 mL
2 cups	packed brown sugar	500 mL
2	eggs	2
½ cup	cold brewed coffee	125 mL
1 cup	chopped nuts	250 mL
1½ cups	raisins	375 mL

1. In a medium bowl, sift together flour, baking soda, salt, cinnamon and nutmeg.

2. In a large bowl, beat butter or margarine, shortening and brown sugar until smooth and creamy. Add eggs, one at a time, beating until incorporated. Beat in coffee. Add flour mixture and blend well. Fold in nuts and raisins.

3. Drop by rounded teaspoonfuls (5 mL), about 2 inches (5 cm) apart, onto baking sheet. Bake in preheated oven for 8 to 10 minutes. Let cool for 2 minutes on sheet, then transfer to wire racks to cool completely.

Tips *Hermits are a spicy and fruity drop cookie, originally from New England.*

Always buy nuts in a store where the turnover is high, as they become rancid quickly. Wrap leftover nuts well and store in the refrigerator or freezer.

Thrifty Hermit Cookies

Makes about 4 dozen
- Preheat oven to 375°F (190°C)
- Baking sheet, greased

3 cups	all-purpose flour	750 mL
2 tsp	baking powder	10 mL
¼ tsp	salt	1 mL
1 tsp	ground allspice	5 mL
1 tsp	ground cinnamon	5 mL
1 tsp	ground nutmeg	5 mL
1 cup	butter or margarine, softened	250 mL
1½ cups	granulated sugar	375 mL
1	egg	1
1 cup	chopped raisins	250 mL

1. In a medium bowl, mix together flour, baking powder, salt, allspice, cinnamon and nutmeg.

2. In a large bowl, beat butter or margarine and sugar until smooth and creamy. Beat in egg until well incorporated. Add flour mixture and mix well. Fold in raisins.

3. Drop by rounded teaspoonfuls (5 mL), about 2 inches (5 cm) apart, onto prepared baking sheet. Bake in preheated oven for 10 to 15 minutes or until golden brown. Let cool for 2 minutes, then transfer to wire racks to cool completely.

Soft Raisin Cookies

Makes about 6 dozen
- Preheat oven to 350°F (180°C)
- Baking sheet, greased

1 cup	water	250 mL
2 cups	raisins	500 mL
3½ cups	all-purpose flour	875 mL
1 tsp	baking powder	5 mL
1 tsp	baking soda	5 mL
1 tsp	salt	5 mL
½ tsp	ground nutmeg	2 mL
½ tsp	ground cinnamon	2 mL
1 cup	shortening, softened	250 mL
1¾ cups	granulated sugar	425 mL
2	eggs	2
1 tsp	vanilla	5 mL

1. In a saucepan, over medium heat, bring water and raisins to a boil. Cook for 3 minutes, remove from heat and let cool. Do not drain.
2. In a medium bowl, mix together flour, baking powder, baking soda, salt, nutmeg and cinnamon.
3. In a large bowl, beat shortening and sugar until smooth and creamy. Beat in eggs, one at a time. Stir in vanilla. Gradually add flour mixture, blending thoroughly. Stir in raisins and liquid.
4. Drop by rounded teaspoonfuls (5 mL), about 2 inches (5 cm) apart, onto prepared baking sheet. Bake in preheated oven for 12 to 15 minutes or until golden brown. Immediately transfer to wire racks to cool.

Cinnamon Raisin Banana Cookies

Makes about 4 dozen
- Preheat oven to 375°F (190°C)
- Baking sheet, lightly greased

2 cups	all-purpose flour	500 mL
¼ tsp	salt	1 mL
1 tsp	ground cinnamon	5 mL
1 cup	raisins	250 mL
½ cup	chopped nuts	125 mL
½ cup	butter or margarine, softened	125 mL
1 cup	granulated sugar	250 mL
2	eggs	2
1 cup	mashed ripe bananas, about 2 to 3 medium	250 mL

1. In a medium bowl, mix together flour, salt, cinnamon, raisins and nuts.
2. In a large bowl, beat butter or margarine and sugar until smooth and creamy. Beat in eggs, one at a time, until incorporated. Stir in banana. Add flour mixture and mix well.
3. Drop by rounded teaspoonfuls (5 mL), about 2 inches (5 cm) apart, onto prepared baking sheet. Bake in preheated oven for 8 to 10 minutes or until golden brown. Immediately transfer to wire racks to cool.

Orange Raisin Butter Cookies

Makes about 6 dozen
- Preheat oven to 400°F (200°C)
- Baking sheet, ungreased

1 cup	water	250 mL
2 cups	raisins	500 mL
4 cups	all-purpose flour	1 L
1 tsp	baking powder	5 mL
1 tsp	baking soda	5 mL
1 tsp	salt	5 mL
1½ tsp	ground cinnamon	7 mL
¼ tsp	ground nutmeg	1 mL
¼ tsp	ground allspice	1 mL
1 cup	shortening or butter, softened	250 mL
1¾ cups	granulated sugar	425 mL
3	eggs	3
2 tsp	vanilla	10 mL
2 tsp	grated orange zest	10 mL

1. In a saucepan, over medium heat, bring raisins and water to a boil. Simmer for 5 minutes. Drain, reserving liquid. Set raisins aside.
2. In a large bowl, mix together flour, baking powder, baking soda, salt, cinnamon, nutmeg and allspice.
3. In another large bowl, beat shortening and sugar until smooth and creamy. Beat in eggs, one at a time, until incorporated. Stir in vanilla.
4. Add flour mixture to creamed mixture alternately with reserved raisin liquid, mixing until well blended. Fold in raisins and orange zest.
5. Drop by tablespoonfuls (15 mL), 2 inches (5 cm) apart, onto baking sheet. Using the bottom of a glass dipped in flour, flatten slightly. Bake in preheated oven for 8 to 10 minutes or until golden brown. Let cool on sheet for 3 minutes, then transfer to wire racks to cool completely.

Tip *To rehydrate raisins that have dried out, place in a sieve and steam over hot water for 3 to 5 minutes.*

Spicy Fig Drops

Makes about 3 dozen
- Preheat oven to 375ºF (190ºC)
- Baking sheet, greased

½ cup	packed dried figs	125 mL
½ cup	shortening	125 mL
¼ cup	granulated sugar	50 mL
½ cup	light (fancy) molasses	125 mL
1	egg, beaten	1
1 tsp	vanilla	5 mL
½ tsp	lemon extract	2 mL
3 cups less 2 tbsp	all-purpose flour	725 mL
1 tsp	baking soda	5 mL
½ tsp	ground cinnamon	2 mL
¼ tsp	ground nutmeg	1 mL
¼ tsp	ground ginger	1 mL
¼ tsp	salt	1 mL

1. In a saucepan, soak figs in boiling water for 10 minutes. Drain, cut off stems and discard. Cut figs into small pieces and set aside.

2. In a saucepan, bring shortening, sugar and molasses to a boil. Remove from heat and let cool to lukewarm. Beat in egg, vanilla and lemon extract.

3. In a large bowl, sift together flour, baking soda, cinnamon, nutmeg, ginger and salt. Stir flour mixture into molasses mixture until well blended. Fold in reserved figs.

4. Drop by rounded teaspoonfuls (5 mL), about 2 inches (5 cm) apart, onto prepared baking sheet. Bake in preheated oven for 12 minutes or until golden brown. Transfer to wire racks to cool.

Tip *To cut sticky foods, such as figs, use kitchen scissors. Rub blades with oil or dip occasionally in hot water.*

Date Nut Cookies

Makes about 5 dozen
- Preheat oven to 375ºF (190ºC)
- Baking sheet, greased

2 cups	all-purpose flour	500 mL
1 tsp	baking soda	5 mL
1 lb	dates, pitted and chopped	500 g
1 cup	shortening, softened	250 mL
1½ cups	lightly packed brown sugar	375 mL
2	eggs	2
2 tsp	vanilla	10 mL
1¼ tsp	ground cinnamon	6 mL
¼ tsp	ground nutmeg	1 mL
1 cup	old-fashioned rolled oats	250 mL
¾ cup	shredded coconut (sweetened or unsweetened)	175 mL
½ cup	chopped nuts	125 mL

1. In a medium bowl, mix together flour and baking soda. Add dates and toss to coat.

2. In a large bowl, beat shortening and brown sugar until smooth and creamy. Add eggs, one at a time, beating until well incorporated. Stir in vanilla, cinnamon and nutmeg until blended. Add oats and flour mixture, mixing until just incorporated. Fold in coconut and nuts.

3. Drop by tablespoonfuls (15 mL), about 2 inches (5 cm) apart, onto prepared baking sheet. Bake in preheated oven for 8 to 10 minutes or until golden brown. Let cool on sheet for 2 minutes, then transfer to wire racks to cool completely.

Mixed Fruit 'n' Nut Drops

Makes about 4 dozen
- Preheat oven to 350ºF (180ºC)
- Mini baking cups or baking sheet, lightly greased

1¼ cups	all-purpose flour	300 mL
½ tsp	baking soda	2 mL
2 cups	quartered pitted dates	250 mL
1 cup	diced candied pineapple	250 mL
1 cup	halved candied cherries	250 mL
½ cup	butter, softened	125 mL
½ cup	packed brown sugar	125 mL
1	egg	1
1 tsp	vanilla	5 mL
½ tsp	ground cinnamon	2 mL
½ cup	chopped walnuts	125 mL
½ cup	chopped pecans	125 mL
½ cup	chopped hazelnuts	125 mL
	Heated corn syrup (optional)	

1. In a large bowl, combine flour, baking soda, dates, pineapple and cherries; toss to coat.

2. In another large bowl, beat butter and brown sugar until smooth and creamy. Beat in egg until incorporated. Stir in vanilla and cinnamon. Add flour mixture and mix well. Fold in nuts.

3. Drop by rounded teaspoonfuls (5 mL) into mini baking cups placed on a baking sheet or directly onto prepared sheet. Bake in preheated oven for 12 to 15 minutes or until tops look dry. Immediately transfer to wire racks to cool. If desired, brush tops lightly with corn syrup.

Frosted Banana Split Drops

Makes about 4 dozen
- Preheat oven to 375°F (190°C)
- Baking sheet, lightly greased

2 cups	all-purpose flour	500 mL
2 tsp	baking powder	10 mL
¼ tsp	baking soda	1 mL
¼ tsp	salt	1 mL
½ tsp	ground cinnamon	2 mL
¼ tsp	ground cloves	1 mL
1 cup	packed brown sugar	250 mL
¼ cup	butter or margarine, softened	50 mL
¼ cup	shortening, softened	50 mL
2	eggs	2
1 cup	mashed ripe bananas, about 2 to 3 medium	250 mL
½ cup	chopped nuts	125 mL
	Chocolate or Vanilla Icing or Fresh Strawberry Frosting	

1. In a medium bowl, mix together flour, baking powder, baking soda, salt, cinnamon and cloves.
2. In a large bowl, beat brown sugar, butter or margarine and shortening until smooth and creamy. Beat in eggs, one at a time, until incorporated. Blend in bananas. Add flour mixture and mix well. Fold in nuts. Cover dough and refrigerate for about 1 hour, until chilled.
3. Drop by rounded teaspoonfuls (5 mL), about 2 inches (5 cm) apart, onto prepared baking sheet. Bake in preheated oven for 8 to 10 minutes or until cookie springs back when lightly touched. Immediately transfer to wire racks to cool completely.
4. Frost with Chocolate Icing (page 548), Fresh Strawberry Frosting (page 547) or Vanilla Icing (page 548).

Orange Nut Cranberry Cookies

Makes about 6 dozen
- Preheat oven to 375°F (190°C)
- Baking sheet, greased

3 cups	all-purpose flour	750 mL
1 tsp	baking powder	5 mL
¼ tsp	baking soda	1 mL
½ tsp	salt	2 mL
½ cup	butter or margarine, softened	125 mL
1 cup	granulated sugar	250 mL
¾ cup	packed brown sugar	175 mL
1	egg	1
¼ cup	milk	50 mL
2 tbsp	orange juice	25 mL
2½ cups	coarsely chopped frozen cranberries	625 mL
¾ cup	chopped nuts	175 mL

1. In a medium bowl, mix together flour, baking powder, baking soda and salt.
2. In a large bowl, beat butter or margarine and sugars until smooth and creamy. Beat in egg until well incorporated. Add milk and orange juice and blend well. Add flour mixture to creamed mixture and mix well. Fold in cranberries and chopped nuts.
3. Drop by rounded teaspoonfuls (5 mL), about 2 inches (5 cm) apart, onto prepared baking sheet. Bake in preheated oven for 10 to 15 minutes or until lightly browned. Immediately transfer to wire racks to cool

Hawaiian Pineapple Drops

Makes about 3 dozen
- Preheat oven to 400°F (200°C)
- Baking sheet, greased

2 cups	all-purpose flour	500 mL
1 tsp	baking powder	5 mL
½ tsp	baking soda	2 mL
¼ tsp	salt	1 mL
½ cup	butter or margarine, softened	125 mL
1 cup	lightly packed brown sugar	250 mL
1	egg	1
1 tsp	vanilla	5 mL
1 cup	crushed pineapple, well drained	250 mL

1. In a medium bowl, mix together flour, baking powder, baking soda and salt.
2. In a large bowl, beat butter or margarine and brown sugar until smooth and creamy. Beat in egg until well incorporated. Stir in vanilla. Add flour mixture and mix well. (Dough will look crumbly.) Add pineapple and mix until well blended.
3. Drop by tablespoonfuls (15 mL), 2 inches (5 cm) apart, onto prepared baking sheet. Bake in preheated oven for 10 to 15 minutes or until golden brown. Immediately transfer to wire racks to cool.

Brandy Lace Rollups

Makes about 2½ dozen

- Preheat oven to 375°F (190°C)
- Baking sheet, lightly greased
- Cake or pastry decorating bag

¾ cup	all-purpose flour	175 mL
½ tsp	ground ginger	2 mL
½ cup	butter or margarine, softened	125 mL
½ cup	corn syrup	125 mL
⅓ cup	packed brown sugar	75 mL
2 tsp	brandy or freshly squeezed lemon juice	10 mL
1 cup	whipping (35%) cream	250 mL
1 tbsp	brandy (optional)	15 mL

1. In a small bowl, mix together flour and ginger.

2. In a saucepan, over medium heat, melt butter or margarine, corn syrup and brown sugar, stirring frequently. Remove from heat and stir in brandy or lemon juice. Add flour mixture, mixing until well blended.

3. Drop by rounded teaspoonfuls (5 mL), about 5 inches (12.5 cm) apart, onto prepared baking sheet. Bake in preheated oven for 6 to 8 minutes or until cookies are a rich brown and have spread into 3- to 4-inch (7.5- to 10-cm) rounds.

4. Let cool for 1 to 3 minutes on sheet. Then, while still warm and working quickly, wrap each cookie around a wooden spoon handle, allowing it to firm up before sliding off. Place roll on a wire rack to cool. If cookies become too crisp to roll, return to preheated oven for about 1 minute to soften. Fill rollups with fresh whipped cream, flavored with brandy, if desired. Use a decorating bag with a plain or fancy tip and pipe the whipped cream into each end of the rollup.

Tip *For ease of rolling, bake rollups one baking sheet at a time. The cookies are likely to harden before they can be rolled if you work with a larger quantity.*

Variation *Brandy Lace Crisps: Leave cookies on baking sheet to cool for 3 to 5 minutes, then transfer to a wire rack. Store in an airtight container away from other cookies.*

Sunny Lemon Yogurt Cookies

Makes about 4 dozen

- Preheat oven to 375°F (190°C)
- Baking sheet, lightly greased

2⅔ cups	all-purpose flour	650 mL
1 tsp	baking powder	5 mL
½ tsp	baking soda	2 mL
1 tsp	salt	5 mL
2	eggs	2
1½ cups	granulated sugar	375 mL
⅓ cup	vegetable oil	75 mL
½ cup	low-fat lemon-flavored yogurt	125 mL
½ tsp	finely grated lemon zest	2 mL
1 tsp	freshly squeezed lemon juice	5 mL
	Confectioner's (icing) sugar, sifted (optional)	
	Lemon Butter Frosting (optional, see recipe, page 547)	

1. In a medium bowl, mix together flour, baking powder, baking soda and salt.

2. In a large bowl, beat eggs, sugar, oil, yogurt, lemon zest and juice until well blended. Add flour mixture and mix well.

3. Drop by rounded teaspoonfuls (5 mL), about 2 inches (5 cm) apart, onto prepared baking sheet. Bake in preheated oven for 10 to 12 minutes or until lightly browned around the edges. Let cool on sheet for 2 minutes, then transfer to wire racks to cool completely. Sprinkle with confectioner's sugar or frost, if desired.

Tip *When a recipe calls for just a few drops of lemon juice, poke holes in an uncut lemon with a fork and squeeze out the required amount. The lemon can go back into the refrigerator and be used several more times.*

Cinnamon Mocha Cappuccino Cookies

Makes about 2½ dozen
- Preheat oven to 375ºF (190ºC)
- Baking sheet, well-greased

2 cups	all-purpose flour	500 mL
1 tsp	baking powder	5 mL
½ tsp	ground cinnamon	2 mL
¾ cup less 1 tbsp	butter or margarine, softened	160 mL
1¼ cups	granulated sugar	300 mL
2	eggs	2
2 tsp	instant cappuccino or other strong coffee powder or granules	10 mL
1 tbsp	boiling water	15 mL
⅓ cup	hot milk	75 mL
1 tsp	vanilla	5 mL
	Sugar-Cinnamon Mix (see recipe, page 543)	
1 oz	semisweet chocolate, grated	30 g

1. In a medium bowl, mix together flour, baking powder and cinnamon.
2. In a large bowl, beat butter or margarine and sugar until smooth and creamy. Add eggs, one at a time, beating until incorporated.
3. In a small bowl, mix together coffee powder, water and hot milk, stirring until coffee dissolves. Stir in vanilla and add to creamed mixture. Add flour mixture and mix thoroughly.
4. Drop by teaspoonfuls (5 mL), about 2 inches (5 cm) apart, onto prepared baking sheet. Sprinkle tops with sugar-cinnamon mix and grated chocolate. Bake in preheated oven for 10 minutes or until bottoms are golden brown. Immediately transfer to wire racks to cool.

Brown Sugar Cookies

Makes about 6 dozen
- Preheat oven to 400ºF (200ºC)
- Baking sheet, lightly greased

3½ cups	all-purpose flour	875 mL
1 tsp	baking soda	5 mL
1 tsp	salt	5 mL
1 cup	shortening, softened	250 mL
2 cups	lightly packed brown sugar	500 mL
2	eggs	2
½ cup	buttermilk	125 mL

1. In a medium bowl, mix together flour, baking soda and salt.
2. In a large bowl, beat shortening and brown sugar until smooth and creamy. Add eggs, one at a time, beating until incorporated. Beat in buttermilk. Add flour mixture and mix well. Cover dough and refrigerate for 1 hour.
3. Drop by teaspoonfuls (5 mL), about 2 inches (5 cm) apart, on prepared baking sheet. Bake in preheated oven for 8 to 10 minutes or until cookie springs back when lightly touched. Immediately transfer to wire racks.

Variations *Coconut Brown Sugar Cookies: Stir in 1 cup (250 mL) shredded coconut before chilling.*

Fruit Nut Brown Sugar Cookies: Stir in 2 cups (500 mL) chopped candied fruit and 1 cup (250 mL) chopped nuts before chilling.

Meringue Dainties

Makes about 3 dozen small meringues
- Preheat oven to 250ºF (120ºC)
- Baking sheet, lined with greased foil

4	egg whites	4
2 tsp	vanilla	10 mL
½ tsp	cream of tartar	2 mL
1 cup	granulated sugar	250 mL

1. Beat egg whites, vanilla and cream of tartar until soft peaks form. Beat in sugar, 2 tbsp (25 mL) at a time, until stiff peaks form.
2. Drop by rounded teaspoonfuls (5 mL), about 2 inches (5 cm) apart, onto prepared baking sheet. Bake in preheated oven for 50 to 60 minutes or until lightly browned. Turn heat off and leave meringues to dry in oven for 30 minutes, then transfer to wire racks.

Variation *Meringue Shells: Shape batter into 3-inch (7.5-cm) mounds and bake for 1 to 1¼ hours. Remove from oven and, using a spoon, scoop out the soft centers. Return meringues to preheated oven 30 minutes, then transfer to wire racks. When cooled, fill centers with whipped cream or your favorite custard.*

Crisp Caramel Wafers

Makes about 2½ dozen

- Preheat oven to 350°F (180°C)
- Baking sheet, lined with parchment or waxed paper

½ cup	all-purpose flour	125 mL
½ tsp	ground cardamom	2 mL
¼ cup	sliced almonds	50 mL
3 tbsp	butter	45 mL
¼ cup	corn syrup	50 mL
¼ cup	packed brown sugar	50 mL
½ tsp	vanilla	2 mL

1. In a bowl, combine flour, cardamom and almonds.
2. In a saucepan, over medium-low heat, bring butter, corn syrup and brown sugar to a boil, stirring constantly. Add vanilla and mix well. Set aside to cool slightly. Add flour mixture and stir until well blended.
3. Drop by rounded teaspoonfuls (5 mL), about 4 inches (10 cm) apart, onto prepared baking sheet. Bake in preheated oven for 6 to 8 minutes or until golden brown. Let cool on sheet for 5 minutes, then transfer to wire racks to cool completely.

Spiced Drop Cookies

Makes about 3½ dozen

- Preheat oven to 350°F (180°C)
- Baking sheet, greased

2¼ cups	all-purpose flour	550 mL
2 tsp	baking soda	10 mL
1 tsp	ground cinnamon	5 mL
½ tsp	ground cloves	2 mL
1 tbsp	ground ginger	15 mL
¼ tsp	salt	1 mL
½ cup	shortening, softened	125 mL
½ cup	granulated sugar	125 mL
1	egg	1
½ cup	light (fancy) molasses	125 mL
⅓ cup	hot strong brewed coffee	75 mL
2 tbsp	anise seeds	25 mL
2 tsp	crushed coriander seeds	10 mL
	Walnut or pecan halves (optional)	

VANILLA GLAZE (OPTIONAL)

2 cups	sifted confectioner's (icing) sugar	500 mL
1 tsp	vanilla	5 mL
	Milk	

1. In a medium bowl, mix together flour, baking soda, cinnamon, cloves, ginger and salt.
2. In a large bowl, cream shortening and sugar until smooth and creamy. Beat in egg until incorporated, then blend in molasses. Add flour mixture to creamed mixture alternately with coffee, mixing well after each addition. Stir in anise and coriander seeds.
3. Drop by rounded teaspoonfuls (5 mL), about 2 inches (5 cm) apart, onto prepared baking sheet. Top with nuts (if using). Bake in preheated oven for 8 to 10 minutes or until golden brown. Immediately transfer to wire racks to cool.
4. *If desired, prepare the glaze:* In a medium bowl, beat together confectioner's sugar, vanilla and enough milk to make the mixture spreadable. Top cookies with glaze.

Traditional Peanut Butter Cookies

Makes about 3 dozen

- Preheat oven to 375°F (190°C)
- Baking sheet, ungreased

1¼ cups	all-purpose flour	300 mL
¾ tsp	baking soda	4 mL
¾ tsp	salt	4 mL
½ cup	shortening, softened	125 mL
¾ cup	smooth peanut butter	175 mL
1¼ cups	firmly packed brown sugar	300 mL
1	egg	1
1 tbsp	vanilla	15 mL
3 tbsp	milk	45 mL

1. In a small bowl, mix together flour, baking soda and salt.
2. In a large bowl, cream shortening, peanut butter and brown sugar until smooth. Beat in egg until incorporated. Mix in vanilla and milk until smooth. Add flour mixture and mix thoroughly.
3. Drop by rounded tablespoonfuls (15 mL), about 2 inches (5 cm) apart, onto baking sheet. Bake in preheated oven for 6 to 8 minutes or until golden brown. Let cool on sheet for 2 to 3 minutes, then transfer to wire racks to cool completely.

Tip *Although these cookies work well as drop cookies, you can also shape them into a 1-inch (2.5 cm) ball and flatten with tines of a fork dipped in flour.*

Poppy Seed Drop Cookies

Makes about 2½ dozen
- Preheat oven to 350°F (180°C)
- Baking sheet, greased

1 cup	poppy seeds	250 mL
½ cup	scalded milk	125 mL
1½ cups	all-purpose flour	375 mL
1 tsp	baking powder	5 mL
Pinch	salt	Pinch
½ tsp	ground cinnamon	2 mL
¼ tsp	ground cloves	1 mL
½ cup	butter, softened	125 mL
½ cup	granulated sugar	125 mL
2 oz	unsweetened chocolate, melted (optional)	60 g

1. In a small bowl, soak poppy seeds in hot milk for 30 minutes. Set aside.
2. In another small bowl, mix together flour, baking powder, salt, cinnamon and cloves.
3. In a large bowl, beat butter and sugar until smooth and creamy. Stir in chocolate (if using), mixing until well blended. Mix in poppy seed mixture. Add flour mixture and mix thoroughly.
4. Drop by rounded teaspoonfuls (5 mL), about 2 inches (5 cm) apart, onto prepared baking sheet. Bake in preheated oven for 20 minutes or until browned. Immediately transfer to wire racks to cool.

Tip *To keep spices fresh for as long as possible, grind your own and keep in jars, sealed tightly away from heat, light and moisture. Stored this way, spices will keep for about a year.*

Classic Sour Cream Drop Cookies

Makes about 5 dozen
- Preheat oven to 425°F (220°C)
- Baking sheet, lightly greased

2¾ cups	all-purpose flour	675 mL
½ tsp	baking powder	2 mL
½ tsp	baking soda	2 mL
½ tsp	salt	2 mL
½ cup	shortening, softened	125 mL
1½ cups	granulated sugar	375 mL
2	eggs	2
1 tsp	vanilla	5 mL
1 cup	sour cream	250 mL

1. In a medium bowl, mix together flour, baking powder, baking soda and salt.
2. In a large bowl, beat shortening and sugar until smooth and creamy. Add eggs, one at a time, beating until well incorporated. Mix in vanilla and sour cream. Gradually add flour mixture, mixing until well blended. Refrigerate for at least 1 hour.
3. Drop by rounded teaspoonfuls (5 mL), about 2 inches (5 cm) apart, onto prepared baking sheet. Bake in preheated oven for 8 to 10 minutes or until lightly browned. Immediately transfer to wire racks to cool.

Variations *Chocolate Sour Cream Drops: Mix in 2 squares (each 1 oz/28 g) melted unsweetened chocolate to the creamed mixture, before adding flour mixture. Fold in 1 cup (250 mL) chopped nuts before chilling dough.*

Fruit Cream Drops: Fold in 1 cup (250 mL) chopped dates or candied fruit before chilling dough.

Almond Sugar Cookie Crisps

Makes about 2½ dozen
- Preheat oven to 350°F (180°C)
- Baking sheet, ungreased

2 cups	all-purpose flour	500 mL
1 tsp	baking soda	5 mL
1 tsp	cream of tartar	5 mL
1 cup	shortening, softened, (butter-flavored, if possible)	250 mL
½ cup	granulated sugar	125 mL
½ cup	packed brown sugar	125 mL
1	egg	1
½ tsp	vanilla	2 mL
½ tsp	almond extract	2 mL

1. In a medium bowl, mix together flour, baking soda and cream of tartar.
2. In a large bowl, beat shortening and sugars until smooth and creamy. Beat in egg until well incorporated. Stir in vanilla and almond extract. Gradually add flour mixture and mix thoroughly.
3. Drop by tablespoonfuls (15 mL), about 2 inches (5 cm) apart, onto baking sheet. Flatten with the bottom of a glass dipped in sugar. Bake in preheated oven for 10 to 12 minutes or until lightly browned. Immediately transfer to wire racks to cool. Recipe can be doubled, if desired.

Tip *Using a glass dipped in water and then sugar to press down and flatten the dough makes cookies thinner and crisper.*

Chocolate Chipit Snackin' Muffins (page 27)

Spiced Carrot Bran Muffins (page 35)

Berry Oat Bran Muffins (page 43)

Peachy Oatmeal Muffins (page 48)

Blueberry Muffins (page 68)

Strawberry Tea Muffins (page 87)

Chili-Pepper Corn Muffins (page 92)

Golden Honey Bran Muffins (page 102)

Deluxe Pizza Muffins (page 111)

Vegetable Corn Muffins (page 115)

Lemon Cream Cuffin Tarts (page 124)

"Candy Apple" Muffins (page 140)

Apple Streusel Pumpkin Muffins (page 152)

Orange Upside-Down Cranberry Muffins (page 157)

Mocha Walnut Frosted Muffins (page 170)

Wholesome Banana Granola Drops (page 176), Hermits (page 185),
Traditional Peanut Butter Cookies (page 191) and Baba Mary's Thimble Cookies (page 520)

Whole Wheat Spice Cookies

Makes about 3 dozen

- Preheat oven to 350°F (180°C)
- Baking sheet, lightly greased

¼ cup	vegetable oil	50 mL
¼ cup	light (fancy) molasses	50 mL
½ cup	granulated sugar	125 mL
¼ cup	packed brown sugar	50 mL
2	eggs	2
½ cup	whole wheat flour	125 mL
1½ cups	all-purpose flour	375 mL
2 tsp	baking soda	10 mL
¼ tsp	salt	1 mL
1 tsp	ground ginger	5 mL
1 tsp	ground cinnamon	5 mL
1 tsp	ground cloves	5 mL

1. In a medium bowl, whisk oil, molasses, sugars and eggs until blended.

2. In a large bowl, mix together flours, baking soda, salt, ginger, cinnamon and cloves. Make a well in the center and add the molasses mixture, mixing until thoroughly blended.

3. Drop by teaspoonfuls (5 mL), about 2 inches (5 cm) apart, onto prepared baking sheets. Bake in preheated oven for 8 to 10 minutes or until cookies are firm to the touch. Let cool on sheets for 5 minutes, then transfer to wire racks to cool completely.

Favorite Pudding Cookies

Makes 6 to 7 dozen

- Preheat oven to 350°F (180°C)
- Baking sheet, ungreased

4 cups	all-purpose flour	1 L
1 tsp	baking soda	5 mL
1 tsp	cream of tartar	5 mL
1 cup	granulated sugar	250 mL
1 cup	confectioner's (icing) sugar, sifted	250 mL
1 cup	vegetable oil	250 mL
1 cup	butter or margarine, softened	250 mL
2	eggs	2
1	package (3½ oz/102 g) instant pudding mix	1
1 tsp	vanilla	5 mL
	Additional granulated sugar	

1. In a medium bowl, combine flour, baking soda and cream of tartar. Mix together.

2. In a large mixer bowl, cream sugar, confectioner's sugar, oil and butter until smooth. Beat in eggs, pudding and vanilla. Add flour mixture, mixing well to blend. Drop by tablespoonfuls (15 mL) onto baking sheet, about 2 inches (5 cm) apart. Flatten each with the bottom of a glass dipped in sugar.

3. Bake in preheated oven for about 15 minutes or until golden brown. Let cool on a wire rack.

Tips *How many cookies you get depends on the size of your spoonfuls!*

You can choose the flavor of instant pudding you prefer. My favorites are lemon and butterscotch.

Hand-Shaped Cookies

Hand-shaped cookies are, as their name suggests, molded into a shape by hand. The dough, which is firmer than drop cookie dough, is usually shaped into a small ball before baking. Often it is flattened slightly and imprinted with a simple pattern made by the tines of a fork or the bottom of a glass.

Nutmeg Pecan Butter Balls

Makes about 2 dozen

- Preheat oven to 350°F (180°C)
- Baking sheet, ungreased

½ cup	butter, softened	125 mL
⅓ cup	confectioner's (icing) sugar, sifted	75 mL
½ tsp	vanilla	2 mL
¼ tsp	ground nutmeg	1 mL
Pinch	salt	Pinch
1 cup	all-purpose flour	250 mL
½ cup	finely chopped pecans, toasted	125 mL
½ cup	coarsely chopped pecans, toasted	125 mL

1. In a large bowl, beat butter and confectioner's sugar until smooth and creamy. Beat in vanilla, nutmeg and salt until well blended. Gradually mix in flour and finely chopped pecans. Wrap dough tightly in plastic wrap and refrigerate for 2 to 3 hours, until firm.

2. Shape dough into 1-inch (2.5 cm) balls and roll in coarsely chopped pecans until coated. Place about 2 inches (5 cm) apart on baking sheet. Bake in preheated oven for 12 to 15 minutes or until browned. Let cool on baking sheets for about 2 minutes, then, being careful to ensure cookies don't break, transfer to wire racks to cool completely.

Cinnamon Pecan Snickerdoodles

Makes about 5 dozen

- Preheat oven to 350°F (180°C)
- Baking sheet, lightly greased

3 cups	all-purpose flour	750 mL
1 tsp	baking powder	5 mL
¼ tsp	salt	1 mL
1 cup	butter, softened (no substitutes)	250 mL
1½ cups	granulated sugar	375 mL
2	eggs	2
1 tsp	vanilla	5 mL
⅓ cup	granulated sugar	75 mL
1 tbsp	ground cinnamon	15 mL
1 cup	almond, pecan or walnut halves	250 mL

1. In a bowl, combine flour, baking powder and salt.

2. In a large bowl, beat butter and 1½ cups (375 mL) sugar until smooth and creamy. Beat in eggs, one at a time. Stir in vanilla. Add flour mixture and mix well.

3. In a small bowl, mix together ⅓ cup (75 mL) sugar and cinnamon.

4. Shape dough into 1-inch (2.5 cm) balls, then roll in cinnamon mixture to coat. Place about 2 inches (5 cm) apart on prepared baking sheet. Press half a nut into the top of each cookie. Bake in preheated oven for 12 to 15 minutes or until golden brown. Immediately transfer to wire racks to cool.

Mexican Wedding Cakes

Makes about 4 dozen

- Preheat oven to 325°F (160°C)
- Baking sheet, ungreased

2 cups	all-purpose flour	500 mL
½ cup	confectioner's (icing) sugar, sifted	125 mL
1 cup	finely chopped pecans, toasted	250 mL
Pinch	salt	Pinch
1 tsp	vanilla	5 mL
1 cup	cold butter (no substitutes), cut into 1-inch (2.5 cm) chunks	500 mL
	Additional confectioner's sugar	

1. In a large bowl, mix together flour, confectioner's sugar, pecans and salt until thoroughly combined. Add vanilla and mix well.

2. Using two knives, a pastry blender or your fingers, cut butter into flour mixture until mixture resembles crumbs. Knead dough gently until it begins to hold together.

3. Shape dough into 1-inch (2.5 cm) balls and place about 2 inches (5 cm) apart on baking sheet. Bake in preheated oven for 25 minutes, until lightly browned. Immediately transfer to wire racks and let cool for 5 minutes. Dip both sides of cookies in confectioner's sugar and return to racks to cool completely.

Tip *To easily make chopped nuts, place pieces in a plastic bag and crush with a rolling pin. Then pour directly into a measuring cup.*

Quick 'n' Easy Butter Nut Cookies

Makes 3 dozen

- Preheat oven to 350°F (180°C)
- Baking sheet, ungreased

1 cup	butter, softened	250 mL
6 tbsp	confectioner's (icing) sugar, sifted	90 mL
2 tsp	vanilla	10 mL
2 cups	sifted cake and pastry flour (no substitutes)	500 mL
1 cup	finely chopped nuts	250 mL
	Confectioner's (icing) sugar, sifted	

1. In a large bowl, beat butter, sugar and vanilla until smooth and creamy. Gradually beat in flour until thoroughly blended. Fold in nuts. Cover and refrigerate for 30 minutes, until firm.

2. Shape dough into 1-inch (2.5 cm) balls. Place about 2 inches (5 cm) apart on baking sheet and flatten slightly with a fork or the bottom of a glass dipped in flour. Bake in preheated oven for 25 minutes or until golden brown. Immediately transfer to wire racks and sprinkle with confectioner's sugar.

Greek Almond Cookies

Makes about 3 dozen

- Preheat oven to 325°F (160°C)
- Baking sheet, ungreased

2 cups	all-purpose flour	500 mL
½ tsp	baking powder	2 mL
1 cup	butter, softened	250 mL
⅓ cup	confectioner's (icing) sugar, sifted	75 mL
1	egg yolk	1
½ tsp	vanilla	2 mL
2 tbsp	brandy	25 mL
½ cup	finely chopped blanched almonds	125 mL

1. In a medium bowl, mix together flour and baking powder.

2. In a large bowl, beat butter and $\frac{1}{4}$ cup (50 mL) of the confectioner's sugar until smooth and creamy. Add egg yolk, vanilla and brandy and beat until very light. Using a spoon, stir in almonds. Stir in flour mixture until a soft dough forms. Cover and refrigerate for 30 minutes, until firm.

3. Form level tablespoonfuls (15 mL) of dough into almond shapes and place about $1\frac{1}{2}$ inches (4 cm) apart on baking sheet. Bake in preheated oven for 25 to 30 minutes or until sandy in color. Immediately transfer to wire racks to cool.

4. Before serving or storing, sprinkle the remaining confectioner's sugar over tops of cookies.

Tip *A Christmas tradition in Greece is to press a whole clove into the center of each cookie before baking.*

Chinese Almond Cookies

Makes 32 balls

- Preheat oven to 350°F (180°C)
- Baking sheet, ungreased

$2\frac{1}{2}$ cups	all-purpose flour	625 mL
$1\frac{1}{2}$ tsp	baking powder	7 mL
1 tsp	ground allspice	5 mL
$\frac{1}{2}$ tsp	ground cloves	2 mL
$\frac{1}{2}$ tsp	salt	2 mL
1 cup	butter or margarine, softened	250 mL
$\frac{3}{4}$ cup	granulated sugar	175 mL
1	egg	1
1 tsp	almond extract	5 mL
$\frac{1}{2}$ cup	finely ground blanched almonds	125 mL
1	egg yolk	1
1 tbsp	water	15 mL
32	whole blanched almonds	32

1. In a medium bowl, mix together flour, baking powder, allspice, cloves and salt.

2. In a large bowl, beat butter or margarine and sugar until light and creamy. Beat in egg. Stir in almond extract. Add flour mixture and mix until blended.

3. Shape dough into 32 balls (see tip) and place about 2 inches (5 cm) apart on baking sheet. Dip the bottom of a glass in flour and flatten balls.

4. In a small bowl, whisk egg yolk with water. Lightly brush tops with mixture, then press an almond into the center of each cookie. Bake in preheated oven for 20 minutes or until lightly browned. Immediately transfer to wire racks to cool.

Tip *To make these cookies even in size, shape the dough into a long roll. Divide the roll in half, quarters and eighths. Divide the smallest pieces into quarters.*

Nutmeg Almond Balls

Makes about $3\frac{1}{2}$ dozen

- Preheat oven to 300°F (150°C)
- Baking sheet, ungreased

1 cup	butter, softened	250 mL
$\frac{1}{2}$ cup	granulated sugar	125 mL
1 tsp	vanilla	5 mL
2 cups	all-purpose flour	500 mL
$\frac{3}{4}$ cup	ground almonds, toasted	175 mL
1 cup	confectioner's (icing) sugar, sifted	250 mL
1 tbsp	ground nutmeg	15 mL

1. In a large bowl, beat butter and sugar until light and creamy. Stir in vanilla. Gradually add flour, mixing until blended. Fold in almonds.

2. Shape dough into 1-inch (2.5 cm) balls. Place about 2 inches (5 cm) apart on baking sheet. Bake in preheated oven for 18 to 20 minutes or until bottoms are lightly browned. Immediately transfer to wire racks to cool completely.

3. In a bowl, combine icing sugar and nutmeg. Gently roll balls in mixture until lightly coated.

Dipped Biscuit Peanut Butter Balls

Makes about 5 dozen

- Preheat oven to 350°F (180°C)
- Baking sheet, ungreased

$\frac{3}{4}$ cup	smooth peanut butter	175 mL
1	can (10 oz/300 mL) sweetened condensed milk	1
1	egg	1
1 tsp	vanilla	5 mL
2 cups	biscuit mix	500 mL
6 oz	semisweet chocolate, melted	175 g
4 tsp	vegetable oil	20 mL

1. In a large bowl, beat peanut butter, milk, egg and vanilla until smooth. Gradually add biscuit mix and mix well. Wrap dough tightly in plastic wrap and refrigerate for 30 minutes, until firm.

2. Shape dough into 1-inch (2.5 cm) balls and place about 2 inches (5 cm) apart on baking sheet. Bake in preheated oven for 10 to 12 minutes or until lightly browned. Immediately transfer to wire racks to cool.

3. In a small bowl, mix melted chocolate with oil. Dip top half of each cookie in warm mixture and place on baking sheet lined with waxed paper. Chill until chocolate has hardened.

Crunchy Peanut Butter Cookies

Makes about 2½ dozen
- Preheat oven to 375°F (190°C)
- Baking sheet, lightly greased

1½ cups	all-purpose flour	375 mL
½ tsp	baking soda	2 mL
¼ tsp	salt	1 mL
½ cup	butter or margarine, softened	125 mL
½ cup	packed brown sugar	125 mL
½ cup	crunchy peanut butter	125 mL
1	egg	1
½ tsp	vanilla	2 mL
½ cup	chopped unsalted peanuts (optional)	125 mL

1. In a small bowl, combine flour, baking soda and salt.

2. In a large bowl, beat butter or margarine, brown sugar and peanut butter until smooth and creamy. Beat in egg and vanilla. Stir in flour mixture and mix until a stiff dough forms.

3. Shape into 1-inch (2.5 cm) balls and place about 2 inches (5 cm) apart on prepared baking sheet. Using a fork, flatten in a criss-cross pattern. Sprinkle with chopped peanuts (if using). Bake in preheated oven for 10 minutes or until lightly browned. Immediately transfer to wire racks to cool.

Mocha Cherry Crackles

Makes about 3½ dozen
- Preheat oven to 325°F (160°C)
- Baking sheet, ungreased

1 cup	butter, softened	250 mL
½ cup	granulated sugar	125 mL
1 tsp	vanilla	5 mL
1 tsp	instant coffee powder or granules	5 mL
¼ cup	unsweetened cocoa powder	50 mL
¼ tsp	salt	1 mL
2 cups	all-purpose flour	500 mL
½ cup	finely chopped maraschino cherries	125 mL
½ cup	finely chopped walnuts or pecans	125 mL
	Additional granulated sugar for coating cookies	

1. In a large bowl, beat butter and sugar until smooth and creamy. Beat in vanilla, then coffee powder, cocoa and salt until well combined. Add flour and mix well until blended. Fold in cherries and walnuts. Wrap dough tightly in plastic wrap and refrigerate for at least 1 hour.

2. Shape dough into 1-inch (2.5 cm) balls and roll in sugar until lightly coated. Place balls about 2 inches (5 cm) apart on baking sheet. Bake in preheated oven for 20 minutes or until tops start to crack. Immediately transfer to wire racks to cool completely.

Iced Lemon Butter Cookies

Makes about 2½ dozen
- Preheat oven to 350°F (180°C)
- Baking sheet, lightly greased

2 cups	all-purpose flour	500 mL
1 cup	confectioner's (icing) sugar, sifted	250 mL
1 tsp	baking powder	5 mL
¼ tsp	salt	1 mL
1 cup	butter, softened	250 mL
1 tsp	lemon extract	5 mL
1 tsp	grated lemon zest	5 mL
1	egg	1
LEMON BUTTER ICING		
1 cup	confectioner's (icing) sugar, sifted	250 mL
1 tbsp	butter, softened	15 mL
2½ tsp	freshly squeezed lemon juice	12 mL

1. In a medium bowl, mix together flour, confectioner's sugar, baking powder and salt.

2. In a large bowl, beat butter, lemon extract, lemon zest and egg until smooth and creamy. Add flour mixture and mix until a sticky batter forms. Wrap tightly in plastic wrap and refrigerate for at least 1 hour, until firm.

3. Shape dough into 1-inch (2.5 cm) balls and place about 2 inches (5 cm) apart on prepared baking sheet. Bake in preheated oven for 12 minutes or until cookie springs back when touched lightly. Let cool for 2 minutes on baking sheet, then transfer to a wire rack to cool completely.

4. *Prepare the icing:* In a small bowl, beat together confectioner's sugar, butter and lemon juice until smooth and creamy. Spread icing on tops of cookies and let harden before storing.

Tip *A medium lemon yields about 2 to 3 tbsp (25 to 45 mL) juice and 1 tbsp (15 mL) grated zest. To always have freshly squeezed juice on hand, pour into ice cube trays and freeze. When frozen, place in plastic bags until ready to use.*

Sugar-Cinnamon Lemon Cookies

Makes about 3 dozen

- Preheat oven to 350°F (180°C)
- Baking sheet, lightly greased

1½ cups	all-purpose flour	375 mL
1 tsp	baking powder	5 mL
¼ tsp	salt	1 mL
1½ tsp	ground cinnamon	7 mL
½ tsp	grated lemon zest	2 mL
½ cup	butter or margarine, softened	125 mL
1 cup	granulated sugar	250 mL
1	egg	1
1 tsp	vanilla	5 mL
	Sugar-Cinnamon Mix (see page 4)	

1. In a small bowl, mix together flour, baking powder, salt, cinnamon and lemon zest.
2. In a large bowl, beat butter or margarine and sugar until smooth and creamy. Beat in egg until well incorporated. Stir in vanilla. Add flour mixture and mix well. Wrap tightly in plastic wrap and refrigerate for 2 hours, until firm.
3. Shape dough into ¾-inch (2 cm) to 1-inch (2.5 cm) balls. Roll in sugar-cinnamon mix to coat. Place balls about 2 inches (5 cm) apart on prepared baking sheet. Bake in preheated oven for 10 minutes or until lightly browned. Let cool on sheet for 2 minutes, then transfer to wire racks to cool completely.

Lemon Thumb Cookies

Makes about 6 dozen

- Preheat oven to 350°F (180°C)
- Baking sheet, greased

2 cups	butter, softened	500 mL
1½ cups	confectioner's (icing) sugar, sifted	375 mL
⅓ cup	freshly squeezed lemon juice	75 mL
4 cups	all-purpose flour	1 L
2 cups	finely chopped walnuts or pecans	500 mL
	Assorted jams, such as grape, raspberry, strawberry, apricot	

1. In a large bowl, cream together butter and confectioner's sugar until smooth. Beat in lemon juice until well blended. Gradually add flour and mix well. Wrap dough tightly in plastic wrap and refrigerate for 2 hours, until firm.
2. Shape dough into 1-inch (2.5 cm) balls and roll in chopped nuts. Place balls about 2 inches (5 cm) apart on prepared baking sheet. Press your thumb in the center of each ball, leaving an indentation, and fill with multicolored jams. Bake in preheated oven for 12 to 15 minutes or until golden brown. Immediately transfer to wire racks to cool.

Tip *When buying lemons, look for fine-textured skin. The lemon will be juicier. If there is a bit of greenish coloring, the juice will be more acidic.*

Rolled Orange Juice Balls

Makes about 3 dozen

- Preheat oven to 350°F (180°C)
- Baking sheet, lightly greased

2½ cups	all-purpose flour	625 mL
1 tbsp	baking powder	15 mL
½ cup	shortening, softened	125 mL
½ cup	granulated sugar	125 mL
3	eggs	3
1 tsp	vanilla	5 mL
½ cup	orange juice	125 mL
	Confectioner's (icing) sugar, sifted	

1. In a medium bowl, mix together flour and baking powder.
2. In a large bowl, beat shortening and sugar until smooth and creamy. Add eggs, one at a time, beating well after each addition. Beat in vanilla. Add flour mixture alternately with orange juice, beating constantly until a soft, sticky dough forms.
3. Scoop out dough 1 tablespoon (15 mL) at a time and roll in confectioner's sugar until it forms a ball. Place balls about 2 inches (5 cm) apart on prepared baking sheet. Repeat with the remaining dough. Bake in preheated oven for 15 minutes or until edges of cookies are lightly browned. Immediately transfer to wire racks to cool.

Tip *If you don't need zest for a particular recipe before squeezing an orange or lemon for juice, grate the peel and freeze it for later use.*

Raspberry Chocolate Chip Crackles

Makes about 4 dozen

- Preheat oven to 300°F (150°C)
- Baking sheet, greased

¼ cup	butter (no substitutes)	50 mL
1	package (10 oz/300 g) raspberry chocolate chips	1
2 cups	all-purpose flour	500 mL
2 tsp	baking powder	10 mL
¼ tsp	salt	1 mL
1½ cups	granulated sugar	375 mL
4	eggs	4
½ cup	finely chopped walnuts	125 mL
	Confectioner's (icing) sugar, sifted	

1. In the top of a double boiler, over hot water, melt butter with 1 cup (250 mL) of the raspberry chocolate chips, stirring until smooth. Remove from hot water and set aside.
2. In a bowl, combine flour, baking powder and salt.
3. In a large bowl, beat sugar with melted butter mixture. Add eggs, one at a time, beating until incorporated. Beat in flour mixture until well blended. Fold in walnuts and the remaining raspberry chocolate chips. Wrap dough tightly in plastic wrap and refrigerate for at least 1 hour.
4. Shape dough into 1-inch (2.5 cm) balls, then roll in confectioner's sugar. Place balls about 2 inches (5 cm) apart on prepared baking sheets. Bake in preheated oven for 15 to 18 minutes or until cracked on the surface but set in the middle. Immediately transfer to wire racks to cool.

Tip *If you don't feel up to making a batch of cookies, try this easy treat. Stack 4 graham wafers on top of each other. Spread chocolate icing between the wafers, over the entire top and down all sides. Set aside to allow icing to harden, then cut into 3 rectangular cookies.*

The Original Dad's Cookie

Makes about 5 dozen

- Preheat oven to 300°F (150°C)
- Baking sheet, ungreased

1 cup	all-purpose flour	250 mL
¾ cup	oat bran	175 mL
1 cup	quick-cooking rolled oats	250 mL
1 tsp	baking powder	5 mL
1 tsp	baking soda	5 mL
1½ tsp	ground cinnamon	7 mL
1 tsp	ground nutmeg	5 mL
1 tsp	ground allspice	5 mL
1 cup	butter or margarine, softened	250 mL
¼ cup	lightly packed brown sugar	50 mL
¾ cup	granulated sugar	175 mL
2 tbsp	light (fancy) molasses	25 mL
1	egg	1
1 tsp	vanilla	5 mL

1. In a medium bowl, mix together flour, oat bran, oats, baking powder, baking soda, cinnamon, nutmeg and allspice.
2. In a large bowl, beat butter or margarine and sugars until smooth. Beat in molasses, egg and vanilla until well blended. Add flour mixture and mix well.
3. Shape dough into 1-inch (2.5 cm) balls and place about 2 inches (5 cm) apart on baking sheet. Using the tines of a fork dipped in flour, flatten. Bake in preheated oven for 15 minutes or until golden brown. Let cool on baking sheet for 2 to 3 minutes, then transfer to wire racks to cool completely.

Coconut Oatmeal Cookies

Makes about 3 dozen

- Preheat oven to 350°F (180°C)
- Baking sheet, lightly greased

1½ cups	all-purpose flour	375 mL
1 tsp	baking powder	5 mL
1 tsp	baking soda	5 mL
1 cup	butter, softened	250 mL
1 cup	granulated sugar	250 mL
½ cup	packed brown sugar	125 mL
2	eggs	2
1 tsp	vanilla	5 mL
1½ cups	quick-cooking rolled oats	375 mL
¾ cup	shredded coconut (sweetened or unsweetened)	175 mL

1. In a small bowl, mix together flour, baking powder and baking soda.
2. In a large bowl, beat butter and sugars until smooth and creamy. Add eggs, one at a time, beating until well incorporated. Stir in vanilla. Add flour mixture and mix well. Stir in oats, then coconut, mixing until thoroughly combined.
3. Shape into 1-inch (2.5 cm) balls and place about 2 inches (5 cm) apart on prepared baking sheet. Using the tines of a fork dipped in flour or your hand, flatten slightly. Bake in preheated oven for 8 to 10 minutes or until golden brown. Immediately transfer to wire racks to cool.

Farm-Style Oatmeal Cookies

Makes about 6 dozen
- Preheat oven to 350°F (180°C)
- Baking sheet, greased

1½ cups	all-purpose flour	375 mL
1 tsp	baking soda	5 mL
1 tsp	ground cinnamon	5 mL
1 cup	shortening, softened	250 mL
1 cup	granulated sugar	250 mL
½ cup	lightly packed brown sugar	125 mL
1	egg, beaten	1
1 tsp	vanilla	5 mL
1½ cups	quick-cooking rolled oats	375 mL
¾ cup	finely crushed walnuts or pecans	175 mL
	Additional granulated sugar	

1. In a small bowl, combine flour, baking soda and cinnamon.
2. In a large bowl, beat shortening and sugars until smooth and creamy. Beat in egg and vanilla. Add flour mixture and mix well. Mix in oats and walnuts or pecans. Wrap dough tightly in plastic wrap and refrigerate for 1 hour.
3. Shape dough into 1-inch (2.5 cm) balls and place about 2 inches (5 cm) apart on prepared baking sheet. Flatten with a fork dipped in granulated sugar. Bake in preheated oven for 10 minutes or until golden brown. Immediately transfer to wire racks to cool.

Tip *To line a baking sheet with parchment or waxed paper, simply cut the paper to fit the sheet and place on top.*

Swedish Thimble Cookies

Makes about 5 dozen
- Preheat oven to 300°F (150°C)
- Baking sheet, lined with parchment or waxed paper

1½ cups	butter, softened	375 mL
¾ cup	packed light brown sugar	175 mL
3	eggs, separated	3
3 cups	sifted all-purpose flour	750 mL
¼ tsp	salt	1 mL
2 cups	finely chopped walnuts	500 mL
	Jam or jelly	

1. In a large bowl, beat butter and brown sugar until smooth and creamy. Beat in egg yolks, one at a time, until well incorporated. Gradually add flour and salt, mixing until all ingredients are well combined. (Dough will be very sticky.) Wrap dough tightly in plastic wrap and refrigerate for 1 hour.
2. Beat egg whites until peaks form. Place walnuts in a small bowl.
3. Shape dough into 1-inch (2.5 cm) balls. Dip each into beaten egg whites, then roll in walnuts to coat. Place balls about 2 inches (5 cm) apart on prepared baking sheets. Using a thimble dipped in flour, make indentations in the center of each ball. Fill with your choice of jam or jelly, using about ¼ tsp (1 mL) each, just enough to fill the indentation.
4. Bake in preheated oven for 15 to 18 minutes or until lightly browned. Let cool on baking sheet for 2 to 3 minutes, then transfer to wire racks to cool completely.

A Honey of a Cookie

Makes about 4 dozen
- Preheat oven to 350°F (180°C)
- Baking sheet, ungreased

3½ cups	all-purpose flour	875 mL
2 tsp	baking soda	10 mL
1 cup	butter or margarine, softened	250 mL
1 cup	packed brown sugar	250 mL
2	eggs	2
6 tbsp	liquid honey	90 mL
1 tsp	vanilla	5 mL

1. In a medium bowl, mix together flour and baking soda.
2. In a large bowl, beat butter and brown sugar until smooth and creamy. Add eggs, one at a time, beating until well incorporated. Beat in honey and vanilla until smooth. Add flour mixture and mix well. (Dough will be very thick.) Wrap dough tightly in plastic wrap and refrigerate until firm, at least 1 hour.
3. Shape dough into 1-inch (2.5 cm) balls and place about 2 inches (5 cm) apart on baking sheet. Bake in preheated oven for 10 to 15 minutes or until golden brown. Immediately transfer to wire racks to cool.

Chocolate Cherry Thumbprint Cookies

Makes about 4 dozen

- Preheat oven to 350°F (180°C)
- Baking sheet, ungreased

1½ cups	all-purpose flour	375 mL
½ cup	unsweetened cocoa powder	125 mL
¼ tsp	baking powder	1 mL
¼ tsp	baking soda	1 mL
½ cup	butter, softened	125 mL
1 cup	granulated sugar	250 mL
1	egg	1
1½ tsp	vanilla	7 mL
1	jar (10 oz/284 mL) maraschino cherries	1
4 tsp	reserved cherry juice	20 mL
¾ cup	mini semisweet chocolate chips	175 mL
½ cup	sweetened condensed milk	125 mL

1. In a medium bowl, sift together flour, cocoa, baking powder and baking soda.

2. In a large bowl, beat butter and sugar until smooth and creamy. Beat in egg, then vanilla until well incorporated. Mix in flour mixture until well blended.

3. Shape dough into 1-inch (2.5 cm) balls and place about 2 inches (5 cm) apart on baking sheet. With your thumb, make an indentation in the center of each ball. Drain cherries and save the juice. Place a cherry in the center of each ball.

4. In a small saucepan, melt chocolate chips and condensed milk, stirring until mixture is smooth. Add cherry juice and mix well. Spoon 1 tsp (5 mL) of mixture over top of cookies, covering the cherry. Bake in preheated oven for 10 to 12 minutes or until golden brown. Transfer to wire racks to cool.

Sesame Seed Cookies

Makes about 2 dozen

- Preheat oven to 350°F (180°C)
- Baking sheet, lightly greased

1½ cups	whole wheat flour	375 mL
1 tsp	baking powder	5 mL
¼ tsp	salt	1 mL
¼ cup	butter or margarine, softened	50 mL
¼ cup	liquid honey	50 mL
¼ cup	sesame paste (tahini)	50 mL
½ tsp	almond extract	2 mL
½ cup	sesame seeds, toasted	125 mL

1. In a small bowl, mix together flour, baking powder and salt.

2. In a large bowl, beat butter or margarine, honey, sesame paste and almond extract until smooth. Add flour mixture and mix well. Stir in sesame seeds.

3. Shape dough into 1-inch (2.5 cm) balls and place about 2 inches (5 cm) apart on prepared baking sheet. Using the tines of a fork dipped in flour, flatten, or using your hands, mold into crescent shapes. (Wet your hands first, if using to mold the dough.) Bake in preheated oven for 10 to 12 minutes or until lightly browned. Immediately transfer to wire racks to cool.

Tips *When a recipe calls for room-temperature or softened butter, grate cold butter. It will soften quickly.*

When measuring spoonfuls of honey or molasses, coating the spoon lightly with oil helps the sticky ingredient to slide off and makes cleanup easier.

Old-Fashioned Spice Balls

Makes about 6 dozen

- Preheat oven to 350°F (180°C)
- Baking sheet, lined with parchment or waxed paper

3 cups	all-purpose flour	750 mL
2 cups	granulated sugar	500 mL
4 tsp	baking soda	20 mL
1 tsp	salt	5 mL
1 tsp	ground cinnamon	5 mL
1 tsp	ground allspice	5 mL
1 tsp	ground ginger	5 mL
2½ cups	old-fashioned rolled oats	625 mL
⅔ cup	shortening, softened	150 mL
½ cup	butter or margarine	125 mL
2	eggs, lightly beaten	2
½ cup	warm corn syrup	125 mL

1. In a large bowl, mix together flour, sugar, baking soda, salt, cinnamon, allspice, ginger and rolled oats. Using two knives, a pastry blender or your fingers, cut in shortening and butter until mixture resembles coarse crumbs. Add eggs and warm syrup (be sure it is warm or dough will not be firm enough) and mix well.

2. Shape dough into 1-inch (2.5 cm) balls and place about 2 inches (5 cm) apart on prepared baking sheet. Bake in preheated oven for 10 to 12 minutes or until golden brown. Immediately transfer to wire racks to cool.

Ginger Snaps

Makes 5 to 6 dozen

- Preheat oven to 350°F (180°C)
- Baking sheet, greased

2 cups	all-purpose flour	500 mL
1 tbsp	baking soda	15 mL
¼ tsp	salt	1 mL
1 tsp	ground cinnamon	5 mL
1 tsp	ground ginger	5 mL
½ tsp	ground cloves	2 mL
¾ cup	shortening, softened	175 mL
1 cup	granulated sugar	250 mL
1	egg	1
¼ cup	light (fancy) molasses	50 mL
	Granulated sugar	

1. In a medium bowl, mix together flour, baking soda, salt, cinnamon, ginger and cloves.

2. In a large bowl, beat shortening and sugar until smooth and creamy. Add egg and beat until well incorporated. Mix in molasses until well blended. Add flour mixture and stir well.

3. Shape dough into 1-inch (2.5 cm) to ¾-inch (2 cm) balls, then roll in granulated sugar. Place on prepared baking sheet, about 2 inches (5 cm) apart. Bake in preheated oven for 10 to 12 minutes, depending upon size of balls. Immediately transfer to wire racks to cool.

Tip *To measure solid shortening, line a measuring cup with plastic wrap and fill it with shortening. It lifts out easily and the cup stays clean.*

Crispy Cheddar Cookies

Makes about 4 dozen smaller or 2½ dozen larger cookies

- Preheat oven to 350°F (180°C)
- Baking sheet, ungreased

1 cup	all-purpose flour	250 mL
½ cup	butter	125 mL
1½ cups	shredded old Cheddar cheese	375 mL
1 cup	crisp rice cereal	250 mL
1	egg, beaten	1

1. In a large bowl, using two knives, a pastry blender or your fingers, combine flour and butter until mixture resembles coarse crumbs. Add cheese, cereal and egg and mix until well blended.

2. Shape dough into either 1-inch (2.5 cm) or ¾-inch (2 cm) balls and place 2 inches (5 cm) apart on baking sheet. Flatten slightly with a fork. Bake in preheated oven for 15 to 17 minutes, depending upon size of balls, until golden brown. Immediately transfer to wire racks to cool.

Chinese Chews

Makes about 2 dozen

- Preheat oven to 350°F (180°C)
- 8-inch (2 L) square baking pan, greased

¼ cup	butter or margarine, softened	50 mL
2	eggs	2
1 tsp	vanilla	5 mL
½ cup	liquid honey	125 mL
½ cup	lightly toasted sesame seeds, divided	125 mL
¼ cup	chopped raisins	50 mL
1 cup	chopped pitted dates	250 mL
½ cup	chopped walnuts	125 mL
¾ cup	whole wheat or all-purpose flour	175 mL
	Confectioner's (icing) sugar, sifted (optional)	

1. In a bowl, beat butter or margarine, eggs, vanilla and honey until light and fluffy. Stir in ¼ cup (50 mL) of the sesame seeds, raisins, dates and walnuts and mix well. Gradually add flour, mixing until thoroughly blended.

2. Using your hands, spread batter into prepared pan. Bake in preheated oven for 20 minutes, until set. Remove from oven and cut into fingers, about 2 by 1½ inches (5 by 4 cm). Using a lifter or a knife, lift out fingers. Let cool very slightly, then shape into balls in the palm of your hands. On a plate, roll in the remaining sesame seeds, then confectioner's sugar (if using) until well coated. Let cool on wire racks.

Tip *If you prefer a sweeter cookie, use only ¼ cup (50 mL) sesame seeds and roll the cookies in ¼ cup (50 mL) confectioner's sugar.*

Cut, Sliced and Sandwich Cookies

Cut Cookies

Sliced Cookies

Sandwich Cookies

Cut Cookies

Although cut cookies are the most fun to make, they are a bit trickier than drop or hand-shaped cookies because the dough must be the right consistency to roll. If it is too wet, it will stick to the rolling pin, and if it is too dry, it will crack. To make it easier to handle, the dough must be chilled, usually for at least an hour and often as long as overnight. If desired, you can wrap the dough tightly in plastic wrap and refrigerate for up to a week. When you're ready to bake, roll the dough out, thinly, and cut your cookies as close together as possible.

● ●

The Ultimate Sugar Cookie

Makes about 50 small cookies
- Preheat oven to 375°F (190°C)
- Baking sheet, ungreased
- Cookie cutters

2 cups	all-purpose flour	500 mL
1½ tsp	baking powder	7 mL
½ tsp	salt	2 mL
1 cup	granulated sugar	250 mL
½ cup	butter, softened	125 mL
1	egg	1
1 tsp	vanilla	5 mL
¼ tsp	each lemon and almond extract (optional)	1 mL
1 tbsp	milk or cream	15 mL
	Granulated or tinted sugar for sprinkling	

1. In a medium bowl, sift together flour, baking powder and salt.
2. In a large bowl, cream sugar and butter until smooth. Beat in egg until well incorporated. Stir in vanilla, lemon extract and almond extract (if using) and milk. Gradually add flour mixture and mix until dough is firm enough to handle. Wrap in plastic wrap and refrigerate for 1 hour.
3. On a lightly floured surface, roll dough out to ⅛-inch (0.25 cm) thickness. Using cookie cutters or a glass dipped in flour, cut out desired shapes. Place about 2 inches (5 cm) apart on baking sheet and sprinkle with sugar. Bake in preheated oven for 8 to 10 minutes or until lightly browned. Immediately transfer to wire racks to cool.

Tip *This is the classic cut cookie. For an extra-special version, add lemon and almond extract along with the vanilla.*

Variations *Sour Cream Cookies: Sift ¼ tsp (1 mL) ground nutmeg and ¼ tsp (1 mL) baking soda with the flour. Reduce baking powder to ½ tsp (2 mL). Substitute ½ tsp (2 mL) lemon extract for the vanilla. Substitute ⅓ cup (75 mL) sour cream for the milk.*

Lemon Sugar Cookies: Substitute 1 tsp (5 mL) lemon extract and 2 tsp (10 mL) grated lemon zest for the vanilla.

Chocolate Sugar Cookies: Add 2 squares (each 1 oz/ 28 g) melted unsweetened chocolate after the egg. If desired, add 1 cup (250 mL) finely chopped nuts to the flour mixture.

Shaped Sugar Cookies: Add ⅓ cup (75 mL) chopped almonds and the grated zest of ½ lemon to the flour mixture. Shape into 1-inch (2.5 cm) balls and flatten with a fork.

● ●

Sugar, Spice 'n' Everything Nice Cookies

Makes about 3 dozen
- Preheat oven to 325°F (160°C)
- Baking sheet, lined with parchment or waxed paper
- Cookie cutters

2 cups + 2 tbsp	all-purpose flour	525 mL
¾ tsp	ground cinnamon	4 mL
1 tsp	ground cardamom	5 mL
1 tsp	ground ginger	5 mL
Pinch	freshly ground black pepper	Pinch
1 cup	butter, softened	250 mL
⅔ cup	packed brown sugar	150 mL
2 tsp	grated lemon zest	10 mL

1. In a medium bowl, sift together flour, cinnamon, cardamom, ginger and black pepper.
2. In a large bowl, beat butter and brown sugar until smooth. Stir in lemon zest. Gradually add flour mixture until a soft dough forms. Shape dough into two flattened disks, wrap tightly in plastic wrap and refrigerate for 1 to 2 hours, until firm.
3. Place one at a time between two sheets of waxed paper and roll out to ¼-inch (0.5 cm) thickness. Using cookie cutters or glass dipped in flour, cut out desired shapes. Place about 2 inches (5 cm) apart on prepared baking sheet. Bake in preheated oven for 8 to 10 minutes or until golden brown. Transfer to wire racks.

Ginger Spice Snaps

Makes about 4 dozen
- Preheat oven to 375°F (190°C)
- Baking sheet, well-greased
- Cookie cutters

4 cups	all-purpose flour	1 L
1 tsp	baking soda	5 mL
1½ tsp	salt	7 mL
½ tsp	ground nutmeg	2 mL
¼ tsp	ground allspice	1 mL
½ tsp	ground cloves	2 mL
1½ tsp	ground ginger	7 mL
½ cup	shortening, softened	125 mL
1 cup	granulated sugar	250 mL
½ cup	water	125 mL
1 cup	dark molasses	250 mL
	Granulated sugar for sprinkling	

1. In a large bowl, mix together flour, baking soda, salt, nutmeg, allspice, cloves and ginger.

2. In another large bowl, cream shortening and sugar until smooth. Add water and molasses and mix well. Stir in flour mixture and mix until well blended and a soft dough forms. Wrap dough tightly in plastic wrap and refrigerate for at least 3 hours.

3. On a lightly floured surface, roll dough out to ¼-inch (0.5 cm) thickness. Using cookie cutters or glass dipped in flour, cut into 3-inch (7.5 cm) circles. Sprinkle with sugar and place about 2 inches (5 cm) apart on prepared baking sheet. Bake in preheated oven for 10 to 12 minutes or until browned. Let cool on sheets for 5 minutes, then transfer to wire racks.

Little Gingerbread People

Makes about 2½ dozen
- Preheat oven to 350°F (180°C)
- Baking sheet, ungreased
- Gingerbread children cookie cutters

2 cups	all-purpose flour	500 mL
1 tsp	baking powder	5 mL
1 tsp	baking soda	5 mL
1 tsp	ground cinnamon	5 mL
1 tsp	ground allspice	5 mL
1½ tsp	ground ginger	7 mL
½ cup	butter, softened	125 mL
½ cup	granulated sugar	125 mL
½ cup	light (fancy) molasses or dark corn syrup	125 mL
1	egg yolk	1
	Colored icings and candies for decoration	

1. In a medium bowl, mix together flour, baking powder, baking soda, cinnamon, allspice and ginger.

2. In a large bowl, beat butter and sugar until smooth and creamy. Beat in molasses or corn syrup (mixture will look curdled) and then egg yolk until incorporated. Gradually add flour mixture, beating well. (Dough will be sticky.) Divide dough into four portions and shape into flattened disks. Wrap tightly in plastic wrap and refrigerate for 3 hours until firm.

3. On a floured surface, roll dough out to ¼-inch (0.5 cm) thickness and cut out figures. Place about 2 inch (5 cm) apart on baking sheets. Bake in preheated oven for 6 to 8 minutes, until slightly firm. Let cool on sheets for 5 minutes, then transfer to wire racks. Decorate cookies with colored icings and candies, as desired.

Nurnbergers

Makes about 5 dozen
- Preheat oven to 400°F (200°C)
- Baking sheet, lightly greased
- Cookie cutters

2¾ cups	all-purpose flour	675 mL
½ tsp	baking soda	2 mL
1 tsp	ground cinnamon	5 mL
½ tsp	ground nutmeg	2 mL
½ tsp	ground allspice	2 mL
¼ tsp	ground cloves	1 mL
⅓ cup	chopped citron	75 mL
½ cup	chopped nuts	125 mL
1 cup	liquid honey	250 mL
¾ cup	packed brown sugar	175 mL
1	egg	1
1 tsp	grated lemon zest	5 mL
1 tbsp	freshly squeezed lemon juice	15 mL
	Blanched almond halves	
	Candied cherries	

SUGAR GLAZE

1 cup	granulated sugar	250 mL
½ cup	water	125 mL

1. In a medium bowl, mix together flour, baking soda, cinnamon, nutmeg, allspice, cloves, citron and nuts.

2. In a small saucepan, heat honey to boiling. Remove from heat and pour into a large bowl to cool thoroughly.

3. Add brown sugar, egg, lemon zest and juice to honey and mix well. Stir in flour mixture and mix until dough forms. Cover and refrigerate for at least 4 hours or preferably overnight.

4. Divide dough into four portions and return three to refrigerator. On a lightly floured surface, roll the first portion to $\frac{1}{4}$-inch (0.5 cm) thickness. Using cookie cutters or a glass dipped in flour, cut into 2-inch (5 cm) rounds and place on prepared baking sheet. Press 5 almond halves, end to end, around the edge of the circle to form a rim and press a candied cherry in the center. Repeat with the remaining dough.

5. Bake in preheated oven for 10 to 12 minutes or until cookie springs back when touched lightly with finger. Immediately transfer to wire racks to cool.

6. *Prepare the glaze:* In a small bowl, beat sugar and water. While cookies are still hot, brush tops lightly.

Tip *Citron is a semi-tropical fruit that looks like a huge lemon. It can be purchased as candied citron especially for baking in specialty stores and supermarkets.*

• •

Maple Syrup Cookies

Makes about 6 dozen
• Preheat oven to 350°F (180°C)
• Baking sheet, greased
• Cookie cutters

3$\frac{1}{2}$ cups	all-purpose flour	875 mL
2 tsp	baking powder	10 mL
$\frac{1}{2}$ tsp	salt	2 mL
1 cup	butter, softened	250 mL
1 cup	firmly packed brown sugar	250 mL
2	eggs	2
1 tsp	vanilla	5 mL
$\frac{1}{3}$ cup	pure maple syrup	75 mL

1. In a medium bowl, combine flour, baking powder and salt.

2. In a large bowl, beat butter and brown sugar until smooth and creamy. Beat in eggs, one at a time, until incorporated. Mix in vanilla and syrup. Add flour mixture in three batches, beating well after each addition. Cover tightly with plastic wrap and refrigerate at least 4 hours.

3. Divide dough into four portions. Place between two sheets of waxed paper. Roll out one portion at a time to $\frac{1}{8}$-inch (0.25 cm) thickness. Using cookie cutters or a glass dipped in flour, cut into desired shapes. Place about 2 inches (5 cm) apart on prepared sheet. Bake in preheated oven for 8 to 10 minutes or until edges are golden brown. Immediately transfer to wire racks.

Tip *For optimum results, bake cookies one sheet at a time. If you do bake two sheets at the same time, place one on the middle rack of your oven and the other on the next-lowest rung. Baking two sheets next to each other affects the heat flow and produces underbaked cookies.*

• •

Danish Jam Squares

Makes about 2$\frac{1}{2}$ dozen
• Preheat oven to 350°F (180°C)
• Baking sheet, lightly greased

2 cups	all-purpose flour	500 mL
1 tbsp	granulated sugar	15 mL
3$\frac{1}{2}$ tsp	baking powder	17 mL
$\frac{1}{2}$ tsp	salt	2 mL
5 tbsp	shortening	75 mL
$\frac{3}{4}$ cup	milk	175 mL
	Jam or jelly of your choice	

1. In a large bowl, mix together flour, sugar, baking powder and salt.

2. Using two knives, a pastry blender or your fingers, work in shortening until mixture resembles coarse crumbs. Gradually stir in enough milk to make a soft dough.

3. On a lightly floured surface, knead dough lightly. Roll into a square about $\frac{1}{8}$-inch (0.25 cm) thick and cut into 2$\frac{1}{2}$-inch (6 cm) squares. Place 1 tsp (5 mL) jam or jelly in the center of each. Bring the four corners to the center and pinch together, making a small, square envelope. Place about 2 inches (5 cm) apart on prepared baking sheet. Bake in preheated oven for 15 to 20 minutes or until golden brown. Transfer to wire racks lined with waxed paper.

Tip *Whenever cookie dough is too sticky to work with, chilling it in the refrigerator for about 20 minutes will firm it up to the right consistency.*

Cinnamon Sugar Diamonds

Makes about 6 dozen

- Preheat oven to 375°F (190°C)
- Baking sheet, greased

1²⁄₃ cups	all-purpose flour	400 mL
½ tsp	baking powder	2 mL
¼ tsp	salt	1 mL
½ cup	butter or margarine, softened	125 mL
1 cup	granulated sugar	250 mL
2	egg yolks	2
1 tsp	vanilla	5 mL
1 tbsp	whipping (35%) cream, plus additional for glazing cookies	1 tbsp
1 tbsp	granulated sugar	15 mL
1 tsp	ground cinnamon	5 mL

1. In a small bowl, mix together flour, baking powder and salt.

2. In a large bowl, beat butter or margarine and sugar until smooth and creamy. Beat in egg yolks until well incorporated. Stir in vanilla and 1 tbsp (15 mL) whipping cream. Add flour mixture and mix well. Cover and refrigerate for several hours or overnight.

3. In a small bowl, mix together sugar and cinnamon. Set aside.

4. On a lightly floured surface, divide dough into three portions. Roll out one portion at a time to ⅛-inch (0.25 cm) thickness. Cut dough into diamond shapes, 3 inches (7.5 cm) long and 1½ inches (4 cm) at widest point. Place about 2 inches (5 cm) apart on prepared baking sheet. Brush tops with additional whipping cream, then with sugar-cinnamon mixture. Bake in preheated oven for 5 to 6 minutes or until lightly browned. Let cool slightly and then transfer to wire racks to cool completely.

Apricot Cream Cheese Kolacky

Makes about 6 dozen

- Preheat oven to 375°F (190°C)
- Baking sheet, ungreased
- Cookie cutters

2 cups	all-purpose flour	500 mL
2 tbsp	granulated sugar	25 mL
2 tsp	baking powder	10 mL
½ tsp	salt	2 mL
1 cup	butter or margarine, softened	250 mL
1 cup + 2 tbsp	cream cheese, softened	275 mL
2	eggs	2
½ cup	apricot or cherry preserves	125 mL

1. In a medium bowl, mix together flour, sugar, baking powder and salt.

2. In a large bowl, beat butter and cream cheese until smooth. Beat in eggs, one at a time, until incorporated. Gradually add flour mixture, mixing until a stiff dough forms. Cover and refrigerate for 3 hours.

3. On a lightly floured surface, divide dough into four portions. Roll each portion to ¼-inch (0.5 cm) thickness. Using a cookie cutter or a glass dipped in flour, cut into circles. Dip your index finger in flour and make a deep indentation in the center of each round. Fill with a scant ¼ tsp (1 mL) preserves. (Do not use too much, as the fruit will spill over.) Place rounds about 2 inches (5 cm) apart on baking sheet. Bake in preheated oven for about 15 minutes or until golden brown. Immediately transfer to wire racks.

Apricot Bundles

Makes about 2 dozen

- Preheat oven to 350°F (180°C)
- Baking sheet, lightly greased

1¼ cups	all-purpose flour	300 mL
½ tsp	baking powder	2 mL
¼ tsp	salt	1 mL
3 tbsp	butter, softened	45 mL
3 tbsp	margarine, softened	45 mL
½ cup	granulated sugar	125 mL
1	egg	1
2 tsp	grated orange zest	10 mL
½ tsp	vanilla	2 mL
APRICOT FILLING		
½ cup	chopped dried apricots	125 mL
⅓ cup	orange juice	75 mL
2 tbsp	light brown sugar	25 mL
	Confectioner's (icing) sugar, sifted	

1. In a small bowl, mix together flour, baking powder and salt.

2. In a large bowl, beat butter, margarine and sugar until smooth and creamy. Beat in egg, orange zest and vanilla until well blended. Add flour mixture and mix until a soft dough forms. Cover tightly with plastic wrap and refrigerate for at least 2 hours.

3. *Prepare the filling:* In a small saucepan, bring apricots, orange juice and brown sugar to a boil. Lower heat, cover and simmer for about 10 minutes, until apricots are soft. Let cool, then purée in food processor. If mixture is too thick, add a little orange juice.

4. On a lightly floured surface, divide dough into three portions. Roll each portion into a 6-inch (15 cm) square and cut into nine 2-inch (5 cm) squares. In a narrow diagonal line, spread a level teaspoonful (5 cm) of filling across each square. Fold the two opposite corners together to make a triangle. Using your fingers or the tines of a fork, press to seal. Repeat with each piece of dough.

5. Place bundles about 2 inches (5 cm) apart on prepared baking sheet. Bake in preheated oven for 10 to 12 minutes. Immediately transfer to wire racks to cool, then sprinkle with confectioner's sugar.

• •

Jam Crescents

Makes about 6½ dozen
- **Preheat oven to 350°F (180°C)**
- **Baking sheet, ungreased**

3¼ cups	all-purpose flour	800 mL
½ tsp	baking powder	2 mL
½ tsp	salt	2 mL
1	envelope (⅓ oz/9 g) vanilla sugar	1
1 cup	butter, softened	250 mL
¼ cup	margarine or shortening, softened	50 mL
3	egg yolks	3
1 cup	sour cream	250 mL
	Plum or seedless raspberry jam	
	Granulated sugar	

1. In a medium bowl, combine flour, baking powder, salt and vanilla sugar.

2. In a large bowl, beat butter, margarine or shortening, egg yolks and sour cream until well blended. Add dry ingredients and beat until a soft dough forms. (If dough is sticky, transfer to a lightly floured board and knead in additional flour until right consistency is achieved.) Form dough into a large ball, then cut in half. Flatten each half into a disk and wrap tightly in plastic wrap. Refrigerate at least 2 hours, until dough is firm.

3. On a lightly floured surface, divide dough into 10 balls. Return nine to the refrigerator until ready to use and roll one ball into an 8-inch (20 cm) circle. Using a knife or a pastry cutter, fluted, if desired, cut into eight pie-shaped wedges.

4. Spread about ½ tsp (2 mL) jam on outer edge of each wedge. Beginning with the outer edge and finishing with the point in the center, roll up to form crescents. Sprinkle generously with sugar and shake off excess. Place, point-side down, about 2 inches (5 cm) apart on baking sheet. Repeat with the remaining dough.

5. Bake in preheated oven for 15 to 17 minutes or until bottom of crescents are golden brown. Immediately transfer to wire racks to cool.

Tip *To ease cleanup when making cut-out cookies, place a piece of plastic wrap loosely over the rolled dough. Using your cookie cutter, press down on the plastic wrap until your shape is cut. Your cookie cutter stays clean because the plastic wrap is between it and the dough.*

Sliced Cookies

Often called refrigerator cookies, sliced cookies are among the easiest and most convenient cookies to make. You can mix the dough, shape it into a roll, wrap tightly in plastic wrap and refrigerate for as long as a week. When you're ready to bake, slice off pieces of dough — only as much as you want — and bake. You can always have warm cookies ready and waiting — even for unexpected guests.

• •

Easy Elephant Ears

Makes about 1 dozen
- **Preheat oven to 425°F (220°C)**
- **Baking sheet, ungreased**

	Granulated sugar	
8 oz	frozen puff pastry, defrosted	250 g

1. Sprinkle a pastry board with a thick layer of sugar. Place puff pastry on top and roll into a neat oblong.

2. Fold one long side of puff pastry inward, like a jellyroll, but stopping at the center. Repeat on the other side, so the two rolls meet in the center. Cut into slices ¼ inch (0.5 cm) thick and press each slice in sugar.

3. Place slices on baking sheet. Bake in preheated oven for 6 to 8 minutes. Turn over and bake for another 6 to 8 minutes or until golden brown.

Variation *Cinnamon Nut Elephant Ears: In a food processor with a metal blade, process ½ cup (125 mL) chopped nuts, 2 tbsp (25 mL) granulated sugar and ½ tsp (2 mL) ground cinnamon until finely ground. Sprinkle dough with mixture before folding.*

The Refrigerator Cookie

Makes about 4 dozen

- Preheat oven to 425°F (220°C)
- Baking sheet, lightly greased

2 cups	all-purpose flour	500 mL
2 tsp	baking powder	10 mL
½ tsp	salt	2 mL
½ cup	shortening, softened	125 mL
¾ cup	granulated sugar	175 mL
½ cup	packed brown sugar	125 mL
1	egg	1
1 tsp	vanilla	5 mL
½ cup	chopped nuts	125 mL

1. In a medium bowl, mix together flour, baking powder and salt.
2. In a large bowl, beat shortening and sugars until smooth and creamy. Beat in egg until well incorporated. Stir in vanilla and nuts. Add flour mixture and mix until a soft dough forms.
3. On a lightly floured surface, divide dough in half. Shape into two long rolls about 2 inches (5 cm) wide. Wrap each tightly in plastic wrap and refrigerate for at least 2 hours, until firm.
4. Remove from wrap and cut dough into slices ¼ inch (0.5 cm) thick. Place about 2 inches (5 cm) apart on prepared baking sheet. Bake in preheated oven for 8 to 10 minutes or until golden brown. Immediately transfer to wire racks to cool.

Variations *Chocolate Refrigerator Cookies: Add 2 squares (each 1 oz/28 g) melted chocolate or ¼ cup (50 mL) unsweetened cocoa powder along with the vanilla.*

Coconut Refrigerator Cookies: Substitute ½ cup (125 mL) flaked or shredded coconut for the nuts.

Spice Refrigerator Cookies: Add 1 tsp (5 mL) each of ground cinnamon, ginger and nutmeg to the dry ingredients.

Easy Icebox Cookies

Makes about 6 dozen

- Preheat oven to 350°F (180°C)
- Baking sheet, lined with parchment or waxed paper

3 cups	all-purpose flour	750 mL
1 tsp	baking soda	5 mL
¼ tsp	salt	1 mL
1 cup	chopped walnuts (optional)	250 mL
1 cup	butter, softened	250 mL
2½ cups	firmly packed light brown sugar	625 mL
2	eggs	2
1 tbsp	vanilla	15 mL

1. In a large bowl, mix together flour, baking soda, salt and walnuts (if using).
2. In another large bowl, beat butter and brown sugar until smooth and creamy. Beat in eggs, one at a time, until incorporated. Stir in vanilla. Add flour mixture and mix well.
3. On a lightly floured surface, divide dough in half. Shape into two rolls about 2 inches (5 cm) wide. Wrap each roll tightly in plastic wrap. Refrigerate at least 3 hours or overnight.
4. Remove from wrap and cut dough into slices ¼ inch (0.5 cm) thick. Place about 2 inches (5 cm) apart on prepared baking sheet. Bake in preheated oven for 12 to 15 minutes, until firm to the touch. Immediately transfer to wire racks to cool completely.

Variations *Almond Icebox Cookies: Substitute 1 cup (250 mL) coarsely chopped slivered almonds for the walnuts.*

Cranberry Icebox Cookies: Add ½ cup (125 mL) chopped, frozen or fresh cranberries along with the walnuts.

Buttery Brown Sugar Slices

Makes about 6 dozen

- Preheat oven to 350°F (180°C)
- Baking sheet, ungreased

3½ cups	all-purpose flour	875 mL
1 tsp	baking soda	5 mL
½ tsp	salt	2 mL
1 cup	butter or margarine, softened	250 mL
2 cups	packed brown sugar	500 mL
2	eggs	2
1 tbsp	vanilla	15 mL
1 cup	finely chopped walnuts (optional)	250 mL

1. In a medium bowl, combine flour, baking soda and salt.
2. In a large bowl, beat butter and brown sugar until smooth and creamy. Beat in eggs, one at a time, until incorporated. Stir in vanilla. Add flour mixture and mix well. Fold in walnuts (if using).
3. On a lightly floured surface, divide dough in half. Shape into two rolls about 2 to 3 inches (5 to 7.5 cm) wide. Wrap each tightly in plastic wrap and refrigerate overnight.

4. Remove from wrap and cut dough into slices ¼ inch (0.5 cm) thick. Place about 2 inches (5 cm) apart on baking sheet. Bake in preheated oven for 10 to 12 minutes or until golden brown. Immediately transfer to wire racks to cool.

• •

Butterscotch Pecan Cookies

Makes about 4 dozen
- Preheat oven to 350°F (180°C)
- Baking sheet, ungreased

1¼ cups	all-purpose flour	300 mL
½ tsp	baking powder	2 mL
¼ tsp	salt	1 mL
6 tbsp	butter or margarine, softened	90 mL
⅔ cup	packed brown sugar	150 mL
1	egg	1
½ tsp	vanilla	2 mL
½ cup	finely chopped pecans	125 mL

1. In a small bowl, combine flour, baking powder and salt.

2. In a large bowl, beat butter and brown sugar until smooth and creamy. Beat in egg until incorporated. Stir in vanilla. Gradually add flour mixture, mixing until well blended. Fold in pecans.

3. On a lightly floured surface, divide dough in half. Shape into two rolls about 2 inches (5 cm) wide. Wrap each log tightly in plastic wrap and refrigerate for at least 2 hours.

4. Remove from wrap and cut dough into slices ¼ inch (0.5 cm) thick. Place about 2 inches (5 cm) apart on baking sheet. Bake in preheated oven for 10 to 12 minutes, until golden brown. Immediately transfer to wire racks to cool.

Variations *Butterscotch Date Cookies: Substitute 2 cups (500 mL) finely chopped pitted dates for the pecans.*

Butterscotch Chews: For a soft, chewy cookie, add ¾ cup (175 mL) crushed cornflakes along with the pecans.

• •

Coffee Break Cinnamon Rolls

Makes 1 dozen
- Preheat oven to 400°F (200°C)
- Jellyroll pan or large baking sheet, lightly greased

1	package (¼ oz/7 g) active dry yeast	1
⅔ cup	warm water	150 mL
2½ cups	biscuit mix	625 mL
¼ cup	packed brown sugar	50 mL
1 tsp	ground cinnamon	5 mL
½ cup	chopped pecans	125 mL
2 tbsp	melted butter	25 mL
TOPPING		
¼ cup	melted butter or margarine	50 mL
⅓ cup	packed brown sugar	75 mL
1 tsp	light corn syrup	5 mL

1. In a medium bowl, dissolve yeast in warm water. Add biscuit mix and beat to form a dough. On a floured surface, knead dough until smooth.

2. In a small bowl, mix together brown sugar, cinnamon and pecans.

3. Roll dough into a 12-inch (30 cm) square and brush with butter. Sprinkle with cinnamon mixture, then roll up like a jellyroll and cut into 12 slices. Place 2 inches (5 cm) apart on prepared pan or sheet and leave in a warm place to rise, about 1 hour. Bake in preheated oven 15 minutes.

4. *Prepare the topping:* In a small saucepan, over low heat, melt butter or margarine. Add brown sugar and corn syrup and, stirring constantly, bring to a boil. Five minutes before baking is completed, pour over rolls. Serve warm.

• •

Cinnamon Roll Slices

Makes about 1 dozen
- Preheat oven to 350°F (180°C)
- Baking sheet, lightly greased

¾ cup	butter or margarine, softened	175 mL
1 cup	granulated sugar	250 mL
1 tsp	baking soda	5 mL
¾ cup	buttermilk	175 mL
3 cups	all-purpose flour	750 mL
	Softened butter to spread	
	Brown sugar	
	Ground cinnamon	

1. In a large bowl, beat butter or margarine and sugar until smooth and creamy. Mix baking soda with buttermilk and stir into mixture. Gradually stir in flour until a dough forms.

2. On a floured surface, roll dough out to ¼-inch (0.5 cm) thickness. Spread with butter, brown sugar and cinnamon. Roll up tightly like a jellyroll, making sure seam is sealed tight, and cut into 1-inch (2.5 cm) slices. Place about 2 inches (5 cm) apart on prepared baking sheet. Bake in preheated oven for 20 to 25 minutes or until lightly browned. Immediately transfer to wire racks to cool.

Mochaccino Cookies

Makes about 3 dozen
- Preheat oven to 350°F (180°C)
- Baking sheet, lightly greased

2 cups	all-purpose flour	500 mL
1/4 tsp	salt	1 mL
1 tsp	ground cinnamon	5 mL
1/2 cup	butter or margarine, softened	125 mL
1/2 cup	shortening, softened	125 mL
1/2 cup	lightly packed brown sugar	125 mL
1/2 cup	granulated sugar	125 mL
1	egg	1
1 tbsp	instant coffee powder or granules, dissolved in 1 tsp (5 mL) hot water	15 mL
2 oz	unsweetened chocolate, melted	60 g
CHOCOLATE DIP		
3 tbsp	shortening	45 mL
1 1/2 cups	semisweet chocolate chips	375 mL

1. In a medium bowl, mix together flour, salt and cinnamon.

2. In a large bowl, beat butter or margarine, shortening and sugars until smooth and creamy. Beat in egg. Add coffee mixture and melted chocolate and mix until thoroughly blended. Stir in flour mixture. Cover and refrigerate for at least 1 hour or until firm.

3. On a lightly floured surface, divide dough in half. Shape into two long logs about 2 to 2 1/2 inches (5 to 6 cm) wide. Wrap each log tightly in plastic wrap and refrigerate at least 2 hours, until firm.

4. When ready to bake, remove from wrap and cut dough into slices 1/4 inch (0.5 cm) thick. Place about 2 inches (5 cm) apart on prepared baking sheet. Bake in preheated oven for 10 to 12 minutes or until edges are firm and bottoms are lightly browned. Immediately transfer to wire racks to cool. When cookies are slightly cooled, dip in chocolate.

5. *Prepare the dip:* In a saucepan, over low heat, stir shortening and chocolate chips until melted and smooth. Using your fingers, dip top half of each cookie in mixture and place on baking sheet lined with waxed paper. Refrigerate until chocolate hardens.

Tip *Pack any chilled cookie dough into juice cans. Seal the open end with foil secured by an elastic band. Keep in refrigerator. When ready to use, cut the end out of the can and push the dough out slowly, cutting slices as you push. Place on baking sheets and bake.*

Fruit and Nut Roly Poly

Makes about 5 dozen
- Preheat oven to 375°F (190°C)
- Baking sheet, greased

4 cups	all-purpose flour	1 L
2 tsp	baking powder	10 mL
1/4 tsp	salt	1 mL
4	eggs	4
1 cup	granulated sugar	250 mL
1 cup	vegetable oil	250 mL
1 tsp	vanilla	5 mL
FILLING		
1 cup	finely chopped walnuts	250 mL
1/4 cup	granulated sugar	50 mL
1/2 cup	peach preserves	125 mL
1 1/4 cups	diced dried fruits and raisins	300 mL
1 tbsp	grated orange zest	15 mL
1/4 cup	fresh orange juice	50 mL
1/4 cup	melted butter or margarine	50 mL
1/4 cup	fine dry bread crumbs	50 mL

1. In a large bowl, sift together flour, baking powder and salt.

2. In another large bowl, beat eggs and sugar until light and fluffy. Beat in oil and vanilla until well blended. Stir in dry ingredients until a soft dough forms. (You may not use the entire flour mixture.)

3. *Prepare the filling:* In a large bowl, mix together walnuts, sugar, peach preserves, dried fruits and raisins, orange zest and juice.

4. On a lightly floured surface, divide dough into four equal portions. Roll one portion into a rectangle about 1/4 inch (0.5 cm) thick. Brush with melted butter or margarine, leaving 1/2-inch (1 cm) border all around. Sprinkle bread crumbs lightly over top and spread one-quarter of the filling over this. Turn ends in and roll dough up like a jellyroll, making sure seam is sealed tight. Repeat with the remaining dough.

5. Place rolls, two at a time, on prepared baking sheet. Bake in preheated oven for 30 to 35 minutes or until nicely browned. Let cool on sheets, then cut into 1/2-inch (1 cm) slices.

Variation *Jam and Nut Roly Poly: On each rolled-out portion of dough, spread your favorite jam, leaving a 1/2-inch (1 cm) border. Sprinkle surface with chopped walnuts. Roll and bake as above. For variety, use different nuts and jam on each portion.*

Chocolate 'n' Vanilla Spirals

Makes about 7 dozen

- Preheat oven to 350°F (180°C)
- Baking sheet, lightly greased

1¼ cups	all-purpose flour	300 mL
¼ tsp	baking powder	1 mL
¼ tsp	salt	1 mL
½ cup	butter or margarine, softened	125 mL
¾ cup	granulated sugar	175 mL
1	egg	1
1 tsp	vanilla	5 mL
1 oz	unsweetened chocolate, melted and cooled	30 g

1. In a small bowl, mix together flour, baking powder and salt.
2. In a large bowl, beat butter or margarine and sugar until smooth and creamy. Beat in egg until well incorporated. Stir in vanilla. Mix in flour mixture until a soft dough forms.
3. On a lightly floured surface, divide dough in half. Add melted chocolate to one of the halves and knead dough until it is uniformly chocolate-colored. Wrap both doughs tightly in plastic wrap and refrigerate for at least 1 hour, until dough is firm.
4. When ready to bake, remove from wrap, place plain dough between two sheets of waxed paper and roll out to a 16- by 6-inch (40 by 15 cm) rectangle. Remove waxed paper from top of plain dough, but leave waxed paper on bottom. Repeat with chocolate dough. Remove waxed paper from top of chocolate dough and invert chocolate onto the plain dough. Using a rolling pin, press together gently. Remove waxed paper from top and trim so both top and bottom are even. Using the waxed paper on the bottom to guide you, and starting from the long edge, roll dough up like a jellyroll, making sure seam is sealed tight. If necessary, roll back and forth on the work surface to make sure the roll is the same diameter from end to end. Wrap tightly in plastic wrap and refrigerate for at least 2 hours or overnight.
5. Place roll, seam-side down, on a cutting board and cut into slices ¼ inch (0.5 cm) thick. Place 2 inches (5 cm) apart on prepared baking sheet. Bake in preheated oven for 10 to 12 minutes or until lightly browned. Immediately transfer to wire racks to cool.

Apricot Cream Cheese Pinwheel Cookies

Makes 4½ to 5 dozen

- Preheat oven to 350°F (180°C)
- Baking sheet, lightly greased

1	package (8 oz/250 g) cream cheese, softened	1
1 cup	butter, softened	250 mL
¼ tsp	salt	1 mL
2 cups	all-purpose flour	500 mL
¾ cup	apricot preserves	175 mL
1 cup	finely chopped walnuts	250 mL

1. In a large bowl, beat cream cheese, butter and salt until smooth and creamy. Gradually add flour and mix until a soft dough forms. Cover and refrigerate overnight.
2. When ready to bake, combine apricot preserves and nuts in a small bowl.
3. On a lightly floured surface, roll dough into a 12- by 14-inch (30 by 35 cm) rectangle. Spread the apricot mixture all over, excluding edges. Beginning on one long side, roll up tightly, like a jellyroll. Ensure seam is sealed tight. Cut log in half, horizontally, and wrap each section tightly in plastic wrap. Refrigerate for at least 30 minutes, until firm.
4. Remove dough from wrap and cut each log into slices ½ inch (1 cm) thick. Place about 1 inch (2.5 cm) apart on prepared baking sheet. Bake in preheated oven for 15 minutes or until golden. Immediately transfer to wire racks.

Tips *Use an electric knife to cut rolled and chilled cookie dough. It makes perfect, even cookies quickly and easily.*

For a fun and quick treat, dip the tips of salted pretzel sticks into melted chocolate and then into sprinkles. Place on a plate or a baking sheet covered in waxed paper until chocolate has set.

Apple Fig Date Log

Makes about 6 dozen
- Preheat oven to 350°F (180°C)
- Baking sheet, greased

5 cups	all-purpose flour	1.25 L
2 tsp	baking powder	10 mL
1 tsp	baking soda	5 mL
½ tsp	salt	2 mL
1 cup	butter, softened	250 mL
1 cup	granulated sugar	250 mL
2	eggs	2
1 cup	sour cream	250 mL
2 tsp	vanilla	10 mL
	Confectioner's (icing) sugar, sifted	
FILLING		
1¾ cups	finely chopped pitted dates	425 mL
1¾ cups	finely chopped figs	425 mL
6	Granny Smith apples, peeled and finely chopped	6
½ cup	freshly squeezed orange juice	125 mL
⅓ cup	granulated sugar	75 mL
1 cup	chopped walnuts	250 mL

1. In a large bowl, combine flour, baking powder, baking soda and salt.
2. In another large bowl, beat butter and sugar until smooth and creamy. Beat in eggs, one at a time, until incorporated. Beat in sour cream and vanilla. Gradually add flour mixture, mixing until well blended. Wrap dough tightly in plastic wrap and refrigerate for at least 1 hour.
3. *Prepare the filling:* In a large pot, over medium heat, combine dates, figs, apples, orange juice and sugar. Cook, covered, stirring occasionally, for 25 minutes, until tender. Remove cover and cook, stirring, until mixture is dry, about 5 minutes. Remove from heat. When cool, mix in walnuts and refrigerate if not using immediately.
4. Divide dough into eight equal portions. On a lightly floured surface, shape one portion into a log, approximately 8 inches (20 cm) long. Roll log into a 10- by 5-inch (25 by 12.5 cm) rectangle. Spread ¾ cup (175 mL) filling down the middle of the rectangle. Fold each side over the filling and pinch together to seal. Place the log, seam-side down, on prepared sheet. Repeat with the remaining dough and filling.
5. Bake in preheated oven for 25 to 30 minutes or until golden brown. Immediately transfer to wire racks to cool. Sift the confectioner's sugar over the logs, then cut into slices ½ inch (1 cm) thick.

Tri-Color Neapolitan Cookies

Makes about 6 dozen
- Preheat oven to 350°F (180°C)
- 9- by 5-inch (2 L) loaf pan, bottom and sides lined with waxed paper
- Baking sheet, ungreased

2½ cups	all-purpose flour	625 mL
½ tsp	baking powder	2 mL
½ tsp	salt	2 mL
1 cup	butter, softened	250 mL
1½ cups	granulated sugar	375 mL
1	egg	1
1 tsp	vanilla	5 mL
½ tsp	almond extract	2 mL
6	drops red food coloring	6
½ cup	chopped walnuts	125 mL
¼ cup	unsweetened cocoa powder	1 mL

1. In a medium bowl, mix together flour, baking powder and salt.
2. In a large bowl, beat butter and sugar until smooth and creamy. Beat in egg until incorporated. Stir in vanilla. Gradually add flour mixture and mix until a soft dough forms.
3. Divide dough into three equal portions. Place one portion in a small bowl. Add almond extract and red food coloring and knead until fully integrated into the dough. Spread this portion evenly over the bottom of the prepared pan. Add nuts to another portion and knead well. Spread this portion evenly over the first layer. Add cocoa to the last portion and knead until it is evenly distributed throughout the dough. Spread this portion over the second layer. Cover with plastic wrap or waxed paper and refrigerate overnight.
4. When ready to bake, remove from pan and cut loaf in half lengthwise. Cut each half into slices ¼ inch (0.5 cm) thick. Place about 2 inches (5 cm) apart on baking sheet. Bake in preheated oven for 10 to 12 minutes or until firm.

Tip *In place of cocoa, add 1 square (1 oz/28 g) melted unsweetened chocolate to the dough.*

Chocolate Chip Pecan Logs

Makes about 4 dozen

- Preheat oven to 350°F (180°C)
- Baking sheet, greased

2 cups	all-purpose flour	500 mL
1/2 tsp	baking powder	2 mL
1/2 tsp	salt	2 mL
1/2 cup	butter, softened	125 mL
4 oz	cream cheese, softened	125 g
1/2 cup	granulated sugar	125 mL
1/2 cup	lightly packed brown sugar	125 mL
1	egg	1
1 tsp	vanilla	5 mL
FILLING		
2/3 cup	semisweet chocolate chips	150 mL
2/3 cup	sweetened condensed milk	150 mL
1/2 cup	chopped pecans	125 mL
	Confectioner's (icing) sugar, sifted	

1. In a medium bowl, mix together flour, baking powder and salt.
2. In a large bowl, beat butter, cream cheese and sugars until smooth and creamy. Beat in egg and vanilla. Add flour mixture and mix until a soft dough forms.
3. On a lightly floured surface, divide dough into four portions. Shape each portion into a log, about 8 inches (20 cm) long. Repeat with the remaining portions. Wrap tightly in plastic wrap and refrigerate for at least 2 hours.
4. *Prepare the filling:* In a small saucepan, over low heat, melt chocolate chips and milk, stirring until smooth. Fold in nuts and set aside.
5. On a well-floured surface, roll each log into a 10- by 5-inch (25 by 12.5 cm) rectangle. Spread one-quarter of the filling down the center of the rectangle, leaving about 1 inch (2.5 cm) at the sides so filling won't spill out. Fold into thirds, each side over the filling, to enclose the filling. Trim ends and pinch to seal.
6. Place logs about 2 inches (5 cm) apart, seam-side down, on prepared baking sheet. Bake in preheated oven for 20 to 25 minutes or until golden brown. Immediately dust with confectioner's sugar, then transfer to wire racks to cool. Once logs are cool, cut into slices 1/2 inch (1 cm) thick.

Double Almond Sticks

Makes about 3 dozen

- Preheat oven to 350°F (180°C)
- Baking sheet, ungreased

1/2 cup	blanched almonds	125 mL
2 tbsp	granulated sugar	25 mL
1 cup	all-purpose flour	250 mL
1/3 cup	granulated sugar	75 mL
1/4 tsp	salt	1 mL
1/2 cup	butter or margarine	125 mL
1	egg yolk	1
1/4 tsp	almond extract	1 mL
1	egg white, lightly beaten	1

1. In a food processor with a metal blade, process almonds until coarsely ground. In a small bowl, mix together 2 tbsp (25 mL) ground almonds with the 2 tbsp (25 mL) sugar and set aside. Set the remaining almonds aside.
2. In a large bowl, mix together flour, 1/3 cup (75 mL) sugar, salt and the reserved almonds. Using two knives, a pastry blender or your fingers, cut in butter until mixture resembles coarse crumbs. Stir in egg yolk and almond extract, mixing until a soft dough forms.
3. On a lightly floured surface, divide dough into six portions. Flour your hands and roll each portion into a long rope about 12 inches (30 cm) long. Brush tops generously with the beaten egg white and sprinkle with the reserved almond-sugar mixture.
4. Cut each rope into sticks 2 inches (5 cm) long. Place about 1 inch (2.5 cm) apart on baking sheet. Bake in preheated oven for 15 minutes. Let cool for 5 minutes, then transfer to wire racks to cool completely.

Tip *To blanch almonds, soak shelled nuts in boiling water for a few minutes. Rinse under cold water and skins will easily slip off.*

Lemon Nutmeg Crisps

Makes about 5 dozen

- Preheat oven to 300°F (150°C)
- Baking sheet, lightly greased

1 cup	all-purpose flour	250 mL
½ tsp	baking powder	2 mL
½ tsp	baking soda	2 mL
½ tsp	salt	2 mL
¼ tsp	ground nutmeg	1 mL
½ cup	butter, softened	125 mL
1½ cups	confectioner's (icing) sugar, sifted	375 mL
1 tbsp	grated lemon zest	15 mL
2	egg whites	2
½ tsp	vanilla	2 mL
¾ cup	ground walnuts	175 mL

1. In a small bowl, mix together flour, baking powder, baking soda, salt and nutmeg.
2. In a large bowl, beat butter, confectioner's sugar and lemon zest until smooth. Beat in egg whites. Stir in vanilla and walnuts. Add flour mixture and mix until a soft dough forms. Refrigerate for 2 to 3 hours, until firm.
3. On a lightly floured surface, shape into two rolls about 2 inches (5 cm) wide. Wrap tightly in plastic wrap and refrigerate for 2 hours.
4. Remove from wrap and cut into slices ¼ inch (0.5 cm) wide. Place about 2 inches (5 cm) apart on prepared baking sheet. Bake in preheated oven for 15 to 18 minutes or until lightly browned. Immediately transfer to wire racks to cool.

Glazed Lemon Braids

Makes about 1½ dozen

- Preheat oven to 350°F (180°C)
- Baking sheet, lightly greased

½ cup	butter or margarine, softened	125 mL
1 cup	granulated sugar	250 mL
1	egg	1
	Zest of 1 lemon	
2 cups	all-purpose flour	500 mL
GLAZE		
1½ cups	confectioner's (icing) sugar, sifted	375 mL
	Juice of 1 lemon	

1. In a large bowl, beat butter and sugar until crumbly. Beat in egg and lemon zest. Gradually add flour, mixing thoroughly after each addition until a soft dough forms.

2. Working with ¼ cup (50 mL) of dough at a time, divide in half. Shape each half into a 7-inch (18 cm) long rope. Entwine the two ropes, as for braiding, then cut in half lengthwise. Place on prepared baking sheet. Repeat with the remaining dough.
3. Chill braids for 30 minutes, then bake in preheated oven until very lightly browned. Immediately transfer to wire racks to cool.
4. *Prepare the glaze:* In a small bowl, mix together confectioner's sugar and lemon juice. Brush over tops of warm cookies. Let set for 20 minutes.

Raspberry Nut Swirls

Makes 3½ dozen

- Preheat oven to 375°F (190°C)
- Baking sheet, lightly greased

1¾ cups	all-purpose flour	425 mL
2 tsp	baking powder	10 mL
¼ tsp	salt	1 mL
½ cup	butter or margarine, softened	125 mL
1 cup	granulated sugar	250 mL
1	egg	1
1 tsp	vanilla	5 mL
½ cup	raspberry jam	125 mL
⅓ cup	finely chopped walnuts or pecans	75 mL

1. In a small bowl, mix together flour, baking powder and salt.
2. In a large bowl, beat butter or margarine and sugar until smooth and creamy. Beat in egg until well incorporated. Stir in vanilla. Gradually add flour mixture, mixing until a dough forms. Turn out on a floured work surface and knead lightly.
3. Place dough between two sheets of waxed paper and roll out to a 12- by 10-inch (30 by 25 cm) rectangle.
4. In a small bowl, mix together jam and nuts. Spread mixture evenly over the dough, leaving a ½-inch (1 cm) border.
5. Starting at the long edge and using the waxed paper on the bottom as a guide, roll up like a jellyroll, making sure seam is sealed tight. Roll back and forth a couple of times to form an even roll. Wrap tightly in plastic wrap and refrigerate at least overnight.
6. When ready to bake, remove from wrap and cut dough into slices ¼ inch (0.5 cm) thick. Place about 2 inches (5 cm) apart on prepared baking sheet. Bake in preheated oven for 10 to 15 minutes or until golden brown. Immediately transfer to wire racks to cool.

Sandwich Cookies

What could be better than a freshly baked cookie? Two freshly baked cookies spread with a mouth-watering filling and pressed together. I hope you'll try some of these delicious treats.

Chocolate Cream Puff Cookies

Makes about 4 dozen puffs
- Preheat oven to 450°F (230°C)
- Baking sheet, ungreased

¼ cup	butter or margarine	50 mL
½ cup	water	125 mL
Pinch	salt	Pinch
½ cup	all-purpose flour	125 mL
2	eggs	2
2 tbsp	grated orange zest	25 mL
CHOCOLATE CREAM FILLING		
½ cup	semisweet chocolate chips	125 mL
2 tbsp	freshly squeezed orange juice	25 mL
⅓ cup	finely chopped almonds	75 mL
½ cup	whipping (35%) cream, whipped	125 mL
	Melted semisweet chocolate (optional)	

1. In a saucepan, over medium heat, bring butter, water and salt to a boil, stirring constantly. Quickly add flour and stir rapidly until mixture leaves the pan and forms a smooth ball. Remove from heat. Beat in eggs, one at a time, until incorporated. Stir in orange zest.
2. Drop batter by level teaspoonfuls (5 mL), about 2 inches (5 cm) apart, onto baking sheet. Bake in preheated oven for 12 to 15 minutes. Immediately transfer to wire racks to cool.
3. *Prepare the filling:* In a saucepan, over low heat, melt chocolate chips. Stir in orange juice, remove from heat and let cool. Fold in almonds and whipped cream.
4. Using a sharp knife, cut puffs in half horizontally. Fill bottom with filling, then replace top. Drizzle melted chocolate over the tops, if desired. Refrigerate until ready to serve.

Chocolate Cream Delights

Makes 18 to 24 sandwiches
- Preheat oven to 400°F (200°C)
- Baking sheet, lightly greased
- Round cookie cutter

2½ cups	all-purpose flour	625 mL
1 tsp	baking powder	5 mL
1 tsp	salt	5 mL
¾ cup	shortening, softened	175 mL
1 cup	granulated sugar	250 mL
2	eggs	2
½ tsp	vanilla	2 mL
3 oz	unsweetened chocolate, melted	90 g
	Granulated sugar	
FILLING		
½ cup	butter, softened	125 mL
1½ cups	confectioner's (icing) sugar, sifted	375 mL
2	egg yolks	2
2 tsp	vanilla	10 mL

1. In a medium bowl, sift together flour, baking powder and salt.
2. In a large bowl, beat shortening and sugar until smooth and creamy. Beat in eggs, one at a time, until incorporated. Stir in vanilla and chocolate. Gradually add flour mixture, mixing until a soft dough forms. Cover tightly and refrigerate for 1 to 2 hours or overnight.
3. On a lightly floured surface, roll out dough to ⅛-inch (0.25 cm) thickness. Using a round cookie cutter or a glass dipped in flour, about 2 inches (5 cm) in diameter, cut out cookies and place about 2 inches (5 cm) apart on prepared baking sheet. Sprinkle generously with sugar and bake in preheated oven for 6 to 8 minutes, until cookies are set. Immediately transfer to wire racks to cool.
4. *Prepare the filling:* In a medium bowl, beat butter and confectioner's sugar until smooth and creamy. Beat in egg yolks and vanilla until well blended.
5. On a work surface, spread filling on one cookie, then top with another to make a sandwich.

Variation *Chocolate Mint Cream Delights: Substitute store-bought or homemade vanilla icing for the filling and beat in ½ tsp (2 mL) peppermint extract and 2 to 3 drops green food coloring.*

Chocolate-Filled Meringues

Makes about 2 dozen sandwiches
- Preheat oven to 250°F (120°C)
- Baking sheet, lined with parchment paper or foil

2	egg whites, at room temperature	2
Pinch	salt	Pinch
½ tsp	vanilla	2 mL
½ cup	granulated sugar	125 mL
1 oz	bittersweet chocolate, melted	30 g

1. In a large bowl, beat egg whites, salt and vanilla until frothy. Gradually add sugar, 2 tbsp (25 mL) at a time, beating until stiff, glossy peaks form.

2. Drop by level teaspoonfuls (5 mL), about 2 inches (5 cm) apart, onto prepared baking sheet and, using a spatula, lightly flatten the tops. Bake in preheated oven for 40 to 45 minutes or until meringue is crisp. Immediately transfer cookies and liner to a wire rack. When completely cool, remove meringues from liner.

3. Spread chocolate over the bottom of one meringue and top with the bottom of another to form a sandwich.

Tip *Don't beat egg whites in plastic bowls, as they retain oils. Use a very clean bowl with no traces of oil.*

Date-Filled Cookies

Makes about 2 dozen sandwiches, depending on size of rounds
- Preheat oven to 325°F (160°C)
- Baking sheet, lightly greased
- Round cookie cutter

1¾ cups	all-purpose flour	425 mL
1 tbsp	baking powder	15 mL
1 tsp	salt	5 mL
1 cup	shortening, softened	250 mL
1 cup	lightly packed brown sugar	250 mL
½ cup	milk	125 mL
2 cups	old-fashioned rolled oats	500 mL
DATE FILLING		
2 cups	chopped pitted dates	500 mL
1 tbsp	grated orange zest	15 mL
¾ cup	freshly squeezed orange juice	175 mL
⅓ cup	water	75 mL

1. In a small bowl, sift flour, baking powder and salt.

2. In a large bowl, beat shortening and brown sugar until smooth and creamy. Add milk and rolled oats and stir until well blended. Add flour mixture and mix until a soft dough forms. Wrap tightly in plastic wrap and refrigerate for 1 to 2 hours, until firm.

3. On a floured surface, roll out dough to ⅛-inch (0.25 cm) thickness. Using a cookie cutter or a glass dipped in flour, cut into rounds. Place about 2 inches (5 cm) apart on prepared baking sheet. Bake in preheated oven for 12 to 15 minutes or until golden brown. Immediately transfer to wire racks to cool.

4. *Prepare the filling:* In a saucepan, over medium heat, bring dates, zest, juice and water to a boil, stirring constantly. Reduce heat to low, cover and simmer, stirring occasionally, for 40 to 50 minutes, until dates are very soft. Remove cover and cook, stirring, for 5 minutes, until mixture becomes a thick paste. Let cool completely.

5. Spread filling over the smooth side of a cooled cookie and top with the smooth side of another cookie to form a sandwich.

Jam-Filled Cottage Cheese Squares

Makes about 4 dozen
- Preheat oven to 425°F (220°C)
- Baking sheet, lightly greased
- Square cookie cutter

1 cup	margarine, softened	250 mL
1 cup	cottage cheese	250 mL
¼ tsp	baking powder	1 mL
2 cups	all-purpose flour	500 mL
	Strawberry jam or red jelly	

1. In a large bowl, beat margarine and cottage cheese until well combined. Stir in baking powder and flour and mix well.

2. Shape dough into a ball, wrap tightly in plastic wrap and refrigerate for 1 hour.

3. On a floured surface, divide dough in half. Roll each half into a rectangle ⅛ inch (0.25 cm) thick. Cut into 2½-inch (6 cm) squares. Place a scant teaspoon (5 mL) jam in the center of each square. Fold corners up to center to make an envelope, pressing all edges together. Place about 2 inches (5 cm) apart on prepared baking sheet. Bake in preheated oven for 12 to 15 minutes or until golden brown. Immediately transfer to wire racks to cool.

Jam-Filled Sandwiches

Makes about 2½ dozen sandwiches
- Preheat oven to 350°F (180°C)
- Baking sheet, greased

⅔ cup	all-purpose flour	150 mL
¾ tsp	baking soda	4 mL
½ tsp	ground cinnamon	2 mL
¾ cup	butter, softened	175 mL
½ cup	granulated sugar	125 mL
1 cup	lightly packed brown sugar	250 mL
1	egg	1
2 tsp	vanilla	10 mL
2 tbsp	water	25 mL
3 cups	old-fashioned rolled oats	750 mL
1½ cups	raspberry jam	375 mL

1. In a small bowl, mix together flour, baking soda and cinnamon.
2. In a large bowl, beat butter and sugars until smooth and creamy. Add egg and beat until incorporated. Stir in vanilla and water. Gradually add flour mixture, beating until well blended. Stir in oats.
3. Drop by level teaspoonfuls (5 mL), about 2 inches (5 cm) apart, onto prepared baking sheet. Bake in preheated oven for 10 to 12 minutes, until golden brown. Immediately transfer to wire racks to cool.
4. When cooled, spread with jam on the smooth side of one cookie and top with the smooth side of another cookie to form a sandwich.

Ice Cream Sandwiches

Oatmeal, chocolate, chocolate chip
or peanut butter cookies
Ice cream, sherbet or frozen yogurt
Chopped nuts, mini chocolate chips
or sprinkles (optional)

1. Place desired number of cookies on work surface, smooth side up. Spread with a generous amount of ice cream or other filling. Top with another cookie, smooth side down, to form a sandwich.
2. For an added treat, roll the edges of the cookie sandwich in chopped nuts, mini chocolate chips or sprinkles or any other type of decorations.
3. Wrap sandwiches tightly in plastic wrap and freeze until ready to serve.

Lemon-Filled Drops

Makes about 2 dozen sandwiches
- Preheat oven to 400°F (200°C)
- Baking sheet, ungreased

2 cups	all-purpose flour	500 mL
¼ tsp	salt	1 mL
1 cup	butter or margarine, softened	250 mL
½ cup	confectioner's (icing) sugar, sifted	125 mL
1 tsp	lemon extract	5 mL
	Confectioner's (icing) sugar for sprinkling	

FILLING

¼ cup	granulated sugar	50 mL
2¼ tsp	cornstarch	11 mL
1 tbsp	butter or margarine	15 mL
1 tsp	grated lemon zest	5 mL
4 tsp	freshly squeezed lemon juice	20 mL
¼ cup	water	50 mL

1. In a medium bowl, mix together flour and salt.
2. In a large bowl, beat butter or margarine and confectioner's sugar until smooth and creamy. Stir in lemon extract. Add dry ingredients and mix until a soft dough forms. Cover tightly and refrigerate for 1 to 2 hours, until firm.
3. Shape dough into 1-inch (2.5 cm) balls and place about 2 inches (5 cm) apart on baking sheet. Flatten slightly with the bottom of a glass dipped in granulated sugar. Bake in preheated oven for 8 to 10 minutes or until lightly browned. Immediately transfer to wire racks to cool.
4. *Prepare the filling:* In a saucepan, combine sugar and cornstarch. Add butter or margarine, lemon zest, lemon juice and water. Cook over medium heat, stirring constantly, until mixture comes to a boil. Boil until mixture thickens, about 1 minute. Set aside to cool.
5. Spread filling over the smooth side of a cooled cookie and top with the smooth side of another cookie to form a sandwich. Sprinkle with confectioner's sugar.

Tip *Drop a bay leaf into your sugar and flour canisters to keep unwanted pests away. It does not change the taste.*

Lemon Raisin-Filled Squares

Makes about 2 dozen sandwiches
- Preheat oven to 375°F (190°C)
- Baking sheet, ungreased
- Square cookie cutter

1	package (8 oz/250 g) cream cheese, softened	1
1/4 cup	butter or margarine, softened	50 mL
1	egg	1
1/4 tsp	vanilla	1 mL
1	package (18 oz/510 g) lemon cake mix	1

RAISIN FILLING

1/2 cup	raisins	125 mL
2 tbsp	water	25 mL
1/4 cup	apricot preserves	50 mL

1. In a large bowl, beat cream cheese and butter or margarine until smooth. Beat in egg until incorporated. Stir in vanilla. Gradually add cake mix, mixing well after each addition, until a stiff dough forms. Wrap dough tightly in plastic wrap and refrigerate for 30 minutes, until chilled.

2. On a floured surface, roll out dough to 1/8-inch (0.25 cm) thickness. Using a square cookie cutter, cut out shapes.

3. *Prepare the filling:* In a saucepan, over medium heat, bring raisins, water and apricot preserves to a boil. Reduce heat to low and simmer until mixture combines, about 5 minutes. Set aside to cool.

4. Place half the squares about 2 inches (5 cm) apart on baking sheet and spoon 1/2 tsp (2 mL) filling on the center of each. Using a sharp knife, cut a 1/2-inch (1 cm) "X" in the center of the remaining squares and place on top of the squares with filling. Press together to seal. Bake in preheated oven for 10 to 12 minutes or until lightly browned.

Chocolate-Dipped Lemon Butter Cookies

Makes about 2 dozen sandwiches
- Preheat oven to 350°F (180°C)
- Baking sheet, ungreased

1 cup	butter, softened	250 mL
1/2 cup	granulated sugar	125 mL
1	egg yolk	1
1 tsp	vanilla	5 mL
2 cups	all-purpose flour	500 mL

LEMON FILLING

2 cups	confectioner's (icing) sugar, sifted	500 mL
1/2 cup	butter, softened	125 mL
2 tbsp	freshly squeezed lemon juice	25 mL

CHOCOLATE DIP

4 oz	semisweet chocolate	125 g
2 tbsp	butter	25 mL
	Finely chopped nuts (optional)	

1. In a large bowl, beat butter and sugar until smooth and creamy. Beat in egg yolk until incorporated. Stir in vanilla. Gradually add flour and mix until well blended.

2. Using your hands, shape into 1-inch (2.5 cm) balls. Flatten with the bottom of a glass dipped in sugar. Place about 2 inches (5 cm) apart on baking sheet. Bake in preheated oven for 10 to 12 minutes or until firm. Immediately transfer to wire racks to cool.

3. *Prepare the filling:* Beat confectioner's sugar, butter and lemon juice until smooth and creamy. Spread filling on the flat surface of one cookie and top with the flat surface of another cookie to form a sandwich.

4. *Prepare the dip:* In a small saucepan, melt chocolate with butter, stirring until smooth. Let cool slightly, then dip half of each cookie into the chocolate. Dip chocolate-coated half in nuts, if desired. Set aside on waxed paper until chocolate hardens.

Tip *Use your slow cooker to melt chocolate in bulk and keep it warm as long as you need to. Break chocolate into chunks or 1-oz (30 g) pieces and turn to Low. Stir occasionally until melted.*

Peanut Butter Mini Turnovers

Makes about 1½ dozen sandwiches
- Preheat oven to 375°F (190°C)
- Baking sheet, ungreased
- 3-inch (7.5 cm) round cookie cutter

2 cups	all-purpose flour	500 mL
1 tsp	baking powder	5 mL
¼ tsp	salt	1 mL
¾ cup	shortening, softened, (butter-flavored, if available)	175 mL
¾ cup	granulated sugar	175 mL
1	egg	1
1½ tsp	vanilla	7 mL
PEANUT BUTTER FILLING		
⅓ cup	smooth peanut butter	75 mL
3 tbsp	confectioner's (icing) sugar, sifted	45 mL
¼ cup	milk	50 mL
2 oz	semisweet chocolate, melted (optional)	60 g

1. In a medium bowl, mix together flour, baking powder and salt.
2. In a large bowl, beat shortening and sugar until smooth and creamy. Beat in egg until incorporated. Stir in vanilla. Gradually add flour mixture, mixing until a soft dough forms.
3. Divide dough in half and wrap each piece tightly in plastic wrap. Refrigerate for 1 to 2 hours, until firm.
4. *Prepare the filling:* In a small bowl, mix together peanut butter, confectioner's sugar and milk until smooth.
5. On a lightly floured surface, roll one piece of dough out to ⅛-inch (0.25 cm) thickness. (Leave the other piece in the refrigerator while you work.) Using a 3-inch (7.5 cm) round cookie cutter dipped in flour, cut into rounds. Place half the rounds about 2 inches (5 cm) apart on baking sheet. Spoon a rounded teaspoonful (5 mL) of filling onto the center of each and, using the back of a spoon, press filling slightly to flatten. Top with the remaining rounds. Using the tines of a fork, lightly press edges of cookies to seal. Repeat with the remaining dough. Bake in preheated oven for 10 to 12 minutes or until edges are lightly browned. Immediately transfer to wire racks to cool. When cookies are cool, drizzle melted chocolate over tops in a zigzag pattern, if desired.

Peanut Butter Jelly Sandwiches

Makes about 2 dozen sandwiches
- Preheat oven to 375°F (190°C)
- Baking sheet, lightly greased

1¼ cups	all-purpose flour	300 mL
½ tsp	baking powder	2 mL
¾ tsp	baking soda	4 mL
¼ tsp	salt	1 mL
½ cup	shortening, softened	125 mL
½ cup	packed brown sugar	125 mL
½ cup	granulated sugar	125 mL
½ cup	smooth peanut butter	125 mL
1	egg	1
	Jam or jelly	

1. In a small bowl, mix together flour, baking powder, baking soda and salt.
2. In a large bowl, beat shortening and sugars until smooth and creamy. Add peanut butter and egg and mix until well blended. Add dry ingredients and mix until a soft dough forms. Cover tightly and refrigerate for 1 hour, until firm.
3. Shape dough into 1-inch (2.5 cm) balls. Place about 2 inches (5 cm) apart on prepared baking sheet. Bake in preheated oven for 10 to 12 minutes or until golden brown. Immediately transfer to wire racks.
4. When cool, place half the cookies on a pan, flat side up, and spread with jam. Top with the remaining cookies, flat side down, to form a sandwich.

Cream Cheese Shortbread Sandwiches

Makes about 16 sandwiches

1	package (8 oz/250 g) cream cheese, softened	1
3 tbsp	granulated sugar	45 mL
2 tbsp	coffee-flavored liqueur	25 mL
½ cup	chopped walnuts	125 mL
32	shortbread cookies, round or oblong, or chocolate wafers	32

1. In a medium bowl, beat cream cheese, sugar and liqueur until smooth and creamy. Fold in nuts.
2. Spread filling between two shortbread cookies or two chocolate wafers until all the cookies are used up. Refrigerate, covered, for 2 hours.

Linzer Cookies

Makes about 2 dozen sandwiches

- Preheat oven to 350°F (180°C)
- Baking sheets, ungreased
- Round or star-shaped cookie cutter and smaller cookie cutter of the same shape

2½ cups	all-purpose flour	625 mL
2 tsp	ground cinnamon	10 mL
½ tsp	ground cloves	2 mL
1 tbsp	grated lemon zest	15 mL
¼ tsp	salt	1 mL
1½ cups	finely ground walnuts	375 mL
1 cup	butter or margarine, softened	250 mL
1 cup	confectioner's (icing) sugar, sifted	250 mL
1	egg	1
1	egg yolk	1
1 tsp	vanilla	5 mL
	Seedless raspberry jam	
	Confectioner's (icing) sugar	

1. In a large bowl, mix together flour, cinnamon, cloves, lemon zest, salt and walnuts.
2. In another large bowl, beat butter or margarine and confectioner's sugar until smooth and creamy. Beat in egg and egg yolk until well incorporated. Stir in vanilla. Gradually add flour mixture, mixing until a soft dough forms. Cover tightly and refrigerate for 2 to 3 hours, until firm.
3. On a floured surface, roll out dough to ⅛-inch (0.25 cm) thickness. Using a round or star-shaped cookie cutter, cut out dough. Place half the cookies on baking sheet. Using a smaller cookie cutter of the same shape that you used above, cut out centers of the remaining cookies and place the cut cookies on baking sheet. Bake in preheated oven for 10 to 12 minutes or until edges are lightly browned. Immediately transfer to wire racks to cool.
4. Spoon about 2 tsp (10 mL) jam onto each whole cookie. Dust confectioner's sugar onto cut cookie, then place on top of cookies with jam filling to form sandwiches.

Tip *Leftover egg yolks or whites can be kept in the refrigerator for 3 to 4 days in airtight containers. Yolks should be covered with cold water to keep them from drying up.*

Apricot Almond Sandwiches

Makes about 15 sandwiches

- Preheat oven to 375°F (190°C)
- Baking sheet, ungreased
- Round cookie cutter

2½ cups	all-purpose flour	625 mL
¼ tsp	baking soda	1 mL
¼ tsp	salt	1 mL
½ cup	shortening, softened	125 mL
1 cup	granulated sugar	250 mL
2	eggs	2
1 tsp	vanilla	5 mL
FILLING		
⅔ cup	granulated sugar	150 mL
⅔ cup	water	150 mL
1 tsp	freshly squeezed lemon juice	5 mL
2 cups	canned apricots, mashed	500 mL
½ cup	finely chopped almonds	125 mL

1. In a medium bowl, mix together flour, baking soda and salt.
2. In a large bowl, beat shortening and sugar until smooth and creamy. Beat in eggs, one at a time, until well incorporated. Stir in vanilla. Gradually add flour mixture, mixing until a soft dough forms. Cover and refrigerate for 1 to 2 hours, until firm.
3. *Prepare the filling:* In a saucepan, over low heat, mix together sugar, water, lemon juice, apricots and almonds. Cook, stirring, until thickened, about 15 minutes. Set aside to cool.
4. On a floured work surface, divide dough in half. One at a time, roll out each half to ⅛-inch (0.25 cm) thickness. Using a round cookie cutter, cut circles in one portion and place 1 inch (2.5 cm) apart on baking sheet. Using the same cutter, cut out the other portion, then, using the open side of a thimble or a pastry cutter, make a small hole in the center and place 1 inch (2.5 cm) apart on sheet. Bake in preheated oven or until edges are lightly browned. Immediately transfer to wire racks to cool.
5. When cool, spread filling on the solid cookie and top with the cut-out cookie.

Grandma's Whoopie Pies

Makes about 2 dozen sandwiches
Preheat oven to 350°F (180°C)
Baking sheet, lightly greased

½ cup	unsweetened cocoa powder	125 mL
½ cup	hot water (not boiling)	125 mL
2⅔ cups	all-purpose flour	650 mL
1 tsp	baking powder	5 mL
1 tsp	baking soda	5 mL
¼ tsp	salt	1 mL
½ cup	shortening, softened	125 mL
1½ cups	granulated sugar	375 mL
2	eggs	2
1 tsp	vanilla	5 mL
½ cup	buttermilk	125 mL
FILLING		
3 tbsp	all-purpose flour	45 mL
Pinch	salt	Pinch
1 cup	milk	250 mL
¾ cup	shortening, softened	175 mL
1½ cups	confectioner's (icing) sugar, sifted	375 mL
2 tsp	vanilla	10 mL

1. In a small bowl, combine cocoa and hot water and mix well. Set aside to cool for 5 minutes.
2. In a medium bowl, sift together flour, baking powder, baking soda and salt.
3. In a large bowl, beat shortening and sugar until smooth and creamy. Add eggs, one at a time, beating until well incorporated. Stir in vanilla. Add cocoa mixture and mix well. Add flour mixture alternately with buttermilk, mixing until thoroughly blended.
4. Drop dough by rounded teaspoonfuls (5 mL), about 2 inches (5 cm) apart, onto prepared baking sheet. Using a spoon or the palm of your hand, flatten slightly. Bake in preheated oven for 10 to 12 minutes until firm. Immediately transfer to wire racks to cool.
5. *Prepare the filling:* In a small saucepan, mix flour and salt. Slowly whisk in milk until smooth. Cook over medium heat, stirring constantly, for 5 to 8 minutes, until thick. Remove from heat, cover and place in refrigerator to cool completely.
6. In a medium bowl, beat shortening, confectioner's sugar and vanilla until smooth and creamy. Add chilled mixture and beat for 5 minutes, until light and fluffy.
7. On a work surface, spread filling over the flat surface of half the cookies. Top with the remaining cookies, flat side down, to form sandwiches. Store in the refrigerator.

Tip *If a recipe calls for buttermilk and you don't have any on hand, add 1 tbsp (15 mL) white vinegar or lemon juice to each cup of regular milk for instant buttermilk.*

Mincemeat Refrigerator Rounds

Makes about 2½ dozen sandwiches
Preheat oven to 400°F (200°C)
Baking sheet, ungreased

2¾ cups	all-purpose flour	675 mL
½ tsp	baking soda	2 mL
1 tsp	salt	5 mL
1 cup	shortening, softened	250 mL
½ cup	granulated sugar	125 mL
½ cup	packed brown sugar	125 mL
2	eggs	2
½ cup	prepared mincemeat	125 mL
¼ cup	chopped nuts	50 mL
2 tbsp	chopped maraschino cherries (optional)	25 mL

1. In a medium bowl, mix together flour, baking soda and salt.
2. In a large bowl, beat shortening and sugars until smooth. Beat in eggs, one at a time, until incorporated. Gradually add dry ingredients, mixing until a soft dough forms.
3. Shape dough into two rolls about 2 inches (5 cm) wide. Wrap tightly in plastic wrap and refrigerate for 3 to 4 hours, until firm.
4. In a small bowl, mix together mincemeat, nuts and cherries (if using).
5. On floured surface, cut dough into slices ⅛ inch (0.25 cm) thick. Place half the slices about 2 inches (5 cm) apart on baking sheet. Place a scant teaspoonful (5 mL) of the mincemeat mixture in the center of each and top with another slice. Bake in preheated oven for 8 to 10 minutes or until golden brown. Immediately transfer to wire racks to cool.

Just Peachy Sandwich Cookies

Makes 2 dozen sandwiches

- Preheat oven to 325°F (160°C)
- Baking sheet, ungreased

²⁄₃ cup	butter or margarine, softened	150 mL
¹⁄₂ cup	confectioner's (icing) sugar, sifted	125 mL
2 tsp	grated lemon zest	10 mL
¹⁄₂ tsp	ground nutmeg	2 mL
1³⁄₄ cups	all-purpose flour	425 mL
PEACH FILLING		
¹⁄₂ cup	peach preserves	125 mL
1 tbsp	granulated sugar	15 mL

1. In a large bowl, beat butter or margarine, confectioner's sugar, lemon zest and nutmeg until smooth and creamy. Gradually stir in flour until thoroughly blended.
2. Shape dough into 1-inch (2.5 cm) balls and place 2 inches (5 cm) apart on baking sheet. Using the bottom of a glass or the tines of a fork dipped in sugar, flatten slightly. Bake in preheated oven for 12 to 15 minutes or until golden brown. Immediately transfer to wire racks to cool.
3. *Prepare the filling:* In a small saucepan, over low heat, bring preserves and sugar to a boil, stirring constantly. Cook, stirring, for 2 minutes, until sugar dissolves and mixture is syrupy. Remove from heat and set aside to cool completely.
4. On a work surface, place half the cookies, flat side up. Spread each with about ¹⁄₂ tsp (2 mL) of the filling. Top with the remaining cookies, flat side down, to form a sandwich. Press together gently. Dab any leftover filling on top of each sandwich as a garnish.

Lacy Oatmeal Sandwiches

Makes about 2 dozen sandwiches

- Preheat oven to 375°F (190°C)
- Baking sheet, lined with buttered foil

²⁄₃ cup	all-purpose flour	150 mL
2 cups	quick-cooking rolled oats	500 mL
²⁄₃ cup	butter or margarine, melted	150 mL
1 cup	granulated sugar	250 mL
¹⁄₄ cup	corn syrup	50 mL
¹⁄₄ cup	milk	50 mL
1 cup	semisweet chocolate chips, melted	250 mL
1 cup	white chocolate chips, melted	250 mL

1. In a medium bowl, mix together flour and oats.
2. In a large bowl, mix together butter or margarine, sugar and corn syrup. Add milk and mix well. Stir in flour mixture and mix thoroughly.
3. Drop batter by level teaspoonfuls (5 mL), about 3 inches (7.5 cm) apart, onto prepared baking sheet and, using the back of a spoon or the tines of a fork, press down slightly on each. Bake in preheated oven for 8 to 10 minutes or until cookies have spread and are browned around the edges. Immediately transfer foil and cookies to wire racks. When cool, peel cookies off the foil.
4. On a work surface, spread a thin layer of semisweet chocolate on the bottom of some cookies and white chocolate on others. Top each with the bottom side of the remaining cookies.

Tip *Drizzle any leftover chocolate over the tops of the cookies for added decoration.*

Biscotti, Shortbread and Holiday Cookies

Biscotti

Shortbread

Holiday Cookies

Biscotti

Crisp and delicious, biscotti are a traditional Italian biscuit, perfect for dunking in a glass of milk or your morning coffee. Most of my biscotti recipes contain butter, which makes them richer and less crunchy than the traditional Italian versions. But because they are baked twice, they are drier than most other cookies.

• •

Coffee House Biscotti

Makes about 3 dozen
- Preheat oven to 350°F (180°C)
- Baking sheet, ungreased

2 cups + 2 tbsp	all-purpose flour	525 mL
1 tsp	baking powder	5 mL
1/4 tsp	salt	1 mL
1/2 cup	butter, softened	125 mL
1 cup	granulated sugar	250 mL
2	eggs	2
1 tsp	vanilla	5 mL
	Grated zest of 1 large lemon	
1 cup	coarsely chopped hazelnuts, toasted	250 mL

1. In a bowl, combine flour, baking powder and salt.
2. In a large bowl, beat butter and sugar until smooth and creamy. Beat in eggs, one at a time, until incorporated. Mix in vanilla and lemon zest. Gradually add flour mixture, mixing until a soft dough forms. Fold in nuts.
3. Divide dough in half. Shape into two rolls about 10 inches (25 cm) long. Place about 2 inches (5 cm) apart on baking sheet. Bake in preheated oven for 30 minutes, until golden.
4. Let cool on sheet for 10 minutes, then transfer to a cutting board and cut into slices 1/2 inch (1 cm) thick. Return to sheet and bake for 10 minutes, until lightly browned. Turn slices over and bake for 10 minutes. Immediately transfer to wire racks.

• •

Italian-Style Biscotti

Makes about 4 dozen
- Preheat oven to 350°F (180°C)
- Baking sheet, lightly greased

3 cups	all-purpose flour	750 mL
2 tsp	baking powder	10 mL
1/2 tsp	salt	2 mL
4	eggs, lightly beaten	4
1 cup	granulated sugar	250 mL
1/2 cup	melted butter	125 mL
2 tsp	vanilla	10 mL
1 tsp	almond extract	5 mL
2 tsp	anise extract	10 mL
3/4 cup	finely chopped blanched almonds	175 mL

1. In a bowl, combine flour, baking powder and salt.
2. In a large bowl, beat eggs, sugar and melted butter until well blended. Add extracts and almonds and mix well. Add dry ingredients and mix until a soft dough forms.
3. On a lightly floured surface, divide dough in half. Shape into two rolls about 12 inches (30 cm) long. Place about 2 inches (5 cm) apart on prepared baking sheet. Bake in preheated oven for 20 minutes or until just beginning to brown around the edges.
4. Let cool on sheet for 10 minutes, then transfer to a cutting board and cut into slices 1/2 inch (1 cm) thick. Place on sheet and bake for 12 minutes. Turn slices over and bake for 5 to 10 minutes, until golden brown.

Tip *Anise extract is available in many supermarkets. If you can't find it there, try a specialty store.*

• •

Cinnamon Oatmeal Biscotti

Makes about 3 dozen
- Preheat oven to 350°F (180°C)
- Baking sheet, greased

2 1/2 cups	all-purpose flour	625 mL
1 cup	quick-cooking rolled oats	250 mL
1 tsp	baking powder	5 mL
1/4 tsp	baking soda	1 mL
2 tsp	ground cinnamon	10 mL
1/4 tsp	salt	1 mL
1 cup	chopped pecans, toasted	250 mL
1/2 cup	butter, softened	125 mL
2/3 cup	packed brown sugar	150 mL
2	eggs	2
1/2 cup	liquid honey	125 mL
2 tsp	vanilla	10 mL

1. In a large bowl, mix together flour, oats, baking powder, baking soda, cinnamon, salt and pecans.
2. In another large bowl, beat butter and brown sugar until smooth and creamy. Beat in eggs, one at a time, until well incorporated. Mix in honey, then vanilla. Add flour mixture and mix until well combined.

3. Divide dough in half. Shape into two rolls about 10 inches (25 cm) long. Place about 2 inches (5 cm) apart on prepared baking sheet. Bake in preheated oven for 30 minutes or until lightly brown.

4. Let cool on sheet for 5 minutes, then transfer to a cutting board and cut into slices ½ inch (1 cm) thick. Stand slices up on sheet and reduce oven heat to 325°F (160°C). Bake for 25 to 30 minutes or until golden brown. Immediately transfer to wire racks to cool.

Tip *If you run out of brown sugar, make your own by mixing 2 tbsp (25 mL) molasses into 1 cup (250 mL) granulated sugar.*

Chocolate Chip Biscotti

Makes about 3½ dozen
- Preheat oven to 350°F (180°C)
- Baking sheet, ungreased

1¾ cups	all-purpose flour	425 mL
2 tsp	baking powder	10 mL
½ cup	semisweet chocolate chips	125 mL
¾ cup	whole unblanched almonds	175 mL
2	eggs	2
⅓ cup	melted butter	75 mL
¾ cup	granulated sugar	175 mL
2 tsp	vanilla	10 mL
1½ tsp	grated orange zest	7 mL
½ tsp	almond extract	2 mL
1	egg white, lightly beaten	1

1. In a large bowl, combine flour, baking powder, chocolate chips and almonds. Make a well in the center.

2. In another bowl, beat eggs, butter, sugar, vanilla, zest and almond extract. Spoon into well and mix until a sticky dough forms.

3. Divide dough in half, then shape into two rolls 10 to 12 inches (25 to 30 cm) long. Place about 2 inches (5 cm) apart on baking sheet. Brush tops with egg white. Bake in preheated oven for 20 minutes.

4. Let cool on baking sheet for 5 minutes, then cut into slices ½ to ¾ inch (1 to 2 cm) thick. Stand cookies upright on sheet and bake for another 20 to 25 minutes or until golden. Immediately transfer to wire racks to cool.

Tip *Chill your rolling pin in the freezer before using so dough will not stick to it.*

Chocolate Almond Biscotti

Makes about 4 dozen
- Preheat oven to 350°F (180°C)
- Baking sheet, greased and floured

2¾ cups	all-purpose flour	675 mL
2½ tsp	baking powder	12 mL
1 tsp	salt	5 mL
½ cup	butter, softened	125 mL
1½ cups	granulated sugar	375 mL
2	eggs	2
3 oz	semisweet chocolate, melted	90 g
1 tbsp	grated orange zest	15 mL
¼ cup	freshly squeezed orange juice	50 mL
3 oz	semisweet chocolate, coarsely chopped	90 g
¾ cup	walnut pieces, toasted	175 mL
¾ cup	whole blanched almonds, toasted	175 mL

1. In a medium bowl, combine flour, baking powder and salt.

2. In a large bowl, beat butter and sugar until smooth and creamy. Add eggs, one at a time, beating until incorporated. Stir in melted chocolate. Add orange zest and juice and mix well. Gradually add flour mixture, mixing until a dough forms. Fold in chocolate and nuts.

3. Divide dough in half. Form two rolls about 2 inches (5 cm) wide. Place at least 2 inches (5 cm) apart on prepared sheet. Bake in preheated oven for 30 minutes.

4. Let cool on baking sheet for 10 minutes, then transfer to a cutting board and cut into slices ½ to ¾ inch (1 to 2 cm) thick. Return to oven and bake for 10 minutes. Turn slices over and bake for 10 minutes. Immediately transfer to wire racks to cool.

Tip *For an added treat, dip one end of the biscotti in additional melted chocolate.*

Chocolate Nut Coffee Biscotti

Makes about 3½ dozen
- Preheat oven to 300°F (150°C)
- Baking sheet, lightly greased and floured

2 cups	all-purpose flour	500 mL
2 cups	unsweetened cocoa powder	500 mL
2 cups	granulated sugar	500 mL
1 tsp	baking powder	5 mL
1 tsp	baking soda	5 mL
6	eggs	6
Pinch	salt	Pinch
¾ cup	brewed coffee or brandy	50 mL
2 tsp	vanilla	10 mL
2 cups	coarsely chopped walnuts, toasted	500 mL

1. In a large bowl, combine flour, cocoa, sugar, baking powder and baking soda. Make a well in the center.
2. In another large bowl, beat eggs and salt. Add coffee and vanilla. Pour into well and mix until a soft dough forms. Fold in walnuts.
3. Divide dough in half. Form into two rolls about 10 inches (25 cm) long. Place about 2 inches (5 cm) apart on prepared baking sheet. Bake in preheated oven for 50 minutes, until loaf looks dry. Transfer to a cutting board and cut into slices ½ inch (1 cm) thick. Return to sheet and bake for 20 minutes. Turn slices over and bake for 20 minutes. Immediately transfer to wire racks.

Apricot Almond Biscotti

Makes about 2½ dozen
- Preheat oven to 325°F (160°C)
- Baking sheet, ungreased

3 cups	all-purpose flour	750 mL
2 tsp	baking powder	10 mL
¼ tsp	salt	1 mL
¾ cup	butter, softened	175 mL
¾ cup	granulated sugar	175 mL
2	eggs	2
1 tsp	almond extract	5 mL
1 tsp	grated orange zest	5 mL
½ cup	blanched chopped almonds, toasted	125 mL
1 cup	finely chopped dried apricots	250 mL

1. In a medium bowl, mix together flour, baking powder and salt.

2. In a large bowl, beat butter and sugar until smooth and creamy. Add eggs, one at a time, beating until well incorporated. Stir in almond extract and orange zest. Add almonds and apricots and mix well. Gradually add flour mixture, mixing until a dough forms.
3. On a lightly floured surface, divide dough in half. Shape into two rolls about 8 inches (20 cm) long. Place at least 2 inches (5 cm) apart on baking sheet. Bake in preheated oven for 30 to 35 minutes or until golden brown.
4. Let cool for 5 minutes on baking sheet, then cut into slices ½ inch (1 cm) thick. Place on baking sheet and return to oven to dry for 15 minutes. Turn slices over and bake for 5 minutes. Immediately transfer to wire racks to cool.

Tip *When cutting the partially cooked dough, always use a sharp knife with a serrated edge and cut in a light sawing motion — otherwise, the cookies will crumble.*

Cherry Nut Biscotti

Makes about 6 dozen
- Preheat oven to 350°F (180°C)
- Baking sheet, greased
- Food processor

2 cups	all-purpose flour	500 mL
1 cup	granulated sugar	250 mL
1 tsp	baking powder	5 mL
2 tsp	grated lime zest	10 mL
¼ cup	cold butter, cut into small pieces	50 mL
¾ cup	dried tart cherries	175 mL
3	eggs	3
1¼ cups	shelled pistachios or nuts of your choice	300 mL

1. In a food processor, combine flour, sugar, baking powder and zest. Pulse until zest is very fine. Add butter and cherries and pulse until cherries are coarsely chopped.
2. In a small bowl, beat eggs lightly. Spoon out 1 tbsp (15 mL) beaten egg and set aside. Add remainder to flour mixture, along with the nuts, and pulse until dough is evenly moistened. (The dough will be sticky.)
3. On a well-floured surface, divide dough into four portions. Shape each into rolls 9 inches (23 cm) long. Place on prepared sheet at least 2 inches (5 cm) apart. Press lightly to flatten and brush with reserved egg. Bake in preheated oven for 25 minutes or until golden brown.

4. Let cool on sheets for about 15 minutes, then transfer to a cutting board. Cut into slices 1/2 inch (1 cm) thick and place upright on sheet. Bake for 15 minutes or until crisp. Immediately transfer to wire racks to cool.

• •

Cranberry Pistachio Biscotti

Makes about 3 dozen
• Preheat oven to 350°F (180°C)
• Baking sheet, greased

3 cups	all-purpose flour	750 mL
1 tbsp	baking powder	15 mL
1/4 tsp	salt	1 mL
3	eggs	3
3/4 cup	granulated sugar	175 mL
1/2 cup	melted butter	125 mL
2 tsp	vanilla	10 mL
1/3 cup	chopped dried cranberries	75 mL
1/2 cup	unsalted pistachios or almonds	125 mL

1. In a medium bowl, combine flour, baking powder and salt.

2. In a large bowl, beat eggs, sugar, butter and vanilla until blended. Gradually add dry ingredients until a sticky dough forms. Using floured hands, work in cranberries and nuts until evenly distributed and dough is smooth.

3. Divide dough in half. Shape into two rolls about 10 inches (25 cm) long. Place about 2 inches (5 cm) apart on prepared baking sheet. Bake in preheated oven for 20 minutes or until browned.

4. Let cool on sheet for 10 minutes, then cut into slices 1/2 to 3/4 inch (1 to 2 cm) thick. Arrange slices upright on baking sheet. Lower oven heat to 300°F (150°C) and bake for 20 to 25 minutes or until firm and dry. Immediately transfer to wire racks.

• •

Lemon Almond Biscotti

Makes about 3 dozen
• Preheat oven to 325°F (160°C)
• Baking sheet, greased

1 3/4 cups	all-purpose flour	425 mL
3/4 cup	granulated sugar	175 mL
1 tbsp	baking powder	15 mL
2 tbsp	finely grated lemon zest	25 mL
3/4 cup	coarsely chopped almonds	175 mL
2	eggs	2
1/3 cup	olive oil	75 mL
1 tsp	vanilla	5 mL
1/2 tsp	almond extract	2 mL

1. In a large bowl, mix together flour, sugar, baking powder, lemon zest and almonds. Make a well in the center.

2. In another bowl, whisk eggs, oil, vanilla and almond extract. Pour into well and mix until a soft, sticky dough forms.

3. Divide dough in half. Shape into two rolls about 10 inches (25 cm) long. Place about 2 inches (5 cm) apart on prepared baking sheet. Bake in preheated oven for 20 minutes.

4. Let cool on sheet for 5 minutes, then cut into slices 1/2 inch (1 cm) thick. Return to sheet and bake for 10 minutes. Turn slices over and bake for 10 minutes. Immediately transfer to wire racks.

• •

Lemon Orange Cocoa Biscotti

Makes about 4 dozen
• Preheat oven to 375°F (190°C)
• Baking sheet, lightly greased

3 cups	all-purpose flour	750 mL
1 cup	granulated sugar	250 mL
5 1/2 tsp	baking powder	27 mL
1/2 tsp	salt	2 mL
3/4 cup	unsweetened cocoa powder	175 mL
1/2 cup	coarsely chopped slivered almonds, toasted	125 mL
1/2 cup	melted butter	125 mL
1/2 cup	water	125 mL
4	eggs	4
1 tsp	vanilla	5 mL
	Grated zest of 3 lemons	
	Grated zest of 2 oranges	

1. In a large bowl, combine flour, sugar, baking powder, salt, cocoa and almonds. Make a well in the center.

2. In another bowl, whisk butter, water, eggs, vanilla, lemon and orange zests. Pour into well and mix until a stiff dough forms.

3. Divide dough in half. Shape into two rolls about 12 by 3 inches (30 by 7.5 cm). Place about 2 inches (5 cm) apart on prepared baking sheet. Bake in preheated oven for 25 to 30 minutes. Immediately cut into slices 1/2 to 3/4 inch (1 to 2 cm) thick.

4. Lower oven heat to 350°F (180°C). Place slices on baking sheet and bake for 10 minutes. Turn slices over and bake for 10 minutes. Immediately transfer to wire racks.

Shortbread

Traditional Scottish shortbread is one of the best-known and best-loved cookies in the world. Served with tea, there are few more satisfying afternoon treats.

Basically, shortbread is some combination of butter and flour, worked together and flavored. Many excellent cooks believe that the best way to "work" the butter into the flour mixture is with your fingers, as it allows you to "feel" the dough as it combines. A food processor, fitted with a metal disk, also does a good job of combining the butter with the flour mixture. If using this method, cut the butter into 1-inch (2.5 cm) cubes. Don't process the dough too much, as it will destroy the "crumb."

Many cooks have shortbread tricks. When making sweet shortbread, some use superfine sugar. Others swear by rice flour. As you bake these shortbreads, you will soon get a feel for what techniques work best for you.

Original Scottish Shortbread

Makes about 3 dozen
- Preheat oven to 300°F (150°C)
- Baking sheet, ungreased
- Cookie cutters

1 cup	butter, softened	250 mL
³⁄₄ cup	granulated or fruit (extra-fine) sugar	175 mL
2¹⁄₂ cups	sifted all-purpose flour	625 mL

1. In a large bowl, beat butter and sugar until smooth. Gradually add flour, mixing thoroughly after each addition. Knead lightly. Wrap tightly in plastic wrap and refrigerate for 1 to 2 hours.

2. On a lightly floured surface, roll out dough to about ¹⁄₂-inch (1 cm) thickness. Using a cookie cutters or a glass dipped in flour, cut into desired shapes and place on baking sheet. Bake in preheated oven for 20 to 25 minutes or until golden brown. Immediately transfer to wire racks to cool.

Variations *Honey Shortbread Cookies: Reduce sugar to ¹⁄₂ cup (125 mL). After beating butter and sugar, add ¹⁄₄ cup (50 mL) liquid honey.*

Butterscotch Shortbread Cookies: Use 1 cup (250 mL) firmly packed brown sugar in place of granulated sugar.

Classic Christmas Shortbread

Makes about 3 dozen
- Preheat oven to 350°F (180°C)
- Baking sheet, lightly greased
- Cookie cutters

1 cup	butter, softened	250 mL
²⁄₃ cup	packed brown sugar	150 mL
2 cups	sifted all-purpose flour	500 mL

1. In a large bowl, cream butter and brown sugar until smooth. Gradually add flour, mixing thoroughly after each addition. Knead lightly.

2. Shape dough into a ball. Roll out on floured working surface to about ¹⁄₄-inch (0.5 cm) thickness. Using cookie cutters or a glass dipped in flour, cut into desired shapes and place on prepared sheet. Bake in preheated oven for 12 to 15 minutes or until golden brown. Immediately transfer to wire racks to cool.

Tip *Dip the ends of plain shortbread cookies into melted chocolate. Let excess drip into saucepan, then place on a baking sheet until chocolate hardens.*

Old-Time Oatmeal Shortbread

Makes about 4 dozen
- Preheat oven to 350°F (180°C)
- Baking sheet, ungreased
- Cookie cutters

1 cup	all-purpose flour	250 mL
¹⁄₂ tsp	baking soda	2 mL
2 cups	quick-cooking rolled oats	500 mL
1 cup	butter, softened	250 mL
¹⁄₂ cup	firmly packed brown sugar	125 mL
1 tsp	vanilla	5 mL

1. In a medium bowl, mix together flour, baking soda and oats.

2. In a large bowl, beat butter, brown sugar and vanilla until smooth and creamy. Gradually add flour mixture, mixing thoroughly after each addition. Knead lightly. Wrap tightly in plastic wrap and refrigerate for at least 2 hours.

3. On a lightly floured surface, roll out dough to ¹⁄₄-inch (0.5 cm) thickness. Using cookie cutters or a glass dipped in flour, cut into desired shapes and place on baking sheet. Bake in preheated oven for 10 to 12 minutes or until golden brown. Immediately transfer to wire racks to cool.

Grandma's Traditional Shortbread

Makes about 2 dozen
- Preheat oven to 300°F (150°C)
- Baking sheet, ungreased
- Cookie cutters

½ cup	confectioner's (icing) sugar	125 mL
½ cup	cornstarch	125 mL
1 cup	all-purpose flour	250 mL
¾ cup	butter, softened	175 mL

1. In a medium bowl, sift together sugar, cornstarch and flour.

2. In a large bowl, cream butter. Using two knives, a pastry blender or your fingers, work flour in until a smooth dough forms. Knead lightly. Wrap dough in plastic wrap and refrigerate for about 30 minutes.

3. On a lightly floured surface, roll out dough to ¼-inch (0.5 cm) thickness. Using cookie cutters or the top of a glass dipped in flour, cut into desired shapes and place on baking sheet. Bake in preheated oven for 15 to 20 minutes or until lightly browned. Immediately transfer to wire racks to cool.

Tip *Give your shortbread a professional look by dipping the shapes into melted white or dark chocolate and then sprinkling the chocolate with finely chopped nuts.*

Ginger Shortbread

Makes 32 bars
- Preheat oven to 300°F (150°C)
- 8-inch (2 L) square baking pan, ungreased

1 cup	butter, softened	250 mL
½ cup	confectioner's (icing) sugar, sifted	125 mL
¼ tsp	salt	1 mL
3 tbsp	finely chopped candied ginger	45 mL
2 cups	all-purpose flour	500 mL

1. In a large bowl, beat butter, confectioner's sugar and salt until smooth and creamy. Mix in ginger until well incorporated. Gradually sift in flour, mixing well after each addition.

2. Press dough into pan and, using a fork, prick deeply all over. Bake in preheated oven for 50 to 60 minutes or until golden brown. Let cool in pan for 5 minutes, then invert onto a cutting board. Using a knife, score 32 bars, 2 by 1 inch (5 by 2.5 cm). When cool enough to handle, using a lifter, transfer to wire racks to cool.

Whipped Shortbread

Makes about 9 dozen
- Preheat oven to 300°F (150°C)
- Baking sheet, ungreased

2 cups	butter, softened	500 mL
1 tsp	vanilla	5 mL
½ cup	cornstarch	125 mL
3 cups	all-purpose flour	750 mL
1 cup	confectioner's (icing) sugar, sifted	250 mL
	Maraschino cherries (optional)	

1. In a large bowl, beat butter until smooth. Stir in vanilla. Add cornstarch, flour and confectioner's sugar and beat until dough is a smooth consistency resembling whipped cream.

2. Drop by teaspoonfuls (5 mL), about 2 inches (5 cm) apart, onto baking sheet. Bake in preheated oven for 15 minutes or until golden brown. Top with a maraschino cherry (if using). Immediately transfer to wire racks to cool.

Chocolate Shortbread

Makes about 2½ to 3 dozen
- Preheat oven to 325°F (160°C)
- Baking sheet, ungreased

¾ cup	all-purpose flour	175 mL
1 tbsp	cornstarch	15 mL
Pinch	salt	Pinch
3 tbsp	unsweetened cocoa powder	45 mL
½ cup	butter, softened	125 mL
½ cup	confectioner's (icing) sugar, sifted	125 mL
½ tsp	vanilla	2 mL

1. In a small bowl, sift together flour, cornstarch, salt and cocoa.

2. In a large bowl, beat butter, confectioner's sugar and vanilla until smooth and creamy. Gradually add flour mixture, mixing thoroughly after each addition. Knead briefly.

3. Shape dough into 1-inch (2.5 cm) balls and place about 2 inches (5 cm) apart on baking sheet. Using the bottom of a glass or the tines of a fork to make a criss-cross pattern, flatten slightly. Bake in preheated oven for 20 minutes or until firm. Let cool slightly, then transfer to wire racks or waxed paper–lined platter to cool completely.

Tip *When your recipe calls for sifting, put the ingredients to be sifted in the mixing bowl and stir them with a whisk. It does an equally good job.*

Refrigerator Nut Shortbread

Makes about 6 dozen
- Preheat oven to 300°F (150°C)
- Baking sheet, ungreased

3 cups	cake and pastry flour	750 mL
½ cup	rice flour	125 mL
¾ cup	granulated sugar	175 mL
1½ cups	butter, softened	375 mL
	Finely chopped almonds or pecans	

1. In a large bowl, combine flours and sugar.
2. In another large bowl, beat butter until smooth. Gradually add flour mixture, mixing thoroughly after each addition. Knead lightly.
3. Divide dough in half and shape into two logs, each about 1½ inches (4 cm) in diameter. Roll logs in nuts until evenly coated. Wrap tightly in plastic wrap and twist ends to seal. Chill in refrigerator for 1 to 2 hours, until firm.
4. Cut dough into ¼-inch (0.5 cm) rounds and place on baking sheet. Bake in preheated oven for 20 to 25 minutes or until golden brown. Let cool on baking sheet for 5 minutes, then transfer to wire racks to cool completely.

Tip *Refrigerator dough cookies are very convenient because you can make the dough ahead of time. When you're ready to bake, you can slice and bake as many cookies as you like.*

Cherry Nut Refrigerator Shortbread

Makes about 3 dozen
- Preheat oven to 375°F (190°C)
- Baking sheet, ungreased

1 cup	all-purpose flour	250 mL
½ cup	confectioner's (icing) sugar, sifted	125 mL
½ cup	cornstarch	125 mL
¾ cup	chopped candied cherries	175 mL
½ cup	chopped pecans	125 mL
¾ cup	butter, softened	175 mL

1. In a medium bowl, mix together flour, confectioner's sugar and cornstarch. Add cherries and pecans and mix thoroughly.
2. In a large bowl, cream butter. Gradually add flour mixture, mixing thoroughly after each addition. Knead lightly. Shape dough into a roll about 1½ inches (4 cm) wide. Wrap tightly in plastic wrap and refrigerate for at least 4 hours.

3. When ready to bake, cut roll into slices ¼ inch (0.5 cm) thick and place on baking sheet. Bake in preheated oven for 8 to 12 minutes or until golden brown. Immediately transfer to wire racks to cool.

Lemon Poppy Seed Shortbread

Makes about 2 dozen
- Preheat oven to 300°F (150°C)
- Baking sheet, ungreased
- Cookie cutters

1 cup	all-purpose flour	250 mL
½ cup	confectioner's (icing) sugar, sifted	125 mL
½ cup	cornstarch	125 mL
2 tbsp	grated lemon zest	25 mL
1 tbsp	poppy seeds	15 mL
¾ cup	butter, softened	175 mL

1. In a medium bowl, mix together flour, sugar, cornstarch, lemon zest and poppy seeds.
2. In a large bowl, cream butter. Gradually add flour mixture, mixing well after each addition. Knead lightly.
3. On a lightly floured surface, roll out dough to ¼-inch (0.5 cm) thickness. Using cookie cutters, cut into desired shapes. Alternately, shape dough into 1-inch (2.5 cm) balls and flatten slightly with a fork and place on baking sheets. Bake in preheated oven for 15 to 20 minutes or until lightly browned. Immediately transfer to wire racks to cool.

Tip *Put lemon and orange zest in water, in a saucepan, and let simmer. You'll have a refreshing, wonderful aroma all through the house.*

Orange Shortbread

Makes about 2 dozen
- Preheat oven to 300°F (150°C)
- Baking sheet, ungreased

1 cup	butter, softened	250 mL
⅓ cup	berry sugar	75 mL
¼ tsp	salt	1 mL
1 tbsp	grated lemon zest	15 mL
2 tbsp	grated orange zest	25 mL
2 cups	all-purpose flour	500 mL

1. In a bowl, beat butter and sugar until smooth and creamy. Add salt and zests and blend in well.

2. Gradually add flour, mixing thoroughly after each addition. Knead lightly. Shape into a roll, wrap tightly in plastic wrap and refrigerate for at least 2 hours or overnight.

3. When ready to bake, cut dough into ¼-inch (0.5 cm) slices and place on baking sheet. Bake in preheated oven for 10 minutes or until lightly browned. Immediately transfer to wire racks to cool.

Tip *Berry, or fruit, sugar is extra-fine granulated sugar, which you can buy at most supermarkets. Many people believe it improves the quality of shortbread.*

• •

Cream Cheese Shortbread

Makes about 3 dozen
- Preheat oven to 375°F (190°C)
- Baking sheet, ungreased
- Cookie cutters

4 oz	cream cheese, softened	125 g
1 cup	butter, softened	250 mL
½ cup	granulated sugar	125 mL
1 tsp	vanilla	5 mL
2 cups	sifted all-purpose flour	500 mL

1. In a large bowl, beat cream cheese and butter until smooth. Add sugar and mix until creamy. Stir in vanilla. Gradually add flour, mixing well after each addition. Knead lightly.

2. On a lightly floured surface, roll out dough to ¼-inch (0.5 cm) thickness. Using a cookie cutter or a glass dipped in flour, cut into desired shapes and place on baking sheet. Bake in preheated oven for 8 to 10 minutes. Immediately transfer to wire racks to cool.

• •

Cheddar Shortbread

Makes 32 bars
- Preheat oven to 425°F (220°C)
- Baking sheet, greased

2 cups	all-purpose flour	500 mL
1 tsp	salt	5 mL
Pinch	cayenne pepper (optional)	Pinch
1 cup	butter or margarine, softened	250 mL
1½ cups	shredded Cheddar cheese	375 mL

1. In a medium bowl, combine flour, salt and cayenne (if using).

2. In a large bowl, cream butter. Beat in cheese, using a spoon, until well blended. Gradually add flour mixture, mixing thoroughly after each addition. Turn out on a floured surface and knead lightly.

3. Shape dough into an 8-inch (20 cm) square and cut into 4- by 1-inch (10 by 2.5 cm) bars. Place on prepared sheet and bake in preheated oven for 25 minutes or until golden brown. Immediately transfer to wire racks to cool.

Variation *Food Processor Method: This method also works well and has the advantage of fully integrating the Cheddar into the dough. Cut butter into 1-inch (2.5 cm) cubes and place in freezer. In a food processor, using the metal blade, add flour, salt and cayenne. Pulse until blended. Add cheese and pulse until well combined. Add chilled butter and pulse just until a dough forms. Turn out on a floured board and knead lightly. Follow Step 3.*

• •

Spicy Shortbread Wedges

Makes 32 wedges
- Preheat oven to 325°F (160°C)
- Two 8-inch (20 cm) round cake pans, ungreased

1 cup	butter, softened	250 mL
1 cup	packed brown sugar	250 mL
2 tbsp	grated orange zest	25 mL
1 tbsp	ground cinnamon	15 mL
¾ tsp	ground cloves	4 mL
2 tbsp	ground ginger	25 mL
1 tsp	baking soda	5 mL
2 cups	all-purpose flour	500 mL
	Granulated sugar	

1. In a large bowl, beat butter, brown sugar, orange zest, cinnamon, cloves, ginger and baking soda until smooth and creamy. Gradually add flour, mixing thoroughly after each addition. Knead lightly.

2. Divide dough in half. Place half in one pan and press evenly over bottom. Repeat with the remaining dough in second pan. Sprinkle tops with granulated sugar and bake in preheated oven for 25 to 30 minutes or until tops look dry and slightly crackled and edges are higher than the centers. Let cool in pans for 5 minutes, then invert onto a cutting board. Cut each cake into 16 wedges.

Tip *If a recipe calls for superfine sugar, whirl regular granulated sugar in a blender until fine.*

Raisin Shortbread Wedges

Makes 16 wedges
- Preheat oven to 350°F (180°C)
- Baking sheet, greased

⅓ cup	orange juice	75 mL
¾ cup	seedless raisins	175 mL
1½ cups	sifted all-purpose flour	375 mL
¼ cup	granulated sugar	50 mL
½ cup	butter, softened	125 mL

1. In a small saucepan, bring orange juice and raisins to a slow boil. Cover and let cool, if possible, overnight.
2. In a medium bowl, mix together flour and sugar.
3. In a large bowl, cream butter. Gradually add flour mixture, mixing thoroughly after each addition. Knead dough thoroughly.
4. Divide dough in quarters and shape into rounds, about ¼ inch (0.5 cm) thick. Place one round on prepared baking sheet and spread cooled raisin mixture over the entire surface. Top with another round, pressing down firmly. Using your fingers dipped in flour, pinch edges together. Prick entire top with a fork. Bake in preheated oven about 20 minutes or until golden. Mark into 8 segments as you would a pie, and when cool, remove from baking sheet.

Tip *Some cooks believe the use of rice flour improves shortbread. Try substituting rice flour for one-fifth of the all-purpose flour in this or any other shortbread recipe.*

Shortbread Wedges with Peanut Butter and Jam

Makes 18 wedges
- Preheat oven to 350°F (180°C)
- 9-inch (23 cm) round pie plate or quiche pan, sprayed with vegetable spray

1¼ cups	all-purpose flour	300 mL
½ tsp	baking powder	2 mL
¼ tsp	salt	1 mL
3 tbsp	butter, softened	45 mL
½ cup	smooth peanut butter	125 mL
½ cup	granulated sugar	125 mL
1	egg	1
½ tsp	vanilla	2 mL
	Grape jam or jelly	

1. In a small bowl, mix together flour, baking powder and salt.

2. In a large bowl, beat butter, peanut butter and sugar until smooth and creamy. Add egg and vanilla and beat until well blended. Gradually add flour mixture, mixing thoroughly after each addition. Knead lightly. Wrap dough tightly in plastic wrap and chill in refrigerator for several hours or overnight.
3. Press dough into bottom of prepared pan. Using a knife, score 18 pie-shaped wedges. (Do not cut all the way to the bottom.) Bake in preheated oven for 10 minutes. Using the tip of a wooden spoon, press random grooves into the dough. Fill with grape jam or jelly and return to the oven for 8 more minutes. Place plate on a wire rack to cool. Cut into 18 wedges.

Holiday Cookies

Many people associate holiday memories with special foods. The Thanksgiving turkey, Christmas pudding, Hanukkah rugelach and special baked goods are, for many, cherished traditions of the holidays. But homemade cookies, bars and squares are more than a holiday treat. They also make an ideal present. Wrapped in pretty paper or presented in elegant tins, they are always appreciated. From Peppermint Candy Canes to Poppy Seed Hamantashen, I hope these recipes will enhance your holiday celebrations.

Chinese New Year Bursts

Makes about 16 bursts
- Deep fryer or Dutch oven

2 cups	all-purpose flour	500 mL
1 tsp	baking powder	5 mL
1 tbsp	shortening, softened	15 mL
⅔ cup	granulated sugar	150 mL
1	egg	1
3 tbsp	water	45 mL
½ cup	sesame seeds	125 mL
8 cups	vegetable oil for frying	2 L

1. In a small bowl, mix together flour and baking powder.
2. In a large bowl, beat shortening and sugar until smooth and creamy. Beat in egg until well incorporated. Add water and mix until well blended. Stir in flour mixture, mixing until a dough forms.
3. On a lightly floured surface, knead dough until soft. Shape into 1½-inch (4 cm) balls.

4. Add water to a bowl and spread sesame seeds on a plate. Dip balls in water, then roll in sesame seeds to coat.
5. Heat oil in deep fryer or Dutch oven to 325ºF (160ºC). Using a slotted spoon, add five or six balls to preheated oil. Cook, turning once, until dough cracks in the center, bursts and is golden brown, about 3 to 5 minutes. Using a slotted spoon, transfer cookies to a paper towel to drain. Repeat with the remaining dough.

Tip *If you don't have a deep-frying thermometer, you can test the temperature of the oil by dropping a small piece of bread into it. If it turns golden in color, the oil is hot enough.*

Chocolate Valentine Hearts

Makes about 3 dozen
- Preheat oven to 300ºF (150ºC)
- 3-inch (7.5 cm) heart-shaped cookie cutter
- Baking sheet, ungreased

1 cup	butter, softened	250 mL
1 cup	confectioner's (icing) sugar, sifted	250 mL
1/3 cup	unsweetened cocoa powder	75 mL
1 1/2 cups	all-purpose flour	375 mL
	Vanilla Icing (see recipe, page 548)	
	Cinnamon hearts for decoration	

1. In a large bowl, cream butter until smooth.
2. In another bowl, sift confectioner's sugar, cocoa and flour. Gradually add to butter and mix until a soft dough forms. If dough is too soft, refrigerate for 30 minutes or until firm.
3. On a lightly floured surface, roll dough to 1/8-inch (0.25 cm) thickness. Using a heart-shaped cookie cutter about 3 inches (7.5 cm) across, cut out cookies.
4. Place about 2 inches (5 cm) apart on baking sheet and bake in preheated oven for 20 to 25 minutes. Let cool on sheet for 5 minutes, then transfer to wire racks to cool completely.
5. Make Vanilla Icing and divide in half. Tint one half with red food coloring. Decorate cookies with red and white icing, cinnamon hearts, whatever strikes your fancy as appropriate for Valentine's Day.

Tip *To use little hearts from leftover cut-outs, lower oven heat to 325ºF (160ºC) and bake for 5 minutes, until lightly browned. Dip in melted chocolate, if desired.*

Cherry Valentine Cookies

Makes about 4 1/2 dozen
- Preheat oven to 375ºF (190ºC)
- Large and small heart-shaped cookie cutters
- Baking sheet, greased

3 1/2 cups	all-purpose flour	875 mL
2 tsp	baking powder	10 mL
1 tsp	baking soda	5 mL
1/2 tsp	salt	2 mL
1/2 cup	shortening, softened	125 mL
1/2 cup	butter or margarine, softened	125 mL
1 cup	granulated sugar	250 mL
1	egg	1
1 tsp	vanilla	5 mL
1/2 cup	milk	125 mL
CHERRY FILLING		
1/2 cup	granulated sugar	125 mL
1 1/2 tbsp	cornstarch	22 mL
1/2 cup	orange juice	125 mL
1 tbsp	butter or margarine	15 mL
12	maraschino cherries, chopped	12
1/4 cup	cherry juice	50 mL
	Additional sugar	

1. In a large bowl, mix together flour, baking powder, baking soda and salt.
2. In another large bowl, beat shortening, butter or margarine and sugar until smooth and creamy. Add egg and beat until well incorporated. Stir in vanilla and milk until well blended. Gradually add flour mixture, mixing until a soft dough forms. Cover and refrigerate for at least 2 hours, until firm.
3. *Prepare the filling:* In a small saucepan, combine sugar, cornstarch, orange juice, butter or margarine, cherries and cherry juice. Bring to a boil over low heat and cook, stirring, for 1 minute. Transfer saucepan to refrigerator and chill until cool.
4. On a lightly floured surface, roll dough out to 1/8-inch (0.25 cm) thickness. Using a heart-shaped cookie cutter about 2 1/2 inches (6 cm) across, cut cookies out. Place half on prepared baking sheet. Spoon 1/2 tsp (2 mL) filling in the center of each. Using a heart-shaped cookie cutter about 1 1/2 inches (4 cm) across, cut hearts out of the remaining cookies. Place cut-out hearts over filled hearts and press together gently.
5. Bake in preheated oven for 8 to 10 minutes or until lightly browned. Immediately transfer to wire racks to cool.

Candied Easter Specials

Makes about 3 dozen
- Preheat oven to 300°F (150°C)
- Round or rectangular cookie cutter
- Baking sheet, greased

2 cups	all-purpose flour	500 mL
1/4 tsp	baking soda	1 mL
Pinch	salt	Pinch
1/2 tsp	ground cinnamon	2 mL
1/4 tsp	ground nutmeg	1 mL
Pinch	ground cloves	Pinch
1 cup	liquid honey	250 mL
1 tbsp	granulated sugar	15 mL
1/4 cup	chopped blanched almonds	50 mL
2 tbsp	butter or margarine, softened	25 mL
1 tbsp	rum or sherry	15 mL
3/4 tsp	grated lemon zest	4 mL
1/2 cup	chopped candied lemon or orange peel	125 mL
	Granulated sugar (optional)	

1. In a medium bowl, sift together flour, baking soda, salt, cinnamon, nutmeg and cloves.
2. In a small saucepan, over low heat, bring honey and sugar to a boil, stirring constantly. Simmer for 5 minutes, then add almonds and simmer for 5 minutes. Set aside to cool.
3. In a large bowl, beat butter or margarine, rum or sherry and lemon zest. Add honey mixture and blend well. Gradually add flour mixture and mix well. Stir in candied peel, mixing until a soft dough forms. Cover and refrigerate for 1 to 2 hours, until firm.
4. On a lightly floured surface, divide dough into three portions. Roll one portion out to 1/4- to 1/2-inch (0.5 to 1 cm) thickness. Using a round or rectangular cookie cutter dipped in flour, cut out shapes. Repeat with the remaining dough.
5. Place cookies about 2 inches (5 cm) apart on prepared baking sheet. Bake in preheated oven for 20 minutes or until browned. Immediately transfer to wire racks to cool. While cookies are still warm, sprinkle with granulated sugar, if desired.

Tip *These cookies are best stored in an airtight container with a slice of apple to keep them moist.*

Poppy Seed Hamantashen

Makes about 3 1/2 dozen
- Preheat oven to 350°F (180°C)
- 3-inch (7.5-cm) round cookie cutter
- Baking sheet, greased

6	eggs	6
1 cup	vegetable oil	250 mL
1 cup	granulated sugar	250 mL
	Juice of 1/2 lemon (or 1/2 cup/ 125 mL orange juice)	
6 cups	all-purpose flour	1.5 L
4 tsp	baking powder	20 mL
1/4 tsp	salt	1 mL
POPPY SEED FILLING		
2 cups	poppy seeds	500 mL
3/4 cup	milk	175 mL
1/2 cup	liquid honey	125 mL
1/4 cup	packed brown sugar	50 mL
Pinch	salt	Pinch
1	egg, beaten	
GLAZE		
1	egg yolk, lightly beaten	1

1. In a medium bowl, whisk together eggs, oil, sugar and juice until blended.
2. In a large bowl, sift together flour, baking powder and salt. Make a well in the center. Pour in egg mixture and, using your hands, mix together until a soft dough forms. Cover and refrigerate for 2 hours or overnight.
3. *Prepare the filling:* In a medium bowl, add boiling water to poppy seeds to cover by 1 inch (2.5 cm). Let stand for 10 minutes, then drain. In a food processor with a metal blade, grind poppy seeds.
4. In a saucepan, combine ground poppy seeds, milk, honey, brown sugar and salt. Cook over low heat for 5 minutes, stirring constantly, until thick. Let cool for 15 minutes, then mix in beaten egg. Set aside.
5. On a lightly floured surface, roll dough into a circle about 1/8 inch (0.25 cm) thick. Using a 3-inch (7.5 cm) cookie cutter, cut out circles. Spoon a heaping tablespoonful (15 mL) of filling in the center of each circle. Moisten the edges lightly with a finger dipped in water and pinch together three edges of the dough to form a triangle, leaving a small opening in the center with some filling showing. It will resemble a three-cornered hat. Or pinch the top together tightly to enclose the filling, if desired.

6. Place triangles on prepared baking sheet. Cover with a cloth and let stand for 1 hour. Then brush tops with egg yolk glaze. Bake in preheated oven for 20 to 25 minutes or until lightly browned. Let cool on sheets, then, using a spatula, lift off very carefully.

Variation *For prune filling, see Olga's Hamantashen, page 523.*

* *

Passover Coconut Macaroons

Makes about 2½ dozen
- Preheat oven to 325°F (160°C)
- Baking sheet, greased and dusted with potato starch

2	egg whites	2
½ cup	granulated sugar	125 mL
1 tbsp	liquid honey	15 mL
2 tbsp	potato starch	25 mL
1¾ cups	finely shredded coconut	425 mL

1. In a clean bowl, beat egg whites until soft peaks form. Add sugar and honey and beat until shiny, stiff peaks form. Gradually fold in potato starch, then coconut.
2. Drop by tablespoonfuls (15 mL), about 2 inches (5 cm) apart, onto prepared baking sheet. Bake in preheated oven for 15 to 18 minutes or until lightly browned. Immediately transfer to wire racks to cool.

Tip *This recipe works best if the coconut is very fine. Add required quantity to a food processor and process to the desired consistency.*

* *

Passover Almond Cookies

Makes about 2½ dozen
- Preheat oven to 300°F (150°C)
- Baking sheet, lightly greased

3	eggs	3
½ cup	granulated sugar	125 mL
1 tbsp	matzo meal	15 mL
2 tbsp	brandy	25 mL
2¼ cups	finely ground almonds or hazelnuts	550 mL
	Halved blanched almonds	

1. In a medium bowl, whisk eggs until light and fluffy. Add sugar and matzo meal and mix well. Stir in brandy. Fold in nuts until well combined.

2. Shape dough into 1-inch (2.5 cm) balls. Place about 2 inches (5 cm) apart on prepared baking sheet and gently press half a nut in the center of each. Bake in preheated oven for 20 minutes or until lightly browned. Immediately transfer to wire racks to cool.

* *

Thanksgiving Pumpkin Spice Cookies

Makes about 6 dozen
- Preheat oven to 375°F (190°C)
- Round cookie cutter or glass, 2 inches (5 cm) in diameter
- Baking sheet, ungreased

4½ cups	all-purpose flour	1.125 L
2 tsp	baking powder	10 mL
1 tsp	baking soda	5 mL
1½ tsp	ground cinnamon	7 mL
½ tsp	ground nutmeg	2 mL
½ tsp	ground ginger	2 mL
1¼ cups	shortening, softened	300 mL
1 cup	packed brown sugar	250 mL
1 cup	granulated sugar	250 mL
2	eggs	2
1 tsp	vanilla	5 mL
1 tsp	finely grated orange zest	5 mL
1	can (14 oz/398 mL) pumpkin purée (not pie filling)	1
	Confectioner's (icing) sugar, sifted	

1. In a large bowl, combine flour, baking powder, baking soda, cinnamon, nutmeg and ginger.
2. In another large bowl, beat shortening and sugars until smooth and creamy. Beat in eggs, one at a time, until incorporated. Stir in vanilla and orange zest. Add half the flour mixture and beat well. Add pumpkin and beat well. Add the remaining flour mixture, beating until well combined and a soft dough forms.
3. Divide dough in half. Wrap each portion tightly in plastic wrap and refrigerate for 3 to 4 hours, until firm.
4. On a lightly floured surface, roll out one portion of dough to ¼-inch (0.5 cm) thickness. Using a cutter dipped in flour, cut into rounds and place about 2 inches (5 cm) apart on baking sheet.
5. Bake in preheated oven for 10 minutes or until browned. Immediately transfer to wire racks to cool. When cool, dust with sifted confectioner's sugar.

Bird's Nest Cookies

Makes about 40 cookies
- Preheat oven to 350°F (180°C)
- Baking sheet, ungreased

3 cups	all-purpose flour	750 mL
1 tsp	baking powder	5 mL
1 tsp	salt	5 mL
1 cup	shortening, softened	250 mL
1 cup	lightly packed brown sugar	250 mL
2	eggs, separated	2
1 tsp	vanilla	5 mL
½ cup	milk	125 mL
1¼ cups	shredded sweetened coconut	300 mL
½ cup	apricot or raspberry jam	125 mL

1. In a medium bowl, mix together flour, baking powder and salt.
2. In a large bowl, beat shortening and sugar until smooth and creamy. Add egg yolks, one at a time, beating until incorporated. Stir in vanilla. Gradually add flour mixture, alternating with milk to form a dough. Shape into 1½-inch (4 cm) balls.
3. In a clean bowl, whisk egg whites. Spread coconut on a plate. One at a time, dip balls into egg whites. Shake off excess, then roll in coconut. Place about 2 inches (5 cm) apart on baking sheet and, using a thimble or your thumb, make a small dent in the center of each. Fill with jam.
4. Bake in preheated oven for 12 to 15 minutes or until lightly browned. Immediately transfer to wire racks to cool.

Christmas Chocolate Log Cookies

Makes 4 dozen
- Preheat oven to 425°F (220°C)
- Baking sheet, ungreased

1⅓ cups	granulated sugar	325 mL
2 tbsp	all-purpose flour	25 mL
Pinch	ground cinnamon	Pinch
2½ cups	ground almonds	625 mL
2	egg whites	2
4 oz	semisweet chocolate, melted	125 g
	Granulated sugar	

1. In a small bowl, mix together sugar, flour, cinnamon and almonds.
2. In a clean bowl, beat egg whites until soft peaks form. Fold in melted chocolate. Gradually add sugar mixture, mixing until a stiff dough forms.

3. On a lightly floured surface, shape dough, 2 tbsp (25 mL) at a time, into logs about 5 inches (12.5 cm) long, then roll in sugar.
4. Place logs about 2 inches (5 cm) apart on baking sheet. Bake in preheated oven for 10 minutes or until browned. Using a lifter, carefully transfer to wire racks to cool.

Holiday Cranberry Cookies

Makes about 3 dozen
- Preheat oven to 375°F (190°C)
- Baking sheet, ungreased

1½ cups	all-purpose flour	375 mL
¾ tsp	baking powder	4 mL
¼ tsp	baking soda	1 mL
¼ tsp	salt	1 mL
¼ cup	butter, softened	50 mL
⅓ cup	packed brown sugar	75 mL
½ cup	granulated sugar	125 mL
1	egg	1
3 tbsp	frozen orange juice concentrate, thawed	45 mL
1 tsp	grated orange zest	5 mL
1½ cups	fresh cranberries, halved (or 1 cup/250 mL dried cranberries)	375 mL
½ cup	chopped pecans or walnuts	125 mL
FROSTING		
¼ cup	butter, softened	50 mL
2 cups	confectioner's (icing) sugar, sifted	500 mL
3 tbsp	frozen orange juice concentrate, thawed	45 mL
1 tsp	vanilla	5 mL
	Pecan or walnut halves (optional)	

1. In a small bowl, mix together flour, baking powder, baking soda and salt.
2. In a large bowl, beat butter and sugars until smooth and creamy. Beat in egg until well incorporated. Stir in concentrate and zest until blended. Gradually add flour mixture and mix until well blended. Fold in cranberries and nuts until thoroughly combined.
3. Drop dough by rounded tablespoonfuls (15 mL), about 2 inches (5 cm) apart, onto baking sheet. Bake in preheated oven for 10 to 12 minutes or until lightly browned. Let cool on baking sheet.
4. *Prepare the frosting:* In a small bowl, beat butter until creamy. Add confectioner's sugar, orange juice and vanilla and mix until smooth. Spread on cooled cookies. Garnish with nuts, if desired.

Glazed Holiday Wreaths

Makes about 2½ dozen
- Preheat oven to 350ºF (180ºC)
- Round cookie cutters or two glasses, 2½ inches (6 cm) and 1 inch (2.5 cm) in diameter
- Baking sheet, ungreased

1¼ cups	all-purpose flour	300 mL
½ cup	confectioner's (icing) sugar, sifted	125 mL
Pinch	salt	Pinch
½ cup	butter, softened	125 mL
½ tsp	vanilla	2 mL
1	egg	1
GLAZE		
1	egg, beaten	1
¼ cup	finely chopped blanched almonds	50 mL
2 tbsp	granulated sugar	25 mL

1. In a small bowl, sift together flour, confectioner's sugar and salt.
2. In a large bowl, beat butter, vanilla and egg until smooth and creamy. Add flour mixture and, using your hands, knead into a dough.
3. Divide dough into three portions. Wrap each tightly in plastic wrap and refrigerate for 1 to 2 hours, until firm.
4. On a lightly floured surface, roll out dough to ⅛-inch (0.25 cm) thickness. Cut out circles with wide cutter, then, using the smaller cutter, cut a circle in the center of each round. Place about 2 inches (5 cm) apart on baking sheet.
5. *Prepare the glaze:* Brush with beaten egg, then top with almonds and sugar.
6. Bake in preheated oven for 10 to 15 minutes, until golden brown. Let cool on baking sheets for 5 minutes, then transfer to wire racks to cool completely.

Cherry Bell Cookies

Makes about 2½ dozen
- Preheat oven to 375ºF (190ºC)
- Baking sheet, ungreased

¾ cup	butter, softened	175 mL
½ cup	granulated sugar	125 mL
1	egg yolk	1
1 tsp	vanilla	5 mL
1¾ cups	all-purpose flour	425 mL
12	maraschino cherries, drained and halved	12

1. In a large bowl, beat butter and sugar until smooth and creamy. Beat in egg yolk and vanilla until well incorporated. Gradually beat in flour until a soft dough forms.
2. On a floured surface, roll dough into a log, 8 by 1½ inches (20 by 4 cm). Wrap tightly in plastic wrap and refrigerate at least 3 hours or overnight.
3. Using a knife, cut log into slices ¼ inch (0.5 cm) wide and place about 2 inches (5 cm) apart on baking sheet. Let dough reach room temperature, then fold two edges of each cookie over the center so they overlap, with one end more pointed and the other a rounded bell shape. Tuck a cherry half into the rounded end to resemble a clapper. Bake in preheated oven for 10 to 12 minutes or until just lightly browned. Immediately transfer to wire racks to cool.

Tip *Make extra dough when making cookies. Roll out and cut, shape and slice, then wrap tightly in plastic wrap and freeze. Unwrap and pop frozen dough into the oven whenever you want warm cookies in a hurry.*

Chocolate Chunk Snowballs

Makes about 5 dozen
- Preheat oven to 350ºF (180ºC)
- Baking sheet, ungreased

2 cups	butter, softened	500 mL
1 cup	confectioner's (icing) sugar, sifted	250 mL
3½ cups	all-purpose flour	875 mL
½ cup	cornstarch	125 mL
6 oz	bittersweet chocolate, coarsely chopped	175 g
1 cup	coarsely chopped pecans, toasted	250 mL
	Confectioner's (icing) sugar, sifted	

1. In a large bowl, beat butter and sugar until smooth and creamy. Gradually stir in flour, then cornstarch, mixing until well blended. Fold in chocolate and pecans.
2. Shape dough into 1-inch (2.5 cm) balls. Place about 2 inches (5 cm) apart on baking sheet. Bake in preheated oven for 15 minutes or until lightly browned. Immediately transfer to wire racks to cool. When cool, dust lightly with confectioner's sugar.

Pfeffernüesse

Makes about 6 dozen

- Preheat oven to 350°F (180°C)
- Baking sheet, ungreased

4 cups	all-purpose flour	1 L
1 tsp	baking soda	5 mL
½ tsp	salt	2 mL
¼ tsp	freshly ground black pepper	1 mL
1 tbsp	ground cinnamon	15 mL
1 tsp	ground nutmeg	5 mL
1 tsp	ground cloves	5 mL
1 tsp	ground allspice	5 mL
1 tbsp	ground cardamom (optional)	15 mL
4 oz	candied orange peel, chopped	125 g
8 oz	citron (see tip, page 205), chopped	250 g
2 tbsp	butter, softened	25 mL
2½ cups	confectioner's (icing) sugar, sifted	625 mL
5	eggs, separated	5
1½ tsp	grated lemon zest	7 mL
	Confectioner's sugar for frosting (optional)	

GLAZE (OPTIONAL)

1 cup	confectioner's (icing) sugar	250 mL
¼ cup	water	50 mL

1. In a large bowl, mix together flour, baking soda, salt, pepper, cinnamon, nutmeg, cloves, allspice, cardamom (if using), orange peel and citron.

2. In another large bowl, beat butter and confectioner's sugar until smooth and creamy. Beat in egg yolks and lemon zest until well blended. Add flour mixture and mix well.

3. In a clean bowl, beat egg whites until peaks form. Fold into flour-butter mixture. Wrap dough tightly in plastic wrap and refrigerate for 2 hours, until firm.

4. Shape dough into 1-inch (2.5 cm) balls and place about 2 inches (5 cm) apart on baking sheet. Bake in preheated oven for 15 minutes or until lightly browned.

5. *If desired, prepare the glaze:* In a small bowl, beat confectioner's sugar with water until smooth and spreadable. Spread lightly over tops of cookies and return to hot oven for 2 minutes. Immediately transfer to wire racks to cool.

Tip *Eggs separate more easily when they are cold. However, egg whites will gain more volume if they are allowed to reach room temperature before being beaten.*

Rum-Glazed Christmas Fruitcake Cookies

Makes about 2 dozen

- Preheat oven to 400°F (200°C)
- 2-inch (5-cm) round cookie cutter, fluted if possible
- Baking sheet, lightly greased

⅔ cup	butter, softened, divided	150 mL
⅓ cup	packed brown sugar	75 mL
½ tsp	ground cinnamon	2 mL
¼ tsp	ground nutmeg	1 mL
½ tsp	ground ginger	2 mL
Pinch	salt	Pinch
1 cup + 2 tbsp	all-purpose flour, divided	275 mL
½ cup	moist dried figs, cut into ½-inch (1 cm) pieces	125 mL
½ cup	large dates, cut into ½-inch (1 cm) pieces	125 mL
½ cup	blanched almonds, toasted and chopped	125 mL
½ cup	coarsely chopped pecans	125 mL
2 tbsp	liquid honey	25 mL
1 tsp	rum	5 mL
1	egg, lightly beaten	1

RUM GLAZE

½ cup	confectioner's (icing) sugar, sifted	125 mL
2 tbsp	dark rum	25 mL

1. In a small bowl, beat 6 tbsp (90 mL) of the butter and brown sugar until smooth and creamy. Add cinnamon, nutmeg, ginger and salt and beat until well combined. Add ¾ cup (175 mL) of the flour and mix until a soft dough forms. Wrap tightly in plastic wrap and refrigerate for 15 to 30 minutes, until firm.

2. In a bowl, combine figs, dates, almonds and pecans.

3. In a clean bowl, beat the remaining butter, honey and rum until smooth and creamy. Gradually beat in egg until incorporated. Add the remaining flour and mix well. Add to fruit mixture, mixing until pieces are completely coated. Set aside.

4. On a lightly floured surface, roll dough out to ¼-inch (0.5 cm) thickness. Using a cookie cutter dipped in flour, cut out rounds and place 2 inches (5 cm) apart on prepared baking sheet. Drop a rounded tablespoonful (15 mL) of the fruit and nut mixture onto each cookie and, using your fingers, shape into mounds. Bake in preheated oven for 10 to 12 minutes, until cookies begin to brown on the top.

5. *Prepare the glaze:* In a bowl, beat confectioner's sugar and rum until smooth. Spread over hot cookies and immediately return to preheated oven to bake for 1 minute, until glaze bubbles. Let cool on baking sheet for 5 minutes, then transfer to wire racks to cool completely.

Tip *Just like Christmas fruitcake, these cookies will be better if they are allowed to mellow for 2 to 3 days after they are baked. Store in an airtight container for up to 2 weeks.*

• •

Springerle Cookies

Makes about 6 dozen
• Preheat oven to 300°F (150°C)
• Springerle rolling pin or molds
• Lightly floured baking sheet

4 cups	all-purpose flour	1 L
1 tsp	baking soda	5 mL
4	eggs	4
2 cups	granulated sugar	500 mL
2 tsp	anise extract	10 mL
2 tbsp	crushed anise seeds	25 mL

1. In a large bowl, mix together flour and baking soda.
2. In another large bowl, beat eggs and sugar until smooth and creamy. Stir in anise extract. Stir in flour, one-third at a time, mixing after each addition, until a stiff dough forms.
3. Divide dough into three portions. On a lightly floured surface, using a plain rolling pin, roll dough out to 1/2-inch (1 cm) thickness. Flour the springerle rolling pin, if using, and roll slowly, only once, over the dough, pressing down firmly to make clear designs. Your cookies will now be about 1/4 inch (0.5 cm) thick. Cut cookies apart on dividing lines. Lift each cookie carefully and transfer to lightly floured baking sheet. Repeat with the remaining dough. Cover with towels and let stand overnight. If using springerle molds, roll the dough a bit thinner with the plain rolling pin and press molds firmly into the dough. Then transfer to floured sheets.
4. Grease a clean baking sheet and sprinkle lightly with anise seeds. Brush excess flour from cookie bottoms and, using a finger dipped in water, moisten bottom of each cookie.

5. Place about 2 inches (5 cm) apart on prepared baking sheet. Bake in preheated oven for 15 minutes, until firm and dry but not browned. Immediately transfer to wire racks to cool. Let cookies mellow in an airtight container for at least 1 week.

• •

Peppermint Candy Canes

Makes about 4 dozen
• Preheat oven to 375°F (190°C)
• Baking sheet, ungreased

2 1/2 cups	all-purpose flour	625 mL
1 tsp	salt	5 mL
1/2 cup	shortening, softened	125 mL
1/2 cup	butter or margarine, softened	125 mL
1 cup	confectioner's (icing) sugar, sifted	250 mL
1	egg	1
1 tsp	vanilla	5 mL
1 tsp	peppermint extract	5 mL
1/2 tsp	red food coloring (or more, as desired)	2 mL

1. In a medium bowl, mix together flour and salt.
2. In a large bowl, beat shortening, butter or margarine and confectioner's sugar until smooth. Beat in egg until well incorporated. Stir in vanilla and peppermint extract and mix well. Gradually add flour mixture and mix until a dough forms.
3. On a lightly floured surface, divide dough into two portions. Knead red food coloring into one portion until well blended. Leave other portion as is.
4. Shape 1 tsp (5 mL) of dough from each half into a rope 4 inches (10 cm) long, rolling back and forth until smooth and even. Place plain rope and a red-colored one side by side. Twist together to make a candy cane. Repeat with the remaining dough.
5. Place canes on baking sheet and, using your hand, curve the top of each to form the handle of a cane. Bake in preheated oven for 8 to 10 minutes or until firm and lightly browned. Immediately transfer to wire racks to cool.

Tip *An egg left at room temperature for 1 hour deteriorates as much as it would if stored for a week in the refrigerator. Eggs should be stored in their carton in the refrigerator, not on the refrigerator door.*

Christmas Fruit Cookies

Makes about 10 dozen
- Preheat oven to 375°F (190°C)
- Baking sheet, ungreased

4 cups	all-purpose flour	1 L
2 tsp	baking powder	10 mL
1/2 tsp	salt	2 mL
3/4 cup	butter or margarine, softened	175 mL
3/4 cup	shortening, softened	175 mL
1 1/4 cups	packed brown sugar	300 mL
2	eggs	2
1 tsp	vanilla	5 mL
1	can (8 oz/227 mL) crushed pineapple, drained	1
1/2 cup	chopped red maraschino cherries	125 mL
1/2 cup	chopped green maraschino cherries	125 mL
1/2 cup	chopped pitted dates	125 mL
1/2 cup	chopped pecans or walnuts	125 mL
1/2 cup	shredded coconut (optional)	125 mL

1. In a large bowl, mix together flour, baking powder and salt.

2. In another large bowl, beat butter or margarine, shortening and brown sugar until smooth and creamy. Beat in eggs, one at a time, until incorporated. Stir in vanilla. Gradually add flour mixture, mixing until well combined. Stir in pineapple, red and green cherries, dates, nuts and coconut (if using). Mix well until thoroughly combined.

3. On a lightly floured surface, divide dough into three portions. Shape each portion into a roll 10 inches (25 cm) long. Wrap each roll tightly in plastic wrap and refrigerate for 2 hours, until firm.

4. On a cutting board, cut dough into slices 1/4 inch (0.5 cm) thick. Place about 2 inches (5 cm) apart on baking sheets. Bake in preheated oven for 8 to 10 minutes or until golden brown. Immediately transfer to wire racks to cool.

Chocolate Thumbprint Cookies

Makes about 3 dozen
- Preheat oven to 325°F (160°C)
- Baking sheet, greased

2 cups	all-purpose flour	500 mL
1/4 cup	unsweetened cocoa powder	50 mL
1 cup	butter, softened	250 mL
1/2 cup	granulated sugar	125 mL
2	eggs	2
1 tsp	vanilla	5 mL
1 cup	finely chopped pecans	250 mL
18	glacé cherries, halved	18
	Semisweet or bittersweet chocolate, melted (optional)	

1. In a medium bowl, mix together flour and cocoa.

2. In a large bowl, beat butter and sugar until smooth and creamy. Beat in eggs, one at a time, until incorporated. Stir in vanilla. Gradually add flour mixture, mixing until well incorporated. Fold in pecans.

3. Shape dough into 1-inch (2.5 cm) balls and press a cherry half into the center. Place about 2 inches (5 cm) apart on prepared baking sheet. Bake in preheated oven for 15 minutes or until golden brown. Immediately transfer to wire racks to cool. When cool, drizzle melted chocolate over tops in a zigzag pattern, if desired.

Mincemeat Drop Cookies

Makes about 4 dozen
- Preheat oven to 350°F (180°C)
- Baking sheet, greased

1 1/2 cups	all-purpose flour	375 mL
1 1/2 tsp	baking soda	7 mL
1/2 tsp	ground cinnamon	2 mL
1/4 tsp	ground nutmeg	1 mL
1/4 tsp	salt	1 mL
1/4 cup	butter or margarine, softened	50 mL
3/4 cup	packed brown sugar	175 mL
2	eggs	2
3/4 cup	mincemeat	175 mL
1 1/2 cups	semisweet chocolate chips	375 mL
1/2 cup	chopped walnuts	125 mL

1. In a small bowl, mix together flour, baking soda, cinnamon, nutmeg and salt.

2. In a large bowl, beat butter or margarine and brown sugar until smooth and creamy. Add eggs, one at a time, beating until well incorporated. Stir in mincemeat. Add flour mixture and mix until thoroughly combined. Fold in chocolate chips and nuts.

3. Drop by tablespoonfuls (15 mL), about 2 inches (5 cm) apart, onto prepared baking sheet. Bake in preheated oven for 10 to 12 minutes or until golden brown. Immediately transfer to wire racks to cool.

Checkerboard Squares

Makes about 6 dozen
- Preheat oven to 375°F (190°C)
- Baking sheet, ungreased

1 cup	butter or margarine, softened	250 mL
½ cup	granulated sugar	125 mL
6 tbsp	packed brown sugar	90 mL
1	egg	1
2 tsp	vanilla	10 mL
1½ tsp	baking powder	7 mL
1⅔ cups	all-purpose flour	400 mL
2 oz	unsweetened chocolate, melted	60 g

1. In a large bowl, beat butter or margarine and sugars until smooth and creamy. Beat in egg until incorporated. Stir in vanilla and baking powder. Gradually add flour, mixing in as much as possible, then stirring in remainder with a wooden spoon.
2. Divide dough in half. Knead melted chocolate into one portion of dough until combined. Divide plain and chocolate doughs in half. Shape each portion into 8-inch (20 cm) logs. (You will have two plain logs and two chocolate logs.) Wrap each tightly in plastic wrap and refrigerate for 2 hours, until firm.
3. On a floured surface, place one plain roll and one chocolate roll side by side. Top the plain roll with another chocolate roll and the chocolate roll with a plain roll. Press logs together firmly so they adhere and, using your hands, square the sides to make a square-shaped log. Wrap tightly in plastic wrap and refrigerate 6 hours, until firm.
4. Using a knife, cut log into slices ¼ inch (0.5 cm) thick. Place about 2 inches (5 cm) apart on baking sheet. Bake in preheated oven for 8 to 10 minutes or until bottoms are lightly browned. Immediately transfer to wire racks to cool.

Double Chocolate Swirl Cookies

Makes 2½ dozen
- Preheat oven to 375°F (190°C)
- Pastry bag with star tip
- Baking sheet, lightly greased
- Large platter or baking sheet, lined with waxed paper

1 tbsp	hot water (not boiling)	15 mL
1½ tsp	instant espresso or coffee powder or granules	7 mL
2¼ cups	all-purpose flour	550 mL
¼ cup	unsweetened cocoa powder	50 mL
1 cup	butter or margarine, softened	250 mL
⅓ cup	firmly packed brown sugar	75 mL
⅓ cup	granulated sugar	75 mL
1	egg	1
1 tsp	vanilla	5 mL
2 oz	semisweet chocolate, melted and cooled	60 g

CHOCOLATE DIP

3 oz	white chocolate, melted	90 g
3 oz	semisweet chocolate, melted	90 g

1. In a cup, mix hot water and coffee powder until coffee dissolves. Set aside to cool.
2. In a medium bowl, mix together flour and cocoa.
3. In a large bowl, beat butter or margarine and sugars until smooth and creamy. Beat in egg until incorporated. Stir in vanilla and melted chocolate until blended. Add coffee and mix well. Gradually add flour mixture, beating until just blended.
4. Using a pastry bag with a star tip, pipe dough onto prepared baking sheet, making a 2-inch (5 cm) circle with a swirled design. Bake in preheated oven for 8 to 10 minutes or until lightly browned. Immediately transfer to wire racks to cool.
5. *Prepare the dip:* Holding a cookie with your fingers, dip top half in white chocolate. Place on a platter or baking sheet lined with waxed paper. Repeat with 13 additional cookies. Drizzle top of the dipped half with semisweet chocolate. Repeat procedure for the remaining cookies, but dip in semisweet chocolate and drizzle with white chocolate.

Hickory Nut Macaroons

Makes about 1½ dozen
- Preheat oven to 325°F (160°C)
- Baking sheet, greased

2	egg whites	2
2 cups	confectioner's (icing) sugar, sifted	500 mL
1 cup	chopped hickory nuts or toasted pecans	250 mL

1. In a clean bowl, beat egg whites until soft peaks form. Add confectioner's sugar, ¼ cup (50 mL) at a time, beating until stiff peaks form. Fold in nuts.
2. Drop by rounded teaspoonfuls (5 mL), about 2 inches (5 cm) apart, onto prepared baking sheet. Bake in preheated oven for 15 minutes or until edges are lightly browned. (Cookies may split around the edges as they bake, which is acceptable.) Immediately transfer to wire racks to cool. Recipe can be doubled.

Chocolate Chip Holiday Stars

Makes about 3 dozen

- Preheat oven to 350°F (180°C)
- Star-shaped cookie cutter
- Baking sheet, ungreased
- Cake decorating tube with a fine tip

2½ cups	all-purpose flour	625 mL
½ tsp	salt	2 mL
1 cup	butter or margarine, softened	250 mL
⅓ cup	granulated sugar	75 mL
½ cup	packed brown sugar	125 mL
1	egg yolk	1
2 tsp	vanilla	10 mL
2 cups	mini semisweet chocolate chips, divided	500 mL
	Vanilla Icing (see recipe, page 548)	

1. In a medium bowl, mix together flour and salt.
2. In a large bowl, beat butter or margarine and sugars until smooth and creamy. Add egg yolk and beat until incorporated. Stir in vanilla. Gradually add flour mixture, mixing until a soft dough forms. Stir in 1½ cups (375 mL) chocolate chips.
3. Divide dough in half. Flatten each half into a disk and wrap tightly in plastic wrap. Cover and refrigerate for 1 to 2 hours, until firm.
4. Place one portion of dough between two sheets of waxed paper and roll out to ¼-inch (0.5 cm) thickness. Using a star cookie cutter, cut into star shapes and place about 2 inches (5 cm) apart on baking sheet. Cover with a clean towel and refrigerate for 10 minutes.
5. Bake in preheated oven for 10 to 12 minutes or until golden brown. Let cool for 5 minutes on sheet, then transfer to wire racks to cool completely.
6. Melt the remaining chocolate chips. Using a cake decorator tube with a fine, straight-line tip, pipe a thin line of chocolate close to outer edge of cookie, following the shape of the star. Repeat with vanilla icing, drawing a second line inside the chocolate outline.

Tip *To decorate cookies with frosting when you don't have a decorator, cut an envelope from one of the top corners to the middle of the bottom of the envelope. Cut a little piece off the corner. Fill with some frosting and squeeze out as you would with a decorator.*

Raspberry Bows

Makes 2 dozen

- Preheat oven to 375°F (190°C)
- Baking sheet, lined with parchment or waxed paper

2¼ cups	all-purpose flour, divided	550 mL
1	package (¼ oz/7 g) quick-rising active dry yeast	1
½ cup	sour cream	125 mL
1 tbsp	water	15 mL
½ cup	butter, softened	125 mL
1	egg	1
	Granulated sugar	
RASPBERRY FILLING		
2 tbsp	butter, softened	25 mL
⅓ cup	raspberry jam	75 mL
¼ cup	plain dry bread crumbs	50 mL
¼ cup	granulated sugar	50 mL
	Confectioner's (icing) sugar, sifted	

1. In a large bowl, combine ½ cup (125 mL) flour with the yeast.
2. In a small saucepan, heat sour cream with water until warm (not hot). Stir into flour mixture. Add butter, egg and as much of the remaining flour as necessary to make a soft dough.
3. Knead dough into a ball. Divide in half and wrap each half tightly in plastic wrap. Refrigerate for 2 to 3 hours.
4. *Prepare the filling:* In a small bowl, mix together butter, jam, bread crumbs and sugar. Set aside.
5. On a work surface sprinkled with granulated sugar, roll one portion of dough into an 18- by 8-inch (45 by 20 cm) rectangle. Spread half of the filling, lengthwise, over half of the dough. Fold dough in half, lengthwise, and trim the edges. Cut crosswise into 12 strips and twist each in the center to form a bow. Repeat with the remaining dough.
6. Place bows about 2 inches (5 cm) apart on prepared baking sheet. Bake in preheated oven for 15 to 20 minutes or until golden brown. Immediately transfer to wire racks. When cool, dust with sifted confectioner's sugar.

Hanukkah Sugar Cookies

Makes about 3 dozen

- Preheat oven to 375°F (190°C)
- Cookie cutters in Hanukkah shapes, such as a dreidel, menorah or Star of David
- Baking sheet, ungreased

2 cups	all-purpose flour	500 mL
1½ tsp	baking powder	7 mL
½ tsp	salt	2 mL
¼ tsp	ground nutmeg	1 mL
¾ cup	butter or margarine, softened	175 mL
1 cup	granulated sugar	250 mL
2	eggs	2
1 tsp	vanilla	5 mL
	Vanilla Icing (optional, see recipe, page 548)	

1. In a medium bowl, mix together flour, baking powder, salt and nutmeg.
2. In a large bowl, beat butter or margarine and sugar until smooth and creamy. Beat in eggs, one at a time, until incorporated. Stir in vanilla. Gradually add flour mixture, mixing until a soft dough forms. Cover tightly and refrigerate for 2 to 3 hours, until firm.
3. On a lightly floured surface, roll dough out to ⅛-inch (0.25 cm) thickness. Using cookie cutters, cut into a variety of Hanukkah shapes.
4. Place 2 inches (5 cm) apart on baking sheet. Bake in preheated oven for 8 to 10 minutes or until lightly browned. Immediately transfer to wire racks to cool. Decorate cookies with icing, if desired.

Tip *Dip cookie cutters in salad oil before cutting out cookies. It will make a cleaner cut and be less sticky.*

Cinnamon-Nut Rugelach

Makes about 4 dozen

- Preheat oven to 375°F (190°C)
- Baking sheet, lined with parchment or waxed paper

1 cup	butter, softened	250 mL
1	package (8 oz/250 g) cream cheese, softened	1
2	eggs	2
1 tsp	salt	5 mL
2½ cups	all-purpose flour	625 mL
CINNAMON-NUT FILLING		
¾ cup	finely chopped raisins	175 mL
⅔ cup	finely chopped walnuts	150 mL
1 cup	granulated sugar	250 mL
½ tsp	ground cinnamon	2 mL
½ cup	melted butter	125 mL

1. In a large bowl, beat butter and cream cheese until smooth. Add eggs, one at a time, beating until incorporated. Mix in salt, then gradually beat in flour until a sticky dough forms. Transfer dough to a lightly floured surface and knead, adding up to ½ cup (125 mL) flour until dough is not sticky.
2. Divide dough into four portions. Wrap each in plastic wrap and refrigerate for 3 to 4 hours, until firm.
3. *Prepare the filling:* In a small bowl, combine raisins and walnuts. Add sugar and cinnamon and mix well. Set aside.
4. On floured surface, roll one portion of dough into a 10-inch (25 cm) circle. Brush with melted butter and sprinkle about ⅓ cup (75 mL) nut mixture over the circle.
5. Using a knife or pastry cutter, cut circle into 12 pie-shaped wedges. Roll up tightly, beginning from the wide edge and finishing with the point in the middle. Bend the rolls slightly inward to form crescents and place, point-side down, about 2 inches (5 cm) apart, on prepared baking sheet. Brush with melted butter. Repeat with the remaining dough.
6. Bake in preheated oven for 20 to 25 minutes or until golden brown. Immediately transfer to wire racks to cool.

Variation *Chocolate-Coconut Filling: In a small bowl, mix together ½ cup (125 mL) finely chopped slivered toasted almonds, ¾ cup (175 mL) sweetened shredded coconut, ½ cup (125 mL) mini semisweet chocolate chips and ¼ cup (50 mL) granulated sugar. Using a spatula, thinly coat a large circle of dough with 2 tbsp (25 mL) apricot preserves. Sprinkle with a quarter of the almond mixture. Proceed with Step 5, above.*

Brownies and Chocolate Bars and Squares

Brownies

Chocolate Bars and Squares

Brownies

The Basic Brownie

Makes 16 brownies
- Preheat oven to 350°F (180°C)
- 8-inch (2 L) square baking pan, greased

¾ cup	all-purpose flour	175 mL
½ tsp	salt	2 mL
½ tsp	baking powder	2 mL
2 oz	unsweetened chocolate	60 g
⅓ cup	shortening or butter, softened	75 mL
1 cup	granulated sugar	250 mL
2	eggs	2
½ cup	chopped walnuts or pecans	125 mL
	Cocoa Frosting (optional, see recipe, page 546)	
	Confectioner's (icing) sugar, for dusting (optional)	

1. In a small bowl, mix together flour, salt and baking powder.

2. In a large saucepan, over low heat, melt chocolate with shortening, stirring until smooth. Remove from heat and set aside to cool slightly.

3. When chocolate mixture has cooled, stir in sugar. Add eggs and beat just until blended. Blend in flour mixture. Stir in nuts.

4. Spread batter evenly in prepared pan. Bake in preheated oven for 30 to 35 minutes or until a tester inserted in the center comes out clean. Place pan on a wire rack to cool completely, then cut into squares. If desired, frost with Cocoa Frosting or your favorite chocolate frosting. Or sift confectioner's sugar over top.

Tip *For a light-textured brownie, beat eggs more thoroughly. For a firmer brownie, beat eggs less.*

Old-Time Brownies

Makes 36 brownies
- Preheat oven to 400°F (200°C)
- Three 12-cup muffin tins, greased or paper-lined

1¾ cups	cake and pastry flour, sifted	425 mL
¾ tsp	baking soda	4 mL
1 tsp	salt	5 mL
1⅓ cups	granulated sugar	325 mL
5	egg yolks	5
2½ oz	unsweetened chocolate, melted	75 g
1 tsp	vanilla	5 mL
1 cup	sour cream	250 mL
1 cup	chopped walnuts	250 mL

1. In a small bowl, mix together flour, baking soda and salt.

2. In a large bowl, beat sugar and egg yolks until thickened. Blend in melted chocolate. Stir in vanilla. Gradually add flour mixture, alternately with sour cream, stirring until just combined. Stir in nuts.

3. Spoon into prepared tins, filling cups about three-quarters full. Bake in preheated oven for about 15 minutes or until a tester inserted in center of a brownie comes out clean. Place pans on a wire rack to cool slightly, then remove from cups and let cool completely on rack.

Tip *To melt chocolate in a microwave, use chocolate chips, chocolate squares (each 1 oz/28 g) or small chunks of chocolate. Place in a microwave-safe bowl, cover tightly with plastic wrap and microwave on High approximately 1 minute per ounce (28 g). (Times will vary depending upon the power of your microwave and the quantity of chocolate used.) Remove from microwave and stir until melted and smooth.*

Low-Fat Brownies

Makes 16 brownies
- Preheat oven to 350°F (180°C)
- 8-inch (2 L) square baking pan, greased

½ cup	cake and pastry flour	125 mL
½ cup	unsweetened cocoa powder	125 mL
¼ tsp	salt	1 mL
¾ cup	granulated sugar	175 mL
6 tbsp	unsweetened applesauce	90 mL
1	egg	1
2	egg whites	2
2 tbsp	vegetable oil	25 mL
1½ tsp	vanilla	7 mL
1 tbsp	chopped walnuts or pecans	15 mL

1. In a small bowl, sift together flour, cocoa and salt.

2. In a large bowl, beat sugar, applesauce, egg, egg whites, oil and vanilla until blended. Blend in flour mixture. Spread batter evenly in prepared pan. Sprinkle walnuts over top. Bake in preheated oven for 25 minutes or until a tester inserted in the center comes out clean. Place pan on a wire rack to cool completely, then cut into squares.

Frypan Brownies

Makes 36 brownies

- Preheat a medium electric skillet to 300°F (150°C), with vent closed

1½ cups	all-purpose flour	375 mL
½ tsp	baking soda	2 mL
Pinch	salt	Pinch
½ cup	butter, margarine or shortening, softened	125 mL
1 cup	packed brown sugar	250 mL
1	egg	1
1½ tsp	vanilla	7 mL
2 oz	unsweetened chocolate, melted and cooled	60 g
½ cup	milk	125 mL
1 tsp	shortening	5 mL
	Chocolate Butter Frosting (optional, see variation, page 544), shredded or flaked coconut or confectioner's (icing) sugar (optional)	

1. In a small bowl, mix together flour, baking soda and salt.

2. In a large bowl, beat butter and brown sugar until smooth and creamy. Beat in egg until incorporated. Stir in vanilla and melted chocolate. Gradually blend in flour mixture alternately with milk, until just incorporated.

3. Brush skillet with shortening. Spread batter evenly over pan. Cover and cook in preheated pan for 25 minutes or until top is no longer sticky. Open vent for the last 5 minutes.

4. Using a spatula, loosen cake around the edges, then invert onto a wire rack. Let cool completely, then cut into squares. If desired, frost with Chocolate Butter Frosting, sprinkle with coconut or dust with confectioner's sugar.

Tip *If you run out of unsweetened chocolate, substitute 3 level tbsp (45 mL) unsweetened cocoa powder and 1 tbsp (15 mL) butter for every 1 oz (28 g) unsweetened chocolate.*

Cake Brownie Mix

Makes 4½ packed cups (1.125 L)

2 cups	granulated sugar	500 mL
1 cup	all-purpose flour	250 mL
¾ cup	unsweetened cocoa powder, sifted	175 mL
1 tsp	baking powder	5 mL
¾ tsp	salt	4 mL
1 cup	shortening, softened	250 mL

1. In a large bowl, mix together sugar, flour, cocoa, baking powder and salt. Using two knives, a pastry blender or your fingers, cut in shortening until mixture resembles coarse crumbs. Store in an airtight container in a cool, dry place.

Brownies from a Mix

Makes 16 brownies

- Preheat oven to 350°F (180°C)
- 8-inch (2 L) square baking pan, greased

2¼ cups	packed Cake Brownie Mix (see recipe, at left)	550 mL
2	eggs, beaten	2
1 tsp	vanilla	5 mL
½ cup	chopped walnuts	125 mL

1. In a large bowl, mix together Cake Brownie Mix, eggs and vanilla until blended. Stir in walnuts.

2. Spread batter evenly in prepared pan. Bake in preheated oven for 30 to 35 minutes or until a tester inserted in the center comes out clean. Place pan on a wire rack to cool completely, then cut into squares.

Tip *If you accidentally break an egg on the floor, sprinkle heavily with salt and leave for 5 to 10 minutes. The dried egg will sweep easily into your dustpan.*

1-2-3 Brownies

Makes 16 brownies

- Preheat oven to 350°F (180°C)
- 8-inch (2 L) square baking pan, greased

1	package (14 oz/425 g) fudge brownie mix	1
⅓ cup	water	75 mL
¼ cup	plain yogurt	50 mL

1. In a large bowl, mix together brownie mix, water and yogurt until well combined. Spread batter evenly in prepared pan. Bake in preheated oven for 25 minutes or until a tester inserted in the center comes out clean. Place pan on a wire rack to cool completely, then cut into squares.

Tip *For a quick and easy chocolate frosting, melt a large bittersweet or milk chocolate bar and spread over cake.*

Original Fudge Brownies

Makes 16 brownies
- Preheat oven to 350°F (180°C)
- 8-inch (2 L) square baking pan, greased

½ cup	butter or margarine	125 mL
2 oz	unsweetened chocolate	60 g
1 cup	granulated sugar	250 mL
2	eggs	2
½ tsp	vanilla	2 mL
½ cup	all-purpose flour	125 mL
Pinch	salt	Pinch
1 cup	chopped walnuts	250 mL

1. In a saucepan, over low heat, melt butter and chocolate, stirring until smooth. Set aside to cool slightly.
2. When chocolate mixture has cooled, stir in sugar. Add eggs and vanilla and mix just until blended. Blend in flour and salt. Stir in nuts.
3. Spread batter evenly in prepared pan. Bake in preheated oven for 30 minutes or until a tester inserted in the center comes out clean. Place pan on a wire rack to cool completely, then cut into squares.

Tip *To line a pan with foil, turn the pan upside down, then smooth the foil around the pan to shape it. Turn the pan over and grease the bottom and sides before placing foil inside the pan. This prevents the foil from shifting.*

Chocolate Fudge Cake Brownies

Makes 16 brownies
- Preheat oven to 325°F (160°C)
- 8-inch (2 L) square baking pan, greased

2 cups	cake and pastry flour, sifted	500 mL
2 tsp	baking powder	10 mL
½ tsp	salt	2 mL
½ cup	butter, margarine or shortening, softened	125 mL
1 cup	granulated sugar	250 mL
1	egg	1
2 oz	unsweetened chocolate, melted	60 g
1 tsp	vanilla	5 mL
¾ cup	milk	175 mL
	No-Cook Fudge Frosting (optional, see recipe, page 546)	

1. In a medium bowl, mix together flour, baking powder and salt.
2. In a large bowl, beat butter and sugar until smooth and creamy. Beat in egg until incorporated. Stir in melted chocolate and vanilla. Gradually blend in flour mixture alternately with milk until just incorporated.
3. Spread batter evenly in prepared pan. Bake in preheated oven for 55 to 60 minutes or until tester inserted in the center comes out clean. Place pan on a wire rack to cool completely. If desired, frost, then cut into squares.

Peanut Butter Brownies

Makes 24 brownies
- Preheat oven to 350°F (180°C)
- 9-inch (2.5 L) square baking pan, greased

¾ cup	smooth peanut butter	175 mL
¼ cup	milk	50 mL
2 cups	packed brown sugar	500 mL
2	eggs	2
1 cup	all-purpose flour	250 mL
FROSTING AND GLAZE		
¾ cup	smooth peanut butter, divided	175 mL
4 oz	semisweet chocolate	125 g

1. In a saucepan, over low heat, melt peanut butter in milk, stirring constantly. Remove from heat and set aside to cool slightly.
2. When mixture has cooled, stir in sugar. Add eggs and beat until just combined. Blend in flour.
3. Spread evenly in prepared pan. Bake in preheated oven for 35 to 40 minutes or until a tester inserted in the center comes out clean. Place pan on a wire rack to cool completely.
4. *Prepare the frosting:* In a saucepan, over low heat, melt ½ cup (125 mL) of the peanut butter with chocolate, stirring constantly, until smooth. Spread evenly over cooled brownies.
5. *Prepare the glaze:* In another saucepan, over low heat, melt the remaining peanut butter, stirring, until smooth. (Alternatively, in a microwaveable bowl, heat peanut butter on High for about 1 minute, until melted.) Spoon over frosting, then swirl with a knife to create a marble effect. Chill until firm, then cut into squares.

Classic Chocolate Nut Brownies

Makes 36 brownies
- Preheat oven to 350°F (180°C)
- 13- by 9-inch (3 L) baking pan, greased

4 oz	unsweetened chocolate	125 g
¾ cup	butter or margarine	175 mL
2 cups	granulated sugar	500 mL
3	eggs	3
1 tsp	vanilla	5 mL
1 cup	all-purpose flour	250 mL
1¼ cups	chopped nuts	300 mL
	Frosting (optional)	

1. In a large saucepan, over low heat, melt chocolate and butter, stirring until smooth. Set aside to cool slightly.
2. When chocolate mixture has cooled, stir in sugar. Add eggs and vanilla and beat until just combined. Blend in flour. Stir in nuts.
3. Spread batter evenly in prepared pan. Bake in preheated oven for 30 to 35 minutes or until a tester inserted in the center comes out clean. Place pan on a wire rack to cool completely. If desired, frost, then cut into squares.

Tip *Plain brownies freeze well wrapped tightly in a double layer of plastic wrap or foil. To avoid condensation, thaw completely before unwrapping.*

Chocolate Pecan Brownies

Makes 24 brownies
- Preheat oven to 350°F (180°C)
- 9-inch (2.5 L) square baking pan, greased

1 cup	all-purpose flour	250 mL
Pinch	salt	Pinch
⅔ cup	chopped pecans	150 mL
½ cup	butter or margarine, softened	125 mL
1 cup	granulated sugar	250 mL
3	eggs	3
2 tsp	vanilla	10 mL
¾ cup	chocolate-flavored syrup	175 mL
	Whole pecans for garnish (optional)	
	Confectioner's (icing) sugar (optional)	

1. In a small bowl, mix together flour, salt and pecans.
2. In a large bowl, beat butter and sugar until smooth and creamy. Add eggs, one at a time, beating until incorporated. Stir in vanilla and chocolate syrup. Blend in flour mixture.

3. Spread batter evenly in prepared pan. Bake in preheated oven for 35 to 40 minutes or until a tester inserted in the center comes out clean. Place pan on a wire rack to cool completely, then cut into squares. Garnish each brownie with a pecan or dust with confectioner's sugar, if desired.

Variation *Chocolate Walnut Brownies: Substitute walnuts for the pecans.*

Chocolate Butter Pecan Brownies

Makes 36 brownies
- Preheat oven to 350°F (180°C)
- 13- by 9-inch (3 L) baking pan, greased

1½ cups	all-purpose flour	375 mL
1 tsp	baking powder	5 mL
1 tsp	salt	5 mL
1 cup	chopped pecans	250 mL
⅔ cup	butter	150 mL
4 oz	unsweetened chocolate	125 g
2 cups	granulated sugar	500 mL
4	eggs	4
FROSTING		
¼ cup	butter	50 mL
2 cups	confectioner's (icing) sugar, sifted	500 mL
3 tbsp	whipping (35%) cream	45 mL
2 tsp	vanilla	10 mL
GLAZE		
1 tbsp	butter	15 mL
1 oz	unsweetened chocolate	30 g

1. In a medium bowl, mix together flour, baking powder, salt and pecans.
2. In a saucepan, over low heat, melt butter and chocolate, stirring until smooth. Remove from heat and set aside to cool slightly.
3. Stir in sugar. Add eggs and beat just until blended. Blend in flour mixture.
4. Spread batter evenly in prepared pan. Bake in preheated oven for 30 to 35 minutes or until a tester inserted in the center comes out clean. Place pan on a wire rack to cool completely.
5. *Prepare the frosting:* In a saucepan, over low heat, melt butter. Remove from heat. Gradually add confectioner's sugar, alternately with cream, beating until smooth. Stir in vanilla. Spread evenly over brownies.
6. *Prepare the glaze:* In another saucepan, or in a microwave, melt butter and chocolate until smooth. Let cool slightly, then drizzle over top of frosting. When cooled, cut into squares.

Rocky Road Brownies

Makes 36 brownies
- Preheat oven to 400ºF (200ºC)
- 13- by 9-inch (3 L) baking pan, greased

BASE

2 cups	all-purpose flour	500 mL
1 tsp	baking soda	5 mL
½ cup	shortening	125 mL
½ cup	butter or margarine	125 mL
1 cup	strong brewed coffee	250 mL
¼ cup	unsweetened cocoa powder, sifted	50 mL
2 cups	granulated sugar	500 mL
2	eggs	2
1 tsp	vanilla	5 mL
½ cup	buttermilk	125 mL

FROSTING

¼ cup	milk	50 mL
½ cup	butter or margarine	125 mL
2 tbsp	unsweetened cocoa powder, sifted	25 mL
1 tsp	vanilla	5 mL
3½ cups	confectioner's (icing) sugar, sifted	875 mL

TOPPING

1 cup	white mini marshmallows	250 mL
½ cup	unsalted peanuts	125 mL
3 oz	semisweet chocolate, melted	90 g

1. *Prepare the base:* In a medium bowl, mix together flour and baking soda.

2. In a large saucepan, over medium heat, bring shortening, butter, coffee and cocoa to a boil, stirring constantly. Remove from heat and set aside to cool slightly.

3. When mixture has cooled, stir in sugar. Beat in eggs and vanilla. Gradually blend in flour mixture, alternately with buttermilk, until just incorporated. Spread evenly in prepared pan. Bake in preheated oven for 35 minutes or until a tester inserted in the center comes out clean.

4. *Prepare the frosting:* In a saucepan, over low heat, heat milk, butter and cocoa, stirring constantly, until steaming (not boiling). Remove from heat. Gradually add confectioner's sugar, beating until mixture is smooth and spreadable. Beat in vanilla. Spread frosting over warm cake.

5. *Prepare the topping:* Sprinkle marshmallows and peanuts evenly over cake. Bake for 2 to 3 minutes, until marshmallows are slightly melted. Drizzle melted chocolate over top. Place pan on a wire rack to cool completely, then cut into squares.

Sour Cream Coffee Brownies

Makes 36 brownies
- Preheat oven to 350ºF (180ºC)
- 13- by 9-inch (3 L) baking pan, greased

BASE

¾ cup	all-purpose flour	175 mL
½ tsp	baking powder	2 mL
¼ tsp	salt	1 mL
¾ cup	butter or margarine, softened	175 mL
6 oz	semisweet chocolate	175 g
1 tbsp	instant coffee powder or granules	15 mL
¾ cup	packed brown sugar	175 mL
2	eggs	2
1 tsp	vanilla	5 mL

CHEESECAKE TOPPING

1	package (8 oz/250 g) cream cheese, softened	1
½ cup	granulated sugar	125 mL
2	eggs	2
1 tsp	vanilla	5 mL
3 tbsp	coffee-flavored liqueur or strong brewed coffee	45 mL
½ tsp	ground cinnamon	2 mL
2 tbsp	all-purpose flour	25 mL

SOUR CREAM TOPPING

1½ cups	sour cream	375 mL
⅓ cup	granulated sugar	75 mL

1. *Prepare the base:* In a small bowl, mix together flour, baking powder and salt.

2. In a large saucepan, over low heat, heat butter, chocolate and coffee powder, stirring until mixture is smooth and melted and coffee has dissolved. Set aside to cool slightly.

3. When mixture has cooled, stir in brown sugar. Add eggs and vanilla and beat until combined. Blend in flour mixture. Spread batter evenly in prepared pan.

4. *Prepare the cheesecake topping:* In a medium bowl, beat cream cheese and sugar until smooth. Beat in eggs, one at a time, until incorporated. Stir in vanilla, liqueur and cinnamon until blended. Blend in flour. Spread evenly over base. Bake for 20 minutes or until top is almost set.

5. *Prepare the sour cream topping:* In a small bowl, mix together sour cream and sugar. Spread carefully over top of brownies. Bake for 10 minutes. Place pan on a wire rack to cool completely, then cut into squares.

Caramel Candy Brownies

Makes 24 brownies
- Preheat oven to 350°F (180°C)
- 9-inch (2.5 L) square baking pan, greased

FILLING

1	bag (14 oz/397 g) soft caramels (about 45)	1
2 tbsp	milk	25 mL

BASE AND TOPPING

4 oz	unsweetened chocolate	125 g
3/4 cup	butter or margarine	175 mL
2 cups	granulated sugar	500 mL
3	eggs	3
1 tbsp	milk	15 mL
1 cup	all-purpose flour	250 mL
1 cup	chopped pecans, divided	250 mL

1. *Prepare the filling:* In a microwave-safe bowl, on Medium power, heat caramels and milk for 3 minutes. Remove from oven and stir until melted and smooth. (Alternatively, heat caramels and milk in a saucepan over low heat, stirring until smooth and melted.) Keep warm while preparing brownie batter.
2. *Prepare the base and topping:* In a large saucepan, over low heat, melt chocolate and butter, stirring constantly, until smooth. Remove from heat and set aside to cool slightly. When mixture has cooled, stir in sugar. Add eggs and beat until just blended. Stir in milk. Blend in flour.
3. Spread half the batter evenly in prepared pan. Spoon filling over batter. Sprinkle 3/4 cup (175 mL) of the nuts over top. Drop the remaining batter by spoonfuls over nuts, then sprinkle with the remaining nuts. Bake in preheated oven for 30 to 35 minutes or until a tester inserted in the centre comes out clean. Place pan on a wire rack to cool completely, then cut into squares.

Coffee Mocha Brownies

Makes 24 brownies
- Preheat oven to 350°F (180°C)
- 9-inch (2.5 L) square baking pan, lightly greased

3 oz	unsweetened chocolate	90 g
1/2 cup	butter	125 mL
2 tsp	instant espresso or coffee powder or granules	10 mL
1 1/4 cups	granulated sugar	300 mL
2	eggs	2
1 tsp	vanilla	5 mL
2/3 cup	all-purpose flour	150 mL
1/2 tsp	salt	2 mL
1/2 cup	coarsely chopped bittersweet chocolate	125 mL
1/2 cup	chopped pecans, toasted	125 mL

1. In a large saucepan, over low heat, melt chocolate, butter and coffee powder, stirring constantly, until mixture is smooth and coffee is dissolved. Set aside to cool slightly.
2. When chocolate has cooled, stir in sugar. Add eggs and vanilla and mix until blended. Blend in flour and salt. Stir in bittersweet chocolate and pecans.
3. Spread evenly in prepared pan. Bake in preheated oven for 25 to 30 minutes or until a tester inserted in the center comes out almost clean but with some moist crumbs. Place pan on a wire rack to cool completely, then cut into squares.

Chocolate Mint Dream Brownies

Makes 36 brownies
- Preheat oven to 350°F (180°C)
- 13- by 9-inch (3 L) baking pan, greased

3/4 cup	butter or margarine	175 mL
1 2/3 cups	semisweet chocolate chips	400 mL
1 1/2 cups	all-purpose flour	375 mL
1/4 tsp	salt	1 mL
1 3/4 cups	granulated sugar	425 mL
6	eggs	6
2 tsp	vanilla	10 mL
12	small chocolate-covered mints	12
1/2 cup	white chocolate chips	125 mL
2 tbsp	whipping (35%) cream	25 mL

1. In a saucepan, over low heat, melt butter and chocolate chips, stirring until smooth. Set aside to cool slightly.
2. In a small bowl, mix together flour and salt.
3. When chocolate mixture has cooled, stir in sugar. Add eggs and vanilla and beat until just blended. Blend in flour mixture.
4. Spread half the batter evenly in prepared pan. Arrange mints evenly over batter, pressing down lightly. Spoon the remaining batter over top. Bake in preheated oven for 30 to 35 minutes or until a tester comes out clean. Place pan on a wire rack to cool completely, then chill for 2 hours.
5. Meanwhile, in a saucepan, over low heat, melt white chocolate chips and cream, stirring constantly, until smooth. Drizzle mixture over top of chilled brownies and cut into squares.

Ice Cream Chocolate Brownies

Makes 20 brownies

- Preheat oven to 350°F (180°C)
- 13- by 9-inch (3 L) baking pan, greased on bottom only

1	package (15½ oz/440 g) brownie mix or brownie mix with chocolate chunks	1
1 cup	crushed peanut brittle	250 mL
6 cups	vanilla ice cream, softened	1.5 L
½ cup	ready-to-serve whipped chocolate frosting	125 mL

1. Prepare brownie mix as directed on package. Spread evenly in prepared pan. Bake in preheated oven for 25 to 30 minutes or until tester inserted in the center comes out clean. Place pan on a wire rack to cool completely.
2. In a clean bowl, fold nut brittle into softened ice cream. Spread evenly over cooled base. Cut into squares.
3. In a saucepan, over low heat, heat frosting until melted, stirring constantly. Drizzle over top of squares in zigzag lines. Serve immediately. Any leftover brownies can be frozen until firm, then wrapped in plastic and stored in the freezer for up to 1 month.

Tip *To prevent ice crystals from forming on ice cream after the carton has been opened, fit a piece of plastic wrap snugly on top of the ice cream before resealing the carton.*

Coconut Macaroon Brownies

Makes 36 brownies

- Preheat oven to 350°F (180°C)
- 13- by 9-inch (3 L) baking pan, greased

BROWNIE BATTER

4 oz	unsweetened chocolate	125 g
¾ cup	butter or margarine	175 mL
2 cups	granulated sugar	500 mL
3	eggs	3
1 tsp	vanilla	5 mL
1 cup	all-purpose flour	250 mL
1 cup	chopped almonds, toasted	250 mL

COCONUT MACAROON BATTER

1	package (8 oz/250 g) cream cheese, softened	1
⅔ cup	granulated sugar	150 mL
2	eggs	2
2 tbsp	all-purpose flour	25 mL
2 cups	flaked coconut (sweetened or unsweetened)	500 mL
1 cup	chopped almonds, toasted	250 mL

CHOCOLATE GLAZE

2 oz	semisweet chocolate, melted	60 g
	Whole almonds (optional)	

1. *Prepare the brownie batter:* In a saucepan over low heat, melt chocolate and butter, stirring constantly, until smooth. Set aside to cool slightly.
2. When chocolate mixture has cooled, stir in sugar. Add eggs and vanilla and mix until blended. Blend in flour. Stir in almonds. Spread batter evenly in prepared pan.
3. *Prepare the coconut macaroon batter:* In a large bowl, beat cream cheese and sugar until smooth. Add eggs, one at a time, beating until incorporated. Blend in flour. Stir in coconut and almonds.
4. Spread coconut macaroon batter evenly over brownie batter and bake for 35 to 40 minutes or until a tester inserted in the center comes out clean. Place pan on a wire rack to cool completely, then drizzle with melted chocolate. Cut into squares and, if desired, place 1 whole almond on top of each.

Chocolate Banana Brownies

Makes 36 brownies

- Preheat oven to 350°F (180°C)
- 13- by 9-inch (3 L) baking pan, greased

1	package (15½ oz/440 g) chocolate chip brownie mix	1
⅔ cup	finely chopped walnuts	150 mL
1 cup	mashed ripe bananas (2 to 3 medium)	250 mL
	Chocolate Butter Frosting (see variation, page 544)	

1. Prepare mix according to package directions. Add walnuts and bananas and mix until blended. Spread batter evenly in prepared pan. Bake in preheated oven for 25 to 30 minutes or until tester inserted in the center comes out clean. Place pan on a wire rack to cool completely. Frost with Chocolate Butter Frosting. Cut into squares.

Tip *If desired, sprinkle top of brownies with some chopped nuts, or when serving, place 2 to 3 thin slices of fresh banana on top.*

Malted Milk Brownies

Makes 36 brownies
- Preheat oven to 350°F (180°C)
- 13- by 9-inch (3 L) baking pan, greased

1½ cups	all-purpose flour	375 mL
½ tsp	baking powder	2 mL
½ tsp	salt	2 mL
4 oz	semisweet chocolate	125 g
2 oz	unsweetened chocolate	60 g
¾ cup	butter or margarine	175 mL
1½ cups	granulated sugar	375 mL
4	eggs, beaten	4
1 tbsp	vanilla	15 mL
TOPPING		
3 tbsp	milk	45 mL
1 tsp	vanilla	5 mL
¾ cup	unsweetened malted milk powder	175 mL
3 tbsp	butter or margarine, softened	45 mL
1 cup	confectioner's (icing) sugar, sifted	250 mL

1. In a bowl, combine flour, baking powder and salt.
2. In a saucepan, over low heat, melt chocolates and butter, stirring constantly, until smooth. Remove from heat and set aside to cool slightly.
3. When mixture has cooled, stir in sugar. Add eggs and vanilla and beat until blended. Blend in flour mixture.
4. Spread batter evenly in prepared pan. Bake in preheated oven for 25 to 30 minutes, until a tester inserted in the center comes out clean. Place pan on a wire rack to cool completely.
5. *Prepare the topping:* In a small bowl, combine milk, vanilla and malted milk powder until blended. In another bowl, cream butter. Gradually add confectioner's sugar, alternately with milk mixture, beating well after each addition until mixture is smooth and spreadable. Spread evenly over cooled brownies. When topping is firm, cut into squares.

Tip *For an added treat, chop malted milk balls or a malted milk chocolate bar and sprinkle over top.*

Unbelievable Orange Brownies

Makes 16 brownies
- Preheat oven to 350°F (180°C)
- 8-inch (2 L) square baking pan, greased

1	orange	1
1	package (14 oz/425 g) fudge brownie mix	1

1. Wash orange, cut into quarters and remove the seeds. In a food processor, process until almost smooth.
2. Prepare brownies as directed on package, but substitute the processed orange for the quantity of water in the package instructions.
3. Bake as directed. Place pan on a wire rack to cool completely, then cut into squares.

Orange Cream Walnut Brownies

Makes 24 brownies
- Preheat oven to 350°F (180°C)
- 9-inch (2.5 L) square baking pan, ungreased

BASE		
½ cup	butter or margarine, softened	125 mL
2 tbsp	confectioner's (icing) sugar, sifted	25 mL
1 cup	all-purpose flour	250 mL
TOPPING		
2 tbsp	all-purpose flour	25 mL
½ tsp	baking powder	2 mL
Pinch	salt	Pinch
2	eggs, beaten	2
1 cup	packed brown sugar	250 mL
½ cup	flaked coconut (sweetened or unsweetened)	125 mL
1 cup	chopped walnuts	250 mL
ORANGE CREAM FROSTING		
1¼ cups	confectioner's (icing) sugar, sifted	300 mL
2 tbsp	butter or margarine, melted	25 mL
1½ tsp	grated orange zest	7 mL
1½ tsp	freshly squeezed orange juice	7 mL

1. *Prepare the base:* In a medium bowl, beat butter and confectioner's sugar until smooth and creamy. Gradually add flour, mixing until a soft dough forms. Press evenly into bottom of pan. Bake in preheated oven for 10 minutes or until golden brown. Place pan on a wire rack to cool for 5 minutes.
2. *Prepare the topping:* In a medium bowl mix together flour, baking powder and salt. Add eggs and brown sugar and beat until just combined. Stir in coconut and nuts. Spoon evenly over baked crust. Bake for 25 minutes or until top is firm. Place pan on a wire rack to cool completely, then frost with Orange Cream Frosting.
3. *Prepare the frosting:* In a small bowl, beat confectioner's sugar, butter and orange juice until blended and smooth. Add zest and mix well. Spread evenly over cooled cake, then cut into squares.

Raspberry Cream Cheese Brownies

Makes 16 brownies

- Preheat oven to 350°F (180°C)
- 8-inch (2 L) square baking pan, greased

FILLING

1	package (8 oz/250 g) cream cheese, softened	1
3 tbsp	granulated sugar	45 mL
1	egg	1
1 tsp	vanilla	5 mL

BASE AND TOPPING

1/2 cup	butter or margarine, softened	125 mL
3/4 cup + 1 tbsp	granulated sugar	190 mL
1	egg	1
3 oz	semisweet chocolate, melted and cooled	90 g
2 oz	unsweetened chocolate, melted and cooled	60 g
1 cup	all-purpose flour	250 mL
Pinch	salt	Pinch
1/4 cup	raspberry jam	50 mL

1. *Prepare the filling:* In a small bowl, beat cream cheese and sugar until smooth. Add egg and beat until incorporated. Stir in vanilla. Set aside.

2. *Prepare the base and topping:* In a large bowl, beat butter and sugar until smooth and creamy. Beat in egg until incorporated. Stir in melted chocolates. Blend in flour and salt. Set aside 1 cup (250 mL) of mixture and spread remainder evenly in prepared pan. Spread filling evenly over batter. Drop reserved batter, by spoonfuls, over filling. Using a teaspoon (5 mL), drop jam on top of batter. Run a knife through the jam and batter to make a zigzag design.

3. Bake in preheated oven for 35 to 40 minutes or until a tester inserted in the center comes out almost clean, but with just a few moist crumbs. Place pan on a wire rack to cool completely, then cut into squares.

Tip *Try substituting carob for chocolate in some of your recipes. Carob is similar to chocolate in flavor but is lower in fat and is caffeine-free.*

Cherry Cream Brownies

Makes 24 brownies

- Preheat oven to 350°F (180°C)
- 9-inch (2.5 L) square baking pan, greased

FILLING

3 oz	cream cheese, softened	90 g
1/4 cup	granulated sugar	50 mL
1	egg	1
1/4 tsp	almond extract	1 mL
1/2 tsp	vanilla	2 mL
1/3 cup	maraschino cherries, drained and chopped	75 mL

BASE AND TOPPING

1/2 cup	all-purpose flour	125 mL
1/2 tsp	baking powder	2 mL
1/4 tsp	salt	1 mL
1/3 cup	unsweetened cocoa powder	75 mL
1/2 cup	butter or margarine, melted	125 mL
1 cup	granulated sugar	250 mL
2	eggs, beaten	2
1 tsp	vanilla	5 mL

1. *Prepare the filling:* In a small bowl, beat cream cheese and sugar until smooth. Beat in egg until incorporated. Stir in almond extract, vanilla and cherries and mix until blended.

2. *Prepare the base and topping:* In a small bowl, mix together flour, baking powder and salt.

3. In a large bowl, sift cocoa into melted butter and mix until smooth. Stir in sugar. Add eggs and vanilla, beating until just combined. Blend in flour mixture.

4. Spread half the batter evenly in prepared pan. Spread filling over top. Drop the remaining batter, by spoonfuls, over filling. Run a knife through the batter and filling to create a marbling effect. Bake in preheated oven for 35 to 40 minutes or until a tester inserted in the centre comes out clean. Place pan on a wire rack to cool completely, then cut into squares.

Black Forest Brownies

Makes 36 brownies

- Preheat oven to 350ºF (180ºC)
- 13- by 9-inch (3 L) baking pan, greased

1	package (14 oz/425 g) fudge brownie mix	1
4 oz	cream cheese, softened	125 g
¼ cup	granulated sugar	50 mL
2	eggs	2
1 tsp	vanilla	5 mL
2 tbsp	all-purpose flour	25 mL
1	can (19 oz/540 mL) cherry pie filling	1
¼ cup	semisweet chocolate chips	50 mL

1. Prepare brownie mix according to package directions. Spread half the batter evenly in prepared pan. Set remainder aside.
2. In a medium bowl, beat cream cheese and sugar until smooth. Beat in eggs, one at a time, until incorporated. Stir in vanilla. Blend in flour. Set aside.
3. Spread pie filling evenly over top of batter in pan. Sprinkle chocolate chips evenly across top. Spoon cream cheese mixture over chocolate chips. Drop the remaining batter by spoonfuls over cream cheese mixture. Using a knife, lightly draw circles in cream cheese and top layer of fudge batters to create marbling effect. Bake in preheated oven for 45 to 50 minutes or until a tester inserted in the centre comes out clean. Place pan on a wire rack to cool completely, then cut into squares.

Cheesecake Swirl Brownies

Makes 16 brownies

- Preheat oven to 350ºF (180ºC)
- 8-inch (2 L) square baking pan, greased

FILLING

4 oz	cream cheese, softened	125 g
2 tbsp	granulated sugar	25 mL
1	egg	1

BASE AND TOPPING

1 cup	all-purpose flour	250 mL
½ cup	unsweetened cocoa powder, sifted	125 mL
¾ cup	granulated sugar	175 mL
½ tsp	baking powder	2 mL
½ cup	mini semisweet chocolate chips	125 mL
¼ cup	chopped walnuts	50 mL
¼ cup	vegetable oil	50 mL
¼ cup	unsweetened applesauce	50 mL
¼ cup	milk	50 mL
1 tsp	vanilla	5 mL
1	egg	1

1. *Prepare the filling:* In a small bowl, beat cream cheese and sugar until smooth. Beat in egg until incorporated. Set aside.
2. *Prepare the base and topping:* In a large bowl, mix together flour, cocoa, sugar and baking powder. Stir in chocolate chips and walnuts.
3. In another small bowl, whisk together oil, applesauce, milk, vanilla and egg until well blended. Add to flour mixture and mix until combined. Reserve 1 cup (250 mL) of mixture for topping and spread remainder evenly in prepared pan. Spread cream cheese filling evenly over batter. Drop reserved batter, by spoonfuls, over filling.
4. Run a knife through the batter at 1-inch (2.5 cm) intervals across the width of the pan, to create a marbling effect. Bake in preheated oven for 25 minutes or until a tester inserted in the center comes out clean. Place pan on a wire rack to cool completely, then cut into squares.

Broadway Blondies

Makes 24 blondies

- Preheat oven to 325ºF (160ºC)
- 9-inch (2.5 L) square baking pan, greased

1½ cups	all-purpose flour	375 mL
1½ tsp	baking powder	7 mL
½ tsp	salt	2 mL
½ cup	butter	125 mL
1½ cups	packed brown sugar	375 mL
2	eggs	2
1½ tsp	vanilla	7 mL
¾ cup	coarsely chopped pecans	175 mL

1. In a bowl, combine flour, baking powder and salt.
2. In a large saucepan, over low heat, melt butter. Gradually add brown sugar, stirring until smooth. Set aside to cool slightly.
3. When butter mixture has cooled, add eggs and vanilla and beat until just blended. Blend in flour mixture. Stir in pecans.
4. Spread batter evenly in prepared pan. Bake in preheated oven for 50 to 60 minutes or until a tester inserted in the center comes out clean. Place pan on a wire rack to cool completely, then cut into squares.

Chocolate Chip Blondies

Makes 30 blondies
- Preheat oven to 350°F (180°C)
- 13- by 9-inch (3 L) baking pan, greased

2 cups	all-purpose flour	500 mL
1 tsp	baking powder	5 mL
¼ tsp	salt	1 mL
⅔ cup	butter, softened	150 mL
2 cups	packed brown sugar	500 mL
2	eggs	2
1 tsp	vanilla	5 mL
1 cup	semisweet chocolate chips	250 mL
1 cup	peanut butter chips	250 mL
½ cup	coarsely chopped walnuts	125 mL
½ cup	coarsely chopped pecans	125 mL

1. In a bowl, combine flour, baking powder and salt.

2. In a large bowl, beat butter and brown sugar until smooth and creamy. Add eggs, one at a time, beating until incorporated. Stir in vanilla. Blend in flour mixture. Stir in chocolate and peanut butter chips, walnuts and pecans.

3. Spread batter evenly in prepared pan. Bake in preheated oven for 30 to 35 minutes or until golden brown. Place pan on a wire rack to cool completely, then cut into squares.

Tip *If you can't live without chocolate, add chocolate chips to a blondie batter.*

Toffee Spice Raisin Blondies

Makes 36 blondies
- Preheat oven to 375°F (190°C)
- 13- by 9-inch (3 L) baking pan, greased

2 cups	all-purpose flour	500 mL
½ tsp	baking soda	2 mL
½ tsp	ground cinnamon	2 mL
½ tsp	ground nutmeg	2 mL
¼ tsp	ground cloves	1 mL
1¼ cups	packed brown sugar	300 mL
1 cup	butter or margarine, softened	250 mL
2	eggs	2
2 tbsp	milk	25 mL
1½ cups	raisins	375 mL

1. In a medium bowl, mix together flour, baking soda, cinnamon, nutmeg and cloves.

2. In a large bowl, beat brown sugar and butter until smooth and creamy. Beat in eggs until incorporated. Stir in milk. Gradually blend in flour mixture. Stir in raisins.

3. Spread batter evenly in prepared pan. Bake in preheated oven for 20 minutes or until a tester inserted in the center comes out clean. Place pan on a wire rack to cool completely, then cut into squares.

Chocolate Bars and Squares

Easy Chocolate Delight Bars

Makes 36 bars
- Preheat oven to 350°F (180°C)
- 13- by 9-inch (3 L) baking pan, greased

BASE

1¼ cups	all-purpose flour	300 mL
1 tsp	baking powder	5 mL
½ cup	butter or margarine, melted	125 mL
1 tsp	granulated sugar	5 mL
1	egg yolk	1
2 tbsp	water	25 mL
2 cups	semisweet chocolate chips or chunks	500 mL

TOPPING

2	eggs	2
¾ cup	granulated sugar	175 mL
6 tbsp	butter, melted	90 mL
2 tsp	vanilla	10 mL
2 cups	finely chopped nuts	500 mL

1. *Prepare the base:* In a small bowl, mix together flour and baking powder.

2. In a large bowl, beat butter, sugar, egg yolk and water until blended. Blend in flour mixture. Press mixture evenly into prepared pan. Bake in preheated oven for 10 minutes. Sprinkle chocolate chips over top and bake for 1 minute or until chocolate begins to melt. Remove from oven and spread chocolate evenly over top of base. Place pan on a wire rack to cool slightly.

3. *Prepare the topping:* Beat eggs, sugar, melted butter and vanilla until smooth and blended. Stir in nuts. Spread over top of chocolate. Bake for 30 to 35 minutes or until a tester inserted in the center comes out clean.

Viennese Chocolate Bars

Makes 36 bars
- Preheat oven to 350°F (180°C)
- 13- by 9-inch (3 L) baking pan, greased

BASE		
1 cup	butter, softened	250 mL
½ cup	granulated sugar	125 mL
2	egg yolks	2
2½ cups	all-purpose flour	625 mL
FILLING		
1	jar (10 oz/284 mL) raspberry jam or jelly	1
1 cup	semisweet chocolate chips	250 mL
TOPPING		
4	egg whites	4
¼ tsp	salt	1 mL
1 cup	granulated sugar	250 mL
2 cups	finely chopped pecans	500 mL

1. *Prepare the base:* In a large bowl, beat butter and sugar until smooth and creamy. Beat in egg yolks until incorporated. Blend in flour. Shape dough into a ball and knead lightly. Press evenly into prepared pan. Bake in preheated oven for 15 to 20 minutes or until lightly browned. Place pan on rack to cool slightly.

2. *Prepare the filling:* Stir jam or jelly until smooth, then spread evenly over base. Sprinkle chocolate chips evenly over top. Set aside.

3. *Prepare the topping:* In a bowl, beat egg whites with salt until frothy. Gradually beat in sugar until stiff peaks form. Fold in pecans. Spread gently over chocolate chips and bake for 25 minutes or until lightly browned. Place pan on a wire rack to cool completely, then cut into bars.

Tip *If you have jam, jelly or syrup that has crystallized, place the bottle in a pan of cold water and heat gently. The crystals will disappear.*

Polish Chocolate Squares (Mazurek)

Makes 36 squares
- Preheat oven to 350°F (180°C)
- 13- by 9-inch (3 L) baking pan, greased

⅓ cup	shortening, softened	75 mL
1½ cups	granulated sugar	375 mL
6	eggs, separated	6
1½ tsp	vanilla	7 mL
6 oz	unsweetened chocolate, melted	175 g
1⅔ cups	dry bread crumbs, divided	400 mL
	Whipped (35%) cream (optional)	

1. In a large bowl, beat shortening and sugar until smooth and creamy. Add egg yolks, one at a time, and beat until incorporated. Stir in vanilla and melted chocolate. Add 1½ cups (375 mL) of the bread crumbs and mix well.

2. In a clean bowl, beat egg whites until soft peaks form. Carefully fold into batter until blended.

3. Dust prepared baking pan with the remaining bread crumbs. Spread batter evenly in pan. Bake in preheated oven for 35 minutes. Place pan on a wire rack to cool completely, then cut into squares. Serve plain or with whipped cream, if desired.

Creole Cake Squares

Makes 16 squares
- Preheat oven to 325°F (160°C)
- 8-inch (2 L) square baking pan, greased

3 tbsp	butter or margarine, melted	45 mL
2 oz	unsweetened chocolate, melted	60 g
1⅓ cups	cake and pastry flour, sifted	325 mL
1¾ tsp	baking powder	9 mL
¼ tsp	salt	1 mL
1 cup	granulated sugar	250 mL
2	eggs	2
½ cup	milk	125 mL
	Butter Frosting (see recipe, page 544)	

1. In a saucepan, over low heat, melt butter and chocolate, stirring until smooth. Set aside to cool slightly.

2. In a small bowl, mix together flour, baking powder and salt.

3. When chocolate mixture has cooled, stir in sugar. Add eggs and beat until just blended. Gradually blend in flour mixture alternately with milk until just incorporated.

4. Spread evenly in prepared pan. Bake in preheated oven for 45 to 50 minutes or until a tester inserted in the center comes out clean. Place pan on a rack to cool completely, then frost with any flavor of Butter Frosting. Cut into squares.

Fudgey Chocolate Oatmeal Bars

Makes 36 bars

- Preheat oven to 350°F (180°C)
- 13- by 9-inch (3 L) baking pan, greased

BASE

3 cups	quick-cooking rolled oats	750 mL
2½ cups	all-purpose flour	625 mL
1 tsp	baking soda	5 mL
1 tsp	salt	5 mL
1 cup	butter or margarine, softened	250 mL
2 cups	packed brown sugar	500 mL
2	eggs	2
2 tsp	vanilla	10 mL

TOPPING

1	can (14 oz/398 mL) sweetened condensed milk	1
2 cups	semisweet chocolate chips	500 mL
2 tbsp	butter or margarine	25 mL
½ tsp	salt	2 mL
2 tsp	vanilla	10 mL
1 cup	chopped walnuts	250 mL

1. *Prepare the base:* In a large bowl, mix together oats, flour, baking soda and salt.
2. In another large bowl, beat butter and brown sugar until smooth and creamy. Beat in eggs until incorporated. Stir in vanilla. Blend in flour mixture. Press two-thirds of mixture evenly into prepared pan. Set remainder aside.
3. *Prepare the topping:* In a saucepan over low heat, combine condensed milk, chocolate chips, butter and salt, stirring until chocolate is melted and mixture is smooth. Remove from heat and stir in vanilla and walnuts. Spread evenly over base, then sprinkle top with reserved base mixture. Bake in preheated oven for 25 to 30 minutes or until top is golden brown. Place pan on a wire rack to cool completely, then cut into bars.

Tip *To freshen stale nuts, spread them on a baking sheet and heat in a 250°F (120°C) oven for 5 to 10 minutes.*

Sour Cream Chocolate Squares

Makes 16 squares

- Preheat oven to 350°F (180°C)
- 8-inch (2 L) square baking pan, greased

1 cup	all-purpose flour	250 mL
¾ tsp	baking soda	4 mL
½ cup	milk	125 mL
½ cup	sour cream	125 mL
¼ cup	butter or margarine	50 mL
2 oz	unsweetened chocolate, chopped	60 g
1 cup	granulated sugar	250 mL
1	egg	1
½ tsp	vanilla	2 mL

FROSTING

2 oz	unsweetened chocolate, melted	60 g
½ cup	sour cream	125 mL
2¼ cups	confectioner's (icing) sugar, sifted	550 mL

1. In a small bowl, mix together flour and baking soda. In a cup, combine milk and sour cream.
2. In a saucepan, melt butter and chocolate, stirring until smooth. Remove from heat and set aside to cool slightly.
3. When mixture has cooled, stir in sugar. Add egg and vanilla and beat until blended. Gradually blend in flour mixture alternately with milk mixture until just incorporated. Spread evenly in prepared pan. Bake in preheated oven for 25 to 30 minutes or until a tester inserted in center comes out clean. Let cool in pan for about 10 minutes, then transfer to a wire rack to cool completely.
4. *Prepare the frosting:* Beat melted chocolate and sour cream until smooth and blended. Gradually beat in confectioner's sugar until smooth and spreadable. Spread frosting over cake and cut into squares.

Tips *To prevent a crust from forming on icings and frostings, press a piece of plastic wrap against their surfaces until ready to use.*

When melting chocolate for any recipe, mix a little flour into the remains of melted chocolate. It gets the last bit of chocolate out of the pan and into the batter.

Buttermilk Chocolate Squares

Makes 36 squares
- Preheat oven to 350°F (180°C)
- 13- by 9-inch (3 L) baking pan, greased

2 oz	unsweetened chocolate, coarsely chopped	60 g
1/2 cup	boiling water	125 mL
2 cups	cake and pastry flour, sifted	500 mL
2 tsp	baking powder	10 mL
1/2 tsp	baking soda	2 mL
1/2 tsp	salt	2 mL
1/2 cup	shortening, softened	125 mL
2 cups	packed brown sugar	500 mL
2	eggs, separated	2
1 tsp	vanilla	5 mL
1/2 cup	buttermilk	125 mL
1/2 cup	water	125 mL
1/2 cup	chopped nuts	125 mL

COCOA FROSTING

6 tbsp	butter, softened	90 mL
1/2 cup	unsweetened cocoa powder, sifted	125 mL
3 1/2 cups	confectioner's (icing) sugar, sifted	875 mL
1/4 cup	milk (approximate)	50 mL
1 1/2 tsp	vanilla	7 mL

1. In a saucepan, over low heat, stir chocolate with boiling water until chocolate is melted and smooth. Set aside to cool for 10 minutes.
2. In a medium bowl, mix together flour, baking powder, baking soda and salt.
3. In a large bowl, beat shortening and brown sugar until smooth and creamy. Beat in egg yolks until incorporated. Stir in vanilla and chocolate mixture. Gradually blend in flour mixture alternately with buttermilk, then water, until just incorporated. Stir in nuts.
4. In a clean bowl, beat egg whites until soft peaks form. Fold into batter, then spread mixture evenly in prepared pan. Bake in preheated oven for 35 to 40 minutes or until a tester inserted in the center comes out clean. Place pan on a wire rack to cool completely.
5. *Prepare the frosting:* In a large bowl, beat butter and cocoa until smooth. Gradually add confectioner's sugar alternately with milk, beating until smooth. (Add just enough milk to make the right consistency for spreading.) Beat in vanilla. Spread evenly over cake. Cut into squares.

Chocolate Macaroon Bars

Makes 36 bars
- Preheat oven to 350°F (180°C)
- 13- by 9-inch (3 L) baking pan, lightly greased

BASE

1/3 cup	butter or margarine, melted	75 mL
1/3 cup	granulated sugar	75 mL
1 1/4 cups	graham wafer crumbs (about 18 wafers)	300 mL
1/4 cup	unsweetened cocoa powder, sifted	50 mL

TOPPING

2 cups	fresh white bread crumbs (about 4 slices)	500 mL
2 2/3 cups	flaked coconut (sweetened or unsweetened)	650 mL
1	can (14 oz/398 mL) sweetened condensed milk	1
2	eggs, lightly beaten	2
2 tsp	vanilla	10 mL
1 cup	mini semisweet chocolate chips	250 mL

1. *Prepare the base:* In a medium bowl, mix together butter, sugar, graham crumbs and cocoa until blended. Press evenly into prepared pan. Bake in preheated oven for 10 minutes.
2. *Prepare the topping:* In a large bowl, mix together bread crumbs, coconut, milk, eggs and vanilla. Stir in chocolate chips. Spread evenly over baked base. Bake for 30 minutes or until lightly browned. Place pan on a wire rack to cool completely, then cut into bars. Store, covered, in refrigerator.

Chocolate Chip Nut Bars

Makes 24 bars
- Preheat oven to 350°F (180°C)
- 9-inch (2.5 L) square baking pan, greased

BASE

1 cup	all-purpose flour	250 mL
1/4 cup	granulated sugar	50 mL
1/3 cup	butter or margarine	75 mL

TOPPING

2 tbsp	butter or margarine	25 mL
1 cup	semisweet chocolate chips	250 mL
1/2 cup	granulated sugar	125 mL
1/2 cup	light corn syrup	125 mL
2	eggs	2
2/3 cup	chopped pecans or walnuts	150 mL

1. *Prepare the base:* In a small bowl, mix together flour and sugar. Using two knives, a pastry blender or your fingers, work butter in until mixture resembles coarse crumbs. Press evenly into prepared pan. Bake in preheated oven for 12 to 15 minutes or until golden brown. Place pan on a rack to cool slightly.

2. *Prepare the topping:* In a large saucepan, over low heat, melt butter and chocolate chips, stirring until smooth. Remove from heat and set aside to cool slightly. When mixture has cooled, beat in sugar and corn syrup. Beat in eggs. Stir in nuts. Spread evenly over base and bake for 25 to 35 minutes or until topping is set. Place pan on a wire rack to cool completely, then cut into bars.

Chocolate Chip Dream Bars

Makes 36 bars
- Preheat oven to 350ºF (180º C)
- 13- by 9-inch (3 L) baking pan, lightly greased

½ cup	butter or margarine, melted	125 mL
1½ cups	graham wafer crumbs (about 22 wafers)	375 mL
1	can (14 oz/398 mL) sweetened condensed milk	1
1 cup	semisweet chocolate chips	250 mL
1 cup	flaked coconut (sweetened or unsweetened)	250 mL
1 cup	chopped nuts	250 mL

1. In a small bowl, mix together butter and graham wafer crumbs. Press evenly into prepared pan. Pour condensed milk over base.

2. Working in layers, sprinkle evenly with chocolate chips, then coconut, then nuts. Using a spatula, press down firmly. Bake in preheated oven for 25 to 30 minutes or until top is golden. Place pan on a wire rack to cool completely, then cut into bars.

Tip *For a healthy snack, combine raisins and nuts left over from baking and chop coarsely.*

Chocolate Marshmallow Squares

Makes 36 squares
- Preheat oven to 350ºF (180ºC)
- 13- by 9-inch (3 L) baking pan, greased

BASE		
2 oz	unsweetened chocolate	60 g
½ cup	butter	125 mL
1 cup	all-purpose flour	250 mL
½ tsp	baking powder	2 mL
¼ tsp	baking soda	1 mL
¼ tsp	salt	1 mL
1 cup	granulated sugar	250 mL
2	eggs	2
1 tsp	vanilla	5 mL
½ cup	unsweetened applesauce	125 mL
TOPPING		
2½ cups	miniature marshmallows, divided	625 mL
GLAZE		
2 tbsp	butter	25 mL
½ cup	granulated sugar	125 mL
2 tbsp	milk	25 mL
¼ cup	semisweet chocolate chips	50 mL

1. *Prepare the base:* In a saucepan, over low heat, melt chocolate and butter, stirring until smooth. Set aside to cool slightly.

2. In a small bowl, mix together flour, baking powder, baking soda and salt.

3. When chocolate mixture has cooled, stir in sugar. Add eggs and vanilla; beat until blended. Stir in applesauce. Blend in flour mixture. Spread evenly in prepared pan. Bake in preheated oven for 20 to 30 minutes or until a tester inserted in the center comes out clean.

4. *Prepare the topping:* Set aside ½ cup (125 mL) of the marshmallows and sprinkle remainder evenly over cake. Bake for 2 minutes or until marshmallows soften.

5. *Prepare the glaze:* In a saucepan, over medium heat, combine butter, sugar and milk. Stir constantly until mixture comes to a boil, then boil for 1 minute. Remove from heat. Stir in chocolate chips and reserved marshmallows until melted and smooth. Immediately drizzle over top of warm cake. Place pan on a wire rack to cool completely, then cut into squares.

Tip *To cut sticky foods (like marshmallows, dates or prunes) easily, use kitchen scissors, dipping them frequently in hot water.*

Chocolate Mallow Sensations

Makes 20 bars
- Preheat oven to 375°F (190°C)
- 8-inch (2 L) square baking pan, greased

FILLING

1 oz	unsweetened chocolate	30 g
2 tbsp	butter or margarine	25 mL
1/3 cup	chopped walnuts	75 mL

BASE

3/4 cup	all-purpose flour	175 mL
1 tsp	baking powder	5 mL
1/2 tsp	salt	2 mL
1 1/4 cups	packed brown sugar	300 mL
2	eggs	2
1/2 cup	flaked coconut (sweetened or unsweetened)	125 mL

TOPPING

20	large marshmallows, halved	20
2 tbsp	butter or margarine	25 mL
2 oz	unsweetened chocolate	60 g
1	egg, lightly beaten	1
1 tsp	vanilla	5 mL
1 cup	confectioner's (icing) sugar, sifted	250 mL

1. *Prepare the filling:* In a saucepan, over low heat, melt chocolate with butter, stirring until smooth. Stir in walnuts. Set aside.
2. *Prepare the base:* In a small bowl, mix together flour, baking powder and salt.
3. In a medium bowl, beat brown sugar and eggs until smooth and creamy. Blend in flour mixture. Spoon half this batter into another medium bowl and stir in coconut. Stir filling into the remaining batter.
4. Spread coconut batter evenly in prepared pan. Spread chocolate-walnut batter evenly over top. Bake in preheated oven for 25 to 30 minutes or until a tester inserted in the center comes out clean.
5. *Prepare the topping:* Remove from oven and arrange marshmallow halves on top. Bake for 2 minutes, until marshmallows are softened. Place pan on a wire rack to cool.
6. In a saucepan, over low heat, melt butter and chocolate, stirring until smooth. Let cool slightly, then beat in egg and vanilla. Gradually add confectioner's sugar, beating until mixture is smooth. Working quickly, spread topping over marshmallow layer. Place pan on a wire rack to cool completely, then cut into bars.

Rocky Road Bars

Makes 36 bars
- Preheat oven to 350°F (180°C)
- 13- by 9-inch (3 L) baking pan, greased

1/2 cup	butter or margarine, melted	125 mL
1 1/2 cups	graham wafer crumbs (about 22 wafers)	375 mL
1 1/2 cups	flaked coconut (sweetened or unsweetened)	375 mL
1 1/2 cups	chopped nuts	375 mL
1 1/2 cups	semisweet chocolate chips	375 mL
1 1/2 cups	miniature marshmallows	375 mL
1	can (10 oz/300 mL) sweetened condensed milk	1
3 oz	semisweet chocolate, melted	90 g

1. In a small bowl, mix together melted butter and graham wafer crumbs. Press evenly into prepared pan. Working in layers, sprinkle coconut, then nuts, then chocolate chips and, finally, marshmallows evenly over base. Drizzle condensed milk evenly over top.
2. Bake in preheated oven for 25 to 30 minutes or until top is golden brown. Remove from oven. Drizzle with melted chocolate. Place pan on a wire rack to cool completely, then cut into bars.

Fudgey Toffee Bars

Makes 36 bars
- Preheat oven to 350°F (180°C)
- 13- by 9-inch (3 L) baking pan, lightly greased

1/2 cup	butter or margarine, melted	125 mL
1 1/2 cups	graham wafer crumbs (about 22 wafers)	375 mL
1	can (10 oz/300 mL) sweetened condensed milk	1
1 cup	toffee bits	250 mL
1 cup	semisweet chocolate chips	250 mL
1 cup	chopped nuts	250 mL

1. In a small bowl, mix together melted butter and graham wafer crumbs. Press evenly into prepared pan.
2. Pour condensed milk evenly over base. Sprinkle an even layer of toffee bits over milk, then a layer of chocolate chips, then a layer of nuts. Using a spatula, firmly press top layer into base.
3. Bake in preheated oven for 20 to 25 minutes or until lightly browned. Place pan on a wire rack to cool completely, then cut into bars.

Gooey Caramel-Pecan Chocolate Bars

Makes 18 bars

- Preheat oven to 425ºF (220ºC)
- 8-inch (2 L) square baking pan, lined with greased foil

BASE

1 cup	all-purpose flour	250 mL
¼ cup	granulated sugar	50 mL
Pinch	salt	Pinch
6 tbsp	cold butter	90 mL
3 tbsp	ice water	45 mL

FILLING

3 tbsp	butter	45 mL
⅓ cup	light corn syrup	75 mL
1⅓ cups	packed brown sugar	325 mL
½ cup	whipping (35%) cream	125 mL
1 tsp	white vinegar	5 mL
Pinch	salt	Pinch
1 tsp	vanilla	5 mL

TOPPING

¾ cup	chopped pecans, toasted (see page 4)	175 mL
3 oz	semisweet chocolate	90 g

1. *Prepare the base:* In a medium bowl, mix together flour, sugar and salt. Using two knives, a pastry blender or your fingers, cut butter in until mixture resembles coarse crumbs. Sprinkle water, 1 tbsp (15 mL) at a time, over mixture, mixing lightly after each addition. (Dough should just be moist enough to hold together.) Press evenly into prepared pan. Bake in preheated oven for 15 to 20 minutes or until golden brown. Place pan on a rack to cool completely.

2. *Prepare the filling:* In a saucepan, over high heat, combine butter, syrup, brown sugar, cream, vinegar and salt. Bring to a boil, reduce heat to low and simmer, stirring constantly, for 5 minutes. Remove from heat and stir in vanilla until bubbling stops (about 20 seconds). Pour filling over cooled base.

3. *Prepare the topping:* Sprinkle top with pecans and set aside to cool. In a small saucepan, over low heat, melt chocolate, stirring until smooth. Let cool slightly, then drizzle over pecans. Chill until chocolate sets. Using foil to lift, transfer to a cutting board and cut into bars.

Chocolate-Lover's Banana Squares

Makes 16 squares

- Preheat oven to 350ºF (180ºC)
- 8-inch (2 L) square baking pan, ungreased

BASE

2 tbsp	butter or margarine	25 mL
½ cup	mashed ripe banana (1 large)	125 mL
1	egg, beaten	1
1 tsp	vanilla	5 mL
¼ cup	water	50 mL
1 cup	all-purpose flour	250 mL
1 tsp	baking powder	5 mL
½ cup	granulated sugar	125 mL
¾ cup	unsweetened cocoa powder, sifted	175 mL
½ tsp	salt	2 mL
¼ tsp	ground cinnamon	1 mL

TOPPING

½ cup	packed brown sugar	125 mL
¼ cup	unsweetened cocoa powder, sifted	50 mL
1¼ cups	boiling water	300 mL

1. *Prepare the base:* In a saucepan, over low heat, melt butter. Remove from heat and stir in banana, egg, vanilla and water until blended. Set aside.

2. In a large bowl, mix together flour, baking powder, sugar, cocoa, salt and cinnamon. Add banana mixture and mix well (batter will be thick). Spread evenly in pan.

3. *Prepare the topping:* In a small bowl, beat brown sugar, cocoa and boiling water until smooth and blended. Pour evenly over base. Bake in preheated oven for 35 to 40 minutes or until a tester inserted in the centre of the cake comes out clean (the fudgey sauce on top will be wet). Place pan on a wire rack to cool for 5 minutes, then cut into squares.

Tips *Score bars or squares that are topped with chocolate as soon as the topping is applied. This prevents the chocolate from cracking later.*

Freeze ripe bananas for later use. Peel them and wrap in plastic wrap. Store them in freezer bags.

Ripen green bananas by wrapping in a wet dish towel and placing in a paper bag.

Chocodamias

Makes 24 bars
- Preheat oven to 350° F (180° C)
- 9-inch (2.5 L) square baking pan, greased

¼ cup	butter or margarine	50 mL
6 oz	semisweet chocolate, divided	175 g
¾ cup	granulated sugar	175 mL
2	eggs	2
1 tsp	vanilla	5 mL
1¼ cups	all-purpose flour	300 mL
½ tsp	baking powder	2 mL
¾ cup	chopped macadamia nuts	175 mL

1. In a large saucepan, over low heat, melt butter and 3 oz (90 g) of the chocolate, stirring until smooth. Set aside to cool slightly. Chop the remaining chocolate into chunks. Set aside.

2. When chocolate mixture has cooled, stir in sugar. Add eggs and vanilla, mixing just until incorporated. Blend in flour and baking powder. Stir in chopped chocolate and nuts. Spread evenly in prepared pan. Bake in preheated oven for 20 to 25 minutes or until a tester inserted in center comes out clean. Place pan on a wire rack to cool completely, then cut into bars.

Cherry Pie Cocoa Bars

Makes 36 bars
- Preheat oven to 350°F (180°C)
- 13- by 9-inch (3 L) baking pan, greased

1¾ cup	all-purpose flour	425 mL
¼ cup	unsweetened cocoa powder, sifted	50 mL
1 cup	granulated sugar	250 mL
1 cup	butter	250 mL
1	egg, lightly beaten	1
1 tsp	almond extract	5 mL
1	can (19 oz/540 mL) cherry pie filling	1
2 cups	semisweet chocolate chips	500 mL
1 cup	chopped almonds	250 mL

1. In a large bowl, combine flour, cocoa and sugar. Using two knives, a pastry blender or your fingers, work butter in until mixture resembles coarse crumbs. Mix in egg and almond extract until blended. Set aside 1 cup (250 mL) of mixture for topping and press remainder evenly into prepared pan. Spoon pie filling evenly over base.

2. In a large bowl, combine chocolate chips, almonds and reserved base mixture. Sprinkle over top of filling. Bake in preheated oven for 35 to 40 minutes, until top is golden. Chill for 2 to 3 hours, then cut into bars.

Raspberry Chocolate Crumb Squares

Makes 24 squares
- Preheat oven to 375°F (190°C)
- 9-inch (2.5 L) square baking pan, ungreased

BASE

1½ cups	quick-cooking rolled oats	375 mL
1½ cups	all-purpose flour	375 mL
½ cup	granulated sugar	125 mL
½ cup	packed brown sugar	125 mL
1 tsp	baking powder	5 mL
Pinch	salt	Pinch
1 cup	butter or margarine	250 mL

TOPPING

1 cup	raspberry jam or preserves	250 mL
1 cup	semisweet chocolate chips	250 mL
¼ cup	chopped almonds	50 mL
3 oz	semisweet chocolate, chopped into small pieces	90 g

1. *Prepare the base:* In a large bowl, mix together oats, flour, sugars, baking powder and salt. Using two knives, a pastry blender or your fingers, cut butter in until mixture resembles coarse crumbs. Set aside 1 cup (250 mL) of mixture and press remainder evenly into prepared pan. Bake in preheated oven for 10 minutes. Place pan on rack to cool slightly.

2. *Prepare the topping:* Stir jam until smooth and spread evenly over warm base. Sprinkle chocolate chips evenly over jam.

3. Combine reserved oat mixture with almonds. Sprinkle evenly over chocolate and gently pat down. Bake for 30 to 35 minutes or until golden brown. Place pan on a wire rack to cool completely.

4. In a saucepan, over low heat, melt chocolate, stirring until smooth. Set aside to cool slightly. When cake has cooled, drizzle melted chocolate over top. Set aside until chocolate sets, then cut into squares.

Tip *Don't overbeat cake batter. Overbeating will remove too much air and make finished cakes flat and heavy.*

Grasshopper Cream Cheese Bars

Makes 16 bars

- Preheat oven to 350°F (180°C)
- 8-inch (2 L) square baking pan, ungreased

BASE

¾ cup	all-purpose flour	175 mL
⅓ cup	unsweetened cocoa powder, sifted	75 mL
⅓ cup	granulated sugar	75 mL
6 tbsp	butter or margarine	90 mL

TOPPING

1	package (8 oz/250 g) cream cheese, softened	1
¼ cup	granulated sugar	50 mL
1	egg	1
½ tsp	peppermint extract	2 mL
4 to 5	drops green food coloring	4 to 5
¼ cup	milk	50 mL

1. *Prepare the base:* In a medium bowl, mix together flour, cocoa and sugar. Using two knives, a pastry blender or your fingers, cut butter in until mixture resembles coarse crumbs. Set aside 1 cup (250 mL) of mixture and press remainder evenly into pan. Bake in preheated oven for 15 minutes or until lightly browned. Place pan on a wire rack to cool slightly.
2. *Prepare the topping:* In a medium bowl, beat cream cheese and sugar until smooth. Beat in egg, peppermint extract and food coloring until blended. Blend in milk. Spread topping evenly over baked base. Sprinkle the remaining base mixture over top and bake for 20 to 25 minutes or until crumbs are golden. Place pan on a wire rack to cool completely, then cut into bars. Store, covered, in refrigerator.

Chocolate Swirl Squares

Makes 16 squares

- Preheat oven to 400°F (200°C)
- 8-inch (2 L) square baking pan, greased

BASE

2 cups	biscuit mix	500 mL
¼ cup	granulated sugar	50 mL
1	egg	1
⅔ cup	milk or water	150 mL
3 tbsp	melted butter or margarine, divided	45 mL
⅓ cup	semisweet chocolate chips, melted	75 mL

TOPPING

¼ cup	granulated sugar	50 mL
⅓ cup	flaked coconut (sweetened or unsweetened)	75 mL
¼ cup	chopped nuts	50 mL

1. *Prepare the base:* In a medium bowl, mix together biscuit mix, sugar, egg, milk and 2 tbsp (25 mL) of the melted butter until blended. Spread evenly in prepared pan. Pour melted chocolate evenly over batter. Run a knife through batter to create a marbling effect.
2. *Prepare the topping:* In a small bowl, mix together sugar, coconut, nuts and the remaining melted butter.
3. Spread mixture evenly over base. Bake in preheated oven for 20 to 25 minutes or until a tester inserted in center comes out clean. Place pan on a wire rack to cool slightly and serve warm or cool completely, then cut into squares.

Mocha Cream Cheese Bars

Makes 24 bars

- Preheat oven to 350°F (180°C)
- 9-inch (2.5 L) square baking pan, greased

BASE

¼ cup	butter or margarine, melted	50 mL
1½ cups	finely crushed chocolate wafers (about 30 wafers)	375 mL

TOPPING

1	package (8 oz/250 g) cream cheese, softened	1
⅔ cup	granulated sugar	150 mL
3	eggs	3
3 tbsp	unsweetened cocoa powder, sifted	45 mL
¼ cup	milk	50 mL
3 tbsp	strong brewed coffee	45 mL

1. *Prepare the base:* In a small bowl, mix together butter and wafers. Press evenly into prepared pan. Set aside.
2. *Prepare the topping:* In a large bowl, beat cream cheese and sugar until smooth. Beat in eggs, one at a time, until incorporated. Add cocoa, milk and coffee, beating until well blended. Spread mixture evenly over base. Bake in preheated oven for 30 to 35 minutes or until set. Place pan on a wire rack to cool completely, then cut into bars. Store, covered, in the refrigerator.

Coffee Mocha Cheesecake Diamonds

Makes 36 diamonds
- Preheat oven to 350°F (180°C)
- 13- by 9-inch (3 L) baking pan, greased

BASE

6 oz	semisweet chocolate	175 g
¾ cup	butter or margarine	175 mL
1 tbsp	instant coffee powder or granules	15 mL
2	eggs	2
¾ cup	packed brown sugar	175 mL
¾ cup	all-purpose flour	175 mL
½ tsp	baking powder	2 mL

CHEESECAKE LAYER

1	package (8 oz/250 g) cream cheese, softened	1
½ cup	granulated sugar	125 mL
2	eggs	2
2 tbsp	strong brewed coffee or coffee-flavored liqueur	25 mL
2 tbsp	all-purpose flour	25 mL

SOUR CREAM TOPPING

1½ cups	sour cream	375 mL
3 tbsp	granulated sugar	45 mL
	Chocolate-covered almonds or espresso beans (optional)	

1. *Prepare the base:* In a saucepan, over low heat, melt chocolate and butter, stirring until smooth. Add coffee powder and mix well. Set aside to cool slightly.
2. In a large bowl, beat eggs and brown sugar. Add cooled chocolate mixture and mix well. Blend in flour and baking powder. Spread evenly in prepared pan. Chill for 10 minutes.
3. *Prepare the cheesecake layer:* In a medium bowl, beat cream cheese and sugar until smooth. Add eggs, one at a time, beating until incorporated. Stir in coffee until blended. Blend in flour. Spread evenly over base. Bake in preheated oven for 20 minutes or until set.
4. *Prepare the topping:* In a small bowl, mix together sour cream and sugar. Spread over warm cheesecake. Bake for 10 minutes. Place pan on a wire rack to cool completely. When cool, cut cake into 6 long strips, then cut strips across on diagonal into diamond shapes. If desired, top each with a chocolate-covered almond or espresso bean.

Marbled Cream Cheese Squares

Makes 24 squares
- Preheat oven to 350°F (180°C)
- 9-inch (2.5 L) square baking pan, greased

FILLING

1	package (8 oz/250 g) cream cheese, softened	1
¼ cup	granulated sugar	50 mL
1	egg	1
2 tbsp	all-purpose flour	25 mL

BASE

¾ cup	butter or margarine	175 mL
4 oz	unsweetened chocolate	125 g
1½ cups	granulated sugar	375 mL
3	eggs	3
1 tbsp	milk	15 mL
1 cup	all-purpose flour	250 mL
1 cup	chopped nuts	250 mL

1. *Prepare the filling:* In a medium bowl, beat cream cheese and sugar until smooth. Beat in egg until incorporated. Blend in flour. Set aside.
2. *Prepare the base:* In a saucepan, over low heat, melt butter and chocolate, stirring until smooth. Set aside to cool slightly.
3. When mixture has cooled, stir in sugar. Beat in eggs until blended. Stir in milk. Blend in flour. Stir in nuts.
4. Spread half the batter evenly in prepared pan. Spread filling evenly over base. Spread the remaining batter evenly over filling. Run a knife through the layers to create a marbling effect. Bake in preheated oven for 35 to 40 minutes or until a tester inserted in the center comes out clean. Let cool completely in pan, then cut into squares.

Tip *When baking cakes, never open the oven door until the minimum time is up or cakes will collapse.*

Chocolate Cookie and Cream Squares

Makes 36 squares
- Preheat oven to 350°F (180°C)
- 13- by 9-inch (3 L) baking pan, ungreased

BASE

2²⁄₃ cups	chocolate cookie crumbs	650 mL
²⁄₃ cup	butter or margarine, melted	150 mL
½ cup	granulated sugar	125 mL

TOPPING

2	packages (each 8 oz/250 g) cream cheese, softened	2
1 cup	granulated sugar	250 mL
4	eggs	4
2 cups	broken chunks chocolate cookies with white cream filling, divided	500 mL
6 oz	semisweet chocolate	175 g
½ cup	whipping (35%) cream	125 mL

1. *Prepare the base:* In a medium bowl, mix together cookie crumbs, butter and sugar. Press evenly into pan. Bake in preheated oven for 8 to 10 minutes. Place pan on a wire rack to cool slightly.
2. *Prepare the topping:* In a large bowl, beat cream cheese and sugar until smooth. Beat in eggs, one at a time, until incorporated. Spread half the mixture evenly over warm base and sprinkle with 1¾ cups (425 mL) of the cookie chunks. Spread the remaining batter over top. Bake for 35 to 40 minutes or until center is almost set. Place pan on a wire rack to cool, then chill for at least 3 hours.
3. In a saucepan, over low heat, stir chocolate and whipping cream until melted and smooth. Pour over chilled cake. Sprinkle the remaining cookie pieces over top. Cut into squares.

Vanilla Fudge Cream Bars

Makes 36 bars
- Preheat oven to 350°F (180°C)
- 13- by 9-inch (3 L) baking pan, ungreased

1	package (18 oz/510 g) dark chocolate or devil's food cake mix	1
½ cup	butter or margarine, melted	125 mL
2	eggs	2
½ cup	chocolate fudge sundae sauce	125 mL
1	container (15 oz/420 g) ready-to-serve vanilla frosting	1
1	package (8 oz/250 g) cream cheese, softened	1

1. In a medium bowl, mix together cake mix, butter, 1 of the eggs and chocolate fudge sauce until blended. (Mixture will be crumbly.) Press evenly into pan.
2. In another medium bowl, beat frosting mix with cream cheese until smooth. Set 1 cup (250 mL) of mixture aside and add 1 egg to remainder in bowl. Beat until blended and smooth. Spread evenly over base.
3. Bake in preheated oven for 30 to 35 minutes or until set. Place pan on a wire rack to cool completely, then frost with reserved cream cheese mixture. Cut into bars. Store, covered, in refrigerator.

Chocolate Chip Meringue Squares

Makes 36 squares
- Preheat oven to 325°F (160°C)
- 13- by 9-inch (3 L) baking pan, lightly greased

2 cups	all-purpose flour	500 mL
1 tsp	baking soda	5 mL
½ cup	butter or margarine, softened	125 mL
½ cup	granulated sugar	125 mL
1½ cups	packed brown sugar, divided	375 mL
2	eggs, separated	2
1 tsp	vanilla	5 mL
1 tbsp	water	15 mL
1 cup	semisweet chocolate chips or pieces	250 mL

1. In a medium bowl, mix together flour and baking soda.
2. In a large bowl, beat butter and granulated sugar and ½ cup (125 mL) of the brown sugar until smooth and creamy. Beat in egg yolks until incorporated. Stir in vanilla and water. Blend in flour mixture. Spread mixture evenly in prepared pan. Sprinkle chocolate chips evenly over top, pressing lightly into the dough.
3. In a clean bowl, beat egg whites until soft peaks form. Gradually beat in the remaining brown sugar until stiff peaks form.
4. Spread evenly over dough. Bake in preheated oven for 30 minutes or until meringue is golden brown. Place pan on a wire rack to cool completely, then cut into squares.

Chocolate Carrot Nut Squares

Makes 36 squares
- Preheat oven to 350ºF (180ºC)
- 13- by 9-inch (3 L) baking pan, greased

2 cups	all-purpose flour	500 mL
1/3 cup	unsweetened cocoa powder, sifted	75 mL
2 tsp	baking powder	10 mL
2 tsp	ground cinnamon	10 mL
1 1/4 tsp	baking soda	6 mL
1 tsp	salt	5 mL
1 1/2 cups	granulated sugar	375 mL
4	eggs, beaten	4
1 1/2 cups	vegetable oil	375 mL
1 tsp	vanilla	5 mL
2 cups	grated carrots	500 mL
1/2 cup	flaked coconut (sweetened or unsweetened)	125 mL
1/2 cup	chopped pecans	125 mL
2 cups	crushed pineapple, drained	500 mL
	Chocolate Butter Frosting (see variation, page 544) or Chocolate Velvet Frosting (see recipe, page 546) (optional)	
	Crushed pineapple (optional)	

1. In a large bowl, mix together flour, cocoa, baking powder, cinnamon, baking soda and salt. Make a well in the center. Add sugar, eggs, oil and vanilla; mix until blended. Stir in carrots, coconut, pecans and pineapple.

2. Spread evenly in prepared pan. Bake in preheated oven for 50 to 55 minutes or until a tester inserted in the center comes out clean. Place pan on a wire rack to cool completely. Frost, if desired, then spread crushed pineapple over top, if desired. Cut into squares.

Mashed Potato Chocolate Squares

Makes 36 squares
- Preheat oven to 350º F (180º C)
- 13- by 9-inch (3 L) baking pan, greased

2 cups	all-purpose flour	500 mL
3 1/2 tsp	baking powder	17 mL
1 tsp	ground cinnamon	5 mL
1/2 tsp	ground nutmeg	2 mL
1/2 tsp	ground mace	2 mL
1/2 tsp	ground cloves	2 mL
2 cups	granulated sugar	500 mL
2/3 cup	butter or margarine, softened	150 mL
4	eggs	4
1 cup	hot mashed potatoes	250 mL
2 oz	unsweetened chocolate, melted	60 g
1/2 cup	milk	125 mL
1 cup	chopped nuts	250 mL
	Chocolate Butter Frosting (see variation, page 544) or Chocolate Velvet Frosting (see recipe, page 546)	

1. In a medium bowl, mix together flour, baking powder, cinnamon, nutmeg, mace and cloves.

2. In a large bowl, beat sugar and butter until smooth and creamy. Beat in eggs, one at a time, until incorporated. Add potatoes and chocolate and mix well. Gradually blend in flour mixture alternately with milk until just incorporated. Stir in nuts.

3. Spread evenly in prepared pan. Bake in preheated oven for 30 to 35 minutes or until a tester inserted in the center comes out clean. Place pan on a wire rack to cool completely, then frost with a chocolate frosting of your choice. Cut into squares.

Black and White Chocolate Bars

Makes 24 bars
- Preheat oven to 350ºF (180ºC)
- 9-inch (2.5 L) square baking pan, lightly greased

1 1/4 cups	all-purpose flour, divided	300 mL
1/3 cup	raisins	75 mL
1/2 cup	chopped walnuts	125 mL
1/2 cup	butter or margarine	125 mL
6 oz	white chocolate, chopped into small chunks, divided	175 g
2/3 cup	granulated sugar	150 mL
3	eggs	3
2 tsp	vanilla	10 mL
4 oz	bittersweet chocolate, chopped into small chunks	125 g

1. In a small bowl, mix together 2 tbsp (25 mL) of the flour, raisins and walnuts. Set aside.

2. In a large saucepan, over low heat, melt butter and half the white chocolate chunks, stirring until smooth. Remove from heat and set aside to cool slightly.

3. When mixture has cooled, stir in sugar. Beat in eggs and vanilla just until blended. Blend in the remaining flour. Stir in raisin-walnut mixture, the remaining white chocolate and the bittersweet chocolate.

4. Spread evenly in prepared pan. Bake in preheated oven for 30 minutes or until a tester inserted in center comes out clean. Place pan on a wire rack to cool completely, then cut into bars.

White Chocolate Dream Bars

Makes 36 bars
- Preheat oven to 350°F (180°C)
- 13- by 9-inch (3 L) baking pan, greased

BASE

2¹⁄₃ cups	all-purpose flour	575 mL
2 cups	old-fashioned rolled oats	500 mL
1 cup	packed brown sugar	250 mL
1 tsp	baking soda	5 mL
1 cup	butter or margarine, melted	500 mL

TOPPING

1¹⁄₂ cups	white chocolate chips	375 mL
1 cup	slivered almonds	250 mL
1 cup	toffee bits	250 mL
1¹⁄₃ cups	caramel sundae sauce	325 mL
¹⁄₃ cup	all-purpose flour	75 mL

1. *Prepare the base:* In a large bowl, mix together flour, oats, brown sugar and baking soda. Add butter and mix thoroughly. Set aside 1 cup (250 mL) of mixture and press remainder evenly into prepared pan. Bake in preheated oven for 12 to15 minutes or until lightly browned. Place pan on a wire rack to cool slightly.

2. *Prepare the topping:* In a medium bowl, combine white chocolate chips, almonds and toffee bits. Sprinkle evenly over base.

3. In a separate bowl, blend caramel sauce with flour. Drizzle over chocolate layer, then sprinkle the remaining base mixture over top. Bake for 20 to 25 minutes or until golden brown. Place pan on a wire rack to cool completely, then cut into bars.

Tip *Dry ingredients — such as baking powder, baking soda and cocoa — sometimes have a tendency to pack down in their containers, so stir to loosen before measuring.*

Raspberry Almond White Triangles

Makes 32 triangles
- Preheat oven to 325°F (160°C)
- 9-inch (2.5 L) square baking pan, greased

¹⁄₂ cup	butter or margarine	125 mL
6 oz	white chocolate, chopped	175 g
¹⁄₂ cup	granulated sugar	125 mL
2	eggs	2
1¹⁄₂ tsp	vanilla	7 mL
¹⁄₄ tsp	salt	1 mL
1 cup	all-purpose flour	250 mL
	Raspberry jam	
1¹⁄₂ cups	white chocolate chips	375 mL
¹⁄₃ cup	sliced almonds	75 mL

1. In a large saucepan, over low heat, melt butter and white chocolate, stirring until smooth. Set aside to cool slightly.

2. When mixture has cooled, stir in sugar. Add eggs and vanilla and beat until just combined. Blend in salt, then flour.

3. Spread half the batter evenly in prepared pan. Bake in preheated oven for 25 minutes or until golden brown. Place pan on a wire rack to cool for 10 minutes.

4. Stir jam until smooth and spread evenly over top of warm cake.

5. Stir white chocolate chips into the remaining batter and drop, by spoonfuls, over jam layer. Sprinkle almonds on top. Bake for 35 to 40 minutes or until lightly browned. Place pan on a wire rack to cool completely. Cut into 16 squares, then cut each square into 2 triangles.

Tip *Use only the size of pan called for in your recipe. The difference between an 8-inch (2 L) square baking pan and a 9-inch (2.5 L) square baking pan can mean the difference between a moist, chewy bar or square and an underbaked, heavy failure.*

Fruit Bars and Squares

Mix-Ahead Bar Mix

Makes about 8 cups (2 L)

4 cups	all-purpose flour	1 L
1 cup	packed brown sugar	250 mL
1 cup	granulated sugar	250 mL
2 tsp	baking powder	10 mL
1½ cups	shortening	375 mL

1. In a large bowl, mix together flour, brown sugar, sugar and baking powder. Using two knives, a pastry blender or your fingers, cut shortening in until mixture resembles coarse crumbs. Store in an airtight container, at room temperature, for up to 6 weeks, or in freezer for up to 6 months.

Apple Cake Bars

Makes 24 bars

- Preheat oven to 350°F (180°C)
- 8-inch (2 L) square baking pan, greased

TOPPING

⅔ cup	packed brown sugar	150 mL
1 tsp	ground cinnamon	5 mL

BASE

1⅓ cups	all-purpose flour	325 mL
¾ cup	granulated sugar	175 mL
1 tbsp	baking powder	15 mL
¼ cup	butter or margarine	50 mL
1	egg, beaten	1
¾ cup	milk	175 mL
1 tsp	vanilla	5 mL
2 to 4	apples, peeled and sliced	2 to 4

1. *Prepare the topping:* In a small bowl, mix together brown sugar and cinnamon. Set aside.

2. *Prepare the base:* In a large bowl, mix together flour, sugar and baking powder. Using two knives, a pastry blender or your fingers, cut butter in until mixture resembles coarse crumbs. Add egg, milk and vanilla and mix well. Spread half evenly in prepared pan. Sprinkle evenly with half the topping mixture. Sprinkle with the remaining base mixture.

3. Arrange apple slices over top of cake, pushing them into the batter. Sprinkle with the remaining topping. Bake in preheated oven for 50 to 60 minutes or until a tester inserted in the center comes out clean. Place pan on a wire rack to cool completely, then cut into bars.

Apple Küchen Bars

Makes 24 bars

- Preheat oven to 375°F (190°C)
- 9-inch (2.5 L) square baking pan, ungreased

BASE

2 cups	all-purpose flour	500 mL
2 tbsp	granulated sugar	25 mL
Pinch	salt	Pinch
¾ cup	butter	175 mL
1	egg, lightly beaten	1

FILLING

⅓ cup	all-purpose flour	75 mL
⅓ cup	packed brown sugar	75 mL
1 tbsp	butter or margarine, softened	15 mL
	Zest of 1 orange	
½ tsp	ground cinnamon	2 mL
5	apples (preferably Granny Smith), peeled and thinly sliced	5

TOPPING

2 tbsp	granulated sugar	25 mL
½ tsp	ground cinnamon	2 mL

1. *Prepare the base:* In a medium bowl, mix together flour, sugar and salt. Using two knives, a pastry blender or your fingers, cut butter in until mixture resembles coarse crumbs. Add egg and mix until a dough forms. Shape into two equal balls; wrap dough tightly in plastic wrap and chill for about 1 hour.

2. On a floured work surface, roll out one portion of the dough to fit the bottom of pan. If necessary, cut dough to fit.

3. *Prepare the filling:* In another bowl, mix together flour, brown sugar, butter, zest, cinnamon and apples. Spread evenly over dough. Roll out the remaining dough as for first portion and place on top of apple mixture, cutting to fit the pan.

4. *Prepare the topping:* In a small bowl, mix together sugar and cinnamon; sprinkle over top of base.

5. Bake in preheated oven for 40 to 50 minutes or until golden brown. Place pan on a wire rack to cool completely, then cut into bars.

Tip *A wet knife does a smoother job of cutting fresh bars, squares or brownies.*

Sliced Apple Bars

Makes 36 bars
- Preheat oven to 375°F (190°C)
- 13- by 9-inch (3 L) baking pan, greased

BASE

4 cups	all-purpose flour	1 L
2 cups	granulated sugar	500 mL
½ tsp	salt	2 mL
1 cup	butter or margarine	250 mL

TOPPING

5 cups	peeled sliced tart apples	1.25 L
1 tsp	ground cinnamon	5 mL

1. *Prepare the base:* In a large bowl, mix together flour, sugar and salt. Using two knives, a pastry blender, or your fingers, cut butter in until mixture resembles coarse crumbs. Scoop out ½ cup (125 mL) of mixture and set aside. Spread half of remainder evenly in prepared pan. Bake in preheated oven for 10 minutes. Place pan on a wire rack to cool slightly.

2. *Prepare the topping:* In a large bowl, mix together apples, cinnamon and reserved base mixture. Spread evenly over warm base. Top with the remaining base mixture. Bake in preheated oven for 30 to 35 minutes or until lightly browned. Place pan on a rack to cool completely, then cut into bars.

Tip *To prevent sliced apples from turning brown, soak them for 10 minutes in moderately salted water after slicing.*

Cinnamon Applesauce Squares

Makes 36 squares
- Preheat oven to 350°F (180°C)
- 13- by 9-inch (3 L) baking pan, greased

BASE AND TOPPING

3 cups	all-purpose flour	750 mL
¼ cup	granulated sugar	50 mL
1 tbsp	baking powder	15 mL
1½ tsp	salt	7 mL
⅓ cup	butter or margarine	75 mL
2	eggs, beaten	2
6 to 8 tbsp	milk	90 to 120 mL

FILLING

2 cups	sweetened applesauce	500 mL
	Ground cinnamon	

GLAZE

1	egg yolk	1
1 tbsp	cold water	15 mL
	Granulated sugar	

1. *Prepare the base and topping:* In a large bowl, mix together flour, sugar, baking powder and salt. Using two knives, a pastry blender or your fingers, cut butter in until mixture resembles coarse crumbs. Add eggs and enough milk to make a dough, mixing lightly with a fork. Form dough into a ball and divide into two equal portions.

2. On a floured work surface, roll one portion into a rectangle, just a bit larger than the pan. Ease pastry into the bottom of prepared pan, bringing the dough a bit up the sides.

3. *Prepare the filling:* Spread applesauce evenly over dough and sprinkle lightly with cinnamon. Roll out the remaining dough as for first portion and place on top of applesauce mixture. Seal the edges.

4. *Prepare the glaze:* Beat egg yolk and water and brush base with the mixture, then sprinkle generously with sugar. Bake in preheated oven for 40 to 45 minutes or until well browned. Place pan on a wire rack and let cool completely, then cut into squares. Serve warm or cooled.

Apricot Crumble Squares

Makes 16 squares
- Preheat oven to 400°F (200°C)
- 8-inch (2 L) square baking pan, ungreased

BASE

2 cups	all-purpose flour	500 mL
½ tsp	baking powder	2 mL
¼ tsp	salt	1 mL
½ cup	butter, softened	125 mL
⅓ cup	granulated sugar	75 mL
1	egg	1
1 tsp	vanilla	5 mL

TOPPING

2 cups	sliced apricots (drained if canned)	500 mL
1 tsp	granulated sugar	5 mL
½ tsp	ground cinnamon	2 mL

1. *Prepare the base:* In a medium bowl, mix together flour, baking powder and salt.

2. In a large bowl, beat butter and sugar until smooth and creamy. Beat in egg and vanilla. Blend in flour mixture, just until a dough forms. Spread dough evenly in pan. Bake in preheated oven for 6 to 7 minutes, until lightly browned.

3. *Prepare the topping:* Arrange apricots evenly over top of base. Sprinkle with sugar and cinnamon.

4. Bake for 10 to 12 minutes or until golden brown. Place pan on a wire rack to cool completely, then cut into squares.

Cream Cheese–Frosted Banana Bars

Makes 36 bars

- Preheat oven to 350°F (180°C)
- 13- by 9-inch (3 L) baking pan, greased

BASE

2 cups	all-purpose flour	500 mL
1 tsp	baking soda	5 mL
Pinch	salt	Pinch
2 cups	granulated sugar	500 mL
½ cup	butter or margarine, softened	125 mL
3	eggs	3
1 tsp	vanilla	5 mL
1½ cups	mashed ripe bananas (3 to 4 large)	375 mL

FROSTING

1	package (8 oz/250 g) cream cheese, softened	1
½ cup	butter or margarine, softened	125 mL
2 tsp	vanilla	10 mL
3½ to 4 cups	confectioner's (icing) sugar, sifted	875 mL to 1 L

1. *Prepare the base:* In a medium bowl, mix together flour, baking soda and salt.

2. In a large bowl, beat sugar and butter until smooth and creamy. Beat in eggs, one at a time, until incorporated. Stir in vanilla, then bananas. Blend in flour mixture. Spread evenly in prepared pan. Bake in preheated oven for 30 to 35 minutes or until a tester inserted in the center comes out clean. Place pan on a wire rack to cool completely.

3. *Prepare the frosting:* Beat cream cheese and butter until smooth and creamy. Stir in vanilla. Gradually beat in confectioner's sugar until smooth and spreadable. Spread over top of cooled cake and cut into bars.

Tip *Protect the finish on nonstick baking pans by using a plastic knife to cut bars or squares.*

Banana Oatmeal Crunch Squares

Makes 36 squares

- Preheat oven to 350°F (180°C)
- 13- by 9-inch (3 L) baking pan, greased

BASE

2 cups	all-purpose flour	500 mL
1 cup	old-fashioned rolled oats	250 mL
2 tsp	baking powder	10 mL
1 tsp	baking soda	5 mL
½ tsp	salt	2 mL
¼ tsp	ground nutmeg	1 mL
½ cup	shortening, softened	125 mL
1¼ cups	granulated sugar	300 mL
2	eggs	2
1 tsp	vanilla	5 mL
¾ cup	buttermilk	175 mL
1½ cups	mashed ripe bananas (4 to 5 medium)	375 mL

TOPPING

¼ cup	shortening	50 mL
¾ cup	packed brown sugar	175 mL
⅓ cup	evaporated milk	75 mL
1½ cups	flaked coconut (sweetened or unsweetened)	375 mL
¾ cup	chopped walnuts	175 mL

1. *Prepare the base:* In a medium bowl, mix together flour, oats, baking powder, baking soda, salt and nutmeg.

2. In a large bowl, beat shortening and sugar until smooth and creamy. Beat in eggs until incorporated. Stir in vanilla. Blend in flour mixture alternately with buttermilk, then bananas, until just incorporated. Spread evenly in prepared pan. Bake in preheated oven for 35 to 40 minutes or until a tester inserted in the center comes out clean. Place pan on a wire rack to cool slightly.

3. *Prepare the topping:* Preheat broiler. In a saucepan, over low heat, melt shortening. Remove from heat and stir in brown sugar, milk, coconut and walnuts. Spread evenly over top of warm cake. Place pan under broiler and broil until top is golden brown. Place pan on a rack to cool completely, then cut into squares.

Tip *To ripen green bananas quickly, wrap them in newspaper.*

Banana Chocolate Chip Oatmeal Bars

Makes 36 bars
- Preheat oven to 350°F (180°C)
- 13- by 9-inch (3 L) baking pan, greased

1 cup	packed brown sugar	250 mL
3/4 cup	butter or margarine, softened	175 mL
1	egg	1
1/2 tsp	salt	2 mL
1 1/4 cups	mashed ripe bananas (4 medium)	300 mL
4 cups	old-fashioned rolled oats	1 L
1/2 cup	semisweet chocolate chips	125 mL
1/2 cup	raisins	125 mL

1. In a large bowl, beat brown sugar and butter until smooth and creamy. Beat in egg, salt and bananas until well combined. Stir in oats, chocolate chips and raisins and mix thoroughly.

2. Spread evenly in prepared pan. Bake in preheated oven for 50 to 60 minutes or until a tester inserted in the center comes out clean. Place pan on a wire rack to cool completely, then cut into bars.

Blueberry Cheesecake Shortbread Bars

Makes 36 bars
- Preheat oven to 350°F (180°C)
- 13- by 9-inch (3 L) baking pan, greased

BASE

2 cups	all-purpose flour	500 mL
1/2 cup	packed brown sugar	125 mL
1/2 tsp	salt	2 mL
3/4 cup	butter	175 mL

TOPPING

2	packages (each 8 oz/250 g) cream cheese, softened	2
3/4 cup	granulated sugar	175 mL
2	eggs	2
1 tsp	vanilla	5 mL
3/4 cup	blueberry preserves	175 mL

1. *Prepare the base:* In a medium bowl, mix together flour, brown sugar and salt. Using two knives, a pastry blender or your fingers, cut butter in until mixture resembles coarse crumbs. Press evenly into prepared pan. Bake in preheated oven for 18 to 20 minutes, until lightly browned.

2. *Prepare the topping:* In a medium bowl, beat cream cheese and sugar until smooth. Add eggs and beat until incorporated. Stir in vanilla.

3. Spread blueberry preserves evenly over hot base. Spread evenly with cream cheese mixture. Bake for 25 to 30 minutes or until slightly puffed. Place pan on a wire rack to cool completely, then cut into bars. Store, covered, in refrigerator.

Blueberry Pie Squares

Makes 36 squares
- Preheat oven to 350°F (180°C)
- 13- by 9-inch (3 L) baking pan, greased

1 cup	butter or margarine, softened	250 mL
1 1/2 cups	granulated sugar	375 mL
4	eggs	4
1 tsp	almond extract	5 mL
2 tsp	baking powder	10 mL
2 cups	all-purpose flour	500 mL
1	can (19 oz/540 mL) blueberry pie filling	1

1. In a large bowl, beat butter and sugar until smooth and creamy. Beat in eggs, one at a time, until incorporated. Stir in almond extract. Blend in baking powder and flour. Spread evenly in prepared pan. Top with large spoonfuls of pie filling, 4 along the length and 4 across the width.

2. Bake in preheated oven for 45 to 50 minutes or until golden brown. (The blueberry filling will sink into the cake while baking.) Place pan on a rack to cool completely, then cut into squares.

Cherry Cheesecake Bars

Makes 24 bars
- Preheat oven to 350°F (180°C)
- 9-inch (2.5 L) square baking pan, greased

BASE

6 tbsp	butter or margarine, melted	90 mL
1 1/2 cups	graham wafer crumbs (about 22 wafers)	375 mL
2 tbsp	granulated sugar	25 mL

TOPPING

1 1/2	packages (each 8 oz/250 g) cream cheese, softened	1 1/2
1/2 cup	granulated sugar	125 mL
2	eggs	2
1 1/2 tsp	vanilla	7 mL
1 cup	cherry pie filling	250 mL

1. *Prepare the base:* In a small bowl, mix together butter, graham crumbs and sugar. Press evenly into prepared pan. Bake in preheated oven for 10 minutes or until golden brown. Place pan on a wire rack to cool.
2. *Prepare the topping:* In a medium bowl, beat cream cheese and sugar until smooth. Beat in eggs until incorporated. Stir in vanilla.
3. Spread evenly over cooled base. Spoon pie filling over cream cheese mixture, then run a knife through the batter to create a marbling effect.
4. Bake for 40 to 45 minutes or until top is almost set. Place pan on a wire rack to cool completely, then store in refrigerator until ready to serve. Cut into bars.

Crabapple Jelly Bars

Makes 24 bars
- Preheat oven to 350°F (180°C)
- 9-inch (2.5 L) square baking pan, greased

BASE

1½ cups	all-purpose flour	375 mL
¼ cup	granulated sugar	50 mL
Pinch	salt	Pinch
1 cup	shredded Cheddar cheese	250 mL
½ cup	finely chopped pecans	125 mL
¾ cup	butter or margarine	175 mL

TOPPING

1 cup	crabapple jelly	250 mL

1. *Prepare the base:* In a large bowl, mix together flour, sugar, salt, cheese and nuts. Using two knives, a pastry blender or your fingers, work butter in until mixture resembles coarse crumbs. Press half of mixture evenly into prepared pan.
2. *Prepare the topping:* Stir crabapple jelly to loosen; spoon evenly over top. Sprinkle with the remaining crumb mixture.
3. Bake in preheated oven for 25 to 30 minutes or until golden brown. Place pan on a wire rack to cool completely, then cut into bars.

Tip *To keep salt easy to pour, add a few grains of rice to the salt shaker.*

Cranberry Streusel Bars

Makes 36 bars
- Preheat oven to 350°F (180°C)
- 13- by 9-inch (3 L) baking pan, lightly greased

BASE

⅓ cup	confectioner's (icing) sugar, sifted	75 mL
¾ cup	butter, softened	175 mL
1½ cups	all-purpose flour	375 mL

FILLING

1	package (8 oz/250 g) cream cheese, softened	1
1	can (10 oz/300 mL) sweetened condensed milk	1
¼ cup	freshly squeezed lemon juice	50 mL
1 tbsp	packed brown sugar	15 mL
2 tbsp	cornstarch	25 mL
1	can (14 oz/398 mL) whole-berry cranberry sauce	1

TOPPING

⅓ cup	all-purpose flour	75 mL
2 tbsp	packed brown sugar	25 mL
¼ cup	butter, softened	50 mL
¾ cup	chopped walnuts	175 mL

1. *Prepare the base:* In a medium bowl, beat confectioner's sugar and butter until smooth and creamy. Gradually blend in flour. Spread evenly in prepared pan. Bake in preheated oven for 15 minutes or until lightly browned. Place pan on a rack to cool slightly.
2. *Prepare the filling:* In another medium bowl, beat cream cheese until smooth. Gradually beat in condensed milk. Stir in lemon juice. Spread mixture evenly over warm base.
3. In another medium bowl, mix together brown sugar and cornstarch. Add cranberry sauce and mix well. Spread over cream cheese layer.
4. *Prepare the topping:* In a clean bowl, mix together flour and brown sugar. Using two knives, a pastry blender, or your fingers, cut butter in until mixture resembles coarse crumbs. Stir in nuts. Sprinkle over cranberry layer. Bake for 30 to 35 minutes or until bubbly and golden brown. Place pan on a rack and cut into bars. Serve warm or cooled.

Tip *If brown sugar is caked and hard, place it in a jar with half an apple. Close lid tight and let stand for 1 day. Remove apple, fluff up sugar with a fork and put lid on tightly until ready to use.*

Deluxe Lemon Bars

Makes 36 bars
- Preheat oven to 350ºF (180ºC)
- 13- by 9-inch (3 L) baking pan, ungreased

BASE

1 cup	butter or margarine, softened	250 mL
1/2 cup	confectioner's (icing) sugar, sifted	125 mL
2 cups	all-purpose flour	500 mL

TOPPING

4	eggs	4
1 1/2 cups	granulated sugar	375 mL
2 tsp	grated lemon zest	10 mL
1/3 cup	freshly squeezed lemon juice	75 mL
1/4 cup	all-purpose flour	50 mL
1/2 tsp	baking powder	2 mL
	Confectioner's (icing) sugar	

1. *Prepare the base:* In a medium bowl, beat butter and confectioner's sugar until smooth and creamy. Gradually blend in flour, just until a soft dough forms. Press evenly into pan. Bake in preheated oven for 20 to 25 minutes or until golden brown.

2. *Prepare the topping:* In another medium bowl, beat eggs, sugar, lemon juice and zest until blended. Gradually blend in flour and baking powder.

3. Spread evenly over base. Bake for 25 minutes. Place pan on a wire rack to cool completely. Sift confectioner's sugar over top and cut into bars.

Tip *Let bars, squares and brownies cool thoroughly before slicing. They will cut more easily and keep their shape better.*

Sour Cream–Topped Lemon Bars

Makes 36 bars
- Preheat oven to 350ºF (180ºC)
- 13- by 9-inch (3 L) baking pan, greased

BASE

1 1/2 cups	all-purpose flour	375 mL
1/2 cup	confectioner's (icing) sugar, sifted	125 mL
1 tsp	grated lemon zest	5 mL
1 tsp	grated orange zest	5 mL
3/4 cup	cold butter or margarine, cut into cubes	175 mL

FILLING

2 cups	granulated sugar	500 mL
1/4 cup	all-purpose flour	50 mL
1 tsp	baking powder	5 mL
4	eggs, beaten	4
2 tsp	grated lemon zest	10 mL
1/3 cup	freshly squeezed lemon juice	75 mL
2 tsp	grated orange zest	10 mL

TOPPING

1/3 cup	granulated sugar	75 mL
2 cups	sour cream	500 mL
1/2 tsp	vanilla	2 mL

1. *Prepare the base:* In a food processor, combine flour and confectioner's sugar. Pulse twice to combine. Add zests and butter and process until mixture begins to form a ball. Press evenly into prepared pan. Bake in preheated oven for 12 to 15 minutes or until lightly browned.

2. *Prepare the filling:* In a bowl, mix together sugar, flour and baking powder. Add eggs, lemon zest and juice and orange zest and mix until blended.

3. Spread mixture evenly over hot base. Bake for 14 to 16 minutes or until set.

4. *Prepare the topping:* In a medium bowl, mix together sugar, sour cream and vanilla. Spread over filling.

5. Bake for 8 to 10 minutes or until set. Place pan on a wire rack to cool completely, then store, covered, in refrigerator. Before serving, cut into bars.

Tip *Use a pastry brush to dislodge pieces of lemon or orange zest from the holes of a grater before washing.*

Lemon Cream Cheese Bars

Makes 36 bars
- Preheat oven to 350º F (180º C)
- 13- by 9-inch (3 L) baking pan, ungreased

BASE

1	package (18 oz/510 g) yellow cake mix	1
1	egg	1
1/3 cup	vegetable oil	75 mL

TOPPING

1	package (8 oz/250 g) cream cheese, softened	1
1/3 cup	granulated sugar	75 mL
1	egg	1
1 tsp	freshly squeezed lemon juice	5 mL

1. *Prepare the base:* In a medium bowl, mix together cake mix, egg and oil until mixture resembles coarse crumbs. Set aside 1 cup (250 mL) of mixture. Press remainder evenly into prepared pan. Bake in preheated oven for 15 minutes.

2. *Prepare the topping:* In another medium bowl, beat cream cheese and sugar until smooth. Add egg and beat until incorporated. Stir in lemon juice.

3. Spread evenly over hot base. Sprinkle with reserved crumb mixture. Bake for 15 minutes or until lightly browned. Place pan on a wire rack to cool completely, then cut into bars.

● ●

Lemon Ginger Bars

Makes 36 bars
- Preheat oven to 350°F (180°C)
- 13- by 9-inch (3 L) baking pan, greased

3 cups	all-purpose flour	750 mL
1½ tsp	baking soda	7 mL
1½ tsp	salt	7 mL
1 tsp	ground cinnamon	5 mL
1 tsp	ground ginger	5 mL
1 cup	shortening, softened	250 mL
1 cup	granulated sugar	250 mL
2	eggs	2
1 cup	light (fancy) molasses	250 mL
1 cup	hot water	250 mL
LEMON SAUCE		
1 cup	water	250 mL
½ cup	granulated sugar	125 mL
2 tsp	cornstarch	10 mL
Pinch	salt	Pinch
Pinch	ground nutmeg	Pinch
2	egg yolks	2
2 tbsp	butter or margarine	25 mL
½ tsp	grated lemon zest	2 mL
2 tbsp	freshly squeezed lemon juice	25 mL

1. In a medium bowl, mix together flour, baking soda, salt, cinnamon and ginger.

2. In a large bowl, beat shortening and sugar until smooth and creamy. Add eggs, one at a time, beating until incorporated. Beat in molasses. Gradually blend in flour mixture alternately with hot water, stirring until just incorporated.

3. Spread evenly in prepared pan. Bake in preheated oven for 35 to 40 minutes or until a tester inserted in the center comes out clean. Place pan on a rack to cool completely, then cut into bars.

4. *Prepare the lemon sauce:* In a saucepan, over medium heat, stir water, sugar, cornstarch, salt and nutmeg until smooth and bubbly. Cook and stir for 2 minutes. Remove from heat.

5. In a small bowl, beat egg yolks with 2 tbsp (25 mL) of the cornstarch mixture. Stir into the remaining cornstarch mixture and return to heat. Cook over low heat, stirring constantly, for 2 minutes. Remove from heat and stir in butter, zest and juice until blended. Serve over warm or cold cake. Store, covered, in refrigerator.

Variation *Top each bar with a dollop of whipped cream cheese and spoon lemon sauce over top.*

● ●

Almond Lemon Bars

Makes about 36 bars
- Preheat oven to 325°F (160°C)
- 2 baking sheets, ungreased

BASE		
1¾ cups	all-purpose flour	425 mL
2 tsp	baking powder	10 mL
¼ tsp	salt	1 mL
½ cup	butter or margarine, softened	125 mL
1 cup	granulated sugar	250 mL
1	egg	1
	Grated zest of 1 lemon	
TOPPING		
	Milk	
¾ cup	sliced almonds	175 mL
GLAZE		
4 tsp	freshly squeezed lemon juice	20 mL
1 cup	confectioner's (icing) sugar, sifted	250 mL

1. *Prepare the base:* In a small bowl, mix together flour, baking powder and salt.

2. In a large bowl, beat butter and sugar until smooth and creamy. Beat in egg and lemon zest until incorporated. Blend in flour mixture.

3. Divide dough into four portions. Shape each portion into a log about 12 inches (30 cm) long. Place two rolls on each sheet, about 4 inches (10 cm) apart. Using your hand, flatten each roll to a width of about 2½ inches (6 cm).

4. *Prepare the topping:* Brush rolls with milk. Sprinkle almonds on top and press lightly into dough. Bake for 12 to 15 minutes or until lightly browned. Place pans on wire racks to cool.

5. *Prepare the glaze:* In a small bowl, beat lemon juice and confectioner's sugar until smooth and spreadable. Drizzle glaze over top of rolls and set aside until set. Cut diagonally into bars.

Lemon Pecan Diamonds

Makes 36 diamonds

- Preheat oven to 350°F (180°C)
- 13- by 9-inch (3 L) baking pan, ungreased

BASE

2 cups	all-purpose flour	500 mL
½ cup	chopped pecans	125 mL
⅓ cup	granulated sugar	75 mL
¼ tsp	salt	1 mL
¾ cup	shortening	175 mL

TOPPING

4	eggs	4
1½ cups	granulated sugar	375 mL
1 tbsp	grated lemon zest	15 mL
½ cup	freshly squeezed lemon juice	125 mL
1 tsp	baking powder	5 mL
	Confectioner's (icing) sugar (optional)	

1. *Prepare the base:* In a food processor, combine flour, pecans, sugar and salt. Pulse twice to combine, then add shortening and process until mixture resembles fine crumbs. Press evenly into pan. Bake in preheated oven for 15 to 18 minutes, until golden brown. Place pan on a wire rack to cool slightly.

2. *Prepare the topping:* In a medium bowl, beat eggs and sugar until blended and thick. Stir in lemon zest and juice. Add baking powder and mix well. Spread mixture evenly over warm base. Bake for 25 minutes or until topping sets. Place pan on a wire rack to cool completely. Sift confectioner's sugar over top, if desired. Cut into diamonds. (For technique, see Coffee Mocha Cheesecake Diamonds, page 264.)

Glazed Lemon Poppy Seed Squares

Makes 16 squares

- Preheat oven to 350°F (180°C)
- 8-inch (2 L) square baking pan, greased

BASE

1½ cups	all-purpose flour	375 mL
¾ tsp	baking soda	4 mL
1 cup	granulated sugar	250 mL
¾ cup	butter, softened	175 mL
3	eggs, separated	3
2 tsp	vanilla	10 mL
¾ cup	sour cream	175 mL
¼ cup	poppy seeds	50 mL
2 tbsp	grated lemon zest	25 mL
2 tbsp	granulated sugar	25 mL

GLAZE

¼ cup	freshly squeezed lemon juice	50 mL
½ cup	granulated sugar	125 mL

TOPPING

1 cup	whipping (35%) cream	250 mL
2 tbsp	granulated sugar	25 mL
1 tsp	lemon extract	5 mL
	Grated lemon zest (optional)	

1. *Prepare the base:* In a small bowl, mix together flour and baking soda.

2. In a large bowl, beat the 1 cup (250 mL) sugar and butter until smooth and creamy. Beat in egg yolks, one at a time, until incorporated. Stir in vanilla. Gradually blend in flour mixture, alternately with sour cream, until just incorporated. Stir in poppy seeds and lemon zest.

3. In a clean bowl, beat egg whites until foamy. Add the 2 tbsp (25 mL) sugar and beat until stiff peaks form. Fold into batter and spread evenly in prepared pan.

4. Bake in preheated oven for 60 to 65 minutes or until a tester inserted in the center comes out clean. Place pan on a wire rack to cool for 10 minutes, then invert cake onto rack with waxed paper placed underneath.

5. *Prepare the glaze:* Mix together lemon juice and sugar until blended. Spoon over warm cake.

6. *Prepare the topping:* In a large bowl, beat cream until frothy. Add sugar and lemon extract and beat until soft peaks form. Spread evenly over glaze. Sprinkle lemon zest over top, if desired. Cut into squares.

Tip *For an attractive dessert, cut lemons in half, scoop out the pulp and hollow out shells. Then fill the shells with scoops of lemon sherbet or fresh fruit salad.*

Lemon Walnut Squares

Makes 16 squares

- Preheat oven to 350°F (180°C)
- 8-inch (2 L) square baking pan, lightly greased

BASE

½ cup	butter	125 mL
¼ cup	confectioner's (icing) sugar, sifted	50 mL
Pinch	salt	Pinch
1 cup	all-purpose flour	250 mL
⅓ cup	finely chopped walnuts	75 mL

TOPPING

¾ cup	granulated sugar	175 mL
2	eggs	2
1 tbsp	grated lemon zest	15 mL
¼ cup	freshly squeezed lemon juice	50 mL
2 tbsp	all-purpose flour	25 mL
½ tsp	baking powder	2 mL
	Confectioner's (icing) sugar (optional)	

1. *Prepare the base:* In a medium bowl, beat butter and sugar until smooth and creamy. Add salt and blend well. Gradually blend in flour, mixing until crumbly. Stir in walnuts. Press evenly into prepared pan. Bake in preheated oven for 20 to 25 minutes or until golden brown. Place pan on a rack to cool slightly.

2. *Prepare the topping:* In a small bowl, beat sugar, eggs, lemon zest and juice until blended. Blend in flour and baking powder. Spoon over baked base. Bake for 25 to 30 minutes or until center is set. Place pan on a rack to cool completely. If desired, sift confectioner's sugar lightly over top. Cut into squares.

Lemon Coconut Tea Squares

Makes 16 squares

- Preheat oven to 350ºF (180ºC)
- 8-inch (2 L) square baking pan, ungreased

BASE

½ cup	butter or margarine, softened	125 mL
⅓ cup	confectioner's (icing) sugar, sifted	75 mL
¾ cup	all-purpose flour	175 mL
⅓ cup	ground almonds	75 mL

TOPPING

2	eggs	2
1 cup	granulated sugar	250 mL
½ tsp	baking powder	2 mL
¼ tsp	salt	1 mL
1 tsp	grated lemon zest	5 mL
2 tbsp	freshly squeezed lemon juice	25 mL
¾ cup	flaked coconut (sweetened or unsweetened)	175 mL

1. *Prepare the base:* In a medium bowl, beat butter and confectioner's sugar until smooth and creamy. Gradually blend in flour just until a soft dough forms. Stir in almonds. Press mixture evenly into pan. Bake in preheated oven for 20 minutes.

2. *Prepare the topping:* In another medium bowl, beat eggs, sugar, baking powder, salt, lemon zest and juice until blended. Stir in coconut.

3. Spread mixture evenly over hot base. Bake for 25 to 30 minutes or until top is golden brown. Place pan on a wire rack to cool completely, then cut into squares.

Coconut Crisp Lemon Squares

Makes 16 squares

- Preheat oven to 350ºF (180ºC)
- 8-inch (2 L) square baking pan, ungreased

BASE

1 cup	all-purpose flour	250 mL
¾ cup	finely crushed saltine crackers (about 18 crackers)	175 mL
½ cup	flaked coconut (sweetened or unsweetened)	125 mL
½ tsp	baking soda	2 mL
½ tsp	salt	2 mL
6 tbsp	butter or margarine, softened	90 mL
¾ cup	packed brown sugar	175 mL

TOPPING

1 cup	water	250 mL
¾ cup	granulated sugar	175 mL
2 tbsp	cornstarch	25 mL
¼ tsp	salt	1 mL
2	egg yolks, beaten	2
½ tsp	grated lemon zest	2 mL
½ cup	freshly squeezed lemon juice	125 mL

1. *Prepare the base:* In a bowl, mix together flour, cracker crumbs, coconut, baking soda and salt.

2. In a large bowl, beat butter and brown sugar until smooth and creamy. Blend in flour mixture. Set aside half of mixture and press remainder evenly into prepared pan. Bake in preheated oven for 10 minutes or until lightly browned. Place pan on a wire rack to cool slightly.

3. *Prepare the topping:* In a saucepan, over medium heat, stir water, sugar, cornstarch and salt until smooth and bubbly. Cook, stirring constantly, for 2 minutes. Remove from heat.

4. In a small bowl, beat egg yolks with 2 tbsp (25 mL) of the cornstarch mixture. Stir into the remaining cornstarch mixture and return to heat. Cook over low heat, stirring constantly, for 2 minutes. Stir in lemon zest and juice.

5. Spread evenly over baked base and sprinkle reserved crumb mixture over top. Bake for 30 minutes or until golden brown. Place pan on a rack to cool completely, then cut into squares.

Tip *A medium-sized lemon yields about 2 to 3 tbsp (25 to 45 mL) of juice and 1 tbsp (15 mL) grated zest.*

Favorite Glazed Lemon Raspberry Bars

Makes 36 bars
- Preheat oven to 350ºF (180ºC)
- 13- by 9-inch (3 L) baking pan, greased

BASE

1½ cups	all-purpose flour	375 mL
½ cup	confectioner's (icing) sugar, sifted	125 mL
¾ cup	butter	175 mL

TOPPING

½ cup	raspberry jam	125 mL
4	eggs	4
1½ cups	granulated sugar	375 mL
½ cup	freshly squeezed lemon juice	125 mL
3 tbsp	all-purpose flour	45 mL
1 tsp	baking powder	5 mL

GLAZE

½ cup	confectioner's (icing) sugar, sifted	125 mL
1 tbsp	butter or margarine, melted	15 mL
1 tbsp	freshly squeezed lemon juice	15 mL

1. *Prepare the base:* In a medium bowl, mix together flour and confectioner's sugar. Using two knives, a pastry blender or your fingers, cut butter in until mixture resembles coarse crumbs. Press evenly into prepared pan. Bake in preheated oven for 15 to 18 minutes, until golden brown.

2. *Prepare the topping:* Stir jam until smooth and spread evenly over warm base.

3. In a medium bowl, beat eggs and sugar until thick. Stir in lemon juice. Blend in flour and baking powder. Spread over jam. Bake for 20 to 25 minutes or until golden brown. Place pan on a rack to cool completely.

4. *Prepare the glaze:* In a small bowl, beat confectioner's sugar, melted butter and lemon juice until smooth. Spread over cooled cake, then cut into bars.

Tip *To sprinkle lemon juice, use a small plastic or glass salt shaker with a non-metallic top.*

"Groovy" Raspberry Lemon Bars

Makes 20 bars
- Preheat oven to 350ºF (180ºC)
- Baking sheet, ungreased

BASE

1 cup	butter, softened	250 mL
½ cup	confectioner's (icing) sugar, sifted	125 mL
1	egg yolk	1
1 tsp	vanilla	5 mL
2½ cups	all-purpose flour	625 mL

FILLING

	Raspberry jam	
½ cup	confectioner's (icing) sugar, sifted	125 mL
2 tsp	milk or whipping (35%) cream	10 mL
2 tsp	freshly squeezed lemon juice	10 mL

1. *Prepare the base:* In a large bowl, beat butter and confectioner's sugar until smooth and creamy. Beat in egg yolk and vanilla until incorporated. Gradually blend in flour. Wrap dough tightly in plastic wrap and refrigerate for at least 1 hour or up to 4 days.

2. When ready to use, divide dough into four portions. Shape each portion into a rope, about ¾ inches (2 cm) wide and 12 inches (30 cm) long. Place ropes on baking sheet, about 2 inches apart. With your little finger, press a groove down the center of each rope. Bake in preheated oven for 10 minutes or until firm to the touch.

3. *Prepare the filling:* Spoon raspberry jam into the grooves, down each rope. Return to preheated oven and bake for 5 to 10 minutes or until golden brown. Place pan on a wire rack.

4. In a small bowl, beat confectioner's sugar, milk and lemon juice until smooth and blended. Drizzle over hot strips. Let cool slightly, then cut, at an angle, into bars. The number of bars will depend on the thickness of the slices.

Tip *If a recipe calls for softened butter (at room temperature) and you are short of time, grate butter into a warm bowl. It will soften in no time.*

Lemon Blueberry Crumb Bars

Makes about 36 bars
- Preheat oven to 375º F (190º C)
- 13- by 9-inch (3 L) baking pan, greased

BASE

3 cups	all-purpose flour	750 mL
2 cups	old-fashioned rolled oats	500 mL
1⅔ cups	packed brown sugar	400 mL
1½ tsp	baking powder	7 mL
1¼ tsp	ground nutmeg	6 mL
½ tsp	salt	2 mL
1 tsp	grated lemon zest	5 mL
1¼ cups	butter or margarine, softened	300 mL
1	egg, beaten	1

TOPPING

1	egg	1
1	can (14 oz/398 mL) sweetened condensed milk	1
2 tsp	grated lemon zest	10 mL
½ cup	freshly squeezed lemon juice	125 mL
2 tbsp	all-purpose flour	25 mL
3 cups	blueberries, thawed if frozen	750 mL

1. *Prepare the base:* In a large bowl, mix together flour, oats, brown sugar, baking powder, nutmeg, salt and lemon zest. Using two knives, a pastry blender or your fingers, cut butter in until mixture resembles coarse crumbs. Set 2 cups (500 mL) aside. Add egg to the remaining mixture and mix until just combined. Spread evenly in prepared pan. Bake in preheated oven for 10 minutes.

2. *Prepare the topping:* In another large bowl, beat egg, condensed milk and lemon juice until smooth and blended. Blend in flour and lemon zest. Stir in blueberries.

3. Spread evenly over base. Sprinkle with reserved crumb mixture. Bake for 40 to 45 minutes or until lightly browned. Place pan on a wire rack to cool completely, then cut into bars.

Tip *A cake will be less likely to stick to the pan if the pan is placed on a cold wet towel upon removal from the oven.*

● ●

Lemon Sunburst Bars

Makes 36 bars

- Preheat oven to 350ºF (180ºC)
- 13- by 9-inch (3 L) baking pan, greased

1 cup	all-purpose flour	250 mL
1 tsp	baking powder	5 mL
¼ tsp	ground cinnamon	1 mL
¼ tsp	ground nutmeg	1 mL
1⅓ cups	packed brown sugar	325 mL
¾ cup	shortening, softened	175 mL
2	eggs	2
½ tsp	vanilla	2 mL
½ tsp	grated lemon zest	2 mL
2 tbsp	freshly squeezed lemon juice	25 mL
1 cup	quick-cooking rolled oats	250 mL
½ cup	chopped walnuts	125 mL
	Lemon Glaze or Lemon Butter Frosting (optional, see recipes, pages 549 and 544)	

1. In a small bowl, mix together flour, baking powder, cinnamon and nutmeg.

2. In a large bowl, beat brown sugar and shortening until smooth and creamy. Beat in eggs, one at a time, until incorporated. Stir in vanilla, lemon zest and juice. Blend in flour mixture. Stir in oats and walnuts.

3. Spread evenly in prepared pan. Bake in preheated oven for 20 to 25 minutes or until golden brown. (If desired, top with Lemon Glaze while still warm, or let cool and frost with Lemon Butter Frosting.) When cool, cut into bars.

● ●

Orange, Lemon and Lime Bars

Makes 36 bars

- Preheat oven to 350ºF (180ºC)
- 13- by 9-inch (3 L) baking pan, lined with greased foil

BASE

¾ cup	butter or margarine, softened	175 mL
½ cup	confectioner's (icing) sugar, sifted	125 mL
1½ cups	all-purpose flour	375 mL

TOPPING

3	eggs	3
1 cup	granulated sugar	250 mL
½ tsp	grated orange zest	2 mL
½ tsp	grated lemon zest	2 mL
½ tsp	grated lime zest	2 mL
2 tbsp	freshly squeezed orange juice	25 mL
2 tbsp	freshly squeezed lemon juice	25 mL
2 tbsp	freshly squeezed lime juice	25 mL
3 tbsp	all-purpose flour	45 mL
½ tsp	baking powder	2 mL
½ tsp	salt	2 mL
1 tbsp	confectioner's (icing) sugar	15 mL

1. *Prepare the base:* In a medium bowl, beat butter and confectioner's sugar until smooth and creamy. Gradually blend in flour, just until dough forms. Press evenly into prepared pan. Bake in preheated oven for 20 to 25 minutes or until lightly browned.

2. *Prepare the topping:* In a medium bowl, beat eggs, sugar, zests and juices until smooth and blended. Blend in flour, baking powder and salt.

3. Spread mixture evenly over hot base. Bake for 15 minutes or until topping is just set and golden brown. Sift confectioner's sugar over top. Place pan on a wire rack to cool completely, then transfer cake, with foil, to a cutting board and cut into bars.

Tip *Before squeezing citrus fruit for juice, grate the peel and freeze it for use in recipes requiring zest.*

Velvet Orange Squares

Makes 16 squares
- Preheat oven to 350°F (180°C)
- 8-inch (2 L) square baking pan, greased

BASE

1²⁄₃ cups	all-purpose flour	400 mL
1 tsp	baking powder	5 mL
½ tsp	baking soda	2 mL
¼ tsp	salt	1 mL
½ cup	butter or margarine, softened	125 mL
1 cup	granulated sugar	250 mL
2	eggs	2
1 tbsp	grated orange zest	15 mL
½ cup	freshly squeezed orange juice	125 mL
½ tsp	lemon extract	2 mL

GLAZE

½ cup	apricot jam	125 mL
½ cup	granulated sugar	125 mL
⅓ cup	water	75 mL
2	oranges, thinly sliced	2
	Granulated sugar	

1. *Prepare the base:* In a small bowl, mix together flour, baking powder, baking soda and salt.
2. In a large bowl, beat butter and sugar until smooth and creamy. Add eggs and beat until incorporated. Stir in orange zest, orange juice and lemon extract. Gradually blend in flour mixture.
3. Spread evenly in prepared pan. Bake in preheated oven for 35 to 40 minutes or until a tester inserted in the center comes out clean. Place pan on a wire rack to cool for 10 minutes. Invert onto rack to cool completely.
4. *Prepare the glaze:* In a saucepan, over low heat, stir jam for 5 to 10 minutes, until melted and smooth. Set aside to cool slightly. In another saucepan, over low heat, combine sugar and water, stirring constantly until sugar is syrupy. Add orange slices and simmer until softened and translucent. Using a slotted spoon, transfer orange slices onto a sheet of waxed paper. Sprinkle lightly with sugar. Let cool just enough to handle, then cut slices into quarters.
5. Spread half the jam over top of cake. Arrange orange pieces evenly over the jam layer, then brush with the remaining jam. Chill for at least 1 hour, then cut into squares.

Variation *If desired, substitute Orange Butter Frosting (page 544) or Easy Orange Frosting (page 548) for the glaze.*

Oatmeal Peach Crumble Squares

Makes 16 squares
- Preheat oven to 375°F (190°C)
- 8-inch (2 L) square baking pan, ungreased

BASE

4 cups	peeled sliced peaches (about 6 peaches)	1 L
1 cup	granulated sugar	250 mL
2 tbsp	freshly squeezed lemon juice	25 mL

TOPPING

3 cups	oatmeal muffin mix	750 mL
¼ tsp	ground nutmeg	1 mL
½ cup	butter or margarine	125 mL

1. *Prepare the base:* In a large bowl, mix together peaches, sugar and lemon juice. Spread evenly in pan.
2. *Prepare the topping:* In another large bowl, combine muffin mix and nutmeg. Using two knives, a pastry blender or your fingers, cut butter in until mixture resembles coarse crumbs.
3. Spoon over fruit. Bake in preheated oven for 40 to 45 minutes or until golden brown. Let cool slightly, then cut into squares.

Tip *These squares are particularly delicious served warm with ice cream.*

Peaches 'n' Cream Dessert Bars

Makes 36 bars
- Preheat oven to 350°F (180°C)
- 13- by 9-inch (3 L) baking pan, greased

BASE

2 cups	graham wafer crumbs	500 mL
⅓ cup	granulated sugar	75 mL
½ cup	sliced almonds	125 mL
6 tbsp	butter, melted	90 mL

FILLING

1½	packages (each 8 oz/250 g) cream cheese, softened	1½
½ cup	granulated sugar	125 mL
2	eggs	2
1 tsp	vanilla	5 mL

TOPPING

2 tbsp	all-purpose flour	25 mL
2 tbsp	cold butter, cut into pieces	25 mL
¼ cup	packed brown sugar	50 mL
½ cup	sliced almonds	125 mL
1 cup	peach jam	250 mL

1. *Prepare the base:* In a medium bowl, mix together graham wafer crumbs, sugar, almonds and melted butter. Press evenly into prepared pan. Bake in preheated oven for 10 minutes or until lightly browned. Place pan on a rack to cool slightly.
2. *Prepare the filling:* In a medium bowl, beat cream cheese and sugar until smooth. Beat in eggs until incorporated. Stir in vanilla.
3. Spread filling evenly over warm base. Bake for 15 minutes, until slightly puffed.
4. *Prepare the topping:* In a small bowl, combine flour, butter, brown sugar and almonds and mix together until crumbly. Set aside.
5. Stir jam until smooth, then spread evenly over filling. Sprinkle topping evenly over jam. Bake for 15 minutes or until hot and bubbly. Place pan on a wire rack to cool completely.

Cinnamon Nut Pear Bars

Makes 24 bars
- Preheat oven to 375° F (190° C)
- 9-inch (2.5 L) square baking pan, greased

BASE

2 cups	biscuit mix	500 mL
1/4 cup	granulated sugar	50 mL
1 tsp	ground cinnamon	5 mL
1	can (28 oz/796 mL) pears, drained and sliced, 1/2 cup (125 mL) liquid reserved	1
1	egg	1
1/2 tsp	vanilla	2 mL

TOPPING

1/4 cup	packed brown sugar	50 mL
1/4 cup	all-purpose flour	50 mL
2 tbsp	butter	25 mL
1/4 cup	chopped walnuts	50 mL

1. *Prepare the base:* In a bowl, mix together biscuit mix, sugar and cinnamon.
2. In a small bowl, whisk together reserved pear juice, egg and vanilla. Add to biscuit mixture, mixing just until a dough forms. Spread evenly in prepared pan. Arrange pears evenly over top.
3. *Prepare the topping:* In a small bowl mix together brown sugar and flour. Using two knives, a pastry blender or your fingers, cut butter in until mixture resembles coarse crumbs. Stir in walnuts.

4. Spoon evenly over pears. Bake in preheated oven for 30 to 35 minutes or until lightly browned around the edges. Place pan on a wire rack to cool completely, then cut into bars.

Tip *For an added touch, thinly slice a fresh pear, leaving the skin on, and place a slice on top of each bar.*

Pineapple Upside-Down Bars

Makes 12 large bars
- Preheat oven to 350°F (180°C)
- 8-inch (2 L) square baking pan, ungreased

2 tbsp	butter or margarine	25 mL
1/2 cup	packed brown sugar	125 mL
1	can (8 oz/227 mL) pineapple slices, drained, 1/2 cup (125 mL) juice reserved	1
4	maraschino cherries	4
1 1/4 cups	all-purpose flour	300 mL
2 tsp	baking powder	10 mL
1/2 tsp	salt	2 mL
1/3 cup	shortening, softened	75 mL
1/2 cup	granulated sugar	125 mL
1	egg	1
1/2 tsp	grated lemon zest (optional)	2 mL

1. In preheated oven, melt butter in baking pan. Remove from oven. Sprinkle brown sugar evenly over pan. Arrange 4 pineapple slices over the sugar and place a cherry in the center of each. Set aside.
2. In a small bowl, mix together, flour, baking powder and salt.
3. In another bowl, beat shortening and granulated sugar until smooth and creamy. Beat in egg until incorporated. Stir in lemon zest (if using). Gradually blend in flour mixture alternately with reserved pineapple juice until just incorporated.
4. Spread mixture evenly over pineapple. Bake in preheated oven for 30 to 35 minutes or until golden. Let stand for about 10 minutes and then invert onto a platter, leaving pan on top for a few minutes to allow the butter–brown sugar liquid to pour onto the cake. Let cool, then cut into bars. Top with whipped cream or ice cream, if desired.

Pineapple Carrot Bars

Makes 36 bars

- Preheat oven to 350°F (180°C)
- 13- by 9-inch (3 L) baking pan, lightly greased

½ cup	all-purpose flour	125 mL
½ cup	whole wheat flour	125 mL
1 tbsp	ground cinnamon	15 mL
1 tsp	baking powder	5 mL
1 tsp	baking soda	5 mL
½ cup	packed brown sugar	125 mL
2 tbsp	vegetable oil	25 mL
1	egg, beaten	1
1 tsp	vanilla	5 mL
¼ cup	milk	50 mL
1 cup	finely grated carrots	250 mL
½ cup	raisins	125 mL
⅔ cup	crushed unsweetened pineapple, drained	150 mL

1. In a large bowl, mix together all-purpose flour, whole wheat flour, cinnamon, baking powder and baking soda. Add brown sugar, oil, egg, vanilla and milk and mix until just blended. Stir in carrots, raisins, and pineapple.

2. Spread evenly in prepared pan. Bake in preheated oven for 25 minutes or until top is golden brown. Place pan on a wire rack to cool completely, then cut into bars. Store, covered, in refrigerator.

Raspberry Oat Granola Bars

Makes 16 bars

- Preheat oven to 375°F (190°C)
- 8-inch (2 L) square baking pan, greased

BASE

⅓ cup	quick-cooking rolled oats	75 mL
17	graham wafers, finely crushed	17
2 tbsp	granulated sugar	25 mL
1	egg white	1
1 tbsp	butter or margarine, melted	15 mL
1 tbsp	fruit juice or water	15 mL
⅓ cup	raisins	75 mL

TOPPING

1½ cups	raspberry jam	375 mL

1. *Prepare the base:* In a medium bowl, mix together oats, graham crumbs, sugar, egg white, butter and fruit juice. Set aside ¼ cup (50 mL) of mixture; stir raisins into the remainder.

2. Spread evenly in prepared pan. Bake in preheated oven for 7 minutes. Place pan on a wire rack to cool completely.

3. *Prepare the topping:* Stir jam until smooth. Spread evenly over cooled base. Sprinkle with reserved crumb mixture. Bake in preheated oven for 30 to 40 minutes or until bubbly. Run a knife around the edges of the pan, then place pan on a rack to cool completely. Cut into bars.

Scrumptious Strawberry Swirls

Makes 24 squares

- Preheat oven to 350°F (180°C)
- 9-inch (2.5 L) square baking pan, ungreased

BASE

2¼ cups	graham wafer crumbs (about 30 wafers)	550 mL
½ cup	butter, melted	125 mL

TOPPING

2	packages (each a 4-serving size) strawberry-flavored gelatin dessert mix	2
1⅓ cups	boiling water	325 mL
2	packages (each 10 oz/300 g) frozen unsweetened strawberries, thawed	2
1	package (10½ oz/300 g) miniature marshmallows	1
½ cup	milk	125 mL
1 cup	whipping (35%) cream, whipped	250 mL

1. *Prepare the base:* In a medium bowl, mix together graham crumbs and melted butter. Press evenly into pan.

2. *Prepare the topping:* In a large bowl, combine gelatin with boiling water and mix until gelatin dissolves. Add strawberries and mix well. Chill until almost set, stirring occasionally.

3. In the top of a double boiler, melt marshmallows in milk, stirring constantly until smooth. Transfer to refrigerator and chill until cold. When gelatin mixture is almost set, fold whipped cream into marshmallow mixture.

4. Alternate layers of marshmallow and gelatin mixtures over base, then run a knife through the layers to create a marbling effect. Refrigerate until ready to serve, then cut into squares.

Tip *If desired, set aside ¼ cup (50 mL) of graham wafer crumb mixture and sprinkle over top.*

Strawberry Rhubarb Meringue Bars

Makes 36 bars

- Preheat oven to 350°F (180°C)
- 13- by 9-inch (3 L) baking pan, ungreased

BASE

1¾ cups	all-purpose flour	425 mL
2 tbsp	confectioner's (icing) sugar, sifted	25 mL
½ cup	butter or margarine	125 mL

FILLING

1½ cups	granulated sugar	375 mL
¼ cup	all-purpose flour	50 mL
¼ tsp	salt	1 mL
6	egg yolks	6
1 cup	evaporated milk	250 mL
2 cups	sliced strawberries, thawed if frozen	500 mL
4 cups	sliced rhubarb (1 inch/2.5 cm thick), thawed if frozen	1 L
½ tsp	freshly squeezed lemon juice	2 mL

TOPPING

6	egg whites	6
½ cup	granulated sugar	125 mL

1. *Prepare the base:* In a medium bowl, mix together flour and confectioner's sugar. Using two knives, a pastry blender or your fingers, cut butter in until mixture resembles coarse crumbs. Press evenly into pan. Bake in preheated oven for 10 to 12 minutes. Place pan on a rack to cool slightly.

2. *Prepare the filling:* In a large bowl, mix together sugar, flour and salt. In another bowl, whisk egg yolks and milk. Add to flour mixture and mix until blended. Stir in strawberries, rhubarb and lemon juice.

3. Spread filling evenly over warm base and bake for 55 to 60 minutes or until filling is firm.

4. *Prepare the topping:* In a clean bowl, beat egg whites until foamy. Gradually add sugar, beating until stiff peaks form.

5. Spread over filling. Bake for 10 minutes or until meringue is nicely browned. Place pan on a wire rack to cool completely, then cut into bars.

Tip *Use only unsweetened strawberries and rhubarb in this recipe.*

Strawberry Rhubarb Crisp Bars

Makes 24 bars

- Preheat oven to 350°F (180°C)
- 9-inch (2.5 L) square baking pan, greased

BASE

½ cup	butter or margarine, melted	125 mL
¼ cup	granulated sugar	50 mL
1½ cups	graham wafer crumbs (about 22 wafers)	375 mL

TOPPING

3 cups	chopped rhubarb (1-inch/ 2.5 cm pieces), thawed if frozen	750 mL
1 cup	granulated sugar	250 mL
3 tbsp	cornstarch	45 mL
Pinch	ground cinnamon	Pinch
½ cup	cold milk	125 mL
1½ tsp	unflavored gelatin	7 mL
1	package (8 oz/250 g) cream cheese, softened	1
2 tbsp	granulated sugar	25 mL
1 cup	sliced fresh strawberries	250 mL

1. *Prepare the base:* In a medium bowl, mix together butter, sugar and crumbs. Set aside one-quarter of the mixture and press remainder evenly into prepared pan. Bake in preheated oven for 10 minutes or until golden brown. Place pan on a rack to cool slightly.

2. *Prepare the topping:* In a saucepan, combine rhubarb, sugar, cornstarch and cinnamon. Cook over low heat, stirring constantly, until sugar dissolves and mixture thickens. Simmer for 5 minutes, until rhubarb is tender. Remove from heat and set aside to cool.

3. In the top of a double boiler, sprinkle gelatin over milk. Let stand for 5 minutes, then stir over hot (not boiling) water until gelatin dissolves. Set aside to cool.

4. In a large bowl, beat cream cheese and sugar until smooth. Gradually add dissolved gelatin mixture and mix until blended. Stir in rhubarb mixture. Spread evenly over baked base. Sprinkle with reserved crumbs. Chill for at least 1 hour, then cut into bars.

Tip *If desired, garnish each bar with sliced strawberries.*

Rhubarb Crisp Squares

Makes 16 squares
- Preheat oven to 350°F (180°C)
- 8-inch (2 L) square baking pan, greased

FILLING

4 cups	chopped rhubarb, thawed if frozen	1 L
1 cup	granulated sugar	250 mL
2 tbsp	cornstarch	25 mL
1 tsp	grated orange zest	5 mL

BASE

1½ cups	all-purpose flour	375 mL
½ cup	packed brown sugar	125 mL
½ cup	chopped pecans	125 mL
1 tsp	ground cinnamon	5 mL
¼ tsp	salt	1 mL
½ cup	butter or margarine, softened	125 mL

1. *Prepare the filling:* In a saucepan, combine rhubarb, sugar, cornstarch and zest. Cook over medium heat, stirring constantly, for 5 minutes or until mixture thickens. Set aside to cool.

2. *Prepare the base:* In a medium bowl, mix together flour, brown sugar, pecans, cinnamon and salt. Using two knives, a pastry blender or your fingers, cut butter in until mixture resembles coarse crumbs. Set aside 1 cup (250 mL) and press remainder evenly in prepared pan.

3. Spread filling evenly over base and sprinkle reserved flour mixture evenly over top. Bake in preheated oven for 35 to 40 minutes or until golden brown. Place pan on a rack to cool completely, then cut into squares.

Tip *Allow bars, squares and brownies to cool completely before cutting. Then use a sharp knife and a gentle, sawing motion to avoid squashing the cake.*

Fresh Fruit Fiesta Bars

Makes 36 bars
- Preheat oven to 375°F (190°C)
- 13- by 9-inch (3 L) baking pan, ungreased

BASE

1¾ cups	all-purpose flour	425 mL
1½ cups	old-fashioned rolled oats	375 mL
½ tsp	ground cinnamon	2 mL
¾ cup	butter or margarine, softened	175 mL
1 cup	packed brown sugar	250 mL

TOPPING

1	can (10 oz/284 mL) mandarin orange segments, drained	1
1	banana, sliced	1
1 cup	cubed peeled apples	250 mL
½ cup	raisins	125 mL
¼ cup	orange juice	50 mL
1 tsp	ground cinnamon	5 mL

1. *Prepare the base:* In a medium bowl, mix together flour, rolled oats, and cinnamon.

2. In a large bowl, beat butter and sugar until smooth and creamy. Blend in flour mixture. Set aside 1¼ cups (300 mL). Press remainder evenly into pan. Bake in preheated oven for 15 minutes.

3. *Prepare the topping:* In a bowl, combine oranges, banana, apples, raisins, orange juice and cinnamon.

4. Spread topping evenly over warm base, leaving a space about ¼ inch (0.5 cm) from the edges. Sprinkle reserved base mixture over top, patting down gently. Bake for 15 to 20 minutes or until golden brown. Place pan on a wire rack to cool completely, then cut into bars.

Mixed Fruit Squares

Makes 30 squares
- Preheat oven to 400°F (200°C)
- Baking sheet, lightly greased

BASE

2 cups	all-purpose flour	500 mL
¾ tsp	salt	4 mL
1 cup	shortening	250 mL
1	egg	1
1 tbsp	white vinegar	15 mL
2 tbsp	cold water	25 mL

FILLING

1 cup	coarsely chopped dried apricots	250 mL
2	pears, peeled and sliced	2
2	apples, peeled and sliced	2
1½ tbsp	all-purpose flour	22 mL
¾ cup	water	175 mL
¼ cup	packed brown sugar	50 mL
¼ tsp	ground cinnamon	1 mL
1 tsp	grated lemon zest	5 mL
1 tbsp	freshly squeezed lemon juice	15 mL
	Confectioner's (icing) sugar	

1. *Prepare the base:* In a medium bowl, combine flour and salt. Using two knives, a pastry blender or your fingers, cut shortening in until mixture resembles coarse crumbs.

2. In another medium bowl, beat egg, vinegar and water just until blended. Blend in flour mixture and stir just until a soft dough forms. Divide dough in half, shaping each half into a ball. Wrap tightly in plastic wrap and chill for 15 to 20 minutes.

3. *Prepare the filling:* In a saucepan, over low heat, combine apricots, pears, apples and flour and stir to blend. Add water, brown sugar, cinnamon, zest and juice. Bring to a boil, stirring frequently, then cover and simmer for 15 minutes or until fruit is tender. Set aside to cool.

4. On a floured work surface, roll out one portion of dough to a 12- by 9-inch (30 by 23 cm) rectangle. Place on prepared baking sheet. Spoon filling evenly over top, leaving a $\frac{1}{2}$-inch (1 cm) border all around. With your fingertips, moisten the edges with a little water.

5. Roll out the remaining dough as for the first. Place on top of the fruit and crimp edges together. Using a knife, make some slashes on the top.

6. Bake in preheated oven for 10 minutes, then lower heat to 350°F (180°C) and bake for 25 to 30 minutes, until golden brown. Place pan on a wire rack to cool slightly and, while still warm, sift confectioner's sugar over top and cut into squares.

Tip *To get every drop of juice from citrus fruits, bring them to room temperature and roll them on the counter before squeezing.*

● ●
Matrimonial Date Bars

Makes 36 bars
- Preheat oven to 325°F (160°C)
- 13- by 9-inch (3 L) baking pan, greased

FILLING

2 cups	chopped pitted dates	500 mL
$\frac{2}{3}$ cup	cold water	150 mL
2 tbsp	packed brown sugar	25 mL
2 tsp	grated orange zest	10 mL
2 tbsp	freshly squeezed orange juice	25 mL
1 tsp	freshly squeezed lemon juice	5 mL

BASE

1$\frac{1}{2}$ cups	all-purpose flour	375 mL
1 tsp	baking powder	5 mL
$\frac{1}{2}$ tsp	baking soda	2 mL
$\frac{1}{4}$ tsp	salt	1 mL
1$\frac{1}{2}$ cups	old-fashioned rolled oats	375 mL
1 cup	packed brown sugar	250 mL
1 cup	butter or margarine	250 mL

1. *Prepare the filling:* In a saucepan, combine dates, water, brown sugar and zest. Cook, stirring, over medium heat until thick and smooth. Remove from heat, then stir in orange and lemon juices. Set aside to cool slightly.

2. *Prepare the base:* In a large bowl, mix together flour, baking powder, baking soda and salt. Stir in oats and brown sugar. Using two knives, a pastry blender or your fingers, cut butter in until mixture resembles coarse crumbs. Set half aside and press remainder evenly into prepared pan.

3. Spread filling evenly over base. Top with the remaining crumb mixture; smooth lightly with your hands. Bake in preheated oven for 30 to 35 minutes, then increase heat to 350°F (180°C) and bake for 5 minutes or until lightly browned. Remove from oven and cut into bars while still hot. Place pan on a wire rack to cool completely.

Tip *To soften brown sugar that has hardened, place sugar in a glass jar with half an apple. Seal tightly and let stand for 1 day. Remove the apple and, using a fork, fluff up sugar. Reseal the jar.*

● ●
Double Date Nut Squares

Makes 36 squares
- Preheat oven to 350°F (180°C)
- 13- by 9-inch (3 L) baking pan, greased

2 cups	boiling water	500 mL
2 cups	chopped pitted dates	500 mL
2 tbsp	baking soda	25 mL
2 tbsp	butter or margarine, softened	25 mL
2 cups	granulated sugar	500 mL
2	eggs	2
2 tsp	vanilla	10 mL
2$\frac{1}{2}$ cups	cake and pastry flour, sifted	625 mL
$\frac{1}{2}$ cup	chopped walnuts	125 mL
	Date Frosting (see recipe, page 548)	

1. In a medium bowl, mix together water, dates and baking soda.

2. In a large bowl, beat butter, sugar, eggs and vanilla until blended. Add date mixture and mix thoroughly. Blend in flour. Stir in walnuts.

3. Spread evenly in prepared pan. Bake in preheated oven for 45 to 50 minutes or until a tester inserted in the center comes out clean. Place pan on a wire rack to cool completely. Frost with Date Frosting, then cut into squares.

Tip *Keep some vegetable oil in a squeeze bottle for when a small amount is needed.*

Wheat Germ Date Bars

Makes 24 bars

- Preheat oven to 350°F (180°C)
- 9-inch (2.5 L) square baking pan, greased

1 1/4 cups	chopped pitted dates (8-oz/250 g package)	300 mL
1 1/4 cups	water	300 mL
BASE		
1 cup	wheat germ	250 mL
1 cup	whole wheat flour	250 mL
1/2 cup	packed brown sugar	125 mL
1/2 cup	butter or margarine, softened	125 mL
TOPPING		
2/3 cup	whole wheat flour	150 mL
1/2 cup	granulated sugar	125 mL
1 tsp	baking powder	5 mL
1/2 tsp	salt	2 mL
2	eggs, beaten	2
1/4 tsp	almond extract	1 mL

1. In a saucepan, over medium heat, bring dates and water to a boil. Reduce heat and simmer, uncovered, for 15 to 20 minutes or until water is absorbed and dates thicken. Set aside.

2. *Prepare the base:* In a medium bowl, mix together wheat germ, whole wheat flour and brown sugar. Using two knives, a pastry blender or your fingers, cut butter in until mixture resembles coarse crumbs. Press 2 cups (500 mL) into prepared pan. Set remainder aside. Bake in preheated oven for 10 minutes. Place pan on a rack.

3. *Prepare the topping:* In another bowl, mix together whole wheat flour, sugar, baking powder and salt. Blend in eggs, almond extract and reserved dates.

4. Spread evenly over hot base. Sprinkle reserved crumb mixture evenly over top, pressing down lightly. Bake for 25 minutes or until topping is set. Place pan on a wire rack to cool completely, then cut into bars.

Chocolate Date Nut Bars

Makes 24 bars

- Preheat oven to 350°F (180°C)
- 9-inch (2.5 L) square baking pan, lightly greased

BASE		
1/2 cup	semisweet chocolate chips or chunks	125 mL
1/2 cup	butter or margarine	125 mL

1/4 cup	granulated sugar	50 mL
1 tbsp	milk	15 mL
1 1/3 cups	all-purpose flour	325 mL
TOPPING		
1/3 cup	granulated sugar	75 mL
2	eggs	2
2 tbsp	all-purpose flour	25 mL
1/2 tsp	baking powder	2 mL
1 cup	finely chopped pitted dates	250 mL
1/2 cup	chopped walnuts	125 mL

1. *Prepare the base:* In a large saucepan, over low heat, melt chocolate and butter. Stir in sugar and milk until blended. Blend in flour. Spread evenly in prepared pan. Bake in preheated oven for 10 minutes. Place pan on a wire rack to cool slightly.

2. *Prepare the topping:* In a medium bowl, beat sugar and eggs until blended. Blend in flour and baking powder. Stir in dates and walnuts.

3. Spread evenly over warm base. Bake for 20 to 25 minutes or until a tester inserted in the center comes out clean. Place pan on a wire rack to cool completely, then cut into bars.

Fig Newton Lattice Bars

Makes 36 bars

- Preheat oven to 375°F (190°C)
- 13- by 9-inch (3 L) baking pan, greased

BASE		
3/4 cups	butter, softened	175 mL
1/3 cup	granulated sugar	75 mL
1	egg	1
2 tsp	vanilla	10 mL
1/4 tsp	salt	1 mL
2 cups	all-purpose flour	500 mL
TOPPING		
1 cup	water	250 mL
1	package (10 oz/300 g) dried figs, stems cut off	1
1 cup	pitted prunes	250 mL
1/3 cup	packed brown sugar	75 mL
2 tbsp	freshly squeezed lemon juice	25 mL

1. *Prepare the base:* In a medium bowl, beat butter and sugar until smooth and creamy. Add egg, vanilla and salt, beating until incorporated. Blend in flour just until a dough forms. Knead lightly, then divide into two pieces, one slightly larger than the other. Wrap smaller piece in plastic wrap and refrigerate. Press larger piece evenly into prepared pan and refrigerate until ready to use.

2. *Prepare the topping:* In a saucepan, over medium heat, combine water, figs, prunes and brown sugar, stirring frequently, until mixture thickens and most of the liquid is absorbed, about 10 minutes. Set aside to cool slightly.

3. In a food processor, process fig mixture with lemon juice until almost smooth. Transfer to a bowl and refrigerate until cool.

4. When ready to bake, spread fig mixture over base. On a floured work surface, divide second piece of dough into two pieces, one slightly larger than the other. Cut the larger piece of dough into 10 equal pieces and, using your hands, roll each into a rope approximately 13 inches (33 cm) long. Repeat with second piece of dough, rolling the 10 pieces into ropes approximately 9 inches (23 cm) long. Top fig mixture with a lattice pattern made from the ropes of dough (see tip, below). Trim excess dough.

5. Bake in preheated oven for 40 minutes or until golden brown. Place pan on a wire rack to cool completely in pan, then cut into bars.

Tip *To make a lattice base or top, place half the dough strips parallel to each other at equal intervals. Weave a cross-strip through the center of the pie or cake in the opposite direction by folding back every other strip. Continue to weave the remaining strips, folding back alternate strips each time a cross-strip is added. Trim ends if necessary.*

• •

Raisin Bars

Makes 24 bars
• Preheat oven to 350°F (180°C)
• 9-inch (2.5 L) square baking pan, greased

2¾ cups	Mix-Ahead Bar Mix (see recipe, page 269)	675 mL
1 cup	raisins	250 mL
¼ tsp	ground cinnamon	1 mL
¼ tsp	ground nutmeg	1 mL
2	eggs, beaten	2
⅓ cup	unsweetened applesauce	75 mL
1 tbsp	milk	15 mL
1 tsp	vanilla	5 mL
	Frosting (optional)	

1. In a large bowl, mix together bar mix, raisins, cinnamon and nutmeg.

2. In another large bowl, beat eggs, applesauce, milk and vanilla. Blend in dry ingredients.

3. Spread evenly in prepared pan. Bake in preheated oven for 20 to 25 minutes or until a tester inserted in the center comes out clean. Place pan on a rack to cool completely. If desired, spread with a frosting, such as Butter Frosting (page 544) or Banana Frosting (page 551), before cutting into bars.

Tip *To freshen raisins that have dried out, place them in a strainer and steam over hot water.*

• •

Full of Prunes Bars

Makes 36 bars
• Preheat oven to 350°F (180°C)
• 13- by 9-inch (3 L) baking pan, greased

BASE
1 cup	chopped pitted prunes	250 mL
2 cups	all-purpose flour	500 mL
1½ cups	granulated sugar	375 mL
½ cup	chopped walnuts	125 mL
1¼ tsp	baking soda	6 mL
1 tsp	salt	5 mL
1 tsp	ground cinnamon	5 mL
1 tsp	ground nutmeg	5 mL
3	eggs, beaten	3
½ cup	vegetable oil	125 mL

TOPPING
½ cup	granulated sugar	125 mL
2 tbsp	all-purpose flour	25 mL
2 tbsp	butter	25 mL

1. *Prepare the base:* In a covered saucepan, over low heat, simmer prunes, with water to cover, for 15 to 20 minutes or until tender. Drain, reserving ⅔ cup (150 mL) of cooking liquid. (If you do not have sufficient liquid, add required amount of water.)

2. In a large bowl, mix together flour, sugar, walnuts, baking soda, salt, cinnamon and nutmeg. Make a well in the center. Add eggs, oil, and reserved prune liquid and mix until blended. Stir in prunes. Spread evenly in prepared pan.

3. *Prepare the topping:* In a small bowl, mix together sugar and flour. Using two knives, a pastry blender or your fingers, cut butter in until mixture resembles coarse crumbs.

4. Sprinkle evenly over base. Bake in preheated oven for 30 to 35 minutes or until a tester inserted in the center comes out clean. Place pan on a wire rack to cool completely, then cut into bars.

Spicy Prune Bars

Makes 24 bars

- Preheat oven to 350°F (180°C)
- 9-inch (2.5 L) square baking pan, greased

1½ cups	all-purpose flour	375 mL
¾ cup	granulated sugar	175 mL
¼ cup	packed brown sugar	50 mL
1 tsp	baking powder	5 mL
½ tsp	baking soda	2 mL
½ tsp	ground cinnamon	2 mL
¼ tsp	salt	1 mL
¼ tsp	ground ginger	1 mL
1	egg, beaten	1
1 tsp	vanilla	5 mL
½ cup	vegetable oil	125 mL
½ cup	cold water	125 mL
½ cup	strained prunes (baby food)	125 mL
½ cup	chopped walnuts	125 mL
GLAZE (OPTIONAL)		
1 tbsp	light (5%) cream	15 mL
Pinch	ground cinnamon	Pinch
½ cup	confectioner's (icing) sugar, sifted	125 mL

1. In a bowl, mix together flour, sugars, baking powder, baking soda, cinnamon, salt and ginger. Make a well in the center. Add egg, vanilla, oil, water and prunes and mix just until incorporated.
2. Spread batter evenly in prepared pan. Sprinkle nuts evenly over top. Bake in preheated oven for 25 to 30 minutes or until a tester inserted in center comes out clean. Place pan on a rack to cool.
3. *If desired, prepare the glaze:* In a bowl, combine cream and cinnamon. Gradually beat in confectioner's sugar. Drizzle over top of cake. When cool, cut into bars.

Jam Crumb Bars

Makes 24 bars

- Preheat oven to 375°F (190°C)
- 9-inch (2.5 L) square baking pan, ungreased

BASE		
1¾ cups	all-purpose flour	425 mL
½ cup	finely chopped nuts	125 mL
¼ cup	butter or margarine, softened	50 mL
½ cup	confectioner's (icing) sugar, sifted	125 mL
¼ tsp	grated lemon zest	1 mL
TOPPING		
¾ cup	jam (any flavor)	175 mL
1 tbsp	all-purpose flour	15 mL

1. *Prepare the base:* In a medium bowl, mix together flour and nuts.
2. In a large bowl, beat butter, confectioner's sugar and lemon zest until smooth and creamy. Blend in flour mixture until crumbly. Set aside one-third of this mixture. Press remainder evenly into pan.
3. *Prepare the topping:* Stir jam until smooth, then spread evenly over base. In a small bowl, mix together reserved base mixture and flour. Sprinkle evenly over jam.
4. Bake in preheated oven for 25 to 30 minutes or until golden brown. Place pan on a wire rack to cool completely, then cut into bars.

Tip *To soften cold butter quickly, place a small heated saucepan upside-down over the dish of butter for several minutes.*

Old-Fashioned Gingerbread Spice Bars

Makes 36 bars

- Preheat oven to 350°F (180°C)
- 13- by 9-inch (3 L) baking pan, greased

2½ cups	all-purpose flour	625 mL
2 tsp	baking powder	10 mL
1 tsp	ground cinnamon	5 mL
1 tsp	ground ginger	5 mL
½ tsp	baking soda	2 mL
½ tsp	salt	2 mL
Pinch	ground cloves	Pinch
½ cup	shortening, softened	125 mL
½ cup	granulated sugar	125 mL
2	eggs	2
1 cup	light (fancy) molasses	250 mL
1 cup	boiling water	250 mL

1. In a medium bowl, mix together flour, baking powder, cinnamon, ginger, baking soda, salt and cloves.
2. In a large bowl, beat shortening and sugar until smooth and creamy. Add eggs, one at a time, beating until incorporated. Beat in molasses. Gradually blend in flour mixture alternately with boiling water until just incorporated.
3. Pour into prepared pan. Bake in preheated oven for 40 to 45 minutes, until a tester inserted in the center comes out clean. Place pan on a wire rack to cool completely, then cut into bars.

Tip *Replace ground spices annually; they lose their flavor over time.*

Chinese Chews (page 201) and
Esther's Famous Komish Bread Cookies (page 525)

Jam Crescents (page 207) and Easy Elephant Ears (page 207)

Lacy Oatmeal Sandwiches (page 222)

Apricot Almond Biscotti (page 226)

Original Scottish Shortbread (page 228)

Peppermint Candy Canes (page 239)
and Checkerboard Squares (page 241)

Classic Chocolate Nut Brownies (page 248)

Rocky Road Brownies (page 249)

Coffee Mocha Cheesecake Diamonds (page 264)

Chocolate Chip Blondies (page 255)

Cinnamon Applesauce Squares (page 270)

Rhubarb Crisp Squares (page 284)

No-Bake Crispy Peanut Butter Squares (page 321)

Delicate Lace Baskets (page 330)

Rainbow Gelatin Squares (page 336)

Orange Ripple Cake (page 351)

Pumpkin Pie Dessert Bars

Makes 36 bars

- Preheat oven to 350°F (180°C)
- 13- by 9-inch (3 L) baking pan, ungreased

BASE

1½ cups	quick-cooking rolled oats	375 mL
1½ cups	packed brown sugar	375 mL
1½ cups	all-purpose flour	375 mL
½ tsp	salt	2 mL
¾ cup	butter	175 mL
1	egg	1

FILLING

3 cups	canned pumpkin purée (not pie filling)	750 mL
¾ cup	packed brown sugar	175 mL
1½ tsp	ground cinnamon	7 mL
¾ tsp	ground nutmeg	4 mL
¾ tsp	ground ginger	4 mL
3	eggs	3
1 cup	evaporated milk	250 mL
¾ cup	chopped pecans	175 mL

1. *Prepare the base:* In a large bowl, mix together oats, brown sugar, flour and salt. Using two knives, a pastry blender or your fingers, cut butter in until mixture resembles coarse crumbs. Add egg and mix well. Set aside 1½ cups (375 mL) of mixture and press remainder evenly in pan. Bake in preheated oven for 20 minutes or until golden brown. Place pan on a rack to cool slightly.
2. *Prepare the filling:* In a large bowl, combine pumpkin, brown sugar, cinnamon, nutmeg and ginger. Add eggs, one at a time and beat until blended. Gradually stir in milk. Pour evenly over baked base.
3. In a small bowl, mix together reserved oat mixture and nuts. Sprinkle evenly over filling. Bake for 30 to 35 minutes or until center is set. Place pan on a wire rack to cool completely, then cut into bars.

Tip *No time to bake it? Fake it! Surprise guests or your family with the aroma of freshly baked cookies, bars, squares or brownies — without baking! Just heat 2 tsp (10 mL) vanilla and ¼ cup (50 mL) water in a metal pan, in a warm oven. No one will ever guess your secret.*

Spiced Pumpkin Bars

Makes 36 bars

- Preheat oven to 350° F (180° C)
- 13- by 9-inch (3 L) baking pan, greased

BASE

1 cup	all-purpose flour	250 mL
½ cup	quick-cooking rolled oats	125 mL
½ cup	packed brown sugar	125 mL
½ cup	cold butter, cut into cubes	125 mL

FILLING

2 cups	scalded milk	500 mL
¾ cup	granulated sugar	175 mL
2 cups	canned pumpkin purée (not pie filling)	500 mL
3	eggs, beaten	3
1 tsp	ground cinnamon	5 mL
½ tsp	salt	2 mL
½ tsp	ground ginger	2 mL
¼ tsp	ground cloves	1 mL

TOPPING

2 tbsp	all-purpose flour	25 mL
1 cup	packed brown sugar	250 mL
1 cup	chopped nuts	250 mL
¼ cup	butter, softened	50 mL

1. *Prepare the base:* In a medium bowl, mix together flour, oats and brown sugar. Using two knives, a pastry blender or your fingers, cut butter in until mixture resembles coarse crumbs. Press evenly into prepared pan. Bake in preheated oven for 12 to 15 minutes or until golden brown.
2. *Prepare the filling:* In a large bowl, mix together milk, sugar and pumpkin. Add eggs, cinnamon, salt, ginger and cloves and mix until thoroughly blended.
3. Spread evenly over baked base. Bake for 15 to 20 minutes or until set.
4. *Prepare the topping:* In another medium bowl, mix together flour, brown sugar and nuts. Using two knives, a pastry blender or your fingers, cut butter in until mixture is crumbly.
5. Sprinkle evenly over hot cake. Bake for 10 to 15 minutes or until topping is golden brown. Place pan on a wire rack to cool completely, then cut into bars.

Pumpkin Cheesecake Bars

Makes 24 bars

- Preheat oven to 375° F (190° C)
- 9-inch (2.5 L) square baking pan, lightly greased

BASE

2 tbsp	butter, melted	25 mL
2 tbsp	pure maple syrup	25 mL
1⅓ cups	graham wafer crumbs	325 mL

TOPPING

½ cup	granulated sugar	125 mL
3	packages (each 8 oz/250 g) cream cheese, softened	3
4	eggs	4
½ cup	pure maple syrup	125 mL
1 tsp	vanilla	5 mL
1⅔ cups	canned pumpkin purée (not pie filling)	400 mL
	Whipped cream (optional)	

1. *Prepare the base:* In a small bowl, mix together butter, syrup and wafer crumbs. Press evenly into prepared pan. Bake in preheated oven for 8 to 10 minutes or until lightly browned. Place pan on a wire rack to cool. Lower oven heat to 350°F (180°C).

2. *Prepare the topping:* In a large bowl, beat sugar and cream cheese until smooth. Add eggs, one at a time, beating until incorporated. Stir in syrup and vanilla. Blend in pumpkin.

3. Pour over base. Bake for 55 to 60 minutes or until center is just set. Run a knife around the edge of the cake, then place pan on a wire rack to cool completely. Chill overnight. When ready to serve, cut into bars. Top with a dollop of whipped cream, if desired.

Raisin Spice Pumpkin Bars

Makes 36 bars

- Preheat oven to 350°F (180°C)
- 13- by 9-inch (3 L) baking pan, greased

2 cups	all-purpose flour	500 mL
2 cups	granulated sugar	500 mL
2 tsp	baking powder	10 mL
1 tsp	baking soda	5 mL
1 tsp	ground cinnamon	5 mL
1 tsp	ground nutmeg	5 mL
½ tsp	salt	2 mL
½ tsp	ground cloves	2 mL
4	eggs, beaten	4
1 cup	vegetable oil	250 mL
2 cups	canned pumpkin purée (not pie filling)	500 mL
½ cup	raisins	125 mL
½ cup	chopped nuts	125 mL

FROSTING (OPTIONAL)

4 oz	cream cheese, softened	125 g
⅓ cup	butter or margarine, softened	75 mL
2 tsp	milk	10 mL
1 tsp	vanilla	5 mL
2 cups	confectioner's (icing) sugar, sifted	500 mL

1. In a large bowl, mix together flour, sugar, baking powder, baking soda, cinnamon, nutmeg, salt and cloves. Make a well in the center. Add eggs, oil and pumpkin and mix until blended. Stir in raisins and nuts.

2. Bake in preheated oven for 30 to 35 minutes or until a tester inserted in the center comes out clean. Place pan on a wire rack to cool completely.

3. *If desired, prepare the frosting:* In a medium bowl, beat cream cheese and butter until smooth. Beat in milk and vanilla. Gradually add confectioner's sugar, beating until smooth and spreadable. Spread frosting over top of cooled cake. Cut into bars.

Carrot Pumpkin Bars

Makes 36 bars

- Preheat oven to 350°F (180°C)
- 13- by 9-inch (3 L) baking pan, greased

BASE

2 cups	all-purpose flour	500 mL
2 tsp	baking powder	10 mL
1½ tsp	ground cinnamon	7 mL
1 tsp	baking soda	5 mL
½ tsp	salt	2 mL
½ tsp	ground ginger	2 mL
Pinch	ground cloves	Pinch
⅓ cup	butter or margarine, softened	75 mL
1 cup	granulated sugar	250 mL
½ cup	packed brown sugar	125 mL
2	eggs	2
2	egg whites	2
1 cup	finely shredded carrots	250 mL
2 cups	pumpkin, cooked and puréed, or canned pumpkin purée (not pie filling)	500 mL

TOPPING

4 oz	light cream cheese, softened	125 g
1/4 cup	granulated sugar	50 mL
1 tbsp	milk	15 mL

1. *Prepare the base:* In a medium bowl, mix together flour, baking powder, cinnamon, baking soda, salt, ginger and cloves.
2. In a large bowl, beat butter, granulated sugar and brown sugar until smooth and creamy. Add eggs and egg whites, beating until incorporated. Stir in carrots and pumpkin. Gradually blend in flour mixture. Spread evenly in prepared pan.
3. *Prepare the topping:* In a small bowl, beat cream cheese and sugar until smooth. Beat in milk.
4. Drop teaspoonfuls of mixture over top of pumpkin batter. Run a knife through batters to create a marbling effect. Bake in preheated oven for 30 to 35 minutes or until a tester inserted in the center comes out clean. Place pan on a wire rack to cool completely, then cut into bars.

Tip *If you prefer, substitute 2 tsp (10 mL) pumpkin pie spice for the cinnamon, ginger and cloves.*

- -

Frosted Carrot Bars

Makes 36 bars
- Preheat oven to 350°F (180°C)
- 13- by 9-inch (3 L) baking pan, greased

1 1/4 cups	all-purpose flour	300 mL
1 cup	granulated sugar	250 mL
1 tsp	baking soda	5 mL
1 tsp	ground cinnamon	5 mL
1/2 tsp	salt	2 mL
1	jar (7 1/2 oz/213 mL) strained carrots (baby food)	1
1	jar (7 1/2 oz/213 mL) strained applesauce (baby food)	1
2 tbsp	vegetable oil	25 mL
2	eggs	2
FROSTING		
3 oz	cream cheese, softened	90 g
1 tsp	milk (approximate)	5 mL
1 tsp	vanilla	5 mL
2 cups	confectioner's (icing) sugar, sifted	500 mL

1. In a large bowl, mix together flour, sugar, baking soda, cinnamon and salt. Add baby foods, oil and eggs and mix until just blended.

2. Spread evenly in prepared pan. Bake in preheated oven for 20 to 25 minutes or until tester inserted in the center comes out clean. Place pan on a wire rack to cool completely, then cut into bars.
3. *Prepare the frosting:* In a medium bowl, beat cream cheese, milk and vanilla until smooth. Gradually add confectioner's sugar, beating until smooth and spreadable, adjusting consistency with more milk if necessary. Drop a spoonful of frosting on top of each bar.

- -

Glazed Zucchini Raisin Bars

Makes 36 bars
- Preheat oven to 350°F (180°C)
- 13- by 9-inch (3 L) baking pan, greased

2 cups	whole wheat flour	500 mL
2 tsp	baking soda	10 mL
3/4 tsp	ground cinnamon	4 mL
1/2 tsp	ground nutmeg	2 mL
1/4 tsp	ground cloves	1 mL
1 cup	raisins	250 mL
1/2 cup	butter or margarine, softened	125 mL
1 1/4 cups	packed brown sugar	300 mL
2	eggs	2
1 tsp	vanilla	5 mL
1 1/2 cups	shredded zucchini	375 mL
LEMON GLAZE		
2 tbsp	butter or margarine, softened	25 mL
1 to 2 tbsp	freshly squeezed lemon juice	15 to 25 mL
1 1/2 cups	confectioner's (icing) sugar, sifted	375 mL

1. In a medium bowl, mix together flour, baking soda, cinnamon, nutmeg, cloves and raisins.
2. In a large bowl, beat butter and brown sugar until smooth and creamy. Beat in eggs, then vanilla, until incorporated. Blend in flour mixture. Stir in zucchini.
3. Spread evenly in prepared pan. Bake in preheated oven for 30 to 35 minutes or until a tester inserted in the center comes out clean. Place pan on a wire rack to cool.
4. *Prepare the glaze:* In a small bowl, beat butter and lemon juice until smooth. Gradually add confectioner's sugar, beating until smooth and spreadable. Spread over warm cake, then cut into bars. Store, covered, in refrigerator.

Tip *If desired, use 1 cup (250 mL) each whole wheat and all-purpose flour.*

Coconut, Nut and Peanut Butter Bars and Squares

Coconut Bars and Squares

Nut and Peanut Butter Bars and Squares

Coconut Bars and Squares

Southern Coconut Squares

Makes 16 squares
- Preheat oven to 375°F (190°C)
- 8-inch (2 L) square baking pan, greased

2 cups	all-purpose flour	500 mL
2½ tsp	baking powder	12 mL
½ tsp	salt	2 mL
⅔ cup	shortening, softened	150 mL
1 cup	granulated sugar	250 mL
3	eggs	3
1 tsp	almond extract	5 mL
⅔ cup	milk	150 mL
1 cup	flaked coconut (sweetened or unsweetened)	250 mL

1. In a medium bowl, mix together flour, baking powder and salt.
2. In a large bowl, beat shortening and sugar until smooth and creamy. Beat in eggs, one at a time, until incorporated. Stir in almond extract. Gradually blend in flour mixture alternately with milk until just incorporated. Stir in coconut.
3. Spread evenly in prepared pan. Bake in preheated oven for 25 minutes or until golden brown. Place pan on a wire rack to cool completely, then cut into squares.

Tip *To prevent coconut from becoming moldy, toast in a skillet until golden, then store in an airtight container.*

Chewy Coconut Squares

Makes 16 squares
- Preheat oven to 350°F (180°C)
- 8-inch (2 L) square baking pan, greased

¼ cup	butter or margarine	50 mL
1 cup	packed brown sugar	250 mL
½ cup	all-purpose flour	125 mL
1 tsp	baking powder	5 mL
½ tsp	salt	2 mL
1	egg, beaten	1
1 tsp	vanilla	5 mL
¾ cup	shredded sweetened coconut	175 mL

1. In a saucepan, over low heat, melt butter with brown sugar, stirring until sugar dissolves. Remove from heat and let cool slightly.
2. In a large bowl, mix together flour, baking powder and salt. Add egg, vanilla and butter mixture and mix until blended. Stir in coconut. Spread evenly in prepared pan. Bake in preheated oven for 20 to 25 minutes or until golden brown. Place pan on a wire rack to cool and cut into squares while slightly warm.

Tip *If your coconut has dried out, sprinkle it with milk and let stand until it softens.*

Coconut Bars Supreme

Makes 24 bars
- Preheat oven to 375°F (190°C)
- 9-inch (2.5 L) square baking pan, greased

BASE		
1¼ cups	all-purpose flour	300 mL
¼ cup	packed brown sugar	50 mL
½ cup	butter, margarine or shortening	125 mL
TOPPING		
2 tbsp	butter, margarine or shortening, melted	25 mL
½ cup	granulated sugar	125 mL
½ cup	corn syrup	125 mL
2	eggs	2
1 tsp	vanilla	5 mL
¼ tsp	ground cinnamon	1 mL
¼ tsp	ground nutmeg	1 mL
⅔ cup	coarsely chopped almonds	150 mL
½ cup	flaked coconut (sweetened or unsweetened)	125 mL

1. *Prepare the base:* In a medium bowl, mix together flour and brown sugar. Using two knives, a pastry blender or your fingers, cut butter in until mixture resembles coarse crumbs. Press evenly into prepared pan. Bake in preheated oven for 15 minutes.
2. *Prepare the topping:* In another medium bowl, beat butter, sugar, syrup, eggs, vanilla, cinnamon and nutmeg until blended. Stir in almonds and coconut.
3. Spread evenly over base. Bake for 20 to 25 minutes or until top is set. Place pan on a wire rack to cool completely, then cut into bars.

Tip *To soften brown sugar, place a slice of soft bread in the package or container and close tightly. In a couple of hours, the sugar will be soft again.*

Golden Butterscotch Triangles

Makes 16 triangles

- Preheat oven to 350°F (180°C)
- 8-inch (2 L) square baking pan, lightly greased

¾ cup	all-purpose flour	175 mL
1 tsp	baking powder	5 mL
¼ tsp	salt	1 mL
¼ cup	butter or margarine	50 mL
1 cup	packed brown sugar	250 mL
1	egg	1
1 tsp	vanilla	5 mL
⅓ cup	flaked coconut (sweetened or unsweetened)	75 mL
⅓ cup	chopped nuts	75 mL

1. In a small bowl, mix together flour, baking powder and salt.
2. In a medium bowl, beat butter and brown sugar until smooth and creamy. Beat in egg until incorporated. Stir in vanilla. Blend in flour mixture. Stir in coconut and chopped nuts.
3. Spread mixture evenly in prepared pan. Bake in preheated oven for 20 to 25 minutes or until lightly browned. Place pan on a wire rack to cool completely, then cut into triangles (see tip, page 301).

Tip *Whenever I make anything flavored with butterscotch, I replace vanilla with almond extract. It seems to enhance the flavor.*

Coconut Dream Squares

Makes 16 squares

- Preheat oven to 350°F (180°C)
- 8-inch (2 L) square baking pan, lightly greased

BASE

½ cup	butter or margarine, softened	125 mL
1 tbsp	packed brown sugar	15 mL
1 cup	all-purpose flour	250 mL
Pinch	salt	Pinch

TOPPING

2 tbsp	all-purpose flour	25 mL
1½ tsp	baking powder	7 mL
Pinch	salt	Pinch
1¼ cups	packed brown sugar	300 mL
2	eggs, beaten	2
¾ cup	chopped walnuts	175 mL
½ cup	shredded coconut (sweetened or unsweetened)	125 mL

1. *Prepare the base:* In a medium bowl, beat butter and brown sugar until smooth and creamy. Blend in flour and salt. Press evenly into prepared pan. Bake in preheated oven for 15 minutes or until lightly browned. Place pan on a wire rack to cool.
2. *Prepare the topping:* In a medium bowl, mix together flour, baking powder and salt. Add brown sugar and eggs and mix until blended. Stir in walnuts and coconut.
3. Spread evenly over cooled base. Bake for 20 to 25 minutes or until golden brown. Place pan on a rack to cool completely, then cut into squares.

Tip *If desired, frost with Butter Frosting (page 544), flavored with 1½ tsp (7 mL) almond extract instead of vanilla, before cutting into squares.*

Double Nut Coconut Bars

Makes 36 bars

- Preheat oven to 350°F (180°C)
- 13- by 9-inch (3 L) baking pan, lined with foil extending over ends

BASE

½ cup	butter or margarine, melted	125 mL
1½ cups	finely crushed graham wafer crumbs (about 22 wafers)	375 mL

TOPPING

1	can (14 oz/398 mL) sweetened condensed milk	1
1 cup	semisweet chocolate chips	250 mL
1½ cups	shredded coconut (sweetened or unsweetened)	375 mL
¾ cup	chopped Brazil nuts	175 mL
¾ cup	chopped cashews	175 mL

1. *Prepare the base:* In a small bowl, mix together butter and wafer crumbs. Press evenly into prepared pan.
2. *Prepare the topping:* Pour condensed milk evenly over crumbs. Working in layers, spread chocolate chips, coconut, Brazil nuts and cashews over crumbs. Using a spatula, press down gently.
3. Bake in preheated oven for 25 to 30 minutes or until coconut is lightly browned. Place pan on a wire rack to cool completely. Transfer cake with foil to a cutting board and cut into bars.

Tip *To keep freshly baked cakes from sticking to wire cooling racks, spray racks with nonstick cooking spray.*

Bridge Mix Coconut Bars

Makes 36 bars

- Preheat oven to 350°F (180°C)
- 13- by 9-inch (3 L) baking pan, ungreased

3 tbsp	butter or margarine, melted	45 mL
½	package (18 oz/510 g) white cake mix	½
¾ cup	semisweet chocolate chips	175 mL
1½ cups	miniature marshmallows	375 mL
1 cup	flaked coconut (sweetened or unsweetened)	250 mL
1 cup	chopped nuts	250 mL
1¼ cups	milk	300 mL

1. Spread melted butter evenly over the bottom of pan. Sprinkle evenly with cake mix, then top with chocolate chips, marshmallows, coconut and nuts. Pour milk evenly over top.
2. Bake in preheated oven for 25 to 30 minutes or until golden brown. Place pan on a wire rack to cool completely, then cut into bars.

Tip *For a richer version of this recipe, substitute 1 can (10 oz/300 mL) sweetened condensed milk for the regular milk.*

Coco-Nut Crumb Bars

Makes 36 bars

- Preheat oven to 350°F (180°C)
- 13- by 9-inch (3 L) baking pan, ungreased

BASE

2 cups	chocolate chip cookie crumbs	500 mL
¼ cup	butter or margarine, melted	50 mL

TOPPING

2 cups	flaked coconut (sweetened or unsweetened)	500 mL
1	can (14 oz/398 mL) sweetened condensed milk	1
2 cups	semisweet chocolate chips	500 mL

1. *Prepare the base:* In a medium bowl, mix together cookie crumbs and melted butter. Press evenly into pan. Bake in preheated oven for 10 minutes.
2. *Prepare the topping:* Remove pan from oven and sprinkle coconut over base. Pour condensed milk over coconut.
3. Bake for 18 to 20 minutes or until coconut begins to brown around the edges of the cake. Place pan on a wire rack to cool.

4. In a saucepan, over low heat, melt chocolate chips, stirring until smooth. Spread melted chocolate evenly over top of coconut. Chill until completely cooled, then cut into bars.

Coconut Fudge Bars

Makes 36 bars

- Preheat oven to 350°F (180°C)
- 13- by 9-inch (3 L) baking pan, greased

BASE

1 cup	all-purpose flour	250 mL
½ cup	chopped walnuts	125 mL
¼ cup	unsweetened cocoa powder, sifted	50 mL
1 cup	butter or margarine, softened	250 mL
1½ cups	granulated sugar	375 mL
3	eggs	3
1 tsp	vanilla	5 mL

TOPPING

1	can (14 oz/398 mL) sweetened condensed milk	1
1 cup	shredded coconut (sweetened or unsweetened)	250 mL

FROSTING

¼ cup	unsweetened cocoa powder	50 mL
2 cups	confectioner's (icing) sugar	500 mL
2 tbsp	butter or margarine, melted	25 mL
⅓ cup	evaporated milk	75 mL
½ tsp	vanilla	2 mL

1. *Prepare the base:* In a small bowl, mix together flour, walnuts and cocoa.
2. In a large bowl, beat butter and sugar until smooth and creamy. Beat in eggs until incorporated. Stir in vanilla. Blend in flour mixture.
3. Spread evenly in prepared pan. Bake in preheated oven for 30 minutes or until tester inserted in the center comes out clean.
4. *Prepare the topping:* In a small bowl, mix together condensed milk and coconut.
5. Spread evenly over hot base. Bake for 20 minutes or until coconut is lightly browned. Place pan on a wire rack to cool slightly.
6. *Prepare the frosting:* Sift together cocoa and confectioner's sugar. Beat in butter, evaporated milk and vanilla until smooth. Spread over warm cake. Chill until cooled completely, then cut into bars.

Tip *Fresh milk cannot be used when evaporated milk is called for in a recipe. But evaporated milk, mixed with an equal amount of water, can be substituted for fresh milk.*

Coconut Chews

Makes 36 bars

- Preheat oven to 350°F (180°C)
- 13- by 9-inch (3 L) baking pan, ungreased

BASE

¾ cup	butter or shortening, softened	175 mL
¾ cup	confectioner's (icing) sugar, sifted	175 mL
1½ cups	all-purpose flour	375 mL

TOPPING

2 tbsp	all-purpose flour	25 mL
½ tsp	baking powder	2 mL
½ tsp	salt	2 mL
1 cup	packed brown sugar	250 mL
2	eggs	2
½ tsp	vanilla	2 mL
½ cup	chopped walnuts	125 mL
½ cup	flaked coconut (sweetened or unsweetened)	125 mL

ORANGE LEMON FROSTING (OPTIONAL)

2 tbsp	butter or margarine, melted	25 mL
1½ cups	confectioner's (icing) sugar, sifted	375 mL
3 tbsp	freshly squeezed orange juice	45 mL
1 tsp	freshly squeezed lemon juice	5 mL

1. *Prepare the base:* In a medium bowl, beat butter and confectioner's sugar until smooth and creamy. Gradually blend in flour until a soft dough forms. Press evenly into pan. Bake in preheated oven for 12 to 15 minutes or until lightly browned.
2. *Prepare the topping:* In a small bowl, mix together flour, baking powder and salt.
3. In another bowl, beat brown sugar, eggs and vanilla until smooth and blended. Blend in flour mixture. Stir in walnuts and coconut. Spread evenly over hot base and bake for 20 minutes, until top is set. Place pan on a wire rack to cool slightly.
4. *If desired, prepare the frosting:* Beat butter, confectioner's sugar, orange juice and lemon juice until smooth and spreadable. Spread frosting over warm cake. When completely cooled, cut into bars.

Apple Pie Coconut Squares

Makes 16 squares

- Preheat oven to 375°F (190°C)
- 8-inch (2 L) square baking pan, greased

BASE

1½ cups	all-purpose flour	375 mL
¼ tsp	salt	1 mL
½ cup	butter or margarine, softened	125 mL
½ cup	packed brown sugar	125 mL
1 tsp	vanilla	5 mL
1⅓ cups	flaked coconut (sweetened or unsweetened)	325 mL

TOPPING

1	can (19 oz/540 mL) apple pie filling	1
1 tbsp	freshly squeezed lemon juice	15 mL
½ tsp	ground cinnamon	2 mL
¼ tsp	ground mace	1 mL

1. *Prepare the base:* In a small bowl, mix together flour and salt.
2. In a large bowl, beat butter and brown sugar until smooth and creamy. Stir in vanilla. Blend in flour mixture. Stir in coconut. Spread half the mixture evenly in prepared pan.
3. *Prepare the topping:* In a clean bowl, mix apple pie filling, lemon juice, cinnamon and mace until blended. Spoon evenly over base. Top with the remaining coconut mixture.
4. Bake in preheated oven for 20 to 25 minutes. Place pan on a rack to cool completely, then cut into squares.

Tip *These squares are also delicious served hot with ice cream.*

Creamy Apricot Coconut Bars

Makes 36 bars

- Preheat oven to 375°F (190°C)
- 13- by 9-inch (3 L) baking pan, greased

BASE

1	package (18 oz/510 g) lemon cake mix, divided	1
¼ cup	packed brown sugar	50 mL
¼ cup	butter or margarine, softened	50 mL
2	eggs	2
¼ cup	water	50 mL
1 cup	flaked coconut (sweetened or unsweetened)	250 mL
1 cup	chopped dried apricots	250 mL

FROSTING

3 oz	cream cheese, softened	90 g
1 tbsp	milk (approximate)	15 mL
Pinch	salt	Pinch
1 tsp	vanilla	5 mL
2½ cups	confectioner's (icing) sugar, sifted	625 mL
Dash	each red and yellow food coloring, mixed to make apricot-orange color	Dash

1. *Prepare the base:* In a large bowl, mix together half the cake mix, brown sugar, butter, eggs and water until blended and smooth. Stir in the remaining cake mix, coconut and apricots. Spread evenly in prepared pan. Bake in preheated oven for 25 to 30 minutes or until a tester inserted in the center comes out clean. Place pan on a wire rack to cool completely.

2. *Prepare the frosting:* In a medium bowl, beat cream cheese, 1 tbsp (15 mL) of milk, salt and vanilla until smooth and creamy. Gradually beat in confectioner's sugar, adding additional milk, 1 tsp (5 mL) at a time, if necessary, until mixture is smooth and spreadable. Beat in coloring, a bit at a time, until desired shade is achieved. Spread evenly over cake. Cut into bars.

Tip *Here's how to protect your frosted cake without having the plastic wrap stick to the frosting. Stick miniature marshmallows on the ends of toothpicks, then stick the toothpicks around the top and sides of the cake, then cover with plastic wrap. After the cake has been unwrapped, the marshmallows make a nice snack.*

Maraschino Coconut Squares

Makes 16 squares
- Preheat oven to 350°F (180°C)
- 8-inch (2 L) square baking pan, lightly greased

BASE

½ cup	butter, softened	125 mL
3 tbsp	confectioner's (icing) sugar, sifted	45 mL
1 cup	all-purpose flour	250 mL

TOPPING

¼ cup	all-purpose flour	50 mL
½ tsp	baking powder	2 mL
¼ tsp	salt	1 mL
½ cup	granulated sugar	125 mL
2	eggs, lightly beaten	2
1 tsp	vanilla	5 mL
¾ cup	chopped walnuts	175 mL
½ cup	flaked coconut (sweetened or unsweetened)	125 mL
½ cup	maraschino cherries, diced and drained	125 mL

1. *Prepare the base:* In a small bowl, cream butter and confectioner's sugar. Blend in flour just until dough forms. Press evenly into prepared pan. Bake in preheated oven for 20 minutes or until edges are lightly browned.

2. *Prepare the topping:* In a medium bowl, mix together flour, baking powder and salt. Add sugar, eggs and vanilla and mix well. Stir in walnuts, coconut and cherries until blended.

3. Spread evenly over baked base. Bake for 25 minutes. Place pan on a wire rack to cool completely, then cut into squares.

Lemon Coconut Squares

Makes 36 squares
- Preheat oven to 325°F (160°C)
- 13- by 9-inch (3 L) baking pan, ungreased

BASE

½ cup	packed brown sugar	125 mL
½ cup	butter, softened	125 mL
1½ cups	all-purpose flour	375 mL

TOPPING

2 tbsp	all-purpose flour	25 mL
½ tsp	baking powder	2 mL
¼ tsp	salt	1 mL
1 cup	granulated sugar, divided	250 mL
3	eggs, separated	3
2 tbsp	grated lemon zest	25 mL
⅓ cup	freshly squeezed lemon juice	75 mL
2 cups	shredded coconut (sweetened or unsweetened)	500 mL

1. *Prepare the base:* In a large bowl, beat brown sugar and butter until smooth and creamy. Gradually add flour, mixing until mixture resembles coarse crumbs. Press evenly into pan. Bake in preheated oven for 10 to 15 minutes or until edges are lightly browned.

2. *Prepare the topping:* In a medium bowl, mix together flour, baking powder, salt and half the sugar. In another bowl, lightly beat egg yolks, lemon zest and juice. Add to flour mixture and mix until blended. Stir in coconut.

3. In a clean bowl, beat egg whites until frothy. Gradually add the remaining sugar and beat until stiff peaks form. Fold into flour mixture until blended.

4. Spread evenly over base. Bake for 20 to 25 minutes or until nearly set. Place pan on a rack to cool completely, then cut into squares.

Tip *To squeeze a few drops of lemon juice without wasting the rest of the lemon, prick the peel at one end of the lemon with a fork, squeeze out the required quantity, then refrigerate the lemon. It will be fresh enough to use several more times.*

Pineapple Coconut Bars

Makes 36 bars

- Preheat oven to 350°F (180°C)
- 13- by 9-inch (3 L) baking pan, greased

BASE

1	package (18 oz/510 g) yellow cake mix	1

FILLING

1	package (4-serving size) vanilla instant pudding mix	1
1 1/4 cups	milk	300 mL
2 cups	drained crushed pineapple	500 mL

TOPPING

1	envelope (1 1/3 oz/42.5 g) whipped topping mix	1
3 oz	cream cheese, softened	90 g
1/4 cup	granulated sugar	50 mL
1/2 tsp	vanilla	2 mL
1/2 cup	flaked coconut, toasted	125 mL

1. *Prepare the base:* Prepare and bake cake mix according to package directions. Place pan on a wire rack to cool.
2. *Prepare the filling:* In a bowl, beat pudding mix and milk. Set aside. When mixture has thickened, fold in pineapple. Spread mixture evenly over cake.
3. *Prepare the topping:* In a medium bowl, prepare whipped topping according to package directions. Set aside.
4. In a medium bowl, beat cream cheese and sugar until smooth. Stir in vanilla. Add 1 cup (250 mL) of whipped topping and beat until blended. Fold in the remaining topping and spread mixture evenly over pudding layer. Sprinkle coconut over top. Cover pan and chill thoroughly (3 to 4 hours), then cut into bars.

Raspberry Coconut Bars

Makes 36 bars

- Preheat oven to 350°F (180°C)
- 13- by 9-inch (3 L) baking pan, ungreased

BASE

1 1/2 cups	all-purpose flour	375 mL
1/4 tsp	salt	1 mL
1/4 cup	granulated sugar	50 mL
3/4 cup	shortening	175 mL
2	egg yolks	2
1/4 tsp	almond extract	1 mL

TOPPING

1 cup	raspberry jam or preserves	250 mL
1/2 cup	flaked coconut (sweetened or unsweetened)	125 mL
2	egg whites	2
1/2 cup	granulated sugar	125 mL

1. *Prepare the base:* In a small bowl, mix together flour and salt.
2. In a large bowl, beat sugar and shortening until smooth and creamy. Beat in egg yolks until incorporated. Stir in almond extract. Blend in flour mixture. Spread evenly in pan. Bake in preheated oven for 15 minutes.
3. *Prepare the topping:* Stir jam or preserves until smooth, then spread evenly over hot base. Sprinkle coconut evenly over top. Set aside.
4. In a clean bowl, beat egg whites until foamy. Gradually beat in sugar until stiff peaks form. Spread evenly over top of coconut. Bake for 25 minutes, until top is lightly browned. Place pan on a wire rack to cool completely, then cut into bars.

Chocolate Coconut Raspberry Squares

Makes 24 squares

- Preheat oven to 350°F (180°C)
- 9-inch (2.5 L) square baking pan, lightly greased

BASE

1/3 cup	granulated sugar	75 mL
1 1/4 cups	all-purpose flour	300 mL
1/2 cup	butter or margarine	125 mL
1	egg yolk	1

TOPPING

1 1/3 cups	raspberry jam or preserves	325 mL
2 cups	flaked coconut (sweetened or unsweetened)	500 mL
1	can (10 oz/300 mL) sweetened condensed milk	1
5 oz	semisweet chocolate	150 g
1 tbsp	butter or margarine	15 mL

1. *Prepare the base:* In a medium bowl, mix together sugar and flour. Using two knives, a pastry blender or your fingers, cut in butter until mixture resembles coarse crumbs. Add egg yolk and mix well. Press evenly into prepared pan. Bake in preheated oven for 18 to 20 minutes or until lightly browned.

2. *Prepare the topping:* Stir jam until smooth and spread over hot base. In a medium bowl, mix together coconut and condensed milk and spread evenly over jam. Bake for 25 minutes or until set. Place pan on a wire rack to cool completely.

3. In a small saucepan, over low heat, melt chocolate and butter, stirring until smooth. Spread evenly over coconut and smooth with a spatula. Chill until set, then cut into squares.

Coconut Nests

Makes 24 squares
- Preheat oven to 350°F (180°C)
- 9-inch (2.5 L) square baking pan, lightly greased

BASE

1 cup	packed brown sugar	250 mL
1 cup	butter or margarine, softened	250 mL
1	egg	1
1 tsp	vanilla	5 mL
2 cups	all-purpose flour	500 mL
1 tsp	salt	5 mL

TOPPING

¼ to ½ cup	raspberry jam	50 to 125 mL
½ cup	shredded coconut (approximate)	125 mL

1. *Prepare the base:* In a bowl, beat sugar and butter until creamy. Beat in egg and vanilla. Gradually mix in flour and salt. Press evenly into prepared pan. Bake in preheated oven for 20 to 25 minutes or until golden brown. Place pan on rack to cool slightly.

2. *Prepare the topping:* Stir jam until smooth and spread over warm base. Sprinkle liberally with coconut until top has a nest-like appearance (you may wish to use more than ½ cup/125 mL of coconut). Place pan on a wire rack to cool completely, then cut into squares.

Coconut Jam Squares

Makes 24 squares
- Preheat oven to 350°F (180°C)
- 9-inch (2.5 L) square baking pan, greased

BASE

1¼ cups	all-purpose flour	300 mL
¼ cup	granulated sugar	50 mL
½ cup	shortening	125 mL

TOPPING

1 cup	raspberry jam	250 mL
2	eggs, beaten	2

2 tsp	vanilla	10 mL
1 cup	granulated sugar	250 mL
½ tsp	baking powder	2 mL
2 cups	flaked coconut (sweetened or unsweetened)	500 mL

1. *Prepare the base:* In a medium bowl, combine flour and sugar. Using two knives, a pastry blender or your fingers, cut shortening in until mixture resembles coarse crumbs. Press evenly into prepared pan.

2. *Prepare the topping:* Stir jam until smooth and spread evenly over base.

3. In a large bowl, beat eggs, vanilla, sugar and baking powder until blended. Stir in coconut. Spread evenly over jam. Bake in preheated oven for 25 to 30 minutes or until golden brown. Place pan on a wire rack to cool completely, then cut into squares. Or serve warm, topped with whipped cream, if desired.

Tip *Other flavors of jam, such as cherry, strawberry, apricot or peach, also work well in this recipe.*

Nut and Peanut Butter Bars and Squares

Grandma's Traditional Almond Squares

Makes 16 squares
- Preheat oven to 350°F (180°C)
- 8-inch (2 L) square baking pan, greased

1 cup	ground almonds	250 mL
¾ cup	all-purpose flour	175 mL
¼ tsp	salt	1 mL
1 cup	granulated sugar	250 mL
1 cup	butter, softened	250 mL
6	egg yolks	6
16	whole blanched almonds	16

1. In a bowl, combine ground almonds, flour and salt.

2. In a large bowl, beat sugar and butter until smooth and creamy. Beat in egg yolks, one at a time, until incorporated. Gradually mix in flour mixture until blended. Spread evenly in prepared pan. Lightly mark off 16 squares and place an almond in the center of each. Bake in preheated oven for 30 to 35 minutes or until golden brown. Place pan on a wire rack to cool slightly, then cut into squares.

Almond Rocca Bars

Makes 24 bars
- Preheat oven to 350°F (180°C)
- 9-inch (2.5 L) square baking pan, greased

BASE

1 cup	butter, softened	250 mL
½ cup	packed brown sugar	125 mL
½ cup	granulated sugar	125 mL
2	egg yolks	2
1 tsp	vanilla	5 mL
1 cup	all-purpose flour	250 mL
1 cup	old-fashioned rolled oats	250 mL

TOPPING

3	milk chocolate bars (each about 1.45 oz/43 g)	3
2 tbsp	butter	25 mL
½ cup	finely chopped almonds	125 mL

1. *Prepare the base:* In a medium bowl, beat butter and sugars until smooth and creamy. Beat in egg yolks until incorporated. Stir in vanilla. Blend in flour and oats.
2. Spread evenly in prepared pan. Bake in preheated oven for 30 to 35 minutes or until browned.
3. *Prepare the topping:* In the top of a double boiler, over hot (not boiling) water, melt chocolate and butter, stirring until smooth. Pour over warm base. Sprinkle almonds evenly over top. Place pan on a wire rack to cool completely, then cut into bars.

Jammin' Almond Bars

Makes 24 bars
- Preheat oven to 375°F (190°C)
- 9-inch (2.5 L) square baking pan, greased

BASE

1¾ cups	old-fashioned rolled oats	425 mL
1 cup	all-purpose flour	250 mL
1 cup	packed brown sugar	250 mL
1 tsp	baking powder	5 mL
¼ tsp	salt	1 mL
¾ cup	butter or margarine, melted	175 mL

TOPPING

¾ cup	raspberry jam	175 mL
½ cup	coarsely chopped almonds	125 mL

1. *Prepare the base:* In a large bowl, mix together oats, flour, brown sugar, baking powder and salt. Add butter and mix until combined. Set aside one-third and press remainder into prepared pan.

2. *Prepare the topping:* Stir jam until smooth and spread evenly over base.
3. In a small bowl, mix together almonds and reserved crumb mixture. Sprinkle over jam layer, pressing down lightly. Bake in preheated oven for 25 to 30 minutes or until golden brown. Place pan on a wire rack to cool completely, then cut into bars.

Dutch Jan Hagels

Makes 36 bars
- Preheat oven to 350°F (180°C)
- 13- by 9-inch (3 L) baking pan, greased

BASE

1¼ cups	all-purpose flour	300 mL
½ cup	granulated sugar	125 mL
½ tsp	ground cinnamon	2 mL
½ cup	butter or margarine, softened	125 mL
1	egg yolk	1

TOPPING

1	egg white	1
¼ cup	granulated sugar	50 mL
½ cup	sliced almonds	125 mL

1. *Prepare the base:* In a medium bowl, mix together flour, sugar and cinnamon. Using two knives, a pastry blender or your fingers, cut butter in until mixture resembles coarse crumbs. Mix in egg yolk until dough forms. Press evenly into prepared pan.
2. *Prepare the topping:* Beat egg white slightly and brush over dough. Sprinkle sugar and almonds over top and press down into dough.
3. Bake in preheated oven for 18 to 20 minutes or until golden brown. Place pan on a wire rack to cool slightly, then cut into bars. Let cool completely before removing from pan.

Tip *When beating ingredients, 150 strokes by hand are equal to 1 minute of beating with an electric mixer.*

Macadamia Nut Triangles

Makes 32 triangles
- Preheat oven to 425°F (220°C)
- 9-inch (2.5 L) square baking pan, greased

BASE

1 cup	all-purpose flour	250 mL
¼ cup	granulated sugar	50 mL
Pinch	salt	Pinch
6 tbsp	butter or margarine	90 mL
3 tbsp	water	45 mL

TOPPING

1¼ cups	macadamia nuts, divided	300 mL
⅔ cup	packed brown sugar	150 mL
1	egg	1
2 tsp	vanilla	10 mL

1. *Prepare the base:* In a small bowl, mix together flour, sugar and salt. Using two knives, a pastry blender, or your fingers, cut butter in until mixture resembles coarse crumbs. Sprinkle with water, 1 tbsp (15 mL) at a time, mixing lightly with a fork until dough is just moist enough to hold together. (You may not need to use all the water.) Press evenly into prepared pan and bake in preheated oven for 15 to 20 minutes or until golden brown. Place pan on a wire rack to cool and reduce oven temperature to 375°F (190°C).

2. *Prepare the topping:* Coarsely chop ½ cup (125 mL) of the nuts and set aside. In food processor, combine the remaining nuts with brown sugar and process until nuts are finely ground. Add egg and vanilla and pulse to blend.

3. Spread topping evenly over base. Sprinkle reserved nuts over top. Bake for 20 minutes. Let cool completely and cut into triangles (see tip, below).

Tip *To cut cake into triangles, cut into 4 long strips. Cut each strip into 4 squares. Cut each square in half on the diagonal to form triangles.*

● ●

Buttermilk Nut Squares

Makes 16 squares
- Preheat oven to 350°F (180°C)
- 8-inch (2 L) square baking pan, greased

BASE

1 cup	all-purpose flour	250 mL
½ tsp	baking powder	2 mL
½ tsp	ground cinnamon	2 mL
¼ tsp	baking soda	1 mL
⅓ cup	butter or margarine, softened	75 mL
½ cup	granulated sugar	125 mL
¼ cup	packed brown sugar	50 mL
1	egg	1
½ cup	buttermilk	125 mL

TOPPING

¼ cup	packed brown sugar	50 mL
¼ cup	finely chopped pecans	50 mL
¼ tsp	ground cinnamon	1 mL
Pinch	ground nutmeg	Pinch

1. *Prepare the base:* In a small bowl, mix together flour, baking powder, cinnamon and baking soda.

2. In a medium bowl, beat butter and sugars until smooth and creamy. Beat in egg until incorporated. Blend in flour mixture alternately with the buttermilk, just until incorporated. Spread evenly in prepared pan.

3. *Prepare the topping:* In a bowl, mix together brown sugar, pecans, cinnamon and nutmeg. Sprinkle evenly over base. Bake in preheated oven for 40 to 45 minutes or until a tester inserted in the center comes out clean. Place pan on a rack to cool completely, then cut into squares.

● ●

Marbled Pistachio Bars

Makes 24 bars
- Preheat oven to 350°F (180°C)
- 9-inch (2.5 L) square baking pan, greased

½ cup	butter or margarine	125 mL
3	eggs	3
1½ cups	granulated sugar	375 mL
½ tsp	vanilla	2 mL
¼ tsp	almond extract	1 mL
1 cup	cake and pastry flour, sifted	250 mL
¼ cup	finely chopped pistachio nuts	50 mL
½ oz	semisweet chocolate, grated	15 g
	Confectioner's (icing) sugar (optional)	
	Vanilla Frosting (optional, see recipe, page 544)	

1. In a saucepan, over low heat, melt butter. Set aside to cool.

2. In a large bowl, beat eggs until foamy. Gradually beat in sugar, beating continually until mixture has tripled in volume, about 15 minutes. Beat in vanilla and almond extract. Fold flour into egg mixture alternately with cooled butter, just until combined. Spread half evenly in prepared pan. Sprinkle half the nuts and half the grated chocolate evenly over top. Spoon the remaining batter over top and sprinkle with the remaining nuts and grated chocolate. Run a knife through the batters to create a marbling effect.

3. Bake in preheated oven for 25 to 30 minutes or until a tester inserted in the center comes out clean. Place pan on a wire rack to cool for 5 minutes, then transfer cake from pan to rack to cool completely. Sift confectioner's sugar lightly over top or frost with Vanilla Frosting. Cut into bars.

Pecan Pie Bars

Makes 36 bars
- Preheat oven to 350°F (180°C)
- 13- by 9-inch (3 L) baking pan, lightly greased

BASE

2 cups	all-purpose flour	500 mL
1/2 cup	granulated sugar	125 mL
3/4 cup	butter or margarine	175 mL

TOPPING

1/4 cup	butter or margarine, melted	50 mL
1 cup	granulated sugar	250 mL
1 cup	corn syrup	250 mL
4	eggs	4
1 2/3 cups	butterscotch chips (10 oz/300 g package)	400 mL
1 1/3 cups	coarsely chopped pecans	325 mL

1. *Prepare the base:* In a medium bowl, mix together flour and sugar. Using two knives, a pastry blender or your fingers, cut butter in until mixture resembles coarse crumbs. Spread evenly in prepared pan. Bake in preheated oven for 15 to 18 minutes or until golden brown.
2. *Prepare the topping:* In a large bowl, beat butter, sugar, syrup and eggs until blended. Stir in butterscotch chips and pecans.
3. Spread evenly over base. Bake for 30 minutes or until set and golden brown. Serve warm or cool completely, then cut into bars.

Tip *These bars are particularly delicious served warm, like pecan pie, with ice cream. If you don't like pecans, use a different kind of nut.*

Caramel Oatmeal Bars

Makes 36 bars
- Preheat oven to 350°F (180°C)
- 13- by 9-inch (3 L) baking pan, greased

BASE

1 1/2 cups	all-purpose flour	375 mL
3/4 cup	packed brown sugar	175 mL
1/2 cup	quick-cooking rolled oats	125 mL
1/2 cup	butter or margarine	125 mL
1	egg, beaten	1
1/2 cup	chopped pecans	125 mL

TOPPING

25	soft caramels	25
1 1/4 cups	milk or sweetened condensed milk	300 mL
1/4 cup	butter or margarine	50 mL

1. *Prepare the base:* In a large bowl, mix together flour, brown sugar and oats. Using two knives, a pastry blender or your fingers, cut butter in until mixture resembles coarse crumbs. Add egg and mix until blended. Stir in pecans. Set aside 1 1/2 cups (375 mL) and press remainder evenly into prepared pan. Bake in preheated oven for 15 to 18 minutes or until lightly browned. Place pan on a rack to cool slightly.
2. *Prepare the topping:* In a saucepan, over low heat, melt caramels in milk and butter, stirring constantly until smooth. Pour over baked base. Sprinkle reserved crumb mixture evenly over top. Bake for 20 to 25 minutes, until bubbly and golden brown. Place pan on a rack to cool completely, then cut into bars.

Caramel Double-Nut Squares

Makes 16 squares
- Preheat oven to 350°F (180°C)
- 8-inch (2 L) square baking pan, greased

3/4 cup	all-purpose flour	175 mL
1 tsp	baking powder	5 mL
1/4 tsp	salt	1 mL
1 cup	packed brown sugar	250 mL
1/4 cup	butter	50 mL
1	egg	1
1 tsp	vanilla	5 mL
1 cup	shredded coconut (sweetened or unsweetened)	250 mL
1/2 cup	ground pecans	125 mL
1/2 cup	chopped walnuts	125 mL

1. In a small bowl, mix together flour, baking powder and salt.
2. In a small saucepan, over medium heat, melt brown sugar and butter, stirring until smooth and blended. Set aside to cool, then beat in egg and vanilla. Gradually blend in flour mixture. Stir in coconut, pecans and walnuts. Spread evenly in prepared pan. Bake in preheated oven for 25 to 30 minutes or until golden brown. Place pan on a rack to cool, then cut into squares.

Walnut Squares

Makes 16 squares
- Preheat oven to 325°F (160°C)
- 8-inch (2 L) square baking pan, greased

BASE

1 cup	all-purpose flour	250 mL
1/2 cup	butter or margarine, softened	125 mL

TOPPING

2	eggs	2
1 cup	packed brown sugar	250 mL
1 tbsp	all-purpose flour	15 mL
1/2 tsp	baking powder	2 mL
1 cup	chopped walnuts	250 mL
1/2 cup	flaked coconut (sweetened or unsweetened) Butter Frosting (optional, see recipe, page 544)	125 mL

1. *Prepare the base:* In a small bowl, mix together flour and butter. Press evenly into prepared pan. Bake in preheated oven for 8 to 10 minutes or until lightly browned. Place pan on a wire rack to cool slightly.

2. *Prepare the topping:* In a medium bowl, beat eggs, brown sugar, flour and baking powder until blended. Stir in nuts and coconut. Spread evenly over warm base. Bake for 20 to 25 minutes or until golden brown. Place pan on a rack to cool completely, then cut into squares. If desired, frost with your favorite Butter Frosting.

Walnut Cheesecake Bars

Makes 36 bars
- Preheat oven to 350ºF (180ºC)
- 13- by 9-inch (3 L) baking pan, greased

BASE

2 cups	all-purpose flour	500 mL
2/3 cup	packed brown sugar	150 mL
1/2 tsp	salt	2 mL
1 cup	finely chopped walnuts	250 mL
2/3 cup	cold butter or margarine, cut into cubes	150 mL

TOPPING

2	packages (each 8 oz/250 g) cream cheese, softened	2
1/2 cup	granulated sugar	125 mL
2	eggs	2
1/4 cup	milk	50 mL
1 tsp	vanilla	5 mL

1. *Prepare the base:* In a large bowl, mix together flour, brown sugar, salt and walnuts. Using two knives, a pastry blender or your fingers, cut butter in until mixture resembles coarse crumbs. Set half aside and press remainder evenly in prepared pan. Bake in preheated oven for 10 to 15 minutes or until lightly browned. Place pan on a wire rack to cool slightly.

2. *Prepare the topping:* In a bowl, beat cream cheese and sugar until smooth. Beat in eggs until incorporated. Stir in milk and vanilla. Spread evenly over warm base. Sprinkle reserved base mixture over top. Bake for 20 to 25 minutes or until just set. Place pan on a rack to cool completely, then cut into bars. Store, covered, in refrigerator.

Sour Cream Coffee Cake Bars

Makes 24 bars
- Preheat oven to 350ºF (180ºC)
- 9-inch (2.5 L) square baking pan, lightly greased

BASE

1 1/2 cups	all-purpose flour	375 mL
1 1/2 tsp	baking powder	7 mL
1 tsp	baking soda	5 mL
Pinch	salt	Pinch
1/2 cup	granulated sugar	125 mL
1/2 cup	butter or margarine, softened	125 mL
2	eggs	2
1 tsp	vanilla	5 mL
1 cup	sour cream	250 mL

TOPPING

1/4 cup	granulated sugar	50 mL
1/4 cup	chopped walnuts	50 mL
2 tsp	ground cinnamon	10 mL

1. *Prepare the base:* In a small bowl, combine flour, baking powder, baking soda and salt.

2. In a large bowl, beat sugar and butter until smooth and creamy. Add eggs and beat until incorporated. Stir in vanilla. Gradually blend in flour mixture alternately with sour cream. Spread half in prepared pan. Set remainder aside.

3. *Prepare the topping:* In a small bowl, mix together sugar, nuts and cinnamon. Sprinkle half evenly over base.

4. Spread reserved batter over nut mixture. Sprinkle the remaining topping evenly over batter. Bake in preheated oven for 40 minutes or until a tester inserted in the center comes out clean. Place pan on a wire rack to cool completely, then cut into squares.

Tip *To prevent freshly baked brownies, bars or squares from sticking to a serving plate, sprinkle a thin layer of sugar evenly over the plate before adding the cake.*

Chinese Nut Chews

Makes 36 bars
- Preheat oven to 350°F (180°C)
- 13- by 9-inch (3 L) baking pan, greased

1 cup	granulated sugar	250 mL
¾ cup	all-purpose flour	175 mL
1 tsp	baking powder	5 mL
¼ tsp	salt	1 mL
3	eggs, beaten	3
1 cup	chopped pitted dates	250 mL
1 cup	chopped walnuts	250 mL
	Confectioner's (icing) sugar	

1. In a large bowl, mix together sugar, flour, baking powder and salt. Add eggs, dates and walnuts and mix well.
2. Spread evenly in prepared pan. Bake in preheated oven for 20 minutes or until top is golden brown. Place pan on a wire rack and cut into bars. Let cool completely, then sift confectioner's sugar over top.

Chocolate Nut Squares

Makes 16 squares
- Preheat oven to 350°F (180°C)
- 8-inch (2 L) square baking pan, lightly greased

BASE

1 cup	all-purpose flour	250 mL
¼ tsp	salt	1 mL
½ cup	butter, softened	125 mL
2 tbsp	confectioner's (icing) sugar, sifted	25 mL
1	egg yolk	1

TOPPING

2 tbsp	all-purpose flour	25 mL
¼ tsp	salt	1 mL
½ cup	packed brown sugar	125 mL
3	eggs	3
⅔ cup	corn syrup	150 mL
1 tbsp	freshly squeezed lemon juice	15 mL
1 cup	semisweet chocolate chips	250 mL
1 cup	chopped pecans or walnuts	250 mL

1. *Prepare the base:* In a small bowl, mix together flour and salt.
2. In a medium bowl, beat butter and confectioner's sugar until smooth and creamy. Beat in egg yolk until incorporated. Blend in flour mixture. Press evenly into prepared pan. Bake in preheated oven for 15 minutes or until golden brown. Place pan on a rack to cool slightly.

3. *Prepare the topping:* In a small bowl, mix together flour and salt. In a large bowl, beat brown sugar, eggs, corn syrup and lemon juice until blended. Blend in flour mixture. Stir in chocolate chips and nuts.
4. Spread topping evenly over top of warm base. Bake for 35 to 40 minutes or until top is set. Place pan on a rack to cool completely, then cut into squares.

Cherry Nut Fingers

Makes 24 bars
- Preheat oven to 350°F (180°C)
- 9-inch (2.5 L) square baking pan, greased

BASE

1¼ cups	all-purpose flour	300 mL
¼ tsp	salt	1 mL
⅔ cup	packed brown sugar	150 mL
½ cup	butter, softened	125 mL
2	egg yolks	2
½ tsp	vanilla	2 mL

TOPPING

2	egg whites	2
2 tbsp	all-purpose flour	25 mL
½ cup	chocolate sundae topping	125 mL
½ cup	shredded coconut (sweetened or unsweetened)	125 mL
½ cup	chopped maraschino cherries	125 mL
½ cup	chopped nuts	125 mL

1. *Prepare the base:* In a small bowl, mix together flour and salt.
2. In a medium bowl, beat brown sugar and butter until smooth and creamy. Beat in egg yolks until incorporated. Stir in vanilla. Blend in flour mixture.
3. Spread evenly in prepared pan. Bake in preheated oven for 15 minutes. Place pan on a wire rack to cool slightly.
4. *Prepare the topping:* In a clean bowl, beat egg whites until soft peaks form. Fold in flour, then chocolate topping, coconut, cherries and nuts.
5. Spread evenly over top of warm base. Bake for 18 to 20 minutes. Place pan on a rack to cool completely, then cut into bars.

Tip *Prefer cake with a finer texture? When baking bars or squares, try adding 2 tbsp (25 mL) boiling water to the creamed butter and sugar mixture.*

Orange Nut Oatmeal Bars

Makes 36 bars

- Preheat oven to 350°F (180°C)
- 13- by 9-inch (3 L) baking pan, greased

BASE

1 1/4 cups	boiling water	300 mL
1 cup	quick-cooking rolled oats	250 mL
1 3/4 cups	all-purpose flour	425 mL
1 tsp	baking powder	5 mL
1 tsp	baking soda	5 mL
1/2 tsp	salt	2 mL
1/2 tsp	ground cinnamon	2 mL
1/2 cup	butter or margarine, softened	125 mL
1/2 cup	packed brown sugar	125 mL
1 cup	granulated sugar	250 mL
2	eggs	2
1 tsp	vanilla	5 mL
1/4 cup	frozen orange juice concentrate, thawed	50 mL

TOPPING

1/2 cup	packed brown sugar	125 mL
1/4 cup	butter or margarine	50 mL
2 tbsp	frozen orange juice concentrate, thawed	25 mL
1 cup	flaked coconut (sweetened or unsweetened)	250 mL
1/2 cup	chopped walnuts	125 mL

1. *Prepare the base:* In a medium bowl, combine boiling water and oats. Set aside.
2. In another medium bowl, mix together flour, baking powder, baking soda, salt and cinnamon.
3. In a large bowl, beat butter and sugars until smooth and creamy. Beat in eggs, one at a time, until incorporated. Stir in vanilla and orange juice concentrate. Gradually blend in flour mixture alternately with oat mixture.
4. Spread evenly in prepared pan. Bake in preheated oven for 40 minutes or until a tester inserted in the center comes out clean. Place pan on a wire rack to cool.
5. *Prepare the topping:* Preheat broiler. In a saucepan, over low heat, stir together brown sugar, butter and orange juice concentrate until dissolved. Increase heat and bring to a boil, stirring constantly; cook for 1 minute. Remove from heat and stir in coconut and nuts. Spread evenly over top of cooled cake and place pan under broiler for 1 to 2 minutes or until golden brown. Place pan on a rack to cool slightly, then cut into bars.

Raspberry Nut Meringue Bars

Makes 24 bars

- Preheat oven to 350°F (180°C)
- 9-inch (2.5 L) square baking pan, greased

BASE

1/2 cup	butter or margarine, softened	125 mL
1/2 cup	confectioner's (icing) sugar, sifted	125 mL
2	egg yolks	2
1 1/4 cups	all-purpose flour	300 mL

FILLING

3/4 cup	raspberry jam	175 mL

TOPPING

2	egg whites	2
Pinch	cream of tartar	Pinch
1/2 cup	granulated sugar	125 mL
1 cup	ground toasted pecans	250 mL

1. *Prepare the base:* In a medium bowl, beat butter and confectioner's sugar until smooth and creamy. Beat in egg yolks until incorporated. Blend in flour. Press evenly into prepared pan. Bake in preheated oven for 10 to 12 minutes or until golden brown. Place pan on a wire rack to cool slightly.
2. *Prepare the filling:* Stir jam until smooth and spread evenly over warm base.
3. *Prepare the topping:* In a clean bowl, beat egg whites and cream of tartar until soft peaks form. Gradually add sugar, beating until stiff peaks form. Fold in nuts.
4. Spread evenly over jam. Bake for 20 to 25 minutes or until lightly browned. Place pan on a rack to cool completely, then cut into bars.

Tips *Always use large eggs for baking, unless a recipe states otherwise.*

To toast nuts in a skillet, stir often over medium heat until nuts become golden brown. To toast nuts in the microwave, spread the nuts out on a paper plate or a shallow dish. Cook on High, 1 1/2 minutes for 1/2 cup (125 mL) nuts and 2 minutes for 1 cup (250 mL) nuts. Stir, then microwave for 2 minutes or until golden.

Variations *Strawberry Nut Meringue Bars: Substitute 3/4 cup (175 mL) strawberry jam for the raspberry.*

Apricot Nut Meringue Bars: Substitute 3/4 cup (175 mL) apricot jam for the raspberry.

Raspberry Hazelnut Bars

Makes 36 bars

- Preheat oven to 350° F (180° C)
- 13- by 9-inch (3 L) baking pan, lightly greased

BASE

1/3 cup	granulated sugar	75 mL
1/2 cup	butter or margarine, softened	125 mL
1	egg	1
2 cups	all-purpose flour	500 mL

TOPPING

3/4 cup	seedless raspberry jam	175 mL
1/2 cup	chopped hazelnuts, toasted	125 mL

1. *Prepare the base:* In a medium bowl, beat sugar and butter until smooth and creamy. Beat in egg until incorporated. Gradually blend in flour just until a dough forms. Spread evenly in prepared pan.
2. *Prepare the topping:* Stir jam until smooth and spread over dough, stopping just short of edges. Sprinkle nuts over top of jam.
3. Bake in preheated oven for 20 to 25 minutes or until golden brown. Place pan on a wire rack to cool completely, then cut into bars.

Banana Cream Walnut Squares

Makes 16 squares

- Preheat oven to 350°F (180°C)
- Baking sheet, greased
- 8-inch (2 L) square baking pan, ungreased

BASE

1 cup	granulated sugar	250 mL
1	egg, beaten	1
1 cup	chopped walnuts	250 mL

TOPPING

1	package (4-serving size) vanilla instant pudding mix	1
1 cup	milk	250 mL
1 cup	sour cream	250 mL
2	bananas, sliced	2

1. *Prepare the base:* In a medium bowl, mix together sugar, egg and nuts until blended. Spread a thin layer on prepared baking sheet. Bake in preheated oven for 18 to 20 minutes or until golden brown. Place pan on a wire rack to cool. When cooled, crush into crumbs. Set aside half and spread remainder evenly in baking pan.

2. *Prepare the topping:* In a medium bowl, beat pudding mix, milk and sour cream until well blended. Fold in bananas. Pour over base and sprinkle with reserved crumbs. Chill for 3 to 4 hours, then cut into squares.

Tip *To toast nuts, spread them in a single layer on a baking sheet. Bake at 350°F (180°C) for 5 to 10 minutes, stirring occasionally until lightly browned.*

Raisin Nut Coffee Cake Bars

Makes 24 bars

- Preheat oven to 350°F (180°C)
- 9-inch (2.5 L) square baking pan, greased

BASE

2 cups	all-purpose flour	500 mL
1 1/2 tsp	baking powder	7 mL
1 tsp	baking soda	5 mL
1/4 tsp	salt	1 mL
1 cup	granulated sugar	250 mL
1/2 cup	butter or margarine, softened	125 mL
2	eggs	2
1 tsp	vanilla	5 mL
1 cup	sour cream	250 mL

FILLING

1 cup	chopped walnuts	250 mL
1/2 cup	granulated sugar	125 mL
1 tsp	ground cinnamon	5 mL
1 1/2 cups	raisins	375 mL

1. *Prepare the base:* In a medium bowl, mix together flour, baking powder, baking soda and salt.
2. In a large bowl, beat sugar and butter until smooth and creamy. Beat in eggs until incorporated. Stir in vanilla and sour cream. Blend in flour mixture. Set half aside and spread remainder evenly in prepared pan.
3. *Prepare the filling:* In a small bowl, mix together nuts, sugar and cinnamon. Sprinkle half evenly over batter in pan. Sprinkle raisins evenly over top. Top with the remaining batter. Sprinkle the remaining nut mixture evenly over top of batter.
4. Bake in preheated oven for 35 to 40 minutes or until a tester inserted in the center comes out clean. Place pan on a wire rack to cool slightly, then cut into bars. Serve warm.

Date Nut Squares

Makes 16 squares
- Preheat oven to 325° F (160° C)
- 8-inch (2 L) square baking pan, greased

6 tbsp	all-purpose flour	90 mL
1 tsp	baking powder	5 mL
1/2 tsp	ground cinnamon	2 mL
1 tsp	grated orange zest	5 mL
3/4 cup	packed brown sugar	175 mL
2	eggs	2
1/2 tsp	vanilla	2 mL
1 cup	chopped pitted dates	250 mL
1 cup	chopped nuts	250 mL
6	maraschino cherries, chopped	6
	Confectioner's (icing) sugar	

1. In a small bowl, mix together flour, baking powder, cinnamon and orange zest.
2. In a large bowl, beat brown sugar, eggs and vanilla until combined. Blend in flour mixture. Stir in dates, nuts and cherries.
3. Spread evenly in prepared pan. Bake in preheated oven for 35 to 40 minutes or until a tester inserted in center comes out clean. Place pan on a wire rack to cool. Sift confectioner's sugar over top, then cut into squares.

Tip *To cut sticky ingredients like dates, prunes or marshmallows, dip kitchen shears in hot water often or rub the blades with vegetable oil.*

Coffee Raisin Nut Bars

Makes 36 bars
- Preheat oven to 350ºF (180ºC)
- 13- by 9-inch (3 L) baking pan, greased

1 1/2 cups	all-purpose flour	375 mL
1/2 tsp	baking powder	2 mL
1/2 tsp	baking soda	2 mL
1/2 tsp	salt	2 mL
1/2 tsp	ground cinnamon	2 mL
1/4 cup	shortening, softened	50 mL
1 cup	packed brown sugar	250 mL
1	egg	1
1/2 cup	hot brewed coffee	125 mL
1/2 cup	raisins	125 mL
1/2 cup	chopped nuts	125 mL
	Coffee Frosting (optional, see recipe, page 551)	

1. In a small bowl, mix together flour, baking powder, baking soda, salt and cinnamon.
2. In a large bowl, beat shortening and brown sugar until smooth and creamy. Add egg and beat until incorporated. Stir in coffee. Blend in flour mixture. Stir in raisins and nuts.
3. Spread evenly in prepared pan. Bake in preheated oven for 20 to 25 minutes or until golden brown. Place pan on a wire rack to cool completely. If desired, frost with Coffee Frosting or a frosting of your choice, then cut into bars.

Carrot Walnut Bars

Makes about 36 bars
- Preheat oven to 350ºF (180ºC)
- 13- by 9-inch (3 L) baking pan, greased

1 1/2 cups	all-purpose flour	375 mL
1 cup	packed brown sugar	250 mL
1 tsp	baking powder	5 mL
1 tsp	ground cinnamon	5 mL
1/2 tsp	baking soda	2 mL
2/3 cup	vegetable oil	150 mL
2	eggs, beaten	2
1 tsp	vanilla	5 mL
1/2 cup	shredded coconut (sweetened or unsweetened)	125 mL
1/2 cup	finely shredded carrots	125 mL
3/4 cup	chopped walnuts	175 mL
	Cream Cheese Frosting (see recipe, page 545)	

1. In a bowl mix together flour, brown sugar, baking powder, cinnamon and baking soda. Make a well in the center. Add oil, eggs and vanilla and mix just until incorporated. Stir in coconut, carrots and walnuts.
2. Spread batter evenly in prepared pan. Bake in preheated oven for 20 to 25 minutes or until a tester inserted in the center comes out clean. Place pan on a wire rack to cool completely.
3. Spread cream cheese frosting over top of cooled cake. Cut into bars. Store, covered, in refrigerator.

Tip *Keep vegetable oil in a squeeze bottle for when small amounts are needed.*

Glazed Walnut Jam Bars

Makes 24 bars

- Preheat oven to 350°F (180°C)
- 9-inch (2.5 L) square baking pan, greased

BASE

1 cup	all-purpose flour	250 mL
1 tsp	baking powder	5 mL
½ cup	shortening, softened	125 mL
1 tbsp	milk	15 mL
1	egg	1

TOPPING

½ cup	raspberry jam	125 mL
2 tbsp	all-purpose flour	25 mL
¼ tsp	salt	1 mL
¼ tsp	baking powder	1 mL
1 cup	packed brown sugar	250 mL
2	eggs	2
1 tsp	vanilla	5 mL
½ cup	flaked coconut (sweetened or unsweetened)	125 mL
1 cup	chopped walnuts	250 mL

GLAZE

1½ cups	confectioner's (icing) sugar, sifted	375 mL
1½ tbsp	freshly squeezed lemon juice	22 mL
1 to 2 tbsp	milk or light (5%) cream	15 to 25 mL

1. *Prepare the base:* In a medium bowl, mix together flour and baking powder. Using two knives, a pastry blender or your fingers, cut shortening in until mixture resembles coarse crumbs. Add milk and eggs; mix just until incorporated. Press evenly into prepared pan.
2. *Prepare the topping:* Stir jam until smooth and spread over base.
3. In a small bowl, mix together flour, salt and baking powder. In another bowl, beat brown sugar, eggs and vanilla until blended. Blend in flour mixture. Stir in coconut and walnuts.
4. Spread evenly over jam and bake in preheated oven for 35 to 40 minutes or until set and golden brown. Place pan on a wire rack to cool.
5. *Prepare the glaze:* In a small bowl, combine confectioner's sugar and lemon juice. Stir in enough milk to make a spreadable consistency. Spread over warm cake. Let cool completely, then cut into bars.

Nutty Mix Bars

Makes 36 bars

- Preheat oven to 350°F (180°C)
- 13- by 9-inch (3 L) baking pan, greased

1	package (18 oz/510 g) yellow cake mix	1
½ cup	crunchy peanut butter	125 mL
1⅔ cups	milk	400 mL
3	eggs	3

NUTTY FROSTING

4¾ cups	confectioner's (icing) sugar, sifted	1.175 L
½ cup	unsweetened cocoa powder, sifted	125 mL
¼ tsp	salt	1 mL
⅓ cup	butter or margarine	75 mL
¼ cup	crunchy peanut butter	50 mL
1 tsp	vanilla	5 mL
⅓ cup	boiling water	75 mL

1. In a large bowl, beat cake mix, peanut butter, milk and eggs until blended and smooth. Spread evenly in prepared pan. Bake in preheated oven for 35 to 40 minutes or until a tester inserted in the center comes out clean. Place pan on a wire rack to cool completely.
2. *Prepare the frosting:* In a large bowl, mix together confectioner's sugar, cocoa and salt. In another large bowl, beat butter, peanut butter and vanilla until smooth and creamy. Beat in boiling water. Gradually add sugar mixture, beating until mixture is smooth and spreadable. Spread frosting on cooled cake, then cut into bars.

Savannah Cake Bars

Makes 36 bars

- Preheat oven to 350° F (180°C)
- 13- by 9-inch (3 L) baking pan, greased

1	package (18 oz/510 g) yellow cake mix	1
½ cup	butter or margarine	125 mL
1 cup	packed brown sugar	250 mL
½ cup	crunchy peanut butter	125 mL
1¼ cups	flaked coconut (sweetened or unsweetened)	300 mL
⅓ cup	half-and-half (10 %) cream	75 mL

1. Prepare and bake cake mix according to package directions. Place pan on a wire rack.

2. In a saucepan, over low heat, melt butter. Remove from heat and add brown sugar, peanut butter, coconut and cream, mixing until well blended. Spread evenly over cake.

3. Preheat broiler. Place cake about 5 to 6 inches (13 to 15 cm) from heat and broil for 1 to 2 minutes or just until frosting bubbles. Place pan on a rack to cool completely, then cut into bars.

Chocolate Chip Granola Bars

Makes 36 bars
- Preheat oven to 325°F (160°C)
- 13- by 9-inch (3 L) baking pan, lined with greased foil

3 cups	old-fashioned rolled oats	750 mL
1 cup	raisins	250 mL
1 cup	sunflower seeds	250 mL
1 cup	chopped peanuts	250 mL
1 cup	semisweet chocolate chips	250 mL
1	can (14 oz/398 mL) sweetened condensed milk	1
½ cup	butter or margarine, melted	125 mL

1. In a large bowl, mix together oats, raisins, sunflower seeds, peanuts and chocolate chips. Add condensed milk and mix thoroughly. Stir in melted butter until blended.

2. Spread evenly in prepared pan. Bake in preheated oven for 25 to 30 minutes or until top is lightly browned. Place pan on a wire rack to cool slightly, then transfer cake, with foil, to a cutting board and cut into bars.

Chunky-Style Peanut Squares

Makes 16 squares
- Preheat oven to 350°F (180°C)
- 8-inch (2 L) square baking pan, greased

1¼ cups	packed brown sugar, divided	300 mL
1 cup	all-purpose flour	250 mL
2 tsp	baking powder	10 mL
½ tsp	salt	2 mL
⅓ cup	crunchy peanut butter	75 mL
½ cup	milk	125 mL
2 tbsp	vegetable oil	25 mL
1 tsp	vanilla	5 mL
1½ cups	hot water	375 mL

1. In a large bowl, mix together ¾ cup (175 mL) of the brown sugar, flour, baking powder and salt. Make a well in the center. Add peanut butter, milk, oil and vanilla and mix just until incorporated.

2. Spread evenly in prepared pan. Sprinkle the remaining brown sugar over top and slowly pour hot water over all. Bake in preheated oven for 45 minutes or until golden brown. Place pan on a wire rack to cool slightly, then cut into squares. Serve warm.

Honey Double-Peanut Bars

Makes 24 bars
- Preheat oven to 400°F (200°C)
- 9-inch (2.5 L) square baking pan, greased

BASE		
2 cups	biscuit mix	500 mL
2 tbsp	granulated sugar	25 mL
⅔ cup	milk	150 mL
1	egg, lightly beaten	1
¼ cup	smooth peanut butter	50 mL
¼ cup	liquid honey	50 mL
TOPPING		
½ cup	biscuit mix	125 mL
½ cup	packed brown sugar	125 mL
½ tsp	ground cinnamon	2 mL
2 tbsp	butter or margarine, softened	25 mL
2 tbsp	smooth peanut butter	25 mL
¼ cup	chopped peanuts	50 mL

1. *Prepare the base:* In a medium bowl, mix together biscuit mix, sugar, milk and egg. Add peanut butter and honey and mix just until blended. (Mixture will not be smooth.) Spread evenly in prepared pan. Set aside.

2. *Prepare the topping:* In a small bowl, mix together biscuit mix, brown sugar and cinnamon. Stir in butter and peanut butter until mixture resembles coarse crumbs. Stir in peanuts.

3. Sprinkle evenly over top of batter. Bake in preheated oven for 20 to 25 minutes or until a tester inserted in the center comes out clean. Place pan on a rack to cool completely, then cut into bars.

Oatmeal Chip Peanut Squares

Makes 16 squares

- Preheat oven to 350°F (180°C)
- 8-inch (2 L) square baking pan, greased

½ cup	packed brown sugar	125 mL
½ cup	corn syrup	125 mL
½ cup	butter or margarine, softened	125 mL
1 tsp	vanilla	5 mL
3 cups	quick-cooking rolled oats	750 mL
½ cup	semisweet chocolate chips	125 mL
¼ cup	smooth peanut butter	50 mL

1. In a large bowl, beat brown sugar, syrup, butter and vanilla until blended and smooth. Stir in oats. Press evenly into prepared pan. Bake in preheated oven for 25 to 30 minutes or until lightly browned. Place pan on a wire rack to cool for 5 minutes.
2. Sprinkle chocolate chips evenly over top, then drop small spoonfuls of peanut butter over top of the chips. Let stand for about 5 minutes, until chips and peanut butter have softened, then run a knife through the topping to create a marbling effect. Chill for 15 to 20 minutes, until topping is firm, then cut into squares.

Tip *If you have forgotten to remove eggs from the refrigerator to allow them to come to room temperature, place them in a bowl of warm water for several minutes.*

Chocolate Raisin Peanut Bars

Makes 36 bars

- Preheat oven to 350°F (180°C)
- 13- by 9-inch (3 L) baking pan, greased

1 cup	all-purpose flour	250 mL
1½ tsp	baking powder	7 mL
½ cup	butter or margarine	125 mL
½ cup	smooth peanut butter	125 mL
1½ cups	granulated sugar	375 mL
2	eggs	2
1 tbsp	vanilla	15 mL
1½ cups	raisins	375 mL
2 oz	semisweet chocolate, melted	60 g

1. In a bowl, combine flour and baking powder.
2. In a large saucepan, over medium heat, stir butter and peanut butter until melted. Remove from heat. Beat in sugar until blended. Add eggs and vanilla and beat until smooth. Blend in flour mixture. Stir in raisins.

3. Spread evenly in prepared pan. Bake in preheated oven for about 25 minutes or until a tester inserted in the center comes out clean. Place pan on a wire rack to cool completely.
4. Drizzle melted chocolate over the top. Let chocolate set, then cut into bars.

Peanut Butterscotch Bars

Makes 36 bars

- Preheat oven to 350°F (180°C)
- 13- by 9-inch (3 L) baking pan, ungreased

BASE

½ cup	packed brown sugar	125 mL
½ cup	butter or margarine, softened	125 mL
1⅓ cups	all-purpose flour	325 mL

TOPPING

⅔ cup	light corn syrup	150 mL
⅔ cup	granulated sugar	150 mL
¾ cup	butterscotch chips	175 mL
½ cup	crunchy peanut butter	125 mL
2 cups	corn flakes cereal	500 mL

1. *Prepare the base:* In a medium bowl, beat brown sugar and butter until smooth and creamy. Blend in flour just until crumbly. Press evenly into pan. Bake in preheated oven for 15 minutes. Place pan on a wire rack to cool slightly.
2. *Prepare the topping:* In a saucepan, over low heat, stir together corn syrup and sugar until dissolved. Increase heat and bring to a boil. Remove from heat and stir in butterscotch chips and peanut butter until chips are melted and mixture is smooth. Stir in corn flakes. Spread evenly over baked base. Let cool completely, then cut into bars.

Caramel Peanut Cup Bars

Makes 36 bars

- Preheat oven to 350°F (180°C)
- 13- by 9-inch (3 L) baking pan, greased

BASE

1	package (18 oz/510 g) yellow cake mix	1
½ cup	butter or margarine, softened	125 mL
1	egg	1
20	miniature peanut butter cups, chopped	20

TOPPING

2½ cups	caramel sundae sauce	625 mL
2 tbsp	cornstarch	25 mL
¼ cup	peanut butter	50 mL
1 cup	chopped salted peanuts, divided	250 mL
1	container (15 oz/450 g) ready-to-serve chocolate frosting	1

1. *Prepare the base:* In a large bowl, mix together cake mix, butter and egg until smooth. Fold in peanut butter cups. Spread mixture evenly in prepared pan. Bake in preheated oven for 18 to 20 minutes or until lightly browned. Place pan on a wire rack to cool slightly.

2. *Prepare the topping:* In a saucepan, over low heat, stir together caramel sauce, cornstarch and peanut butter. Increase heat and bring to a boil; cook, stirring constantly, for 2 minutes, until smooth. Remove from heat. Stir in ½ cup (125 mL) of the peanuts and spread evenly over warm base.

3. Bake for 6 to 8 minutes or until almost set. Place pan on a rack to cool completely. Spread frosting over top. Sprinkle with the remaining peanuts. Chill at least 1 hour before cutting into bars.

• •

Peanut Butter Chews

Makes 16 squares
- Preheat oven to 350°F (180°C)
- 9-inch (2.5 L) square baking pan, greased

BASE

½ cup	butter or margarine, softened	125 mL
½ cup	packed brown sugar	125 mL
1 cup	all-purpose flour	250 mL

FILLING

½ cup	semisweet chocolate pieces	125 mL

TOPPING

1 cup	smooth peanut butter	250 mL
5 cups	miniature marshmallows	1.25 L
½ cup	packed brown sugar	125 mL
¼ cup	table (18%) cream	50 mL
¼ cup	halved maraschino cherries	50 mL
4 cups	dry chow mein noodles	1 L

1. *Prepare the base:* In a small bowl, beat butter and brown sugar until smooth and creamy. Blend in flour. Press evenly into prepared pan. Bake in preheated oven for 15 to 20 minutes or until golden brown. Place pan on a wire rack.

2. *Prepare the filling:* Sprinkle chocolate pieces evenly over hot base.

3. *Prepare the topping:* In the top of a double boiler, over low heat, melt peanut butter and marshmallows. Add brown sugar and cream, stirring constantly until melted and blended. Remove top of double boiler from heat. Stir in cherries and noodles. Spread evenly over chocolate layer. Place pan on a rack to cool completely, then cut into squares.

• •

Peanut Butter Chip Bars

Makes 36 bars
- Preheat oven to 350°F (180°C)
- 13- by 9-inch (3 L) baking pan, ungreased

BASE

1⅓ cups	graham wafer crumbs (about 18 wafers)	325 mL
1¼ cups	all-purpose flour	300 mL
½ cup	granulated sugar	125 mL
1 cup	butter or margarine, melted	250 mL

TOPPING

¾ cup	unsweetened cocoa powder	175 mL
1¼ cups	sweetened condensed milk	300 mL
1	package (10 oz/300 g) peanut butter chips	1
1 cup	flaked coconut (sweetened or unsweetened)	250 mL
¾ cup	chopped peanuts, divided	175 mL

1. *Prepare the base:* In a large bowl, combine crumbs, flour and sugar. Add butter and mix well. Press evenly into pan. Bake in preheated oven for 15 to 20 minutes or until golden brown. Place pan on a rack.

2. *Prepare the topping:* In a large bowl, sift cocoa. Gradually stir in condensed milk until blended. Add peanut butter chips, coconut and ½ cup (125 mL) of the peanuts and mix well.

3. Spread evenly over hot base. Sprinkle the remaining peanuts over top. Bake for 20 to 25 minutes or until topping is set. Place pan on a wire rack to cool completely, then cut into bars.

Tip *Most bars, squares and brownies should be cooled completely before cutting. But when the filling is sticky, you should run a knife around the edge of the pan as soon as you remove it from the oven.*

Chocolate Chip Peanut Butter Squares

Makes 16 squares

- Preheat oven to 350°F (180°C)
- 8-inch (2 L) square baking pan, lightly greased

1 cup	all-purpose flour	250 mL
1 tsp	baking powder	5 mL
¼ tsp	salt	1 mL
½ cup	smooth peanut butter	125 mL
⅓ cup	butter or margarine, softened	75 mL
½ cup	packed brown sugar	125 mL
½ cup	granulated sugar	125 mL
2	eggs	2
1 tsp	vanilla	5 mL
1 cup	semisweet chocolate chips	250 mL

1. In a small bowl, mix together flour, baking powder and salt.
2. In a large bowl, beat peanut butter, butter and sugars until smooth and creamy. Beat in eggs until incorporated. Stir in vanilla. Gradually blend in flour mixture. Stir in chocolate chips.
3. Spread evenly in prepared pan. Bake in preheated oven for 30 to 35 minutes, until golden brown. Place pan on a rack to cool completely.

Tip *Allow cakes to cool completely before frosting, then cut into squares.*

Chocolate-Drizzled Peanut Butter Bars

Makes 36 bars

- Preheat oven to 350°F (180°C)
- 13- by 9-inch (3 L) baking pan, lightly greased

1½ cups	all-purpose flour	375 mL
1 tsp	baking powder	5 mL
¼ tsp	salt	1 mL
1 cup	packed brown sugar	250 mL
½ cup	granulated sugar	125 mL
½ cup	butter or margarine, softened	125 mL
¼ cup	smooth peanut butter	50 mL
2	eggs	2
1 tsp	vanilla	5 mL
½ cup	chopped unsalted peanuts	125 mL
24	miniature peanut butter cups, quartered	24
CHOCOLATE DRIZZLE		
¼ cup	semisweet chocolate chips	50 mL
1 tsp	butter or margarine	5 mL

1. In a bowl, combine flour, baking powder and salt.
2. In a large bowl, beat sugars, butter and peanut butter until smooth. Beat in eggs, one at a time, until incorporated. Stir in vanilla. Blend in flour mixture. Stir in peanuts. Spread evenly in prepared pan. Sprinkle pieces of peanut butter cups over batter and press down slightly. Bake in preheated oven for 20 to 25 minutes or until a tester inserted in the center of cake comes out clean. Place pan on a wire rack to cool slightly.
3. *Prepare the chocolate drizzle:* In the top of a double boiler, over hot (not boiling) water, melt chocolate chips with butter, stirring until smooth. Drizzle over top of warm cake. Let cool completely, then cut into bars.

Tip *To determine if an egg is fresh, place it in a large bowl filled with water. A fresh egg will sink; a stale one will float.*

Peanut Butter Marshmallow Treats

Makes 36 bars

- Preheat oven to 325°F (160°C)
- 13- by 9-inch (3 L) baking pan, greased

BASE		
1½ cups	packed brown sugar	375 mL
½ cup	butter, softened	125 mL
½ cup	peanut butter (smooth or crunchy)	125 mL
2	eggs	2
1 tsp	vanilla	5 mL
1½ cups	quick-cooking rolled oats	375 mL
1 cup	all-purpose flour	250 mL
TOPPING		
3 cups	miniature marshmallows	750 mL
FROSTING		
¼ cup	smooth peanut butter	50 mL
¼ cup	butter or margarine, softened	50 mL
2 tbsp	milk	25 mL
1 tsp	vanilla	5 mL
1⅓ cups	confectioner's (icing) sugar, sifted	325 mL

1. *Prepare the base:* In a large bowl, beat brown sugar, butter and peanut butter until smooth. Beat in eggs, then vanilla, until blended. Blend in oats and flour. Press evenly into prepared pan. Bake in preheated oven for 25 to 30 minutes or until lightly browned around the edges.
2. *Prepare the topping:* Sprinkle marshmallows evenly over base. Bake for 1 to 2 minutes or until marshmallows puff up slightly. Place pan on a wire rack to cool completely.

3. *Prepare the frosting:* In a small bowl, beat peanut butter, butter, milk and vanilla until smooth and creamy. Gradually add confectioner's sugar, beating until mixture is smooth and spreadable. Spread evenly over marshmallow layer, then cut into bars.

• •

Butterscotch Peanut Butter Krunchies

Makes 30 squares
- Preheat oven to 350°F (180°C)
- 13- by 9-inch (3 L) baking pan, ungreased

BASE

1⅓ cups	all-purpose flour	325 mL
½ cup	packed brown sugar	125 mL
½ cup	butter or margarine	125 mL

TOPPING

⅔ cup	granulated sugar	150 mL
⅔ cup	light corn syrup	150 mL
½ cup	crunchy peanut butter	125 mL
1 cup	butterscotch chips	250 mL
2 cups	corn flakes cereal	500 mL

1. *Prepare the base:* In a medium bowl, mix flour and brown sugar. Using two knives, a pastry blender or your fingers, cut butter in until mixture resembles coarse crumbs. Press evenly into pan. Bake in preheated oven for 15 minutes or until lightly browned. Place pan on a wire rack to cool slightly.

2. *Prepare the topping:* In a saucepan, over low heat, stir together sugar and syrup until dissolved. Increase heat and bring to boil. Remove from heat. Add peanut butter and butterscotch chips, stirring until chips are melted and mixture is smooth. Stir in corn flakes until blended. Spread evenly over baked base. Place pan on a rack to cool completely, then cut into squares.

• •

Peanut Butter 'n' Jelly Bars

Makes 36 bars
- Preheat oven to 350°F (180°C)
- 13- by 9-inch (3 L) baking pan, greased

BASE

2 cups	all-purpose flour	500 mL
1 tbsp	baking powder	15 mL
1 tsp	salt	5 mL
1½ cups	granulated sugar	375 mL
⅓ cup	shortening, softened	75 mL
2	eggs	2
⅓ cup	peanut butter	75 mL
1 cup	milk	250 mL

TOPPING

1 cup	red currant jelly	250 mL
1	container (15 oz/450 g) ready-to-serve vanilla frosting	1
½ cup	chopped peanuts	125 mL

1. *Prepare the base:* In a medium bowl, mix together flour, baking powder and salt.

2. In a large bowl, beat sugar and shortening until smooth and creamy. Add eggs and beat until incorporated. Beat in peanut butter. Gradually blend in flour mixture alternately with milk, just until incorporated.

3. Spread evenly in prepared pan. Bake in preheated oven for 45 to 50 minutes, until a tester inserted into center comes out clean. Place pan on a wire rack to cool.

4. *Prepare the topping:* Stir jelly until smooth and spread evenly over top of cake. When cake has cooled completely, frost. Sprinkle chopped peanuts over top and cut into bars.

• •

Shortbread Peanut Butter Favorites

Makes 16 squares
- Preheat oven to 350°F (180°C)
- 9-inch (2.5 L) square baking pan, lightly greased

2 cups	cake and pastry flour, sifted	500 mL
½ tsp	baking powder	2 mL
Pinch	salt	Pinch
½ cup	crunchy peanut butter	125 mL
¾ cup	confectioner's (icing) sugar, sifted	175 mL
¾ cup	unsalted butter, softened	175 mL
1	egg	1
½ tsp	vanilla	2 mL
½ cup	coarsely chopped salted peanuts	125 mL

1. In a medium bowl, mix together flour, baking powder and salt.

2. In another bowl, beat peanut butter, confectioner's sugar and butter until blended. Beat in egg until incorporated. Stir in vanilla. Gradually blend in flour mixture.

3. Spread evenly in prepared pan. Press peanuts into the surface of the batter. Bake in preheated oven for 25 to 30 minutes or until a tester inserted in the center comes out clean. Place pan on a wire rack to cool completely, then cut into squares.

No-Bake Cookies, Bars and Squares

No-Bake Cookies, Bars and Squares

What could be easier than making cookies, bars and squares that you don't even have to bake? Some of these tasty treats require a bit of stovetop cooking; others are just mixed, shaped and chilled. All are simple, fail-proof, fun and delicious.

Almond-Coated Chocolate Fig Balls

Makes about 4 dozen

2³⁄₄ cups	trimmed dried figs	675 mL
¼ cup	water	50 mL
½ cup	bourbon, divided	125 mL
3¼ cups	crushed vanilla wafers (about 68 cookies)	800 mL
1 cup	confectioner's (icing) sugar, sifted	250 mL
1 cup	ground almonds or pecans, divided	250 mL
3 tbsp	all-purpose flour	45 mL
¼ tsp	ground cinnamon	1 mL
1 cup	mini semisweet chocolate chips	250 mL
2 tbsp	light corn syrup	25 mL
¼ cup	granulated sugar	50 mL

1. In a saucepan, combine figs, water and half the bourbon. Bring to a boil over low heat, then simmer, covered, for 10 minutes. Set aside to cool.
2. In a large bowl, mix together vanilla wafers, confectioner's sugar, half the almonds, flour, cinnamon and chocolate chips.
3. In a food processor, combine cooled fig mixture, corn syrup and the remaining bourbon. Process until figs are puréed and mixture is smooth. Add to vanilla wafer mixture and mix until blended.
4. In a small bowl, mix the remaining almonds with granulated sugar.
5. Shape dough into 1-inch (2.5 cm) balls, then roll in the sugar-nut mixture. Place in an airtight container and let mellow for at least 24 hours.

No-Bake Granola Peanut Treats

Makes about 3 dozen
- Large platter or baking sheet, lined with waxed paper

6 cups	miniature marshmallows	1.5 L
¼ cup	butter or margarine	50 mL
½ cup	smooth or crunchy peanut butter	125 mL
4 cups	granola cereal	1 L
1 cup	semisweet chocolate chips	250 mL

1. In a saucepan, over low heat, melt marshmallows and butter or margarine, stirring until mixture is smooth. Remove from heat. Add peanut butter and mix well. Stir in granola and chocolate chips.
2. Shape mixture into 1-inch (2.5 cm) balls and place on platter or prepared baking sheet. Refrigerate until firm.

Chocolate Haystacks

Makes about 3 dozen
- Large platter or baking sheet, lined with waxed paper

6 oz	semisweet chocolate	175 g
1 cup	mini butterscotch chips	250 mL
2 cups	dried chow mein noodles	500 mL
1 cup	salted peanuts	250 mL
1 cup	miniature marshmallows	250 mL

1. In the top of a double boiler, over hot water, melt chocolate and butterscotch chips, stirring constantly, until smooth. Add noodles, peanuts and marshmallows, stirring until well coated with chocolate mixture.
2. Drop by rounded teaspoonfuls (5 mL) onto platter or prepared baking sheet. Refrigerate until firm.

Tip *To freshen up stale marshmallows, store them in an airtight container with a slice of fresh bread.*

Crispy Caramel Haystacks

Makes about 2 dozen
- Large platter or baking sheet, lined with waxed paper

2½ cups	miniature marshmallows	625 mL
3 tbsp	butter or margarine	45 mL
2 cups	dried chow mein noodles	500 mL
12	soft caramels	12
1 tbsp	water	15 mL
2 tbsp	smooth or crunchy peanut butter	25 mL

1. In a large saucepan, over low heat, melt marshmallows and butter or margarine, stirring constantly, until smooth. Add noodles and stir until well coated.
2. Drop mixture by teaspoonfuls (5 mL) onto platter or prepared baking sheet.
3. In a saucepan, over low heat, melt caramels in water, stirring until smooth. Add peanut butter and mix well. Drizzle caramel mixture over haystacks. Refrigerate until firm.

No-Bake Peanut Butter Rice Chews

Makes about 3 dozen

- Large platter or baking sheet, lined with waxed paper

²/₃ cup	corn syrup	150 mL
²/₃ cup	smooth peanut butter	150 mL
½ cup	lightly packed brown sugar	125 mL
2½ cups	crisp rice cereal	625 mL
1 cup	shredded coconut (sweetened or unsweetened)	250 mL
½ cup	chopped nuts	125 mL

1. In a large saucepan, over low heat, combine corn syrup, peanut butter and brown sugar, stirring constantly, until sugar is dissolved. Remove from heat. Stir in rice cereal, coconut and nuts until thoroughly blended.

2. Drop mixture by tablespoonfuls (15 mL) onto prepared baking sheet and refrigerate until firm.

No-Bake Cocoa Orange Balls

Makes about 2½ dozen

- Small baking cups (optional)

¼ cup	unsweetened cocoa powder, sifted	50 mL
1 cup	confectioner's (icing) sugar, sifted	250 mL
1 cup	graham wafer crumbs (about 14 crackers)	250 mL
2 tbsp	corn syrup	25 mL
1 tsp	vanilla	5 mL
¼ cup	frozen orange juice concentrate, thawed	50 mL
	Cocoa powder or confectioner's sugar for coating	

1. In a large bowl, mix together cocoa, confectioner's sugar and graham wafer crumbs. Make a well in the center.

2. In a small bowl, combine corn syrup, vanilla and orange juice concentrate. Add to cocoa mixture and stir until blended. Cover and refrigerate for 30 minutes.

3. Shape mixture into 1-inch (2.5 cm) balls and roll in cocoa or confectioner's sugar. Place in baking cups for decoration, if desired. Store in the refrigerator, but bring to room temperature before serving.

Barnyard Cow Pies

Makes about 2 dozen

- Large platter or baking sheet, lined with waxed paper

2 cups	milk chocolate chips	500 mL
1 tbsp	shortening	15 mL
½ cup	raisins	125 mL
½ cup	chopped slivered almonds	125 mL

1. In the top of a double boiler, over hot water, melt chocolate chips with shortening, stirring constantly, until smooth. Remove from heat. Stir in raisins and almonds until well blended.

2. Drop by tablespoonfuls (15 mL) onto platter or prepared baking sheet and refrigerate until firm.

Chocolate Rum Balls

Makes 2½ dozen

1 cup	vanilla wafer crumbs (about 20 cookies)	250 mL
1½ cups	chopped pecans	375 mL
1 cup	confectioner's (icing) sugar, sifted	250 mL
¼ cup	unsweetened cocoa powder	50 mL
2 tbsp	corn syrup	25 mL
¼ cup	dark rum	50 mL
½ cup	fine granulated sugar	125 mL

1. In a large bowl, mix together wafer crumbs, pecans, confectioner's sugar and cocoa. Stir in syrup and rum until well blended.

2. Shape dough into 1-inch (2.5 cm) balls and roll in sugar. Store in tightly covered container.

Tip *To ease cleanup when measuring 1-cup (250 mL) quantities of messy ingredients such as honey or syrup, use 8-oz (250 mL) paper cups in place of glass measuring cups. When through, just throw them away.*

Chocolate-Covered Peanut Graham Balls

Makes about 2 dozen

- Large platter or baking sheet, lined with waxed paper

3 tbsp	butter, softened	45 mL
½ cup	smooth peanut butter	125 mL
1 cup	confectioner's (icing) sugar, sifted	250 mL
1 cup	graham wafer crumbs (about 14 wafers)	250 mL
8 oz	semisweet chocolate, melted	250 g

1. In a medium bowl, beat butter, peanut butter and confectioner's sugar until smooth. Add wafer crumbs and mix until well blended.
2. Shape mixture into 1-inch (2.5 cm) balls and place on platter or prepared baking sheet. Refrigerate 30 minutes, until firm.
3. Using a spoon or your fingers, dip balls in melted chocolate and roll around until all surfaces are covered. Return to baking sheet and refrigerate until chocolate sets. Store, tightly covered, in refrigerator.

Fruit 'n' Nut Snowballs

Makes about 5 dozen

4 cups	all-bran cereal	1 L
1 cup	pitted prunes	250 mL
1²⁄₃ cups	raisins	400 mL
1½ cups	dried apricots	375 mL
2 cups	chopped pecans	500 mL
	Confectioner's (icing) sugar	

1. Place cereal and prunes in a food processor and process until cereal is crumbled. Add raisins, apricots and pecans and process until fruit is finely chopped.
2. Shape mixture into 1-inch (2.5 cm) balls, then roll in confectioner's sugar. Store in a tightly covered container. Before serving, roll again in confectioner's sugar.

Tip *To keep dried fruit fresh after the package has been opened, place in an airtight container and refrigerate. To soften hardened fruit, soak in hot water or juice.*

Pineapple Snowballs

Makes about 3 dozen
• Large platter or baking sheet, lined with waxed paper

4 oz	cream cheese, softened	125 g
2½ cups	confectioner's (icing) sugar, sifted	625 mL
1 cup	vanilla wafer crumbs (about 20 cookies)	250 mL
¼ tsp	salt	1 mL
½ cup	crushed pineapple, drained	125 mL
½ cup	quartered miniature marshmallows	125 mL
	Shredded coconut	

1. In a large bowl, beat cream cheese until smooth. Gradually add sugar, mixing until creamy. Stir in wafer crumbs and salt and mix well. Add pineapple, then marshmallows, stirring until well combined. Cover and refrigerate for 1 hour.

2. Shape mixture into 1-inch (2.5 cm) balls and roll in coconut until well coated. Place on platter or prepared baking sheet and refrigerate until firm.

Rocky Road Specials

Makes about 2 dozen
• Large platter or baking sheet, lined with waxed paper

8 oz	semisweet chocolate	250 g
1 cup	miniature marshmallows	250 mL
1 cup	chopped walnuts	250 mL
⅓ cup	white chocolate, coarsely chopped, about 2 oz (60 g)	75 mL

1. In top of a double boiler, over hot water, melt semisweet chocolate, stirring occasionally, until smooth. Remove pot from hot water and let stand for 10 to 15 minutes, until chocolate has cooled slightly. Stir in marshmallows, walnuts and white chocolate until well blended.
2. Drop by rounded tablespoonfuls (15 mL) onto platter or prepared baking sheet and refrigerate until chocolate has set.

Tip *To freshen up stale marshmallows, store them in an airtight container with a slice of fresh bread.*

Stovetop Cookies

Makes about 2 dozen

½ cup	chopped pitted dates	125 mL
2	eggs, beaten	2
¾ cup	granulated sugar	175 mL
1 tsp	vanilla	5 mL
Pinch	salt	Pinch
1 cup	crisp rice cereal	250 mL
1 cup	coarsely crushed corn flakes cereal	250 mL
	Flaked or shredded coconut	

1. In a heavy skillet, over low heat, stirring constantly, cook dates, eggs and sugar for 8 minutes. Remove from heat. Stir in vanilla and salt, then rice cereal and corn flakes. Mix together until well blended.
2. Wet hands and roll dough into balls or fingers. On a plate, roll balls in coconut until well coated.

Tip *To color coconut, add food coloring to 1 tsp (5 mL) water and toss the coconut until evenly colored.*

Stovetop Sugarplum Gems

Makes about 2½ dozen

- Large platter or baking sheet, lined with waxed paper

½ cup	cooking dates, cut into thin strips	125 mL
½ cup	dried apricots, cut into thin strips	125 mL
3 tbsp	water	45 mL
2 tbsp	liquid honey	25 mL
1 tsp	grated orange zest	5 mL
2 tbsp	freshly squeezed orange juice	25 mL
¼ cup	finely chopped pecans	50 mL
¾ cup	shredded coconut (sweetened or unsweetened)	175 mL
	Confectioner's (icing) sugar	

1. In a saucepan, combine dates, apricots, water, honey and orange juice. Cover and cook over medium heat until simmering. Reduce heat to low and, stirring constantly, cook for 10 minutes, until fruit is very tender and liquid has evaporated. (If liquid evaporates before the fruit softens, add about 1 tbsp/15 mL water.) Remove from heat and set aside until mixture is lukewarm, then process in a food processor until mixture is a fairly smooth paste.
2. Transfer mixture to a bowl and stir in orange zest and pecans, mixing until well blended.
3. Spread coconut out on a shallow dish. Pinch off a rounded teaspoonful (5 mL) of dough and, using the palms of your hands, roll into a ball. Drop into coconut and roll until well coated. Repeat with the remaining dough.
4. Place on platter or prepared baking sheet and sprinkle with confectioner's sugar.

Tip *If shredded or flaked coconut dries out, sprinkle with milk and let stand until it softens to the desired consistency. If you won't be using coconut for a while, to prevent it from becoming moldy, toast in a skillet, then store.*

Chocolate Peppermint Bars

Makes 18 long bars

- 9-inch (2.5 L) square baking pan, greased

BASE

¼ cup	butter or margarine, melted	50 mL
1¼ cups	vanilla wafer crumbs (about 28 cookies) filling	300 mL

FILLING

4 cups	peppermint-flavored ice cream, softened	1 L

TOPPING

2 oz	unsweetened chocolate	60 g
½ cup	butter or margarine	125 mL
3	eggs, separated	3
1 tsp	vanilla	5 mL
1½ cups	confectioner's (icing) sugar, sifted	375 mL
½ cup	chopped pecans	125 mL

1. *Prepare the base:* In a small bowl, mix together butter and crumbs. Set aside ¼ cup (50 mL) and press remainder evenly into prepared pan.
2. *Prepare the filling:* Spread softened ice cream evenly over top of base, then freeze until solid.
3. *Prepare the topping:* In a large saucepan, over low heat, melt butter and chocolate, stirring until smooth. Set aside to cool slightly, then beat in egg yolks. Stir in vanilla. Gradually add confectioner's sugar, beating until blended and smooth. Fold in nuts.
4. In a clean bowl, beat egg whites until soft peaks form. Gently fold into chocolate mixture until combined, then spread mixture over top of ice cream. Sprinkle reserved base mixture over top and freeze. When ready to serve, cut into bars.

Tip *Raw eggs can be a potentially dangerous source of salmonella. To reduce this food-safety risk, add egg yolk to butter and chocolate in Step 3 and cook over low heat. Use pasteurized egg whites in Step 4.*

Hawaiian Cheesecake Bars

Makes 24 bars

- 9-inch (2.5 L) square baking pan, ungreased

BASE

1 cup	graham wafer crumbs (about 14 wafers)	250 mL
¼ cup	granulated sugar	50 mL
¼ cup	butter or margarine, melted	50 mL

TOPPING

1	can (20 oz/568 mL) pineapple chunks packed in juice	1
1	package (4-serving size) lemon-flavored gelatin dessert mix	1
1	package (8 oz/250 g) cream cheese, softened	1

1. *Prepare the base:* In a small bowl, mix together wafer crumbs, sugar and butter until blended. Press evenly into pan. Chill until firm.

2. *Prepare the topping:* Drain pineapple, reserving juice. Cover pineapple and refrigerate until ready to use. Add water to the juice to make 1 cup (250 mL). In a saucepan, over medium heat, bring to a boil.

3. In a heatproof bowl, combine lemon gelatin and boiling liquid. Stir until gelatin dissolves. Set half aside. Add cream cheese to remainder and beat until smooth and blended. Spread evenly over base. Chill until set.

4. Arrange pineapple chunks over top and spoon reserved gelatin mixture over top of pineapple. Refrigerate until set, then cut into bars.

• •

Ice Cream Peanut Krispies

Makes 12 bars

• 13- by 9-inch (3 L) baking pan, greased with butter

½ cup	peanut butter (smooth or crunchy)	125 mL
½ cup	corn syrup	125 mL
4 cups	crisp rice cereal (cocoa-flavored, if desired)	1 L
2 cups	chocolate or vanilla ice cream	500 mL

1. In a large bowl, beat peanut butter and corn syrup until smooth and creamy. Stir in cereal and mix until well coated. Press evenly into prepared pan. Chill until firm.

2. When ready to serve, cut cake into 12 large bars. Place a slice of ice cream on half the bars, then top with the remaining bars. Cut each bar in half. Store in freezer.

• •

No-Bake Eatmore Bars

Makes 36 bars

• 13- by 9-inch (3 L) baking pan, lightly greased

¾ cup	packed brown sugar	175 mL
¾ cup	liquid honey	175 mL
¾ cup	smooth peanut butter	175 mL
½ cup	unsweetened cocoa powder, sifted	125 mL
1¼ cups	quick-cooking rolled oats	300 mL
2½ cups	crisp rice cereal	625 mL
1 cup	chopped peanuts	250 mL
1 cup	chopped mixed dried fruit (such as dates, raisins, apples, apricots, cranberries, etc.)	250 mL

1. In a saucepan, over low heat, combine brown sugar, honey and peanut butter. Cook, stirring, until sugar dissolves and mixture is smooth. Stir in cocoa.

2. In a large bowl, mix together oats, cereal, peanuts and dried fruit. Add brown sugar mixture and mix until blended (mixture will be a bit crumbly). Press batter evenly into prepared pan. Chill until set, then cut into bars.

• •

The Ultimate Nanaimo Bar

Makes 24 bars

• 9-inch (2.5 L) square baking pan, greased with butter

BASE

½ cup	butter, melted	125 mL
¼ cup	granulated sugar	50 mL
1	egg, beaten	1
⅓ cup	unsweetened cocoa powder, sifted	75 mL
1 tsp	vanilla	5 mL
2 cups	graham wafer crumbs (about 30 wafers)	500 mL
1 cup	shredded coconut (sweetened or unsweetened)	250 mL
½ cup	chopped walnuts	125 mL

FILLING

¼ cup	butter, softened	50 mL
2 tbsp	vanilla custard powder or vanilla instant pudding mix	25 mL
2 tbsp	milk (approximate)	25 mL
2 cups	confectioner's (icing) sugar, sifted	500 mL

TOPPING

4 oz	unsweetened chocolate	125 g
1 tbsp	butter	15 mL

1. *Prepare the base:* In a small bowl, mix together melted butter, sugar, egg, cocoa and vanilla until blended.

2. In a large bowl, mix together crumbs, coconut and walnuts. Add butter mixture and mix well. Press evenly into prepared pan. Chill for at least 1 hour.

3. *Prepare the filling:* In a medium bowl, cream butter. Beat in custard powder, milk and confectioner's sugar until blended. If mixture is too thick, add a few drops more milk. Spread evenly over base and chill for 30 minutes or until firm.

4. *Prepare the topping:* In a saucepan, over low heat, melt chocolate and butter, stirring until smooth. Spread evenly over topping, then cut into bars. Store, covered, in the refrigerator.

Tip *Classic Nanaimo Bars are made with Bird's Custard Powder. If you can't find it, substitute an equal quantity of vanilla instant pudding powder (sold in tins).*

Puffed Wheat Bars

Makes about 40 bars

- 13- by 9-inch (3 L) baking pan, greased

½ cup	butter or margarine	125 mL
½ cup	corn syrup	125 mL
1 cup	packed brown sugar	250 mL
2 tbsp	unsweetened cocoa powder, sifted	25 mL
1 tsp	vanilla	5 mL
½ cup	salted peanuts	125 mL
8 cups	puffed wheat cereal	2 L

1. In a saucepan, over low heat, bring butter, corn syrup, brown sugar and cocoa to a boil. Cook, stirring for 3 minutes. Remove from heat. Stir in vanilla. Stir in peanuts and puffed wheat.

2. Press evenly into prepared pan. Set aside until firm, then cut into bars.

Noble Napoleons

Makes 36 bars

- 13- by 9-inch (3 L) baking pan, lined with waxed paper

BASE

40	graham wafers, divided	40
1	package (6 oz/170 g) chocolate pudding and pie filling (not instant pudding)	1
2 cups	milk	500 mL
1 cup	whipping (35%) cream, whipped	250 mL

TOPPING

2 tbsp	butter or margarine	25 mL
1 cup	semisweet chocolate chips	250 mL

FROSTING

1 tbsp	butter or margarine, softened	15 mL
1 tbsp	milk	15 mL
¾ cup	confectioner's (icing) sugar, sifted	175 mL

1. *Prepare the base:* In prepared pan, place half of the graham wafers in a single layer, cutting end pieces to fit. Set aside.

2. Prepare pudding mix according to package directions, using 2 cups (500 mL) of milk. Place a layer of plastic wrap directly on pudding (to prevent a skin from forming) and chill.

3. When pudding is chilled, fold in whipped cream. Spread evenly over wafers in pan. Cover with the remaining graham wafers, cutting as necessary to cover top completely. Chill for several hours or overnight.

4. *Prepare the topping:* In a saucepan, over low heat, melt butter and chocolate chips. Spread evenly over top layer of graham wafers. Chill until chocolate is firm.

5. *Prepare the frosting:* Mix together butter, milk and confectioner's sugar until blended and smooth. Using a cake decorator's bag, or any appropriate method, make a checkerboard design over top of chocolate. Chill until set.

6. Before serving, leave at room temperature for about 15 minutes, then cut into bars. Store, covered, in refrigerator.

Blueberry and White Chocolate Squares

Makes 16 squares

- 8-inch (2 L) square baking pan, lined with foil extending over ends

BASE

¼ cup	butter or margarine, melted	50 mL
2 cups	amaretti cookie crumbs	500 mL

TOPPING

1½ cups	blueberries, fresh or individually frozen and thawed	375 mL
⅓ cup	whipping (35%) cream	75 mL
8 oz	white chocolate, finely chopped	250 g

1. *Prepare the base:* In a medium bowl, mix together butter and cookie crumbs. Press evenly into prepared pan

2. *Prepare the topping:* Sprinkle blueberries evenly over base.

3. In a large saucepan, heat whipping cream to boiling. Remove from heat and add chocolate, stirring until melted and smooth.

4. Spoon evenly over blueberries. Chill for 2 hours or until firm. Transfer cake, with foil, to a cutting board and cut into squares.

Honey Nut Chocolate Squares

Makes 16 squares

- 8- or 9-inch (2 or 2.5 L) square baking pan, greased

1 cup	smooth peanut butter	250 mL
¾ cup	liquid honey	175 mL
1 tsp	vanilla	5 mL
3 cups	crisp rice cereal	750 mL
1 cup	salted peanuts	250 mL
1 cup	semisweet chocolate chips	250 mL

1. In a saucepan, over medium heat, bring peanut butter and honey to a boil, stirring until smooth. Remove from heat and stir in vanilla. Add cereal, peanuts and chocolate chips and mix well.
2. Press evenly into prepared pan. Chill for 1 hour, until firm. Cut into squares.

• •

Raspberry Patch Shortcake

Makes 30 squares
- 13- by 9-inch (3 L) baking pan, ungreased

1	pound cake (about 10 oz/300 g), cut into 12 slices	1
1/3 cup	cranberry juice	75 mL
2 cups	fresh whole raspberries	500 mL
2	packages (each a 4-serving size) vanilla instant pudding mix	2
2 1/2 cups	milk	625 mL
4 cups	whipped topping, divided	1 L

1. Line pan with sliced cake. Drizzle cranberry juice evenly over top. Spread raspberries evenly over top.
2. Prepare pudding according to package directions, using 2 1/2 cups (625 mL) of milk for both packages. Fold in 1 cup (250 mL) of the whipped topping and spoon over the raspberries. Spread the remaining topping evenly over top. Chill for at least 1 hour. Cut into squares.

• •

Luscious Lemon Squares

Makes 12 large squares
- 13- by 9-inch (3 L) baking pan, ungreased

BASE

1/4 cup	butter or margarine, melted	50 mL
1 1/4 cups	graham wafer crumbs (about 18 wafers)	300 mL

FILLING

3/4 cup	boiling water	175 mL
1	package (6 oz/170 g) lemon-flavored gelatin dessert mix	1
1/4 cup	freshly squeezed lemon juice	50 mL
1/4 cup	liquid honey	50 mL
1	can (14 oz/385 mL) chilled evaporated milk	1
1 tsp	grated lemon zest	5 mL

1. *Prepare the base:* In a small bowl, mix together butter and wafer crumbs. Set aside 1/4 cup (50 mL) and press remainder into pan.

2. *Prepare the filling:* In a heatproof bowl, combine boiling water and gelatin, stirring until gelatin is completely dissolved. Add lemon juice and honey. Set aside to cool.
3. In another bowl, beat evaporated milk until stiff. Gently fold in lemon zest, then gelatin mixture. Spoon over base and sprinkle the reserved crumbs evenly over top. Chill for 4 hours or until set. Cut into squares.

• •

Chocolate Peanut Krispies

Makes 30 squares
- 13- by 9-inch (3 L) baking pan, lightly greased

2/3 cup	smooth peanut butter	150 mL
2 cups	semisweet chocolate chips	500 mL
3 cups	miniature marshmallows	750 mL
6 cups	crisp rice cereal	1.5 L

1. In a large saucepan, over low heat, melt peanut butter and chocolate chips, stirring constantly until smooth. Remove from heat. Stir in marshmallows and cereal, mixing until combined.
2. Press evenly into prepared pan and chill until firm, about 1 hour. Cut into squares and store, covered, in refrigerator.

• •

No-Bake Crispy Peanut Butter Squares

Makes 16 squares
- 8-inch (2 L) square baking pan, lightly greased

1 cup	smooth peanut butter	250 mL
1/4 cup	butter or margarine	50 mL
1/2 cup	packed brown sugar	125 mL
1/2 cup	corn syrup	125 mL
1 tsp	vanilla	5 mL
Pinch	salt	Pinch
2 cups	corn flakes cereal	500 mL
1 cup	crispy rice cereal	250 mL

1. In a saucepan, over low heat, stir together peanut butter, butter, brown sugar and corn syrup until blended and smooth. Remove from heat and stir in vanilla and salt.
2. In a large bowl, mix together cereals. Add peanut butter mixture and mix well.
3. Press evenly into prepared pan. Chill for 6 hours or until firm. Cut into squares.

Coconut Date Refrigerator Squares

Makes 16 squares

• 8-inch (2 L) square baking pan, ungreased

BASE

½ cup	finely chopped pitted dates	125 mL
⅓ cup	granulated sugar	75 mL
½ cup	butter or margarine	125 mL
⅓ cup	unsweetened cocoa powder, sifted	75 mL
1	egg	1
1 tsp	vanilla	5 mL
2 cups	graham wafer crumbs (about 30 wafers)	500 mL
1 cup	shredded coconut (sweetened or unsweetened)	250 mL
½ cup	chopped walnuts	125 mL

FILLING

⅓ cup	butter or margarine	75 mL
2 tbsp	vanilla custard powder	25 mL
¼ cup	milk	50 mL
2 cups	confectioner's (icing) sugar, sifted	500 mL

TOPPING

1 tbsp	butter or margarine	15 mL
4 oz	semisweet chocolate	125 g

1. *Prepare the base:* In a saucepan, combine dates, sugar, butter and cocoa. Cook, stirring, over medium heat until butter melts. Remove from heat and stir in egg and vanilla until blended. Add crumbs, coconut and nuts and mix well. Press evenly into pan. Chill for 2 to 3 hours.
2. *Prepare the filling:* In a medium bowl, cream butter. Beat in custard powder, milk and confectioner's sugar until blended and smooth. Spread evenly over chilled base. Chill for 30 minutes.
3. *Prepare the topping:* In a small saucepan, melt chocolate and butter over low heat, stirring constantly, until smooth. Spread over chilled layers. Chill until chocolate hardens, then cut into squares.

Tip *Raw eggs can be a potentially dangerous source of salmonella. To reduce this food-safety risk, use pasteurized egg in Step 1.*

Coconut Custard Icebox Bars

Makes 36 bars

• 13- by 9-inch (3 L) baking pan, ungreased

BASE

¼ cup	granulated sugar	50 mL
¼ cup	unsweetened cocoa powder, sifted	50 mL
½ cup	butter or margarine	125 mL
2 cups	graham wafer crumbs (about 30 wafers)	500 mL
1	egg, beaten	1
1 tsp	vanilla	5 mL
1 cup	flaked coconut (sweetened or unsweetened)	250 mL
½ cup	finely ground walnuts	125 mL

TOPPING

¼ cup	butter or margarine, softened	50 mL
3 tbsp	custard powder	45 mL
Pinch	salt	Pinch
2 cups	confectioner's (icing) sugar, sifted	500 mL
3 tbsp	boiling water	45 mL

FROSTING (OPTIONAL)

6 oz	semisweet chocolate	175 g
1 tbsp	butter	15 mL

1. *Prepare the base:* In a large saucepan, over low heat, stir together sugar, cocoa and butter until butter is melted and sugar dissolves. Remove from heat and sprinkle graham crumbs over top. Let stand for 1 minute, then stir until blended. Stir in egg and vanilla. Stir in coconut and walnuts. Spread mixture evenly in pan. Chill until firm (about 30 minutes).
2. *Prepare the topping:* In a medium bowl, beat butter, custard powder and salt until creamy. Gradually add confectioner's sugar, beating until mixture resembles coarse crumbs. Slowly add boiling water, beating until mixture is smooth and spreadable. Spread over base and chill for 30 minutes or until topping has hardened.
3. *If desired, prepare the frosting:* In a small saucepan, over low heat, melt chocolate and butter, stirring until melted and smooth. Drizzle over cake. Chill until chocolate is firm. Cut into bars.

Tip *Raw eggs can be a potentially dangerous source of salmonella. To reduce this food-safety risk, use pasteurized egg in Step 1.*

Specialty Cookies, Bars and Squares

Specialty Cookies, Bars and Squares

In this chapter I've collected recipes for cookies, bars and squares that are a bit unusual. They may be special because they are put to extraordinary uses, such as being shaped into cups or cones and packed with a filling or, like Best Spritz Cookies, they are pressed into interesting patterns and designs using an uncommon technique. Try browsing through this chapter when you're in the mood to make cookies, bars and squares but feel you want something different.

Cookie Cups

Makes 1 dozen cookie cups
- Preheat oven to 350°F (180°C)
- Baking sheet, greased
- Small custard cups, inverted, or overturned muffin tin, brushed with butter

1/2 cup	all-purpose flour	125 mL
1/2 cup	granulated sugar	125 mL
Pinch	salt	Pinch
1	egg	1
1	egg white	1
1 tsp	orange-flavored liqueur	5 mL
1 tsp	grated orange zest	5 mL
3 tbsp	butter or margarine, melted	45 mL
1/4 cup	sliced blanched almonds, toasted	50 mL
	Pudding, mousse or fresh fruit for filling	
	Whipped cream	

1. In a small bowl, combine flour, sugar and salt.
2. In a medium bowl, whisk together egg, egg white, liqueur and zest. Gradually stir in flour mixture and mix until blended and smooth. Fold in toasted almonds.
3. Drop batter by heaping tablespoons (15 mL), 4 inches (10 cm) apart and 4 inches (10 cm) from the edge, onto prepared baking sheet. Bake only two cookies at a time in preheated oven for 5 to 7 minutes or until edges are lightly browned.
4. Working quickly, with a spatula, drape warm cookies, one at a time, over the inverted cups and press down lightly with your hand to make a cup shape. When cookies become firm, about 30 minutes, lift gently and place on a wire rack to cool.
5. *To serve:* Fill cookie cups with pudding, mousse or fresh fruit topped with whipped cream.

Apricot Cheddar Pillows

Makes about 3 dozen
- Preheat oven to 400°F (200°C)
- Baking sheet, ungreased
- Round cookie cutter

2 cups	all-purpose flour	500 mL
1/2 tsp	salt	2 mL
1/3 cup	butter	75 mL
2/3 cup	shortening	150 mL
1 cup	crumbled old Cheddar cheese	250 mL
1 to 2 tbsp	cold water	15 to 25 mL
1/2 cup	apricot jam	125 mL

1. In a large bowl, mix together flour and salt. Using two knives, a pastry blender or your fingers, cut in butter and shortening until mixture resembles coarse crumbs. Mix in crumbled cheese. If necessary, add enough cold water to dough to achieve a pastry-like consistency. Knead lightly and refrigerate for at least 30 minutes.
2. On a lightly floured surface, roll dough out to 1/8-inch (0.25 cm) thickness. Using a round cookie cutter or glass dipped in flour, cut out circles. Place a level teaspoonful (5 mL) apricot jam in the center of each round. Fold dough in half to form a semi-circle. Seal edges with the tines of a fork. Place about 1/2 inch (1 cm) apart on baking sheet. Bake in preheated oven for 12 to 15 minutes or until golden brown. Immediately transfer to wire racks to cool.

Rice Pudding Bars

Makes 24 bars
- Preheat oven to 325°F (160°C)
- 9-inch (2.5 L) square baking pan, greased

2	eggs	2
1/3 cup	packed brown sugar	75 mL
1/2 tsp	ground cinnamon	2 mL
1/2 tsp	vanilla	2 mL
1 cup	milk	250 mL
1 cup	cooked rice	250 mL
1/4 cup	raisins	50 mL

1. In a medium bowl, beat eggs, brown sugar, cinnamon, vanilla and milk until well blended. Stir in rice and raisins.
2. Spread evenly in prepared pan. Bake in preheated oven for 40 to 45 minutes or until firm. Place pan on a wire rack and cut into bars.

Chocolate Puffs

Makes 4 puffs

- Preheat oven to 375°F (190°C)
- Baking sheet, ungreased

1	package (8 oz/235 g) refrigerated crescent rolls	1
1	milk chocolate or bittersweet chocolate bar (4 oz/100 g), broken into 4 equal pieces	1

1. On a floured surface, separate dough into 4 rectangles and press the perforated seams together to form a seamless piece. Place a piece of chocolate in the center of each rectangle. Fold up the sides of dough to cover the chocolate, making certain the chocolate is totally enclosed and won't leak out. Pinch the seams together to form a new rectangle about 4$\frac{1}{2}$ by 2$\frac{1}{2}$ inches (11 by 6 cm). Repeat with the remaining dough. Place about 2 inches (5 cm) apart on baking sheet.

2. Bake in preheated oven for 10 to 12 minutes or until golden brown. Let cool on sheet for a few minutes, then transfer to a serving plate.

Peak Frean Vanilla Napoleons

Makes 8 Napoleons

1	package (4-serving size) vanilla pudding and pie filling mix	1
1$\frac{1}{2}$ cups	milk	375 mL
$\frac{1}{2}$ cup	confectioner's (icing) sugar, sifted	125 mL
1 tbsp	water	15 mL
$\frac{1}{4}$ tsp	vanilla	1 mL
24	Peak Frean Nice cookies	24
1 oz	unsweetened chocolate, melted	30 g

1. Prepare pudding following package directions, but using only 1$\frac{1}{2}$ cups (375 mL) milk. Let cool, stirring frequently.

2. In a small bowl, mix together sugar, water and vanilla to make a glaze.

3. Place eight cookies on a work surface. Spread tops with the glaze. Using a spoon, drizzle with chocolate in thin horizontal lines about $\frac{1}{2}$ inch (1 cm) apart. Draw a knife across the lines in the opposite direction (vertically) to make a design. Set aside.

4. Place eight more cookies on work surface. Spread each with pudding. Top with eight more cookies and spread with pudding. Top with glazed cookies. Refrigerate for 6 hours.

Almond Cookie Cones

Makes 6 cones

- Preheat oven to 400°F (200°C)
- Baking sheet, lightly oiled and lined with parchment or waxed paper

2 tbsp	corn syrup	25 mL
4 tsp	pure maple syrup	20 mL
2 tbsp	butter, softened	25 mL
4 tsp	liquid honey	20 mL
$\frac{1}{2}$ cup	granulated sugar	125 mL
3 tbsp	whipping (35%) cream	45 mL
1 tsp	all-purpose flour	5 mL
$\frac{3}{4}$ cup	ground almonds	175 mL
WHITE CHOCOLATE CREAM FILLING		
3 oz	white chocolate, chopped	90 g
$\frac{3}{4}$ cup	whipping (35%) cream, divided	175 mL

1. In a medium saucepan, combine syrups, butter, honey, sugar, cream and flour. Bring to a boil and, over medium heat, cook, stirring, for about 5 minutes. Remove from heat and stir in almonds.

2. Using a ladle or large spoon, drop one-sixth of the batter onto prepared baking sheet to form a round cookie. Repeat two more times, so there are three cookies on the sheet, leaving enough room between each cookie to allow for considerable spreading.

3. Bake in preheated oven for 5 to 6 minutes, until cookies are golden. Let cool on sheet for 3 minutes, then carefully loosen the edges with a spatula or knife. Lift cookie and wrap it around well-greased handles of several spoons held together to form a cone. Let cool, then slide off gently. Or place lacy side of a cooled cookie on a foil-lined baking sheet and heat in a 350°F (180°C) oven for 2 to 3 minutes, until it softens slightly. Remove from foil, one cookie at a time, and roll, lacy side out, to form cones. Repeat with the remaining batter.

4. *Prepare the filling:* In a small saucepan, over low heat, melt chocolate and $\frac{1}{4}$ cup (50 mL) of the cream, stirring until smooth. Set aside to cool. In a small bowl, beat remaining cream until soft peaks form. Fold in chocolate mixture and refrigerate until ready to use. When ready to serve, spoon about 2 tbsp (25 mL) mixture into each cornucopia.

Tip *Fill the cones with plain whipped cream or whipped cream mixed with chopped strawberries.*

Almond Crescents

Makes about 4 dozen
- Preheat oven to 350°F (180°C)
- Baking sheet, lined with parchment or waxed paper

2 cups	cake and pastry flour	500 mL
½ cup	confectioner's (icing) sugar, sifted	125 mL
1 cup	butter, softened	250 mL
1 tsp	vanilla	5 mL
1 cup	finely chopped almonds	250 mL
	Confectioner's (icing) sugar, sifted	

1. In a medium bowl, sift flour and confectioner's sugar.

2. In a large bowl, cream butter until smooth. Add vanilla and mix well. Stir in flour mixture until well blended. Fold in almonds. Refrigerate dough for at least 4 hours, until firm.

3. On a lightly floured surface, shape 1 tbsp (15 mL) dough into a roll 2 to 2½ inches (5 to 6 cm) long. Bend ends inward to form a crescent shape. Repeat with the remaining dough. Place about 2 inches (5 cm) apart on prepared baking sheet. Bake in preheated oven for 12 to 15 minutes, until firm to the touch and golden brown. Transfer to wire racks to cool, then sprinkle with confectioner's sugar.

Tip *To coat crescents with confectioner's sugar, sift sugar onto a clean baking sheet until it forms a thin layer. Arrange crescents on sugar and sift additional confectioner's sugar over tops. Let stand until cool.*

Sugar-Coated Walnut Crescents

Makes about 3 dozen
- Preheat oven to 300°F (150°C)
- Baking sheet, lined with parchment or waxed paper

1½ cups	butter, softened	375 mL
2 tbsp	confectioner's (icing) sugar, sifted	25 mL
1	egg yolk, beaten	1
1 cup	finely chopped walnuts	250 mL
3¼ cups	all-purpose flour	800 mL
	Additional confectioner's (icing) sugar, sifted, for coating	

1. In a large bowl, cream butter and confectioner's sugar until smooth. Add beaten egg yolk and chopped walnuts. Mix together until well blended. Gradually add flour and mix until a soft dough forms. Cover and refrigerate for 1 hour, until firm.

2. On a lightly floured surface, form dough into 1¼-inch (3 cm) balls. Shape each into a tapered log about 3 inches (7.5 cm) long. Bend each end inward to form a crescent. Place about 2 inches (5 cm) apart on prepared baking sheet. Bake in preheated oven for 35 to 40 minutes, until lightly browned on the bottom and almost firm to the touch. Let cool slightly on sheet. Coat with confectioner's sugar.

Swedish Rosettes

Makes about 6 dozen
- Rosette iron
- Deep fryer or Dutch oven

1 cup	all-purpose flour	250 mL
2 tbsp	granulated sugar	25 mL
Pinch	salt	Pinch
2	eggs	2
1 cup	milk	250 mL
	Vegetable oil for frying	
¾ cup	confectioner's (icing) sugar, sifted	175 mL

1. In a medium bowl, mix together flour, sugar and salt. Make a well in the center.

2. In a small bowl, whisk eggs and milk until blended. Gradually spoon into well, stirring until blended and smooth. Cover and chill in refrigerator for 1 hour.

3. In a deep fryer or Dutch oven, heat oil to 375°F (190°C). Dip rosette iron into hot oil for about 1 minute. Tap off excess oil and dip iron into batter until about three-quarters of it is submerged in the batter. However, do not allow batter to cover the top of the iron. If the batter won't stick, the iron is probably too hot, so let it cool slightly.

4. Return iron to oil and fry until the rosette slips off the iron. Continue cooking the rosette for 35 to 40 seconds or until golden. If rosette does not come off iron, loosen sides gently with a knife. With a slotted spoon, transfer the rosette from the oil to paper towels to drain. Repeat, stirring the batter each time before dipping, until all batter is used up. When cooled, sprinkle rosettes with confectioner's sugar.

Tip *Rosette irons can be purchased at kitchen accessory stores.*

Sugar-Cinnamon Twists

Makes 4 dozen twists

- Preheat oven to 350°F (180°C)
- Baking sheets, greased

1	package (¼ oz/7 g) active dry yeast	1
¾ cup	warm water, divided	175 mL
¼ cup	butter or margarine, softened	50 mL
¼ cup	granulated sugar	50 mL
1	egg	1
4 to 4½ cups	all-purpose flour, divided	1 to 1.125 L
1½ tsp	salt	7 mL
½ cup	warm milk	125 mL
FILLING		
½ cup	packed brown sugar	125 mL
4 tsp	ground cinnamon	20 mL
¼ cup	melted butter or margarine	50 mL

1. In a large bowl, combine yeast and ¼ cup (50 mL) of the water. Stir until dissolved.
2. Add butter, sugar, egg, 2 cups (500 mL) of the flour, salt, the remaining water and milk. Beat for 2 to 3 minutes, until blended. Gradually add more flour, mixing until a soft dough forms.
3. On a floured surface, knead dough for 6 to 8 minutes, until smooth and elastic. Place dough in a greased bowl, turning to ensure that all sides of the dough are greased. Cover and let rise in a warm place for about 1 hour, until dough doubles in size. Punch down, then roll out to a 16- by 12-inch (40 by 30 cm) rectangle.
4. *Prepare the filling:* In a small bowl, mix together brown sugar and cinnamon. Brush dough with melted butter or margarine, then sprinkle with sugar-cinnamon mixture.
5. Let dough rest for 5 minutes, then cut lengthwise into 3 strips, 16 by 4 inches (40 by 10 cm). Cut each strip into 16 pieces, 4 by 1 inches (10 by 2.5 cm). Twist each strip and place on prepared sheets. Cover with a cloth and let rise for about 30 minutes, until doubled in size.
6. Bake in preheated oven for 5 minutes or until golden brown. Immediately transfer to wire racks to cool.

Tip *If your recipe calls for eggs at room temperature and you forgot to remove them from the refrigerator, place them in warm water for several minutes.*

Cinnamon Pretzels

Makes 16 pretzels

- Preheat oven to 350°F (180°C)
- Baking sheet, greased

1	package (16 oz/500 g) hot roll mix with yeast or frozen pizza dough, thawed	1
¾ cup	warm water	175 mL
⅓ cup	granulated sugar	75 mL
3	egg yolks	3
1 tsp	grated orange zest (optional)	5 mL
¼ cup	freshly squeezed orange juice	50 mL
2 tbsp	melted butter	25 mL
1 tsp	ground cinnamon	5 mL
1 tsp	vanilla	5 mL
TOPPING		
2 tbsp	granulated sugar	25 mL
½ tsp	ground cinnamon	2 mL

1. In a large bowl, mix the hot roll mix with yeast package, or the frozen pizza dough, with water, sugar, 2 egg yolks, orange zest (if using), orange juice, butter, cinnamon and vanilla. Mix together until well blended and a soft dough forms.
2. On a lightly floured surface, knead dough for 5 minutes, until smooth and elastic. Cover and let rest for 5 minutes.
3. Divide dough into 16 portions. Roll each portion out into a 6-inch (15 cm) long rope. Place one portion on prepared sheet.
4. Shape into a heart shape. Twist dough ends twice where they meet and attach ends to the curved bottom of the heart to form a pretzel shape. Repeat with the remaining dough.
5. In a small bowl, whisk the remaining egg yolk with 1 tbsp (15 mL) water. Brush over top of pretzels.
6. *Prepare the topping:* In another small bowl, mix together sugar and cinnamon. Sprinkle over pretzels. Let rise for 10 minutes.
7. Bake in preheated oven for 20 minutes or until golden brown. Immediately transfer to wire racks to cool.

Tip *Leftover egg yolks or whites can be kept in the refrigerator for 3 to 4 days in airtight containers. Yolks should be covered with cold water to keep them from drying up.*

Homemade Ladyfingers

Makes about 20 ladyfingers

- Preheat oven to 350°F (180°C)
- Baking sheet, greased
- Pastry bag

2	egg yolks	2
½ tsp	vanilla	2 mL
Pinch	salt	Pinch
3	egg whites, at room temperature	3
⅓ cup	granulated sugar	75 mL
⅓ cup	all-purpose flour	75 mL
3 tbsp	granulated sugar	45 mL

1. In a medium bowl, whisk together egg yolks, vanilla and salt until thick and pale yellow in color.

2. In a clean bowl, beat egg whites until soft peaks form. Gradually add the ⅓ cup (75 mL) sugar, beating until stiff peaks form. Fold into egg yolk mixture, then gradually fold in flour until well combined.

3. Fill a pastry bag with batter. Pipe fingers, about 4 to 5 inches (10 to 12.5 cm) long and 2 inches (5 cm) apart, onto prepared baking sheet. Sprinkle lightly with the 3 tbsp (45 mL) sugar. Bake in preheated oven for 10 to 12 minutes or until lightly browned. Immediately transfer to wire racks to cool.

Tip *Ladyfinger tins are molds that ladyfingers are baked in. Spoon the mixture into each mold and bake as above.*

Special Wonton Cookies

Makes 2 dozen

- Deep fryer or Dutch oven

1½ cups	packed brown sugar	375 mL
1 cup	chopped dried apricots	250 mL
1½ cups	chopped prunes	375 mL
1 cup	chopped almonds	250 mL
1½ cups	flaked or shredded coconut (sweetened or unsweetened)	375 mL
24	wonton squares	24
	Vegetable oil for frying	

1. In a large bowl, mix together brown sugar, apricots, prunes, almonds and coconut.

2. Lay half the wonton squares out on a work surface. Place about 2 tsp (10 mL) filling in the center of each. Moisten edges with water and fold in half to form a triangle. Press edges together firmly to seal. Repeat until all wrappers are filled. Cover filled wontons with a cloth to keep moist.

3. Fill a deep fryer or Dutch oven with oil to a depth of about 1½ inches (4 cm). Heat to 360°F (185°C). Using a slotted spoon, drop four wontons at a time into the hot oil and cook, turning, until golden brown. Lift out with the slotted spoon and drain on paper towel.

Tips *Wonton wrappers, or squares of dough, can be purchased at most major grocery stores.*

Next time you buy vegetable oil, don't pull off the silver seal. Instead, cut a small slit in it. It makes it much easier to pour without spilling.

Fortune Cookies

Makes about 2 dozen

- Preheat oven to 300°F (150°C)
- Baking sheet, greased
- Muffin tin, ungreased

½ cup	all-purpose flour	125 mL
1 tbsp	cornstarch	15 mL
¼ cup	granulated sugar	50 mL
Pinch	salt	Pinch
¼ cup	vegetable oil	50 mL
2	egg whites	2
1 tsp	almond extract	5 mL

1. In a medium bowl, mix together flour, cornstarch, sugar and salt. Make a well in the center.

2. In a small bowl, whisk oil, egg whites and almond extract. Pour into well and stir until mixture is blended and smooth.

3. Spoon a heaping teaspoonful (5 mL) batter onto prepared baking sheet. Using the back of a spoon, spread into a 3-inch (7.5 cm) circle. Make three other circles. (Cookies will spread, so bake only four at a time.) Bake in preheated oven for 10 minutes or until golden brown.

4. Working quickly, one cookie at a time, and using a wide spatula, flip cookies from baking sheet onto a sheet of waxed paper. Place a paper fortune in the center and fold cookie in half. Gently bring tips of cookie together to form a slight crease or bend in the middle. Place cookie in an ungreased muffin cup to cool and to hold its shape. Repeat with the remaining dough.

Tips *Before beginning these cookies, make up about 24 paper fortunes, about 2- by ½-inches (5 by 1 cm), with clever little sayings, to place inside.*

If a cookie cools before you can form it, heat in a preheated 300°F (150°C) oven for about 1 minute.

Cookie Cards

Makes about 18 name cards, depending on the size of cookie cutter used

- Preheat oven to 375ºF (190ºC)
- Rectangular cookie cutter, preferably with fluted edges
- Baking sheet, ungreased
- Drinking straw
- Cookie cutter

2¼ cups	all-purpose flour	550 mL
1½ tsp	baking powder	7 mL
¼ tsp	salt	1 mL
¾ cup	shortening, softened	175 mL
1 cup	granulated sugar	250 mL
2	eggs	2
1 tsp	vanilla	5 mL
	Icings	
	Cake decorator for printing names	
	Strands of red shoestring licorice, colored ribbon, wool or string	

1. In a medium bowl, mix together flour, baking powder and salt.
2. In a large bowl, beat shortening and sugar until smooth and creamy. Add eggs, one at a time, beating until well incorporated. Stir in vanilla. Gradually add flour mixture and mix until a dough forms.
3. On a lightly floured surface, roll dough out to ⅛-inch (0.25 cm) thickness. Using a cookie cutter dipped in flour, cut out shapes and place 2 inches (5 cm) apart on sheet. Using a drinking straw, punch two holes into the dough on one long side of the rectangle. Bake in preheated oven for 6 to 8 minutes or until lightly browned. Immediately transfer to wire racks to cool.
4. Decorate and print names on with icing.
5. *To make place cards:* Place two cookies together and thread a ribbon or licorice through the holes. Make a bow or a knot in the back and stand cards up. These cookies are a unique and fun way to make place cards.

Tip *Chill your rolling pin in the freezer before using so the dough won't stick to it.*

Oatmeal Pecan Turnovers

Makes 16 turnovers

- Preheat oven to 375ºF (190ºC)
- Baking sheet, greased

2½ cups	all-purpose flour	625 mL
1 tsp	baking powder	5 mL
½ tsp	baking soda	2 mL
1 tsp	salt	5 mL
2 cups	old-fashioned rolled oats	500 mL
½ cup	chopped pecans	125 mL
½ cup	butter or margarine, softened	125 mL
1 cup	packed brown sugar	250 mL
1	egg	1
1 tsp	vanilla	5 mL
½ cup	milk	125 mL
1	package (8 oz/250 g) cream cheese, softened	1
1 cup	fruit pie filling	250 mL
	Confectioner's (icing) sugar, sifted	

1. In a medium bowl, mix together flour, baking powder, baking soda, salt, oats and pecans.
2. In a large bowl, beat butter or margarine and brown sugar until smooth and creamy. Beat in egg until incorporated. Stir in vanilla and milk. Mix in dry ingredients until well blended and a soft dough forms. Cover and refrigerate for 30 minutes.
3. Place dough between two sheets of waxed paper and roll out to ¼-inch (0.5 cm) thickness. Remove paper and cut into 4-inch (10 cm) squares. Spoon 1 tbsp (15 mL) cream cheese onto half of each square. Top with 1 tbsp (15 mL) fruit pie filling. Fold into a triangle and press edges with the tines of a fork dipped in flour to seal.
4. Place about 2 inches (5 cm) apart on prepared baking sheet. Bake in preheated oven for 20 to 25 minutes, until crispy and golden brown. Transfer to wire racks to cool. Sprinkle with confectioner's sugar.

Tip *Don't waste milk that is just about to pass its "best before" date. Pour the milk into an ice cube tray and freeze. These cubes can be added to hot liquids such as coffee or hot chocolate.*

Best Spritz Cookies

Makes about 7 dozen

- Preheat oven to 400°F (200°C)
- Cookie press
- Baking sheet, ungreased

1 cup	butter, softened	250 mL
1 cup	granulated sugar	250 mL
1	egg	1
1/4 tsp	salt	1 mL
2 tsp	vanilla	10 mL
2 1/4 cups	all-purpose flour	550 mL

1. In a large bowl, beat butter and sugar until smooth and creamy. Beat in egg until well incorporated. Stir in salt and vanilla. Add flour and beat until blended. If dough is too soft, cover and chill in refrigerator for about 30 minutes, until firm.

2. Pack dough into cookie press and press cookies onto baking sheet about 1 inch (2.5 cm) apart. Bake in preheated oven for 6 to 8 minutes or until edges are lightly browned. Let cool on sheet for 5 minutes, then transfer to wire racks to cool completely.

Variations *Lemon Spritz: Omit egg and vanilla and add 1/4 cup (50 mL) frozen lemonade concentrate.*

Cinnamon Spritz: Substitute 1 1/3 cups (325 mL) lightly packed brown sugar for the granulated sugar. Add 1 tsp (5 mL) cinnamon.

Chocolate Spritz: Add 2 squares (each 1 oz/28 oz) melted unsweetened chocolate.

Fancy Lattice Cookies

Makes about 2 1/2 dozen

- Preheat oven to 350°F (180°C)
- Baking sheet, ungreased
- Cookie cutter

2/3 cup	all-purpose flour	150 mL
1/4 tsp	ground cinnamon	1 mL
1/4 tsp	ground cloves	1 mL
1/4 tsp	ground nutmeg	1 mL
1	package (18 oz/510 g) refrigerated sugar cookie dough	1
	Seedless raspberry jam	
	Confectioner's (icing) sugar, sifted	

1. In a large bowl, mix together flour, cinnamon, cloves and nutmeg. Add sugar cookie dough and knead together until well combined.

2. Place dough between two sheets of waxed paper and roll out to 1/8-inch (0.25 cm) thickness. Remove top sheet and, using a cookie cutter or a glass dipped in flour, cut out 2-inch (5 cm) rounds. Shape the remaining scraps of dough into a disk and set aside.

3. Place rounds about 1 inch (2.5 cm) apart on baking sheet. Spread each with 1/2 tsp (2 mL) jam.

4. Place disk of scrap dough between two sheets of waxed paper and roll out to 1/8-inch (0.25 cm) thickness. Cut dough into 2- by 1/4-inch (5 by 0.5 cm) strips. Place strips over the jam on each cookie to form a lattice pattern, two strips horizontally and two strips intertwined vertically. Trim to fit.

5. Bake in preheated oven for 15 minutes or until golden brown. Let cool on sheet for 2 minutes, then transfer to wire racks to cool completely. Sprinkle with confectioner's sugar.

Delicate Lace Baskets

Makes 6 baskets

- Preheat oven to 300°F (150°C)
- Baking sheet, greased
- 4-inch (10 cm) diameter bowl, brushed with melted butter

1/4 cup	butter	50 mL
1/4 cup	granulated sugar	50 mL
2 1/2 tbsp	dark molasses	32 mL
1/4 tsp	ground cinnamon	1 mL
Pinch	ground ginger	Pinch
1/2 tbsp	vanilla	7 mL
1/3 cup	all-purpose flour	75 mL
	Pudding, mousse or ice cream for filling	

1. In a saucepan, over medium heat, melt butter with sugar, molasses, cinnamon and ginger, stirring until mixture is smooth. Stir in vanilla, then flour, until blended.

2. Using a large spoon, drop 2 1/2 tbsp (32 mL) batter, about 4 inches (10 cm) apart, onto prepared baking sheet. (Cookies will spread, so bake only three at a time.) Bake in preheated oven for 18 minutes. Let cool on sheet for 30 seconds, then, using a wide spatula, lift cookies up and carefully shape over the bottom of prepared bowl. Let cool on bowl until cookie is firm, then gently lift off. Repeat with the remaining batter.

3. Fill cooled baskets with pudding, mousse or ice cream.

Blueberry Graham Cheesecake Bars

Makes 24 bars

- Preheat oven to 300°F (150°C)
- 9-inch (2.5 L) square baking pan, ungreased

BASE

1¼ cups	graham wafer crumbs (about 16 wafers)	300 mL
½ cup	butter or margarine, softened	125 mL
¼ cup	granulated sugar	50 mL

FILLING

1	package (8 oz/250 g) cream cheese, softened	1
½ cup	granulated sugar	125 mL
2	eggs	2
1 tsp	vanilla	5 mL
	Ground cinnamon	

TOPPING

1	can (19 oz/540 mL) blueberry pie filling	1
2 tbsp	freshly squeezed lemon juice	25 mL

1. *Prepare the base:* In a small bowl, mix together crumbs, butter and sugar. Press evenly into pan. Set aside.

2. *Prepare the filling:* In a medium bowl, beat cream cheese and sugar until smooth. Beat in eggs and vanilla until blended.

3. Spread evenly over base. Bake in preheated oven for 30 minutes. Sprinkle cinnamon over top and place pan on a wire rack to cool.

4. *Prepare the topping:* In a small bowl, mix together blueberry pie filling and lemon juice. Spread over warm cake. Chill thoroughly, then cut into bars.

Coffee Lovers' Bars

Makes 24 bars

- Preheat oven to 350°F (180°C)
- 9-inch (2.5 L) square baking pan, greased

2 tsp	instant coffee powder or granules	10 mL
2 tbsp	boiling water	25 mL
½ cup	all-purpose flour	125 mL
½ cup	unsweetened cocoa powder, sifted	125 mL
½ cup	butter or margarine, softened	125 mL
1 cup	granulated sugar	250 mL
2	eggs	2
1 tsp	vanilla	5 mL

FROSTING

2 tbsp	butter or margarine, softened	25 mL
4 oz	cream cheese, softened	125 g
2 tsp	instant coffee powder or granules	10 mL
1 tsp	vanilla	5 mL
1½ cups	confectioner's (icing) sugar, sifted	375 mL
	Unsweetened cocoa powder	

1. In a cup, mix coffee powder with boiling water until dissolved. Set aside.

2. In a small bowl, mix together flour and cocoa.

3. In a large bowl, beat butter and sugar until smooth and creamy. Beat in eggs and vanilla just until blended. Blend in flour mixture.

4. Spread evenly in prepared pan. Bake in preheated oven for 20 to 25 minutes or until tester inserted in center comes out clean. Place pan on a wire rack to cool completely.

5. *Prepare the frosting:* In a medium bowl, beat butter, cream cheese, coffee powder and vanilla until smooth and blended. Gradually add confectioner's sugar, beating until frosting is smooth and spreadable. Spread evenly over cake. Sift cocoa lightly over top, then cut into bars.

Cola Honey Cake Bars

Makes 36 bars

- Preheat oven to 325°F (160°C)
- 13- by 9-inch (3 L) baking pan, greased

4 cups	all-purpose flour	1 L
2 tsp	baking powder	10 mL
1 tsp	ground cinnamon	5 mL
½ tsp	baking soda	2 mL
½ tsp	ground cloves, nutmeg or allspice	2 mL
4	eggs	4
1 cup	granulated sugar	250 mL
½ cup	vegetable oil	125 mL
1½ cups	liquid honey	375 mL
1 cup	cola	250 mL
½ cup	raisins (optional)	125 mL

1. In a large bowl, mix together flour, baking powder, cinnamon, baking soda and cloves.

2. In another large bowl, beat eggs, sugar, oil and honey until smooth and blended. Gradually blend in flour mixture, alternately with cola, just until incorporated. Stir in raisins (if using).

3. Spread evenly in prepared pan. Bake in preheated oven for 50 to 60 minutes or until tester inserted in center comes out clean. Place pan on a rack to cool completely, then cut into bars.

Powdered Poppy Seed Squares

Makes 16 squares

- Preheat oven to 350ºF (180ºC)
- 8-inch (2 L) square baking pan, greased

1 cup	poppy seeds	250 mL
1 cup	milk	250 mL
2 cups	all-purpose flour	500 mL
2 tsp	baking powder	10 mL
1/2 tsp	salt	2 mL
1/2 cup	butter, softened	125 mL
1 cup	granulated sugar	250 mL
2	eggs, separated	2
1/2 tsp	almond extract	2 mL
	Confectioner's (icing) sugar	

1. In a small bowl, combine poppy seeds and milk. Let stand for 1 hour.
2. In a medium bowl, mix together flour, baking powder and salt.
3. In a large bowl, beat butter and sugar until smooth and creamy. Beat in egg yolks until incorporated. Stir in almond extract. Gradually blend in flour mixture alternately with poppy seed mixture, just until incorporated.
4. In a clean bowl, beat egg whites until soft peaks form. Fold into batter.
5. Spread evenly in prepared pan. Bake in preheated oven for 40 to 45 minutes or until a tester inserted in the center comes out clean. Place pan on a wire rack to cool completely, then sift confectioner's sugar over top. Cut into squares.

Dainty Petit-Four Bars

Makes 36 bars

- Preheat oven to 350º F (180º C)
- 13- by 9-inch (3 L) baking pan, lightly greased

2 cups	cake and pastry flour	500 mL
1 tbsp	baking powder	15 mL
1/4 tsp	salt	1 mL
1/4 cup	shortening, softened	50 mL
1/4 cup	butter or margarine, softened	50 mL
1 1/4 cups	granulated sugar, divided	300 mL
1/2 tsp	vanilla	2 mL
1/4 tsp	almond extract	1 mL
3/4 cup	milk	175 mL
6	egg whites	6
FROSTING		
1 1/2 cups	hot water	375 mL
3 cups	granulated sugar	750 mL
1/4 tsp	cream of tartar	1 mL
1 tsp	vanilla	5 mL
2 1/4 cups	confectioner's (icing) sugar, sifted	550 mL

1. In a medium bowl, sift together flour, baking powder and salt.
2. In a large bowl, beat shortening, butter and 1 cup (250 mL) of the sugar until smooth and creamy. Beat in vanilla and almond extract. Blend in flour mixture, alternately with milk, just until incorporated.
3. In a clean bowl, beat egg whites until foamy. Gradually add the remaining sugar, beating until stiff peaks form. Fold into batter.
4. Bake in preheated oven for 35 to 40 minutes or until a tester inserted in center comes out clean. Place pan on a rack to cool for 5 minutes, then remove cake and let cool completely on rack.
5. *Prepare the frosting:* In a saucepan, over low heat, stir together water, sugar and cream of tartar until mixture resembles a thin syrup. Let cool until lukewarm, then beat in vanilla and confectioner's sugar until smooth and spreadable. Cut cake into bars or diamond shapes. Spoon frosting over cakes.

Tip *For a special touch, tint the frosting with food coloring and place a nut or candy decoration on top of each bar.*

Lebkuchen (Honey Cake Bars)

Makes 36 bars

- Preheat oven to 350º F (180º C)
- Two 9-inch (2.5 L) square baking pans, greased

2 cups	all-purpose flour	500 mL
1 1/2 tsp	ground cinnamon	7 mL
1/2 tsp	baking soda	2 mL
1/2 tsp	ground ginger	2 mL
1/2 tsp	ground nutmeg	2 mL
1/4 tsp	salt	1 mL
1/4 tsp	ground cloves	1 mL
1/2 cup	raisins	125 mL
1/2 cup	chopped blanched almonds	125 mL
1 cup	liquid honey	250 mL
3/4 cup	packed brown sugar	175 mL
1	egg	1
1 tsp	grated lemon zest	5 mL
3 tbsp	freshly squeezed lemon juice, divided	45 mL
1 cup	confectioner's (icing) sugar, sifted	250 mL
	Candied red cherries, halved	

1. In a medium bowl, mix together flour, cinnamon, baking soda, ginger, nutmeg, salt and cloves. Stir in raisins and almonds.
2. In a large saucepan, over medium heat, bring honey and brown sugar to a boil, stirring constantly, until sugar dissolves. Let cool, then beat in egg, lemon zest and 1 tbsp (15 mL) of the lemon juice. Blend in flour mixture. Chill overnight.
3. Divide dough in half and spread evenly in prepared pans. Bake in preheated oven for 30 minutes or until firm. Place pans on wire racks, score into bars and press a cherry half, cut side down, in the center of each bar.
4. Meanwhile, in a bowl, beat confectioner's sugar with the remaining lemon juice until smooth and blended. Drizzle glaze over top of cake. Let cool completely, then cut into bars.

Tip *If you prefer, substitute 1 tbsp (15 mL) pumpkin pie spice for the cinnamon, ginger, nutmeg and cloves.*

Raisin Spice Hermit Bars

Makes 36 bars
- Preheat oven to 375° F (190° C)
- 13- by 9-inch (3 L) baking pan, lined with greased foil

2 cups	all-purpose flour	500 mL
2/3 cup	packed brown sugar	150 mL
2 tsp	ground cinnamon	10 mL
1 1/2 tsp	ground ginger	7 mL
1/2 tsp	baking soda	2 mL
1/2 tsp	salt	2 mL
6 tbsp	butter or margarine, melted	90 mL
2	eggs	2
2/3 cup	light (fancy) molasses	150 mL
2 tsp	vanilla	10 mL
3/4 cup	dark seedless raisins	175 mL

1. In a medium bowl, mix together flour, brown sugar, cinnamon, ginger, baking soda and salt.
2. In a large bowl, beat butter, eggs, molasses and vanilla until blended. Blend in flour mixture. Stir in raisins.
3. Spread evenly in prepared pan. Bake in preheated oven for 20 to 25 minutes or until edges are golden brown. Place pan on a wire rack to cool completely. Transfer cake, with foil, to a cutting board and cut into bars.

Tip *To plump raisins, soak them in orange juice and store in refrigerator.*

Orange Raisin Bars

Makes 24 bars
- Preheat oven to 350°F (180°C)
- 9-inch (2.5 L) square baking pan, lightly greased

BASE		
2 cups	all-purpose flour	500 mL
1 cup	granulated sugar	250 mL
1 tsp	baking powder	5 mL
1 cup	butter or margarine	250 mL
1	egg, beaten	1
FILLING		
1 1/3 cups	raisins	325 mL
3/4 cup	granulated sugar	175 mL
2 tbsp	all-purpose flour	25 mL
1 cup	boiling water	250 mL
1/2 tsp	orange juice	2 mL
Pinch	salt	Pinch

1. *Prepare the base:* In a large bowl, mix together flour, sugar and baking powder. Using two knives, a pastry blender or your fingers, cut butter in until mixture resembles coarse crumbs. Mix in egg just until dough forms. Form dough into a ball, then divide in half. Press one portion into prepared pan. Set other aside.
2. *Prepare the filling:* In a saucepan, over low heat, stir together raisins, sugar, flour and boiling water until sugar is dissolved. Increase heat and bring to a boil. Reduce heat to simmer and cook, stirring constantly, for 5 to 8 minutes or until thickened. Remove from heat. Stir in orange juice and salt. Set aside to cool slightly.
3. Spread filling evenly over dough. On lightly floured work surface, press the remaining dough to make a 9-inch (23 cm) square and place over the raisin filling. (Disregard any small holes in the dough.) Bake in preheated oven for 25 to 35 minutes or until lightly browned. Place pan on a wire rack to cool completely, then cut into bars.

Tips *For a more pronounced orange flavor, increase amount of orange juice in filling to 1 tsp (5 mL).*

To prevent cakes from becoming soggy, always cool them in their pans, on a wire rack, so the bottom of the pan will be cooled by circulating air.

Strawberry Cheesecake Bars

Makes 36 bars

- Preheat oven to 375°F (190°C)
- 13- by 9-inch (3 L) baking pan, greased

BASE

¾ cup	butter or margarine, softened	175 mL
⅓ cup	light corn syrup	75 mL
¼ cup	granulated sugar	50 mL
2 cups	all-purpose flour	500 mL
½ tsp	salt	2 mL

TOPPING

2	packages (each 8 oz/250 g) cream cheese, softened	2
3	eggs	3
2 tsp	vanilla	10 mL
1 cup	light corn syrup	250 mL
¾ cup	strawberry jam	175 mL

1. *Prepare the base:* In a medium bowl, beat butter, corn syrup and sugar until smooth. Blend in flour and salt until a dough forms. Press evenly into prepared pan.
2. *Prepare the topping:* In another medium bowl, beat cream cheese, eggs and vanilla until smooth and creamy. Beat in corn syrup.
3. Spread evenly over dough. Bake in preheated oven for 35 to 40 minutes or until lightly browned and topping is set. Place pan on a wire rack.
4. Stir jam until smooth. Spread evenly over hot topping. Let cool for 30 minutes, then chill 3 hours, or overnight, before cutting into bars. Store, covered, in the refrigerator.

Greek Baklava Diamonds

Makes 28 diamonds

- Preheat oven to 350°F (180°C)
- 13- by 9-inch (3 L) baking pan, ungreased

BASE

3½ cups	finely chopped walnuts	875 mL
½ cup	granulated sugar	125 mL
1 tsp	ground cinnamon	5 mL
2	packages (each 8 oz/250 g) refrigerated crescent rolls	2

GLAZE

2 tbsp	butter or margarine	25 mL
¼ cup	granulated sugar	50 mL
2 tbsp	freshly squeezed lemon juice	25 mL
½ cup	liquid honey	125 mL

1. *Prepare the base:* In a large bowl, mix together nuts, sugar and cinnamon.
2. On a work surface, separate each package of dough into two long rectangles. Line bottom of pan with half, spreading ½ inch (1 cm) up the sides. Spread evenly with nut mixture. Place the remaining dough on top, pressing down. Using the dough edges and the perforations in the dough as guidelines, take a sharp knife and score the dough five times lengthwise and seven times diagonally to make diamond-shaped pieces.
3. *Prepare the glaze:* In a saucepan, over medium-high heat, combine butter, sugar, lemon juice and honey. Bring to a boil. Remove from heat and spoon half evenly over top of the dough.
4. Bake in preheated oven for 25 to 30 minutes or until golden brown. Spoon the remaining glaze over hot pastry. Place pan on a wire rack to cool completely, then cut into diamonds.

Tip *To keep honey or molasses from sticking to a measuring cup, grease the cup first — or, if the recipe calls for oil, measure that first.*

Butterscotch Pudding Bars

Makes 36 bars

- Preheat oven to 350°F (180°C)
- 13- by 9-inch (3 L) baking pan, ungreased

BASE

1 cup	all-purpose flour	250 mL
½ cup	chopped pecans	125 mL
½ cup	butter	125 mL

FILLING

1 cup	confectioner's (icing) sugar, sifted	250 mL
1	package (8 oz/250 g) cream cheese, softened	1
3 cups	frozen whipped topping, thawed, divided	750 mL

TOPPING

2	packages (each a 4-serving size) butterscotch instant pudding mix	2
3½ cups	milk	875 mL
¼ cup	chopped pecans	50 mL

1. *Prepare the base:* In a medium bowl, mix together flour and pecans. Using two knives, a pastry blender or your fingers, cut butter in until mixture resembles coarse crumbs. Press evenly into pan. Bake in preheated oven for 15 to 20 minutes or until lightly browned. Place pan on a wire rack to cool.

2. *Prepare the filling:* In a medium bowl, beat sugar and cream cheese until smooth. Fold in 1 cup (250 mL) of the whipped topping and spread evenly over baked base.
3. *Prepare the topping:* In another medium bowl, beat pudding mix and milk until blended and smooth. Spoon over filling. Chill for 15 to 20 minutes, until set. Top with the remaining whipped topping and pecans. Chill for 2 hours. Cut into bars.

Tip *Plastic wrap will cling better to the rim of a bowl or pan if you moisten the rim with a few drops of water.*

Frosted Chocolate Nut Bars

Makes 36 bars
- Preheat oven to 350°F (180°C)
- 13- by 9-inch (3 L) baking pan, greased

2 cups	all-purpose flour	500 mL
1/2 tsp	salt	2 mL
2 cups	granulated sugar	500 mL
1 cup	butter or margarine, softened	250 mL
4	eggs	4
1 tbsp	vanilla	15 mL
2 cups	chopped walnuts	500 mL
2 oz	unsweetened chocolate, melted	60 g
FROSTING		
1 cup	milk	250 mL
5 tbsp	all-purpose flour	75 mL
1 cup	confectioner's (icing) sugar, sifted	250 mL
1 cup	butter or margarine, softened	250 mL
2 tsp	vanilla	10 mL

1. In a small bowl, mix together flour and salt.
2. In a large bowl, beat sugar and butter until smooth and creamy. Beat in eggs until incorporated. Stir in vanilla. Blend in flour mixture. Stir in nuts.
3. Set aside half the batter and spread remainder evenly in prepared pan. Blend melted chocolate into reserved batter. Spread carefully over the batter in the pan. Bake in preheated oven for 30 to 35 minutes or until a tester inserted in the center comes out clean. Place pan on a wire rack to cool completely.
4. *Prepare the frosting:* In a saucepan, whisk milk and flour until smooth. Cook, stirring constantly, over medium heat until thickened (about 10 minutes). Remove from heat and set aside.
5. In a medium bowl, beat sugar, butter and vanilla until smooth and blended. Gradually add milk mixture, beating until smooth and spreadable. Spread frosting over top of cake. Cut into bars.

Spicy Oatmeal Bars with Citrus Glaze

Makes 36 bars
- Preheat oven to 375°F (190°C)
- 13- by 9-inch (3 L) baking pan, greased

1 3/4 cups	all-purpose flour	425 mL
1 1/2 tsp	baking soda	7 mL
3/4 tsp	ground cinnamon	4 mL
1/4 tsp	ground nutmeg	1 mL
1/4 tsp	ground cloves	1 mL
1/2 cup	butter or margarine, softened	125 mL
1 cup	packed brown sugar	250 mL
2	eggs	2
1 tsp	vanilla	5 mL
1 cup	unsweetened applesauce	250 mL
1 1/2 cups	quick-cooking rolled oats	375 mL
1 cup	raisins	250 mL
1/2 cup	chopped walnuts	125 mL
CITRUS GLAZE		
1/2 cup	confectioner's (icing) sugar, sifted	125 mL
2 tsp	water	10 mL
2 tsp	freshly squeezed lemon juice	10 mL

1. In a small bowl, mix together flour, baking soda, cinnamon, nutmeg and cloves.
2. In a large bowl, beat butter and brown sugar until smooth and creamy. Beat in eggs until incorporated. Stir in vanilla. Gradually blend in flour mixture, alternately with applesauce, until just incorporated. Stir in oats, raisins and walnuts.
3. Spread evenly in prepared pan. Bake in preheated oven for 30 to 35 minutes or until a tester inserted in the center comes out clean. Place pan on a wire rack to cool.
4. *Prepare the glaze:* In a small bowl, beat confectioner's sugar, water and juice until smooth and spreadable. Drizzle glaze over top of warm cake. Let cool completely, then cut into bars.

Tip *For a quick dessert, take 1 can of refrigerated biscuit dough and separate the biscuits. Dip each biscuit in melted butter, then in a mixture of 1 tsp (5 mL) ground cinnamon and 3/4 cup (175 mL) granulated sugar. Place biscuits in a greased baking pan, sides touching, and bake in a preheated 450°F (230°C) oven for 10 minutes or until golden brown. Place pan on a wire rack to cool completely, then cut into squares.*

Trail Mix Squares

Makes 16 squares
- Preheat oven to 325°F (160°C)
- 8-inch (2 L) square baking pan, greased

1 cup	all-purpose flour	250 mL
1 tsp	baking powder	5 mL
¾ cup	packed brown sugar	175 mL
½ cup	butter or margarine, softened	125 mL
2	eggs	2
1 tsp	vanilla	5 mL
½ cup	trail mix, chopped	125 mL
½ cup	semisweet chocolate chips	125 mL

1. In a small bowl, combine flour and baking powder.
2. In a medium bowl, beat brown sugar and butter until smooth and creamy. Beat in eggs until incorporated. Stir in vanilla. Blend in flour mixture. Stir in trail mix and chocolate chips.
3. Spread evenly in prepared pan. Bake in preheated oven for 30 to 35 minutes or until a tester inserted in the center comes out clean. Place pan on a wire rack to cool completely, then cut into squares.

Krispie Toffee Triangles

Makes 32 triangles
- Preheat oven to 350°F (180°C)
- 8-inch (2 L) square baking pan, greased

BASE		
½ cup	all-purpose flour	125 mL
¼ tsp	baking soda	1 mL
Pinch	salt	Pinch
⅓ cup	butter or margarine, melted	75 mL
⅓ cup	packed brown sugar	75 mL
¾ cup	crisp rice cereal	175 mL
FILLING		
½ cup	butter or margarine	125 mL
1¼ cups	sweetened condensed milk	300 mL
½ cup	packed brown sugar	125 mL
TOPPING		
½ cup	semisweet chocolate chips	125 mL
1¼ cups	crisp rice cereal	300 mL

1. *Prepare the base:* In a medium bowl, mix together flour, baking soda and salt. Make a well in the center. Add melted butter, brown sugar and rice cereal and mix until blended. Press evenly into prepared pan. Bake in preheated oven for 10 to 12 minutes or until lightly browned. Place pan on a wire rack.

2. *Prepare the filling:* In a saucepan, over low heat, stir together butter, condensed milk and brown sugar until sugar is dissolved. Increase heat and bring to a boil, stirring constantly; boil for 5 minutes. Spoon evenly over baked base.
3. *Prepare the topping:* In another saucepan, over low heat, melt chocolate chips. Stir in cereal and mix until well coated. Spread evenly over filling. Chill for at least 3 hours, then cut into 16 squares. Cut each square in half diagonally to form two triangles.

Tip *After placing batter in your baking pan, bang the pan on the counter two or three times. This will get rid of any large air pockets that will create holes in the cake.*

Rainbow Gelatin Squares

Makes 30 squares
- 13- by 9-inch (3 L) baking pan, greased

CLEAR LAYERS		
4	packages (each a 4-serving size) gelatin dessert mix, assorted flavors	4
3 cups	boiling water, divided	750 mL
3 cups	cold water, divided	750 mL
CREAMY LAYERS		
3	packages (each a 4-serving size) gelatin dessert mix, assorted flavors	3
2¼ cups	boiling water, divided	300 mL
¾ cup	cold water, divided	175 mL
1½ cups	evaporated milk, divided	375 mL
4 cups	frozen whipped topping, thawed	1 L
	Sliced fresh strawberries (optional)	

1. *Prepare the clear layers:* In a small bowl, combine gelatin dessert mix with ¾ cup (175 mL) boiling water, stirring until completely dissolved. Add ¾ cup (175 mL) cold water and mix thoroughly. Pour into prepared baking pan and refrigerate for 35 to 40 minutes or until almost set.
2. *Prepare the creamy layers:* In another small bowl, combine gelatin dessert mix with ¾ cup (175 mL) boiling water, stirring until completely dissolved. Add ¼ cup (50 mL) cold water and ½ cup (125 mL) evaporated milk; mix thoroughly. Spoon over chilled clear layer and refrigerate until almost set.
3. Repeat clear and creamy layers, making seven in all, chilling each layer before adding another.
4. When all layers are completed and gelatin is set, cut into squares. Decorate squares with topping and garnish with sliced strawberries (if using).

Glazed Boston Cream Bars

Makes 24 bars

- Preheat oven to 350°F (180°C)
- 9-inch (2.5 L) square baking pan, lightly greased

CAKE

1⅓ cups	all-purpose flour	325 mL
1½ tsp	baking powder	7 mL
¼ tsp	salt	1 mL
3	egg whites	3
½ cup	granulated sugar, divided	125 mL
¼ cup	butter or margarine, softened	50 mL
2 tsp	vanilla	10 mL
⅔ cup	skim milk	150 mL

FILLING

1½ cups	skim milk	375 mL
1	package (4-serving size) vanilla instant pudding mix	1

CHOCOLATE GLAZE

3 tbsp	granulated sugar	45 mL
2 tbsp	unsweetened cocoa powder, sifted	25 mL
1¼ tsp	cornstarch	6 mL
⅓ cup	skim milk	75 mL
½ tsp	vanilla	2 mL

1. *Prepare the cake:* In a small bowl, mix together flour, baking powder and salt.
2. In a clean bowl, beat egg whites until frothy. Gradually beat in half the sugar until stiff peaks form.
3. In a large bowl, beat the remaining sugar and butter until smooth and creamy. Stir in vanilla. Gradually blend in flour mixture, alternately with milk, just until incorporated. Stir in one-third of the egg white mixture until well blended, then fold in the remainder.
4. Spread evenly in prepared pan. Bake in preheated oven for 35 minutes or until a tester inserted in the center comes out clean. Place pan on a wire rack to cool for 10 minutes, then turn cake out onto rack to cool completely.
5. *Prepare the filling:* Prepare pudding according to the instructions on the package but use 1½ cups (375 mL) of milk. Chill for 30 minutes or until thickened.
6. *Prepare the glaze:* In a saucepan, combine sugar, cocoa, cornstarch and milk. Bring to a boil over medium heat and cook for 1 to 2 minutes, stirring constantly, until slightly thickened. Remove from heat and stir in vanilla. Let cool in refrigerator for about 20 minutes.
7. Using a serrated knife, cut the cake in half horizontally and place the bottom piece, cut side up, on a plate. Spoon filling evenly over top. Top with second layer, cut side down. Spoon glaze over top, allowing some to drip down the sides. Chill for 3 to 4 hours, until glaze hardens, then cut into bars.

Tip *To determine whether an egg is fresh, immerse it in a pan of cool, salted water. If it sinks, it is fresh. If it rises to the top, it has passed its peak and is best discarded.*

Orange Nut Dessert Layers

Makes 24 squares

- Preheat oven to 375°F (190°C)
- 13- by 9-inch (3 L) baking pan, ungreased

BASE

1½ cups	all-purpose flour	375 mL
½ cup	packed brown sugar	125 mL
¼ tsp	salt	1 mL
1 tbsp	grated orange zest	15 mL
½ cup	butter or margarine	125 mL

FILLING

1 cup	semisweet chocolate chips	250 mL

TOPPING

¼ cup	all-purpose flour	50 mL
½ tsp	baking powder	2 mL
¼ tsp	salt	1 mL
2	eggs	2
1 cup	packed brown sugar	250 mL
1 tsp	vanilla	5 mL
1½ cups	chopped walnuts	375 mL

1. *Prepare the base:* In a medium bowl, mix together flour, brown sugar, salt and orange zest. Using two knives, a pastry blender or your fingers, cut butter in until mixture resembles coarse crumbs. Press evenly into pan. Bake in preheated oven for 10 minutes. Place pan on a rack.
2. *Prepare the filling:* Sprinkle chocolate over hot base. Let stand for about 2 minutes or until chocolate softens. Using a knife, spread evenly over base.
3. *Prepare the topping:* In a small bowl, mix together flour, baking powder and salt. In another bowl, beat eggs, brown sugar and vanilla until blended. Blend in flour mixture. Stir in walnuts.
4. Spread mixture evenly over chocolate. Bake for 20 minutes or until top is firm and golden brown. Place pan on a rack to cool completely, then cut into squares.

Chocolate Peanut Butter Coconut Gems

Makes 24 squares

- Preheat oven to 325°F (160°C)
- 13- by 9-inch (3 L) baking pan, ungreased

BASE

1½ cups	graham wafer crumbs (about 22 wafers)	375 mL
½ cup	butter or margarine, melted	125 mL

FILLING

1⅓ cups	flaked coconut (sweetened or unsweetened)	325 mL
1	can (10 oz/300 mL) sweetened condensed milk	1

TOPPING

½ cup	smooth peanut butter	125 mL
1½ cups	semisweet chocolate chips	375 mL

1. *Prepare the base:* In a small bowl, mix together crumbs and melted butter. Press evenly into pan.

2. *Prepare the filling:* Sprinkle coconut evenly over base. Pour condensed milk evenly over coconut.

3. Bake in preheated oven for 20 to 25 minutes or until lightly browned.

4. *Prepare the topping:* In a saucepan, over low heat, melt peanut butter and chocolate chips, stirring until smooth. Spread evenly over filling. Place pan on a wire rack to cool for 30 minutes, then chill thoroughly. Cut into squares.

Old-Fashioned Butter Tart Bars

Makes about 24 bars

- Preheat oven to 350°F (180°C)
- 9-inch (2.5 L) square baking pan, ungreased

BASE

1 cup	all-purpose flour	250 mL
2 tbsp	granulated sugar	25 mL
½ cup	butter or margarine, softened	125 mL

FILLING

1½ cups	packed brown sugar	375 mL
1 cup	chopped walnuts	250 mL
½ cup	raisins	125 mL
3	eggs, beaten	3
3 tbsp	all-purpose flour	45 mL
½ tsp	baking powder	2 mL
1 tsp	vanilla	5 mL

1. *Prepare the base:* In a small bowl, mix together flour and sugar. Using two knives, a pastry blender or your fingers, cut butter in until mixture resembles coarse crumbs. Press evenly into pan. Bake in preheated oven for 15 to 18 minutes or until golden brown. Place pan on a wire rack.

2. *Prepare the filling:* In a medium bowl, combine brown sugar, walnuts and raisins. Add eggs, flour, baking powder and vanilla and beat until well blended.

3. Spread evenly over hot base and bake for 20 to 25 minutes or until golden brown. Place pan on a wire rack to cool completely. (The filling may seem a bit jiggly at first but will become firm when completely cooled.) Cut into bars.

Buttermilk Spice Squares

Makes 16 squares

- Preheat oven to 350°F (180°C)
- 8-inch (2 L) square baking pan , greased

2½ cups	cake and pastry flour, sifted	625 mL
2 tsp	baking powder	10 mL
2 tsp	ground cinnamon	10 mL
½ tsp	baking soda	2 mL
½ tsp	ground cloves	2 mL
¼ tsp	ground allspice	1 mL
¼ tsp	ground nutmeg	1 mL
¼ tsp	ground mace	1 mL
½ cup	butter or shortening, softened	125 mL
1 cup	packed brown sugar	250 mL
2	eggs	2
1 cup	buttermilk	250 mL

1. In a medium bowl, mix together flour, baking powder, cinnamon, baking soda, cloves, allspice, nutmeg and mace.

2. In a large bowl, beat butter and brown sugar until smooth and creamy. Beat in eggs until incorporated. Gradually blend in flour mixture, alternately with buttermilk, just until incorporated.

3. Spread evenly in prepared pan. Bake in preheated oven for 45 to 50 minutes or until a tester inserted in the center comes out clean. Place pan on a wire rack to cool completely, then cut into squares.

Tip *If you don't have any buttermilk, here's an easy substitute: For each cup of buttermilk needed, just add 1 tbsp (15 mL) lemon juice to 1 cup (250 mL) regular milk and stir well.*

Cinnamon Raisin Bars

Makes 24 bars

- Preheat oven to 350º F (180ºC)
- 9-inch (2.5 L) square baking pan, greased

3 cups	raisins	750 mL
1½ cups	all-purpose flour	375 mL
1 tsp	baking soda	5 mL
1 tsp	salt	5 mL
1 tsp	ground cinnamon	5 mL
1 tsp	ground nutmeg	5 mL
1 cup	packed brown sugar	250 mL
½ cup	butter or margarine, softened	125 mL
3	eggs	3

1. In a saucepan, over medium heat, add sufficient water to cover raisins. Bring to a boil and cook for 5 minutes. Remove from heat and strain cooking liquid into a 1-cup (250 mL) measure. Add water, if required, to make 1 cup (250 mL) of liquid. Set raisins and liquid aside.
2. In a medium bowl, mix together flour, baking soda, salt, cinnamon and nutmeg.
3. In a large bowl, beat brown sugar and butter until smooth and creamy. Beat in eggs until incorporated. Gradually blend in flour mixture, alternately with reserved raisin liquid, until just incorporated. Stir in reserved raisins.
4. Spread evenly in prepared pan. Bake in preheated oven for 35 to 40 minutes or until a tester inserted in the center comes out clean. Place pan on a wire rack to cool completely, then cut into bars.

Coffee Bran Squares

Makes 16 squares

- Preheat oven to 350ºF (180ºC)
- 8-inch (2 L) square baking pan, lightly greased

½ cup	all-bran cereal	125 mL
1 cup	cold strong brewed coffee	250 mL
1 cup	granulated sugar	250 mL
1 cup	whole wheat flour	250 mL
½ cup	all-purpose flour	125 mL
1 tsp	baking soda	5 mL
1 tsp	ground cinnamon	5 mL
½ tsp	salt	2 mL
½ tsp	ground nutmeg	2 mL
¼ tsp	ground cloves	1 mL
¼ cup	vegetable oil	50 mL
1 tsp	vanilla	5 mL
1 tbsp	white vinegar	15 mL

1. In a small bowl, mix together cereal and coffee. Let stand for 2 minutes or until coffee is almost completely absorbed.
2. In a medium bowl, mix together sugar, flours, baking soda, cinnamon, salt, nutmeg and cloves.
3. In a large bowl, whisk together oil, vanilla and vinegar. Stir in cereal mixture until blended. Blend in flour mixture.
4. Spread evenly in prepared pan. Bake in preheated oven for 35 to 40 minutes or until a tester inserted in center comes out clean. Place pan on a wire rack to cool completely, then cut into squares.

Honey Cake Spice Bars

Makes 36 bars

- Preheat oven to 375ºF (190ºC)
- 13- by 9-inch (3 L) baking pan, lightly greased

2 tbsp	packed brown sugar	25 mL
4 tbsp	vegetable oil	60 mL
¼ cup	water	50 mL
¼ cup	liquid honey	50 mL
¾ cup	frozen apple juice concentrate, thawed	175 mL
2	eggs	2
½ cup	ground almonds	125 mL
2¼ cups	all-purpose flour	550 mL
1½ tsp	baking powder	7 mL
1 tsp	ground cinnamon	5 mL
½ tsp	ground ginger	2 mL
¼ tsp	ground allspice	1 mL

1. In a saucepan, combine brown sugar, oil, water, honey and apple juice concentrate. Bring to a boil and remove from heat. Set aside to cool. Add eggs and mix to blend.
2. In a large bowl, mix together almonds, flour, baking powder, cinnamon, ginger and allspice. Make a well in the center. Add apple juice mixture and stir until blended. Shape dough into a ball, wrap tightly in plastic wrap and chill for 2 hours.
3. Press dough evenly into prepared pan. Bake in preheated oven for 25 to 30 minutes or until golden brown. Place pan on a wire rack to cool completely, then cut into bars.

Tip *For a decorative touch, use a sharp knife to gently score center of each bar before baking and place a whole blanched almond in each. Bake as directed.*

Peachy Topped Bars

Makes 12 bars
- Preheat oven to 400°F (200°C)
- 8-inch (2 L) square baking pan, greased

BASE

1½ cups	all-purpose flour	375 mL
¼ cup	granulated sugar	50 mL
2 tsp	baking powder	10 mL
½ tsp	salt	2 mL
1	egg	1
3 tbsp	butter or shortening, melted	45 mL
½ cup	milk	125 mL

PEACH TOPPING

1½ cups	thinly sliced peaches	375 mL
2 tbsp	granulated sugar	25 mL
½ tsp	ground cinnamon	2 mL

1. *Prepare the base:* In a medium bowl, mix together flour, sugar, baking powder and salt. Make a well in the center.
2. In a small bowl, beat egg, butter and milk until blended. Add to flour mixture and mix until just incorporated. Spread evenly in prepared pan.
3. *Prepare the topping:* In a small bowl, mix together peaches, sugar and cinnamon.
4. Spread evenly over batter. Cover pan with aluminum foil and bake in preheated oven for 10 minutes. Remove foil, bake for 15 minutes, cool and cut into bars.

Tip *To ripen fruits such as peaches, nectarines or plums, place the unripe fruit in a brown paper bag, close the bag and keep it on your kitchen counter or in an area away from direct sunlight or cold. It will be ripe in 1 to 3 days.*

Scottish Cottage Pudding Squares

Makes 16 squares
- Preheat oven to 350°F (180°C)
- 8-inch (2 L) square baking pan, greased

1¾ cups	all-purpose flour	425 mL
2½ tsp	baking powder	12 mL
½ tsp	salt	2 mL
¼ cup	shortening, softened	50 mL
1 cup	granulated sugar	250 mL
1	egg	1
½ tsp	vanilla	2 mL
¼ tsp	almond extract	1 mL
1 tbsp	grated orange zest	15 mL
⅔ cup	milk	150 mL

1. In a small bowl, mix together flour, baking powder and salt.
2. In a large bowl, beat shortening and sugar until smooth and creamy. Beat in egg until incorporated. Stir in vanilla, almond extract and orange zest. Blend in flour mixture alternately with milk, until just incorporated.
3. Spread evenly in prepared pan. Bake in preheated oven for 30 to 35 minutes or until a tester inserted in the center comes out clean. Cut into squares immediately and serve while still hot.

Tip *These squares are even more delicious with a lemon or orange sauce.*

Plantation Marble Squares

Makes 16 squares
- Preheat oven to 350°F (180°C)
- 8-inch (2 L) square baking pan, greased

2 cups	cake and pastry flour, sifted	500 mL
2 tsp	baking powder	10 mL
¼ tsp	salt	1 mL
½ cup	butter or margarine, softened	125 mL
1 cup	granulated sugar	250 mL
2	eggs	2
½ cup	milk	125 mL
1 tsp	ground cinnamon	5 mL
½ tsp	ground nutmeg	2 mL
½ tsp	ground cloves	2 mL
2 tbsp	light (fancy) molasses	25 mL

1. In a medium bowl, mix together flour, baking powder and salt.
2. In a large bowl, beat butter and sugar until smooth and creamy. Beat in eggs until incorporated. Gradually blend in flour mixture alternately with milk, until just incorporated.
3. Divide batter into two bowls. Stir cinnamon, nutmeg, cloves and molasses into one of the bowls; spread mixture evenly in prepared pan. Drop batter from the remaining bowl, by spoonfuls, over top. Run a knife through batters to create a marbling effect.
4. Bake in preheated oven for 45 to 50 minutes or until a tester inserted in the center comes out clean. Place pan on a wire rack to cool completely, then cut into squares.

Tip *If desired, frost with a butter frosting (see recipes, page 544), then sprinkle with nuts and/or raisins.*

Dutch Crumb Squares

Makes 16 squares

- Preheat oven to 350°F (180°C)
- 8-inch (2 L) square baking pan, greased

2½ cups	cake and pastry flour, sifted	625 mL
½ tsp	baking soda	2 mL
½ tsp	salt	2 mL
½ cup	butter or margarine, softened	125 mL
¾ cup	packed brown sugar	175 mL
1 cup	seedless raisins, ground in a food processor	250 mL
1	egg, beaten	1
¾ cup	buttermilk	175 mL
2 tbsp	granulated sugar	25 mL
Pinch	ground cinnamon	Pinch

1. In a medium bowl, mix together flour, baking soda and salt.
2. In a large bowl, beat butter and brown sugar until smooth and creamy. Gradually blend in flour mixture. Set aside ¾ cup (175 mL). To the remaining mixture, add raisins, egg and buttermilk, beating until well blended.
3. Spread evenly in prepared pan. Sprinkle with reserved crumb mixture, then with sugar and cinnamon. Bake in preheated oven for 20 to 25 minutes or until a tester inserted in the center comes out clean. Place pan on a wire rack to cool completely, then cut into squares.

Tip *When working with a sticky or fluffy batter, wet your spatula, or hands, before patting or spreading the batter in the pan.*

Poppy Seed Squares

Makes 16 squares

- Preheat oven to 350°F (180°C)
- 8-inch (2 L) square baking pan, greased

1 cup	poppy seeds	250 mL
1 cup	milk	250 mL
2 cups	all-purpose flour	500 mL
2 tsp	baking powder	10 mL
½ tsp	salt	2 mL
½ cup	butter or margarine, softened	125 mL
1 cup	granulated sugar	250 mL
2	eggs, separated	2
	Grated zest of 1 orange (or ½ tsp/2 mL almond extract)	
	Confectioner's (icing) sugar	

1. In a small bowl, combine poppy seeds and milk. Let stand for 1 hour.
2. In a medium bowl, mix together flour, baking powder and salt.
3. In a large bowl, beat butter and sugar until smooth and creamy. Beat in egg yolks until incorporated. Blend in flour mixture alternately with poppy seed mixture, mixing just until incorporated. Stir in orange zest.
4. In a clean bowl, beat egg whites until stiff. Fold gently into batter.
5. Spread evenly in prepared pan. Bake in preheated oven for about 45 minutes or until a tester inserted in the center comes out clean. Place pan on a rack to cool completely. Sift confectioner's sugar over top. Cut into squares.

Pink Lemonade Bars

Makes 12 bars

- Preheat oven to 325°F (160°C)
- 8-inch (2 L) square baking pan, ungreased

BASE

2 cups	vanilla wafer crumbs (about 40 cookies)	500 mL
½ cup	butter or margarine, melted	125 mL

TOPPING

¾ cup	water	175 mL
½	can (12 oz/355 mL) frozen pink lemonade concentrate	½
48	miniature marshmallows	48
1 cup	whipping (35%) cream	250 mL

1. *Prepare the base:* In a medium bowl, mix together crumbs and butter. Set aside ½ cup (125 mL) and press remainder evenly into bottom and halfway up the sides of pan. Bake in preheated oven for 15 minutes. Place pan on a wire rack to cool completely.
2. *Prepare the topping:* In a saucepan, combine water and lemonade concentrate. Heat over low heat until lemonade thaws and mixture is hot. Stir in marshmallows until melted and smooth. Chill for 3 to 4 hours or overnight, until mixture is thick and syrupy.
3. In a medium bowl, whip cream until stiff. Fold gently into marshmallow mixture until blended. Spoon into cooled base. Sprinkle the remaining crumb mixture evenly over top. Freeze for 3 to 4 hours or until firm. Cut into bars. Let stand at room temperature for about 30 minutes before serving. Store, covered, in the freezer.

Cakes

General Cakes

Pound Cakes

Coffee Cakes

Loaf Cakes

Angel Food Cakes

Chiffon Cakes

Sponge Cakes

Layer Cakes and Tortes

Fancy and Specialty Cakes

Cheesecakes

General Cakes

White Sheet Cake

Serves 16 to 20
- Preheat oven to 375°F (190°C)
- 17- by 11- by 1-inch (45 by 29 by 2.5 cm) rimmed baking sheet, greased, and bottom lined with parchment paper

4 cups	all-purpose flour	1 L
4 tsp	baking powder	20 mL
½ tsp	salt	2 mL
¾ cup	butter, margarine or shortening, softened	175 mL
2 cups	granulated sugar	500 mL
6	egg whites	6
½ tsp	vanilla	2 mL
½ tsp	almond extract (optional)	2 mL
¾ cup	water	175 mL
¾ cup	milk	175 mL

1. In a medium bowl, sift together flour, baking powder and salt.
2. In a large mixer bowl, cream butter until smooth. Gradually add in sugar, beating until light and fluffy. Add egg whites, one at a time, beating well after each addition. Stir in vanilla and almond extract (if using). Stir in flour mixture alternately with water and milk, making 3 additions of flour and 1 each of water and milk, until mixture is smooth. Pour into prepared baking pan, smoothing top.
3. Bake in preheated oven for 30 to 35 minutes or until cake top springs back when touched lightly with fingertip. Let cool in pan on a wire rack.

Tip *These sheet cakes can be cut into 2-inch squares to serve, or made fancy by using cookie cutters to make individual shapes. They can be frosted or left plain. Decorate as desired.*

Variations *Lemon Sheet Cake: Omit almond extract and replace with 2 tsp (10 mL) lemon extract.*

Chocolate Sheet Cake: Add ½ cup (125 mL) unsweetened cocoa powder, sifted, to the dry ingredients before baking.

Mom's War Cake

Serves 8 to 10
- Preheat oven to 350°F (180°C)
- 9-inch (2.5 L) square metal baking pan, greased and floured

2 cups	water	500 mL
2 cups	granulated sugar (or 1 cup/250 mL granulated and 1 cup/250 mL packed brown sugar)	500 mL
1 cup	raisins	250 mL
⅔ cup	lard or shortening	150 mL
2 tsp	ground cinnamon	10 mL
1 tsp	ground cloves	5 mL
½ tsp	ground nutmeg	2 mL
½ tsp	salt	2 mL
⅓ cup	cold water or brewed coffee	75 mL
2 tsp	baking soda	10 mL
4 cups	all-purpose flour	1 L
1 tsp	baking powder	5 mL
1 cup	chopped nuts (optional)	250 mL

1. In a large saucepan, bring to a boil the 2 cups (500 mL) of water, sugar, raisins, lard, cinnamon, cloves, nutmeg and salt. Boil for about 5 minutes or until the lard is smooth and melted. Set aside to cool.
2. In a small bowl, mix together cold water and baking soda and add to the mixture in the saucepan.
3. Mix in flour and baking powder until blended. Add chopped nuts (if using) and mix well. Spoon into prepared baking pan, spreading evenly.
4. Bake in preheated oven for 30 minutes or until a toothpick inserted in the center comes out clean and dry. Let cool in pan on a wire rack for 10 minutes, then remove from pan to cool completely on wire rack.

Tips *To keep a cake fresh for several days longer, place an apple cut in half in the cake box.*

If you wish to have an icing for this cake, warm 2 tbsp (25 mL) evaporated milk in a small saucepan, add ½ to ¾ tsp (2 to 4 mL) lemon extract and 1 cup (250 mL) confectioner's (icing) sugar and mix until the right consistency for spreading. Spread over top of cake when both cake and icing are cooled.

Easy Coconut Snowball Cake

Serves 12 to 16

- Preheat oven according to cake mix instructions
- Two 9-inch (2.5 L) square metal baking pans, greased and floured

1	package (18 oz/510 g) yellow cake mix	1

FILLING

2 cups	granulated sugar	500 mL
2 cups	sour cream	500 mL
¼ cup	orange juice (optional)	50 mL
1½ cups	flaked coconut (sweetened or unsweetened)	375 mL
1	carton (8 oz/250 mL) whipped topping	1
1	can (10 oz/284 mL) mandarin orange segments, drained	1

1. In a large bowl, prepare cake mix according to package directions. Pour batter into the two prepared baking pans and bake as directed on the package. Let cool in pans for 10 minutes, then remove onto wire racks to cool completely.
2. *Prepare the filling:* In a medium bowl, mix together sugar, sour cream and orange juice (if using) until well blended. Add coconut and mix well. The mixture will be soft. Set aside 1 cup (250 mL) of this filling.
3. Split each cake layer horizontally. Place one layer on a plate and spread about one-third of the filling over top. Top with another cake layer and one-third of the filling. Repeat with the third layer and top with the fourth layer.
4. Fold the reserved 1 cup (250 mL) of filling into the whipped topping and frost top and sides of cake. Decorate with mandarin orange segments.

Tip *Frosting spreads easier and frosted cakes are easier to cut when you dip your knife in cold water.*

Graham Streusel Cake

Serves 12 to 16

- Preheat oven to 350°F (180°C)
- 13- by 9-inch (3 L) metal baking pan, greased and floured

STREUSEL TOPPING

2 cups	graham wafer crumbs (about 25 whole wafers)	500 mL
¾ cup	firmly packed brown sugar	175 mL
¾ cup	butter or margarine, melted	175 mL
1½ tsp	ground cinnamon	7 mL

CAKE

1⅔ cups	graham wafers, finely crushed (about 20 whole wafers)	400 mL
¼ cup	all-purpose flour	50 mL
1½ tsp	baking powder	7 mL
¼ tsp	salt	1 mL
½ cup	butter, margarine or shortening, softened	125 mL
1 cup	granulated sugar	250 mL
½ tsp	vanilla	2 mL
3	eggs, separated, at room temperature	3
¾ cup	milk	175 mL
½ cup	chopped nuts (optional)	125 mL

1. *Prepare the topping:* In a small bowl, mix together graham crumbs, brown sugar, melted butter and cinnamon until well combined.
2. *Prepare the cake:* In a medium bowl, combine graham wafer crumbs, flour, baking powder and salt.
3. In a large mixer bowl, cream butter until smooth. Gradually add sugar and vanilla and beat on medium speed until blended. Beat in egg yolks until light and fluffy. Beat in flour mixture alternately with milk, making 3 additions of flour and 2 of milk, on low speed until mixed. Stir in nuts (if using).
4. In a small mixer bowl with clean beaters, on high speed, beat egg whites until stiff peaks form. Gently fold into the batter until thoroughly blended. Spoon into prepared baking pan, spreading evenly. Sprinkle streusel topping evenly over batter.
5. Bake in preheated oven for 45 to 50 minutes or until a toothpick inserted in the center comes out clean and dry. Let cool in pan on a wire rack for 10 minutes, then remove to wire rack to cool completely.

Poppy Seed Bundt Cake

Serves 12 to 16
- Preheat oven to 350°F (180°C)
- 10-inch (3 L) Bundt pan, greased and floured

¾ cup	milk	175 mL
½ cup	poppy seeds	125 mL
2 cups	all-purpose flour	500 mL
2 tsp	baking powder	10 mL
Pinch	salt	Pinch
¾ cup	butter or margarine, softened	175 mL
1½ cups	granulated sugar	375 mL
5	eggs, separated	5
	Confectioner's (icing) sugar	

1. In a small bowl, soak poppy seeds in milk and let stand for 1 hour or overnight.

2. In a medium bowl, combine flour, baking powder and salt.

3. In a large mixer bowl, cream butter and sugar until smooth. Beat in egg yolks, one at a time, on medium speed until light and fluffy. Add poppy seed mixture and mix until well blended. Beat in flour mixture on low speed until well blended.

4. In a small mixer bowl with clean beaters, on high speed, beat egg whites until stiff peaks form. Gently fold into batter, blending thoroughly. Spoon into prepared baking pan.

5. Bake in preheated oven for 50 to 60 minutes or until a toothpick inserted in the center comes out clean and dry. Let cool in pan on a wire rack for 20 to 30 minutes. Remove from pan and let cool completely on wire rack. Sift confectioner's sugar over top or decorate as desired.

Old-Fashioned Chocolate Cake

Serves 12 to 16
- Preheat oven to 350°F (180°C)
- 10-inch (4 L) tube pan, greased and dusted with unsweetened cocoa powder

2¾ cups	all-purpose flour	675 mL
2 tsp	baking soda	10 mL
½ tsp	baking powder	2 mL
½ tsp	salt	2 mL
2 cups	boiling water	500 mL
1 cup	unsweetened cocoa powder, sifted	250 mL
1 cup	butter or margarine, softened	250 mL
2½ cups	granulated sugar	625 mL
1½ tsp	vanilla	7 mL
4	eggs	4

CHOCOLATE FROSTING

1 cup	butter or margarine	250 mL
1 cup	semisweet chocolate pieces or chips	250 mL
½ cup	light (5%) cream	125 mL
2½ cups	confectioner's (icing) sugar	625 mL

1. In a medium bowl, sift together flour, baking soda, baking powder and salt.

2. In another bowl, whisk together boiling water and cocoa until smooth. Let cool to room temperature.

3. In a large mixer bowl, beat butter, sugar, vanilla and eggs on high speed. Beat in flour mixture alternately with cocoa mixture, making 3 additions of flour and 2 of cocoa, on low speed until well blended. Do not overbeat.

4. Pour into prepared baking pan and tap pan lightly on counter to get rid of any air bubbles that may have formed.

5. Bake in preheated oven for 60 to 70 minutes or until a toothpick inserted in the center comes out clean and dry. Let cool in pan on a wire rack for 10 minutes. Loosen around edges of cake with a spatula or knife, then invert onto wire rack or plate to cool completely.

6. *Prepare the frosting:* In a medium saucepan, over low heat, combine butter, chocolate and cream, stirring until smooth. Remove from heat and add confectioner's sugar. Transfer to a small bowl, place bowl over ice and whisk until frosting is of the right consistency for spreading. Frost sides and top of cake, swirling with a knife or spatula to decorate.

Dutch Chocolate Mayo Cake

Serves 12 to 16
- Preheat oven to 350°F (180°C)
- 13- by 9-inch (3 L) metal baking pan, greased and floured

2 cups	all-purpose flour	500 mL
¾ cup	unsweetened cocoa powder, sifted	175 mL
1¼ tsp	baking soda	6 mL
¼ tsp	baking powder	1 mL
3	eggs	3
1½ cups	granulated sugar	375 mL
1 tsp	vanilla	5 mL
1 cup	real mayonnaise	250 mL
1¼ cups	water	300 mL

1. In a bowl, combine flour, cocoa powder, baking soda and baking powder.

2. In a large mixer bowl, on high speed, beat eggs, sugar and vanilla. Add mayonnaise and beat on low speed until well combined. Beat in flour mixture alternately with water, making 3 additions of flour and 2 of water, beating only until well blended.

3. Spoon into prepared baking pan. Bake in preheated oven for 35 to 40 minutes or until cake springs back when touched lightly with fingertip. Let cool in pan on a wire rack for 10 minutes, then remove to wire rack to cool completely.

Tip *If desired, frost with your favorite frosting or dust with confectioner's sugar.*

Easy Chocolate Caramel Pecan Cake

Serves 12 to 16

- Preheat oven according to cake mix instructions
- 13- by 9-inch (3 L) metal baking pan, greased

¼ cup	evaporated milk	50 mL
½ cup	butter or margarine	125 mL
60	vanilla caramels	60
1	package (18 oz/510 g) chocolate cake mix	1
1 cup	chopped pecans or walnuts	250 mL
1 cup	semisweet chocolate chips (optional)	250 mL

1. In a small saucepan, over low heat, melt milk, butter and caramels, stirring until smooth. Set aside.

2. In a large mixer bowl, prepare cake mix as directed on the package. Pour half of the batter into the prepared baking pan and bake in preheated oven for 15 minutes.

3. Remove from oven and pour the caramel mixture over top of cake, spreading evenly. Sprinkle pecans over the caramel and then the chocolate chips (if using) over top of the nuts.

4. Pour the remaining batter over top, spreading evenly. Bake at 350°F (180°C) for 25 to 35 minutes or until a toothpick inserted in the center comes out clean and dry. Let cool in pan on a wire rack.

Tips *Frost with a chocolate frosting, if desired.*

Bake any type of cake mix, cut it into small or large squares, and serve hot with a caramel sauce. To make this sauce, combine a jar of caramel ice cream topping and ⅓ cup (75 mL) milk over low heat.

Turnover Chocolate Pecan Cake

Serves 12 to 16

- Preheat oven to 350°F (180°C)
- 10-inch (3 L) Bundt pan, buttered and dusted with cocoa powder

1¾ cups	sifted cake and pastry flour	425 mL
2 tsp	baking powder	10 mL
Pinch	salt	Pinch
¼ cup	firmly packed light brown sugar	50 mL
⅔ cup	butter or margarine, softened, divided	150 mL
¼ cup	whipping (35%) cream	50 mL
⅔ cup	light corn syrup	150 mL
1 cup	chopped pecans	250 mL
1⅓ cups	granulated sugar	325 mL
2	eggs, separated	2
1 tsp	vanilla	5 mL
3 oz	unsweetened chocolate, melted	90 g
1 cup	milk	250 mL

1. In a medium bowl, combine flour, baking powder and salt.

2. In a small saucepan, mix together brown sugar and ¼ cup (50 mL) of the butter, stirring over low heat until bubbly. Add cream and corn syrup, stirring constantly to boiling. Remove from heat and stir in pecans. Spoon into prepared baking pan and set aside.

3. In a large mixer bowl, cream the remaining butter and granulated sugar until smooth. Beat in egg yolks, vanilla and chocolate, beating on medium speed until thoroughly blended. Stir in flour mixture alternately with milk, making 3 additions of flour and 2 of milk, until well blended.

4. In small mixer bowl with clean beaters, beat egg whites on high speed until stiff peaks form. Fold into the batter gently until well blended.

5. Pour batter over nut mixture in pan. Bake in preheated oven for 45 to 50 minutes or until a toothpick inserted in the center comes out clean and dry.

6. Place pan on a wire rack and loosen around the edges of the cake with a knife or spatula. Place a serving plate over top of pan and invert, gently shaking to remove the cake. Remove pan. If any of the nut mixture is still clinging to the pan, scrape back onto cake with a rubber spatula. Leave on plate to cool completely before serving.

Chocolate Chunk Banana Snackin' Cake

Serves 6 to 8

- Preheat oven to 350°F (180°C)
- 8-inch (2 L) square metal baking pan, buttered

1½ cups	all-purpose flour	375 mL
¾ tsp	baking soda	4 mL
3 oz	semisweet chocolate, chopped	90 g
½ cup	granulated sugar	125 mL
½ cup	butter or margarine, softened	125 mL
1 tsp	vanilla	5 mL
2	eggs	2
¼ cup	sour cream	50 mL
1 cup	mashed ripe bananas (about 4 medium)	250 mL

1. In a bowl, combine flour, baking soda and chocolate.

2. In a large mixer bowl, cream sugar and butter until smooth. Beat in vanilla and eggs, one at a time, beating until light and fluffy. Add sour cream, beating to blend well. Stir in flour mixture alternately with the mashed bananas, making 3 additions of flour and 2 of bananas, just until moistened and thoroughly combined.

3. Spoon into prepared baking pan. Bake in preheated oven for 30 to 35 minutes or until a toothpick inserted in the center comes out clean and dry. Let cool in pan on a wire rack.

Tip *Frost with your favorite chocolate or mocha frosting, if desired.*

German Chocolate Cake

Serves 10 to 12

- Preheat oven to 350°F (180°C)
- Two 9-inch (23 cm) round metal cake pans, greased and lightly dusted with unsweetened cocoa powder

4 oz	sweetened baking chocolate	125 g
½ cup	water	125 mL
1½ cups	all-purpose flour	375 mL
¾ tsp	baking soda	4 mL
¼ tsp	salt	1 mL
¾ cup	butter, margarine or shortening, softened	175 mL
1 cup	granulated sugar	250 mL
1 tsp	vanilla	5 mL
3	eggs	3
¾ cup	buttermilk or sour cream	175 mL

PECAN FROSTING

1	egg	1
⅔ cup	evaporated milk	150 mL
⅔ cup	granulated sugar	150 mL
¼ cup	butter or margarine	50 mL
1⅓ cups	flaked coconut (sweetened or unsweetened)	325 mL
½ cup	chopped pecans	125 mL

1. In a small saucepan, over low heat, stir chocolate and water until chocolate has melted. Set aside to cool.

2. In a bowl, combine flour, baking soda and salt.

3. In a large mixer bowl, on medium speed, cream butter until smooth. Add sugar and beat until light and fluffy. Beat in vanilla and eggs on low speed until blended, and then beat on medium for about 2 minutes. Stir in chocolate mixture. Beat in flour mixture alternately with the buttermilk, making 3 additions of flour and 2 of buttermilk, on low speed until well blended.

4. Pour batter evenly into prepared pans. Bake in preheated oven for 35 to 40 minutes or until a toothpick inserted in the center comes out clean and dry. Let cool in pans on wire racks for 10 minutes and then remove and let cool completely on wire racks.

5. *Prepare the frosting:* In a saucepan, over medium heat, lightly beat the egg. Add the milk, sugar and butter, stirring until thickened and bubbly, about 10 minutes. Remove from heat and add coconut and pecans. Cover and let cool completely before frosting cake. Place one cake layer on serving plate. Spread about one-third of the frosting evenly over top and top with the second cake. Frost sides and top with the remaining frosting.

Turnover Apple Cake

Serves 6 to 8

- Preheat oven to 400°F (200°C)
- 9-inch (23 cm) round or 9-inch (2.5 L) square metal baking pan, well-buttered

TOPPING

½ cup	granulated sugar	125 mL
1 tsp	ground cinnamon	5 mL
4	Granny Smith apples, peeled and thinly sliced	4

CAKE

2 cups	biscuit mix	500 mL
2 tbsp	granulated sugar	25 mL

1 tsp	ground cinnamon	5 mL
1/4 tsp	ground nutmeg	1 mL
1	egg	1
2/3 cup	milk	150 mL

1. *Prepare the topping:* In a medium bowl, toss sugar, cinnamon and apples, mixing well to coat. Spoon into prepared baking pan.
2. *Prepare the cake:* In a large mixer bowl, combine biscuit mix, sugar, cinnamon, nutmeg, egg and milk. Beat on low speed until blended, then on medium speed until thoroughly blended. Pour over top of apple mixture, spreading evenly.
3. Bake in preheated oven for 25 to 30 minutes or until a toothpick inserted in the center comes out clean and dry. Let cool in pan on a wire rack for 5 to 10 minutes, then invert onto a serving plate and let cool completely or serve slightly warm.

Tip *If desired, top with ice cream or a dollop of whipped cream.*

Easy Apple Pie Dump Cake

Serves 12 to 16
- Preheat oven to 400°F (200°C)
- 13- by 9-inch (3 L) metal baking pan, lightly greased

1	can (20 oz/590 mL) apple pie filling	1
1/2 tsp	ground cinnamon	2 mL
1	package (18 oz/510 g) yellow or white cake mix	1
1/2 cup	butter or margarine, melted	125 mL
	Ice cream or whipped cream	

1. In a medium bowl, mix together apple pie filling and cinnamon. Pour into prepared baking pan.
2. Spread dry cake mix over top. Pour the melted butter evenly over the cake mix.
3. Bake in preheated oven for 40 to 45 minutes or until golden brown. Serve warm with ice cream or whipped cream.

Variations *Pumpkin Dump Cake: Use a yellow cake mix. Omit apple pie filling and cinnamon and replace with 1 can (20 oz/590 mL) pumpkin pie filling. Stir 1 cup (250 mL) chopped nuts into the pumpkin filling.*

Cherry Pineapple Dump Cake: Use a yellow cake mix. Omit apple pie filling and cinnamon. Use 1/2 can (10 oz/300 mL) cherry pie filling and 1/2 can (10 oz/ 300 mL) crushed pineapple, undrained.

Blueberry Dump Cake: Use a yellow cake mix. Omit apple pie filling and cinnamon. Use 1 can (20 oz/ 590 mL) blueberry pie filling.

Spiced Pear Gingerbread Cake

Serves 8 to 10
- Preheat oven to 350°F (180°C)
- 9-inch (23 cm) round or 9-inch (2.5 L) square metal baking pan, greased

3 cups	all-purpose flour	750 mL
1 tbsp	ground ginger	15 mL
1/2 tsp	ground cinnamon	2 mL
1/4 tsp	salt	1 mL
1/4 tsp	ground cloves	1 mL
2 tsp	baking soda	10 mL
1 cup	boiling water	250 mL
1 cup	butter or margarine, softened	250 mL
1/2 cup	firmly packed brown sugar	125 mL
1	egg	1
1 cup	light (fancy) molasses	250 mL
2 tbsp	packed brown sugar	25 mL
1	can (14 oz/398 mL) pear halves, drained and cut into quarters (or 2 large pears, peeled and sliced)	1

1. In a medium bowl, sift together flour, ginger, cinnamon, salt and cloves.
2. In another bowl, dissolve the baking soda in the boiling water and set aside.
3. In a large mixer bowl, cream butter and 1/2 cup (125 mL) brown sugar until smooth. Beat in egg until mixture is light and fluffy. Stir in molasses and blend well. Stir in flour mixture alternately with baking soda mixture, making 3 additions of flour and 2 of baking soda, until well blended. Pour into prepared baking pan. Sprinkle with 2 tbsp (25 mL) brown sugar and arrange pear slices over top.
4. Bake in preheated oven for 60 to 65 minutes or until a toothpick inserted in the center comes out clean and dry. Let cool in pan on a wire rack for 10 minutes, then remove onto wire rack and let cool slightly. Best when served warm.

Tip *To soften brown sugar that has become hard, put a slice of soft bread in the package and close the bag tightly. The sugar will be soft again in a few hours.*

Blueberry Streusel Cake

Serves 8 to 10

- Preheat oven to 350°F (180°C)
- 9-inch (23 cm) round metal baking pan or springform pan, greased and floured

STREUSEL TOPPING

1/3 cup	all-purpose flour	75 mL
1/4 cup	packed brown sugar	50 mL
1 tsp	ground cinnamon	5 mL
3 tbsp	butter or margarine, softened	45 mL

CAKE

2 cups	all-purpose flour	500 mL
1 tsp	baking powder	5 mL
1/4 tsp	baking soda	1 mL
Pinch	salt	Pinch
1/4 cup	butter or margarine, softened	50 mL
1 cup	granulated sugar	250 mL
	Grated zest of 1 lemon	
1 tsp	vanilla	5 mL
2	eggs	2
1 cup	sour cream	250 mL
1 cup	fresh blueberries, washed and dried (or frozen, thawed and drained)	250 mL

1. *Prepare the topping:* In a small bowl, mix together flour, brown sugar and cinnamon. Cut in butter with a fork, or by hand, until mixture is crumbly. Set aside.

2. *Prepare the cake:* In a medium bowl, sift together flour, baking powder, baking soda and salt.

3. In a large mixer bowl, cream butter and sugar until smooth. Add lemon zest and vanilla. Beat in eggs, on medium speed, until light and fluffy. Beat in flour mixture alternately with sour cream, making 3 additions of flour and 2 of sour cream, on low speed until well blended. Pour into prepared baking pan. Sprinkle blueberries over top of batter. Sprinkle streusel topping evenly over blueberries.

4. Bake in preheated oven for 60 minutes or until a toothpick inserted in the center comes out clean and dry. Let cool in pan on a wire rack for 10 minutes, then remove onto a plate or wire rack to cool completely.

Tip *If you have rust marks on your baking pans that just won't come off, pour some cola into them and soak overnight. The pans should be free of rust the next morning.*

Lemon Blueberry Cake

Serves 12 to 16

- Preheat oven to 350°F (180°C)
- 13- by 9-inch (3 L) metal baking pan, greased and floured

3 cups	all-purpose flour	750 mL
2 tsp	baking powder	10 mL
1/2 tsp	salt	2 mL
3/4 cup	butter, margarine or shortening, softened	175 mL
2 cups	granulated sugar	500 mL
4	eggs	4
1 tsp	vanilla	5 mL
1 tsp	grated lemon zest	5 mL
1 tsp	freshly squeezed lemon juice	5 mL
1 cup	milk	250 mL
1 1/2 cups	fresh blueberries (or frozen blueberries, thawed and drained)	375 mL

1. In a medium bowl, combine flour, baking powder and salt.

2. In a large mixer bowl, on medium speed, cream butter and sugar until smooth. Add eggs, one at a time, beating until light and fluffy. Beat in vanilla, lemon juice and lemon zest until blended. Beat in flour mixture alternately with milk, making 3 additions of flour and 2 of milk, on low speed until well combined.

3. Fold in blueberries and spoon into prepared baking pan. Bake in preheated oven for 50 to 60 minutes or until toothpick inserted in the center comes out clean and dry. Let cool completely in pan on a wire rack.

Crusted Lemon Poppy Seed Cake

Serves 12 to 16

- Preheat oven to 350°F (180°C)
- 10-inch (3 L) Bundt pan, well-greased

1/4 cup	fine dry bread crumbs	50 mL
2 1/4 cups	sifted cake and pastry flour	550 mL
1/2 cup	poppy seeds	125 mL
1 tsp	baking powder	5 mL
1/2 tsp	salt	2 mL
3	eggs	3
1 1/2 cups	granulated sugar	375 mL
3/4 cup	butter or margarine, softened	175 mL
1 tbsp	grated lemon zest	15 mL
2 tbsp	freshly squeezed lemon juice	25 mL
2/3 cup	milk	150 mL

1. Dust greased pan evenly with the dry bread crumbs. When cake is baked and removed from pan, this will form a lovely brown crust.
2. In a medium bowl, combine flour, poppy seeds, baking powder and salt.
3. In a large mixer bowl, combine eggs, sugar and butter, and beat on high speed for 3 to 5 minutes, until well beaten and smooth. Slowly beat in lemon juice and lemon zest. Beat in flour mixture alternately with milk, making 3 additions of flour and 2 of milk, on low speed just until blended.
4. Pour into prepared baking pan. Bake in preheated oven for 50 to 55 minutes or until a toothpick inserted in center comes out clean. Let cool in pan on a wire rack for about 10 minutes and then loosen cake around the edges with a knife or spatula and invert onto wire rack to cool completely.

Orange Ripple Cake

Serves 8 to 10
- Preheat oven to 375°F (190°C)
- 9-inch (2.5 L) square or 9-inch (23 cm) round metal baking pan, greased

RIPPLE MIXTURE

½ cup	granulated sugar	125 mL
2 tbsp	unsweetened cocoa powder, sifted	25 mL
2 tsp	ground cinnamon	10 mL

CAKE

2 cups	all-purpose flour	500 mL
2½ tsp	baking powder	12 mL
¼ tsp	baking soda	1 mL
Pinch	salt	Pinch
1 cup	granulated sugar	250 mL
½ cup	butter or margarine, softened	125 mL
2	eggs, beaten	2
½ cup	chopped nuts	125 mL
1 tbsp	grated orange zest	15 mL
1 cup	sour cream	250 mL

1. *Prepare the ripple mixture:* In a small bowl, combine sugar, cocoa powder and cinnamon, mixing until well combined. Set aside.
2. *Prepare the cake:* In another bowl, sift together flour, baking powder, baking soda and salt.
3. In a large mixer bowl, cream sugar and butter until smooth. Beat in eggs until light and fluffy. Stir in nuts and orange zest, and mix well. Stir in flour mixture alternately with sour cream, making 3 additions of flour and 2 of sour cream, on low speed, mixing until well blended.

4. Spread half of the batter into the prepared baking pan. Sprinkle ripple mixture over batter. Top with the remaining batter, spreading evenly. Bake in preheated oven for 40 to 45 minutes or until a toothpick inserted in the center comes out clean and dry. Let cool in pan on a wire rack for 10 minutes. Remove from pan and let cool completely on wire rack.

Tip *If desired, frost with your favorite chocolate frosting after removing cake from the pan.*

Coconut Apricot Cake

Serves 6 to 8
- Preheat oven to 375°F (190°C)
- 8-inch (20 cm) round or 8-inch (2 L) square metal baking pan, ungreased

1 cup	all-purpose flour	250 mL
¾ cup	granulated sugar	175 mL
1¼ tsp	baking powder	6 mL
Pinch	salt	Pinch
6 tbsp	butter or margarine	90 mL
⅔ cup	packed brown sugar	150 mL
1¼ cups	flaked coconut (sweetened or unsweetened)	300 mL
1 tbsp	light corn syrup	15 mL
1¼ cups	canned apricot halves, drained	300 mL
¼ cup	shortening, softened	50 mL
1	egg	1
½ cup	milk	125 mL
½ tsp	vanilla	2 mL

1. In a large mixer bowl, sift together flour, granulated sugar, baking powder and salt.
2. In a small saucepan, melt butter over low heat. Remove from heat and stir in brown sugar, coconut and corn syrup. Pat evenly onto bottom and sides of baking pan.
3. Place apricot halves, cut side up, over top of coconut mixture.
4. To the flour mixture, add shortening, egg, milk and vanilla, beating on low speed until blended. Beat for another 2 to 3 minutes on medium speed. Spoon over the apricots.
5. Bake in preheated oven for 45 to 50 minutes or until golden. Let cool in pan on a wire rack for 2 to 3 minutes and invert onto a serving plate.

Tip *If desired, serve warm with whipped cream or ice cream.*

Sour Cream Peach Küchen

Serves 8 to 10

- Preheat oven to 350°F (180°C)
- 10-inch (25 cm) springform pan or 10-inch (4 L) tube pan, greased

NUT TOPPING

1 tbsp	all-purpose flour	15 mL
1/3 cup	packed brown sugar	75 mL
1/2 tsp	ground cinnamon	2 mL
1/3 cup	chopped pecans	75 mL
1 tbsp	butter or margarine, melted	15 mL

CAKE

2 cups	all-purpose flour	500 mL
2 tsp	baking powder	10 mL
1/2 tsp	baking soda	2 mL
1/2 tsp	salt	2 mL
1 cup	granulated sugar	250 mL
1/2 cup	butter or margarine, softened	125 mL
1 tsp	vanilla	5 mL
3	eggs	3
1 1/3 cups	sour cream	325 mL
1	can (28 oz/796 mL) sliced peaches, drained	1

1. *Prepare the topping:* In a small bowl, combine flour, brown sugar, cinnamon, pecans and butter. Set aside.

2. *Prepare the cake:* In a medium bowl, sift together flour, baking powder, baking soda and salt.

3. In a large mixer bowl, cream sugar, butter and vanilla until smooth. Beat in eggs, one at a time, beating well until light and fluffy. Stir in flour mixture alternately with sour cream, making 3 additions of flour and 2 of sour cream, on low speed until well blended.

4. Pour into prepared baking pan, spreading evenly. Bake in preheated oven for 40 minutes.

5. Arrange peach slices on top in a circular, or pinwheel, pattern. Sprinkle nut topping over top. Bake for 15 to 20 minutes or until golden. Let cool slightly in pan on a wire rack and serve warm, or cool completely.

Tip *When your baking seems to brown too quickly on top and is not completely done in the center, place a pan of water on the rack above it. On the contrary, if the bottom browns too quickly, place a pan of water on the rack underneath.*

Pineapple Upside-Down Cake

Serves 8 to 10

- Preheat oven to 350°F (180°C)
- 9-inch (23 cm) round metal baking pan

2 tbsp	butter or margarine	25 mL
1/3 cup	firmly packed brown sugar	75 mL
1 tbsp	water	15 mL
1	can (14 oz/398 mL) pineapple slices, drained	1
4	maraschino cherries, cut in half	4
1 1/3 cups	all-purpose flour	325 mL
2/3 cup	granulated sugar	150 mL
2 tsp	baking powder	10 mL
1	egg	1
2/3 cup	milk	150 mL
1/4 cup	butter or margarine, softened	50 mL
1 tsp	vanilla	5 mL

1. Put the 2 tbsp (25 mL) butter in baking pan, and put the pan in the oven while preheating to melt the butter. Remove from oven and stir in the brown sugar and water.

2. Arrange pineapple slices over top and place a halved cherry, cut side down, in the center of each slice.

3. In a medium bowl, mix together flour, sugar and baking powder.

4. In a large mixer bowl, combine egg, milk, butter and vanilla, beating on low speed until blended. Beat in flour mixture on medium speed for 2 to 3 minutes, until thoroughly combined. Spoon into baking pan over the fruit, spreading evenly.

5. Bake in preheated oven for 30 to 35 minutes or until a toothpick inserted in the center comes out clean and dry. Let cool in pan on a wire rack for 5 to 10 minutes, loosen around the sides with a knife and then invert onto a serving plate. Best when served slightly warm.

Tips *Use any reserved pineapple juice to sprinkle over sliced apples or bananas to prevent discoloring without adding a strong flavor.*

You can also cut the pineapple slices in half and place a halved cherry in the center of each.

Streusel Sugar Plum Cake

Serves 8 to 10

- Preheat oven to 350°F (180°C)
- 9-inch (23 cm) springform pan, greased

STREUSEL TOPPING

½ cup	packed brown sugar	125 mL
1 tbsp	all-purpose flour	15 mL
2 tsp	ground cinnamon	10 mL
2 tbsp	butter or margarine, melted	25 mL

CAKE

1½ cups	all-purpose flour	375 mL
1 tsp	baking powder	5 mL
⅔ cup	granulated sugar	150 mL
¼ cup	butter or margarine, softened	50 mL
2	eggs, separated	2
½ cup	milk	125 mL
2 cups	canned plums, drained and halved (or fresh plums)	500 mL

GLAZE (OPTIONAL)

1	jar (4 oz/114 mL) strained plum (or plum-apple) baby food	1
1 cup	confectioner's (icing) sugar	250 mL
2 tbsp	milk	25 mL

1. *Prepare the topping:* In a small bowl, mix together brown sugar, flour and cinnamon. Add melted butter and mix well until crumbly.
2. *Prepare the cake:* In a medium bowl, mix together flour and baking powder.
3. In a large mixer bowl, cream sugar and butter until smooth. Add egg yolks and beat on medium speed until light and fluffy. Beat in flour mixture alternately with milk, making 3 additions of flour and 2 of milk, on low speed until well blended.
4. In a small mixer bowl with clean beaters, on high speed, beat egg whites until stiff peaks form. Fold into the batter, gently, until well combined. Spoon into prepared baking pan. Arrange plum halves on top, cut side down. Sprinkle streusel topping evenly over top of plums. Bake in preheated oven for 45 to 50 minutes or until top is golden brown. Let cool completely in pan on a wire rack.
5. *If desired, prepare the glaze:* In a small bowl, combine plum baby food, confectioner's sugar and milk, and mix well until smooth and of the right consistency for spreading. Drizzle over cooled cake.

Strawberry Cream Shortcake

Serves 12 to 16

- Preheat oven to 350°F (180°C)
- 13- by 9-inch (3 L) metal baking pan, greased

1	package (3 oz/90 g) strawberry gelatin powder	1
1	package (16 oz/475 g) frozen sweetened sliced strawberries, thawed (or 2 cups/500 mL fresh strawberries, washed and sliced)	1
1 cup	miniature white marshmallows	250 mL
2¼ cups	all-purpose flour	550 mL
1 tbsp	baking powder	15 mL
¼ tsp	salt	1 mL
1½ cups	granulated sugar	375 mL
½ cup	shortening, softened	125 mL
3	eggs	3
1 tsp	vanilla	5 mL
1 cup	milk	250 mL
	Whipped cream	
	Fresh strawberries	

1. In a small bowl, combine gelatin and strawberries. Set aside.
2. Sprinkle the marshmallows into prepared baking pan, spreading evenly.
3. In a bowl, mix together flour, baking powder and salt.
4. In a large mixer bowl, cream sugar and shortening until smooth. Beat in eggs, one at a time, until light and fluffy. Add vanilla. Beat in flour mixture alternately with milk on low speed, making 3 additions of flour and 2 of milk, until well blended. Pour batter over the marshmallows in pan. Spoon strawberry mixture over top of batter.
5. Bake in preheated oven for 45 to 50 minutes or until a toothpick inserted into the center comes out clean and dry. Let cool on a wire rack. To serve, top each slice with a dollop of whipped cream and a whole fresh strawberry.

Tip *An easy way to measure shortening is to fill a 2-cup (500 mL) liquid measuring cup with 1 cup (250 mL) of cold water. Add the shortening — for ½ cup (125 mL) of shortening, the water level will rise to 1½ cups (375 mL).*

Special Holiday Fruitcake

Makes 7 or 8 small cakes

- Preheat oven to 300°F (150°C)
- Seven or eight 12-oz (375 mL) cans, greased and floured

2½ cups	(approx.) all-purpose flour, divided	625 mL
2 tsp	salt	10 mL
2 tsp	ground allspice	10 mL
2 tsp	ground cinnamon	10 mL
1 tsp	ground cloves	5 mL
1 tsp	baking powder	5 mL
1½ cups	chopped nuts	375 mL
1 cup	chopped candied pineapple	250 mL
1 cup	whole candied cherries	250 mL
1 cup	raisins	250 mL
1 cup	chopped dates or figs	250 mL
½ cup	candied orange peel	125 mL
½ cup	flaked coconut (sweetened or unsweetened)	125 mL
4	eggs	4
1½ cups	packed brown sugar	375 mL
1 cup	vegetable oil	250 mL
1 cup	orange juice	250 mL
	Red wine or brandy	

1. In a medium bowl, sift together 2 cups (500 mL) of the flour, salt, allspice, cinnamon, cloves and baking powder and mix well.
2. In another bowl, combine nuts, pineapple, cherries, raisins, dates, orange peel and coconut. Spoon in enough flour to dredge the fruit, about ½ cup (125 mL), or more as required.
3. In a large mixer bowl, combine eggs, brown sugar and oil, and beat on medium speed until well blended. Stir in flour mixture alternately with orange juice, making 3 additions of flour and 2 of juice, until well combined. Fold in the dredged fruit mixture until well incorporated into the batter.
4. Spoon into the prepared cans, filling three-quarters full, and bake in preheated oven for 90 minutes or until a toothpick inserted in center comes out clean and dry. Let cool completely in the cans on a rack, then remove from cans. Wrap each cake in a cloth soaked with wine. Then wrap each in tin foil. Store in a cool place for 2 to 3 weeks. Remoisten the cloths once or twice during this time. To serve, chill for easier slicing, then cut into slices.

Tip *To prevent fruit from rising to the top of a cake, dredge it in flour before adding to the batter.*

Date (Matrimony) Cake

Serves 12 to 16

- Preheat oven to 400°F (200°C)
- 13- by 9-inch (3 L) metal baking pan, greased

DATE FILLING		
1 cup	chopped dates	250 mL
1 cup	boiling water	250 mL
½ cup	firmly packed brown sugar	125 mL
CAKE		
2 cups	quick-cooking rolled oats	500 mL
1 cup	firmly packed brown sugar	250 mL
1 cup	all-purpose flour, sifted	250 mL
1 tsp	baking soda	5 mL
½ tsp	salt	2 mL
1 cup	butter or margarine, softened	250 mL

1. *Prepare the filling:* In a medium saucepan, over medium heat, combine dates, boiling water and brown sugar, stirring until mixture becomes thick, about 5 to 6 minutes. Set aside to cool.
2. *Prepare the cake:* In a large bowl, combine oats, brown sugar, flour, baking soda and salt. Cut in butter with two knives, a pastry blender or your fingers until mixture resembles coarse crumbs. Spread a little over half of the oat mixture into the prepared baking pan, packing down firmly with your hand.
3. Spoon filling, by teaspoonfuls (5 mL), carefully over the oat layer in pan. Top with the remaining oat mixture and pat lightly with your hand.
4. Bake in preheated oven for 25 to 30 minutes or until golden brown. Let cool completely in pan on a wire rack.

Tips *Dates, marshmallows and any sticky ingredients can be cut easily with scissors dipped in hot water.*

When greasing a baking pan, if the shortening is cold and not spreading easily, turn your baking pan upside down and hold it under the hot water tap for just a few seconds. When the pan feels warm, the shortening will spread easily.

Raisin Spice Cake

Serves 12 to 16

- Preheat oven to 350°F (180°C)
- 13- by 9-inch (3 L) metal baking pan, greased and floured

2 cups	all-purpose flour	500 mL
2 tsp	ground cinnamon	10 mL
2 tsp	ground allspice	10 mL
1 tsp	baking soda	5 mL
½ tsp	ground nutmeg	2 mL
½ tsp	ground cloves	2 mL
¼ tsp	salt	1 mL
½ cup	butter or margarine, softened	125 mL
2 cups	firmly packed brown sugar	500 mL
3	eggs	3
1 cup	sour cream or buttermilk	250 mL
¾ cup	raisins	175 mL
	Cream Cheese Frosting (see recipe, page 545) or other favorite frosting	

1. In a medium bowl, sift together flour, cinnamon, allspice, baking soda, nutmeg, cloves and salt.
2. In a large mixer bowl, cream butter and brown sugar until light and fluffy. Add eggs, one at a time, beating well on medium speed after each addition. Beat in flour mixture alternately with sour cream, making 3 additions of flour and 2 of sour cream, on low speed until well combined. Stir in raisins. Mix well.
3. Pour into prepared baking pan, spreading evenly. Bake in preheated oven for 45 to 50 minutes or until a toothpick inserted in the center comes out clean and dry. Let cool in pan on a wire rack for 10 minutes. Remove from pan and let cool completely on wire rack.
4. Frost with Cream Cheese Frosting or another favorite.

Tips *To rehydrate dried-out raisins, steam them over hot water for a few minutes.*

Frosting spreads easier and frosted cakes are easier to cut when you dip your knife in cold water.

Carrot Spice Cake

Serves 12 to 16

- Preheat oven to 350°F (180°C)
- 13- by 9-inch (3 L) metal baking pan, lightly greased

1½ cups	all-purpose flour	375 mL
1 cup	whole wheat flour	250 mL
4 tsp	baking powder	20 mL
2 tsp	baking soda	10 mL
1 tsp	ground cinnamon	5 mL
½ tsp	ground nutmeg	2 mL
¼ tsp	ground cloves	1 mL
1 cup	butter or margarine, melted	250 mL
2	eggs, lightly beaten	2
1 cup	liquid honey	250 mL
1 cup	vegetable oil	250 mL
½ cup	freshly squeezed lemon juice	125 mL
2 cups	grated carrots (about 4 medium)	500 mL
½ cup	chopped nuts (optional)	125 mL
	Cream Cheese Frosting (see recipe, page 545)	
	Chopped nuts (optional)	

1. In a large bowl, combine all-purpose and whole wheat flours, baking powder, baking soda, cinnamon, nutmeg and cloves.
2. In a medium bowl, whisk together butter, eggs, honey, oil and lemon juice. Add this mixture to the flour mixture and mix until thoroughly combined. Stir in grated carrots and then chopped nuts (if using) and mix well.
3. Spoon into prepared baking pan, spreading evenly, and bake in preheated oven for 50 to 60 minutes or until toothpick inserted in the center comes out clean and dry. Let cool completely in pan on a wire rack.
4. Frost with Cream Cheese Frosting and sprinkle more chopped nuts (if using) over top.

Tip *To prevent the cake from sliding on the plate while you are carrying it, drizzle a bit of frosting in a circle where the cake will rest on the plate before transferring the cake from the pan. This will hold the cake in place.*

Carrot Streusel Crumb Cake

Serves 6 to 8

- Preheat oven to 350°F (180°C)
- 9-inch (2.5 L) square metal baking pan, greased and floured

STREUSEL CRUMB TOPPING

1/3 cup	lightly packed brown sugar	75 mL
3 tbsp	all-purpose flour	45 mL
1 tsp	ground cinnamon	5 mL
1/3 cup	chopped nuts (pecans or walnuts)	75 mL
3 tbsp	butter or margarine, melted	45 mL

CAKE

2 cups	all-purpose flour	500 mL
2 tsp	baking powder	10 mL
1/2 tsp	baking soda	2 mL
1/2 tsp	salt	2 mL
1/2 tsp	ground cinnamon	2 mL
1/2 tsp	ground nutmeg	2 mL
1/4 tsp	ground cloves	1 mL
1/4 tsp	ground ginger	1 mL
1/2 cup	butter or shortening, softened	125 mL
1 1/2 cups	firmly packed brown sugar	375 mL
3/4 cup	mashed cooked carrots (about 2 medium)	175 mL
3/4 cup	milk, divided	175 mL
2	eggs	2

1. *Prepare the topping:* In a small bowl, mix together brown sugar, flour, cinnamon and nuts until combined. Stir in melted butter to form a crumbly mixture. Set aside.
2. *Prepare the cake:* In another bowl, combine flour, baking powder, baking soda, salt and spices.
3. In a large mixer bowl, on medium speed, cream butter and brown sugar until smooth. Beat in carrots and 1/2 cup (125 mL) of the milk and continue beating for 2 to 3 minutes. Add eggs and the remaining milk and beat for 2 minutes, until well blended.
4. Stir in flour mixture and beat for 2 minutes, until mixed thoroughly. Spoon into prepared baking pan.
5. Sprinkle topping over batter evenly. Bake in preheated oven for 45 to 50 minutes or until toothpick inserted in center comes out clean and dry. Let cool completely in pan on a wire rack.

Pineapple Carrot Cake

Serves 12 to 16

- Preheat oven to 350°F (180°C)
- 10-inch (4 L) tube pan, greased and floured

2 cups	all-purpose flour	500 mL
1 tbsp	ground cinnamon	15 mL
2 tsp	baking soda	10 mL
1 tsp	ground cloves	5 mL
1/2 tsp	salt	2 mL
3	eggs	3
1 1/2 cups	vegetable oil	375 mL
1 3/4 cups	granulated sugar	425 mL
2 cups	grated carrots (about 4 medium)	500 mL
1 cup	chopped walnuts	250 mL
1	can (8 oz/227 mL) crushed pineapple, drained	1
3/4 cup	shredded coconut (sweetened or unsweetened), toasted (optional)	175 mL

CREAM CHEESE FROSTING

6 oz	cream cheese, softened	175 g
1/2 cup	butter or margarine, softened	125 mL
2 tsp	vanilla	10 mL
4 1/2 cups	confectioner's (icing) sugar, sifted	1.125 L

1. In a medium bowl, sift together flour, cinnamon, baking soda, cloves and salt.
2. In a large mixer bowl, combine eggs, oil and sugar and beat on medium speed until well blended. Add flour mixture and mix until well combined. Stir in carrots, walnuts and pineapple and mix until well blended.
3. Pour into prepared cake pan, smoothing top. Bake in preheated oven for 1 hour or until a toothpick inserted in the center comes out clean and dry. Let cool in pan on a wire rack for 10 minutes, then remove from pan to cool completely on wire rack.
4. *Prepare the frosting:* In a small mixer bowl, cream together cream cheese, butter and vanilla, beating on medium speed until light and fluffy. Gradually add half of the confectioner's sugar, beating well. Beat in the remainder of the confectioner's sugar gradually, until you reach the right spreading consistency.
5. If desired, split cake into two layers. Spread about one-third of the frosting on the bottom layer and top with top layer. Cover complete cake, top and sides, with the cream cheese frosting. If you do not split the cake, cover completely with frosting. Either way, you can sprinkle coconut over top and sides, if desired.

Lemon-Glazed Pumpkin Cake

Serves 12 to 16
- Preheat oven to 350ºF (180ºC)
- 10-inch (4 L) tube pan, greased

2 cups	all-purpose flour	500 mL
2 tsp	baking powder	10 mL
2 tsp	baking soda	10 mL
2 tsp	ground cinnamon	10 mL
1 tsp	ground nutmeg	5 mL
1 tsp	pumpkin pie spice	5 mL
½ tsp	salt	2 mL
4	eggs	4
2 cups	granulated sugar	500 mL
1 cup	vegetable oil	250 mL
2 cups	canned pumpkin purée (not pie filling)	500 mL

LEMON GLAZE

1½ cups	confectioner's (icing) sugar	375 mL
1 tsp	grated lemon zest	5 mL
2 to 3 tbsp	freshly squeezed lemon juice	25 to 45 mL

1. In a medium bowl, sift together flour, baking powder, baking soda, cinnamon, nutmeg, pumpkin pie spice and salt.
2. In a large mixer bowl, cream eggs and sugar until smooth and fluffy. Add oil and pumpkin and beat on medium speed until well blended.
3. Add flour mixture to the creamed mixture, beating until thoroughly combined. Do not overbeat. Spoon into prepared baking pan.
4. Bake in preheated oven for 45 to 55 minutes or until a toothpick inserted in the center comes out clean and dry. Let cool in pan on a wire rack for 10 minutes. Loosen around edges of cake with a knife or spatula and invert onto wire rack to cool completely.
5. *Prepare the glaze:* In a small bowl, combine confectioner's sugar, zest and enough lemon juice for a glazing consistency. Mix together to blend. Drizzle over cooled cake.

Tips *To get more juice from a lemon, pop it into the microwave and cook on high for 15 seconds, then cool before squeezing. You can also roll the lemon back and forth on the countertop until slightly softened.*

If desired, you could add ½ cup (125 mL) raisins and/or ½ cup (125 mL) chopped nuts to the batter before baking.

Pound Cakes

Traditional Pound Cake

Serves 12 to 16
- Preheat oven to 325ºF (160ºC)
- 10-inch (3 L) Bundt pan, greased and floured

1½ cups	butter, softened	375 mL
4 cups	confectioner's (icing) sugar, sifted	1 L
1 tsp	vanilla	5 mL
6	eggs	6
2¾ cups	cake and pastry flour, sifted	675 mL
	Confectioner's (icing) sugar (optional)	

1. In a large mixer bowl, cream butter until smooth. Slowly add confectioner's sugar, beating well after each addition, and then add vanilla, beating until light and fluffy.
2. Add eggs, one at a time, beating well after each addition, until blended.
3. Stir in cake flour gradually until thoroughly blended, but do not overmix.
4. Pour into prepared baking pan and tap pan lightly on the table or counter to get rid of any air bubbles that may have formed.
5. Bake in preheated oven for 80 minutes or until a toothpick inserted in the center comes out clean and dry. Let cool in pan on a wire rack for 5 to 10 minutes, loosen cake from the edges with a spatula or knife, invert, and let cool completely on a rack. Sprinkle with more confectioner's sugar over top, if desired.

Tip *To make an authentic, rich pound cake, always use butter instead of margarine.*

Variations *Cinnamon Nut Pound Cake: Before baking, add 1 tsp (5 mL) ground cinnamon, ¼ tsp (1 mL) ground nutmeg and ½ cup (125 mL) finely chopped nuts to the batter, mixing well.*

Pound Cake Kabobs: Cut a pound cake into 1½-inch (4 cm) cubes. Spear each on a fork and dip in melted currant jelly or in sweetened condensed milk. Then roll in flaked coconut to cover. Thread on skewers and toast over very hot coals, turning often.

Easy Banana Pound Cake

Serves 12 to 16

- Preheat oven to 350°F (180°C)
- 10-inch (3 L) Bundt pan, greased and floured

1	package (18 oz/510 g) yellow cake mix	1
½ cup	water	125 mL
⅓ cup	vegetable oil	75 mL
4	eggs	4
1	package (4-serving size) instant vanilla pudding mix	1
½ tsp	ground cinnamon	2 mL
½ tsp	ground nutmeg	2 mL
1½ cups	mashed ripe bananas (4 to 5 medium)	375 mL
	Confectioner's (icing) sugar (optional)	

1. In a large mixer bowl, combine cake mix, water, oil and eggs. Mix together on medium speed until blended.
2. Stir in pudding mix, cinnamon and nutmeg. Add mashed bananas and mix well until thoroughly blended. Pour into prepared baking pan, smoothing top.
3. Bake in preheated oven for 55 to 60 minutes or until a toothpick inserted in the center comes out clean and dry. Let cool in pan on a wire rack for 20 to 25 minutes, and then remove to cool completely on wire rack. Dust with confectioner's sugar, if desired.

Cranberry Pound Cake

Serves 12 to16

- Preheat oven to 350°F (180°C)
- 10-inch (3L) Bundt pan, greased and floured

3 cups	all-purpose flour	750 mL
1 tsp	baking powder	5 mL
Pinch	salt	Pinch
1¼ cups	butter or margarine, softened	300 mL
2½ cups	granulated sugar	625 mL
5	eggs	5
1 tsp	almond extract or vanilla	5 mL
1 cup	evaporated milk	250 mL
2 cups	chopped fresh cranberries (or frozen, thawed)	500 mL
	Confectioner's (icing) sugar (optional)	

1. In a medium bowl, mix together flour, baking powder and salt.
2. In a large mixer bowl, cream butter and sugar until smooth. Beat in eggs, one at a time, beating on medium speed after each addition. Add almond extract and beat until light and fluffy.
3. Stir in flour mixture alternately with milk, making 3 additions of flour and 2 of milk, mixing gently until blended. Gently fold in cranberries until all ingredients are well combined. Pour into prepared baking pan.
4. Bake in preheated oven for 75 minutes or until a toothpick inserted in the center comes out clean and dry. Let cool in pan on a wire rack for 10 minutes, then remove and let cool completely on a wire rack. Sprinkle confectioner's sugar over top, if desired.

Tip *Freeze cranberries before chopping or grinding them to ease cleanup.*

Raspberry Ice Cream Pound Cake

Serves 10 to 12

- Preheat oven to 325°F (160°C)
- 9- by 5-inch (1.5 L) metal loaf pan, greased

2¾ cups	cake and pastry flour, sifted	675 mL
2 tsp	baking powder	10 mL
¼ tsp	salt	1 mL
1 cup	granulated sugar	250 mL
1 cup	butter or margarine, softened	250 mL
1½ tsp	vanilla	7 mL
3	eggs	3
⅔ cup	milk	150 mL
2 cups	vanilla ice cream	500 mL
	Raspberry jam	

1. In a medium bowl, sift together flour, baking powder and salt.
2. In a large mixer bowl, cream sugar and butter on medium speed until smooth. Beat in vanilla, and then eggs, one at a time, until well blended.
3. Stir in flour mixture alternately with milk, making 3 additions of flour and 2 of milk, on low speed, mixing well until thoroughly combined. Spoon into prepared baking pan.
4. Bake in preheated oven for 70 to 75 minutes or until a toothpick inserted in the center comes out clean and dry. Let cool on a wire rack. Meanwhile, soften ice cream in refrigerator just until soft enough to spread.

5. Slice cake into 3 layers. Place first layer on a freezer-safe plate and spread jam evenly and thickly on top. Cover with second layer of cake and spread ice cream over top. Top with the remaining layer and spread jam thickly and evenly over top. Freeze until firm, and then slice and serve.

Pumpkin Pound Cake

Serves 16 to 20
- Preheat oven to 350°F (180°C)
- Two 9- by 5-inch (2 L) metal loaf pans, greased and floured

3 cups	all-purpose flour	750 mL
1/2 tsp	salt	2 mL
1/2 tsp	baking powder	2 mL
1 tsp	ground cinnamon	5 mL
1/4 tsp	ground cloves	1 mL
1/2 tsp	ground ginger	2 mL
1 1/2 cups	butter or margarine, softened	375 mL
2 1/2 cups	granulated sugar	625 mL
1 tsp	vanilla	5 mL
6	eggs	6
1 cup	canned or cooked pumpkin purée (not pie filling)	250 mL

1. In a medium bowl, combine flour, salt, baking powder, cinnamon, cloves and ginger.
2. In a large mixer bowl, cream butter, sugar and vanilla on medium speed until smooth. Beat in eggs, one at a time, beating after each addition, until well blended.
3. Beat in flour mixture alternately with pumpkin, making 3 additions of flour and 2 of pumpkin, on low speed, beating only until well combined. Spoon into the two prepared baking pans, dividing evenly.
4. Bake in preheated oven for 60 to 70 minutes or until a toothpick inserted in the center comes out clean and dry. Let cool in pans on a wire rack for 10 minutes, and then remove to wire racks to cool completely.

Tip *For a special treat, and to use up leftover pound cake slices, melt about 1/4 cup (50 mL) of butter in a skillet and fry slices on each side to brown. Place slices on a plate and top each slice with a spoonful of strawberry jam and a dollop of whipped topping.*

Chocolate-Glazed Pound Cake

Serves 12 to 16
- Preheat oven to 350°F (180°C)
- 10-inch (3 L) Bundt or 10-inch (4 L) tube baking pan, greased and floured

3 cups	all-purpose flour	750 mL
Pinch	salt	Pinch
1 tsp	baking powder	5 mL
1/2 cup	sifted unsweetened cocoa powder	125 mL
2 2/3 cups	granulated sugar	650 mL
1 1/4 cups	butter, softened	300 mL
5	eggs	5
1 tsp	vanilla	5 mL
1 cup	evaporated milk	250 mL
GLAZE		
2 tbsp	butter or margarine	25 mL
1/2 cup	semisweet chocolate chips	125 mL
1 1/4 cups	confectioner's (icing) sugar	300 mL
1/2 tsp	vanilla	2 mL
3 to 4 tbsp	milk	45 to 50 mL

1. In a medium bowl, combine flour, salt, baking powder and cocoa.
2. In a large mixer bowl, cream sugar and butter on medium speed until smooth. Beat in eggs, one at a time, beating after each addition. Add vanilla and beat until well blended.
3. Stir in flour mixture alternately with the milk, making 3 additions of flour and 2 of milk, mixing after each addition until well combined. Spoon into prepared baking pan.
4. Bake in preheated oven for 70 to 75 minutes or until a toothpick inserted in the center comes out clean and dry. Let cool in pan on a wire rack for 10 minutes, then loosen edges of cake with a narrow spatula or knife and invert onto wire rack or plate to cool completely.
5. *Prepare the glaze:* Melt butter and chocolate chips in a small saucepan over low heat. Remove from heat and add confectioner's sugar, vanilla and 3 tbsp (45 mL) milk. Whisk until blended and smooth, adding more milk as necessary to make a drizzling consistency. Drizzle over cooled cake.

Tip *You could omit glaze and dust top of cake with confectioner's sugar.*

Variation *Chocolate Chip Pound Cake: Omit cocoa and fold 2 cups (500 mL) of semisweet chocolate chips into the batter until well combined. Bake as above. Dust top with confectioner's sugar when cooled, if desired.*

Marble Pound Cake

Serves 8 to 10

- Preheat oven to 325°F (160°C)
- 9-inch (2.5 L) square metal baking pan or 9- by 5-inch (2 L) metal loaf pan, greased and floured

2¼ cups	cake and pastry flour, sifted	550 mL
1 tsp	baking powder	5 mL
1 tsp	salt	5 mL
¾ cup	butter or margarine, softened (preferably butter)	175 mL
1¼ cups	granulated sugar	300 mL
½ cup	milk	125 mL
1 tsp	grated lemon zest	5 mL
1 tbsp	freshly squeezed lemon juice	15 mL
3	eggs	3
	Confectioner's (icing) sugar (optional)	
MARBLING		
1 oz	unsweetened chocolate, melted	30 g
1 tbsp	granulated sugar	15 mL
2 tbsp	boiling water	25 mL

1. In a medium bowl, combine flour, baking powder and salt.
2. In a large mixer bowl, cream butter and sugar on medium speed, beating until light and fluffy. Add milk, lemon zest and juice, and continue beating for 2 to 3 minutes, until blended. Add eggs, one at a time, beating well after each addition, until well blended.
3. Gradually add flour mixture to creamed mixture, beating on low speed for about 2 to 3 minutes, until smooth. Transfer half of the batter into a separate bowl.
4. *Prepare the marbling:* In a small bowl, mix together melted chocolate, sugar and boiling water. Stir the chocolate mixture into one bowl of the batter and mix well.
5. Spoon into prepared baking pan by alternating spoonfuls of light and dark batter, making a checkerboard effect. With a knife or narrow spatula, gently stir through the batter, making a marbling effect.
6. Bake in preheated oven for about 75 minutes or until a toothpick inserted in the center comes out clean and dry. Let cool in pan on a wire rack for 10 minutes, remove from pan and let cool completely on wire rack. Sift confectioner's sugar over top, if desired.

Tip *Cut a pound cake into slices, arrange in a circle around edge of serving plate, and place scoops of chocolate, strawberry and vanilla ice cream in the center so that everyone can pick their favorite flavor to top their slice of cake.*

Variation *Chocolate Swirl Pound Cake: Do not mix marbling ingredients into half of the batter. Instead spoon half of the batter into the prepared pan, spoon chocolate mixture over top, spreading evenly, and top with the remaining batter. Bake as above.*

Coffee Cakes

Babka

Serves 16 to 20

- Two 8-inch (2 L) square metal baking pans, well greased

1	envelope (¼ oz/7 g) active dry yeast or 1 cake (1 oz/30 g) compressed yeast	1
1 cup	warm milk, divided	250 mL
¾ cup	granulated sugar, divided	175 mL
¼ tsp	salt	1 mL
3¾ cups	all-purpose flour, divided	925 mL
½ cup	butter, softened	125 mL
3	eggs, well beaten	3
1 tbsp	grated lemon zest	15 mL
½ cup	raisins	125 mL
¼ cup	butter, melted	50 mL
STREUSEL TOPPING		
½ cup	firmly packed brown sugar	125 mL
½ cup	chopped nuts	125 mL
¼ cup	all-purpose flour	50 mL
3 tbsp	butter, melted	45 mL
1½ tsp	ground cinnamon	7 mL

1. In a small bowl, sprinkle yeast (or mash, if using compressed yeast) over ¼ cup (50 mL) of the warm milk. If using dry yeast, let stand for 10 minutes or until foamy. Then add the remaining milk, 1 tsp (5 mL) of the sugar and 1 cup (250 mL) of the flour. Beat well and let rise until the mixture is at least 1½ times the original size and is spongy, about 30 minutes.
2. In a large mixer bowl, cream the softened butter and the remaining sugar on medium speed until smooth. Beat in the eggs and the yeast mixture, beating until thoroughly blended.

3. Add lemon zest, raisins and the remaining flour, beating on low speed. Mix well until batter is smooth and thick. Cover and let rise in a warm, draft-free place until doubled in size, about 1½ hours.

4. When dough is doubled, stir to deflate bubbles. Divide batter in half and place each half in the prepared baking pans, pressing out to edges with a moistened spatula. Cover and let rise again until doubled in size, about 1 hour.

5. Preheat oven to 375°F (190°C).

6. *Prepare the topping:* In another bowl, mix together brown sugar, chopped nuts, flour, melted butter and cinnamon until mixture resembles coarse crumbs. Brush dough with melted butter, if desired. Sprinkle streusel topping over top.

7. Bake in preheated oven for 45 to 50 minutes or until lightly browned. Let cool completely in pans on wire racks.

Chocolate Swirl Coffee Cake

Serves 6 to 8

- Preheat oven to 400°F (200°C)
- 8- or 9-inch (20 or 23 cm) round metal baking pan, greased

2 cups	biscuit mix	500 mL
¼ cup	granulated sugar	50 mL
1	egg	1
⅔ cup	milk	150 mL
2 tbsp	butter or margarine, melted	25 mL
½ cup	semisweet chocolate pieces or chips, melted	125 mL

1. In a large mixer bowl, combine biscuit mix, sugar, egg, milk and butter. Beat on medium speed until thoroughly combined.

2. Pour into prepared baking pan, smoothing top. Spoon the melted chocolate over top and cut through the batter several times with a knife for a swirl or marbled effect.

3. Bake in preheated oven for 20 to 25 minutes or until a toothpick inserted in the center comes out clean and dry. Let cool completely in pan on a wire rack.

Variation *Cherry Swirl Coffee Cake: Omit chocolate and replace with 1 can (19 oz/540 mL) cherry pie filling. If desired, top with a streusel topping (see above) and sprinkle ¼ cup (50 mL) sliced almonds over top.*

Glazed Lemon Coffee Cake

Serves 12 to 16

- Preheat oven to 350°F (180°C)
- 10-inch (4 L) tube pan, greased and floured

SUGAR-CINNAMON MIXTURE

½ cup	lightly packed brown sugar	125 mL
1 tbsp	ground cinnamon	15 mL

CAKE

1¾ cups	cake and pastry flour	425 mL
2 tsp	baking powder	10 mL
1 tsp	baking soda	5 mL
1 cup	evaporated milk	250 mL
1 tsp	grated lemon zest	5 mL
2 tbsp	freshly squeezed lemon juice	25 mL
½ cup	butter or margarine, softened	125 mL
1 cup	granulated sugar	250 mL
2	eggs, well beaten	2

LEMON GLAZE

1¾ cups	confectioner's (icing) sugar, sifted	425 mL
2 tbsp	freshly squeezed lemon juice	25 mL

1. *Prepare the sugar-cinnamon mixture:* In a small bowl, mix together brown sugar and cinnamon. Set aside.

2. *Prepare the cake:* In a medium bowl, sift together flour and baking powder.

3. In another bowl, combine baking soda, milk and lemon juice. Mix well.

4. In a large mixer bowl, cream butter and sugar on medium speed until light and fluffy. Add eggs and lemon zest, beating on low until blended. Beat in flour mixture alternately with the milk mixture, making 3 additions of flour and 2 of milk, on low speed, beating until well combined.

5. Pour half of the batter into prepared baking pan. Sprinkle half the sugar-cinnamon mixture over top. Spoon on the remaining batter and sprinkle the remaining sugar-cinnamon over top.

6. Bake in preheated oven for 45 to 50 minutes or until a toothpick inserted in the center comes out clean and dry. Let cool in pan on a wire rack for 10 minutes, and then remove from pan to cool completely on wire rack.

7. *Prepare the glaze:* In a small bowl, mix together confectioner's sugar and lemon juice until the right consistency for drizzling. Spread over top of cooled cake and drizzle over the edges.

Apple Crumb Coffee Cake

Serves 12 to 16

- Preheat oven to 350°F (180°C)
- 10-inch (3 L) Bundt pan, greased and floured

CRUMB TOPPING

1¼ cups	firmly packed brown sugar	300 mL
¾ cup	all-purpose flour	175 mL
½ cup	cold butter or margarine, cut into small chunks	125 mL
2 tsp	ground cinnamon	10 mL
1 cup	chopped nuts (optional)	250 mL

CAKE

3¼ cups	all-purpose flour	800 mL
1½ tsp	baking powder	7 mL
¾ tsp	baking soda	4 mL
¾ cup	butter or margarine, softened	175 mL
1¼ cups	granulated sugar	300 mL
3	eggs	3
2 tsp	vanilla	10 mL
2 cups	low-fat plain yogurt	500 mL
2	apples (such as Golden Delicious), peeled, cored and chopped	2

1. *Prepare the topping:* In a medium bowl, combine brown sugar, flour, butter and cinnamon. Use a pastry blender or fork to mix until mixture is coarse and crumbly and the butter is well incorporated. Stir in the nuts (if using) and mix well. Set aside.
2. *Prepare the cake:* In another bowl, combine flour, baking powder and baking soda.
3. In a large mixer bowl, cream butter and sugar on medium speed until smooth and fluffy. Beat in eggs, one at a time, beating well after each addition. Add vanilla and yogurt and beat on low speed until blended. Beat in flour mixture, beating on low speed until well blended.
4. Spoon half the batter into the prepared baking pan. Sprinkle evenly with ¼ cup (50 mL) of the crumb topping, then the apples, and then ½ cup (125 mL) of the crumb topping. Spoon on the remaining batter and top with the remaining crumb topping.
5. Bake in preheated oven for 55 to 60 minutes or until a toothpick inserted in the center comes out clean and dry. Let cool in pan on a wire rack for 10 minutes. Put a large plate over top and carefully invert. Remove pan. Place another plate on top of cake and invert so that crumb topping is facing up. Let cool completely.

Banana Chip Coffee Cake

Serves 12 to 16

- Preheat oven to 350°F (180°C)
- 13- by 9-inch (3 L) metal baking pan, greased

TOPPING

½ cup	firmly packed brown sugar	125 mL
1½ tsp	ground cinnamon	7 mL

CAKE

3 cups	all-purpose flour	750 mL
2 tsp	baking powder	10 mL
2 tsp	baking soda	10 mL
2	eggs	2
1¾ cups	granulated sugar	425 mL
1 cup	butter or margarine, softened	250 mL
1 tsp	vanilla	5 mL
2 cups	mashed ripe bananas (about 6 medium)	500 mL
1 cup	sour cream	250 mL
1 cup	semisweet chocolate chips	250 mL

1. *Prepare the topping:* In a small bowl, combine brown sugar and cinnamon and mix well to blend.
2. *Prepare the cake:* In a medium bowl, sift together flour, baking powder and baking soda.
3. In a large mixer bowl, beat eggs, sugar and butter on medium speed until smooth. Add vanilla and bananas. Mix until smooth and well blended.
4. Stir in flour mixture alternately with sour cream, making 3 additions of flour and 2 of sour cream, mixing until well incorporated.
5. Spoon half of the batter into the prepared baking pan. Sprinkle half of the topping mixture over batter and then half of the chocolate chips. Spoon on the remaining batter. Sprinkle on the remaining topping mixture, and then top with the remaining chocolate chips.
6. Bake in preheated oven for 50 to 55 minutes or until a toothpick inserted in the center comes out clean and dry. Let cool completely in pan on a wire rack before removing to a serving plate.

Tip *If you have left your cake in the pan for too long, and it just won't come out, try dipping the pan quickly in hot water (like a gelatin mold), or put in a slow oven, 250°F (120°C), for 3 to 5 minutes. If all else fails, leave cake in pan and decorate with frosting, then slice.*

Blueberry Streusel Coffee Cake

Serves 8 to 10

- Preheat oven to 350ºF (180ºC)
- 9-inch (23 cm) springform pan, greased

STREUSEL TOPPING

½ cup	lightly packed brown sugar	125 mL
2 tbsp	butter or margarine, melted	25 mL
1 tbsp	all-purpose flour	15 mL
2 tsp	ground cinnamon	10 mL

CAKE

2 cups	all-purpose flour	500 mL
1 tsp	baking powder	5 mL
1 tsp	baking soda	5 mL
¼ tsp	salt	1 mL
¾ cup	granulated sugar	175 mL
¾ cup	butter or margarine, softened	175 mL
1	egg	1
1 tsp	vanilla	5 mL
1 cup	sour cream or buttermilk	250 mL
2 cups	blueberries, fresh (or well-drained, thawed frozen blueberries)	500 mL

1. *Prepare the topping:* In a small bowl, mix together brown sugar, melted butter, flour and cinnamon until blended and crumbly.
2. *Prepare the cake:* In a medium bowl, combine flour, baking powder, baking soda and salt.
3. In a large mixer bowl, cream sugar and butter on medium speed until smooth. Add egg, vanilla and sour cream and beat on low speed until well blended. Beat in flour mixture on low speed until well blended.
4. Pour about two-thirds of the batter into the prepared baking pan, spreading evenly. Top with blueberries. Spoon the remaining batter evenly over blueberry filling. Sprinkle streusel topping over top.
5. Bake in preheated oven for 60 to 70 minutes or until a toothpick inserted in the center comes out clean and dry. Let cool completely in pan on a wire rack before removing cake.

Tip *If your cake falls but still tastes great, cut it into squares and serve with a sauce, or dip squares in melted chocolate for instant petit fours.*

Raspberry Cream Coffee Cake

Serves 8 to 10

- Preheat oven to 350ºF (180ºC)
- 9-inch (23 cm) springform pan, greased

¾ cup	cold butter or margarine	175 mL
2¼ cups	all-purpose flour	550 mL
½ cup	granulated sugar	125 mL
½ tsp	baking powder	2 mL
½ tsp	baking soda	2 mL
¾ cup	sour cream	175 mL
1	egg	1
1 tsp	grated lemon zest	5 mL
½ cup	raspberry jam	125 mL

CREAM CHEESE FILLING

1	package (8 oz/250 g) cream cheese, softened	1
1	egg	1
⅓ cup	granulated sugar	75 mL

1. In a large bowl, combine butter, flour and sugar, cutting in the butter with a pastry blender or two knives until mixture resembles coarse crumbs. Take 1 cup (250 mL) of this crumb mixture and set aside.
2. Stir baking powder and baking soda into the remaining crumb mixture.
3. In a small bowl, whisk together sour cream, egg and zest. Add to the crumb mixture and mix just until moistened and blended. Spoon into prepared baking pan, spreading over bottom and part way up the sides.
4. *Prepare the filling:* In a small mixer bowl, combine cream cheese, egg and sugar on medium speed and beat until well blended. Pour over the batter in the pan. Spoon jam carefully over the filling. Sprinkle the reserved crumb mixture over top.
5. Bake in preheated oven for 45 to 50 minutes or until cake is golden brown and filling is firmly set. Let cool completely in pan on a wire rack.

Strawberry Rhubarb Coffee Cake

Serves 12 to 16

- Preheat oven to 350ºF (180ºC)
- 13- by 9-inch (3 L) metal baking pan, greased

FILLING

3 cups	small chunks fresh rhubarb	750 mL
1	package (10 oz/300 g) frozen unsweetened strawberries	1
2 tbsp	freshly squeezed lemon juice	25 mL
1 cup	granulated sugar	250 mL
1/3 cup	cornstarch	75 mL

TOPPING

3/4 cup	granulated sugar	175 mL
1/2 cup	all-purpose flour	125 mL
1/4 cup	butter or margarine, softened	50 mL

CAKE

3 cups	all-purpose flour	750 mL
1 cup	granulated sugar	250 mL
1 tsp	baking powder	5 mL
1 tsp	baking soda	5 mL
1 tsp	salt	5 mL
1 cup	butter or margarine, softened	250 mL
1 cup	buttermilk	250 mL
1 tsp	vanilla	5 mL
2	eggs, lightly beaten	2

1. *Prepare the filling:* Combine rhubarb and strawberries in a saucepan over low heat and cook, covered, for 5 to 6 minutes, until thoroughly heated. Add lemon juice and mix well. Mix together sugar and cornstarch and stir into mixture. Cook until thick, about 5 minutes, and set aside to cool to room temperature, about 10 to 15 minutes.
2. *Prepare the topping:* In a small bowl, combine sugar and flour. Cut in butter to make fine crumbs. Set aside.
3. *Prepare the cake:* In a large bowl, combine flour, sugar, baking powder, baking soda and salt. Cut in butter with a pastry blender or two knives until mixture resembles fine crumbs.
4. In another bowl, whisk buttermilk, vanilla and eggs until well combined. Stir into flour mixture just until moistened and thoroughly blended.
5. Spoon half of the batter into prepared baking pan. Spoon filling over top of batter in pan. Top with the remaining batter. Swirl through with a knife or spoon. Sprinkle topping evenly over batter.
6. Bake in preheated oven for 40 to 45 minutes or until top becomes golden brown. Let cool completely in pan on a wire rack.

Loaf Cakes

Nut Loaf

Serves 8 to 10

- Preheat oven to 350ºF (180ºC)
- 9- by 5-inch (2 L) metal loaf pan, well greased and floured

3 cups	all-purpose flour	750 ml
1 tbsp	baking powder	15 mL
1/4 tsp	salt	1 mL
1 cup	butter or margarine, softened	250 mL
1 3/4 cups	granulated sugar	425 mL
3	eggs, separated	3
1 tsp	vanilla	5 mL
1/4 cup	milk	50 mL
1 cup	chopped nuts (pecans or walnuts)	250 mL

1. In a medium bowl, sift together flour, baking powder and salt.
2. In a large mixer bowl, cream butter and sugar on medium speed until smooth. Add egg yolks and vanilla and beat until light and fluffy.
3. Stir in flour mixture alternately with milk, making 3 additions of flour and 2 of milk, until well blended.
4. In a small mixer bowl, with clean beaters, beat egg whites on high speed until stiff peaks form. Fold into batter gently. Add nuts, folding until well combined. Pour into prepared baking pan.
5. Bake in preheated oven for 50 to 60 minutes or until a toothpick inserted in the center comes out clean and dry. Let cool in pan on a wire rack for 10 minutes, then remove onto wire rack to cool completely.

Variation *Cranberry Nut Loaf: Use chopped pecans and add 1 cup (250 mL) cranberries to the nuts. Change granulated sugar to 1 cup (250 mL) granulated sugar and 3/4 cup (175 mL) firmly packed brown sugar.*

Banana Nut Loaf

Serves 8 to 10

- Preheat oven to 350ºF (180ºC)
- 9- by 5-inch (2 L) metal loaf pan, greased

2 cups	all-purpose flour	500 mL
3/4 cup	granulated sugar	175 mL
1 tsp	baking powder	5 mL
1/2 tsp	baking soda	2 mL
1/4 tsp	salt	1 mL

2	eggs	2
1 tsp	vanilla	5 mL
¼ cup	buttermilk	50 mL
¼ cup	butter or margarine, melted and cooled	50 mL
1½ cups	mashed ripe bananas (about 4 to 5 medium)	375 mL
¾ cup	chopped nuts	175 mL

1. In a medium bowl, combine flour, sugar, baking powder, baking soda and salt.
2. In a large bowl, whisk together eggs, vanilla, buttermilk and butter until well blended.
3. Gradually stir in flour mixture. Stir in mashed bananas and mix until just moistened and blended. Do not overmix. Fold in chopped nuts and mix well. Pour into prepared baking pan, spreading evenly.
4. Bake in preheated oven for 50 to 60 minutes or until a toothpick inserted in the center comes out clean and dry. Let cool in pan on a wire rack for 10 minutes. Loosen around edges of cake with a knife or spatula. Remove onto wire rack to cool completely.

Tip *If desired, replace nuts with ¾ cup (175 mL) semisweet chocolate chips, or use both nuts and chocolate chips (½ cup/125 mL each).*

Lemon Tea Loaf

Serves 8 to 10

- Preheat oven to 350°F (180°C)
- 9- by 5-inch (2 L) metal loaf pan, greased and floured

1½ cups	all-purpose flour	375 mL
1 tsp	baking powder	5 mL
Pinch	salt	Pinch
1 tbsp	grated lemon zest	15 mL
½ cup	butter or margarine, softened	125 mL
1 cup	granulated sugar	250 mL
2	eggs	2
½ cup	milk	125 mL
LEMON SYRUP		
1¾ cup	confectioner's (icing) sugar, sifted	425 mL
2 tbsp	freshly squeezed lemon juice	25 mL

1. In a medium bowl, combine flour, baking powder, salt and lemon zest.
2. In a large mixer bowl, cream butter and sugar on medium speed until smooth. Beat in eggs, one at a time, beating until blended and light and fluffy.

3. Stir in flour mixture alternately with milk, making 3 additions of flour and 2 of milk, until thoroughly combined. Pour into prepared baking pan.
4. Bake in preheated oven for 45 to 50 minutes or until a toothpick inserted in the center comes out clean and dry. Let cool in pan on a wire rack for 10 minutes and then remove to a wire rack.
5. *Prepare the lemon syrup:* In a small bowl, mix together sugar and lemon juice.
6. Pierce the top of the loaf all over with a fork and drizzle lemon syrup over top. Let loaf cool completely before serving.

Raspberry Swirl Loaf

Serves 8 to 10

- Preheat oven to 350°F (180°C)
- 9- by 5-inch (2 L) metal loaf pan, greased and floured

1½ cups	all-purpose flour	375 mL
¾ cup	firmly packed brown sugar	175 mL
2 tsp	baking powder	10 mL
1 tsp	ground cardamom	5 mL
½ cup	butter or margarine	125 mL
2	eggs	2
¾ cup	buttermilk	175 mL
6 tbsp	seedless raspberry jam	90 mL

1. In a large bowl, combine flour, brown sugar, baking powder and cardamom and mix well. Cut in butter with a pastry blender or two knives to form coarse crumb mixture.
2. In a small bowl, combine eggs and buttermilk and whisk until blended. Stir into flour mixture until well combined.
3. Spoon about one-third of the batter onto the bottom of the prepared baking pan. Drop 2 tbsp (25 mL) of the jam in two long strips lengthwise (1 tbsp/15 mL each) over the batter in the bottom of the pan. Swirl through with a knife or spatula.
4. Top with another third of the batter, dropping another 2 tbsp (25 mL) of jam over top of that layer. Swirl through again with a knife or spatula. Top with the remaining batter and the remaining 2 tbsp (25 mL) of jam and swirl one more time with a knife.
5. Bake in preheated oven for 40 to 50 minutes or until a toothpick inserted in the center comes out clean and dry. Let cool in pan on a wire rack for 10 minutes and then remove onto wire rack to cool completely.

Glazed Chocolate Pumpkin Loaf

Serves 16 to 20
- Preheat oven to 350°F (180°C)
- Two 9- by 5-inch (2 L) metal loaf pans, greased and floured

3⅓ cups	all-purpose flour	825 mL
3 cups	granulated sugar	750 mL
2 tsp	baking soda	10 mL
1 tsp	salt	5 mL
1 tsp	ground cinnamon	5 mL
1 tsp	ground nutmeg	5 mL
4	eggs, lightly beaten	4
1 cup	vegetable oil	250 mL
⅔ cup	water	150 mL
2 cups	canned or cooked pumpkin purée (not pie filling)	500 mL
½ cup	chopped nuts	125 mL
4 oz	semisweet chocolate, melted and cooled	125 g

ICING SUGAR GLAZE

1½ cups	confectioner's (icing) sugar, sifted	375 mL
4 to 6 tsp	cold water	20 to 30 mL
1 oz	semisweet chocolate, melted and cooled	30 g
2 to 4 tsp	hot water	10 to 20 mL

1. In a large bowl, combine flour, sugar, baking soda, salt, cinnamon and nutmeg, and mix together thoroughly.

2. In a medium bowl, whisk together eggs, oil, water and pumpkin until well blended. Pour into the flour mixture, mixing just until well blended. Fold in nuts.

3. Transfer 2 cups (500 mL) of batter to a small bowl, add the melted chocolate and mix well.

4. Spoon half the remaining plain batter into the two prepared baking pans, one-quarter in each. Spoon chocolate batter over top, half in each pan. Spoon the remaining plain batter, half in each pan, over the chocolate batter.

5. Bake in preheated oven for 60 to 65 minutes or until a toothpick inserted in the center comes out clean and dry. Let cool in pans on a wire rack for 10 minutes, and then remove onto wire rack to cool completely.

6. *Prepare the glaze:* In a small bowl, mix together confectioner's sugar and cold water until the right drizzling consistency. Transfer half to a separate bowl. To one bowl, stir in chocolate and enough of the hot water for it to be the right consistency for drizzling.

7. Drizzle white glaze in a zigzag pattern on top of one loaf, and do the same with the chocolate glaze on the second loaf. Or do a zigzag pattern with white and chocolate glaze on each loaf. If not using both loaves immediately, they can be frozen for up to 6 months, well wrapped first in plastic wrap, then in a freezer bag.

Tips *Cooled, unglazed loaf can be wrapped (sliced or unsliced) and frozen for up to 1 month. Thaw (wrapped) in refrigerator overnight. Glaze before serving.*

Make a special pumpkin ice cream sundae: soften 2 cups (500 mL) of vanilla or butter pecan ice cream just slightly, stir in 1 can (19 oz/540 mL) of pumpkin purée, then cinnamon and nutmeg. Spoon into custard cups, sprinkle with some graham wafer crumbs, and then place in freezer for an hour.

Easy Baked Alaska Loaf

Serves 8 to 10
- Preheat oven according to cake mix instructions
- 9-inch (2.5 L) square metal baking pan, greased and floured

1	package (18 oz/510 g) chocolate cake mix	1
1	brick (1 quart/1 L) strawberry or Neapolitan ice cream (or any other favorite flavor); keep in freezer	1

WHITE FLUFFY FROSTING

¼ tsp	cream of tartar	1 mL
2	egg whites	2
1 tbsp	water	15 mL
2 tbsp	light corn syrup	25 mL
1½ tsp	vanilla	7 mL
½ tsp	lemon extract	2 mL
2½ cups	confectioner's (icing) sugar, sifted	625 mL

1. Prepare chocolate cake mix according to the directions on the package. Pour batter into prepared baking pan.

2. Bake in preheated oven for time indicated on cake mix package. Let cake cool in pan for about 10 minutes. Remove from pan and let cool completely on a wire rack.

3. Cut off top of cake to make flat, if necessary. Cut cake to ½-inch (1 cm) larger than the brick of ice cream on all sides and place on an ovenproof serving plate.

4. *Prepare the frosting:* In a medium mixer bowl, beat cream of tartar and egg whites on high speed until firm peaks form. In a small bowl, mix water, corn syrup, vanilla and lemon extract. Add to the egg white mixture, alternating with the confectioner's sugar and beating well after each addition, until frosting is creamy, stiff and easy to spread.

5. Remove ice cream from freezer. Place in center of the trimmed cake layer. Quickly spread the frosting over the ice cream and cake, making sure that you seal the edges of the cake all around.

6. Raise temperature in oven to 500°F (260°C) and place frosted loaf into hot oven for 4 to 5 minutes or until the meringue-type frosting is golden brown. Serve immediately.

Tip *To cut a 2-quart (2 L) brick of ice cream to fit this cake, open up one end and top of box and stand ice cream brick vertically on remaining closed end. Cut in half lengthwise. Freeze remaining ice cream for another use.*

Angel Food Cakes

Getting a light, tender cake will depend on how much you beat the egg whites, how gently you fold in the flour mixture and the temperature at which you bake the cake. Sift the dry ingredients two or three times. Bring egg whites to room temperature before beating for the best volume. Do not underbeat or overbeat the egg whites. The egg whites should be stiff enough to form soft peaks but still be moist and glossy. It is also best to use a fine granulated sugar.

● ●

Traditional Angel Food Cake

Serves 10 to 12

- Preheat oven to 350°F (180°C)
- 10-inch (4 L) metal tube pan, ungreased

1½ cups	confectioner's (icing) sugar	375 mL
1 cup	cake and pastry flour	250 mL
Pinch	salt	Pinch
10	egg whites, at room temperature (about 1¼ cups/300 mL)	10
1½ tsp	cream of tartar	7 mL
¾ cup	granulated sugar	175 mL
1 tsp	vanilla	5 mL
1 tsp	almond extract (optional)	5 mL

1. In a medium bowl, sift together confectioner's sugar, flour and salt.

2. In a large, clean mixer bowl, on high speed, beat egg whites and cream of tartar until foamy. Gradually add the granulated sugar, beating until stiff peaks form. Sift one-third of the flour mixture over the egg whites and fold in gently. Fold in the remaining flour mixture, in two more portions, folding lightly just until well blended. Fold in vanilla and almond extract (if using). Spoon into baking pan. Tap pan on counter lightly to get rid of any air bubbles. Smooth top of batter.

3. Bake in preheated oven for 40 minutes or until lightly browned and top of cake springs back when touched lightly with fingertip. Immediately invert pan and, using hole in tube, hang upside down on an inverted funnel, neck of a bottle or a wire rack until cooled completely.

4. With a long thin knife or metal spatula, loosen around the edges, and then remove cake from pan. Decorate as desired.

Variations *Pineapple Angel Food Cake:* Add 19-oz (540 mL) can crushed pineapple and its juice to the batter with vanilla (omit almond extract), mixing in until well combined, and bake as above.

Coconut and Strawberry Angel Cake: Beat 2 cups (500 mL) whipping (35%) cream and ¼ cup (50 mL) confectioner's sugar on high speed until stiff peaks form. Spread over the sides and top of the plain angel food cake. Sprinkle ¼ cup (500 mL) toasted shredded sweetened coconut over the frosting. Arrange sliced strawberries on top (about 2 cups/500 mL). Chill cake for at least 30 minutes or for up to 4 hours.

Angel Cake Loaf: Spoon batter into 2 ungreased 9- by 5-inch (2 L) metal loaf pans and bake in preheated oven for 25 to 30 minutes, then proceed as above.

Burnt Sugar Angel Cake

Serves 10 to 12

- Preheat oven to 375°F (190°C)
- 10-inch (4 L) metal tube pan, ungreased

2 cups	granulated sugar, divided	500 mL
1/2 cup	water	125 mL
1 cup	cake and pastry flour	250 mL
1/4 tsp	salt	1 mL
12	egg whites, at room temperature (about 1 1/2 cups/375 mL)	12
1 1/2 tsp	cream of tartar	7 mL
1 cup	chopped pecans, toasted	250 mL
1 1/2 tsp	vanilla	7 mL
	Pecan halves	

BURNT SUGAR FROSTING

1 cup	confectioner's (icing) sugar, sifted	250 mL
2 tbsp	butter or margarine, softened	25 mL
2 tbsp	milk	25 mL

1. In a small saucepan, cook 3/4 cup (175 mL) of the sugar until melted, stirring constantly, until golden brown. Stir in water, bring to a boil and boil for 5 to 10 minutes or until mixture is syrupy and caramel-colored and reduced to about 1/3 cup (75 mL). Set aside to cool to room temperature, about 10 to 15 minutes.

2. In a bowl, sift together another 3/4 cup (175 mL) of the sugar and the cake flour and salt. Sift three or four times.

3. In a large, clean mixer bowl, on high speed, beat egg whites and cream of tartar until soft peaks form. Gradually beat in 1/4 cup (50 mL) of the syrup mixture. Add the remaining sugar, by spoonfuls, beating until stiff peaks form. Sift one-third of the flour mixture over the egg whites and fold in gently. Fold in the remaining flour mixture in two portions, folding lightly just until well blended. Fold in chopped pecans and vanilla. Pour into baking pan. Tap pan on counter lightly to get rid of any air bubbles. Smooth top of batter.

4. Bake in preheated oven for 35 to 40 minutes or until a toothpick inserted in the center comes out clean and dry. Immediately invert pan and, using hole in tube, hang upside down on an inverted funnel, the neck of a bottle or a wire rack, and let cool completely. With a long thin knife or metal spatula, loosen around the edges and then remove cake from pan. Place on serving plate.

5. *Prepare the frosting:* In a medium bowl, mix confectioner's sugar, butter, the remaining syrup mixture and milk. Mix well and spoon over top of cake, allowing it to drip onto the sides. Decorate top with pecan halves or as desired.

Tip *To slice an angel food cake easily, freeze the whole cake overnight before frosting. The cake doesn't get squished by the knife and it slices up nicely.*

Three-Egg Angel Cake

Serves 10 to 12

- Preheat oven to 350°F (180°C)
- 10-inch (4 L) metal tube pan, ungreased

1 cup	all-purpose flour	250 mL
2 tsp	baking powder	10 mL
1/2 tsp	cream of tartar	2 mL
3/4 cup	granulated sugar	175 mL
2/3 cup	milk	150 mL
3	egg whites	3
Pinch	salt	Pinch
1/2 tsp	vanilla	2 mL
1/2 tsp	almond extract (optional)	2 mL

1. In a large bowl, sift together flour, baking powder and cream of tartar. Sift three or four more times.

2. In a small saucepan, heat sugar and milk over medium heat until steaming. Remove from heat.

3. In a large, clean mixer bowl, on high speed, beat egg whites and salt until stiff peaks form. Slowly add the hot milk mixture, beating until well blended. Set aside to cool.

4. Fold sifted flour mixture into egg white mixture. Fold in vanilla and almond extract (if using) until well combined. Pour into baking pan, smoothing top.

5. Bake in preheated oven for 30 to 35 minutes or until cake springs back when touched lightly with fingertip. Immediately invert pan and, using hole in tube, hang upside down on an inverted funnel, the neck of a bottle or a wire rack, and let cool completely. With a long thin knife or metal spatula, loosen around the edges and then remove cake from pan. Decorate as desired.

Tips *An easy way to frost an angel food cake, or any cake, is to thaw 2 cups (500 mL) frozen whipped topping. Fold in 1 package of any flavor gelatin powder. It mixes up in seconds and tastes great.*

After you have beaten the egg whites to perfection, keep foam cakes light and airy by folding in the dry ingredients with a rubber spatula, using a circular motion and never stirring.

Frosted Chocolate Angel Food Cake

Serves 10 to 12

- Preheat oven to 350°F (180°C)
- 10-inch (4 L) metal tube pan, ungreased

½ cup	sifted unsweetened cocoa powder	125 mL
⅓ cup	hot water	75 mL
1½ cups	granulated sugar, divided	375 mL
¾ cup	cake and pastry flour	175 mL
¼ tsp	salt	1 mL
12	egg whites, at room temperature (about 1½ cups/375 mL)	12
1 tsp	cream of tartar	5 mL
1 tsp	vanilla	5 mL
COCOA FROSTING		
¾ cup	confectioner's (icing) sugar	175 mL
3 tbsp	sifted unsweetened cocoa powder	45 mL
2 cups	whipping (35%) cream	500 mL
1 tsp	vanilla	5 mL

1. In a small bowl, combine cocoa powder and hot water until well blended. Let cool completely.
2. In another bowl, sift together ¾ cup (175 mL) of the sugar, the flour and salt.
3. In a large, clean mixer bowl, on high speed, beat egg whites and cream of tartar until foamy. Gradually add the remaining sugar, by spoonfuls, beating until stiff peaks form. Sift one-third of the flour mixture over the egg whites and fold in gently. Fold in the remaining flour mixture in two portions, folding lightly just until well blended. Fold in vanilla.
4. Take 1 cup (250 mL) of the egg white mixture and stir into the cocoa mixture. Mix well and then gently fold this cocoa mixture into the remaining egg white mixture, folding until well blended. Spoon into the baking pan. Tap pan lightly on counter to remove any air bubbles. Smooth top of batter.
5. Bake in preheated oven for 45 to 50 minutes or until a toothpick inserted in the center comes out clean and dry. Immediately invert pan and, using hole in tube, hang upside down on an inverted funnel, the neck of a bottle or a wire rack, and let cool completely. With a long thin knife or metal spatula, loosen around the edges and then remove cake from pan.
6. *Prepare the frosting:* In a mixer bowl, sift together confectioner's sugar and cocoa powder. Add whipping cream and vanilla and beat on medium speed until stiff and of spreading consistency. Cut cake in half horizontally and place bottom layer on a serving plate, cut side up. Spread evenly with about one-third of the frosting. Top with second layer, cut side down, and frost top and sides.

Tip *Sprinkle icing sugar or some chopped nuts over top, or alternating strips of both to create a pattern.*

Lemon Swirl Angel Cake

Serves 10 to 12

- Preheat oven to 375°F (190°C)
- 10-inch (4 L) metal tube pan, ungreased

1½ cups	granulated sugar, divided	375 mL
1 cup	cake and pastry flour	250 mL
¼ tsp	salt	1 mL
12	egg whites, at room temperature (about 1½ cups/375 mL)	12
1½ tsp	cream of tartar	7 mL
6	egg yolks	6
1 tbsp	grated lemon zest	15 mL
1½ tsp	vanilla	7 mL
½ tsp	almond extract (optional)	2 mL

1. In a medium bowl, sift together ¾ cup (175 mL) of the sugar, the flour and salt.
2. In a large, clean mixer bowl, on high speed, beat egg whites and cream of tartar until foamy. Gradually add the remaining sugar, by spoonfuls, beating until stiff peaks form.
3. In a small mixer bowl, beat egg yolks until lemon-colored and very thick. Fold in lemon zest, vanilla and almond extract (if using).
4. Sift one-third of the flour mixture over the egg whites and fold in gently. Fold in the remaining flour mixture in two portions, folding lightly just until well blended. Spoon half of this batter into another bowl and gently fold in the egg yolk mixture. Spoon the plain batter and the egg yolk batter alternately in spoonfuls around the baking pan and in layers. Cut through batters with a knife or thin spatula, making a swirl pattern.
5. Bake in preheated oven for 40 to 45 minutes or until top springs back when touched lightly. Immediately invert pan and, using hole in tube, hang upside down on an inverted funnel, the neck of a bottle or a wire rack, and let cool completely. With a long thin knife or metal spatula, loosen around the edges and then remove cake from pan.

Tip *If desired, make a lemon glaze (see recipe, page 549) and drizzle over top and sides of cooled cake.*

Surprise Angel-Sponge Cake

Serves 10 to 12
Preheat oven to 375°F (190°C)
10-inch (4 L) metal tube pan, ungreased

1½ cups	granulated sugar, divided	375 mL
1 cup	cake and pastry flour	250 mL
¼ tsp	salt	1 mL
11	egg whites (about 1⅓ cups/325 mL)	11
1¼ tsp	cream of tartar	6 mL
4	egg yolks, well beaten	4
1 tsp	grated orange zest	5 mL
2 tbsp	freshly squeezed orange juice	25 mL
2 tbsp	cake and pastry flour, sifted	25 mL
½ tsp	vanilla	2 mL

1. In a medium bowl, sift together ½ cup (125 mL) of the sugar, 1 cup (250 mL) cake flour and salt.

2. In a large, clean mixer bowl, on high speed, beat egg whites and cream of tartar until soft peaks form. Gradually add the remaining sugar, by spoonfuls, beating until stiff peaks form. Sift one-third of the flour mixture over the egg whites and fold in gently. Fold in the remaining flour mixture in two portions, folding lightly just until well blended. Transfer half of batter to another bowl. Set both aside.

3. In a small mixer bowl, combine egg yolks, orange zest and orange juice and beat until lemon-colored and very thick. Fold this mixture and the 2 tbsp (25 mL) cake flour into one bowl of batter. Fold the vanilla into the other bowl of batter. Spoon batters alternately in spoonfuls around the baking pan. Tap pan lightly on counter to remove any air bubbles. Smooth top of batter.

4. Bake in preheated oven for 35 to 40 minutes or until a toothpick inserted into the center comes out clean and dry. Immediately invert pan and, using hole in tube, hang upside down on an inverted funnel, the neck of a bottle or a wire rack, and let cool completely. With a long thin knife or metal spatula, loosen around the edges and then remove cake from pan. Decorate as desired.

Tip *If you need eggs at room temperature but have forgotten to remove them from the refrigerator, put them in warm water for several minutes before cracking.*

Chiffon Cakes

The method for baking chiffon cakes uses some of the method for baking angel food cakes and some of the method for baking sponge cakes. Be sure to read recipe instructions before baking.

Traditional Chiffon Cake

Serves 12 to 16
• Preheat oven to 325°F (160°C)
• 10-inch (4 L) metal tube pan, ungreased

6	eggs, separated	6
½ tsp	salt	2 mL
1½ cups	granulated sugar, divided	375 mL
½ cup	warm water	125 mL
1½ cups	all-purpose flour, divided	375 mL
1 tsp	vanilla	5 mL
½ tsp	cream of tartar	2 mL

1. In a large mixer bowl, beat egg yolks and salt for 2 to 3 minutes, until lemon-colored and thick. Beat in 1 cup (250 mL) of sugar gradually and continue beating. Gradually add the water and beat until mixture is frothy.

2. Slowly beat in ¾ cup (175 mL) of the flour and vanilla until blended. Beat in the remaining flour and blend well.

3. In a clean mixer bowl, with clean blades, on high speed, beat egg whites and cream of tartar until soft peaks form. Gradually add the remaining sugar, by spoonfuls, beating until stiff peaks form. Fold egg white mixture into the egg yolk mixture, gently, until well combined. Spoon into baking pan. Tap pan lightly on counter to remove any air bubbles. Smooth top of batter.

4. Bake in preheated oven for 55 to 60 minutes or until top springs back when touched lightly with fingertip. Immediately invert pan and, using hole in tube, hang upside down on an inverted funnel, the neck of a bottle or a wire rack, and let cool completely. With a long thin knife or metal spatula, loosen around the edges and then remove cake from pan. Serve plain or decorate as desired.

Variation *Banana Chiffon Cake: Add 1 cup (250 mL) of mashed, ripe bananas to the egg yolk mixture before combining with egg whites.*

Glazed Chocolate Chiffon Cake

Serves 12 to 16

- Preheat oven to 325°F (160°C)
- 10-inch (4 L) metal tube pan, ungreased

2¼ cups	cake and pastry flour	550 mL
1¾ cups	granulated sugar	425 mL
1 tbsp	baking powder	15 mL
1 tsp	salt	5 mL
½ cup	vegetable oil	125 mL
5	egg yolks, beaten	5
¾ cup	cold water	175 mL
1 tsp	vanilla	5 mL
7	egg whites	7
½ tsp	cream of tartar	2 mL
3 oz	semisweet chocolate, grated	90 g
CHOCOLATE GLAZE		
4 oz	semisweet chocolate, chopped	125 g
¼ cup	whipping (35%) cream	50 mL
1 tsp	vanilla	5 mL

1. In a large bowl, sift together flour, sugar, baking powder and salt. Make a well in the center. Pour oil, egg yolks, water and vanilla into well. Mix well until blended.
2. In a large, clean mixer bowl, with clean blades, on high speed, beat egg whites and cream of tartar until stiff peaks form. Slowly and gently fold into batter. Quickly fold in the grated chocolate. Pour into baking pan. Tap pan lightly on counter to remove any air bubbles. Smooth top of batter.
3. Bake in preheated oven for 55 minutes. Increase temperature to 350°F (180°C) and bake for another 10 to 15 minutes or until top springs back when touched lightly with fingertip. Immediately invert pan and, using hole in tube, hang upside down on an inverted funnel, the neck of a bottle or a wire rack, and let cool completely. With a long thin knife or metal spatula, loosen around the edges and then remove cake from pan.
4. *Prepare the glaze:* In a small saucepan, combine chocolate and whipping cream, stirring on low heat until chocolate is completely melted. Stir in vanilla. Drizzle immediately over top and sides of cooled cake.

Tip *To substitute all-purpose flour for cake flour in a recipe, remove 2 tbsp (25 mL) of flour from every cup of all-purpose flour, and add 2 tbsp (25 mL) cornstarch.*

Maple Nut Chiffon Cake

Serves 12 to 16

- Preheat oven to 325°F (160°C)
- 10-inch (4 L) metal tube pan, ungreased

2¼ cups	cake and pastry flour	550 mL
¾ cup	granulated sugar	175 mL
¾ cup	packed brown sugar	175 mL
1 tbsp	baking powder	15 mL
1 tsp	salt	5 mL
½ cup	vegetable oil	125 mL
5	egg yolks	5
¾ cup	cold water	175 mL
2 tsp	maple extract	10 mL
8	egg whites	8
½ tsp	cream of tartar	2 mL
1 cup	finely chopped walnuts or other nuts	250 mL
	Buttercream Frosting (optional, see recipe, page 550)	

1. In a large mixer bowl, sift together flour, granulated sugar, brown sugar, baking powder and salt.
2. In another bowl, whisk oil, egg yolks, water and maple extract, beating until smooth.
3. Add egg mixture to the flour mixture and beat on low speed until well blended.
4. In a small, clean mixer bowl, with clean beaters, on high speed, beat egg whites and cream of tartar until very stiff peaks form. Fold into the batter, gently, until blended. Fold in nuts. Spoon into baking pan. Tap pan lightly on counter to remove any air bubbles. Smooth top of batter.
5. Bake in preheated oven for 55 minutes. Increase heat to 350°F (180°C) and bake for an additional 10 to 15 minutes or until top springs back when touched lightly with fingertip. Immediately invert pan and, using hole in tube, hang upside down on an inverted funnel, the neck of a bottle or a wire rack, and let cool completely. With a long thin knife or metal spatula, loosen around the edges and then remove cake from pan.
6. Frost, if desired, with Buttercream Frosting or another frosting.

Tip *When baking calls for mostly egg whites, drop the yolks into a pan of boiling, salted water and cook for about 10 minutes, until firm. You'll have hard-boiled egg yolks to use in sandwiches or salads.*

Sponge Cakes

The method for baking sponge cakes is the same as that for angel food cakes when it comes to beating and folding in the egg whites, but be sure to follow the method used in your particular recipe. Remove your cake from the pan as soon as it is cool if you want a nice brown crust. If you leave it in the pan too long, the crust will cling to the pan.

● ●

Traditional Sponge Cake

Serves 12 to 16
- Preheat oven to 325°F (160°C)
- 10-inch (4 L) metal tube pan, ungreased

1¾ cups	all-purpose flour	425 mL
1½ cups	granulated sugar, divided	375 mL
2½ tsp	baking powder	12 mL
4	eggs, separated	4
1 tsp	vanilla	5 mL
1 cup	milk	250 mL
2 tbsp	butter or margarine, softened	25 mL

1. In a medium bowl, sift together flour, 1 cup (250 mL) of the sugar and baking powder.
2. In a large, clean mixer bowl, on high speed, beat egg whites until foamy. Gradually add the remaining sugar, by spoonfuls, beating until sugar is dissolved and stiff peaks form.
3. In another mixer bowl, on high speed, beat egg yolks and vanilla until lemon-colored and thick.
4. In a small saucepan, over medium heat, heat milk and butter until the butter is melted, but do not bring to a boil. Gradually beat into the egg yolk mixture. Add flour mixture and beat on low speed until well blended. Fold into the egg white mixture, blending until well combined. Pour into baking pan.
5. Bake in preheated oven for 55 to 60 minutes or until top of cake springs back when touched lightly with fingertip. Immediately invert pan and, using hole in tube, hang upside down on an inverted funnel, the neck of a bottle or a wire rack, and let cool completely. With a long thin knife or metal spatula, loosen around the edges and then remove cake from pan.

Tip *I often use a Bundt pan for this particular cake, and do not invert the pan to cool. I leave the cake in the pan for 20 to 25 minutes to cool and then remove from the pan to cool completely on a wire rack.*

● ●

Chocolate Sponge Cake Roll

Serves 10 to 12
- Preheat oven to 350°F (180°C)
- 15- by 10-inch (38 by 25 cm) rimmed baking sheet, greased and lined with greased waxed or parchment paper

⅓ cup	sifted unsweetened cocoa powder	75 mL
⅓ cup	all-purpose flour	75 mL
½ tsp	baking powder	2 mL
¼ tsp	salt	1 mL
4	eggs	4
¾ cup	granulated sugar	175 mL
1 tsp	vanilla	5 mL
	Unsweetened cocoa powder	
CHOCOLATE CREAM FILLING		
1	package (4 oz/125 g) chocolate whipped dessert mix	1
½ cup	milk	125 mL
½ cup	water	125 mL
½ cup	whipping (35%) cream	125 mL

1. In a medium bowl, sift together cocoa powder, flour, baking powder and salt.
2. In a large mixer bowl, beat eggs until thick and lemon-colored. Gradually add sugar, a spoonful at a time, and vanilla, beating for about 10 to 12 minutes, until very thick. Gently fold in flour mixture until blended. Spoon into prepared baking pan, spreading evenly.
3. Bake in preheated oven for 20 to 25 minutes or until cake springs back when touched lightly with fingertip. Let cool in pan on a wire rack for about 10 minutes. Cut off a ¼-inch (0.5 cm) strip from the edges of cake. Invert cake onto a clean tea towel sprinkled with unsweetened cocoa powder and remove the waxed paper. Starting at the narrow end, roll up cake and wrap in towel. Set aside to cool completely on a wire rack.
4. *Prepare the filling:* In a bowl, mix dessert mix with the milk and water and follow the directions on the package. Chill in refrigerator for at least 30 minutes or until ready to serve.
5. When ready to serve, in a small mixer bowl, beat the whipping cream until stiff. Spoon half of the chilled chocolate dessert into another small bowl and beat until smooth. Gently fold in the whipped cream until well combined.

6. Unroll cake carefully and spread chocolate cream filling over top, spreading evenly. Reroll, using the towel as a guide. Remove towel and place roll on a serving plate. Whisk the remaining chocolate dessert until smooth and frost the roll, top and sides.

Tip *You could decorate by sprinkling confectioner's (icing) sugar or shaving chocolate curls over top, or any other decoration desired.*

Variation *Lemon Sponge Cake Roll: Omit cocoa powder and chocolate cream filling ingredients. Separate eggs into yolks and whites. Add 2 tbsp (25 mL) lemon juice and 1 tsp (5 mL) lemon extract to the egg yolks. Fold the flour mixture into the egg yolk mixture, as above. Beat the egg whites with ½ tsp (2 mL) cream of tartar until stiff and fold into the batter, as above. Bake and cool as directed. Fill with crabapple jelly or any other jam or jelly you desire.*

Orange Sponge Cake

Serves 12 to 16
- Preheat oven to 350°F (180°C)
- 10-inch (4 L) metal tube pan, ungreased

1¾ cups	sifted all-purpose flour	425 mL
¼ tsp	salt	1 mL
6	eggs, separated, at room temperature	6
1½ cups	granulated sugar, divided	375 mL
1 tbsp	grated orange zest	15 mL
6 tbsp	freshly squeezed orange juice	90 mL
	Confectioner's (icing) sugar	

1. In a medium bowl, sift together flour and salt and set aside.
2. In a large, clean mixer bowl, on medium speed, beat egg whites until foamy. Gradually beat in ½ cup (125 mL) of the sugar, a spoonful at a time, beating until stiff peaks form.
3. In a small mixer bowl, on high speed, beat egg yolks until lemon-colored and thick, about 2 to 3 minutes. Do not underbeat. Beat in the remaining sugar gradually until mixture is smooth and blended.
4. Beat in flour mixture alternately with orange juice, making 3 additions of flour and 2 of orange juice, on low speed, just to blend. Add orange zest. Gently fold into egg white mixture until well combined. Pour into baking pan.

5. Bake in preheated oven for 50 to 55 minutes or until top springs back when touched lightly with fingertip. Immediately invert pan and, using hole in tube, hang upside down on an inverted funnel, the neck of a bottle or a wire rack, and let cool completely. With a long thin knife or metal spatula, loosen around the edges and then remove cake from pan. Sift confectioner's sugar over top.

Tip *Decorate with an orange frosting (see variation, page 552) or orange glaze, or leave plain and serve with sherbet or a raspberry sauce.*

Sabbath Sponge Cake

Serves 12 to 16
- Preheat oven to 325°F (160°C)
- 10-inch (4 L) metal tube pan, ungreased

½ cup	cake flour	125 mL
Pinch	salt	Pinch
7	eggs, separated	7
	Grated zest of 1 lemon	
	Juice of 1 lemon	
¾ cup	fine granulated sugar, divided	175 mL
½ tsp	cream of tartar	2 mL
	Confectioner's (icing) sugar (optional)	

1. In a medium bowl, sift flour and salt two to three times.
2. In a large mixer bowl, on high speed, beat the egg yolks until lemon-colored and thick. Beat in lemon zest, lemon juice and half the sugar.
3. In a clean mixer bowl, with clean beaters, on high speed, beat egg whites and cream of tartar until soft peaks form. Gradually add the remaining sugar, by spoonfuls, beating until stiff peaks form.
4. Fold egg white mixture gently into egg yolk mixture. Sift the flour mixture over top and fold in. Pour into baking pan.
5. Bake in preheated oven for 55 to 60 minutes or until top springs back when touched lightly with fingertip. Immediately invert pan and, using hole in tube, hang upside down on an inverted funnel, the neck of a bottle or a wire rack, and let cool completely. With a long thin knife or metal spatula, loosen around the edges and then remove cake from pan.

Tip *This cake is usually topped with confectioner's (icing) sugar sprinkled over top.*

Layer Cakes and Tortes

• •

Butterscotch Layer Cake

Serves 12 to 16
- Preheat oven to 375°F (190°C)
- Two 9-inch (23 cm) round metal cake pans, greased and floured

2¼ cups	all-purpose flour	550 mL
1 tsp	baking soda	5 mL
1 tsp	salt	5 mL
½ tsp	baking powder	2 mL
⅔ cup	chopped butterscotch candies	150 mL
¼ cup	water	50 mL
1 cup	granulated sugar	250 mL
½ cup	butter or margarine, softened	125 mL
3	eggs	3
1 cup	buttermilk or sour cream	250 mL
COCONUT TOPPING		
½ cup	granulated sugar	125 mL
⅔ cup	evaporated milk	150 mL
1 tbsp	cornstarch	15 mL
⅓ cup	butterscotch pieces	75 mL
2 tbsp	butter or margarine	25 mL
1 cup	flaked coconut (sweetened or unsweetened)	250 mL
½ cup	chopped nuts	125 mL
	Whipped cream or whipped topping	

1. In a medium bowl, sift together flour, baking soda, salt and baking powder.
2. In a small saucepan, over low heat, stir butterscotch and water, stirring constantly, until the pieces melt. Set aside to cool to room temperature, about 10 to 15 minutes.
3. In a large mixer bowl, on medium speed, cream sugar and butter until smooth. Add eggs, one at a time, beating after each addition, until well blended. Stir in cooled butterscotch mixture and mix well. Add flour mixture to creamed mixture alternately with the buttermilk, making 3 additions of flour and 2 of buttermilk, beating on low speed until well incorporated. Spoon into prepared baking pans, dividing evenly.
4. Bake in preheated oven for 25 to 30 minutes or until a toothpick inserted in the center comes out clean and dry. Let cool in pans on wire racks for 10 minutes, then remove from pans onto wire racks to cool completely.

5. *Prepare the topping:* In a medium saucepan, combine sugar, evaporated milk and cornstarch. Cook over medium heat, stirring until boiling and thickened. Remove from heat and stir in the butterscotch and butter, stirring until these have melted. Add coconut and nuts and mix well. Let cool.
6. Spread the topping on each cake layer, dividing evenly. Place one cake layer on a serving plate. Top with the other cake layer. Frost the sides of the cake with whipped cream. Pipe some whipped cream around top edge of layered cake, making a border about ½ inch (1 cm) wide all around the top edges. Keep refrigerated until ready to serve.

Tip *When a recipe calls for flaked coconut, it means dried coconut. It is used in recipes where fresh coconut would add unwanted additional moisture.*

• •

Classic Red Devil's Cake

Serves 12 to 16
- Preheat oven to 350°F (180°C)
- Two 8-inch (20 cm) round metal cake pans, lightly greased and floured

2½ cups	cake and pastry flour	625 mL
½ cup	unsweetened cocoa powder	125 mL
1½ tsp	baking soda	7 mL
1 tsp	salt	5 mL
1¾ cups	granulated sugar, divided	425 mL
½ cup	butter or margarine or shortening, softened	125 mL
1 tsp	vanilla	5 mL
1 tsp	red food coloring	5 mL
3	eggs, separated	3
1⅓ cups	water	325 mL
WHITE FROSTING		
1 cup	milk	250 mL
⅓ cup	all-purpose flour	75 mL
1 cup	granulated sugar	250 mL
1 cup	butter or margarine, softened	250 mL
2 tsp	vanilla	10 mL

1. In a medium bowl, sift together flour, cocoa, baking soda and salt.
2. In a large mixer bowl, on medium speed, cream 1 cup (250 mL) of the sugar and butter until smooth. Add vanilla, red food coloring and then egg yolks, one at a time, beating after each addition.

3. Add flour mixture to creamed mixture alternately with the water, making 3 additions of flour and 2 of water, beating on low speed until well blended.

4. In a small mixer bowl, with clean beaters, on high speed, beat egg whites until soft peaks form. Gradually add the remaining ¾ cup (175 mL) of sugar, by spoonfuls, and beat until stiff peaks form. Gently fold into batter until well blended. Spoon into the two prepared baking pans, dividing evenly.

5. Bake in preheated oven for 35 to 45 minutes or until a toothpick inserted in the center comes out clean and dry. Let cool in pans on wire racks for 10 minutes, and then remove from pans onto wire racks to cool completely.

6. *Prepare the frosting:* In a small saucepan, whisk milk and flour to blend. Bring to a boil over medium heat, stirring for 2 to 3 minutes or until thickened. Cover and chill in refrigerator for at least 30 minutes.

7. In small mixer bowl, cream sugar and butter until smooth. Add the chilled milk mixture and beat for about 8 to 10 minutes or until fluffy. Add vanilla and mix well. Spread one-third of the frosting on one cake layer, top with the other cake layer and frost top and sides.

Tip *Dust the layers of your cake lightly with confectioner's (icing) sugar before spreading on the filling to keep it from soaking into the cake.*

• •

Mom's Sour Cream Chocolate Layer Cake

Serves 12 to 16
- Preheat oven to 350°F (180°C)
- Two 8- or 9-inch (20 cm or 23 cm) round metal cake pans, greased and lightly floured

2 cups	cake and pastry flour	500 mL
1¼ tsp	baking soda	6 mL
1 tsp	salt	5 mL
1 cup	water	250 mL
½ cup	butter or margarine	125 mL
4 oz	unsweetened chocolate, chopped	125 g
2 cups	granulated sugar	500 mL
1 cup	sour cream	250 mL
2	eggs	2
1½ tsp	vanilla	7 mL

CHOCOLATE SOUR CREAM FROSTING

1 cup	semisweet chocolate chips or pieces	250 mL
¼ cup	butter or margarine	50 mL
½ cup	sour cream	125 mL
2½ cups	confectioner's (icing) sugar, sifted	625 mL

1. In a large mixer bowl, sift together flour, baking soda and salt.

2. Combine water, butter and chocolate in the top of a double boiler over simmering water, and heat until mixture is completely melted. Remove from heat and set aside to cool.

3. In another bowl, on medium speed, beat sugar, sour cream, eggs and vanilla until well blended. Stir in cooled chocolate mixture and beat until blended.

4. Pour chocolate mixture into flour mixture gradually and beat until smooth. Batter will be thin. Pour into prepared pans.

5. Bake in preheated oven for 35 to 40 minutes or until top springs back when lightly touched, or a toothpick inserted in center comes out clean and dry. Let cool in pans on wire racks for 10 minutes. Run a knife around edges to loosen cakes from pan. Remove from pans and let cool completely on wire racks.

6. *Prepare the frosting:* In a saucepan, over low heat, combine chocolate pieces and butter. Melt, stirring constantly. Set aside to cool for about 5 minutes.

7. Add sour cream and mix to blend. Gradually add the confectioner's sugar and beat until smooth and of the right consistency for spreading.

8. Place one cake layer on plate. Slice a small piece off of the top to make surface flat. Spread evenly with one-third of the frosting. Top with second cake layer. Spread the remaining frosting over top and sides of layered cake.

Tip *If your cake layer has sunk in the center, cut a circle out of the center of each layer. Stack your layers and frost as usual, thereby making a ring cake. You could fill the center with chopped fresh fruit or some whipped cream.*

Hungarian Dobos Torte

Serves 12 to 16

- Preheat oven to 350°F (180°C)
- Three 8-inch (20 cm) round metal cake pans, greased and floured

6	eggs, separated	6
2/3 cup	granulated sugar, divided	150 mL
1 cup	sifted all-purpose flour	250 mL
CHOCOLATE CREAM		
2 cups	milk	500 mL
1 tsp	vanilla	5 mL
6	egg yolks	6
3/4 cup	granulated sugar	175 mL
1/3 cup	all-purpose flour, sifted	75 mL
Pinch	salt	Pinch
2 oz	unsweetened chocolate, melted	60 g
CARAMEL TOPPING		
1/2 cup	granulated sugar	125 mL

1. In a large mixer bowl, on high speed, beat egg whites until frothy. Gradually add 1/3 cup (75 mL) of the sugar, by spoonfuls, beating until stiff, glossy peaks form.

2. In a small mixer bowl, beat egg yolks until frothy. Add the remaining sugar gradually, beating on high speed for about 5 to 6 minutes or until mixture becomes lemon-colored and very thick. Fold gently into egg white mixture to blend. Then fold in the sifted flour, gently, just until blended. Spoon into the three prepared baking pans, dividing evenly.

3. Bake in preheated oven for 30 to 40 minutes or until a toothpick inserted in the center comes out clean and dry. Let cool in pans on wire racks for 10 minutes, then remove from pans onto wire racks to cool completely.

4. Slice each layer cake in half so that you have 6 layers, and slice off tops to flatten.

5. *Prepare the chocolate cream:* In a double boiler, over medium heat, heat milk just until steaming and bubbles form around edge of pan. In a mixer bowl, beat vanilla and egg yolks until foamy. Gradually add sugar and beat on high speed until lemon-colored and thick. Add the flour and salt, beating until blended. Beat in melted chocolate. Mix in scalded milk slowly. Return entire mixture to the double boiler and cook over simmering water, stirring constantly, for about 20 to 25 minutes, until thick. Strain, cover and refrigerate until completely cooled.

6. Set about one-third of the Chocolate Cream aside. Divide the remaining two-thirds into four equal portions, spread it evenly over each of four cake layers and stack, so that you have five stacked layers with cream between. Use the Chocolate Cream you set aside to frost over top and sides. Set in refrigerator to chill for at least 30 minutes.

7. *Prepare the topping:* In a heavy skillet, over medium heat, melt sugar until golden. Spoon this quickly onto the remaining cake layer, spreading evenly. With a sharp, greased knife, mark into 8 or 12 wedges, cutting right through the sugar so that, when the topping hardens, this marking will make it easier to cut the cake.

8. Place this top onto chilled cake layers and chill until ready to serve.

Tip *The original, correct way to make this torte is to grease and flour baking sheets with six 8-inch (20 cm) rounds by tracing around an 8-inch (20 cm) layer cake pan. If using the baking sheet method, divide the batter into six portions and spread about 3/4 cup (175 mL) into each round traced on baking sheets. Try to put two rounds on each sheet, and bake each separately at 350°F (180°C) for about 10 minutes, until lightly browned or cake springs back when touched lightly with your fingertip. Remove from sheets and let cool on wire racks.*

Meringue Blitz Torte

Serves 12 to 16

- Preheat oven to 350°F (180°C)
- Two 8-inch (20 cm) round metal cake pans, greased and floured

MERINGUE TOPPING		
4	egg whites	4
1 cup	granulated sugar	250 mL
CAKE		
1 cup	all-purpose flour	250 mL
1 tsp	baking powder	5 mL
Pinch	salt	Pinch
3/4 cup	confectioner's (icing) sugar	175 mL
1/2 cup	butter or margarine, softened	125 mL
4	egg yolks	4
1/4 cup	milk	50 mL
1/2 cup	sliced almonds	125 mL
2 tbsp	granulated sugar	25 mL
2 cups	ready-to-serve vanilla pudding	500 mL

1. *Prepare the topping:* In a small mixer bowl, beat egg whites until foamy. Add the sugar, 1 tbsp (15 mL) at a time, beating until mixture is glossy and stiff peaks form. Set aside.
2. *Prepare the cake:* In a medium bowl, sift together flour, baking powder and salt.
3. In a large mixer bowl, combine the confectioner's sugar, butter, egg yolks and milk. Beat on low speed for 1 minute, until blended.
4. Add flour mixture to the butter mixture and beat on medium speed for another 2 to 3 minutes, until well blended. Spoon batter into each prepared baking pan, dividing evenly.
5. Spread half of the meringue mixture on top of the batter in each pan, then sprinkle half of the almonds on top of each. Sprinkle the granulated sugar on top of the almonds in each pan.
6. Bake in preheated oven for 30 to 35 minutes or until meringue is set and golden brown. Let cool in pans for 10 minutes, then turn out on racks with meringue sides up and let cool completely.
7. When cooled, place one cake on a serving plate, meringue side up, and spread the vanilla pudding evenly over top. Place the second cake on top of the pudding. Chill until ready to serve.

● ●

Mocha Hazelnut Torte

Serves 12 to 16

- Preheat oven to 350°F (180°C)
- Three 9-inch (23 cm) round metal cake pans, lightly greased and floured

4 tsp	instant coffee powder or granules	20 mL
1¼ cups	milk	300 mL
3 cups	cake and pastry flour	750 mL
⅓ cup	sifted unsweetened cocoa powder	75 mL
1 tbsp	baking powder	15 mL
1 tsp	salt	5 mL
1½ cups	granulated sugar	375 mL
¾ cup	butter or margarine, softened	175 mL
6	egg yolks	6
MERINGUE TOPPING		
6	egg whites	6
¾ cup	granulated sugar	175 mL
½ cup	chopped or sliced hazelnuts	125 mL
CREAM FILLING		
1½ cups	whipping (35%) cream	375 mL
¼ cup	strong brewed coffee	50 mL

GLAZE		
2 oz	semisweet chocolate, melted and cooled	60 g

1. Mix together coffee powder and milk until dissolved. Set aside.
2. In a medium bowl, sift together cake flour, cocoa, baking powder and salt.
3. In a large mixer bowl, on medium speed, beat sugar and butter until smooth. Add egg yolks, one at a time, beating after each addition, until light and fluffy. Add flour mixture alternately with coffee mixture, making 3 additions of flour and 2 of coffee, beating on low speed until moistened and blended. Then beat on medium speed for 3 to 5 minutes, until well blended. Pour batter into the three prepared baking pans, dividing evenly.
4. *Prepare the topping:* In a large, clean bowl, beat egg whites until soft peaks form. Gradually add sugar, by spoonfuls, beating until stiff peaks form. Spread lightly over top of the batter in each pan, dividing evenly. Sprinkle the hazelnuts over top in each pan.
5. Bake in preheated oven for 35 to 40 minutes or until topping is a golden brown. Let cool in pans on wire racks for 20 to 25 minutes and remove from pans onto wire racks to cool completely.
6. *Prepare the filling:* In a mixer bowl, beat cream and coffee until stiff peaks form. Spread half of filling gently over the meringue side of one cake layer. Top with a second layer, meringue side up, and spread the remaining filling on top. Top this with the remaining cake layer, with meringue side facing up.
7. Drizzle the melted chocolate over top and let it run down sides. Chill for at least 30 minutes or until ready to serve.

Tip *When whipping (35%) cream does not seem to whip properly, add 3 to 4 drops of lemon juice or ½ tsp (2 mL) unflavored gelatin. Always use glass or metal mixing bowls to whip cream, and be sure that your beaters are thoroughly cleaned before whipping.*

Peach Cream Torte

Serves 10 to 12

- Preheat oven to 375°F (190°C)
- 9-inch (23 cm) springform pan

1 cup	all-purpose flour, sifted	250 mL
¼ cup	granulated sugar	50 mL
6 tbsp	butter or margarine	90 mL
1	egg yolk, lightly beaten	1
2 cups	milk	500 mL
1	package (6 oz/175 g) coconut cream pudding mix	1
4	firm ripe peaches, peeled, halved and pitted	4
	Water	
1 tsp	vanilla	5 mL
1½ cups	whipping (35%) cream	375 mL
GLAZE		
1½ tsp	cornstarch	7 mL
2 tbsp	light corn syrup	25 mL
1½ tsp	freshly squeezed lemon juice	7 mL

1. In a medium bowl, sift together flour and sugar. Cut in butter with two knives or a pastry blender until mixture resembles coarse crumbs. Add beaten egg yolk and mix until a smooth, soft dough is formed and leaves side of bowl clean. Press into the bottom and up the side of baking pan, about 1½ inches (4 cm) high. Do not prick this shell.

2. Bake in preheated oven for 20 to 25 minutes or until golden brown. Let cool completely in pan, on a wire rack.

3. In a saucepan, over low heat, combine milk and pudding mix. Cook, following package directions, until thickened. Spoon into a large bowl, cover with plastic wrap and chill for about 2 hours.

4. Place peaches in a single layer in a skillet. Add water to cover. Bring to a boil and then reduce to simmer for 2 to 3 minutes, until peaches are tender. Reserve 6 tbsp (90 mL) of this liquid in a small bowl. Drain the rest and set peaches aside to cool.

5. *Prepare the glaze:* In a small saucepan, over low heat, cook reserved liquid, cornstarch and corn syrup, stirring until mixture boils and becomes thick. Remove from heat and stir in lemon juice.

6. In a small mixer bowl, beat vanilla and whipping cream until stiff peaks form. Fold gradually into chilled pudding mixture in large bowl. Blend thoroughly and spoon over pastry in springform pan. Arrange peach halves, rounded side up, in a circle on top. Spoon glaze over top of peaches.

Fancy and Specialty Cakes

Boston Cream Pie

Serves 12 to 16

- Preheat oven to 350°F (180°C)
- Two 9-inch (23 cm) round metal cake pans, lightly greased

2	eggs, separated	2
1½ cups	granulated sugar, divided	375 mL
2¼ cups	cake and pastry flour	550 mL
1 tbsp	baking powder	15 mL
1 tsp	salt	5 mL
⅓ cup	vegetable oil	75 mL
1½ tsp	vanilla	7 mL
1 cup	milk, divided	250 mL
CUSTARD FILLING		
⅓ cup	granulated sugar	75 mL
2 tbsp	all-purpose flour	25 mL
1 tbsp	cornstarch	15 mL
¼ tsp	salt	1 mL
1½ cups	milk	375 mL
1	egg	1
1	egg yolk	1
1 tsp	vanilla	5 mL
CHOCOLATE GLAZE		
1 oz	unsweetened chocolate, chopped	30 g
1 tbsp	butter or margarine	15 mL
1 cup	confectioner's (icing) sugar, sifted	250 mL
½ tsp	vanilla	2 mL
3 to 4 tsp	boiling water or milk	15 to 20 mL

1. In a small, clean mixer bowl, beat the egg whites until soft peaks form. Add ½ cup (125 mL) of the sugar, slowly, and continue beating until stiff peaks form.

2. In the large mixer bowl, sift together cake flour, baking powder, salt and the remaining sugar. Add the oil, vanilla and ½ cup (125 mL) of the milk and beat on medium speed for about 2 minutes. Gradually add the egg yolks and the remaining milk, and beat for another 2 minutes.

3. Fold in the beaten egg white mixture only until well blended. Spoon into prepared cake pans, dividing equally.

4. Bake in preheated oven for 25 to 30 minutes or until a toothpick inserted in center comes out clean and dry. Let cool in pans on wire racks for 10 minutes. Remove from pans and place on wire racks to cool completely.

5. *Prepare the filling:* In a medium saucepan, over medium heat, combine sugar, flour, cornstarch and salt. Slowly add the milk and cook until it boils and becomes thickened. Continue cooking for another 2 to 3 minutes. In a small bowl, combine the egg, egg yolk and vanilla and beat with a fork to mix. Pour a few spoonfuls of the hot mixture into the egg mixture and then add this mixture to the saucepan, stirring constantly until mixture comes to a boil again. Remove from heat, cover with lid, foil or waxed paper, and set aside to cool to room temperature, about 10 to 15 minutes.

6. *Meanwhile, prepare the glaze:* In a small saucepan, over low heat, combine chocolate and butter, stirring until completely melted. Remove from heat and stir in the confectioner's sugar and vanilla. Stir in the boiling water, one spoonful at a time, until the glaze is the right consistency to spread over top of the cake.

7. Place one cake layer on a plate. If necessary, cut off a bit from the top to make it flat and even. Spread custard filling evenly over top. Place second cake layer on top of the custard. Spread the chocolate glaze over top and allow it to drizzle over the sides. Chill in refrigerator until glaze sets.

Tip *To cool a cake that has just come out of the oven, place the pan on a wet towel. Your cake will not stick to the pan if you cool it this way.*

• •

Lady Baltimore Cake

Serves 12 to 16
- Preheat oven to 350°F (180°C)
- Two 9-inch (23 cm) round metal cake pans, greased on bottom, then lined with waxed paper that has been greased and floured

2¹/₂ cups	sifted cake and pastry flour	625 mL
1 tbsp	baking powder	15 mL
¹/₂ tsp	salt	2 mL
2 cups	granulated sugar	500 mL
³/₄ cup	shortening, softened	175 mL
1 tsp	vanilla	5 mL
¹/₄ tsp	lemon extract	1 mL
¹/₂ cup	milk	125 mL
¹/₂ cup	water	125 mL
6	egg whites	6
LADY BALTIMORE FILLING		
¹/₂ cup	finely chopped pecans	125 mL
¹/₃ cup	chopped raisins	75 mL
¹/₃ cup	chopped dried figs	75 mL
3 tbsp	chopped drained maraschino cherries	45 mL
2 tsp	grated orange zest	10 mL
PINK MOUNTAIN CREAM FROSTING		
1 cup	granulated sugar	250 mL
¹/₃ cup	light corn syrup	75 mL
¹/₄ cup	maraschino cherry liquid	50 mL
¹/₄ tsp	salt	1 mL
4	egg whites	4
Pinch	cream of tartar	Pinch
¹/₂ tsp	vanilla	2 mL
	Red food coloring	

1. In a medium bowl, sift together flour, baking powder and salt.

2. In a large mixer bowl, with clean beaters, on medium speed, cream sugar and shortening until smooth. Beat in vanilla and lemon extract until light and fluffy.

3. Add flour mixture to creamed mixture alternately with the milk and water, making 3 additions of flour and 1 each of milk and water, on low speed, beating well after each addition.

4. In a small, clean mixer bowl, with clean beaters, on high speed, beat egg whites until stiff peaks form. Fold into batter, gently, until well blended. Pour into prepared baking pans, dividing evenly.

5. Bake in preheated oven for 25 to 30 minutes or until center springs back when touched lightly with a fingertip. Let cool in pan on wire racks for 10 minutes, loosen around edges with a knife and turn out onto wire racks to cool completely.

6. *Prepare the filling:* In a medium bowl, combine pecans, raisins, figs, cherries and zest, and toss to mix well.

7. *Prepare the frosting:* In a small saucepan, over medium heat, combine sugar, corn syrup, cherry liquid and salt. Heat to boiling and boil gently until a small amount of the syrup mixture falls threadlike from a spoon. In a large, clean mixer bowl, with clean beaters, beat egg whites and cream of tartar. Pour the hot syrup mixture onto egg whites, very slowly, in a thin stream, beating on high speed until stiff and glossy. Beat in vanilla and a few drops of the red food coloring. Fold in the filling mixture and mix well.

8. Place one layer of cake on a serving plate. Spread filling over top. Place second cake layer on top of the first. Frost sides and top of cake with the remaining frosting. Decorate further as desired.

Tip *If desired, substitute water for the cherry liquid and omit the red food coloring for a white frosting.*

Black Forest Cake

Serves 12 to 16

- Preheat oven to 325°F (160°C)
- Two 9-inch (23 cm) round metal cake pans, ungreased

¾ cup	sifted cake and pastry flour	175 mL
¼ cup	sifted unsweetened cocoa powder	50 mL
¼ tsp	salt	1 mL
5	eggs, separated	5
½ tsp	cream of tartar	2 mL
⅔ cup	granulated sugar, divided	150 mL
3 tbsp	water	45 mL
1 tsp	vanilla	5 mL

CHERRY FILLING

2½ cups	canned sweetened black cherries, with juice	625 mL
3 tbsp	granulated sugar	45 mL
2½ tbsp	cornstarch	32 mL
1 tbsp	cherry liqueur or brandy (kirsch)	15 mL

CHOCOLATE BUTTERCREAM FILLING

½ cup	granulated sugar	125 mL
Pinch	salt	Pinch
2 tbsp	water	25 mL
1	egg white	1
Pinch	cream of tartar	Pinch
½ tsp	vanilla	2 mL
⅓ cup	butter, softened	75 mL
1 oz	semisweet chocolate, melted and cooled	30 g

CHOCOLATE CREAM FROSTING

3 tbsp	granulated sugar	45 mL
3 tbsp	sifted unsweetened cocoa powder	45 mL
1 cup	whipping (35%) cream	250 mL
1 tsp	vanilla	5 mL
	Chocolate shavings or curls	
	Whole maraschino cherries, stemmed	

1. In a medium bowl, mix together flour, cocoa powder and salt.

2. In a small, clean mixer bowl, beat the egg whites and cream of tartar until frothy. Beat in ⅓ cup (75 mL) of the sugar until stiff peaks are formed.

3. In a large mixer bowl, beat the egg yolks and the remaining sugar until light and fluffy. Stir in the water and vanilla. Sift flour mixture over this egg yolk mixture in thirds, gently folding in after each addition. Then gently fold in the egg white mixture and blend well. Pour into the two baking pans, dividing evenly

4. Bake in preheated oven for 30 to 35 minutes or until a toothpick inserted in the center comes out clean and dry. Invert pans onto wire racks and let cool for 10 minutes. Remove from pans and let cool completely.

5. *Prepare the cherry filling:* Remove pits from the cherries, if necessary. In a medium saucepan, combine sugar and cornstarch. Stir in the cherries and their juice and cook over medium heat, stirring until mixture comes to a boil and is clear and thickened. Cover and cook over low heat for 5 minutes, stirring occasionally. Remove from heat to cool. Stir in the liqueur. Let cool completely.

6. *Prepare the chocolate buttercream filling:* In another saucepan, over medium heat, combine sugar, salt and water. Stir until sugar is dissolved, then let boil, without stirring, until a small amount of this syrup forms a soft ball when dropped into water.

7. In a clean mixer bowl, with clean beaters, beat the egg white and cream of tartar until soft peaks form. Slowly pour the hot, syrupy mixture into the egg white mixture in a thin stream, beating until mixture becomes thick. Let cool slightly, then beat in vanilla. Let cool completely.

8. In another bowl, cream butter until smooth. Beat in egg white mixture, by spoonfuls, and then the melted chocolate, blending well. Let cool or chill until the right consistency, if necessary.

9. Place one cake layer on a serving plate. Spread a 1-inch (2.5 cm) border of buttercream filling around the edge of the cake and then spread the remainder in a 1¼-inch (4 cm) circle in the center. Spread the cooled cherry mixture between the buttercream border and center. Place second cake layer on top, pressing down gently.

10. *Prepare the frosting:* In a small mixer bowl, beat sugar, cocoa, cream and vanilla until stiff peaks form. Do not overbeat. Frost top and sides of cake. Decorate with chocolate shavings and cherries, or any other desired decoration. Refrigerate for at least 1 hour or until chilled, or for up to 1 day.

Tip *1½ cans (each 14 oz/398 mL) of cherries is about 2½ cups (625 mL). Drain extra cherries from second can and pat dry to use as garnish, if desired.*

Tres Leches Cake

Serves 12 to 16

- Preheat oven to 350°F (180°C)
- 13- by 9-inch (3 L) metal baking pan, greased and floured

1½ cups	all-purpose flour	375 mL
1 tsp	baking powder	5 mL
1 cup	granulated sugar	250 mL
½ cup	butter or margarine, softened	125 mL
½ tsp	vanilla	2 mL
5	eggs	5
1 cup	milk (whole/homogenized)	250 mL
1 cup	sweetened condensed milk	250 mL
¾ cup	evaporated milk	175 mL
⅓ cup	liqueur or brandy (optional)	75 mL
TOPPING		
1 cup	granulated sugar	250 mL
1½ cups	whipping (35%) cream	375 mL
1 tsp	vanilla	5 mL

1. In a large bowl, combine flour and baking powder. Set aside.

2. In a large mixer bowl, on medium speed, cream sugar and butter until smooth. Beat in vanilla and then eggs, one at a time, beating well after each addition.

3. Gradually, by spoonfuls, add flour mixture to the creamed mixture, on low speed, mixing until well combined. Pour into prepared baking pan, spreading evenly.

4. Bake in preheated oven for 30 to 35 minutes or until a toothpick inserted in the center comes out clean and dry. Pierce top of cake with a fork or skewer in about 10 places. Let cool completely in pan on a wire rack.

5. In another bowl, combine milk, condensed milk, evaporated milk and liqueur (if using). Pour over top of the cooled cake and let soak in while chilling for at least 2 hours.

6. *Prepare the topping:* In a small bowl, whisk sugar, whipping cream and vanilla until thick. Spread over top of cake. Store in refrigerator until ready to serve (up 1 week).

Tip *If you want leftover whipped cream to retain its lightness, height and texture for a day or more, add 1 tsp (5 mL) of light corn syrup to each 1 cup (250 mL) of cream while whipping.*

Passover Wine Cake

Serves 10 to 12

- Preheat oven to 350°F (180°C)
- 10-inch (3 L) Bundt pan, heavily greased

½ cup	matzo cake meal	125 mL
¼ cup	potato starch or cornstarch	50 mL
6	eggs, separated, at room temperature	6
1 cup	granulated sugar, divided	250 mL
1 tsp	vanilla	5 mL
¼ cup	vegetable oil	50 mL
½ cup	apricot preserves	125 mL
2 tbsp	freshly squeezed lemon juice	25 mL
WINE SAUCE		
¼ cup	granulated sugar	50 mL
2 tbsp	water	25 mL
2 tbsp	freshly squeezed lemon juice	25 mL
¼ cup	sweet white wine	50 mL

1. In a small bowl, combine cake meal and potato starch.

2. In a small, clean mixer bowl, beat egg whites until foamy. Gradually add ½ cup (125 mL) of the sugar and beat until stiff peaks form.

3. In a large mixer bowl, beat egg yolks, vanilla and the remaining sugar until mixture is thick. Gently fold in egg white mixture and then the starch mixture. Drizzle the oil over the batter and mix gently into batter until well incorporated. Spoon into prepared baking pan.

4. Bake in preheated oven for 35 to 40 minutes or until a toothpick inserted in the center comes out clean and dry. Let cool in pan on a wire rack for 10 minutes, and then remove and place on wire rack to cool completely.

5. *Prepare the wine sauce:* In a small saucepan, combine sugar, water and lemon juice, bring to a simmer over low heat, and simmer for 2 to 3 minutes. Remove from heat and stir in wine.

6. Place cake on a serving plate and spoon wine sauce over cake until it is absorbed. Combine the apricot preserves and lemon juice and heat until melted, then brush over cake.

Tip *Cooling cakes in their pans on a rack will prevent sogginess, because the bottom of the pans will be cooled by the air.*

Sally Lunn Cake

Serves 12 to 16

- Preheat oven to 400°F (200°C)
- 10-inch (3 L) Bundt pan, greased and floured

3½ cups	all-purpose flour, divided	875 mL
¼ cup	granulated sugar	50 mL
1	package (¼ oz/7 g) quick-rise (instant) yeast (or 2¼ tsp/11 mL)	1
1 tsp	salt	5 mL
1 cup	milk	250 mL
½ cup	butter or margarine, cut into chunks	125 mL
¼ cup	water	50 mL
3	eggs, at room temperature	3

1. In a large mixer bowl, combine 1 cup (250 mL) of the flour, sugar, yeast and salt. Set aside.

2. In a medium saucepan, over low heat, combine milk, butter and water until liquids are warm, but butter does not need to melt.

3. Add butter mixture to flour mixture, beating on medium speed for about 2 to 3 minutes. Add eggs and another 1 cup (250 mL) of flour, beating on high speed for 2 to 3 minutes. Stir in enough of the remaining flour to make a stiff batter. Cover and let rise in a warm place for about 1 hour or until doubled in size.

4. Stir down and spoon into prepared baking pan. Cover and let rise in a warm place for about 45 minutes or until doubled in size again.

5. Bake in preheated oven for 30 to 35 minutes or until top is golden brown. Remove from pan onto a wire rack and let cool completely, or serve when just warm.

Tip *To test if yeast is still good, dissolve a bit of it in ¼ cup (50 mL) of warm water that has about 1 tsp (5 mL) of sugar dissolved in it. It should start bubbling in a few minutes. If it doesn't, or is slow, throw it away.*

Petits Fours

Makes about 54 tiny cakes

- Preheat oven to 350°F (180°C)
- 13- by 9-inch (3 L) metal baking pan, greased and floured

2 cups	sifted cake and pastry flour	500 mL
1 tbsp	baking powder	15 mL
¼ tsp	salt	1 mL
¼ cup	butter or margarine, softened	50 mL
¼ cup	shortening	50 mL

1¼ cups	granulated sugar, divided	300 mL
½ tsp	vanilla	2 mL
¼ tsp	almond extract	1 mL
¾ cup	milk	175 mL
6	egg whites	6

1. In a medium bowl, sift together flour, baking powder and salt.

2. In a large mixer bowl, cream butter and shortening until smooth. Gradually add 1 cup (250 mL) of the sugar, vanilla and almond extract, and beat until light and fluffy. Beat in flour mixture alternately with the milk, making 3 additions of flour and 2 of milk, on low speed, beating well after each addition.

3. In a small, clean mixer bowl, with clean beaters, beat egg whites until foamy. Gradually beat in the remaining sugar and beat until soft peaks form. Fold gently into the batter. Pour into prepared baking pan.

4. Bake in preheated oven for 40 to 45 minutes or until a toothpick inserted in the center comes out clean and dry. Let cool in pan on a wire rack for 10 minutes, then remove from pan and let cool completely on wire rack.

5. Cut cooled cake into 1½-inch (4 cm) squares or diamonds. Place squares into paper baking cups and decorate as desired.

Tip *To measure solid shortening, line your measuring cup with plastic wrap and then fill it with shortening. To remove the shortening, lift out with the plastic wrap. It will come out easily, and the cup will still be clean.*

Cheesecakes

Classic Cheesecake

Serves 12 to 16

- Preheat oven to 325°F (160°C)
- 9-inch (23 cm) springform pan, greased

GRAHAM CRUST

1½ cups	graham wafer crumbs (about 18 whole wafers)	375 mL
⅓ cup	confectioner's (icing) sugar	75 mL
½ cup	butter or margarine, melted	125 mL
1 tsp	ground cinnamon (optional)	5 mL

FILLING

1 lb	creamed cottage cheese	500 g
2	packages (each 8 oz/250 g) cream cheese, softened	2

1 1/2 cups	granulated sugar	375 mL
4	eggs, lightly beaten	4
3 tbsp	all-purpose flour	45 mL
3 tbsp	cornstarch	45 mL
1 tsp	vanilla	5 mL
1 tsp	grated lemon zest	5 mL
1 1/2 tbsp	freshly squeezed lemon juice	22 mL
2 cups	sour cream	500 mL
1/2 cup	butter or margarine, melted	125 mL
	Canned or fresh fruit	

1. *Prepare the crust:* In a bowl, combine graham crumbs, sugar, butter and cinnamon (if using). Press into the bottom of prepared baking pan.

2. *Prepare the filling:* In a large mixer bowl, on high speed, beat cottage cheese and cream cheese. Add sugar gradually and then beat in eggs, one at a time, beating after each addition.

3. Add the flour, cornstarch, vanilla, lemon zest and lemon juice, and beat on low speed until blended. Add the sour cream and melted butter and continue beating just until smooth and well blended. Pour over crust, spreading evenly.

4. Bake in preheated oven for 70 minutes or until firm around the edges and center is set. Let cool on a wire rack for 20 to 25 minutes, then chill in refrigerator for 3 hours or overnight. Before serving, run a spatula around the sides of cake, then release the clasp and remove. Leave bottom of pan in place and transfer to a serving plate.

5. When ready to serve, top with fruit, such as peach slices or raspberries, kiwi and strawberries.

Tip *Another method is to set aside sour cream and bake the cheesecake for 65 minutes. Remove from oven and spread the sour cream evenly over top. Return to oven and bake for another 5 minutes. Then proceed as above. To prevent cracking on top, let the sour cream come to room temperature first and place a shallow pan, half full of water, underneath on the lower rack while baking.*

● ●

New York–Style Cheesecake

Serves 10 to 12

- Preheat oven to 375°F (190°C)
- 9-inch (23 cm) springform pan, greased

CRUST

1/4 cup	finely chopped walnuts	50 mL
1/2 tsp	ground cinnamon	2 mL
1 3/4 cups	graham wafer crumbs (about 20 whole wafers)	425 mL
1/2 cup	butter or margarine, melted	125 mL

FILLING

3	packages (each 8 oz/250 g) cream cheese, softened	3
1 cup	granulated sugar	250 mL
2 tbsp	all-purpose flour	25 mL
1 tsp	vanilla	5 mL
1/2 tsp	finely grated lemon zest (optional)	1 mL
2	eggs	2
1	egg yolk	1
1/4 cup	milk	50 mL

1. *Prepare the crust:* In a bowl, combine walnuts, cinnamon and wafer crumbs. Mix well and stir in butter. Set aside 1/4 cup (50 mL), if you wish to use as topping. Press the remaining mixture on the bottom of the pan, spreading evenly and pressing about 2 inches up the sides. Set aside.

2. *Prepare the filling:* In a large mixer bowl, combine cream cheese, sugar, flour, vanilla and lemon zest (if using). Beat on medium speed until well combined. Reduce speed to low and add eggs and egg yolk until blended. Mix in milk. Pour over crust in pan and sprinkle the reserved crumb mixture evenly over top, if desired.

3. Bake in preheated oven for 40 to 50 minutes, until firm around the edges and center is set.

4. Let cool in pan on a wire rack for 15 minutes, then run a knife around edge to loosen the crust from the pan. Let cool a bit longer, about 30 minutes, and then remove sides of pan. Cover and chill in refrigerator for 4 to 6 hours before serving.

Variations *Fruit Topping: Before chilling, spread 1 can (19 oz/540 mL) of blueberry, cherry or any other flavor of pie filling over top.*

Streusel Topping: Spread a streusel topping (see recipe, page 543) over top of filling and then bake as above.

Raspberry Sauce: Combine 1 1/2 cups (375 mL) frozen raspberries, 1/4 cup (50 mL) granulated sugar, 1 tsp (5 mL) lemon juice and, if desired, 1 tbsp (15 mL) raspberry liqueur in a blender. Blend until smooth. Pour mixture into a sieve over a bowl to remove seeds. Spread evenly over top of filling and then bake as above.

Praline Topping: In a heavy skillet, cook 1/2 cup (125 mL) granulated sugar over medium heat until melted and dark golden. Stir in 1/3 cup (75 mL) whole blanched almonds until well coated. Lightly grease a baking sheet and pour mixture onto it. Set aside to cool completely, then break into pieces and place into a plastic bag. Roll with a rolling pin until coarsely crushed. Spread over top of cheesecake before chilling.

Caramel Apple Cheesecake

Serves 10 to 12

- Preheat oven to 400°F (200°C)
- 9-inch (23 cm) springform pan, lightly greased

CRUST

1½ cups	all-purpose flour	375 mL
¼ cup	granulated sugar	50 mL
½ cup	butter or margarine, softened	125 mL
1	egg yolk	1

FILLING

2 tbsp	butter or margarine	25 mL
2	apples (Granny Smith or any type preferred), peeled, thinly sliced	2
1½ tsp	milk	7 mL
20	soft vanilla caramels	20
½ cup	granulated sugar	125 mL
2	packages (each 8 oz/250 g) cream cheese, softened	2
1 tsp	vanilla	5 mL
2	eggs	2
½ cup	finely chopped pecans, hazelnuts or other nut	125 mL
	Vanilla ice cream (optional)	

1. *Prepare the crust:* In a small bowl, combine flour, sugar, butter and the egg yolk. Mix well and then press into bottom and about 1 inch (2.5 cm) up the sides of prepared baking pan. Bake in preheated oven for 15 minutes or until golden. Let cool completely. Reduce oven temperature to 325°F (160°C).

2. *Prepare the filling:* In a large skillet, melt butter. Add apples and cook over low heat until tender. Arrange apples on top of baked crust.

3. In a small saucepan, over low heat, combine milk and caramels, and cook until melted. Drizzle this mixture over the apples.

4. In a large mixer bowl, on medium speed, cream sugar and cream cheese until smooth. Add vanilla and beat in eggs, one at a time, beating until well blended. Spoon over the caramel-apple mixture.

5. Bake for 30 to 35 minutes or until firm around the edges and center is set. Let cool in pan for 20 to 25 minutes. Run a spatula around the sides of cake, then release the clasp and remove. Leave bottom of springform in place and let cool completely.

6. Chill in refrigerator for at least 30 minutes or until ready to serve. Sprinkle the nuts over top. Place a scoop of vanilla ice cream over each slice of cake, if desired.

Speedy Blueberry Cheesecake

Serves 6 to 8

- Preheat oven to 300°F (150°C)
- 9-inch (2.5 L) square baking pan or dish, ungreased

CRUST

½ cup	butter or margarine, softened	125 mL
¾ cup	granulated sugar, divided	175 mL
1¼ cups	finely crushed graham wafer crumbs (about 16 whole wafers)	300 mL

FILLING

2	eggs	2
1 tsp	vanilla	5 mL
1	package (8 oz/250 g) cream cheese, softened	1
Pinch	ground cinnamon	Pinch

TOPPING

1	can (19 oz/540 mL) blueberry pie filling	1
2 tbsp	freshly squeezed lemon juice	25 mL
	Whipped topping	

1. *Prepare the crust:* In a small bowl, combine butter, ¼ cup (50 mL) of the sugar and the graham wafer crumbs. Press into bottom of baking pan, evenly and firmly.

2. *Prepare the filling:* In a large mixer bowl, on medium speed, beat eggs until thick and pale yellow in color. Add the remaining sugar, vanilla and cream cheese, and beat until smooth and blended. Spoon over crumb crust.

3. Bake in preheated oven for 30 to 35 minutes or until firm around the edges and center is set. Let cool in pan on a wire rack, sprinkle cinnamon over top, and let cool completely.

4. *Prepare the topping:* In a small bowl, mix blueberry pie filling and lemon juice to blend. Pour over top of the cheesecake, spreading evenly, and chill in refrigerator for 3 to 4 hours, or preferably overnight. To serve, top a slice with a dollop of whipped topping.

Tip *Most cakes can be frozen for up to 6 months if completely cooled and not frosted, and if wrapped tightly in plastic wrap and then in foil. Cheesecakes and butter cakes are the best choices, because the higher the fat content, the better they take to the deep freeze. Thaw overnight in the refrigerator.*

Apple Crumb Coffee Cake (page 362)

Glazed Chocolate Pumpkin Loaf (page 366)

Traditional Angel Food Cake (Coconut and Strawberry variation, page 367)

Mom's Sour Cream Chocolate Layer Cake (page 375)

Mini Cheesecakes (page 388)

Pumpkin Cupcakes with Lemon Cream Cheese Frosting (page 399)

Old-Fashioned Cookie Sheet Apple Pie (page 410)

Southern Pecan Pie (page 432)

Lemon Tarts with Raspberry Glaze (page 435)

Tropical Fruit Crunch (page 446)

Apple Cream Cheese Turnovers (page 457)

Traditional Cream Scones (page 462)

Perfect Baked Custard (page 471)

Easy Mocha Mousse (page 481)

Clafloutis (page 490), made
with plums instead of apples

Bread Pudding with Lemon Sauce (page 501)

Deluxe Lemon Cheesecake

Serves 12 to 16
- Preheat oven to 350°F (180°C)
- 10-inch (25 cm) springform pan, greased

CRUST

2½ cups	crushed gingersnap cookies (about 40 cookies)	625 mL
⅓ cup	butter or margarine, melted	75 mL

FILLING

¾ cup	granulated sugar	175 mL
4	packages (each 8 oz/250 g) cream cheese, softened	4
4	eggs	4
2 tsp	freshly squeezed lemon juice	10 mL
1 tsp	vanilla	5 mL

1. *Prepare the crust:* In a small bowl, mix together cookie crumbs and butter. Mix well and press onto the bottom and up the sides of the prepared baking pan.

2. *Prepare the filling:* In a large mixer bowl, on medium speed, cream sugar and cream cheese. Add eggs, lemon juice and vanilla, and beat until smooth and well blended. Pour over crust, spreading evenly.

3. Bake in preheated oven for 45 to 55 minutes or until firm around the edges and center is set. Turn off oven, leave door ajar, and let cake cool for about 1 hour. Let cool completely in pan on a wire rack. Run a spatula around the sides of cake, then release the clasp and remove. Leave bottom of springform in place and chill in refrigerator for several hours before serving.

Tip *To minimize cracking in cheesecakes, put a shallow pan half full of hot water on the rack below your cake during baking. Then turn oven off, leave door ajar, and let cheesecake stand in oven for about 30 minutes. Remove from oven and refrigerate overnight.*

Cool Key Lime Cheesecake

Serves 10 to 12
- Preheat oven to 375°F (190°C)
- 9-inch (23 cm) springform pan, greased

CRUST

1¾ cups	graham wafer crumbs (about 20 whole wafers)	425 mL
¼ cup	granulated sugar	50 mL
½ cup	butter or margarine, melted	125 mL

FILLING

¾ cup	granulated sugar	175 mL
3	packages (each 8 oz/250 g) cream cheese, softened	3
3 tbsp	all-purpose flour	45 mL
1 cup	sour cream	250 mL
3	eggs	3
1 tbsp	grated Key lime zest (optional)	15 mL
⅔ cup	freshly squeezed Key lime juice	150 mL
1 tsp	vanilla	5 mL
	Drop of green food coloring (optional)	
	Whipping (35%) cream, whipped (optional)	
	Key limes, thinly sliced (optional)	

1. *Prepare the crust:* In a small bowl, combine wafer crumbs, sugar and melted butter. Mix well until crumbly. Press firmly onto the bottom and about 1½ inches (3.5 cm) up the sides of your prepared baking pan. Bake in preheated oven for 8 minutes or until golden. Let cool completely. Reduce oven temperature to 325°F (160°C).

2. *Prepare the filling:* In a large mixer bowl, on medium speed, cream sugar and cream cheese until smooth. Beat in flour and sour cream until well blended. Add eggs, one at a time, beating until well blended. Stir in lime zest (if using), lime juice, vanilla and food coloring (if using). Mix well. Pour over crust, spreading evenly.

3. Bake for 50 to 60 minutes or until firm around the edges and center is almost set. Let cool completely in pan on a wire rack. Run a spatula around the sides of cake, then release the clasp and remove. Leave bottom of springform in place and chill in refrigerator for several hours or overnight before serving. Garnish with dollops of whipped cream and very thin slices of key lime, if desired.

Tip *Key limes, grown mainly in Florida, are smaller and have a more yellow color than the more common Persian lime. Key limes can be found at specialty produce markets. To substitute for Key lime juice, use half Persian lime juice and half lemon juice.*

Layered Chocolate-Vanilla Cheesecake

Serves 10 to 12
- Preheat oven to 325°F (160°C)
- 9-inch (23 cm) springform pan, greased

CRUST

1¼ cups	graham wafer crumbs (about 16 whole wafers)	300 mL
⅓ cup	butter or margarine, melted	75 mL

FILLING

½ cup	granulated sugar	125 mL
2	packages (each 8 oz/250 g) cream cheese, softened	2
4	eggs	4
½ cup	whipping (35%) cream	125 mL
1 tbsp	cornstarch	15 mL
1 tsp	grated lemon zest	5 mL
1 tbsp	freshly squeezed lemon juice	15 mL
1 tsp	vanilla	5 mL
3 tbsp	unsweetened cocoa powder	45 mL
	Chocolate curls or shavings (optional)	

1. *Prepare the crust:* In a bowl, combine wafer crumbs and butter. Set aside ¼ cup (50 mL) of the crumb mixture for garnish, if desired. Press the remaining crumb mixture firmly onto bottom of prepared baking pan. Bake in preheated oven for 10 minutes or until golden. Let cool completely.

2. *Prepare the filling:* In a large mixer bowl, on medium speed, cream sugar and cream cheese until smooth. Add eggs, one at a time, beating well after each addition. Beat in whipping cream, cornstarch, lemon zest, lemon juice and vanilla, beating until smooth and thoroughly blended.

3. Place about one-third of the mixture in a small bowl. Sift cocoa powder over top and then fold in until well blended.

4. Spread half of the remaining vanilla mixture over top of crust. Top with the cocoa mixture, spreading evenly. Then spread the remaining vanilla mixture over top of the cocoa mixture.

5. Bake in preheated oven for 50 to 60 minutes or until firm around the edges and center is set. Turn off oven and keep oven door ajar to let cake cool for about 1 hour. Remove from oven and then chill in refrigerator for at least 6 to 8 hours before serving. Before serving, run a spatula around the sides of cake, then release the clasp and remove. Leave bottom of springform in place and transfer over to a serving plate.

6. If desired, to garnish, spread the reserved crumb mixture around edge of top of cake in a strip about 1 inch (2.5 cm) deep and place chocolate curls or shavings (if using) in the middle.

Tip *Here's how to make chocolate curls: For each square of chocolate you use, place square in microwave, on Defrost, for 1 minute, until slightly soft. Draw a vegetable peeler over the flat bottom surface and carefully lift curls with a toothpick. Place curls right onto your cake or on a plate to use when ready.*

All Chocolate Cheesecake

Serves 10 to 12
- Preheat oven to 350°F (180°C)
- 9-inch (23 cm) springform pan, lightly greased

CHOCOLATE CRUST

1 cup	finely crushed chocolate wafer crumbs (about 25 wafers)	250 mL
2 tbsp	granulated sugar	25 mL
3 tbsp	butter or margarine, melted	45 mL

CHOCOLATE FILLING

¾ cup	granulated sugar	175 mL
3	packages (each 8 oz/250 g) cream cheese, softened	3
1 tsp	vanilla	5 mL
3	eggs	3
3 oz	white chocolate, melted and cooled	90 g
2 tbsp	raspberry liqueur or syrup (optional)	25 mL
3 oz	semisweet chocolate, melted and cooled	90 g
	White and semisweet chocolate curls or shavings	

CHOCOLATE GLAZE

6 oz	semisweet chocolate, chopped	175 g
¾ cup	whipping (35%) cream	175 mL

1. *Prepare the crust:* In a small bowl, mix together wafer crumbs, sugar and melted butter until blended and crumbly. Press firmly onto bottom of your prepared baking pan. Bake in preheated oven for 10 minutes or until golden. Let cool completely. Increase oven temperature to 425°F (220°C).

2. *Prepare the filling:* In a large mixer bowl, on medium speed, cream sugar and cream cheese until smooth. Add vanilla and then eggs, one at a time, beating well after each addition. Place half of this batter in another bowl and stir in the melted white chocolate and liqueur (if using) and set aside.

3. To the remaining batter, add the melted semisweet chocolate and stir until well blended. Spoon this chocolate batter into the crust, spreading evenly. Slowly spoon the white chocolate batter over top, spreading evenly.

4. Bake for 10 minutes, then lower heat to 250°F (120°C) and bake for 35 to 40 minutes or until firm around the edges and center is set. Set on a wire rack and let cool completely in the pan. Run a spatula around the sides of cake, then release the clasp and remove. Leave bottom of springform in place and transfer over to a serving plate.

5. *Prepare the glaze:* In a small saucepan, over low heat, heat chocolate and whipping cream, stirring until melted and smooth. Spread over top of cake to cover completely and allow mixture to drizzle over the sides.

6. Garnish with white and semisweet chocolate curls or shavings. Chill in refrigerator for at least 30 minutes or until ready to serve.

No-Bake Mocha Cheesecake

Serves 12 to 16
- 13- by 9-inch (3 L) metal baking pan, lightly greased

CRUST

1¼ cups	finely crushed chocolate wafer cookies (about 36 wafers)	300 mL
¼ cup	granulated sugar	50 mL
⅓ cup	butter or margarine, melted	75 mL

FILLING

2	packages (each 8 oz/250 g) cream cheese, softened	2
1	can (10 oz/300 mL) sweetened condensed milk	1
⅔ cup	chocolate syrup	150 mL
2 tbsp	instant coffee powder or granules	25 mL
1 tbsp	hot water	15 mL
1 cup	whipping (35%) cream, whipped	250 mL

1. *Prepare the crust:* In a small bowl, mix together wafer crumbs, sugar and melted butter until mixture is crumbly. Set aside ¼ cup (50 mL) of the crumb mixture for garnish. Spread the remaining crumb mixture evenly onto bottom of prepared baking pan. Chill in refrigerator.

2. *Prepare the filling:* In a large mixer bowl, on medium speed, beat cream cheese until smooth. Add milk and chocolate syrup, beating just until well blended.

3. In another bowl, dissolve the coffee powder in the water. Stir into cheese mixture and mix well.

Gently fold in the whipped cream until mixture is well combined.

4. Pour into crust in pan, cover, and freeze for 6 to 8 hours, until firm. Sprinkle the reserved crumb mixture over top. Freeze for up to 6 months. Serve frozen.

Eggnog Cheesecake

Serves 12 to 16
- Preheat oven to 325°F (160°C)
- 9-inch (23 cm) springform pan, lightly greased

CRUST

1¾ cups	graham wafer crumbs (about 20 whole wafers)	425 mL
¼ cup	granulated sugar	50 mL
½ cup	butter or margarine, melted	125 mL

FILLING

1 cup	granulated sugar	250 mL
4	packages (each 8 oz/250 g) cream cheese, softened	4
3 tbsp	all-purpose flour	45 mL
½ tsp	ground nutmeg	2 mL
3 tbsp	rum	45 mL
1 tsp	vanilla	5 mL
2	eggs	2
1 cup	whipping (35%) cream	250 mL
4	egg yolks	4
	Whipped cream	
	Ground cinnamon or nutmeg	

1. *Prepare the crust:* In a small bowl, combine wafer crumbs, sugar and melted butter. Mix well until mixture is crumbly. Press firmly onto bottom and up the sides of prepared baking pan. Bake in preheated oven for 10 minutes or until golden. Let cool completely.

2. *Prepare the filling:* In a large mixer bowl, on medium speed, beat sugar and cream cheese until smooth. Add flour, nutmeg, rum and vanilla, and beat until well blended. Add the eggs, one at a time, beating after each addition, until blended. Beat in the whipping cream and egg yolks until well combined. Pour over crust, spreading evenly.

3. Bake for 70 to 75 minutes or until firm around the edges and the center is almost set. Let cool completely in pan on a wire rack. Run a spatula around the sides of cake, then release the clasp and remove. Leave bottom of springform in place and chill in refrigerator for 4 to 5 hours or overnight.

4. Garnish with whipped cream and then sprinkle with cinnamon or nutmeg, or decorate as desired.

Tropical Pineapple Cheesecake

Serves 12 to 16
- Preheat oven to 350°F (180°C)
- 13- by 9-inch (3 L) metal baking pan, lightly greased

CRUST

1 cup	finely crushed graham wafer crumbs (about 14 whole wafers)	250 mL
¼ cup	packed brown sugar	50 mL
½ tsp	ground cinnamon	2 mL
½ cup	butter or margarine, melted	125 mL

FILLING

1 cup	granulated sugar	250 mL
2	packages (each 8 oz/250 g) cream cheese, softened	2
5	eggs, separated	5
1	can (19 oz/540 g) crushed pineapple, well-drained	1

TOPPING

2 tbsp	granulated sugar	25 mL
2 cups	sour cream	500 mL
1 tsp	vanilla	5 mL

1. *Prepare the crust:* In a small bowl, combine wafer crumbs, brown sugar, cinnamon and melted butter. Reserve ¼ cup (50 mL) and set aside. Spread the remaining crumb mixture evenly onto bottom of prepared baking pan.
2. *Prepare the filling:* In a large mixer bowl, on medium speed, cream sugar, cream cheese and egg yolks until smooth.
3. In a small, clean mixer bowl, with clean beaters, beat the egg whites on high speed until stiff peaks form. Fold gently into the creamed mixture. Fold in pineapple and blend thoroughly. Pour onto crust, spreading evenly, and bake in preheated oven for 30 minutes. Sprinkle some of the reserved crumbs over top.
4. *Prepare the topping:* In a small bowl, combine sugar, sour cream and vanilla and mix with a fork or spoon. Spoon over top of cake. Sprinkle the remainder of reserved crumb mixture over top.
5. Reduce oven temperature to 300°F (150°C) and bake for another 5 to 10 minutes. Let cool in pan on a wire rack and then chill in refrigerator for at least 30 minutes or until ready to serve. Cut into squares.

Tip *To make sour cream last longer, turn its container upside down in the refrigerator. This prevents air from filling the top.*

Mini Cheesecakes

Makes 12 mini cheesecakes
- Preheat oven to 300°F (150°C)
- 12-cup muffin pan, lined with paper baking cups

12	chocolate wafer cookies	12
¾ cup	granulated sugar	175 mL
2	packages (each 8 oz/250 g) cream cheese, softened	2
1 tsp	vanilla	5 mL
2	eggs	2
1 cup	canned fruit pie filling (peach, blueberry, cherry)	250 mL

1. Place 1 chocolate wafer in the bottom of each muffin cup. Trim wafers to fit into bottom of cups, if necessary.
2. In a large mixer bowl, on medium speed, cream sugar and cream cheese until smooth. Add vanilla and then eggs, and beat until smooth and well blended. Spoon into muffin cups, over the wafer, filling each cup about three-quarters full.
3. Bake in preheated oven for 20 to 25 minutes or until set. Let cool in cups on a wire rack for about 20 minutes, and then remove carefully and let cool completely. Store in refrigerator for up to 3 days. Just before serving, top each cheesecake with a spoonful of pie filling.

Cupcakes

Everyday Cupcakes

Makes 12 cupcakes
- Preheat oven to 350ºF (180ºC)
- 12 muffin cups, greased or paper-lined

1²⁄₃ cups	sifted cake and pastry flour	400 mL
1½ tsp	baking powder	7 mL
1 cup	granulated sugar	250 mL
½ cup	butter or margarine, softened (or shortening)	125 mL
2	eggs, well beaten	2
½ cup	milk	125 mL
1 tsp	vanilla (or lemon extract)	5 mL

1. In a large bowl, sift together cake flour and baking powder.
2. In a medium mixer bowl, on medium speed, cream sugar and butter until light and fluffy. Beat in eggs.
3. Add flour mixture to creamed mixture alternately with the milk, a small amount at a time, beating after each addition. Add vanilla. Pour into prepared muffin cups, filling three-quarters full.
4. Bake in preheated oven for 20 to 25 minutes or until a toothpick inserted into the center of a cupcake comes out clean and dry. Let cool on a wire rack. Frost with your favorite frosting.

Tip *To substitute all-purpose flour for cake flour in a recipe, remove 2 tbsp (25 mL) of flour from every cup of all-purpose flour, and add 2 tbsp (25 mL) cornstarch.*

Traditional Vanilla Cupcakes

Makes 12 cupcakes
- Preheat oven to 375ºF (190ºC)
- 12 muffin cups, paper-lined

½ cup	butter (no substitute), softened	125 mL
2	eggs	2
½ cup	milk	125 mL
1 tsp	vanilla	5 mL
2 cups	sifted cake and pastry flour	500 mL
¾ cup	granulated sugar	175 mL
2 tsp	baking powder	10 mL
½ tsp	salt	2 mL

1. In a large mixer bowl, cream butter and eggs. Add milk and vanilla and beat on low speed until blended.

2. In a medium bowl, sift together cake flour, sugar, baking powder and salt. Add to creamed mixture and beat on medium speed until smooth and well blended. Spoon into prepared muffin cups, filling about three-quarters full.
3. Bake in preheated oven for 15 to 20 minutes or until a toothpick inserted in the center of a cupcake comes out clean and dry. Let cool in pan for 10 minutes, then remove and place on a wire rack to cool completely.

Tip *Because the cupcakes are a neutral vanilla, you can use any type of frosting — even a vanilla frosting with a few drops of food coloring. Or make a rainbow of cupcakes with different colors of frosting.*

Angel Food Cupcakes

Makes 24 cupcakes
- Preheat oven to 375ºF (190ºC)
- 24 muffin cups, lined with paper baking cups

12	egg whites (use large eggs)	12
1½ tsp	cream of tartar	7 mL
¼ tsp	salt	1 mL
1 cup	granulated sugar	250 mL
2 tsp	vanilla	10 mL
1 cup	cake and pastry flour	250 mL
½ cup	confectioner's (icing) sugar, sifted	125 mL
	Can of prepared frosting	

1. In a large mixer bowl, on medium speed, beat egg whites, cream of tartar and salt until mixture is foamy. Turn speed up to high and continue beating until soft peaks form. Gradually add sugar, by spoonfuls, then vanilla, beating until stiff, glossy peaks form.
2. In a small bowl, combine flour and confectioner's sugar. Sift over the beaten egg whites and fold into mixture until flour is well incorporated and no longer visible.
3. Spoon batter into prepared muffin cups, filling to top, and bake in preheated oven for 20 to 25 minutes or until a toothpick inserted in the center of a cupcake comes out clean and dry.
4. Remove from pan and let cool on a wire rack. When completely cooled, frost with your favorite frosting or sprinkle some confectioner's sugar over tops of cupcakes.

Tip *To make cupcakes and muffins uniform in size, use a ¼-cup (50 mL) measuring cup to fill each muffin cup, making each cup three-quarters full.*

Coconut Chiffon Cupcakes

Makes 30 cupcakes

- Preheat oven to 400°F (200°C)
- 30 muffin cups, lined with paper baking cups

2¼ cups	cake and pastry flour	550 mL
1½ cups	granulated sugar, divided	375 mL
1 tbsp	baking powder	15 mL
1 tsp	salt	5 mL
⅓ cup	vegetable oil	75 mL
1 cup	milk, divided	250 mL
1½ tsp	vanilla	7 mL
2	eggs, separated	2
1 cup	flaked or shredded coconut (sweetened or unsweetened)	250 mL

1. In a large mixer bowl, sift together flour, 1 cup (250 mL) of the sugar, baking powder and salt. Mix until well combined and make a well in the center. Add the oil, ½ cup (125 mL) of the milk and vanilla and beat, on medium speed, for 1 to 2 minutes, until blended.
2. Add the remaining milk and the egg yolks and beat for another 1 to 2 minutes.
3. In a small, clean mixer bowl, with clean beaters, on high speed, beat the egg whites until soft peaks form. Gradually add the remaining sugar, by spoonfuls, beating until stiff peaks form.
4. Fold egg white mixture into the batter, gently, until fully blended. Spoon into muffin cups, filling about three-quarters full. Sprinkle coconut on top of each.
5. Bake in preheated oven for 15 minutes or until golden and a toothpick inserted in the center of a cupcake comes out clean and dry. Let cool completely in pans on wire racks.

Spicy Cupcakes

Makes 12 cupcakes

- Preheat oven to 350°F (180°C)
- 12 muffin cups, greased or paper-lined

¼ cup	granulated sugar	50 mL
¼ cup	shortening or butter, softened	50 mL
1	egg	1
½ cup	unsulfured molasses	125 mL
½ cup	boiling water	125 mL
1¼ cups	all-purpose flour	300 mL
1 tsp	baking soda	5 mL
1 tsp	ground cinnamon	5 mL
½ tsp	ground nutmeg	2 mL
¼ tsp	ground cloves	1 mL
Pinch	salt	Pinch

1. In a large mixer bowl, cream sugar and shortening. Add egg and beat until smooth and blended.
2. In a small bowl, mix together molasses and boiling water.
3. In a medium bowl, combine flour, baking soda, cinnamon, nutmeg, cloves and salt. Mix together to blend. Add flour mixture to the creamed mixture alternately with the molasses mixture, beating well after each addition. Spoon into prepared muffin cups, filling about three-quarters full.
4. Bake in preheated oven for 18 to 20 minutes or until a toothpick inserted in the center of a cupcake comes out clean and dry. Let cool in pan for 5 minutes, then remove onto wire rack to cool completely.

Peanut Butter 'n' Jelly Cupcakes

Makes 24 cupcakes

- Preheat oven to 375°F (190°C)
- 24 muffin cups, paper-lined

2 cups	all-purpose flour	500 mL
2 tsp	baking powder	10 mL
½ tsp	salt	2 mL
½ cup	peanut butter, at room temperature	125 mL
⅓ cup	butter or shortening, softened	75 mL
1 tsp	vanilla	5 mL
1½ cups	firmly packed brown sugar	375 mL
2	eggs	2
¾ cup	milk	175 mL
½ cup	jelly or jam (your favorite)	125 mL

1. In a medium bowl, mix together flour, baking powder and salt until blended.
2. In a large mixer bowl, on medium speed, beat peanut butter, butter and vanilla until smooth. Gradually add brown sugar, beating until light and fluffy. Add eggs one at a time, beating after each addition.
3. Add flour mixture to creamed mixture alternately with the milk, mixing well. Spoon batter into prepared muffin cups, filling about half full. Drop a teaspoonful of the jelly into the center of each cup and top with the remaining batter.
4. Bake in preheated oven for 20 to 25 minutes or until a toothpick inserted into the center of a cupcake comes out clean and dry. Remove from pan immediately and let cool completely on a wire rack.

Cupcake Cones

Makes 24 cupcake cones
- Preheat oven to 350°F (180°C)
- 24 flat-bottom ice cream cones, placed in muffin cups

2 cups	all-purpose flour	500 mL
2½ tsp	baking powder	12 mL
½ tsp	salt	2 mL
1½ cups	firmly packed brown sugar	375 mL
⅓ cup	butter or margarine, softened	75 mL
½ cup	creamy peanut butter, at room temperature	125 mL
1 tsp	vanilla	5 mL
2	eggs	2
	White frosting	
½ cup	chopped peanuts or sprinkles	125 mL

1. In a large bowl, combine flour, baking powder and salt and mix well.
2. In a large mixer bowl, cream together brown sugar, butter and peanut butter until smooth. Beat in vanilla and then eggs. Add to flour mixture alternately with the milk, beating only until well incorporated. Spoon about 3 tbsp (45 mL) of the batter into each cone, leaving about ½ inch (1 cm) at the top of each cone.
3. Bake in preheated oven for 30 minutes or until a toothpick inserted in the center of a cupcake comes out clean and dry. Leave cones in pan for 10 minutes, then remove onto wire rack to cool completely.
4. Frost with a favorite white frosting and sprinkle peanuts or sprinkles over tops.

Creamy Cookie Cupcakes

Makes 24 cupcakes
- Preheat oven to 350°F (180°C)
- 24 muffin cups, greased or paper-lined

1	package (18 oz/510 g) white cake mix	1
⅓ cup	vegetable oil	75 mL
3	eggs, lightly beaten	3
10	cream-filled sandwich cookies, either vanilla or chocolate, cut into ¼-inch (0.5 cm) chunks	10
FROSTING		
2 tbsp	butter or margarine	25 mL
2 oz	unsweetened chocolate, chopped	60 g
1 cup	sifted confectioner's (icing) sugar	250 mL
¼ cup	milk	50 mL

1. Prepare cake mix according to directions on package, but mix with the oil and eggs. Add cookie chunks and stir until well incorporated.
2. Bake in preheated oven according to cupcake directions on package, but check cupcakes about 10 minutes before the suggested time. Let cool in cups for 10 minutes and then remove onto wire rack and let cool completely.
3. *Prepare the frosting:* In a small saucepan, over low heat, melt the butter and chocolate. Set aside to cool. Gradually whisk in confectioner's sugar until well blended. Beat in just enough milk until mixture is of an icing consistency. Spread over tops of cupcakes.

Rich Chocolate Cupcakes

Makes 12 cupcakes
- Preheat oven to 375°F (190°C)
- 12 muffin cups, greased or paper-lined

½ cup	butter or shortening	125 mL
1 cup	granulated sugar	250 mL
2	egg yolks	2
2 cups	all-purpose flour	500 mL
2 tsp	baking powder	10 mL
¼ tsp	baking soda	1 mL
¼ tsp	salt	1 mL
¾ cup	milk	175 mL
1 tsp	vanilla	5 mL
3 oz	unsweetened chocolate	90 g
2	egg whites	2
WHITE FLUFFY FROSTING		
1 lb	confectioner's (icing) sugar, sifted (about 3½ to 4 cups/875 mL to 1 L)	500 g
½ cup	unsalted butter or margarine, softened	125 mL
⅓ cup	milk	75 mL
¼ tsp	almond extract	1 mL

1. In a large mixer bowl, cream butter until smooth. Gradually add sugar, beating until fluffy.
2. In a small bowl or cup, beat the egg yolks well. Add to creamed mixture, beating until mixture is light and fluffy.
3. In a medium bowl, sift together flour, baking powder, baking soda and salt. Add to creamed mixture alternately with the milk, stirring only until well blended. Add vanilla and the melted chocolate and mix well.
4. In a small mixer bowl, beat egg whites until stiff peaks form. Fold into batter. Spoon into prepared muffin cups, filling about three-quarters full.

5. Bake in preheated oven for 20 to 25 minutes or until a toothpick inserted in the center comes out clean and dry. Let cool completely on a wire rack.

6. *Prepare the frosting:* In a small mixer bowl, beat confectioner's sugar, butter, milk and almond extract until smooth, about 3 to 5 minutes. Spread onto tops of cupcakes.

Variation *Instead of the white fluffy frosting, prepare your favorite chocolate frosting. Dip the tops of each cupcake into the chocolate frosting and sprinkle crushed nuts, grated white chocolate or any other decoration over top.*

- -

Chocolate Chip Instant Cupcakes

Makes 12 cupcakes

- Preheat oven to 375°F (190°C)
- 12 muffin cups, greased or paper-lined

1	package (18 oz/510 g) yellow cake mix	1
1	package (3 oz/90 g) instant vanilla pudding mix	1
4	eggs	4
1 cup	water	250 mL
½ cup	vegetable oil	125 mL
1 cup	mini or regular semisweet chocolate chips (about 6 oz/175 g) Can of prepared frosting (optional)	250 mL

1. In a large mixer bowl, combine cake mix, pudding mix, eggs, water and oil and beat on low speed until blended. Continue beating on medium speed for 5 minutes or until well incorporated.

2. Stir or fold in chocolate chips until well blended. Spoon into prepared muffin cups, filling three-quarters full.

3. Bake in preheated oven for 15 to 20 minutes or until a toothpick inserted in the center comes out clean and dry. Let cool in pan for 10 minutes, then remove onto wire rack to cool completely. Frost with prepared frosting, if desired, or leave plain.

Tip *To make cupcakes and muffins uniform in size, use a ¼-cup (50 mL) measuring cup to fill each muffin cup, making each cup three-quarters full.*

- -

Cream Cheese Chocolate Surprise

Makes 12 to 18 cupcakes

- Preheat oven to 350°F (180°C)
- 12 to 18 muffin cups, greased or paper-lined

1½ cups	all-purpose flour	375 mL
1 cup	granulated sugar	250 mL
¼ cup	unsweetened cocoa powder	50 mL
1 tsp	baking soda	5 mL
½ tsp	salt	2 mL
1 cup	water	250 mL
⅓ cup	vegetable oil	75 mL
1 tbsp	white vinegar	15 mL
1 tsp	vanilla	5 mL
	Sifted confectioner's (icing) sugar (optional)	
FILLING		
⅓ cup	granulated sugar	75 mL
1	package (8 oz/250 g) cream cheese, softened	1
1	egg	1
Pinch	salt	Pinch
1 cup	semisweet chocolate pieces or chips (about 6 oz/175 g)	250 mL

1. In a large bowl, combine flour, sugar, cocoa, baking soda and salt. Mix to blend and make a well in the center.

2. In a small bowl, whisk water, oil, vinegar and vanilla. Pour into flour mixture and stir until well blended.

3. *Prepare the filling:* In a medium mixer bowl, on medium speed, cream sugar and cream cheese until smooth. Beat in the egg and salt, beating until well incorporated. Stir in chocolate pieces and mix well.

4. Spoon batter into prepared muffin cups, filling only half full. Drop 1 tbsp (15 mL) of the filling over top, then top with the remaining batter.

5. Bake in preheated oven for 25 to 30 minutes or until a toothpick inserted into the center of a cupcake comes out clean and dry. Let cool in pan for 10 minutes, then remove onto wire rack to cool completely. Dust tops with confectioner's sugar, if desired.

Tip *You could use a chocolate cake mix with the filling instead.*

Chocolate Volcano Cupcakes

Makes 8 cupcakes
- Preheat oven to 350°F (180°C)
- Eight ¾-cup (175 mL) custard cups, greased and placed on a baking sheet

1 cup	all-purpose flour	250 mL
¼ tsp	salt	1 mL
1 cup	butter, softened	250 mL
½ cup	granulated sugar	125 mL
3	eggs	3
3	egg yolks	3
1 tsp	vanilla	5 mL
2 cups	semisweet chocolate chips, melted (about 12 oz/375 g)	500 mL
1 cup	ground pecans, toasted (optional)	250 mL
4 oz	white chocolate, cut into 8 pieces	125 g
	Sifted confectioner's (icing) sugar (optional)	

1. In a small bowl, mix together flour and salt.
2. In a large mixer bowl, cream butter and sugar until smooth. Add eggs, egg yolks and vanilla, beating on low speed. Beat in melted chocolate until well blended.
3. Add flour mixture to creamed mixture and stir in pecans (if using). Spoon into prepared custard cups and bake in preheated oven for 10 minutes.
4. Remove from oven and push one piece of the white chocolate into the center of each cupcake. Return to oven and bake for 15 to 20 minutes or until a toothpick inserted into a cupcake comes out clean and dry.
5. Remove from oven and let stand in cups for about 5 minutes. Run a knife around the edges of the custard cups and slowly invert each custard cup onto individual serving plates. Sprinkle some confectioner's sugar over tops, if desired.

Brownie Pecan Cupcakes

Makes 12 cupcakes
- Preheat oven to 350°F (180°C)
- 12 muffin cups, greased or paper-lined

½ cup	butter or margarine	125 mL
3 oz	unsweetened chocolate	90 g
2	eggs	2
1 cup	granulated sugar	250 mL
1½ tsp	vanilla	7 mL
⅔ cup	all-purpose flour	150 mL
¼ tsp	baking powder	1 mL
¼ cup	milk	50 mL
½ cup	finely chopped pecans or walnuts	125 mL

1. In a small saucepan, over low heat, melt butter and chocolate, stirring until melted. Remove from heat and set aside to cool.
2. In a medium mixer bowl, on high speed, beat eggs until frothy. Gradually beat in sugar until mixture is pale yellow in color and thick. Lower speed to low and add chocolate mixture and vanilla.
3. In a small bowl, mix together flour and baking powder. Beat flour mixture into egg mixture alternately with the milk. Stir in nuts. Spoon into prepared muffin cups, filling about three-quarters full.
4. Bake in preheated oven for 20 to 25 minutes or until a toothpick inserted in the center comes out only slightly wet. Let cool in pan for about 10 minutes, remove and let cool completely on a wire rack.

Devil's Food Cupcakes

Makes 18 cupcakes
- Preheat oven to 400°F (200°C)
- 18 muffin cups, lined with paper baking cups

2¼ cups	sifted cake and pastry flour	550 mL
1 tsp	baking powder	5 mL
1 tsp	baking soda	5 mL
1 tsp	salt	5 mL
⅔ cup	butter or margarine, softened	150 mL
2 cups	granulated sugar	500 mL
1¼ cups	milk	300 mL
3	eggs	3
1 tsp	red food coloring	5 mL
3 oz	unsweetened chocolate, melted	90 g

1. In a medium bowl, sift together flour, baking powder, baking soda and salt.
2. In a large mixer bowl, cream butter and sugar until smooth. Beat in flour mixture on low speed. Add milk, eggs and food coloring and beat on medium speed until well blended. Stir in melted chocolate and beat for another 2 to 3 minutes, until thoroughly combined.
3. Spoon into muffin cups, filling three-quarters full. Bake in preheated oven for 18 to 20 minutes or until a toothpick inserted in the center of a cupcake comes out clean and dry.
4. Let cool in muffin cups for 5 minutes, then remove from muffin cups and let cool completely on a wire rack. Decorate as desired.

Fudge Nut Cupcakes

Makes 18 to 24 cupcakes
- Preheat oven to 375°F (190°C)
- 18 to 24 muffin cups, greased or paper-lined

1⅓ cups	sifted all-purpose flour	325 mL
1 tsp	baking soda	5 mL
½ tsp	salt	2 mL
2 oz	unsweetened chocolate	60 g
1⅓ cups	lightly packed brown sugar, divided	325 mL
⅓ cup	milk	75 mL
⅓ cup	butter, or shortening, softened	75 mL
1 tsp	vanilla	5 mL
2	eggs	2
½ cup	milk	125 mL
½ cup	chopped nuts	125 mL

1. In a medium bowl, sift together flour, baking soda and salt.
2. In a small saucepan, over low heat, cook chocolate, half the brown sugar and the ⅓ cup (75 mL) milk, stirring until chocolate melts. Set aside to cool.
3. In a large mixer bowl, cream the remaining brown sugar, butter and vanilla until light and fluffy. Beat in eggs, one at a time, beating well after each addition. Add flour mixture alternately with the ½ cup (125 mL) of milk, beating well after each addition. Stir in chocolate mixture and then the nuts until well incorporated.
4. Spoon into prepared muffin cups, filling three-quarters full, and bake in preheated oven for 15 to 20 minutes or until a toothpick inserted in the center of a cupcake comes out clean and dry. Let cool for 10 minutes in pan, remove and place on a wire rack to cool completely.

Tip *To melt chocolate in the microwave, use chocolate chips, chocolate squares (each 1 oz/30 g) or small chunks of chocolate. Place in a microwave-safe bowl, cover tightly with plastic wrap and microwave on High for approximately 1 minute per ounce (30 g). (Times will vary depending on the power of your microwave and the quantity of chocolate used.) Remove from microwave and stir until smooth.*

Frosted Fudgey Cocoa Cupcakes

Makes 20 cupcakes
- Preheat oven to 375°F (190°C)
- 20 muffin cups, paper-lined

1¼ cups	all-purpose flour	300 mL
¾ cup	unsweetened cocoa powder	175 mL
1 tbsp	baking powder	15 mL
½ tsp	salt	2 mL
1¼ cups	granulated sugar	300 mL
½ cup	butter or margarine, softened	125 mL
3	eggs	3
1 tsp	vanilla	5 mL
⅔ cup	milk	150 mL
FUDGEY FROSTING		
⅓ cup	butter or margarine	75 mL
⅓ cup	unsweetened cocoa powder	75 mL
½ tsp	vanilla	2 mL
3 cups	sifted confectioner's (icing) sugar	750 mL
¼ cup	milk	50 mL

1. Sift together flour, cocoa, baking powder and salt.
2. In a large mixer bowl, cream sugar and butter until smooth. Beat in eggs, one at a time, beating well after each addition. Add vanilla. Add the cocoa mixture alternately with the milk and blend on low speed, combining lightly after each addition.
3. Spoon into prepared muffin cups evenly and bake in preheated oven for 20 to 25 minutes or until a toothpick inserted in the center of a cupcake comes out clean and dry. Let cool completely on a wire rack.
4. *Prepare the frosting:* In a small saucepan, melt the butter. Remove from heat and stir in the cocoa and vanilla. Stir in the confectioner's sugar alternately with the milk, stirring only until frosting is smooth and of spreading consistency. Spread frosting on tops of cooled cupcakes and decorate further if desired.

Tip *If you have a lot of leftover frosting, use it up making sandwich cookies from plain ones.*

Mini Cocoa Cupcakes

Makes 24 mini cupcakes

- Preheat oven to 350°F (180°C)
- 24 mini muffin cups, greased

1/3 cup	all-purpose flour	75 mL
3 tbsp	unsweetened cocoa powder	45 mL
1/2 tsp	ground cinnamon	2 mL
5	egg whites	5
1/2 tsp	cream of tartar	2 mL
2/3 cup	superfine granulated sugar	150 mL
TOPPING		
1/3 cup	semisweet chocolate chips (about 2 oz/60 g)	75 mL
3 tbsp	whipping (35%) cream	45 mL

1. In a medium bowl, sift flour, cocoa and cinnamon and mix to blend.
2. In a large mixer bowl, on medium speed, beat egg whites and cream of tartar until frothy. Add sugar, one spoonful at a time, beating for about 5 minutes, until mixture forms glossy, stiff peaks.
3. Fold half of the flour mixture into the egg whites. Gradually fold in the remaining flour mixture until well incorporated. Spoon into prepared muffin cups, using a teaspoon or a melon ball scoop, filling each to the top.
4. Bake in preheated oven for 15 to 20 minutes or until puffy and a toothpick inserted into the center comes out dry. Let cool in pan for 5 minutes and then remove onto wire rack to cool completely.
5. *Prepare the topping:* In a small saucepan, over low heat, cook chocolate chips and cream, whisking until melted and smooth. Dip tops of the mini cupcakes into the melted chocolate mixture, then stand upright on a baking sheet or waxed paper.

Cocoa-Cola Cupcakes

Makes 12 cupcakes

- Preheat oven to 350°F (180°C)
- 12 muffin cups, greased or paper-lined

2 cups	all-purpose flour	500 mL
1 1/4 cups	granulated sugar	300 mL
1/2 cup	unsweetened cocoa powder	125 mL
1/2 tsp	salt	2 mL
1/2 tsp	baking soda	2 mL
2/3 cup	milk	150 mL
1/2 cup	vegetable oil	125 mL
3	eggs	3
1/2 tsp	vanilla	2 mL
1	bottle or can (12 oz/355 mL) cola	1

1. In a large bowl, combine flour, sugar, cocoa, salt and baking soda. Mix well to blend. Make a well in the center.
2. In a small bowl, whisk milk, oil, eggs and vanilla. Add cola and whisk until blended. Pour into flour mixture and mix until well incorporated. Spoon into prepared muffin cups.
3. Bake in preheated oven for 30 to 35 minutes or until a toothpick inserted into the center of a cupcake comes out clean and dry. Let cool on a wire rack.

Coconut Cupcakes

Makes 24 cupcakes

- Preheat oven to 400°F (200°C)
- 24 muffin cups, greased or paper-lined

2 1/4 cups	sifted cake and pastry flour	550 mL
1 1/2 cups	granulated sugar, divided	375 mL
1 tbsp	baking powder	15 mL
1 tsp	salt	5 mL
1 cup	milk, divided	250 mL
1/3 cup	vegetable oil	75 mL
1 1/2 tsp	vanilla	7 mL
2	eggs, separated	2
1 1/3 cups	flaked sweetened coconut	325 mL
	Can of prepared frosting	

1. In a large mixer bowl, sift together cake flour, 1 cup (250 mL) of the sugar, baking powder and salt. Mix well.
2. In a small bowl, combine 1/2 cup (125 mL) of the milk, oil and vanilla. Pour into flour mixture and stir with a spoon until blended. Then beat on medium speed for about 2 minutes, scraping sides of bowl. Add the remaining milk and the egg yolks and beat for another 2 minutes.
3. In a small mixer bowl, beat egg whites until soft peaks form. Gradually add the remaining sugar, beating until stiff peaks form. Gently fold into batter.
4. Spoon into prepared muffin cups, filling about three-quarters full. Top with the coconut. Bake in preheated oven for 12 to 15 minutes or until a toothpick inserted in the center comes out clean and dry. Frost with a creamy frosting, such as cream cheese frosting.

Lemon Cupcakes

Makes 18 cupcakes

- Preheat oven to 350°F (180°C)
- 18 muffin cups, lined with paper baking cups

2¾ cups	cake flour	675 mL
1½ cups	granulated sugar	375 mL
2½ tsp	baking powder	12 mL
½ tsp	salt	2 mL
4	eggs	4
¾ cup	buttermilk	175 mL
2 tbsp	grated lemon zest	25 mL
2 tbsp	freshly squeezed lemon juice	25 mL
1 cup	butter or margarine, softened	250 mL

1. In a medium bowl, combine flour, sugar, baking powder and salt.
2. In a large mixer bowl, on medium speed, beat together eggs, buttermilk, lemon zest and lemon juice until well combined. Add half of flour mixture and the butter to the egg mixture, and beat on low speed until well blended. Add the remaining flour mixture and beat until well blended.
3. Spoon into muffin tins until three-quarters full. Bake in preheated oven for 18 to 20 minutes or until a toothpick inserted in the center of a cupcake comes out clean and dry. Let cool completely on a wire rack.

Tip *If desired, frost with your favorite frosting or drizzle with a lemon glaze.*

Grandma's Lemon Cupcakes

Makes 24 to 30 cupcakes

- Preheat oven to 350°F (180°C)
- 24 to 30 muffin cups, greased or paper-lined

3½ cups	all-purpose flour	875 mL
2 tsp	baking powder	10 mL
1 tsp	baking soda	5 mL
½ tsp	salt	2 mL
1¾ cups	granulated sugar	425 mL
1 cup	butter or margarine, softened	250 mL
1 tsp	vanilla	5 mL
3	eggs	3
2 tsp	grated lemon zest	10 mL
2 cups	sour cream	500 mL

1. In a medium bowl, mix together flour, baking powder, baking soda and salt until blended.

2. In a large mixer bowl, on medium-high speed, cream sugar, butter and vanilla until smooth and fluffy. Add eggs one at a time, beating well after each addition. Add lemon zest and mix well.
3. Add flour mixture to creamed mixture alternately with the sour cream, beating until well incorporated and blended. Spoon into prepared muffin cups, filling about three-quarters full.
4. Bake in preheated oven for 25 to 30 minutes or until a toothpick inserted in the center of a cupcake comes out clean and dry. Let cool in pan for 5 to 10 minutes, then remove onto wire rack and let cool completely.

Banana Cupcakes

Makes 12 cupcakes

- Preheat oven to 400°F (200°C)
- 12 muffin cups, greased or paper-lined

1 cup	granulated sugar	250 mL
½ cup	butter or margarine, softened	125 mL
2	eggs	2
1 tsp	vanilla	5 mL
1¾ cups	all-purpose flour	425 mL
½ tsp	salt	2 mL
½ tsp	baking powder	2 mL
½ tsp	baking soda	2 mL
3	large ripe bananas, cut into 1-inch (2.5 cm) chunks	3
⅓ cup	sour cream	75 mL

1. In a large mixer bowl, cream sugar and butter until light and fluffy. Add eggs one at a time, beating after each addition. Beat in vanilla.
2. In a medium bowl, sift together flour, salt, baking powder and baking soda.
3. In a blender or food processor, purée bananas and sour cream until smooth.
4. Add flour mixture and banana mixture alternately to the egg mixture, stirring only until blended and moistened. Spoon into prepared muffin cups.
5. Bake in preheated oven for 15 to 20 minutes or until a toothpick inserted into the center of a cupcake comes out clean and dry. Let cool in pan for 10 minutes, then remove onto wire rack to cool completely.

Tip *If you have a lot of overripe bananas, don't throw them away. Save them by peeling, slicing and puréeing them in the blender with a few drops of lemon juice to prevent browning. Freeze in zippered freezer bags and keep handy for future recipes.*

Candy Apple Cupcakes

Makes 12 cupcakes
- Preheat oven to 350°F (180°C)
- 12 muffin cups, greased or paper-lined

1⅓ cups	all-purpose flour	325 mL
1½ tsp	ground cinnamon	7 mL
1 tsp	baking powder	5 mL
½ tsp	baking soda	2 mL
½ tsp	salt	2 mL
½ tsp	ground nutmeg	2 mL
Pinch	ground cloves	Pinch
¾ cup	granulated sugar	175 mL
⅓ cup	butter or margarine, softened	75 mL
2	eggs	2
1 tsp	vanilla	5 mL
¾ cup	sweetened applesauce (or use 2 apples, peeled and chopped)	175 mL

TOPPING

20	caramels	20
3 tbsp	milk	45 mL
1 cup	finely chopped pecans or walnuts	250 mL
12	Popsicle sticks	12

1. In a large bowl, combine flour, cinnamon, baking powder, baking soda, salt, nutmeg and cloves. Mix well.

2. In a large mixer bowl, on medium speed, cream sugar and butter. Add eggs and vanilla and beat until well mixed.

3. Add flour mixture alternately with applesauce into the egg mixture and mix until just blended and moistened. Do not overmix.

4. Spoon into prepared baking cups and bake in preheated oven for 25 minutes or until a toothpick inserted in the center of a cupcake comes out clean and dry. Let cool in pan for 10 minutes, then remove from pan and let cool completely on a wire rack.

5. *Prepare the topping:* In a small saucepan, over low heat, cook caramels and milk until smooth. Spread over tops of cupcakes. Sprinkle chopped nuts over top. Insert a Popsicle stick into the center of each cupcake.

Tip *To make a delicious instant frosting for cupcakes, top each one with a marshmallow about 2 minutes before taking them out of the oven. The marshmallows will melt onto the cupcakes and become frosting. Then decorate as you wish with sprinkles, shaved chocolate, etc.*

Maraschino Cherry Cupcakes

Makes 12 cupcakes
- Preheat oven to 350°F (180°C)
- 12 muffin cups, greased or paper-lined

¾ cup	granulated sugar	175 mL
½ cup	butter or margarine, softened	125 mL
2	eggs	2
1⅓ cups	all-purpose flour	325 mL
1 tsp	baking powder	5 mL
¼ cup	syrup from jar of maraschino cherries	50 mL
¼ cup	milk	50 mL
1 tsp	vanilla	5 mL
¼ tsp	almond extract	1 mL
¼ cup	drained and finely chopped maraschino cherries (about 15 to 20 cherries)	50 mL

1. In a large mixer bowl, cream sugar and butter until light and fluffy. Beat in eggs, one at a time, just until blended.

2. In a small bowl, whisk flour and baking powder until blended.

3. In another small bowl, combine cherry syrup, milk, vanilla and almond extract.

4. Beat flour mixture into creamed mixture alternately with the cherry syrup mixture, beating on low just until blended. Stir in cherries and mix well. Spoon into prepared muffin cups, filling about three-quarters full.

5. Bake in preheated oven for 20 to 25 minutes or until golden brown and a toothpick inserted in the center comes out clean and dry. Let cool in pan for 10 minutes, then remove and let cool completely on a wire rack.

Frozen Fruit Cupcakes

Makes 18 cupcakes
- 18 muffin cups, paper-lined

1	can (10 oz/284 mL) mandarin orange segments, drained	1
1	jar (12 oz/375 mL) maraschino cherries, drained	1
½ cup	granulated sugar	125 mL
1	package (8 oz/250 g) cream cheese, softened	1
1	can (8 oz/227 mL) crushed pineapple, drained	1
½ cup	chopped nuts (pecans or other)	125 mL

| 1 cup | frozen whipped topping, thawed (about 8 oz/250 g) | 250 mL |

1. Set aside 18 orange segments and 9 halved cherries, then chop the remaining cherries.
2. In a large mixer bowl, on medium speed, cream sugar and cream cheese until smooth and fluffy. Add the pineapple, pecans and chopped cherries and mix until well incorporated. Fold in the whipped topping and the remaining orange segments.
3. Spoon mixture into the prepared muffin cups. Top each with a reserved cherry half and orange segment. Freeze in freezer until firm. Remove from freezer about 10 minutes before serving.

• •

Pumpkin Cupcakes with Lemon Cream Cheese Frosting

Makes 12 cupcakes
- Preheat oven to 350°F (180°C)
- 12 muffin cups, greased or paper-lined

1¼ cups	granulated sugar	300 mL
1¼ cups	canned pumpkin purée (not pie filling)	300 mL
½ cup	vegetable oil	125 mL
2	eggs	2
1⅓ cups	all-purpose flour	325 mL
2 tsp	ground cinnamon	10 mL
1½ tsp	baking powder	7 mL
½ tsp	baking soda	2 mL
½ tsp	salt	2 mL
½ tsp	ground ginger	2 mL
LEMON CREAM CHEESE FROSTING		
1	package (8 oz/250 g) cream cheese, softened	1
1 cup	sifted confectioner's (icing) sugar Finely grated zest of 1 lemon	250 mL
2 to 3 tbsp	freshly squeezed lemon juice	25 to 45 mL

1. In a large bowl, whisk together sugar, pumpkin, oil and eggs until well blended.
2. In a small bowl, mix together flour, cinnamon, baking powder, baking soda, salt and ginger. Add flour mixture to pumpkin mixture and mix well. Spoon into prepared muffin cups, filling about three-quarters full.
3. Bake in preheated oven for 18 to 20 minutes or until a toothpick inserted in the center of a cupcake comes out clean and dry. Let cool in pan for 10 minutes, then remove onto wire rack to cool completely.

4. *Prepare the frosting:* In a small mixer bowl, beat cream cheese and confectioner's sugar until smooth. Add lemon zest and juice and continue to beat until smooth and blended. Swirl the tops of each cupcake with frosting.

• •

Caramel Zucchini Cupcakes

Makes 20 to 24 cupcakes
- Preheat oven to 350°F (180°C)
- 20 to 24 muffin cups, greased or paper-lined

2½ cups	all-purpose flour	625 mL
2 tsp	baking powder	10 mL
2 tsp	ground cinnamon	10 mL
1 tsp	salt	5 mL
1 tsp	baking soda	5 mL
½ tsp	ground cloves	2 mL
1¼ cups	granulated sugar	300 mL
½ cup	vegetable oil	125 mL
½ cup	freshly squeezed orange juice	125 mL
3	eggs	3
1 tsp	almond extract	5 mL
1½ cups	shredded zucchini	375 mL
CARAMEL FROSTING		
1 cup	firmly packed brown sugar	250 mL
½ cup	butter or margarine	125 mL
¼ cup	milk	50 mL
1 tsp	vanilla	5 mL
1¾ cups	sifted confectioner's (icing) sugar	425 mL

1. In a medium bowl, combine flour, baking powder, cinnamon, salt, baking soda and cloves. Whisk together until well blended.
2. In a large mixer bowl, on medium speed, combine sugar, oil, orange juice, eggs and almond extract, beating just to blend.
3. Add the flour mixture to the egg mixture and mix until well incorporated. Add zucchini and mix well. Spoon into prepared muffin cups, filling about three-quarters full.
4. Bake in preheated oven for 20 to 25 minutes or until a toothpick inserted in the center of a cupcake comes out clean and dry. Let cool in pan for 10 minutes, then remove onto wire rack to cool completely.
5. *Prepare the frosting:* In a medium saucepan, over medium heat, combine brown sugar, butter and milk and bring to a boil, stirring for 2 minutes. Remove from heat, add vanilla, mix well and let cool until lukewarm. Whisk in the confectioner's sugar, beating until mixture is of the right spreading consistency. Spread over tops of cupcakes.

Chocolate Walnut Carrot Cupcakes

Makes 18 cupcakes
- Preheat oven to 350°F (180°C)
- 18 muffin cups, lined with paper baking cups

2 cups	all-purpose flour	500 mL
2 cups	granulated sugar	500 mL
⅓ cup	unsweetened cocoa powder, sifted	75 mL
1 tsp	baking powder	5 mL
1 tsp	baking soda	5 mL
1 tsp	ground cinnamon	5 mL
4	eggs	4
1 cup	vegetable oil	250 mL
3 cups	finely grated carrots (about 6 medium)	750 mL
¾ cup	chopped walnuts	175 mL

1. In a large mixer bowl, combine flour, sugar, cocoa powder, baking powder, baking soda and cinnamon.
2. In another bowl, whisk eggs and oil. Stir in carrots and walnuts and mix well. Add to flour mixture and beat on medium speed until thoroughly combined.
3. Spoon into prepared muffin cups until three-quarters full. Bake in preheated oven for 18 to 20 minutes or until toothpick inserted in center of a cupcake comes out clean and dry. Remove from muffin cups and let cool on a wire rack until completely cooled.

Tip *Frost with your favorite frosting, if desired, and sprinkle some chopped nuts over top.*

Rice Cupcakes

Makes 14 to 16 cupcakes
- Preheat oven to 400°F (200°C)
- 14 to 16 muffin cups, greased or paper-lined

2	eggs	2
¼ cup	packed brown sugar	50 mL
1 cup	cooked white rice	250 mL
1 cup	all-purpose flour	250 mL
1 tbsp	baking powder	15 mL
¼ tsp	salt	1 mL
¾ cup	milk	175 mL
2 tbsp	butter or margarine, melted	25 mL
½ tsp	vanilla	2 mL

1. In a large mixer bowl, beat eggs. Add brown sugar and beat well. Stir in the rice and mix to blend.
2. In a small bowl, combine flour, baking powder and salt. Stir into egg and rice mixture, mixing until well blended. Add the melted butter and vanilla and beat until well combined. Spoon into prepared muffin cups, filling about three-quarters full.
3. Bake in preheated oven for 25 to 30 minutes or until a toothpick inserted in the center of a cupcake comes out clean and dry. Let cool on a wire rack.

Pies and Tarts

Pie Pastry and Crusts

Fruit Pies

continued on next page

Chocolate Pies

Other Pies

Tarts

Pie Pastry and Crusts

To mix and roll out the dough, follow the steps in "Making a Perfect Pie Crust," page 9, unless otherwise directed.

● ●

Single-Crust Plain Pastry

Makes enough for one 9-inch (23 cm) single-crust pie
- Preheat oven to 450°F (230°C)
- 9-inch (23 cm) pie plate

1½ cups	all-purpose flour	375 mL
½ tsp	salt	2 mL
½ cup	cold shortening, cubed	125 mL
2 to 4 tbsp	cold water	25 to 50 mL

1. In a large bowl, sift together flour and salt. Cut in the shortening with a pastry blender or two knives until mixture resembles coarse meal.
2. Sprinkle 1 tbsp (15 mL) of the water over part of the flour mixture and toss lightly with a fork. Push this to the side of the bowl. Repeat this procedure, using just enough water until all of the flour mixture is moistened. Form dough into a ball. Flatten slightly into a circle and wrap in plastic wrap. Chill in refrigerator for about 30 minutes.
3. On a lightly floured surface, roll the dough out and transfer to the pie plate. Turn edges under and flute or crimp as desired. Refrigerate for about 15 minutes or until chilled.
4. If a baked pie shell is needed, prick the bottom and sides well with a fork so that your pastry does not puff up while baking. If your recipe requires the filling and crust to be baked together, do not prick the pastry. Just add the filling and bake as directed.
5. Bake in preheated oven for 10 to 12 minutes or until golden brown.

Tip *To add great flavor and color to a plain pastry crust, add 1 tbsp (15 mL) of minced fresh parsley to the flour mixture before cutting in the butter.*

Variations *Poppy Seed Pastry: Add 1 tsp (5 mL) poppy seeds to the flour mixture before adding the water.*

Pecan Pastry: Add 3 tbsp (45 mL) finely chopped pecans to the flour mixture before adding the water.

Lemon Pastry: Add ½ tsp (2 mL) grated lemon zest to the flour mixture, and substitute 1 tbsp (15 mL) lemon juice for 1 tbsp (15 mL) of the water.

● ●

Double-Crust Pie Pastry

Makes enough for one 9-inch (23 cm) double-crust pie or twenty-four 2½-inch (6 cm) tarts
- 9-inch (23 cm) pie plate

2 cups	all-purpose flour	500 mL
1 tsp	salt	5 mL
¾ cup	cold shortening, cubed	175 mL
3 to 5 tbsp	cold water	45 to 75 mL

1. In a large bowl, combine flour and salt. Cut in shortening, using a pastry blender or two knives, until mixture resembles coarse crumbs or large peas.
2. Sprinkle with cold water, 1 tbsp (15 mL) at a time, tossing lightly with a fork. Add just enough water, a spoonful at a time, to form dough into a ball.
3. Divide dough in half. Shape each half into a ball and flatten slightly into a circle with the palm of your hand. Wrap each separately in plastic wrap and chill in refrigerator for 15 to 30 minutes for easier rolling.
4. On lightly floured surface, roll half the dough out and transfer it to the pie plate. To repair any tears, moisten edges and press together. Trim edge even with pie plate. Dampen edges of dough and fill with desired filling .
5. Roll out the remaining dough 1 inch (2.5 cm) larger than the pie plate and place on top of filling. Fold under and flute or crimp as desired. Cut slits in top to allow steam to escape.
6. Bake as directed in recipe.

Tips *Get a rich, flaky, melt-in-your-mouth pie crust by substituting the same amount of sour cream for any water in the recipe.*

It is best to make your pie dough the day before and let it rest overnight in the refrigerator. You will find you have a much better dough, and there will be less shrinkage.

All-Purpose No-Fail Pie Pastry

Makes enough for two 9-inch (23 cm) double-crust pies and one 9-inch (23 cm) single-crust pie

4 cups	all-purpose flour	1 L
1 tbsp	granulated sugar	15 mL
2 tsp	salt	10 mL
1¾ cups	shortening (no substitutes), at room temperature	425 mL
½ cup	water	125 mL
1 tbsp	white or cider vinegar	15 mL
1	egg	1

1. In a large bowl, combine flour, sugar and salt. Mix with a fork to blend. Add the shortening and mix again with the fork, or a pastry blender, until mixture is crumbly.
2. In another bowl, whisk water, vinegar and egg. Pour into flour mixture and mix together until moistened and blended.
3. Divide dough into five portions and shape each portion with your hands into a flat, round patty. Wrap each separately in plastic wrap. Chill in refrigerator for at least 30 minutes or freeze in an airtight container for up to 3 months. Thaw in refrigerator before using.

Variations *Lemon-Lime Soda Pie Pastry: Use 5½ cups (1.375 L) flour, ¾ tsp (4 mL) baking soda, ½ tsp (2 mL) salt, 1 lb (500 g) cold shortening and 1 can (12 oz/340 mL) cold lemon-lime soda in place of the above ingredients, then follow the same instructions.*

Brown Sugar Pastry: Use 5½ cups (1.375 L) flour, 1¼ tsp (6 mL) salt, 1 tsp (5 mL) baking powder, 1 lb (500 g) lard, 1 egg (lightly beaten with a fork), 2 tbsp (25 mL) packed brown sugar and 1 tbsp (15 mL) vinegar. Proceed as above, but put egg into a 1-cup (250 mL) measuring cup, add the brown sugar and vinegar, and then fill with cold water to the top. Then add to the flour and lard mixture.

Flaky Double-Crust Pastry

Makes enough for one 9-inch (23 cm) double-crust pie

- 9-inch (23 cm) deep-dish pie plate

2 cups	cake and pastry flour	500 mL
¾ tsp	salt	4 mL
¼ tsp	granulated sugar	1 mL
⅔ cup	cold shortening, cut in chunks	150 mL
1 tsp	white vinegar or lemon juice	5 mL
3 tbsp	ice water	45 mL

1. In a large bowl, combine flour, salt and sugar, and mix well to blend. Cut in the chunks of shortening, using a pastry blender or two knives, until the mixture resembles small peas.
2. Sprinkle the vinegar and ice water over the flour mixture, one spoonful at a time. Stir with a fork.
3. Press together with your hand until particles begin to cling and can be formed into a rough ball that cleans the bowl. If the dough is too dry, break open the ball and sprinkle a few more drops of water, then press together again. Dough should not be wet and sticky.
4. Divide dough in half, with a little more in one portion. The larger half will be used for the bottom crust, and the other for the top crust. Flatten each slightly into a round circle and wrap separately in waxed paper. Chill in freezer until dough is firm but still pliable, about 15 minutes.
5. Set the larger portion on a floured surface, lightly flour your rolling pin and roll out the dough into a circle wide enough to fit your pie plate. Press down lightly into the plate and trim off excess. Dampen the edge and fill with the filling.
6. Roll out the remaining dough 1 inch (2.5 cm) larger than the pie plate and place on top of filling. Fold under and flute or crimp as desired. Cut slits in top to allow steam to escape.
7. Bake as directed in recipe.

Tip *This pastry is too fragile for deep tarts such as Classic Butter Tarts, Chocolate Butter Tarts or Old-Fashioned Chess Tarts.*

Dry Pastry Mix

Makes enough for six 9-inch (23 cm) single-crust pies

6 cups	all-purpose flour	1.5 L
1 tbsp	salt	15 mL
1 lb	lard or shortening, cut into cubes	500 g

1. In a large bowl, combine the flour and salt. Cut in the lard with a pastry blender or two knives until mixture resembles coarse crumbs.
2. Cover and keep on a cupboard shelf until ready to use, or for up to 1 month.
3. Use 2 cups (500 mL) of the mix (unsifted) and 2½ tbsp (32 mL) of water for a single-crust pie.
4. For a double-crust pie, use 2⅔ cups (650 mL) of the mix and ¼ cup (50 mL) of water.

Rich Pastry

Makes enough for two 9-inch (23 cm) single-crust pies

• Two 9-inch (23 cm) pie plates

½ cup	butter	125 mL
¼ cup	shortening	50 mL
3 tbsp	granulated sugar	45 mL
1 tsp	grated lemon zest	5 mL
2 cups	all-purpose flour	500 mL

1. In a large bowl, cream butter, shortening and sugar until smooth. Add lemon zest.
2. Stir in flour gradually until well blended and shape into a ball.
3. Divide dough in half. Press each into the bottom and up the sides of the pie plates.
4. If not using immediately, wrap in plastic and keep chilled in refrigerator for up to 2 days, or freeze for up to 3 months. Before using pastry, bring to room temperature. If frozen, thaw in refrigerator.
5. Bake as directed in recipe.

Egg Yolk Pastry

Makes enough for three 9-inch (23 cm) double-crust pies or six 9-inch (23 cm) single-crust pies

5 cups	sifted all-purpose flour	1.25 L
4 tsp	granulated sugar	20 mL
½ tsp	salt	2 mL
½ tsp	baking powder	2 mL
1½ cups	lard or shortening	375 mL
2	egg yolks	2
	Cold water	

1. In a large bowl, combine flour, sugar, salt and baking powder. Cut in lard with a pastry blender or two knives until mixture is crumbly.
2. In a measuring cup, beat egg yolks lightly with a fork, then beat in enough cold water to bring the measure to just under 1 cup (250 mL).
3. Sprinkle the egg yolk and water mixture over the flour mixture, 1 tbsp (15 mL) at a time, tossing with the fork, just until dough is moist and will hold together.
4. Divide into six even balls and press each into a flat, round patty. Wrap in plastic wrap and chill for at least 30 minutes or freeze for up to 3 months. Thaw in refrigerator overnight before rolling, if necessary.
5. Roll out dough as directed in recipe.

Hot-Water Pastry

Makes enough for one 9-inch (23 cm) double-crust pie

½ cup	shortening	125 mL
½ cup	boiling water	125 mL
2¾ cups	all-purpose flour	675 mL
½ tsp	baking powder	2 mL
½ tsp	salt	2 mL

1. In a small bowl, melt shortening with the boiling water. Set aside to cool.
2. In a large bowl, sift together flour, baking powder and salt, mixing until well blended. Add cooled shortening mixture and mix well until mixture is very moist.
3. Divide dough in half and press each into a flat, round patty. Wrap in plastic wrap and chill in refrigerator for several hours or overnight before rolling.

Tip *Chill your rolling pin in the freezer before using so the dough won't stick to it.*

Oil Pastry

Makes enough for one 9-inch (23 cm) double-crust pie

2½ cups	all-purpose flour	625 mL
1 tsp	baking powder	5 mL
3	eggs	3
1 cup	granulated sugar	250 mL
⅔ cup	vegetable oil	150 mL

1. In a large bowl, combine flour and baking powder until blended.
2. In another bowl, whisk eggs and sugar until well blended. Add oil and beat until thoroughly blended.
3. Add egg mixture to flour mixture, stirring until mixture forms a dough.
4. Follow recipe instructions.

Tip *Reroll any scraps of leftover pie dough and cut into shapes. Sprinkle with sugar and ground cinnamon and bake at 475ºF (240ºC) for 8 to 10 minutes or until lightly browned.*

Cheese Pastry

Makes enough for one 9-inch (23 cm) double-crust pie

2 cups	all-purpose flour	500 mL
1 tsp	salt	5 mL
¾ cup	shortening	175 mL
⅓ cup	shredded Cheddar cheese	75 mL
5 to 6 tbsp	cold water	75 to 90 mL

1. In a large bowl, combine flour and salt and mix with a fork. Cut in shortening, using a pastry blender or two knives, until mixture resembles coarse crumbs.
2. Stir in the cheese. Sprinkle water, 1 tbsp (15 mL) at a time, into the mixture, mixing lightly with a fork after each addition.
3. Shape mixture into a ball with your hands, then divide dough into two portions and shape each into a flat, round patty. Wrap in plastic wrap or waxed paper, and chill until ready to use. Roll out as directed in recipe.

Cornmeal Pastry

Makes enough for one 9-inch (23 cm) single-crust pie

1 cup	all-purpose flour	250 mL
½ cup	cornmeal	125 mL
½ tsp	salt	2 mL
½ cup	shortening	125 mL

1. In a medium bowl, combine flour, cornmeal and salt.
2. Cut in shortening with a pastry blender or two knives until mixture resembles coarse crumbs.
3. Sprinkle with water, 1 tbsp (15 mL) at a time, stirring with a fork until mixture forms a dough. Pat dough into a ball and press into a flat, round patty. Wrap in plastic wrap or waxed paper, and chill until ready to use. Roll out as directed in recipe.

Tip *Chill your rolling pin in the freezer before using so the dough won't stick to it.*

Lemon Juice Pastry

Makes enough for two 9-inch (23 cm) single-crust pies or twenty-four 2½-inch (6 cm) tarts

3 cups	sifted cake and pastry flour	750 mL
1 cup	shortening	250 mL
1	egg, lightly beaten	1
3 tbsp	freshly squeezed lemon juice	45 mL
1 tsp	salt	5 mL
2 tbsp	ice water	25 mL

1. In a medium bowl, sift flour again. Cut in shortening and mix until mixture resembles coarse crumbs.
2. Add in egg and lemon juice and blend. Add salt to the ice water and gradually add this to the mixture until it holds together to form a dough.
3. Shape dough into a ball and press into a flat, round patty. Wrap in plastic wrap or waxed paper, and chill in refrigerator for 2 hours. Roll out pastry as directed in recipe.

Tip *This pastry is best used for tarts and fancy pies*

Sour Cream Pastry

Makes enough for three 9-inch (23 cm) single-crust pies

3 cups	all-purpose flour	750 mL
1 tsp	baking powder	5 mL
Pinch	salt	Pinch
1 cup	butter, softened	250 mL
¼ cup	granulated sugar	50 mL
1	egg yolk	1
½ cup	sour cream	125 mL

1. In a medium bowl, sift flour, baking powder and salt. Mix to blend.
2. In a large mixer bowl, cream butter and sugar until smooth and blended. Add egg yolk and beat. Add sour cream, beating until well blended.
3. Add flour mixture to batter, stirring until well combined. Knead into a smooth ball. Divide dough into three equal parts and press each into a flat, round patty. Wrap in plastic and chill for at least 30 minutes.
4. Roll out as directed in recipe. Dough can be wrapped and frozen for up to 3 months. If you are only using one pie crust, the extra dough may be frozen until needed.

Sweet Dough Crust

Makes enough for two 9-inch (23 cm) single-crust pies or twenty-four 2½-inch (6 cm) tarts

1	egg, separated	1
Pinch	cream of tartar	Pinch
½ cup	butter, softened	125 mL
¼ cup	granulated sugar	50 mL
¼ tsp	salt	1 mL
2 cups	sifted all-purpose flour	500 mL
	Milk	

1. In a small mixer bowl, beat egg white and cream of tartar just until foamy.

2. In a warm bowl, with a wooden spoon, mash butter into a smooth paste. Stir in the sugar and salt. Gradually stir in the flour, mashing until mixture resembles fine particles.

3. Add the egg yolk and egg white mixture to the flour mixture, and work it with your hands or wooden spoon until soft dough forms. Shape dough into a ball, adding a little milk, if necessary, to soften dough enough to be manageable. Press into a flat, round patty.

4. If not using immediately, wrap in plastic and keep chilled in refrigerator for up to 2 days, or freeze for up to 3 months. Before using pastry, bring to room temperature. If frozen, thaw in refrigerator.

Chocolate Crumb Crust

Makes one 9-inch (23 cm) single pie crust
- Preheat oven to 350°F (180°C)
- 9-inch (23 cm) pie pan

1¼ cups	finely crushed chocolate wafer crumbs (about 30 wafers)	300 mL
¼ cup	packed brown sugar	50 mL
¼ cup	butter or margarine, melted	50 mL

1. In a medium bowl, combine cookie crumbs, brown sugar and melted butter. Mix until well blended.

2. Press firmly onto the bottom and sides of the pie plate.

3. Bake in preheated oven for 8 to 10 minutes or until lightly browned. Let cool.

Coconut Crumb Crust

Makes one 9-inch (23 cm) single pie crust
- Preheat oven to 375°F (190°C)
- Baking sheet
- 9-inch (23 cm) pie plate

1 cup	flaked coconut (sweetened or unsweetened)	250 mL
1 cup	vanilla wafer crumbs (about 25 cookies)	250 mL
2 tbsp	butter or margarine, softened	25 mL
2 tbsp	granulated sugar	25 mL

1. Spread the flaked coconut on the baking sheet and bake in preheated oven for 10 minutes, until lightly browned. Stir once or twice during baking. Let cool.

2. In a medium bowl, combine coconut, crumbs, melted butter and sugar. Mix well until thoroughly combined.

3. Press firmly into bottom and sides of pie plate, making a small rim. Bake in preheated oven for 6 to 8 minutes or until golden brown. Let cool.

Graham Cracker Crust

Makes one 9-inch (23 cm) single pie crust
- Preheat oven to 350°F (180°C)
- 9-inch (23 cm) pie plate

1½ cups	finely crushed graham wafer crumbs (about 18 whole wafers)	375 mL
3 tbsp	granulated sugar	45 mL
⅓ cup	butter or margarine, melted	75 mL

1. In a medium bowl, combine wafer crumbs, sugar and melted butter. Mix well to blend. Set aside about 2 to 3 tbsp (25 to 45 mL) for topping.

2. Press the remaining mixture onto bottom and sides of pie plate.

3. Bake in preheated oven for 10 minutes or until firm. You can also chill in refrigerator until firm. Either method will work well.

Tip *To make your graham wafer crust even more special, use half graham wafer crumbs and half vanilla, chocolate or shortbread cookie crumbs, or any other favorite cookies.*

Corn Flake Crust

Makes one 9-inch (23 cm) single pie crust
- 9-inch (23 cm) pie plate

1 cup	corn flakes cereal crumbs	250 mL
1/4 cup	granulated sugar	50 mL
1/2 tsp	ground cinnamon (optional)	2 mL
1/4 cup	butter or margarine, melted	50 mL

1. In a bowl, combine crumbs, sugar, cinnamon (if using) and melted butter. Mix well.
2. Press firmly into pie plate. Chill.

Gingersnap Crust

Makes one 9-inch (23 cm) single pie crust
- Preheat oven to 375°F (190°C)
- 9-inch (23 cm) pie plate, greased

1 1/2 cups	fine gingersnap crumbs (about 24 gingersnaps)	375 mL
1/4 cup	butter or margarine, softened	50 mL

1. In a medium bowl, combine crumbs and butter until well mixed.
2. Press into bottom and sides of prepared pie pan.
3. Bake in preheated oven for about 8 minutes. Let cool.

Vanilla Wafer Crumb Crust

Makes one 9-inch (23 cm) single pie crust
- Preheat oven to 350°F (180°C)
- 9-inch (23 cm) pie pan, greased

1 1/3 cups	finely crushed vanilla wafers (about 38 cookies)	325 mL
2 tbsp	granulated sugar	25 mL
1/2 tsp	vanilla	2 mL
1/3 cup	unsalted butter, melted	75 mL

1. In a medium bowl, combine cookie crumbs, sugar and vanilla until blended.
2. Add melted butter and mix together until well blended.
3. Press firmly into bottom and sides of prepared pie pan. Bake in preheated oven for 8 minutes or until lightly browned. Let cool.

Tip *To shape a graham wafer or cookie crust evenly, heap the crumb mixture into your 9-inch (23 cm) pie plate and press an 8-inch (20 cm) pie plate on top, into the crumbs. This is a much easier and quicker method than pressing by hand.*

Crunchy Oatmeal Crust

Makes one 9-inch (23 cm) single pie crust
- Preheat oven to 375°F (190°C)
- 9-inch (23 cm) pie plate, greased

1 cup	quick-cooking rolled oats	250 mL
1/3 cup	sifted all-purpose flour	75 mL
1/3 cup	packed brown sugar	75 mL
1/4 tsp	salt	1 mL
Pinch	ground cinnamon (optional)	Pinch
Pinch	ground nutmeg (optional)	Pinch
1/3 cup	butter or margarine	75 mL

1. In a medium bowl, combine oats, flour, brown sugar and salt, and cinnamon and nutmeg (if using). Mix together well.
2. Cut in butter until mixture resembles coarse crumbs. Press into prepared pie plate.
3. Bake in preheated oven for 15 minutes or until golden brown. Let cool.

Poppy Seed Crust

Makes one 9-inch (23 cm) single pie crust
- 9-inch (23 cm) pie plate

1 1/3 cups	all-purpose flour	325 mL
1 tbsp	poppy seeds	15 mL
1/4 tsp	salt	1 mL
1/2 cup	shortening	125 mL
3 tbsp	cold water	45 mL

1. In a medium bowl, combine flour, poppy seeds and salt. Cut in shortening until mixture resembles coarse crumbs.
2. Add water, 1 tbsp (15 mL) at a time, tossing with a fork until dough forms a ball. Press into a flat, round patty. Refrigerate for at least 30 minutes.
3. Roll out as directed in recipe.

Zwieback Crust

Makes one 9-inch (23 cm) single pie crust
- 9-inch (23 cm) pie plate, buttered on the bottom only

1 cup	zwieback crumbs (about 6 biscuits)	250 mL
1/4 cup	confectioners' (icing) sugar	50 mL
2 tbsp	butter or margarine, melted	25 mL

1. In a bowl, combine crumbs, sugar and butter.
2. Press firmly into bottom and sides of prepared pie plate. Chill until set.

Shortbread Crust

Makes one 9-inch (23 cm) single pie crust or eighteen 2½-inch (6 cm) tart shells
- Preheat oven to 300°F (150°C)
- 9-inch (23 cm) pie plate or 14 to 18 tart tins

1 cup	butter or margarine, softened	250 mL
½ cup	granulated sugar	125 mL
2 cups	all-purpose flour	500 mL
Pinch	salt	Pinch

1. In a large bowl, cream butter and sugar until smooth. Add flour and salt and work in with your fingers to form a dough.

2. Press into bottom and sides of pie plate and bake in preheated oven for 30 to 40 minutes or until golden brown. Let cool.

Walnut Crumb Crust

Makes one 9-inch (23 cm) single pie crust
- Preheat oven to 350°F (180°C)
- 9-inch (23 cm) pie plate

1 cup	finely crushed graham wafer crumbs (about 14 whole wafers)	250 mL
½ cup	finely chopped walnuts	125 mL
¼ tsp	salt	1 mL
¼ cup	butter or margarine, softened	50 mL
1 tbsp	liquid honey	15 mL

1. In a bowl, combine wafer crumbs, walnuts and salt. Mix in butter and honey until combined.

2. Press into bottom and sides of pie plate and bake in preheated oven for 6 to 8 minutes or until lightly browned. Let cool.

Whole Wheat Crust

Makes one 9-inch (23 cm) single pie crust
- Preheat oven to 450°F (230°C)
- 9-inch (23 cm) pie plate

1¼ cups	whole wheat flour	300 mL
½ tsp	salt	2 mL
½ cup	shortening	125 mL
	Cold water	

1. In a medium bowl, mix together flour and salt. Cut in shortening with a pastry blender or two knives until mixture resembles coarse crumbs.

2. Add water, 1 tbsp (15 mL) at a time, just until mixture holds together and forms a dough. Shape into a ball. Press into a flat, round patty.

3. Roll out and transfer to pie plate. Bake in preheated oven for 10 to 12 minutes or until lightly browned. Let cool.

Regular Pastry for Tarts

Makes twenty-four 2½-inch (6 cm) tart shells
- Preheat oven to 475°F (245°C)
- 4 tart or muffin pans, fluted or unfluted, or 24 tart tins

1. Use your favorite recipe for a double-crust pie.

2. Roll out thin, then cut into twenty-four 2½-inch (6 cm) rounds, using the rim of a glass or a cookie cutter.

3. Line tart or muffin tins with the rounds of dough.

4. If the shells are to be baked before filling, prick the bottoms with a fork and bake in preheated oven for 8 to 10 minutes or until golden brown. If the shells are to be filled before baking, follow the instructions in your recipe.

Tip *Freeze unbaked tart shells for handy future baking. Cut your pastry into 5-inch (12.5 cm) circles, prick thoroughly with a fork and stack with waxed paper between each circle. Wrap securely in foil and freeze. When ready to use, place the frozen circles of dough over inverted muffin cups. Bake in preheated oven for 8 to 10 minutes, then fill as desired.*

Icing Sugar Pastry for Tarts

Makes twelve 2½-inch (6 cm) tart shells
- Preheat oven to 350°F (180°C)
- 2 tart or muffin pans, fluted or unfluted, or 12 tart tins

2 cups	cake and pastry flour	500 mL
½ cup	confectioner's (icing) sugar	125 mL
½ tsp	salt	2 mL
1 cup	shortening, softened	250 mL
1	egg, lightly beaten	1
1 tsp	vanilla (or other flavoring)	5 mL

1. In a medium bowl, combine flour, sugar and salt. Mix to blend.

2. Add shortening, egg and vanilla, and mix until thoroughly combined.

3. Press into bottoms and sides of tart or muffin tins.

4. If the shells are to be baked before filling, prick bottoms with a fork and bake in preheated oven for 10 to 15 minutes or until golden brown. If baking first is not necessary, follow recipe instructions.

Meringue Pie Shells

Makes 8 small pie shells
- Preheat oven to 275°F (140°C)
- Baking sheet, lined with foil or waxed paper or parchment paper

3	egg whites, at room temperature	3
1/4 tsp	cream of tartar	1 mL
1 tsp	vanilla	5 mL
Pinch	salt	Pinch
1 cup	granulated sugar	250 mL
1/4 cup	flaked coconut (sweetened or unsweetened, optional)	50 mL

1. In a mixer bowl, beat egg whites and cream of tartar. Add vanilla and salt and beat until frothy. Add sugar gradually, and beat until stiff, but not dry, peaks form.

2. Fold in coconut (if using). Drop meringue in eight 3- to 3½-inch (7.5 to 8.5 cm) rounds onto prepared baking sheet, at least 2 inches (5 cm) apart. Press the middle of each round with the back of a spoon to make a shell, pushing around the edges to make soft sides.

3. Bake in preheated oven for 1 hour. Turn off the oven, keep the door closed and leave shells inside to dry for 1 hour. Fill as desired.

Fruit Pies

Deep-Dish Apple Pie

Serves 8 to 10
- Preheat oven to 425°F (220°C)
- 9-inch (2.5 L) square metal baking pan

	Pastry for a 9-inch (23 cm) single-crust pie	
12 cups	tart cooking apples (Granny Smith or any other type preferred), peeled and thinly sliced (8 to 10 apples)	3 L
1½ cups	granulated sugar	375 mL
½ cup	all-purpose flour	125 mL
1 tsp	ground cinnamon	5 mL
1 tsp	ground nutmeg	5 mL
1/4 tsp	salt	1 mL
2 tbsp	butter or margarine	25 mL

1. In a large bowl, combine apples, sugar, flour, cinnamon, nutmeg and salt. Toss together to mix well.

2. Spoon into baking pan. Dot over top with the butter. Place the pastry crust over top, make some slits near center, and fold edges under, just inside the edge of pan.

3. Bake in preheated oven for 1 hour or until juice begins to bubble through the slits in the crust and apples are tender. Serve warm.

Old-Fashioned Cookie Sheet Apple Pie

Serves 6 to 8
- Preheat oven to 400°F (200°C)
- Rimmed baking sheet, lightly greased and dusted with flour

CHEDDAR CRUST

2 cups	all-purpose flour	500 mL
½ tsp	salt	2 mL
½ cup	cold butter, cut into cubes	125 mL
1 cup	shredded old (sharp) Cheddar cheese	250 mL
½ cup	milk	125 mL

FILLING

5	Granny Smith apples, peeled and sliced	5
1/4 cup	granulated sugar	50 mL
1 tbsp	all-purpose flour	15 mL
½ tsp	ground cinnamon	2 mL
Pinch	salt	Pinch
2 tbsp	butter or margarine	25 mL

GLAZE

1	egg	1
2 tbsp	milk	25 mL
	Confectioner's (icing) sugar (optional)	

1. *Prepare the crust:* In a large bowl, combine flour and salt, and mix with a fork. Cut in butter with a pastry blender or two knives until mixture resembles coarse crumbs. Stir in the cheese. Sprinkle milk, 1 tbsp (15 mL) at a time, into the mixture, mixing lightly with a fork after each addition. Shape mixture into a ball with your hands. Chill in refrigerator.

2. *Prepare the filling:* In a large bowl, combine apples, sugar, flour, cinnamon and salt, and mix well to coat.

3. Flatten pastry out onto the prepared baking sheet. Roll out to 1/4-inch (0.5 cm) thickness and trim to make a 14-inch (35 cm) square. Roll out the trimmings and cut into strips.

4. Arrange apples in rows over the crust, overlapping slightly, and leaving an empty border about 2 inches (5 cm) wide at the edges. Dot apple mixture with butter. Fold the border edges over the filling and pinch the corners to seal. Place the strips of dough over top in a crisscross pattern.

5. *Prepare the glaze:* In a small bowl, whisk the egg and milk, and brush over top of the pastry.

6. Bake in preheated oven for 30 to 35 minutes or until crust is golden brown and apples are tender. Sprinkle with confectioner's sugar before serving, if desired.

Upside-Down Apple Pie

Serves 8 to 10
- Preheat oven to 375°F (190°C)
- 9-inch (23 cm) deep-dish pie plate

CRUST

1¼ cups	all-purpose flour	300 mL
½ tsp	salt	2 mL
¼ cup	cold butter or margarine	50 mL
2 tbsp	cold shortening	25 mL
4 to 5 tbsp	ice water	50 to 75 mL

APPLE FILLING

6	tart cooking apples, peeled and sliced	6
¾ cup	granulated sugar	175 mL
¼ cup	firmly packed brown sugar	50 mL
2 tbsp	all-purpose flour	25 mL
½ tsp	ground cinnamon	2 mL
¼ tsp	ground nutmeg	1 mL
¼ tsp	salt	1 mL
2 tbsp	butter or margarine, melted	25 mL
½ cup	chopped walnuts	125 mL
⅓ cup	packed brown sugar	75 mL

1. *Prepare the crust:* In a large bowl, sift together flour and salt. Cut in the chilled butter and shortening with a pastry blender or two knives until mixture resembles coarse meal. Sprinkle the ice water, 1 tbsp (15 mL) at a time, into the mixture, mixing lightly with a fork after each addition. Form dough into a ball and flatten slightly. Wrap in plastic. Chill in refrigerator for 1 hour or overnight.

2. *Prepare the filling:* In a large bowl, combine apples, granulated sugar, the ¼ cup (50 mL) of brown sugar, flour, cinnamon, nutmeg and salt. Mix well until blended.

3. Pour the melted butter over bottom of pie pan. Spread chopped walnuts over top and sprinkle the ⅓ cup (75 mL) brown sugar over the walnuts. Pour in apple mixture and spread evenly in pan.

4. On a lightly floured surface, roll out pastry to fit over filling. Place pastry over top of the apple mixture, turn edges under and crimp and seal to the edge of the pie plate. With a fork, prick the dough in several places.

5. Bake in preheated oven for 30 to 40 minutes or until pastry is nicely browned and apples are tender. Let cool in pie plate for about 5 minutes. Then invert onto a rimmed serving plate and remove the pie pan.

Tips *When preparing apples for an apple pie, use the small end of a melon baller to neatly and easily scoop out the core from apples that have been halved.*

Delicious when served warm with ice cream.

Traditional Apple Pandowdy

Serves 6
- Preheat oven to 425°F (220°C)
- 8-inch (20 cm) pie plate

	Pastry for an 8-inch (20 cm) double-crust pie	
1	can (20 oz/600 g) apple slices, drained	1
½ cup	firmly packed brown sugar	125 mL
3 tbsp	butter or margarine, melted	45 mL
5 to 6 tbsp	pure maple syrup, divided	75 to 90 mL

1. In a medium bowl, mix together apple slices and brown sugar to blend.

2. On lightly floured surface, roll out half of pastry and fit into pie plate. Spoon apple mixture onto bottom crust. Dot with the butter and top with 3 tbsp (45 mL) of the syrup.

3. Roll out the remaining pastry to fit over filling. Place top crust over the filling and make slits in the crust to allow steam to escape. Seal and crimp or flute the edges.

4. Bake in preheated oven for 15 minutes, then remove from the oven and make crisscross cuts about 1 inch (2.5 cm) apart through the top crust and filling. Drizzle the remaining syrup over top and bake for another 25 minutes. If crust browns too quickly, place a strip of foil around edge. Best when served warm.

Impossible Apple Pie

Serves 6 to 8

- Preheat oven to 375°F (190°C)
- 9-inch (23 cm) pie plate, greased

1	can (19 oz/540 mL) apple pie filling	1
1 tsp	ground cinnamon	5 mL
1 cup	all-purpose flour	250 mL
½ cup	firmly packed brown sugar	125 mL
1 tsp	baking powder	5 mL
¼ tsp	salt	1 mL
1	egg	1
1 tsp	vanilla	5 mL
½ cup	butter or margarine, melted	125 mL

1. Spoon pie filling into prepared pie plate. Sprinkle cinnamon over top.
2. In a medium bowl, combine flour, sugar, baking powder and salt. Mix well.
3. In a small bowl, whisk egg and vanilla. Add to flour mixture and stir until mixture becomes crumbly. Sprinkle evenly over apple filling. Drizzle melted butter over top.
4. Bake in preheated oven for 30 minutes or until golden brown and crisp. Serve warm with scoop of vanilla ice cream or whipped topping.

Applecot Lattice Pie

Serves 6 to 8

- Preheat oven to 425°F (220°C)
- 9-inch (23 cm) pie plate

	Pastry for a 9-inch (23 cm) double-crust pie	
⅓ cup	granulated sugar	75 mL
2 tbsp	all-purpose flour	25 mL
1 cup	milk	250 mL
4	egg yolks, divided	4
½ tsp	vanilla	2 mL
4 cups	tart cooking apples, peeled and sliced (about 2 lbs/1 kg)	1 L
1 tbsp	freshly squeezed lemon juice	15 mL
2 tbsp	butter or margarine	25 mL
2 tbsp	granulated sugar	25 mL
Pinch	ground nutmeg	Pinch
¾ cup	apricot preserves	175 mL
1 tbsp	water	15 mL

1. In a small saucepan, combine the ⅓ cup (75 mL) sugar and flour, and mix to blend. Stir in milk and bring to a boil, stirring constantly. Reduce heat and simmer, stirring, until mixture is slightly thickened, about 1 to 2 minutes.
2. In a small bowl, whisk 3 of the egg yolks lightly, then stir in vanilla. Whisk some of the hot mixture into this and then pour back into the saucepan and stir to blend. Set aside to cool.
3. Sprinkle the apples with lemon juice. In a skillet, over low heat, combine butter, the 2 tbsp (25 mL) sugar and nutmeg. Add the apples and sauté, stirring, until apples are almost tender, about 5 minutes. Remove from heat.
4. In a small saucepan, melt the apricot preserves.
5. On lightly floured surface, roll out half of pastry and fit into pie plate. Spoon the egg yolk filling into the bottom crust. Arrange the apple slices on top, piling up slightly in the center. Spread melted preserves over top.
6. Roll out the remaining pastry and cut into strips to make a lattice top (see tip, below). Bring the overhang of bottom pastry up over the ends of the strips and crimp edges. Whisk the final egg yolk with water and brush over top of lattice, but not the edges. Bake in preheated oven for 40 to 45 minutes or until golden brown. Let cool completely.

Tip *To make a lattice top, roll out pastry and cut into ten ½-inch (1 cm) strips. Arrange five pastry strips, about 1½ inches (3.5 cm) apart, over your filling. Fold back every other strip. Place another strip across, then unfold strips. To finish, fold back the alternate strips and place next strip the same distance from the other strip. Unfold strips and continue weaving until lattice top is completed.*

Pear Crumble Pie

Serves 6 to 8

- Preheat oven to 400°F (200°C)
- 9-inch (23 cm) pie plate

	Pastry for a 9-inch (23 cm) single-crust pie	
½ cup	granulated sugar	125 mL
2 tbsp	quick-cooking tapioca	25 mL
1 tsp	ground cinnamon	5 mL
¼ tsp	ground nutmeg	1 mL
¼ tsp	salt	1 mL
6	firm ripe pears, peeled and sliced (about 6 cups/1.5 L)	6
1 tbsp	fresh lemon juice	15 mL
TOPPING		
½ cup	all-purpose flour	125 mL
⅓ cup	granulated sugar	75 mL

¼ cup	old-fashioned rolled oats	50 mL
1 tsp	ground cinnamon	5 mL
3 tbsp	butter or margarine, softened	45 mL
CARAMEL PECAN SAUCE (OPTIONAL)		
10	soft vanilla caramels	10
3 tbsp	milk	45 mL
¼ cup	chopped pecans	50 mL

1. On a lightly floured surface, roll out pastry and fit into pie plate.
2. In a bowl, combine sugar, tapioca, cinnamon, nutmeg and salt. Place pears in a large bowl and sprinkle with lemon juice. Add dry mix to pears and mix, gently, just to blend. Let stand for 15 to 20 minutes, then spoon into prepared pastry crust.
3. *Prepare the topping:* In a small bowl, combine flour, sugar, oats, cinnamon, and butter. Mix with a fork until mixture resembles coarse crumbs. Sprinkle evenly over top of pear filling.
4. Bake in preheated oven for 45 to 50 minutes or until golden brown.
5. *If desired, prepare the caramel pecan sauce:* Melt caramels into milk in a saucepan over low heat. Stir in chopped pecans. Drizzle over pie and continue baking for 10 minutes or until lightly browned. Let cool on a wire rack. Best when served warm.

• •

Pear Apple Crunch Pie

Serves 6 to 8
- Preheat oven to 400°F (200°C)
- 9-inch (23 cm) pie plate

	Pastry for a 9-inch (23 cm) single-crust pie	
⅓ cup	granulated sugar	75 mL
2 tbsp	all-purpose flour	25 mL
1 tsp	ground cinnamon	5 mL
¼ tsp	salt	1 mL
1	can (14 oz/398 mL) pear halves, drained and sliced	1
3	Granny Smith apples, peeled and sliced	3
½ tsp	grated lemon zest	2 mL
1 tbsp	freshly squeezed lemon juice	15 mL
½ cup	raisins	125 mL
NUT TOPPING		
½ cup	firmly packed brown sugar	125 mL
¼ cup	all-purpose flour	50 mL
½ tsp	salt	2 mL
¼ cup	butter or margarine, softened	50 mL
½ cup	chopped walnuts (or other nuts)	125 mL

1. On a lightly floured surface, roll out pastry and fit into pie plate.
2. In a large bowl, combine sugar, flour, cinnamon and salt. Mix to blend. Add pear and apple slices and toss to blend. Stir in lemon zest, lemon juice and raisins, and mix thoroughly. Spoon mixture into prepared pastry pie shell.
3. *Prepare the topping:* In a bowl, combine brown sugar, flour and salt. Cut in the butter with a fork until mixture resembles coarse crumbs. Stir in chopped walnuts. Sprinkle over top of filling.
4. Bake in preheated oven for 15 minutes. Cover with foil and bake for 25 to 30 minutes or until apples are tender and top is golden brown. Let cool on a wire rack.

• •

Classic Blueberry Pie

Serves 6 to 8
- Preheat oven to 400°F (200°C)
- 9-inch (23 cm) pie plate

	Pastry for a 9-inch (23 cm) double-crust pie	
4 cups	fresh or frozen blueberries	1 L
¾ cup	granulated sugar	175 mL
3 tbsp	all-purpose flour	45 mL
½ tsp	grated lemon zest	2 mL
Pinch	salt	Pinch
½ tsp	ground cinnamon (optional)	2 mL
½ tsp	ground nutmeg (optional)	2 mL
2 tsp	freshly squeezed lemon juice	10 mL
1 tbsp	butter or margarine, softened	15 mL

1. In a large bowl, combine blueberries, sugar, flour, lemon zest and salt. Add cinnamon and nutmeg (if using). Mix together well until thoroughly blended.
2. On a lightly floured surface, roll out half of pastry and fit into pie plate. Spoon blueberry mixture into bottom pie crust. Sprinkle with lemon juice and dot with butter.
3. Roll out the remaining pastry to fit over filling. Cut several slits near the center to allow steam to escape, and place over fruit filling. Trim, seal and flute edges or press with a fork all around.
4. Bake in preheated oven for 35 to 40 minutes or until top is golden brown. Let cool on a wire rack. Serve warm or cold.

Tip *When making a juicy berry pie, sprinkle the bottom crust lightly with sugar and flour mixed in equal proportions.*

Cranapple Pie

Serves 6 to 8

- Preheat oven to 450°F (230°C)
- 9-inch (23 cm) pie plate

	Pastry for a 9-inch (23 cm) double-crust pie	
6 cups	Granny Smith apples, peeled and thinly sliced (about 5 apples)	1.5 L
1 cup	fresh or frozen cranberries	250 mL
¾ cup	granulated sugar	175 mL
3 tbsp	all-purpose flour	45 mL
1 tsp	ground cinnamon	5 mL
1 tbsp	freshly squeezed lemon juice	15 mL

1. In a large bowl, combine apples and cranberries.
2. In a small bowl, combine sugar, flour and cinnamon. Sprinkle over the apples and cranberries, and mix well until fruit is coated.
3. On lightly floured surface, roll out half of pastry and fit into pie plate. Spoon filling into bottom crust in pie plate, spreading evenly, as it will seem very full. Sprinkle the lemon juice over top.
4. Roll out the remaining pastry to fit over filling. Make some slits in the top of your second crust and place over top. Be sure to seal and then crimp or flute the edges.
5. Bake in preheated oven for 10 minutes. Reduce temperature to 350°F (180°C) and bake for another 40 to 50 minutes or until crust is golden brown and apples are tender.

Cranberry Cherry Crumb Pie

Serves 6 to 8

- Preheat oven to 375°F (190°C)
- 9-inch (23 cm) pie plate

	Pastry for a 9-inch (23 cm) single-crust pie	
2 cups	fresh or frozen cranberries	500 mL
1	can (19 oz/540 mL) cherry pie filling	1
2 tbsp	cornstarch	25 mL
1 tbsp	lightly packed brown sugar	15 mL
1	package (8 oz/250 g) cream cheese, softened	1
1	can (10 oz/284 mL) sweetened condensed milk	1
¼ cup	freshly squeezed lemon juice	50 mL

TOPPING

½ cup	all-purpose flour	125 mL
⅓ cup	packed brown sugar	75 mL
1 tsp	ground cinnamon	5 mL
½ cup	butter or margarine, softened	125 mL
½ cup	chopped nuts (optional)	125 mL

1. In a large bowl, combine cranberries, cherry pie filling, cornstarch and brown sugar. Mix well until thoroughly combined.
2. In a mixer bowl, beat cream cheese until light and fluffy. Add milk and lemon juice gradually, beating until smooth and blended.
3. On a lightly floured surface, roll out pastry and fit into pie shell. Spoon cream cheese mixture into prepared pie crust. Spoon fruit mixture over cheese mixture, spreading evenly.
4. *Prepare the topping:* In a medium bowl, combine flour, brown sugar and cinnamon, and mix to blend. Add butter and mix with a fork until mixture resembles coarse crumbs. Mix in nuts (if using). Sprinkle over top of fruit mixture.
5. Bake in preheated oven for 50 to 55 minutes or until golden brown. Let cool on a wire rack.

Fresh Gooseberry Pie

Serves 6 to 8

- Preheat oven to 450°F (230°C)
- 9-inch (23 cm) pie plate

	Pastry for a 9-inch (23 cm) double-crust pie	
3 cups	fresh gooseberries, divided	750 mL
3 tbsp	quick-cooking tapioca	45 mL
1½ cups	granulated sugar	375 mL
¼ tsp	salt	1 mL
2 tbsp	butter or margarine, softened	25 mL

1. In a large bowl, crush about ½ cup (125 mL) of the gooseberries and add the tapioca, sugar and salt. Put into a large saucepan.
2. Add the remaining whole berries to the crushed mixture. Cook over medium heat, stirring, until mixture thickens.
3. On a lightly floured surface, roll out half of pastry and fit into pie plate. Spoon gooseberry mixture into bottom pie crust and dot with the butter.
4. Roll out the remaining pastry to fit over filling. Make several slits in the top crust to allow steam to escape. Place over top of filling and trim, seal and flute or crimp edge.

5. Bake in preheated oven for 10 minutes. Reduce heat to 350°F (180°C) and continue baking for 30 to 35 minutes, until top crust is lightly browned. Let cool slightly on a wire rack and serve warm, or cool completely.

Tip *To determine when a fruit pie is done, bake until the top crust is golden brown and insert a paring knife into one of the slits in your top crust. If the knife can easily pierce a piece of the fruit, it is soft and tender, and the filling is bubbly, your pie is done.*

• •

Raspberry Swirl Cream Pie

Serves 6 to 8

• 9-inch (23 cm) pie plate

	Graham Cracker Crust (see recipe, page 407), baked and cooled	
1	package (3 oz/90 g) raspberry-flavored gelatin	1
½ cup	milk	125 mL
8 oz	white, regular size marshmallows	250 g
2 cups	frozen whipped topping, thawed	500 mL
1	package (10 oz/300 g) frozen whole raspberries, thawed and drained	1

1. Prepare gelatin as directed on the package. Chill in refrigerator until partially set.

2. In a small saucepan, over low heat, combine milk and marshmallows, stirring constantly, until melted, smooth and well blended. Set aside to cool. Then fold in whipped topping.

3. Fold raspberries into partially set gelatin. Spoon gelatin mixture into pie crust. Top with marshmallow mixture and swirl through with a knife or spatula for a marbled effect. Chill in refrigerator for 5 hours, or preferably overnight.

• •

Chocolate Raspberry Pie

Serves 6 to 8

• 9-inch (23 cm) pie plate

	Chocolate Crumb Crust (see recipe, page 407), baked and cooled	
3 tbsp	granulated sugar	45 mL
1 tbsp	cornstarch	15 mL
2 cups	fresh raspberries	500 mL
⅓ cup	granulated sugar	75 mL
1	package (8 oz/250 g) cream cheese, softened	1
½ tsp	vanilla	2 mL
½ cup	whipping (35%) cream	125 mL
3 tbsp	butter or margarine	45 mL
2 oz	semisweet chocolate, chopped	60 g

1. In a small saucepan, over medium heat, stir together the 3 tbsp (45 mL) sugar and the cornstarch.

2. Add raspberries and bring to a boil, stirring constantly. Boil for 2 to 3 minutes or until thickened. Let cool for 15 minutes. Then spoon into prepared pie crust and place in refrigerator.

3. In a large mixer bowl, on medium speed, cream sugar, cream cheese and vanilla until smooth, light and fluffy.

4. In a small mixer bowl, on high speed, beat whipping cream until stiff peaks form. Fold whipped cream into creamed mixture, and spread evenly over raspberry layer in crust. Cover with waxed paper and chill in refrigerator for 1 to 2 hours.

5. In a small saucepan, over low heat, melt butter and chocolate. Let cool for 5 minutes. Pour over top of chilled pie. Cover loosely and set in refrigerator to chill for 3 hours or overnight. Garnish with raspberries, if desired.

• •

Saskatoon Berry Pie

Serves 6 to 8

• Preheat oven to 375°F (190°C)
• 9-inch (23 cm) pie plate

	Pastry for a 9-inch (23 cm) double-crust pie	
5 cups	Saskatoon berries	1.25 L
1 tbsp	quick-cooking tapioca	15 mL
½ to ¾ cup	granulated sugar	125 to 175 mL

1. On a lightly floured surface, roll out half of pastry and fit into pie plate. Spread berries over bottom of pie crust. Sprinkle tapioca and then sugar to taste over top of berries.

2. Roll out the remaining pastry to fit over filling. Make several slits near the center of top crust. Place over top of berries. Trim overhang, fold under to fit rim, and seal, fluting edges.

3. Bake in preheated oven for 40 to 45 minutes, until fruit is bubbly and top is golden brown. Let cool on a wire rack.

Tip *For even browning on double-crust pies, brush a beaten egg white or milk on the crust prior to baking.*

Double Strawberry Pie

Serves 6

- 9-inch (23 cm) pie plate

	9-inch (23 cm) single-crust pie shell, baked and cooled	
1	package (3 oz/90 g) strawberry-flavored gelatin	1
1 cup	boiling water	250 mL
1	package (1 lb/500 g) frozen sliced strawberries	1

1. In a bowl, dissolve gelatin in the boiling water. Stir until completely dissolved.

2. Add frozen strawberries, stirring to break berries apart. When mixture is partially set, spoon into prepared pie crust. Chill in refrigerator until completely set.

Tip *Serve with whipped cream, ice cream or whatever you desire.*

Strawberry Baked Alaska Pie

Serves 8

- 9-inch (23 cm) pie plate

	9-inch (23 cm) single-crust pie shell, baked and well chilled	
1 cup	strawberry jam or sundae topping, divided	250 mL
6 cups	strawberry ice cream, softened to room temperature	1.5 L

MERINGUE TOPPING

	egg whites	
3	egg whites	3
Pinch	cream of tartar	Pinch
¼ cup	granulated sugar	50 mL
	Fresh strawberries	

1. Set aside about ¼ cup (50 mL) of the strawberry jam. Spread the remaining strawberry jam evenly over bottom of pie crust.

2. In a mixer bowl, beat ice cream until creamy and smooth. Spread over strawberry jam, mounding ice cream in the center. Freeze until firm, about 2 hours.

3. Preheat oven to 450°F (230°C).

4. *Prepare the topping:* In a small mixer bowl, on high speed, beat egg whites and cream of tartar until frothy. Gradually add sugar, a spoonful at a time, beating until stiff peaks form. Spread evenly over ice cream in crust, right to the edges, to seal pie.

5. Bake in preheated oven for 5 minutes, until meringue is lightly browned. Heat the reserved strawberry jam in a small saucepan over low heat for 2 to 3 minutes, until the right consistency to drizzle. Drizzle over the meringue and serve garnished with fresh strawberries.

Strawberry Marshmallow Pie

Serves 6 to 8

- 9-inch (23 cm) pie plate

	Graham Cracker Crust (see recipe, page 407), baked and cooled	
¾ cup	orange juice	175 mL
1½ cups	white miniature marshmallows	375 mL
1½ cups	whipping (35%) cream, whipped	375 mL
2 cups	sliced fresh strawberries	500 mL
	Whipped cream (optional)	
	Fresh strawberries (optional)	

1. In a double boiler, heat orange juice over simmering water. Add marshmallows, stirring constantly, until melted. Set aside to cool, then chill in refrigerator until partially set, stirring occasionally, about 30 minutes.

2. Fold in the whipped cream, then the strawberries, until thoroughly combined.

3. Spoon into prepared pie crust and chill in refrigerator for at least 1 hour or for up to 1 day. Garnish with whipped cream and whole strawberries, if desired.

Strawberry Peach Pie

Serves 6 to 8

- Preheat oven to 425°F (220°C)
- 9-inch (23 cm) pie plate and baking sheet

	Pastry for a 9-inch (23 cm) double-crust pie	
½ cup	granulated sugar	125 mL
½ cup	all-purpose flour	125 mL
1 tsp	ground cinnamon	5 mL
¼ tsp	ground nutmeg	1 mL
4	peaches, cut in thin slices	4
3 cups	strawberries, hulled and sliced	750 mL
3 tbsp	freshly squeezed lemon juice	45 mL
1	egg	1
1 tbsp	water	15 mL

1. In a small bowl, combine sugar, flour, cinnamon and nutmeg. Mix to blend.

2. In a large bowl, combine peach and strawberry slices. Add dry mixture to the fruit mixture. Toss to combine. Add lemon juice and stir to blend well.
3. On a lightly floured surface, roll out half of pastry and fit into pie plate. Beat egg and water and brush some of it inside bottom pie crust. Spoon fruit mixture into pastry shell.
4. Roll out the remaining pastry to fit over filling and cut into ten ½-inch (1 cm) wide strips to form a lattice crust (see tip, page 412). Brush lattice top with the remaining egg glaze. Place pie plate on a baking sheet to catch any overflowing juice.
5. Bake in preheated oven for 10 minutes. Reduce oven temperature to 350°F (180°C) and bake for another 45 to 50 minutes, until bubbly and crust is golden brown. Let cool on a wire rack.

Glazed Strawberry Pear Pie

Serves 6

• 9-inch (23 cm) pie plate

	9-inch (23 cm) single-crust pie shell, baked and cooled	
2	cans (each 14 oz/398 mL) pear halves	2
1	package (10 oz/300 g) frozen strawberries, thawed	1
2 tbsp	cornstarch	25 mL
¼ cup	currant jelly	50 mL
	Whipped cream (optional)	
	Fresh strawberries (optional)	

1. Drain pears and strawberries and reserve the juices.
2. Slice pears and arrange with the strawberries in prepared pie crust.
3. Pour reserved pear juice and strawberry juice into a measuring cup to equal 1 cup (250 mL). Pour into a saucepan, and add cornstarch and jelly. Cook over low heat, stirring constantly, until mixture bubbles and thickens. Spoon over fruit in crust. Let cool to set, and serve garnished with whipped cream and fresh strawberries, if desired.

Glazed Strawberry Tart

Serves 6 to 8

• 8-inch (20 cm) round metal cake pan, lined with foil, or tart pan with removable bottom

CRUST

1 cup	sifted all-purpose flour	250 mL
3 tbsp	granulated sugar	45 mL
¼ tsp	salt	1 mL
6 tbsp	butter or margarine, chilled	90 mL
1 tsp	grated lemon zest (optional)	5 mL
1	egg white	1

FILLING

¼ cup	granulated sugar	50 mL
3 tbsp	all-purpose flour	45 mL
Pinch	salt	Pinch
¾ cup	light (5%) cream	175 mL
4	egg yolks, beaten	4
⅓ cup	whipping (35%) cream, whipped	75 mL
2 tbsp	orange-flavored liqueur	25 mL
2 cups	whole fresh strawberries	500 mL

GLAZE

½ cup	currant jelly	125 mL
1 tbsp	orange-flavored liqueur	15 mL

1. *Prepare the crust:* In a bowl, combine flour, sugar and salt. Cut in butter with a pastry blender or two knives until mixture resembles coarse crumbs. Stir in lemon zest (if using) and egg white, mixing until a dough forms and leaves bowl clean.
2. Set aside one-third of the dough and press the remaining dough into bottom of prepared pan. Press the reserved one-third dough around the sides to make a rim about 1¼ inches (3 cm) high. Prick crust with a fork and freeze for 1½ hours.
3. Preheat oven to 375°F (190°C). Bake crust for 25 to 30 minutes or until golden brown. Let cool in pan on a wire rack, and when cooled, remove to a serving plate, using foil to lift out of pan. Discard foil.
4. *Prepare the filling:* In a medium saucepan, combine sugar, flour and salt. Stir in cream and cook over medium heat, stirring constantly, until mixture has boiled for about 1 minute and has thickened. Stir half of this hot mixture into the bowl of beaten egg yolks, and then stir this mixture back into saucepan. Cook, stirring, for another 1 to 2 minutes, until mixture becomes thick again. Chill in refrigerator.
5. Fold whipped cream and liqueur into chilled filling. Spread evenly into bottom of crust on plate. Arrange the strawberries, standing upright, on top of filling.
6. *Prepare the glaze:* In a small saucepan, melt the currant jelly and stir in the liqueur. Let cool to room temperature, about 10 to 15 minutes, and then brush over berries. Chill tart in refrigerator for at least 30 minutes or until ready to serve.

Concord Grape Pie

Serves 6 to 8

- Preheat oven to 375°F (190°C)
- 9-inch (23 cm) pie plate

	Pastry for a 9-inch (23 cm) single-crust pie	
¾ cup	granulated sugar	175 mL
⅓ cup	all-purpose flour	75 mL
¼ tsp	salt	1 mL
4 cups	Concord grapes (about 1½ lbs/750 g)	1 L
2 tbsp	butter or margarine, melted	25 mL
1 tbsp	freshly squeezed lemon juice	15 mL
TOPPING		
½ cup	granulated sugar	125 mL
½ cup	all-purpose flour	125 mL
¼ cup	butter or margarine, softened	50 mL

1. In a large bowl, combine sugar, flour and salt.
2. Slip skins from grapes by pressing grape between your fingers, gently. Skins should slip off easily. Set skins aside.
3. In a large saucepan, bring skinned grapes to a boil. Reduce heat and simmer, uncovered, for about 5 minutes. Place this pulp into a sieve to remove the seeds. Add the reserved grape skins to this pulp. Let cool to room temperature, about 10 to 15 minutes. Stir grape mixture, melted butter and lemon juice into the dry mixture. Mix well until thoroughly blended.
4. On a lightly floured surface, roll out pastry and fit into pie plate. Spoon filling into crust.
5. Bake in preheated oven for 20 minutes.
6. *Prepare the topping:* In a bowl, combine sugar and flour. Add butter and stir with a fork until mixture resembles coarse crumbs. Sprinkle evenly over pie and bake for another 20 to 25 minutes or until topping is golden brown. Let cool on a wire rack.

Quick 'n' Easy Lemon Pie

Serves 6 to 8

- 8-inch (20 cm) round metal cake pan

	9-inch (23 cm) single-crust pie shell, baked and cooled	
2¼ cups	water, divided	550 mL
1	envelope (¼ oz/7 g) unflavored gelatin	1
1	package (7 oz/212 g) lemon pie filling and pudding mix	1
½ cup	granulated sugar	125 mL
⅔ cup	evaporated milk	150 mL
2 tbsp	freshly squeezed lemon juice	25 mL

1. In a large saucepan, combine ½ cup (125 mL) of the water and gelatin to soften. Stir in pudding mix, sugar and the remaining water. Cook over medium heat, stirring, until mixture comes to a boil and thickens. Transfer to a bowl and chill until mixture mounds from a spoon.
2. Pour the milk into the cake pan and chill in freezer until soft ice crystals form around the edges, about 10 to 15 minutes. Transfer to a small mixer bowl and whip until stiff. Add lemon juice and beat until very stiff. Fold into cooled pudding. If necessary, beat until mixture is smooth.
3. Spoon into prepared pie crust and chill for about 2 hours or until firm and set.

Lemon Ice Cream Pie

Serves 6 to 8

- 9-inch (23 cm) pie plate

	9-inch (23 cm) single-crust pie shell, baked and cooled	
6 tbsp	butter or margarine	90 mL
1¼ cups	granulated sugar, divided	300 mL
1 tsp	grated lemon zest	5 mL
⅓ cup	freshly squeezed lemon juice	75 mL
Pinch	salt	Pinch
2	eggs	2
2	egg yolks	2
2 cups	vanilla ice cream, softened	500 mL
2	egg whites	2

1. In a medium saucepan, over low heat, melt butter and stir in 1 cup (250 mL) of the sugar, lemon juice and a pinch of salt.
2. In a small bowl, whisk eggs and egg yolks, then stir into the butter mixture. Stir until mixture is boiling, then remove from heat and chill for at least 30 minutes.
3. Spread the ice cream into the pastry shell and top with the chilled lemon mixture. Freeze until firm.
4. Preheat oven to 500°F (260°C). In a small mixer bowl, on high speed, beat egg whites and a pinch of salt until soft peaks form. Gradually add the remaining sugar, by spoonfuls, and beat until stiff peaks form. Fold in lemon zest and spread over frozen pie, sealing edges.
5. Bake in preheated oven for 3 minutes or until top becomes lightly browned. For best results, serve immediately.

Lemon Cream Cheese Pie

Serves 6 to 8

- Preheat oven to 350°F (180°C)
- 9-inch (23 cm) deep-dish pie plate

	Pastry for a 9-inch (23 cm) deep-dish single-crust pie	

CHEESE LAYER

¼ cup	granulated sugar	50 mL
1	package (8 oz/250 g) cream cheese, softened	1
1	egg	1

LEMON LAYER

2	eggs	2
2 tsp	grated lemon zest	10 mL
⅓ cup	freshly squeezed lemon juice	75 mL
½ cup	corn syrup	125 mL
2 tbsp	butter or margarine, melted	25 mL
1 tbsp	cornstarch	15 mL
	Whipped topping (optional)	
	Lemon zest (optional)	

1. On a lightly floured surface, roll out pastry and fit into pie plate.
2. *Prepare the cheese layer:* In a mixer bowl, cream sugar and cream cheese until smooth. Add the egg and blend well. Spread over prepared pie shell.
3. *Prepare the lemon layer:* In a mixer bowl, beat eggs until frothy. Add lemon zest, lemon juice, corn syrup, butter and cornstarch, beating until well blended. Pour over cheese layer.
4. Bake in preheated oven for 50 to 55 minutes or until set and golden brown. Let cool on a wire rack. Decorate with whipped topping and a strip of lemon zest, if desired.

Tips *When baking a pie with a very wet filling, brush the pie crust with a beaten egg before baking. The egg will help seal the crust during baking and keep it from getting soggy.*

Before squeezing a lemon, lime or orange for juice, grate the peel and freeze it for use in later recipes.

Perfect Lemon Meringue Pie

Serves 6 to 8

- Preheat oven to 450°F (230°C)
- 9-inch (23 cm) pie plate

	Pastry for a 9-inch (23 cm) single-crust pie	
1¾ cups	granulated sugar	425 mL
¼ cup	cornstarch	50 mL
3 tbsp	all-purpose flour	45 mL
¼ tsp	salt	1 mL
2 cups	water	500 mL
4	egg yolks, lightly beaten	4
1 tbsp	grated lemon zest	15 mL
½ cup	freshly squeezed lemon juice (about 1½ lemons)	125 mL
1 tbsp	butter	15 mL

MERINGUE

4	egg whites	4
¼ tsp	cream of tartar	1 mL
½ cup	granulated sugar	125 mL

1. On a lightly floured surface, roll out pastry and fit into pie plate. Prick bottom of crust with a fork and bake in preheated oven for 8 to 10 minutes or until golden brown. Let cool on a wire rack. Reduce oven temperature to 400°F (200°C).
2. In a medium saucepan, combine sugar, cornstarch, flour and salt, mixing well to blend. Add the water gradually, and stir until mixture is smooth. Bring to a boil over medium heat, stirring constantly, and boil for 1 minute, until mixture is shiny and clear.
3. Quickly stir some of the hot mixture into the beaten egg yolks and then pour back into the remaining hot mixture. Return to heat, stir and cook over low heat for 5 minutes, until thick.
4. Remove from heat and add lemon zest, lemon juice and butter, stirring until well blended. Pour into baked pie shell.
5. *Prepare the meringue:* In a mixer bowl, on medium speed, beat egg whites and cream of tartar until foamy. Gradually beat in the sugar, 2 tbsp (25 mL) at a time. Then beat on high until stiff peaks form. Spread meringue over hot filling, carefully sealing to the edge of the crust and swirling the top decoratively with a spatula.
6. Bake for 7 to 9 minutes or until meringue is golden brown. Let cool completely on a wire rack for 3 hours.

Tip *If you sprinkle a little granulated sugar over your meringue before browning, it will produce a topping that will cut more easily.*

Variation *Lime Meringue Pie: Substitute lime zest and juice for the lemon, and add a few drops of green food coloring to the filling just before pouring it into the pie shell.*

Lemon Pear Pie

Serves 6 to 8

- Preheat oven to 400°F (200°C)
- 9-inch (23 cm) pie plate

	Pastry for 9-inch (23 cm) double-crust pie	
1	egg, lightly beaten	1
1 cup	granulated sugar	250 mL
1 tbsp	butter or margarine	15 mL
1 tsp	grated lemon zest	5 mL
¼ cup	freshly squeezed lemon juice	50 mL
2	cans (each 14 oz/398 mL) pear halves, drained and diced	2

1. In a small saucepan, over low heat, combine egg, sugar, butter, lemon zest and lemon juice. Cook, stirring constantly, until mixture bubbles and is thick. Remove from heat.
2. On a lightly floured surface, roll out half of pastry and fit into pie plate. Arrange diced pears in bottom of pie crust. Top with the lemon mixture.
3. Roll out the remaining pastry to fit over filling. Make several slits in top crust, near the center, and place over filling. Trim overhang, turn edges under, flush with rim, and flute or crimp edge.
4. Bake in preheated oven for 30 to 35 minutes or until top crust is golden brown. Let cool on a wire rack.

Tip *For a flaky top for your pies, brush the top crust with a little water.*

Fluffy Whipped Lime Pie

Serves 6 to 8

- 8- or 9-inch (20 or 23 cm) pie plate

	Graham Cracker Crust (see recipe, page 407), baked and cooled	
1 cup	sour cream	250 mL
1	can (10 oz/300 mL) sweetened condensed milk	1
2 tbsp	freshly squeezed lime juice	25 mL
5	drops green food coloring (optional)	5
2 cups	frozen whipped topping, thawed	500 mL

1. In a large bowl, combine sour cream, milk, lime juice and food coloring (if using). Gently fold in whipped topping until well combined.
2. Spoon into prepared pie crust. Chill in refrigerator for 12 hours or overnight before serving.

Classic Key Lime Pie

Serves 6 to 8

- Preheat oven to 350°F (180°C)
- 9-inch (23 cm) pie plate

	Coconut Crumb Crust (see recipe, page 407) or Graham Cracker Crust (see recipe, page 407), baked and cooled	
3	eggs, separated	3
1	can (10 oz/300 mL) sweetened condensed milk	1
1 tsp	grated Key lime zest	5 mL
½ cup	freshly squeezed Key lime juice (about 4 Key limes)	125 mL
¼ tsp	cream of tartar	1 mL
	Graham wafer crumbs (optional)	
	Whipped cream (optional)	
	Toasted flaked coconut (sweetened or unsweetened), (optional)	
	Key lime slices or extra zest	

1. In a large mixer bowl, combine egg yolks, milk, lime zest and lime juice, beating until blended.
2. In a small mixer bowl, with clean beaters, on high speed, beat egg whites and cream of tartar until stiff, but not dry, peaks form. Fold gently into egg yolk mixture and spoon into prepared pie crust. Sprinkle wafer crumbs over top, if desired.
3. Bake in preheated oven for about 25 minutes or until center is set. Let cool on a wire rack. Garnish with whipped cream or coconut, if desired, and lime slices or zest.

Mandarin Orange Cream Pie

Serves 6 to 8

- 9-inch (23 cm) pie plate

	Graham Cracker Crust (see recipe, page 407), baked and cooled	
1	can (10 oz/284 mL) mandarin orange segments	1
1	package (8 oz/250 g) cream cheese, softened	1
	Water	
1	package (3 oz/90 g) orange-flavored gelatin	1
8 oz	frozen whipped topping, thawed	250 g

1. Drain the orange segments and reserve the juice. Place about half of the orange segments and the cream cheese in a bowl. Mix well to combine.
2. Put the reserved juice in a measuring cup and add enough water to make 1 cup (250 mL). Pour into a small saucepan and bring to a boil. Add the gelatin and stir until completely dissolved.
3. Add gelatin mixture to the cream cheese mixture and chill in refrigerator until almost set. Fold in whipped topping, gently, until well blended. Spoon into prepared pie crust and arrange the remaining orange segments over top. Chill in refrigerator until completely set.

Black Forest Cherry Pie

Serves 6 to 8

- 9-inch (23 cm) pie plate

	9-inch (23 cm) single-crust pie shell, baked and cooled	
2/3 cup	granulated sugar	150 mL
3 tbsp	cornstarch	45 mL
1/4 tsp	salt	1 mL
2 cups	milk	500 mL
2	eggs, lightly beaten	2
2 tbsp	butter or margarine	25 mL
1 tsp	vanilla	5 mL
2 oz	semisweet chocolate, melted	60 g
2 cups	drained canned dark sweet cherries, halved	500 mL
1/2 cup	whipping (35%) cream	125 mL

1. In a medium saucepan, combine sugar, cornstarch and salt. Gradually stir in milk and cook over low heat until mixture is bubbly, then cook for 2 minutes. Stir a small amount of this mixture into the eggs and then return to saucepan and cook for 2 minutes.
2. Remove from heat and stir in the butter and vanilla, mixing until blended. Stir 1/2 cup (125 mL) of the egg mixture into melted chocolate. Spread evenly onto bottom of prepared crust.
3. Cover the hot egg mixture with plastic wrap or waxed paper. Let cool for 25 to 30 minutes.
4. Place cherry halves, cut side down, onto layer of chocolate in crust, setting aside 8 halves. When egg mixture is cooled, spread it on top of the cherries. Chill in refrigerator until firm.
5. In a small mixer bowl, on high speed, beat whipping cream until stiff peaks form. Spoon on top of pie and use the reserved cherry halves to decorate.

Supreme Lattice Cherry Pie

Serves 6 to 8

- Preheat oven to 425°F (220°C)
- 9-inch (23 cm) pie plate

	Pastry for a 9-inch (23 cm) double-crust pie	
4 cups	frozen pitted tart red cherries, thawed, juice reserved	1 L
3/4 cup	granulated sugar	175 mL
2 1/2 tbsp	cornstarch	32 mL
Pinch	salt	Pinch
1/4 cup	butter or margarine, melted	50 mL
6	drops almond extract	6

1. On lightly floured surface, roll out half of pastry and fit into pie plate.
2. Drain cherries, reserving 1 cup (250 mL) juice.
3. In a medium saucepan, over low heat, combine sugar, cornstarch and salt. Slowly stir in cherry juice and cook until smooth. Keep stirring until mixture becomes thick and clear. Remove from heat and add butter and almond extract, and stir until smooth and well blended. Let cool to room temperature, 10 to 15 minutes.
4. Add cherries to cooled cornstarch mixture, mix well, and pour into bottom of your prepared crust.
5. Roll out the remaining pastry to fit over filling. Cut into 10 strips, 1/2 inch (1 cm) wide. Top with lattice crust (see tip, below) and crimp edges high. To keep top from browning too quickly, place a strip of foil loosely around edge of pie.
6. Bake in preheated oven for 35 to 40 minutes or until top is golden brown. Remove the foil about 10 minutes before the end of baking time. Let cool on a wire rack.

Tips *To make a lattice top, roll out pastry and cut into ten 1/2-inch (1 cm) strips. Arrange five pastry strips, about 1 1/2 inches (3.5 cm) apart, over your filling. Fold back every other strip. Place another strip across, then unfold strips. To finish, fold back the alternate strips and place next strip the same distance from the other strip. Unfold strips and continue weaving until lattice top is completed.*

Use a pizza cutter when cutting strips of dough for a lattice crust.

Mile-High Apricot Meringue Pie

Serves 6 to 8
- Preheat oven to 325°F (160°C)
- 9-inch (23 cm) pie plate

	9-inch (23 cm) single-crust pie shell, baked and cooled	
2 cups	granulated sugar	500 mL
3 tbsp	cornstarch	45 mL
¼ tsp	salt	1 mL
1½ cups	water	375 mL
1½ cups	chopped dried apricots (about 12 oz/375 g)	375 mL
4	egg yolks, lightly beaten	4
2 tbsp	butter or margarine, softened	25 mL
MERINGUE TOPPING		
4	egg whites	4
¼ tsp	cream of tartar	1 mL
½ cup	granulated sugar	125 mL

1. In a medium bowl, mix together the sugar, cornstarch and salt.
2. In a medium saucepan, over medium heat, bring water and apricots to a boil. Reduce heat to low, and simmer for about 10 to 12 minutes or until apricots are softened.
3. Add the sugar mixture to the apricot mixture and, stirring, bring to a boil. Reduce heat and cook for 1 to 2 minutes, until mixture is thickened. Remove from heat, add a small amount into the egg yolks and then pour back into saucepan. Bring to a gentle boil, stirring constantly, for about 1 to 2 minutes or until mixture is glossy and clear. Remove from heat and stir in the butter until it dissolves.
4. *Prepare the topping:* In a small mixer bowl, beat egg whites and cream of tartar until soft peaks form. Gradually add sugar, by spoonfuls, and beat on high speed until stiff peaks form.
5. Spoon hot filling into prepared pie crust. Spoon meringue over top, spreading evenly, and sealing the edges of the crust.
6. Bake in preheated oven for 30 minutes or until meringue is golden brown. Let cool for 10 minutes on a wire rack and then chill in refrigerator for several hours.

Tip *When you bake a pie topped with meringue, always spread the meringue so that it extends out to the edge of your crust. This will prevent the meringue from pulling away and coming up short during baking.*

Nectarine Pie

Serves 6 to 8
- Preheat oven to 425°F (220°C)
- 9-inch (23 cm) pie plate

	Pastry for a 9-inch (23 cm) double-crust pie	
4 cups	peeled, sliced fresh nectarines	1 L
½ cup	granulated sugar	125 mL
¼ cup	all-purpose flour	50 mL
¼ cup	firmly packed brown sugar	50 mL
1 tsp	grated lemon zest	5 mL
1 tsp	freshly squeezed lemon juice	5 mL
½ tsp	ground cinnamon	2 mL
Pinch	salt	Pinch
2 tbsp	butter or margarine	25 mL
1 tbsp	milk, half-and-half (10%) cream or table (18%) cream	15 mL
	Whipped topping (optional)	

1. On a lightly floured surface, roll out half of pastry and fit into pie plate.
2. Place fruit in a large bowl. Sprinkle with granulated sugar, flour, brown sugar, lemon zest, lemon juice, cinnamon and salt. Toss lightly to combine. Spoon into bottom crust and dot with butter.
3. Roll out the remaining pastry to fit over filling. Make several slits near the center of the top crust and place over top of filling. Trim overhang, turn edges under flush with rim and flute or crimp edge all around. Brush top with milk.
4. Bake in preheated oven for 45 to 50 minutes or until juices are bubbly and top crust is golden brown. Serve with whipped topping, if desired.

Old-Fashioned Fresh Peach Pie

Serves 6 to 8
- Preheat oven to 425°F (220°C)
- 9-inch (23 cm) pie plate

	Pastry for a 9-inch (23 cm) double-crust pie	
1 cup	granulated sugar	250 mL
¼ cup	all-purpose flour	50 mL
½ tsp	ground cinnamon	2 mL
Pinch	ground nutmeg	Pinch
9	fresh peaches, sliced (about 9 cups/2.25 L)	9
1 tsp	freshly squeezed lemon juice	5 mL
2 tbsp	butter or margarine, softened	25 mL

1. On a lightly floured surface, roll out half of pastry and fit into pie plate.
2. In a small bowl, combine sugar, flour, cinnamon and nutmeg. Mix to blend. In a large bowl, mix peaches and lemon juice. Add dry mixture to peaches. Spoon into bottom crust. Dot with butter.
3. Roll out the remaining pastry to fit over filling. Cut into 10 strips, about 1/2 inch (1 cm) wide. Moisten rim of bottom crust with water and place strips to form a lattice top (see tip, page 421). Pinch to make a stand-up edge and then flute.
4. Bake in preheated oven for 40 to 45 minutes or until filling is bubbly and crust is golden brown. Let cool on a wire rack.

Peaches 'n' Cream Pie

Serves 6 to 8
• 9-inch (23 cm) pie plate

	9-inch (23 cm) single-crust pie shell, baked and cooled	
1	package (8 oz/250 g) cream cheese, softened	1
2 tbsp	milk	25 mL
2 tbsp	granulated sugar	25 mL
1/4 tsp	almond extract	1 mL
2	packages (each 10 oz/300 g) frozen sliced peaches, drained (reserve juice)	2

GLAZE

1/4 cup	granulated sugar	50 mL
1 tbsp	cornstarch	15 mL
2/3 cup	reserved peach juice	150 mL
1 tbsp	freshly squeezed lemon juice	15 mL
1 tbsp	butter or margarine	15 mL

1. In a medium bowl, combine cream cheese and milk. Mix well until smooth and blended. Add sugar and almond extract, and mix until well blended. Spoon onto prepared pie crust. Chill in refrigerator for at least 30 minutes.
2. Arrange peach slices on top of cream cheese mixture.
3. *Prepare the glaze:* In a saucepan, combine sugar, cornstarch, reserved juice and lemon juice. Cook over medium heat, stirring, until mixture is clear and thick. Stir in butter until dissolved, about 2 to 3 minutes. Set aside to cool to room temperature, about 10 to 15 minutes.
4. When glaze has cooled, pour over peach slices.

Peach Custard Pie

Serves 6 to 8
• Preheat oven to 375°F (190°C)
• 9-inch (23 cm) pie plate

	9-inch (23 cm) single-crust pie shell, baked and cooled	
1	can (19 oz/540 mL) peach pie filling	1
1 cup	drained crushed canned pineapple	250 mL
1	package (8 oz/250 g) cream cheese, softened	1
1 cup	sour cream	250 mL
2	eggs, lightly beaten	2
1/3 cup	granulated sugar	75 mL
	Ground nutmeg (optional)	

1. In a bowl, mix together pie filling and pineapple. Spoon into prepared pie crust.
2. In a mixer bowl, beat cream cheese and sour cream until smooth. Beat in eggs and sugar until blended and smooth. Spoon over peach mixture. Sprinkle some nutmeg over top, if desired.
3. Bake in preheated oven for 30 to 35 minutes or until top is golden brown. Let cool on a wire rack.

Peach Melba Pie

Serves 6 to 8
• 9-inch (23 cm) pie plate

	Graham Cracker Crust (see recipe, page 407), baked and cooled	
1	package (3 oz/90 g) peach-flavored gelatin	1
2/3 cup	boiling water	150 mL
2 cups	ice cubes	500 mL
2 cups	frozen whipped topping, thawed	500 mL
1 cup	fresh peaches, sliced and dipped in lemon juice (about 2 peaches)	250 mL
3 tbsp	raspberry jam	45 mL

1. In a bowl, dissolve gelatin in boiling water, stirring until completely dissolved. Add ice cubes and stir until mixture starts to thicken, about 3 minutes. Remove any unmelted ice. Immediately fold in whipped topping and beat until well blended.
2. Arrange peach slices on prepared baked crust. Spoon gelatin mixture over top of peaches.
3. In a small bowl, stir jam to soften and then drizzle over pie. Use a knife or spatula to make swirls or a marbling effect. Chill in refrigerator for several hours, until firm.

Peach Streusel Pie

Serves 6 to 8

- Preheat oven to 375°F (190°C)
- 9-inch (23 cm) pie plate

	Crunchy Oatmeal Crust (see recipe, page 408)	
1	can (19 oz/540 mL) peach pie filling	1
½ cup	raisins	125 mL
½ tsp	ground cinnamon	2 mL
STREUSEL TOPPING		
⅓ cup	quick-cooking rolled oats	75 mL
¼ cup	all-purpose flour	50 mL
¼ cup	firmly packed brown sugar	50 mL
3 tbsp	butter or margarine, softened	45 mL

1. In a medium bowl, combine pie filling, raisins and cinnamon. Mix together to blend. Spoon into prepared pie crust.
2. *Prepare the topping:* Combine oats, flour and brown sugar, mixing to blend. Cut in butter with a fork until mixture resembles coarse crumbs. Sprinkle over top of peach mixture.
3. Bake in preheated oven for 25 to 30 minutes or until topping is golden brown.

Plum and Peach Galette

Serves 8 to 10

- Preheat oven to 400°F (200°C)
- Baking sheet

CRUST		
1¼ cups	all-purpose flour	300 mL
2 tbsp	granulated sugar	25 mL
¼ tsp	salt	1 mL
½ cup	unsalted butter, chilled	125 mL
3 tbsp	ice water	45 mL
FILLING		
1 cup	granulated sugar	250 mL
2 tbsp	quick-cooking tapioca	25 mL
¼ tsp	salt	1 mL
1 tsp	ground cinnamon	5 mL
1 tsp	grated lemon zest	5 mL
4 cups	peeled, sliced red or purple plums	1 L
4 cups	peeled, sliced peaches	1 L
2 tsp	freshly squeezed lemon juice	10 mL
1 tsp	ground mace (optional)	5 mL
1	egg	1
	Granulated sugar	

1. *Prepare the crust:* In a large bowl, combine flour, sugar and salt, and mix to blend. Cut in butter with a pastry blender or two knives until mixture resembles coarse crumbs. Add ice water, 1 tbsp (15 mL) at a time, until dough is of right consistency. Then shape into a round disk, wrap in plastic wrap and chill in refrigerator for at least 1 hour.
2. *Prepare the filling:* In a large bowl, combine sugar, tapioca, salt, cinnamon, lemon zest, plums, peaches, lemon juice and mace (if using). Mix together well and let stand for about 20 minutes.
3. On a lightly floured surface, roll out dough to form a circle, about 14 inches (35 cm) in diameter. Place on baking sheet. Place fruit mixture in center and spread over dough, leaving a border of 2 inches (5 cm). Fold the border in toward the center of the fruit filling, leaving the filling exposed in the center. Make an egg wash by lightly beating egg in a small bowl. Brush egg wash over folded border and sprinkle granulated sugar over top.
4. Bake in preheated oven for about 45 to 50 minutes or until crust is golden brown and fruit is tender. Let tart cool on the baking sheet for 1 to 2 hours, and then place onto a serving plate. Best when served warm.

Spicy Tart Plum Pie

Serves 6 to 8

- Preheat oven to 425°F (220°C)
- 9-inch (23 cm) pie plate

	Pastry for a 9-inch (23 cm) double-crust pie	
1¾ cups	granulated sugar	425 mL
½ cup	all-purpose flour	125 mL
1 tsp	grated lemon zest	5 mL
½ tsp	ground cinnamon	2 mL
¼ tsp	ground nutmeg	1 mL
Pinch	salt	Pinch
4 cups	pitted, quartered red or purple plums (about 6)	1 L
2 tbsp	butter or margarine	25 mL

1. On a lightly floured surface, roll out half of pastry and fit into pie plate.
2. In a small bowl, combine sugar, flour, lemon zest, cinnamon, nutmeg and salt. Mix well to blend thoroughly. Sprinkle 2 tbsp (25 mL) of this mixture over bottom of prepared crust.

3. Arrange one-quarter of the plums over the sugar mixture. Sprinkle with ½ cup (125 mL) of the sugar mixture. Repeat with the remaining plums and sugar mixture to make 3 more layers of each. Dot with the butter.

4. Roll out remaining pastry to fit over filling. Cut several slits near the center of top crust. Cover top of pie and trim, seal and flute or crimp edges.

5. Bake in preheated oven for 10 minutes. Reduce oven temperature to 350ºF (180ºC) and bake for 40 to 45 minutes or until juices bubble up and the top is golden brown. Let cool on a wire rack.

Tip *To avoid leakage from fruit pies, sprinkle fine dry bread crumbs on the bottom crust before adding filling.*

• •

Old-Fashioned Banana Cream Pie

Serves 6 to 8

• 9-inch (23 cm) pie plate

	9-inch (23 cm) single-crust pie shell, baked and cooled	
4	firm ripe bananas (not green)	4
1 cup	whipping (35%) cream	250 mL
½ to 1 tsp	granulated sugar (optional)	2 to 5 mL

1. Slice bananas and pile into prepared cooled pie crust. Fill pie crust as full as you like.

2. In a small mixer bowl, beat whipping cream until stiff peaks form. Add granulated sugar (if using) while beating.

3. Spoon scoops of whipped cream over top of bananas, piling as high as you like. Keep in refrigerator until ready to serve.

Tip *This seems almost too easy, but I remember when my mom used to make this pie. With real whipped cream, not frozen whipped topping, this pie seems to melt in your mouth.*

• •

Banana Split Pie

Serves 6 to 8

• 9-inch (23 cm) pie plate

	9-inch (23 cm) single-crust pie shell, baked and cooled	
3	firm ripe bananas	3
1 tbsp	freshly squeezed lemon juice	15 mL
2 cups	strawberry ice cream, slightly softened	500 mL
1 cup	frozen whipped topping, thawed Maraschino cherries, whole or halved	250 mL
2 tbsp	finely chopped walnuts	25 mL

CHOCOLATE SAUCE

1 cup	semisweet chocolate pieces	250 mL
⅔ cup	evaporated milk	150 mL
½	jar (1 cup/250 mL) marshmallow crème	½

1. Slice bananas into thin slices and place in a bowl. Sprinkle lemon juice over top. Arrange as desired on bottom of prepared pie crust.

2. In a bowl, stir ice cream to soften sufficiently and to make smooth. Spread over top of banana slices. Freeze until firm.

3. Spread whipped topping over the ice cream. Top with maraschino cherries, either whole or halved. Sprinkle nuts over top. Place in freezer until firm. When ready to serve, leave at room temperature for 30 minutes.

4. *Prepare the chocolate sauce:* In a saucepan, over low heat, combine chocolate and milk. Cook, stirring, until well blended. Whisk in half the jar of marshmallow crème, beating until mixture is thoroughly combined. Drizzle over each slice of pie.

• •

Coconut Pineapple Cream Pie

Serves 6 to 8

• 9-inch (23 cm) pie plate

	Coconut Crumb Crust (see recipe, page 407), baked and cooled	
1	package (3 oz/90 g) vanilla tapioca pudding mix	1
1	package (3 oz/90 g) lemon-flavored gelatin	1
1¼ cups	milk	300 mL
⅓ cup	frozen unsweetened pineapple juice concentrate, thawed	75 mL
1	package (2 oz/60 g) dessert topping mix	1
¾ cup	well-drained canned crushed pineapple	175 mL

1. In a medium saucepan, mix pudding mix and gelatin. Stir in milk and cook over medium heat until mixture boils. Remove from heat and stir in pineapple juice concentrate. Chill in refrigerator until partially set.

2. Prepare the dessert topping mix according to package instructions. Fold into the pudding mixture. Fold in pineapple, gently, until mixture is thoroughly combined.

3. Spoon into coconut crust and chill in refrigerator for 5 to 6 hours or overnight.

Old-Fashioned Rhubarb Custard Pie

Serves 6 to 8

- Preheat oven to 400°F (200°C)
- 9-inch (23 cm) pie plate

	Pastry for a 9-inch (23 cm) single-crust pie	
2	eggs, lightly beaten	2
3/4 cup	granulated sugar	175 mL
3 tbsp	all-purpose flour	45 mL
1 tsp	ground cinnamon	5 mL
4 cups	chopped fresh rhubarb	1 L

1. On a lightly floured surface, roll out pastry and fit into pie plate. Brush pastry with a tiny bit of the beaten eggs, just enough to coat the bottom.
2. In a mixer bowl, combine eggs, sugar, flour and cinnamon. Beat on high speed until mixture becomes thick.
3. Place rhubarb in the pie shell, and pour egg mixture over the rhubarb, spreading evenly to the edges.
4. Bake in preheated oven for 30 to 35 minutes or until top is lightly browned. Let cool on a wire rack.

Tip *If you want your pie to have a sugary top, remove the pie from the oven 5 minutes before it is done, sprinkle with granulated sugar, and return it to the oven.*

Sour Cream Rhubarb Pie

Serves 6 to 8

- Preheat oven to 450°F (230°C)
- 9-inch (23 cm) pie plate

	Pastry for a 9-inch (23 cm) single-crust pie	
1 cup	granulated sugar	250 mL
1/3 cup	all-purpose flour	75 mL
3/4 cup	sour cream	175 mL
4 cups	chopped fresh rhubarb	1 L
TOPPING		
1/2 cup	packed brown sugar	125 mL
1/2 cup	all-purpose flour	125 mL
1/4 cup	butter or margarine, softened	50 mL

1. On a lightly floured surface, roll out pastry and fit into pie plate.
2. In a large bowl, combine granulated sugar, flour and sour cream. Add rhubarb and toss until well combined and coated. Spoon into prepared pie crust.

3. *Prepare the topping:* In a small bowl, combine brown sugar and flour. Cut in butter with a fork, mixing until mixture is crumbly. Sprinkle over top of pie filling.
4. Bake in preheated oven for 15 minutes. Reduce heat to 350°F (180°C) and continue baking for another 35 to 40 minutes or until fruit is tender and top is lightly browned. Let cool on a wire rack for about 20 to 25 minutes before serving.

Pumpkin Purée

Having a good recipe for pumpkin purée can make a real difference to many pumpkin recipes. To make 2 cups (500 mL) of purée, use a 3-lb (1.5 kg) ripe pumpkin. Wash the pumpkin well and cut in half. Scoop out seeds and fibers and then cut into quarters. Place pieces into a baking dish. Set dish in a pan of hot water and bake at 350°F (180°C) for 45 minutes or until tender. Scrape the pulp from the pumpkin rind. Place pulp in a blender or food processor and purée.

Old-Fashioned Pumpkin Pie

Serves 6 to 8

- Preheat oven to 425°F (220°C)
- 9-inch (23 cm) pie plate

	Pastry for a 9-inch (23 cm) single-crust pie	
3/4 cup	granulated sugar or packed brown sugar	175 mL
2 cups	Pumpkin Purée (see recipe, above) or canned (not pie filling)	500 mL
1	can (14 oz/398 mL) evaporated milk	1
2	eggs, lightly beaten	2
1 tsp	ground cinnamon	5 mL
1/2 tsp	ground nutmeg	2 mL
1/2 tsp	ground ginger	2 mL
1/2 tsp	salt	2 mL
1/4 tsp	ground cloves	1 mL
	Whipped cream or topping (optional)	

1. On a lightly floured surface, roll out pastry and fit into pie plate.
2. In a large bowl, combine sugar, pumpkin, milk and eggs. Mix together until well combined. Add cinnamon, nutmeg, ginger, salt and cloves, and mix well. Spoon into prepared pastry shell, spreading evenly.

3. Bake in preheated oven for 15 minutes. Reduce oven temperature to 350°F (180°C) and bake for another 45 to 50 minutes or until a knife inserted in the center comes out clean and dry. Let cool on a wire rack. Decorate with whipped cream or topping, or as desired.

Tips *If your pumpkin filling contains milk or cream, warm it slightly so that the filling sets more quickly, and bake your pie as soon as you have added the filling to the crust. Too much time standing before baking allows the filling to soak into the pastry, causing a soggy crust.*

I always love pumpkin pie with whipped cream or ice cream! In place of the spices, you can also use 2 tsp (10 mL) of pumpkin pie spice.

Lite Pumpkin Pie with Phyllo Crust

Serves 6 to 8
- Preheat oven to 350°F (180°C)
- 9-inch (23 cm) pie plate, lightly coated with non-stick cooking spray

PHYLLO CRUST

4	sheets phyllo pastry	4
	Non-stick cooking spray	

FILLING

1/2 cup	firmly packed brown sugar	125 mL
1 tbsp	cornstarch	15 mL
1 tsp	ground cinnamon	5 mL
1 tsp	ground ginger	5 mL
1/4 tsp	ground cloves	1 mL
Pinch	salt	Pinch
1 1/2 cups	Pumpkin Purée (see recipe, page 426) or canned (not pie filling)	375 mL
1	can (14 oz/398 mL) fat-free evaporated milk	1
1/2 cup	liquid egg substitute	125 mL
1 tsp	vanilla	5 mL

1. *Prepare the crust:* Cut each sheet of phyllo pastry in half across the short side, to make 8 sheets. Place one sheet on work surface with a short side facing you. Spray lightly with cooking spray. Starting at the left edge of the first sheet, place another sheet in the same direction, overlapping 1 inch (2.5 cm) to the right of the left edge, and spray lightly with cooking spray. Repeat with the remaining sheets, placing each 1 inch (2.5 cm) to the right of the left edge of the previous sheet and spraying lightly. This will form a large rectangle.

2. Carefully fit rectangle of pastry into prepared pie plate, pressing to the bottom gently. Starting at one corner, roll edges down and around, to form a ridge around the plate. Bake in preheated oven for 8 to 10 minutes or until golden brown. If bottom starts to puff up halfway through baking, press it down gently with a wooden spoon. Let cool completely on a wire rack.

3. *Prepare the filling:* In a large bowl, combine brown sugar, cornstarch, cinnamon, ginger, cloves and salt. Mix together to blend. In another bowl, combine pumpkin purée, milk, egg substitute and vanilla. Beat until thoroughly combined. Add the pumpkin mixture to the brown sugar mixture and beat until well blended.

4. Spoon into cooled phyllo crust and bake for 50 to 60 minutes or until knife inserted in the center comes out clean and dry. Let cool completely on a wire rack. Garnish as desired.

Tip *Fruit pies will slice more attractively if you add 1 to 2 tbsp (15 to 25 mL) of cornstarch into the dry filling ingredients. It gives the filling more body and, therefore, it slices much better.*

Crustless Pumpkin Pie

Serves 6 to 8
- Preheat oven to 350°F (180°C)
- 9-inch (23 cm) pie plate, greased

1/2 cup	biscuit mix	125 mL
3/4 cup	granulated sugar	175 mL
2 1/2 tsp	pumpkin pie spice	12 mL
1	can (14 oz/398 mL) evaporated milk	1
2	eggs	2
2 cups	Pumpkin Purée (see recipe, page 426) or canned (not pie filling)	500 mL
2 tbsp	butter or margarine, softened	25 mL
2 tsp	vanilla	10 mL

1. In a large mixer bowl, mix together biscuit mix, sugar and spice, until blended.

2. Add milk, eggs, pumpkin, butter and vanilla. Beat on medium speed until blended. Then beat on high speed for 2 minutes, until thoroughly blended. Spoon into prepared pie plate.

3. Bake in preheated oven for 50 to 55 minutes or until knife inserted in the center comes out clean and dry. Let cool on a wire rack.

Tip *To prepare your own pumpkin pie spice, mix together 1 tsp (5 mL) ground cinnamon, 1/4 tsp (1 mL) ground nutmeg, 1/4 tsp (1 mL) ground ginger and a pinch of ground cloves. Store in an airtight container.*

Caramel Pecan Pumpkin Pie

Serves 8 to 10
- Preheat oven to 375°F (190°C)
- 9-inch (23 cm) pie plate

	Pastry for a 9-inch (23 cm) single-crust pie	
¾ cup	granulated sugar	175 mL
1 tbsp	all-purpose flour	15 mL
1 tsp	finely grated lemon zest	5 mL
½ tsp	ground cinnamon	2 mL
¼ tsp	ground nutmeg	1 mL
¼ tsp	salt	1 mL
Pinch	ground allspice	Pinch
½ tsp	vanilla	2 mL
2 cups	Pumpkin Purée (see recipe, page 426) or canned (not pie filling)	500 mL
2	eggs, lightly beaten	2
¼ cup	milk	50 mL
TOPPING		
2 tbsp	butter or margarine, softened	25 mL
½ cup	firmly packed brown sugar	125 mL
½ cup	chopped pecans	125 mL

1. On a lightly floured surface, roll out pastry and fit into pie plate.
2. In a small bowl, combine sugar, flour, zest, cinnamon, nutmeg, salt, allspice and vanilla.
3. In a large bowl, combine pumpkin, eggs and milk. Mix well to blend. Add dry mixture to pumpkin mixture. Stir until mixture is well combined and spoon into pie crust.
4. Bake in preheated oven for 25 minutes. If edges seem to be browning too quickly, cover the edge with a strip of tin foil.
5. *Prepare the topping:* In a small bowl, combine butter, brown sugar and pecans. Mix well. Sprinkle evenly over top of pie and bake for another 20 to 25 minutes or until golden brown and bubbly and a knife inserted in the center comes out clean and dry. Let cool on a wire rack until cool to the touch. Chill in refrigerator for at least 30 minutes or until ready to serve.

Tip *To prevent the crust of a pumpkin pie from becoming soggy, use only enough water to allow the dough to clump into a ball. Too much moisture can contribute to a soggy crust.*

Double-Creamy Pumpkin Pie

Serves 8 to 10
- 9-inch (23 cm) pie plate

	Graham Cracker Crust (see recipe, page 407), baked and cooled	
CREAM FILLING		
4 oz	cream cheese, softened	125 g
1 tbsp	granulated sugar	15 mL
1 tbsp	milk	15 mL
1½ cups	frozen whipped topping, thawed	375 mL
PUMPKIN FILLING		
1 cup	cold milk	250 mL
2 cups	Pumpkin Purée (see recipe, page 426) or canned (not pie filling)	500 mL
2	packages (each a 4-serving size) vanilla instant pudding	500 mL
1 tsp	ground cinnamon	5 mL
½ tsp	ground ginger	2 mL
¼ tsp	ground cloves	1 mL
	Whipped topping (optional)	
	Ground cinnamon or nutmeg (optional)	
	Nuts (optional)	

1. *Prepare the cream filling:* In a large mixer bowl, on low speed, combine cream cheese and sugar. Add milk and beat until smooth and blended. Slowly fold in whipped topping, and blend well. Spoon into crust in pie plate, spreading evenly.
2. *Prepare the pumpkin filling:* In a large bowl, whisk milk, pumpkin, pudding mix, cinnamon, ginger and cloves until mixture is thick. Spread over cream cheese layer.
3. Chill in refrigerator for 4 to 5 hours or until set. Garnish with a dollop of whipped topping sprinkled with cinnamon or nutmeg, or nuts, if desired.

Tip *If you have a large amount of leftover pumpkin pie spice, especially at holiday time, sprinkle on sweet potatoes or carrots.*

Chocolate Pies

• •

Chocolate Chip Cookies 'n' Cream Pie

Serves 6 to 8

• Preheat oven to 375°F (190°C)
• 9-inch (23 cm) pie plate, greased and lightly sugared

6 oz	unsweetened chocolate, chopped	175 g
2 tbsp	water	25 mL
8 oz	slice-and-bake chocolate chip cookie dough (½ roll)	250 g
2 cups	vanilla ice cream, slightly softened	500 mL

1. In a small saucepan, melt chocolate and water. Set aside to cool to room temperature, about 10 to 15 minutes.
2. Slice the cookie dough into ⅛-inch (0.25 cm) thick slices. Line bottom and sides of prepared pie plate by slightly overlapping each slice of cookie dough.
3. Bake in preheated oven for 8 to 10 minutes or until lightly browned. Let cool completely in plate on a wire rack.
4. Arrange scoops of ice cream over bottom of pie crust, then drizzle over top with the melted chocolate mixture. Serve immediately, or wrap and freeze for up to 6 months. If frozen, leave at room temperature for 20 minutes before serving.

• •

Chocolate Cream Pie

Serves 8

• 9-inch (23 cm) pie plate

	9-inch (23 cm) single-crust pie shell, baked and cooled	
1 cup	granulated sugar	250 mL
¼ cup	cornstarch	50 mL
¼ tsp	salt	1 mL
2¾ cups	milk	675 mL
3	egg yolks	3
1 tbsp	butter or margarine, softened	15 mL
1 tsp	vanilla	5 mL
3 oz	unsweetened chocolate, coarsely chopped	90 g
	Whipped topping	
	Chocolate shavings or curls (optional)	

1. In a medium saucepan, combine sugar, cornstarch and salt and mix to blend. Over medium heat, whisk in milk until mixture is smooth, and, stirring constantly, bring to a boil. Boil for 1 to 2 minutes, stirring gently, until slightly thickened. Remove from heat.
2. In a small bowl, beat egg yolks and slowly whisk in about ½ to 1 cup (125 to 250 mL) of the hot milk mixture and pour that back into the saucepan. Whisk constantly and return to a boil. Boil for 1 to 2 minutes, until thick.
3. Remove from heat and whisk in butter and vanilla, then the chocolate, and whisk until mixture is blended and completely smooth.
4. Pour into baked pastry crust and let cool for 15 to 20 minutes on a wire rack. Cover the filling with a piece of plastic wrap or foil and chill in refrigerator for 5 hours, or overnight. When ready to serve, spread whipped topping either around the edge of pie or over the complete pie. Garnish with chocolate shavings, if desired.

Variation *Black Forest Pie: Take 1 can (19 oz/540 mL) of cherry pie filling and divide in half. Before spooning chocolate filling into pie crust, fold in half of the cherry pie filling and then refrigerate as above. Just before serving, top with the remaining half of cherry pie filling. Garnish with whipped topping, if desired.*

• •

Chocolate Ice Cream Pie

Serves 8 to 10

• 9-inch (23 cm) pie plate

	Chocolate Crumb Crust (see recipe, page 407), baked and cooled	
4 cups	vanilla ice cream, slightly softened	1 L
4 cups	chocolate ice cream, slightly softened	1 L
	Chocolate shavings or curls	

1. Place vanilla ice cream in a bowl and mix lightly until softened and smooth. Using an ice cream scoop, place a row of scoops around the edge of pie shell.
2. Place chocolate ice cream in a bowl and mix lightly until softened and smooth. Arrange two rows of scoops of chocolate ice cream inside the row of vanilla scoops.
3. Use the remaining vanilla ice cream to fill up the center of pie.
4. Freeze until firm, about 4 to 5 hours. Sprinkle chocolate shavings or curls over top of pie.

Triple-Layer Chocolate Graham Pie

Serves 6 to 8

- 9-inch (23 cm) pie shell

	Graham Cracker Crust (see recipe, page 407), baked and cooled	
2	packages (each a 4-serving size) instant chocolate pudding	2
2 cups	cold milk	500 mL
8 oz	frozen whipped topping, thawed	250 g
	Chocolate curls (optional)	

1. In a large bowl, mix the packages of instant pudding to blend. Add milk and whisk for 1 to 2 minutes, until well blended.

2. Spoon 1½ cups (375 mL) of this mixture into prepared pie crust, spreading evenly.

3. Into the remaining pudding mixture, add half of the whipped topping and mix to blend. Spoon this mixture over the first layer. Top with the remaining whipped topping.

4. Chill in refrigerator for 5 hours or until set. Garnish with chocolate curls, if desired.

Fudge Brownie Pie à la Mode

Serves 6 to 8

- Preheat oven to 350°F (180°C)
- 8-inch (20 cm) pie plate, lightly greased

	8-inch (20 cm) single-crust pie shell, baked and cooled	
½ cup	all-purpose flour	125 mL
⅓ cup	unsweetened cocoa powder, sifted	75 mL
¼ tsp	salt	1 mL
2	eggs, beaten	2
1 cup	granulated sugar	250 mL
½ cup	butter or margarine, melted	125 mL
½ cup	chopped nuts	125 mL
1 tsp	vanilla	5 mL
	Vanilla ice cream	

FUDGE SAUCE

¾ cup	granulated sugar	175 mL
½ cup	unsweetened cocoa powder	125 mL
½ cup	evaporated milk	125 mL
⅓ cup	light corn syrup	75 mL
⅓ cup	butter or margarine	75 mL
1 tsp	vanilla	5 mL

1. In a small bowl, mix together flour, cocoa powder and salt to blend.

2. In a mixer bowl, combine eggs, sugar and melted butter. Add flour mixture to egg mixture and beat on low speed until combined. Add nuts and vanilla and mix well to thoroughly combine. Spoon into prepared pie crust.

3. Bake in preheated oven for 25 to 30 minutes or until filling is almost set when pie is jiggled slightly. Let cool completely on a wire rack.

4. *Prepare the fudge sauce:* In a small saucepan, mix together sugar and cocoa powder. Stir in milk and corn syrup. Bring to a boil over medium heat, stirring constantly, and boil for 1 to 2 minutes. Remove from heat and stir in butter and vanilla. Keep warm.

5. Serve each wedge of pie topped with a scoop of vanilla ice cream and with hot fudge sauce drizzled over top.

Chocolate Pecan Pie

Serves 6 to 8

- Preheat oven to 350°F (180°C)
- 9-inch (23 cm) pie plate

	9-inch (23 cm) single-crust pie shell, baked and cooled	
½ cup	granulated sugar	125 mL
⅔ cup	corn syrup	150 mL
2 oz	unsweetened chocolate, chopped	60 g
2 tbsp	butter or margarine, softened	25 mL
2	eggs	2
½ tsp	vanilla	2 mL
Pinch	salt	Pinch
½ cup	coarsely chopped pecans	125 mL
¾ cup	pecan halves	175 mL

1. In a small saucepan, combine sugar and corn syrup, and cook over medium heat until dissolved. Remove from heat and add chocolate and butter, stirring until melted. Let cool slightly.

2. In a small bowl, whisk eggs, vanilla and salt. Add to sugar mixture and mix until well blended.

3. Sprinkle the chopped pecans evenly over the bottom of prepared crust. Spoon in filling, spreading evenly. Arrange pecan halves over top.

4. Bake in preheated oven for 25 minutes or until filling is set when pie is jiggled slightly. Let cool completely on a wire rack.

Tip *To determine whether an egg is fresh, immerse it in a pan of cool, salted water. If it sinks, it is fresh. If it rises to the surface, throw it away.*

Chocolate Mint Pie

Serves 6 to 8
9-inch (23 cm) pie plate

	Chocolate Crumb Crust (see recipe, page 407)	
1½ cups	sweetened condensed milk	375 mL
1½ tsp	peppermint extract	7 mL
5 to 10	drops green food coloring (optional)	5 to 10
2 cups	whipped topping or whipping (35%) cream, whipped	500 mL
	Chocolate curls or chocolate mints, crumbled (optional)	

1. In a large bowl, combine condensed milk, peppermint extract and food coloring (if using).

2. Fold in whipped topping, gently, until well combined. Spoon into prepared pie crust, cover, and freeze for several hours, until firm. Decorate with chocolate curls or chocolate mints, if desired.

Chocolate Orange Pie

Serves 6 to 8
• 9-inch (23 cm) pie plate

	Chocolate Crumb Crust (see recipe, page 407), baked and cooled	
6 oz	white chocolate, finely chopped	175 g
¼ cup	butter or margarine	50 mL
¼ cup	whipping (35%) cream	50 mL
2 tbsp	grated orange zest	25 mL
1 tbsp	orange liqueur or orange juice	15 mL
6	chocolate cookies or wafers	6
TOPPING		
8 oz	bittersweet chocolate, finely chopped	250 g
½ cup	whipping (35%) cream	125 mL
¼ cup	butter or margarine	50 mL
¼ cup	almonds, toasted and chopped	50 mL
	Whipped cream or topping	
	Orange segments	
	Grated orange zest (optional)	

1. In a double boiler, over hot but not boiling water, melt the white chocolate, butter and whipping cream. Stir until smooth. Remove from heat, fold in orange zest and liqueur and mix to blend. Spoon into prepared pie crust.

2. Break the 6 chocolate wafers, by hand, into coarse chunks and sprinkle over top of filling. Chill in refrigerator until firm.

3. *Prepare the topping:* In the double boiler, over hot but not boiling water, melt the bittersweet chocolate, whipping cream and butter. Remove from heat and fold in the nuts. Spoon over chilled white chocolate layer. Chill in refrigerator until firm. Garnish with whipped cream and orange segments, and orange zest, if desired.

Other Pies

Lazy Day Grasshopper Pie

Serves 6 to 8
• 9-inch (23 cm) pie plate

25 to 30	chocolate wafer cookies (about 6 oz/175 g)	25 to 30
1	jar (2 cups/500 mL) marshmallow crème	1
¼ cup	milk	50 mL
4	drops peppermint extract	4
	Green food coloring	
1 cup	whipping (35%) cream, whipped, or frozen whipped topping, thawed	250 mL

1. Line the bottom of pie plate with the cookies, filling in spaces with pieces of cookie. Then line the sides with half cookies, close together or overlapping.

2. In a mixer bowl, combine marshmallow crème, peppermint extract and 5 to 6 drops (or more, if you like) of food coloring. Beat on medium speed until fluffy.

3. Fold in the whipped cream, slowly but thoroughly. Spoon into cookie crust and place in freezer for 8 hours, or preferably overnight. Garnish with more whipped cream, or crumble a few cookie wafers and sprinkle over top. Decorate with stand-up pieces of cookie.

Tip *To transport a pie, place an empty pie plate on top as a cover. This works great with any pie, and especially with meringue pies.*

Southern Pecan Pie

Serves 8 to 10

- Preheat oven to 350°F (180°C)
- 9-inch (23 cm) pie plate

	Pastry for a 9-inch (23 cm) single-crust pie	
1 cup	firmly packed dark brown sugar	250 mL
3	eggs, lightly beaten	3
1 cup	light corn syrup	250 mL
1/3 cup	butter or margarine, melted	75 mL
1 tsp	vanilla	5 mL
1/2 tsp	salt	2 mL
1 1/4 cups	pecan halves	300 mL
	Whipped topping (optional)	

1. On a lightly floured surface, roll out pastry and fit into pie plate.

2. In a large bowl, whisk together brown sugar, eggs, corn syrup, butter, vanilla and salt until well blended. Spoon into pie crust, spreading evenly. Sprinkle with the pecan halves over top.

3. Bake in preheated oven for 45 to 50 minutes or until a toothpick inserted in the center of the pie comes out clean and dry. Let cool completely on a wire rack. Decorate with whipped topping, or as desired.

Shoo-Fly Pie

Serves 6 to 8

- Preheat oven to 375°F (190°C)
- 9-inch (23 cm) pie plate

	Pastry for a 9-inch (23 cm) single-crust pie	
1 1/2 cups	all-purpose flour	375 mL
1/2 cup	granulated sugar	125 mL
1/2 tsp	baking soda, divided	2 mL
1/4 cup	butter or margarine	50 mL
1/2 cup	light (fancy) molasses	125 mL
1/2 cup	hot water	125 mL

1. On a lightly floured surface, roll out pastry and fit into pie plate.

2. In a large bowl, combine flour, sugar and half the baking soda. Cut in the butter by hand, or mixing with a fork, until mixture resembles coarse crumbs.

3. In another bowl, combine molasses, hot water and the remaining baking soda. Mix well. Spoon one-third of the molasses mixture into pie crust.

Sprinkle with one-third of the flour mixture. Repeat layers, ending with the flour mixture.

4. Bake in preheated oven for 40 to 45 minutes or until lightly browned. Let cool completely on a wire rack.

Maple Sugar Pie

Serves 6 to 8

- Preheat oven to 375°F (190°C)
- 9-inch (23 cm) pie plate

	9-inch (23 cm) single-crust pie shell, baked and cooled	
2/3 cup	firmly packed brown sugar	150 mL
2/3 cup	pure maple syrup	150 mL
2 tbsp	unsalted butter	45 mL
3	eggs	3
1/4 tsp	vanilla	1 mL
	Pinch of salt	
	Whipped cream or ice cream (optional)	

1. In the top of a double boiler, over simmering water, combine brown sugar, maple syrup and butter. Cook until melted. Remove from heat. Let cool slightly.

2. Add eggs, beating in one at a time. Then add vanilla and salt and mix until well blended. Spoon into prepared pie crust.

3. Bake in preheated oven for 25 to 30 minutes, until browned. Let cool completely on a wire rack. Serve with whipped cream or ice cream, or as desired.

Coconut Meringue Pie

Serves 6 to 8

- Preheat oven to 350°F (180°C)
- 9-inch (23 cm) pie plate

	9-inch (23 cm) single-crust pie shell, baked and cooled	
2/3 cup	granulated sugar	150 mL
1/4 cup	cornstarch	50 mL
1/4 tsp	salt	1 mL
2 cups	milk	500 mL
3	egg yolks, lightly beaten	3
1 cup	flaked coconut (sweetened or unsweetened)	250 mL
2 tbsp	butter or margarine	25 mL
1/2 tsp	vanilla	2 mL

MERINGUE TOPPING

3	egg whites	3
1/4 tsp	cream of tartar	1 mL
1/3 cup	granulated sugar	75 mL
1/2 cup	toasted flaked coconut (sweetened or unsweetened)	125 mL

1. In a medium saucepan, combine sugar, cornstarch and salt. Cook over low heat. Add milk gradually and bring to a boil on medium heat. Stirring constantly, cook for 2 minutes or until mixture is thickened.

2. Place egg yolks in a small bowl. Stir in about 1 cup (250 mL) of the hot mixture and pour this mixture back into the saucepan. Bring to a boil, stirring constantly, and boil gently for 2 to 3 minutes, until thick. Remove from heat.

3. Stir in coconut, butter and vanilla, and mix until all of the butter is melted. Spoon into prepared pie crust.

4. *Prepare the topping:* In a small, clean mixer bowl, on high speed, beat egg whites and cream of tartar until frothy. Gradually beat in sugar, one spoonful at a time, until stiff peaks form. Spread over filling, sealing edges to crust.

5. Bake in preheated oven for 15 minutes or until top is lightly browned. Let cool completely on a wire rack and then chill in refrigerator until serving. Top with toasted coconut.

Tip *If you want to bake a meringue pie ahead of time, the pie will freeze, but the meringue doesn't. It is best to freeze the pie without the meringue, then put a meringue on the pie and bake it the day you will serve it.*

• •

Passover Cheese Pie

Serves 8 to 10
• Preheat oven to 350°F (180°C)
• 9- or 10-inch (23 or 25 cm) deep-dish pie plate

CRUST

3 tbsp	granulated sugar	45 mL
1/2 tsp	salt	2 mL
1/2 cup	shortening, softened	125 mL
1 1/2 cups	matzo meal	375 mL
1 tbsp	water	15 mL

FILLING

1 cup	cottage cheese (creamed or dry)	250 mL
1	package (8 oz/250 g) cream cheese, softened	1
3	eggs, separated	3
3/4 cup	granulated sugar	175 mL
1 cup	sour cream	250 mL
1 tbsp	potato starch	15 mL
1 tsp	grated lemon zest	5 mL

1. *Prepare the crust:* In a medium bowl, cream sugar, salt and shortening until smooth. Add the matzo meal and mix well to blend thoroughly. Stir in water gradually. Spoon into prepared pie plate and pat down.

2. *Prepare the filling:* In a large mixer bowl, beat cottage and cream cheeses until smooth and fluffy. Add egg yolks and sugar and beat until smooth and blended. Stir in sour cream, potato starch and lemon zest. Mix well.

3. In a small, clean mixer bowl, with clean beaters, on high speed, beat egg whites until stiff peaks form, but whites are not dry. Fold into cheese mixture, slowly but thoroughly. Spoon into pie plate.

4. Bake in preheated oven for 1 hour or until a knife inserted in the middle comes out clean and dry. Let cool completely on a wire rack.

• •

Eggnog Pie

Serves 6 to 8
• 9-inch (23 cm) pie plate

	9-inch (23 cm) single-crust pie shell, baked and cooled	
1	envelope (1/4 oz/7 g) unflavored gelatin	1
1	package (3 oz/90 g) no-bake custard mix	1
1/4 tsp	ground nutmeg	1 mL
2 1/4 cups	milk	550 mL
2 tbsp	rum (or 1 tsp/5 mL rum extract)	25 mL
4 oz	frozen whipped topping, thawed	125 g
	Peaches or other fruit (optional)	

1. In a medium saucepan, combine gelatin, custard mix and nutmeg. Add milk and, stirring constantly, bring to a boil over medium heat. Remove from heat.

2. Stir in rum and mix to blend. Transfer to a bowl and place plastic wrap directly on the surface. Chill in refrigerator until partially set.

3. Fold in whipped topping and chill again, if necessary, until mixture mounds.

4. Spoon into prepared pie crust and chill in refrigerator for 4 to 5 hours or until firm. Garnish with peach slices or other fruit, or sprinkle a bit of nutmeg over top.

Tarts

●●●●●●●●●●●●●●●●●●●●●●●●●●●●

Classic Butter Tarts

Makes 24 tarts
Preheat oven to 425°F (220°C)
Baking sheet, if necessary

24	2½- by 1-inch (6 by 2.5 cm) tart shells (see recipe, page 409), unbaked	24
¾ cup	packed brown sugar	175 mL
¼ cup	butter or margarine, softened	50 mL
¼ cup	corn syrup	50 mL
1 tbsp	freshly squeezed lemon juice	15 mL
1 tsp	vanilla	5 mL
2	eggs	2
¾ cup	raisins	175 mL

1. In a large mixer bowl, cream brown sugar and butter until smooth. Add corn syrup, lemon juice and vanilla, beating to blend. Beat in eggs, one at a time, beating after each addition just until combined.

2. Sprinkle raisins equally onto the bottom of each tart shell. Spoon batter over raisins. If you are using individual tart tins, place them on a baking sheet.

3. Bake in preheated oven for 5 minutes. Then reduce oven temperature to 350°F (180°C) and bake for another 8 minutes or until filling is set and pastry is golden brown. Let cool in pans on a wire rack for 10 minutes. Carefully loosen around edges with a knife and remove from pans. Let tarts cool completely on a wire rack.

Tip *To make tarts using muffin pans, use twelve 3- by 1½-inch (7.5 by 4 cm) tart shells. Increase baking time at 350°F (180°C) to about 15 minutes. Let cool in pans for 15 minutes before removing tarts.*

●●●●●●●●●●●●●●●●●●●●●●●●●●●●

Chocolate Butter Tarts

Makes 24 tarts
● Preheat oven to 450°F (230°C)
● Baking sheet, if necessary

24	2½- by 1-inch (6 by 2.5 cm) tart shells (see recipe, page 409), unbaked	24
¾ cup	packed brown sugar	175 mL
¼ cup	corn syrup	50 mL
2 tbsp	butter or margarine, softened	25 mL
1 tsp	white vinegar	5 mL
1 tsp	vanilla	5 mL
1	egg	1
3 oz	bittersweet chocolate, chopped	90 g
1 oz	bittersweet chocolate, melted	30 g

1. In a large mixer bowl, combine brown sugar, corn syrup, butter, vinegar, vanilla and egg. Beat until blended.

2. Sprinkle equal amounts of chopped chocolate into the bottom of each tart shell. Spoon filling over chocolate until shells are about three-quarters full. If you are using individual tart tins, place them on a baking sheet.

3. Bake in preheated oven for 5 minutes, then reduce oven temperature to 350°F (180°C) and bake for another 12 to 15 minutes, until filling is bubbly and pastry is lightly browned. Let cool in pans on a wire rack for 10 minutes. Carefully loosen around edges with a knife and remove from pans. Let tarts cool completely on a wire rack. Drizzle melted chocolate over tops.

●●●●●●●●●●●●●●●●●●●●●●●●●●●●

Old England Chess Tarts

Makes 24 tarts
● Preheat oven to 450°F (230°C)
● Baking sheet, if necessary

24	2½- by 1-inch (6 by 2.5 cm) tart shells (see recipe, page 409), with fluted edges, unbaked	24
1 cup	firmly packed brown sugar	250 mL
½ cup	butter or margarine, softened	125 mL
2	eggs	2
¾ cup	chopped dates	175 mL
¾ cup	chopped walnuts	175 mL
½ cup	raisins	125 mL
1 tsp	grated lemon zest	5 mL
½ cup	sour cream	125 mL
	Walnut halves (optional)	
	Sour cream (optional)	

1. In a large mixer bowl, cream brown sugar and butter until softened and smooth. Beat in eggs, one at a time, beating after each addition. Stir in dates, chopped walnuts, raisins, lemon zest and the ½ cup (125 mL) sour cream.

2. Spoon into prepared tart shells, dividing evenly. If you are using individual tart tins, place them on a baking sheet.

3. Bake in preheated oven for 5 minutes. Reduce oven temperature to 350°F (180°C) and bake for 12 to 15 minutes or until filling is firm and shells are lightly browned. Let cool in pans on a wire rack for 10 minutes. Carefully loosen around edges with a knife and remove from pans. Let tarts cool completely on a wire rack.

4. Garnish with a dollop of sour cream and a walnut half, if desired.

Tip *To remove baked tarts easily when you're using individual tart tins, press up from the bottom of the foil cup.*

● ●

Blueberry Tarts

Makes 24 tarts
- Preheat oven to 375°F (190°C)
- Baking sheet, if necessary

24	2¹/₂- by 1-inch (6 by 2.5 cm) tart shells (see recipe, page 409), unbaked	24
¹/₃ cup	packed brown sugar	75 mL
1 tbsp	all-purpose flour	15 mL
¹/₂ cup	corn syrup	125 mL
1 tsp	vanilla	5 mL
1 tsp	freshly squeezed lemon juice	5 mL
1	egg, lightly beaten	1
3 tbsp	butter or margarine, melted	45 mL
1¹/₂ cups	fresh blueberries	375 mL

1. In a small bowl, mix together brown sugar and flour.

2. In a large bowl, combine corn syrup, vanilla, lemon juice and egg. Beat just until blended. Add dry mixture to corn syrup mixture. Add melted butter and mix well until thoroughly combined. Spoon berries into prepared tart shells equally. Spoon in egg mixture and fill each shell to the top. If you are using individual tart tins, place them on a baking sheet.

3. Bake in preheated oven for 15 minutes or until filling is bubbly and crust is lightly browned. Let cool completely in pan on a wire rack. The filling will become firm as tarts cool.

● ●

Lemon Tarts with Raspberry Glaze

Makes 24 tarts

24	2¹/₂- by 1-inch (6 by 2.5 cm) tart shells (see recipe, page 409), baked	24
1	can (19 oz/540 mL) lemon pie filling	1
1 cup	sour cream	250 mL
1	package (10 oz/300 g) frozen raspberries, thawed	1

RASPBERRY GLAZE

2 tbsp	granulated sugar	25 mL
1 tbsp	cornstarch	15 mL

1. In a small bowl, mix pie filling and sour cream. Chill in refrigerator, for at least 30 minutes.

2. Drain raspberries and reserve ²/₃ cup (150 mL) of the liquid.

3. *Prepare the glaze:* In a small saucepan, mix sugar and cornstarch. Gradually add the reserved raspberry liquid and cook over medium heat, stirring constantly, until mixture thickens and boils. Transfer to a bowl, cover, and chill in refrigerator.

4. Fill prepared tart shells with lemon mixture and top with a few raspberries. Spoon about 1 tbsp (15 mL) of the raspberry glaze over top of each.

● ●

Neapolitan Ice Cream Tarts

Makes twelve 3-inch (7.5 cm) tarts
- 2 muffin tins or tart pans
- Baking sheet

2 cups	all-purpose flour	500 mL
1 cup	unsweetened cocoa powder, sifted	250 mL
2 tbsp	packed brown sugar	25 mL
¹/₂ tsp	salt	2 mL
1 cup	butter or margarine, softened	250 mL
2	eggs, lightly beaten	2
	Neapolitan ice cream	
	Raspberries or blueberries (optional)	

1. In a large mixer bowl, mix together flour, cocoa powder, brown sugar and salt. Add butter and mix well until mixture resembles coarse crumbs. Add eggs and mix well until blended and mixture forms a dough. Roll into a ball and wrap in plastic wrap. Chill in refrigerator for about 1 hour, until firm.

2. Preheat oven to 450°F (230°C). Place ball of dough onto a floured surface and roll out into a thin sheet. Using a round cookie cutter or the top of a glass, cut into circles about 3.5 inches (9 cm) in diameter. Turn muffin tin(s) upside down. Fit circles over the backs of cups, making pleats so the dough will fit closely. Prick with a fork, thoroughly, to prevent puffing of dough. Place tins upside down on a baking sheet.

3. Bake in preheated oven for 8 to 10 minutes or until lightly browned. Let cool completely on muffin pans, on baking sheet, on a wire rack.

4. Just before serving, place a scoop of Neapolitan ice cream in each tart. Top with a handful of berries, if desired.

Cobblers, Crumbles and Crisps

Cobblers

Crumbles

Crisps

Cobblers

Apple Cinnamon Cobbler

Serves 6

- Preheat oven to 400ºF (200ºC)
- 8-inch (20 cm) round cake pan, lightly greased

1 cup	granulated sugar	250 mL
2 tbsp	all-purpose flour	25 mL
1 tsp	ground cinnamon	5 mL
¼ tsp	ground nutmeg	1 mL
6 cups	peeled, sliced, tart apples	1.5 L
BISCUIT TOPPING		
1 cup	all-purpose flour	250 mL
2 tbsp	granulated sugar	25 mL
1½ tsp	baking powder	7 mL
¼ tsp	salt	1 mL
¼ cup	shortening or butter	50 mL
1	egg, lightly beaten	1
¼ cup	milk	50 mL
½ tsp	vanilla	2 mL

1. In a large saucepan, over medium heat, combine sugar, flour, cinnamon and nutmeg. Add apples and toss until well blended and coated. Cook, stirring, until apples are almost tender, about 7 to 8 minutes. Spoon into prepared cake pan.
2. *Prepare the topping:* In a large bowl, combine flour, sugar, baking powder and salt. Cut in shortening until mixture resembles coarse crumbs. Add egg, milk and vanilla and mix well to blend.
3. Drop dough by spoonfuls onto apple mixture and bake in preheated oven for 20 to 25 minutes or until topping is golden brown. Let cool slightly .

Cran-Apple Cobbler

Serves 6

- Preheat oven to 375ºF (190ºC)
- 9-inch (23 cm) round cake pan or pie plate, greased

4½ cups	peeled, cored, coarsely chopped cooking apples	1.125 L
1½ cups	fresh or frozen cranberries	375 mL
½ cup	granulated sugar	125 mL
2 tbsp	all-purpose flour	25 mL
1 tsp	grated orange zest (optional)	5 mL
¾ cup	freshly squeezed orange juice	175 mL
TOPPING		
¾ cup	all-purpose flour	175 mL
2 tbsp	granulated sugar	25 mL
1 tsp	baking powder	5 mL
Pinch	salt	Pinch
¼ cup	cold butter or margarine	50 mL
¼ cup	milk	50 mL

1. In a large saucepan, combine apples, cranberries, sugar, flour, orange zest (if using) and orange juice; bring to a boil. Reduce heat, cover and simmer for 3 minutes, stirring, until apples are nearly tender. Spoon into prepared baking pan and set aside.
2. *Prepare the topping:* In a bowl, combine flour, sugar, baking powder and salt. Cut in butter with a pastry blender or two knives until crumbly. Add milk and stir until a soft dough forms. Drop dough by spoonfuls over the hot apple mixture.
3. Bake, uncovered, in preheated oven for 35 minutes or until topping is golden brown.

Fresh Blueberry Cobbler

Serves 6 to 8

- Preheat oven to 350ºF (180ºC)
- 9- or 10-inch (23 or 25 cm) pie plate, lightly greased

1 cup	all-purpose flour	250 mL
½ cup	granulated sugar	125 mL
1 tsp	baking powder	5 mL
¼ tsp	salt	1 mL
1	egg	1
¼ cup	butter or margarine, melted	50 mL
¼ cup	milk	50 mL
1 tsp	vanilla	5 mL
BLUEBERRY TOPPING		
3 cups	fresh blueberries (about 1 lb/500 g)	750 mL
¼ cup	granulated sugar	50 mL
½ tsp	ground cinnamon	2 mL
1 tsp	freshly squeezed lemon juice (optional)	5 mL
1 tbsp	butter or margarine	15 mL

1. In a large bowl, combine flour, sugar, baking powder and salt. Make a well in the center.
2. In a small bowl, whisk egg, melted butter, milk and vanilla. Pour into the flour mixture, stirring only until blended and moistened, as for a pie dough. Spoon into prepared pie dish and spread evenly to cover bottom.
3. *Prepare the topping:* In a large bowl, toss blueberries, sugar, cinnamon and lemon juice (if using) until well mixed. Spread over dough and dot with the butter.
4. Bake in preheated oven for 45 to 50 minutes or until juice bubbles up. Best when served warm.

Quick 'n' Easy Blueberry Cobbler

Serves 6
- Preheat oven to 400°F (200°C)
- 9-inch (2.5 L) square baking pan, ungreased

1	package (14 oz/400 g) blueberry muffin mix	1
1	can (19 oz/540 mL) blueberry pie filling	1
1 tbsp	freshly squeezed lemon juice	15 mL
1 tsp	ground cinnamon	5 mL

1. Open the can of blueberries that comes in the muffin mix package and drain, setting aside the liquid.
2. In a small saucepan, combine the reserved liquid, pie filling, lemon juice and cinnamon and heat to boiling. Remove from stove and pour into baking pan.
3. Prepare the muffin mix as directed on the package, but pour the finished batter onto the hot pie filling mixture, spreading evenly, or drop muffin mixture by spoonfuls onto hot filling.
4. Bake in preheated oven for 25 to 30 minutes or until top is golden brown. Serve warm or at room temperature.

Warm Raspberry Pear Cobbler

Serves 6 to 8
- Preheat oven to 350°F (180°C)
- 13- by 9-inch (3 L) baking dish, ungreased

1	package (10 oz/300 g) frozen raspberries, thawed, drained, reserve liquid	1
1/3 cup	granulated sugar	75 mL
2 tsp	cornstarch	10 mL
1/2 tsp	ground cinnamon	2 mL
3 cups	peeled, sliced pears (about 3 medium)	750 mL
TOPPING		
1 cup	all-purpose flour	250 mL
1/2 cup	granulated sugar	125 mL
1 tsp	baking powder	5 mL
1/4 tsp	salt	1 mL
1	egg, lightly beaten	1
3/4 cup	sour cream	175 mL
2 tbsp	butter or margarine, melted	25 mL

1. Put reserved raspberry liquid into a measuring cup and add enough water to make 1 cup (250 mL).

2. In a large saucepan, combine sugar, cornstarch, cinnamon and the 1 cup (250 mL) of raspberry liquid. Cook over medium heat until bubbly. Add the pears and raspberries and mix well until heated through. Spoon into baking dish and set aside.
3. *Prepare the topping:* In a medium bowl, combine flour, sugar, baking powder and salt. Mix together. In a small bowl, whisk egg, sour cream and butter and stir into flour mixture. Mix until well blended. Drop by spoonfuls onto fruit mixture.
4. Bake in preheated oven for 25 to 30 minutes or until topping is golden brown.

Tip *Serve warm with whipped topping or ice cream.*

Strawberry Rhubarb Cobbler

Serves about 9
- Preheat oven to 450°F (230°C)
- 9-inch (2.5 L) square baking dish, ungreased

1	package (20 oz/600 g) sliced frozen rhubarb, thawed	1
1	package (10 oz/300 g) frozen strawberries, thawed	1
1/2 to 3/4 cups	granulated sugar	125 to 175 mL
TOPPING		
2 cups	all-purpose flour	500 mL
2 tbsp	granulated sugar	25 mL
1 tbsp	baking powder	15 mL
1 tsp	salt	5 mL
2/3 cup	milk	150 mL
1/3 cup	vegetable oil	75 mL
	Butter or margarine	
1 tsp	ground cinnamon	5 mL
2 tbsp	granulated sugar	25 mL

1. In a large bowl, combine rhubarb, strawberries and sugar, mixing well. Pour into baking dish.
2. *Prepare the topping:* In another large bowl, mix together flour, sugar, baking powder and salt. Make a well in the center. Add milk and oil and stir until mixture forms a ball of dough. Divide dough into 9 biscuits and place biscuits atop the fruit in the baking dish. Make an indentation in each biscuit and dot with butter.
3. In a small bowl, mix together sugar and cinnamon. Sprinkle the cinnamon-sugar mixture over top.
4. Bake in preheated oven for 25 minutes or until topping is golden brown. Serve warm or at room temperature.

Old-Fashioned Cherry Cobbler

Serves 6

- Preheat oven to 400°F (200°C)
- 9-inch (2.5 L) square baking dish, ungreased

6 cups	stemmed pitted sweet or sour cherries	1.5 L
1 cup	granulated sugar	250 mL
¼ cup	cornstarch	50 mL
2 tbsp	freshly squeezed orange juice or cherry brandy	25 mL
2 tsp	freshly squeezed lemon juice	10 mL
TOPPING		
1 cup	all-purpose flour	250 mL
1½ tsp	baking powder	7 mL
¼ tsp	salt	1 mL
¼ cup	cold butter or shortening, cut into pieces	50 mL
⅓ cup	milk	75 mL
1 tsp	vanilla	5 mL

1. Place cherries in a large bowl.
2. In a small bowl, mix together sugar and cornstarch. Stir in orange juice and lemon juice. Pour into bowl of cherries and stir until well mixed. Place mixture into baking dish.
3. *Prepare the topping:* In another small bowl, mix together flour, baking powder and salt. Cut in butter, using a pastry blender or two knives, until mixture is crumbly. Add milk and vanilla and mix just until you have a thick dough.
4. Drop the dough by spoonfuls onto the fruit mixture and, with the back of a spoon, smooth out dough until even and touching the sides of the pan.
5. Bake in preheated oven for 25 to 30 minutes or until fruit filling is bubbling and the top is golden brown. Let stand for 10 to 15 minutes before serving.

Tip *If using frozen cherries, thaw and drain well before combining with the other ingredients.*

Variation *For a delightful addition, mix together about ⅓ to ½ cup (75 to 125 mL) of blanched sliced almonds and 2 tsp (10 mL) of granulated sugar and sprinkle over dough before baking.*

Saucy Nectarine Cobbler

Serves 6 to 8

- 8-inch (2 L) square baking dish, ungreased

2 cups	all-purpose flour	500 mL
¼ tsp	salt	1 mL
½ cup	shortening, chilled	125 mL
⅓ cup	ice water	75 mL
FILLING		
8	fresh nectarines	8
¾ to 1 cup	granulated sugar	175 to 250 mL
¼ cup	cornstarch (optional)	50 mL
¼ cup	butter or margarine	50 mL
SAUCE (OPTIONAL)		
1 cup	water	250 mL
⅔ cup	granulated sugar	150 mL
2 tsp	cornstarch	10 mL
½ tsp	ground nutmeg	2 mL
¼ tsp	ground cinnamon (optional)	1 mL
Pinch	salt	Pinch
3 to 4 tbsp	peach-flavored brandy (optional)	45 to 60 mL

1. In a medium bowl, mix together flour and salt. Cut in shortening with a pastry blender or two knives until mixture is crumbly. Add the ice water and mix until a ball of dough that holds together is formed. Wrap in plastic wrap and chill in refrigerator for 3 to 4 hours or overnight.
2. Set aside one-quarter of the dough and roll out the remaining dough to fit the bottom and sides of baking dish. Preheat oven to 425°F (220°C).
3. *Prepare the filling:* Slice nectarines and place in a large bowl with sugar and cornstarch. Toss until well combined. Spoon fruit mixture into pastry-lined pan. Dot with butter.
4. Roll out the reserved dough, cut into strips and place on fruit in a lattice pattern, sealing edges. Bake in preheated oven for 35 to 40 minutes or until filling is bubbly and top crust is lightly browned.
5. *If desired, prepare the sauce:* In a small saucepan, over medium heat, bring water to a boil. Stir in sugar, cornstarch, nutmeg, cinnamon and salt and bring back to a boil, stirring constantly. Cook until thickened and then remove from heat. Add brandy (if using).
6. Serve cobbler warm, Drizzle warm sauce (if using) over top.

Individual Peach Cobblers

Serves 4

- Preheat oven to 400°F (200°C)
- Four ¾-cup (175 mL) custard cups, buttered

2 tbsp	cold water	25 mL
1 tbsp	cornstarch	15 mL
1	can (14 oz/398 mL) sliced peaches, with juice	2
¼ tsp	ground cinnamon	1 mL
TOPPING		
1 cup	biscuit mix	250 mL
4 tsp	granulated sugar	20 mL
¼ cup	milk	50 mL
2 tbsp	vegetable oil	25 mL

1. In a medium saucepan, mix together cold water and cornstarch until smooth. Add the peaches and bring to a boil, stirring, over medium heat until mixture becomes thickened, about 2 to 3 minutes. Spoon into prepared custard cups.

2. *Prepare the topping:* In a medium bowl, mix together biscuit mix and sugar until blended. Add milk and oil, stirring just until moistened and blended. Drop by small spoonfuls over each hot peach filling, then sprinkle with cinnamon.

3. Bake in preheated oven for 20 to 25 minutes or until filling is bubbly and topping is golden brown.

Tip *Serve warm with ice cream or whipped cream.*

Lazy Day Peach Cobbler

Serves 4 to 6

- Preheat oven to 375°F (190°C)
- 8-inch (2 L) square baking dish, ungreased

1	package (14 oz/400 g) oatmeal muffin mix	1
¼ tsp	ground nutmeg	1 mL
½ tsp	ground cinnamon (optional)	2 mL
½ cup	butter or margarine	125 mL
FILLING		
4 cups	peeled, sliced fresh peaches (about 6 medium)	1 L
¾ cup	granulated sugar	175 mL
2 tbsp	freshly squeezed lemon juice	25 mL

1. In a medium bowl, mix together oatmeal mix, nutmeg and cinnamon (if using). Cut in the butter with a pastry blender or two knives until mixture resembles coarse crumbs. Set aside.

2. *Prepare the filling:* In a large bowl, combine peaches, sugar and lemon juice. Mix well and spoon into baking dish.

3. Spoon crumbly mixture over peach mixture. Bake in preheated oven for 40 to 50 minutes or until topping is golden brown.

Tip *Serve warm or cool, topped with ice cream or whipped topping.*

Skillet Peach Cobbler

Serves 4 to 6

2	cans (each 14 oz/398 mL) sliced peaches, with juice	2
3 tbsp	cornstarch	45 mL
3 tbsp	packed brown sugar	45 mL
2 tbsp	butter or margarine	25 mL
½ tsp	ground ginger	2 mL
DUMPLINGS		
1 cup	biscuit mix	250 mL
⅓ cup	milk	75 mL
1 tbsp	packed brown sugar	15 mL

1. In a skillet, combine peaches, cornstarch, brown sugar, butter and ginger. Cook over low heat until mixture becomes thickened.

2. *Prepare the dumplings:* In a medium bowl, mix together biscuit mix, milk and brown sugar until well blended.

3. Drop by spoonfuls onto bubbly peach mixture and cook, uncovered, for about 10 to 12 minutes. Cover and continue cooking for another 10 to 15 minutes, until top is fluffy and lightly browned. Spoon into serving bowls.

Tip *Serve warm with whipped topping or ice cream.*

Jiffy Cobbler

Serves 6 to 8

- Preheat oven to 350°F (180°C)
- 8-inch (2 L) square baking pan, lightly greased

2	cans (each 19 oz/540 mL) prepared peach pie filling	2
2 cups	fresh blueberries (about 12 oz/ 375 g) (optional)	500 mL
1	package (18 oz/510 g) yellow cake mix	1
½ cup	butter or margarine, melted	125 mL
½ cup	chopped nuts (pecans, almonds, or walnuts)	125 mL

1. In a large bowl, mix together peach pie filling and blueberries (if using) and spoon onto bottom of prepared baking pan. Sprinkle cake mix over fruit.
2. Drizzle melted butter over cake mix and sprinkle chopped nuts over top.
3. Bake in preheated oven for 45 to 50 minutes or until top is golden brown.

Variations *Use apple pie filling and spice cake mix.*

Use blueberry pie filling and lemon cake mix.

Use cherry pie filling and chocolate cake mix.

Use any pie filling you may have on hand and combine with any cake mix on hand.

You can also add other berries or fruits, mixed with the pie filling.

Fresh Plum Cobbler

Serves 6

- Preheat oven to 400ºF (200ºC)
- 8-cup (2 L) shallow casserole dish, greased

3 cups	sliced fresh plums (about 6 medium)	750 mL
¾ cup	pineapple chunks (fresh or canned)	175 mL
1 cup	granulated sugar	250 mL
¼ cup	cornstarch	50 mL
1 tbsp	butter or margarine	15 mL
BISCUIT TOPPING		
4 tsp	granulated sugar	20 mL
½ tsp	ground cinnamon	2 mL
1	roll (12 oz/340 g) refrigerated buttermilk biscuits	1
1 tbsp	butter or margarine, melted	15 mL

1. In a large bowl, combine plums, pineapple, sugar and cornstarch. Mix until well blended. Spoon into prepared casserole dish and dot with butter. Bake, uncovered, in preheated oven for 15 minutes.
2. *Prepare the topping:* In a small bowl, mix together sugar and cinnamon. Separate biscuits and cut into quarters. Place biscuit pieces over hot plum mixture, brush melted butter over biscuits and sprinkle cinnamon-sugar mixture over top.
3. Return to oven and bake for another 25 to 30 minutes or until top is golden brown.

Apricot Cobbler

Serves 6

- Preheat oven to 400ºF (200ºC)
- 11- by 7-inch (2 L) baking dish, greased

¾ cup	granulated sugar	175 mL
1 tbsp	cornstarch	15 mL
½ tsp	ground cinnamon	2 mL
Pinch	ground nutmeg	Pinch
1 cup	water	250 mL
1 tbsp	butter or margarine	15 mL
3	cans (each 14 oz/398 mL) apricot halves, drained	3
BISCUIT TOPPING		
1 cup	all-purpose flour	250 mL
4 tsp	granulated sugar	20 mL
1½ tsp	baking powder	7 mL
½ tsp	salt	2 mL
2 tbsp	shortening or butter	25 mL
⅓ cup	milk	75 mL

1. In a large saucepan, mix together sugar, cornstarch, cinnamon and nutmeg. Add water and bring to a boil over medium heat. Boil, stirring, for about 1 minute, then reduce the heat. Add butter and apricots, stirring just until heated through. Spoon into prepared baking dish.
2. *Prepare the topping:* In a medium bowl, mix together flour, sugar, baking powder and salt. Cut in shortening with a pastry blender or two knives until mixture is crumbly. Stir in milk, just until moistened. Drop by spoonfuls over apricot mixture.
3. Bake in preheated oven for 30 to 35 minutes or until topping is golden brown and a toothpick inserted into the topping comes out clean and dry. Serve warm or at room temperature.

Orange Marmalade Cobbler

Serves 2 to 3
- Preheat oven to 400°F (200°C)
- 4-cup (1 L) casserole dish, greased

½ cup	cold water	125 mL
¼ cup	orange marmalade	50 mL
2 tbsp	frozen orange juice concentrate	25 mL
2 tbsp	granulated sugar	25 mL
1 tbsp	cornstarch	15 mL
2 tsp	butter or margarine	10 mL
½ cup	biscuit mix	125 mL
Pinch	ground nutmeg	Pinch
3 tbsp	milk	45 mL

1. In a small saucepan, over medium heat, combine cold water, marmalade and orange juice concentrate. Stir in sugar and cornstarch and stir until thickened. Add butter and stir until butter is melted. Pour into prepared casserole dish.

2. In a small bowl, combine biscuit mix and nutmeg. Add milk, stirring just until blended and moistened. Drop by spoonfuls over orange mixture.

3. Bake in preheated oven for 20 to 25 minutes or until top is golden brown. Best when served warm.

Tip *If you don't have a 4-cup (1 L) casserole dish, you can use a 6-cup (1.5 L) casserole dish instead.*

Hawaiian Pineapple Cobbler

Serves 6
- Preheat oven to 350°F (180°C)
- 9-inch (2.5 L) square baking pan or 9-inch (23 cm) pie plate, greased

⅓ cup	biscuit mix	75 mL
1 cup	granulated sugar	250 mL
1 tsp	grated lemon zest	5 mL
4 cups	fresh pineapple chunks (about 1 small pineapple)	1 L
TOPPING		
¾ cup	biscuit mix	175 mL
⅔ cup	granulated sugar	150 mL
1	egg, lightly beaten	1
¼ cup	butter or margarine, melted	50 mL

1. In a large bowl, mix together biscuit mix, sugar and zest. Add the pineapple chunks and mix to blend. Spoon into prepared baking pan.

2. *Prepare the topping:* In a medium bowl, mix together biscuit mix, sugar and egg and sprinkle over fruit. Drizzle melted butter over top.

3. Bake in preheated oven for 40 to 45 minutes or until topping is browned. Serve warm or at room temperature.

Canned Fruit Cookie Cobbler

Serves 6
- Preheat oven to 375°F (190°C)
- 6-cup (1.5 L) casserole dish, ungreased

1	can (19 oz/540 mL) fruit, such as raspberries, sliced peaches or sweetened cherries, drained, reserve liquid	1
1 tbsp	butter or margarine	15 mL
1 cup	reserved canned fruit syrup	250 mL
2 tbsp	all-purpose flour	25 mL
1	roll (18 oz/510 g) prepared sugar cookie dough	1

1. Spoon drained fruit into casserole dish.

2. In a small saucepan, melt the butter. Stir in syrup and flour and cook over low heat until mixture thickens. Pour thickened mixture over the fruit.

3. Crumble cookie dough over fruit, covering thickly and completely.

4. Bake, uncovered, in preheated oven for 20 to 25 minutes or until juices are bubbly and the cookie crust is golden brown and crisp.

Chocolate Nut Cobbler

Serves 6 to 8
- Preheat oven to 350°F (180°C)
- 13- by 9-inch (3 L) baking dish

5 to 6 tbsp	butter or margarine	75 to 90 mL
1½ cups	granulated sugar, divided	375 mL
1 cup	self-rising flour	250 mL
½ cup	chopped nuts (pecans, almonds or other)	125 mL
½ cup	milk	125 mL
⅓ cup	unsweetened cocoa powder, divided	75 mL
1 tsp	vanilla	5 mL
1½ cups	boiling water	375 mL
	Fudge sundae topping	

1. Melt the butter in the baking dish in preheated oven. Remove from oven when melted.
2. In a large bowl, mix together 1/2 cup (125 mL) of the granulated sugar, flour, nuts, milk, 2 tbsp (25 mL) of the cocoa and vanilla, mixing until well blended. Spoon mixture into baking dish over the melted butter. Do not stir or mix.
3. In a small bowl, mix together the remaining sugar and the remaining cocoa and sprinkle this mixture over the batter. Again do not stir or mix.
4. Pour the boiling water over top; again do not stir or mix. Bake in preheated oven for 25 to 30 minutes or until golden brown. Set aside to cool slightly, just until warm. When serving, spoon some fudge sundae topping over top.

Cobbler Cake with Applesauce

Serves 6 to 8
- Preheat oven to 400°F (200°C)
- 9-inch (23 cm) round cake pan, greased

2 cups	sifted all-purpose flour	500 mL
1/4 cup	granulated sugar	50 mL
1 tbsp	baking powder	15 mL
1 tsp	salt	5 mL
1/3 cup	cold butter or shortening	75 mL
1	egg	1
1/2 cup	milk	125 mL
APPLESAUCE		
6 tbsp	butter or margarine	90 mL
1/3 cup	firmly packed brown sugar	75 mL
1/2 cup	sweetened applesauce	125 mL
1 tbsp	corn syrup	15 mL
3/4 tsp	ground cinnamon	4 mL

1. In a large bowl, sift together flour, sugar, baking powder and salt. Cut in the butter with a pastry blender, or crumble with your hands, until mixture resembles coarse crumbs.
2. In a small bowl, combine egg and milk and beat until blended. Pour into flour mixture and stir only until blended. Do not overmix.
3. *Prepare the applesauce:* In a small bowl, cream butter and brown sugar until light and smooth. Stir in applesauce, corn syrup and cinnamon and mix well.

4. Drop cake mixture by spoonfuls into prepared cake pan. Spoon the applesauce mixture over dough and bake in preheated oven for 30 to 35 minutes or until the cake pulls away from the side of the pan. Cut into wedges and serve warm.

Tip *When your recipe calls for sifting, put the ingredients to be sifted in the mixing bowl and stir them with a whisk. It does an equally good job.*

Rhubarb Cobblecake

Serves 4 to 6
- Preheat oven to 350°F (180°C)
- 8-inch (2 L) square baking pan, well greased

2 cups	trimmed, diced rhubarb (about 10 oz/300 g)	500 mL
2/3 cup	liquid honey	150 mL
1 tbsp	all-purpose flour	15 mL
1 tsp	ground cinnamon	5 mL
1 tsp	grated orange zest	5 mL
TOPPING		
1 cup	all-purpose flour	250 mL
2 tsp	baking powder	10 mL
1/2 tsp	salt	2 mL
1/4 cup	butter or shortening	50 mL
1	egg, lightly beaten	1
3 tbsp	milk	45 mL
2 tbsp	liquid honey	25 mL

1. In a large bowl, mix together rhubarb, honey, flour, cinnamon and zest. Pour into prepared baking pan.
2. *Prepare the topping:* In another large bowl, combine flour, baking powder and salt. Cut in butter with a pastry blender or two knives until mixture is crumbly.
3. In a small bowl, mix together egg, milk and honey. Pour into flour mixture and stir only until mixture is moistened and blended or until you have a stiff batter. Drop batter by spoonfuls onto rhubarb mixture.
4. Bake in preheated oven for 30 to 35 minutes or until topping is golden brown. Serve warm.

Crumbles

• •

Apple Crumble

Serves 6

- Preheat oven to 350°F (180°C)
- 6-cup (1.5 L) casserole dish, greased

¼ cup	water	50 mL
1 tsp	ground cinnamon	5 mL
7	large apples, peeled and thinly sliced	7
TOPPING		
¾ cup	all-purpose flour	175 mL
¾ cup	old-fashioned rolled oats	175 mL
½ cup	granulated sugar	125 mL
½ cup	butter or margarine	125 mL

1. In a large bowl, mix together water and cinnamon. Add apples and toss together until well mixed. Pour into prepared casserole dish.
2. *Prepare the topping:* In a medium bowl, combine flour, oats and sugar. Cut in butter or margarine with a pastry blender or two knives until mixture resembles coarse crumbs. Spoon over apple mixture.
3. Bake in preheated oven for 45 to 50 minutes or until topping is golden brown.

Tip *Serve warm, with Quick Custard Sauce (page 555), ice cream or whipped cream.*

Variation *You could use ¼ cup (50 mL) oat bran and ½ cup (125 mL) of quick-cooking oats instead of the ¾ cup (175 mL) of rolled oats.*

• •

Canned Apple Crunch

Serves 6

- Preheat oven to 350°F (180°C)
- 8-inch (2 L) square baking pan, greased

1	package (12 oz/350 g) shortbread cookies, finely crushed	1
½ cup	firmly packed brown sugar, divided	125 mL
1	can (19 oz/540 mL) pie-sliced apples, well-drained	1
2 tbsp	butter or margarine	25 mL
¼ cup	granulated sugar	50 mL
1 tsp	ground cinnamon	5 mL

1. In a medium bowl, combine cookie crumbs and half the brown sugar. Mix well. Press about one-third of the crumb mixture into prepared baking pan.

2. Place apples in a blender and process until smooth. Pour into another medium bowl and add the remaining brown sugar.
3. In a small bowl, mix together sugar and cinnamon.
4. Spoon about half of the apple mixture over the crumb mixture in pan. Spoon in another third of the crumb mixture. Spoon in the remaining apple mixture and then top with the remaining crumb mixture. Dot with butter and sprinkle sugar-cinnamon mixture lightly over top.
5. Bake in preheated oven for 25 to 30 minutes or until firm and golden brown.

Tip *Serve warm, with Quick Custard Sauce (page 555).*

• •

Apple Rhubarb Oat Crumble

Serves 6

- Preheat oven to 350°F (180°C)
- 8- or 9-inch (2 or 2.5 L) square baking pan, ungreased

1½ cups	apples, peeled and diced (about 1½ medium)	375 mL
1 cup	frozen rhubarb, diced	250 mL
½ cup	lightly packed brown sugar	125 mL
2 tbsp	all-purpose flour	25 mL
1 tsp	ground cinnamon	5 mL
½ tsp	ground nutmeg	2 mL
¼ tsp	salt	1 mL
1 cup	sour cream	250 mL
TOPPING		
1½ cups	quick-cooking rolled oats	375 mL
½ cup	granulated sugar	125 mL
½ cup	chopped nuts (optional)	125 mL
2 tbsp	all-purpose flour	25 mL
¾ cup	butter or margarine, melted	175 mL

1. In a large bowl, combine apples and rhubarb. Add brown sugar, flour, cinnamon, nutmeg and salt and mix together to blend. Add sour cream and mix until well blended. Spoon into baking pan.
2. *Prepare the topping:* In another large bowl, combine oats, sugar, nuts (if using) and flour. Stir in melted butter and mix until mixture resembles coarse crumbs. Sprinkle over apple-rhubarb mixture.
3. Bake in preheated oven for 25 to 30 minutes or until apples are fork-tender and top is golden brown.

Apple Pear Crumble

Serves 4 to 6

- Preheat oven to 350°F (180°C)
- 6-cup (1.5 L) casserole dish, greased

½ cup	old-fashioned rolled oats	125 mL
⅓ cup	all-purpose flour, sifted	75 mL
¼ cup	ground almonds	50 mL
2 tbsp	butter or margarine	25 mL
3	apples (such as Granny Smith), cored and chopped	3
2	pears, cored and chopped	2
¼ cup	raisins (optional)	50 mL
2 tsp	lemon zest (optional)	10 mL
3 tbsp	freshly squeezed lemon juice	45 mL
½ cup	packed brown sugar	125 mL
½ tsp	ground allspice	2 mL

1. In a small bowl, mix together oats, flour and almonds. Cut in butter, using your hands or a pastry blender. Set aside.

2. Place apples, pears, raisins (if using), lemon zest (if using) and lemon juice into prepared casserole dish.

3. In another small bowl, mix together brown sugar and allspice. Sprinkle over fruit in baking dish. Then sprinkle oat mixture over top.

4. Bake in preheated oven for 25 to 30 minutes or until fruit is tender and top is golden brown.

Cran-Apple Almond Crumble

Serves 8 to 10

- Preheat oven to 400°F (200°C)
- 13- by 9-inch (3 L) baking dish, greased

1 cup	granulated sugar, divided	250 mL
4 tsp	grated orange zest	20 mL
1 cup	freshly squeezed orange juice	250 mL
1½ cups	fresh or frozen, thawed cranberries (about 6 oz/175 g)	375 mL
2 tbsp	butter or margarine	25 mL
2 tbsp	liquid honey	25 mL
2 tbsp	pure maple syrup	25 mL
5	Granny Smith apples, peeled and cut into ½-inch (1 cm) slices	5
2 tbsp	quick-cooking tapioca	25 mL
TOPPING		
1½ cups	all-purpose flour	375 mL
¾ cup	firmly packed brown sugar	175 mL
2 tsp	ground cinnamon	10 mL
½ tsp	ground nutmeg	2 mL
½ cup	cold butter or margarine	125 mL
3 tbsp	almond paste	45 mL
1 cup	slivered almonds, toasted (optional)	250 mL

1. In a medium saucepan, over medium heat, combine ¾ cup (175 mL) of the sugar, orange zest and juice and bring to a boil. Lower heat to simmer and cook uncovered, stirring, for about 5 to 6 minutes. Add cranberries and continue to simmer for 10 minutes or until the berries begin popping. Remove from heat.

2. In a large saucepan, melt the butter and add honey, syrup and the remaining sugar. Pour in apples and cook over medium heat for about 5 minutes. Remove from heat and pour into the cranberry mixture. Sprinkle tapioca over top and mix until well blended. Set aside for 15 minutes. Spoon into prepared baking dish.

3. *Prepare the topping:* In a medium bowl, combine flour, brown sugar, cinnamon and nutmeg. Cut in butter and almond paste until mixture resembles coarse crumbs.

4. Sprinkle topping over cranberry mixture and sprinkle almonds (if using) over top. Bake in preheated oven for 20 minutes or until bubbly and golden brown.

Turnover Cranberry Crumble

Serves 6

- Preheat oven to 325°F (160°C)
- 8-inch (2 L) square baking dish, greased

3 cups	fresh or frozen, thawed cranberries (about 12 oz/375 g)	750 mL
1¾ cups	granulated sugar, divided	425 mL
½ cup	chopped nuts (pecans or other)	125 mL
2	eggs	2
1 cup	all-purpose flour	250 mL
½ cup	butter or margarine, melted	125 mL

1. Spoon cranberries into prepared baking dish and sprinkle with ¾ cup (175 mL) of the sugar and chopped nuts. Toss together until well blended.

2. In a large mixer bowl, combine eggs, flour, melted butter and the remaining sugar and beat until blended and smooth. Spread evenly over cranberry mixture.

3. Bake in preheated oven for 55 to 60 minutes or until golden brown. Run a knife around the edges of the dish and invert immediately onto a serving platter. Serve warm.

Raspberry and Pear Crumble

Serves 6
- Preheat oven to 350°F (180°C)
- 8-inch (2 L) square baking dish, ungreased

4 cups	peeled, sliced pears (about 4 medium)	1 L
2 cups	frozen raspberries (about 12 oz/375 g)	500 mL
1/3 cup	lightly packed brown sugar	75 mL
2 tbsp	all-purpose flour	25 mL
1/2 tsp	ground nutmeg	2 mL
TOPPING		
3/4 cup	all-purpose flour	175 mL
3/4 cup	quick-cooking rolled oats	175 mL
3/4 cup	lightly packed brown sugar	175 mL
1/3 cup	butter or margarine, melted	75 mL

1. In a large bowl, combine pears, raspberries, brown sugar, flour and nutmeg and toss together gently to blend. Spoon into baking dish.
2. *Prepare the topping:* In another large bowl, combine flour, oats and brown sugar and mix well. Drizzle in the melted butter and mix together until mixture is crumbly. Sprinkle topping over fruit mixture.
3. Bake in preheated oven for 45 to 50 minutes or until bubbly, golden brown and fruit is tender.

Pineapple Coconut Crumble

Serves 6
- Preheat oven to 350°F (180°C)
- Rimmed baking sheet
- 8-cup (2 L) casserole dish, ungreased

1 cup	flaked sweetened coconut	250 mL
2	cans (each 19 oz/540 mL) pineapple chunks, drained, juice reserved (or use 5 cups/ 1.25 L fresh pineapple)	2
1/4 cup	reserved pineapple juice	50 mL
1 cup	all-purpose flour	250 mL
2/3 cup	firmly packed brown sugar	150 mL
1/4 tsp	baking powder	1 mL
1/2 cup	butter or margarine, melted and cooled	125 mL
1 cup	coarsely chopped macadamia (or other) nuts	250 mL

1. Spread coconut on baking sheet and bake in preheated oven for 10 minutes or until lightly browned. Set aside to cool. Keep the oven heated to 350°F (180°C).
2. Spoon pineapple chunks and the reserved liquid into casserole dish. Cover tightly and bake for 15 to 20 minutes or until hot.
3. In a medium bowl, combine flour, brown sugar and baking powder and mix well. Add the butter and mix with your fingers until evenly moistened. Add the coconut and nuts and stir to form a large clump. Break into small pieces and scatter evenly over the hot pineapple.
4. Bake for 30 to 35 minutes or until golden brown and bubbly and fruit is tender. Serve warm or at room temperature.

Tropical Fruit Crunch

Serves 6
- Preheat oven to 375°F (190°C)
- 8-cup (2 L) casserole dish, ungreased

2 cups	fresh fruit (see tip, below), peeled, cored and cut into 1-inch (2.5 cm) chunks	500 mL
	Juice of 1/2 lime	
1/2 to 3/4 cup	granulated sugar	125 to 175 mL
2 tbsp	quick-cooking tapioca	25 mL
TOPPING		
1 cup	sifted all-purpose flour	250 mL
1/2 cup	granulated sugar	125 mL
1/2 cup	packed brown sugar	125 mL
2/3 cup	cold butter or margarine, cut into small chunks	150 mL
1/3 cup	shredded sweetened coconut	75 mL
1/2 cup	chopped nuts (optional)	125 mL

1. In a large bowl, combine the prepared fruit. Sprinkle with lime juice and toss gently to coat.
2. In a small bowl, mix together sugar and tapioca. Toss in with the fruit. Spoon fruit into casserole dish.
3. *Prepare the topping:* In a large bowl, mix together flour, sugar and brown sugar. Cut in butter with a pastry blender or two knives until mixture resembles coarse crumbs. Stir in coconut and nuts (if using) and sprinkle evenly over fruit.
4. Bake in preheated oven for 40 to 45 minutes or until bubbly and topping is golden brown.

Tips *For the fruit, use 1 ripe pineapple, 2 small mangos and 1 large ripe banana, or any other suitable fruits, such as papaya, melons, etc.*

Peach Crumble

Serves 6
- Preheat oven to 350°F (180°C)
- 6-cup (1.5 L) casserole dish, buttered

1 cup	all-purpose flour	250 mL
¾ cup	packed brown sugar, divided	175 mL
¼ tsp	salt	1 mL
¼ cup	butter or margarine	50 mL
6	peaches, peeled, pitted and thinly sliced	6
¼ tsp	ground mace	1 mL

1. In a medium bowl, combine flour, ½ cup (125 mL) of the brown sugar and salt and mix well. Cut in butter with your hands or a pastry blender until mixture is crumbly. Set aside.
2. In a large bowl, combine peach slices, the remaining brown sugar and mace and toss to blend. Spoon into prepared casserole dish. Spread flour mixture over peaches and pat down lightly.
3. Bake in preheated oven for 40 to 45 minutes or until golden brown.

Crisps

Mom's Old-Fashioned Apple Crisp

Serves 4 to 6
- Preheat oven to 375°F (190°C)
- 8- or 9-inch (2 or 2.5 L) square baking dish, greased

4 cups	peeled, cored and sliced tart apples (about 4 medium)	1 L
¾ cup	firmly packed brown sugar	175 mL
½ cup	quick-cooking rolled oats	125 mL
½ cup	all-purpose flour	125 mL
1½ tsp	ground cinnamon	7 mL
¼ tsp	ground allspice (optional)	1 mL
Pinch	ground nutmeg	Pinch
⅓ cup	cold butter or margarine	75 mL

1. Place apple slices into prepared baking dish.
2. In a medium bowl, combine brown sugar, oats, flour, cinnamon, allspice and nutmeg. Cut in butter with a pastry blender or two knives until mixture resembles coarse crumbs. Spoon evenly over apples.
3. Bake in preheated oven for 30 to 35 minutes or until apples are tender and topping is golden brown.

Cheesy Apple Crisp

Serves 6
- Preheat oven to 375°F (190°C)
- 6-cup (1.5 L) casserole dish, buttered

6 to 8	Granny Smith apples, peeled, cored and sliced	6 to 8
½ cup	water	125 mL
¾ cup	granulated sugar (more or less, depending on tartness of apples)	175 mL
⅔ cup	all-purpose flour	150 mL
½ cup	butter or margarine	125 mL
½ cup	shredded Cheddar cheese (sharp or according to taste, about 2 oz/60 g)	125 mL
1½ tsp	ground cinnamon	7 mL

1. Place apple slices in prepared casserole dish. Pour water over apple slices.
2. In a large bowl, combine sugar and flour. Cut in butter with a pastry blender or two knives until mixture resembles coarse crumbs. Stir in cheese and cinnamon, mixing together well. Sprinkle over apple slices.
3. Bake in preheated oven for 40 to 45 minutes or until apples are tender and top is golden brown.

Microwave Apple Graham Crisp

Serves 6
- 8-cup (2 L) microwave-safe casserole dish, greased

6 to 8	tart apples, peeled, cored and sliced	6 to 8
1 cup	graham cracker crumbs (about 12 wafers)	250 mL
½ cup	packed brown sugar	125 mL
½ cup	all-purpose flour	125 mL
1½ tsp	ground cinnamon	7 mL
½ tsp	ground nutmeg	2 mL
½ cup	butter or margarine, melted	125 mL

1. Place apple slices into prepared casserole dish.
2. In a medium bowl, combine graham cracker crumbs, brown sugar, flour, cinnamon and nutmeg and mix together until well incorporated. Stir in melted butter and mix well. Sprinkle over apple slices.
3. Microwave, uncovered, on High for 12 minutes or until apples become tender. Best when served warm.

Scrumptious Apple Crisp

Serves 8 to 10

- Preheat oven to 375°F (190°C)
- 13- by 9-inch (3 L) baking dish or 9-inch (2.5 L) square baking dish, ungreased

6 to 8	apples, peeled, cored and cut into slices Ground cinnamon Granulated sugar	6 to 8
TOPPING		
1½ cups	lightly packed brown sugar	375 mL
1 cup	all-purpose flour	250 mL
1 tsp	baking powder	5 mL
¼ tsp	salt	1 mL
1	egg	1
¼ cup	butter or margarine, melted	50 mL

1. Layer apple slices in baking dish. After each layer, sprinkle cinnamon and sugar to taste over top before adding another layer.

2. *Prepare the topping:* In a medium bowl, mix together brown sugar, flour, baking powder, salt and egg. Mix well until blended. Sprinkle over the apples, then drizzle the melted butter over top.

3. Bake in preheated oven for 35 to 40 minutes or until topping is golden brown and crisp.

Tip *Best when served warm with ice cream or any other topping.*

Variation *Use 2 cans (each 19 oz/540 mL) of apple pie filling mixed with 1 tsp (5 mL) freshly squeezed lemon juice and 1 tsp (5 mL) ground cinnamon. Then add the topping and bake as above.*

Quick Apple Brown Betty

Serves 6 to 8

- Preheat oven to 350°F (180°C)
- 9-inch (2.5 L) square baking dish, buttered

2½ cups	canned apple pie filling	625 mL
1	package (18 oz/510 g) spice cake mix	1
6 tbsp	butter or margarine, melted	90 mL

1. Spoon pie filling into prepared baking dish. Sprinkle cake mix evenly over filling. Drizzle with melted butter.

2. Bake in preheated oven for 45 minutes or until topping is golden brown. Serve either warm or cold.

Apple Nut Crisp

Serves 6 to 8

- Preheat oven to 350°F (180°C)
- 13- by 9-inch (3 L) baking dish, greased

6 to 8	tart apples, peeled, cored and sliced	6 to 8
¼ cup	packed brown sugar	50 mL
2 tsp	ground cinnamon	10 mL
TOPPING		
2 cups	firmly packed brown sugar	500 mL
1 cup	butter or margarine, softened	250 mL
2	eggs	2
2 cups	all-purpose flour	500 mL
1 cup	finely chopped walnuts, divided	250 mL

1. Place apple slices into prepared baking dish. Sprinkle the brown sugar and cinnamon over top.

2. *Prepare the topping:* In a large mixer bowl, cream brown sugar and butter. Add eggs, beating after each egg. Stir in the flour and ½ cup (125 mL) of the walnuts. Spread mixture over apples. Sprinkle the remaining walnuts over top.

3. Bake in preheated oven for 45 to 50 minutes or until topping is golden brown and apples are tender. Serve warm.

Very Berry Apple Crisp

Serves 6 to 8

- Preheat oven to 375°F (190°C)
- 8- or 9-inch (2 or 2.5 L) square baking dish, ungreased

6	Granny Smith apples, peeled, cored and cut into bite-size chunks	6
2 cups	berries (your choice of blueberries, strawberries, cranberries, raspberries or others), fresh or frozen	500 mL
¾ cup	granulated sugar (more or less, depending on tartness of apples)	175 mL
2 tbsp	all-purpose flour	25 mL
1 to 2 tsp	ground cinnamon	5 to 10 mL
½ tsp	ground nutmeg	2 mL
TOPPING		
¾ cup	old-fashioned rolled oats	175 mL
2 tbsp	lightly packed brown sugar	25 mL
2 tbsp	all-purpose flour	25 mL
3 tbsp	butter or margarine, softened	45 mL

1. In a large bowl, combine apples, berries, sugar, flour, cinnamon and nutmeg. Toss together until well incorporated. Spoon into baking dish.

2. *Prepare the topping:* In a small bowl, combine oats, brown sugar and flour. Add butter and stir until moist and crumbly. Sprinkle topping over apple mixture.

3. Bake in preheated oven for 50 to 60 minutes or until filling is bubbly and topping is golden brown. Serve warm or at room temperature.

Tip *Use one type of berries or combine them as you please.*

• •

Cran-Apple Pecan Crisp

Serves 6

- Preheat oven to 350°F (180°C)
- 9-inch (2.5 L) square baking dish, greased

3 cups	peeled, cored and chopped Granny Smith apples (about 3 medium)	750 mL
2 cups	fresh or frozen, thawed cranberries (about 8 oz/250 g)	500 mL
1 cup	granulated sugar	250 mL
3 tbsp	all-purpose flour	45 mL
TOPPING		
1½ cups	quick-cooking rolled oats	375 mL
½ cup	all-purpose flour	125 mL
½ cup	firmly packed brown sugar	125 mL
½ cup	butter or margarine, melted	125 mL
⅓ cup	chopped pecans	75 mL

1. In a large bowl, toss together apples, cranberries, sugar and flour. Spoon into prepared baking dish.

2. *Prepare the topping:* In the same bowl, combine oats, flour and brown sugar. Mix well and stir in melted butter and then pecans until well blended and crumbly. Sprinkle topping over apples.

3. Bake in preheated oven for 50 to 60 minutes or until topping is golden brown and the fruit is tender. Serve warm.

• •

Fruit Jam Apple Betty

Serves 6

- Preheat oven to 350°F (180°C)
- 9-inch (2.5 L) square baking dish, buttered

2 cups	peeled, cored and chopped apples (about 2 medium)	500 mL
½ cup	fruit jam or marmalade (orange, pineapple, rhubarb or other)	125 mL
3 cups	fresh bread crumbs (about 6 slices)	750 mL
2 tbsp	butter or margarine, softened	25 mL
	Light brown sugar	
	Ground nutmeg	

1. In a medium bowl, mix together apples and jam. Set aside.

2. In a large bowl, mix together bread crumbs and butter until crumbly. Sprinkle a layer of crumbs into prepared baking dish. Top with some of the apple-jam mixture. Sprinkle a little nutmeg and brown sugar over top. Repeat with another layer of each.

3. Bake in preheated oven for 35 to 45 minutes or until golden brown.

Tip *To make fresh bread crumbs, process bread slices in a food processor or blender until crumbs are the desired size. Store in an airtight container in the refrigerator for up to 1 week or in the freezer for up to 6 months.*

• •

Spiced Pear Crisp

Serves 8

- Preheat oven to 350°F (180°C)
- 9-inch (2.5 L) square baking dish, ungreased

8 to 10	ripe pears, peeled, cored and sliced	8 to 10
2 tbsp	freshly squeezed lemon juice	25 mL
¾ cup	packed brown sugar, divided	175 mL
2 tsp	ground ginger	10 mL
¼ tsp	ground nutmeg	1 mL
¼ tsp	ground cloves	1 mL
1 cup	all-purpose flour	250 mL
½ cup	whole wheat flour	125 mL
½ tsp	salt	2 mL
½ cup	butter or margarine, cut into pieces	125 mL

1. Place pear slices in a large bowl and toss with the lemon juice. Add ¼ cup (50 mL) of the brown sugar, ginger, nutmeg and cloves and stir until well blended. Spoon into baking dish.

2. In another large bowl, mix together flours, salt and the remaining brown sugar. Cut in butter with a pastry blender or two knives until mixture resembles coarse crumbs. Sprinkle over pear mixture, spreading evenly.

3. Bake in preheated oven for 45 to 50 minutes or until topping is golden brown and filling is bubbly. Serve warm.

Traditional Raspberry Crisp

Serves 6 to 8

- Preheat oven to 350°F (180°C)
- 9-inch (2.5 L) square baking dish, greased

4 cups	fresh or frozen raspberries (about 1½ lbs/750 g)	1 L
⅓ cup	granulated sugar	75 mL
3 tbsp	all-purpose flour	45 mL
TOPPING		
¾ cup	quick-cooking rolled oats	175 mL
⅓ cup	firmly packed brown sugar	75 mL
⅓ cup	all-purpose flour	75 mL
¼ cup	cold butter or margarine	50 mL

1. In a medium bowl, toss together raspberries, sugar and flour. Spoon into prepared baking dish.
2. *Prepare the topping:* In a large bowl, combine oats, brown sugar and flour. Cut in butter, using a fork, your fingertips or a pastry blender, until mixture is crumbly. Sprinkle over fruit mixture.
3. Bake in preheated oven for 25 to 30 minutes or until top is golden brown.

Strawberry Rhubarb Crisp

Serves 6

- Preheat oven to 350°F (180°C)
- 12-cup (3 L) casserole dish, ungreased

2 lbs	fresh rhubarb, cut into ½-inch (1 cm) pieces (about 7 cups/1.75 L)	1 kg
1½ lbs	fresh strawberries, hulled and sliced in half lengthwise	750 g
	Grated zest of 1 orange	
	Juice of ½ orange	
⅔ cup	granulated sugar	150 mL
3 tbsp	all-purpose flour	45 mL
TOPPING		
1 cup	old-fashioned rolled oats	250 mL
¾ cup	all-purpose flour	175 mL
¾ cup	firmly packed brown sugar	175 mL
1 tsp	ground cinnamon	5 mL
Pinch	ground nutmeg	Pinch
½ cup	cold butter or margarine, cut into cubes	125 mL

1. In a large bowl, combine rhubarb, strawberries, orange zest and juice. Toss together until well blended.

2. In a small bowl, mix together sugar and flour. Stir into the fruit mixture, mixing until well incorporated. Spoon into casserole dish.
3. *Prepare the topping:* In a medium bowl, combine oats, flour, brown sugar, cinnamon and nutmeg. Cut in butter cubes with your fingertips or a pastry blender until mixture resembles coarse crumbs. Sprinkle topping over fruit, spreading evenly.
4. Bake in preheated oven for 30 to 35 minutes or until fruit filling is bubbly and topping is golden brown. Let cool before serving.

Bumbleberry Crisp

Serves 8

- Preheat oven to 350°F (180°C)
- 13- by 9-inch (3 L) baking dish, buttered

1½ cups	peeled, cored and chopped tart apples (about 1½ medium)	375 mL
1½ cups	finely chopped rhubarb, fresh or frozen (about 10 oz/300 g)	375 mL
1½ cups	fresh or frozen blueberries (about 10 oz/300 g)	375 mL
1½ cups	fresh or frozen raspberries (about 10 oz/300 g)	375 mL
¾ cup	granulated sugar	175 mL
¼ cup	quick-cooking tapioca	50 mL
1½ tsp	ground cinnamon	7 mL
TOPPING		
½ cup	firmly packed brown sugar	125 mL
½ cup	all-purpose flour	125 mL
⅓ cup	butter or margarine	75 mL
½ cup	old-fashioned rolled oats	125 mL
¼ cup	sliced almonds (optional)	50 mL

1. In a large bowl, combine apples, rhubarb, blueberries and raspberries. Add sugar, tapioca and cinnamon and toss together until well blended. Spoon into prepared baking dish.
2. *Prepare the topping:* In a medium bowl, combine brown sugar and flour. Cut in butter by hand, using your fingertips so that mixture is crumbly. Mix in rolled oats and almonds (if using). Sprinkle topping over fruit mixture, spreading evenly.
3. Bake in preheated oven for 40 to 45 minutes or until topping is golden brown and fruit is bubbly. Serve warm.

Lemon Coconut Crisp

Serves 6
- Preheat oven to 350°F (180°C)
- 8-inch (2 L) square baking pan, ungreased

CRUST

¾ cup	packed brown sugar	175 mL
6 tbsp	butter or margarine, softened	90 mL
18	saltine crackers, finely crushed	18
1 cup	all-purpose flour	250 mL
½ cup	flaked sweetened coconut	125 mL
½ tsp	salt	2 mL
½ tsp	baking soda	2 mL

FILLING

¾ cup	granulated sugar	175 mL
2 tbsp	cornstarch	25 mL
¼ tsp	salt	1 mL
1 cup	hot water	250 mL
2	egg yolks, lightly beaten	2
½ tsp	grated lemon zest	2 mL
½ cup	freshly squeezed lemon juice	125 mL

1. *Prepare the crust:* In a large bowl, cream brown sugar and butter until smooth. Add crushed crackers, flour, coconut, salt and baking soda and stir until well mixed. Press half of this mixture into baking pan and bake in preheated oven for 10 minutes. Set aside to cool. Keep the oven heated to 350°F (180°C).
2. *Prepare the filling:* In a medium saucepan, over low heat, combine sugar, cornstarch and salt. Gradually stir in hot water. Cook, stirring constantly, until mixture is boiling and thick; boil for about 2 to 3 minutes. Remove from heat.
3. In a small bowl, beat egg yolks lightly. Add a small amount of the hot cornstarch mixture into the egg yolks and return this egg mixture back to saucepan. Bring to a boil, stirring constantly, then remove from heat. Stir in the lemon zest and juice and spoon over baked crumb crust. Top with the remaining crumb mixture.
4. Bake for 30 to 35 minutes or until top is golden brown.

Tip *Serve warm with whipped topping or a sauce.*

Favorite Peach Crisp

Serves 6 to 8
- Preheat oven to 350°F (180°C)
- 9-inch (2.5 L) square baking dish, greased

CRUST

1 cup	all-purpose flour	250 mL
½ cup	firmly packed brown sugar	125 mL
Pinch	salt	Pinch
½ cup	butter or margarine, softened	125 mL

FILLING

¾ cup	granulated sugar	175 mL
¼ cup	cornstarch	50 mL
2	cans (each 14 oz/398 mL) sliced peaches, drained, reserving juice	2

TOPPING

1½ cups	old-fashioned rolled oats	375 mL
½ cup	firmly packed brown sugar	125 mL
¼ cup	all-purpose flour	50 mL
⅓ cup	butter or margarine, softened	75 mL

1. *Prepare the crust:* In a medium bowl, combine flour, brown sugar and salt. Cut in butter by hand, using your fingertips or a fork, until mixture resembles coarse crumbs. Pat down into prepared baking dish and bake in preheated oven for 15 minutes. Keep the oven heated to 350°F (180°C).
2. *Prepare the filling:* In a medium saucepan, bring sugar, cornstarch and reserved juice to a boil, stirring constantly, and boil for 2 minutes or until thickened. Remove from heat and stir in peach slices. Spoon into baked crust.
3. *Prepare the topping:* In a large bowl, combine oats, brown sugar and flour. Cut in butter with a fork or pastry blender until mixture resembles coarse crumbs. Sprinkle over filling.
4. Bake for 25 to 30 minutes or until topping is golden brown and fruit is bubbly.

Plum Good Apricot Crisp

Serves 8 to 10

- Preheat oven to 400°F (200°C)
- 13- by 9-inch (3 L) baking dish, ungreased

1½ lbs	fresh plums, pitted and quartered	750 g
1 lb	fresh apricots, pitted and quartered	500 g
½ cup	granulated sugar (or to taste)	125 mL
3 tbsp	all-purpose flour	45 mL
TOPPING		
¾ cup	all-purpose flour	175 mL
⅓ cup	light brown sugar, packed	75 mL
¼ cup	old-fashioned rolled oats	50 mL
¼ cup	chopped nuts	50 mL
1 tbsp	granulated sugar	15 mL
½ tsp	ground cinnamon	2 mL
¼ cup	butter or margarine	50 mL

1. Spoon plums and apricots into baking dish. Sprinkle sugar and flour over fruit.
2. *Prepare the topping:* In a large bowl, combine flour, brown sugar, oats, nuts, sugar and cinnamon. Cut in butter with a pastry blender or two knives until mixture resembles coarse crumbs (or process in food processor). Spread topping over the fruit, spreading evenly.
3. Bake in preheated oven for 35 to 40 minutes or until topping is golden brown and fruit is tender and bubbly. Serve warm.

Springtime Fruit Crisp

Serves 8 to 12

- Preheat oven to 350°F (180°C)
- 13- by 9-inch (3 L) baking dish, buttered

4	apples, peeled, cored and thinly sliced	4
2 lbs	fresh rhubarb, chopped (about 7 cups/1.75 L)	1 kg
4	ripe medium mangos, pitted, chopped and peeled into ½-inch (1 cm) chunks	4
1	small pineapple, peeled, cut into quarters, cored and chopped into bite-size chunks	1
1 cup	golden raisins	250 mL
½ cup	chopped nuts (pecans, or other)	125 mL
1½ cups	packed brown sugar, divided	375 mL
1½ cups	all-purpose flour, divided	375 mL
2 tsp	ground cinnamon, divided	10 mL
¾ cup	butter or margarine, softened	175 mL

1. In a large bowl, combine apples, rhubarb, mango and pineapple and mix well. Add raisins and nuts and toss together until well blended.
2. In a small bowl, mix together ½ cup (125 mL) of the brown sugar, ¼ cup (50 mL) of the flour and half the cinnamon. Sprinkle over bowl of fruit and toss and mix until well incorporated and blended.
3. Pour fruit mixture into prepared baking dish, pressing fruit down with your hands to pack mixture down tightly.
4. Combine the remaining flour, brown sugar and cinnamon. Cut in butter with your fingertips, a fork or a pastry blender until mixture resembles coarse crumbs. Sprinkle over mixture in baking dish.
5. Bake in preheated oven for 1 to 1½ hours or until golden brown and fruit is tender and bubbly. Let stand for about 10 minutes before serving.

Zucchini Oat Crisp

Serves 6 to 8

- Preheat oven to 375°F (190°C)
- 9-inch (2.5 L) square baking dish, greased

2	zucchini, peeled and cut into slices	2
2 cups	all-purpose flour	500 mL
1 cup	quick-cooking rolled oats	250 mL
¾ cup	packed brown sugar	175 mL
⅔ cup	butter or margarine, softened	150 mL
⅓ cup	freshly squeezed lemon juice	75 mL
⅓ cup	granulated sugar	75 mL
1½ tsp	ground cinnamon	7 mL

1. Put zucchini slices in a medium saucepan and add enough water just to cover. Cook over medium heat until tender. Drain and set aside.
2. In a large bowl, combine flour, oats and brown sugar. Cut in butter with a pastry blender until mixture resembles coarse crumbs. Pat half of this crumb mixture into bottom of prepared baking dish and bake in preheated oven for 10 minutes. Remove from oven.
3. Place cooked zucchini slices on baked crust. Sprinkle lemon juice, sugar and cinnamon over filling. Top with the remaining crumb mixture.
4. Bake for another 30 to 35 minutes or until topping is golden brown. Serve warm.

Popovers, Turnovers and Scones

Popovers

Turnovers

Scones

Popovers

To make scrumptious popovers, use a heavy cast-iron popover pan. If you do not have a special pan, use a metal muffin pan or individual glass custard cups. The pans or cups should be filled about half full. If you use custard cups, they should be placed on a baking sheet for easier handling. Spray the cups with nonstick cooking spray.

Popover batter can be prepared in a bowl by whisking the ingredients together until blended and smooth and the consistency of the batter is similar to heavy cream. Be careful not to overbeat or the popovers may not rise as high as they should. If you are not planning to make the popovers immediately, store batter in a covered container in the refrigerator for 3 to 4 hours or overnight. Stir before using.

Do not open the oven door to peek during baking, and do not underbake, as this could cause the popovers to collapse. Be patient, and you will be rewarded with puffy, delicious popovers.

Baked popovers are moist inside from the steam that makes them rise and be puffy, so about 5 minutes before popovers are done, remove them from the oven and quickly prick each in two or three places with a fork or a pointed knife to let the steam escape. Turn the oven off and return popovers to the oven for the remaining time.

Basic Popovers

Makes 8 popovers
- Preheat oven to 425°F (220°C)
- Popover pan

1 cup	all-purpose flour	250 mL
½ tsp	salt	2 mL
2	eggs	2
1 cup	milk	250 mL
1 tbsp	butter or margarine, melted (or shortening)	15 mL

1. In a large bowl, sift together flour and salt. Make a well in the center.
2. In a medium bowl, whisk eggs, milk and melted butter until blended and smooth. Pour into the well in the flour mixture and whisk until batter is smooth.
3. Grease and flour 8 cups in the popover pan, 2 in each row. Spoon batter into prepared cups, filling each about half full. Fill the empty cups with about the same amount of cold water.

4. Bake in preheated oven for 35 minutes. Remove from oven, prick each popover in two or three places with a fork or a pointed knife to let steam escape and return to oven for 5 minutes or until crisp, popped and a deep golden brown. Serve immediately.

Tip *If you don't have a popover pan, use eight ¾-cup (175 mL) custard cups.*

Sage Butter Popovers

Makes 6 popovers
- Preheat oven to 450°F (230°C)
- Popover pan

1¼ cups	all-purpose flour	300 mL
½ tsp	crumbled dried sage	2 mL
¼ tsp	salt	1 mL
¼ tsp	freshly ground black pepper	1 mL
3	eggs	3
1¼ cups	milk, at room temperature	300 mL
SAGE BUTTER		
½ cup	butter, softened	125 mL
½ tsp	crumbled dried sage	2 mL
¼ tsp	freshly ground black pepper	1 mL

1. In a large bowl, combine flour, sage, salt and pepper. Make a well in the center.
2. In a medium bowl, whisk eggs and milk until frothy and pale in color, about 2 minutes. Pour into the well in the flour mixture and stir just until blended.
3. Grease and flour 6 alternating cups in the popover pan. Spoon batter into prepared cups, filling each about half full. Fill the empty cups with about the same amount of cold water.
4. Bake in preheated oven for 15 minutes, then reduce heat to 350°F (180°C) and bake for another 25 minutes. Remove from oven, prick each popover in two or three places with a fork or a pointed knife to let steam escape and return to oven for 5 minutes or until puffed and golden brown.
5. *Prepare the sage butter:* In a small mixer bowl, combine butter, sage and pepper, beating on low speed until light and fluffy.
6. Serve hot popovers with sage butter.

Tip *If you don't have a popover pan, use six ¾-cup (175 mL) custard cups.*

Mom's Golden Popovers

Makes 9 to 10 popovers

- Preheat oven to 450°F (230°C)
- 2 popover pans

1 cup	all-purpose flour	250 mL
Pinch	salt	Pinch
3	eggs	3
1 cup	milk	250 mL

1. In a large bowl, mix together flour and salt. Make a well in the center.
2. In a medium bowl, whisk together eggs and milk until blended and smooth. Pour into the well in the flour mixture and whisk just until blended.
3. Grease and flour 5 cups in one popover pan and 4 to 5 cups in the other. Spoon batter into prepared cups, filling about half full. Fill the empty cups with about the same amount of cold water.
4. Bake in preheated oven for 15 minutes. Reduce oven temperature to 350°F (180°C) and, without opening the oven door, bake for another 10 minutes. Remove from oven, prick each popover in two or three places with a fork or a pointed knife to let steam escape and return to oven for 5 minutes or until firm and golden brown. Serve immediately.

Tip *If you don't have a popover pan, use nine to ten ¾-cup (175 mL) custard cups.*

Light Popovers

Makes 6 popovers

- Preheat oven to 475°F (240°C)
- Popover pan

2	eggs	2
1 cup	all-purpose flour	250 mL
1 cup	milk	250 mL
½ tsp	salt	2 mL
1 tbsp	vegetable oil	15 mL

1. In a medium mixer bowl, beat eggs. Add flour, milk and salt and beat for 1 to 2 minutes. Add the oil and beat for another minute. Do not overbeat.
2. Grease and flour 6 alternating cups in the popover pan. Spoon batter into prepared cups, filling each about half full. Fill the empty cups with about the same amount of cold water.

3. Bake in preheated oven for 15 minutes, then reduce oven temperature to 350°F (180°C) and bake for another 25 minutes. Remove from oven, prick each popover in two or three places with a fork or a pointed knife to let steam escape and return to oven for 5 minutes or until firm and golden brown. Serve immediately.

Tips *If you don't have a popover pan, use six ¾-cup (175 mL) custard cups.*

If you prefer popovers that are dry inside, leave popovers in turned-off oven, with door ajar, for about 30 minutes after they are finished baking.

Sweet Jam 'n' Butter Popovers

Makes 12 popovers

- Preheat oven to 450°F (230°C)
- Popover pan, greased and floured

4	eggs	4
2 cups	milk	500 mL
2 cups	all-purpose flour	500 mL
2 tsp	granulated sugar	10 mL
1 tsp	salt	5 mL
1 tsp	grated orange zest	5 mL
½ tsp	ground nutmeg	2 mL

1. In a large mixer bowl, beat eggs and milk until well blended. Add flour, sugar, salt, zest and nutmeg and beat just until well blended.
2. Spoon batter into prepared popover pan, filling each cup about half full.
3. Bake in preheated oven for 15 minutes, then reduce oven temperature to 350°F (180°C) and bake for another 15 minutes. Remove from oven, prick each popover in two or three places with a fork or a pointed knife to let steam escape and return to oven for 5 minutes or until puffed and golden brown. Serve immediately.

Tips *If you don't have a popover pan, use twelve ¾-cup (175 mL) custard cups.*

These taste great with your favorite jam and butter, or with honey.

Popovers for Two

Makes 4 popovers
- Preheat oven to 425°F (220°C)
- Popover pan

½ cup	all-purpose flour	125 mL
¼ tsp	salt	1 mL
2	eggs	2
½ cup	milk	125 mL

1. In a medium bowl, mix together flour and salt. Make a well in the center.
2. Add eggs and milk to the well in the flour mixture and whisk together just until blended.
3. Grease and flour 4 cups in the popover pan, 1 in each row. Spoon batter into prepared cups, filling each about half full. Fill the empty cups with about the same amount of cold water.
4. Bake in preheated oven for 20 minutes. Remove from oven, prick each popover in two or three places with a fork or a pointed knife to let steam escape and return to oven for 5 minutes or until puffed and golden brown. Serve immediately.

Tip *If you don't have a popover pan, use four ¾-cup (175 mL) custard cups.*

Orange Popovers

Makes 8 popovers
- Preheat oven to 450°F (230°C)
- Popover pan

4	eggs	4
1 cup	milk	250 mL
¾ cup	all-purpose flour	175 mL
¾ cup	whole wheat flour	175 mL
¼ cup	water	50 mL
¼ cup	frozen orange juice concentrate, thawed	50 mL
4 tsp	butter or margarine, melted	20 mL
½ tsp	salt	2 mL

1. In a large bowl, whisk eggs and milk. Add flours, water, orange juice concentrate, melted butter and salt and whisk until well blended and smooth.
2. Grease and flour 8 cups in the popover pan, 2 in each row. Spoon batter into prepared cups, filling

each about half full. Fill the empty cups with about the same amount of cold water.

3. Bake in preheated oven for 20 minutes, reduce oven temperature to 350°F (180°C) and bake for another 15 minutes. Remove from oven, prick each popover in two or three places with a fork or a pointed knife to let steam escape and return to oven for 5 minutes or until puffy and golden brown. Serve warm.

Tip *If you don't have a popover pan, use eight ¾-cup (175 mL) custard cups.*

Cheesy Breakfast Popovers

Makes 8 popovers
- Preheat oven to 450°F (230°C)
- Popover pan

1 cup	all-purpose flour	250 mL
½ tsp	salt	2 mL
2	eggs	2
1 cup	milk	250 mL
½ cup	shredded Cheddar or Gouda cheese (about 2 oz/60 g)	125 mL

1. In a large bowl, mix together flour and salt. Make a well in the center.
2. In a small bowl, whisk eggs and milk until frothy. Pour into the well in the flour mixture and whisk just until blended. Do not overbeat. Add cheese and stir until well mixed.
3. Grease and flour 8 cups in the popover pan, 2 in each row. Spoon batter into prepared cups, filling each about half full. Fill the empty cups with about the same amount of cold water.
4. Bake in preheated oven for 25 minutes. Remove from oven, prick each popover in two or three places with a fork or a pointed knife to let steam escape and return to oven for 5 minutes or until puffed and golden brown. Serve immediately.

Tips *If you don't have a popover pan, use eight ¾-cup (175 mL) custard cups.*

These popovers are delicious alone or with scrambled eggs.

Turnovers

Easy Apple Spice Turnovers

Makes 12 turnovers
• Large skillet or deep fryer

1	package (double crust) pie crust mix	1
1	can (19 oz/540 mL) pie-sliced apples, drained	1
3 tbsp	packed brown sugar	45 mL
½ tsp	ground allspice	2 mL
	Vegetable oil for frying	
	Sifted confectioner's (icing) sugar	

1. Prepare pie crust mix according to package instructions. Divide dough in half. Roll out each half on a floured work surface to ¼-inch (0.5 cm) thickness. Cut out 12 rounds with a 4-inch (10 cm) cookie cutter.

2. In a medium bowl, combine apples, brown sugar and allspice and toss together to coat. Spread 2 tbsp (25 mL) of this apple mixture over half of each pastry round, fold the other half of the round evenly over the filling half and press all around the edges with a fork to seal.

3. Pour oil into skillet or fryer, about 1 inch (2.5 cm) deep, and bring to medium heat or to 350°F (180°C). Drop turnovers one at a time into the hot fat and cook for about 5 minutes, turning often, until golden brown. Remove from pan, drain well on paper towel and let cool slightly. Dust with confectioner's sugar and serve while still warm.

Apple Cinnamon Turnovers

Makes 24 turnovers
• Preheat oven to 350°F (180°C)
• Large baking sheet, lightly greased

24	wonton wrappers	24
2	apples, peeled, cored and finely diced	2
1 tbsp	packed brown sugar	15 mL
1 tsp	ground cinnamon	5 mL
1 tsp	freshly squeezed lemon juice	5 mL
	Sifted confectioner's (icing) sugar (optional)	

1. Place wonton wrappers on a flat work surface.

2. In a medium bowl, toss together apples, brown sugar, cinnamon and lemon juice until well blended. Drop by teaspoonfuls onto center of each wrapper. Wet your fingers with water and moisten the edges of wrappers. Fold one corner over filling to make a triangle and press sides together firmly with your fingers or a fork to seal.

3. Place turnovers on prepared baking sheet and bake in preheated oven for 15 to 20 minutes or until golden brown. Place on serving plate to cool slightly and dust with confectioner's sugar, if desired.

Apple Cream Cheese Turnovers

Makes 24 turnovers
• 2 baking sheets, greased

¾ cup	butter or margarine, softened	175 mL
1	package (8 oz/250 g) cream cheese, softened	1
1	egg, separated	1
2 tbsp	cold water	25 mL
2 cups	all-purpose flour	500 mL
6	apples, peeled, cored and thinly sliced	6
⅔ cup	granulated sugar	150 mL
2 tsp	ground cinnamon	10 mL
	Additional granulated sugar (optional)	

1. In a large mixer bowl, cream butter and cream cheese until soft and smooth.

2. In a small bowl, whisk egg yolk (refrigerate the egg white) and cold water and add to creamed mixture. Gradually add flour and beat until well blended. Shape dough into a ball, wrap in plastic wrap and chill in refrigerator for about 1 hour. Meanwhile, preheat the oven to 375°F (190°C).

3. In a medium saucepan, over medium-high heat, combine apples, sugar and cinnamon, toss together and bring to a boil. Lower heat to low, cover and simmer for about 10 minutes or until apples are tender. Remove from heat.

4. Roll out pastry on a floured work surface to ⅛-inch (0.25 cm) thickness. Cut out 24 rounds with a 4-inch (10 cm) cookie cutter. Place 2 tbsp (25 mL) of apple mixture on half of each circle. Brush around the edges with water and then fold pastry over filling and press around edges with a fork to seal.

5. In a small bowl, whisk egg white and 1 tbsp (15 mL) water and brush over each turnover. Sprinkle granulated sugar over tops, if desired.

6. Place 12 turnovers on each prepared baking sheet and bake in preheated oven for 20 to 25 minutes or until golden brown. Let cool on wire racks.

Raspberry Turnovers

Makes 12 turnovers
- Preheat oven to 450°F (230°C)
- Baking sheet, ungreased

1	sheet or block frozen puff pastry, thawed (about 8.5 oz/255 g)	1
¾ cup	red raspberry jam	175 mL
1	egg, lightly beaten	1
	Granulated sugar	

1. Unfold pastry and roll out to a rectangle 15 inches (38 cm) wide and 20 inches (50 cm) long. Cut lengthwise into 3 pieces, then crosswise into 4 pieces, making twelve 5-inch (12.5 cm) squares in all.
2. Place 1 tbsp (15 mL) jam in the middle of each square and brush the edges with beaten egg. Fold dough over, making triangles, and press down on the edges with your thumb or a fork to seal. Brush tops with the remaining egg and place turnovers on baking sheet.
3. Bake in preheated oven for 15 minutes, then reduce oven temperature to 350°F (180°C) and bake for 25 to 30 minutes or until tops are golden brown. Sprinkle with sugar.

Tip *To make a puffy, crisp turnover, use French pastry.*

Strawberry Mock Turnovers

Makes 12 turnovers
- Preheat oven to 400°F (200°C)
- Baking sheet, lightly greased

2 cups	hulled, washed and chopped fresh strawberries (about 12 oz/375 g)	500 mL
6 to 8 tbsp	strawberry preserves	90 to 120 mL
	Grated zest of 1 lemon	
12	slices soft white sandwich bread	12
6 tbsp	butter or margarine, melted	90 mL
	Sifted confectioner's (icing) sugar (optional)	

1. In a medium bowl, mix together strawberries, preserves and zest until well blended.
2. Remove crusts from bread slices and flatten each slice with a rolling pin. Spoon 1 tbsp (15 mL) strawberry mixture in the center of each flattened slice of bread and fold over to form a triangle. Brush both sides of each turnover with the melted butter and place turnovers on prepared baking sheet.

3. Bake in preheated oven for about 5 minutes, then turn over and bake for another 5 to 6 minutes or until golden brown. Let cool on a wire rack and dust with confectioner's sugar, if desired.

Tip *I use the same bread slices and method to make mock blintzes, replacing the strawberry filling with cottage cheese filling, or any other blintz filling.*

Apricot Turnovers

Makes 10 turnovers
- Preheat oven to 400°F (200°C)
- Baking sheet, lightly greased

1	package (8 oz/250 g) cream cheese, softened	1
½ cup	apricot jam	125 mL
10	slices white sandwich bread, crusts removed	10
	Milk or light (5%) cream	
	Granulated sugar	
	Flaked sweetened coconut (optional)	

1. In a small bowl, mix together cream cheese and jam until blended.
2. Spread 2 tbsp (25 mL) of this mixture on each slice of bread and fold each slice diagonally. Press edges together firmly with fingers or a fork to seal well.
3. Place turnovers on prepared baking sheet, brush each with milk and sprinkle with sugar and coconut, if desired.
4. Bake in preheated oven for 10 to 12 minutes or until golden brown.

Jam and Nut Half Moons

Makes about 5 dozen turnovers
- Preheat oven to 350°F (180°C)
- Baking sheet, ungreased

1 cup	jam (your favorite, apricot, berry or other)	250 mL
¾ cup	chopped nuts (walnuts or other)	175 mL
½ cup	raisins	125 mL
3	eggs	3
¾ cup	granulated sugar	175 mL
½ cup	shortening, softened	125 mL
½ cup	milk	125 mL
	Grated zest of 1 orange and 1 lemon	
¼ cup	freshly squeezed orange juice	50 mL
¼ cup	freshly squeezed lemon juice	50 mL

1 tsp	vanilla	5 mL
4½ cups	all-purpose flour (approx.)	1.125 L
2 tsp	baking powder	10 mL
	Sifted confectioner's (icing) sugar (optional)	

1. In a small bowl, mix together jam, nuts and raisins and set aside.
2. In a large mixer bowl, beat eggs and sugar until light and fluffy. Add shortening and beat until well blended and smooth. Add milk, zests, juices and vanilla and beat until thoroughly blended. Slowly beat in about half of the flour, then the baking powder. Stir in the remaining flour with a wooden spoon or your hands until a soft dough forms. If dough is a bit sticky, add a few tablespoons of flour until the right consistency.
3. Place dough on a floured work surface and tear off evenly sized pieces, about 1½ inches (4 cm) each, and roll each out into a 4-inch (10 cm) round. Use a 4-inch (10 cm) cookie cutter to trim each, if you want an exact measurement.
4. Spread a rounded teaspoon of the jam mixture over one half of each round, but not to the edges, then fold over opposite half so that edges meet, like a half moon. Press down with your fingers or crimp with a fork to seal. Place half moons on baking sheet.
5. Bake in preheated oven for 25 to 30 minutes or until golden brown. Let cool on a wire rack. Sprinkle with confectioner's sugar, if desired.

Tip *For a vanilla icing, use 1 cup (250 mL) confectioner's (icing) sugar and 4 tsp (20 mL) water, mixing until smooth. If a chocolate icing is desired, add about 1 tbsp (15 mL) unsweetened cocoa powder to the vanilla icing. Drizzle half moons with either or both.*

Mini Chocolate Puff Turnovers

Makes 9 mini turnovers
- Preheat oven to 425ºF (220ºC)
- Baking sheet, lightly greased

1	sheet or block frozen puff pastry, thawed (about 8.5 oz/255 g)	1
4 oz	semisweet chocolate, broken into chunks	125 g
1	egg, lightly beaten	1
	Sifted confectioner's (icing) sugar	

1. Place the puff pastry on a floured work surface and trim or roll into a 9-inch (23 cm) square. Cut sheet into nine 3-inch (7.5 cm) squares.

2. Place a chunk of chocolate near one corner, brush two sides of the square with some of the egg and then fold dough over diagonally to cover the chocolate chunk. Pinch edges with your fingers or a fork to seal and place turnovers on prepared baking sheet. Brush tops with the remaining egg.
3. Bake in preheated oven for 10 to 15 minutes or until golden brown. Let cool slightly, then dust with confectioner's sugar.

Tip *This recipe calls for 1 sheet of puff pastry. Because a package of puff pastry contains many sheets, use as many as you like and adjust the amount of chocolate accordingly.*

Special Breakfast Turnovers

Makes about 2 dozen turnovers
- Preheat oven to 450ºF (230ºC)
- Baking sheet, lightly greased

4 oz	cream cheese, softened	125 g
1	egg yolk	1
⅓ cup	peach preserves	75 mL
2 cups	all-purpose flour	500 mL
1 tbsp	granulated sugar	15 mL
1 tbsp	baking powder	15 mL
½ tsp	cream of tartar	2 mL
¼ tsp	salt	1 mL
½ cup	butter or margarine	125 mL
¾ cup	milk or light (5%) cream	175 mL

1. In a small mixer bowl, beat cream cheese and egg yolk until smooth. Mix in peach preserves.
2. In a large bowl, combine flour, sugar, baking powder, cream of tartar and salt. Cut in butter until mixture resembles coarse crumbs. Add milk and stir with a fork until mixture is just blended and moistened. Place dough on a lightly floured surface and knead gently until the dough is nearly smooth. Cut in half and roll out one half to ⅛-inch (0.25 cm) thickness and cut into circles with a 4-inch (10 cm) cookie cutter, rerolling scraps.
3. Place a heaping teaspoonful (5 mL) of cream cheese filling onto the center of each circle. Brush the edge of half of each circle with water, then fold over opposite side to form a half moon. Press edges with a fork to seal, and make two small slits in each. Repeat with the remaining dough and filling.
4. Place turnovers on prepared baking sheet and bake in preheated oven for 10 to 15 minutes or until golden brown. Let cool slightly on a wire rack, then serve warm.

Mushroom and Broccoli Turnovers

Makes 4 dozen turnovers
- Baking sheet, greased

1/3 cup	butter or margarine, softened	75 mL
1	package (8 oz/250 g) cream cheese, softened	1
1 cup	all-purpose flour	250 mL
2 1/2 cups	small broccoli florets	625 mL
1 1/2 cups	finely chopped fresh mushrooms	375 mL
1 1/2 cups	shredded old Cheddar cheese (about 6 oz/175 g)	375 mL
	Ground nutmeg	
	Freshly ground black pepper	
1/4 cup	Dijon mustard	50 mL
1	egg, lightly beaten, mixed with 1 tbsp (15 mL) water	1

1. In a large mixer bowl, on medium speed, cream butter and cream cheese, beating until softened and blended. Add flour and beat until a soft dough forms. Divide dough in half, form into two balls and cover each with plastic wrap. Chill in refrigerator for 1 to 2 hours. Meanwhile, preheat oven to 400°F (200°C).
2. In a large saucepan, blanch broccoli in boiling water for 2 minutes. Drain well and place on paper towels, patting dry and then chopping florets.
3. In a large bowl, combine the chopped broccoli, mushrooms and cheese. Season to taste with nutmeg and pepper.
4. On a well floured work surface, roll out each portion of dough to 1/8-inch (0.25 cm) thickness. Cut out circles with a 3-inch (7.5 cm) cookie cutter, rerolling scraps. Spread mustard on each circle, leaving a 1/2-inch (1 cm) border around the edges. Place a teaspoonful (5 mL) of broccoli mixture onto one side of each circle.
5. Brush egg wash around the edges of each circle. Fold each in half and press down with a fork to seal. Make two small slits in each to allow steam to escape. Brush tops with the remaining egg mixture. Repeat with the remaining dough and filling.
6. Place turnovers on prepared baking sheet and bake in preheated oven for 15 to 20 minutes or until golden brown. Let cool slightly on a wire rack and serve warm.

Spinach Feta Turnovers

Makes about 9 dozen turnovers
- Preheat oven to 375°F (190°C)
- Baking sheet, lightly greased

36	sheets frozen phyllo pastry, thawed (about 1 1/2 packages, each 16 oz/454 g)	36
2	eggs, lightly beaten	2
1	package (10 oz/284 g) fresh spinach, chopped	1
3/4 cup	feta cheese, finely crumbled (about 6 oz/175 g)	175 mL
1/4 cup	chopped fresh dill (optional)	50 mL
2 tsp	dried onion flakes	10 mL
1/4 tsp	freshly ground black pepper	1 mL
1/4 cup	butter or margarine, melted	50 mL

1. Place phyllo sheets on a work surface and cover with a damp tea towel to prevent them from drying out.
2. In a large bowl, whisk eggs. Mix in spinach, cheese, dill (if using), onion flakes and pepper.
3. Stack two sheets of phyllo dough together. Cut crosswise into 6 strips about 3 inches (7.5 cm) wide. With a pastry brush, lightly brush each strip with melted butter. Spoon 1 tsp (5 mL) spinach filling about 1 inch (2.5 cm) away from bottom of each strip. Fold one bottom corner over filling to form a triangle. Fold in this manner to end of strip, folding end flap underneath. Brush tops with more of the melted butter. Cut a small slit in the top of each. Repeat with more sheets of phyllo dough until all the spinach filling is used up.
4. Place turnovers on prepared baking sheet and bake in preheated oven for 10 to 15 minutes or until tops are golden brown. Serve hot.

Tempting Sweet Potato Turnovers

Makes 12 turnovers
- Preheat oven to 425°F (220°C)
- 2 baking sheets, greased

2 1/2 cups	all-purpose flour	625 mL
1 tsp	baking powder	5 mL
1/2 tsp	salt	2 mL
3/4 cup	butter-flavored shortening	175 mL
6 tbsp	cold water	90 mL
FILLING		
1	can (19 oz/540 mL) crushed pineapple, drained	1

2 cups	mashed sweet potatoes (no butter or milk added)	500 mL
1 1/4 cups	granulated sugar	300 mL
1 tsp	grated lemon zest	5 mL
1 tsp	grated orange zest	5 mL
1/2 tsp	ground cinnamon	2 mL
1/4 tsp	ground allspice	1 mL
1/4 tsp	ground ginger (optional)	1 mL
	Milk	
	Granulated sugar	

1. In a medium bowl, combine flour, baking powder and salt. Cut in shortening with a pastry blender or two knives until mixture resembles coarse crumbs. Add cold water, 1 tbsp (15 mL) at a time, stirring until a ball of soft dough forms.
2. Place dough on a floured work surface and divide into 12 pieces. Roll each piece into a 6-inch (15 cm) circle.
3. *Prepare the filling:* In a large saucepan, over low heat, combine pineapple, sweet potatoes, sugar, zests, cinnamon, allspice and ginger and cook, stirring, until thickened, about 10 to 12 minutes. Set aside to cool.
4. Place 1/4 cup (50 mL) of cooled filling onto half of each circle. Fold dough over filling and press edges with your fingers or a fork to seal. Place turnovers onto prepared baking sheets. Brush with some milk and sprinkle with granulated sugar. Cut slits in tops to allow steam to escape.
5. Bake in preheated oven for 15 to 20 minutes or until golden brown. Serve hot or warm with a meal.

• •

Puffy Turkey Turnovers

Makes 8 turnovers
• Preheat oven to 375°F (190°C)
• 2 baking sheets, greased or lined with parchment paper

1 1/2 cups	cubed cooked turkey (about 1 lb/500 g)	375 mL
2/3 cup	shredded Swiss cheese (about 4 oz/125 g)	150 mL
3 tbsp	Dijon mustard	45 mL
1	package (14 oz/397 g) frozen puff pastry, thawed	1
1	egg, lightly beaten	1
1 tbsp	milk	15 mL

1. In a large bowl, combine turkey, cheese and mustard and mix together to blend.
2. On a lightly floured surface, roll out half of the pastry to a 9-inch (23 cm) square, then cut into 4 squares. Repeat with the other half. Place 1/4 cup (50 mL) of the turkey mixture in the center of each square.
3. In a small bowl, whisk egg and milk. Brush over edges of squares. Fold in half diagonally to form a triangle and press down on edges with a fork to seal. Place on prepared baking sheets. Brush lightly with the remaining egg mixture.
4. Bake in preheated oven for 25 to 30 minutes or until tops are golden brown.

• •

Bacon Turnovers

Makes 25 to 30 turnovers
• Preheat oven to 425°F (220°C)
• Baking sheet, greased

8 oz	sliced bacon	250 g
1	large onion, diced	1
3	envelopes (each 1/4 oz/7 g) active dry yeast	3
1/2 cup	warm water	125 mL
1 cup	warm milk	250 mL
1/2 cup	butter or margarine, melted	125 mL
1 1/2 tsp	salt	7 mL
1	egg, lightly beaten	1

1. In a skillet, cook bacon until well done. Transfer to a medium bowl, crumble bacon, add onion and mix together. Set aside.
2. In a large mixer bowl, dissolve yeast in the warm water. Add milk, butter and salt and beat until blended and smooth and a soft dough is formed. Place dough on a floured work surface and knead for 5 to 6 minutes or until smooth and elastic. Transfer dough to a greased bowl and turn once so that top is also greased. Cover and set aside in a warm place to rise for about 25 to 30 minutes or until double in size, then punch dough down and place on floured work surface again.
3. Cut dough into 25 to 30 pieces. Take each piece and roll it out into a circle, 3 inches (7.5 cm) in diameter if you want mini turnovers, or 4 inches (10 cm) for a regular turnover. Put 1 1/2 to 2 tsp (7 to 10 mL) of the bacon mixture on one side of each circle. Fold dough over the filling and press down on edges with your fingers or a fork to seal.
4. Place turnovers on prepared baking sheet, leaving room between each. Cover with a towel and let rise in a warm place until double in size, about 15 to 20 minutes. Brush tops of each with the beaten egg.
5. Bake in preheated oven for 10 to 15 minutes or until golden brown. Let cool slightly.

Scones

Old-Fashioned Scones

Makes 16 scones
- Preheat oven to 400°F (200°C)
- Baking sheet, ungreased

2 cups	all-purpose flour	500 mL
1/2 cup	granulated sugar	125 mL
1 tsp	cream of tartar	5 mL
1/2 tsp	salt	2 mL
1/2 tsp	baking soda	2 mL
1/4 cup	shortening or butter	50 mL
1	egg	1
1/2 cup	milk	125 mL
1 tsp	vanilla	5 mL
3/4 cup	raisins (optional)	175 mL
	Additional milk and granulated sugar	

1. In a large bowl, combine flour, sugar, cream of tartar, salt and baking soda. Cut in shortening with a pastry blender or two knives until mixture resembles coarse crumbs.
2. In a small bowl, whisk egg, milk and vanilla until blended. Pour into flour mixture and stir until mixture forms a dough. Fold in raisins (if using).
3. Place dough on a floured work surface and divide into 4 portions. Place each portion on baking sheet and pat down with the palm of your hand. With a knife, score an X into each round to mark out 4 wedges.
4. Brush each portion with milk and sprinkle with sugar. Bake in preheated oven for 15 to 20 minutes or until golden brown. Let cool on a wire rack and cut into wedges as marked.

Tip *Serve these delicious scones warm, with butter, jam or cream cheese — or all three!*

Golden Tea Scones

Makes about 12 scones
- Preheat oven to 450°F (230°C)
- Baking sheet, buttered

2 cups	all-purpose flour	500 mL
4 tsp	baking powder	20 mL
1 tbsp	granulated sugar	15 mL
1/2 tsp	salt	2 mL
2 tbsp	cold butter or shortening	25 mL
1 cup	cold milk	250 mL
1	egg, lightly beaten, mixed with 1 tbsp (15 mL) water (optional)	1

1. In a large bowl, sift together flour, baking powder, sugar and salt. Cut in butter with a pastry blender or two knives until mixture is crumbly. Add milk and mix with a fork until blended, moistened and a soft dough forms.
2. Place dough on a floured work surface and knead gently about 5 to 6 times. Roll out dough into a circle 1/2 inch (1 cm) thick and cut out rounds, using a 2-inch (5 cm) round cookie cutter, rerolling scraps. Place rounds onto prepared baking sheet. Brush tops with egg wash (if using).
3. Bake in preheated oven for 12 to 15 minutes or until golden brown. Let cool slightly on a wire rack and serve warm.

Tip *To dress up your scones, add to the crumbly mixture 1/2 cup (125 mL) chopped pecans or raisins, or 1/2 cup (125 mL) chopped candied cherries or other dried fruit.*

Traditional Cream Scones

Makes 8 scones
- Preheat oven to 450°F (230°C)
- Baking sheet, ungreased

2 cups	all-purpose flour	500 mL
2 tbsp	granulated sugar	25 mL
1 tbsp	baking powder	15 mL
Pinch	salt	Pinch
1/4 cup	shortening or butter	50 mL
2	eggs	2
1/2 cup	half-and-half (10%) cream	125 mL
	Additional granulated sugar (optional)	

1. In a large bowl, combine flour, sugar, baking powder and salt. Cut in shortening with a pastry blender or your fingers until mixture resembles coarse crumbs.
2. Break eggs into a small bowl, reserving a little of the white. Whisk eggs and stir in the cream. Add to the flour mixture, stirring with a fork until a soft dough forms.
3. Place dough on a floured work surface, knead for about 30 seconds and roll into an oblong 3/4 inch (1.5 cm) thick. Cut into triangles, or into diamonds by making diagonal cuts in one direction and then in the other direction. Mix the reserved egg white with 1 tsp (5 mL) water and brush over tops. Sprinkle with granulated sugar, if desired.
4. Bake in preheated oven for 12 to 15 minutes or until golden brown. Let cool slightly on a wire rack.

Tip *These scones are popular in England, at tea time, served with clotted cream and strawberry jam.*

Old-Time Scottish Scones

Makes 8 scones

- Griddle, ungreased

2 cups	all-purpose flour	500 mL
2 tsp	granulated sugar	10 mL
1½ tsp	baking powder	7 mL
¼ tsp	salt	1 mL
1½ tbsp	shortening	22 mL
1 cup	milk	250 mL
Pinch	baking soda	Pinch

1. In a large bowl, sift together flour, sugar, baking powder and salt. Cut in shortening with a pastry blender or your fingers until mixture resembles coarse crumbs.
2. In a small bowl, mix together milk and baking soda. Pour into flour mixture and mix together with a fork until blended, moistened and a soft dough forms.
3. Turn out dough onto a floured work surface, knead lightly 5 to 6 times and roll into a circle about ½ inch (1 cm) thick. Cut into 8 wedges.
4. Bake on griddle, over medium heat, turning over to brown both sides. Turn each scone on edge to brown the edges.

Tip *Serve hot, split in half, with butter and your favorite jam.*

Buttermilk Scones

Makes 12 scones

- Preheat oven to 400°F (200°C)
- Baking sheet, greased

2 cups	all-purpose flour	500 mL
¼ cup	granulated sugar	50 mL
1 tbsp	baking powder	15 mL
1 tsp	salt	5 mL
½ tsp	baking soda	2 mL
½ tsp	ground cinnamon (optional)	2 mL
¼ cup	cold butter or margarine	50 mL
2	eggs, lightly beaten	2
⅓ cup	buttermilk	75 mL

1. In a large bowl, combine flour, sugar, baking powder, salt, baking soda and cinnamon. Mix well to blend. Cut in butter with a pastry blender or two knives until mixture resembles coarse crumbs.
2. In a small bowl, lightly whisk eggs and buttermilk just to blend. Sir into flour mixture until a soft dough forms.

3. Place dough on a floured work surface and knead lightly 5 times. Divide dough in half. With the palm of your hand, pat each portion into a 7-inch (18 cm) circle and cut each into 6 wedges.
4. Place wedges on prepared baking sheet and bake in preheated oven for 10 to 12 minutes or until golden brown. Let cool slightly on a wire rack and serve warm.

Southern Cornmeal Scones

Makes 6 to 8 scones

- Preheat oven to 425°F (220°C)
- Baking sheet, lightly greased

1 cup	all-purpose flour	250 mL
½ cup	yellow cornmeal	125 mL
¼ cup	freshly grated Parmesan cheese	50 mL
2 tsp	baking powder	10 mL
½ tsp	baking soda	2 mL
½ tsp	crumbled dried sage	2 mL
¼ tsp	salt	1 mL
¼ cup	cold butter or margarine	50 mL
¾ cup	buttermilk	175 mL
	Additional freshly grated Parmesan cheese (optional)	

1. In a large bowl, combine flour, cornmeal, cheese, baking powder, baking soda, sage and salt. Mix well to blend. Work in butter with your fingers or a pastry blender until mixture resembles coarse crumbs. Add buttermilk and stir until just blended and moistened and a soft dough is formed.
2. Place dough on a floured work surface, knead 10 times and place on prepared baking sheet. With the palm of your hand, pat down into a 6-inch (15 cm) circle. Score into 6 to 8 wedges with the point of a sharp knife, but do not cut through. Sprinkle tops with extra Parmesan cheese (if using).
3. Bake in preheated oven for 20 minutes or until golden brown. Let cool slightly on a wire rack, cut into wedges as marked and serve warm.

Tip *You can use ½ cup (125 mL) all-purpose flour and ½ cup (125 mL) whole wheat flour in this recipe in place of the 1 cup (250 mL) all-purpose flour.*

Sour Cream Scones

Makes 16 scones
- Preheat oven to 400°F (200°C)
- Baking sheet, ungreased

2¼ cups	cake and pastry flour	550 mL
¼ cup	granulated sugar	50 mL
2½ tsp	baking powder	12 mL
½ tsp	salt	2 mL
½ tsp	baking soda	2 mL
1	egg	1
1 cup	sour cream	250 mL
¼ tsp	vanilla	1 mL

1. In a large bowl, combine flour, sugar, baking powder, salt and baking soda, mixing until blended. Make a well in the center.
2. In a small bowl, whisk egg, sour cream and vanilla. Pour into the well in the flour mixture and stir with a fork until blended, just moistened and a soft dough is formed.
3. Turn out dough onto a floured work surface and knead gently about 5 to 10 times, working in a little more cake flour if the dough is too sticky. Divide dough in half and, with the palm of your hand, pat down each portion into a 6-inch (15 cm) circle about ½ inch (1 cm) in thickness. Cut each circle into 8 wedges and place wedges on baking sheet, leaving about 2 inches (5 cm) between each.
4. Bake in preheated oven for 15 minutes or until golden brown. Let cool slightly on a wire rack and serve warm.

Oatmeal Scones

Makes 8 scones
- Preheat oven to 400°F (200°C)
- Baking sheet, greased

1½ cups	all-purpose flour	375 mL
1 cup	old-fashioned rolled oats	250 mL
½ tsp	salt	2 mL
¼ cup	butter or margarine, softened	50 mL
¾ cup	buttermilk	175 mL

1. In a large bowl, combine flour, oats and salt. Mix well to blend. Cut in butter with a pastry blender or two knives until mixture resembles coarse crumbs. Stir in buttermilk, mixing just until blended and moistened and a soft dough is formed.

2. Place dough on a floured work surface and knead lightly a few times. Divide dough in half and roll each half into a circle ½ inch (1 cm) thick. Place on prepared baking sheet.
3. Bake in preheated oven for 12 to 15 minutes or until golden brown. Let cool slightly on a wire rack and then cut each circle into 4 wedges.

Tip *Serve hot or warm, with butter, jam or honey.*

Chunky Chocolate Scones

Makes about 8 to 12 scones
- Preheat oven to 400°F (200°C)
- Baking sheet, lightly greased

2 cups	all-purpose flour	500 mL
¼ cup	granulated sugar	50 mL
1 tbsp	baking powder	15 mL
½ tsp	salt	2 mL
¼ tsp	ground nutmeg	1 mL
6 tbsp	cold butter or margarine, cut into chunks	90 mL
5 oz	bittersweet baking chocolate, coarsely chopped into chunks	150 g
2	eggs	2
¼ cup	buttermilk	50 mL
2 tsp	vanilla	10 mL
	Beaten egg or milk, for glaze (optional)	

1. In a large bowl, combine flour, sugar, baking powder, salt and nutmeg and mix together to blend. Cut in butter with a pastry blender or two knives until mixture resembles coarse crumbs. Stir in chocolate chunks.
2. In a small bowl, whisk together eggs, buttermilk and vanilla. Add to flour mixture and stir just until blended and a soft dough forms.
3. Place dough on a floured work surface, knead 3 to 4 times and roll out into a circle about ¾ to 1 inch (1.5 to 2.5 cm) thick. Cut out 3-inch (7.5 cm) rounds with a cookie cutter and place rounds on prepared baking sheet, rerolling scraps. Brush tops with beaten egg (if using).
4. Bake in preheated oven for 15 to 20 minutes or until golden brown. Let cool slightly on a wire rack and serve warm.

Tip *Try substituting carob for chocolate in some of your recipes. Carob is similar to chocolate in flavor but is lower in fat and is caffeine-free.*

Crusty Cheddar Cheese Scones

Makes 12 scones

- Preheat oven to 425°F (220°C)
- Baking sheet, greased

3 cups	all-purpose flour	750 mL
2 tbsp	granulated sugar	25 mL
4 tsp	baking powder	20 mL
½ tsp	baking soda	2 mL
½ tsp	salt	2 mL
½ cup	cold butter or margarine, cut into cubes	125 mL
2 cups	shredded Cheddar cheese (about 8 oz/250 g)	500 mL
1	egg	1
1 cup	milk	250 mL
1 tbsp	white vinegar	15 mL

1. In a large bowl, combine flour, sugar, baking powder, baking soda and salt. Mix together to blend. Cut in butter with a pastry blender or two knives until mixture resembles coarse crumbs. Stir in cheese and mix well.

2. In a small bowl, whisk together egg, milk and vinegar. Add to flour mixture and mix gently with a fork until blended and moistened.

3. Spoon into 12 mounds on prepared baking sheet, leaving 2 inches (5 cm) between each.

4. Bake in preheated oven for 15 to 18 minutes or until golden brown. Let cool slightly on a wire rack and serve warm.

Cheese 'n' Apple Scones

Makes 8 scones

- Preheat oven to 450°F (230°C)
- Baking sheet, greased

1 cup	shredded Cheddar cheese (about 4 oz/125 g)	250 mL
1 cup	peeled, cored and diced apples (about 1 medium)	250 mL
1¾ cups	all-purpose flour	425 mL
2 tbsp	granulated sugar	25 mL
1½ tsp	baking powder	7 mL
½ tsp	salt	2 mL
¼ tsp	baking soda	1 mL
⅓ cup	butter or margarine, cold	75 mL
1 cup	buttermilk	250 mL

1. In a medium bowl, mix together cheese and apples to blend.

2. In a large bowl, combine flour, sugar, baking powder, salt and baking soda. Cut in butter with a pastry blender or two knives until mixture resembles coarse crumbs. Add buttermilk and mix together just until blended and moistened. Fold in the cheese-apple mixture.

3. Place dough on a floured work surface and knead 10 times. With the palm of your hand, pat dough into a 9-inch (23 cm) circle, then cut circle into 8 wedges. Separate the wedges and place them on the prepared baking sheet.

4. Bake in preheated oven for 15 minutes or until golden brown. Let cool slightly on a wire rack and serve warm.

Traditional Blueberry Scones

Makes about 12 scones

- Preheat oven to 375°F (190°C)
- Baking sheet, lightly greased

2¼ cups	all-purpose flour	550 mL
½ cup	granulated sugar	125 mL
2 tsp	baking powder	10 mL
½ tsp	salt	2 mL
½ tsp	ground cinnamon	2 mL
¼ tsp	ground ginger	1 mL
	Finely grated zest of 1 orange (optional)	
¼ cup	cold butter, cut into cubes	50 mL
1 cup	half-and-half (10%) cream	250 mL
1 cup	fresh or frozen, well-drained blueberries (about 6 oz/175 g)	250 mL
1	egg, lightly beaten (optional)	1

1. In a large bowl, combine flour, sugar, baking powder, salt, cinnamon, ginger and zest (if using). Cut in butter with a pastry blender or two knives until mixture resembles coarse crumbs.

2. In a medium bowl, mix together cream and blueberries and stir into flour mixture, mixing just until blended and a soft dough forms.

3. Place dough on a floured work surface, knead 10 to 12 times and roll out into a circle ½ inch (1 cm) thick. Use a 2- or 3-inch (5 or 7.5 cm) cookie cutter, or the top of a glass, floured, to cut out scones, rerolling scraps. Brush tops of scones with beaten egg (if using).

4. Bake in preheated oven for 15 to 20 minutes or until golden brown. Let cool slightly on a wire rack and serve warm.

Cranberry Yogurt Scones

Makes 8 scones
- Preheat oven to 425°F (220°C)
- Baking sheet, lightly greased

1¾ cups	all-purpose flour	425 mL
2 tsp	baking powder	10 mL
1 tsp	baking soda	5 mL
½ tsp	salt	2 mL
1 cup	fresh or frozen cranberries (about 4 oz/125 g)	250 mL
1½ cups	plain yogurt	375 mL
1 tbsp	vegetable oil	15 mL
2 tsp	grated lemon zest	10 mL
1 tsp	vanilla	5 mL

1. In a large bowl, combine flour, baking powder, baking soda and salt. Mix well to combine. Add cranberries and mix together. Make a well in the center.

2. In a medium bowl, combine yogurt, oil, zest and vanilla. Mix together to blend. Pour into the well in the flour mixture and stir with a fork until well combined and a soft dough forms.

3. Place dough on a floured work surface and knead 5 or 6 times, until dough holds together well. Roll into a circle ½ to ¾ inch (1 to 1.5 cm) thick. Cut into 8 wedges and place wedges on prepared baking sheet.

4. Bake in preheated oven for 15 to 18 minutes or until golden brown. Let cool slightly on a wire rack and serve warm.

Glazed Lemon Scones

Makes 8 to 12 scones
- Preheat oven to 400°F (200°C)
- Baking sheet, ungreased

2 cups	all-purpose flour	500 mL
¼ cup	granulated sugar	50 mL
4 tsp	baking powder	20 mL
½ tsp	salt	2 mL
½ cup	butter or shortening	125 mL
1 tbsp	grated lemon zest	15 mL
1	egg	1
½ cup	milk	125 mL
¼ cup	freshly squeezed lemon juice	50 mL
GLAZE		
½ cup	confectioner's (icing) sugar, sifted	125 mL
4 tsp	freshly squeezed lemon juice	20 mL
3 to 4	drops yellow food coloring (optional)	3 to 4

Grated lemon zest, for garnish
Slivered almonds, for garnish

1. In a large bowl, combine flour, sugar, baking powder and salt. Work in butter with your fingers or a pastry blender until mixture resembles coarse crumbs. Stir in lemon zest and blend.

2. In a small bowl, whisk egg, milk and lemon juice. Pour into flour mixture and mix until blended and moistened and a soft dough is formed.

3. Place dough on a floured work surface, knead 15 to 20 times and roll into a circle ¾ inch (1.5 cm) thick. Place on baking sheet. Score into 8 to 12 wedges with the point of a sharp knife.

4. Bake in preheated oven for 15 minutes or until golden brown. Let cool slightly on a wire rack, cut into wedges as marked and serve warm.

5. *Prepare the glaze:* In a small bowl, mix together confectioner's sugar, lemon juice and food coloring (if using). Drizzle over warm scones and sprinkle with zest and almonds.

Poppy Seed Orange Scones

Makes about 16 scones
- Preheat oven to 375°F (190°C)
- Baking sheet, lightly greased

2 cups	all-purpose flour	500 mL
¼ cup	granulated sugar	50 mL
1 tbsp	baking powder	15 mL
½ tsp	salt	2 mL
¼ cup	cold butter or margarine, cut into small cubes	50 mL
¼ cup	poppy seeds	50 mL
	Finely grated zest of 1 orange	
1	egg	1
⅔ cup	half-and-half (10%) cream or milk	150 mL
	Additional granulated sugar (optional)	

1. In a large bowl, combine flour, sugar, baking powder and salt. Mix together to blend. Cut in butter, using a pastry blender or your fingertips, until mixture resembles coarse crumbs. Stir in poppy seeds and zest.

2. In a small bowl, whisk egg and cream until blended. Stir into flour mixture, mixing just until blended, moistened and a soft dough forms. Form dough into a ball.

3. Place dough on a lightly floured work surface, knead about 10 times and roll out to a circle ½ inch (1 cm) thick. Cut out rounds with a 2-inch (5 cm) round cookie cutter or an inverted glass and place on prepared baking sheet, rerolling scraps. Sprinkle with the additional sugar, if desired.

4. Bake in preheated oven for 15 to 18 minutes or until golden brown. Let cool slightly on a wire rack.

• •

Scrumptious Chocolate 'n' Orange Scones

Makes 16 scones

- Preheat oven to 425°F (220°C)
- Baking sheet, ungreased

3 cups	buttermilk pancake mix	750 mL
2 tbsp	grated orange zest	25 mL
1½ cups	whipping (35%) cream	375 mL
6 tbsp	unsweetened cocoa powder	90 mL
6 tbsp	chopped milk chocolate	90 mL

1. In a large bowl, combine pancake mix and zest. Gradually stir in cream, just until moistened and a soft dough forms. Form into a ball and divide dough in half. Leave one portion as is; to the other portion add cocoa and mix into dough.
2. Place both doughs on a floured work surface. Gently knead 3 tbsp (45 mL) chopped chocolate into each portion, kneading about 5 to 6 times. Roll out each portion to a circle ¾ inch (1.5 cm) thick. Cut out 8 rounds from each dough, using a 2-inch (5 cm) cookie cutter, rerolling scraps.
3. Place rounds about 1 inch (2.5 cm) apart on baking sheet and bake in preheated oven for 10 to 12 minutes or until golden brown. Let cool slightly on a wire rack and serve warm.

Tip *When serving, mix the chocolate and plain scones for a colorful plate or basket.*

• •

Chocolate Chip Banana Scones

Makes 8 scones

- Preheat oven to 425°F (220°C)
- 9-inch (2.5 L) square baking dish or a baking sheet, greased

2 cups	all-purpose flour	500 mL
⅔ cup	granulated sugar	150 mL
½ cup	semisweet chocolate chips (about 3 oz/90 g)	125 mL
1 tbsp	baking powder	15 mL
1 tsp	salt	5 mL
½ cup	cold butter or margarine, cut into cubes	125 mL
1	egg	1
¾ cup	whipping (35%) cream	175 mL

1	very ripe large banana, mashed well	1
	Additional granulated sugar (optional)	

1. In a large bowl, combine flour, sugar, chocolate chips, baking powder and salt. Mix well to blend. Cut in butter with a pastry blender or two knives until mixture resembles coarse crumbs.
2. In a bowl, whisk egg and cream until frothy. Stir in banana until well blended. Add to flour mixture and mix until moistened and a soft dough forms.
3. Place dough on a floured work surface and, with the palm of your hand, pat into an 8-inch (20 cm) circle. Place onto prepared baking dish or sheet and sprinkle with additional sugar, if desired.
4. Bake in preheated oven for 15 to 20 minutes or until golden brown. Let cool slightly on a wire rack and serve warm. Cut into 8 wedges.

• •

Festive Fruit Scones

Makes 12 scones

- Preheat oven to 400°F (200°C)
- Large baking sheet, lightly greased

2 cups	all-purpose flour	500 mL
3 tbsp	granulated sugar	45 mL
2 tsp	baking powder	10 mL
¼ tsp	salt	1 mL
6 tbsp	cold butter or margarine, cut into small chunks	90 mL
1 cup	chopped dried fruit (about 5 oz/150 g)	250 mL
2	eggs	2
½ cup	buttermilk	125 mL
	Additional buttermilk	
	Brown sugar	

1. In a large bowl, combine flour, sugar, baking powder and salt and mix well. Cut in butter with a pastry blender or two knives until mixture resembles coarse crumbs. Stir in dried fruit.
2. In a small bowl, whisk eggs and buttermilk to blend. Pour into flour mixture, stirring with a fork just until combined and moistened and a soft dough forms.
3. Spoon into 12 mounds on prepared baking sheet, leaving about 2 inches (5 cm) between each. Brush with buttermilk and sprinkle with brown sugar.
4. Bake in preheated oven for 15 minutes or until golden brown. Let cool slightly on a wire rack and serve warm.

Tip *For the dried fruit, I use ½ cup (125 mL) dried cherries and ½ cup (125 mL) dried apricots.*

Giant Filled Apricot Scone

Serves 6 to 8
- Preheat oven to 400°F (200°C)
- Baking sheet, greased

2	eggs	2
¼ cup	sour cream	50 mL
1 tbsp	milk	15 mL
⅔ cup	finely chopped dried apricots (about 4 oz/125 g)	150 mL
½ cup	quick-cooking rolled oats	125 mL
1½ cups	all-purpose flour	375 mL
¼ cup	granulated sugar	50 mL
2½ tsp	baking powder	12 mL
¼ tsp	salt	1 mL
⅓ cup	cold butter or margarine, cut into cubes	75 mL
	Additional granulated sugar (optional)	

FILLING

1 tbsp	quick-cooking rolled oats	15 mL
3 tbsp	packed brown sugar	45 mL
1 tbsp	butter or margarine, softened	15 mL

1. In a small bowl, beat eggs. Set aside 1 tbsp (15 mL). Whisk in sour cream and milk. Stir in apricots and mix well.
2. In a large bowl, combine oats, flour, sugar, baking powder and salt. Mix well to blend. Cut in butter with a pastry blender or two knives until mixture resembles coarse crumbs. Pour in apricot mixture, mixing well until a dough forms.
3. *Prepare the filling:* In another small bowl, mix together oats, brown sugar and butter until well combined.
4. Place dough on a floured work surface and knead 12 times. Divide dough in half. With the palm of your hand, pat each portion into an 8-inch (20 cm) circle. Place one circle onto prepared baking sheet and sprinkle filling evenly over top. Place second circle over the filling and brush top with the reserved beaten egg. Sprinkle sugar over top, if desired. Using the point of a sharp knife, mark out 6 to 8 wedges, but do not cut.
5. Bake in preheated oven for 15 to 20 minutes or until top is golden brown. Let cool slightly on a wire rack until warm. When ready to serve, follow markings and cut into wedges.

Super Raisin Nut Scones

Makes 8 scones
- Preheat oven to 375°F (190°C)
- Baking sheet, ungreased

2 cups	all-purpose flour	500 mL
½ cup	granulated sugar	125 mL
2 tsp	baking powder	10 mL
⅓ cup	butter or margarine	75 mL
2	eggs	2
¼ cup	milk or table (18%) cream	50 mL
½ cup	chopped nuts (pecans, hazelnuts, walnuts or other)	125 mL
½ cup	raisins	125 mL

1. In a large bowl, combine flour, sugar and baking powder. Mix to blend and then cut in butter with a pastry blender or your fingertips until mixture resembles coarse crumbs.
2. In a small bowl, whisk eggs and milk and pour into flour mixture, stirring with a fork just until blended, moistened and a soft dough is formed. Stir in nuts and raisins and form dough into a ball.
3. Place dough on a floured work surface and cut into 8 portions. Shape each portion into a round ball and place on baking sheet. Using a sharp knife, slash an X in the center of each.
4. Bake in preheated oven for 15 minutes or until golden brown. Let cool slightly on a wire rack and serve warm.

Tip *Delicious when served with Maple Butter (page 541).*

Spicy Pumpkin Scones

Makes about 16 scones
- Preheat oven to 400°F (200°C)
- Baking sheet, ungreased

2 cups	all-purpose flour	500 mL
½ cup	packed brown sugar	125 mL
2 tsp	baking powder	10 mL
1 tsp	ground cinnamon	5 mL
½ tsp	baking soda	2 mL
¼ tsp	ground nutmeg	1 mL
¼ tsp	ground allspice	1 mL
Pinch	salt	Pinch
¼ cup	butter or margarine	50 mL
½ cup	raisins	125 mL
1	egg, lightly beaten	1

3/4 cup	canned pumpkin purée (not pie filling)	175 mL
2 tbsp	buttermilk	25 mL
1	egg white, lightly beaten	1

1. In a large bowl, combine flour, brown sugar, baking powder, cinnamon, baking soda, nutmeg, allspice and salt. Cut in butter with a pastry blender or two knives until mixture resembles coarse crumbs. Mix in raisins.

2. In a small bowl, mix egg, pumpkin and buttermilk. Add to flour mixture and mix until blended and a soft dough forms. Turn out dough onto a floured work surface and roll into a circle 3/4 inch (1.5 cm) thick. Cut out rounds using a 2-inch (5 cm) round cookie cutter or the top of an inverted glass and place on baking sheet, rerolling scraps.

3. Brush tops with the beaten egg white and bake in preheated oven for 12 to 15 minutes or until golden brown. Let cool slightly on a wire rack and serve warm.

Potato Scones

Makes 16 scones
- Baking sheet, floured

3/4 cup	sour cream	175 mL
1/4 cup	butter or margarine	50 mL
2 tbsp + 1 tsp	granulated sugar	30 mL
1/2 tsp	baking soda	2 mL
1/4 tsp	ground mace	1 mL
1/2 cup	cold mashed potatoes	125 mL
1	envelope (1/4 oz/7 g) active dry yeast	1
1/2 cup	lukewarm water	125 mL
3 cups	all-purpose flour, divided	750 mL
1/2 tsp	salt	2 mL

1. In a medium saucepan, over low heat, scald sour cream (see tip, page 471). Add butter, the 2 tbsp (25 mL) sugar, baking soda and mace and stir just until blended. Remove from heat and stir in the mashed potatoes. Mix well.

2. In a large bowl, dissolve the yeast and 1 tsp (5 mL) sugar in the lukewarm water. Mix yeast into the creamed potato mixture and add 1 1/2 cups (375 mL) of the flour. Sift the salt and the remaining flour and add to yeast mixture. Stir until well blended, moistened and a soft dough forms.

3. Place dough on a floured work surface and knead until smooth and elastic. Place dough into a greased bowl, cover with a towel or plastic wrap and let rise to double the size, about 45 minutes. Then punch down, cover and let rise for another 10 minutes.

4. Divide dough into 4 equal parts. Roll each out into a 9-inch (23 cm) circle. Dust each with flour and cut each into 4 triangular scones. Place well apart on prepared baking sheet, cover with a towel or plastic wrap and let rise, in a warm spot, for about 45 minutes. Meanwhile, preheat oven to 375°F (190°C).

5. Bake in preheated oven for 15 minutes or until golden brown. Serve hot.

Onion-Topped Herb Scones

Makes 8 scones
- Preheat oven to 425°F (220°C)
- Baking sheet, lightly greased

2 tbsp	butter or margarine	25 mL
2	onions, thinly sliced	2
3/4 tsp	dried thyme, divided	3 mL
1 3/4 cups	all-purpose flour (or half all-purpose and half whole wheat)	425 mL
1 tbsp	granulated sugar	15 mL
1 tbsp	chopped chives or green onion	15 mL
1 tbsp	chopped fresh parsley	15 mL
1/2 tsp	salt	2 mL
1/4 cup	cold butter, cut into chunks	50 mL
1 cup	plain yogurt	250 mL

1. In a skillet, over medium heat, melt butter and add onions, cooking about 5 minutes, until tender. Stir in 1/4 tsp (1 mL) of the thyme and cook for 1 to 2 minutes. Remove from heat and set aside.

2. In a large bowl, combine flour, sugar, chives, parsley, salt and the remaining thyme. Mix together and then cut in butter, using your fingers or a pastry blender, until mixture resembles coarse crumbs. Stir in yogurt and, with a fork, mix until blended and moistened and a soft dough forms.

3. Place dough on a floured work surface and knead 5 to 6 times, until smooth. With the palm of your hand, pat down to an 8-inch (20 cm) circle about 1 inch (2.5 cm) thick. Score 8 wedges on surface of dough. Spread the reserved onion mixture evenly over top.

4. Bake in preheated oven for 20 minutes or until golden brown. Let cool slightly on a wire rack, cut into wedges as marked and serve warm.

Custards, Crème Brûlée and Flans

Custards

When baking custards, to minimize the possibility of curdling, place custard cups in a 13- by 9-inch (3 L) baking pan on the oven rack, then pour hot water into the pan until water reaches halfway up the cups. Then slide into oven and bake as directed. Do not overbake, as custards will set as they cool. The point of a knife inserted in the center will come out clean when the custard is set and done.

A stirred custard is cooked in a double boiler over hot but not boiling water. Stir constantly.

When preparing crème brûlée, use light (5%) cream instead of milk, cool and chill, then broil for about 5 minutes, until custard has a bubbly brown crust.

Perfect Baked Custard

Serves 12
- Preheat oven to 350°F (180°C)
- Twelve ¾-cup (175 mL) custard cups or ramekins
- Two 13- by 9-inch (3 L) baking pans

6	eggs, lightly beaten	6
⅔ cup	granulated sugar	150 mL
2 tsp	vanilla	10 mL
Pinch	salt	Pinch
5 cups	milk, scalded	1.25 L
	Ground cinnamon	
	Ground nutmeg	

1. In a large bowl, whisk together eggs, sugar, vanilla and salt. Gradually stir in milk, just until well blended. Spoon into custard cups. Sprinkle tops with cinnamon and nutmeg.
2. Place custard cups in baking pans set on oven racks. Pour hot water into each pan until it reaches halfway up the cups. Bake in preheated oven for 45 to 50 minutes or until custard is set and a knife inserted near the center comes out clean. Remove cups to wire rack to cool. Serve warm or chilled.

Tips *Milk, cream and sour cream are scalded when bubbles form around the edge of the pan as you heat it.*

If you put both pans in the oven at the same time, place them on different racks, and make sure one is not directly above the other. Put one on the right side of its rack and the other on the left.

This custard can be stored in the refrigerator, in the cups, covered with plastic wrap, for up to 1 week.

Custard Pie

Serves 6 to 8
- Preheat oven to 400°F (200°C)
- Baking sheet

	9-inch (23 cm) unbaked pastry shell	
2½ cups	milk	625 mL
4	eggs, lightly beaten	4
½ cup	granulated sugar	125 mL
½ tsp	vanilla	2 mL
¼ tsp	salt	1 mL
Pinch	almond extract	Pinch
	Ground nutmeg	

1. Chill pie shell in refrigerator while preparing recipe.
2. In a medium saucepan, scald milk (see tip, left). Remove from heat.
3. In a large bowl, whisk eggs, sugar, vanilla, salt and almond extract. Gradually stir in scalded milk. Pour into chilled pie shell and sprinkle nutmeg over top. Place pie shell on baking sheet.
4. Bake in preheated oven for 25 to 30 minutes or until custard is set and a knife inserted near the center comes out clean. Let cool on a wire rack, then chill in refrigerator for 3 to 4 hours or overnight.

Old-Time Vanilla Custards

Serves 4
- Preheat oven to 350°F (180°C)
- Four ¾-cup (175 mL) custard cups or ramekins
- 13- by 9-inch (3 L) baking pan

2	eggs, lightly beaten	2
2 cups	milk	500 mL
6 tbsp	packed brown sugar	90 mL
1½ tsp	vanilla	7 mL
Pinch	salt (optional)	Pinch
	Ground nutmeg	

1. In a small mixer bowl, combine eggs, milk, brown sugar, vanilla and salt (if using). Beat on medium speed until well blended. Spoon into custard cups and sprinkle with nutmeg.
2. Place cups in baking pan set on oven rack and pour in hot water until it reaches halfway up the cups. Bake in preheated oven for 30 to 35 minutes or until custard is set and a knife inserted near the center comes out clean. Remove cups to wire rack to cool. Serve warm or chilled.

Stirred Almond Custard

Serves 8
- Double boiler
- Eight ¾-cup (175 mL) custard cups or ramekins

6	egg yolks, lightly beaten	6
3 cups	milk	750 mL
1¼ cups	granulated sugar	300 mL
1½ tsp	unflavored gelatin powder, mixed with ⅓ cup (75 mL) milk	7 mL
1 tsp	vanilla	5 mL
1 tsp	almond extract	5 mL
2 cups	whipping (35%) cream, whipped	500 mL
1 to 2	bananas, sliced	1 to 2
½ cup	sliced almonds, toasted	125 mL

1. In the top of a double boiler, over hot but not boiling water, combine egg yolks, milk and sugar. Cook over medium heat for 10 minutes, stirring constantly, until mixture thickens enough to coat the back of a metal spoon.

2. In a small saucepan, over low heat, heat the gelatin-milk mixture until gelatin is dissolved. Stir this mixture into the egg mixture and chill until partially set. Stir in vanilla and almond extract. Fold in the whipped cream and spoon into custard cups.

3. Chill in refrigerator until set, about 45 to 50 minutes. Garnish with banana slices and sprinkle with almonds.

Microwave Egg Custard

Serves 4

3	eggs	3
½ cup	granulated sugar	125 mL
1 tsp	vanilla	5 mL
Pinch	salt	Pinch
1½ cups	milk	375 mL
	Ground nutmeg and/or cinnamon	

1. Whisk eggs in a 4-cup (1 L) microwave-safe dish. Add sugar, vanilla and salt and whisk until well blended.

2. In a small microwave-safe dish, scald milk on High for 2 to 3 minutes. Slowly stir into egg mixture. Cover with plastic wrap and microwave on Low for about 10 minutes. Remove cover and sprinkle with nutmeg or cinnamon, or both.

Tip *When cooling custards in the refrigerator, put a piece of plastic wrap over top to prevent a skin from forming.*

Grandma's Egg Custard

Serves 6 to 8
- Double boiler

2 cups	whole milk or light (5%) cream	500 mL
5	egg yolks	5
¼ cup	granulated sugar	50 mL
1 tsp	vanilla	5 mL

1. In a heavy saucepan, scald milk (see tip, page 471). Remove from heat.

2. In a large mixer bowl, on low speed, beat egg yolks and sugar until blended. Gradually beat in hot milk and pour mixture into top of double boiler over simmering, not boiling, water. Cook, stirring constantly, for about 10 to 12 minutes or until the mixture thickens enough to coat the back of a metal spoon. Remove from heat and stir in vanilla.

3. Spoon into individual dessert or parfait glasses, filling each about three-quarters full, and serve.

Variation *Spoon custard over fresh fruit, or place dessert glasses in refrigerator to chill and serve cold.*

Velvety Chocolate Custard

Serves 6
- Preheat oven to 325°F (160°C)
- Six ⅔-cup (150 mL) custard cups or ramekins
- 13- by 9-inch (3 L) baking pan

2 cups	milk	500 mL
½ cup	semisweet chocolate chips (about 3 oz/90 g)	125 mL
3	eggs, lightly beaten	3
¼ cup	granulated sugar	50 mL
1 tsp	vanilla	5 mL
Pinch	salt	Pinch

1. In a medium saucepan, over low heat, cook milk and chocolate chips, stirring constantly until chocolate is melted. Set aside to cool slightly.

2. In a medium bowl, whisk together eggs, sugar, vanilla and salt. Gradually stir in the chocolate mixture. Pour into custard cups.

3. Place cups in baking pan set on oven rack and pour in hot water until it reaches halfway up the cups. Bake in preheated oven for 40 to 45 minutes or until custard is set and a knife inserted near the center comes out clean. Remove cups to wire rack to cool. Invert onto serving dishes and garnish as desired.

Baked Coconut Custard

Serves 6

- Preheat oven to 325°F (160°C)
- Six ¾-cup (175 mL) custard cups or ramekins
- 13- by 9-inch (3 L) baking pan

4	eggs	4
⅓ cup	granulated sugar	75 mL
½ tsp	salt	2 mL
½ tsp	vanilla	2 mL
3 cups	milk	750 mL
1 cup	flaked sweetened coconut	250 mL
	Ground nutmeg	

1. In a large bowl, whisk eggs. Add sugar, salt and vanilla and blend well. Gradually add milk and mix well to incorporate. Stir in coconut. Spoon into custard cups, dividing equally. Sprinkle with nutmeg.
2. Place cups in baking pan set on oven rack and pour in boiling water until it reaches halfway up the cups. Bake in preheated oven for 35 to 40 minutes or until custard is set and a knife inserted near the center comes out clean. Remove cups to wire rack to cool.

Tip *Serve with your favorite sauce (see Sauces, pages 553–555).*

Cherry-Topped Lemon Custard Cake

Serves 10 to 12

- 13- by 9-inch (3 L) baking dish, ungreased

1	angel food cake, either prepared or baked from a mix according to instructions	1
1	package (3½ oz/102 g) instant lemon pudding mix	1
1½ cups	cold milk	375 mL
1 cup	sour cream	250 mL
1	can (19 oz/540 mL) cherry pie filling (or any other flavor)	1

1. Tear angel food cake into bite-size pieces and place in baking dish.
2. In a large mixer bowl, on medium speed, beat pudding mix, milk and sour cream for about 2 to 3 minutes, until thickened. Spread over cake in pan. Top with pie filling, spreading evenly. Chill for 1 to 2 hours or until ready to serve.

Rhubarb Meringue Custard

Serves 8 to 12

- Preheat oven to 350°F (180°C)
- 13- by 9-inch (3 L) baking dish, ungreased

CRUST

2 cups	all-purpose flour	500 mL
½ cup	butter or margarine, softened	125 mL
2 tbsp	granulated sugar	25 mL

FILLING

6	egg yolks	6
2 cups	granulated sugar	500 mL
1 cup	whipping (35%) cream	250 mL
¼ cup	all-purpose flour	50 mL
¼ tsp	salt	1 mL
5 cups	chopped fresh rhubarb (about 1½ lbs/750 g)	1.25 L

MERINGUE

6	egg whites	6
1 tsp	vanilla	5 mL
¼ tsp	salt	1 mL
¾ cup	granulated sugar	175 mL

1. *Prepare the crust:* In a small mixer bowl, on low speed, beat flour, butter and sugar for about 2 minutes, scraping sides of bowl often, until mixture resembles coarse crumbs. Press into bottom of prepared baking dish and bake in preheated oven for 15 minutes. Raise oven temperature to 400°F (200°C).
2. *Prepare the filling:* In a large mixer bowl, on medium speed, beat egg yolks well. Add sugar, whipping cream, flour and salt and beat for 2 minutes, until smooth. Stir in rhubarb, mixing well. Pour over hot baked crust and bake for 45 to 55 minutes or until filling is firm to the touch.
3. *Prepare the meringue:* In a clean small mixer bowl, on high speed, beat egg whites for 2 minutes or until soft peaks form. Add vanilla and salt; continue beating and gradually add sugar, beating until stiff peaks form. Spread over hot filling and seal around the edges.
4. Bake for another 6 to 8 minutes or until meringue is lightly browned. Let cool completely on a wire rack before serving.

Tip *For the best volume, bring egg whites to room temperature before beating. If you have forgotten to remove eggs from the refrigerator to allow them to come to room temperature, place them in a bowl of warm water for several minutes.*

Blueberry Custard

Serves 4

1½ cups	half-and-half (10%) cream	375 mL
½ cup	granulated sugar	125 mL
2 tbsp	all-purpose flour	25 mL
1 tsp	grated lemon zest	5 mL
Pinch	salt	Pinch
3	egg yolks	3
2 tbsp	butter or margarine	25 mL
1 tbsp	vanilla	15 mL
1 tbsp	cornstarch	15 mL
1	can (16 oz/500 mL) blueberries, drained, juice reserved	1

1. In a medium saucepan, combine cream, sugar, flour, lemon zest and salt. Cook over medium heat and bring to a boil, stirring, for about 2 to 3 minutes, until mixture becomes bubbly and thickened. Remove from heat.
2. In a small bowl, beat egg yolks lightly, then stir in a small amount of the hot mixture. Pour back into hot mixture and, over low heat, bring to a gentle boil, stirring constantly. Remove from heat and stir in butter and vanilla. Spoon into 4 individual custard cups or dessert dishes and set aside to cool.
3. In a small saucepan, over medium heat, bring cornstarch and reserved blueberry juice to a boil. Stir for 2 minutes or until mixture thickens. Spoon blueberries equally over custard, then spoon cornstarch mixture over top. Serve warm.

Nectarine Custard

Serves 8

- Preheat oven to 325°F (160°C)
- Eight ¾-cup (175 mL) custard cups or ramekins
- 13- by 9-inch (3 L) baking pan

3 cups	milk	750 mL
4 cups	peeled, thinly sliced ripe nectarines (about 4 medium)	1 L
3	eggs	3
3 tbsp	granulated sugar	45 mL
1 tsp	vanilla	5 mL
Pinch	salt	Pinch

1. In a medium saucepan, scald milk (see tip, page 471). Remove from heat.
2. Spoon nectarine slices into custard cups, dividing equally.

3. In a large bowl, whisk eggs and stir in sugar, vanilla and salt. Slowly blend in scalded milk. Strain mixture over the nectarines, dividing equally.
4. Place cups in baking pan set on oven rack and pour in boiling water until it reaches halfway up the cups. Bake in preheated oven for 45 to 50 minutes or until custard is set and a knife inserted near the center comes out clean. Remove cups to wire rack to cool. Serve warm or chilled.

Honey Custard Cups

Serves 6

- Preheat oven to 325°F (160°C)
- Six ¾-cup (175 mL) custard cups or ramekins
- 13- by 9-inch (3 L) baking pan

3 cups	milk	750 mL
4	eggs	4
⅓ cup	liquid honey	75 mL
1 tsp	vanilla	5 mL
Pinch	salt	Pinch
	Ground nutmeg	

1. In a medium saucepan, on low heat, slowly scald milk (see tip, page 471). Remove from heat.
2. In a large bowl, whisk eggs. Whisk in honey, vanilla and salt. Stir in scalded milk until well blended. Strain into a large measuring cup and pour into custard cups. Sprinkle with nutmeg.
3. Place cups in baking pan set on a wire rack and pour in boiling water until it reaches halfway up the cups. Bake in preheated oven for 35 to 40 minutes or until custard is set and a knife inserted near the center comes out clean. Remove cups to wire rack to cool. Serve warm or chilled.

Apple Custard Cups

Serves 6

- Preheat oven to 350°F (180°C)
- Six ¾-cup (175 mL) custard cups or ramekins
- 13- by 9-inch (3 L) baking pan

¾ cup	firmly packed brown sugar	175 mL
2 tbsp	butter or margarine, softened	25 mL
1 tsp	ground cinnamon	5 mL
6	baking apples, peeled and cored	6
2	eggs	2
2 cups	milk, scalded (see tip, page 471)	500 mL
⅓ cup	granulated sugar	75 mL
½ tsp	vanilla	2 mL
Pinch	salt	Pinch

1. In a small bowl, mix together brown sugar, butter and cinnamon.
2. Place the apples in the custard cups. Spoon the sugar mixture into the centers of the apples, dividing equally.
3. In a medium bowl, whisk eggs, milk, sugar, vanilla and salt until well blended. Spoon into each apple, dividing equally.
4. Place custard cups in baking pan set on oven rack and pour in hot water until it reaches halfway up the cups. Bake in preheated oven for 45 to 55 minutes or until custard is set and a knife inserted in the center comes out clean. Remove cups to wire rack to cool. Serve warm or cool.

Banana Custard Pudding

Serves 4

½ cup	granulated sugar	125 mL
1 tbsp	cornstarch	15 mL
Pinch	salt	Pinch
1½ cups	milk	375 mL
3	egg yolks, lightly beaten	3
1 tsp	vanilla	5 mL
1	firm medium banana, sliced	1
	Whipped topping (optional)	

1. In a medium saucepan, over medium heat, combine sugar, cornstarch and salt. Slowly add milk and bring to a boil, stirring constantly. Boil for about 2 minutes. Stir a small amount into the egg yolks and pour egg mixture back into saucepan. Continue cooking and stirring until mixture is thickened. Remove from heat and stir in vanilla.
2. Transfer to a medium glass bowl and chill in refrigerator for 1 hour. When ready to serve, fold in banana slices. Garnish with whipped topping and 1 to 2 banana slices, if desired.

Rice Custard and Fruit

Serves 6
- Double boiler
- Six ¾-cup (175 mL) custard cups or ramekins

2 cups	milk	500 mL
4	egg yolks	4
¼ cup	granulated sugar	50 mL
Pinch	salt	Pinch
1 to	cooked white rice	250 to
1½ cups		375 mL
½ tsp	vanilla	2 mL
	Sliced almonds, toasted	
1	package (10 oz/300 g) frozen fruit (such as strawberries or raspberries), thawed	1

1. In a medium saucepan, scald milk (see tip, page 471). Remove from heat.
2. In top of double boiler, over simmering but not boiling water, whisk egg yolks, sugar and salt. Gradually beat in scalded milk and stir until mixture thickens enough to coat the back of a metal spoon, about 10 minutes. Stir in rice and vanilla.
3. Spoon into custard cups and top with almonds. Serve warm or chilled, topped with fruit.

Sweet Potato Custard

Serves 8
- Preheat oven to 350°F (180°C)
- 12-cup (3 L) casserole dish, ungreased
- 13- by 9-inch (3 L) baking pan

½ cup	golden raisins	125 mL
2 tbsp	hot water	25 mL
1 tbsp	brandy extract or brandy	15 mL
1½ lbs	sweet potatoes, peeled and sliced (about 3 cups/750 mL)	750 g
4	small eggs, beaten	4
1 cup	milk	250 mL
½ cup	evaporated milk	125 mL
1½ tbsp	granulated sugar	22 mL
1 tsp	ground cinnamon	5 mL
¼ tsp	ground nutmeg	1 mL
¼ tsp	ground mace	1 mL

1. In a small bowl, combine raisins, hot water and brandy extract. Mix well and set aside.
2. Overlap potato slices in the bottom of casserole dish. Drain the raisin mixture, reserving the liquid, and sprinkle raisins over potato slices.
3. In a medium bowl, combine the reserved raisin liquid, eggs, milk, evaporated milk, sugar, cinnamon, nutmeg and mace. Mix together until well blended and pour evenly over the potato slices and raisins.
4. Place casserole dish into baking pan set on oven rack and pour in hot water until it reaches halfway up the dish. Bake in preheated oven for 50 to 60 minutes or until a knife inserted near the center comes out clean and the custard is set. Remove casserole dish from pan of water and let cool on a wire rack. Serve warm.

Vegetable Cheese Custard

Serves 6 to 8
- Preheat oven to 350°F (180°C)
- 6-cup (1.5 L) casserole dish, ungreased
- 13- by 9-inch (3 L) baking pan

2	packages (each 10 oz/300 g) frozen mixed vegetables	2
2 cups	milk	500 mL
1 tbsp	grated onion	15 mL
1 tsp	dried parsley flakes	5 mL
½ tsp	salt	2 mL
4	eggs, lightly beaten	4
1	package (8 oz/250 g) processed American (or other) cheese, shredded	1

1. In a large saucepan, cook vegetables according to instructions on package. Drain and spoon into casserole dish.
2. In a medium saucepan, combine milk, onion, parsley and salt and cook until milk is scalded (see tip, page 471). Slowly stir in eggs.
3. Sprinkle shredded cheese over vegetables and pour egg mixture over top.
4. Place casserole dish in baking pan and pour in boiling water until it reaches halfway up the dish. Bake in preheated oven for 45 to 50 minutes or until custard is set and a knife inserted near the center comes out clean. Remove casserole dish from pan of water and let cool on a wire rack. Serve warm.

Pepper Corn Custard

Serves 4 to 6
- Preheat oven to 350°F (180°C)
- 6-cup (1.5 L) casserole dish, greased

4	eggs	4
¾ cup	sour cream	175 mL
½ cup	shredded old Cheddar cheese (about 2 oz/60 g)	125 mL
½ tsp	salt	2 mL
Pinch	freshly ground black pepper	Pinch
½	red bell pepper, chopped	½
2½ cups	corn kernels (about 3 cobs)	625 mL

1. In a medium bowl, whisk eggs until well beaten. Add sour cream, cheese, salt and black pepper, whisking until well incorporated.
2. Sprinkle red pepper and corn into prepared casserole dish. Spoon egg mixture over top.
3. Bake in preheated oven for 1 hour or until slightly puffed and top is golden brown. Let cool slightly on a wire rack and serve with a salad, or as desired.

Crème Brûlée

Serves 6
- Six ½-cup (125 mL) custard cups or ramekins
- Jellyroll pan or rimmed baking sheet

2 cups	whipping (35%) cream	500 mL
4	egg yolks	4
¼ cup	granulated sugar	50 mL
½ tsp	vanilla	2 mL
3 tbsp	packed brown sugar	45 mL
	Fresh seasonal fruit	

1. In a medium saucepan, heat cream over medium heat to scalding (until tiny bubbles form around the edges).
2. In a heavy medium saucepan, combine egg yolks and sugar and whisk until well blended. Gradually stir in scalded cream and cook, stirring, over medium-low heat, until mixture has thickened enough to coat the back of a metal spoon, about 12 to 15 minutes. Do not boil. Stir in vanilla.
3. Pour mixture into custard cups, dividing equally. Place in refrigerator for 3 to 4 hours or until well chilled. An hour or two before ready to serve, preheat the broiler.
4. Put the brown sugar in a small strainer and press with the back of a spoon so that it comes through the sieve and over the creamed mixture in the cups.
5. Place the cups on the jellyroll pan and set under broiler for 2 to 3 minutes, just until sugar melts. Return to refrigerator and chill for 1 to 2 hours or until the melted sugar forms a crisp crust over the custard. (If you do this too long before serving, the sugar will lose its crispness.)
6. To serve, place each cup on a serving plate. Cut fresh seasonal fruit into slices or chunks and spoon over top.

Individual Caramel Flans

Serves 4
- Preheat oven to 325°F (160°C)
- Four ¾-cup (175 mL) custard cups or ramekins
- 9-inch (2.5 L) square baking dish

⅔ cup	granulated sugar, divided	150 mL
3	eggs	3
1½ cups	milk	375 mL
1 tsp	vanilla	5 mL
	Ground cinnamon or nutmeg (optional)	

1. In a heavy skillet, over medium-high heat, cook ⅓ cup (75 mL) of the sugar to caramelize. Do not stir, but shake pan a few times to heat evenly. When sugar begins to melt, reduce heat to low and cook, stirring as needed, until all of the sugar is melted and golden, about 5 minutes. Divide the mixture equally among the custard cups, tilting the cups to coat the bottoms evenly. Set aside for 10 minutes.
2. Meanwhile, in a small mixer bowl, on medium speed, beat eggs, milk, the other ⅓ cup (75 mL) sugar and vanilla until well blended but not foamy. Spoon into custard cups, dividing equally. Sprinkle some cinnamon or nutmeg, or both, over top.
3. Place cups in baking dish set on oven rack and pour in boiling water until it reaches halfway up the cups. Bake in preheated oven for 30 to 45 minutes or until custard is set and a knife inserted near the center comes out clean. Remove cups to wire rack to cool completely. Cover tightly with plastic wrap and chill in refrigerator for 3 to 4 hours or overnight.
4. When ready to serve, loosen edges with a knife, invert a serving plate over the top of each cup, then flip cup and plate. Remove the cups to leave individual caramel flans on the serving plates.

Variation *Substitute an equal amount of brown sugar for the second ⅓ cup (75 mL) of granulated sugar.*

Pumpkin Loaf Flan

Serves 8 to 10
- Preheat oven to 350°F (180°C)
- 9- by 5-inch (2 L) glass loaf pan, ungreased
- 13- by 9-inch (3 L) baking pan

1⅓ cups	granulated sugar, divided	325 mL
¼ cup	water	50 mL
6	eggs	6
2 cups	canned pumpkin purée (not pie filling)	500 mL
2 cups	whipping (35%) cream	500 mL
1 tsp	ground cinnamon	5 mL
½ tsp	salt	2 mL
½ tsp	ground ginger	2 mL
¼ tsp	ground allspice	1 mL
	Whipped topping (optional)	

1. In a heavy skillet, combine ⅔ cup (150 mL) of the sugar and the water. Bring to a boil, stirring until sugar is dissolved. Cook syrup, swirling pan but not stirring, until mixture is a deep caramel. Pour into loaf pan and tilt pan to coat the bottom evenly. Set aside to harden.
2. In a large mixer bowl, on medium speed, beat eggs, pumpkin, whipping cream, the remaining sugar, cinnamon, salt, ginger and allspice, beating until mixture is well combined. Pour into loaf pan evenly.
3. Place in baking pan set on oven rack and pour in hot water until it reaches halfway up the sides of the loaf pan. Bake in preheated oven for 75 minutes or until a knife inserted near the center comes out clean. Remove loaf pan to wire rack to cool. Cover tightly with plastic wrap and chill overnight.
4. When ready to serve, run a knife around the edge of loaf pan, invert a platter over the pan, then flip over the platter and pan. Remove the loaf pan. Cut into slices to serve, topped with whipped topping, if desired.

Mousses and Puddings

Mousses

Puddings

Bread Puddings

Steamed Puddings

Mousses

Divine Chocolate Mousse

Serves 6

1 cup	granulated sugar, divided	250 mL
¼ cup	water	50 mL
4 oz	unsweetened chocolate, chopped	125 g
1 tbsp	strong brewed coffee	15 mL
3	egg whites (see tip, below)	3
½ cup	frozen whipped topping, thawed	125 mL
	Mint leaves	
	Berries	

1. In a small saucepan, over low heat, combine ¾ cup (175 mL) of the sugar and the water and stir until sugar is dissolved. Remove from heat and add the chocolate. Whisk until chocolate is completely melted and smooth. Add the coffee and whisk to blend. Pour mixture into a large bowl.

2. In a small mixer bowl, on high speed, beat egg whites until soft peaks form. Slowly add the remaining sugar and continue beating until stiff, but not dry, peaks form. Fold about one-quarter of the beaten egg whites into the chocolate mixture. Then fold in the remaining beaten egg whites. Fold in whipped topping until well blended.

3. Spoon into 6 individual dessert dishes and cover each tightly with plastic wrap. Chill in refrigerator for 3 to 4 hours. Garnish with a dollop of whipped topping and mint leaves or berries, or as desired.

Tip *This recipe contains raw egg whites. If the food safety of raw egg whites is a concern for you, substitute 6 tbsp (90 mL) pasteurized egg whites, found in the refrigerated egg section of most supermarkets. Alternatively, omit egg whites and increase whipped topping to 1½ cups (375 mL).*

Kahlúa Chocolate Mousse

Serves 4
• Double boiler

3 oz	semisweet chocolate	90 g
¼ cup	butter or margarine	50 mL
¼ cup	Kahlúa liqueur, divided	50 mL
2	egg yolks	2
1½ tsp	granulated sugar	7 mL
1 cup	whipping (35%) cream	250 mL

1. In a small saucepan, over low heat, melt chocolate and butter. Stir in half the Kahlúa and mix to blend. Set aside.

2. In the top of a double boiler, whisk egg yolks and the remaining Kahlúa. Add sugar and whisk until slightly thickened and color lightens. Place over boiling water and stir until thickened, about 10 to 12 minutes. Remove top of double boiler and set in a large bowl or pan of cold water. Beat until mixture is thick, about 3 to 5 minutes. Add chocolate mixture to egg mixture and mix together until well blended.

3. In a small mixer bowl, beat whipping cream until stiff peaks form. Fold into the chocolate mixture. Spoon into 4 individual dessert dishes or glasses and chill in refrigerator for 3 to 4 hours or until ready to serve. Garnish as desired.

White Chocolate Mousse

Serves 4
• Double boiler

3 oz	white chocolate	90 g
2	egg yolks	2
½	package (3 oz/85 g) unflavored gelatin	½
1 cup	whipping (35%) cream, whipped	250 mL

1. Melt chocolate in double boiler, over low heat, stirring until smooth and creamy.

2. In a small mixer bowl, on medium speed, beat egg yolks until light and fluffy. Add melted chocolate until blended.

3. In a small bowl, dissolve the gelatin in 6 tbsp (90 mL) hot water. Pour into chocolate mixture and whisk gently until blended. Chill in refrigerator for 2 to 4 hours or until mixture mounds slightly.

4. Fold whipped cream into chocolate mixture, whisking just until blended. Spoon into 4 individual dessert dishes and chill in refrigerator for 3 to 4 hours, or overnight.

Tip *Garnish with your favorite sauce (see Sauces, pages 553–555), or with seasonal fruit.*

Easy Mocha Mousse

Serves 4
- Small bowl, chilled

6 oz	semisweet chocolate	175 g
1/2 cup	strong brewed coffee	125 mL
2 cups	whipping (35%) cream	500 mL
2 tbsp	confectioner's (icing) sugar, sifted	25 mL
MOCHA WHIPPED TOPPING		
1/2 cup	whipping (35%) cream	125 mL
1 tbsp	confectioner's (icing) sugar, sifted	15 mL
1 tsp	instant coffee powder or granules	5 mL
1/4 tsp	vanilla	1 mL

1. In a small saucepan, over low heat, combine chocolate and coffee, stirring until melted and smooth. Remove from heat and pour into chilled bowl for faster cooling.

2. In a small mixer bowl, on high speed, beat cream, slowly adding the confectioner's sugar and beating until soft peaks form. Fold into chocolate mixture. Spoon into 4 individual dessert dishes and chill in refrigerator for 3 to 4 hours or overnight.

3. *Prepare the topping:* In a small mixer bowl, combine whipping cream, confectioner's sugar, coffee powder and vanilla and beat on high speed until firm peaks form. Spoon over chilled mousse to garnish.

Choco-Raspberry Mousse Dessert

Serves 6 to 8
- Preheat oven to 350°F (180°C)
- 9-inch (2.5 L) square baking dish, greased

3 oz	unsweetened chocolate	90 g
1/2 cup	butter or margarine, softened	125 mL
3	eggs, lightly beaten	3
1 cup	granulated sugar	250 mL
1 tsp	vanilla	5 mL
2/3 cup	all-purpose flour	150 mL
1/2 tsp	baking powder	2 mL
Pinch	salt	Pinch
MOUSSE TOPPING		
1	package (10 oz/300 g) frozen raspberries in syrup, thawed	1
1	envelope (1/4 oz/7 g) unflavored gelatin powder	1
1/2 cup	granulated sugar	125 mL
2 tbsp	freshly squeezed lemon juice	25 mL
1 1/4 cups	whipping (35%) cream	300 mL

1. In a medium saucepan, over low heat, combine chocolate and butter and stir constantly until melted and smooth. Remove from heat and stir in eggs, sugar and vanilla, stirring until well blended.

2. In a medium bowl, mix together flour, baking powder and salt until combined. Pour in chocolate mixture and mix well. Spoon into prepared baking dish, spreading evenly, and bake at 350°F (180°C) for 25 to 30 minutes or until set. Set aside to cool.

3. *Prepare the topping:* Drain raspberries, reserving the syrup. Cut the raspberries into halves or pieces. Add water to the reserved syrup to make 1 1/4 cups (300 mL) of liquid.

4. In a medium saucepan, combine gelatin and sugar. Add raspberry liquid and lemon juice and bring to a boil, stirring constantly until dissolved. Remove from heat and chill in refrigerator for 2 to 4 hours or until mixture begins to set.

5. In a small mixer bowl, on high speed, beat whipping cream until stiff peaks form.

6. In a large bowl, whisk gelatin mixture well until light. Fold in whipped cream and then raspberries and spoon over chocolate base in baking dish. Chill in refrigerator for 1 to 2 hours, until set.

Tips *For a change, use frozen strawberries in syrup, or any other frozen berries, in place of the raspberries.*

If desired, whip an additional 3/4 cup (175 mL) whipping cream and use to decorate the top of the dessert.

Frozen Strawberry Mousse

Serves 4 to 6
- 9-inch (2.5 L) square baking dish

1	package (10 oz/300 g) frozen sweetened strawberries	1
1/2 cup	granulated sugar	125 mL
1/2 cup	sour cream	125 mL
1 tsp	vanilla	5 mL
	Fresh strawberries	

1. In a food processor or blender, combine strawberries, sugar, sour cream and vanilla and process until blended and smooth. Spoon into baking dish, cover tightly with plastic wrap and place in the freezer until frozen.

2. When ready to serve, spoon into 4 to 6 individual dessert dishes. Garnish with fresh strawberries, whole or sliced.

Pineapple Nut Mousse

Serves 6

1 cup	water	250 mL
1	package (3 oz/85 g) pineapple or lemon gelatin powder	1
1 cup	canned crushed pineapple, with liquid	250 mL
Pinch	salt (optional)	Pinch
1 cup	whipping (35%) cream, whipped	250 mL
¼ cup	chopped nuts (pecans or other)	50 mL

1. In a medium saucepan, bring water to a boil. Stir in gelatin until completely dissolved. Add crushed pineapple and salt (if using) and mix together. Spoon into a medium bowl and chill in refrigerator until slightly thickened.

2. Gently fold in whipped cream and nuts until well combined. Spoon into 6 individual dessert dishes, dividing equally, and chill in refrigerator until firm. Garnish as desired.

Lemon Mousse with Fresh Berries

Serves 8

• Double boiler

2	eggs	2
6	egg yolks	6
1 cup	granulated sugar	250 mL
1½ tbsp	grated lemon zest	22 mL
¾ cup	freshly squeezed lemon juice	175 mL
2 cups	whipping (35%) cream, divided	500 mL
	Assorted berries, tossed with granulated sugar	

1. In a double boiler, over simmering water, combine eggs, egg yolks, sugar, lemon zest and lemon juice. Mix well. Whisk until mixture thickens, then transfer to a large bowl. Chill in refrigerator, whisking occasionally, until cool.

2. In a small mixer bowl, on high speed, beat 1½ cups (375 mL) of the whipping cream until firm peaks form. Fold one-third of the whipped cream into the lemon mixture just to lighten, then fold in the remaining whipped cream.

3. Spoon berry-sugar mixture into 8 individual dessert dishes, dividing equally. Spoon lemon mixture over top.

4. In the small mixer bowl, on high speed, beat the remaining whipping cream until stiff peaks form. Spoon over each dish.

Refreshing Lemon-Lime Mousse

Serves 6

½ cup	granulated sugar	125 mL
2 tbsp	cornstarch	25 mL
Pinch	salt	Pinch
3	egg yolks	3
⅔ cup	milk	150 mL
1½ tsp	grated lemon zest	7 mL
¼ cup	freshly squeezed lemon juice	50 mL
½ tsp	grated lime zest	2 mL
1 tbsp	freshly squeezed lime juice	15 mL
1 cup	whipping (35%) cream	250 mL
	Lemon or lime slices	
	Additional grated lemon or lime zest, for garnish (optional)	

1. In a medium saucepan, mix together sugar, cornstarch and salt.

2. In a small bowl, whisk together egg yolks and milk and add to the sugar mixture. Add lemon and lime juices and whisk until blended and smooth. Cook over medium heat, stirring until mixture comes to a boil. Then cook and stir for 2 minutes. Stir in the grated lemon and lime zests and cover tightly with plastic wrap. Chill in refrigerator until completely cooled.

3. In a small mixer bowl, whip cream until firm peaks form. Fold into cooled mixture. Spoon into 6 individual dessert dishes and garnish with lemon or lime slices and zests, if desired.

Quick 'n' Easy Orange Mousse

Serves 6

• 4-cup (1 L) glass dessert bowl

1	can (10 oz/284 g) mandarin orange segments	1
1	package (3 oz/85 g) orange gelatin powder	1
1 cup	boiling water	250 mL
1	can (6 oz/160 mL) evaporated milk, chilled	1

1. Drain the mandarin orange segments, reserving liquid. Add enough water to the liquid to bring it to 1 cup (250 mL).

2. In a medium bowl, dissolve gelatin in boiling water, stirring until completely dissolved. Add the reserved orange liquid and mix well. Let cool in refrigerator until slightly thickened.

3. In another medium bowl, whisk chilled milk, then beat with an electric beater until thick. Stir in slightly thickened gelatin and whisk to blend.
4. Arrange some of the mandarin orange segments in bottom of dessert bowl. Spoon gelatin mixture over top. Garnish with the remaining orange segments. Chill in refrigerator until ready to serve.

Pumpkin Pie Mousse

Serves 6

1	envelope (¼ oz/7 g) unflavored gelatin powder	1
¾ cup	firmly packed brown sugar	175 mL
1½ tsp	ground cinnamon	7 mL
¼ tsp	ground nutmeg	1 mL
¼ tsp	ground ginger	1 mL
1½ cups	canned pumpkin purée (not pie filling)	375 mL
1 cup	evaporated milk	250 mL
3	egg whites (see tip, below)	3
Pinch	salt	Pinch
	Grated lemon zest (optional)	

1. In a medium saucepan, over medium heat, combine gelatin, brown sugar, cinnamon, nutmeg and ginger. Mix together. Stir in pumpkin and milk and cook for about 10 minutes, stirring constantly, until gelatin is completely dissolved. Spoon into a large bowl and set aside to cool until mixture mounds when dropped from a spoon.
2. In a small mixer bowl, on medium speed, beat egg whites and salt until stiff peaks form. Fold into pumpkin mixture, mixing until well combined. Spoon into 6 individual dessert dishes. Cover tightly with plastic wrap and chill in refrigerator for 3 to 4 hours or overnight. Garnish with grated zest, if desired.

Tip *This recipe contains raw egg whites. If the food safety of raw egg whites is a concern for you, substitute 6 tbsp (90 mL) pasteurized egg whites, found in the refrigerated egg section of most supermarkets. Alternatively, omit egg whites and use 1 cup (250 mL) frozen whipped topping, thawed.*

Creamy Apricot Mousse

Serves 6 to 8
• Double boiler

1 cup	dried apricots (about 8 oz/250 g)	250 mL
2 tbsp	cold water	25 mL
1	envelope (¼ oz/7 g) unflavored gelatin powder	1
2	egg yolks	2
¾ cup	granulated sugar	175 mL
2 tbsp	freshly squeezed orange juice	25 mL
2 cups	whipping (35%) cream	500 mL
	Fresh apricots, halved, for garnish	

1. Place the apricots in a small saucepan and add enough water just to cover by about 1 inch (2.5 cm). Set aside for 30 minutes.
2. In a small bowl, combine cold water and gelatin to soften.
3. Place saucepan with apricots over medium-high heat and heat to boiling. Reduce heat and simmer, uncovered, for about 25 minutes or until apricots become tender.
4. Place hot apricots and water in a food processor with the softened gelatin and process until smooth. Let stand to cool to room temperature.
5. In another small bowl, whisk egg yolks, sugar and orange juice until well mixed. Transfer mixture to the top of double boiler, over simmering water, and whisk until mixture is hot to the touch and slightly thickened. Do not overcook. Set aside and whisk until slightly cool.
6. In a small mixer bowl, beat whipping cream until stiff peaks form.
7. In a large bowl, mix together the cooled egg mixture and apricot mixture and fold in the whipped cream. Spoon into individual dessert dishes or glasses. Garnish with a fresh apricot half, or as desired.

Variation *Substitute an equal amount of orange liqueur for the orange juice.*

Puddings

When you are making pudding that calls for either sugar and flour or sugar and cornstarch, it is best to mix the sugar with the flour or cornstarch before mixing them with the other ingredients. This method will always produce a smooth pudding.

● ●

Phyllo Cups

Makes 12 phyllo cups
- Preheat oven to 375°F (190°C)
- 12-cup muffin tin, ungreased

3	sheets phyllo pastry	3
¼ cup	butter, melted	50 mL
2 tbsp	granulated sugar	25 mL

1. Place 1 sheet of phyllo on a flat work surface. Cover the remaining sheets with a damp towel to prevent them from drying out.

2. Brush the phyllo sheet generously with one-third of the melted butter. Lay a second sheet over top and brush with another third of the butter. Place the third sheet on top and, with a rolling pin, press the three layers firmly together, forming a rectangle. Brush the top with the remaining butter and sprinkle sugar over top.

3. Cut rectangle in half lengthwise, then cut each half into 3 equal rectangles and press into the cups of the muffin tin.

4. Bake in preheated oven for 7 to 10 minutes or until crisp and golden brown. Let cool on a wire rack. When ready to serve, fill with prepared pudding and garnish as desired.

Tip *Rather than use custard cups or dessert dishes, a fancy, decorative way to serve puddings is to bake phyllo cups, spoon the pudding into the cup and then top with fruit, whipped topping or any other desired garnish.*

● ●

Old-Fashioned Cottage Pudding

Serves 6 to 8
- Preheat oven to 350°F (180°C)
- 8-inch (2 L) square baking dish, buttered

1 cup	granulated sugar	250 mL
¼ cup	shortening	50 mL
1	egg	1
¼ tsp	lemon extract	1 mL
1¾ cups	sifted all-purpose flour	425 mL
2½ tsp	baking powder	12 mL
½ tsp	salt	2 mL
⅔ cup	milk	150 mL

1. In a large mixer bowl, cream sugar and shortening until smooth. Add egg and lemon extract and beat well.

2. In a medium bowl, sift together flour, baking powder and salt. Add to creamed mixture alternately with the milk, beating after each addition. Spoon into prepared baking dish.

3. Bake in preheated oven for 30 to 35 minutes or until pudding is set and top is golden brown. Let cool slightly on a wire rack and serve warm.

Tip *This pudding tastes great with a lemon sauce, such as the one on page 501.*

● ●

Quick Pudding Cake

Serves 12 to 16
- 13- by 9-inch (3 L) baking pan

1	package (18 oz/510 g) double-layer cake mix	1
2	packages (each 4 oz/113 g) instant pudding mix	2
1 cup	confectioner's (icing) sugar, sifted	250 mL
4 cups	cold milk	1 L

1. Prepare cake mix as directed on the package (or prepare a homemade cake as per your recipe). As soon as cake is removed from oven, poke holes down through the cake to the pan using a plastic drinking straw or the round handle of a wooden spoon. Use a gentle turning motion to make large enough holes. Set cake aside.

2. In a large mixer bowl, mix together pudding mix and sugar. Slowly add the milk and stir to combine. Beat for 1 minute, on low speed, and immediately pour one-half of the thin pudding evenly over the top of warm cake so that it falls into the holes to make the stripes.

3. Let the remaining pudding thicken slightly, then spoon over the cake, using a swirling motion as you would when frosting a cake. Chill in refrigerator for at least 1 hour or until ready to serve.

Tip *This recipe is a quick, easy way to make a plain cake into a moist, delicious pudding cake. It's great because you can use any plain homemade cake, or any flavor cake mix, and any flavor pudding mix.*

Last-Minute Pudding Loaf Cake

Serves 10 to 12
- Preheat oven to 350ºF (180ºC)
- 9- by 5-inch (2 L) loaf pan, greased

1	package (18 oz/510 g) cake mix	1
1	package (4 oz/113 g) instant pudding mix	1
4	eggs, lightly beaten	4
1/3 cup	vegetable oil	75 mL

1. In a large mixer bowl, mix cake mix and pudding mix together. Make a well in the center. Add eggs, 1 cup (250 mL) cold water and oil and beat on low speed, just until moist, blended and smooth. Pour into prepared baking pan.
2. Bake in preheated oven for 50 to 55 minutes or until a toothpick inserted in the center of cake comes out clean and dry. Let cool on a wire rack.

Tip *Here's another quick recipe that can be made with any flavor cake mix and pudding mix.*

English Bakewell Pudding

Serves 6 to 8
- Preheat oven to 425ºF (220ºC)
- 9-inch (23 cm) pie plate or wide, shallow dish, ungreased

8 oz	puff pastry, thawed if frozen (a little more than 1/2 package)	250 g
1 cup	strawberry jam	250 mL
1/3 cup + 2 tbsp	granulated sugar	100 mL
1/3 cup + 2 tbsp	butter	100 mL
4	egg yolks	4
2	egg whites, beaten	2
1/2 tsp	almond extract	2 mL

1. Roll out the puff pastry on a floured work surface. Line pie plate with the pastry. Spread a thick layer of jam over pastry, using whatever amount you desire.
2. In a medium bowl, cream the sugar and butter. Add egg yolks, egg whites and almond extract, beating just until well blended. Spread over jam.
3. Bake in preheated oven for 15 minutes, then reduce oven temperature to 350ºF (180ºC) and bake for an additional 20 minutes, until pudding is set and top is golden brown. Let cool on a wire rack.

Old-Fashioned Indian Pudding

Serves 6 to 8
- Preheat oven to 325ºF (160ºC)
- 8-cup (2 L) casserole dish, buttered

1/2 cup	yellow cornmeal	125 mL
5 cups	milk, divided	1.25 L
1/2 cup	granulated sugar	125 mL
1/2 cup	light (fancy) molasses	125 mL
1/4 cup	butter or margarine	50 mL
1 tsp	salt	5 mL
1 tsp	pumpkin pie spice	5 mL

1. In a large, heavy saucepan, over medium-low heat, combine cornmeal, 2 cups (500 mL) of the milk, sugar, molasses, butter, salt and pumpkin pie spice. Stir to blend, heating slowly to boiling. Reduce heat to low and simmer for about 5 minutes, stirring constantly, until thick and creamy. Pour into prepared baking dish. Add another 2 cups (500 mL) milk and stir to blend well.
2. Bake in preheated oven for 1 hour. Remove from oven and stir in the remaining milk. Bake for 2 hours longer or until pudding sets.

Tip *Best when served warm with ice cream.*

Variation *Some of the original recipes use 1 tsp (5 mL) ground ginger instead of the pumpkin pie spice.*

Traditional Yorkshire Pudding

Serves 12
- Preheat oven to 450ºF (230ºC)
- 12-cup muffin tin, greased

1 cup	all-purpose flour	250 mL
1/2 tsp	salt	2 mL
2	eggs	2
1 cup	milk	250 mL
1 tsp	butter	5 mL

1. In a large mixer bowl, sift together flour and salt. Add eggs and beat well. Beat in about one-third of the milk and the butter, beating until batter is stiff. Let stand for a few minutes, then gradually add the remaining milk and beat until well blended.
2. Put muffin tin into oven to heat up for a few minutes. Remove from oven. Spoon batter into hot muffin cups and bake in preheated oven for 30 to 35 minutes or until puffed and golden brown. Serve immediately.

Layered Pudding Squares

Serves 12 to 16

- Preheat oven to 350ºF (180ºC)
- 13- by 9-inch (3 L) baking pan, ungreased

2 cups	all-purpose flour	500 mL
1 cup	cold butter or margarine	250 mL
1	package (8 oz/250 g) cream cheese, softened	1
1 cup	confectioner's (icing) sugar, sifted	250 mL
1 cup	frozen whipped topping, thawed	250 mL
2	packages (each 3½ oz/102 g) vanilla pudding mix	2
4	ripe bananas	4
2	packages (each 3 oz/85 g) strawberry gelatin powder	2

1. Place flour in a medium bowl and cut in the butter with a pastry blender or fork until mixture is crumbly. Set aside about ½ cup (125 mL) of this crumb mixture and press the remaining mixture into baking pan. Bake in preheated oven for 18 to 20 minutes or until golden brown. Set on a wire rack to cool.
2. In a small mixer bowl, beat cream cheese and confectioner's sugar until smooth. Gently fold in the whipped topping. Spread evenly over cooled crust.
3. Prepare vanilla pudding mix according to package directions. Set aside to cool.
4. Slice 2 bananas and spread over cream cheese mixture. Spread cool vanilla pudding over bananas. Top with the reserved crumb mixture. Chill in refrigerator for 1 hour.
5. Prepare gelatin according to package directions. Chill in refrigerator for 30 minutes or until partially set.
6. Pour gelatin over crumbs. Slice the remaining bananas and spread over gelatin. Chill in refrigerator for at least 2 hours or until ready to serve. Cut into squares.

Old-Fashioned Vanilla Pudding

Serves 6

3 cups	milk	750 mL
¾ cup	granulated sugar	175 mL
3 tbsp	cornstarch	45 mL
2	eggs, well beaten	2
1 tbsp	butter or margarine	15 mL
1½ tsp	vanilla	7 mL

1. In a large saucepan, over medium heat, combine milk with sugar and cornstarch. Stir and cook until bubbly, then stir and cook for 2 more minutes. Remove from heat.
2. Gradually stir 1 cup (250 mL) of the hot milk mixture into the beaten eggs, then pour into the saucepan. Cook over medium heat until nearly bubbly, but do not boil. Reduce heat to low and cook, stirring constantly, for another 3 minutes. Remove from heat.
3. Stir in the butter and vanilla and mix until well blended. Spoon into 6 individual dessert dishes, cover each tightly with plastic wrap and chill in refrigerator for 4 to 5 hours or overnight.

Caramel Nut Pudding

Serves 4 to 6

2 cups	cold milk	500 mL
1½ cups	packed brown sugar	375 mL
1 tbsp	butter or margarine	15 mL
3 tbsp	cornstarch	45 mL
1 tsp	vanilla	5 mL
½ cup	chopped walnuts	125 mL

1. In a small saucepan, over low heat, scald milk (see tip, page 471). Remove from heat.
2. In a large saucepan, over low heat, combine brown sugar and butter and stir well until melted and quite brown. Add the scalded milk and stir in the cornstarch. Remove from heat and whisk until well beaten. Add vanilla and stir in walnuts.
3. Spoon into individual dessert dishes or glasses and set aside to cool slightly.

Tip *Garnish with a dollop of whipped topping and sprinkle additional chopped nuts over top.*

Frozen Butterscotch Dessert

Serves 20 to 24

1 gallon	vanilla ice cream, softened	3.8 L
1 cup	whipping (35%) cream	250 mL
1	package (3½ oz/102 g) butterscotch pudding mix	1
	Semisweet chocolate chips	

1. In a large bowl, blend together ice cream and whipping cream. Add pudding and chocolate chips and mix in to blend well. Freeze for at least 3 hours or until ready to serve.

Butterscotch Pudding

Serves 4 to 6
- Double boiler

¾ cup	packed brown sugar	175 mL
2 tbsp	butter or margarine	25 mL
2½ cups	cold milk, divided	625 mL
⅓ cup	cornstarch	75 mL
1	egg, beaten	1

1. In the top of double boiler, over medium heat, combine brown sugar and butter and stir until caramelized and brown. Add 2 cups (500 mL) of the milk, stirring until dissolved.
2. In a small bowl, mix cornstarch with the remaining milk and add to the brown sugar mixture. Stir until thickened. Add a little of this hot mixture to the beaten egg, then pour it into the pudding. Cook, stirring, for 2 minutes. Remove from heat.
3. Spoon into a glass serving bowl or individual dessert dishes and set aside to cool slightly. Cover tightly with plastic wrap so a film won't form on top of the pudding.

Tip *Serve with whipped cream or any other topping.*

Gingerbread Pudding with Peachy Sauce

Serves 6 to 8
- Preheat oven to 350ºF (180ºC)
- 8-inch (2 L) square baking dish, greased and lightly floured

1	package (14½ oz/400 g) gingerbread cake mix	1
¾ cup	water	175 mL
½ cup	prepared mincemeat	125 mL
PEACH SAUCE		
1	can (14 oz/398 mL) sliced peaches	1
¼ cup	granulated sugar	50 mL
1 tbsp	cornstarch	15 mL
¼ tsp	salt	1 mL
2 tbsp	butter or margarine	25 mL
¼ tsp	grated lemon zest	1 mL
1 tbsp	freshly squeezed lemon juice	15 mL
½ cup	prepared mincemeat	125 mL

1. In a large mixer bowl, combine gingerbread mix and water, beating on medium speed for 2 to 3 minutes. Add mincemeat, beating until blended. Spoon into prepared baking dish.
2. Bake in preheated oven for 35 to 40 minutes or until top is golden brown. Let cool slightly on a wire rack and cut into squares.
3. *Prepare the peach sauce:* Drain the peaches, reserving the liquid. Add enough water to bring liquid to 1 cup (250 mL). In a medium saucepan, combine sugar, cornstarch and salt. Stir in the peach liquid and cook over medium heat, stirring constantly, until mixture becomes bubbly and thickened. Add butter, lemon zest and lemon juice. Stir in the peaches and mincemeat until well blended. Spoon over the warm gingerbread squares.

Divine Chocolate Pudding

Serves 4

⅔ cup	unsweetened cocoa powder	150 mL
2 tbsp	cornstarch	25 mL
2¼ cups	milk, divided	550 mL
2	egg whites	2
½ cup	granulated sugar	125 mL
Pinch	salt	Pinch
1 tsp	vanilla	5 mL
4	strawberries	4
	Mint leaves	

1. In a large bowl, mix together cocoa and cornstarch until blended. Whisk in ¾ cup (175 mL) of the milk until mixture is completely smooth.
2. In a small bowl, lightly whisk egg whites. Set aside.
3. In a large heavy saucepan, over high heat, whisk the remaining milk, sugar and salt. Bring to a boil, whisking constantly, over high heat. Reduce heat to medium-high and add cocoa mixture. Bring to a boil, whisking constantly, for 3 minutes. Remove pan from heat and reduce heat to medium-low.
4. Whisk 1 cup (250 mL) of the hot cocoa mixture into the bowl of egg whites and then pour into the pan. Cook for 2 minutes, whisking constantly, but do not bring to a boil. Remove from heat. Add vanilla and mix until well blended and smooth.
5. Spoon into 4 individual dessert dishes and set aside to cool to room temperature. Cover tightly with plastic wrap and chill in refrigerator for 1 hour. When ready to serve, place a whole strawberry and a mint leaf on each.

Microwave Chocolate Pudding

Serves 4

- 4-cup (1 L) microwave-safe bowl
- Four ¾-cup (175 mL) custard cups or ramekins

¾ cup	granulated sugar	175 mL
2 tbsp	cornstarch	25 mL
2 cups	milk	500 mL
2 oz	unsweetened chocolate, chopped	60 g
½ tsp	vanilla	2 mL
Pinch	salt	Pinch

1. In microwave-safe bowl, mix together sugar and cornstarch. Gradually stir in milk until well blended. Add the chopped chocolate and mix well.

2. Microwave, uncovered, on High for 5 minutes. Whisk thoroughly to blend in the chocolate. Microwave on High for 2 to 3 minutes, until boiling and thickened.

3. Stir in vanilla and salt. Spoon into custard cups and set aside to cool to room temperature.

Tip *Garnish with whipped cream or fresh fruit, or as desired.*

Chocolate Puddin' Pie

Serves 6 to 8

- Preheat oven to 350°F (180°C)
- 9-inch (23 cm) glass pie plate, ungreased

1½ cups	chocolate wafer cookie crumbs (about 35 wafers)	375 mL
¼ cup	butter or margarine, melted	50 mL
⅔ cup	granulated sugar	150 mL
3½ tbsp	unsweetened cocoa powder	52 mL
3½ tbsp	cornstarch	52 mL
2 cups	milk	500 mL
⅓ cup	semisweet chocolate chips (about 2 oz/60 g)	75 mL
1½ tsp	vanilla	7 mL
	Whipped topping	

1. In a small bowl, mix together cookie crumbs and butter until well blended. Set aside 2 to 3 tbsp (25 to 45 mL) of this crumb mixture for a topping, if desired, and press the remaining mixture firmly into bottom and sides of pie plate. Bake in preheated oven for 10 minutes, then set aside to cool on a wire rack.

2. In a medium saucepan, over medium heat, whisk sugar, cocoa and cornstarch. Slowly add the milk, whisking to combine. Stir constantly until mixture comes to a boil and thickens. Boil for 2 minutes, stirring constantly. Remove from heat. Add chocolate chips and vanilla and stir until chips have melted and mixture is smooth.

3. Spoon filling evenly into cooled pie crust. Cover tightly with plastic wrap to prevent a skin from forming over the top. Chill in refrigerator for at least 1 hour. When ready to serve, swirl whipped topping over top.

Tip *If you don't have a glass pie plate, any pie plate will do.*

Chocolate Meringue Crumb Pudding

Serves 6 to 8

- Preheat oven to 325°F (160°C)
- Double boiler
- 8-inch (2 L) square baking dish, greased

½ cup	fresh bread crumbs (about 1 slice)	250 mL
½ cup	fresh cake crumbs (see tip, below)	250 mL
2 cups	milk, divided	500 mL
1½ oz	unsweetened chocolate, melted and cooled	45 g
¾ cup	granulated sugar	175 mL
3	egg yolks	3
2 tbsp	butter or margarine, melted	25 mL
¼ tsp	salt	1 mL
½ tsp	vanilla	2 mL
MERINGUE TOPPING		
3	egg whites	3
½ cup	confectioner's (icing) sugar, sifted	125 mL

1. In a small bowl, mix together bread crumbs and cake crumbs.

2. In the top of a double boiler, combine 1½ cups (375 mL) of the milk and crumbs. Stir in melted chocolate and sugar. Cook over boiling water until the mixture forms a smooth paste.

3. In a small bowl, whisk egg yolks and the remaining milk. Add butter and salt and whisk until thickened. Stir egg mixture into the hot mixture and cook, stirring constantly, over medium-low heat, until mixture is thickened. Remove from heat. Add vanilla and stir to blend. Spoon mixture into prepared baking dish.

4. Bake in preheated oven for 25 to 30 minutes or until set. Set aside to cool on a wire rack. Raise oven temperature to 425°F (220°C).

5. *Prepare the topping:* In a small mixer bowl, on medium speed, beat egg whites to form soft peaks. Slowly add the confectioner's sugar and beat on high speed until stiff peaks form.

6. When the pudding has cooled slightly, spread the meringue evenly over top. Bake at 425°F (220°C) for about 5 to 6 minutes or until meringue is golden brown. Chill for 3 to 4 hours or overnight.

Tip *To make your cake crumbs, you can use any kind of prepared cake you prefer.*

• •

Graham Wafer Chocolate Pudding

Serves 8 to 10

• 8-inch (2 L) square glass baking dish, ungreased

1½ cups	cornstarch	375 mL
1⅓ cups	granulated sugar	325 mL
6 tbsp	unsweetened cocoa powder	90 mL
Pinch	salt	Pinch
5½ cups	milk	1.375 L
1 tbsp	vanilla	15 mL
1 tbsp	butter or margarine (optional)	15 mL
30	graham wafers (honey or chocolate), divided	30
	Whipped topping or ice cream	

1. In a medium saucepan, combine cornstarch, sugar, cocoa and salt. Mix to blend. Stir in milk until smooth. Cook over medium heat to a rolling boil, stirring constantly. Boil for 1 minute, no more, and remove from heat. Stir in vanilla and butter (if using) until well combined and smooth.

2. Line baking pan with graham wafers. Spoon one-third of pudding mixture over top. Make two more layers each of wafers and pudding. Crumble the remaining graham wafers over top. Serve warm with a dollop of whipped topping or ice cream.

• •

Upside-Down Mocha Pudding

Serves 4 to 6

• Preheat oven to 350°F (180°C)
• 6-cup (1.5 L) casserole dish, buttered

1 cup	sifted all-purpose flour	250 mL
¾ cup	granulated sugar, divided	175 mL
3 tbsp	instant coffee powder or granules	45 mL
1½ tsp	baking powder	7 mL
Pinch	salt	Pinch
1	egg, lightly beaten	1
½ cup	milk	125 mL
¼ cup	butter or margarine, melted and cooled	50 mL
½ cup	unsweetened cocoa powder	125 mL
1¼ cups	boiling water	300 mL

1. In a large bowl, combine flour, ½ cup (125 mL) of the sugar, coffee powder, baking powder and salt.

2. In a small bowl, whisk egg, milk and butter. Add to flour mixture, mixing until blended and smooth. Spoon into prepared casserole dish.

3. In another small bowl, mix together cocoa and the remaining sugar. Sprinkle over batter and pour the boiling water slowly over top.

4. Bake in preheated oven for 30 to 35 minutes or until center springs back when lightly touched. Set on a wire rack to cool slightly. Spoon into individual dessert dishes, spooning some of the sauce over each. Serve warm.

• •

Coconut Meringue Pudding

Serves 6 to 8

• Preheat oven to 350°F (180°C)
• 8-inch (2 L) square baking dish, ungreased

1¼ cup	granulated sugar, divided	300 mL
¼ cup	cornstarch	50 mL
3 cups	milk	750 mL
4	eggs, separated	4
1 cup	flaked sweetened coconut	250 mL
1 tsp	vanilla	5 mL

1. In a heavy saucepan, over medium heat, mix together ¾ cup (175 mL) of the sugar and cornstarch. Add milk and cook, stirring, until mixture becomes bubbly and thick. Cook for another 2 minutes, then remove from heat.

2. In a small bowl, whisk egg yolks. Stir in 1 cup (250 mL) of the hot milk mixture, then pour into saucepan. Cook and stir until mixture is boiling gently, then continue cooking and stirring for 2 minutes. Remove pan from heat and set aside to cool to lukewarm. Add coconut and vanilla and stir until blended. Spoon into baking dish.

3. In a small mixer bowl, beat egg whites until soft peaks form. Gradually add the remaining sugar and beat on high speed until stiff peaks form. Spread evenly over pudding, right to the edges so that pudding is sealed in.

4. Bake in preheated oven for 10 to 15 minutes or until set and top is golden brown. Best when served at room temperature.

Clafoutis

Serves 6 to 8

- Preheat oven to 375°F (190°C)
- 10-inch (3 L) quiche dish, buttered

4	eggs	4
½ cup	milk	125 mL
¼ cup	whipped topping	50 mL
2 tsp	vanilla	10 mL
½ tsp	ground cinnamon	2 mL
¼ tsp	ground nutmeg	1 mL
⅔ cup	self-rising flour	150 mL
2 tbsp	granulated sugar	25 mL
4 cups	small apples, peeled, cored and thinly sliced	1 L
1 tbsp	freshly squeezed lemon juice	15 mL
2 tsp	packed brown sugar (optional)	10 mL
	Confectioner's (icing) sugar (optional)	

1. In a large mixer bowl, combine eggs, milk, whipped topping, vanilla, cinnamon and nutmeg, beating on medium speed until well blended and smooth. Add flour, then sugar, and continue beating until the mixture is thick and smooth.
2. Arrange apple slices in prepared baking dish in a single layer; sprinkle with lemon juice. Pour batter mixture evenly over apples and sprinkle with brown sugar (if using).
3. Bake in preheated oven for 35 to 40 minutes or until golden brown. Serve warm or at room temperature and sprinkle with confectioner's sugar, if desired.

Variation *A clafoutis is a French fruit pudding. This recipe is great with any type of seasonal fruit you prefer.*

Apple Almond Pudding Cake

Serves 6

- Preheat oven to 375°F (190°C)
- 8-inch (2 L) square baking dish, buttered

4 cups	peeled, halved, cored, grated apples (about 4 medium)	1 L
1 cup	granulated sugar, divided	250 mL
2 cups	zwieback crumbs (about 12 biscuits)	500 mL
½ cup	whole blanched almonds, finely ground	125 mL
½ cup	butter or margarine, melted	125 mL

1. In a large bowl, toss together the apples and half the sugar.
2. In another large bowl, mix the zwieback crumbs with the remaining sugar. Add ground almonds and melted butter and mix to blend well.
3. In prepared baking dish, make layers of apple mixture and crumb mixture, starting and ending with apple mixture.
4. Bake in preheated oven for 45 to 50 minutes or until golden brown and apples are tender. Serve warm.

Applesauce Noodle Pudding

Serves 6 to 8

- Preheat oven to 350°F (180°C)
- 8-inch (2 L) square baking dish, greased

¼ cup	shortening or butter	50 mL
8 oz	fine noodles, cooked and drained	250 g
3	eggs	3
½ cup	dry or fresh bread crumbs, divided	125 mL
¼ cup	granulated sugar	50 mL
1½ tsp	ground cinnamon	7 mL
3 cups	sweetened applesauce	750 mL

1. In a skillet, melt shortening. Add the noodles and sauté until browned.
2. In a large mixer bowl, combine eggs, ¼ cup (50 mL) of the bread crumbs, sugar and cinnamon, beating until blended. Stir in noodles and mix well.
3. In the prepared baking dish, alternate layers of noodle mixture and applesauce, starting and ending with the noodles. Sprinkle the remaining bread crumbs over top.
4. Bake in preheated oven for 25 to 30 minutes or until golden brown.

Apple Raisin Pudding

Serves 6 to 8

- Preheat oven to 350°F (180°C)
- 8-cup (2 L) casserole dish, greased

1 cup	all-purpose flour	250 mL
1 tsp	ground cinnamon	5 mL
¾ tsp	baking soda	4 mL
¼ tsp	ground nutmeg	1 mL
Pinch	salt	Pinch
¾ cup	granulated sugar	175 mL
½ cup	shortening or butter, softened	125 mL
1	egg, lightly beaten	1

1 tsp	vanilla	5 mL
1½ cups	chopped apples (best with Spartan or McIntosh, about 2 small)	375 mL
1 cup	raisins	250 mL
1 tbsp	milk or table (18%) cream	15 mL

1. In a medium bowl, combine flour, cinnamon, baking soda, nutmeg and salt, mixing well to blend.

2. In a large bowl, cream sugar and shortening until light and fluffy. Add egg and vanilla and blend well. Add flour mixture and stir just until blended.

3. Lightly fold in apples, raisins and milk just until well combined. Transfer to prepared casserole dish.

4. Bake, uncovered, in preheated oven for 50 to 60 minutes or until golden brown. Serve warm with your favorite sauce (see Sauces, pages 553–555), if desired.

Grandma's Pear Pudding

Serves 6

- Preheat oven to 350ºF (180ºC)
- 6-cup (1.5 L) casserole dish, ungreased

½ cup	butter or margarine, divided	125 mL
1 cup	all-purpose flour, divided	250 mL
1	can (28 oz/796 mL) pear halves, drained and sliced, juice reserved	1
1 cup	packed brown sugar, divided	250 mL
½ tsp	ground ginger	2 mL
¼ tsp	salt	1 mL
¼ tsp	almond extract	1 mL
½ cup	quick-cooking rolled oats	125 mL

1. In a medium saucepan, over low heat, melt 2 tbsp (25 mL) of the butter and slowly stir in 2 tbsp (25 mL) of the flour. Cook for about 1 minute, stirring constantly. Gradually stir in the reserved pear juice. Remove from heat and let cool, stirring constantly until mixture is thick and smooth. Stir in ¼ cup (50 mL) of the brown sugar, ginger, salt, almond extract and sliced pears. Spoon into casserole dish.

2. In a medium bowl, combine the remaining flour and brown sugar. Cut in the remaining butter until crumbly. Add oats and mix together well. Sprinkle over pears.

3. Bake in preheated oven for 35 to 40 minutes or until bubbly and topping is golden brown. Set aside to cool slightly on a wire rack and serve warm.

Layered Blueberry Crumb Pudding

Serves 4 to 6

- Preheat oven to 350ºF (180ºC)
- 11- by 7-inch (2 L) baking dish, ungreased

1 cup	wafer crumbs (about 6 wafers, zwieback, graham wafer or other)	250 mL
¼ cup	granulated sugar	50 mL
½ tsp	ground cinnamon	2 mL
3 tbsp	butter or margarine	45 mL
2 cups	fresh or frozen, well-drained blueberries (about 12 oz/375 g) Whipped topping or ice cream	500 mL

1. In a small bowl, mix together wafer crumbs, sugar and cinnamon until well blended. Cut in butter, using a pastry blender or two knives, until the mixture resembles coarse crumbs.

2. Spoon 1 cup (250 mL) of the blueberries into baking dish, top with half of the crumb mixture, then repeat layers.

3. Bake in preheated oven for 25 to 30 minutes or until golden brown. Serve warm. Cut into squares and top with whipped topping or ice cream.

Raspberry Tapioca Pudding

Serves 6

1	package (10 oz/300 g) frozen sweetened raspberries, thawed	1
1	strip lemon peel (1 inch/2.5 cm)	1
1 cup	red grape juice	250 mL
⅓ cup	granulated sugar	75 mL
¼ cup	quick-cooking tapioca	50 mL
½ cup	whipping (35%) cream	125 mL
2 tbsp	confectioner's (icing) sugar, sifted	25 mL

1. Pour raspberries into a strainer and reserve the juice, but throw away the seeds. Add enough water to the juice to make it 2 cups (500 mL). Pour into a large saucepan. Add lemon peel, grape juice and sugar. Bring to a boil over medium heat, then reduce heat to low and simmer, uncovered, for 10 minutes.

2. Remove the lemon peel and add the tapioca. Cook, stirring constantly, for 10 minutes. Spoon into 6 individual serving dishes, cover each tightly with plastic wrap and chill in refrigerator for 4 to 5 hours or until set.

3. In a small mixer bowl, on high speed, beat whipping cream and confectioner's sugar until soft peaks form. Spoon over puddings.

Lemon Sponge Pudding

Serves 4 to 6

- Preheat oven to 325°F (160°C)
- 8-cup (2 L) casserole dish, greased

1 cup	granulated sugar	250 mL
3 tbsp	butter or margarine, softened	45 mL
1/3 cup	all-purpose flour	75 mL
3	eggs, separated	3
1 cup	milk	250 mL
1 tsp	lemon zest	5 mL
3 tbsp	freshly squeezed lemon juice	45 mL

1. In a large bowl, cream sugar and butter until light and fluffy. Add flour and mix to blend.
2. In a small bowl, beat egg yolks well. Stir in milk, lemon zest and lemon juice, mixing until well blended. Pour into creamed mixture and mix well.
3. In a small mixer bowl, on high speed, beat egg whites until stiff peaks form. Gently fold into lemon mixture until well combined. Spoon into prepared casserole dish.
4. Bake in preheated oven for 50 to 60 minutes or until a tester comes out clean when inserted into the cake layer that forms on top. Be sure to avoid the pudding layer on the bottom when testing.

Lemon Pudding Cups

Serves 8

- Preheat oven to 325°F (160°C)
- Eight 3/4-cup (175 mL) custard cups, ungreased
- 13- by 9-inch (3 L) baking pan

1 cup	granulated sugar	250 mL
1/4 cup	sifted all-purpose flour	50 mL
2 tbsp	vegetable oil	25 mL
Pinch	salt	Pinch
2 tbsp	grated lemon zest	25 mL
1/3 cup	freshly squeezed lemon juice	75 mL
3	eggs, separated	3
1 1/2 cups	milk, scalded (see tip, at right)	375 mL
	Whipped topping	

1. In a medium bowl, combine sugar, flour, oil and salt. Add lemon zest and juice and mix well until blended.
2. In a small bowl, whisk egg yolks and milk. Pour into lemon mixture.

3. In a small mixer bowl, on high speed, beat egg whites until firm peaks form. Fold into lemon mixture. Spoon into custard cups, dividing equally. Place cups in baking pan set on oven rack and pour in hot water to a depth of about 1 inch (2.5 cm).
4. Bake in preheated oven for 35 to 40 minutes or until a tester comes out clean when inserted into the cake layer that forms on top. Be sure to avoid the pudding layer on the bottom when testing. Serve warm or chilled. Top with a dollop of whipped topping.

Tip *Milk, cream and sour cream are scalded when bubbles form around the edge of the pan as you heat it.*

Orange Surprise Pudding

Serves 6

- Preheat oven to 325°F (160°C)
- Six 3/4-cup (175 mL) custard cups, buttered
- 13- by 9-inch (3 L) baking pan

2	eggs, separated	2
1/2 cup	granulated sugar, divided	125 mL
1/4 cup	butter or margarine, softened	50 mL
1/4 cup	frozen orange juice concentrate, thawed, undiluted	50 mL
1/2 tsp	vanilla	2 mL
2 tbsp	all-purpose flour	25 mL
1/4 tsp	salt	1 mL
1 cup	milk	250 mL

1. In a small mixer bowl, on medium-high speed, beat egg whites until foamy. Add 2 tbsp (25 mL) of the sugar, one spoonful at a time, beating until firm peaks form.
2. In a medium bowl, cream the remaining sugar and butter until light and fluffy. Add egg yolks, orange juice and vanilla, beating until well blended. Stir in flour and salt, then slowly stir in milk. Gently fold in beaten egg whites until fluffy and smooth. Spoon into prepared custard cups. Place cups in baking pan set on oven rack and pour in boiling water to a depth of about 1 inch (2.5 cm).
3. Bake in preheated oven for 25 to 30 minutes or until top springs back when lightly touched with fingertip. Run a knife around the edges and invert onto serving dishes. Best served warm, but also delicious served cold.

Tip *Eggs separate more easily when they are cold.*

Tart Red Cherry Pudding

Serves 6 to 8

- Preheat oven to 350°F (180°C)
- 9-inch (2.5 L) square baking pan, greased

1	egg, lightly beaten	1
1 cup	canned tart red cherries, with juice	250 mL
½ cup	coarsely chopped nuts	125 mL
1 tbsp	butter or margarine, melted	15 mL
1 cup	all-purpose flour	250 mL
1 cup	granulated sugar	250 mL
1 tsp	baking soda	5 mL
½ tsp	salt	2 mL

1. In a medium bowl, combine egg, cherries, nuts and butter. Mix well.
2. In another medium bowl, mix together flour, sugar, baking soda and salt. Add to the cherry mixture, stirring until well blended. Spoon into prepared baking pan.
3. Bake in preheated oven for 35 to 40 minutes or until lightly browned. Serve warm.

Self-Saucing Plum Pudding

Serves 6 to 8

- Preheat oven to 350°F (180°C)
- 8-cup (2 L) casserole dish, greased

1 cup	all-purpose flour	250 mL
⅓ cup	granulated sugar	75 mL
1 tsp	baking powder	5 mL
1 tsp	baking soda	5 mL
¼ tsp	salt	1 mL
1½ cups	coarsely chopped red or purple plums (about 3 medium)	375 mL
½ cup	milk	125 mL
2 tbsp	butter or margarine, melted	25 mL
1 cup	unsweetened apple juice	250 mL
½ cup	water	125 mL
½ cup	packed brown sugar	125 mL
1 tsp	ground cinnamon	5 mL
¼ tsp	ground nutmeg	1 mL

1. In a large bowl, combine flour, sugar, baking powder, baking soda and salt. Add plums and mix together until well combined.
2. In a small bowl, mix together milk and butter. Add to flour mixture and stir just until blended. Spoon into prepared casserole dish and set aside.
3. In a medium saucepan, over medium heat, combine apple juice and water and bring to a boil. Stir in brown sugar, cinnamon and nutmeg, stirring until sugar is dissolved. Remove from heat. Pour hot mixture over batter in casserole dish.
4. Bake in preheated oven for 30 to 35 minutes or until topping is golden brown and firm to the touch. Serve hot or warm.

Banana Cream Pudding

Serves 6 to 8

- 8-cup (2 L) glass bowl (as you would use for trifle)

⅔ cup	firmly packed brown sugar	150 mL
⅓ cup	all-purpose flour	75 mL
2 cups	milk	500 mL
2	egg yolks, beaten	2
2 tbsp	butter or margarine	25 mL
1 tsp	vanilla	5 mL
1 cup	whipping (35%) cream, whipped	250 mL
6	ripe but firm bananas, sliced	6
⅓ cup	chopped nuts (optional)	75 mL

1. In a medium saucepan, over medium heat, mix together brown sugar and flour. Stir in milk and, stirring constantly, cook until bubbly and thickened. Continue cooking for 1 minute, then remove from heat.
2. Take a cupful (250 mL) of the hot mixture and stir into the beaten egg yolks; return this mixture to the saucepan. Bring to a boil and boil gently for 3 minutes, stirring constantly. Remove from heat. Add the butter and vanilla and stir until blended and smooth. Set aside to cool, stirring occasionally. When at room temperature, fold in the whipped cream.
3. Spoon about one-third of the pudding into the glass bowl. Spread half of the sliced bananas over top. Repeat the layers and top with the remaining pudding. Sprinkle the chopped nuts over top, if desired, or add a few extra slices of banana for decoration, or both. Cover tightly with plastic wrap and chill in refrigerator for at least 1 to hour or until ready to serve.

Tip *Leftover whipped cream will retain its lightness and texture for a day or more, refrigerated, if you add 1 tsp (5 mL) light corn syrup to each ½ pint cream. You won't notice any more sweetness with this addition.*

Passover Pineapple Pudding

Serves 8 to 10

- Preheat oven to 350°F (180°C)
- 8-cup (2 L) round soufflé dish, greased

²/₃ cup	butter or margarine	150 mL
1¼ cups + 1 tbsp	granulated sugar	315 mL
8	eggs	8
2	cans (each 19 oz/540 mL) crushed pineapple, drained slightly	2
4 cups	matzo farfel (see tip, below), soaked in water	1 L
½ tsp	ground cinnamon	2 mL

1. In a large saucepan, melt butter. Remove from heat and mix in sugar. Add eggs, one at a time, mixing well each time. Stir in pineapple, mixing well to blend. Fold in matzo farfel and cinnamon and spoon into prepared soufflé dish.

2. Bake in preheated oven for 1 hour or until golden brown. Serve warm.

Tip *Matzo farfel is available in Jewish delis.*

Pineapple Pudding with Butterscotch Sauce

Serves 6 to 8

- Preheat oven to 350°F (180°C)
- 9-inch (2.5 L) square baking dish, lightly greased

2	eggs	2
1 cup	granulated sugar	250 mL
1 cup	chopped nuts	250 mL
1 cup	canned crushed pineapple, drained, juice reserved	250 mL
¾ cup	all-purpose flour	175 mL
1 tsp	baking powder	5 mL
¼ tsp	salt	1 mL
BUTTERSCOTCH SAUCE		
1	egg	1
1 cup	packed brown sugar	250 mL
¼ cup	water	50 mL
¼ cup	reserved pineapple juice	50 mL
¼ cup	butter or margarine	50 mL
2 cups	whipped topping	500 mL

1. In a large bowl, whisk together eggs and sugar until light and frothy. Stir in nuts and pineapple, mixing until well blended.

2. In a small bowl, sift together flour, baking powder and salt. Add to the egg mixture and mix until well combined. Spoon into prepared baking dish and bake in preheated oven for 35 to 40 minutes or until golden brown. Set on a wire rack to cool. Cut into squares.

3. *Prepare the butterscotch sauce:* In a medium saucepan, combine egg, brown sugar, water, pineapple juice and butter. Cook over low heat until dissolved and smooth. Set aside to cool, then add whipped topping. Spoon over pudding cake squares. Place a dollop of whipped topping on top, if desired.

Danish Rhubarb Pudding

Serves 6

2 lbs	rhubarb, cut into ½-inch (1 cm) pieces (about 7 cups/1.75 mL)	1 kg
¾ cup	granulated sugar, divided	175 mL
1½ tsp	vanilla, divided	7 mL
3 tbsp	cornstarch, mixed with 3 tbsp to ¼ cup (45 to 50 mL) cold water	45 mL
1 cup	whipping (35%) cream	250 mL

1. In a large saucepan, over medium heat, combine rhubarb, 1½ cups (375 mL) cold water and ½ cup (125 mL) of the sugar. Simmer until rhubarb is soft. Stir in ½ tsp (2 mL) of the vanilla and the cornstarch-water mixture and cook, stirring constantly, until sauce is transparent and thick. Spoon into a glass serving bowl, cover and chill in refrigerator for 3 to 4 hours or overnight.

2. In a small mixer bowl, on high speed, beat whipping cream until soft peaks form. Add the remaining sugar and vanilla and beat until stiff. Spoon over pudding.

Tip *You could also spoon the pudding into 6 individual serving dishes and top each with whipped cream.*

Norwegian Prune Pudding

Serves 8

- Eight ¾-cup (175 mL) custard cups or ramekins

⅓ cup	granulated sugar, divided	75 mL
2 cups	fresh bread crumbs (about 4 slices)	500 mL
¼ cup	butter or margarine	50 mL
1	jar (27 oz/767 g) stewed prunes	1
½ tsp	ground cinnamon	2 mL
Pinch	ground nutmeg	Pinch
2 cups	whipping (35%) cream	500 mL

1. In a small bowl, mix 2 tbsp (25 mL) of the sugar with the bread crumbs.

2. In a small skillet, melt the butter. Add the crumb mixture and sauté over low heat, stirring constantly, until mixture is browned and crispy. Set aside to cool on a wire rack.

3. Drain the prunes, setting aside ¼ cup (50 mL) of the liquid, and remove the pits.

4. In a large bowl, combine the prunes, reserved prune liquid, 1 tbsp (15 mL) of the sugar, cinnamon and nutmeg. Mix together to blend well.

5. In a small mixer bowl, on high speed, beat whipping cream and the remaining sugar until stiff peaks form.

6. Layer the crumb mixture, prune mixture and whipped cream in the custard cups, beginning and ending with cream. Chill in refrigerator for at least 3 hours or until ready to serve.

Western Raisin Nut Pudding

Serves 6 to 8
- Preheat oven to 350°F (180°C)
- 8-inch (2 L) square baking pan, ungreased

2 cups	water	500 mL
2 tbsp	butter or margarine	25 mL
1¾ cups	firmly packed brown sugar, divided	425 mL
1¼ cups	biscuit mix	300 mL
⅓ cup	water	75 mL
1 tsp	vanilla	5 mL
1 cup	raisins	250 mL
½ cup	chopped nuts	125 mL

1. In a medium saucepan, over medium heat, combine water, butter and 1 cup (250 mL) of the brown sugar. Bring to a boil, stirring, and boil for 5 minutes. Pour into baking pan.

2. In a large bowl, mix together biscuit mix, the remaining brown sugar, water and vanilla. Add raisins and chopped nuts and mix well until thoroughly combined. Spoon over brown sugar mixture in pan.

3. Bake in preheated oven for 40 to 45 minutes or until set and golden brown. The batter will sink into the liquid and spread out as it bakes.

Tip *Serve with your favorite sauce (see Sauces, pages 553–555).*

Oatmeal Raisin Pudding

Serves 8
- Preheat oven to 350°F (180°C)
- 8-inch (2 L) square baking dish, greased

2¼ cups	quick-cooking rolled oats	550 mL
¾ cup	packed brown sugar	175 mL
⅔ cup	raisins	150 mL
1½ tsp	ground cinnamon	7 mL
½ tsp	salt	2 mL
2	eggs	2
3½ cups	milk	875 mL
1 tbsp	vegetable oil	15 mL
1 tsp	vanilla	5 mL

1. In a large bowl, combine oats, brown sugar, raisins, cinnamon and salt. Make a well in the center.

2. In another large bowl, whisk eggs, milk, oil and vanilla until blended. Pour into the well in the oat mixture, stirring until well combined. Spoon into prepared baking dish.

3. Bake in preheated oven for 50 to 60 minutes or until firmly set. Serve warm, cutting into squares or rectangles.

Date Nut Pudding

Serves 4 to 6
- Preheat oven to 300°F (150°C)
- 6-cup (1.5 L) casserole dish, buttered

2	eggs	2
¾ cup	granulated sugar	175 mL
2 tbsp	all-purpose flour	25 mL
1 tsp	baking powder	5 mL
1 cup	chopped dates (about 6 oz/175 g)	250 mL
1 cup	chopped walnuts	250 mL
	Ground cinnamon	
	Vanilla ice cream or whipped topping	

1. In a large mixer bowl, on medium speed, beat eggs well. Gradually beat in sugar until mixture thickens.

2. In a medium bowl, sift together flour and baking powder. Add dates and walnuts and mix well to blend. Pour into egg mixture and mix on medium speed until well combined. Spoon into prepared baking pan and sprinkle cinnamon over top.

3. Bake in preheated oven for 30 to 35 minutes or until set and top is golden brown. Let cool on a wire rack and serve with vanilla ice cream or whipped topping (or any other desired topping).

Quick Pumpkin Patch Pudding

Serves 8

1	package (5 oz/135 g) vanilla instant pudding and pie filling mix	1
1½ cups	evaporated milk	375 mL
1	can (14 oz/398 mL) pumpkin purée (not pie filling)	1
1 tsp	pumpkin pie spice	5 mL
2 cups	whipping (35%) cream, whipped, or vanilla ice cream	500 mL

1. In a large mixer bowl, combine pudding mix and milk and beat according to package directions. Chill in refrigerator for 5 minutes.
2. Stir in pumpkin purée and pumpkin pie spice until well mixed. Spoon into 8 individual dessert dishes or glasses and chill in refrigerator for 15 minutes or until ready to serve. Top each with a dollop of whipped cream or ice cream.

Russian Cheese Pudding

Serves 4 to 6

- Preheat oven to 300°F (150°C)
- 6-cup (1.5 L) casserole dish, greased

4	egg yolks, hard-boiled	4
2 cups	dry cottage cheese (about 1 lb/500 g)	500 mL
3	eggs, separated	3
1 cup	granulated sugar	250 mL
¼ cup	butter, melted	50 mL
½ cup	raisins	125 mL
3 tbsp	all-purpose flour	45 mL
½ tsp	vanilla	2 mL
Pinch	salt	Pinch

1. Over a medium bowl, put hard-boiled egg yolks and cheese through a fine sieve.
2. In a large bowl, whisk together raw egg yolks, sugar and butter, beating until well blended. Add the egg-cheese mixture and mix well. Stir in raisins, flour, vanilla and salt. Mix well until thoroughly blended.
3. In a small mixer bowl, beat egg whites until stiff peaks form. Fold into mixture gently. Spoon into prepared casserole dish.
4. Bake in preheated oven for 35 to 45 minutes or until golden brown. Place on a wire rack to cool slightly.

Cheese 'n' Raisins Pudding

Serves 6 to 8

- Preheat oven to 325°F (160°C)
- 6-cup (1.5 L) casserole dish, buttered

12 oz	cottage cheese, drained	375 g
4 oz	cream cheese, softened	125 g
3	eggs, separated	3
1 cup	granulated sugar	250 mL
Pinch	salt	Pinch
3	egg yolks, hard-boiled and finely chopped	3
½ cup	raisins	125 mL
⅓ cup	butter or margarine, melted	75 mL
3 tbsp	all-purpose flour	45 mL
1 tsp	vanilla	5 mL

1. Over a medium bowl, push the cottage cheese and cream cheese through a sieve. Set aside.
2. In a large mixer bowl, on medium speed, beat raw egg yolks. Add sugar and salt and beat until thick and light in color. Stir in boiled egg yolks, raisins, butter, flour, vanilla and the sieved cheese mixture. Mix together until well blended.
3. In a small mixer bowl, on high speed, beat egg whites until stiff but not dry. Fold gently into the egg-cheese mixture until thoroughly combined. Spoon into prepared casserole dish.
4. Bake in preheated oven for 30 to 35 minutes or until firm and golden brown. Place on a wire rack to cool slightly.

Tip *Don't beat egg whites in plastic bowls, as plastic retains oil. Use a very clean bowl with no traces of oil and very clean beaters.*

Rice Pudding (Kugel)

Serves 6 to 8

- Preheat oven to 375°F (190°C)
- 8-cup (2 L) casserole dish, well greased

4 cups	water	1 L
1½ cups	long-grain rice	375 mL
1½ tsp	salt	7 mL
6	eggs	6
⅓ cup	granulated sugar	75 mL
½ cup	raisins	125 mL
⅓ cup	shortening or margarine, melted	75 mL

1. In a large saucepan, over medium-low heat, bring water, rice and salt to a boil, then cook for 10 minutes. Drain any remaining liquid.

2. In a large mixer bowl, beat eggs and sugar until well blended. Stir in rice, raisins and shortening and mix together until thoroughly blended. Pour into prepared casserole dish.

3. Bake in preheated oven for 25 to 30 minutes or until set and nicely browned. Serve hot or warm, cut into squares.

Tip *A great substitute for potatoes or plain cooked rice!*

• •

Traditional Baked Rice Pudding

Serves 4 to 6
- Preheat oven to 250ºF (120ºC)
- 6-cup (1.5 L) glass casserole dish, buttered

2¼ cups	milk	550 mL
½ cup	long-grain rice	125 mL
⅓ cup	granulated sugar	75 mL
¼ tsp	salt	1 mL
Pinch	ground cinnamon or nutmeg	Pinch
2 tbsp	raisins (optional)	25 mL
1 tsp	vanilla	5 mL

1. In prepared baking dish, combine milk, rice, sugar and salt. Fold in cinnamon until just blended.

2. Bake, uncovered, in preheated oven for 30 minutes. Remove from oven and mix well, then bake for another 30 minutes. Stir in raisins and vanilla and bake for 1½ hours or until rice is tender and most of the milk is absorbed.

Tip *Serve warm or cold, plain or with some cream.*

• •

Hawaiian Rice Pudding with Pineapple Sauce

Serves 6

4 cups	milk, divided	1 L
3 cups	cooked long-grain rice	750 mL
⅔ cup	granulated sugar	150 mL
½ tsp	salt	2 mL
4 oz	cream cheese, softened	125 g
2	eggs	2
1 tsp	vanilla	5 mL
PINEAPPLE SAUCE		
¼ cup	packed brown sugar	50 mL
1 tbsp	cornstarch	15 mL
1 tbsp	butter or margarine	15 mL
Pinch	salt	Pinch
1	can (19 oz/540 mL) pineapple chunks, drained, juice reserved	1
½ tsp	vanilla	2 mL

1. In a large saucepan, over medium heat, combine 3½ cups (825 mL) of the milk, rice, sugar and salt. Bring to a boil and cook for 15 to 20 minutes, stirring often, until mixture is creamy and thick.

2. In a medium bowl, beat cream cheese until smooth. Whisk in eggs and the remaining milk, beating until well blended. Stir into rice mixture and cook over medium heat for 3 minutes. Stir in vanilla and spoon into 6 individual dessert dishes, dividing equally.

3. *Prepare the pineapple sauce:* In a medium saucepan, over medium heat, combine brown sugar, cornstarch, butter, salt and reserved pineapple juice. Bring to a boil and cook for 2 minutes, stirring constantly, until mixture is thickened. Remove from heat and stir in pineapple chunks and vanilla.

4. Spoon sauce over each pudding dish. Let cool slightly on a wire rack before serving.

• •

Hint of Orange Creamy Rice Pudding

Serves 4
- Double boiler

½	orange	½
2 cups	milk, scalded (see tip, page 492)	500 mL
¼ cup	long-grain rice	50 mL
¼ cup	granulated sugar	50 mL
¼ tsp	salt	1 mL
1	egg yolk, lightly beaten	1
½ cup	light (5%) cream	125 mL
¼ tsp	vanilla	1 mL

1. Pare the orange half so that the peel is in one long continuous spiral.

2. In the top of a double boiler, over gently boiling water, combine orange peel, milk, rice, sugar and salt. Cook for about 15 minutes, stirring occasionally, until rice is tender. Remove the orange peel.

3. In a small bowl, whisk egg yolk and cream. Stir in a small amount of the hot mixture, then pour into hot mixture and blend thoroughly. Cover and continue cooking for 45 to 50 minutes, stirring several times, until mixture thickens. Remove from heat and stir in vanilla.

4. Spoon into 4 individual dessert dishes or glasses. Serve warm or chilled.

Tip *Top each dish with a dollop of whipped cream or sprinkle some granulated sugar and cinnamon on top.*

Country Corn Pudding

Serves 6 to 8

- Preheat oven to 350°F (180°C)
- 8-cup (2 L) casserole dish, buttered
- Roasting pan

2 tbsp	butter or margarine	25 mL
1	onion, chopped	1
4 cups	corn kernels, well drained	1 L
2 tbsp	yellow cornmeal	25 mL
2 tbsp	all-purpose flour	25 mL
4	eggs	4
3 cups	milk or half-and-half (10%) cream	750 mL
2 tbsp	chopped fresh parsley	25 mL
1 tsp	Worcestershire sauce	5 mL
¾ tsp	mustard powder	4 mL
½ tsp	salt	2 mL

1. In a skillet, over medium heat, melt the butter. Stir in chopped onion and sauté until softened, about 5 minutes.

2. In prepared casserole dish, mix together corn, cornmeal and flour. Mix well to blend. Add the onion mixture and mix to blend.

3. In a large bowl, whisk eggs, milk, parsley, Worcestershire sauce, mustard and salt. Mix well and then add to corn mixture, stirring until well combined. Place casserole dish into roasting pan set on oven rack and pour in hot water until it reaches halfway up the sides of the baking dish.

4. Bake in preheated oven for 50 to 55 minutes or until pudding is just set and the top is golden brown. Let cool in the roasting pan for about 10 minutes, then remove casserole dish to wire rack. Serve hot or warm.

Matzo Meal Pudding

Serves 4 to 6

- Preheat oven to 350°F (180°C)
- 8-cup (2 L) casserole dish, buttered

2	eggs	2
½ cup	granulated sugar	125 mL
2 cups	milk	500 mL
¼ cup	butter, melted	50 mL
1 cup	matzo meal (available at Jewish delis)	250 mL
2 tbsp	brandy	25 mL
½ tsp	salt	2 mL

1. In a large mixer bowl, on medium speed, beat eggs and sugar well until light and fluffy. Stir in milk and butter, mixing together to blend. Add matzo meal, brandy and salt, beating well to blend. Spoon into prepared casserole dish.

2. Bake in preheated oven for 1 hour or until top is golden brown and pudding is set.

Tip *Serve this pudding as a side dish in place of rice or potatoes.*

Cabbage Pudding (Kugel)

Serves 6 to 8

- 8-cup (2 L) casserole dish, greased

¼ cup	shortening or butter	50 mL
4 cups	finely shredded cabbage (about 6 oz/175 g)	1 L
1 cup	boiling water	250 mL
8	slices white bread, crusts removed	8
4	eggs, separated	4
½ cup	sifted all-purpose flour	125 mL
½ cup	blanched almonds, ground	125 mL
¼ cup	raisins	50 mL
2 tsp	freshly squeezed lemon juice	10 mL
1 tsp	salt	5 mL

1. In a skillet, over low heat, melt shortening. Add cabbage and cook for 45 to 50 minutes, stirring often. Chill for 3 to 4 hours or overnight. Meanwhile, preheat oven to 350°F (180°C).

2. Pour boiling water into a large bowl and add the bread slices. Soak bread for about 5 minutes, drain and mash.

3. In another large bowl, combine egg yolks, flour, almonds, raisins, lemon juice and salt. Add the bread and mix until well blended and very smooth. Add the cabbage and mix together lightly.

4. In a small mixer bowl, beat egg whites on high speed until stiff peaks form. Carefully fold egg whites into cabbage mixture until thoroughly blended. Pour into prepared casserole dish.

5. Bake in preheated oven for 30 to 35 minutes or until set and golden brown. Let cool on a wire rack.

Tip *In any recipe that calls for separated eggs, remember this rule: eggs separate more easily when they are very cold, but whipped egg whites gain more volume if they are at room temperature.*

Potato Pudding (Kugel)

Serves 6 to 8

- Preheat oven to 375°F (190°C)
- 6-cup (1.5 L) casserole dish, greased

6	large potatoes, peeled	6
2	egg yolks, lightly beaten	2
1	onion, grated	1
1/4 cup	matzo meal (available at Jewish delis)	50 mL
1 1/2 tsp	salt	7 mL
1 tsp	baking powder	5 mL
1/4 tsp	freshly ground black pepper	1 mL
1/4 cup	butter or shortening, melted, divided	50 mL
2	egg whites	2

1. Grate the potatoes into a large bowl of salted water. Drain well.
2. In the same large bowl, combine potatoes, egg yolks, onion, matzo meal, salt, baking powder and pepper. Add half the melted butter and mix together until well combined.
3. In a small mixer bowl, on high speed, beat egg whites until stiff peaks form. Carefully fold into potato mixture until well blended. Spoon into prepared casserole dish and spoon the remaining melted butter over top.
4. Bake in preheated oven for 1 hour or until set and golden brown on top.

Tip *Serve hot or warm alongside chicken or meat dishes.*

Sour Cream Noodle Pudding

Serves 10 to 12

- Preheat oven to 350°F (180°C)
- 13- by 9-inch (3 L) baking dish, ungreased

1	package (12 oz/375 g) medium noodles or broad egg noodles	1
3	eggs	3
1/2 cup	milk	125 mL
1 cup	sour cream	250 mL
1 cup	creamy cottage cheese (about 8 oz/250 g)	250 mL
4 oz	cream cheese, softened	125 g
1/4 cup	unsalted butter, melted, divided	50 mL
1 cup	raisins (golden or dark)	250 mL
1/2 tsp	ground cinnamon	2 mL
	Salt	

1. In a large saucepan, bring salted water to a boil. Add noodles and cook until just tender, about 10 minutes. Drain and set aside.
2. In a large bowl, whisk eggs and milk. Add the sour cream, cottage cheese, cream cheese and half the butter. Add the noodles, raisins, cinnamon and salt to taste. Mix together until well blended.
3. Grease baking dish with the remaining butter. Pour in the noodle mixture, spreading evenly.
4. Bake in preheated oven for 45 to 50 minutes or until top is lightly browned and pudding is set. Let cool for 5 to 10 minutes on a wire rack, then cut into squares for serving.

Tip *If not serving immediately, cool pudding completely in baking dish, cover tightly with plastic wrap and refrigerate.*

Sweet Potato Rum Pudding

Serves 6 to 8

- Preheat oven to 300°F (150°C)
- 8-cup (2 L) shallow casserole dish, buttered

2 1/2 cups	milk	625 mL
3	sweet potatoes or yams, peeled	3
3	eggs	3
1 cup	granulated sugar	250 mL
1/2 cup	slivered blanched almonds	125 mL
2 tsp	ground cinnamon	10 mL
2 tbsp	butter or margarine	25 mL
1/2 cup	rum or bourbon	125 mL

1. Pour milk into prepared casserole dish. Grate the sweet potatoes directly into the milk to prevent darkening.
2. In a medium bowl, whisk eggs; gradually add sugar, beating until blended. Stir in almonds and cinnamon and mix together well. Spoon into potato mixture and mix together until well blended. Dot with butter.
3. Bake in preheated oven for about 1 1/2 hours, until golden brown and pudding is set. When ready to serve, spoon the rum over top.

Tip *Delicious served with turkey or ham!*

Bread Puddings

Bread puddings were originally made to use up stale bread, but it wasn't long before they became a favorite comfort food. In most recipes you have the option of using any kind of bread, including challah or raisin bread, cakes, bread rolls or even doughnuts, or a combination of these. They should be day-old and broken or cut into pieces or cubes.

• •

Traditional Bread Pudding

Serves 6

• Preheat oven to 350°F (180°C)
• 8-cup (2 L) casserole dish, buttered
• 13- by 9-inch (3 L) baking pan

2	eggs, beaten	2
1/4 cup	granulated sugar	50 mL
1 tsp	vanilla	5 mL
1/2 tsp	salt	2 mL
1/4 tsp	ground nutmeg	1 mL
4 cups	milk, scalded (see tip, page 492)	1 L
3	slices day-old bread, cut into cubes (about 2 cups/500 mL)	3

1. In a large bowl, combine eggs, sugar, vanilla, salt and nutmeg. Mix well to blend. Add scalded milk and mix until thoroughly blended.
2. Stir in bread cubes and mix until well combined. Pour into prepared casserole dish. Place casserole dish in baking pan set on oven rack and pour in hot water to a depth of about 1 inch (2.5 cm).
3. Bake in preheated oven for 45 to 50 minutes or until a knife inserted in the center comes out clean and dry. Let cool on a wire rack.

Tip *Serve warm with whipped cream or your favorite sauce (see Sauces, pages 553–555).*

• •

Special Bread Pudding Cake

Serves 10 to 12

• 10-inch (25 cm) springform pan, oiled, with outside covered with foil to seal
• Roasting pan

6	eggs	6
4 cups	milk	1 L
1 1/2 cups	granulated sugar	375 mL
3 tbsp	vanilla	45 mL
1 tbsp	ground cinnamon	15 mL
1 tbsp	ground nutmeg	15 mL
2 tsp	minced orange zest	10 mL
2	large loaves (each 1 lb/450 g) French bread, cut into 1/2-inch (1 cm) cubes	2
1 cup	raisins	250 mL
1 cup	chopped pecans	250 mL

1. In a large bowl, whisk together eggs, milk and sugar to blend. Add vanilla, cinnamon, nutmeg and zest and whisk until thoroughly blended.
2. Press one layer of bread cubes into the bottom of prepared springform pan so that there are no empty spaces between. Sprinkle some of the raisins and pecans on top.
3. Spoon one-third of the egg mixture over raisins and pecans and carefully press down into the bread cubes with your fingertips. Repeat layers until all of the bread cubes and egg mixture are used up. (Some of the egg custard mixture may be left over once the pan is filled, but continue to add it, a little at a time, pressing firmly into the bread cubes until all of the mixture is used up.) For best results, chill in refrigerator overnight. Meanwhile, preheat oven to 375°F (190°C).
4. Place springform pan in roasting pan set on oven rack and pour in water to a depth of about 1 inch (2.5 cm). Bake in preheated oven for 1 to 1 1/2 hours or until a toothpick inserted in the center comes out clean and dry. Let cool slightly on a wire rack and cut into slices.

Tip *Serve warm or cold, with ice cream or your favorite sauce (see Sauces, pages 553–555).*

• •

Mock Bread Pudding

Serves 6

• Preheat oven to 350°F (180°C)
• Six 3/4-cup (175 mL) custard cups or ramekins

1	egg	1
1 1/2 cups	milk	375 mL
1/2 cup	granulated sugar	125 mL
2 tbsp	butter or margarine, melted	25 mL
3 cups	granola cereal (with or without raisins)	750 mL

1. In a large bowl, whisk together egg, milk, sugar and butter until thoroughly blended. Add cereal and mix well. Spoon into custard cups.
2. Bake in preheated oven for 20 to 25 minutes or until pudding is not liquid in the center but is still a bit jiggly. Serve warm.

Custard Bread Pudding

Serves 6 to 8

- Preheat oven to 350°F (180°C)
- 8-cup (2 L) casserole dish, buttered
- 13- by 9-inch baking pan

6	eggs	6
4 cups	warm milk	1 L
½ cup	granulated sugar	125 mL
½ tsp	ground nutmeg	2 mL
½ tsp	salt	2 mL
¼ tsp	vanilla	1 mL
2	day-old cinnamon buns, cubed	2

1. In a large bowl, whisk eggs and milk. Whisk in sugar, nutmeg, salt and vanilla until well blended.
2. Place cubed buns in prepared casserole dish and stir in egg mixture until well combined. Place in baking pan set on oven rack and pour in hot water until it reaches halfway up the sides of dish.
3. Bake in preheated oven for 50 to 60 minutes or until a knife inserted in the center comes out clean and dry and pudding is firm to the touch. Let cool on a wire rack.

Bread Pudding with Vanilla Sauce

Serves 6

- Preheat oven to 350°F (180°C)
- 6-cup (1.5 L) casserole dish, greased

2 cups	milk	500 mL
¼ cup	butter or margarine	50 mL
6	slices raisin bread, cut into cubes (about 4 cups/1 L)	6
2	eggs, lightly beaten	2
½ cup	granulated sugar	125 mL
1 tsp	vanilla	5 mL
½ tsp	ground nutmeg	2 mL
VANILLA SAUCE		
½ cup	firmly packed brown sugar	125 mL
½ cup	granulated sugar	125 mL
½ cup	butter or margarine	125 mL
½ cup	whipping (35%) cream	125 mL
1 tsp	vanilla	5 mL

1. In a saucepan, over medium heat, cook milk and butter for 5 minutes or until butter is melted.
2. Put bread cubes in a large bowl. Pour milk mixture over bread and let stand for 10 minutes. Then add eggs, sugar, vanilla and nutmeg and mix to blend. Spoon into prepared casserole dish.

3. Bake in preheated oven for 45 to 50 minutes or until center of pudding is set.
4. *Prepare the vanilla sauce:* In a saucepan, over medium heat, combine brown sugar, granulated sugar, butter and cream. Cook for 5 to 8 minutes, stirring often, until mixture comes to a boil and thickens. Stir in vanilla. Serve over warm pudding.

Bread Pudding with Lemon Sauce

Serves 4 to 6

- Preheat oven to 350°F (180°C)
- 6-cup (1.5 L) casserole dish, greased
- 13- by 9-inch (3 L) baking pan

3	slices day-old bread, crusts removed, cut into cubes (about 2 cups/500 mL)	3
2 cups	milk	500 mL
¼ cup	granulated sugar	50 mL
3 tbsp	butter	45 mL
Pinch	salt	Pinch
2	eggs	2
½ tsp	vanilla	2 mL
LEMON SAUCE		
½ cup	granulated sugar	125 mL
1 tbsp	cornstarch	15 mL
Pinch	salt	Pinch
1 cup	water	250 mL
1 to 2 tsp	grated lemon zest	5 to 10 mL
2 tbsp	butter	25 mL
1 tbsp	freshly squeezed lemon juice	15 mL
1 to 2	drops yellow food coloring (optional)	1 to 2

1. Spoon the bread cubes into prepared casserole dish. Set aside.
2. In a saucepan, over low heat, heat milk, sugar, butter and salt just until butter has melted.
3. In a bowl, whisk eggs and vanilla. Whisk in the heated milk mixture until well blended. Spoon over bread cubes. Place in baking pan set on oven rack and pour in water to a depth of 1 inch (2.5 cm).
4. Bake, uncovered, in preheated oven for 40 to 50 minutes or until a knife inserted near the edge of the pan comes out clean and dry. Let cool on a wire rack.
5. *Prepare the lemon sauce:* In a medium saucepan, over medium heat, combine sugar, cornstarch and salt and mix to blend. Stir in water and zest and bring to a boil, cooking and stirring for 2 minutes. Remove from heat and add butter, lemon juice and food coloring (if using). Stir until well blended. Serve warm or cold over pudding.

Bread Pudding with Rum Sauce

Serves 6 to 8

- Preheat oven to 350°F (180°C)
- 8-cup (2 L) casserole dish, buttered

¼ cup	butter or margarine, softened	50 mL
4	slices day-old bread, crusts removed	4
2	eggs, lightly beaten	2
2½ cups	milk	625 mL
½ cup	packed brown sugar	125 mL
½ cup	raisins	125 mL
1 tsp	vanilla	5 mL
Pinch	salt	Pinch
½ tsp	granulated sugar	2 mL
½ tsp	ground cinnamon	2 mL
RUM SAUCE		
1½ cups	granulated sugar	375 mL
1½ cups	corn syrup	375 mL
2 cups	light (5%) cream, divided	500 mL
½ cup	butter or margarine	125 mL
3 tbsp	light rum	45 mL
½ tsp	vanilla	2 mL

1. Butter the bread slices and cut into cubes. Put cubes into prepared casserole dish.
2. In a large bowl, combine eggs, milk, brown sugar, raisins, vanilla and salt. Mix together to blend thoroughly. Spoon over bread cubes and sprinkle sugar and cinnamon on top.
3. Bake in preheated oven for 45 to 50 minutes or until browned.
4. *Prepare the rum sauce:* In a large saucepan, over medium heat, combine sugar, corn syrup, half the cream and the butter. Bring to a boil and cook without stirring to the firm-ball stage, 245°F (118°C) on a candy thermometer. Lower the heat and add the remaining cream. Cook for another 15 to 20 minutes or until golden brown. Remove from heat, add the rum and vanilla and mix well. Serve over warm or cold pudding.

Egg Bread 'n' Butter Pudding

Serves 6

- Preheat oven to 350°F (180°C)
- 8-inch (2 L) square baking dish, buttered
- 13- by 9-inch baking pan

3	eggs	3
⅔ cup	granulated sugar	150 mL
Pinch	salt	Pinch
2 cups	milk	500 mL

3 tbsp	butter or margarine, melted	45 mL
2 tsp	vanilla	10 mL
1½ tsp	ground cinnamon	7 mL
Pinch	ground nutmeg	Pinch
	Finely grated zest of 1 lemon or orange	
6	slices stale egg bread (challah), cut into cubes (about 4 cups/1 L)	6
½ cup	raisins (optional)	125 mL

1. In a large bowl, whisk together eggs, sugar and salt until smooth. Add milk, butter, vanilla, cinnamon, nutmeg and zest. Mix thoroughly until well blended.
2. Place bread cubes in prepared baking dish. Pour egg mixture over top and mix well to coat all of the bread. Sprinkle with raisins (if using). Place baking dish in baking pan set on oven rack and pour in hot water until it reaches halfway up the sides of baking dish.
3. Bake in preheated oven for 55 to 60 minutes or until golden brown and set in the center. Let cool on a wire rack.

Chocolate Bread Pudding

Serves 6 to 8

- Preheat oven to 350°F (180°C)
- 8-cup (2 L) soufflé dish or casserole dish, buttered

4 oz	semisweet chocolate, cut into pieces	125 g
3 cups	milk, divided	750 mL
½ cup	granulated sugar	125 mL
¼ cup	butter or margarine	50 mL
8	slices egg bread (challah) or white, cut into cubes (about 5 cups/1.25 L)	8
2 tsp	vanilla	10 mL
1 tsp	ground cinnamon	5 mL
3	eggs, lightly beaten	3
½ cup	ground nuts, toasted (optional)	125 mL
	Whipped cream	
	Shaved chocolate or chocolate curls	

1. In a large saucepan, over low heat, combine chocolate, 2 cups (500 mL) of the milk, sugar and butter, stirring constantly until butter and chocolate are melted. (Or use a microwave-safe dish and microwave on High for 9 minutes.)
2. Remove from heat and stir in bread cubes, the remaining milk, vanilla and cinnamon. Add the eggs and stir until thoroughly blended. Stir in nuts (if using). Let stand for 5 minutes, stir, then spoon into prepared soufflé dish.

3. Bake in preheated oven for 45 to 50 minutes or until a knife inserted in the center comes out clean and dry. Serve warm topped with whipped cream and shaved chocolate.

• •

Spicy Wheat Germ Pudding

Serves 6
- Preheat oven to 350°F (180°C)
- Six ¾-cup (175 mL) custard cups, buttered
- 13- by 9-inch (3 L) baking pan

3 cups	fresh white bread crumbs (about 6 slices)	750 mL
3 cups	milk, scalded (see tip, page 492)	750 mL
3 tbsp	butter or margarine	45 mL
⅓ cup	wheat germ	75 mL
1 tsp	ground cinnamon	5 mL
¼ tsp	ground nutmeg	1 mL
Pinch	salt	Pinch
3	eggs	3
⅓ cup	firmly packed brown sugar	75 mL
1 tsp	vanilla	5 mL

1. In a large bowl, combine crumbs, milk and butter and mix well. Stir in wheat germ, cinnamon, nutmeg and salt and mix together well. Let stand for 5 minutes, then beat until smooth.
2. In another large bowl, whisk eggs slightly. Add brown sugar, vanilla and bread mixture and mix thoroughly to blend. Set aside for 15 minutes, then spoon into prepared custard cups. Place cups in baking pan set on oven rack and pour in hot water to a depth of about 1 inch (2.5 cm).
3. Bake in preheated oven for 45 to 50 minutes or until set and firm to the touch. Serve warm.

• •

Whole Wheat–Apple Bread Pudding

Serves 8
- Preheat oven to 375°F (190°C)
- 9-inch (2.5 L) square baking dish, lightly greased

8	slices 100% whole wheat bread, toasted and cut in half diagonally	8
¼ cup	granulated sugar	50 mL
1½ tsp	ground cinnamon	7 mL
2	eggs	2
2 cups	skim or 1% milk	500 mL
1 tbsp	packed brown sugar	15 mL
1½ tsp	vanilla	7 mL
2	large apples, cored and diced	2
	Vanilla frozen yogurt	

1. Place half of the toasted bread slices in prepared baking dish.
2. In a small bowl, mix together sugar and cinnamon.
3. In a medium bowl, whisk eggs, milk, brown sugar and vanilla until well blended.
4. Sprinkle half of the cinnamon mixture and half of the apples over toasted bread in baking dish. Repeat the layers. Spoon egg mixture over top.
5. Bake, uncovered, in preheated oven for 45 to 55 minutes or until set and a knife inserted in the center comes out clean and dry. Set aside to cool slightly on a wire rack, then cut into squares. When ready to serve, top each square with a scoop of frozen yogurt.

• •

Slow Cooker Apple Bread Pudding

Serves 8 to 10
- Slow cooker, greased

8	slices raisin bread, cut into cubes (about 5 cups/1.25 mL)	8
2	tart apples, peeled and sliced	2
1 cup	chopped pecans, toasted	250 mL
1 cup	granulated sugar	250 mL
1½ tsp	ground cinnamon	7 mL
½ tsp	ground nutmeg	2 mL
3	eggs, beaten	3
2 cups	half-and-half (10%) cream	500 mL
¼ cup	butter or margarine, melted	50 mL
¼ cup	unsweetened apple juice	50 mL

1. In a large bowl, combine bread cubes, apples and pecans. Mix well to blend. Spoon into prepared slow cooker.
2. In the same bowl, combine sugar, cinnamon and nutmeg, mixing to blend. Add eggs, cream, butter and apple juice, mixing until thoroughly blended. Spoon over bread mixture.
3. Cook, covered, on low setting for 3 to 4 hours or until a knife inserted in the center comes out clean and dry. Serve warm or cold.

Apples 'n' Cheese Bread Pudding

Serves 4 to 6

- Preheat oven to 350°F (180°C)
- 6-cup (1.5 L) casserole dish, greased

2 tbsp	butter or margarine	25 mL
4	slices white bread, cut into cubes (about 3 cups/750 mL)	4
1	tart apple, peeled and thinly sliced	1
1 cup	shredded Monterey Jack cheese (about 4 oz/125 g)	250 mL
1/4 cup	raisins (optional)	50 mL
1 cup	milk	250 mL
1/4 cup	packed brown sugar	50 mL
1/2 tsp	ground cinnamon	2 mL
2	eggs, beaten	2

1. In a skillet, on low heat, melt butter. Add bread cubes and mix to coat cubes with butter. Cook, stirring, until cubes are toasted to a golden brown.

2. Spoon bread cubes into prepared casserole dish with the apple slices, cheese and raisins (if using) and mix together thoroughly.

3. In the same skillet, combine milk with brown sugar and cinnamon and scald (see tip, page 511). Remove from heat.

4. In a small bowl, whisk eggs. Pour the scalded milk mixture into the eggs, then spoon the egg mixture over the bread mixture.

5. Bake in preheated oven for 50 to 60 minutes or until browned and firm to the touch. Let cool on a wire rack.

Apple Raisin Bread Pudding

Serves 6 to 8

- Preheat oven to 375°F (190°C)
- 8- by 4-inch (1.5 L) glass loaf pan, ungreased

7	slices raisin bread, toasted	7
1	can (19 oz/540 mL) apple pie filling	1

1. Remove crusts from bread and cut 1 slice into 3 strips.

2. Line the bottom of the loaf pan with 2 slices of bread and 1 strip of bread. Spoon about 2/3 cup (150 mL) of the apple pie filling over top. Repeat with two more layers.

3. Bake in preheated oven for 40 to 45 minutes or until browned. Serve warm.

Tip *Serve with your favorite sauce (see Sauces, pages 553–555).*

Apple Pie Raisin Bread Pudding

Serves 8 to 12

- Preheat oven to 350°F (180°C)
- 12-cup (3 L) casserole dish, buttered

3	eggs, well beaten	3
1	can (14 oz/398 mL) evaporated milk	1
1 cup	milk	250 mL
3/4 cup	granulated sugar	175 mL
1/2 tsp	ground cinnamon	2 mL
1/4 tsp	ground nutmeg	1 mL
1	can (19 oz/540 mL) apple pie filling	1
6 cups	fresh bread crumbs (about 12 slices)	1.5 L
1 cup	raisins	250 mL

1. In prepared dish, combine eggs, evaporated milk, milk, sugar, cinnamon and nutmeg. Add pie filling, bread crumbs and raisins and mix thoroughly. Set aside for about 10 minutes to allow bread crumbs to become saturated.

2. Bake in preheated oven for 40 to 45 minutes or until golden brown and a knife inserted in the center comes out clean and dry. Let cool on a wire rack.

Applesauce Bread Pudding

Serves 8

- Preheat oven to 325°F (160°C)
- 11- by 7-inch (2 L) baking dish, greased

10	slices French bread (or other), cut into cubes (about 6 cups/1.5 L), divided	10
1	jar (28 oz/796 mL) chunky-style sweetened applesauce	1
Pinch	ground nutmeg	Pinch
2	eggs	2
2 cups	milk	500 mL
1/2 cup	granulated sugar	125 mL
1/2 tsp	vanilla	2 mL
1/2 tsp	ground cinnamon	2 mL

1. Spoon half the bread cubes into prepared baking dish. Spoon applesauce over top and sprinkle with nutmeg. Top with the remaining bread cubes.

2. In a medium bowl, whisk eggs, milk, sugar and vanilla until well blended. Spoon over bread and sprinkle cinnamon over top.

3. Bake, uncovered, in preheated oven for 50 to 60 minutes or until a knife inserted near the center comes out clean and dry. Let cool on a wire rack.

Baked Pear Bread Pudding

Serves 6

- Preheat oven to 350°F (180°C)
- 8-inch (2 L) square baking pan, greased

6	slices day-old egg or French bread, cut into cubes (about 4 cups/1 L)	6
1 cup	peeled and chopped ripe pears (about 1 medium)	250 mL
¼ cup	raisins or dried cranberries (optional)	50 mL
2	eggs, beaten	2
2	cans (each 14 oz/398 mL) evaporated milk	2
⅔ cup	firmly packed brown sugar	150 mL
4 tsp	vanilla	20 mL
2 tsp	ground cinnamon	10 mL
½ tsp	ground nutmeg	2 mL
½ tsp	salt	2 mL

1. Place bread cubes, pears and raisins (if using) into prepared baking pan.
2. In a medium bowl, whisk together eggs, milk, brown sugar, vanilla, cinnamon, nutmeg and salt, beating until well blended. Spoon over bread mixture and toss lightly to coat. Let stand for 5 to 8 minutes or until liquid is absorbed. Press down on bread cubes with a spatula to make sure all of the liquid has been absorbed.
3. Bake in preheated oven for 45 to 55 minutes or until firm and golden brown on top. Serve warm.

Creamy Blueberry Bread Pudding

Serves 6

- 8-cup (2 L) casserole dish, greased

4	slices day-old Italian bread (or French, brioche or other), cut into cubes (about 3 cups/750 mL)	4
2	egg yolks	2
½ cup	whipping (35%) cream	125 mL
6 tbsp	milk	90 mL
¼ cup	granulated sugar	50 mL
¼ cup	butter or margarine, melted	50 mL
½ tsp	ground cinnamon	2 mL
½ tsp	vanilla	2 mL
¼ tsp	ground nutmeg	1 mL
1 cup	fresh or frozen blueberries (about 6 oz/175 g)	250 mL
	Sifted confectioner's (icing) sugar	

1. Place bread cubes into prepared casserole dish.
2. In a large bowl, whisk egg yolks, whipping cream, milk, sugar, butter, cinnamon, vanilla and nutmeg until thoroughly blended. Add blueberries and stir until blended. Spoon over bread cubes, cover tightly with plastic wrap and chill in refrigerator for 30 minutes. Meanwhile, preheat oven to 350°F (180°C).
3. Bake, uncovered, in preheated oven for 25 to 30 minutes or until golden brown and a knife inserted in the center comes out clean and dry. Sprinkle with confectioner's sugar.

Cornbread Cranberry Bread Pudding

Serves 6 to 8

- Preheat oven to 350°F (180°C)
- 6-cup (1.5 L) casserole dish, greased

8	slices cornbread (or other), cut into cubes (about 5 cups/1.25 L)	8
2	eggs	2
1 cup	whole-berry cranberry sauce	250 mL
2 tsp	grated orange zest	10 mL
1 cup	freshly squeezed orange juice	250 mL
1 cup	milk	250 mL
½ cup	granulated sugar	125 mL
½ cup	chopped walnuts	125 mL
½ tsp	ground cardamom	2 mL
½ tsp	vanilla	2 mL
¼ tsp	ground ginger	1 mL

1. Place cornbread cubes into prepared casserole dish.
2. In a large bowl, whisk eggs, then stir in cranberry sauce, orange zest, orange juice, milk, sugar, walnuts, cardamom, vanilla and ginger. Mix well until thoroughly combined. Pour over cornbread cubes and mix well, tossing to coat cubes. Let stand for 15 to 20 minutes, stirring occasionally, until liquid is absorbed.
3. Bake in preheated oven for 45 to 50 minutes or until golden brown and a knife inserted in the center comes out clean and dry. Let cool on a wire rack.

Raspberry Bread Pudding

Serves 6

Preheat oven to 400°F (200°C)

6-cup (1.5 L) casserole dish, buttered

6	slices day-old French bread (or other), crusts removed, cut into cubes (about 4 cups/1 L)	6
3	eggs	3
½ cup	granulated sugar	125 mL
2 cups	milk	500 mL
1 cup	fresh or frozen, partially thawed raspberries (about 6 oz/175 g)	250 mL
1 tbsp	butter or margarine, cut into small chunks	15 mL
	Additional granulated sugar	

1. Arrange bread cubes in prepared casserole dish.
2. In a small mixer bowl, on medium speed, beat eggs until foamy. Beat in sugar and then add milk and beat until well blended. Pour over bread in casserole dish. Place spoonfuls of the raspberries in several places over egg mixture. Press down with a spatula until bread is well moistened. Dot with butter and sprinkle with granulated sugar.
3. Bake in preheated oven for 40 to 50 minutes or until a knife inserted in the center comes out clean and dry. Serve warm or at room temperature.

Tip *Serve with whipped topping or your favorite sauce (see Sauces, pages 553–555).*

Strawberry Apricot Bread Pudding

Serves 6 to 8

- Preheat oven to 350°F (180°C)
- 8-cup (2 L) casserole dish, buttered
- 13- by 9-inch (3 L) baking pan

10	slices white bread (or other), cut into cubes (about 6 cups/1.5 L)	10
2	eggs	2
2	egg yolks	2
¾ cup	granulated sugar, divided	175 mL
1 tbsp	butter or margarine, melted	15 mL
2 tsp	vanilla	10 mL
½ tsp	ground cinnamon	2 mL
Pinch	salt	Pinch
4 cups	milk	1 L
2	egg whites	2
1 cup	apricot preserves, divided	250 mL
½ cup	strawberry preserves	125 mL

1. Place bread cubes in prepared casserole dish.
2. In a large bowl, whisk eggs, egg yolks, ½ cup (125 mL) of the sugar, butter, vanilla, cinnamon and salt until blended. Stir in milk. Pour over bread cubes in casserole dish. Let stand for 15 to 20 minutes or until bread has absorbed milk mixture. Place casserole dish in baking pan set on oven rack and pour in boiling water to a depth of about 1 inch (2.5 cm).
3. Bake in preheated oven for 45 to 50 minutes or until center is almost set and a knife inserted near the edge comes out clean and dry.
4. Meanwhile, in a small mixer bowl, on high speed, beat the egg whites until foamy. Add the remaining sugar, 1 tbsp (15 mL) at a time, beating until stiff peaks form.
5. Remove casserole dish from pan and spoon half the apricot preserves over the hot pudding. With a pastry bag, press puffs of the beaten egg white mixture on top of pudding, close together so that no pudding is visible. Place back in baking pan and bake for another 10 minutes or until the peaks of the egg whites are golden brown. Set aside to cool completely on a wire rack.
6. In a small saucepan, over low heat, melt the remaining apricot preserves. In another small saucepan, over low heat, melt the strawberry preserves. Strain each through a sieve and set aside to cool slightly. When ready to serve, drizzle some of each melted preserve over top of the pudding.

Touch of Lemon Bread Pudding

Serves 6

- Preheat oven to 350°F (180°C)
- Baking sheet
- 6-cup (1.5 L) casserole dish, buttered
- 13- by 9-inch (3 L) baking pan

6	slices day-old bread, cut into cubes (about 4 cups/1 L)	6
3	eggs, lightly beaten	3
3 cups	milk	750 mL
½ cup	granulated sugar	125 mL
½ cup	raisins	125 mL
2 tbsp	butter or margarine, melted	25 mL
¼ tsp	salt	1 mL
	Grated zest of 1 lemon	
	Ground nutmeg	

1. Arrange bread cubes on baking sheet in a single layer. Bake in preheated oven for 10 minutes to dry them.

2. In a large bowl, combine eggs, milk, sugar, raisins, butter, salt and zest. Mix well until sugar is dissolved.

3. Place bread cubes in a large bowl. Pour milk mixture over top and mix well. Let stand for 10 minutes to soak. Spoon into prepared casserole dish. Sprinkle nutmeg over top. Place casserole dish in baking pan set on oven rack and pour in hot water to a depth of about 1 inch (2.5 cm).

4. Bake, uncovered, in preheated oven for 55 to 60 minutes or until set and a knife inserted in the center comes out clean and dry. Remove casserole dish from pan and set aside to cool slightly on a wire rack. Serve warm.

Orange Marmalade Bread Pudding

Serves 6

- Preheat oven to 300°F (150°C)
- 6-cup (1.5 L) casserole dish, ungreased
- 13- by 9-inch (3 L) baking pan

6	slices white bread (about 4 cups/1 L)	6
	Butter or margarine for spreading	
	Orange marmalade for spreading	
2	eggs	2
¼ cup	granulated sugar	50 mL
3 cups	milk, scalded (see tip, page 511)	750 mL
Pinch	salt	Pinch

1. Spread each bread slice with butter, then marmalade. Cut the slices into cubes or finger-length pieces and place them in casserole dish.

2. In a medium bowl, whisk eggs and sugar until sugar is blended and dissolved. Add scalded milk and salt and whisk to blend. Pour over the bread pieces, mixing thoroughly to coat bread. Place casserole dish in baking pan set on oven rack and pour in hot water until it reaches halfway up the sides of casserole dish.

3. Bake in preheated oven for 40 to 50 minutes or until pudding is firm in the center and golden brown. Remove casserole dish from pan and set aside to cool slightly on a wire rack. Serve warm or cold.

Variation *Use any flavor of marmalade or jam you prefer.*

Peaches 'n' Cream Bread Pudding

Serves 6

- Preheat oven to 350°F (180°C)
- 6-cup (1.5 L) casserole dish, greased
- 13- by 9-inch (3 L) baking pan

2 tbsp	granulated sugar	25 mL
2 tsp	ground cinnamon	10 mL
2 cups	canned peaches, drained and diced	500 mL
3½ cups	whipping (35%) cream	875 mL
½ cup	half-and-half (10%) cream	125 mL
6	eggs	6
1 cup	granulated sugar	250 mL
1 tbsp	vanilla	15 mL
1 tsp	ground cinnamon	5 mL
Pinch	ground nutmeg	Pinch
4	slices egg bread (challah, sourdough, or French), cut into cubes (about 3 cups/750 mL)	4
½ cup	raisins (optional)	125 mL

1. In a medium bowl, mix together the 2 tbsp (25 mL) sugar and cinnamon until blended. Add peaches and toss to coat.

2. In a large saucepan, over low heat, mix together whipping cream and half-and-half cream, stirring constantly, until simmering.

3. In a large bowl, whisk eggs. Spoon a little of the heated cream slowly into the eggs, whisking well so the mixture does not curdle, then stir in the remaining cream. Stir in the 1 cup (250 mL) sugar, vanilla, cinnamon and nutmeg. Mix well.

4. Put bread cubes, peach mixture and raisins (if using) into prepared casserole dish. Pour the cream mixture over top and let stand for 15 minutes or until cream has completely soaked into the bread. Place casserole dish in baking pan set on oven rack and pour in hot water until it reaches halfway up the sides of casserole dish.

5. Bake in preheated oven for 45 to 50 minutes or until browned and firm. Remove casserole dish from pan and set aside to cool on a wire rack. Serve warm.

Banana Bread Pudding

Serves 6 to 8
- Preheat oven to 375°F (190°C)
- 8-cup (2 L) casserole dish, greased

¼ cup	butter or margarine, melted	50 mL
6	slices day-old sourdough bread (or French or other), cut into cubes (about 4 cups/1 L)	6
3	eggs, lightly beaten	3
2 cups	milk	500 mL
½ cup	granulated sugar	125 mL
2 tsp	vanilla	10 mL
1 tsp	ground cinnamon	5 mL
¼ tsp	ground nutmeg	1 mL
¼ tsp	salt	1 mL
1	firm banana, sliced	1

1. In a medium bowl, toss together butter and bread cubes. Pour into prepared casserole dish.

2. In the same bowl, combine eggs, milk, sugar, vanilla, cinnamon, nutmeg and salt. Mix thoroughly to blend, then gently add the banana and fold to combine. Spoon mixture over bread cubes and stir gently, just enough to coat bread.

3. Bake, uncovered, in preheated oven for 40 to 45 minutes or until firm and a knife inserted in the center comes out clean and dry. Let cool slightly on a wire rack.

Tip *Serve warm with whipped topping or your favorite sauce (see Sauces, pages 553–555).*

Variation *Mash a ripe banana and mix it in with the milk mixture.*

Fresh Fruit Bread Pudding

Serves 4 to 6
- Preheat oven to 350°F (180°C)
- 6-cup (1.5 L) soufflé dish or baking dish, greased

4	slices white bread (or other), cut into cubes (about 3 cups/750 mL)	4
1 cup	fresh raspberries (about 6 oz/175 g)	250 mL
1 cup	fresh blueberries (about 6 oz/175 g) or any other fruit	250 mL
2	eggs	2
1 cup	milk	250 mL
2 tbsp	packed brown sugar	25 mL
	Whipped topping or ice cream	

1. In a large bowl, mix together bread cubes, raspberries and blueberries. Toss together well and pour into prepared soufflé dish.

2. In a small bowl, whisk together eggs, milk and brown sugar. Pour over bread and fruit mixture.

3. Bake in preheated oven for 20 to 30 minutes or until a knife inserted in the center comes out clean. Let cool on a wire rack and serve with whipped topping or ice cream.

Rhubarb Puff Pudding

Serves 6 to 8
- Preheat oven to 350°F (180°C)
- 11- by 7-inch (2 L) baking dish, greased

8	slices day-old French bread, cut into cubes (about 5 cups/1.25 L)	8
3 cups	sliced fresh or frozen rhubarb (about 15 oz/450 g)	750 mL
3	eggs	3
1	can (14 oz/398 mL) evaporated milk	1
1 cup	water	250 mL
½ cup	granulated sugar	125 mL
1 tsp	grated orange zest	5 mL
1 tsp	ground cinnamon	5 mL
1 tsp	vanilla	5 mL
¼ cup	packed brown sugar	50 mL
	Whipped cream	

1. Place bread cubes and rhubarb in prepared baking dish and mix together to blend.

2. In a large bowl, whisk together eggs, evaporated milk, water, sugar, zest, cinnamon and vanilla until thoroughly combined. Pour evenly over bread mixture and let stand for 10 to 15 minutes or until bread has absorbed egg mixture.

3. Bake in preheated oven for 50 to 60 minutes or until set and a knife inserted in center comes out clean and dry. Remove from oven and sprinkle brown sugar evenly over top. Put under broiler and broil for 1 to 2 minutes or until brown sugar melts and the top is golden brown. Watch very closely. Serve warm with whipped cream.

Tip *Leftover whipped cream will retain its lightness and texture for a day or more, refrigerated, if you add 1 tsp (5 mL) light corn syrup to each ½ pint cream. You won't notice any more sweetness with this addition.*

Cinnamon Raisin Bread Pudding

Serves 12 to 16

- Preheat oven to 350°F (180°C)
- 13- by 9-inch (3 L) glass baking dish, greased

6	eggs	6
8 cups	milk	2 L
½ cup	granulated sugar	125 mL
2 tbsp	vanilla	25 mL
1½ tbsp	ground cinnamon	22 mL
½ tsp	ground nutmeg	2 mL
1½	loaves (each 1 lb/450 g) cinnamon raisin bread	1½
2 tbsp	pure maple syrup	25 mL

1. In a large bowl, whisk together eggs, milk, sugar, vanilla, cinnamon and nutmeg.
2. Arrange 8 slices of bread in the bottom of prepared baking dish. Cut each remaining slice of bread diagonally in half and place in baking dish, overlapping slices.
3. Spoon egg mixture evenly over bread and press down with a spatula. Set aside for 15 to 20 minutes or until bread slices have absorbed most of the egg mixture.
4. Bake in preheated oven for 50 to 60 minutes or until golden brown, set and a knife inserted in the center comes out clean and dry. If topping begins to brown too quickly, cover loosely with a piece of foil for the last 15 minutes of baking.
5. Brush the top of the pudding with maple syrup and serve warm, or chill in refrigerator for 3 to 4 hours or overnight and serve cold.

Pumpkin Bread Puddings

Serves 4

- Bake at 350°F (180°C)
- Four ¾-cup (175 mL) custard cups or ramekins, greased
- 13- by 9-inch (3 L) baking pan

1	egg	1
1 cup	table (18%) or half-and-half (10%) cream	250 mL
¾ cup	cooked pumpkin purée, cooled	175 mL
⅓ cup	packed brown sugar	75 mL
1 tsp	ground cinnamon	5 mL
½ tsp	vanilla	2 mL
¼ tsp	ground nutmeg	1 mL
5	slices raisin bread, cut into cubes (about 3½ cups/875 mL)	5

1. In a large bowl, whisk together egg, cream, pumpkin, brown sugar, cinnamon, vanilla and nutmeg until thoroughly combined.
2. Stir in bread cubes and toss together with egg mixture to coat. Let stand for 5 to 10 minutes or until bread softens slightly and has absorbed egg mixture. Spoon into prepared baking cups. Place cups in baking pan set on oven rack and pour in hot water until it reaches halfway up the sides of cups.
3. Bake in preheated oven for 20 to 25 minutes or until a knife inserted into the center comes out clean and dry. Remove cups from pan and set aside to cool on a wire rack. Serve warm or cold.

Tip *Serve with whipped topping, ice cream or your favorite sauce (see Sauces, pages 553–555).*

Old-Time Tomato Bread Pudding

Serves 6

- Preheat oven to 375°F (190°C)
- 8-cup (2 L) glass casserole dish, lightly greased
- 13- by 9-inch (3 L) baking pan

2 cups	canned diced tomatoes	500 mL
½ cup	firmly packed brown sugar	125 mL
½ cup	water	125 mL
1 tbsp	freshly squeezed lemon juice	15 mL
¼ tsp	salt	1 mL
Pinch	freshly ground black pepper	Pinch
6	slices white bread (or French or sourdough), cut into cubes (about 4 cups/1 L)	6
⅔ cup	butter or margarine, melted	150 mL

1. In a medium saucepan, over medium-low heat, combine tomatoes, brown sugar, water, lemon juice, salt and pepper. Simmer, covered, for 5 to 6 minutes.
2. Spread bread cubes evenly in prepared casserole dish. Spoon melted butter over bread cubes and mix together until well combined. Pour tomato mixture over bread, but do not stir. Place casserole dish in baking pan set on oven rack and pour in hot water until it reaches halfway up the sides of casserole dish.
3. Bake in preheated oven for 55 to 60 minutes or until top of pudding is browned. Remove casserole dish from pan and serve immediately.

Tip *If you prefer, you can purée the tomatoes before adding them to the saucepan.*

Special Sage Bread Pudding

Serves 6 to 8
- Preheat oven to 350°F (180°C)
- 9- or 10-inch (23 or 25 cm) pie plate, lightly greased

6	slices day-old bread, cut into cubes (about 4 cups/1 L)	6
1 to 2 tbsp	vegetable oil	15 to 25 mL
1	stalk celery, chopped	1
1	onion, peeled and chopped	1
1	clove garlic, minced	1
1 tbsp	chopped fresh sage (or 1½ tsp/7 mL dried)	15 mL
½ tsp	salt	2 mL
¼ tsp	freshly ground black pepper	1 mL
2 cups	sliced mushrooms (optional)	500 mL
3	eggs, lightly beaten	3
1½ cups	vegetable or chicken broth	375 mL
2	green onions, thinly sliced	2

1. Spread bread cubes evenly in prepared pie plate. Set aside.
2. In a skillet, over low heat, heat 1 tbsp (15 mL) oil. Add celery, onion, garlic, sage, salt and pepper. Cook, stirring, for about 5 minutes. Increase heat to medium-high. If you are using mushrooms, add another 1 tbsp (15 mL) of oil, then mushrooms, and mix together well. Cook for about 5 minutes, until browned. Pour over bread cubes.
3. In a small bowl, whisk eggs and broth. Spoon over bread cubes. Spread green onions over top.
4. Bake in preheated oven for 40 to 50 minutes or until golden brown and a knife inserted near the edge comes out clean and dry. Let stand for about 15 minutes before slicing and serving.

Bacon and Egg Bread Pudding

Serves 8 to 10
- 12-cup (3 L) casserole dish, buttered

8	English muffins, split in half, toasted and buttered	8
5	thin slices Swiss cheese, cut in half crosswise	5
10	thin slices American cheese	10
10	slices Canadian-style bacon	10
6	eggs	6
3 cups	milk	750 mL
¼ tsp	salt	1 mL
Pinch	freshly ground black pepper	Pinch
	Chopped fresh parsley	

1. On a cutting board, place 5 muffin halves, split side up. Make sandwiches with 1 Swiss cheese slice, 1 American cheese slice and 1 slice of bacon and top with another half muffin, split side down. Cut each sandwich in half.
2. Place the remaining 6 muffin halves, split side up, on the bottom of prepared casserole dish, cutting to fit. Chop the remaining bacon and sprinkle over arranged muffin halves. Top with the remaining cheese slices, alternating slices and overlapping.
3. Place sandwich halves over cheeses, overlapping slightly with the cut sides facing down. Be sure to keep the sandwiches intact.
4. In a large bowl, whisk together eggs, milk, salt and pepper. Pour over sandwiches, spreading evenly and pressing sandwiches with a spatula or the back of a wooden spoon so that the egg mixture is absorbed. Cover tightly with foil and chill in refrigerator for at least 3 hours or until ready to bake. Meanwhile, preheat oven to 350°F (180°C).
5. Bake, uncovered, in preheated oven for 50 to 60 minutes or until nicely browned. Garnish with parsley. Let stand for 15 minutes before serving.

Spinach and Cheese Bread Pudding

Serves 8
- Preheat oven to 375°F (190°C)
- 13- by 9-inch (3 L) baking dish, lightly greased

6	eggs	6
2 cups	1% milk	500 mL
¼ tsp	dried thyme	1 mL
¼ tsp	salt	1 mL
¼ tsp	freshly ground black pepper	1 mL
Pinch	ground nutmeg	Pinch
8	slices firm white bread (or egg bread), cut into cubes (about 5 cups/1.25 L)	8
1	package (10 oz/300 g) frozen spinach, thawed, squeezed dry and chopped	1
1 cup	shredded Monterey Jack cheese	250 mL

1. In a large bowl, whisk together eggs, milk, thyme, salt, pepper and nutmeg. Carefully fold in bread cubes, spinach and cheese until well incorporated. Spoon into prepared baking dish.
2. Bake in preheated oven for 25 minutes or until golden brown, puffed and a knife inserted in the center comes out clean and dry. Let stand for 5 to 10 minutes and serve warm.

Steamed Puddings

These puddings require a little more effort, but they are well worth it. People used to make steamed puddings mainly on holidays, but all of the many different kinds are delicious and can be enjoyed all year round.

Steamed pudding is made in a well-buttered or oiled pudding mold, or in a container of your choice, such as an ovenproof bowl. The mold should not be filled to the top, but about three-quarters full to allow room for expansion. The mold must be covered; if your mold does not have a cover, use a double thickness of foil and tie it down with a string.

In most recipes, the mold is set into a large pot, such as a Dutch oven, with a tightly fitting cover. Set the pot on a burner and place the covered mold in the pot, raised slightly with a rack, a canning jar ring or crumpled-up foil shaped like a small round plate placed beneath it. Pour boiling water into the pot until it reaches halfway up the sides of the mold. Let the water in the pot boil gently, over low heat, and follow the instructions in the recipe.

Steamed Bread Pudding

Serves 8 to 10
- Preheat oven to 350°F (180°C)
- 8-cup (2 L) pudding mold, well buttered or oiled
- 13- by 9-inch (3 L) baking pan

5	eggs, beaten	5
2 cups	milk, divided	500 mL
1/3 cup	pure maple syrup	75 mL
1/3 cup	unsweetened apple juice	75 mL
1/4 tsp	ground nutmeg	1 mL
10	slices white bread (or other), cut into cubes (about 6 cups/1.5 L)	10
6	dates, pitted and chopped	6
1/2 cup	raisins	125 mL

1. In a medium bowl, combine eggs, half the milk, syrup, apple juice and nutmeg, whisking until blended and smooth.
2. In a small saucepan, scald the remaining milk (see tip, at right). Stir into the egg mixture.
3. Put bread cubes, dates and raisins into prepared mold, filling about three-quarters full, and toss well to coat. Spoon in the milk mixture and press down lightly with a spatula to make sure bread mixture is coated. Place mold in baking pan set on oven rack and pour in boiling water until it reaches halfway up the sides of mold. Cover pan loosely with foil.

4. Bake in preheated oven for 55 to 60 minutes or until set. Remove mold from pan and set on a wire rack to cool, then loosen sides of pudding with a knife and invert onto a serving plate. Cut into slices and serve warm.

Tip *Milk, cream and sour cream are scalded when bubbles form around the edge of the pan as you heat it.*

Buttermilk Crumb Pudding

Serves 4 to 6
- 6-cup (1.5 L) pudding mold, well buttered or oiled
- Large pot

1 cup	granulated sugar	250 mL
3 tbsp	butter or shortening	45 mL
2 cups	fresh bread crumbs, toasted	500 mL
1 cup	raisins	250 mL
1 1/2 tsp	ground nutmeg	7 mL
1 cup	buttermilk or sour cream	250 mL
1 tsp	baking soda	5 mL

1. In a large mixer bowl, cream sugar and butter until light and fluffy. Stir in bread crumbs, raisins and nutmeg, mixing until well blended.
2. In a small bowl, mix together buttermilk and baking soda until smooth. Pour into creamed mixture and mix thoroughly. Spoon into prepared mold, filling about three-quarters full, and cover.
3. Place mold onto a rack set in large pot and pour boiling water into pot until it reaches halfway up the sides of mold. Cover pot. Keep water boiling over low heat and steam pudding for 45 to 50 minutes or until pudding is firm to the touch and a knife or wooden skewer inserted in the center comes out clean and dry. Be sure water is at a continuous low boil.
4. Remove mold from pot and set on a wire rack to cool, then loosen sides of pudding with a knife and invert onto a serving plate. Cut into slices and serve warm.

Tip *Serve with whipped cream or your favorite sauce (see Sauces, pages 553–555).*

Steamed Coffee Pudding

Serves 6

- 6-cup (1.5 L) pudding mold, well buttered or oiled
- Large pot

½ cup	granulated sugar	125 mL
½ cup	butter or margarine, softened	125 mL
2	eggs, beaten	2
1½ cups	all-purpose flour	375 mL
½ cup	raisins	125 mL
¼ cup	strong brewed coffee	50 mL
1 tbsp	milk	15 mL
1½ tsp	baking powder	7 mL

1. In a large mixer bowl, on medium speed, cream sugar and butter until light and smooth. Beat in the eggs until light and fluffy. Stir in flour, raisins, coffee, milk and baking powder until well blended. Pour into prepared mold, filling three-quarters full, and cover.

2. Place mold onto a rack set in large pot and pour boiling water into pot until it reaches halfway up the sides of mold. Cover pot. Keep water boiling over low heat and steam pudding for 1 to 1½ hours or until pudding is firm to the touch and a knife or wooden skewer inserted in the center comes out clean and dry. Be sure water is at a continuous low boil.

3. Remove mold from pot and set on a wire rack to cool slightly (about 10 minutes), then loosen sides of pudding with a knife and invert onto a serving plate. Cut into slices and serve warm.

Graham Wafer Steamed Pudding

Serves 6

- Six ¾-cup (175 mL) custard cups, well buttered or oiled
- Large pot

2 cups	graham wafer crumbs (about 24 wafers)	500 mL
1 tsp	baking powder	5 mL
Pinch	salt	Pinch
⅓ cup	granulated sugar	75 mL
¼ cup	shortening or butter, softened	50 mL
1	egg, separated	1
1 tsp	vanilla	5 mL
⅔ cup	milk	150 mL

1. In a medium bowl, mix together wafer crumbs, baking powder and salt until well blended.

2. In a large mixer bowl, on medium speed, cream sugar and shortening. Add egg yolk and vanilla, beating until well blended. Stir in crumb mixture alternately with the milk, mixing thoroughly.

3. In a small mixer bowl, on high speed, beat the egg white until stiff peaks form. Fold into mixture. Spoon mixture evenly into prepared custard cups and cover tightly with aluminum foil.

4. Place cups onto a rack set in large pot and pour boiling water into pot up to the level of the rack. Make sure water is not touching cups. Cover pot. Keep water boiling gently over low heat and steam puddings for 30 minutes or until puddings are firm to the touch and a knife or wooden skewer inserted in the center comes out clean and dry. Be sure water is at a continuous low boil.

5. Remove cups from pot and set on a wire rack to cool slightly (about 10 minutes), then loosen sides of puddings with a knife and invert cups into glass serving dishes. Serve warm.

Tip *Serve with whipped topping, ice cream or your favorite sauce (see Sauces, pages 553–555).*

Steamed Chocolate Pudding

Serves 6 to 8

- 6-cup (1.5 L) pudding mold, well buttered or oiled
- Large pot

1 cup	granulated sugar	250 mL
½ cup	butter or margarine, softened	125 mL
2	egg yolks	2
2 cups	all-purpose flour	500 mL
2 tsp	baking powder	10 mL
Pinch	salt	Pinch
½ cup	milk	125 mL
2 oz	unsweetened chocolate	60 g
¼ cup	boiling water	50 mL
2	egg whites	2
1 tsp	vanilla	5 mL

1. In a large mixer bowl, on medium speed, cream sugar and butter until fluffy. Beat in egg yolks until light and fluffy.

2. In a medium bowl, sift together flour, baking powder and salt. Add to creamed mixture alternately with the milk.

3. In a small bowl, melt chocolate in boiling water.

4. In a small mixer bowl, on high speed, beat egg whites until stiff peaks form. Fold melted chocolate, egg whites and vanilla into the creamed mixture until thoroughly blended. Spoon into prepared pudding mold.

5. Place mold onto a rack set in large pot and pour boiling water into pot until it reaches halfway up the sides of mold. Cover pot. Keep water boiling over low heat and steam pudding for 2 hours or until pudding is firm to the touch and a knife or wooden skewer inserted in the center comes out clean and dry. Be sure water is at a continuous low boil.

6. Remove mold from pot and set on a wire rack to cool, then loosen sides of pudding with a knife and invert onto a serving plate. Cut into slices and serve warm.

Applesauce Gingerbread Steamed Pudding

Serves 10

- Ten ¾-cup (175 mL) custard cups, well buttered or oiled
- Large pot

1	package (14½ oz/400 g) gingerbread cake mix	1
1 cup	sweetened applesauce	250 mL
¼ cup	water	50 mL
1 cup	raisins	250 mL
	Warmed applesauce or whipped topping	

1. In a large mixer bowl, on medium speed, combine gingerbread mix, applesauce and water, beating for about 2 to 3 minutes or until well blended, scraping sides of bowl often. Stir in raisins. Spoon mixture evenly into prepared custard cups and cover tightly with aluminum foil.

2. Place cups onto a rack set in large pot and pour boiling water into pot up to the level of the rack. Make sure water is not touching cups. Cover pot. Keep water boiling gently over low heat and steam puddings for 30 minutes or until puddings are firm to the touch and a knife or wooden skewer inserted in the center comes out clean and dry. Be sure water is at a continuous low boil.

3. Remove cups from pot and set on a wire rack to cool slightly (about 10 minutes), then loosen sides of puddings with a knife and invert cups into glass serving dishes. Serve warm with some warmed applesauce or whipped topping.

Tip *If gingerbread cake mix is not available, substitute 1 package (18 oz/510 g) spice cake mix. The flavor will be a little more mild.*

Christmas Pudding

Serves 12 to 16

- 10-cup (2.5 L) pudding mold, well buttered or oiled
- Large pot

3	eggs, well beaten	3
2 cups	ground suet	500 mL
1 cup	firmly packed brown sugar	250 mL
⅓ cup	currant jelly	75 mL
¼ cup	fruit juice	50 mL
1 cup	all-purpose flour	250 mL
1½ tsp	ground cinnamon	7 mL
1 tsp	salt	5 mL
1 tsp	baking soda	5 mL
¾ tsp	ground mace	4 mL
¼ tsp	ground nutmeg	1 mL
1½ cups	fresh or dry bread crumbs	375 mL
1½ cups	raisins, cut up	375 mL
1½ cups	currants	375 mL
¾ cup	finely chopped candied citron	175 mL
½ cup	finely chopped walnuts	125 mL
⅓ cup	candied orange peel	75 mL
⅓ cup	candied lemon peel	75 mL

1. In a large bowl, combine eggs, suet, brown sugar, jelly and fruit juice. Set aside.

2. In another large bowl, combine flour, cinnamon, salt, baking soda, mace and nutmeg. Mix well to blend. Stir in bread crumbs, raisins, currants, citron, walnuts, orange peel and lemon peel. Add egg mixture and mix thoroughly until well blended. Spoon into prepared pudding mold, filling three-quarters full, and cover.

3. Place mold onto a rack set in large pot and pour boiling water into pot up to the level of the rack. Cover pot. Keep water boiling over low heat and steam pudding for 3 to 4 hours or until pudding is firm to the touch and a knife or wooden skewer inserted in the center comes out clean and dry. Be sure water is at a continuous low boil.

4. Remove mold from pot and set on a wire rack to cool slightly (about 10 minutes), then loosen sides of pudding with a knife and invert onto a serving plate. Cut into slices and serve warm.

Tip *Serve with your favorite sauce (see Sauces, pages 553–555).*

Steamed Apple Carrot Pudding

Serves 8 to 10

- 8-cup (2 L) pudding mold, well buttered or oiled
- Large pot

1	egg, lightly beaten	1
½ cup	granulated sugar or packed brown sugar	125 mL
½ cup	butter or shortening	125 mL
½ cup	grated carrot	125 mL
½ cup	grated potato	125 mL
½ cup	peeled, cored and grated apple	125 mL
	Grated lemon zest (optional)	
1½ tbsp	freshly squeezed lemon juice	22 mL
1⅔ cups	all-purpose flour, divided	400 mL
1 tsp	baking powder	5 mL
1 tsp	ground cinnamon	5 mL
½ tsp	baking soda	2 mL
¼ tsp	ground nutmeg	1 mL
Pinch	salt	Pinch
½ cup	raisins	125 mL
½ cup	dried fruit, chopped	125 mL
⅓ cup	chopped nuts (almonds or walnuts)	75 mL
1 tbsp	lemon zest (optional)	15 mL

1. In a large mixer bowl, on medium speed, cream egg, sugar and butter, beating until light and fluffy. Stir in carrot, potato, apple and lemon juice and mix well to blend.

2. In a small bowl, sift together 1½ cups (375 mL) flour, baking powder, cinnamon, baking soda, nutmeg and salt. Mix well. Add flour mixture to creamed mixture, mixing until thoroughly blended.

3. In the same small bowl, toss raisins and dried fruit with the remaining flour. Shake off excess flour and add to mixture with nuts and lemon zest (if using). Spoon into prepared mold, filling three-quarters full, and cover.

4. Place mold onto a rack set in large pot and pour boiling water into pot until it reaches halfway up the sides of mold. Cover pot. Keep water boiling over low heat and steam pudding for about 3 hours or until pudding is firm to the touch and a knife or wooden skewer inserted in the center comes out clean and dry. Be sure water is at a continuous low boil.

5. Remove mold from pot and set on a wire rack to cool, then loosen sides of pudding with a knife and invert onto a serving plate. Cut into slices and serve warm.

Traditional Steamed Plum Pudding

Serves 16 to 20

- 10-cup (2.5 L) pudding mold, well buttered or oiled and sprinkled with granulated sugar
- Large pot

⅔ cup	chopped candied citron	150 mL
2 cups	raisins	500 mL
1¾ cups	chopped walnuts	425 mL
1 cup	chopped dried figs	250 mL
1 cup	chopped dried apricots	250 mL
1 cup	chopped pitted dates	250 mL
4	eggs	4
1 cup	firmly packed light brown sugar	250 mL
2½ cups	fresh white bread crumbs (about 5 slices)	625 mL
½ cup	ground suet	250 mL
½ cup	corn syrup or light molasses	125 mL
½ cup	brandy	125 mL
1 cup	all-purpose flour	250 mL
1 tbsp	pumpkin pie spice	15 mL
1 tsp	salt	5 mL

1. In a large bowl, combine citron, raisins, walnuts, figs, apricots and dates.

2. In a large mixer bowl, on high speed, beat eggs and brown sugar until fluffy, about 2 to 3 minutes. Lower speed and mix in bread crumbs, suet, corn syrup and brandy until well blended.

3. In a small bowl, sift together flour, pumpkin pie spice and salt. Stir into egg mixture, mixing well, and pour over the fruits and nuts, mixing until combined and well blended. Tap any excess sugar out of prepared mold, spoon in pudding mixture, filling three-quarters full, and cover.

4. Place mold onto a rack set in large pot and pour boiling water into pot until it reaches halfway up the sides of mold. Cover pot. Keep water boiling gently over low heat and steam for 5 to 6 hours or until pudding is firm to the touch and a knife or wooden skewer inserted into the center comes out clean and dry. Be sure water is at a continuous low boil.

5. Remove mold from pot and set aside to cool in mold for about 30 minutes, then loosen sides of pudding with a knife and invert onto a serving plate. Cut into slices and serve warm.

Tips *You will need about 6 oz (175 g) each of the figs, apricots and dates.*

Serve with your favorite sauce (see Sauces, pages 553–555).

Old-Fashioned Steamed Cranberry Pudding

Serves 8 to 10

- 8-cup (2 L) pudding mold, well buttered or oiled
- Large pot

⅔ cup	granulated sugar	150 mL
2 tbsp	shortening or butter, softened	25 mL
1	egg	1
2 cups	all-purpose flour	500 mL
4 tsp	baking powder	20 mL
Pinch	salt	Pinch
1 cup	milk	250 mL
1 cup	chopped fresh cranberries (about 4 oz/125 g)	250 mL
1 tsp	finely grated orange zest	1 tsp
1	orange, peeled, sectioned and finely chopped	1

1. In a large mixer bowl, on medium speed, cream sugar and shortening. Beat in egg until smooth and fluffy.

2. In a medium bowl, combine flour, baking powder and salt, mixing to blend. Add flour mixture to creamed mixture alternately with the milk, beating on low speed just until incorporated. Gently fold in cranberries, orange zest and orange, stirring until well blended. Pour into prepared pudding mold, filling three-quarters full, and cover.

3. Place mold onto a rack set in large pot and pour boiling water into pot to a depth of 1 inch (2.5 cm). Cover pot. Keep water boiling over low heat and steam for 1 to 1½ hours or until pudding is firm to the touch and a knife or wooden skewer inserted in the center comes out clean and dry. Be sure water is at a continuous low boil.

4. Remove mold from pot and set on a wire rack to cool slightly (about 10 minutes), then loosen sides of pudding with a knife and invert onto a serving plate. Cut into slices and serve warm.

Tip *Serve with whipped cream or your favorite sauce (see Sauces, pages 553–555).*

Special Sliced Jellyroll Pudding

Serves 10 to 12

- 10-cup (2.5 L) heatproof mixing bowl, well buttered or oiled and sprinkled with granulated sugar
- Large pot

1	jellyroll, cut into 7 slices, each ½ inch (1 cm) thick	1
⅓ cup	butter or margarine	75 mL
⅔ cup	sifted all-purpose flour	150 mL
1 cup	milk	250 mL
4	eggs, separated	4
¼ cup	granulated sugar	50 mL
1 tsp	vanilla	5 mL
Pinch	salt	Pinch

1. Tap out any excess sugar from the prepared bowl and line the bottom and sides with jellyroll slices.

2. In a medium saucepan, over low heat, melt butter. Remove from heat and add flour, then stir in milk slowly. Return to heat and cook for 2 to 3 minutes, stirring constantly, until the batter forms a thick, smooth ball that follows the spoon around the pan. Remove from heat. Add egg yolks, one at a time, beating with each addition. Add sugar, vanilla and salt and beat until well blended.

3. In a small mixer bowl, on high speed, beat egg whites until soft peaks form. Fold into the batter until well incorporated. Spoon over top of jelly-roll slices and cover.

4. Place bowl onto a rack set in large pot and pour boiling water into pot to about one-third the depth of the bowl. Cover pot. Keep water boiling gently over low heat and steam pudding for 2 hours or until pudding is firm to the touch and a knife or wooden skewer inserted in the center comes out clean and dry. Be sure water is at a continuous low boil.

5. Remove bowl from pot and let cool in bowl for 5 to 10 minutes, then loosen sides of pudding with a knife and invert onto a serving plate. Cut into slices and serve warm.

Tip *Serve with a favorite sauce, such as lemon sauce (see recipe, page 501).*

Date Nut Steamed Pudding

Serves 6 to 8

- 6-cup (1.5 L) pudding mold, well buttered or oiled
- Large pot

½ cup	granulated sugar	125 mL
3 tbsp	butter or margarine, softened	45 mL
1	egg	1
1 cup	freshly squeezed orange juice	250 mL
¼ cup	orange marmalade	50 mL
1 tbsp	grated lemon zest	15 mL
1 tsp	vanilla	5 mL
1½ cups	sifted all-purpose flour	375 mL
1 tsp	baking powder	5 mL
¾ tsp	baking soda	4 mL
½ tsp	ground cinnamon	2 mL
½ tsp	salt	2 mL
Pinch	ground mace	Pinch
1 cup	chopped pitted dates (about 6 oz/175 g)	250 mL
1 cup	chopped walnuts	250 mL
½ cup	chopped candied cherries (optional)	125 mL

1. In a large mixer bowl, on medium speed, cream together sugar and butter until smooth. Add egg, orange juice, marmalade, lemon zest and vanilla, beating until well combined.
2. In a large bowl, sift together flour, baking powder, baking soda, cinnamon, salt and mace. Mix to blend. Stir in dates, walnuts and cherries (if using). Spoon into egg mixture and mix together until combined. Pour into prepared mold, filling three-quarters full, and cover.
3. Place mold onto a rack set in large pot and pour boiling water into pot until it reaches halfway up the sides of mold. Cover pot. Keep water boiling gently over low heat and steam pudding for 2 to 2½ hours or until pudding is firm to the touch and a knife or wooden skewer inserted in the center comes out clean and dry. Be sure water is at a continuous low boil.
4. Remove mold from pot and set on a wire rack to cool slightly (about 10 minutes), then loosen sides of pudding with a knife and invert onto a serving plate. Cut into slices and serve warm.

Steamed Pumpkin Pie Pudding

Serves 6 to 8

- 8-cup (2 L) pudding mold, well buttered or oiled
- Large pot

1½ cups	all-purpose flour	375 mL
½ cup	instant mashed potato powder	125 mL
2 tsp	pumpkin pie spice	10 mL
1 tsp	salt	5 mL
1 tsp	baking soda	5 mL
¾ cup	firmly packed brown sugar	175 mL
¼ cup	butter or margarine, softened	50 mL
3	eggs, separated	3
1 tsp	grated orange zest	5 mL
1 tsp	vanilla	5 mL
¾ cup	freshly squeezed orange juice	175 mL
1 cup	canned pumpkin purée (not pie filling)	250 mL
½ cup	chopped walnuts	125 mL

1. In a medium bowl, sift together flour, potato powder, pumpkin spice, salt and baking soda.
2. In a large mixer bowl, on medium speed, cream brown sugar and butter until fluffy. Beat in eggs, zest and vanilla until well blended. Add flour mixture alternately with the orange juice, beating well after each addition. Gently fold in pumpkin and walnuts. Spoon into prepared pudding mold, filling three-quarters full, and cover.
3. Place mold onto a rack set in large pot and pour boiling water into pot until it reaches halfway up the sides of mold. Cover pot. Keep water boiling gently over low heat and steam pudding for 2 hours or until pudding is firm to the touch and a knife or wooden skewer inserted into the center comes out clean and dry. Be sure water is at a continuous low boil.
4. Remove mold from pot and set on a wire rack to cool slightly (about 10 minutes), then loosen sides of pudding with a knife and invert onto a serving plate. Cut into wedges and serve warm.

Tip *Serve with whipped topping, a scoop of vanilla ice cream or your favorite sauce (see Sauces, pages 553–555).*

Mom's Carrot Pudding

Serves 6 to 8

- 6-cup (1.5 L) pudding mold, well buttered or oiled
- Large pot

1 cup	packed brown sugar	250 mL
½ cup	butter or margarine, softened	125 mL
1 cup	grated carrot (1 to 2 medium)	250 mL
1 cup	grated potato (1 to 2 medium), divided	250 mL
⅔ cup	raisins	150 mL
½ cup	currants or other dried fruit	125 mL
2 tbsp	all-purpose flour	25 mL
1 cup	all-purpose flour	250 mL
1 tsp	ground cinnamon	5 mL
½ tsp	ground nutmeg	2 mL
½ tsp	ground cloves	2 mL
1 tsp	baking soda	5 mL

1. In a large bowl, cream together brown sugar and butter until light and fluffy. Add carrot and half the potato and mix well. Sprinkle the raisins and currants with the 2 tbsp (25 mL) flour and stir into carrot mixture until well blended.
2. In a small bowl, sift together the 1 cup (250 mL) flour, cinnamon, nutmeg and cloves and add to the carrot mixture.
3. In another small bowl, dissolve the baking soda in the remaining potato and add to the carrot mixture. Mix together just until blended. Pour into prepared pudding mold, filling three-quarters full, and cover.
4. Place mold onto a rack set in large pot and pour boiling water into pot until it reaches halfway up the sides of mold. Cover pot. Keep water boiling over low heat and steam pudding for 3 hours or until pudding is firm to the touch and a knife or wooden skewer inserted in the center comes out clean and dry. Be sure water is at a continuous low boil.
5. Remove mold from pot and set on a wire rack to cool slightly (about 10 minutes), then loosen sides of pudding with a knife and invert onto a serving plate. Cut into slices and serve warm.

Tip *Serve with your favorite sauce (see Sauces, pages 553–555).*

Steamed Spicy Mincemeat Pudding

Serves 6 to 8

- 4-cup (1 L) pudding mold, well buttered or oiled
- Large pot

1	egg	1
1 cup	firmly packed brown sugar	250 mL
⅓ cup	butter or margarine	75 mL
1 cup	sifted all-purpose flour	250 mL
1 tsp	baking powder	5 mL
½ tsp	salt	2 mL
½ cup	milk	125 mL
1 cup	prepared mincemeat (from a jar)	250 mL
½ cup	dry bread crumbs	125 mL
½ cup	chopped walnuts	125 mL

1. In a large mixer bowl, on medium speed, combine egg, brown sugar and butter, beating until smooth and fluffy.
2. In a small bowl, sift flour, baking powder and salt. Add flour mixture to egg mixture alternately with the milk, beating well after each addition. Gently stir in mincemeat, bread crumbs and walnuts, just until well blended. Spoon into prepared pudding mold, filling three-quarters full, and cover.
3. Place mold onto a rack set in large pot and pour boiling water into pot until it reaches halfway up the sides of mold. Cover pot. Keep water boiling gently over low heat and steam pudding for 1 hour or until pudding is firm to the touch and a knife or wooden skewer inserted into the center comes out clean and dry. Be sure water is at a continuous low boil.
4. Remove mold from pot and set on a wire rack to cool slightly (about 10 minutes), then loosen sides of pudding with a knife and invert onto a serving plate. Cut into slices and serve warm.

Tip *When your recipe calls for sifting, put the ingredients to be sifted in the mixing bowl and stir them with a whisk. It does an equally good job.*

Esther's Favorites

Esther's Favorite Cookies

Esther's Favorite Bars and Squares

Esther's Favorite Cakes

Esther's Favorite Pies

Esther's Favorite Cookies

Mama's Homemade Cookies

Makes about 5 dozen
- Preheat oven to 350ºF (180ºC)
- Baking sheet, ungreased

4 cups	all-purpose flour	1 L
1 tsp	baking soda	5 mL
¼ tsp	salt	1 mL
3	eggs	3
½ cup	vegetable oil	125 mL
1 cup	granulated sugar	250 mL
1 tsp	vanilla	5 mL
½ cup	milk	125 mL

1. In a large bowl, mix together flour, baking soda and salt. Make a well in the center.
2. In a separate bowl, whisk eggs, oil, sugar, vanilla and milk. Pour into well and mix thoroughly.
3. Drop by rounded teaspoonfuls (5 mL), 2 inches (5 cm) apart, onto baking sheet. Bake in preheated oven for about 20 minutes or until golden brown. Immediately transfer to wire racks to cool.

Shauna's Bow Knots

Makes about 3 dozen
- Deep fryer or Dutch oven

2	eggs	2
3 tbsp	granulated sugar	45 mL
1 tbsp	sour cream	15 mL
½ tsp	brandy	2 mL
½ tsp	any flavor liqueur	2 mL
1¾ cups	all-purpose flour (approx.), divided	425 mL
	Vegetable oil for frying	
	Confectioner's (icing) sugar, sifted	

1. In a bowl, beat eggs and sugar until light and fluffy. Add sour cream, brandy and liqueur, mixing until well blended. Gradually add 1⅓ cups (325 mL) flour, in three portions, beating after each addition.
2. On a floured surface, knead in as much of the remaining flour as required so dough is not sticky. Cover with a clean tea towel and let rest for 20 to 25 minutes.
3. Divide dough into four rolls. Place three pieces under a damp towel and roll one piece into a rectangle about ¼ inch (0.5 cm) thick. Using a knife, cut into strips, 1 by 4 inches (2.5 by 10 cm). Cut a slit almost through the middle of the long side of the strip and take the two ends of each strip and pull them through the slit. Repeat with the remaining dough.
4. Fill a deep fryer or Dutch oven with oil to a depth of about 2 inches (5 cm). Heat to 375ºF (190ºC). Add bows, a few at a time, and fry just until light golden brown (this will only take a few seconds). Lift out with a slotted spoon and drain on paper towel. Dust heavily with confectioner's sugar.

Mildred's Sour Cream Kiffles

Makes 32 kiffles
- Preheat oven to 350ºF (180ºC)
- Baking sheet, greased

1	package (¼ oz/7 g) active dry yeast	1
6 cups	all-purpose flour	1.5 L
6 tbsp	granulated sugar	90 mL
1 tsp	salt	5 mL
1 cup	butter	250 mL
1 cup	margarine	250 mL
4	eggs, beaten	4
1 cup	sour cream	250 mL
2 cups	Sugar-Cinnamon Mix (see recipe, page 543)	500 mL

1. In a small bowl, proof yeast according to package instructions.
2. In a large bowl, mix together flour, sugar and salt. Using two knives, a pastry blender or your fingers, cut in butter and margarine until mixture resembles coarse crumbs. Make a well in the center. Add eggs, sour cream and dissolved yeast and mix well. Cover and refrigerate overnight.
3. Divide dough into four parts. Knead one part until soft, then, on a work surface sprinkled with sugar-cinnamon mix, roll into a large circle, turning at least once so both sides will be coated with the sugar-cinnamon mixture. Using a knife or a pastry cutter, fluted if desired, cut into 8 pie-shaped wedges and spread with sugar-cinnamon mix. Beginning with the outer edge and finishing with the point in the center, roll up. Turn ends slightly towards each other to form a crescent. Repeat with the remaining dough.
4. Place crescents 2 inches (5 cm) apart on prepared baking sheet, cover with a clean tea towel and set in a warm place to rise until double in size, approximately 1 hour. Bake in preheated oven for 20 minutes or until golden brown. Immediately transfer to wire racks to cool.

Baba Mary's Thimble Cookies

Makes about 4 dozen
- Preheat oven to 300°F (150°C)
- Baking sheet, ungreased

1 cup	butter, softened	250 mL
1/2 cup	lightly packed brown sugar	125 mL
2	egg yolks	2
2 cups	all-purpose flour	500 mL
2	egg whites, lightly beaten	2
1 cup	chopped walnuts	250 mL
	Jam or jelly	

1. In a large bowl, beat butter and brown sugar until smooth and creamy. Beat in egg yolks until well incorporated. Gradually add flour and mix until well blended.

2. Shape dough into 1-inch (2.5 cm) balls. Drop balls into egg whites and then into walnuts. Place about 1 inch (2.5 cm) apart on baking sheet and, using a fork, flatten slightly. Using a thimble or your thumb, make an indentation in the center of each cookie and fill with jam or jelly. Bake in preheated oven for 15 to 20 minutes or until golden brown. Immediately transfer to wire racks to cool.

Tip *Rinse hot baking sheet under cold water to cool completely before baking any more cookies.*

Lisa's Cinnamon Nut Crescents

Makes about 6 1/2 dozen
- Preheat oven to 350°F (180°C)
- Foil-lined baking sheet, greased

1	package (1/4 oz/7 g) active dry yeast	1
2 tbsp	granulated sugar	25 mL
1/2 cup	warm water	125 mL
3 cups	all-purpose flour	750 mL
1/2 tsp	salt	2 mL
3	egg yolks	3
1/2 cup	whipping (35%) cream	125 mL
1 tsp	vanilla	5 mL
1 cup	butter or margarine, softened	250 mL
FILLING		
2	egg whites	2
1 3/4 cups	finely chopped walnuts, toasted	425 mL
3/4 cup	granulated sugar	175 mL
Pinch	salt	Pinch

SUGAR-CINNAMON MIX

3/4 cup	granulated sugar	175 mL
3 tbsp	ground cinnamon	45 mL

1. In a small bowl, dissolve yeast and 2 tbsp (25 mL) sugar in warm water.

2. In a large bowl, combine flour and salt. Add yeast mixture, mixing until blended, then mix in egg yolks, cream and vanilla. Beat in butter, spoonfuls at a time, until well blended and a dough forms. Wrap tightly in plastic wrap and refrigerate for at least 3 hours or overnight, until dough is firm.

3. *Prepare the filling:* In a clean bowl, beat egg whites until soft peaks form. Fold in walnuts, sugar and salt. Set aside.

4. *Prepare the sugar-cinnamon mix:* In a small bowl, mix sugar and cinnamon.

5. Divide dough into 10 balls and return nine to refrigerator until ready to use. On a work surface, sprinkled with a heaping tablespoonful (15 mL) sugar-cinnamon mixture, roll one dough ball into an 8-inch (20 cm) circle, turning at least once so both sides will be coated with the sugar-cinnamon mixture. Using a knife or a pastry cutter, fluted, if desired, cut into 8 pie-shaped wedges. Place 1 tsp (5 mL) walnut filling on the outer edge of each wedge. Beginning with the outer edge and finishing with the point in the center, roll up to form crescents. Repeat with the remaining dough.

6. Place, point side down, on prepared sheet and bake in preheated oven for 12 to 15 minutes, until puffy and browned. Immediately transfer to wire racks to cool.

Betty's Nothings

Makes about 3 dozen
- Preheat oven to 425°F (220°C)
- Baking sheet, greased

3	eggs	3
1 tbsp	granulated sugar	15 mL
Pinch	salt	Pinch
1/2 cup	vegetable oil	125 mL
1 cup	all-purpose flour	250 mL

1. In a large bowl, beat eggs, sugar and salt until light and fluffy. Continue beating, gradually adding oil, alternately with flour. Mix well.

2. Drop by teaspoonfuls (5 mL), about 2 inches (5 cm) apart, onto prepared baking sheet. Bake in preheated oven for 20 to 25 minutes or until lightly browned. Immediately transfer to wire racks to cool.

Mom's Peanut Butter Cookies

Makes about 2 dozen
- Preheat oven to 350°F (180°C)
- Baking sheet, lightly greased

1 cup	all-purpose flour	250 mL
1 tsp	baking soda	5 mL
¼ tsp	salt	1 mL
½ cup	shortening, softened	125 mL
½ cup	granulated sugar	125 mL
½ cup	lightly packed brown sugar	125 mL
1	egg	1
½ cup	peanut butter (smooth or crunchy)	125 mL
¼ tsp	vanilla	1 mL

1. In a bowl, combine flour, baking soda and salt.

2. In a large bowl, beat shortening and sugars until smooth and creamy. Beat in egg until incorporated. Stir in peanut butter and vanilla. Gradually add flour mixture, mixing until a soft dough forms.

3. Shape dough into 1-inch (2.5 cm) balls. Place about 2 inches (5 cm) apart on prepared baking sheet and, using the tines of a fork, press to flatten. Bake in preheated oven for 12 to 15 minutes. Immediately transfer to wire racks to cool.

Helen's Mon Cookies

Makes about 3 dozen
- Preheat oven to 350°F (180°C)
- Baking sheet, ungreased

1½ to	all-purpose flour	375 to
2 cups		500 mL
1 tsp	baking powder	5 mL
1 cup	old-fashioned rolled oats	250 mL
½ cup	shortening, softened	125 mL
¼ to	vegetable oil	50 to
½ cup		125 mL
¾ cup	packed brown sugar	175 mL
1	egg	1
¼ cup	poppy seeds	50 mL

1. In a bowl, combine flour, baking powder and oats.

2. In a large bowl, cream together shortening, oil and brown sugar. Mix in egg and poppy seeds until well blended. Add flour mixture and mix well.

3. Drop by rounded teaspoonfuls (5 mL), about 2 inches (5 cm) apart, onto baking sheet. Flatten slightly with a fork. Bake in preheated oven for 10 minutes, until golden brown. Transfer to wire racks to cool.

Betty's Cornflake Macaroons

Makes about 2½ dozen
- Preheat oven to 350°F (180°C)
- Baking sheet, well-greased

2	egg whites	2
½ tsp	vanilla	2 mL
1 cup	lightly packed brown or granulated sugar	250 mL
2 cups	crushed corn flakes cereal	500 mL
½ cup	chopped nuts	125 mL
1 cup	shredded coconut (sweetened or unsweetened)	250 mL

1. Beat egg whites and vanilla until soft peaks form. Gradually beat in sugar until stiff peaks form. Gently fold in corn flakes, nuts and coconut.

2. Drop by rounded teaspoonfuls (5 mL), about 2 inches (5 cm) apart, onto prepared baking sheet. Bake in preheated oven for 15 to 20 minutes or until delicately browned. Immediately transfer to wire racks to cool.

Lisa's Chocolate Chip Cookies

Makes about 2 dozen
- Preheat oven to 375°F (190°C)
- Baking sheet, ungreased

1 cup	all-purpose flour	250 mL
½ tsp	baking soda	2 mL
½ tsp	salt	2 mL
½ cup	shortening or butter, softened	125 mL
½ cup	granulated sugar	125 mL
¼ cup	firmly packed brown sugar	50 mL
1	egg	1
1 tsp	vanilla	5 mL
1	package (10 oz/300 g) mini semisweet chocolate chips	1

1. In a bowl, combine flour, baking soda and salt.

2. In a large bowl, beat shortening and sugars until smooth and creamy. Beat in egg until incorporated. Stir in vanilla. Fold in chocolate chips. Add flour mixture and mix thoroughly.

3. Drop by rounded teaspoonfuls (5 mL), about 2 inches (5 cm) apart, onto baking sheet. Bake in preheated oven for 8 to 10 minutes or until lightly browned. Immediately transfer to wire racks to cool.

Cecille's One-Bowl Chocolate Cookies

Makes about 1½ dozen large cookies
- Preheat oven to 350°F (180°C)
- Baking sheet, ungreased

1 lb	semisweet chocolate, divided	500 g
¾ cup	firmly packed brown sugar	175 mL
¼ cup	butter or margarine, softened	50 mL
2	eggs	2
1 tsp	vanilla	5 mL
¼ tsp	baking powder	1 mL
½ cup	all-purpose flour	125 mL
2 cups	chopped nuts (optional)	500 mL

1. Coarsely chop half the chocolate and set aside.

2. In a large bowl, in a microwave, melt the remaining chocolate. Add brown sugar, butter, eggs and vanilla, beating until smooth. Stir in baking powder, then flour, and mix until well blended. Fold in reserved chocolate and nuts (if using), mixing until well combined.

3. Using a ¼-cup (50 mL) measure, drop by cupfuls onto baking sheet. Bake in preheated oven for 12 to 13 minutes, until cookies are puffed and soft to touch. Let cool on baking sheet for 1 minute, then transfer to wire racks to cool completely.

Tip *If you do not have enough baking sheets when baking cookies, use a baking pan instead. Turn it over and set the cookies on the bottom.*

Aunty Giza's Lemon Cookies

Makes about 4 dozen
Preheat oven to 350°F (180°C)
Baking sheet, lightly greased

1¾ cups	all-purpose flour	425 mL
1 tsp	baking powder	5 mL
¼ tsp	salt	1 mL
⅔ cup	shortening, softened	150 mL
¾ cup	granulated sugar	175 mL
2	egg yolks	2
	Zest and juice of ½ lemon	
½ cup	orange juice	125 mL
2 tsp	red wine (optional)	10 mL
	Egg whites	
	Halved nuts (optional)	

1. In a small bowl, mix together flour, baking powder and salt.

2. In a large bowl, beat shortening and sugar until smooth and creamy. Beat in egg yolks until incorporated. Stir in lemon zest and juice, orange juice and wine (if using). Add flour mixture and mix until a dough forms.

3. Cut dough in half. Shape into 1-inch (2.5 cm) balls and, using your finger, press down on each to flatten slightly. Place about 1-inch (2.5 cm) apart on prepared baking sheet. Brush egg white on top of each cookie and place a nut (if using) in the center. Bake in preheated oven for 20 minutes or until golden brown. Immediately transfer to wire racks to cool.

Baba Mary's Jam Delights

Makes about 4 dozen
- Preheat oven to 350°F (180°C)
- Baking sheet, lined with parchment or waxed paper

2 cups	all-purpose flour	500 mL
2 tsp	baking powder	10 mL
Pinch	salt	Pinch
¾ cup	shortening	175 mL
½ cup	granulated sugar	125 mL
2	eggs	2
	Jam, any flavor, for filling	

1. In a medium bowl, sift together flour, baking powder and salt.

2. In a large bowl, beat shortening and sugar until smooth and creamy. Add eggs, one at a time, beating after each addition. Gradually mix in flour mixture until well blended.

3. Shape dough into 1-inch (2.5 cm) balls and place on prepared baking sheet. Using a thimble or your thumb, make an indentation in the center of each cookie and fill with jam. Bake in preheated oven for 15 minutes or until golden brown. Immediately transfer to wire racks to cool.

Shirley's Meringue Cookies

Makes about 2 dozen
- Preheat oven to 250°F (120°C)
- Baking sheet, lined with waxed paper

½ cup	granulated sugar	125 mL
3 tbsp	potato flour or cornstarch	45 mL
3	egg whites	3
1 cup	semisweet chocolate chips	250 mL

1. In a small bowl, mix together sugar and potato flour or cornstarch.

2. In a large, clean bowl, beat egg whites until soft peaks form. Gradually add sugar mixture to egg whites, beating until stiff, glossy peaks form. Fold in chocolate chips.

3. Drop by teaspoonfuls (5 mL), about 2 inches (5 cm) apart, onto prepared baking sheet. Bake in preheated oven for 55 to 60 minutes or until lightly browned. Immediately transfer to wire racks to cool.

Tip *Potato flour is available in the baking section of supermarkets.*

Variation *Coconut Meringues: Substitute 1 cup (250 mL) sweetened shredded coconut for the chocolate chips.*

• •

Olga's Hamantashen

Makes about 2 dozen
- Preheat oven to 350ºF (180ºC)
- Cookie cutter or glass, 2 to 3 inches (5 to 7.5 cm) in diameter
- Baking sheet, lightly greased

PRUNE FILLING

1 cup	pitted prunes	250 mL
1 cup	raisins	250 mL
	Juice of 1 lemon	
	Juice of 1 orange	
½ cup	granulated sugar	125 mL
2 tsp	vanilla	10 mL
3 tbsp	apricot jam or other jam	45 mL
1 cup	finely crushed walnuts	250 mL

DOUGH

⅔ cup	shortening, softened	150 mL
1 tsp	salt	5 mL
3 tbsp	liquid honey	45 mL
3	eggs	3
1 tsp	baking powder	5 mL
3 cups	all-purpose flour	750 mL

TOPPING

1	egg	1
2 tbsp	milk	25 mL
Pinch	granulated sugar	Pinch

1. *Prepare the filling:* In a medium bowl, cover prunes and raisins with boiling water and leave to soak overnight, until softened. Drain.

2. In a food processor or using a mincer, process prunes and raisins until smooth. Transfer to a medium bowl. Add lemon juice, orange juice, sugar, vanilla, jam and walnuts and mix well. Set aside.

3. *Prepare the dough:* In a large bowl, cream shortening, salt and honey until smooth. Beat in eggs, one at a time, mixing until well incorporated. Stir in baking powder, then gradually add flour, mixing until a soft dough forms. Cover with a damp towel.

4. On a lightly floured surface, divide dough in half. Return one half to bowl and cover. Roll other half out to a ¼-inch (0.5 cm) thickness. Using a cookie cutter dipped in flour, cut out circles. Spoon a heaping teaspoonful (5 cm) of filling in the center of each circle. Moisten the edges lightly with a finger dipped in water and pinch together three edges of the dough to form a triangle, leaving a small opening in the center with some filling showing. It will resemble a three-cornered hat.

5. *Prepare the topping:* In a small bowl, beat the egg, milk and sugar. Brush top of each triangle with the mixture.

6. Place triangles on prepared baking sheet and bake in preheated oven for 15 to 20 minutes, until nicely browned. Let cool on sheet and, using a spatula, lift off very carefully.

• •

Colleen's Goosnargh Cakes

Makes 40 cookies
- Preheat oven to 300ºF (150ºC)
- Baking sheet, ungreased

1 tbsp	coriander seeds	15 mL
1 tbsp	caraway seeds	15 mL
2 cups	butter, softened	500 mL
¼ cup	confectioner's (icing) sugar, sifted	50 mL
3¾ cups	all-purpose flour	925 mL
	Confectioner's (icing) sugar, sifted	

1. Place seeds in a plastic bag and, using a rolling pin, crush finely.

2. In a large bowl, beat butter and confectioner's sugar until smooth and creamy. Add seeds and mix well. Gradually add flour, mixing well after each addition. (You may not need all the flour because dough should be moist, not dry.)

3. On a floured work surface, roll dough out to ¾-inch (2 cm) thickness. Using a small glass, about 2 inches (5 cm) in diameter, cut out cookies. Place 2 inches (5 cm) apart on baking sheet and bake in preheated oven for 30 to 45 minutes, until just dry. Do not brown. Cookies should be white. Immediately transfer to wire racks to cool. When cool, sprinkle liberally with confectioner's sugar and pat to press down.

Aunty Giza's Rosettes

Makes about 2 dozen
- Round cookie cutters, 2 inches (5 cm), 1 inch (2.5 cm) and ½ inch (1 cm) in diameter
- Deep fryer or Dutch oven

1 cup	all-purpose flour	250 mL
1 tbsp	granulated sugar	15 mL
¼ tsp	salt	1 mL
4	egg yolks, beaten	4
1	whole egg, beaten	1
1 tsp	freshly squeezed lemon juice	5 mL
	Vegetable oil for frying	
	Confectioner's (icing) sugar, sifted	
	Glacé cherries, each cut into three or four pieces, or red jam or jelly	

1. In a large bowl, mix together flour, sugar and salt. Make a well in the center. Add egg yolks, egg and lemon juice and mix until well blended.

2. On a floured surface, roll dough out to ⅛-inch (0.25 cm) thickness and, using the three cutters, make as many complete sets of different-sized circles as possible. Slit the edge of each round in five places to make petals. Combine three different-sized circles by placing the largest on the bottom and the smallest on the top. Using your finger, press hard in the center to stick layers together.

3. In a deep fryer or Dutch oven, heat oil to 375°F (190°C). Working with four to six rosettes at a time, fry cookies, turning once, to a golden brown. Using a slotted spoon, lift out carefully and drain on paper towel. While still warm, dust with confectioner's sugar. Place a piece of glacé cherry or ¼ tsp (1 mL) red jam or jelly in the center of each rosette.

Tip *For the smallest cookie cutter, use the top from a narrow-mouthed container, such as ketchup bottle.*

Sima's Passover Cookies

Makes about 2 dozen
- Preheat oven to 350°F (180°C)
- Baking sheet, lightly greased

2	eggs	2
½ cup	vegetable oil	125 mL
2 tbsp	potato starch	25 mL
1 tbsp	freshly squeezed lemon juice	15 mL
¾ cup	granulated sugar	175 mL
1 cup	cake meal	250 mL
¾ cup	ground almonds, divided	175 mL
½ cup	Sugar-Cinnamon Mix (see recipe, page 543)	125 mL

1. In a large bowl, beat together eggs and oil. Add potato starch and lemon juice and mix well. Add sugar and cake meal, mixing until blended. Fold in ½ cup (125 mL) of the almonds.

2. Roll dough into 1-inch (2.5 cm) balls. Mix the remaining almonds with sugar-cinnamon mix and roll the ball in this mixture to coat. Flatten a little, if desired.

3. Place about 2 inches (5 cm) apart on prepared baking sheet. Bake for 10 to 12 minutes, until golden brown. Immediately transfer to wire racks to cool.

Felicia's Mandelbrot

Makes about 3 dozen
- Preheat oven to 350°F (180°C)
- Baking sheet, lightly greased

2¾ cups	all-purpose flour	675 mL
4 tsp	baking powder	20 mL
½ tsp	salt	2 mL
3	eggs	3
1 cup	granulated sugar	250 mL
6 tbsp	vegetable oil	90 mL
	Grated zest of 1 lemon	
½ tsp	vanilla	2 mL
⅓ cup	coarsely chopped blanched almonds	75 mL

1. In a medium bowl, sift together flour, baking powder and salt.

2. In a large bowl, beat eggs, sugar, oil, zest and vanilla until thoroughly blended. Stir egg mixture into flour mixture and mix well. Fold in almonds and mix until a soft dough forms.

3. On a well-floured surface, divide dough in half. Shape into two long rolls about 3 inches (7.5 cm) wide. Place at least 2 inches (5 cm) apart on prepared sheet. Bake in preheated oven for 40 to 50 minutes, until lightly browned and a toothpick inserted into center of one of the rolls comes out clean and dry. Remove from oven and turn off heat.

4. On a cutting board, cut hot rolls into slices about ½ inch (1 cm) thick. Place on baking sheet and, leaving heat off, return to oven to dry for 25 minutes.

Shauna's Shortbread Cookies

Makes about 2 dozen

- Preheat oven to 300°F (150°C)
- Baking sheet, ungreased

1½ cups	sifted cake and pastry flour	375 mL
½ cup	cornstarch	125 mL
½ tsp	salt	2 mL
1 cup	butter, softened	250 mL
⅔ cup	lightly packed brown sugar	150 mL
½ cup	glacé cherries (optional)	125 mL
½ cup	chopped almonds (optional)	125 mL

1. In a bowl, combine flour, cornstarch and salt.
2. In a large bowl, beat butter and brown sugar until smooth and creamy. Stir in cherries (if using) and almonds (if using). Gradually add flour mixture, mixing thoroughly after each addition, until a soft dough forms. Knead lightly.
3. On a lightly floured board, knead dough until cracks appear on the surface. Roll out to about ¼-inch (0.5 cm) thickness. Using a knife or a cookie cutter, cut into small oblongs and place on baking sheet. Bake in preheated oven for 20 to 25 minutes or until golden brown. Immediately transfer to wire racks to cool.

Cecille's Passover Komish Bread

Makes 4½ dozen

- Preheat oven to 325°F (160°C)
- 9-inch (2.5 L) square baking pan, greased

3	eggs	3
¾ cup	granulated sugar	175 mL
¾ cup	vegetable oil	175 mL
1 to 2 tsp	ground cinnamon	5 to 10 mL
¾ cup	cake meal	175 mL
¼ cup	matzo meal	50 mL
2 tbsp	potato starch	25 mL
½ cup	chopped walnuts	125 mL

1. In a large bowl, beat eggs and sugar until thick and pale. Beat in oil until well incorporated. Mix in cinnamon to taste, cake meal, matzo meal and potato starch until well blended. Fold in nuts.
2. Using a spatula, scrape batter into prepared pan and bake in preheated oven for 50 to 60 minutes, until a toothpick inserted in the center comes out clean and dry. Let cool in pan for 30 minutes, then cut into slices ½ inch (1 cm) thick. Place on wire racks.

3. Increase oven heat to 350°F (180°C) and return rack of slices to oven to dry for 30 minutes. Remove from oven and let cool completely before serving.

Tip *When you buy vegetable oil, instead of removing the protective seal, cut a small slit in it. You'll be able to pour the oil through it without spilling.*

Esther's Famous Komish Bread Cookies

Makes about 4 dozen

- Preheat oven to 350°F (180°C)
- Baking sheet, greased

3 cups	all-purpose flour	750 mL
½ tsp	salt	2 mL
1 tsp	baking powder	5 mL
1 to 2 tsp	ground cinnamon	5 to 10 mL
3	eggs	3
1 cup	granulated sugar	250 mL
1 cup	vegetable oil	250 mL
1 tsp	vanilla	5 mL
1 cup	semisweet chocolate chips	250 mL
SUGAR-CINNAMON MIX		
½ cup	granulated sugar	125 mL
2 tsp	ground cinnamon	10 mL

1. In a medium bowl, mix together flour, salt, baking powder and cinnamon.
2. In a large bowl, beat eggs, sugar and oil until blended. Mix in vanilla. Add dry ingredients and mix well. Fold in chocolate chips.
3. On a floured surface, divide dough into three portions. Shape into three rolls about 2 to 3 inches (5 to 7.5 cm) wide. Place at least 2 inches (5 cm) apart on prepared baking sheet. Bake in preheated oven for 30 to 35 minutes, until lightly browned and a toothpick inserted into center of one of the rolls comes out clean and dry. Remove from oven and turn off heat.
4. *Prepare the sugar-cinnamon mix:* In a small bowl, mix sugar and cinnamon.
5. On a cutting board, cut hot rolls into slices about ½ inch (1 cm) thick. Dip each slice in sugar-cinnamon mix until well coated. Place on baking sheet, and leaving heat off, return to oven to dry for 20 to 25 minutes.

Tip *Vary the quantity of cinnamon according to your taste. I probably use more than most people, as I love cinnamon.*

Esther's Rugelach

Makes about 4 dozen
Preheat oven to 350°F (180°C)
Baking sheet, lined with parchment or waxed paper

2 cups	all-purpose flour	500 mL
¼ cup	granulated sugar	50 mL
1 cup	butter, softened	250 mL
1	package (8 oz/250 g) cream cheese, softened	1
¼ cup	melted butter	50 mL
FILLING		
½ cup	granulated sugar	125 mL
1 tbsp	ground cinnamon	15 mL
¾ cup	finely chopped walnuts	175 mL
½ cup	raisins (optional)	125 mL

1. In a large bowl, mix together flour and ¼ cup (50 mL) sugar. Using your fingers, work the butter and cream cheese together to form a dough. (You can also do this in a food processor.)

2. Divide dough into four sections. Wrap tightly in plastic wrap and refrigerate for at least 4 hours.

3. *Prepare the filling:* In a medium bowl, mix together ½ cup (125 mL) sugar, cinnamon, walnuts and raisins (if using).

4. On a floured surface, using a floured rolling pin, roll one portion of dough into a 10-inch (25 cm) circle. Brush with 1 tbsp (15 mL) melted butter, then spread one-quarter of the filling evenly over circle.

5. Using a knife or a pastry wheel, cut circle into 12 pie-shaped wedges. Beginning at the wide edge, with the filling inside, roll tightly, finishing with the point in the middle. Curve the rolls slightly to form a crescent and place, point side down, on prepared baking sheet. Repeat with the remaining dough.

6. Bake in preheated oven for 25 to 30 minutes or until delicately browned. Transfer to wire racks to cool.

Variation *Raspberry Hazelnut Rugelach: In a small bowl, mix together ½ cup (125 mL) raspberry jam and ½ cup (125 mL) finely chopped toasted hazelnuts. Spread over circle after brushing with butter. Sprinkle lightly with granulated sugar.*

Esther's Favorite Bars and Squares

Baba Mary's Honey Diamonds

Makes 36 diamonds
- Preheat oven to 350°F (180°C)
- 13- by 9-inch (3 L) baking pan, greased

2 cups	all-purpose flour	500 mL
½ tsp	baking soda	2 mL
½ tsp	ground cinnamon	2 mL
¼ tsp	salt	1 mL
¼ cup	butter or shortening, softened	50 mL
1 cup	packed brown sugar	250 mL
2	eggs	2
⅓ cup	liquid honey	75 mL
½ cup	milk	125 mL
	Butter Frosting (see recipe, page 544)	
½ cup	ground nuts	125 mL

1. In a medium bowl mix together flour, baking soda, cinnamon and salt.

2. In a large bowl, beat butter and sugar until smooth and creamy. Add eggs and beat until incorporated. Stir in honey. Gradually blend in flour mixture alternately with milk until just incorporated.

3. Spread evenly in prepared pan. Bake in preheated oven for 35 to 40 minutes or until a tester inserted in the center comes out clean. Place pan on a wire rack to cool completely.

4. Frost generously with Butter Frosting, then sprinkle with nuts. Cut lengthwise into 6 strips; cut crosswise at an angle into 6 strips to make diamonds.

Shirley's Cornmeal Squares (Malai Cake)

Makes 30 squares
- Preheat oven to 350°F (180°C)
- 13- by 9-inch (3 L) baking pan, greased

1 cup	all-purpose flour	250 mL
1 tbsp	baking powder	15 mL
1 tsp	salt	5 mL
½ cup	yellow cornmeal	125 mL
2 cups	water	500 mL
½ cup	butter or margarine, melted	125 mL
6	eggs, separated	6
2 cups	creamed cottage cheese	500 mL
2 cups	sour cream	500 mL
½ cup	granulated sugar	125 mL

1. In a small bowl, mix together flour, baking powder and salt.
2. In the top of a double boiler, combine cornmeal and water. Cook over low heat until mixture thickens. Stir in butter until melted. Set aside to cool.
3. In a large bowl, beat egg yolks, cottage cheese, sour cream and sugar until blended. Blend in flour mixture, alternating with cornmeal mixture, just until incorporated.
4. In a clean bowl, beat egg whites until stiff peaks form. Fold into batter. Spoon into prepared baking pan, spreading evenly. Bake in preheated oven for 55 to 60 minutes or until golden brown. Place pan on a wire rack to cool completely, or cool slightly and serve warm. Cut into squares.

Tip *This cake is delicious when served warm with sour cream and strawberries.*

• •

Cecille's Walnut Squares

Makes 30 squares
- Preheat oven to 325°F (160°C)
- 13- by 9-inch (3 L) baking pan, ungreased

BASE

1½ cups	all-purpose flour	375 mL
1 tbsp	packed brown sugar	15 mL
Pinch	baking powder	Pinch
½ cup	butter or margarine	125 mL

TOPPING

1¼ cups	finely chopped walnuts, divided	300 mL
2	eggs	2
¾ cup	packed brown sugar	175 mL
2 tbsp	all-purpose flour	25 mL
Pinch	baking powder	Pinch
1 tsp	vanilla	5 mL
	Butter Frosting (see recipe, page 544)	

1. *Prepare the base:* In a bowl, mix together flour, brown sugar and baking powder. Using two knives, a pastry blender or your fingers, cut butter in until mixture resembles coarse crumbs. Press evenly into pan. Bake in preheated oven for 15 to 20 minutes or until golden brown. Place pan on a wire rack to cool slightly.
2. *Prepare the topping:* Set aside ½ cup (125 mL) of the chopped walnuts. In a bowl, beat eggs and brown sugar until blended. Blend in flour, baking powder and vanilla. Stir in the remaining walnuts.

3. Spread evenly over warm base. Bake for 15 to 20 minutes, until golden brown. Place pan on a wire rack to cool completely. Frost with Butter Frosting and sprinkle reserved walnuts over top. Cut into squares.

Tip *To soften brick-hard brown sugar, transfer it to a paper bag and place in a 350°F (180°C) oven until the bag is warm. Then crush with a rolling pin and spread out on a baking sheet to cool.*

• •

Mama's Icebox Cake Bars

Makes 24 bars
- 13- by 9-inch (3 L) baking pan, ungreased

1	package (4-serving size) gelatin dessert mix, any flavor	1
1	package (14 oz/400 g) whole graham wafers	1

WALNUT FILLING

1 cup	graham wafer crumbs (about 14 wafers)	250 mL
1 cup	finely chopped walnuts	250 mL
	Grated zest of 1 lemon	
½ cup	packed brown sugar	125 mL

SOUR CREAM FILLING

1½ cups	sour cream	375 mL
½ cup	packed brown sugar	125 mL
2 tsp	freshly squeezed lemon juice	10 mL
1 tsp	vanilla	5 mL

1. Prepare gelatin according to package directions, allowing to set partially. Gelatin should be firm enough to spread.
2. *Prepare the walnut filling:* In a medium bowl, mix together wafer crumbs, walnuts, zest and brown sugar.
3. *Prepare the sour cream filling:* In another medium bowl, mix sour cream, brown sugar, lemon juice and vanilla until thoroughly blended.
4. Line bottom of pan with half of the whole graham wafers. Spoon half of sour cream filling over top, spreading evenly. Place the remaining graham wafers on top and spread evenly with remaining sour cream filling.
5. Spoon half the walnut filling evenly over sour cream layer; spread evenly with the partially set gelatin. Spoon the remaining walnut filling over top, spreading evenly. Chill for 3 to 4 hours, until cold and set. Cut into bars before serving.

Lisa's Midas Squares

Makes 16 squares

- 8-inch (2 L) square baking pan, ungreased

BASE

1 cup	smooth peanut butter	250 mL
½ cup	cane sugar syrup (golden syrup)	125 mL
½ cup	packed brown sugar	125 mL
2 cups	corn flakes cereal, lightly crushed	500 mL
1 cup	crisp rice cereal	250 mL

FROSTING

½ cup	packed brown sugar	125 mL
3 tbsp	milk	45 mL
1 tbsp	margarine, softened	15 mL
1 cup	confectioner's (icing) sugar, sifted	250 mL
½ tsp	vanilla	2 mL

1. *Prepare the base:* In a saucepan, over low heat, stir peanut butter, syrup and brown sugar until sugar dissolves and mixture is smooth. Stir in corn flakes and rice cereal. Press firmly and evenly into pan.
2. *Prepare the frosting:* In a small bowl, beat brown sugar, milk, margarine, icing sugar and vanilla until smooth and spreadable. Spread over base. Chill for 3 hours or overnight. Cut into squares.

Cecille's Cookie Bars

Makes 36 bars

- Preheat oven to 350°F (180°C)
- 13- by 9-inch (3 L) baking pan, greased

BASE

1½ cups	crushed corn flakes cereal	375 mL
3 tbsp	granulated sugar	45 mL
½ cup	butter or margarine, melted	125 mL

TOPPING

1 cup	semisweet chocolate chips	250 mL
1⅓ cups	flaked coconut (sweetened or unsweetened)	325 mL
1 cup	coarsely chopped walnuts	250 mL
1	can (10 oz/300 mL) sweetened condensed milk	1

1. *Prepare the base:* In a bowl, combine corn flakes, sugar and butter. Press firmly into prepared pan.
2. *Prepare the topping:* Spread chocolate chips evenly over base. Sprinkle with coconut, then with nuts . Pour condensed milk evenly over nuts.
3. Bake in preheated oven for 25 minutes or until edges are lightly browned. Place pan on a wire rack to cool completely, then cut into bars.

Felicia's Passover Mocha Nut Bars

Makes 24 bars

- Preheat oven to 350°F (180°C)
- 9-inch (2.5 L) square baking pan, greased

2 oz	bittersweet chocolate	60 g
½ cup	butter or margarine	125 mL
2	eggs	2
1 cup	granulated sugar	250 mL
½ tsp	salt	2 mL
½ cup	sifted cake meal (Passover)	125 mL
1 cup	chopped nuts	250 mL

1. In a saucepan, over low heat, melt chocolate and butter, stirring until smooth. Set aside.
2. In a medium bowl, beat eggs, sugar and salt until blended and thick. Add cake meal and mix well. Blend in chocolate mixture. Stir in nuts.
3. Spread evenly in prepared pan. Bake in preheated oven for 25 to 30 minutes or until a tester inserted in the center comes out clean. Place pan on a wire rack to cool completely, then cut into bars.

Betty's Sour Cream Chocolate Chip Bars

Makes 36 bars

- Preheat oven to 350°F (180°C)
- 13- by 9-inch (3 L) baking pan, greased

BASE

1⅓ cups	all-purpose flour	325 mL
1½ tsp	baking powder	7 mL
1 tsp	baking soda	5 mL
1 tsp	ground cinnamon	5 mL
Pinch	salt	Pinch
6 tbsp	butter or margarine, softened	90 mL
1 cup	granulated sugar	250 mL
2	eggs	2
½ tsp	vanilla	2 mL
1 cup	sour cream	250 mL

TOPPING

1 cup	semisweet chocolate chips	250 mL
1 tbsp	granulated sugar	15 mL

1. *Prepare the base:* In a small bowl, mix together flour, baking powder, baking soda, cinnamon and salt.
2. In a large bowl, beat butter and sugar until smooth and creamy. Beat in eggs. Stir in vanilla. Blend in flour mixture alternately with sour cream until just incorporated. Spread evenly in prepared pan.

3. *Prepare the topping:* Sprinkle chocolate chips evenly over top. Sprinkle sugar over chocolate chips.
4. Bake in preheated oven for 30 to 35 minutes or until a tester inserted in the center comes out clean. Place pan on a wire rack to cool completely, then cut into bars.

• •

Wendy's Chocolate Chip Cream Cheese Bars

Makes 36 bars

- Preheat oven to 350°F (180°C)
- 13- by 9-inch (3 L) baking pan, greased

1	package (18 oz/510 g) refrigerated chocolate chip cookie dough, softened	1
2	packages (each 8 oz/250 g) cream cheese, softened	2
1 cup	granulated sugar	250 mL
2	eggs	2
1½ tsp	vanilla	7 mL
1	package (18 oz/510 g) refrigerated chocolate chip cookie dough, chilled	1

1. Spread cookie dough evenly in prepared pan.
2. In a bowl, beat cream cheese and sugar until smooth. Beat in eggs, one at a time,. Stir in vanilla. Spread evenly over dough.
3. On a cutting board, cut chilled dough into very thin slices. Completely cover cream cheese mixture with thin cookie slices. (Place dough in freezer for 15 minutes to make slicing easier.) Bake in preheated oven for 40 minutes or until golden brown. Place pan on a wire rack to cool completely. Store in refrigerator, then cut into bars.

• •

Colleen's "Sex in a Pan"

Makes 30 squares

- Preheat oven to 350°F (180°C)
- 13- by 9-inch (3 L) baking pan, greased

BASE

1 cup	all-purpose flour	250 mL
½ cup	chopped almonds or pecans	125 mL
3 tbsp	granulated sugar	45 mL
½ cup	butter or margarine	125 mL

FILLING

1	package (8 oz/250 g) cream cheese, softened	1
1 cup	confectioner's (icing) sugar, sifted	250 mL
2 cups	frozen whipped topping (thawed) or whipped (35%) cream, divided	500 mL

TOPPING

2	packages (each a 4-serving size) chocolate or caramel instant pudding mix	2
1	package (4-serving size) vanilla instant pudding mix	1
4 cups	milk	1 L
	Grated chocolate, chopped nuts or cherries for garnish (optional)	

1. *Prepare the base:* In a bowl, combine flour, nuts and sugar. Using two knives, a pastry blender or your fingers, cut butter in until mixture resembles coarse crumbs. Press evenly into prepared pan. Bake in preheated oven for 12 to 15 minutes or until browned. Place pan on a wire rack to cool completely.
2. *Prepare the filling:* In another bowl, beat cream cheese and confectioner's sugar until smooth and creamy. Fold in 1 cup (250 mL) of the whipped topping. Spread evenly over cooled base.
3. *Prepare the topping:* In a large bowl, beat puddings and milk until blended and smooth. Spread evenly over cream cheese mixture. Spread with the remaining whipped topping. If desired, garnish with chocolate, nuts or cherries. Chill until ready to serve. Cut into squares.

• •

Christine's Chocolate Nut Bars

Makes 24 bars

9-inch (2.5 L) square baking pan, greased

1 cup	corn syrup	250 mL
1 cup	packed brown sugar	250 mL
1 cup	smooth peanut butter	250 mL
2 tbsp	butter or margarine	25 mL
1 tsp	vanilla	5 mL
Pinch	salt	Pinch
4 cups	crisp rice cereal	1 L
2 cups	peanuts	500 mL
	Chocolate frosting (see recipes, pages 546)	

1. In a large saucepan, over low heat, stir together corn syrup, brown sugar, peanut butter and butter until sugar is dissolved. Increase heat and bring to a boil; cook, stirring constantly, until melted and smooth. Remove from heat. Stir in vanilla and salt. Stir in cereal and peanuts until blended.
2. Press evenly into prepared pan. Chill until firm. Frost and cut into bars.

Felicia's Apple Squares

Makes 30 squares
- Preheat oven to 350°F (180°C)
- 13- by 9-inch (3 L) baking pan, greased

BASE

2 cups	all-purpose flour	500 mL
1 cup	granulated sugar	250 mL
1 tsp	baking powder	5 mL
½ cup	butter or margarine, melted	125 mL
2	egg yolks, beaten	2

TOPPING

9	apples (about 3 lbs/1.5 kg), peeled and coarsely grated	9
2 tsp	packed brown sugar	10 mL
1 tsp	freshly squeezed lemon juice	5 mL
2 tbsp	cold butter or margarine, cut into tiny chunks	25 mL
1 tsp	granulated sugar	5 mL

1. *Prepare the base:* In a large bowl, mix together flour, sugar and baking powder. Add butter and egg yolks and mix until crumbly. Set aside 1 cup (250 mL) and press remainder evenly into prepared pan.

2. *Prepare the topping:* In a large bowl, mix together apples, brown sugar and lemon juice. Spread evenly over base. Sprinkle reserved crumb mixture over top. Sprinkle with butter chunks, then sugar.

3. Bake in preheated oven for 45 to 50 minutes or until golden brown. Place pan on a wire rack to cool completely, then cut into squares.

Olga's Blueberry Cake Squares

Makes 30 squares
- Preheat oven to 350°F (180°C)
- 13- by 9-inch (3 L) baking pan, greased

BASE

2½ cups	all-purpose flour	625 mL
1 tbsp	baking powder	15 mL
½ tsp	salt	2 mL
2	eggs	2
1 cup	granulated sugar	250 mL
3 tbsp	water	45 mL
1 tsp	vanilla	5 mL
1	can (19 oz/540 mL) blueberry pie filling	1

TOPPING

1 tbsp	butter, softened	15 mL
2 tbsp	all-purpose flour	25 mL

1 tbsp	granulated sugar	15 mL
1	egg yolk	1

1. *Prepare the base:* In a medium bowl, mix together flour, baking powder and salt.

2. In a large bowl, beat eggs, sugar, water and vanilla until blended. Gradually blend in flour mixture. Set half aside and spread remainder evenly in prepared pan. Spread pie filling evenly over top.

3. On a floured work surface, divide the remaining dough into 14 portions. Shape each into a rope, half to fit vertically across the cake and half to fit horizontally. Place over cake.

4. *Prepare the topping:* In a small bowl mix butter, flour, sugar and egg yolk until mixture is crumbly.

5. Sprinkle topping evenly over cake. Bake in preheated oven for 55 to 60 minutes or until golden brown. Place pan on a rack to cool completely, then cut into squares.

Arlene's Pineapple Cheesecake Squares

Makes 16 squares
- Preheat oven to 350° F (180° C)
- 8-inch (2 L) square baking pan, lightly greased

BASE

2½ cups	finely crushed graham wafer crumbs (about 36 wafers)	625 mL
¼ cup	butter, melted	50 mL

TOPPING

2	packages (each 8 oz/250 g) cream cheese, softened	2
½ cup	granulated sugar	125 mL
3	eggs	3
1 tsp	vanilla	5 mL
10	maraschino cherries, finely chopped	10
½ cup	drained crushed pineapple	125 mL

1. *Prepare the base:* In a medium bowl, mix together wafer crumbs and butter. Set aside ¾ cup (175 mL) and press remainder evenly into prepared pan.

2. *Prepare the topping:* In a large bowl, beat cream cheese and sugar until smooth. Beat in eggs, one at a time, until incorporated. Stir in vanilla. Stir in cherries and pineapple.

3. Spread evenly over base. Sprinkle reserved crumb mixture evenly over top. Bake in preheated oven for 35 minutes or until just set. Place pan on a wire rack to cool completely, then chill for 4 hours, or longer, before cutting into squares.

Sima's Pineapple Squares

Makes 30 squares

- Preheat oven to 375°F (190°C)
- 13- by 9-inch (3 L) baking pan, greased

TOPPING

3 cups	crushed pineapple, drained, 2 tbsp (25 mL) juice reserved	750 mL
1/2 cup	granulated sugar	125 mL
2 tbsp	cornstarch	25 mL
1 tbsp	butter	15 mL

BASE

1 1/2 cups	all-purpose flour	375 mL
2 tsp	baking powder	10 mL
Pinch	salt	Pinch
2	eggs	2
3/4 cup	granulated sugar	175 mL
1/2 cup	vegetable oil	125 mL
1/2 cup	orange juice	125 mL
1/4 cup	water	50 mL

1. *Prepare the topping:* In the top of a double boiler, over simmering (not boiling) water, combine pineapple and sugar. In a small bowl, mix cornstarch with reserved pineapple juice. Add to sugar mixture along with butter. Cook, stirring frequently, until mixture thickens. Set aside.

2. *Prepare the base:* In a large bowl, mix together flour, baking powder and salt. Make a well in the center. In another bowl, beat eggs, sugar, oil, orange juice and water. Pour into well and mix until just blended. (Batter will be thin.) Set aside one-half of the batter and pour remainder into prepared pan.

3. Spoon pineapple mixture evenly over batter. Drop the remaining batter, by spoonfuls, over pineapple, leaving spaces in the form of vertical and horizontal lines between the dollops of batter. Bake in preheated oven for 25 minutes, then reduce heat to 350° F (180° C) and bake for 10 minutes, until golden brown. Place pan on a wire rack to cool completely, then cut into squares.

Christine's Lemon Squares

Makes 16 squares

- Preheat oven to 350°F (180°C)
- 8-inch (2 L) square baking pan, lightly greased

BASE

1/2 cup	butter or margarine, softened	125 mL
1/4 cup	confectioner's (icing) sugar, sifted	50 mL
1/2 tsp	salt	2 mL
1 cup	all-purpose flour	250 mL

TOPPING

2	eggs, beaten	2
1 cup	granulated sugar	250 mL
2 tbsp	all-purpose flour	25 mL
1 1/2 tsp	grated lemon zest	7 mL
2 tbsp	freshly squeezed lemon juice	25 mL
	Confectioner's (icing) sugar	

1. *Prepare the base:* In a small bowl, beat butter and confectioner's sugar until smooth and creamy. Beat in salt, then gradually blend in flour until a soft dough forms. Press evenly into prepared pan. Bake in preheated oven for 20 minutes or until lightly browned. Place pan on a wire rack to cool slightly.

2. *Prepare the topping:* In a small bowl, mix together eggs, sugar, 2 tbsp (25 mL) flour, zest and juice until blended.

3. Spoon evenly over warm base. Bake for 20 to 25 minutes. Remove from oven and sift confectioner's sugar over top. Place pan on a wire rack to cool completely, then cut into squares.

Betty's Fruit Cocktail Squares

Makes 16 squares

- Preheat oven to 350°F (180°C)
- 8-inch (2 L) square baking pan, greased

BASE

1 cup	all-purpose flour	250 mL
1 tsp	baking soda	5 mL
1/4 tsp	salt	1 mL
3/4 cup	granulated sugar	175 mL
1	egg, beaten	1
2 cups	canned fruit cocktail, partially drained	500 mL

TOPPING

1/3 cup	packed brown sugar	75 mL
1 tsp	ground cinnamon	5 mL

1. *Prepare the base:* In a small bowl, mix together flour, baking soda and salt.

2. In a large bowl, mix together, sugar, egg and fruit cocktail. Blend in flour mixture. Spread evenly in prepared pan.

3. *Prepare the topping:* In a small bowl, mix together brown sugar and cinnamon.

4. Sprinkle evenly over top of cake. Bake in preheated oven for 40 to 45 minutes, until golden brown. Place pan on a wire rack to cool completely, then cut into squares.

Jeanette's Filled Coffee Cake Squares

Makes 30 squares
- Preheat oven to 350°F (180°C)
- 13- by 9-inch (3 L) baking pan, greased

BASE

3 cups	all-purpose flour	750 mL
2 tsp	baking powder	10 mL
½ tsp	salt	2 mL
½ cup	butter or margarine, softened	125 mL
2 cups	granulated sugar	500 mL
4	eggs	4
1 tsp	vanilla	5 mL
1 cup	milk	250 mL

FILLING

1 cup	packed brown sugar	250 mL
2 tbsp	butter, softened	25 mL
2 tbsp	all-purpose flour	25 mL
1 cup	chopped nuts	250 mL
1 tsp	ground cinnamon	5 mL

1. *Prepare the base:* In a medium bowl, mix together flour, baking powder and salt.
2. In a large bowl, beat butter and sugar until smooth and creamy. Beat in eggs, one at a time, until incorporated. Stir in vanilla. Gradually blend in flour mixture, alternately with milk, until just incorporated. Set half aside and spread remainder evenly in prepared pan.
3. *Prepare the filling:* In a medium bowl, beat brown sugar and butter until smooth and creamy. Blend in flour, nuts and cinnamon.
4. Spoon half the filling over batter in pan. Spread reserved batter evenly over filling. Spread the remaining filling evenly over batter. Bake in preheated oven for 40 to 50 minutes or until a tester inserted in the center comes out clean. Place pan on a wire rack to cool completely, then cut into squares.

Colleen's Fruit Cake Squares

Makes 30 squares
- Preheat oven to 400°F (200°C)
- 13- by 9-inch (3 L) baking pan, greased

1½ cups	water	375 mL
1½ cups	raisins	375 mL
2 tsp	baking soda	10 mL
3 cups	all-purpose flour	750 mL
1 tsp	ground cinnamon	5 mL
1 tsp	ground nutmeg	5 mL
1 tsp	ground ginger	5 mL
2 cups	granulated sugar	500 mL
1 cup	vegetable oil	250 mL
3	eggs	3
2 tsp	vanilla	10 mL
½ cup	chopped nuts (optional)	125 mL
½ cup	semisweet chocolate chips (optional)	125 mL

1. In a saucepan, over low heat, stir together water, raisins and baking soda. Increase heat and bring to a boil. Cook, stirring occasionally, for 5 minutes. Set aside to cool.
2. In a large bowl, mix together flour, cinnamon, nutmeg and ginger. Make a well in the center.
3. In another large bowl, beat sugar, oil, eggs and vanilla until blended. Stir in raisin mixture. Pour into flour mixture and stir just until incorporated. Stir in nuts (if using) and chocolate chips (if using).
4. Spread evenly in prepared pan. Bake in preheated oven for 1 hour and 10 minutes or until a tester inserted in the center comes out clean. Place pan on a wire rack to cool completely, then cut into squares.

Esther's Favorite Cakes

Mom's Icebox Cake

Serves 6 to 8
- 9-inch (2.5 L) square metal baking pan, ungreased

3 oz	gelatin, any flavor	90 g
1 cup	graham wafer crumbs (about 12 whole wafers)	250 mL
1 cup	chopped walnuts	250 mL
½ cup	packed brown sugar	125 mL
	Grated zest of 1 lemon	
	Whole graham wafers	

FILLING

½ cup	packed brown sugar	125 mL
1½ cups	sour cream	375 mL
2 tsp	freshly squeezed lemon juice	10 mL
1 tsp	vanilla	5 mL

1. Prepare gelatin as directed on package. Chill in refrigerator until set.
2. In a medium bowl, combine graham crumbs, walnuts, brown sugar and lemon zest. Mix well until thoroughly combined.

3. *Prepare the filling:* In another bowl, combine brown sugar, sour cream, lemon juice and vanilla. Mix well until thoroughly blended.

4. Arrange whole graham wafers on bottom of baking pan. Spread half of the filling mixture evenly on top of wafers. Place another layer of whole graham wafers on top of filling. Top with the remaining filling mixture, spreading evenly.

5. Spoon half of the crumb mixture on top of the filling mixture. Spread the gelatin over top and then spread the remaining crumb mixture on top of the gelatin. Chill in refrigerator for at least 30 minutes or until ready to serve. Store any remaining cake in the refrigerator.

Tip *Originally, a creative cook quickly put together a reasonable facsimile of a cake by alternating layers of cookies and flavored whipped cream. This creation was placed in an old-fashioned icebox to mellow, hence the name icebox cake.*

Christine's Honey Cake

Serves 10 to 12

- Preheat oven to 325°F (160°C)
- 9- by 5-inch (2 L) metal loaf pan, greased and floured

3 cups	all-purpose flour	750 mL
1 tsp	baking powder	5 mL
1 tsp	ground cinnamon	5 mL
1 tsp	ground allspice	5 mL
1 cup	cold strong brewed coffee	250 mL
1 tsp	baking soda	5 mL
1¼ cups	packed brown sugar	300 mL
1 cup	liquid honey	250 mL
4	eggs, at room temperature	4
¾ cup	vegetable oil	175 mL

1. In a medium bowl, sift together flour, baking powder, cinnamon and allspice. In a small bowl, combine coffee with baking soda and mix well.

2. In a large mixer bowl, on medium speed, beat together brown sugar and honey. Add the eggs and beat well. Beat in oil until blended.

3. Stir in flour mixture alternately with the coffee mixture, making 3 additions of flour and 2 of coffee, until well blended. Pour into prepared baking pan.

4. Bake in preheated oven for 1 hour or until a toothpick inserted in the center comes out clean and dry. Let cool completely in pan on a wire rack.

Betty's Carrot Cake

Serves 12 to 16

- Preheat oven to 375°F (190°C)
- 10-inch (4 L) tube pan, ungreased

3 cups	all-purpose flour	750 mL
1 tbsp	baking powder	15 mL
1 tsp	salt	5 mL
½ tsp	baking soda	2 mL
4	eggs	4
2 cups	granulated sugar	500 mL
1 cup	vegetable oil	250 mL
1 tsp	vanilla	5 mL
2 cups	grated carrots (about 4 medium)	500 mL
½ cup	chopped nuts	125 mL
TOPPING		
½ cup	packed brown sugar	125 mL
2 tbsp	butter or margarine, softened	25 mL
2 tbsp	milk	25 mL
¼ cup	chopped nuts	50 mL

1. In a medium bowl, combine flour, baking powder, salt and baking soda.

2. In a large mixer bowl, combine eggs, sugar, oil and vanilla. Beat on medium speed until well combined.

3. Add flour mixture to egg mixture, mixing until well blended. Fold in carrots and chopped nuts. Pour batter into baking pan.

4. Bake in preheated oven for 45 minutes or until tester inserted in the center comes out just slightly moist.

5. *Prepare the topping:* Cream together brown sugar and butter until smooth. Add milk and nuts and mix well.

6. Remove cake from oven, spread topping over top of cake, and bake for 15 minutes or until tester inserted in center of cake comes out clean and dry and topping is golden. Immediately invert pan and, using hole in tube, hang upside down on an inverted funnel, the neck of a bottle or a wire rack, and let cool completely. With a long thin knife or metal spatula, loosen around the edges and then remove cake from pan. Place on serving plate.

Tip *When spreading topping on a hot cake, it is not as important to spread it evenly, as it melts and forms a glaze when put back into oven.*

Felicia's Apple Cake

Serves 12 to 16
- Preheat oven to 350°F (180°C)
- 13- by 9-inch (3 L) metal baking pan, greased

1¾ cups	all-purpose flour	425 mL
2 tsp	baking powder	10 mL
Pinch	salt	Pinch
2	eggs	2
¾ cup	granulated sugar	175 mL
¾ cup	vegetable oil	175 mL
½ cup	cold water	125 mL
1	can (21 oz/625 mL) apple pie filling	1
	Cinnamon sugar	

1. In a medium bowl, sift together flour, baking powder and salt.
2. In a large mixer bowl, on medium speed, beat eggs until well beaten. Add the sugar slowly, beating until blended. Beat in oil. Add flour mixture alternately with water, making 3 additions of flour and 2 of water, beating on low speed until well blended.
3. Spread about half, or a little more, of the batter on the bottom of your prepared baking pan. Spread apple pie filling over top, in spoonfuls, evenly. Top with the remaining batter, spreading evenly, to cover apple filling. Sprinkle cinnamon-sugar mixture over top of cake.
4. Bake in preheated oven for 45 to 55 minutes or until a toothpick inserted in the center comes out clean and dry. Let cool completely in pan on a wire rack.

Mildred's Banana Cake

Serves 8 to 10
- Preheat oven to 350°F (180°C)
- 9- by 5-inch (2 L) metal loaf pan, greased and floured

2 cups	all-purpose flour	500 mL
2 tsp	baking powder	10 mL
¼ tsp	salt	1 mL
1 tsp	baking soda	5 mL
⅓ cup	buttermilk or sour cream	75 mL
1 cup	granulated sugar	250 mL
½ cup	butter or margarine, softened	125 mL
2	eggs, well beaten	2
1 cup	mashed ripe bananas,	250 mL
1 tsp	vanilla	5 mL

1. In a medium bowl, sift together flour, baking powder and salt. In a small bowl, dissolve the baking soda in the buttermilk. Set aside.
2. In a large mixer bowl, on medium speed, cream sugar and butter until light and fluffy. Add beaten eggs, beating until blended. Add bananas and vanilla, beating until well blended.
3. Beat in flour mixture alternately with the buttermilk mixture on low speed, making 3 additions of flour and 2 of buttermilk, mixing until thoroughly combined. Spoon into prepared baking pan.
4. Bake in preheated oven for 50 to 55 minutes or until a toothpick inserted in the center comes out clean and dry. Let cool in pan on a wire rack for 10 minutes, and remove from pan onto wire rack to cool completely.

Esther's Chocolate Pound Cake

Serves 8 to 10
- Preheat oven to 325°F (160°C)
- 9- by 5-inch (2 L) metal loaf pan, greased and dusted with unsweetened cocoa powder

2 cups	all-purpose flour	500 mL
1 tsp	baking soda	5 mL
1½ cups	firmly packed brown sugar	375 mL
½ cup	butter or margarine, softened	125 mL
2	eggs	2
1 cup	sour cream	250 mL
1 tsp	vanilla	5 mL
2 oz	unsweetened chocolate, melted and cooled	60 g

1. In a medium bowl, combine flour and baking soda.
2. In a large mixer bowl, on medium speed, cream brown sugar and butter until smooth and blended. Add eggs, one at a time, beating well after each addition. Gradually add flour mixture, on low speed, beating until well combined. Add sour cream and vanilla and beat until well blended. Add chocolate and continue beating until thoroughly combined. Pour into prepared baking pan.
3. Bake in preheated oven for 60 to 70 minutes or until a toothpick inserted in the center comes out clean and dry. Let cool in pan for 10 minutes, then loosen around edges with a knife and remove carefully from pan onto wire rack to cool completely.

Baba Mary's Favorite Chocolate Roll

Serves 10 to 12

- Preheat oven to 350°F (180°C)
- 15- by 10-inch (38 by 25 cm) rimmed baking sheet, greased and floured

5	eggs, separated	5
1 cup	sifted confectioner's (icing) sugar	250 mL
3 tbsp	unsweetened cocoa powder, sifted	45 mL
1 tsp	vanilla	5 mL
	Chocolate Buttercream Filling (optional, see recipe, page 380)	
	Sweetened whipping (35%) cream, whipped (optional)	
	Confectioner's (icing) sugar (optional)	
	Chocolate sauce (optional)	

1. In a clean mixer bowl, on high speed, beat egg whites until foamy. Gradually add sugar, a spoonful at a time, until stiff peaks form. Add cocoa powder.
2. In another bowl, beat egg yolks until lemon-colored and thick. Add vanilla and blend.
3. Fold egg yolk mixture gently into the egg white mixture until well combined. Spoon batter into prepared baking pan, spreading evenly with a spatula.
4. Bake in preheated oven for 20 minutes or until top springs back when lightly touched. Spread a damp tea towel over cake and let cool in pan on a wire rack for 15 minutes.
5. Sprinkle a clean tea towel with cocoa powder. When cake has almost cooled, remove damp towel and loosen edges carefully with a spatula. Invert onto cocoa-dusted towel. Roll up the cake, jellyroll-style, using the towel as a guide, and set aside to cool completely.
6. When completely cooled, unroll and spread with any filling you desire, such as Chocolate Buttercream Filling or sweetened whipped cream. Reroll and place on a serving plate. Sprinkle with confectioner's sugar, if desired, or drizzle a hot or cold chocolate sauce over top.

Esther's Sour Cream Coffee Cake

Serves 12 to 16

- Preheat oven to 350°F (180°C)
- 10-inch (3 L) Bundt pan, lightly greased

1½ cups	all-purpose flour	375 mL
1½ tsp	baking powder	7 mL
1 cup	sour cream	250 mL
1 tsp	baking soda	5 mL
1 cup	granulated sugar	250 mL
¼ cup	butter or margarine, softened	50 mL
2	eggs, lightly beaten	2
1 tbsp	vanilla	15 mL
TOPPING		
½ cup	chopped nuts	125 mL
¼ cup	granulated sugar	50 mL
½ tsp	ground cinnamon	2 mL
1 to 1½ tbsp	butter	15 to 22 mL

1. In a medium bowl, combine flour and baking powder. In a small bowl, mix sour cream and baking soda. Set aside.
2. In a large mixer bowl, cream sugar, butter and eggs until smooth and fluffy. Add sour cream mixture to the egg mixture and beat on low speed until well blended.
3. Stir flour mixture into creamed mixture. Add vanilla and mix well until combined. Pour into prepared baking pan.
4. *Prepare the topping:* In a small bowl, combine nuts, sugar and cinnamon. Sprinkle evenly over top of batter and dot with butter.
5. Bake in preheated oven for 45 to 50 minutes or until a toothpick inserted in the center comes out clean and dry. Turn off oven and keep door ajar, allowing cake to remain in oven until slightly cooled, about 15 to 20 minutes. Remove cake from pan onto a wire rack to cool completely.

Tip *If your recipe calls for chopped nuts, put whole nuts in a plastic bag and roll them with a rolling pin. Then just pour them from the bag into your mixing bowl.*

Arlene's Pumpkin Pecan Cake

Serves 12 to 16
- Preheat oven to 350°F (180°C)
- 10-inch (3 L) Bundt pan, greased and floured

1	package (18 oz/510 g) spice cake mix	1
1 cup	canned pumpkin purée (not pie filling)	250 mL
½ cup	vegetable oil	125 mL
1	package (4-serving size) vanilla instant pudding mix	1
3	eggs	3
1 tsp	ground cinnamon	5 mL
½ cup	water	125 mL
½ cup	chopped pecans	125 mL
	Whipped cream or ice cream (optional)	

1. In a large mixer bowl, combine cake mix, pumpkin, oil and pudding mix, beating until blended. Add eggs, one at a time, beating well after each addition. Beat in cinnamon and water, beating until well blended.
2. Fold in pecans, gently, and mix until thoroughly combined. Pour into prepared baking pan.
3. Bake in preheated oven for 40 to 45 minutes or until a toothpick inserted in the center comes out clean and dry. Let cool in pan on a wire rack for 10 minutes, then turn out of pan onto wire rack to cool completely. Serve with whipped cream or ice cream, if desired.

Tip *If your whipping cream won't whip, chill the bowl, beaters and cream. You can also set the bowl into a larger bowl of ice while you whip. If that doesn't work, gradually whip in 3 to 4 drops of lemon juice.*

Mom's Chocolate Chip Chiffon Cake

Serves 12 to 16
- Preheat oven to 325°F (160°C)
- 10-inch (4 L) tube pan, ungreased, or a 10-inch (3 L) Bundt pan, lightly greased

2¼ cups	sifted cake and pastry flour	550 mL
1⅓ cups	granulated sugar	325 mL
1 tbsp	baking powder	15 mL
1 tsp	salt	5 mL
¾ cup	cold water	175 mL
½ cup	vegetable oil	125 mL
5	egg yolks	5
2 tsp	vanilla	10 mL
8	egg whites	8
½ tsp	cream of tartar	2 mL
3 oz	unsweetened chocolate, grated	90 g

1. In a large mixer bowl, sift together flour, sugar, baking powder and salt. Mix well and make a well in the center. Pour in water, oil, egg yolks and vanilla. Beat on medium speed for about 3 minutes, and then on high speed for another 2 minutes, until mixture bubbles.
2. In a clean mixer bowl with clean beaters, beat egg whites and cream of tartar on high speed until stiff peaks form. Gently fold into egg yolk mixture until well incorporated. Do not stir.
3. Sprinkle the grated chocolate over top of batter, gently folding in with few strokes. Pour into prepared baking pan. Tap pan lightly on counter to remove any air bubbles. Smooth top of batter.
4. Bake in preheated oven for 55 minutes, then increase temperature to 350°F (180°C) and bake for another 10 to 15 minutes or until cake springs back when lightly touched. Immediately invert pan and, using hole in tube, hang upside down on an inverted funnel, the neck of a bottle or a wire rack, and let cool completely. With a long thin knife or metal spatula, loosen around the edges and then remove cake from pan.

Shauna's Passover Chiffon Cake

Serves 12 to 16
- Preheat oven to 325°F (160°C)
- 10-inch (4 L) tube pan, ungreased

3 tbsp	unsweetened cocoa powder	45 mL
½ cup	hot water	125 mL
10	eggs, separated, at room temperature	10
1½ cups	granulated sugar	375 mL
½ cup	vegetable oil	125 mL
1 tsp	vanilla	5 mL
½ tsp	cream of tartar	2 mL
¾ cup	matzo cake meal	175 mL
¼ cup	potato starch	50 mL

1. In a small bowl, mix together cocoa powder and hot water.
2. In a large mixer bowl, combine egg yolks, cocoa mixture, sugar, oil and vanilla, beating until well blended.

3. In another large mixer bowl, with clean beaters, on high speed, beat egg whites and cream of tartar until stiff peaks form. Fold gently into the egg yolk mixture until well combined. Gently fold in cake meal, and then potato starch, until thoroughly blended. Spoon into baking pan. Tap pan lightly on counter to remove any air bubbles. Smooth top of batter.

4. Bake in preheated oven for 75 minutes or until cake springs back when lightly touched. Immediately invert pan and, using hole in tube, hang upside down on an inverted funnel, the neck of a bottle or a wire rack, and let cool completely. With a long thin knife or metal spatula, loosen around the edges and then remove cake from pan.

Ann's Cheesecake Torte

Serves 10 to 12
- 9-inch (23 cm) springform pan, greased

1	package (6½ oz/200 g) chocolate wafers	1
2 tbsp	butter or margarine, melted	25 mL
1	package (8 oz/250 g) cream cheese, softened	1
1 cup	confectioner's (icing) sugar, sifted	250 mL
2 cups	frozen whipped topping, thawed	500 mL
1	can (14 oz/398 mL) crushed pineapple, well drained	1
1	can (19 oz/540 mL) cherry pie filling	1

1. Set aside 14 chocolate wafers. Crush the remaining wafers and put into a small bowl. Add the butter and mix well. Press firmly onto bottom of prepared baking pan. Stand the reserved 14 wafers on end around the pan.

2. In a large mixer bowl, on medium speed, beat cream cheese and confectioner's sugar until smooth and blended. Fold in whipped topping, gently, until well combined. Fold in pineapple. Spoon into baking pan.

3. Wrap pan in foil and freeze until it feels firm, at least 2 to 3 hours or overnight. About 2 hours before serving, spread cherry pie filling evenly over top and remove springform ring. Keep in fridge until ready to serve.

Tip *Keep a plastic sandwich bag in your shortening container, or close by, and use like a mitten to grease baking pans and sheets. I also use the wrappers from the shortening or butter to grease pans.*

Sima's Cheesecake

Serves 12 to 16
- Preheat oven to 350°F (180°C)
- 13- by 9-inch (3 L) metal baking pan, greased

¾ cup	granulated sugar	175 mL
½ cup	butter, melted	125 mL
2	eggs	2
	Juice of 1 orange	
	Grated zest from ½ lemon	
1 tsp	vanilla	5 mL
2½ cups	all-purpose flour	625 mL
¼ cup	milk	50 mL

CHEESE FILLING

½ cup	granulated sugar	125 mL
1 lb	pressed cottage cheese	500 g
2	packages (each 8 oz/250 g) cream cheese, softened	2
1	egg	1
⅓ cup	butter, melted	75 mL
	Juice of ½ lemon	
1 tsp	vanilla	5 mL

1. In a large mixer bowl, combine sugar, butter, eggs, orange juice and lemon zest. Beat on medium speed until well blended. Stir in vanilla, then flour alternately with the milk, making 3 additions of flour and 2 of milk. Mix until soft dough is formed. Set aside one-quarter of the dough. Press the remaining dough onto bottom and up sides of prepared baking pan.

2. *Prepare the filling:* In a large mixer bowl, combine sugar, pressed cheese and cream cheese. Beat on low speed until blended. Add egg, butter, lemon juice and vanilla, and mix until well blended. Spoon cheese filling over top of dough.

3. Roll out reserved dough into 10 long strips, about ½ inch (1 cm) wide. Arrange strips over top of cheese filling in a lattice pattern (see tip, below).

4. Bake in preheated oven for 50 to 60 minutes, until golden brown. Let cool completely in pan on a wire rack.

Tip *To make a lattice top, roll out pastry and cut into ten ½-inch (1 cm) strips. Arrange five pastry strips, about 1½ inches (3.5 cm) apart, over your filling. Fold back every other strip. Place another strip across, then unfold strips. To finish, fold back the alternate strips and place next strip the same distance from the other strip. Unfold strips and continue weaving until lattice top is completed.*

Esther's Favorite Pies

● ●

Esther's Mock Apple Pie

Serves 6 to 8
- Preheat oven to 400°F (200°C)
- 9-inch (23 cm) pie plate

	Pastry for a 9-inch (23 cm) single-crust pie	
1 cup	granulated sugar	250 mL
2 tsp	cream of tartar	10 mL
2 cups	water	500 mL
30	whole Ritz crackers	30
1 tbsp	freshly squeezed lemon juice	15 mL
½ tsp	ground cinnamon	2 mL

CRUMB TOPPING

30	Ritz crackers, finely rolled into crumbs	30
½ cup	lightly packed brown sugar	125 mL
⅓ cup	butter or margarine, melted	75 mL

1. On a lightly floured surface, roll out pastry and fit into pie plate.
2. In a medium saucepan, combine sugar, cream of tartar and water. Bring to a boil over medium heat. Add the crackers and keep boiling for 5 to 6 minutes. Spoon into pie crust and sprinkle over top with lemon juice and cinnamon.
3. *Prepare the topping:* In a bowl, mix together cracker crumbs, brown sugar and melted butter until well blended. Sprinkle over top.
4. Bake in preheated oven for 15 minutes, then reduce heat to 350°F (180°C) and continue baking for another 15 to 20 minutes or until topping is browned. Best when served warm.

● ●

Mildred's Streusel-Topped Apple Pie

Serves 6 to 8
- Preheat oven to 450°F (230°C)
- 9-inch (23 cm) pie plate

	Frozen or homemade 9-inch (23 cm) deep-dish pie shell, baked and cooled	

FILLING

5	apples, peeled and sliced	5
⅓ cup	firmly packed brown sugar	75 mL
1 tbsp	cornstarch	15 mL
½ tsp	ground cinnamon	2 mL

STREUSEL TOPPING

1 cup	all-purpose flour	250 mL
½ cup	granulated sugar	125 mL
½ cup	butter or margarine, softened	125 mL

1. *Prepare the filling:* In a large bowl, toss together apples, brown sugar, cornstarch and cinnamon. Mix well and spoon into pie shell.
2. *Prepare the topping:* In another bowl, combine flour and sugar. Cut in butter until mixture resembles coarse crumbs. Sprinkle over the apple mixture.
3. Bake in preheated oven for 10 minutes. Reduce oven temperature to 350°F (180°C) and continue baking for about 40 to 45 minutes or until apples are tender. Serve warm.

● ●

Esther's Strawberry Swirl Pie

Serves 12 to 16
- Preheat oven to 350°F (180°C)
- 13- by 9-inch (3 L) glass baking dish, ungreased

CRUST

2¼ cups	graham wafer crumbs (about 30 whole wafers)	550 mL
½ cup	butter or margarine, melted	125 mL

FILLING

6 cups	miniature white marshmallows (about 10 oz/300 g)	1.5 L
½ cup	milk	125 mL
1	package (6 oz/175 g) strawberry-flavored gelatin	1
1⅓ cups	boiling water	325 mL
2	packages (each 10 oz/300 g) frozen strawberries, thawed, including juice	2
1 cup	whipping (35%) cream, whipped	250 mL
	Graham wafer crumbs (optional)	

1. *Prepare the crust:* In a small bowl, mix together wafer crumbs and melted butter. Press firmly onto bottom of prepared baking dish. Bake in preheated oven for 10 minutes. Let cool.
2. In the top of a double boiler, over hot water, melt the marshmallows with the milk, stirring until melted. Let cool.
3. *Prepare the filling:* In a large bowl, combine the strawberry gelatin with the boiling water. Mix well. Add the thawed strawberries. Stir until blended and let cool in refrigerator until partially jelled, about 20 minutes, stirring occasionally.

4. When gelatin mixture is almost set, fold whipped cream into marshmallow mixture. Spread half of the marshmallow mixture over crust and top with half of the strawberry mixture. Repeat layers with the remaining filling, swirling with a spatula to make a marble effect. Sprinkle lightly with additional wafer crumbs, if desired. Chill in refrigerator for at least 1 hour or until set.

● ●

Bernice's Apricot Parfait Pie

Serves 6 to 8

- 9-inch (23 cm) pie plate

	Graham Cracker Crust (see recipe, page 407)	
1	can (13 oz/385 g) apricot nectar	1
1	package (3 oz/90 g) orange-flavored gelatin	1
2 cups	vanilla ice cream	500 mL
	Whipping (35%) cream, whipped	
	Chocolate curls	

1. In a small saucepan, bring apricot nectar to a boil. Remove from heat and stir in the orange gelatin.
2. Cut ice cream into chunks and add to gelatin until all of the ice cream melts. Chill in refrigerator until mixture mounds slightly when dropped from a spoon.
3. Pour into prepared crust and chill until set. Top with whipped cream and chocolate curls. Serve cold.

Tip *You could line pan with peach slices, tangerine or orange slices before filling.*

● ●

Poffy's Rhubarb Strawberry Pie

Serves 6 to 8

- Preheat oven to 400°F (200°C)
- 9-inch (23 cm) pie plate

	Pastry for a 9-inch (23 cm) double-crust pie	
3	soda crackers, crushed	3
1	egg	1
1 cup	granulated sugar	250 mL
3 cups	chopped rhubarb	750 mL
2 cups	chopped fresh strawberries	500 mL
	Granulated sugar	

1. On a lightly floured surface, roll out half of pastry and fit into pie plate. Spread crushed soda cracker crumbs evenly onto bottom pie crust.
2. In a large bowl, whisk egg. Add sugar and whisk to blend. Stir in rhubarb and strawberries and mix well. Spoon into pie crust.
3. Roll out the remaining pastry to fit over filling. Cut several slits in top crust near the center to allow steam to escape, and place over fruit filling. Trim, seal and flute edges or press with a fork all around. Sprinkle a little granulated sugar over the top.
4. Bake in preheated oven for 20 minutes, then reduce oven temperature to 350°F (180°C) and continue baking for 1 hour. Let cool completely on a wire rack.

● ●

Colleen's Rhubarb Crisp

Serves 6 to 8

- Preheat oven to 375°F (190°C)
- 9-inch (2.5 L) square glass baking dish, buttered

2 lbs	rhubarb, cut into ½-inch (1 cm) pieces (about 7 cups/1.75 L)	1 kg
1	egg, lightly beaten	1
¾ cup	granulated sugar	175 mL
2 tbsp	all-purpose flour	25 mL
½ tsp	ground cinnamon	2 mL
TOPPING		
¾ cup	old-fashioned rolled oats	175 mL
⅓ cup	packed brown sugar	75 mL
¼ cup	all-purpose flour	50 mL
1 tsp	ground cinnamon	5 mL
¼ cup	cold butter or margarine	50 mL

1. In a large bowl, toss together rhubarb, egg, sugar, flour and cinnamon until well incorporated and blended. Pour into prepared baking dish.
2. *Prepare the topping:* In a small bowl, combine oats, brown sugar, flour and cinnamon. Cut in butter with a fork or pastry blender until mixture resembles coarse crumbs. Sprinkle over rhubarb mixture.
3. Bake in preheated oven for 40 minutes or until topping is golden brown.

Tip *Serve warm with whipped topping or ice cream.*

Spreads, Toppings, Frostings and Sauces

Muffin Spreads and Toppings

Frostings and Glazes

For Bars and Squares

For Cakes

Sauces

Muffin Spreads and Toppings

There are numerous ways to add flavor, variety and a little intrigue to your muffins. Warm sliced muffins are delicious topped with any of the following recipes. Whether added before or after baking, toppings make an extra special treat.

Some of the following recipes may seem to yield a large amount, but you will want to have plenty on hand to serve with different flavors of muffins.

Toppings you can sprinkle on top of muffins before baking:
- Sesame or poppy seeds
- Shredded Cheddar cheese
- Sugar mixed with lemon or orange zest

> **Tip** *For a quick topping for muffins, place a soft caramel candy in the bottom of each muffin tin. Pour batter over top. Bake as usual and then invert. You'll have a delicious caramel sauce!*

Toppings you can sprinkle on top of muffins after baking:
- Marmalade, jelly or jam
- Dip tops in melted butter and then in sugar or cinnamon
- Confectioner's (icing) sugar
- Chocolate sauce: In a bowl, blend together 1 can sweetened condensed milk, 2 oz (60 g) semisweet chocolate, 2 tbsp (25 mL) butter and 1 tsp (5 mL) butter. Heat over low heat.

> **Tip** *For a quick and easy sweet spread that is terrific on muffins (or toast), combine equal amounts of softened butter or margarine and honey. Add a little vanilla. Start with a smaller amount, like ¼ tsp (1 mL), and increase, if desired.*

Cinnamon Butter

Makes about ½ cup (125 mL)

3 tbsp	butter, softened	45 mL
½ cup	confectioner's (icing) sugar	125 mL
¼ tsp	ground cinnamon	1 mL

1. In a bowl, cream together butter, sugar and cinnamon. Chill.

Maple Butter

Makes about ½ cup (125 mL)

½ cup	confectioner's (icing) sugar	125 mL
1 to 2 tsp	milk	5 to 10 mL
1 tsp	pure maple syrup	5 mL

1. In a small bowl, mix together sugar, milk and maple syrup and beat until smooth enough to spread.

Sweet Orange Butter

Makes about 1 cup (250 mL)

¼ cup	butter, softened	50 mL
½ cup	confectioner's (icing) sugar	125 mL
	Grated zest of ½ orange	
	Juice of ½ orange	

1. In a bowl, mix together butter and sugar. Add juice and zest. Mix well and serve.

> **Tip** *For lump-free confectioner's sugar, try sifting it through a tea strainer.*

Honey Peach Butter

Makes about 1 cup (250 mL)

½ cup	butter, softened	125 mL
6 tbsp	peach preserves	90 mL
2 tsp	liquid honey	10 mL

1. In a bowl, beat butter until fluffy. Mix in peach preserves and honey.

> **Tip** *Keep honey or molasses from sticking to the measuring cup by greasing cup first. If recipe calls for vegetable oil, measure that first.*

Special Fruit Butter

Makes about 2 cups (500 mL)

1 cup	puréed baby fruit (any flavor)	250 mL
1 cup	butter, softened	250 mL
2 tbsp	confectioner's (icing) sugar	25 mL

1. In a bowl, beat together puréed fruit and butter. Beat in sugar. Chill and serve.

Creamy Berry Spread

Makes about 2 cups (500 mL)

| 1 cup | strawberries or raspberries | 250 mL |
| 1 | package (8 oz/250 g) light cream cheese, softened | 1 |

1. In a bowl, mash strawberries.

2. In another bowl, beat cream cheese until fluffy. Stir in mashed berries. Spread on sliced muffins or toast.

Strawberry Cream Cheese Spread

Makes about ⅔ cup (150 mL)

| 4 oz | low-fat cream cheese | 125 g |
| 2 tbsp | strawberry jam | 25 mL |

1. In a small bowl, mash cream cheese until softened. Stir in jam and mix well.

Variations *Orange Cream Cheese Spread: Replace jam with 1 tbsp (15 mL) thawed frozen orange juice concentrate and 1 tbsp (15 mL) liquid honey.*

Cinnamon Date Cream Cheese Spread: Replace jam with 2 tbsp (25 mL) finely chopped dates and ¼ tsp (1 mL) ground cinnamon.

Cinnamon Raisin Cream Cheese Spread: Replace jam with 2 tbsp (25 mL) chopped raisins and ¼ tsp (1 mL) ground cinnamon.

Lemon Swirl Spread

Makes about 5 cups (1.25 L)

3 oz	cream cheese, softened	90 g
½ cup	butter, softened	125 mL
4 cups	confectioner's (icing) sugar	1 L
1 tsp	vanilla	5 mL
2 tsp to	grated lemon zest	10 to
1 tbsp		15 mL
3 tbsp	freshly squeezed lemon juice	45 mL

1. In a bowl, beat together cream cheese, butter, sugar, vanilla, zest and juice until fluffy and spreadable. If necessary, add more lemon juice, 1 tsp (5 mL) at a time. Store in refrigerator up to 1 week.

Tip *This makes a large amount, so halve the recipe if you're not planning on using much.*

Plum Cheese Spread

Makes about 1¾ cups (425 mL)

1	package (8 oz/250 g) cream cheese, softened	1
½ cup	shredded mild Cheddar cheese	125 mL
2 tbsp	mayonnaise or plain yogurt	25 mL
2 tbsp	plum sauce	25 mL

1. In a blender or food processor, cream together cream cheese and Cheddar cheese until smooth. Add mayonnaise and plum sauce and purée until creamy and thick, but not hard.

Special Holiday Spread

Makes about 4 cups (1 L)

1 cup	raisins	250 mL
⅓ cup	rum	75 mL
1	package (8 oz/250 g) cream cheese, softened	1
2 cups	shredded sharp Cheddar cheese	500 mL
¼ tsp	ground cinnamon	1 mL
¼ tsp	ground ginger	1 mL

1. In a saucepan, over low heat, combine raisins and rum. Heat slowly just until hot. Let cool for 15 to 20 minutes.

2. In a large bowl, cream together cream cheese, Cheddar cheese, cinnamon and ginger. Drain raisins, reserving rum. Pour rum into cheese mixture and mix until well blended and smooth. Fold in raisins.

3. Put mixture into jar or container. Store, covered, in refrigerator up to 3 weeks.

Sugar-Cinnamon Mix

Makes about ⅓ cup (75 mL)

⅓ cup	granulated sugar	75 mL
1½ tsp	ground cinnamon	7 mL
1 tbsp	margarine, melted	15 mL

1. In a bowl, combine sugar, cinnamon and margarine. Sprinkle over batter. Bake as directed in muffin recipe.

Streusel Topping

Makes about 2 cups (500 mL)

⅓ cup	butter or margarine, softened	75 mL
⅓ cup	granulated sugar	75 mL
½ cup	all-purpose flour	125 mL
1 cup	ground dry cake or bread crumbs	250 mL
1 tsp	ground cinnamon	5 mL

1. In a bowl, cream butter while gradually adding sugar. Mix well. Add flour, crumbs and cinnamon, stirring until well mixed and crumbly.

2. Spoon topping over batter. Bake as directed in muffin recipe.

Nut Crunch Topping

Makes about ½ cup (125 mL)

¼ cup	firmly packed brown sugar	50 mL
¼ cup	chopped walnuts	50 mL
1 tbsp	all-purpose flour	15 mL
1 tbsp	margarine, softened	15 mL
1 tsp	ground cinnamon	5 mL

1. In a bowl, combine brown sugar, walnuts, flour, margarine and cinnamon. Sprinkle over batter. Bake as directed in muffin recipe.

Tip *This recipe can also be used as a filling for muffins.*

Lemon Glaze Topping

Makes about 1 cup (250 mL)

1 cup	confectioner's (icing) sugar	250 mL
2 tsp to 1 tbsp	grated lemon zest	10 to 15 mL
4 to 5 tsp	freshly squeezed lemon juice	20 to 25 mL

1. In a bowl, combine sugar and lemon zest. Add lemon juice gradually, mixing well until desired consistency is reached.

Crunchy Broiled Topping

Makes about 2 cups (500 mL)

¼ cup	butter, softened	50 mL
⅔ cup	firmly packed brown sugar	150 mL
½ cup	finely chopped nuts	125 mL
½ cup	whole wheat flakes cereal	125 mL
3 tbsp	milk	45 mL

1. In a bowl, cream together butter and brown sugar. Add nuts and cereal, mixing well. Stir in milk, mixing until well blended.

2. Spread evenly over muffins, hot from the oven. Put under broiler for 3 minutes or until topping is bubbling and slightly browned.

Toffee Coffee Topping

Makes about 3 cups (750 mL)

1 cup	packed brown sugar	250 mL
2 tbsp	cornstarch	25 mL
Pinch	salt	Pinch
1¾ cups	hot strong brewed coffee	425 mL
2 tbsp	butter or margarine	25 mL
2 tsp	vanilla	10 mL

1. In a heavy saucepan, over low heat, combine brown sugar, cornstarch and salt. Add coffee and cook, stirring, until thickened. Remove from heat. Add butter and vanilla, stirring until well blended. Drizzle warm over muffins.

Chocolate, Sour Cream and Coconut Topping

Makes about 2 cups (500 mL)

1 cup	semisweet chocolate pieces	250 mL
1 cup	sour cream	250 mL
¼ cup	toasted flaked coconut (sweetened or unsweetened)	50 mL
1 tsp	vanilla	5 mL

1. In top of a double boiler over hot water, melt chocolate. Add sour cream, stirring until well blended. Add coconut and vanilla and mix well.

Peach Walnut Topping

Makes about 1¾ cups (425 mL)

1 cup	peach preserves	250 mL
1 tbsp	butter or margarine	15 mL
	Juice of 1 orange	
¼ cup	chopped walnuts	50 mL

1. In a small saucepan, over low heat, combine peach preserves, butter and orange juice. Cook, stirring, until heated and blended. Stir in walnuts. Serve warm.

Whipped Cream Topping

Makes about 1 cup (250 mL)

1 cup	whipping (35%) cream	250 mL
2 to 4 tbsp	confectioner's (icing) sugar	25 to 50 mL

1. In a bowl, beat together cream and sugar until stiff.

Variations

Grand Marnier Whipped Cream Topping: To unbeaten cream add 1 to 2 tbsp (15 to 25 mL) confectioner's (icing) sugar and 2 tbsp (25 mL) orange liqueur. Beat until stiff.

Mocha Whipped Cream Topping: To unbeaten cream add ¼ cup (50 mL) confectioner's (icing) sugar, 3 tbsp (45 mL) unsweetened cocoa powder, 1 tsp (5 mL) instant coffee powder or granules and ½ tsp (2 mL) vanilla. Beat until stiff.

Peppermint Whipped Cream Topping: To unbeaten cream add 2 tbsp (25 mL) confectioner's (icing) sugar, a drop of green food coloring and ¼ tsp (1 mL) peppermint extract. Beat until stiff.

Strawberry Whipped Cream Topping: To unbeaten cream add a drop of red food coloring and 2 tbsp (25 mL) strawberry jam. Beat until stiff.

Frostings and Glazes for Bars and Squares

Butter Frosting

Makes enough for a 13- by 9-inch (3 L) pan

⅓ cup	butter, softened	75 mL
4 cups	confectioner's (icing) sugar, sifted	1 L
1½ tsp	vanilla	7 mL
2 tbsp	light (5%) cream or milk (approximate)	25 mL

1. In a large bowl, cream butter. Slowly add about half the sugar, blending well. Beat in vanilla and gradually blend in the remaining sugar. Add only enough cream to make the right spreading consistency.

Variations *Chocolate Butter Frosting: When adding vanilla, also add 2 squares (each 1 oz/28 g) unsweetened chocolate, melted and cooled, and mix to blend.*

Lemon Butter Frosting: To creamed butter, add ½ tsp (2 mL) grated lemon zest. Replace light cream with lemon juice, only enough to make frosting the right spreading consistency.

Mocha Coffee Butter Frosting: To creamed butter, add ¼ cup (50 mL) unsweetened cocoa powder and ½ tsp (2 mL) instant coffee powder or granules.

Orange Butter Frosting: To creamed butter, add 2 tsp (10 mL) grated orange zest and replace light cream with 2 tbsp (25 mL) orange juice.

Pineapple Butter Frosting: Omit vanilla and light cream, and add ⅓ cup (75 mL) pineapple juice and ⅔ cup (150 mL) granulated sugar. Combine the butter, juice and sugar in a small saucepan and heat until sugar is dissolved. Remove from heat and gradually beat in the confectioner's sugar, just enough to give a good spreading consistency.

Vanilla Frosting

Makes enough for an 8- or 9-inch (2 or 2.5 L) pan

3 cups	confectioner's (icing) sugar, sifted	750 mL
⅓ cup	butter or margarine, softened	75 mL
2 tbsp	milk	25 mL
1½ tsp	vanilla	7 mL

1. In a large bowl, with an electric mixer, cream confectioner's sugar and butter. Stir in milk and vanilla and beat until smooth and the right consistency for spreading.

White Fluffy Frosting

Makes enough for an 8- or 9-inch (2 or 2.5 L) pan

2	egg whites	2
1/4 tsp	cream of tartar	1 mL
2 1/2 tbsp	water	32 mL
2 tbsp	light corn syrup	25 mL
1 1/2 tsp	vanilla	7 mL
1/2 tsp	lemon extract	2 mL
2 cups	confectioner's (icing) sugar, sifted	500 mL

1. In a medium bowl, with an electric mixer, beat egg whites and cream of tartar until stiff peaks form.

2. In another bowl, whisk together water, syrup, vanilla and lemon extract.

3. Add to the egg white mixture alternately with the confectioner's sugar, beating well after each addition, until creamy and stiff and easy to spread.

Tip *Raw eggs can be a potentially dangerous source of salmonella. To reduce food-safety risk, use pasteurized egg whites in this recipe.*

Make-Ahead Whipped Cream Frosting

Makes enough for an 8- or 9-inch (2 or 2.5 L) pan

1/2 tsp	unflavored gelatin powder	2 mL
1 tbsp	cold water	15 mL
1 cup	whipping (35%) cream	250 mL
Pinch	salt	Pinch
1/2 tsp	vanilla	2 mL
1 tbsp	granulated sugar (optional)	15 mL

1. In a small bowl, sprinkle gelatin over the water. Set bowl in 1 inch (2.5 cm) of hot water in a saucepan. Let stand until gelatin dissolves. Remove and let mixture cool for 1 minute.

2. In the small bowl of an electric mixer, whip the cream until almost stiff, then add dissolved gelatin mixture, salt, vanilla and sugar (if using). Continue beating until stiff peaks form. Cover and chill in refrigerator.

3. Before spreading, beat with a spoon to blend.

Tip *This recipe will keep for up to 4 days in the refrigerator without separating. Be sure to use very fresh cream.*

Variation *Chocolate-Dotted Whipped Frosting: Grate 1 square (1 oz/28 g) semisweet chocolate (about 1/4 cup/ 50 mL) and fold into frosting; cover and chill in refrigerator.*

Cream Cheese Frosting

Makes enough for a 13- by 9-inch (3 L) pan

6 oz	cream cheese, softened	175 g
1/2 cup	butter or margarine, softened	125 mL
2 tsp	vanilla	10 mL
4 1/2 to 5 cups	confectioner's (icing) sugar, sifted	1.125 L to 1.25 L

1. In a large bowl, beat together cream cheese, butter and vanilla until light and fluffy. Gradually add 2 cups (500 mL) of the sugar, beating well. Gradually beat in as much of the remaining sugar as required to make the right consistency for spreading.

Tip *To keep cake crumbs from getting into your frosting, first spread cake with a thin layer of frosting and let it set. Then frost as usual.*

Rocky Road Frosting

Makes enough for an 8- or 9-inch (2 or 2.5 L) pan

2 oz	unsweetened chocolate	60 g
2 cups	miniature marshmallows, divided	500 mL
1/4 cup	water	50 mL
1/4 cup	butter or margarine	50 mL
2 cups	confectioner's (icing) sugar, sifted	500 mL
1 tsp	vanilla	5 mL
1/2 cup	chopped walnuts	125 mL

1. In a small saucepan, combine chocolate, half the marshmallows, water and butter. Cook over low heat, stirring constantly, until blended. Remove from heat and let cool slightly.

2. Slowly beat in confectioner's sugar, then vanilla. Beat until smooth and thick, about 2 minutes. Stir in the remaining marshmallows and the nuts; mix until well combined.

Tips *To remove lumps from confectioner's sugar, press through a sieve, or sift until smooth.*

To keep frosting from hardening in the bowl, cover it with a damp towel.

Cocoa Frosting

Makes enough for an 8- or 9-inch (2 or 2.5 L) pan

3 tbsp	butter or margarine, softened	45 mL
1/3 cup	unsweetened cocoa powder	75 mL
2 cups	confectioner's (icing) sugar, sifted	500 mL
3 tbsp	milk	45 mL
1/2 tsp	vanilla	2 mL
1/4 tsp	salt	1 mL

1. In a small bowl, with an electric mixer, cream together butter and cocoa until smooth and blended. Stir in confectioner's sugar alternately with milk, blending until smooth and of the right consistency for spreading. Stir in vanilla and salt.

Chocolate Chip Frosting

Makes enough for a 13- by 9-inch (3 L) pan

1 1/2 cups	granulated sugar	375 mL
1/2 cup	butter or margarine	125 mL
1/3 cup	evaporated milk	75 mL
1/2 cup	semisweet chocolate chips	125 mL

1. In a small saucepan, over low heat, combine sugar, butter and milk until sugar is dissolved. Increase heat and bring to boil; cook, stirring constantly, for 1 minute. Add chocolate chips and stir until melted. Let cool slightly before using.

Chocolate Velvet Frosting

Makes enough for a 13- by 9-inch (3 L) pan

1 1/2 cups	granulated sugar	375 mL
1/4 tsp	salt	1 mL
6 tbsp	cornstarch	90 mL
1 1/2 cups	boiling water	375 mL
3 oz	unsweetened chocolate	90 g
1/4 cup	butter or margarine	50 mL
1 tsp	vanilla	5 mL

1. In a saucepan, over low heat, combine sugar, salt and cornstarch. Stir in the boiling water until well blended. Cook, stirring constantly, until mixture thickens. Add chocolate and butter; cook, stirring until melted. Remove from heat. Stir in vanilla.

2. Pour into a bowl and chill, stirring several times, until thick enough to spread.

Tip *Need a garnish? Sprinkle bars or squares with sugar and spice, or glaze with a thin mixture of orange juice and confectioner's sugar.*

No-Cook Fudge Frosting

Makes enough for an 8- or 9-inch (2 or 2.5 L) pan

1 cup	confectioner's (icing) sugar, sifted	250 mL
3 tbsp	milk	45 mL
1	egg	1
1 tsp	vanilla	5 mL
2 oz	unsweetened chocolate, melted and cooled slightly	60 g
3 tbsp	butter or margarine, softened	45 mL

1. In a small bowl, combine confectioner's sugar, milk, egg and vanilla, stirring constantly until blended. Stir in melted chocolate, then butter, beating well after each addition. Chill for 10 minutes in refrigerator.

2. Place bowl in ice water. Beat frosting over ice water until the right consistency for spreading.

Tip *Raw eggs can be a potentially dangerous source of salmonella. To reduce this food-safety risk, use a pasteurized egg.*

Caramel Frosting

Makes enough for a 13- by 9-inch (3 L) pan

1 1/2 cups	packed brown sugar	375 mL
1/2 cup	granulated sugar	125 mL
1 cup	milk	250 mL
1 tbsp	butter or margarine	15 mL

1. In a saucepan, over medium-low heat, combine brown sugar, granulated sugar and milk; cook until sugar is dissolved. Increase heat and bring to a boil; cook until syrup forms a soft ball in cold water. Add butter and stir until melted. Remove from heat. Let cool to lukewarm. Beat until thick and creamy and of right consistency for spreading.

Tip *For a different topping or spread, place caramel candies in the bottom of your baking pan before pouring in batter. Bake as usual, then invert the cake, spread melted caramel evenly over top of cake; cool and cut into bars or squares.*

Fresh Strawberry Frosting

Makes enough for an 8- or 9-inch (2 or 2.5 L) pan

1 cup	fresh, ripe strawberries	250 mL
½ tsp	freshly squeezed lemon juice	2 mL
1½ cups	confectioner's (icing) sugar, sifted	375 mL

1. In a medium bowl, mash strawberries with a fork. Add lemon juice and mix until blended. Gradually add confectioner's sugar, beating briskly with a whisk or a hand beater until fluffy. Add up to an additional ½ cup (125 mL) confectioner's sugar, if necessary, until mixture is the right consistency for spreading.

Tip *To keep cake crumbs from getting into your frosting, first spread cake with a thin layer of frosting and let it set. Then frost as usual.*

Strawberry Buttercream Frosting

Makes enough for an 8- or 9-inch (2 or 2.5 L) pan

¼ cup	butter or margarine, softened	50 mL
4 oz	cream cheese, softened	125 g
⅓ cup	mashed fresh strawberries	75 mL
2 cups	confectioner's (icing) sugar, sifted	500 mL

1. In a medium bowl, with an electric mixer, cream butter and cream cheese until fluffy. Beat in strawberries. Stir in the confectioner's sugar and beat until the right consistency for spreading.

Lemon Butter Frosting

Makes enough for an 8- or 9-inch (2 or 2.5 L) pan

1½ cups	confectioner's (icing) sugar, sifted	375 mL
2 tbsp	butter or margarine, softened	25 mL
1 tbsp	milk	15 mL
½ tsp	grated lemon zest	2 mL
1 tsp	freshly squeezed lemon juice	5 mL

1. In a small bowl, mix together confectioner's sugar, butter or margarine, milk, lemon zest and juice until smooth and spreadable.

Creamy Lemon Frosting

Makes enough for a 13- by 9-inch (3 L) pan

¼ cup	butter or margarine, softened	50 mL
¼ cup	shortening, softened	50 mL
¼ tsp	salt	1 mL
1	egg	1
3 cups	confectioner's (icing) sugar, sifted	750 mL
¼ cup	light corn syrup	50 mL
3 tbsp	freshly squeezed lemon juice	45 mL

1. In a large bowl, beat butter and shortening until creamy. Beat in salt and egg. Gradually beat in confectioner's sugar, then slowly add corn syrup and lemon juice, beating until fluffy and spreadable.

Tip *To remove lumps from confectioner's sugar, press through a sieve, or sift until smooth.*

Pink Lemonade Frosting

Makes enough for a 13- by 9-inch (3 L) pan

½ cup	frozen pink lemonade concentrate, thawed	125 mL
3½ to 4 cups	confectioner's (icing) sugar, sifted	825 mL to 1 L
2	egg whites	2
Pinch	salt	Pinch

1. In a large bowl, with an electric mixer, combine concentrate, confectioner's sugar, egg whites and salt. Beat on high speed until thick enough to spread.

Tip *Raw eggs can be a potentially dangerous source of salmonella. To reduce this food-safety risk, use pasteurized egg whites.*

Quick Banana Frosting

Makes enough for an 8- or 9-inch (2 or 2.5 L) pan

1	ripe banana, mashed	1
½ tsp	almond extract	2 mL
2 cups	confectioner's (icing) sugar, sifted	500 mL

1. In a medium bowl, beat banana, almond extract and confectioner's sugar until blended and spreadable.

Easy Orange Frosting

Makes enough for an 8- or 9-inch (2 or 2.5 L) pan

2	egg whites	2
1¼ cups	granulated sugar	300 mL
¼ cup	frozen orange juice concentrate, thawed	50 mL
1 tbsp	light corn syrup	15 mL

1. In the top of a double boiler over simmering (not boiling) water, combine egg whites, sugar, concentrate and syrup. Cook, beating constantly with an electric mixer on high speed for about 10 minutes or until frosting forms stiff peaks. Remove from heat. Let cool slightly.

Tip *If your frosting becomes hard or too stiff while beating, just add a little lemon juice.*

Date Frosting

Makes enough for a 13- by 9-inch (3 L) pan

1	package (8 oz/250 g) pitted dates, chopped	1
1 cup	boiling water	250 mL
1 cup	granulated sugar	250 mL
½ cup	butter or margarine	125 mL
½ cup	chopped pecans	125 mL

1. In a saucepan, combine dates, boiling water, granulated sugar and butter; cook over medium heat, stirring constantly, for about 20 minutes or until mixture is very thick. Remove from heat; stir in pecans. Let cool to lukewarm.

Vanilla Icing

Makes enough for a 13- by 9-inch (3 L) pan

⅓ cup	butter or margarine, softened	75 mL
3 cups	confectioner's (icing) sugar, sifted	750 mL
1½ tsp	vanilla	7 mL
2 tbsp	milk or cream	25 mL

1. In a medium bowl, beat butter and confectioner's sugar until smooth and blended. Stir in vanilla and milk and beat until mixture is smooth and the right consistency for spreading.

Penuche Nut Icing

Makes enough for an 8- or 9-inch (2 or 2.5 L) pan

1 cup	packed brown sugar	250 mL
¼ cup	milk	50 mL
¼ cup	shortening	50 mL
½ tsp	vanilla	2 mL
¼ tsp	salt	1 mL
½ cup	chopped nuts	125 mL

1. In a saucepan, over medium-low heat, combine brown sugar, milk, shortening and salt. Slowly bring to a rolling boil, stirring constantly, and boil for 2 minutes.

2. Remove from heat and beat with an electric mixer until lukewarm. Add the vanilla and beat until thick enough to spread. If too thick, add a little cream. Stir in nuts.

Tip *To keep frosting from hardening in the bowl, cover it with a damp towel.*

Chocolate Icing

Makes enough for a 13- by 9-inch (3 L) pan

3 oz	unsweetened chocolate	90 g
1½ tsp	butter	7 mL
5 tbsp	milk	75 mL
3½ cups	confectioner's (icing) sugar, sifted	875 mL
1 tsp	vanilla	5 mL

1. In the top of a double boiler, combine chocolate, butter and milk until melted and smooth.

2. Transfer to a large bowl and gradually beat in confectioner's sugar, then vanilla, until smooth and creamy.

Tip *For easier handling of icings and frostings when decorating cookies or cakes, use a squeeze bottle with a pointed tip, like your ketchup and mustard squeeze bottles.*

Orange Butter Icing

Makes enough for an 8- or 9-inch (2 or 2.5 L) pan

3 tbsp	butter or margarine, softened	45 mL
1½ cups	confectioner's (icing) sugar, sifted	375 mL
2 tsp	grated orange zest	10 mL
1 tbsp	freshly squeezed orange juice	15 mL

1. In a medium bowl, beat butter or margarine and sugar until smooth and creamy. Stir in orange zest and juice. Beat until smooth and the right consistency for spreading.

Vanilla Glaze

Makes enough for a 13- by 9-inch (3 L) pan

1 cup	granulated sugar	250 mL
½ tsp	baking soda	2 mL
½ cup	buttermilk	125 mL
1 tbsp	light corn syrup	15 mL
½ cup	butter or margarine	125 mL
1 tsp	vanilla	5 mL

1. In a saucepan, over low heat, combine sugar, baking soda, buttermilk, syrup and butter. Heat slowly, stirring constantly, to boiling. Continue cooking for 2 minutes. Remove from heat. Stir in vanilla.

Apricot Brandy Glaze

Makes enough for a 13- by 9-inch (3 L) pan

1	jar (12 oz/340 mL) apricot preserves	1
¼ cup	apricot brandy	50 mL

1. In a small saucepan, over low heat, cook apricot preserves until very warm. Add apricot brandy and cook, stirring, for 1 to 2 minutes. Remove from heat. Strain through a fine sieve and let cool.

Lemon Glaze

Makes enough for a 13- by 9-inch (3 L) pan

1 cup	confectioner's (icing) sugar, sifted	250 mL
4 tsp	freshly squeezed lemon juice	20 mL

1. In a small bowl, mix together confectioner's sugar and lemon juice until smooth and blended.

Variation *Pineapple Glaze: Add another ½ cup (125 mL) confectioner's sugar and replace lemon juice with ¼ cup (50 mL) pineapple juice.*

Praline Topping

Makes enough for an 8- or 9-inch (2 or 2.5 L) pan

1 cup	chopped nuts	250 mL
½ cup	packed brown sugar	125 mL
¼ cup	butter or margarine, melted	50 mL
3 tbsp	whipping (35%) cream	45 mL

1. In a small bowl, combine nuts, brown sugar, butter and cream. Mix together until well blended.

2. Spread evenly over a hot or cooled cake and broil about 3 inches (7.5 cm) from the heat for 1 to 2 minutes or until pale brown.

Broiled Topping

Makes enough for an 8- or 9-inch (2 or 2.5 L) pan

½ cup	packed brown sugar	125 mL
¼ cup	butter or margarine, softened	50 mL
3 tbsp	evaporated milk	45 mL
½ cup	shredded coconut or chopped nuts	125 mL
1 tbsp	grated orange zest (optional)	15 mL

1. In a small bowl, mix together brown sugar, butter, milk, coconut and orange zest (if using).

2. Spread mixture evenly over cake before cutting into squares or bars, then put under broiler for 2 to 3 minutes or until topping is bubbly and golden brown.

Tip *This is especially good with a butter, chocolate, orange or carrot cake.*

Brown Sugar Meringue

Makes enough for an 8- or 9-inch (2 or 2.5 L) pan

2	egg whites	2
1 tbsp	freshly squeezed lemon juice	15 mL
1 cup	packed brown sugar	250 mL

1. In a small bowl, with an electric mixer, beat egg whites until doubled in volume. Beat in lemon juice. Beat in brown sugar, 1 tbsp (15 mL) at a time, until meringue stands in firm peaks.

2. Spread over cake and bake in a 350°F (180°C) oven for about 10 minutes or until meringue is browned. Place pan on a rack to cool completely.

Tip *Meringues are often called "angel crust" because of their gossamer texture.*

Frostings and Glazes for Cakes

Basic Frosting Base

Makes about 2¼ cups (550 mL)

3 cups	confectioner's (icing) sugar, sifted	750 mL
½ cup	butter or margarine, softened	125 mL
¼ cup	milk (approx.)	50 mL
½ tsp	vanilla	2 mL

1. In a large mixer bowl, combine sugar, butter, milk and vanilla. Beat on medium speed until smooth. Add more milk, if necessary, 1 tsp (5 mL) at a time, so that frosting is fairly thin but of spreading consistency.

Tips *To frost a cake easily, place cake on a plate and then on a lazy Susan.*

To this basic recipe, you can add whatever you desire, such as melted chocolate, food coloring, nuts, etc.

Seven-Minute Frosting

Makes about 2 cups (500 mL)

1½ cups	granulated sugar	375 mL
¼ tsp	cream of tartar (or use 2 tsp/ 10 mL light corn syrup)	1 mL
2	egg whites	2
⅓ cup	cold water	75 mL
Pinch	salt	Pinch
1 tsp	vanilla	5 mL

1. In the top of a double boiler, before placing on stove, combine sugar, cream of tartar, egg whites, cold water and salt. Beat with a hand mixer or whisk to blend.

2. Place over boiling water and cook, whisking constantly, until mixture forms stiff peaks, about 7 minutes.

3. Remove from the boiling water and pour into a mixing bowl. Add vanilla and whisk for 2 to 3 minutes or until mixture is the right consistency for spreading.

Variations *Chocolate Fluff Frosting: Fold in 2 oz (60 g) of unsweetened chocolate, melted and cooled, just before spreading on cake.*

Brown Sugar Frosting: Substitute brown sugar for the granulated sugar and, if desired, replace vanilla with ½ tsp (2 mL) maple extract.

Brown Butter Frosting

Makes about 1¾ cups (425 mL)

¼ cup	butter or margarine	50 mL
2 cups	sifted confectioner's (icing) sugar	500 mL
2 tbsp	half-and-half (10%) or table (18%) cream	25 mL
1 tsp	vegetable oil	5 mL
1 tsp	vanilla	5 mL
	Hot water	

1. Put butter in a medium saucepan, over low heat, and heat slowly until liquid bubbles up, is very foamy, and then settles and is golden brown, about 3 to 5 minutes. Remove from heat and add sugar, cream, oil and vanilla. Stir until right consistency for spreading. If mixture is too thick, add some hot water.

Buttercream Frosting

Makes about 1 cup (250 mL)

¼ cup	butter, softened	50 mL
1½ cups	sifted confectioner's (icing) sugar	375 mL
1 tsp	vanilla	5 mL
2 to 3 tbsp	whipping (35%) cream	25 to 45 mL

1. In a mixer bowl, cream butter until smooth. Gradually add in sugar and vanilla and beat until light and fluffy. If necessary, add a little cream, a spoonful at a time, until mixture is of the right consistency.

Variations *Chocolate Buttercream Frosting: Add 2 oz (60 g) melted unsweetened chocolate to the recipe. If desired, add some chopped nuts.*

Orange Buttercream Frosting: Add grated zest and juice of ½ orange and 1½ tsp (7 mL) of lemon juice. If mixture is too thin, add a little more confectioner's sugar and beat well.

Caramel Candy Frosting

Makes about 3½ cups (875 mL)

28	soft vanilla caramels (8 oz/250 g)	28
½ cup	water	125 mL
½ cup	butter or margarine, softened	125 mL
Pinch	salt	Pinch
4 cups	sifted confectioner's (icing) sugar	1 L
¼ cup	chopped walnuts (optional)	50 mL

1. In the top of a double boiler, over boiling water, melt caramels in water, stirring constantly. Let cool to room temperature, about 10 to 15 minutes.
2. In a large mixer bowl, cream butter, add salt, and then add confectioner's sugar alternately with the caramel mixture, making 4 additions of sugar and 3 of caramel, beating on low speed until smooth and creamy. Stir in walnuts (if using). Chill until of the right consistency for spreading.

White Chocolate Buttercream Frosting

Makes about 1¾ cups (425 mL)

6 oz	white chocolate, chopped	175 g
¼ cup	milk, half-and-half (10%) cream or table (18%) cream	50 mL
1 cup	cold, unsalted butter, cut into chunks	250 mL
1 cup	confectioner's (icing) sugar	250 mL

1. In a small saucepan, melt white chocolate in milk, over low heat, stirring just until melted. Let cool for about 15 minutes, until just warm to the touch.
2. In a large mixer bowl, cream butter until soft and smooth. Gradually add sugar and blend. Add cooled chocolate and beat on high speed until smooth and fluffy, about 2 to 3 minutes.

Coffee Frosting

Makes about 1½ cups (375 mL)

2 cups	sifted confectioner's (icing) sugar, divided	500 mL
½ cup	butter or margarine, softened	125 mL
3 tbsp	coffee-flavored liqueur	45 mL
2 tbsp	milk	25 mL
1 tbsp	instant coffee powder or granules	15 mL

1. In a small mixer bowl, cream 1 cup (250 mL) of the confectioner's sugar and butter until smooth and fluffy.
2. In a measuring cup, mix together liqueur, milk and coffee powder until blended. Add to the creamed mixture alternately with the remaining confectioner's sugar, beating until smooth.

Tip *To prevent crust from forming on prepared icings and frostings, press a piece of plastic wrap against the surface until ready to use.*

Fluffy Mocha Frosting

Makes about 1½ cups (375 mL)

2¾ cups	confectioner's (icing) sugar	675 mL
¼ cup	unsweetened cocoa powder, sifted	50 mL
6 tbsp	butter or margarine, softened	90 mL
2 tbsp	milk	25 mL
2 tbsp	cold strong brewed coffee	25 mL
1 tsp	vanilla	5 mL

1. In a large mixer bowl, on low speed, cream sugar, cocoa powder and butter until smooth. Gradually add milk, coffee and vanilla, beating until well blended.

Cherry Frosting

Makes about 2 cups (500 mL)

3 cups	confectioner's (icing) sugar, sifted	750 mL
⅓ cup	butter or margarine, softened	75 mL
2 tbsp	chopped drained maraschino cherries	25 mL
2 tbsp	milk	25 mL
1½ tsp	vanilla	7 mL
2	drops red food coloring	2

1. In a large mixer bowl, cream sugar and butter until smooth. Stir in cherries, milk, vanilla and food coloring. Beat on medium speed until the right consistency for spreading.

Banana Frosting

Makes about 2½ cups (625 mL)

½ cup	butter or margarine, softened	125 mL
½ cup	mashed ripe bananas (1 to 2 medium)	125 mL
3½ cups	sifted confectioner's (icing) sugar	875 mL
1 tbsp	freshly squeezed lemon juice	15 mL
1 tsp	vanilla	5 mL

1. In a large mixer bowl, cream butter and bananas until blended. Gradually add the sugar, lemon juice and vanilla, and mix well. Chill until mixture is the right consistency for spreading.

Variation *Banana Filling: Chop 2 bananas with a little pulverized sugar and lemon juice and mix together. Spread in between layers of cake and cover top and sides with Banana Frosting.*

Coconut Frosting and Filling

Makes about 2½ cups (625 mL)

⅔ cup	granulated sugar	150 mL
Pinch	salt	Pinch
1	can (6 oz/175 mL) evaporated milk	1
¼ cup	butter or margarine	50 mL
1	egg, lightly beaten	1
1⅓ cups	flaked coconut (sweetened or unsweetened)	325 mL
½ cup	chopped pecans	125 mL
1 tsp	vanilla	5 mL

1. In a medium saucepan, over medium heat, combine sugar, salt, milk, butter and egg. Cook and stir until mixture thickens and begins to boil, 12 to 15 minutes. Remove from heat. Stir in coconut, pecans and vanilla, and mix well. Let cool completely before frosting or filling cake.

Cream Filling

Makes about 2 cups (500 mL)

½ cup	granulated sugar	125 mL
⅓ cup	all-purpose flour	75 mL
½ tsp	salt	2 mL
2 cups	milk	500 mL
2	eggs, lightly beaten	2
1 tsp	vanilla	5 mL

1. In a medium saucepan, over medium heat, combine sugar, flour and salt. Slowly stir in milk and cook until mixture boils and thickens, then cook for 2 minutes. Stir a little of this hot mixture into the eggs, then stir back into remaining hot mixture and bring just to boiling, stirring constantly until thick. Remove from heat. Add vanilla and set aside to cool.

Variations *Chocolate Filling: Add 1½ oz (45 g) of unsweetened chocolate, chopped, with the milk. Increase the sugar to ¾ cup (175 mL).*

Lemon Filling: Substitute ⅔ cup (150 mL) water for the milk. Add 1 tbsp (15 mL) grated lemon zest and 2 tbsp (25 mL) lemon juice to the sugar mixture. Omit the vanilla.

Butterscotch Filling: Use ⅔ cup (150 mL) packed brown sugar instead of the granulated sugar. Add ¼ cup (50 mL) butter with the vanilla.

Lemon Butter Icing

Makes about 1¼ cups (300 mL)

½ cup	butter, softened	125 mL
1¾ cups	sifted confectioner's (icing) sugar	425 mL
1 tbsp	grated lemon zest	15 mL
1 tbsp	freshly squeezed lemon juice	15 mL

1. In a large mixer bowl, cream butter until soft and smooth. Gradually add sugar, lemon zest and lemon juice, and beat on low speed, just until well blended.

Variation *Orange Butter Frosting: Substitute orange juice and zest for the lemon juice and zest.*

Chocolate Glaze

Makes about 1½ cups (375 mL)

¼ cup	unsweetened cocoa powder	50 mL
3 tbsp	water	45 mL
2 tbsp	butter or shortening	25 mL
2 tbsp	light corn syrup	25 mL
2 cups	sifted confectioner's (icing) sugar	500 mL
¼ tsp	vanilla	1 mL

1. In a medium saucepan, over low heat, combine cocoa powder, water, butter and corn syrup, stirring until butter melts and mixture is smooth. Remove from heat and gradually beat in sugar and vanilla. If mixture is too thick to drizzle, add another spoonful of water.

Dark Chocolate Glaze

Makes about ⅔ cup (150 mL)

2 oz	unsweetened chocolate, chopped	60 g
⅓ cup	granulated sugar	75 mL
¼ cup	water	50 mL
1 tsp	butter	5 mL
1 tbsp	milk	15 mL

1. In a double boiler, over hot water, melt chocolate.

2. In a small saucepan, combine sugar and water, and bring to a boil. Boil for 1 minute, stirring constantly.

3. Put melted chocolate in a mixer bowl. Slowly stir in sugar mixture, then the butter. Add milk and beat on low speed until of drizzling consistency. While glaze is still warm, drizzle over cake.

Sauces

Mock Vanilla Ice Cream Sauce

Makes about 2 cups (500 mL)

1	egg (see tip, page 554)	1
3 tbsp	granulated sugar	45 mL
Pinch	salt	Pinch
¼ cup	butter or margarine, melted	50 mL
½ tsp	vanilla	2 mL
¾ cup	whipping (35%) cream	175 mL

1. In a medium mixer bowl, on medium speed, beat egg, sugar and salt until fluffy but thickened. Beat in butter, a little bit at a time, until blended. Stir in vanilla.

2. In a small mixer bowl, on high speed, beat whipping cream until stiff peaks form. Fold into the egg mixture thoroughly until well combined. Chill in refrigerator until ready to serve.

Tip *Delicious on puddings and any other dessert that's great with real vanilla ice cream.*

Fresh Strawberry Sauce

Makes about 2 cups (500 mL)

¼ cup	margarine (no substitute)	50 mL
1½ cups	confectioner's (icing) sugar, sifted	375 mL
¼ cup	crushed fresh strawberries (about 3 berries)	50 mL

1. In a medium mixer bowl, on medium speed, cream margarine until fluffy. Beat in confectioner's sugar, a little bit at a time, until blended and smooth. Add strawberries and continue beating until mixture is blended and smooth.

2. Cover tightly with plastic wrap and chill in refrigerator for 3 to 4 hours or overnight.

Tip *This is a great, classic sauce for steamed puddings.*

Melba Sauce

Makes about 1 cup (250 mL)

1	package (10 oz/300 g) frozen red raspberries, thawed	1
⅔ cup	granulated sugar	150 mL
Pinch	cream of tartar	Pinch

1. Place raspberries into a sieve set over a medium saucepan and press through, throwing away the seeds.

2. Add sugar and cream of tartar to raspberries and cook over medium-high heat to boiling, stirring constantly. Cook for about 3 minutes or until the mixture is slightly thickened. Remove from heat and spoon into a bowl. Cover tightly with plastic wrap and chill in refrigerator for 3 to 4 hours or overnight.

Tip *Usually served on peaches and ice cream, but also delicious on puddings.*

Fruit Cocktail Sauce

Makes about 2 cups (500 mL)

1	can (14 oz/398 mL) fruit cocktail, drained, liquid reserved	1
1 tbsp	cornstarch	15 mL
1½ tsp	grated lemon zest	7 mL
2 tbsp	freshly squeezed lemon juice	25 mL

1. In a small saucepan, mix together 3 tbsp to ¼ cup (45 to 50 mL) of the reserved fruit liquid and cornstarch. Whisk until smooth and blended. Stir in the remaining fruit liquid and the lemon juice.

2. Bring to a boil over medium heat, stirring constantly, and boil for 3 minutes or until sauce thickens. Remove from heat. Stir in lemon zest and fruit cocktail. Best when served warm.

Tip *Wonderful served with all types of desserts, especially custards and puddings.*

Burnt Sugar Sauce

Makes about 2 cups (500 mL)

1½ cups	granulated sugar	375 mL
1 cup	boiling water	250 mL

1. In a medium saucepan, over low heat, cook the sugar, stirring constantly with a wooden spoon, until the sugar is melted and becomes a golden syrup. Remove from heat.

2. Gradually, very slowly, add the water and stir until blended. Return saucepan to heat and continue cooking, over low heat, stirring constantly, until sauce is syrupy and smooth. The sauce will be thin but will get thicker as it cools.

Tip *This is a great sauce for custards.*

Choice Pudding Sauce

Makes about 3 cups (750 mL)
Double boiler

1 cup	packed brown sugar	250 mL
½ cup	butter or margarine	125 mL
2	egg whites, lightly beaten (see tip, below)	2
1 cup	whipping (35%) cream	250 mL

1. In the top of a double boiler, combine brown sugar and butter and cook over simmering water until the sugar is dissolved. Remove top of double boiler and add the beaten egg whites. Set aside to cool.

2. In a small mixer bowl, on high speed, beat whipping cream until stiff peaks form. Fold into the cooled mixture.

Tips *A perfect sauce for any pudding or custard.*

This recipe contains raw eggs. If the food safety of raw eggs is a concern for you, substitute ¼ cup (50 mL) pasteurized eggs, found in the refrigerated egg section of most supermarkets. Alternatively, omit egg whites and use ⅔ cup (150 mL) frozen whipped topping, thawed.

Instant Pudding Sauce

Makes about 4 cups (1 L)

1	package (4 oz/113 g) instant pudding mix (chocolate, vanilla or any other)	1
3 cups	milk	750 mL
¼ cup	confectioner's (icing) sugar, sifted	50 mL
1 tsp	vanilla	5 mL
½ cup	whipping (35%) cream, whipped	125 mL

1. In a large mixer bowl, combine pudding mix, milk, confectioner's sugar and vanilla. Beat on medium speed for 1 to 2 minutes or until well blended and smooth. Fold in the whipped cream until well combined.

2. Cover tightly with plastic wrap and chill in refrigerator for at least 1 hour or until ready to serve.

Tip *Especially good served on baked or steamed puddings.*

Foamy Pudding Sauce

Makes about 3 cups (750 mL)

1	egg (see tip, below)	1
⅓ cup	butter or margarine, melted	75 mL
1½ cups	confectioner's (icing) sugar, sifted	375 mL
1 tsp	vanilla	5 mL
1 tsp	rum extract	5 mL
1 cup	whipping (35%) cream	250 mL

1. In a medium mixer bowl, on medium speed, beat egg until thick. Add butter, beating until well blended. Mix in confectioner's sugar, vanilla and rum extract , stirring until well combined and smooth.

2. In a small mixer bowl, on high speed, beat whipping cream until stiff peaks form. Fold into egg mixture. Cover tightly with plastic wrap and chill in refrigerator for 3 to 4 hours or overnight.

Tip *Raw eggs can be a potentially dangerous source of salmonella. To reduce this food-safety risk, use a pasteurized egg.*

Christmas Pudding Sauce

Makes about 3 cups (750 mL)
Double boiler

¾ cup	butter or margarine	175 mL
1 cup	granulated sugar	250 mL
¼ cup	all-purpose flour	50 mL
2	eggs, separated (see tip, below)	2
1 cup	hot milk	250 mL

1. In a large mixer bowl, cream butter until smooth. Add sugar and flour and beat until well blended.

2. In a small bowl, whisk the egg yolks until well beaten. Add to creamed mixture with the hot milk. Pour mixture into top of double boiler and cook over simmering water until mixture thickens. Set aside to cool.

3. In a small mixer bowl, on high speed, beat the egg whites until stiff peaks form. When ready to serve pudding, fold in the beaten egg whites.

Tip *This recipe contains raw egg whites. If the food safety of raw egg whites is a concern for you, substitute 6 tbsp (90 mL) pasteurized egg whites, found in the refrigerated egg section of most supermarkets. Alternatively, omit egg whites and add ⅔ cup (150 mL) frozen whipped topping, thawed.*

Quick Custard Sauce

Makes about 4 cups (1 L)

1	package (4 oz/113 g) instant vanilla pudding mix	1
4 cups	milk	1 L
2 tbsp	granulated sugar	25 mL
1 tbsp	butter or margarine	15 mL
½ tsp	vanilla	2 mL

1. In a medium saucepan, over medium heat, combine pudding mix, milk, sugar, butter and vanilla. Cook according to the directions on the pudding package. Remove from heat.

2. Spoon into a bowl, cover tightly with plastic wrap and set aside to cool. Can be served warm or cold.

Sour Cream Custard Sauce

Makes about 2 cups (500 mL)

½ cup	granulated sugar	125 mL
2 tbsp	cornstarch	25 mL
¼ tsp	salt	1 mL
1½ cups	milk	375 mL
4	eggs, well beaten	4
½ cup	sour cream	125 mL
1½ tsp	vanilla	7 mL

1. In a medium saucepan, over medium heat, combine sugar, cornstarch and salt. Slowly stir in milk, mixing until smooth. Bring to a boil, stirring constantly. Stir a small amount of this hot mixture into the beaten eggs and return all to the saucepan, stirring constantly. Cook for 2 to 3 minutes. Remove from heat. Mix in sour cream and vanilla and mix well to blend.

2. Place saucepan in ice water and stir for 5 minutes. Transfer to a medium bowl, cover tightly with plastic wrap and chill in refrigerator for 3 to 4 hours or overnight.

Eggnog Sauce

Makes about 2¾ cups (675 mL)

5	egg yolks	5
⅔ cup	granulated sugar	150 mL
½ tsp	grated fresh nutmeg	2 mL
2 cups	light (5%) cream	500 mL
1 tbsp	rum or brandy	15 mL
2 tsp	vanilla	10 mL

1. In a medium bowl, whisk egg yolks, sugar and nutmeg.

2. In a medium saucepan, over medium heat, scald cream, heating until small bubbles form around the edges. Pour into egg mixture, whisking until blended, and return to saucepan. Continue cooking over medium heat, stirring constantly, until mixture is thickened.

3. Pour into a strainer set over a medium bowl and stir in the rum and vanilla. Cover tightly with plastic wrap and chill in refrigerator for 3 to 4 hours or overnight. Serve cold, or warm by microwaving on Medium for 3 minutes.

Tip *Great with custards and puddings.*

Index

Library and Archives Canada Cataloguing in Publication

Brody, Esther
    1500 best bars, cookies, muffins, cakes & more / Esther Brody.

Includes index.
ISBN-10: 0-7788-0194-2
ISBN-13: 978-0-7788-0194-8

    1. Cake. 2. Muffins. 3. Baking. I. Title. II. Title: One thousand five hundred best bars, cookies, muffins, cakes & more.

TX763.B875 2008   641.8'65   C2008-902462-1